ASPEN PUBLISHERS

Individual Retirement Account Answer Book

Sixteenth Edition

by Martin Fleisher and Jo Ann Lippe

The continuing popularity and importance of individual retirement accounts as retirement vehicles underscores the necessity for attorneys, accountants, financial planners, and insurance advisors to keep abreast of legislative and regulatory developments in this area. *Individual Retirement Account Answer Book* is the source most practitioners rely on for the most comprehensive, authoritative coverage of traditional IRAs, Roth IRAs, SIMPLE IRAs, SEP IRAs, and Coverdell Education Savings Accounts.

Highlights of the Sixteenth Edition

The Sixteenth Edition brings practitioners up to date on congressional and administrative agency actions affecting all IRAs and the Coverdell ESA, including:

- The Worker, Retiree, and Employer Recovery Act of 2008 [Pub. L. No. 110-458], the Tax Extenders and Alternative Minimum Tax Relief Act of 2008 [Pub. L. No. 110-343], and the Heroes Earnings Assistance and Relief Tax Act of 2008 [Pub. L. No. 110-245], under which:

  - The minimum distribution rules are suspended for 2009.

  - As of 2010, qualified plans must allow nonspouse beneficiaries to roll over (and thus convert) inherited interests to IRAs—making obsolete the IRS position in Notice 2007-7, Q&A-15, that allowing such transfers was voluntary.

  - Bankruptcy payments made to replace retirement income lost by eligible airline workers when their defined benefit plans were terminated or frozen may be rolled over to Roth IRAs.

  - An eligible individual's ability to exclude from income certain charitable contributions made directly from an IRA is extended through 2009.

  - Settlement payments received in the *Exxon Valdez* litigation may be rolled over to IRAs.

- Disaster relief is provided to victims of storms in the Midwestern Disaster Area during 2008, so they may withdraw up to $100,000 from IRAs without incurring the 10 percent additional tax, income from the withdrawal is deferred for up to three years, and payments may be rolled back within three years.

- Military death gratuities and payments received under the Service-members' Group Life Insurance Program may be rolled over to Roth IRAs and Coverdell ESAs.

- An update on the status of estate tax legislation—estate tax rates and the estate tax exemption amount are likely to be frozen at their 2009 levels.

- Strategies for Roth IRA conversions—by owners and beneficiaries—and how the planning landscape is rapidly changing in favorable ways.

- Recent court decisions of significance:

  - *Sharma v. Commissioner,* T.C. Summ. Op. 2008-98 (Aug. 7, 2008). For purposes of the first-time homebuyer exception to the 10 percent additional tax, state law controls the time at which a present ownership interest is acquired in mortgaged real property.

  - *Benz v. Commissioner,* 132 T.C. No. 15 (May 11, 2009). The Tax Court holds that an IRA distribution made for qualified higher education expenses does not modify a series of substantially equal periodic payments for purposes of the 10 percent additional tax.

  - *Dart v. Commissioner,* T.C. Summ. Op. 2008-158 (Dec. 16, 2008). The Tax Court holds that the Social Security Administration's grant of disability benefits establishes disability as of the application date, so IRA distributions commencing from the application date may qualify for the disability exception to the 10 percent additional tax—there is no need to wait until the benefits are actually granted.

  - *Kowsh v. Commissioner,* T.C. Memo. 2008-204 (Aug. 28, 2008). The Tax Court holds that qualification for benefits under a private disability insurance policy is not sufficient to establish disability for purposes of the exception to the 10 percent additional tax.

  - *Evers v. Commissioner,* T.C. Summ. Op. 2008-140 (Nov. 3, 2008). The Tax Court holds that the medical expenses exception to the 10 percent additional tax does not apply to IRA funds in one year to repay a loan of proceeds used in another year to pay for medical expenses.

  - *Jankelovits v. Commissioner,* T.C. Memo. 2008-285 (Dec. 22, 2008). The Tax Court refuses to cure a defective rollover transaction because the defect (a beneficiary's failure to use a direct trustee-to-trustee transfer to transfer assets) concerns a fundamental element of the statutory requirements.

- IRS guidance and private letter rulings important to IRAs:

  - Notice 2009-9 [2009-5 I.R.B. 419], explaining how owners and beneficiaries are affected by the waiver of RMDs for 2009.

  - Private Letter Ruling 200846028 (Nov. 14, 2008), in which the IRS holds a trust must actually be named on IRA beneficiary form for look-through rule to apply; phrase "as stated in wills" does not designate a beneficiary, so five-year distribution rule applies.

  - The IRS warns it will closely scrutinize retirement plan transactions for illegal circumvention of contribution limits and rules governing taxation of distributions. [News Release 2009-41, *Beware of IRS' "Dirty Dozen" Tax Scams* (Apr. 13, 2009); and IRS Memorandum, *Guidelines Regarding Rollovers as Business Start-Ups* (Oct. 1, 2008)]

  - Private Letter Ruling 200852034 (Dec. 26, 2008), in which the IRS distinguishes between payments to replace IRA losses from breach of a fiduciary duty (restorative payments not subject to contribution limits) and payments to replace losses due to market fluctuations (to which IRA contribution limits apply).

10/09

For questions concerning this shipment, billing, or other customer service matters, call our Customer Service Department at 1-800-234-1660.

For toll-free ordering, please call 1-800-638-8437.

ASPEN PUBLISHERS

Individual Retirement Account Answer Book

Sixteenth Edition

Martin Fleisher
Jo Ann Lippe

Wolters Kluwer
Law & Business

AUSTIN   BOSTON   CHICAGO   NEW YORK   THE NETHERLANDS

This publication is designed to provide accurate and authoritative information in regard to the subject matter covered. It is sold with the understanding that the publisher is not engaged in rendering legal, accounting, or other professional services. If legal advice or other professional assistance is required, the services of a competent professional person should be sought.

—From a *Declaration of Principles* jointly adopted by
a Committee of the American Bar Association and
a Committee of Publishers and Associations

Printed in the United States of America

1 2 3 4 5 6 7 8 9 0

ISBN 978-0-7355-8454-9

About Wolters Kluwer Law & Business

Wolters Kluwer Law & Business is a leading provider of research information and workflow solutions in key specialty areas. The strengths of the individual brands of Aspen Publishers, CCH, Kluwer Law International and Loislaw are aligned within Wolters Kluwer Law & Business to provide comprehensive, in-depth solutions and expert-authored content for the legal, professional and education markets.

CCH was founded in 1913 and has served more than four generations of business professionals and their clients. The CCH products in the Wolters Kluwer Law & Business group are highly regarded electronic and print resources for legal, securities, antitrust and trade regulation, government contracting, banking, pension, payroll, employment and labor, and healthcare reimbursement and compliance professionals.

Aspen Publishers is a leading information provider for attorneys, business professionals and law students. Written by preeminent authorities, Aspen products offer analytical and practical information in a range of specialty practice areas from securities law and intellectual property to mergers and acquisitions and pension/benefits. Aspen's trusted legal education resources provide professors and students with high-quality, up-to-date and effective resources for successful instruction and study in all areas of the law.

Kluwer Law International supplies the global business community with comprehensive English-language international legal information. Legal practitioners, corporate counsel and business executives around the world rely on the Kluwer Law International journals, loose-leafs, books and electronic products for authoritative information in many areas of international legal practice.

Loislaw is a premier provider of digitized legal content to small law firm practitioners of various specializations. Loislaw provides attorneys with the ability to quickly and efficiently find the necessary legal information they need, when and where they need it, by facilitating access to primary law as well as state-specific law, records, forms and treatises.

Wolters Kluwer Law & Business, a unit of Wolters Kluwer, is headquartered in New York and Riverwoods, Illinois. Wolters Kluwer is a leading multinational publisher and information services company.

ASPEN PUBLISHERS SUBSCRIPTION NOTICE

This Aspen Publishers product is updated on a periodic basis with supplements to reflect important changes in the subject matter. If you purchased this product directly from Aspen Publishers, we have already recorded your subscription for the update service.

If, however, you purchased this product from a bookstore and wish to receive future updates and revised or related volumes billed separately with a 30-day examination review, please contact our Customer Service Department at 1-800-234-1660 or send your name, company name (if applicable), address, and the title of the product to:

ASPEN PUBLISHERS
7201 McKinney Circle
Frederick, MD 21704

Important Aspen Publishers Contact Information

- To order any Aspen Publishers title, go to *www.aspenpublishers.com* or call 1-800-638-8437.

- To reinstate your manual update service, call 1-800-638-8437.

- To contact Customer Care, e-mail *customer.care@aspenpublishers .com*, call 1-800-234-1660, fax 1-800-901-9075, or mail correspondence to Order Department, Aspen Publishers, PO Box 990, Frederick, MD 21705.

- To review your account history or pay an invoice online, visit *www.aspenpublishers.com/payinvoices*.

Preface

Individual Retirement Account Answer Book is designed to provide quick, accurate, and timely answers to questions pertaining to traditional IRAs that concern accountants, attorneys, financial planners, mutual fund brokers, insurance advisors, and other pension professionals. It also contains discussions of the Roth IRA and Coverdell Education Savings Account (ESA), which continue to be powerful tools for retirement and estate planning and for achieving other long-range financial goals.

To further clarify existing and new legislation, regulations, and rulings that affect traditional IRAs, Roth IRAs, SEP IRAs, SIMPLE IRAs, and Coverdell ESAs, the book includes practice pointers, worksheets, and numerous examples. Useful addresses and telephone numbers are also provided. Because some federal forms discussed in this volume may have been replaced after preparation of the current edition began, we encourage subscribers to visit the IRS's Web site (*www.irs.gov*) and inquire at local or district IRS offices to obtain the most recent versions of the forms and publications cited in this book.

Format. The question-and-answer format provides specific, concise responses to hundreds of practical questions—a boon for professionals who need clear, concise, and authoritative answers. Citations to authority are provided as research aids for those who wish to pursue particular subjects in greater detail.

Numbering System. Within each chapter, questions are numbered consecutively (e.g., Q 2:1, Q 2:2, Q 2:3).

List of Questions. The list of questions that follows the Contents helps the reader locate areas of immediate interest. A series of subheadings helps to group and organize the questions by topic within each chapter. The list is similar to a detailed table of contents, providing both the question number and the page on which the question appears.

Examples and Practice Pointers. Throughout the chapters, numerous examples are presented to illustrate important concepts. In many chapters, useful information for practitioners is presented in the form of practice pointers.

Appendix. For the convenience of subscribers, IRS Publication 590, *Individual Retirement Arrangements (IRAs)* for preparing 2008 returns is reproduced in Appendix A, immediately following chapter 14.

Tables. At the back of the book are tables of statutes and authorities (private letter rulings, Internal Revenue Code and Treasury regulations sections, revenue rulings, revenue procedures, IRS announcements and notices, ERISA sections, and DOL opinion letters). A table of cases is also provided. All references in the tables are to question numbers, not page numbers.

Index. A comprehensive Index is provided as a further aid to locating specific information. All references in the Index are to question numbers, not page numbers.

We hope that the detailed and updated coverage of IRAs provided in this edition proves invaluable for professionals who are advising their clients about the retirement planning opportunities afforded by traditional and Roth IRAs and the Coverdell ESA.

Martin Fleisher
Jo Ann Lippe

About the Authors

Martin Fleisher, JD, is an attorney with a solo practice in New York City specializing in the areas of pensions and employee benefits. Before he established his own practice, he was associated with Kramer, Levin, Naftalis & Frankel, also in New York City. He is a graduate of Swarthmore College and the New York University School of Law.

Jo Ann Lippe, JD, MS, is an attorney in Nashville, Tennessee, specializing in tax law. Before settling in Nashville, she practiced law in New York City with Kramer, Levin, Naftalis & Frankel, and in Salt Lake City with Parsons Behle & Latimer. Ms. Lippe also served as Of Counsel to Trauger & Tuke in Nashville. She is a graduate of Tufts University, Harvard University, and the New York University School of Law.

Anthony P. Curatola, PhD, is the Joseph F. Ford Professor of Accounting at Drexel University in Philadelphia. Dr. Curatola has held a variety of leadership positions, including current national service with the Institute of Management Accountants. He is a member of the Pension Editorial Advisory Board of Wolters Kluwer Law & Business.

Dr. Curatola has been called on to provide information to the House Judiciary Committee concerning the source tax law, and he is a regular contributor to numerous journals, including *The Tax Advisor, TAXES, Oil and Gas Tax Quarterly, National Public Accountant, Benefits Quarterly, Tax Executive, Journal of Pension Planning and Compliance*, and *Tax Notes*. He has also completed sponsored research for the Louisiana Accounting and Education Foundation and the International Foundation of Employee Benefit Plans.

Acknowledgments

Individual Retirement Account Answer Book, Sixteenth Edition, is the product of the hard work and dedication of many people.

We are indebted to Professor Anthony P. Curatola for his fine work on chapter 14 of this edition, and former authors Steven G. Lockwood, Gary S. Lesser, and Susan D. Diehl for their major contributions to earlier editions of this work.

We are especially grateful to Donald R. Levy, the original author of *Individual Retirement Account Answer Book*, not only for having the vision to launch and develop this topic but, more importantly, for recognizing and developing young talent to continue his fine work.

We gratefully acknowledge the guidance, encouragement, and skills of the professionals at Wolters Kluwer Law & Business who have made this edition possible: May Wu, Senior Managing Editor for Business Compliance, and Paul Christman, Senior Manuscript Editor. Our thanks also go to Indexing Partners for expert preparation of the endmatter tables and the index.

Martin Fleisher expresses his great appreciation to his wife, Andrea, for her patience and support. Jo Ann Lippe is grateful to Doug and Jianmei Perkins for graciously tolerating her work on this edition during the family's season in Italy.

The authors are extremely grateful to Ellen Bruck for her substantial contributions to this project.

Contents

CHAPTER 7
Disclosure, Filings, Penalties, and Withholding 7-1

CHAPTER **8**

Estate and Tax Planning for Traditional IRAs 8-1

CHAPTER 13

Contents

APPENDIX **A**

TABLES

Contents

List of Questions

Chapter 1 Introduction to IRAs

Coverdell ESA

SIMPLE IRA

SEP IRA

Health Savings Account

Financial Planning

Roth IRA Versus Traditional IRA

Conversions

Attractive Uses of IRAs

Benefit of Establishing an IRA Early

Investment Options

Chapter 2 Adopting a Traditional IRA or a Roth IRA

Chapter 3 Contributions to Traditional and Roth IRAs

Special Rules for Traditional IRA Contributions

Deducting Traditional IRA Contributions

Active Participation Rules

Excess Contributions

Saver's Tax Credit for IRA Contributions

Chapter 4 Distributions from Traditional IRAs

Minimum Distributions During the IRA Owner's Lifetime

General Rule—Death Before the Required Beginning Date

Determining Which General Rule Applies

Distributions After the Beneficiary's Death

Beneficiaries

The Beneficiary Designation

Exception for Qualified Higher Education Expenses

Q 4:139 What are qualified higher education expenses? **4-50**

Q 4:140 When must education expenses be incurred for a distribution
to qualify for the exception? **4-50**

Q 4:141 May an IRA owner use the qualified higher education expenses
exception for members of his or her family? **4-50**

Q 4:142 What is an eligible educational institution for purposes of
qualified higher education expenses? **4-51**

Q 4:143 Do other tax-favored education programs reduce the amount
of education expenses available for penalty-free distributions
from an IRA? **4-51**

Qualified Health Savings Account Funding Distributions

Q 4:144 What is the one-time-only exclusion from income for a qualified
HSA funding distribution? **4-51**

Q 4:145 Who is an eligible individual? **4-52**

Q 4:146 What is the dollar limitation on a qualified HSA funding
distribution? **4-52**

Q 4:147 If the exception for changed coverage applies and a second
qualified HSA funding distribution is made, how is the testing
period determined? **4-53**

Q 4:148 What happens if the transferor ceases to be an eligible
individual at some point during the testing period? **4-53**

Q 4:149 To what year is a qualified HSA funding distribution
attributable? **4-53**

Q 4:150 May an individual contribute a qualified HSA funding
distribution to another person's HSA? **4-53**

Q 4:151 Can any type of IRA be the source of a qualified HSA funding
distribution? **4-54**

Q 4:152 May an individual combine amounts from two or more IRAs to
make a qualified HSA funding distribution? **4-54**

Q 4:153 How must funds be transferred to the HSA? **4-54**

Q 4:154 How does a qualified HSA funding distribution affect an
owner's basis in the IRA? **4-54**

Q 4:155 Is the IRA trustee or custodian required to verify that a
distribution meets the requirements for a qualified HSA
funding distribution? **4-55**

Q 4:156 Is a qualified HSA funding distribution subject to withholding? . . . **4-55**

Exception for Qualified Reservist Distributions

Q 4:157 To what distributions does the qualified reservist exception
apply? **4-55**

Special Tax Relief for Disaster Victims

Chapter 5 Roth IRA Distributions

Distributions in General

Qualified Distributions

Chapter 6 Rollovers

Rollovers from IRAs to Qualified Plans

Rollovers from Designated Roth Accounts to Roth IRAs

Rollovers from IRAs to Health Savings Accounts

Chapter 7 Disclosure, Filings, Penalties, and Withholding

Chapter 8 Estate and Tax Planning for Traditional IRAs

Chapter 9 Estate and Tax Strategies for Roth IRAs

Conversion Strategies

General

Strategies for Reducing MAGI (before 2010)

Strategies for Reducing Income Tax

Strategies for Reducing Estate Tax

Chapter 10 Income and Estate Planning Concerns for Large IRA Balances

Distributions

After the Traditional IRA Owner's Required Beginning Date

Before the IRA Owner Attains Age 59½

Prototypes

Individually Designed Forms

Approval for Combined Plans and Prior Plans

Participation

Eligible Employees

Rollovers, Conversions, and Recharacterizations

Miscellaneous Rules

Chapter 12 SIMPLE IRA Arrangements

Basic Concepts

Qualified Salary Reduction Arrangement

Establishing a SIMPLE

Employer Eligibility

Contributions

Employee Elections

Chapter 13 Coverdell Education Savings Account

Reporting

Chapter 14 State Tax Rules Regarding IRAs

Tax on Post-1995 Distributions Received from Traditional IRAs by Former Residents

Tax on Pre-1996 Distributions Received from Traditional IRAs by Former Residents

Chapter 1

Introduction to IRAs

Martin Fleisher, Esq.
Jo Ann Lippe, Esq.

An individual retirement account or annuity (IRA) was once viewed primarily as a personal retirement plan or a tax shelter. However, the Roth IRA and the Coverdell education savings account (Coverdell ESA)—along with a significantly revitalized traditional IRA—have greatly diversified the benefits of an IRA. This chapter provides an introductory overview of the various types of IRAs and explains their principal uses. IRAs are now used to accumulate funds for education expenses, first-home purchases, medical expenses, and general savings, as well as for retirement savings. Simplified employee pension plan (SEP) IRAs and savings incentive match plan for employees (SIMPLE) IRAs have extended the concept of the IRA to employer-sponsored plans. Further evidence of the evolution of the IRA can be found in the fact that its core concept—a tax deduction—does not apply to either Roth IRA or Coverdell ESA contributions. Finally, some of the best features of IRAs are combined in the health savings account (HSA), which is not a retirement account but a special purpose savings account for qualifying individuals who are covered by a high-deductible health plan.

Types of IRAs

Q 1:1   What is meant by the acronym "IRA"?

Historically, the acronym "IRA" referred to an individual retirement arrangement (account or annuity) established and maintained by an individual for his or her own benefit. Over time, Congress has expanded the use of the term *IRA* to describe any type of individual savings plan receiving federal tax benefits. The tax-favored status of an IRA—and the rules that accompany that status—is what distinguishes any type of IRA from a general savings plan.

Q 1:2   What are the different types of IRAs?

There are six types of accounts commonly referred to as IRAs. In two instances, the term *IRA* is a misnomer, and the term's definition is stretched in others. Nonetheless, for purposes of the discussion herein and in acknowledgment of popular usage, the following are categorized as IRAs.

Traditional IRA. An individual may make annual contributions to a traditional IRA (deductible or nondeductible) until the year in which he or she attains age 70½. For 2009, the maximum contribution is either $5,000 ($6,000 for individuals age 50 or older) or the individual's total earned income for the year, if less. The dollar limit is subject to increase in future years to reflect changes in the cost of living.

Whether a contribution is deductible depends on (1) whether the IRA owner (or his or her spouse) is an active participant in a retirement plan and (2) the IRA owner's adjusted gross income (AGI) (see chapter 3). Earnings in a traditional IRA grow tax deferred, but minimum amounts must be withdrawn at least annually after the IRA owner attains age 70½ or dies. Amounts may be withdrawn earlier, but a penalty is imposed if the IRA owner is younger than age 59½ and no exception applies.

Roth IRA. A Roth IRA is a type of nondeductible IRA and the dollar contribution limits for a Roth IRA are the same as those for a traditional IRA. One distinguishing feature of a Roth IRA is that distributions are potentially tax free. Also, the Roth IRA is more accessible than the traditional IRA: a Roth IRA owner may take a distribution of the principal amount at any time and for any reason without penalty (an exception applies for Roth IRAs containing assets converted from a traditional IRA). Roth IRA earnings may be withdrawn tax free before the owner attains age 59½ if they are used to pay for higher education or a first home or on account of disability. Annual contributions can continue even after the IRA owner attains age 70½ (if he or she has earned income), and minimum distributions need not occur during the IRA owner's lifetime.

Coverdell ESA. A Coverdell ESA allows an individual to make a contribution on behalf of a child to save for the child's education. The maximum annual contribution that may be made on behalf of any child is $2,000. The Coverdell ESA is not an IRA per se in that its sole purpose is to save for a child's education expenses—not for retirement.

Simplified Employee Pension Plan. A simplified employee pension (SEP) plan is an employer retirement plan that allows an employer to make contributions into the traditional IRAs of its employees. Although a SEP is not an IRA, traditional IRAs that receive employer SEP contributions are often referred to as SEP IRAs. Eligibility and contribution amounts are governed by the laws and regulations covering SEPs, which are similar to those governing retirement plans. [I.R.C. § 408(k)] Once an employer makes a contribution into a traditional IRA, the traditional IRA rules apply.

SIMPLE IRA. A SIMPLE IRA is a special type of IRA that may receive only employer contributions and employee salary deferrals. (SIMPLE is an acronym for savings incentive match plan for employees.) A SIMPLE is very similar in concept to a SEP; in fact, it replaced the salary reduction SEP (SARSEP), except for certain grandfathered plans. Once assets are in a SIMPLE IRA, the traditional IRA rules apply, with one significant exception: the 10 percent premature distribution penalty is increased to 25 percent for the first two years of participation. [I.R.C. § 72(t)(6)]

Health Savings Account. An HSA is not a retirement account, but an individual savings account with IRA-like features: a federal tax deduction may be taken at the time of contribution, earnings grow tax deferred, and qualified distributions may be taken tax free. [I.R.C. § 223]

Q 1:3 What is an individual retirement annuity?

An *individual retirement annuity* is a type of traditional IRA or Roth IRA that is issued by an insurance company qualified to do business under the laws of the jurisdiction where the contract is sold. [Treas. Reg. § 1.408-3(a)]

Q 1:4 What are the tax benefits of an IRA?

All types of IRAs share one common tax characteristic: their earnings grow tax deferred. From that common base, the tax benefits of the various IRAs diverge.

An IRA owner may be eligible for a tax deduction for contributions to a traditional IRA, but distributions from a deductible traditional IRA are generally subject to taxation. In contrast, a Roth IRA and a Coverdell ESA allow for tax-free distributions if certain conditions are met. An employer is permitted to take a tax deduction for contributions made pursuant to a SEP or a

SIMPLE IRA; distributions from a traditional IRA containing SEP contributions or from a SIMPLE IRA are subject to taxation.

Traditional IRA

Q 1:5   What is a traditional IRA?

The term *traditional IRA* simply refers to an IRA that is not a Roth IRA or a SIMPLE IRA; it also refers to a SEP IRA. Most major financial institutions and forms providers have used the term *traditional* to identify a deductible or nondeductible IRA. The Internal Revenue Service (IRS) adopted that terminology in its instructions to Form 1099-R, Distributions From Pensions, Annuities, Retirement or Profit-Sharing Plans, IRAs, Insurance Contracts, etc., and Form 5498, IRA Contribution Information, and uses it in the Roth IRA regulations. [Treas. Reg. § 1.408A-8]

Nondeductible IRA. A nondeductible IRA is a traditional IRA whose contributions are not deductible for federal income tax purposes. Individuals choose to make nondeductible contributions because earnings grow tax deferred. Nondeductible contributions are reported on Form 8606, Nondeductible IRAs, which is attached to the IRA owner's tax return.

Spousal IRA. This term refers to the special way in which a husband and wife who file a joint return are able to determine their separate *IRA contribution limits.* For this purpose, their earned income is taken into account on an aggregate basis (see Qs 3:10–3:17).

Q 1:6   When must distributions from a traditional IRA be taken?

In general, an IRA owner has complete control over when to take a distribution from an IRA. Two important exceptions exist to that general rule: attainment of age 70½ and death. Complex rules apply regarding minimum distributions from a traditional IRA, which must begin following either of those occurrences (see chapter 4). Distributions may also be required in the case of an excess contribution to an IRA. [I.R.C. § 401(a)(9)]

Q 1:7   How is a distribution from a traditional IRA taxed?

A distribution from a traditional IRA is subject to taxation on the full amount of the distribution—unless the distribution includes the return of nondeductible contribution amounts. The return of a nondeductible contribution is not a taxable event, because no tax deduction was allowed at the time of the contribution.

Q 1:8   Is a penalty imposed on an early withdrawal from a traditional IRA?

Yes. Although an IRA owner may access his or her assets in a traditional IRA at any time, the IRS imposes a 10 percent penalty on early withdrawals. [I.R.C. § 72(t)] Several exceptions allow a traditional IRA owner to avoid the premature distribution penalty: attainment of age 59½, death, disability, qualified higher education expenses, qualified first-time home purchase, substantially equal periodic payments, medical expenses in excess of certain amounts, and health insurance for unemployed individuals (see chapters 4 and 5).

Also, members of the military reserves ordered or called to active duty on or after September 11, 2001 for a period of at least 180 days or for an indefinite period, may receive IRA distributions from the time of the order or call date until the close of active duty without being liable for the 10 percent additional tax (see Q 4:157). [I.R.C. § 72(t)(2)(G), as amended by § 107 of the Heroes Earnings Assistance and Relief Tax Act of 2008, Pub. L. No. 110-205, 122 Stat. 713 (May 22, 2008)] Finally, pursuant to relief granted to persons who suffered economic losses due to the May 4, 2007, Kansas storms and tornadoes, the 10 percent premature distribution penalty does not apply to "qualified recovery assistance distributions" received from an IRA or other qualified plan. Such distributions must be received on or after May 4, 2007, and before January 1, 2009 (see Qs 4:158–4:166). [I.R.C. § 1400Q, as amended by § 15345 of the Food, Conservation, and Energy Act of 2008, Pub. L. No. 110-234]

> **Note.** *Qualified hurricane distributions* were also exempt from the early distribution penalty pursuant to relief granted in 2004 after the devastation of hurricanes Katrina, Rita, and Wilma. The exemption is now irrelevant for planning purposes because all such distributions had to be made before 2007, but a person who received a qualified hurricane distribution may still be eligible to roll it over tax free or may still have to report deferred income from the distribution on his or her current income tax return (see Qs 4:158–4:166). [I.R.C. § 1400Q]

Roth IRA

Q 1:9   What is a Roth IRA?

A *Roth IRA* is a type of individual retirement arrangement that is sometimes referred to as a "back-ended" IRA—because its tax benefits occur at the time of distribution rather than at the time of contribution. Unlike contributions to a traditional IRA, contributions to a Roth IRA are never tax deductible; however, federal income tax on earnings is at least deferred, and qualified distributions are free from federal income tax.

> **Note.** Congress created the Roth IRA because it was concerned about the low national savings rate. The theory was that individuals might be more likely to save for retirement or for certain special purposes, including the purchase of a first home, if funds set aside in a tax-favored account could be withdrawn without tax after a reasonable holding period. [Joint Comm. on Taxation, *General Explanation of Tax Legislation Enacted in 1997* (JCS-23-97)]
>
> The Roth IRA is named in honor of the late Sen. William V. Roth (R-Del.), a longtime proponent of IRAs and the legislator instrumental in the passage of the Roth IRA law.

Q 1:10   Does the Roth IRA replace the nondeductible IRA?

No, technically the Roth IRA does not replace the nondeductible IRA (see Q 1:5). However, because distributions from a Roth IRA are completely tax free as long as certain conditions are satisfied (see Q 5:10), the only individuals who should consider making nondeductible IRA contributions (from which distributions are only partially tax free) are those with incomes above the limits for the Roth IRA. Basically, the Roth IRA effectively replaces the nondeductible IRA for most eligible individuals.

Q 1:11   What types of contributions may be made to a Roth IRA?

An eligible individual may make two types of contributions to a Roth IRA: an annual contribution and a conversion contribution. (See Qs 3:83–3:86, 3:87–3:110.)

A conversion contribution is made by moving assets from a traditional IRA to a Roth IRA. Although current tax is paid on the conversion amount, the amounts in the Roth IRA attributable to the conversion receive the same favorable tax treatment as amounts contributed directly to the Roth IRA.

Q 1:12   May a Roth IRA contain both annual and conversion contributions?

Yes, a Roth IRA owner may combine annual and conversion contributions in the same Roth IRA. It should be noted that the law still treats conversion contributions differently from annual contributions, requiring a separate accounting. Both annual and conversion contributions must be accounted for on Form 8606 at the time of a distribution.

Caution. One reason for keeping conversion and annual contributions separate relates to the return of excess contributions. Commingling the two types of contributions complicates the calculation of earnings on excess contributions and can result in adverse tax consequences.

Roth IRA Versus Traditional IRA

Q 1:13   Do the rules that apply to the traditional IRA apply to the Roth IRA?

Although specific exceptions exist, the Roth IRA generally follows the same rules as the traditional IRA. [I.R.C. § 408A(a)]

Q 1:14   What are some of the similarities between the Roth IRA and the traditional IRA?

Highlighted below are some key areas in which the rules for the Roth IRA are the same as or similar to the rules for the traditional IRA.

Cash Contributions. Contributions to both a Roth IRA and a traditional IRA must be made in cash.

Contribution Deadline. Contributions to a Roth IRA must be made by the same date that applies to contributions to a traditional IRA—the due date for filing the IRA owner's tax return, not including extensions.

Contribution Amount. The maximum contribution that may be made is the same for the Roth IRA and the traditional IRA. For 2009, the limit is $5,000 ($6,000 for individuals age 50 or older); this figure is subject to annual cost-of-living increases (see Q 1:2). The contribution limit is coordinated between the Roth IRA and the traditional IRA so that the aggregate contributions for any year do not exceed the maximum amount.

Disclosure Requirements. The Roth IRA and the traditional IRA are subject to the same regulations on mandatory disclosure by the trustee or custodian. However, the actual disclosures for the two types of accounts will differ.

Earned Income. An individual must earn an income to be eligible to establish either a Roth IRA or a traditional IRA, and the individual's annual contribution is limited to the lesser of the otherwise applicable dollar maximum or the individual's earned income. However, if married individuals file a joint return, their earned income is considered in the aggregate to determine how much may be contributed to each spouse's IRA (see Qs 3:10–3:117).

Exceptions to 10 Percent Penalty for Premature Distributions. The Roth IRA and the traditional IRA are subject to the same exceptions to the 10 percent premature distribution penalty, but the distribution rules for a Roth IRA and a traditional IRA are quite different.

Investments. The investment options available to the traditional IRA are the same as those available to the Roth IRA. The Roth IRA is also subject to prohibitions against investing in life insurance or collectibles, pledging the account as security for a loan, commingling the assets with other property except in a common trust fund or a common investment fund, and engaging in a prohibited transaction (see Qs 1:47–1:54).

IRS Reporting. The IRS forms that are used to report Roth IRA contributions and distributions are the same as those used to report traditional IRA contributions and distributions.

Movement of Assets Between Like Accounts. The rules applicable to moving assets from a Roth IRA to a new Roth IRA are the same as those that apply when assets of a traditional IRA are moved to a new traditional IRA via a rollover or transfer.

Spousal IRA Rules. The Roth IRA and the traditional IRA follow similar rules regarding the ability to make contributions on behalf of lesser-compensated spouses.

Tax-Deferred Growth of Earnings. The earnings in both a Roth IRA and a traditional IRA avoid federal income taxes while protected in the IRA. At the time of distribution, however, the Roth IRA earnings are generally tax free while the traditional IRA earnings are subject to taxation.

Trustee or Custodial Requirements. The requirements for a trustee or a custodian of a traditional IRA also apply to a trustee or custodian of a Roth IRA.

Q 1:15   What are some of the key differences between the Roth IRA and the traditional IRA?

The Roth IRA and the traditional IRA are more alike than different, but there are significant differences.

Access to Funds. Assets in a Roth IRA are generally more accessible to the IRA owner than are assets in a traditional IRA (see Q 5:3).

Age-Limited Contributions. Annual contributions to a traditional IRA must cease beginning with the year in which the IRA owner attains age 70½. No age limit applies for annual contributions a Roth IRA.

Eligibility. The eligibility rules for the Roth IRA and the traditional IRA are quite different (see Qs 3:2, 3:3).

IRS Penalties. Although the Roth IRA and the traditional IRA are subject to many of the same penalties imposed by the IRS, significant differences also exist (see chapters 4 and 5).

Movement of Assets Between Different Types of Plans. The rules for rollovers and transfers from various types of retirement plans to a Roth IRA differ from those for rollovers and transfers to a traditional IRA. A Roth IRA may receive assets converted from a traditional SEP or SIMPLE IRA. A traditional IRA may receive assets directly from any qualified plan, but a Roth IRA may receive assets only from a designated Roth account within a qualified plan. However, the Roth IRA, unlike the traditional IRA, may not receive assets directly from a qualified plan (see chapter 6).

Required Minimum Distributions. The Roth IRA is not subject to the required minimum distribution (RMD) rules that apply to the traditional IRA when the IRA owner attains age 70½ (although Roth IRA beneficiaries must still meet RMD rules) (see chapter 4 and Qs 5:49, 5:51–5:53).

Tax Treatment of Contributions. Contributions to a Roth IRA are never tax deductible, whereas a tax deduction may be allowed for a contribution to a traditional IRA (see chapter 3).

Taxation of Distributions. Distributions from a Roth IRA meeting certain qualification requirements are free from federal income taxes, whereas distributions from a traditional IRA are subject to federal income tax (see Qs 4:1–4:7, 5:1–5:8).

Coverdell ESA

Q 1:16   What is a Coverdell ESA?

A *Coverdell education savings account* (formerly known as an Education IRA) is a vehicle that an individual may use to save for a child's education on a tax-favored basis. Contributions to the Coverdell ESA may be made only on behalf of an already-born child under the age of 18. (The age limit does not apply to special needs beneficiaries.) The Coverdell ESA is a back-ended IRA, similar to the Roth IRA, for which no deduction is allowed for contributions.

The Coverdell ESA's principal tax advantages are the tax-free growth of its earnings and the ability to take tax-free withdrawals for education expenses.

Note. The Coverdell ESA, although not a retirement account, is referred to as an IRA because it borrows many of its design features and rules from the traditional IRA.

Q 1:17 May a Coverdell ESA ever be used as a retirement account?

No. The Coverdell ESA is not a retirement planning tool because any assets remaining in a Coverdell ESA must be fully distributed by the time the beneficiary reaches age 30, except for a special needs beneficiary. [I.R.C. § 530(b)(1)(E)]

Q 1:18 What are some key similarities between the Coverdell ESA and the traditional IRA or the Roth IRA?

The key areas in which the rules for the Coverdell ESA are the same as or substantially similar to the rules for the traditional IRA or the Roth IRA are as follows:

Cash Contributions. Contributions to a Coverdell ESA, like contributions to a traditional IRA and a Roth IRA, must be made in cash.

Investments. Although the investment rules for the Coverdell ESA are not fully explained in the law, the permitted investment vehicles appear to be the same as those allowed for the traditional IRA and the Roth IRA, which include certificates of deposit, time accounts, stocks, mutual funds, bonds, other securities, and most other investment vehicles. Like the traditional IRA and the Roth IRA, a Coverdell ESA may not be invested in life insurance, be pledged as security for a loan, have its assets commingled with other property except in a common investment fund, or take part in prohibited transactions (see Qs 1:47–1:54).

IRS Reporting. Like trustees and custodians of traditional IRAs and Roth IRAs, trustees and custodians of Coverdell ESAs use Form 1099-R and Form 5498-ESA for information reporting. An individual taxpayer uses Form 5498 for reporting traditional IRAs and Roth IRAs (see chapter 7).

Movement of Assets Between Like Accounts. Assets in a Coverdell ESA may be moved to a new Coverdell ESA via a rollover or transfer. The rules that apply to the rollover or transfer of assets in a Coverdell ESA are similar to those that apply to a rollover or transfer of assets from a traditional IRA to a new traditional IRA and from a Roth IRA to a new Roth IRA (see chapter 6).

Tax-Deferred Growth of Earnings. Earnings in the Coverdell ESA, traditional IRA, and Roth IRA all grow with federal income tax deferred while invested in the IRA. At the time of distribution, earnings in the Coverdell ESA (and the Roth IRA) may be free from federal income tax.

Trustee or Custodial Requirements. Assets in a Coverdell ESA must be held by a trustee or custodian—the same requirement that applies to the Roth IRA and the traditional IRA. The rules for becoming a Coverdell ESA trustee or custodian are the same as those for becoming a traditional IRA or Roth IRA trustee or custodian (see Qs 2:13–2:17).

Q 1:19   What are some of the key differences between the Coverdell ESA and the traditional IRA or the Roth IRA?

The Coverdell ESA has little relationship to the traditional IRA or the Roth IRA, as follows.

Contribution Amount. Contributions to a Coverdell ESA are limited to $2,000 per child per year *from all donors combined.*

Eligibility. The dollar thresholds and the eligibility rules for the Coverdell ESA and the traditional or Roth IRA are quite different. The amount that joint filers of income tax returns can contribute to a Coverdell ESA is gradually reduced if the filers' modified adjusted gross income (MAGI) is more than $190,000 but less than $220,000. No contributions are permitted for joint filers with MAGI of $220,000 or above. In addition to the income limits on the contributor, the designated beneficiary must meet eligibility rules (i.e., be under age 18 unless he or she is a special needs beneficiary).

Full Distribution at Age 30. The Coverdell ESA provides for a mandatory full distribution when the designated beneficiary (except for a special needs beneficiary) attains age 30, a rule not applicable to the Roth IRA or the traditional IRA. (The traditional IRA requires distributions to commence at age 70½.)

Movement of Assets Between Different Plan Types. Assets in a Coverdell ESA may never be moved to a Roth IRA, traditional IRA, or qualified retirement plan; they may be moved only to another Coverdell ESA.

Parties to the Agreement. Unlike the Roth IRA or the traditional IRA, the Coverdell ESA will generally be established by one person for the benefit of another. Indeed, in many cases, a third party may control the account.

Purpose of the Account. The Coverdell ESA is not a retirement savings account; unlike the traditional IRA or the Roth IRA, the Coverdell ESA is used exclusively to save for education expenses.

Rollover to a New Designated Beneficiary. Assets in a Coverdell ESA may be rolled over to another Coverdell ESA for the benefit of a new designated beneficiary. Neither a traditional IRA nor a Roth IRA may be rolled over to anyone else, except to the spouse of the IRA owner in the case of the owner's death or divorce (see chapter 6).

Tax Treatment of Contributions. Contributions to a Coverdell ESA are not tax deductible. Such contributions, however, count as part of the $11,000 annual gift tax exclusion for the contributor.

Tax Treatment of Distributions. Distributions from a Coverdell ESA are tax free only if used for qualified education expenses; other distributions are subject to a pro rata return of principal and earnings. Principal and earnings are similarly prorated when distributed from a nondeductible traditional IRA, but all distributions from a deductible traditional IRA are fully taxable. The Roth IRA allows for all contributions to be returned before earnings.

SIMPLE IRA

Q 1:20   What is a SIMPLE IRA?

A *SIMPLE IRA* is a type of IRA that may receive only contributions made pursuant to a savings incentive match plan for employees (SIMPLE). For the most part, other than the rules on contributions, the same rules apply to a SIMPLE IRA as do to a traditional IRA. The significant exception is that the 10 percent premature distribution penalty associated with IRAs is increased to 25 percent for the first two years of participation in a SIMPLE (see chapter 12).

Q 1:21   What are SIMPLE contributions?

SIMPLE contributions are contributions made pursuant to an employer's savings incentive match plan for employees, under which employees are allowed to defer a portion of their compensation. The employer also makes contributions—either a matching contribution or an employer nonelective contribution.

A SIMPLE IRA shares the underlying concept of a 401(k) plan; one of its distinguishing features, however, is that a SIMPLE IRA does not maintain a collective trust. Instead, all SIMPLE contributions must be made into the participants' SIMPLE IRAs established by or for each participant.

SEP IRA

Q 1:22   What are SEP contributions?

SEP contributions are contributions made by an employer into an IRA pursuant to an employer's simplified employee pension plan (see chapter 11). It is important to note that even though SEP contributions are made into traditional IRAs, the rules governing IRA contributions do not apply.

Q 1:23   What is a SEP IRA?

A *SEP IRA* is an IRA that receives employer contributions made pursuant to a SEP. The only distinction between a SEP IRA and a traditional IRA is that the trustee or custodian receiving the contributions must report the type of IRA appropriately. Once the assets are properly placed in the IRA, a SEP IRA follows the same rules as a traditional IRA.

Note. Many an IRA owner makes his or her annual contributions into the same IRA into which the owner's employer makes the SEP contribution.

Health Savings Account

Q 1:24   What is a health savings account?

A health savings account (HSA) is a tax-favored savings account that may be used to accumulate funds for qualified medical expenses. An individual must be covered by a high-deductible health plan (HDHP) to make HSA contributions, but that coverage need not be in effect when the funds are withdrawn. The individual's employer may also contribute to the HSA.

Q 1:25   How is an HSA similar to an IRA?

HSAs, like IRAs, are established as trust or custodial accounts. Contributions to an HSA are subject to an annual maximum, and are tax deductible (as may be true for traditional IRA contributions). The range of investments for HSAs is similar to that for IRAs, and earnings are also allowed to grow untaxed. Withdrawals from an HSA may be excluded from income (similar to a Roth IRA), but only if the funds are used to pay for qualified medical expenses. Finally, like the SEP IRA and the SIMPLE IRA (see Qs 1:20–1:23), an HSA belongs to the individual for whom it is established even after employment is terminated.

Q 1:26   How is an HSA different from an IRA?

A different set of contribution limits applies to the HSA. Most important, though, is that the HSA is the only truly tax-free savings vehicle, with contributions that are tax deductible, earnings that grow untaxed, and distributions that are excluded from income—provided the applicable requirements are met.

Financial Planning

Roth IRA Versus Traditional IRA

Q 1:27   Which provides the better tax and other benefits—the Roth IRA or the traditional IRA?

Factors to consider when choosing between a Roth IRA and a traditional IRA include the following:

1. *Eligibility*. It is much more likely that an individual will be eligible for the Roth IRA, with its higher income limits, than for the deductible traditional IRA. Of course, some individuals may not be eligible for either a deductible traditional IRA or a Roth IRA; for them, the only option is a nondeductible IRA.

2. *Future tax bracket (at time of distribution).* An individual who expects his or her tax bracket to be lower in retirement (frequently the case) may prefer the deductible traditional IRA to the Roth IRA.

3. *Age.* An individual over age 70½ who has earned income may make contributions to a Roth IRA—but not to a traditional IRA.

4. *Reason for saving.* The Roth IRA allows for easier and earlier access to contribution amounts than does a traditional IRA. A Roth IRA owner may access his or her contribution amounts free of tax and penalty, even if he or she is not making the withdrawal for a qualified reason. Any withdrawal from a traditional IRA is subject to taxes and penalty (unless an exception to the penalty applies). Accordingly, a Roth IRA may be a better vehicle for an individual who wants to save for the long term but also wants an emergency fund. The Roth IRA also provides more estate planning opportunities than a traditional IRA because distributions are not required during the Roth IRA owner's lifetime.

5. *Current financial situation.* The better an individual's current financial position, the more the individual may be willing to forgo a current deduction in exchange for a future tax break. The contrary is also true: if an individual has an immediate, urgent need for the current tax deduction, the attractions of a traditional IRA may outweigh those of a Roth IRA.

6. *Miscellaneous factors.* Obviously, many other factors—some beyond an individual's control—will help determine which type of IRA should be established. For instance, are taxes expected to go up or down in the next 10, 20, or 30 years? Do state taxes in the taxpayer's state of residence apply to his or her Roth IRA?

Practice Pointer. The "pay taxes now or later" evaluation is an oversimplification of the basic difference between the Roth IRA and the deductible traditional IRA because, as has just been shown, many other factors come into play.

Q 1:28   What resources are available to help an individual choose between a Roth IRA and a traditional IRA?

Financial planners, accountants, and attorneys are likely to be in the best position to help an individual decide between the Roth IRA and the traditional IRA (and to determine whether to convert a traditional IRA into a Roth IRA). Software is available to aid in the determination, as well. A number of banks, insurance companies, mutual funds, and other financial organizations offer the use of IRA "calculators" free on their Web pages or make the software available for a nominal charge; many institutions also provide worksheets as tools for completing comparison calculations.

Q 1:29   Is the Roth IRA a better choice than the nondeductible traditional IRA when either is available to be chosen?

The Roth IRA is *always* a better choice than the nondeductible traditional IRA. The Roth IRA has the advantage that contribution amounts are returned tax free and penalty free first, before earnings are returned. On the other hand, the nondeductible IRA rules require that each distribution consist of a ratio of taxable and nontaxable earnings. Furthermore, if the proper conditions are satisfied, the Roth IRA enjoys tax-free growth of earnings instead of the merely tax-deferred earnings that exist in a nondeductible IRA (see Qs 1:5, 1:9).

Q 1:30   Over a long period of time and with constant tax rates, does the Roth IRA achieve better results than the deductible traditional IRA?

No. The assets actually available for distribution on an after-tax basis will be identical for a Roth IRA and a deductible traditional IRA over any period when the taxpayer's bracket remains constant.

Example. Kate has $5,000 in pretax dollars to contribute to an IRA for 2009, but she is unsure whether the Roth IRA or the deductible traditional IRA (she is eligible for both) is a better choice for her. Kate is in the 28 percent tax bracket and expects to be in that tax bracket at the time she takes distributions from her IRA. Accordingly, she may contribute $5,000 to a traditional IRA or $3,600 ($5,000 reduced by a 28% income tax rate) to a Roth IRA. If Kate's tax bracket remains unchanged, the results for each IRA will be identical.

Assumptions	
a. Annual contribution amount	$5,000 (traditional IRA)/ $3,600 (Roth IRA)
b. The number of years before Kate plans to retire	20
c. The annual return Kate anticipates from her investments	8%
d. Preretirement federal tax rate	28%
e. Postretirement federal tax rate	28%
f. Full distribution at retirement	
g. Contribution at end of year	

$180,000
$175,000
$170,000
$165,000
$160,000
$155,000
$150,000
$145,000

$177,923	$177,923
Roth IRA	Deductible IRA

Q 1:31   **Over a long period of time and with a lower tax bracket at the time of distribution, does the Roth IRA achieve better results than the deductible traditional IRA?**

No. The deductible traditional IRA provides better results than the Roth IRA when an individual's tax bracket is expected to drop at the time of distribution.

Example. The facts are the same as those in the example in Q 1:30, except that Kate is currently in the 33 percent tax bracket and expects to be in the 28 percent bracket at the time of distribution. In that case, the deductible traditional IRA would be the better choice.

Assumptions

a. Annual contribution amount $5,000 (traditional IRA)/ $3,350 (Roth IRA)

b. The number of years before Kate plans to retire   20

c. The annual return Kate anticipates from her investments   8%

d. Preretirement federal tax rate   33%

e. Postretirement federal tax rate   28%

f. Full distribution at retirement

g. Contribution at end of year

$190,000
$185,000
$180,000
$175,000
$170,000
$165,000
$160,000
$155,000
$150,000
$145,000
$140,000

$177,923

$165,567

Roth IRA   Deductible IRA

Q 1:32   Over a long period of time and with a higher tax bracket at the time of distribution, does the Roth IRA achieve better results than the deductible traditional IRA?

Generally, the Roth IRA will provide better results than the deductible traditional IRA when the IRA owner's tax bracket is higher at the time of distribution.

Example. The facts are the same as those in the example in Q 1:30, except that Kate is currently in the 15 percent tax bracket and expects to be in the 28 percent bracket at retirement. In this case, the Roth IRA is the better choice for Kate.

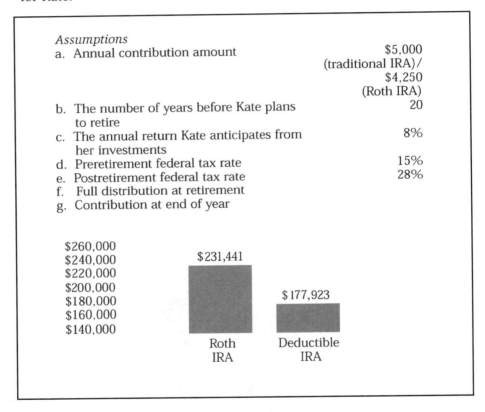

Assumptions

a. Annual contribution amount — $5,000 (traditional IRA)/ $4,250 (Roth IRA)

b. The number of years before Kate plans to retire — 20

c. The annual return Kate anticipates from her investments — 8%

d. Preretirement federal tax rate — 15%

e. Postretirement federal tax rate — 28%

f. Full distribution at retirement

g. Contribution at end of year

Roth IRA: $231,441

Deductible IRA: $177,923

Q 1:33   Is a $5,000 contribution to a Roth IRA a bigger investment than a $5,000 contribution to a deductible traditional IRA?

Yes. A $5,000 contribution to a Roth IRA represents after-tax dollars. The $5,000 deductible traditional IRA contribution really represents an amount less than $5,000 because the federal government will collect its taxes due on the $5,000 at the time of distribution. Accordingly, an individual who wants the largest tax-deferred benefits will elect to establish a Roth IRA.

Example. Leo, whose primary objective is to save as much as possible for his retirement, is trying to decide whether to establish a deductible traditional IRA or a Roth IRA. If Leo makes a $5,000 deductible traditional IRA contribution, he will receive a current tax benefit, but the assets in the IRA will be subject to taxation at the time of distribution. In a sense, Leo's contribution for retirement is less than $5,000 because of the future tax obligation; that is, if Leo is, for instance, in the 28 percent tax bracket at the time of distribution, his $5,000 contribution in reality represents only $3,600 that he can use in retirement. The earnings Leo will make on the $5,000 could also be viewed as less than fully available for his retirement because of the future tax obligation on the earnings. A $5,000 Roth IRA contribution, however, represents after-tax dollars and is a full $5,000. Also, all the earnings on the $5,000 will be available to Leo on a tax-free basis.

Conversions

Q 1:34   What are the significant factors used to determine whether a conversion from a traditional IRA to a Roth IRA is desirable?

Significant factors used to evaluate whether a conversion from a traditional IRA to a Roth IRA is a wise choice for an IRA owner are: (1) the owner's current tax rate, (2) the owner's predicted tax rate at the time of distribution, and (3) the owner's ability or desire to pay the taxes currently.

Note. Conversions are subject to eligibility requirements in 2009, but these are eliminated as of 2010. Tax deferral is available for conversions that occur in 2010, the transition year. (See Q 3:92.)

Q 1:35   Do assets converted from a traditional IRA to a Roth IRA become more accessible?

Yes. One reason an IRA owner may choose to convert a traditional IRA to a Roth IRA is to have easier and earlier access to his or her savings. The assets in a traditional IRA generally are not available without penalty until the owner attains age 59½. The contribution amount (the conversion amount) in a Roth IRA, on the other hand, is available free of tax and penalty after five years (see chapters 2 and 5). Thus, the owner of a traditional IRA who is younger than age 59½ can gain earlier access to his or her IRA funds by converting to a Roth IRA.

Example. Randall, age 40, has a traditional IRA valued at $30,000 and works for a company that provides excellent retirement benefits. Because he does not need his traditional IRA for retirement, Randall decides to use its assets to buy a pleasure boat. If he takes a distribution from his traditional IRA, he will owe taxes, plus a 10 percent penalty. Instead, he chooses to convert his traditional IRA into a Roth IRA. He still has to pay taxes, but he avoids the 10 percent penalty. (If Randall waits five years, he may withdraw the full $30,000 from his Roth IRA tax and penalty free. Any earnings in the account would have to remain in the Roth IRA, however, or they would be subject to taxes and penalties.)

Q 1:36 Does it make financial sense to convert a traditional IRA to a Roth IRA and then use IRA assets to pay the taxes on the conversion?

In general, no. If an IRA owner cannot afford to pay the taxes that result from a conversion to a Roth IRA without using IRA assets, converting is not as a rule desirable. In addition to reducing the size of the retirement fund, the amount used to pay the taxes will be subject to a 10 percent penalty. The imposition of that penalty makes it unlikely that the Roth IRA would be superior to the traditional IRA when the taxes are paid from IRA assets.

Q 1:37 Over a long savings horizon and with a constant tax rate, does the conversion of a traditional IRA to a Roth IRA result in more dollars available for retirement?

Yes. The conversion of a traditional IRA to a Roth IRA will result in more after-tax assets being available for retirement, when the IRA owner's tax bracket remains constant and he or she has the ability to pay the taxes on the conversion from funds outside the IRA.

Example. Jean converts her $100,000 deductible traditional IRA to a Roth IRA. Jean is in the 28 percent tax bracket and expects to remain in that tax bracket at the time of distribution; she also has $28,000 in other savings earning 8 percent interest. Jean's savings are enough to pay the taxes she owes on the $100,000 conversion. She expects that she will retire in 30 years and will not need to access her Roth IRA before that date. As shown, the Roth IRA will give Jean more assets as a lump-sum distribution after 30 years.

Assumptions	
a. Conversion amount	$100,000
b. The number of years before Jean plans to retire	30
c. The annual return Jean anticipates from her investments	8%
d. Preretirement federal tax rate	28%
e. Postretirement federal tax rate	28%
f. Full distribution	
g. Contribution at end of year	

$1,500,000		
$1,450,000	$1,446,711	
$1,400,000		$1,367,820
$1,350,000		
$1,300,000		
$1,250,000		
$1,200,000		
	Roth IRA	Deductible IRA and other

Q 1:38   If an IRA owner's tax bracket drops at the time of distribution, does a conversion from a traditional IRA to a Roth IRA still result in more assets being available at the time of retirement?

Perhaps. If an IRA owner's tax bracket drops at the time of distribution, the conversion to a Roth IRA may, after the fact, appear to have been the less desirable choice. Given a sufficiently long period of time, however, the conversion probably will result in more after-tax assets being available for retirement as long as sufficient assets exist outside the IRA to pay the conversion tax.

Q 1:39   Why would an IRA owner want to convert a traditional IRA to a Roth IRA if doing so creates immediate tax liability?

Although conversion to a Roth IRA requires payment of taxes at the time of conversion, tax liability is avoided in the future. A taxpayer's goals may make avoidance of future tax liability advantageous (see Q 3:99).

Q 1:40   Is a conversion to a Roth IRA more desirable when the traditional IRA contains nondeductible contributions?

Yes. The larger the percentage of nondeductible contributions contained in a traditional IRA, the more desirable it is to convert to a Roth IRA because no taxes are owed on the conversion of nondeductible contributions. Only the earnings and the return of deductible contributions will be subject to federal income taxes. Furthermore, the Roth IRA allows for tax-free growth of earnings, whereas the traditional IRA provides for only tax-deferred growth.

Note. An IRA owner is not allowed to convert only the nondeductible contributions. A pro rata share of taxable and nontaxable amounts will be considered converted if an individual does not convert his or her entire traditional IRA balance.

Attractive Uses of IRAs

Q 1:41   What are some of the most attractive uses of an IRA?

The traditional IRA, the Roth IRA, and the Coverdell ESA provide some or all of the following features:

- A convenient depository and a disciplined method for annual savings
- A tax deduction in the case of some traditional IRA contributions
- A way to achieve tax-free (Roth IRA and Coverdell ESA) or tax-deferred (traditional IRA) growth of assets
- Tax-sheltered annuity arrangements and a means to continue tax-deferred growth of untaxed distributions from qualified plans (traditional IRA)
- A supplemental source of retirement income
- A source for emergency funds

- A source of funds for a child's education
- A source of funds for a first home
- A vehicle for pursuing several investment options
- A way to retain transferability
- An opportunity to maintain individual control of retirement funds or other funds
- An instrument for completing an individual's financial plan

Q 1:42   Why are any of the IRA types a convenient place for annual savings?

IRAs can be established quite easily, with little more effort than is required to open a checking account at a bank. Regular deposit of contributions through payroll deduction is usually simple to arrange. A taxpayer may even direct the IRS to deposit all or part of a tax refund directly to a traditional, Roth, or SEP IRA—but not a SIMPLE IRA (see Q 3:44). When it comes to savings, however, the tax benefits of an IRA are the key considerations. An IRA owner enjoys tax-deferred growth of assets in each type of IRA and may qualify for up-front tax deductions to a traditional IRA. Contributions to a Roth IRA or Coverdell ESA are not tax deductible, but distributions are tax free if taken for a qualified reason. It must be remembered, however, that distributions from all three types of IRAs may be assessed a penalty—in most cases, 10 percent—if assets are withdrawn prematurely or for nonqualified reasons and that the penalty could cancel out any tax benefit received from the IRA.

> **Example 1.** Ronald contributes $5,000 to a traditional IRA and claims a tax deduction for that amount. Because his marginal income tax rate is 25 percent, Ronald saves $1,250 in taxes. The IRA grows at the rate of 9 percent per year. After eight years, and before he reaches age 59½, Ronald withdraws the entire balance of $9,963 ($5,000 × 1.09 to the eighth power). After paying taxes, Ronald is left with $6,476 ($9,963, less income taxes of $2,491 and a 10 percent penalty of $996).

> Had Ronald invested in a non-IRA account, he would have been able to save only $3,750 ($5,000, less $1,250 in taxes). After taxes were paid on the interest earned each year, the account would have grown at the rate of 6.75 percent (0.09 × (1.0 − 0.25)). After eight years, Ronald would have accumulated $6,324 ($3,750 × 1.0675 to the eighth power), with all taxes paid, in his non-IRA bank account.

> Thus, Ronald earns $152 more in spendable income by establishing an IRA, even though he has to pay the 10 percent premature distribution penalty.

> **Example 2.** The facts are the same as those in Example 1, except that Ronald contributes $3,750 to a Roth IRA instead of contributing to a traditional IRA. He will receive no tax deduction; however, he hopes to enjoy the tax-free use of his earnings in the future. After eight years, Ronald is forced to withdraw the entire balance of $7,472 ($3,750 × 1.09 to the eighth power) before he

meets an exception to the 10 percent premature distribution penalty. Ronald must pay a 10 percent penalty on the earnings portion of the distribution; the original contribution amount of $3,750 is not subject to any penalty. Ronald's penalty amount is $372. Also, Ronald must pay taxes in the amount of $931 on the earnings of $3,722. That leaves Ronald with $6,169 ($7,472 − $372 penalty − $931 taxes). Had Ronald placed his $3,750 in a regular savings account, it would have grown at an effective rate of 6.75 percent. At the end of eight years he would have had $6,324. The $6,324 would have been already fully taxed and not subject to penalty. Accordingly, Ronald would have been better off placing his assets in a regular savings account, by $154.

Q 1:43 How may a traditional IRA or Roth IRA be useful as a depository for accumulated retirement money from qualified plans?

Since 1986, holding rollover assets from qualified plans has been one of the primary uses of the traditional IRA. It is frequently the case that after retirement or termination of employment with a company, an individual will want to move assets from a qualified retirement plan to an IRA to more directly control the investment and distribution of those assets while avoiding the full tax consequences of taking the assets directly. A rollover to a traditional IRA is useful for maintaining a retirement fund that has already been developed under another plan; to avoid 20 percent mandatory withholding on the distribution, a rollover can be made directly from the plan to the IRA (see chapter 6).

Many 401(k) and 403(b) plans now include a qualified Roth IRA contribution program. This feature allows participants to elect the designation of part or all of their elective deferrals to the plan as after-tax Roth contributions. [I.R.C. § 402A; Prop. Treas. Reg. § 1.402A-1] The resulting *designated Roth IRA account* (DRAC) is an account within the qualified plan, not a Roth IRA. DRAC assets may, however, be rolled over to a Roth IRA, where they are exempted from the lifetime minimum distribution requirements and generally less favorable basis recovery rules that apply to qualified plan distributions. The rollover may produce some unfavorable consequences, so caution is warranted (see Qs 6:103–6:106).

Q 1:44 How is an IRA useful as a depository for emergency funds?

The Roth IRA serves as an excellent depository for emergency funds because the Roth IRA owner may take a distribution of his or her annual contribution amounts at any time and for any reason tax free and penalty free (see Qs 5:24, 5:42). In some cases, however, earnings must remain in the account in order to avoid taxes and penalties. The traditional IRA is not as well suited to emergency savings because distributions are subject to taxes and penalties.

Q 1:45   How is an IRA useful as a way to retain transferability?

One of the most valuable features of the traditional IRA, the Roth IRA, and the Coverdell ESA is the ability they afford the IRA owner to transfer his or her investments without any penalty. The transfer may be effected either by a trustee to another trustee or by a rollover. Trustee-to-trustee transfers are unlimited in amount and frequency. A rollover may be accomplished only once a year, but *each* IRA has the once-a-year opportunity—and an individual may have as many separate IRAs as he or she wishes to create. [I.R.C. § 408(d)(4)(B); Treas. Reg. § 1.408-4(b)(4)(ii)] (The rules limiting rollovers to once annually apply separately to the traditional IRA, the Roth IRA, and the Coverdell ESA; the one-year period starts on the day that the amount is received from the IRA making the distribution.)

Benefit of Establishing an IRA Early

Q 1:46   What is the advantage of establishing an IRA as early as possible?

The advantage of beginning IRA savings as early as possible, and thus lengthening the deferral period, is best demonstrated by an example. It should be noted that, although the following example assumes a traditional IRA, the principle of tax deferral on earnings also applies to the Roth IRA and the Coverdell ESA. Further, the Roth IRA and the Coverdell ESA have the advantage that qualified distributions will be tax free.

> **Example.** Ed begins to make annual contributions to a traditional IRA when he is age 22. He invests $5,000 each year for nine years until he reaches age 30, and then never adds another penny. The IRA grows at 10 percent each year. At retirement (age 65), as shown in the accompanying table, Ed has $2,098,890 in his account. Lisa, who is the same age as Ed, waits until she is age 35 to begin making annual IRA contributions. She also defers $5,000 and continues doing so until she reaches age 65. Lisa never catches up with Ed, even though Ed does not contribute money after his nine deposits and even though Lisa contributes $110,000 more than Ed does. Ed ends up with more than twice as much as Lisa.

IRA Deposits and Accumulations

Ed			Lisa	
Deposit	*Accumulation*	*Age*	*Deposit*	*Accumulation*
5,000	5,500	22	0	0
5,000	11,550	23	0	0
5,000	18,205	24	0	0
5,000	25,526	25	0	0
5,000	33,578	26	0	0
5,000	42,436	27	0	0

IRA Deposits and Accumulations (*cont'd*)

	Ed			Lisa	
Deposit	*Accumulation*	*Age*	*Deposit*	*Accumulation*	
5,000	52,179	28	0	0	
5,000	62,897	29	0	0	
5,000	74,687	30	0	0	
0	82,156	31	0	0	
0	90,371	32	0	0	
0	99,409	33	0	0	
0	109,349	34	0	0	
0	120,284	35	5,000	5,500	
0	132,313	36	5,000	11,550	
0	145,544	37	5,000	18,205	
0	160,098	38	5,000	25,526	
0	176,108	39	5,000	33,578	
0	193,719	40	5,000	42,436	
0	213,091	41	5,000	52,179	
0	234,400	42	5,000	62,897	
0	257,840	43	5,000	74,687	
0	283,624	44	5,000	87,656	
0	311,987	45	5,000	101,921	
0	343,185	46	5,000	117,614	
0	377,504	47	5,000	134,875	
0	415,254	48	5,000	153,862	
0	456,780	49	5,000	174,749	
0	502,458	50	5,000	197,724	
0	552,703	51	5,000	222,996	
0	607,974	52	5,000	250,795	
0	668,771	53	5,000	281,375	
0	735,648	54	5,000	315,012	
0	809,213	55	5,000	352,014	
0	890,134	56	5,000	392,715	
0	979,148	57	5,000	437,487	
0	1,077,063	58	5,000	486,735	
0	1,184,769	59	5,000	540,909	
0	1,303,246	60	5,000	600,500	
0	1,433,570	61	5,000	666,050	

IRA Deposits and Accumulations (*cont'd*)

	Ed			Lisa	
Deposit	*Accumulation*	*Age*	*Deposit*	*Accumulation*	
0	1,576,927	62	5,000	738,155	
0	1,734,620	63	5,000	817,470	
0	1,908,082	64	5,000	904,717	
0	2,098,890	65	5,000	1,000,689	

Investment Options

Q 1:47   What are the investment options for traditional and Roth IRAs?

Investments permissible for traditional and Roth IRAs include the following:

- Certificates of deposit (CDs);
- Savings accounts;
- Money market mutual funds;
- Mutual funds;
- Stocks, bonds, annuities; and
- A substantial number of other investment vehicles.

In addition, IRAs are allowed to hold certain U.S. government-issued gold and silver coins and certain state-issued coins, including U.S. government-issued gold, silver, platinum, and palladium coins, as well as gold, silver, platinum, and palladium bullion meeting certain standards of fineness. [I.R.C. § 408(m)]

Q 1:48   Are IRA trustees and custodians required to offer precious metals as investment options?

No. Most trustees and custodians are unlikely to offer those precious metals as investment options. Investments in gold, silver, platinum, and palladium are optional for IRA trustees and custodians.

Q 1:49   Are there any special rules that must be met for institutions offering investment by an IRA in precious metals?

Yes. Any gold, silver, platinum, or palladium bullion must be kept in the physical possession of the IRA trustee or custodian. [I.R.C. § 408(m)(3)] This requirement adds to the expense of allowing precious metals as an investment option, and the trustee or custodian can charge a fee to cover the cost of handling such metals. As an alternative to direct acquisition of the bullion, the IRA may acquire shares of an investment that tracks the price of the bullion in the physical market. [*See* Priv. Ltr. Rul. 200732026 (Oct. 8, 2007).]

Q 1:50   May IRAs be invested in life insurance?

No. Individuals are prohibited from investing in life insurance in their IRAs. [I.R.C. § 408(e)(5)]

Q 1:51   May IRA assets be invested in collectibles?

No part of the funds in an IRA may be invested in collectibles, including any work of art, rug or antique, metal or gem, stamp or coin, alcoholic beverage, or other tangible property specified by the IRS. [I.R.C. § 408(m)] There is an exception for certain coins and bullion (see Q 1:47). If an individual uses IRA assets to purchase a collectible, the amount so used will be treated as a distribution.

Q 1:52   May IRA assets be pledged as security for a loan?

No. If during any taxable year the owner of an IRA uses the account or any portion thereof as security for a loan, the portion so used is treated as a distribution to that individual. [I.R.C. § 408(e)(4)]

Q 1:53   May the assets in an IRA be forfeited?

No. The Code provides that the assets in an IRA are nonforfeitable. [I.R.C. § 408(a)(4); *see also* IRS Form 5305-R, Article III.]

Q 1:54   Are IRAs subject to the prohibited transaction rules?

Yes. IRAs are subject to the rules against prohibited transactions (see chapter 4). Generally, a prohibited transaction occurs when a disqualified person (often the IRA owner) engages in a transaction involving the IRA. [I.R.C. § 4975] The consequences of engaging in a prohibited transaction are that the IRA will lose its tax exemption as of the first day of the year of the transaction and the account will be treated as distributing all of its assets on that day. [I.R.C. § 408(e)]

Because disqualified person status may be indirectly attributed, fiduciaries of an IRA must tread carefully when directing the IRA's investment. Disqualified persons include, among others, the IRA owner if he or she exercises investment discretion over the IRA, as well as the spouse, ancestors, and lineal descendants of the owner and any spouse of a lineal descendant. A corporation is considered a disqualified person if at least 50 percent of either the combined voting power or the value of its stock is owned by disqualified persons. Based on these considerations, the Department of Labor (DOL) opined in 2006 that an IRA's investment, at the direction of its owner, in notes to be issued by a corporation, the majority owners of which were the IRA owner's son-in-law and daughter, would be a prohibited transaction. [ERISA Adv. Op. 2006-09A]

In another 2006 opinion, the DOL concluded that a transaction by an entity in which an IRA has invested can be a prohibited transaction even though the entity does not itself hold any plan assets. The opinion considered a limited liability company's (LLC) lease of property to an S corporation on terms that an independent expert had determined were at least as favorable to the LLC as an arm's-length transaction. A husband and wife owned the majority of the S corporation, and the husband's IRA owned 49 percent of the LLC. The other 51 percent of the LLC was owned by the comptroller of the S corporation. Since the IRA had invested in the LLC with the understanding that the LLC would engage in the transaction with a party in interest, the DOL found that the lease would be a prohibited transaction. [ERISA Adv. Op. 2006-01A]

Q 1:55 May an IRA owner's personal securities transactions be matched with acquisitions made through his or her IRA to find that a wash sale has occurred?

Yes. The IRS's position is that Code Section 1091—the wash sale rule—*may* apply to an individual's sale of securities at a loss if there is an acquisition of substantially identical securities within 30 days before or after the sale by his or her IRA (traditional or Roth). At the very least, the IRS will consider the transaction a wash sale if the IRA owner caused the IRA to acquire the replacement securities. [Rev. Rul. 2008-5 (2008-3 I.R.B. 271)]

Code Section 1091 is applied by matching a taxpayer's sales of stock or securities at a loss with the taxpayer's purchases of substantially identical stock or securities within the proscribed period of time. If a matching pair of transactions is identified (a so-called *wash sale*), the taxpayer is denied a deduction for the loss, the basis in the sold securities is added to the taxpayer's basis in the replacement securities, and the holding period for the replacement securities includes the holding period for the securities that the taxpayer sold. In effect, recognition of the loss is deferred until the replacement securities are sold. [I.R.C. § 1091(d)]

If the wash sale occurs in the context of an IRA, however, the IRA owner never recognizes the loss. The IRA owner does not hold the replacement securities, so the basis in the securities that were sold is simply lost. It cannot be used to increase the owner's basis in the IRA. Worse still, a wash sale transaction involving an IRA might be a prohibited transaction (see Q 1:54); Revenue Ruling 2008-5 expressly warns that conclusions should not be drawn from the IRS's failure to consider that issue in the ruling. [Rev. Rul. 2008-5 (2008-3 I.R.B. 271)]

Bankruptcy and Debtor Issues

Q 1:56 Are traditional and Roth IRAs protected in bankruptcy?

Yes. Federal law developments have provided substantial protection for the IRAs of debtors in bankruptcy.

First, the Supreme Court held that a debtor's retirement savings (including IRAs) must be excluded from the bankruptcy estate to the extent the funds are reasonably needed to support the debtor and any dependents. [Rousey v. Jacoway, 544 U.S. 320 (2005)] The decision placed IRAs on the same footing as other qualified retirement plans—meaning they are shielded from creditors to an equal extent—but left bankruptcy courts to make a factual determination in each case as to the amount of funds needed to satisfy the reasonable support standard.

Soon after the *Rousey* decision, the Bankruptcy Abuse Prevention and Consumer Protection Act of 2005 (BAPCPA) was enacted. BAPCPA contains provisions that address the protection of retirement savings, including IRAs in bankruptcy, and largely supersedes the ruling in *Rousey*.

Finally, in 2008, the Third Circuit Court of Appeals held that an IRA need not be in present payment status (e.g., because the debtor is younger than age 59½) to satisfy the reasonable support requirement for bankruptcy petitions that are governed by pre-BAPCPA law. [*In re Krebs*, 2008 WL 2079956 (3d Cir. May 19, 2008)]

Note. The debtor, Susan Marie Krebs, had filed her bankruptcy petition before the effective date of BAPCPA. Present payment status is irrelevant for cases governed by BAPCPA (see Q 1:57).

Q 1:57   How does BAPCPA affect the treatment of IRAs in bankruptcy?

BAPCPA provides a qualified bankruptcy exemption for traditional and Roth IRAs of $1 million, plus any amount attributable to rollovers. The cap is indexed to the consumer price index and may be increased by the bankruptcy court in the interest of justice, leaving the courts room to stretch the boundaries of the exemption under the appropriate set of facts. These amounts will be protected from creditors regardless of need and regardless of state law considerations—though it is not clear whether state laws that afford greater protection to IRAs (e.g., unlimited protection without the $1 million cap) apply. However, given the modest level of contributions permitted annually ($5,000, or $6,000 for individuals age 50 or older), only the rare non-rollover IRA will be able to accumulate $1 million or more. For all practical purposes, most taxpayers will have an unlimited exemption.

BAPCPA also resolves the issue of how rollovers and contributions are treated in bankruptcy. The bankruptcy exemption is not lost when distributions from qualified retirement plans are directly rolled over to other qualified plans or IRAs. Unlimited protection is available for these amounts because the $1 million cap does not apply to amounts rolled over to IRAs from qualified retirement plans. As discussed in chapter 6, rollovers must occur within 60 days of the distribution. However, a debtor cannot avoid the cap on amounts in an IRA by rolling over IRA proceeds from one IRA into a second IRA. That is because rollovers from an IRA are not listed in Bankruptcy Code Section 522(n) among the rollovers whose assets do not apply toward the $1 million cap. [BAPCPA § 224(a)]

Q 1:58   How does BAPCPA apply to SEPs and SIMPLE plans?

SEPs and SIMPLE plans for employees receive unlimited protection in a bankruptcy filing because the $1 million cap does not apply to these retirement vehicles (see Qs 1:2, 1:20–1:23).

Q 1:59   Does BAPCPA apply to "deemed IRAs"?

An area of uncertainty relates to amounts held in "deemed IRAs" set up by employers in connection with retirement plans; see discussion of deemed IRAs in Qs 2:62, 2:63. The IRS generally permits employers to hold assets relating to IRAs in a single trust that also includes the assets of the qualified plan, or, alternatively, to keep the deemed IRAs in a separate trust. [Treas. Reg. § 1.408(q)-1] Because a deemed IRA, though associated with a qualified plan, is treated like an IRA for most purposes, it is unclear whether a bankruptcy court would apply the $1 million cap to it or will apply the unlimited exemption for retirement accounts.

Q 1:60   Does bankruptcy protection apply to Coverdell ESAs?

Yes, more limited protection exists for Coverdell ESAs (see Qs 1:16–1:19 and chapter 13). Funds contributed to a Coverdell ESA more than 720 days before the bankruptcy filing are excluded from the bankruptcy estate and are, therefore, protected from creditors. Between 720 days and 365 days before the bankruptcy filing, all amounts contributed for the same designated beneficiary are aggregated and protected only up to $5,000. Amounts contributed less than 365 days before the bankruptcy filing are not protected. [BAPCPA § 224(a)]

Q 1:61   Can the IRS exact a levy on IRAs to collect payment for taxes owed?

Yes, but the agency's official policy is to do so only in "flagrant" cases and not if "the taxpayer is dependent on the funds in the retirement account (or will be dependent in the near future)." [IRS Manual § 5.11.6.2 (Mar. 15, 2005)] An IRA distribution made pursuant to a levy is subject to normal taxation rules, except that the 10 percent penalty on early distributions does not apply. [I.R.C. § 72(t)(2)(A)(vii)]

Chapter 2

Adopting a Traditional IRA or a Roth IRA

Martin Fleisher, Esq.
Jo Ann Lippe, Esq.

The procedure for adopting either a traditional IRA or a Roth IRA is a relatively simple one for the average taxpayer. The trustee or custodian, however, must follow comprehensive regulations and use specific forms to properly establish an IRA. This chapter discusses the rules for adopting a traditional IRA and a Roth IRA (in part by answering some common account-opening questions), reviews the duties of the IRA trustee or custodian, and analyzes the IRA documentation requirements.

Common Account-Opening Questions

Q 2:1   What does it mean to adopt an IRA?

To adopt an IRA is to complete the documentation legally required to make an IRA contribution. The term *establish* is used synonymously with the term *adopt* in this discussion of IRAs.

Q 2:2   When must an IRA be adopted?

An IRA must be adopted no later than the tax filing date (with no extensions) for the individual wishing to adopt an IRA for the taxable year in which the IRA is made effective. [I.R.C. § 408(d)(4)(A)]

> **Example.** Larry is a calendar-year taxpayer. To adopt an IRA for 2009, Larry must adopt the IRA no later than April 15, 2010 (whether or not he obtains an extension for filing his tax return). All of his IRA contributions must also be made by that date.

Q 2:3   May an individual adopt an IRA without making a contribution?

Yes. Adopting—or establishing—an IRA is a procedure that is legally independent of funding an IRA. In practice, of course, an individual usually establishes and funds his or her IRA simultaneously. Nonetheless, the distinction can become important when determining what legal requirements must be met. For instance, an IRA trustee or custodian is required to provide a disclosure statement upon *establishment* of an IRA. If an IRA owner makes an initial contribution to the IRA after it is established, no additional IRA disclosure is necessary.

Q 2:4   How is a traditional IRA or a Roth IRA established?

To establish (adopt) either a traditional IRA or a Roth IRA, a taxpayer must use the four following documents:

1. *IRA Agreement.* The IRA agreement/contract is effected by completing a form approved by the Internal Revenue Service (IRS) for the appropriate type of IRA issued by an IRS-approved IRA trustee or custodian. The same general rules regarding trustee and disclosure issues and model forms apply to the establishment of either form of IRA; however, some of the specifics of establishment (i.e., eligibility and documentation) are different. There are different types of IRA agreements in the IRS Form 5305 series of model documents:
   - IRS Form 5305, *Traditional Individual Retirement Trust Account*
   - IRS Form 5305-A, *Traditional Individual Retirement Custodial Account*
   - IRS Form 5305-R, *Roth Individual Retirement Trust Agreement*
   - IRS Form 5305-RA, *Roth Individual Retirement Custodial Agreement*
   - IRS Form 5305-RB, *Roth Individual Retirement Annuity Endorsement*

2. *The Application.* An individual generally signs an application, which can be a separate document or part of an IRA agreement/contract. The application captures certain information for an IRA custodian or trustee for accurate reporting; the information includes the IRA owner's name, address, date of birth, and Social Security number or appropriate tax identification number, the contribution amount and type, and the death benefit information.

3. *The Plain Language Disclosure.* A new IRA owner must receive a plain-language disclosure statement or nontechnical written version of the IRA rules and regulations. A financial organization may create its own plain-language disclosure or use one drafted by a document provider, or use IRS Publication 590, *Individual Retirement Arrangements (IRAs)* 2008 [reproduced in Appendix A].

4. *The Financial Disclosure.* An IRA owner must also receive a financial disclosure statement. To the extent that it can reasonably be made, the financial disclosure is a projection of future values of an IRA based on the type of contribution made at establishment (i.e., regular, rollover, or transfer contribution) and a fixed contribution amount of $1,000.

Pursuant to Code Section 6693(a), a $50 penalty is applied to each IRA custodian or trustee that fails to provide a copy of an IRA agreement, a plain-language disclosure, or a financial disclosure to a taxpayer establishing an IRA. [Treas. Reg. § 1.408-6(d)(4)(ix)]

Q 2:5 What additional disclosure should be included in the investment documentation presented?

The type of investment(s) a new IRA owner chooses for his or her first contribution or any later contributions can require additional disclosures or agreements. IRA investments may be deposit investments (e.g., money market accounts and certificates of deposits) or nondeposit investments (e.g., mutual funds, annuities, stocks and bonds) depending on the policy of the IRA custodian or trustee.

Some important investment documentation may include the following:

- Ownership of IRA investments should reflect the investment relationship between an IRA owner and his or her IRA custodian or trustee—for example, "ABC Credit Union, custodian of John Doe's IRA" or "XYZ Bank, trustee of Jane Doe's IRA"

- Each investment selected may have its own specific information disclosures, like a mutual fund's prospectus or annual report

- The Truth-in-Savings Act applies to all deposit investments, including IRA deposit investments, held by or offered to consumers at banks and savings associations, and those held by or offered to members at credit unions

- Under an Interagency Statement developed in 1994 by the Office of the Comptroller of the Currency, the Federal Reserve Board, the Federal

Deposit Insurance Corporation (FDIC), and the Office of Thrift Supervision, a *non*deposit investment policy should also inform IRA owners that nondeposit investments are not insured by the Federal Deposit Insurance Corporation; are subject to investment risks, including possible loss of the amounts invested; are not deposits or other obligations of the IRA custodian or trustee; and are not guaranteed by the IRA custodian or trustee

Q 2:6   What institutions may sponsor an IRA?

The Internal Revenue Code (Code) permits a variety of institutions to sponsor an IRA, including banks, other financial institutions, and mutual funds. Life insurance companies may sponsor IRAs, but they may not offer life insurance or endowment contracts as investment options. An IRA may also be established by or through a stockbroker or credit union. [I.R.C. §§ 408(a), 408(n); Treas. Reg. §§ 1.408-2(b), 1.408-2(e)]

Though not required by the IRA rules, a financial institution must also apply its Customer Identification Program (CIP) when a new IRA is established. CIP rules require a financial organization to verify the identity of any individual establishing a new account. Each financial institution must have a written policy that meets the minimum CIP requirements and provides the following:

- Procedures for verifying the identity of a customer opening a new account;
- Recordkeeping procedures;
- Procedures for checking a customer's name against federal government lists of known or suspected terrorists or terrorist organizations; and
- Procedures for notifying customers of an existing CIP.

[68 Fed. Reg. 25,090 (May 9, 2003); 31 C.F.R. § 103.121]

Most financial institutions have blanket CIP policies and procedures applied uniformly to all new accounts, including IRAs. A financial institution should incorporate its CIP procedures into its IRA establishment procedure and retain CIP documentation as part of each IRA file or separate from the IRA file.

Q 2:7   Are IRAs covered by federal deposit insurance?

The Federal Deposit Insurance Corporation (FDIC) approved final rules that raised (for the first time in 25 years) the deposit insurance coverage on certain retirement accounts at banks or savings institutions from $100,000 to $250,000, effective April 1, 2006. [12 C.F.R. § 330.14] The increase was triggered by new legislation—the Federal Deposit Reform Act of 2005 [Pub. L. No. 109-171, 120 Stat. 41 (2005)] and the Federal Deposit Insurance Reform Conforming Amendments Act of 2005. [Pub. L. No. 109-173, 120 Stat. 3618] The basic insurance coverage for other deposit accounts was temporarily raised to $250,000 until December 31, 2009, although many commentators believe that the new $250,000 limit will be permanent for all accounts.

Under the new FDIC regulation, up to $250,000 in deposit insurance is provided for the money a taxpayer holds in a variety of retirement accounts, primarily traditional and Roth IRAs, at a given insured institution. In addition, IRAs and other retirement accounts that are protected, under the new rules, up to $250,000 are insured separately from other accounts at the same institution that continue to be insured up to at least $100,000. The new legislation also established a method by which the FDIC will consider an increase in the insurance limits on all deposit accounts (including retirement accounts) every five years, starting in 2011, based in part on inflation. [*See* 71 Fed. Reg. 82 (Apr. 28, 2006).]

Q 2:8   How many IRAs may an individual establish?

There is no legal limit on the number of IRAs that an individual may establish. However, because the maximum contribution amount applies in the aggregate to all IRAs, an individual cannot circumvent this limitation by establishing multiple IRAs.

> **Example.** Dan understands the benefits of the IRA, but he believes in diversification of institutions as well as investments. He established a traditional IRA at ABC Bank in 2006, another traditional IRA at XYZ Credit Union in 2007, and another at Big Mutual Funds in 2008. In 2009 Dan opened two new IRAs, one traditional and one Roth IRA. As long as he contributes no more than his annual maximum (currently $5,000, or $6,000 if he is age 50 or over by December 31, 2009), Dan has not violated any rule by opening multiple IRAs.

> **Note.** Many trustees and custodians impose minimum dollar limits or charge a fee for each IRA to discourage individuals from opening multiple IRAs.

Q 2:9   May IRA investments be made jointly with another person?

No. Joint IRA investments are not permitted. For example, it is not permissible for a husband and wife to hold a jointly owned certificate of deposit in a joint IRA account. [I.R.C. § 408(a); Treas. Reg. § 1.408-2(b)]

Q 2:10   May an IRA investment be commingled with the IRA owner's other investments?

No. Assets in an IRA may not be combined with the IRA owner's other assets. [I.R.C. § 408(a)(5); Treas. Reg. § 1.408-2(b)(5)]

Q 2:11   How often should IRA documents be reviewed?

Apart from an annual financial review, IRA documents should be reviewed whenever a change is made in the designated beneficiary. A traditional IRA should also be reviewed before the IRA owner reaches age 70$\frac{1}{2}$ or when a major life event occurs, such as retirement or the incurrence of large expenses. Of course, the documents should be reviewed when the IRA owner dies or when the trustee (or custodian) proposes amendments.

Q 2:12   Is an IRA a qualified plan?

No. To be a qualified plan, a plan must be sponsored by an employer and meet the requirements of Code Section 401(a). An IRA does *not* meet those requirements.

Trustees and Custodians

Q 2:13   Who may serve as a trustee or custodian of a traditional IRA or a Roth IRA?

Generally, a bank is required to be the trustee or custodian of an IRA, but the IRS may approve another entity to serve in that capacity (see Q 2:14). [Treas. Reg. § 1.408-2(b)(2)]

The term *bank* is broadly defined as follows:

1. A bank, a trust company, or a domestic savings and loan association [I.R.C. § 408(n)(1)]
2. A corporation that, under the laws of the state of its incorporation or under the laws of the District of Columbia, is subject to both the supervision of, and examination by, the authority in such jurisdiction in charge of the administration of the banking laws [I.R.C. § 408(n)(3)]
3. An insured credit union [I.R.C. § 408(n)(2); Federal Credit Union Act § 101(6), 12 U.S.C. § 1752]

Note. Although a bank is required to be the trustee or custodian of an IRA, the trust instrument may grant the IRA owner the power to control the investment of the trust funds either by directing investments (including reinvestments, disposals, and exchanges) or by disapproving proposed investments (including reinvestments, disposals, and exchanges). In some cases, the IRA document may contain provisions permitting the IRA owner to appoint a third party (e.g., a registered investment advisor) to invest and reinvest the assets of the trust.

Q 2:14   What are the criteria for IRS approval of a noninstitutional trustee or custodian of an IRA?

The trustee or custodian of an IRA may be an entity other than a bank if that entity demonstrates to the satisfaction of the IRS that the manner in which the entity will administer IRA trusts will be consistent with the requirements of Code Section 408. The IRS imposes a user fee of $14,500 for ruling on a request to become a nonbank trustee (a "nonbank bank"). [Rev. Proc. 2009-8, § 6.01(8), 2009-1 I.R.B. 229; Treas. Reg. § 1.408-2(e)]

Q 2:15   What is the difference between a trustee and a custodian for purposes of an IRA?

For purposes of an IRA, there is little, if any, difference between a trustee and a custodian. The official IRA documents state that a trustee handles the account of a grantor; a custodian holds the assets for a depositor. For a traditional IRA, a trustee uses Form 5305, Individual Retirement Trust Account; a custodian uses Form 5305-A, Individual Retirement Custodial Account. However, Form 5305 and Form 5305-A are nearly identical. For a Roth IRA, a trustee uses Form 5305-R, Roth Individual Retirement Trust Account; a custodian uses Form 5305-RA, Roth Individual Retirement Custodial Account. Because the same types of institutions are eligible to serve as trustees and custodians of IRAs, it is clear that the difference in nomenclature is historical in nature and is not pertinent to IRS requirements for IRAs. The definition of the term *trustee* in Code Section 408(n) includes custodians. [Treas. Reg. § 1.408-2(d); Priv. Ltr. Rul. 9116011 (Jan. 17, 1991)]

For purposes of the discussion herein, a custodial account is treated as a trust, and the custodian of such an account is treated as the trustee thereof if the account satisfies the requirements of an IRA (except that it is not a trust) and if the assets of the account are held by a bank or person that is approved by the IRS (see Q 2:14).

It should be noted that custodians may, and often do, agree to act only at the direction of the IRA owner, whereas trustees may be given discretion to make investments on behalf of their clients.

Q 2:16   May an IRA owner serve as trustee or custodian of an IRA?

Generally, no. Unlike a qualified plan, an IRA may not have an individual serve as its trustee or custodian unless the IRS approves (see Q 2:13). IRS approval of an individual as an IRA trustee or custodian is extremely unlikely.

Q 2:17   May regular trustee or custodian fees be assessed against an IRA?

If provided for in the IRA plan document, a trustee or custodian is entitled to make charges against the account. In such a case, the document should specify the order of liquidation; for example, to cover its fees, the trustee (or custodian) may provide for liquidating assets starting with the assets that were most recently purchased.

Traditional IRA Documentation

Q 2:18   How is a traditional IRA established?

An individual establishes a traditional IRA with a document that is an IRS approved model, an IRS-approved prototype, or an individually designed plan. An IRS model document is automatically approved by the IRS. Although receipt of a favorable opinion letter, a prototype document, or an individually designed document is not required as a condition of receiving favorable tax treatment, it is nevertheless advisable to submit such documents to the IRS for approval. [Rev. Proc. 2009-4, 2009-1 I.R.B. 118; Rev. Proc. 98-59, 1998-2 C.B. 727] In all cases, the document must be completed and signed by both the individual adopting the IRA and a qualified organization that has agreed to serve as the IRA trustee or custodian (see Qs 2:20, 2:22).

Q 2:19   May a traditional IRA be revoked?

Yes. A traditional IRA may be revoked by the IRA owner within seven days of the receipt of the required explanation of basic information from the trustee, custodian, or annuity issuer (see chapter 7); the full amount contributed must be returned if the account is revoked. Information on the right to revoke is not required when the trustee, custodian, or annuity issuer supplies a disclosure statement and a copy of the governing instrument to the prospective IRA owner at least seven days before the IRA is established. The governing instrument need not contain information pertaining to the benefiting individual provided that the instrument is complete in all other respects. [Treas. Reg. § 1.408-6(d)(4)(ii)(A)(2)]

Note. If an IRA is timely revoked, no amount may be deducted for sales commissions, administrative expenses, or fluctuations in market value. [Treas. Reg. § 1.408-6(d)(4)(ii)(A)(2)] On the other hand, unless the IRA document provides otherwise, investment gains do not have to be distributed from an IRA that is revoked.

Practice Pointer. To protect themselves from having to restore investment losses upon revocation, some IRA trustees do not allow initial contributions to be invested in anything other than a government-guaranteed investment or security until the seven-day revocation period has expired.

IRS-Approved Model

Q 2:20   How is an IRS-approved model document used to establish a traditional IRA?

The IRS has created a model trust account agreement (Form 5305, Individual Retirement Trust Account) and a model custodial account agreement (Form 5305-A, Individual Retirement Custodial Account) that meet the requirements of Code Section 408(a) for individuals who wish to adopt an IRA program. The forms are not filed with the IRS, and user fees do not apply. Either model may also be used to establish a traditional IRA for a nonworking spouse, sometimes called a *spousal IRA* (see Q 1:5). The person establishing the IRA (the nonworking spouse, in the case of a spousal IRA) should complete and sign the appropriate instrument.

Note. Special forms are required to establish a SIMPLE (savings incentive match plan for employees) IRA (see chapter 12).

A sponsor of programs, an employer, or an association of employees that uses Form 5305 or Form 5305-A need not submit its program to the IRS even if it reproduces the provisions of either form on its own letterhead or in pamphlets that omit all references to the IRS and its form. (The model forms may be reproduced and reduced in size for passbook purposes.)

Q 2:21 How must amendments to Form 5305 or Form 5305-A be disclosed to an IRA owner?

Form 5305 and Form 5305-A are periodically reissued by the IRS, and significant changes are usually noted. If either form is amended, the IRA sponsor must deliver or mail a new form to the IRA owner within 30 days of the later of the adoption of or the effective date of the amendment. [Treas. Reg. § 1.408-6(d)(4)(ii)(C)]

IRS-Approved Prototype

Q 2:22 How is a prototype IRA established?

Prototype IRAs are offered by many organizations as pre-approved alternatives to the model IRA. They may contain more options and elections than those available under either of the IRS model documents. Frequently, documents contain several beneficiary designation options that may be more suitable for an individual's financial and estate planning needs.

An individual establishes a prototype IRA by completing and executing the IRA document agreement. For the IRA to be valid, it must be accepted by the trustee or custodian.

Q 2:23 How does a prototype plan obtain IRS approval?

An institution that offers IRAs to its clients may seek a ruling from the IRS approving a standard IRA plan (with various options designed to tailor the IRA to individual needs). The same process is followed to obtain approval of an employer-sponsored IRA. The submission is done on Form 5306, Application for Approval of Prototype or Employer-Sponsored Individual Retirement Account, (most recently revised in October 2006).

Form 5306 must be accompanied by the plain-language disclosure statement to be used or, alternatively, the applicant must certify that each participant will be furnished with a copy of IRS Publication 590, *Individual Retirement Arrangements (IRAs)* 2008 (see Appendix A). The type of funding entity—trust, custodial account, insurance company annuity contract, or insurance company endowment policy—must be indicated. For company contracts or policies, the contract or policy number must be provided. A copy of the plan document—a trust agreement, a custodial account, or an insurance company document—in which reference has been made to the provisions or requirements that are mandated for the particular kind of prototype (see Qs 2:24, 2:25, 2:54, and 2:55) must also accompany the application. Further, if the sponsoring organization applying for a ruling is other than an employer or an employee association, it must affirm that it is one of the following types of sponsoring organizations:

- Insurance company
- Trade or professional organization
- Savings and loan association that qualifies as a bank
- Bank
- Regulated investment company
- Federally insured credit union
- Approved nonbank trustee

The IRS imposes a user fee of $3,000 for the initial approval or subsequent amendment of a prototype IRA document (or $200 for a word-for-word adoption of a mass submitter's prototype). [Rev. Proc. 2009-8, § 6.04(02), 2009-1 I.R.B. 229]

Q 2:24 What specific items does Form 5306 require to be included in a prototype document for a traditional IRA?

Form 5306 lists 15 specific items that the prototype submitter is required to address. Twelve of the items apply to a traditional IRA plan and must be included in the prototype, with reference on the form to the article (or section) in which each item appears. The other three items must be marked "not applicable" on the form. The IRS offers sample language for the mandatory items in a "List of Required Modifications and Information Package" for traditional IRAs, last revised in June 2007 and available on the IRS Web site (see *www.irs.gov/pub/irs-tege/tira_lrm.pdf*). The IRS encourages prototype drafters to use the LRM, but cautions that some language may not be appropriate in all cases. [Form 5306, Part II; LRM for traditional IRAs, p. 1 (June 2007)] The 15 items, shown here with sample language that is based on the LRM, are:

1. The exclusive benefit provision. [I.R.C. § 408(a)]

   The account is established for the exclusive benefit of the individual or his or her beneficiaries.

2. Provision that contributions other than rollovers must be in cash and not exceed the maximum limit. [I.R.C. §§ 72(t)(2)(G), 219(b), 408(a)(1), 408(d)(3)(G), 408(p)(1)(B), 408(p)(2)(A)(iv)]

(a) Except in the case of a rollover contribution (as permitted by Code Sections 402(c), 402(e)(6), 403(a)(4), 403(b)(8), 403(b)(10), 408(d)(3), and 457(e)(16)) or a contribution made in accordance with the terms of a simplified employee pension (SEP) as described in Code Section 408(k), no contributions will be accepted unless they are in cash, and the total of such contributions shall not exceed:

- $3,000 for any taxable year beginning in 2002 through 2004;
- $4,000 for any taxable year beginning in 2005 through 2007; and
- $5,000 for any taxable year beginning in 2008 and years thereafter.

After 2008, the limit will be adjusted by the Secretary of the Treasury for cost-of-living increases under Code Section 219(b)(5)(D). Such adjustments will be in multiples of $500.

(b) In the case of an individual who is 50 or older, the annual cash contribution limit is increased by:

- $500 for any taxable year beginning in 2002 through 2005; and
- $1,000 for any taxable year beginning in 2006 and years thereafter.

(c) In addition to the amounts described in paragraphs (a) and (b) above, an individual may make a repayment of a qualified reservist distribution described in Code § 72(t)(2)(G) during the 2-year period beginning on the day after the end of the active duty period or by August 17, 2008, if later.

(d) In addition to the amounts described in paragraphs (a) and (c) above, an individual who was a participant in a § 401(k) plan of a certain employer in bankruptcy described in Code § 219(b)(5)(C) may contribute up to $3,000 for taxable years beginning after 2006 and before 2010 only. An individual who makes contributions under this paragraph (d) may not also make contributions under paragraph (b).

(e) No contributions will be accepted under a SIMPLE IRA plan established by any employer pursuant to § 408(p). Also, no transfer or rollover of funds attributable to contributions made by a particular employer under its SIMPLE IRA plan will be accepted from a SIMPLE IRA, that is, an IRA used in conjunction with a SIMPLE IRA plan, prior to the expiration of the 2-year period beginning on the date the individual first participated in that employer's SIMPLE IRA plan.

3. Provision acknowledging the prohibition of investment by an IRA in collectibles or a statement informing participants in the IRA plan that investment in collectibles will be a taxable distribution. [I.R.C. § 408(m)]

If the trust acquires collectibles within the meaning of Code Section 408(m) after December 31, 1981, trust assets will be treated as a distribution in an amount equal to the cost of such collectibles.

(This provision is *not* required if the IRA precludes any investments that could be construed as collectibles. It should be noted that Code Section 408(m)(3) provides an exception to the rule for certain gold and silver coins.)

4. Prohibition of investment by an individual retirement account in life insurance contracts. [I.R.C. § 408(a)(3)]

    No part of the trust funds will be invested in life insurance contracts.

5. Statement of required distributions commencing before death (see Qs 2:31–2:32). [I.R.C. § 408(a)(6), Treas. Reg. § 1.408-8]

    (a) Notwithstanding any provision of this IRA to the contrary, the distribution of the individual's interest in the account shall be made in accordance with the requirements of Code § 408(a)(6) and the regulations thereunder, the provisions of which are herein incorporated by reference. If distributions are made from an annuity contract purchased from an insurance company, distributions thereunder must satisfy the requirements of Q&A-4 of § 1.401(a)(9)-6 of the Income Tax Regulations, rather than paragraphs (b), (c) and (d) below and [reference to IRA provision for distributions at death]. The required minimum distributions calculated for this IRA may be withdrawn from another IRA of the individual in accordance with Q&A-9 of § 1.408-8 of the Income Tax Regulations.

    (b) The entire value of the account of the individual for whose benefit the account is maintained will commence to be distributed no later than the first day of April following the calendar year in which such individual attains age 70½ (the "required beginning date") over the life of such individual or the lives of such individual and his or her designated beneficiary.

    (c) The amount to be distributed each year, beginning with the calendar year in which the individual attains age 70½ and continuing through the year of death, shall not be less than the quotient obtained by dividing the value of the IRA, as determined under [reference to IRA provision for distributions at death], as of the end of the preceding year by the distribution period in the Uniform Lifetime Table in Q&A-2 of § 1.401(a)(9)-9 of the Income Tax Regulations, using the individual's age as of his or her birthday in the year. However, if the individual's sole designated beneficiary is his or her surviving spouse and such spouse is more than

10 years younger than the individual, then the distribution period is determined under the Joint and Last Survivor Table in Q&A-3 of § 1.401(a)(9)-9, using the ages as of the individual's and spouse's birthdays in the year.

(d) The required minimum distribution for the year the individual attains age 70½ can be made as late as April 1 of the following year. The required minimum distribution for any other year must be made by the end of such year.

6. Statement of required distributions commencing after death (see Qs 2:33–2:34). [I.R.C. § 408(a)(6), Treas. Reg. § 1.408-8]

(a) Death On or After Required Beginning Date. If the individual dies on or after the required beginning date, the remaining portion of his or her interest will be distributed at least as rapidly as follows:

(1) If the designated beneficiary is someone other than the individual's surviving spouse, the remaining interest will be distributed over the remaining life expectancy of the designated beneficiary, with such life expectancy determined using the beneficiary's age as of his or her birthday in the year following the year of the individual's death, or over the period described in paragraph (a)(3) below if longer.

(2) If the individual's sole designated beneficiary is the individual's surviving spouse, the remaining interest will be distributed over such spouse's life or over the period described in paragraph (a)(3) below if longer. Any interest remaining after such spouse's death will be distributed over such spouse's remaining life expectancy determined using the spouse's age as of his or her birthday in the year of the spouse's death, or, if the distributions are being made over the period described in paragraph (a)(3) below, over such period.

(3) If there is no designated beneficiary, or if applicable by operation of paragraph (a)(1) or (a)(2) above, the remaining interest will be distributed over the individual's remaining life expectancy determined in the year of the individual's death.

(4) The amount to be distributed each year under paragraph (a)(1), (2) or (3), beginning with the calendar year following the calendar year of the individual's death, is the quotient obtained by dividing the value of the IRA as of the end of the preceding year by the remaining life expectancy specified in such paragraph. Life expectancy is determined using the Single Life Table in Q&A-1 of § 1.401(a)(9)-9 of the Income Tax Regulations. If distributions are being made to a surviving spouse as the sole designated beneficiary, such spouse's remaining life expectancy for a year is the number in the Single Life Table corresponding to such spouse's age in the year. In all other cases, remaining life expectancy for a year is

the number in the Single Life Table corresponding to the beneficiary's or individual's age in the year specified in paragraph (a)(1), (2) or (3) and reduced by 1 for each subsequent year.

(b) Death Before Required Beginning Date. If the individual dies before the required beginning date, his or her entire interest will be distributed at least as rapidly as follows:

(1) If the designated beneficiary is someone other than the individual's surviving spouse, the entire interest will be distributed, starting by the end of the calendar year following the calendar year of the individual's death, over the remaining life expectancy of the designated beneficiary, with such life expectancy determined using the age of the beneficiary as of his or her birthday in the year following the year of the individual's death, or, if elected, in accordance with paragraph (b)(3) below.

(2) If the individual's sole designated beneficiary is the individual's surviving spouse, the entire interest will be distributed, starting by the end of the calendar year following the calendar year of the individual's death (or by the end of the calendar year in which the individual would have attained age 70½, if later), over such spouse's life, or, if elected, in accordance with paragraph (b)(3) below. If the surviving spouse dies before distributions are required to begin, the remaining interest will be distributed, starting by the end of the calendar year following the calendar year of the spouse's death, over the spouse's designated beneficiary's remaining life expectancy determined using such beneficiary's age as of his or her birthday in the year following the death of the spouse, or, if elected, will be distributed in accordance with paragraph (b)(3) below. If the surviving spouse dies after distributions are required to begin, any remaining interest will be distributed over the spouse's remaining life expectancy determined using the spouse's age as of his or her birthday in the year of the spouse's death.

(3) If there is no designated beneficiary, or if applicable by operation of paragraph (b)(1) or (b)(2) above, the entire interest will be distributed by the end of the calendar year containing the fifth anniversary of the individual's death (or of the spouse's death in the case of the surviving spouse's death before distributions are required to begin under paragraph (b)(2) above).

(4) The amount to be distributed each year under paragraph (b)(1) or (2) is the quotient obtained by dividing the value of the IRA as of the end of the preceding year by the remaining life expectancy specified in such paragraph. Life expectancy is determined using the Single Life Table in Q&A-1 of § 1.401(a)(9)-9 of the Income Tax Regulations. If distributions are being made to a surviving spouse as the sole designated beneficiary, such spouse's remaining life expectancy for a

year is the number in the Single Life Table corresponding to such spouse's age in the year. In all other cases, remaining life expectancy for a year is the number in the Single Life Table corresponding to the beneficiary's age in the year specified in paragraph (b)(1) or (2) and reduced by 1 for each subsequent year.

(c) The "value" of the IRA includes the amount of any outstanding rollover, transfer and recharacterization under Q&As-7 and -8 of § 1.408-8 of the Income Tax Regulations.

(d) If the sole designated beneficiary is the individual's surviving spouse, the spouse may elect to treat the IRA as his or her own IRA. This election will be deemed to have been made if such surviving spouse makes a contribution to the IRA or fails to take required distributions as a beneficiary.

7. Nonforfeitability provision. [I.R.C. § 408(a)(4)]

   The interest of an individual in the balance of his or her account is nonforfeitable at all times.

8. Nontransferability provision.

   (This provision is required *only* for individual retirement annuity contracts (see Q 2:25).)

9. Provision governing the application of premium refunds, for any annuity that provides for participation in dividends.

   (This provision is required *only* for individual retirement annuity contracts (see Q 2:25).)

10. Provision acknowledging the prohibition against commingling of assets. [I.R.C. § 408(a)(5)]

    The assets of the trust will not be commingled with other property except in a common trust fund or common investment fund.

11. Provision acknowledging the prohibition against requiring fixed premiums for an individual retirement annuity.

    (This provision is required *only* for individual retirement annuities (see Q 2:25).)

12. Requirement for separate accounting for the interest of each individual under an account or annuity established by an employer or employee association. [Treas. Reg. § 1.408-2(c)(3)]

    Separate records will be maintained for the interest of each individual.

    (This provision is required *only* in IRAs that are sponsored by employers or employee associations.)

13. Requirement that trustees or insurers furnish annual calendar-year reports concerning the status of the account or annuity. [Treas. Reg. §§ 1.408-5, 1.408-8]

> The trustee of an individual retirement account shall furnish annual calendar-year reports concerning the status of the account and such information concerning required minimum distributions as is prescribed by the Commissioner of Internal Revenue.

14. Provision that there be substitution for a nonbank trustee or custodian when the Commissioner of Internal Revenue issues a notification. [Treas. Reg. § 1.408-2(e)(6)(v)]

> The nonbank trustee or custodian shall substitute another trustee or custodian if the nonbank trustee or custodian receives notice from the Commissioner of Internal Revenue that such substitution is required because it has failed to comply with the requirements of Treasury Regulations Section 1.408-2(e).

> (This provision is required *only* in IRAs that are sponsored by nonbank trustees or custodians.)

15. Provision describing the type of compensation used for computing deductible limits. [I.R.C. § 219(f)(1); Treas. Reg. § 1.219-1(c)(1)]

> Compensation means wages, salaries, professional fees, or other amounts derived from or received for personal services actually rendered (including, but not limited to, commissions paid to salespersons, compensation for services on the basis of a percentage of profits, commissions on insurance premiums, tips, and bonuses) and includes earned income, as defined in Code Section 401(c)(2) (reduced by the deduction the self-employed individual takes for contributions made to a self-employed retirement plan). For purposes of this definition, Code Section 401(c)(2) shall be applied as if the term *trade or business* for purposes of Code Section 1402 included service described in subsection (c)(6). Compensation does not include amounts derived from or received as earnings or profits from property (including but not limited to interest and dividends) or amounts not includable in gross income. Compensation also does not include any amount received as a pension or annuity or as deferred compensation. The term *compensation* shall include any amount includable in the individual's gross income under Code Section 71 with respect to a divorce or separation instrument described in subparagraph (A) of Code Section 71(b)(2).

(This provision, used for computing deductible limits, is *not required* for receipt of a favorable opinion letter.)

Caution. The IRS warns that the information and sample provisions included in the LRM may not be appropriate in all cases. Acceptability may depend on the context in which the provisions are used.

Q 2:25 Does the IRS offer sample language for a prototype IRA that specifically applies to an individual retirement annuity?

Yes. Part B of the LRM for traditional IRAs (June 2007) contains sample language that specifically applies to individual retirement annuity contracts (see Q 2:40). The sample provisions shown in Q 2:24 are based on Part A of the LRM, which does not apply to such contracts.

Q 2:26 What form does the IRS approval of a prototype IRA take, and what weight does that approval carry?

When the IRS approves a prototype IRA, it issues an opinion letter stating that the *form* of the prototype is acceptable under the Code. Such a letter is similar to a determination letter issued by the IRS for a qualified retirement plan.

Approval of the form of the prototype IRA means only that it will be acceptable if, in operation, it complies with all of the following rules:

1. The terms of the program are followed.
2. There are no prohibited transactions.
3. The trustee or custodian is a qualified bank or has been approved by the IRS.
4. The required plain-language disclosure statement is provided to each participant.
5. Each adopting individual is provided with annual reports of transactions.
6. The sponsoring institution's telephone number is provided to those adopting the plan.
7. Those adopting the plan are advised to contact the sponsoring institution if there are questions about the plan's operation.
8. A copy of the opinion letter is provided to each affected person.

It is important to note that the IRS provides three caveats to its approval of a prototype IRA:

1. Future changes in the Code or regulations may require further amendments or revisions.
2. The IRS has not evaluated the program and does not guarantee contributions or investments made.
3. No opinion is expressed regarding the existence or absence of prohibited transactions.

Q 2:27 To make IRS approval more likely, should Form 5305 and Form 5305-A be consulted when designing a prototype IRA?

Yes. There are two general approaches to designing a prototype IRA, either of which is likely to ensure IRS approval. One is to design a prototype plan that includes the requirements set forth in Form 5305 and Form 5305-A but that has more than eight articles, thus allowing for more provisions of particular concern to the IRA owner. The second is to repeat Article I through Article VII of Form 5305 (or Form 5305-A) and then place all other matters in Article VIII of the prototype.

Preparation of New Plan Documents

Q 2:28　Must a new IRA plan document be prepared for each contribution?

No. Forms 5305, 5305-A, 5305-R, and 5305-RA provide for further contributions, as do nearly all prototypes.

Note. A trustee (or custodian) of a traditional IRA established by a rollover from a qualified plan, a 403(b) annuity, or a custodial account plan may require that a new document be signed in order for the IRA owner to make additional contributions—a sensible rule that prevents the commingling of annual contributory assets with IRA assets rolled over from qualified plans. (If such assets are commingled, an individual may not roll the qualified plan assets back into a qualified plan.)

Q 2:29　When must new IRA plan documents be prepared, and are IRS filings required for the new documents?

Although a new plan document is not required for each contribution to one IRA, it is not possible to have more than one traditional IRA (or Roth IRA) without preparing a new plan document. The trustee (or custodian) generates additional IRS filings for each IRA (see chapter 7) and sends the IRA owner other IRS forms (e.g., Form 1099-R and Form 5498). The IRA owner, however, does not have to file the IRA plan document with the IRS; instead, the document should be kept in the owner's records.

Caution. Even if the same trustee (or custodian) is used, maintaining more than one traditional IRA (or Roth IRA) affects recordkeeping and could complicate minimum distribution calculations and nondeductible contribution cost basis determinations. Indeed, maintaining too many IRAs could become a significant inconvenience.

Beneficiary Election

Q 2:30　What is the most important election made in a traditional IRA plan document?

The most important election made in a traditional IRA plan document is the beneficiary designation. Such an election allows the IRA owner to make certain that distributions are made to a specific individual or individuals (or a trust) upon the owner's death. In the absence of a beneficiary designation, the IRA will be paid to the owner's estate. The beneficiary designation may be changed at any time before the IRA owner's death. Spousal consent is required in community/marital property states if an IRA owner names a beneficiary other than his or her spouse.

Distribution Provisions

Q 2:31   What distribution provisions are included in the model IRA forms and generally appear in IRS-approved prototype IRAs?

IRS model IRA forms and IRS-approved prototype IRAs generally provide a restatement of the Code and Treasury regulations concerning IRA distribution requirements (see Q 2:24 and chapter 4).

Many IRA trustees and custodians add distribution requirements to their IRA plan documents to meet the needs of their organization. For example, the number of distributions allowed each year may be limited or a minimum distribution amount may be required. In addition, many trustees and custodians include default provisions for the IRA owner (or beneficiary) who fails to make a required election (e.g., an election that must be made when the owner dies or reaches age 70½); that is, the trustees and custodians deem that a certain election is made if the owner (or beneficiary) makes no affirmative election by a certain date.

Q 2:32   What is a common approach to drafting a required minimum distribution provision for a traditional IRA?

It is common practice for the drafter of a traditional IRA plan document to simply restate the Code and Treasury regulations concerning minimum distributions (those required to be made after an IRA owner reaches age 70½). [Treas. Reg. §§ 1.401(a)(9)-1, 1.401(a)(9)-4] (See Q 2:24 and chapter 4.)

Q 2:33   To what extent may an IRA owner specify the distribution pattern to be followed after his or her death and accordingly control the beneficiary's choices?

If the spouse of an IRA owner is the beneficiary of the IRA, imposing a form of distribution may be ineffective because the spouse is permitted to make a rollover to his or her own IRA. However, if the beneficiary is a nonspouse who inherits the IRA before the owner was required to receive distributions, the owner may effectively determine whether the beneficiary may continue the IRA for five years or for the life expectancy of the beneficiary or terminate the IRA immediately. (See chapter 4 regarding inheritance after distributions have commenced.)

Q 2:34   What do the IRS model IRA forms require if an IRA owner dies after distributions have begun?

The IRS model IRA forms require that upon the death of an IRA owner for whom distributions have begun, distributions continue to be made in accordance with the beneficiary designation and at least as rapidly as the election made under the minimum distribution provision. It should be noted, however, that if the surviving spouse is the beneficiary, he or she may reconstitute the IRA as his or her own. [I.R.C. § 408(a)(6); Priv. Ltr. Rul. 9649045 (Sept. 11, 1996)]

Additional Provisions

Q 2:35 May a nonspouse beneficiary of an IRA change the IRA trustee (or custodian)?

Yes. A nonspouse beneficiary of an IRA may change the IRA trustee (or custodian) unless such action was prohibited by the IRA owner.

Q 2:36 Do model Forms 5305 and 5305-A allow for any variation of their terms?

Yes. Both Form 5305 and Form 5305-A, used to establish a traditional IRA, contain a blank section captioned "Article VIII" for the purpose of adding other provisions. Those additional provisions must comply with applicable requirements of state law and the Code.

Article VIII is frequently used to insert provisions for payment of the fees of the trustee (or custodian). The article is also used to include provisions for the resignation of the trustee (or custodian) and the right to appoint a successor. When an IRS model IRA form is sponsored by a financial institution, provisions concerning investments and arbitration of securities law issues are often inserted in Article VIII (see Qs 2:37, 2:38).

Caution. Any additions to an IRA plan via Article VIII of Form 5305 or Form 5305-A should be limited to defined, clearly permissible alternatives after a careful study of the law. [Rev. Proc. 92-38, 1992-1 C.B. 859]

Q 2:37 If extensive use is made of Article VIII when using Form 5305 or Form 5305-A to establish a traditional IRA, should IRS approval be sought?

Approval for the use of Article VIII in Form 5305 or Form 5305-A need not be sought under normal circumstances. If the drafter of a typical IRA plan document follows the precedents of law, including letter rulings (which, although not binding, are quite informative), there should be no need for further IRS approval.

Practice Pointer. It is always possible to seek a letter ruling regarding the use of Article VIII in a special situation or if the IRA is part of a larger program for which approval is desired.

Q 2:38 What language does the IRS suggest be added to Form 5305 and Form 5305-A?

In the instructions to Form 5305 and Form 5305-A, the IRS suggests including language regarding investment powers, voting rights, exculpatory provisions, amendment and termination, removal of the trustee, trustees' fees, state-law requirements, acceptance of cash only, treatment of excess contributions, and prohibited transactions with the grantor. Additional pages may be added to the form and should be used if necessary to complete the agreement. Other items, such as detailed reporting requirements, may be provided in supplemental documents, which must also comply with the Code (see chapter 7).

Q 2:39   Has the IRS approved plan language specifically for an individual retirement annuity contract, other than what is contained in Form 5305 and Form 5305-A?

Yes. The approved language appears in Part B of the LRM for traditional IRAs. [*See www.irs.gov/pub/irs-tege/tira_lrm.pdf.*]

Q 2:40   What plan language has the IRS approved for prototype individual retirement annuities?

The IRS has published certain language that it has approved for use in drafting an individual retirement annuity contract. The following clauses are based on material contained in the section of the "List of Required Modifications and Information Package" (June 2007) that pertains to traditional individual retirement annuity contracts:

1. The exclusive benefit provision. [I.R.C. § 408(b)]

   The contract is established for the exclusive benefit of the individual or his or her beneficiaries.

2. Provision that contributions other than rollovers must be in cash and not exceed the maximum limit. [I.R.C. §§ 72(t)(2)(G), 219(b), 408(b)(2), 408(d)(3)(G), 408(p)(1)(B), 408(p)(2)(A)(iv)]

   (a) Except in the case of a rollover contribution (as permitted by Internal Revenue Code §§ 402(c), 402(e)(6), 403(a)(4), 403(b)(8), 403(b)(10), 408(d)(3) and 457(e)(16)) or a contribution made in accordance with the terms of a Simplified Employee Pension (SEP) as described in § 408(k), no contributions will be accepted unless they are in cash, and the total of such contributions shall not exceed:

   • $3,000 for any taxable year beginning in 2002 through 2004;

   • $4,000 for any taxable year beginning in 2005 through 2007; and

   • $5,000 for any taxable year beginning in 2008 and years thereafter.

   After 2008, the limit will be adjusted by the Secretary of the Treasury for cost-of-living increases under Code § 219(b)(5)(D). Such adjustments will be in multiples of $500.

   (b) In the case of an individual who is 50 or older, the annual cash contribution limit is increased by:

- $500 for any taxable year beginning in 2002 through 2005; and
- $1,000 for any taxable year beginning in 2006 and years thereafter.

(c) In addition to the amounts described in paragraphs (a) and (b) above, an individual may make a repayment of a qualified reservist distribution described in Code § 72(t)(2)(G) during the 2-year period beginning on the day after the end of the active duty period or by August 17, 2008, if later.

(d) In addition to the amounts described in paragraphs (a) and (c) above, an individual who was a participant in a § 401(k) plan of a certain employer in bankruptcy described in Code § 219(b)(5)(C) may contribute up to $3,000 for taxable years beginning after 2006 and before 2010 only. An individual who makes contributions under this paragraph (d) may not also make contributions under paragraph (b).

(e) No contributions will be accepted under a SIMPLE IRA plan established by any employer pursuant to § 408(p). Also, no transfer or rollover of funds attributable to contributions made by a particular employer under its SIMPLE IRA plan will be accepted from a SIMPLE IRA, that is, an IRA used in conjunction with a SIMPLE IRA plan, prior to the expiration of the 2-year period beginning on the date the individual first participated in that employer's SIMPLE IRA plan.

3. Statement of required distributions commencing before death (see Qs 2:31–2:32). [I.R.C. § 408(b)(3), Treas. Reg. § 1.408-8]

(a) Notwithstanding any provision of this IRA to the contrary, the distribution of the individual's interest in the IRA shall be made in accordance with the requirements of Code § 408(b)(3) and the regulations thereunder, the provisions of which are herein incorporated by reference. If distributions are not made in the form of an annuity on an irrevocable basis (except for acceleration), then distribution of the interest in the IRA (as determined under section [reference to IRA provision that defines "interest" in the IRA]) must satisfy the requirements of Code § 408(a)(6) and the regulations thereunder, rather than paragraphs (b), (c) and (d) below and section [reference to IRA provision for distributions at death].

(b) The entire interest of the individual for whose benefit the contract is maintained will commence to be distributed no later than the first day of April following the calendar year in which such individual attains age 70½ (the "required beginning date") over (a) the life of such individual or the lives of such individual and his or her designated beneficiary or (b) a period certain not extending beyond the life expectancy of such individual or the joint and last survivor expectancy of such individual and his or her designated beneficiary. Payments must be made in periodic payments at intervals of no longer than 1 year and must be either nonincreasing or they may increase only as provided in Q&As-1 and -4 of § 1.401(a)(9)-6 of the Income Tax Regulations. In addition, any distribution must satisfy the incidental benefit requirements specified in Q&A-2 of § 1.401(a)(9)-6.

(c) The distribution periods described in paragraph (b) above cannot exceed the periods specified in § 1.401(a)(9)-6 of the Income Tax Regulations.

(d) The first required payment can be made as late as April 1 of the year following the year the individual attains age 70½ and must be the payment that is required for one payment interval. The second payment need not be made until the end of the next payment interval.

4. Statement of required distributions commencing after death (see Qs 2:33–2:34). [I.R.C. § 408(b)(3), Treas. Reg. § 1.408-8]

(a) Death On or After Required Distributions Commence. If the individual dies on or after required distributions commence, the remaining portion of his or her interest will continue to be distributed under the contract option chosen.

(b) Death Before Required Distributions Commence. If the individual dies before required distributions commence, his or her entire interest will be distributed at least as rapidly as follows:

(1) If the designated beneficiary is someone other than the individual's surviving spouse, the entire interest will be distributed, starting by the end of the calendar year following the calendar year of the individual's death, over the remaining life expectancy of the designated beneficiary, with such life expectancy determined using the age of the beneficiary as of his or her birthday in the year following the year of the individual's death, or, if elected, in accordance with paragraph (b)(3) below.

(2) If the individual's sole designated beneficiary is the individual's surviving spouse, the entire interest will be distributed, starting by the end of the calendar year following the calendar year of the individual's death (or by the end of the calendar year in which the individual would have attained age 70½, if later), over such spouse's life, or, if elected, in accordance with paragraph (b)(3) below. If the surviving spouse dies before required distributions commence to him or her, the remaining interest will be distributed, starting by the end of the calendar year following the calendar year of the spouse's death, over the spouse's designated beneficiary's remaining life expectancy determined using such beneficiary's age as of his or her birthday in the year following the death of the spouse, or, if elected, will be

distributed in accordance with paragraph (b)(3) below. If the surviving spouse dies after required distributions commence to him or her, any remaining interest will continue to be distributed under the contract option chosen.

(3) If there is no designated beneficiary, or if applicable by operation of paragraph (b)(1) or (b)(2) above, the entire interest will be distributed by the end of the calendar year containing the fifth anniversary of the individual's death (or of the spouse's death in the case of the surviving spouse's death before distributions are required to begin under paragraph (b)(2) above).

(4) Life expectancy is determined using the Single Life Table in Q&A-1 of § 1.401(a)(9)-9 of the Income Tax Regulations. If distributions are being made to a surviving spouse as the sole designated beneficiary, such spouse's remaining life expectancy for a year is the number in the Single Life Table corresponding to such spouse's age in the year. In all other cases, remaining life expectancy for a year is the number in the Single Life Table corresponding to the beneficiary's age in the year specified in paragraph (b)(1) or (2) and reduced by 1 for each subsequent year.

(c) The "interest" in the IRA includes the amount of any outstanding rollover, transfer and recharacterization under Q&As-7 and -8 of § 1.408-8 of the Income Tax Regulations and the actuarial value of any other benefits provided under the IRA, such as guaranteed death benefits.

(d) For purposes of paragraphs (a) and (b) above, required distributions are considered to commence on the individual's required beginning date or, if applicable, on the date distributions are required to begin to the surviving spouse under paragraph (b)(2) above. However, if distributions start prior to the applicable date in the preceding sentence, on an irrevocable basis (except for acceleration) under an annuity contract meeting the requirements of § 1.401(a)(9)-6 of the Income Tax Regulations, then required distributions are considered to commence on the annuity starting date.

(e) If the sole designated beneficiary is the individual's surviving spouse, the spouse may elect to treat the IRA as his or her own IRA. This election will be deemed to have been made if such surviving spouse makes a contribution to the IRA or fails to take required distributions as a beneficiary.

5. Nonforfeitability provision. [I.R.C. § 408(b)(4)]

   The interest of the individual is nonforfeitable.

6. Nontransferability provision. [I.R.C. § 408(b)(1)]

   This contract is nontransferable by the individual.

7. Provision for the application of premium refunds. [I.R.C. § 408(b)(2)]

Any refund of premiums (other than those attributable to excess contributions) will be applied, before the close of the calendar year following the year of the refund, toward the payment of future premiums or the purchase of additional benefits.

(This provision is required for annuities that provide for participation in dividends.)

8. Provision for interruption of premium payments. [I.R.C. § 408(b)(2), Prop. Treas. Reg. § 1.408-3(f)]

   If the premium payments are interrupted, the contract will be reinstated at any date prior to maturity upon payment of a premium to the Company, and the minimum premium amount for reinstatement shall be—(not to exceed $50), however, the Company may at its option either accept additional future payments or terminate the contract by payment in cash of the then present value of the paid up benefit if no premiums have been received for two full consecutive policy years and the paid up annuity benefit at maturity would be less than $20 per month.

9. Requirement that trustees or issuers furnish annual calendar-year reports. [Treas. Reg. §§ 1.408-5, 1.408-8]

   The issuer of an individual retirement annuity shall furnish annual calendar year reports concerning the status of the annuity and such information concerning required minimum distributions as is prescribed by the Commissioner of Internal Revenue.

10. Provision describing the type of compensation used for computing deductible limits. [I.R.C. § 219(f)(1), Treas. Reg. § 1.219-1(c)(1)]

    Compensation means wages, salaries, professional fees, or other amounts derived from or received for personal services actually rendered (including, but not limited to commissions paid salesmen, compensation for services on the basis of a percentage of profits, commissions on insurance premiums, tips, and bonuses) and includes earned income, as defined in Code § 401(c)(2) (reduced by the deduction the self-employed individual takes for contributions made to a self-employed retirement plan). For purposes of this definition, § 401(c)(2) shall be applied as if the term trade or business for purposes of § 1402 included service described in subsection (c)(6). Compensation does not include amounts derived from or received as earnings or profits from property (including but not limited to interest and dividends) or amounts not includible in gross income. Compensation also does not include any amount received as a pension or annuity or as deferred compensation. The term "compensation" shall include any amount includible in the individual's gross income under § 71 with respect to a divorce or separation instrument described in subparagraph (A) of § 71(b)(2).

Caution. The IRS warns that the information and sample provisions included in the LRM may not be appropriate in all cases. Acceptability may depend on the context in which the provisions are used.

Roth IRA Account-Opening Questions

Q 2:41 What identification is necessary to open a Roth IRA?

The IRA trustee (or custodian) must obtain the potential Roth IRA owner's name, address, date of birth, and Social Security number or individual taxpayer identification number when a Roth IRA is being established. The trustee (or custodian) is allowed to collect that information in a manner convenient to the trustee (or custodian).

Q 2:42 Must an individual be a U.S. citizen to establish a Roth IRA?

No, an individual need not be a U.S. citizen to establish a Roth IRA. Generally, a resident alien who is subject to U.S. federal income tax, has a Social Security number or an individual taxpayer identification number, and meets the eligibility requirements may establish a Roth IRA.

Q 2:43 Who must sign the Roth IRA agreement?

Both the Roth IRA owner and the trustee (or custodian) must sign the Roth IRA agreement. A spouse's signature may also be necessary if the Roth IRA owner lives in a community property state and names someone other than the owner's spouse as beneficiary.

Q 2:44 What financial institutions are authorized to accept Roth IRA contributions?

Any financial institution authorized to accept traditional IRA contributions will automatically be approved to accept Roth IRA contributions. Any other institution must submit an application to the IRS for approval to serve as a trustee or custodian for a Roth IRA (see Q 2:14).

Q 2:45 How many Roth IRAs may an individual establish?

There is no limit on the number of Roth IRAs an individual may establish; however, the overall combined annual contribution to multiple IRAs is limited to the same amount as the maximum contribution to a single IRA.

Q 2:46 May a Roth IRA be revoked?

Yes. A Roth IRA owner has the right to revoke a Roth IRA within seven days after receiving the disclosure statement for it. The revocation procedures for the

Roth IRA are the same as those for the traditional IRA (see Q 2:19). [I.R.C. § 408A]

Note. When a Roth IRA or a traditional IRA is revoked, the trustee (or custodian) must return the full amount of the contribution, without adjustment for such items as sales commissions, administrative expenses, or fluctuation in market value. [Treas. Reg. § 1.408-6(d)(4)(ii)(A)(2)]

Roth IRA Documentation

Q 2:47   How is a Roth IRA established?

A Roth IRA is established as a trust or custodial account in the same manner as a traditional IRA (see Q 2:4). An IRS model Roth document or a prototype document can be used, along with a plain-language disclosure (and, in some cases, a financial projection). After the Roth IRA is established, the financial institution must provide the owner with an amended plain-language disclosure statement that reflects any significant legislative or regulatory changes or updates of its policies and procedures. An amendment is usually required within 30 days of the effective date of a change. The financial organization must be able to demonstrate that it provided the required documents to the owner of a traditional IRA or Roth IRA, but it need not retain a copy of the disclosure in the IRA owner's file. [Treas. Reg. § 1.408-6]

Q 2:48   Does the IRS provide model forms for establishing Roth IRAs?

Yes. The IRS provides two model forms that may be used to establish Roth IRAs: Form 5305-R, Roth Individual Retirement Trust Account, and Form 5305-RA, Roth Individual Retirement Custodial Account.

Q 2:49   What is the benefit of using an IRS model Roth IRA form?

As with a traditional IRA, the benefit of using an IRS model form to establish a Roth IRA is that the form is automatically pre-approved. Therefore, the individual adopting a Roth IRA does not need to submit the form to the IRS for approval.

Note. Trustees and custodians using either of the IRS model Roth IRA forms are not required to submit any application or user fee to the IRS.

Q 2:50   What is the difference between the two IRS model Roth IRA forms?

The two IRS model Roth IRA forms are nearly identical. The only difference is that Form 5305-R uses the term *trustee* to describe the financial institution accepting the contribution and the term *grantor* to describe the contributor, while Form 5305-RA uses the terms *custodian* and *depositor,* respectively.

Caution. The question of whether nontrust departments should use the trust agreement (Form 5305-R) to establish Roth IRAs has generated some debate among professionals in the industry.

Q 2:51   What do the IRS model Roth IRA forms contain?

The IRS model Roth IRA forms, Forms 5305-R and 5305-RA, have the same appearance and organization as the IRS model forms for traditional IRAs, Forms 5305 and 5305-A, because the IRS duplicated as much language as possible from the traditional IRA forms when it created the model Roth IRA forms.

The IRS model Roth IRA forms contain the following:

1. A place to enter the name, address, date of birth, and Social Security number of the person establishing the Roth IRA;
2. A place to enter the name and address of the trustee (or custodian);
3. A place to enter the amount of the contribution;
4. The legal language set forth in eight articles;
5. Signature lines; and
6. Instructions on how to use the form.

Q 2:52   May a trustee or custodian modify the IRS model Roth IRA forms?

No. The language in the IRS model Roth IRA forms must not be changed. However, the IRS allows a trustee or a custodian to add articles to the model agreements following the IRS model language. The additional language may begin in "Article IX" and continue through additional articles as necessary. It may include definitions, investment powers, voting rights, exculpatory provisions, amendment and termination provisions, provisions regarding withdrawal of (custodian) fees from the account, state law requirements, beginning date of distributions, the cash-only requirement, treatment of excess contributions, prohibited transactions with the grantor or depositor, and other issues of importance to the trustee or custodian. [General Instructions to Form 5305-R and Form 5305-RA]

Q 2:53   May a trustee or custodian create its own prototype Roth IRA document?

Yes. The IRS allows a trustee or a custodian to draft prototype Roth IRA documents. The advantage of a prototype Roth IRA document is that it allows a trustee (or custodian) to tailor the language in the document to meet specific needs.

Drafters use Form 5306, Application for Approval of Prototype or Employer Sponsored Individual Retirement Arrangement (last revised in October 2006), to apply for approval of the prototype Roth IRA.

Q 2:54   What specific items does Form 5306 require to be included in a prototype Roth IRA document?

The same 15 items that Form 5306 requires for the application for approval of a traditional IRA prototype plan must likewise be addressed when applying for approval of a Roth IRA prototype plan. The 12 items that are required in a Roth IRA prototype must be marked on the form to refer to the plan article (or section) in which each item appears. [Form 5306, Part II] In its LRM for Roth IRAs, the IRS offers sample language for prototype Roth IRAs, which drafters are encouraged to use. The most recent version of the LRM, revised in May 2007, is available on the IRS Web site (see *http://www.irs.gov/pub/irs-tege/rira_lrm.pdf*). Among other changes, the new LRM completely revises the suggested language for post-death distributions. The IRS warns that some language in the LRM may not be appropriate in all cases. [Roth IRA LRM, p. 1 (May 2007)] The 15 items, shown here with sample language based on the LRM, are:

1. The exclusive benefit provision. [I.R.C. §§ 408A and 408(a)]

    The account is established for the exclusive benefit of the individual or his or her beneficiaries.

2. Provision that contributions other than rollovers must be in cash and not exceed the maximum limit. [I.R.C. §§ 219(b), 219(f)(1), 408(d)(3)(G), 408(p)(1)(B), 408(p)(2)(A)(iv), 408A(c), 408A(d)(6) and 408A(e) and Treas. Reg. §§ 1.219-1(c)(1) and 1.408A-3, -4 and -5]

    (a) Maximum Permissible Amount. Except in the case of a qualified rollover contribution or a recharacterization (as defined in (f) below), no contribution will be accepted unless it is in cash and the total of such contributions to all the individual's Roth IRAs for a taxable year does not exceed the applicable amount (as defined in (b) below), or the individual's compensation (as defined in (h) below), if less, for that taxable year. The contribution described in the previous sentence that may not exceed the lesser of the applicable amount or the individual's compensation is referred to as a "regular contribution." However, notwithstanding the dollar limits on contributions, an individual may make a repayment of a qualified reservist distribution described in Code § 72(t)(2)(G) during the 2-year period beginning on the day after the end of the active duty period or by August 17, 2008, if later. A "qualified rollover contribution" is a rollover contribution of a distribution from an IRA that meets the requirements of Code § 408(d)(3), except the one-rollover-per-year rule of Code § 408(d)(3)(B) does not apply if the rollover contribution is from an IRA other than a Roth IRA (a "non-Roth IRA"). For taxable years beginning after 2005, a qualified rollover contribution includes a rollover from a designated Roth account described in Code § 402A; and for taxable years beginning after 2007, a qualified rollover contribution also includes a rollover from an eligible retirement plan described in § 402(c)(8)(B). Contributions may be limited under (c) through (e) below.

(b) Applicable Amount. The applicable amount is determined under (i) or (ii) below:

> (i) If the individual is under age 50, the applicable amount is $3,000 for any taxable year beginning in 2002 through 2004, $4,000 for any taxable year beginning in 2005 through 2007 and $5,000 for any taxable year beginning in 2008 and years thereafter. After 2008, the $5,000 amount will be adjusted by the Secretary of the Treasury for cost-of-living increases under Code § 219(b)(5)(D). Such adjustments will be in multiples of $500.

> (ii) If the individual is 50 or older, the applicable amount under paragraph (i) above is increased by $500 for any taxable year beginning in 2002 through 2005 and by $1,000 for any taxable year beginning in 2006 and years thereafter.

> (iii) If the individual was a participant in a § 401(k) plan of a certain employer in bankruptcy described in Code § 219(b)(5)(C), then the applicable amount under paragraph (i) above is increased by $3,000 for taxable years beginning after 2006 and before 2010 only. An individual who makes contributions under this paragraph (iii) may not also make contributions under paragraph (ii).

(c) Regular Contribution Limit. The maximum regular contribution that can be made to all the individual's Roth IRAs for a taxable year is the smaller amount determined under (i) or (ii) below.

> (i) The maximum regular contribution is phased out ratably between certain levels of modified adjusted gross income ("modified AGI," defined in (g) below) in accordance with the following table:

Filing Status	Full Contribution	Phase-out Range	No Contribution
		Modified AGI (for 2008)	
Single or Head of Household	$101,000 or less	$101,000–$116,000	$116,000 or more
Joint Return or Qualifying Widow(er)	$159,000 or less	$159,000–$169,000	$169,000 or more
Married, Filing Separate Return	$0	$0–$10,000	$10,000 or more

If the individual's modified AGI for a taxable year is in the phase-out range, the maximum regular contribution determined under this table for that taxable year is rounded up to the next multiple of $10 and is not reduced below $200. After 2006, the dollar amounts above will be adjusted by the Secretary of the Treasury for cost-of-living increases under Code § 408A(c)(3). Such adjustments will be in multiples of $1,000.

(ii) If the individual makes regular contributions to both Roth and non-Roth IRAs for a taxable year, the maximum regular contribution that can be made to all the individual's Roth IRAs for that taxable year is reduced by the regular contributions made to the individual's non-Roth IRAs for the taxable year.

(d) Qualified Rollover Contribution Limit. A rollover from a non-Roth IRA cannot be made to this IRA if, for the year the amount is distributed from the non-Roth IRA, (i) the individual is married and files a separate return, (ii) the individual is not married and has modified AGI in excess of $100,000 or (iii) the individual is married and together the individual and the individual's spouse have modified AGI in excess of $100,000. For purposes of the preceding sentence, a husband and wife are not treated as married for a taxable year if they have lived apart at all times during that taxable year and file separate returns for the taxable year. For taxable years beginning after 2009, the limits in this paragraph (d) do not apply to qualified rollover contributions.

(e) SIMPLE IRA Limits. No contributions will be accepted under a SIMPLE IRA plan established by any employer pursuant to Code § 408(p). Also, no transfer or rollover of funds attributable to contributions made by a particular employer under its SIMPLE IRA plan will be accepted from a SIMPLE IRA, that is, an IRA used in conjunction with a SIMPLE IRA plan, prior to the expiration of the 2-year period beginning on the date the individual first participated in that employer's SIMPLE IRA plan.

(f) Recharacterization. A regular contribution to a non-Roth IRA may be recharacterized pursuant to the rules in § 1.408A-5 of the Income Tax Regulations as a regular contribution to this IRA, subject to the limits in (c) above.

(g) Modified AGI. For purposes of (c) and (d) above, an individual's modified AGI for a taxable year is defined in Code § 408A(c)(3) and does not include any amount included in adjusted gross income as a result of a rollover from an eligible retirement plan other than a Roth IRA (a "conversion").

(h) Compensation. For purposes of (a) above, compensation is defined as wages, salaries, professional fees, or other amounts derived from or received for personal services actually rendered (including, but not limited to commissions paid salesmen, compensation for services on the basis of a percentage of profits, commissions on insurance premiums, tips, and bonuses) and includes earned income, as defined in § 401(c)(2) (reduced by the deduction the self-employed individual takes for contributions made to a self-employed retirement plan). For purposes of this definition, Code § 401(c)(2) shall be applied as if the term trade or business for purposes of Code § 1402 included service described in subsection (c)(6). Compensation does not include amounts derived from or received as earnings or profits from property (including but not limited to interest and dividends) or amounts not includible in gross income. Compensation also does not include any amount received as a pension or annuity or as deferred compensation. The term "compensation" shall include any amount includible in the individual's gross income under Code § 71 with respect to a divorce or separation instrument described in subparagraph (A) of Code § 71(b)(2). In the case of a married individual filing a joint return, the greater compensation of his or her spouse is treated as his or her own compensation, but only to the extent that such spouse's compensation is not being used for purposes of the spouse making a contribution to a Roth IRA or a deductible contribution to a non-Roth IRA.

3. Provision acknowledging the prohibition of investment by an IRA in collectibles or a statement informing participants in the IRA plan that investment in collectibles will be a taxable distribution. [I.R.C. § 408(m)]

   If the trust acquires collectibles within the meaning of Code § 408(m) after December 31, 1981, trust assets will be treated as a distribution in an amount equal to the cost of such collectibles.

   (This provision is *not* required if the IRA precludes any investments that could be construed as collectibles. It should be noted that Code Section 408(m)(3) provides an exception to the rule for certain gold and silver coins.)

4. Prohibition of investment by an individual retirement account in life insurance contracts. [I.R.C. § 408(a)(3)]

   No part of the trust funds will be invested in life insurance contracts.

5. Statement of required distributions commencing before death. [I.R.C. § 408A(c)(5)]

   No amount is required to be distributed prior to the death of the individual for whose benefit the account was originally established.

6. Statement of required distributions commencing after death. [I.R.C. §§ 408(a)(6) and 408A(c)(5) and Treas. Reg. §§ 1.408-8 and 1.408A-6]

   (a) Notwithstanding any provision of this IRA to the contrary, the distribution of the individual's interest in the account shall be made in accordance with the requirements of Code § 408(a)(6), as modified by Code § 408A(c)(5), and the regulations thereunder, the provisions of which are herein incorporated by reference. If distributions are made from an annuity contract purchased from an insurance company, distributions thereunder must satisfy the requirements of § 1.401(a)(9)-6 of the Income Tax Regulations (taking into account Code § 408A(c)(5)), rather than the distribution rules in paragraphs (b), (c) and (d) below.

(b) Upon the death of the individual, his or her entire interest will be distributed at least as rapidly as follows:

(i) If the designated beneficiary is someone other than the individual's surviving spouse, the entire interest will be distributed, starting by the end of the calendar year following the calendar year of the individual's death, over the remaining life expectancy of the designated beneficiary, with such life expectancy determined using the age of the beneficiary as of his or her birthday in the year following the year of the individual's death, or, if elected, in accordance with paragraph (b)(iii) below.

(ii) If the individual's sole designated beneficiary is the individual's surviving spouse, the entire interest will be distributed, starting by the end of the calendar year following the calendar year of the individual's death (or by the end of the calendar year in which the individual would have attained age 70½, if later), over such spouse's life, or, if elected, in accordance with paragraph (b)(iii) below. If the surviving spouse dies before distributions are required to begin, the remaining interest will be distributed, starting by the end of the calendar year following the calendar year of the spouse's death, over the spouse's designated beneficiary's remaining life expectancy determined using such beneficiary's age as of his or her birthday in the year following the death of the spouse, or, if elected, will be distributed in accordance with paragraph (b)(iii) below. If the surviving spouse dies after distributions are required to begin, any remaining interest will be distributed over the spouse's remaining life expectancy determined using the spouse's age as of his or her birthday in the year of the spouse's death.

(iii) If there is no designated beneficiary, or if applicable by operation of paragraph (b)(i) or (b)(ii) above, the entire interest will be distributed by the end of the calendar year containing the fifth anniversary of the individual's death (or of the spouse's death in the case of the surviving spouse's death before distributions are required to begin under paragraph (b)(ii) above).

(iv) The amount to be distributed each year under paragraph (b)(i) or (ii) is the quotient obtained by dividing the value of the IRA as of the end of the preceding year by the remaining life expectancy specified in such paragraph. Life expectancy is determined using the Single Life Table in Q&A-1 of § 1.401(a)(9)-9 of the Income Tax Regulations. If distributions are being made to a surviving spouse as the sole designated beneficiary, such spouse's remaining life expectancy for a year is the number in the Single Life Table corresponding to such spouse's age in the year. In all other cases, remaining life expectancy for a year is the number in the Single Life Table corresponding to the beneficiary's age in the year specified in paragraph (b)(i) or (ii) and reduced by 1 for each subsequent year.

(c) The "value" of the IRA includes the amount of any outstanding rollover, transfer and recharacterization under Q&As-7 and -8 of § 1.408-8 of the Income Tax Regulations.

(d) If the sole designated beneficiary is the individual's surviving spouse, the spouse may elect to treat the IRA as his or her own IRA. This election will be deemed to have been made if such surviving spouse makes a contribution to the IRA or fails to take required distributions as a beneficiary.

7. Nonforfeitability provision. [I.R.C. § 408(a)(4)]

   The interest of an individual in the balance in his or her account is nonforfeitable at all times.

8. Nontransferability provision.

   (This provision is required only for Roth individual retirement annuity contracts (see Q 2:55).)

9. Provision governing the application of premium refunds, for any annuity that provides for participation in dividends.

   (This provision is required only for Roth individual retirement annuity contracts (see Q 2:55).)

10. Provision acknowledging the prohibition against commingling of assets. [I.R.C. § 408(a)(5)]

    The assets of the trust will not be commingled with other property except in a common trust fund or common investment fund.

11. Provision acknowledging the prohibition against requiring fixed premiums for an individual retirement annuity.

    (This provision is required only for Roth individual retirement annuity contracts (see Q 2:55).)

12. Requirement for separate accounting for the interest of each individual under an account or annuity established by an employer or employee association. [Treas. Reg. §§ 1.408-2(c)(3), 1.408A-2]

    Separate records will be maintained for the interest of each individual.

    (This provision is required *only* in Roth IRAs that are sponsored by the employer or employee association.)

13. Requirement that trustees or insurers furnish annual calendar-year reports concerning the status of the account or annuity. [I.R.C. §§ 408(i), 408A(d)(3)(D); Treas. Reg. §§ 1.408-5, 1.408-8]

   > The trustee of a Roth individual retirement account shall furnish annual calendar-year reports concerning the status of the account and such information concerning required minimum distributions as is prescribed by the Commissioner of Internal Revenue.

14. Provision that there be substitution for a nonbank trustee or custodian when the Commissioner of Internal Revenue issues a notification. [Treas. Reg. § 1.408-2(e)(6)(v)]

   > (This provision is required *only* in IRA accounts that are sponsored by non-bank trustees or custodians.)

15. Provision describing the type of compensation used for computing deductible limits.

   > (This provision does not apply to Roth IRAs.)

Caution. The IRS warns that the information and sample provisions included in the LRM may not be appropriate in all cases. Acceptability may depend on the context in which the provisions are used.

Q 2:55 Does the IRS offer sample language for a prototype Roth IRA that specifically applies to a Roth individual retirement annuity?

Yes. The following clauses are based on Part B of the LRM for Roth IRAs (May 2007) which contains sample language that specifically applies to individual retirement annuity contracts (see *http://www.irs.gov/pub/irs-tege/rira_lrm.pdf*). The sample provisions shown in Q 2:54 are based on Part A of the LRM, which does not apply to such contracts.

1. The exclusive benefit provision. [I.R.C. §§ 408A and 408(b)]

   > The contract is established for the exclusive benefit of the individual or his or her beneficiaries.

2. Provision that contributions other than rollovers must be in cash and not exceed the maximum limit. [I.R.C. §§ 72(t)(2)(G), 219(b), 219(f)(1), 408(d)(3)(G), 408(p)(1)(B), 408(p)(2)(A)(iv), 408A(c), 408A(d)(6) and 408A(e)]

   > (a) Maximum Permissible Amount. Except in the case of a qualified rollover contribution or a recharacterization (as defined in (f) below), no contribution will be accepted unless it is in cash and the total of such contributions to all the individual's Roth IRAs for a taxable year does not exceed the applicable amount (as defined in (b) below), or the individual's compensation (as defined in (h) below), if less, for that taxable year. The contribution described in the

previous sentence that may not exceed the lesser of the applicable amount or the individual's compensation is referred to as a "regular contribution." However, notwithstanding the dollar limits on contributions, an individual may make a repayment of a qualified reservist distribution described in Code § 72(t)(2)(G) during the 2-year period beginning on the day after the end of the active duty period or by August 17, 2008, if later. A "qualified rollover contribution" is a rollover contribution of a distribution from an IRA that meets the requirements of Code § 408(d)(3), except the one-rollover-per-year rule of § 408(d)(3)(B) does not apply if the rollover contribution is from an IRA other than a Roth IRA (a "nonRoth IRA"). For taxable years beginning after 2005, a qualified rollover contribution includes a rollover from a designated Roth account described in Code § 402A; and for taxable years beginning after 2007, a qualified rollover contribution also includes a rollover from an eligible retirement plan described in § 402(c)(8)(B). Contributions may be limited under (c) through (e) below.

(b) Applicable Amount. The applicable amount is determined below:

(i) If the individual is under age 50, the applicable amount is $3,000 for any taxable year beginning in 2002 through 2004, $4,000 for any taxable year beginning in 2005 through 2007 and $5,000 for any taxable year beginning in 2008 and years thereafter. After 2008, the $5,000 amount will be adjusted by the Secretary of the Treasury for cost-of-living increases under Code § 219(b)(5)(D). Such adjustments will be in multiples of $500.

(ii) If the individual is 50 or older, the applicable amount under paragraph (i) above is increased by $500 for any taxable year beginning in 2002 through 2005 and by $1,000 for any taxable year beginning in 2006 and years thereafter.

(iii) If the individual was a participant in a § 401(k) plan of a certain employer in bankruptcy described in Code § 219(b)(5)(C), then the applicable amount under paragraph (i) above is increased by $3,000 for taxable years beginning after 2006 and before 2010 only. An individual who makes contributions under this paragraph (iii) may not also make contributions under paragraph (ii).

(c) Regular Contribution Limit. The maximum regular contribution that can be made to all the individual's Roth IRAs for a taxable year is the smaller amount determined under (i) or (ii) below.

(i) The maximum regular contribution is phased out ratably between certain levels of modified adjusted gross income ("modified AGI," defined in (g) below) in accordance with the following table:

Filing Status	Full Contribution	Phase-out Range	No Contribution
		Modified AGI (for 2008)	
Single or Head of Household	$101,000 or less	$101,000–$116,000	$116,000 or more
Joint Return or Qualifying Widow(er)	$159,000 or less	$159,000–$169,000	$169,000 or more
Married, Filing Separate Return	$0	$0–$10,000	$10,000 or more

If the individual's modified AGI for a taxable year is in the phase-out range, the maximum regular contribution determined under this table for that taxable year is rounded up to the next multiple of $10 and is not reduced below $200. After 2006, the dollar amounts above will be adjusted by the Secretary of the Treasury for cost-of-living increases under Code § 408A(c)(3). Such adjustments will be in multiples of $1,000.

(ii) If the individual makes regular contributions to both Roth and nonRoth IRAs for a taxable year, the maximum regular contribution that can be made to all the individual's Roth IRAs for that taxable year is reduced by the regular contributions made to the individual's nonRoth IRAs for the taxable year.

(d) Qualified Rollover Contribution Limit. A rollover from an eligible retirement plan other than a Roth IRA or a designated Roth account cannot be made to this IRA if, for the year the amount is distributed from the other plan, (i) the individual is married and files a separate return, (ii) the individual is not married and has modified AGI in excess of $100,000 or (iii) the individual is married and together the individual and the individual's spouse have modified AGI in excess of $100,000. For purposes of the preceding sentence, a husband and wife are not treated as married for a taxable year if they have lived apart at all times during that taxable year and file separate returns for the taxable year. For taxable years beginning after 2009, the limits in this paragraph (d) do not apply to qualified rollover contributions.

(e) SIMPLE IRA Limits. No contributions will be accepted under a SIMPLE IRA plan established by any employer pursuant to § 408(p). Also, no transfer or rollover of funds attributable to contributions made by a particular employer under its SIMPLE IRA plan will be accepted from a SIMPLE IRA, that is, an IRA used in conjunction with a SIMPLE IRA plan, prior to the expiration of the 2-year period beginning on the date the individual first participated in that employer's SIMPLE IRA plan.

(f) Recharacterization. A regular contribution to a nonRoth IRA may be recharacterized pursuant to the rules in § 1.408A-5 of the regulations as a regular contribution to this IRA, subject to the limits in (c) above.

(g) Modified AGI. For purposes of (c) and (d) above, an individual's modified AGI for a taxable year is defined in Code § 408A(c)(3)(C)(i) and does not include any amount included in adjusted gross income as a result of a rollover from an eligible retirement plan other than a Roth IRA (a "conversion").

(h) Compensation. For purposes of (a) above, compensation is defined as wages, salaries, professional fees, or other amounts derived from or received for personal services actually rendered (including, but not limited to commissions paid salesmen, compensation for services on the basis of a percentage of profits, commissions on insurance premiums, tips, and bonuses) and includes earned income, as defined in Code § 401(c)(2) (reduced by the deduction the self-employed individual takes for contributions made to a self-employed retirement plan). For purposes of this definition, § 401(c)(2) shall be applied as if the term trade or business for purposes of § 1402 included service described in subsection (c)(6). Compensation does not include amounts derived from or received as earnings or profits from property (including but not limited to interest and dividends) or amounts not includible in gross income. Compensation also does not include any amount received as a pension or annuity or as deferred compensation. The term "compensation" shall include any amount includible in the individual's gross income under § 71 with respect to a divorce or separation instrument described in subparagraph (A) of § 71(b)(2). In the case of a married individual filing a joint return, the greater compensation of his or her spouse is treated as his or her own compensation, but only to the extent that such spouse's compensation is not being used for purposes of the spouse making a contribution to a Roth IRA or a deductible contribution to a nonRoth IRA.

3. Statement of required distributions commencing before death. [I.R.C. § 408A(c)(5)]

   No amount is required to be distributed prior to the death of the individual for whose benefit the contract was originally established.

4. Statement of required distributions commencing after death. [I.R.C. §§ 408(b)(3), 408A(c)(5); Treas. Reg. §§ 1.408-8 and 1.408A-6]

   (a) Notwithstanding any provision of this IRA to the contrary, the distribution of the individual's interest in the IRA shall be made in accordance with the requirements of Code § 408(b)(3), as modified by § 408A(c)(5), and the regulations thereunder, the provisions of which are herein incorporated by reference. If distributions are not made in the form of an annuity on an irrevocable basis (except for acceleration), then distribution of the interest in the IRA (as determined under section [reference to IRA provision that defines "interest" in the IRA]) must satisfy the requirements of Code § 408(a)(6), as modified by § 408A(c)(5), and the regulations thereunder, rather than the distribution rules in paragraphs (b), (c), (d) and (e) below.

(b) Upon the death of the individual, his or her entire interest will be distributed at least as rapidly as follows:

(i) If the designated beneficiary is someone other than the individual's surviving spouse, the entire interest will be distributed, starting by the end of the calendar year following the calendar year of the individual's death, over the remaining life expectancy of the designated beneficiary, with such life expectancy determined using the age of the beneficiary as of his or her birthday in the year following the year of the individual's death, or, if elected, in accordance with paragraph (b)(iii) below.

(ii) If the individual's sole designated beneficiary is the individual's surviving spouse, the entire interest will be distributed, starting by the end of the calendar year following the calendar year of the individual's death (or by the end of the calendar year in which the individual would have attained age 70½, if later), over such spouse's life, or, if elected, in accordance with paragraph (b)(iii) below. If the surviving spouse dies before required distributions commence to him or her, the remaining interest will be distributed, starting by the end of the calendar year following the calendar year of the spouse's death, over the spouse's designated beneficiary's remaining life expectancy determined using such beneficiary's age as of his or her birthday in the year following the death of the spouse, or, if elected, will be distributed in accordance with paragraph (b)(iii) below. If the surviving spouse dies after required distributions commence to him or her, any remaining interest will continue to be distributed under the contract option chosen.

(iii) If there is no designated beneficiary, or if applicable by operation of paragraph (b)(i) or (b)(ii) above, the entire interest will be distributed by the end of the calendar year containing the fifth anniversary of the individual's death (or of the spouse's death in the case of the surviving spouse's death before distributions are required to begin under paragraph (b)(ii) above).

(iv) Life expectancy is determined using the Single Life Table in Q&A-1 of § 1.401(a)(9)-9 of the Income Tax Regulations. If distributions are being made to a surviving spouse as the sole designated beneficiary, such spouse's remaining life expectancy for a year is the number in the Single Life Table corresponding to such spouse's age in the year. In all other cases, remaining life expectancy for a year is the number in the Single Life Table corresponding to the beneficiary's age in the year specified in paragraph (b)(i) or (ii) and reduced by 1 for each subsequent year.

(c) The "interest" in the IRA includes the amount of any outstanding rollover, transfer and recharacterization under Q&As-7 and -8 of § 1.408-8 of the Income Tax Regulations and the actuarial value of any other benefits provided under the IRA, such as guaranteed death benefits.

(d) For purposes of paragraph (b)(ii) above, required distributions are considered to commence on the date distributions are required to begin to the surviving spouse under such paragraph. However, if distributions start prior to the applicable date in the preceding sentence, on an irrevocable basis (except for acceleration) under an annuity contract meeting the requirements of § 1.401(a)(9)-6 of the Income Tax Regulations, then required distributions are considered to commence on the annuity starting date.

(e) If the sole designated beneficiary is the individual's surviving spouse, the spouse may elect to treat the IRA as his or her own IRA. This election will be deemed to have been made if such surviving spouse makes a contribution to the IRA or fails to take required distributions as a beneficiary.

5. Nonforfeitability provision. [I.R.C. § 408(b)(4)]

    The interest of the individual is nonforfeitable.

6. Nontransferability provision. [I.R.C. § 408(b)(1)]

    This contract is nontransferable by the individual.

7. Provision governing the application of premium refunds. [I.R.C. § 408(b)(2)]

    Any refund of premiums (other than those attributable to excess contributions) will be applied, before the close of the calendar year following the year of the refund, toward the payment of future premiums or the purchase of additional benefits.

    (This provision is required for annuities that provide for participation in dividends.)

8. Provision for interruption of premium payments. [I.R.C. § 408(b)(2); Prop. Treas. Reg. § 1.408-3(f)]

    If the premium payments are interrupted, the contract will be reinstated at any date prior to maturity upon payment of a premium to the insurance company, and the minimum premium amount for reinstatement shall be—(not to exceed $50), however, the insurance company may at its option either accept additional future payments or terminate the contract by payment in cash of the then present value of the paid up benefit if no premiums have been received for two full consecutive policy years and the paid up annuity benefit at maturity would be less than $20 per month.

9. Requirement that trustees or issuers furnish annual calendar-year reports. [I.R.C. §§ 408(i), 408A(d)(3)(D); Treas. Reg. §§ 1.408-5, 1.408-8]

> The issuer of a Roth individual retirement annuity shall furnish annual calendar year reports concerning the status of the annuity and such information concerning required minimum distributions as is prescribed by the Commissioner of Internal Revenue.

Caution. The IRS warns that the information and sample provisions included in the LRM may not be appropriate in all cases. Acceptability may depend on the context in which the provisions are used.

Q 2:56 May one document serve to establish either a Roth IRA or a traditional IRA?

Yes, one document may be used to establish a Roth IRA or a traditional IRA. A trustee or custodian that wants to combine those two IRAs into one document must develop its own prototype form, because the IRS model forms for Roth and traditional IRAs are separate and may not be combined (unless submitted as a prototype).

The IRS will permit a prototype sponsor to combine a Roth IRA and a traditional IRA in the same document as long as (1) a separate trust, custodial account, or annuity is established for each type of contribution and (2) the document, as completed by the owner, clearly indicates whether it is to be used as a traditional IRA or as a Roth IRA. [Rev. Proc. 98-59, 1998-2 C.B. 729; Ann. 97-122, 1997-50 I.R.B. 63]

> **Practice Pointer.** A prototype document could use a check-box system to distinguish traditional IRA contributions from Roth IRA contributions.

Q 2:57 What must be included in the disclosure statement for a Roth IRA?

The IRS requires that the trustee (or custodian) of a Roth IRA provide the IRA owner with a plain-language disclosure explaining the Roth IRA. [Forms 5305-R, 5305-RA] The Treasury regulations governing disclosures were written for traditional IRAs but apply to Roth IRAs as well until they are revised by the IRS. Currently, the disclosure statement must provide a concise explanation of the following:

- Statutory requirements for the Roth IRA
- Income tax consequences of contributions (including nondeductibility), distributions, and rollovers
- Eligibility requirements
- Procedures for revocation of the account

- Prohibited transaction rule
- Rule against borrowing money from an IRA
- Rule against pledging the account as security for a loan
- Estate and gift tax consequences
- Penalties on premature distributions and other tax penalties
- Beneficiary minimum distribution requirements
- Excess contribution rules
- Form 5329, Additional Taxes on Qualified Plans (Including IRAs) and Other Tax-Favored Accounts
- That the document has been approved as to form by the IRS, but that IRS approval does not represent a determination of the merits of the account
- That further information is available at a district office of the IRS

[Treas. Reg. § 1.408-6(d)(4)]

Q 2:58 What is a financial disclosure statement for a Roth IRA?

Like the financial disclosure statement for a traditional IRA, the financial disclosure statement for a Roth IRA illustrates the growth of the assets in the account. The projections must make a number of assumptions and then project the growth of the account over each of the first five years and as of the Roth IRA owner's attainment of ages 60, 65, and 70. [Rev. Rul. 86-78, 1986-1 C.B. 208]

Q 2:59 When is a financial disclosure statement required for a Roth IRA?

Treasury regulations require a financial disclosure statement for a Roth IRA if the rate of growth in the Roth IRA can be reasonably projected or is guaranteed. [Treas. Reg. § 1.408-6(d)(4)(v)] For example, if an individual opened a Roth IRA and selected a fixed-rate certificate of deposit offered by a bank insured by the Federal Deposit Insurance Corporation (FDIC) as an initial investment, that investment growth can be reasonably projected; therefore, a disclosure statement is required.

Q 2:60 Is a conversion of a traditional IRA to a Roth IRA separately accounted for on the IRS model Roth IRA forms?

No. The IRS has revised the model Roth IRA forms so that there is no special designation for Roth conversion IRAs.

Payroll Deduction IRA

Q 2:61   How is a payroll deduction IRA established?

The IRS encourages employers to allow employees to establish payroll deduction IRAs. An employee establishes (and contributes to) a payroll deduction IRA (traditional or Roth) by direct deposit through payroll deduction. [Ann. 99-2, 1999-1 C.B. 305]

Deemed IRA

Q 2:62   What is a deemed IRA?

A *deemed IRA* is an account that a qualified employer maintains separately under a retirement plan to receive employees' voluntary contributions, making it possible for employees to do one-stop saving for retirement. This separate account may be treated as a traditional IRA or as a Roth IRA. If it meets the requirements of an IRA, it is subject only to the rules governing IRAs and none of the qualified plan rules or limits will apply. Note that a SIMPLE IRA and a SEP IRA may not be used as a deemed IRA.

A qualified employer plan may be a qualified pension plan, a profit-sharing plan, a stock bonus plan (Section 401(a) plan), a qualified employee annuity plan (Section 403(a) plan), a tax-sheltered annuity plan (Section 403(b) plan), or a deferred compensation plan (Section 457(b) plan) maintained by a state, a political subdivision of a state, or an agency or instrumentality of a state or political subdivision of a state. [I.R.C. § 408(q); IRS Publication 590, *Individual Retirement Arrangements (IRAs)* 2008; see Appendix A.]

Q 2:63   In what way is a deemed IRA treated differently from other IRAs?

Unlike other IRAs, a deemed IRA is not required to create a separate trust for each individual account. Rather, all deemed IRAs under a qualified employer plan may be held in a single trust as long as that trust is separate from the trust that holds other assets of the plan, there is separate accounting for each deemed IRA, and each deemed IRA complies with the requirements applicable to its type, whether traditional or Roth. [Prop. Treas. Reg. § 1.408(q)-1(f)(2)]

If the portion of the employer plan that is not a deemed IRA fails to satisfy its qualification requirements, the deemed IRA is not considered to be a deemed IRA. However, the account or annuity that was intended to be a deemed IRA may still be treated as a traditional or Roth IRA if it satisfies the applicable IRA requirements. Employer plans that fail to satisfy the applicable qualification requirements may correct the qualification failure using the Employee Plans Compliance Resolutions System (EPCRS) or another administrative practice. [Rev. Proc. 2006-27, 2006-22 I.R.B. 945; *modified by* Rev. Proc. 2007-49, 2007-30 I.R.B. 141; *modified and superseded by* Rev. Proc. 2008-50, 2008-35 I.R.B. 464]

Chapter 3

Contributions to Traditional and Roth IRAs

Martin Fleisher, Esq.
Jo Ann Lippe, Esq.

For both traditional and Roth IRAs, the annual contribution limit is $5,000 for contributions made for 2009 and years thereafter. Taxpayers who are age 50 or older by the end of the year may contribute an additional $1,000.

Contributions may be apportioned among IRAs in any fashion as long as the annual limit is not exceeded and as long as the individual meets the eligibility requirements. A married couple filing jointly may contribute a total of $10,000 ($12,000 if each spouse is age 50 or older), even if one of the spouses is not working. Contributions to the Coverdell education savings account (Coverdell ESA) (see chapter 13), are considered separately and do not count against the annual limit.

Everyone under age 70½ who has compensation (i.e., wages or self-employment income) is eligible to contribute to a traditional IRA. The only question is whether the contribution is deductible. If an individual is considered an active participant in an employer-sponsored retirement plan, his or her eligibility to deduct the IRA contribution begins to be phased out at certain income levels. For an individual who is not an active participant but whose spouse is, different income levels apply.

Roth IRA contributions are never deductible. To be eligible for a Roth IRA, an individual must (1) have compensation and (2) have adjusted gross income that does not exceed certain levels.

Prior to the contribution deadline for any year, contributions that were originally designated as one type (e.g., as Roth IRA contributions) may be recharacterized (along with their earnings) as being another type (e.g., as traditional IRA contributions). Recharacterization is essentially a bookkeeping function and does not trigger a tax, although it may affect the deductibility of a contribution. Subject to restrictions, a traditional IRA may also be converted to a Roth IRA, but conversions (unlike recharacterizations) are taxable.

Certain individuals may be able to claim a credit for a percentage of contributions made to a traditional or Roth IRA, as well as for a percentage of salary reduction contributions made to a SEP or SIMPLE IRA. (The tax credit also applies to salary reduction contributions to qualified plans, Section 403(b) annuities, or eligible deferred compensation plans of state and local governments, which are not covered by this book.) Eligibility for the credit is restricted to individuals who are at least age 18 and whose adjusted gross income is below certain limits, excluding students and individuals claimed as an exemption on someone else's return.

Overview

Q 3:1   Do the traditional IRA and the Roth IRA follow the same rules concerning eligibility and contributions?

No. Although many of the contribution rules for the traditional IRA also apply to the Roth IRA, the overall rules are different.

Q 3:2   What contribution and eligibility rules do the traditional IRA and the Roth IRA share?

Both the traditional IRA and the Roth IRA must comply with the following rules concerning eligibility and contributions:

1. *Contribution amount.* An individual's annual contributions to traditional and Roth IRAs are subject, on an aggregate basis, to a single contribution limit (see Qs 3:4, 3:5).

2. *Contribution deadline.* Traditional and Roth IRA contributions must be made by the IRA owner's tax filing due date, not including extensions. [I.R.C. § 219(f)(3)]

3. *Spousal IRA rules.* Similar rules regarding the ability to make contributions on behalf of lesser-compensated spouses apply to traditional and Roth IRAs (see Qs 3:10 to 3:17). [I.R.C. § 219(c)]

Q 3:3   What contribution rules are unique to either the traditional IRA or the Roth IRA?

The following rules are unique to either the traditional IRA or the Roth IRA:

1. *Tax deductibility.* Roth IRA contributions are never deductible; traditional IRA contributions can be deductible if certain conditions are satisfied.

2. *Age 70½ eligibility limitation.* Individuals who have attained age 70½ by the end of the taxable year for which the contribution is made are not eligible to make traditional IRA contributions [I.R.C. §§ 219(d)(1), 408(o)]; this limitation does not apply to the Roth IRA.

3. *Income limits.* The Roth IRA rules place maximum income limits on eligibility; the traditional IRA rules do not.

4. *Rollover contributions.* Although many of the rollover rules are identical for Roth and traditional IRAs, some key differences exist. The most important is that all qualified plan amounts may be rolled over to traditional IRAs, but only amounts from "designated Roth accounts" (DRACs) within qualified plans may be rolled over to Roth IRAs. Roth IRAs may, however, receive conversion contributions (rollovers) from traditional IRAs (see Qs 3:84–3:102).

Contribution Amount

Q 3:4   How much may an individual who is under age 50 contribute for one taxable year to a traditional IRA, a Roth IRA, or both?

For 2009, the maximum annual contribution to a traditional IRA (whether or not deductible), a Roth IRA, or a combination of the two, by an individual who is under age 50 is the lesser of $5,000 or the individual's compensation. This limit is subject to annual increase by a cost-of-living adjustment (COLA) that is applied in $500 increments, but the limit for 2009 is unchanged from 2008. [I.R.C. § 219(b)(5); Rev. Proc. 2007-66, 2007-45 I.R.B. 970]

> **Example.** Alan, who is single and age 47, lives in a religious community and earns a salary of only $3,500 per year, but he has investment income of $15,000 per year. Because Alan's taxable compensation is $3,500, the most he can contribute to an IRA is $3,500. If Alan receives a raise to $5,500 in 2009, his maximum contribution would be $5,000.

Married couples who take advantage of the special spousal rules (see Qs 3:10–3:17) may contribute a maximum of $10,000 for 2009 (assuming both spouses are under age 50), or their total compensation if less. The total may be allocated between spouses in any proportion as long as neither spouse is credited with more than $5,000. [I.R.C. § 219(b)(5)(A)]

Special rules allow a small number of individuals to contribute larger amounts to traditional and Roth IRAs. Under the Pension Protection Act of 2006 [Pub. L. No. 109-280, 120 Stat. 780] (PPA), certain employees of bankrupt companies may contribute larger amounts for 2006 through 2009 only (see Qs 3:31–3:32). A provision of the Heroes Act of 2008 [Pub. L. No. 110-245, § 109] allows military gratuities and payments received under the Servicemembers Group Life Insurance (SGLI) program to be contributed. Finally, pursuant to the Tax Extenders and AMT Relief Act of 2008 [Pub. L. No. 110-343], some settlement payments received in the *Exxon Valdez* litigation may now be contributed to IRAs (see Q 3:33).

Q 3:5   How much may an individual who is age 50 or older contribute to a traditional IRA, a Roth IRA, or both for one taxable year?

An individual who is at least age 50 by the end of a year is permitted to make an additional "catch-up" contribution of $1,000 for the year. Unlike the underlying contribution limit, this catch-up amount is not subject to cost-of-living adjustment. Table 3-1 shows the resulting contribution limits that apply to individuals who attain age 50 or older during the contribution year.

Table 3-1. Contribution Limits with Catch-Up Amounts

Year	General Contribution Limit	Additional Catch-up Contribution
2009	$5,000	$1,000
2010 and later	$5,000 plus adjustment, if any*	$1,000

---

* Cost-of-living increases apply in $500 increments.

Example. Mel will be age 50 on December 31, 2009, and, therefore, he is eligible to make a $6,000 contribution for 2009. Mel's wife, Dorothy, will reach age 50 on January 2, 2010. Since the deadline for making 2009 IRA contributions is April 15, 2010, Dorothy may already be age 50 when she makes her 2009 contribution. Nonetheless, her 2009 IRA contribution is limited to $5,000.

Q 3:6 May an individual make both a traditional IRA and a Roth IRA contribution for the same tax year?

Yes. An individual may contribute to both a traditional IRA and a Roth IRA in the same tax year, up to the maximum contribution amounts described above (see Qs 3:4, 3:5) as long as the Roth IRA contribution does not exceed the maximum prescribed for the individual's modified adjusted gross income (MAGI) (see Q 3:71). [I.R.C. § 219(b)(1)]

Example 1. Barbara is single, age 48, works full time, and has MAGI of $58,000 in 2009 for purposes of making a traditional IRA contribution. She determines that she is eligible to deduct $2,500 (see Qs 3:64–3:66). Barbara decides to make a $2,500 traditional IRA contribution and takes the $2,500 deduction. She may also make up to a $2,500 Roth IRA contribution in order to take advantage of her $5,000 combined contribution limit.

Example 2. Chuck is under age 50, married, and an active retirement plan participant. He files a joint income tax return, and has MAGI of $165,000. He calculates his maximum Roth IRA contribution as $3,000. Chuck may make a $3,000 Roth IRA contribution and an additional $2,000 nondeductible IRA contribution. His wife may do the same.

Q 3:7 Does creating multiple IRAs increase an individual's annual contribution limit?

No. Although an individual may split his or her contributions among multiple IRAs, the annual contribution limit remains unaffected. [I.R.C. § 219(b)(1)]

Q 3:8 If less than the maximum IRA contribution is made for a taxable year, may the balance be carried forward to another year?

No. The IRA contribution limit is applied annually and may not be increased even if a contribution has been forgone in an earlier year. A contribution in excess of the limit in any year may, however, be corrected by contributing less than would otherwise have been permitted in the later year (subject to penalty). Even in that case, no more than the maximum contribution may be claimed for the subsequent year.

> **Example.** Andrea was entitled to contribute to her traditional IRA and deduct $1,000 in 2008 and $1,500 in 2009 (the amounts of her taxable compensation for those years). Andrea actually contributed $1,400 for 2008 and therefore had a $400 excess contribution subject to a 6 percent (or $24) excise tax. [See chapter 7 and IRS Publication 590, *Individual Retirement Arrangements (IRAs)* 2008, in Appendix A, for a full discussion of the excise tax on excess contributions.]
>
> Andrea could have corrected the 2008 excess contribution of $400 in 2009 and avoided the excise tax that year by making a 2009 contribution of only $1,100 (the allowable deductible contribution of $1,500 minus the $400 excess amount from 2008 that she wished to treat as a deductible contribution in 2009). Andrea could have deducted $1,500 in 2009 (the $1,100 actually contributed plus the $400 excess from 2008). But this correction does not avoid the excise tax for 2008.

For a fuller discussion of the treatment of excess contributions, see Q 7:36.

Q 3:9 Is a payment of either traditional IRA or Roth IRA account fees from outside sources treated as a contribution to the IRA?

The answer depends on the type of fee charged and the source of funds used for payment. Annual maintenance fees paid to an IRA trustee or custodian using money outside the IRA are not treated as IRA contributions. If such fees are paid from funds in the IRA, however, and the participant reimburses the account for the payment, the reimbursement is treated as a regular IRA contribution.

Brokerage commissions charged on a transactional basis (i.e., with respect to purchases or sales of securities held in an IRA) are considered expenses of the account, so if non-IRA funds are used to pay the commissions, the payments are treated as IRA contributions. By contrast, management fees calculated as a percentage of an IRA's total asset value are (like annual maintenance fees) not deemed to be IRA contributions when paid from non-IRA sources. [*See* Rev. Rul. 86-142, 1986-2 C.B. 60; Priv. Ltr. Rul. 200507021 (Feb. 18, 2005).]

Some financial institutions offer IRA accounts in which all the services are covered by a single "wrap" fee. In Private Letter Ruling 200507021 (Feb. 18, 2005), the IRS concluded that if the wrap fee is calculated as a percentage of the assets under management and bears no relation to the number of transactions executed (and such number is unlimited), then payment of the wrap fee using non-IRA funds is not deemed to be a contribution to the IRA.

In the foregoing cases, any amount deemed to be an IRA contribution counts toward the IRA owner's contribution limit for the year and must be reported on Form 5498 (see Q 7:154). Moreover, any deemed contribution that causes the contribution limit to be exceeded for the year is also subject to the 6 percent penalty for excess contributions. [Priv. Ltr. Rul. 200507021 (Feb. 18, 2005)]

Limit for Spousal IRA Contributions

Q 3:10   What is a spousal IRA contribution?

A *spousal IRA* contribution is a contribution to a traditional or Roth IRA that one spouse makes on behalf of the other spouse. The rule allows a spouse without sufficient compensation to establish an IRA and receive an IRA contribution. [I.R.C. § 219(c)(1)]

Q 3:11   What are the eligibility rules for spousal contributions to a traditional or Roth IRA?

To be able to take advantage of the spousal IRA rules for either a traditional or a Roth IRA, a couple must meet the following requirements:

1. They must file a joint federal income tax return.
2. The receiving spouse must have less compensation than the spouse making the contribution (or no compensation) (see Qs 3:18–3:30 for the definition of compensation).

[I.R.C. § 219(c)(2); Treas. Reg. § 1.408A-3, Q&A-4]

Q 3:12   Can a same-sex married couple make use of the spousal IRA rules?

Generally no. As discussed above (see Q 3:11), to be able to take advantage of the spousal IRA rules, the couple must file a joint federal income tax return. To be able to do so, the individuals must be legally married under federal law. The Defense of Marriage Act (DOMA), which defines marriage as a union between a man and a woman, does not permit a same-sex couple that is legally married under state law to file a joint tax return. [Pub. L. No. 104-199, 110 Stat. 2419 (1996)]

However, if a member of a heterosexual couple has a gender change, the IRS presumably would continue to allow the couple to take advantage of the spousal IRA rules. An IRS spokesman declined to comment to the media on transgender issues. [*Through Sickness, Health and Sex Change*, The New York Times, Style, p. 7 (Apr. 27, 2008)]

Q 3:13   How much may a couple contribute to an IRA using the spousal rules?

For 2009, the total combined contribution a couple may make to both their Roth IRAs and their traditional IRAs is the lesser of $10,000 or the couple's combined compensation for the year (with an additional $1,000 permitted for each spouse who is age 50 or over by the end of the year) (see Qs 3:2, 3:5). The spouses may divide the total contribution in any manner they choose, as long as no more than $5,000, plus a catch-up of $1,000 if applicable, is contributed on behalf of each spouse to any type of IRA or combination of IRAs. [I.R.C. § 219(c)(1)]

> **Example 1.** Jason and Ellen, both age 45, are married and file a joint federal income tax return. Jason works as a swimming coach and earns $30,000. Ellen does not work outside the home and has no compensation. Jason may make a $5,000 contribution to his own Roth IRA and a $5,000 contribution to a Roth IRA for Ellen.

> **Example 2.** Felix and Gloria are 60 years old and married. They file a joint federal income tax return. Felix has compensation of $10,000, and Gloria has compensation of $2,000. If neither Felix nor Gloria contributes to a traditional IRA, each may contribute $6,000 to a Roth IRA in 2009. That is because the couple is allowed to split their combined compensation of $12,000 so that each can make a Roth IRA contribution.

Q 3:14   Other than the eligibility requirement, is a spousal IRA different from a regular contributory IRA?

No. Once the contribution is made, the spousal IRA is treated as an IRA for the spouse receiving the contribution. The spouse making the contribution enjoys no special control over the IRA. The trustee or custodian receiving the contribution treats the spousal IRA in the same manner as any regular contributory IRA.

Q 3:15   What rules apply to a spousal IRA based on the age of the spouse?

If one spouse (the first spouse) is age 70½ or older, the other spouse (the second spouse) may contribute as much as $6,000 to a Roth spousal IRA, but nothing at all to a traditional spousal IRA, for the benefit of the first spouse. The second spouse may contribute as much as $6,000 to either type of spousal IRA for a first spouse who is at least age 50 but younger than age 70½, or as much as $5,000 to either type of spousal IRA for a first spouse who is younger than age 50. The age of the contributing spouse does not matter, but the couple must file jointly for any tax year for which a spousal IRA contribution is made. [I.R.C. § 219(d)(1); IRS Publication 590, *Individual Retirement Arrangements (IRAs)* 2008 (see Appendix A)] The amounts stated apply to contributions for 2009.

Q 3:16   May a traditional spousal IRA or Roth spousal IRA be created as a joint account held by a husband and wife?

No. Each spouse must establish a separate IRA. Joint accounts are not allowed.

Q 3:17   May a spouse receive a spousal IRA contribution for one year and make a regular IRA contribution for the next year?

Yes. The spousal IRA rules are designed to expand the eligibility of IRAs to spouses who earn little or no income. If a spouse receives a spousal contribution for one year because he or she has no compensation in that year and in the next year has compensation, the spouse may make his or her own contribution for the second year. The spouse may alternate between receiving and making contributions. There is no need to open a new IRA; the same IRA may receive both types of contributions. (Of course, traditional and Roth IRA contributions must be kept separate.)

Compensation Defined

Q 3:18   How is compensation determined for purposes of IRA contributions?

In general, *compensation* refers to monies received in exchange for personal services, as opposed to investment or pension income. The rules that apply to the determination of compensation are entirely separate from the traditional IRA deduction rules under which MAGI is determined. [I.R.C. § 219(f)(1); Treas. Reg. § 1.408A-3, Q&A-4]

Q 3:19   Are the compensation rules the same for the traditional IRA and the Roth IRA?

Yes. Both the traditional IRA and the Roth IRA follow the same rules regarding the determination of compensation for eligibility to make a contribution.

Q 3:20   What types of payment are specifically included in compensation for purposes of IRA contributions?

Amounts received as wages, salaries, tips, professional fees, commissions, and bonuses, and other amounts received for personal services, are specifically included in compensation. [I.R.C. § 219(f)(1); Treas. Reg. § 1.408A-3, Q&A-4] [IRS Publication 590, *Individual Retirement Arrangements (IRAs)* 2008 (see Appendix A)]

As of 2009, differential pay also specifically qualifies as compensation under the IRA contribution rules. Differential pay is the supplement some employers pay an employee during a period (extending more than 30 days) of active duty in the U.S. uniformed services, representing some or all of the wages that would have been paid if the individual were performing services for the employer. Unlike combat pay (see Q 3:27), differential pay is taxable and subject to withholding. [I.R.C. §§ 219(f)(1), 3401(h)]

Q 3:21　What amounts are excluded from compensation for purposes of IRA contributions?

Rental, interest, and dividend income, as well as foreign earned income and housing cost amounts that are excluded from U.S. income under Code Section 911, are excluded from compensation for purposes of IRA contributions. Other exclusions include pension or annuity income, deferred compensation, and income from a partnership for which an individual does not provide services that are a material income-producing factor. [I.R.C. § 219(f)(1); IRS Publication 590, *Individual Retirement Arrangements (IRAs)* 2008 (see Appendix A)]

Q 3:22　Are alimony and separate maintenance payments considered compensation for purposes of IRA contributions?

Yes. Taxable alimony and separate maintenance payments are considered compensation and may be contributed to an IRA, as long as such amounts are within the contribution limits. Thus, a divorced taxpayer may contribute as much as $5,000 of received alimony ($6,000 if he or she is age 50 or older) even if he or she is not working. [I.R.C. §§ 71(b)(2), 219(f)(1)]

Q 3:23　Is self-employment income included in compensation for purposes of IRA contributions?

It can be. If a taxpayer's personal services are a material income-producing factor, net earnings from a trade or business (whether it is operated as a sole proprietorship or a partnership) are included in compensation for purposes of IRA contributions.

Self-employment income is reduced by contributions that are made on the taxpayer's behalf to any retirement plan other than the IRA. The deduction allowed for half of the taxpayer's self-employment taxes also reduces the taxpayer's eligible compensation. Earnings from self-employment may be included even if no self-employment tax was payable because of religious beliefs. [IRS Publication 590, *Individual Retirement Arrangements (IRAs)* 2008 (see Appendix A)]

Q 3:24　What effect does a net loss from self-employment have on a taxpayer's ability to contribute to an IRA?

The fact that a taxpayer has a net loss from self-employment does not affect an individual's ability to contribute to an IRA if the individual has wages reportable on Form W-2, Wage and Tax Statements. [Rev. Rul. 79-286, 1979-2 C.B. 121]

> **Example.** In 2009, John, age 40, was self-employed and had a $10,000 net loss from his plumbing business. He also worked part time as a clerk in a hardware store and earned W-2 wages of $9,500. John has compensation and is eligible to make either a traditional IRA contribution or a Roth IRA contribution, or both.

Q 3:25   Are disability payments considered compensation for purposes of IRA contributions?

No. Even when disability payments are subject to ordinary federal income tax and FICA (Social Security) tax, they are considered annuity payments rather than compensation. Therefore, such payments may not support an IRA contribution. [Priv. Ltr. Rul. 8331069 (May 3, 1983)]

Q 3:26   May an individual who is employed by his or her spouse claim wages received from the spouse to be compensation for purposes of IRA contributions?

Whether wages received from a spouse may be claimed as compensation for purposes of IRA contributions depends on whether the employment is bona fide.

In one case that involved a farm operation, the wife was compensated in only a single year and was paid in livestock, which she sold for slightly more than $2,000. Although a joint return was filed, Schedule F, Profit or Loss from Farming, showed the farm operation as the husband's business. The wife's services valued out at less than $5 an hour. The IRS allowed a deduction for the proceeds realized on the sale of the livestock, which the wife received as "compensation" and which she then offset by a separate $2,000 IRA (the maximum IRA contribution for years before 2002). The transaction was reported on Form W-2, and the business was also taxed on the profit realized on the sale of the livestock. [Priv. Ltr. Rul. 9202003 (Oct. 9, 1991)]

In an earlier case, the IRS ruled otherwise. There, too, a joint return was filed. The wife performed bookkeeping services in connection with certain investments that the husband had placed in a joint tenancy with her. The IRS said that if separate returns had been filed, the taxpayers could have prevailed in deducting both the cash compensation (husband) and the IRA contribution (wife). They still, however, would have had the burden of proving that the facts and circumstances showed substance in the overall transaction. [Priv. Ltr. Rul. 8535001 (May 3, 1985)]

Q 3:27   Does compensation include combat pay earned by members of the armed forces that is excluded from federal income tax?

Yes, for tax years 2004 and later due to a change in the law. [See I.R.C. § 219(f)(7).] Prior to 2006, a member of the U.S. armed forces who had no taxable income for a year because of pay exclusion for service in a combat zone was not eligible to contribute to an IRA, and needed to remove such contributions that were wrongfully made. [Notice 99-30, 1999-1 C.B. 1135; Notice 2002-17, 2002-1 C.B. 567; Notice 2003-21, 2003-1 C.B. 818] Legislation enacted in 2006, however, treats tax-free combat pay as compensation for purposes of the IRA contribution rules, so recipients who are otherwise eligible may now contribute to IRAs (most likely, Roth IRAs, because the combat pay is tax free). Individuals who earned combat pay in 2004 or 2005 have until May 28, 2009, to make retroactive IRA contributions for such years. [The Heroes Earned Retirement Opportunities (HERO) Act, Pub. L. No. 109-227, 120 Stat. 385 (May 29, 2006)]

Q 3:28   Does compensation include deferred compensation?

No. In general, payments that are not made within two and one-half months after the close of a taxable year during which significant services are performed are considered deferred compensation. [*See* I.R.C. § 404(b)(2); Priv. Ltr. Rul. 8519051 (Feb. 13, 1985).]

Code Section 219(f)(1) specifically excludes pension, annuity, and deferred compensation payments from compensation that may be considered when determining an individual's eligibility to make contributions to an IRA.

Q 3:29   May severance payments support an IRA contribution?

Whether severance payments may support an IRA contribution depends on when the payments are made. Severance payments that are not completed within two and one-half months after the close of the taxable year during which significant services are performed will likely be considered deferred compensation and, therefore, may not serve as the basis for IRA contributions. [Priv. Ltr. Rul. 8519051 (Feb. 13, 1985)]

Q 3:30   Is there any safe harbor regarding the compensation requirements for contributions to a traditional IRA or a Roth IRA?

Yes. For administrative convenience, the IRS will accept the amount properly shown in box 1 of Form W-2 (wages, tips, and other compensation), less any amount shown in box 11 of Form W-2 (nonqualified plans), as compensation for the purpose of IRA eligibility. [Rev. Proc. 91-18, 1991-1 C.B. 522]

Special Contribution Limits

Q 3:31   Did the Pension Protection Act temporarily increase IRA contribution limits for certain individuals who lost retirement savings due to corporate malfeasance?

Yes, certain employees of bankrupt companies may increase their regular IRA contributions by $3,000 annually for 2007 through 2009. However, such individuals may not also make the catch-up contribution described in Q 3:5. [I.R.C. §§ 25B, 219]

Q 3:32   To which individuals do the special IRA limits apply?

To qualify for the special IRA limits, a taxpayer must have participated in a Section 401(k) plan under which the employer matched at least 50 percent of the employee's contributions to the plan with stock of the employer. In addition, in a taxable year preceding the taxable year of an additional contribution to the IRA (1) the employer (or any controlling corporation of the employer) must have been a debtor in a bankruptcy and (2) the employer or any other person must have been subject to an indictment or conviction resulting from business transactions related to the bankruptcy. The taxpayer must also have been a participant in the 401(k) plan on the date six months before the bankruptcy case was filed. [I.R.C. §§ 25B, 219]

> **Note.** This rule was specifically tailored to assist individuals whose retirement savings were lost in the collapse of the Enron Corporation during the 1990s.

Q 3:33   Do other special rules temporarily increase the IRA contribution limits in specified circumstances?

Yes, in effect. Subject to restrictions, the following may be transferred into IRAs as qualified rollover contributions and are not subject to the ordinary contribution limits:

1. Qualified reservist distributions
2. Military gratuities and payments received under the Servicemembers Group Life Insurance (SGLI) Program
3. Payments received in settlement of the *Exxon Valdez* litigation
4. Payments received by employees of airlines that filed for bankruptcy after September 11, 2001 and before 2007.

(See Qs 6:78–6:81.)

Contributions Versus Restorative Payments

Q 3:34   Do the regular contribution limits apply to payments that are deposited to an IRA to restore losses in the account?

It depends. Restorative payments, which are made to replace IRA losses resulting from breach of fiduciary duty, fraud, or federal or state securities violations, are not treated as regular contributions and as such may be deposited into the IRA without regard for the normal contribution limits. By contrast, payments that make up for losses due to market fluctuations or poor investment returns are treated as contributions, not restorative payments, and the usual contribution limits apply. [*See* Priv. Ltr. Rul. 200852034 (Dec. 26, 2008).]

Contribution Deadline

Q 3:35   When must IRA contributions be made?

Contributions to traditional and Roth IRAs must be made during the tax year to which they relate or in the following year before the due date for filing the individual's income tax return (not including extensions). For most taxpayers that is April 15 (or the following Monday, if April 15 falls on a Saturday or Sunday) of the year following the tax year of the contribution.

Q 3:36 When a calendar-year taxpayer makes a contribution between January 1 and April 15, for which year is the contribution made?

A taxpayer must indicate whether a contribution made between January 1 and April 15 applies to the previous year, to the current year, or in stated portions to each. The taxpayer should instruct the IRA trustee (or custodian) how to report such a contribution to the Internal Revenue Service (IRS). The IRA trustee or custodian must report it to the IRS accordingly. [I.R.C. § 408A(d)(7); Treas. Reg. § 1.408A-3, Q&A-2] For example, if an individual wants to take a deduction for the preceding year (as is often the case), the sponsor (i.e., the trustee, custodian, or annuity issuer) must be so advised. Otherwise, the sponsor can assume, and report to the IRS, that the contribution is for the current year (the year the sponsor received it). [IRS Publication 590, *Individual Retirement Arrangements (IRAs)* 2008 (see Appendix A)]

More than one contribution may be made between January 1 and April 15. If that happens, the same rules regarding designation apply.

Note. It is possible to contribute the full amount that is allowed for two consecutive years within a single calendar year. Of course, that can be the case only if no other contributions have been or will be made for either of the years.

A timely contribution that the taxpayer elects to treat as made for the previous year is deemed to have been made on the last day of the tax year to which it relates. [I.R.C. § 219(c)(1)(F)(3)]

Q 3:37 Is an IRA contribution received after the tax filing due date timely made?

Possibly. The IRS ruled that a bank could have accepted as timely a mail payment that was postmarked April 12 even though it was not received until April 16. For purposes of determining the timeliness of payments, the U.S. Postal Service is treated as an agent, and its cancellation mark is accepted as evidence under general contract law. [Priv. Ltr. Rul. 8611090 (Dec. 20, 1985)] The IRS has further ruled that Code Section 7502(a)(1), which provides that the date of the U.S. postmark is deemed to be the date of payment, applies under Code Section 219(f)(3). [Priv. Ltr. Rul. 8707084 (Nov. 20, 1986)]

Practice Pointer. It would be prudent, even if not legally required, for an individual to follow up with the addressee if the normal confirmation of an IRA contribution is not provided within a reasonable time.

Q 3:38   May IRA contributions be delayed for individuals serving in the U.S. armed forces or in support of such forces in designated combat areas?

Yes, IRA contributions may be made later than otherwise required by individuals serving in the U.S. armed forces or in support of such forces in designated combat or hazardous duty areas. The extended contribution period for these individuals includes the time spent in the designated area plus at least 180 days. [I.R.C. § 7508] The IRA trustee or custodian simply includes the amount of the contribution on Form 5498, IRA Contribution Information, for the year in which it was made, and one of the following designations in the appropriate box of the form, followed by the year and amount:

- "AF" (Allied Force) for the Kosovo area;
- "JE" (Joint Endeavor) for the Persian Gulf area;
- "EF" (Enduring Freedom) for Afghanistan, Uzbekistan, Kyrgyzstan, Pakistan, Tajikistan, Jordan, and Somalia; or
- "IF" (Iraqi Freedom) for the Arabian Peninsula Areas (the Persian Gulf, the Red Sea, the Gulf of Oman, the portion of the Arabian Sea that lies north of 10 degrees north latitude and west of 68 degrees east longitude, the Gulf of Aden, and the total land areas of Iraq, Kuwait, Saudi Arabia, Oman, Bahrain, Qatar, the United Arab Emirates, and the airspace above such locations.

Example. In January 2010, Janelle, a member of the U.S. armed forces who has served in the Iraqi Freedom area since October 2008, makes a $5,000 IRA contribution for the tax year 2008. The custodian of her IRA will enter "IF 2008 5000" on Form 5498, IRA Contribution Information, in the blank box to the left of box 10.

[*See* IRS Publication 3, *Armed Forces' Tax Guide 2008,* which provides more information on benefits available to members of the armed forces serving in combat zones and qualified hazardous duty areas.]

A special rule allows military personnel who received tax-free combat pay in 2004 or 2005 to make retroactive contributions for such years, if they do so by May 28, 2009 (see Q 3:27).

Q 3:39   May an IRA contribution be made after the tax return that reports the contribution has been filed?

Possibly. If a tax return is filed before the regular filing deadline, it is possible for an IRA contribution to be made after the actual filing. If the taxpayer expects to contribute no later than the filing deadline, it is appropriate to report a deduction for traditional IRA contributions. Failure to follow through on time could, however, subject the taxpayer to penalties under Code Section 6651. [Rev. Rul. 84-18, 1984-1 C.B. 88]

Q 3:40   What happens when a contribution is made to an IRA after the individual's tax filing due date?

The rule that a taxpayer is deemed to have made an IRA contribution on the last day of the tax year does not allow for a delay based on an extended filing date (either automatic or requested and approved).

If a taxpayer makes a contribution after the due date for filing his or her return and the return has already been filed, the taxpayer has two choices:

1. The taxpayer may file an amended return reversing the deduction (if applicable) and pay the tax; or

2. The taxpayer may file an amended return indicating that the contribution is being made in the current year on a return that is expected to be filed in the following year.

Penalties may be imposed, depending on the promptness with which the corrective measures are accomplished. [Rev. Rul. 84-18, 1984-1 C.B. 88]

Q 3:41   Can a tax return preparer be liable for approving a traditional IRA deduction claim for a contribution that is not yet made?

It depends. The rules that apply to tax return preparers are discussed in General Counsel Memorandum 39422. The rules provide that a preparer is not required to follow up with the taxpayer to confirm that the contribution is completed in a timely manner. However, the preparer must not have knowledge that the taxpayer is not likely to make the proposed contribution on time. If a follow-up is standard procedure in the preparer's practice, the preparer could be held liable for not reporting such a failure to the IRS.

Practice Pointer. If a tax return is filed shortly before its due date, the preparer should inquire when the taxpayer plans to make an IRA contribution for which a deduction has been claimed.

Q 3:42   Is there any requirement that, once started, IRA contributions must be continued annually?

No, there is no requirement that IRA contributions must be continued annually. Furthermore, there is no requirement that the same IRA be used for all contributions. A taxpayer may choose to establish new IRAs for subsequent contributions. If overcontributions are being corrected, a taxpayer may choose the IRAs from which he or she will take the excess. Similarly, if other corrective measures are taken (e.g., delaying the deduction until another year), the taxpayer may determine which IRA or IRAs will receive a contribution and which will not to avoid overcontributions in the current year.

Q 3:43   How do the traditional IRA and the Roth IRA differ from qualified plans with regard to the timing requirements?

IRAs are less flexible than other retirement plans (i.e., qualified plans) in that extended tax return filing dates do not afford extended contribution deadlines. On the other hand, a taxpayer wishing to establish an IRA does not have to do so until his or her regular filing due date. [I.R.C. § 219(f)(3)] This is in contrast to the rules that apply to qualified plans, which require that a plan must be established no later than the end of the tax year for which a deduction is being claimed.

Direct Deposit of Tax Refunds to IRAs

Q 3:44   Can a federal income tax refund be directly deposited into an IRA?

Yes. A taxpayer may direct the deposit of a tax refund into one, two, or three separate accounts at banks or other financial institutions. Traditional, Roth, and SEP IRAs (but not SIMPLE IRAs) and Coverdell ESAs may be designated to receive refunds, along with a broad range of other accounts such as checking and savings accounts, health savings accounts (HSAs), and Archer Medical Savings Accounts (MSAs).

A taxpayer who desires a direct deposit of the tax refund into a single account (IRA or other) would provide the routing and account numbers directly on his or her Form 1040. To direct the deposit into two or three accounts, the taxpayer must file Form 8888, Direct Deposit of Refund to More Than One Account. On Lines 1 to 3 of Form 8888, the taxpayer lists the different accounts and indicates how the refund should be allocated among them. A receiving account must be in the taxpayer's name (or the spouse's name, in the case of a joint return). Taxpayers may not request partial payment of a refund by check and the remainder by direct deposit to another account.

Some banks and financial institutions do not permit deposit of joint refunds to individual accounts. If a deposit is rejected for this reason, the IRS will mail the refund check to the taxpayer.

The direct deposit and split-refund options do not change the IRA contribution deadlines or limits in any way. Taxpayers need to verify that the deposit is timely made and instruct the IRA trustee or custodian regarding the year to which it should be assigned. Absent such instruction, the trustee or custodian will apply the contribution to the current year.

Q 3:45   In 2008, did the IRS deposit some economic stimulus payments directly into IRAs?

Yes. Most taxpayers were eligible to receive an economic stimulus payment in 2008 from the U.S. Treasury. [I.R.C. § 6428] In making the payment (really an advance refund of the income tax payable for 2008), the IRS followed any refund instruction that the taxpayer had designated on his or her 2007 income tax return if the instruction was for deposit to a single financial account. The account so designated may have been an IRA, Coverdell ESA, HSA, or other tax-favored account.

Nonetheless, the IRS recognized that some taxpayers may have wanted to receive the economic stimulus payment in cash, rather than by direct deposit. Without special tax relief, the withdrawal of a stimulus payment from an IRA or Coverdell ESA would subject the taxpayer to tax and penalties. Consequently, the IRS announced in 2008 that it would allow certain taxpayers to withdraw (by a specified time)—free of Code restrictions that might otherwise have applied—part or all of an economic stimulus payment that was directly deposited into a tax-favored account. For a stimulus payment that was directly deposited into a traditional IRA or a Roth IRA, a withdrawal qualifies for this relief if it occurs by the deadline for filing the taxpayer's 2008 income tax return (including extensions). [Ann. 2008-44, 2008-20 I.R.B. 982; IRS Publication 970, *Tax Benefits for Education,* 2008]

> **Caution.** If the stimulus payment was directly deposited into a Coverdell ESA, a different deadline applies for tax-free withdrawal (see Q 13:34).

(See Qs 4:22 and 5:92 regarding distribution of the economic stimulus payment without adverse tax consequences.)

Q 3:46   How are contributions affected if the deposited tax refund is adjusted due to math errors on the return?

If a refund is increased or decreased because math errors were made on the return, the contribution of the tax refund is also adjusted. Adjustments are made first to any deposits to the account on Line 3, next to any deposits to the account on Line 2, and finally to deposits to the account on Line 1. If the taxpayer appeals a refund decrease and prevails, the IRS will deposit the resulting refund in the first account listed. [General Instructions for Form 8888, Direct Deposit of Refund to More Than One Account]

> **Example 1.** Annette prepares her 2009 income tax return and determines she is due a refund of $500. She is still eligible to contribute $350 to her Roth IRA account, so she uses Form 8888 to instruct the IRS to deposit $350 of the refund to her Roth IRA (Line 1), and the remaining $150 to her checking account (Line 2). The IRS corrects a math error on the return and increases the refund to $600. The $100 increase is added to the deposit to the checking account on Line 2.

> **Example 2.** Cecil's 2009 return shows that he is due a $300 refund. He files Form 8888 requesting the IRS to deposit $100 to his traditional IRA (Line 1), $100 to a mutual fund account holding nonretirement assets (Line 2), and $100 to his checking account (Line 3). The IRS determines there is a math error and reduces the refund to $150. It deposits nothing to the checking account,

$50 to the mutual fund account, and $100 to the IRA. If Cecil appeals the adjustment and his calculation is upheld, the resulting refund of $150 would be deposited to his IRA. If the larger deposit causes an excess contribution to be made, Cecil must withdraw the excess or amend his return.

Q 3:47   How are contributions affected if the refund is offset by other obligations of the taxpayer?

It depends on the reason for the offset. A refund that is offset because federal taxes are past due is applied in the same manner as a refund reduction attributable to math errors (see Q 3:46). Refunds are also subject to offset by the Treasury Department's Financial Management Service if certain other amounts are past due (e.g., outstanding state income tax, child support, spousal support, or certain federal nontax debts such as student loans). Those past due amounts are collected from the accounts listed on Form 8888 based on their bank routing numbers, in order from lowest to highest. [General Instructions for Form 8888, Direct Deposit of Refund to More Than One Account]

Special Rules for Traditional IRA Contributions

Deducting Traditional IRA Contributions

Q 3:48   What determines the deductibility of traditional IRA contributions?

Whether an individual may deduct a traditional IRA contribution depends on

1. The individual's or the individual's spouse's status as an active participant in an employer-sponsored retirement plan (see Qs 3:49–3:64);
2. The individual's MAGI (see Q 3:65); and
3. The individual's filing status (see Q 3:66).

Active Participation Rules

Q 3:49   If an individual is not an active participant in an employer-sponsored retirement plan, what income limits apply to the deductibility of traditional IRA contributions?

None. No income limits apply to the deductibility of traditional IRA contributions for an individual who is not an active participant in an employer-sponsored retirement plan.

Note. If an individual's spouse is an active participant in an employer-sponsored retirement plan, the individual's ability to deduct a traditional IRA contribution may be affected (see Q 3:60).

Example. Jane, age 32, and Kevin, age 35, are married and file a joint federal income tax return. Kevin is a homemaker and has no income from any source. Jane earns $1 million a year as a spokeswoman for a nationwide health club. Jane is considered self-employed and is not eligible to participate in the health club's retirement plan. Jane has not established a retirement plan of her own, other than an IRA. She may make and deduct a $5,000 contribution to her traditional IRA because she is not an active participant in a retirement plan. She could also make and deduct a $5,000 contribution on behalf of Kevin.

Q 3:50 When is an individual an active participant in an employer-sponsored retirement plan?

In general, an individual is an active participant in an employer-sponsored retirement plan if he or she receives an allocation under a defined contribution plan or is not excluded from participation under the terms of a defined benefit plan. [Notice 87-16, 1987-1 C.B. 446; *clarified by* Notice 89-25, 1989-1 C.B. 662; *modified by* Notice 98-49, 1998-2 C.B. 365]

Q 3:51 What types of plans are considered employer-sponsored retirement plans?

Employer-sponsored retirement plans include the following:

- Qualified pension, profit sharing, stock bonus, and money purchase plans (including 401(k) plans, target benefit plans, and employee stock ownership plans (ESOPs))
- Simplified employee pension plans (SEPs) and salary reduction SEPs (SARSEPs)
- Savings incentive match plans for employees (SIMPLEs)
- Qualified annuity plans
- Section 403(b) tax-sheltered annuity plans
- Governmental plans not covered by Code Section 457 (federal judges are considered covered)

Although SEPs are not qualified plans under Code Section 401(a), the fact that funding takes place through an IRA rather than through a retirement plan does not change their status as employer-sponsored retirement plans for purposes of the rules that cap deductibility of IRA contributions. Even if the employee adds personal IRA contributions to the SEP IRA, the plan remains an employer-sponsored retirement plan. Indeed, the creation of a SEP may make an individual's regular IRA contributions nondeductible, even if there are no other employer-sponsored retirement plans and even though the contributions could have been deductible if the SEP had not been created.

A SIMPLE follows the same rule: An employee electing to defer a portion of his or her compensation into the SIMPLE is considered an active participant. Any employer contributions to the SIMPLE for an employee also make that employee an active participant. [I.R.C. § 219(g)(5)]

Q 3:52   How may an individual verify that he or she is an active participant in an employer-sponsored retirement plan?

Form W-2 provides a box labeled "Retirement Plan" that the employer must mark if the employee is an active participant in an employer-sponsored retirement plan for IRA purposes. If a taxpayer is not certain that the box has been correctly marked (or correctly left unmarked), the IRS suggests that the taxpayer contact the employer for further information. It might also be advisable for the taxpayer to check with his or her tax advisor.

Q 3:53   What is the year of active participation when an individual's tax year and the plan year of the employer-sponsored retirement plan are not the same?

If an individual is a calendar-year taxpayer (as is almost always the case), the year of active participation for purposes of determining the deductibility of an IRA contribution is the calendar year in which the plan year ends. [Notice 87-16, 1987-1 C.B. 446; Priv. Ltr. Rul. 8919064 (Feb. 16, 1989)]

Example. Meg's employer maintains a 401(k) profit sharing plan with a plan year that runs from July 1 to June 30. In the plan year ending June 30, 2008, Meg had not met the length-of-service requirements for participation in the plan. Beginning July 1, 2008, however, Meg elected to defer part of her salary into the plan. Meg terminated employment on December 31, 2008, to attend medical school. Because Meg was ineligible to participate in the plan during the plan year ending June 30, 2008, she was not an active participant for calendar year 2008 (the calendar year in which the plan year ends). Therefore, Meg may make a deductible IRA contribution for 2008 even though she could have made substantial 401(k) deferrals during the last six months of the year. Meg will, however, be considered an active participant for the 2009 calendar year, because she contributed to the 401(k) plan during the plan year ending June 30, 2009.

Q 3:54   What rules apply to an employee's active participation in a defined contribution plan?

Defined contribution plans include 401(k) plans, profit sharing plans, thrift saving plans, stock bonus plans, and money purchase plans.

Active participation begins during the plan year in which a contribution or allocation is made to the employee's account. If the plan requires that an allocation be made as of the end of each plan year, the employee is deemed, for purposes of an IRA, to be a participant for the IRA tax year within which that employer plan year ends. That is so even if the employment ends before the IRA tax year ends but the plan allocation is not made until the following year. The fact that the employer's contribution is delayed until the next tax year of the employee does not extend participation until that next year. [Notice 87-16, 1987-1 C.B. 446] IRS Publication 590, *Individual Retirement Arrangements*

(IRAs) 2008, provides an example of a money purchase pension plan (see Appendix A).

> **Example.** On December 30, 2008, Olivia terminates employment with Woolf, Inc., the sponsor of a money purchase plan. The final allocation for the 2008 plan year is made on June 30, 2009. Woolf remits its money purchase plan contribution for the year ending June 30, 2009, on February 15, 2010 (its tax return filing due date). Olivia's participation continues into the 2009 IRA tax year but does not extend into 2010.

Q 3:55   What rules apply to an employee's active participation in a defined benefit plan?

Defined benefit plans, which include pension plans and annuity plans, work somewhat differently from defined contribution plans because employer contributions are not allocated to individual accounts. If an employee has met the eligibility requirements (usually, one year of service and attainment of age 21), he or she is deemed to have participated for purposes of the IRA contribution deduction rules even though no benefit accruals have begun.

> **Example.** The facts are the same as those in the example in Q 3:54, except that Woolf's plan is a defined benefit plan. Olivia's 2009 IRA deduction is limited by the active participation rules, but her 2010 IRA deduction is not. [Notice 87-16, 1987-1 C.B. 446; Treas. Reg. § 1.219-2(b)]

A defined benefit plan may condition the accrual of benefits for a particular year on the participant either having worked a minimum number of hours, or having earned a minimum amount of compensation, during the plan year. The two thresholds seem similar, but yield distinctly different results when determining whether a person failing to meet one of them is an active participant. If benefit accrual is conditioned on earning a minimum amount of compensation, an otherwise eligible individual who earns less than that amount in a particular plan year is not considered an active participant for that year. [Treas. Reg. § 1.219-2(b)(1)] On the other hand, if the benefit is conditioned on working a minimum number of hours, an individual who is otherwise eligible is considered to be an active participant even if he or she works too few hours to accrue a benefit. [*See* William Edward Colombell, T.C. Summary Op. 2006-184.]

Q 3:56   If an employee refuses to make contributions, do the active participation rules still apply?

If the plan is a contributory defined benefit plan, the active participation rules still apply. For such a plan, an employee's refusal to contribute will not eliminate active participation for IRA contribution deduction purposes. In contrast, because benefit entitlement is not established until contributions are made to an individual's defined contribution plan account, active participation rules do not apply unless the employer contributes to the employee's account. [Notice 87-16, 1987-1 C.B. 446]

Thus, if an employee does not make any elective deferrals into the employer's 401(k) plan, the employee may not be considered an active participant. The determination is based on whether the employee received any contributions to the plan. If the employer made a profit-sharing contribution on behalf of the employee, the employee would be considered an active participant.

Note. Even if an employee shares only in a nominal amount of forfeitures made to a plan for the year, the employee is considered an active participant.

Q 3:57 Are the active participation rules affected if an employee is not vested in accruals?

No. Active participation in either a defined contribution plan or a defined benefit plan is not affected by whether the employee's benefits under the plan are vested. The fact that termination of employment would result in the loss of benefits does not prevent an individual from being considered an active participant for purposes of the IRA contribution deduction rules. The same rule applies to participation in a plan for U.S. government employees. [Priv. Ltr. Rul. 8725094 (Mar. 30, 1987)] It should be noted that the IRA itself is at all times 100 percent vested.

Q 3:58 Will nonvested termination of participation in an eligible retirement plan before the end of the year avoid the issue of nondeductible IRA contributions?

No. Participation in an eligible retirement plan during any part of the year is deemed sufficient to raise the issue of whether IRA contributions may be deducted. In a case on this point, employee contributions were withdrawn during the year. At the end of the year there was nothing left to distribute, because employer contributions had been forfeited. Had the forfeiture occurred under a regular vesting schedule rather than as a result of participant withdrawal of funds, the result would not have been different. The Tax Court rejected the end of the plan year test, although there were no benefits remaining from earlier in the year. Participation during any part of the year determines the matter even if it is subsequently and retroactively eliminated. [Wartes v. Commissioner, T.C. Memo 1993-84]

The rule remains the same if the active participant is the spouse and not the individual claiming the deduction. Participation for at least part of the year by either spouse is sufficient to limit IRA contribution deductibility. In *Wartes*, the joint MAGI was sufficient to disallow the entire deduction. The spouses argued that, in view of the forfeiture from the qualified plan, there was no possibility of a double tax benefit from the qualified plan and the IRA. The Tax Court held that Code Section 219(g) does not allow such issues to be considered. [*See also* Baumann's v. Commissioner, T.C. Memo 1995-313.]

Q 3:59   Do the active participation rules apply to a U.S. military retirement plan?

It would seem that the active participation rules do apply to a U.S. military retirement plan. In *Morales-Caban v. Commissioner* [T.C. Memo 1993-466], the Tax Court held that a U.S. Air Force retirement plan was to be treated as an employer-sponsored retirement plan. Thus, a husband and wife participating in the plan were subject to IRA contribution deductibility limits. The taxpayers argued that they were not active participants in a retirement plan—the Air Force plan was a "gift" to be awarded after 20 years of service that was unlikely to be attained because of defense force downsizing. The Tax Court rejected this argument. (But see Q 3:60 regarding military reservists.)

Q 3:60   What types of retirement plan participation are not treated as "active"?

An individual may be covered under the following types of plans without affecting the deductibility of his or her IRA contributions:

1. Social Security and railroad retirement coverage or benefits;
2. Benefit payments from an employer retirement plan when the individual is no longer employed [Notice 87-16, 1987-1 C.B. 446];
3. Benefits from membership in the U.S. Armed Forces reserve units when service does not exceed 90 days in a year [I.R.C. § 219(g)(6)(A)]; and
4. Volunteer firefighter benefits when retirement income from U.S. or local plans, accrued as of the start of the IRA tax year, does not exceed $1,800 annually (payable at retirement). [I.R.C. § 219(g)(6)(B)]

[IRS Publication 590, *Individual Retirement Arrangements (IRAs)* 2008 (see Appendix A)]

Q 3:61   Will participation by one spouse in a qualified plan cause the other spouse to be deemed an active participant even though he or she is not covered by the plan?

Yes. If one spouse is an active participant in a qualified plan, the other spouse is also considered an active participant. This rule is not as harsh as it sounds, because if one spouse is considered an active participant solely by attribution from the other spouse, special higher income thresholds apply (see Qs 3:62, 3:66). [I.R.C. § 219(g)(7)]

Q 3:62   What are the income thresholds for the deductibility of traditional IRA contributions for an individual who is an active participant merely by attribution from his or her spouse?

If an individual is not an active participant except by attribution from the individual's spouse, the individual's ability to deduct his or her traditional IRA contribution begins to be phased out at $166,000 of MAGI. A joint return must be filed to take advantage of the higher income threshold. The ability to deduct any portion of the contribution at all is completely phased out at MAGI of $176,000 (see Q 3:66).

Example. Michael and Natalie are married and file a joint federal income tax return for 2009. Michael is an active participant in a 401(k) plan sponsored by his employer. Natalie, age 35, is a homemaker and is not an active participant in a retirement plan except by attribution from Michael. With MAGI of $80,000, Natalie may receive a spousal contribution and deduct up to $5,000 because she is an active participant only by attribution from Michael, and her MAGI is below the $166,000 threshold.

Q 3:63   How is the status of an individual who is an active participant by attribution from a spouse affected by remarriage, divorce without remarriage, or death during the year?

To be considered a spouse, a party must be married at the end of the IRA tax year. If there was more than one marriage during that year, the marriage that is in place at the end of the year is the only one that applies. If divorce occurs without remarriage, the IRA taxpayer is deemed to be single for the entire year. If the spouse who is actually covered by the employer plan dies during the IRA tax year and the surviving spouse files a joint return with the deceased spouse (through the executor or administrator), the decedent's coverage before death will affect the survivor's IRA deduction position exactly as if the decedent had lived with the marriage intact until the end of the year. [I.R.C. § 6013; IRS Publication 590, *Individual Retirement Arrangements (IRAs)* 2008 (see Appendix A)]

Q 3:64   Can a spouse avoid the active participation rules by filing a separate income tax return?

Not usually. Filing separate income tax returns has no effect on the active participation rules, with one exception. If the spouses live apart from each other throughout the entire tax year, each may file as a single taxpayer. [I.R.C. § 219(g)(4); IRS Publication 590, *Individual Retirement Arrangements (IRAs)* 2008 (see Appendix A)]

Modified Adjusted Gross Income

Q 3:65   How is modified adjusted gross income determined?

Modified adjusted gross income is adjusted gross income (AGI), which can be determined from the front page of Form 1040 or 1040A, with the following amounts added back:

- IRA deduction
- Student loan interest deduction

- Savings bond excluded interest (shown on Form 8815, Exclusion of Interest From Series EE and I U.S. Savings Bonds Issued After 1989)
- Employer-paid adoption expenses (shown on Form 8839, Qualified Adoption Expenses)
- Foreign earned income exclusion
- Foreign housing exclusion or deduction
- Deduction for qualified tuition and related expenses

[I.R.C. § 219(g)(3)]

Q 3:66   What are the MAGI thresholds for eligibility to deduct a traditional IRA contribution?

For 2009, the MAGI thresholds for eligibility to deduct a traditional IRA contribution are as indicated in Table 3-2. [IRS News Release IR-2008-118 (Oct. 16, 2008); Notice 2008-102, 2008-45 I.R.B. 1106] For later years, the phaseout ranges will be increased in $1,000 increments by COLAs. [*See* I.R.C. § 219(g).]

Individuals who are active participants (see Qs 3:50–3:64) in retirement plans should locate their MAGI in Table 3-2 under the appropriate filing status. Individuals with MAGI below the "Low End" amount are entitled to a full deduction for their eligible traditional IRA contribution amount. Individuals with MAGI above the "High End" amount may not deduct any traditional IRA contribution amount. Individuals whose MAGI falls between the Low End and High End figures are in the phaseout range and must calculate their maximum contribution amount (see Qs 3:67, 3:68).

Table 3-2. MAGI Phaseout Ranges for Traditional IRAs

Filing and Active Participant Status	Low End	High End
Single, active participant	$ 55,000	$ 65,000
Married filing jointly, active participant	$ 89,000	$109,000
Married filing separately, active participant	$ 0	$ 10,000
Married filing jointly, not an active participant, but spouse is	$166,000	$176,000

Q 3:67   How is a deduction for a traditional IRA contribution affected when MAGI is more than the full-deduction level but less than the no-deduction level?

The following eight rules apply to a traditional IRA contribution that falls between the full-deduction and no-deduction levels:

1. The reduction in the deduction applies ratably. For example, a contribution will be 50 percent deductible if MAGI falls at the midpoint of the

range; that is, a $5,000 contribution to a traditional IRA will be deductible in the amount of $2,500 and nondeductible in the amount of $2,500. [I.R.C. § 219(g)(2)(A)]

2. The deduction amount is rounded up to the next $10 when it is not a multiple of 10. [I.R.C. § 219(g)(2)(C)]

3. If any amount remains deductible, $200 is the minimum deductible amount. [I.R.C. § 219(g)(2)(B)]

4. In the case of a spousal IRA, the $200 minimum applies to the total deduction on the return. In the case of a joint return when both spouses have compensation and each contributes to his or her own IRA, the $200 minimum applies separately to each. [IRS Publication 590, *Individual Retirement Arrangements (IRAs)* 2008 (see Appendix A)]

5. If the reduction applies so that one spouse has overdeducted (on an earlier filed return) and the other has contributed less than the maximum deductible, no transfer of deduction limit is permitted between the spouses. [IRS Publication 590, *Individual Retirement Arrangements (IRAs)* 2008 (see Appendix A)] (It would seem that with more careful planning—or replanning, if it is not too late—a different allocation of contributions could produce a higher total deductible amount if desired.)

6. A head of household follows the single taxpayer rules for reductions in IRA deductible limits. [I.R.C. § 219(g)(3)]

7. Qualifying widowers or widows follow the married taxpayer rules for reductions in IRA deductible limits. [I.R.C. § 219(g)(3)]

8. A Section 501(c)(18) plan is considered an employer plan if the taxpayer made deductible contributions during the year. Such a plan, a special type of tax-exempt trust, must have been (a) created before June 25, 1959, and (b) funded only by employee contributions. The deduction limit is reduced by any contributions to such a plan that the taxpayer made during the year. [I.R.C. § 219(g)(5)]

Of course, a taxpayer may elect to deduct less than the permitted deduction for an IRA contribution and increase the nondeductible portion correspondingly. The taxpayer may also elect to contribute only the deductible amount. In the case of a spousal IRA, each spouse determines the deductible amount separately (or the spouses determine the deductible amount for one spouse, and the other spouse's amount will be the same).

Q 3:68   Is there a formula for calculating the amount of a partial deduction for a traditional IRA contribution?

Yes. If MAGI is within the phaseout range shown in Table 3-2 (see Q 3:66), the partial deduction for a contribution to a traditional IRA is calculated as below. The IRS provides a slightly different formula for arriving at the same number. [IRS Publication 590, *Individual Retirement Arrangements (IRAs)* 2008 (see Appendix A)] An individual with sufficient compensation may still contribute the full amount ($5,000, or $6,000 if age 50 or older, for 2009), either as a nondeductible traditional IRA contribution or as a Roth IRA contribution if MAGI falls within the Roth IRA contribution income limits (see Qs 3:73–3:81).

1. Start with MAGI.
2. Subtract the amount in line 1 from:
   a. $65,000 if single and an active participant (see Qs 3:50–3:64);
   b. $109,000 if the individual is married, filing jointly, and an active participant;
   c. $10,000 if married filing separately and an active participant; or
   d. $176,000 if the individual is married filing jointly, and not an active participant but spouse is.
3. Divide the result in line 2 by $10,000 ($20,000 if filing a joint return and the individual is an active participant).
4. Multiply the maximum contribution limit (before reduction by this adjustment but after reduction for any contributions to Roth IRAs) by the result in line 3.
5. The result, rounded up to the nearest $10, is the reduced contribution limit. If the reduced contribution limit is more than $0 but less than $200, increase the limit to $200.

Example. Janet and Bernard file a joint return and have combined MAGI of $98,200 for 2009. Each is age 55, earns more than $5,000 compensation, and contributes $6,000 to a traditional IRA. Janet is an active participant in her employer's retirement plan, so her deduction is calculated as follows:

1. Combined MAGI = $98,200
2. $109,000 – $98,200 = $10,800
3. $10,800 ÷ $20,000 = 0.54
4. $6,000 (contribution limit) × 0.54 = $3,240.

Bernard's contribution is fully deductible because the couple's combined MAGI is below his phaseout range.

Q 3:69 How are Social Security benefits treated when determining MAGI for purposes of IRA contribution deductibility?

When deductibility depends on MAGI, 50 percent of an individual's Social Security benefits is included in determining that figure. The taxability of Social Security benefits is then recalculated, taking into account the portion of the IRA contribution that is determined to be deductible. (The entire process is illustrated in Worksheets 1, 2, and 3 of Appendix B in IRS Publication 590, *Individual Retirement Arrangements (IRAs)* 2008 (see Appendix A).)

Q 3:70   May IRA contributions be deducted only by taxpayers who do not claim a standard deduction?

No. Deductions for IRA contributions have no relationship to the manner in which other deductions are taken. They are a direct adjustment to adjusted gross income in full and are in no way affected by the pattern of other deductions.

Q 3:71   May nondeductible IRA contributions be recharacterized as deductible at some later time?

Yes. The tax-deductible status of an IRA contribution is not determined until the individual files an income tax return.

Q 3:72   May a deductible IRA contribution be designated as nondeductible?

Yes. A taxpayer may elect to treat a deductible contribution as nondeductible by filing Form 8606, Nondeductible IRAs, and including the designated amount with any other nondeductible contributions for that year.

Generally, a taxpayer who is not eligible to make a Roth IRA contribution might take such action to reduce the taxable amount of his or her distributions. This might occur if it is anticipated that tax rates will be higher at a later time, and the taxpayer concludes that it is better to pay taxes now. If deductible IRA contributions are repeatedly designated as nondeductible, however, the loss of tax deductions might outweigh any tax differential.

In almost all instances, an individual will make a Roth IRA contribution instead of a nondeductible traditional IRA contribution if he or she is eligible.

Special Rules for Roth IRA Contributions

Roth IRA Eligibility

Q 3:73   What eligibility rules apply to the Roth IRA?

To establish and make annual contributions to a Roth IRA, an individual must have MAGI below certain levels and must have compensation. [I.R.C. §§ 219(b), 408A(c)] Failure to meet either requirement could lessen or eliminate an individual's eligibility to make a Roth IRA contribution. Different eligibility rules exist for converting a traditional IRA to a Roth IRA (see Qs 3:92–3:116).

Q 3:74   May a married couple establish a joint Roth IRA?

No. The Roth IRA is an individual account. However, special spousal rules are available for married couples, making it easier for both spouses to establish a Roth IRA (see Q 3:20).

Q 3:75   May a minor establish a Roth IRA?

Yes. Any minor meeting the eligibility requirements may establish a Roth IRA under federal law. (The compensation requirement, however, is often a problem for minors.)

Practice Pointer. Most states have laws governing contractual relationships with a minor (to protect the minor). Such laws may prevent or make it undesirable for a trustee or custodian to open a Roth IRA for a minor. If the trustee or custodian agrees to accept a minor's Roth IRA contribution, in most instances the trustee or custodian should require a parent's or guardian's signature in place of or in addition to the minor's signature.

Q 3:76   What is modified adjusted gross income for purposes of determining eligibility for the Roth IRA?

For determining eligibility to make a Roth IRA contribution, certain modifications are applied to the adjusted gross income (AGI) figure from an individual's federal income tax return.

MAGI for a Roth IRA is AGI with the following added back:

- Traditional IRA deduction
- Student loan interest deduction
- Income from U.S. savings bonds used to pay for higher education (shown on Form 8815)
- Foreign earned income exclusion
- Foreign housing exclusion or deduction [I.R.C. § 135]
- Employer-reimbursed adoption expenses (shown on Form 8839)
- Deduction for qualified tuition and related expenses
- Income from a Roth IRA conversion (see Qs 3:111–3:116)

[I.R.C. § 408A(c)(3); Treas. Reg. § 1.408A-3, Q&A-5]

Note. The modifications made to AGI for Roth IRAs differ slightly from those made to AGI for traditional IRAs (see Q 3:65).

Q 3:77   What is compensation for purposes of the Roth IRA?

The definition of *compensation* for purposes of the Roth IRA is the same as that for purposes of the traditional IRA (see Qs 3:17–3:30). [Treas. Reg. § 1.408A-3, Q&A-4]

The requirement that an individual have compensation in order to contribute to a Roth IRA prevents many retired or otherwise nonworking individuals from making Roth IRA contributions.

Q 3:78   What are the Roth IRA MAGI limits?

To be eligible to make a regular or spousal contribution to a Roth IRA, an individual's MAGI must be below certain limits. Different limits apply depending on an individual's federal income tax filing status. [I.R.C. § 408A(c)(3)]

Married, Filing Jointly. Married spouses filing a joint return with MAGI of $166,000 or less are each entitled to make up to a full $5,000 Roth IRA contribution ($6,000 if age 50 or over). Married joint filers with MAGI of more than $166,000 and less than $176,000 are each able to make a partial Roth IRA contribution. The range between $166,000 and $176,000 is called the phaseout range because the ability to make a Roth IRA contribution is phased out as the MAGI level increases; that is, married joint filers with MAGI of $176,000 or more are not eligible to make Roth IRA contributions. Married couples filing jointly with MAGI falling within the phaseout range determine the amount of their contribution by using a reduced Roth IRA contribution calculation (see Q 3:79).

Married, Filing Jointly, and Lived with Spouse at Any Time During the Year. A married individual who files separately and did not live apart from his or her spouse for the entire year is automatically placed into a phaseout range of $0 to $10,000. If such an individual has any MAGI at all, he or she begins to lose the ability to make a Roth IRA contribution. After an individual's MAGI reaches $10,000, that individual is no longer eligible to make any Roth IRA contribution.

All Other Filers. Anyone else (i.e., single filers, and married persons who file separately and lived apart from their spouses for the entire year) having MAGI of $105,000 or less may make up to a full $5,000 Roth IRA contribution ($6,000 if age 50 or over). If the filer's MAGI is more than $105,000 but less than $120,000, he or she may make a partial Roth IRA contribution. Single filers with MAGI above $116,000 are not eligible to make a Roth IRA contribution. [*See* I.R.S. News Release IR-2008-118 (Oct. 16, 2008); Notice 2008-102, 2008-45 I.R.B. 1106; IRS Publication 590, *Individual Retirement Arrangements (IRAs)* 2008 (see Appendix A).]

Table 3-3 summarizes the income limits based on the contributor's filing status.

Table 3-3. Roth IRA MAGI Limits

MAGI	Single; or Married, Filing Separately, and Living Apart from Spouse for Entire Year	Married, Filing Jointly	Married, Filing Separately, and Living with Spouse At Least Part of Year
Less than $10,000	Full Contribution	Full Contribution	Partial Contribution
$10,000–$105,000	Full Contribution	Full Contribution	No Contribution

Table 3-3. Roth IRA MAGI Limits (*cont'd*)

MAGI	Single; or Married, Filing Separately, and Living Apart from Spouse for Entire Year	Married, Filing Jointly	Married, Filing Separately, and Living with Spouse At Least Part of Year
$105,001–$119,999	Partial Contribution	Full Contribution	No Contribution
$120,000–$166,000	No Contribution	Full Contribution	No Contribution
$166,001–$175,999	No Contribution	Partial Contribution	No Contribution
$176,000 or more	No Contribution	No Contribution	No Contribution

Example 1. Peter, who is single and age 40, has MAGI of $60,000 for 2009. He earned $50,000 as a professional artist and another $10,000 from investments. Peter has compensation of more than $5,000 and MAGI of less than $105,000. Accordingly, he may make up to a $5,000 contribution to a Roth IRA for 2009.

Example 2. Quentin is married and files a joint federal income tax return. His compensation is $80,000. His MAGI (including his wife's income) is $200,000. Quentin makes above the $176,000 income limit for married couples filing jointly, so neither he nor his wife may make a Roth IRA contribution for the tax year.

Example 3. Robert, who earns $92,000 as a pilot, is married and files a joint federal income tax return. His wife, Sarah, earns $80,000 at her job as a computer programmer. Robert and Sarah's MAGI is $172,000 (including investment income). Robert and Sarah fall within the phaseout range and must calculate the amount they are eligible to contribute to a Roth IRA (see Q 3:79).

Example 4. Tim and Ursula are married but file separately and they do not live together during the year. Tim's MAGI is $6,000. He is eligible to make a partial Roth IRA contribution because his MAGI falls within the phaseout range for married individuals filing separately. Ursula's MAGI is $130,000. Her MAGI exceeds the limits for married couples filing separately, so she is ineligible to make a Roth IRA contribution.

Q 3:79   If an individual's income falls in the phaseout range, what is the maximum Roth IRA contribution?

If MAGI is within the phaseout range as determined in Table 3-3 (see Q 3:78), the reduced contribution limit is determined as follows:

1. Start with MAGI.

2. Subtract the amount in line 1 from
   a. $176,000 if filing a joint return;
   b. $10,000 if the individual is married, filing a separate return, and lived with his or her spouse at any time during the year; or
   c. $120,000 for all other individuals.
3. Divide the result in line 2 by $15,000 ($10,000 if filing a joint return or if married filing a separate return and living apart the entire year).
4. Multiply the maximum contribution limit (before reduction by this adjustment but after reduction for any contributions to traditional IRAs) by the result in line 3.
5. The result, rounded up to the nearest $10, is the reduced contribution limit. If the reduced contribution limit is more than $0 but less than $200, increase the limit to $200.

Example. Janet is single, age 45, with taxable compensation of $112,000. She wants to make the maximum allowable contribution to her Roth IRA for 2009. Her MAGI for 2009 is $109,000. She has not contributed to any traditional IRA, so her contribution limit before the MAGI reduction is $5,000. Janet calculates her reduced Roth IRA contribution of $4,000 as follows:

1. MAGI = $109,000
2. $120,000 − $109,000 = $11,000
3. $11,000 ÷ $15,000 = 0.733
4. $5,000 (contribution limit before adjustment) × 0.733 = $3,667
5. Janet's reduced Roth IRA contribution limit is $3,670.

[IRS Publication 590, *Individual Retirement Arrangements (IRAs)* 2008, at page 63 (see Appendix A)]

Q 3:80   Are there any special rules for performing the Roth IRA partial contribution calculation?

Yes. Two special rules apply when the Roth IRA partial contribution is performed:

1. *Minimum $200 contribution.* An individual is allowed to contribute $200 to a Roth IRA if the result from the partial contribution calculation is more than $0 but less than $200.
2. *Rounding up to the nearest $10.* An individual is allowed to round the contribution amount up to the next highest $10 increment when using the calculation formula above (see Q 3:79). The calculation formula in the Code is more complicated, and the rounding occurs at an earlier stage in the calculation—but with the same result.

[I.R.C. § 408A(c)(3)(A); Treas. Reg. § 1.408A-3, Q&A-3]

Q 3:81 Does active participation in another retirement plan affect eligibility to make contributions to a Roth IRA?

No. An individual may actively participate in an employer-sponsored retirement plan or any type of plan without affecting his or her eligibility to make a Roth IRA contribution. Having compensation and having MAGI within the income limits are the only factors that determine eligibility to make a Roth IRA contribution. A contribution to a traditional IRA, however, will directly affect an individual's eligibility to make a Roth IRA contribution. [IRS Publication 590, *Individual Retirement Arrangements (IRAs)* 2008 (see Appendix A)]

> **Example.** Yvonne, age 65, is single and works for Zane Advertising Company, which offers a 401(k) plan. Yvonne defers 10 percent of her $70,000 income ($7,000) into the 401(k) plan. She has no other source of income. Yvonne's active participation in Zane's 401(k) plan does not change her ability to make up to a $6,000 Roth IRA contribution for 2009.

Q 3:82 Have the Roth IRA eligibility rules effectively been liberalized for 2010 and later years?

Not directly. Prior to 2010, income limits restrict both regular contributions and conversion contributions to a Roth IRA. Starting in 2010, the income limits on conversions no longer apply, so it should be possible for a high-income individual to make a nondeductible contribution to a traditional IRA and then, in a later year, convert the assets to a Roth IRA and pay tax only on the converted earnings. (See Qs 3:88, 3:92.)

Roth IRA Annual Contributions

Q 3:83 Is there a minimum contribution amount for the Roth IRA?

No. An individual is permitted to make as small a contribution to a Roth IRA as he or she wishes; however, the IRA trustee or custodian may require a minimum contribution to its accounts. That disparity may become significant because individuals may want to establish a Roth IRA with a minimum amount to start the five-year holding period as soon as possible (see chapter 5).

If an individual whose MAGI is in the phaseout range (see Q 3:78) is eligible to make a Roth IRA contribution of more than $0 but less than $200, the individual may make up to a $200 contribution (see Q 3:80). That rule does not require that the individual make a $200 contribution. [I.R.C. § 219(g)(2)(B)]

Q 3:84 May a Roth IRA contribution be made in securities or other property?

No. Roth IRA annual contributions must be made in cash. A person with 100 shares of XYZ stock worth $3,000 would not be allowed to contribute the stock to a Roth IRA. That person would have to sell the stock and contribute the cash proceeds. Assets rolled over or converted from another Roth IRA or from a traditional IRA, however, may be moved in-kind. [I.R.C. § 219(e)(1)]

Q 3:85   May an individual over age 70½ make a Roth IRA contribution?

Yes. No age limit exists for making a Roth IRA contribution—a significant difference between the Roth IRA and the traditional IRA. Of course, an individual over age 70½ must have compensation to be eligible to make a Roth IRA contribution. [I.R.C. § 408A(c)(4)]

Example. Cecilia is single and 74 years old. She has been required to take minimum distributions from her traditional IRA for the last four years and has been prohibited from making any additional contributions to that IRA. Cecilia works part time as a storyteller at the local library and earns more than $10,000 (i.e., at least $6,000 and not more than $105,000) per year. She is eligible to make a $6,000 Roth IRA contribution.

Q 3:86   May an individual combine a Roth IRA contribution with a traditional IRA contribution?

No. Contributions to a Roth IRA must be maintained in a separate trust, custodial account, or annuity, apart from contributions to a traditional IRA. Separate accounting within a single trust, custodial account, or annuity is not permitted. [Ann. 97-122, 1997-50 I.R.B. 63]

Conversion Contributions

Q 3:87   What is a conversion?

The term *conversion* refers to the movement of assets from a traditional, SEP, or SIMPLE IRA into a Roth IRA. Individuals may convert such IRAs into Roth IRAs if they meet certain eligibility requirements (see Q 3:92) and comply with certain rules. [I.R.C. § 408A(c)(3)(B)] (For a discussion of conversion strategies, see chapter 9.)

The term is less frequently used to describe the changing of a traditional IRA contribution into a Roth IRA contribution before the individual's tax return filing due date. Such a *contribution conversion,* or *recharacterization,* is a different type of conversion (see Qs 3:120–3:136).

Q 3:88   Are all holders of traditional IRAs, SEP IRAs, or SIMPLE IRAs eligible to convert them to Roth IRAs?

As of 2010, any non-beneficiary owner of a traditional, SEP, or SIMPLE IRA is eligible to convert the account to a Roth IRA. Conversions during or before 2009, however, are only allowed if the holder satisfies income eligibility requirements.

Note. A favorable transition rule that only applies to conversions completed during 2010 spreads the inclusion of income from such conversions over several years (see Q 3:112).

Caution. Conversions from a SIMPLE IRA are not allowed until the holder has completed at least two years of participation in the SIMPLE IRA plan. (See Q 3:119.)

Q 3:89 May an individual who is receiving required minimum distributions from a traditional IRA make a conversion?

Yes. An individual receiving required minimum distributions (RMDs) from a traditional IRA may convert that IRA to a Roth IRA. Such an individual may wish to do so simply to avoid RMDs or because it makes financial sense. [IRS Publication 590, *Individual Retirement Arrangements (IRAs)* 2008 (see Appendix A)]

Practice Pointer. Individuals who wish to use their IRAs for estate planning purposes should consider the potential benefits of converting for beneficiaries. The disadvantage of converting is that, in most cases, a conversion will accelerate the taxation of the traditional IRA.

Example. Andrew, age 71, has a $40,000 balance in his traditional IRA. He is taking RMDs over his remaining life expectancy of 15 years and already has taken his RMD for 2009. If he also converts in 2009, Andrew would be relieved of future RMD obligations, but would accelerate his tax payments because he would have to pay taxes in one year rather than over his life expectancy. Conversion may nonetheless be desirable to Andrew for a number of reasons. He may not need the assets in the traditional IRA and may prefer that they continue to grow tax-deferred for his beneficiaries. By converting, Andrew can pay the taxes at his tax rate, which may be lower than that of his beneficiaries, and the assets can remain in a tax-deferred account for the rest of his life and for the life expectancy of the oldest beneficiary.

Q 3:90 May the amount of a required minimum distribution be converted?

No, RMD amounts may not be rolled over into an IRA and therefore cannot be converted to a Roth IRA. [I.R.C. § 408(d)(3)(E); Treas. Reg. § 1.408A-4, Q&A-6]

If a minimum distribution is required for a year with respect to an IRA, the first dollars distributed during that year are treated as consisting of the RMD until an amount equal to the RMD for that year has been distributed. Thus, in a year for which a minimum distribution is required (including the calendar year in which the individual attains age 70½), an individual may not convert the assets of a traditional IRA (or any portion of those assets) to a Roth IRA if the RMD from the traditional IRA for the year has not been distributed.

Example. Lydia, age 75, is subject to the RMD rules for her traditional IRA. She decides to convert her traditional IRA to a Roth IRA in 2009. Lydia would like to convert her total balance of $25,000; however, she has not yet taken her RMD for 2009, which is calculated at $1,700. Lydia must first take a distribution of the $1,700; she then may convert the balance of $23,300.

If an RMD amount is contributed to a Roth IRA, it is treated as having been distributed from the traditional IRA and then contributed as a regular contribution to a Roth IRA. [Treas. Reg. § 1.408A-4, Q&A-6]

Q 3:91　May an individual taking substantially equal periodic payments from a traditional IRA make a conversion?

Yes. An individual taking substantially equal periodic payments from his or her traditional IRA may convert the traditional IRA to a Roth IRA and then continue the series of payments from the Roth IRA.

The conversion amount is not subject to the 10 percent premature distribution penalty, and the conversion is not considered a modification of the substantially equal periodic payment stream. [Treas. Reg. § 1.408A-4, Q&A-12] If, however, the original series of substantially equal periodic payments does not continue to be distributed in the same manner from the Roth IRA after the conversion, the series of payments will have been modified. If that modification occurs within five years of the first payment or before the individual becomes disabled or attains age 59½, the individual will be subject to the recapture tax of Code Section 72(t)(4)(A). [Treas. Reg. § 1.408A-4, Q&A-12]

Distributions from the Roth IRA that are part of the original series of substantially equal periodic payments will be nonqualified distributions from the Roth IRA until they meet the requirements for being a qualified distribution. The 10 percent premature distribution penalty will not apply to the extent that the nonqualified distributions are part of a series of substantially equal periodic payments.

Individuals under age 59½ may elect to take substantially equal periodic payments from their traditional IRAs as a way of avoiding the 10 percent premature distribution penalty. This exception requires that an individual continue the periodic payments for five years or until the individual reaches age 59½, whichever period is longer. Individuals failing to maintain the periodic payments for the required time period must retroactively pay the 10 percent premature distribution penalty on all previous distributions that were meant to meet the exception.

Eligibility Requirements for Pre-2010 Conversions

Q 3:92　What eligibility requirements apply to IRA conversions that are completed before or during 2009?

All conversions prior to 2010 are subject to two eligibility requirements: (1) for the year of conversion, MAGI cannot exceed $100,000; and (2) married individuals must file a joint income tax return in the year of the conversion. Prior to 2010, married taxpayers filing separate returns are not allowed to convert a traditional IRA to a Roth IRA (unless the spouses have lived apart for the entire tax year). [I.R.C. § 408A(c)(3)(B)(ii); Treas. Reg. § 1.408A-3, Q&A 3(b)]

Q 3:93   Does the $100,000 limit apply to a married individual's income on a combined basis?

Yes. The $100,000 limit for a conversion (see Q 3:92) applies whether an individual is married or single. Because married individuals must file a joint income tax return to be eligible to convert, a married couple must add their incomes together to determine whether they meet the $100,000 limit. [Treas. Reg. § 1.408A-4, Q&A-2]

Example. Willow is single in 2009 and makes $85,000 working as a writer for a major magazine. With few other sources of income, she has MAGI of less than $100,000, and meets the eligibility requirements for conversion in 2008. Willow meets Yves in 2010; they intend to marry in December 2010. Yves works as a technician and makes $35,000. The couple's combined MAGI for 2010 will place them above the $100,000 limit. If they delay their marriage until 2011, Willow and Yves may convert their traditional IRAs to Roth IRAs in 2010. Otherwise, they will not be eligible to convert their traditional IRAs to Roth IRAs in 2010.

Q 3:94   How can an individual know if he or she meets the $100,000 limit before the end of the year?

The rule that an individual must have MAGI of no more than $100,000 (see Q 3:92) to be eligible to make a conversion can be a problem if an individual does not know what his or her MAGI will be until after the end of the year. In most cases, however, individuals will know whether their income will be above or below the $100,000 limit.

Practice Pointer. Individuals who anticipate being near the $100,000 limit may want to wait until closer to the end of the year before deciding whether to make a conversion.

Q 3:95   Does the amount converted count as income for purposes of the $100,000 limit?

No. An individual may determine his or her MAGI for purposes of determining eligibility for a conversion without considering any increase in the individual's taxable income caused by the conversion. [Treas. Reg. § 1.408A-3, Q&A-5] (For purposes of income taxes, however, the conversion amount must be included as taxable income.)

Example. Carl has MAGI of $80,000, and he decides to convert his $100,000 traditional IRA to a Roth IRA in 2009. Carl must include $100,000 as *income* for 2009. He does not, however, have to include the $100,000 for the purpose of meeting the $100,000 eligibility requirement.

Q 3:96   Are required minimum distributions counted toward the $100,000 limit?

No. RMDs do not count toward the $100,000 limit for a conversion (see Q 3:92). [I.R.C. § 408A(c)(3)(C)(i)]

Q 3:97   Are there steps an individual can take to reduce MAGI below the $100,000 limit?

Yes. Individuals who want to convert a traditional IRA to a Roth IRA but whose MAGI is close to the $100,000 limit can take steps to reduce their income for the year of the conversion. Common methods for reducing income include (1) fully funding a qualified retirement plan (e.g., making the maximum deferral to a 401(k) plan); (2) delaying the sale of appreciated stock or property; (3) investing in nondividend-paying stocks or tax-exempt securities; (4) deferring bonuses or the exercise of stock options; and (5) reducing salary.

Practice Pointer. Individuals who are considering ways of reducing their income or changing the timing of income should consult with their tax and legal advisors.

Q 3:98   What happens if an individual makes a conversion and then discovers that his or her income exceeded the $100,000 limit?

An individual who makes a conversion but discovers that his or her income exceeds the $100,000 limit may recharacterize the contribution as a traditional IRA contribution. [I.R.C. § 408A(d)(6)] That recharacterization takes place without tax or penalty (see Q 3:120).

Example. Joe makes $55,000 as a foreman at a candy factory. He converted his traditional IRA into a Roth IRA in April because he thought he was eligible. In November Joe wins $1 million in the lottery. His income now exceeds $100,000, so he is not eligible to convert his traditional IRA to a Roth IRA. Joe may, however, switch back to the traditional IRA without paying taxes or penalties on the amount switched back.

Conversion of Nondeductible Traditional IRA Contributions

Q 3:99   May a traditional IRA that contains nondeductible contributions be converted to a Roth IRA?

Yes. Nondeductible contributions in a traditional IRA may be converted to a Roth IRA. The return of the after-tax nondeductible contributions in the traditional IRA will not be taxable as part of the conversion. That makes the conversion of nondeductible contributions particularly desirable because such contributions can be converted without any tax impact in the year of the conversion. [I.R.C. §§ 408A(d)(3)(A)(i), 408A(d)(3)(C); Treas. Reg. § 1.408A-4, Q&A-7]

Example. In 2009, Frank converts his only IRA, a traditional IRA with a $20,000 balance, to a Roth IRA. Since Frank made a total of $8,000 in nondeductible contributions to the traditional IRA, his taxable amount on conversion is $12,000 ($20,000 less his nondeductible contributions of $8,000).

Q 3:100 May an individual convert only the nondeductible portion of a traditional IRA?

No. Individuals may not convert only their nondeductible contributions. If that were possible, however, it would be an extremely popular option.

Distributions from a traditional IRA that contains nondeductible contributions are apportioned by a ratio. Part of the distribution is a return of the nondeductible contribution and part is a return of taxable contributions and taxable earnings. The IRS requires taxpayers to file Form 8606 to determine the taxable portion of a distribution from a traditional IRA containing nondeductible contributions. [I.R.C. § 408A(d)(4)(B)]

Q 3:101 How is Form 8606 filed?

An individual converting all or a portion of a traditional IRA to a Roth IRA must complete and file Form 8606 to determine the taxable and nontaxable portions of the amount converted. The form is filed as an attachment to the individual's personal income tax return.

Q 3:102 If all nondeductible contributions are kept in a separate IRA, may just that IRA (along with earnings) be converted?

No. All IRAs are treated as one IRA for the purposes of taxation of distributions. Accordingly, an individual who separated nondeductible contributions from deductible contributions is no more able to convert just the nondeductible contributions than someone who mixed together deductible and nondeductible contributions. [Treas. Reg. § 1.408A-6, Q&A-9]

Mechanics of Conversion

Q 3:103 What is the deadline for a conversion?

A conversion of a traditional IRA to a Roth IRA must be completed before the end of the calendar year of the conversion. A conversion may, however, occur in any tax year. Accordingly, if an individual misses a particular tax year, the individual could convert in the next tax year (as long as the individual meets the eligibility requirements, if applicable, in the next tax year). [I.R.C. § 408A(d)(6)]

Q 3:104   May only a portion of a traditional IRA be converted?

Yes, only a portion of a traditional IRA may be converted. Many individuals, especially those with large traditional IRA balances, may benefit from a conversion but cannot afford the taxes. An individual who is unsure of whether conversion is the right choice may simply convert a portion of his or her traditional IRA or IRAs. [Treas. Reg. § 1.408A-4, Q&A-1]

Q 3:105   May the conversion be spread over a number of years?

Yes. For financial planning and tax reasons it may make sense for some individuals to spread the conversion of a traditional IRA to a Roth IRA over a number of years. The law allows individuals to complete a conversion in any year in which they are eligible and have traditional IRA assets to convert. [I.R.C. § 408A(d)(3)] Each conversion is treated as a separate tax transaction, but through proper financial planning a comprehensive tax strategy can be devised.

Example. Constance is living on a low, fixed income and is in the lowest tax bracket. She would like to convert her $200,000 traditional IRA to a Roth IRA, but she is concerned about the tax impact of such a large conversion. After discussing the situation with her tax advisor, Constance decides to convert $10,000 in 2009 and then convert $10,000 per year for the next 19 years. She also plans to convert any growth in the traditional IRA over the same period. Following such a strategy, Constance will be able to pay taxes on the converted amount each year at a lower rate. Although it will take longer for her to move all her traditional IRA assets into Roth IRAs, Constance feels the 20-year plan is the best solution.

Q 3:106   How is a conversion completed?

Three methods are available to convert a traditional IRA to a Roth IRA. To convert the interest of a nonspouse beneficiary, however, the second method (direct trustee-to-trustee transfer) must be used and the receiving account must be denominated as an inherited Roth IRA (see Q 4:88). [Notice 2008-30, Q&A-7, 2008-12 I.R.B. 638]:

1. *Rollover.* An amount distributed from a traditional IRA is contributed (rolled over) to a Roth IRA within 60 days after the distribution unless it is eligible for an extension of the rollover period (see chapter 6).
2. *Transfer to new trustee.* The trustee of the traditional IRA directly transfers an amount from it to the trustee of the Roth IRA.
3. *Internal transfer.* An amount in a traditional IRA is transferred to a Roth IRA maintained by the same trustee.

[Treas. Reg. § 1.408A-4, Q&A-1]

Note. The IRS clarified that a conversion must be reported as a taxable distribution and should not be treated as a trustee-to-trustee transfer from a reporting perspective. [Treas. Reg. § 1.408A-4, Q&A-1; *see also* Instructions for IRS Forms 1099, 1098, 5498, and W-2G (2008).]

Q 3:107 Is a conversion treated as a rollover or as a transfer?

Regardless of how the transaction is actually completed, a conversion is treated as a rollover of traditional IRA assets into a Roth IRA for reporting and taxation purposes. [Treas. Reg. § 1.408A-4, Q&A-1] The assets are treated as a distribution from the traditional IRA and then as a rollover contribution into the Roth IRA.

The Code also provides for the conversion of traditional IRAs to Roth IRAs without the IRA owner's actually taking a distribution of the assets. This occurs when an individual authorizes his or her existing IRA trustee or custodian to convert the account to a Roth IRA. The transaction is considered a rollover even though the assets never moved outside of the trustee's or custodian's control. Conversions under the same trustee or custodian are considered rollovers although the assets are moved directly between the traditional IRA and the Roth IRA as a convenience to the IRA owner.

> **Example.** Max receives a brochure from Mutual Funds, Inc., advertising the Roth IRA and, in particular, the benefits of converting to a Roth IRA. Max has a traditional IRA with Big Bank. Max completes the conversion form included in the marketing material and returns it to Mutual Funds. Mutual Funds forwards the form to Big Bank. The form requests Big Bank to send Max's IRA assets directly to Mutual Funds. Big Bank forwards the assets and treats the conversion as a taxable distribution. Mutual Funds treats the contribution as a rollover conversion contribution.

Q 3:108 Does the 60-day rule for rollovers apply to rollover conversions?

Yes. Assets distributed from a traditional IRA must be rolled over into a Roth IRA within 60 days of receipt unless the transaction is eligible for an extension of the rollover period (see chapter 6). [I.R.C. § 408A(e)]

If the assets move directly between trustees or custodians and the taxpayer never actually receives a distribution, it is less clear that the 60-day rule applies. An argument can be made that the 60-day rule applies only when the taxpayer actually receives a distribution of the assets.

> **Practice Pointer.** A cautious approach would be to complete all conversions within 60 days, regardless of the form of the transaction.

Q 3:109 May an individual convert a traditional IRA to a Roth IRA if he or she has already completed a rollover in the last 12 months?

Yes. Although conversions are considered rollovers, the rule limiting traditional IRA rollovers to one every 12 months does not apply to conversions. [I.R.C. § 408A(e)]

> **Example 1.** Ken rolled over his only traditional IRA from ABC Bank to XYZ Credit Union on March 10, 2009. Ken decides in April 2009 that he would like

to convert his traditional IRA to a Roth IRA. The one rollover per 12 months rule does not prevent Ken from completing the conversion.

Example 2. Sally has $100,000 in a traditional IRA invested in a mutual fund that she would like to convert to a Roth IRA. She understands that the conversion is a taxable distribution, and she does not want to risk converting the entire amount at one time. Like everyone else, Sally is unsure whether the market is going up or down over the next 12 months. She decides to convert one-twelfth of $100,000 for each month of the year so as to obtain a rough yearly average of the stock price. That is permissible because there is no limit on the number of conversions that can be made in one year.

Q 3:110   May individuals convert, recharacterize, and then convert again?

Yes, subject to restrictions (see Q 3:83).

Tax Consequences of Conversion

Q 3:111   What are the tax consequences of a conversion?

An individual who converts a traditional IRA to a Roth IRA must pay income taxes on the taxable portion of the distribution from the traditional IRA. The Roth IRA is a nondeductible IRA, and taxing the distribution from the traditional IRA creates an account that contains after-tax dollars. [Treas. Reg. § 1.408A-4, Q&A-7]

Q 3:112   What transition rule particularly favors conversions completed during 2010?

The legislation that eliminates the eligibility requirements for conversions after 2009 (see Q 3:88) also includes a favorable transition rule that applies only to conversions completed during 2010. Under this special rule, half the gross income resulting from a 2010 conversion is included in income in 2011 and half in 2012 (unless the individual elects not to have the rule apply). An income acceleration rule applies if any converted amounts are distributed before 2012. [I.R.C. § 408A(d)(3)]

Example. In March 2010, Jane has a traditional IRA balance of $20,000, consisting of tax-deductible contributions plus earnings. She converts her traditional IRA to a Roth IRA, which results in $20,000 of conversion income. If none of the converted amount is distributed before 2012, the conversion income will be included in taxable income as follows: none in 2010, $10,000 in 2011, and $10,000 in 2012.

Q 3:113   Why would an individual want to convert if he or she would have to pay taxes now?

The conversion accelerates tax, but an individual may prefer to pay lower taxes now to avoid higher taxes in the future. In both the Roth IRA and the traditional IRA, earnings grow tax deferred. However, a qualified distribution from a Roth IRA is tax free, while a distribution from a traditional IRA is taxable (see chapters 4 and 5).

Example. Betty has $10,000 in a traditional IRA that she rolled over from a qualified plan from her previous job. If she converts the traditional IRA to a Roth IRA in 2011, she will have to include $10,000 in taxable income in 2011. She will, however, have $10,000 in her Roth IRA. With an 8 percent return over the next 25 years, Betty will accumulate $77,727. That amount is completely tax free in the Roth IRA, but only tax deferred in the traditional IRA. Accordingly, Betty may decide that paying some taxes today is beneficial to avoid taxes in the future.

Q 3:114   What tax rate applies to the conversion amount?

The amount converted from a traditional IRA to a Roth IRA is taxed at the IRA owner's marginal income tax rate in the year the income is included in compensation.

Example. Clark is single and has taxable income of $25,000 for 2009. His income places him in the 15 percent tax bracket. Clark converts his $60,000 deductible IRA to a Roth IRA in 2009; accordingly, he must include an additional $60,000 in income that year. Adding the $60,000 to his 2009 income will push Clark into the 28 percent marginal tax bracket in 2009.

Q 3:115   Is a conversion an exception to the 10 percent premature distribution penalty?

Yes. An individual who converts a traditional IRA to a Roth IRA is not subject to the 10 percent premature distribution penalty normally associated with distributions before age 59½. [I.R.C. § 408A(d)(3)]

Q 3:116   How is a conversion taxed if one of the account assets is an annuity contract, or if an IRA annuity is converted?

Generally, an amount equal to the fair market value of the annuity contract on the date of conversion is deemed to be distributed from the traditional IRA and then transferred to the Roth IRA by means of a rollover contribution. However, if the conversion is accomplished by surrendering the annuity for its cash value and reinvesting the entire cash proceeds in a Roth IRA, and all contractual rights are extinguished in the surrender, then only the cash proceeds are deemed to be distributed. [Temp. Treas. Reg. § 1.408A-4T, Q&A-14] (See Q 4:20.)

Withholding on Conversions

Q 3:117 Are conversions subject to withholding?

A conversion is treated as a distribution. Accordingly, withholding applies unless waived by the IRA owner. [Treas. Reg. § 1.408A-6, Q&A-13] Most individuals waive withholding because they want to convert the entire amount and then elect to pay applicable taxes from funds held outside the IRA.

Additionally, any amount withheld and not converted will not enjoy the automatic exception to the 10 percent premature distribution penalty available to conversion amounts (see Q 3:115). An individual who elects withholding may, however, make up for the amount withheld out of other assets so as to complete the conversion in the full amount of the distribution and avoid the 10 percent penalty. For example, a taxpayer who converts a $10,000 traditional IRA to a Roth IRA and elects to have $1,000 (10 percent of the $10,000) withheld for federal income tax purposes must add $1,000 to the Roth IRA within 60 days to avoid a 10 percent penalty on the $1,000 withheld.

Practice Pointer. *Some* method of withholding is probably warranted for most individuals completing conversions, especially in the case of large conversion amounts. An individual may find it more convenient to increase his or her payroll withholding or to use estimated quarterly withholding amounts to compensate for the increased tax liability caused by the conversion than to request withholding from the IRA.

Conversions of SEPs and SIMPLE IRAs

Q 3:118 May an individual convert a SEP to a Roth IRA?

Yes. A traditional IRA that receives SEP contributions is commonly referred to as a *SEP IRA*, a term that often confuses taxpayers. It may be better to think of the SEP as the plan authorizing an employer to make contributions to its employees' traditional IRAs. Once the assets are contributed to the traditional IRA, the traditional IRA rules apply. Accordingly, a taxpayer with a traditional IRA that contains SEP contributions can convert that IRA to a Roth IRA. [Treas. Reg. § 1.408A-4, Q&A-4(a)]

Example 1. HighTech, Inc. provides a SEP as the retirement plan for its employees. HighTech contributed $35,000 to Sam's IRA over the years, and, with earnings, Sam currently has a balance of $50,000 in his traditional IRA (SEP IRA). Sam wishes to convert that IRA to a Roth IRA. He can convert the entire $50,000 balance (or less) in 2009 as long as his MAGI (or, if Sam is married, the couple's combined MAGI as shown on a jointly filed return) does not exceed $100,000 in the year of conversion. If he converts in 2010 or later, he can do so regardless of MAGI.

Example 2. Sam, from Example 1, converts the entire balance of $50,000. Shortly after the conversion, HighTech announces that it will be making its annual SEP contribution and that Sam will be receiving a contribution of $3,000. Sam requests that HighTech make his contribution directly to his

Roth IRA. HighTech must refuse that request and make the $3,000 contribution to a traditional IRA. Immediately after the $3,000 is placed in a traditional IRA, Sam may convert the traditional IRA to a Roth IRA.

Q 3:119   May an individual convert a SIMPLE IRA to a Roth IRA?

Eventually. Contributions made pursuant to a SIMPLE IRA plan must be made to a SIMPLE IRA. Accordingly, the annual contributions may not be made to a Roth IRA. Once the contribution is placed in a SIMPLE IRA, however, the SIMPLE IRA may be converted to a Roth IRA—but not during the initial two-year participation period required for a SIMPLE IRA. SIMPLE IRAs are subject to a 25 percent premature distribution penalty instead of the 10 percent penalty applicable to traditional IRAs during the initial two-year period. After the two-year period has elapsed, the SIMPLE IRA is basically a traditional IRA. [Treas. Reg. § 1.408A-4, Q&A-4(b)]

> **Example.** Confetti, Inc. offers a SIMPLE IRA plan to its employees allowing them to defer a portion of their income into a SIMPLE IRA. Paula, a new participant in Confetti's SIMPLE IRA plan, wants her assets in a Roth IRA instead of the SIMPLE IRA. Confetti cannot make the contribution directly to a Roth IRA and must continue to make the contributions to a SIMPLE IRA. After the SIMPLE IRA has been open two years, Paula may convert the SIMPLE IRA to a Roth IRA; however, she must maintain the SIMPLE IRA in order to receive future employer SIMPLE contributions.

Recharacterization of IRA Contributions

Q 3:120   May a traditional IRA contribution be recharacterized as a Roth IRA contribution?

Yes. An IRA owner may elect to have a contribution that was originally made to a traditional IRA recharacterized as a Roth IRA contribution. To accomplish the recharacterization, the original contribution, plus allocable earnings, must be moved to a Roth IRA by means of a trustee-to-trustee transfer, and the transfer must occur by the due date (including extensions) of the IRA owner's income tax return for the year for which the contribution was made.

The recharacterization causes the contribution to be treated as though it were made directly to the transferee IRA. Consequently, if a traditional IRA contribution is recharacterized as a Roth contribution, no deduction is allowed for the contribution, and no income is generated by the trustee-to-trustee transfer. [I.R.C. § 408A(d)(6)]

> **Note.** The term *recharacterize* describes the process of switching from one type of IRA to another.

> **Example.** On January 15, 2010, Joan made a $5,000 traditional IRA contribution for the prior year, 2009. Two months later, she received a brochure

from her banker explaining the benefits of the Roth IRA. Joan decides she would rather open a Roth IRA. The law allows her to recharacterize her 2009 traditional IRA contribution (including earnings) as a Roth IRA contribution for 2009. No taxes or penalties will apply. Of course, Joan may not claim a deduction for any traditional IRA contribution because she recharacterized it as a Roth IRA contribution.

Q 3:121   May a Roth IRA contribution be recharacterized as a traditional IRA contribution?

Yes. It is also possible to recharacterize a Roth IRA contribution as a traditional IRA contribution. The recharacterization is accomplished in the same way—i.e., through a trustee-to-trustee transfer of the contribution, plus allocable earnings, from the Roth IRA to the traditional IRA, which must occur on or before the due date (including extensions) of the tax return for the year for which the contribution was made. [I.R.C. § 408A(d)(6)] The trustee-to-trustee transfer does not generate any income, but in this case the recharacterized contribution (now treated as made to a traditional IRA) may be eligible for a tax deduction.

Q 3:122   How is the election to recharacterize an IRA contribution made?

The election to recharacterize a traditional IRA contribution as a Roth IRA contribution (or vice versa) is made by notifying, on or before the date of the transfer, both the trustee of the initial IRA and the trustee of the new IRA how the individual has elected to treat the contribution for federal income tax purposes.

The notification of the election to recharacterize must include the following information:

1. The type and amount of the contribution to the initial IRA that is to be recharacterized;
2. The date on which the contribution was made to the initial IRA and the year for which it was made;
3. A direction to the trustee or custodian of the initial IRA to transfer, in a trustee-to-trustee transfer, the amount of the contribution and net income allocable to the contribution to the trustee or custodian of the new IRA;
4. The names of the trustee or custodian of the initial IRA and the trustee or custodian of the new IRA; and
5. Any additional information needed to make the transfer.

[Treas. Reg. § 1.408A-5, Q&A-6]

Q 3:123   Can the recharacterization deadline be extended?

Yes. Two kinds of extensions are available: automatic and discretionary.

The recharacterization deadline is automatically extended—to the date that is six months after the unextended due date of the tax return for the year of the contribution—if three requirements are met:

1. The IRA owner timely filed a tax return for the year of the contribution,

2. The owner completes the election procedure (see Q 3:122) during the six-month extension period, and

3. If necessary, the owner files an amended tax return for the contribution year.

[Treas. Reg. § 30.9100-2(b); IRS Ann. 99-57, 1999-24 I.R.B. 50 (June 14, 1999)]

Note. The automatic extension does not really change the deadline in many cases, because an automatic six-month extension of the return filing date is also generally available. However, it may be useful to an individual who files a return by April 15, or who files a return on extension but before October 15, and later decides to recharacterize.

Individuals may also apply to the IRS for a discretionary waiver of the recharacterization deadline. Such waivers are only granted in letter rulings, so the procedures and fees that are generally attendant to ruling requests have to be followed. To obtain the waiver, an individual must show that he or she acted in good faith, and that the granting of relief would not prejudice any IRS interests. [Treas. Reg. § 301.9100-3] Many favorable recharacterization rulings have been granted on this basis. [*See, e.g.,* Priv. Ltr. Rul. 200331004 (Aug. 1, 2003); Priv. Ltr. Rul. 200909073 (Feb. 27, 2009).]

Q 3:124   Is recharacterizing a traditional IRA as a Roth IRA a conversion?

No. A conversion is a taxable rollover of assets from a traditional IRA to a Roth IRA, and until 2010 an individual must meet eligibility requirements in order to convert (see Q 3:92). Changing the contribution type before the tax return filing due date, on the other hand, does not require that the individual meet the conversion eligibility requirements. [I.R.C. § 408A(d)(6)]

The opportunity to recharacterize one type of IRA as another is designed to accommodate individuals who make mistakes, change their minds, or find themselves ineligible for one type of IRA and therefore want to switch to the other.

Example. Ann, a married joint filer, age 53, made a $6,000 traditional IRA contribution in January 2009 for the 2009 tax year. She anticipated that she would be eligible to deduct the contribution, but she received an unexpectedly large bonus in April 2009 that pushed her MAGI above the deduction limits. Ann decides to recharacterize the $6,000 contribution (along with earnings of $150) as a Roth IRA contribution before her tax return filing due date. She therefore transfers the entire $6,150 to a Roth IRA. The transaction is *not* a conversion, and Ann does not have to pay taxes on the $6,150. She is not allowed to take a deduction on her income tax return for the traditional IRA contribution. Ann may complete the transaction even if her MAGI exceeds $100,000 (the eligibility limit for conversions), as long as it is less than $166,000 (the eligibility limit for Roth IRA contributions).

Q 3:125   May the conversion of a traditional IRA be recharacterized?

Yes. The ability to recharacterize the conversion of a traditional IRA is important if the IRA owner completes a conversion and then discovers that he or she is not eligible to convert because of the income limit or his or her filing status. [Treas. Reg. § 1.408A-4, Q&A-3]

Moreover, the transaction may be recharacterized even if eligibility is not a problem. For instance, if, upon further review, the IRA owner decides that paying taxes on the conversion amount is not in his or her interest, he or she could move the assets back to a traditional IRA.

Example 1. On January 1, 2009, Pam converted her traditional IRA to a Roth IRA. On April 10, 2009, Pam discovers that her MAGI for 2009 exceeded $100,000 and that, therefore, she was ineligible to convert her traditional IRA to a Roth IRA. Pam may transfer back the assets in the Roth IRA (including earnings) to a traditional IRA before her tax return filing due date.

Example 2. In 2009, Linda converted the entire amount in her traditional IRA to a Roth IRA. Soon after, Linda learns that her MAGI for 2009 exceeded $100,000, and that, therefore, she was ineligible to make a conversion in that year. Accordingly, before the due date (plus extensions) for filing her federal income tax return for 2009, Linda decides to recharacterize the conversion contribution. She instructs the trustee of the Roth IRA to transfer directly the amount of the contribution, plus net income, to the trustee of a new traditional IRA. Linda notifies both trustees that she is recharacterizing her Roth IRA. On her federal income tax return for 2009, Linda treats the original amount of the conversion as having been contributed to the traditional IRA and not to the Roth IRA. For federal income tax purposes, the original conversion amount is treated as a contribution to the second traditional IRA, and the conversion is disregarded. (The result is the same as if the conversion amount had been transferred in a tax-free transfer to another Roth IRA before the recharacterization.) [Treas. Reg. § 1.408A-5, Q&A-9, Q&A-10]

Q 3:126   How is net income that is attributable to an IRA contribution that is being recharacterized treated?

The net income attributable to an IRA contribution that is being recharacterized must be transferred along with the contribution. [Treas. Reg. § 1.408A-5, Q&A-2]

If the amount of the contribution being recharacterized was contributed to a separate IRA, and no distributions or additional contributions have been made from or to that IRA, then the entire account balance of that IRA is recharacterized, and the attributable net income (or loss) is the difference between the amount of the original contribution and the amount transferred.

If the IRA contribution was not kept separate, the net income attributable to the contribution is calculated as described below (see Q 3:127).

Q 3:127   How is net income calculated for recharacterized contributions?

The net income or loss attributable to recharacterized contributions is calculated as follows:

1. Enter the amount of the IRA contribution to be recharacterized.
2. Enter the fair market value of the IRA immediately prior to the recharacterization, increased by any distributions, transfers, or recharacterizations made while the contribution was in the account. This is the "adjusted closing balance."
3. Enter the fair market value of the IRA immediately prior to the time the contribution being recharacterized was made, increased by the amount of such contribution and any other contributions, transfers, or recharacterizations made while the contribution was in the account. This is the "adjusted opening balance."
4. Subtract the amount in line 3 from line 2.
5. Divide line 4 by line 3. Enter the result as a decimal (rounded to at least three places).
6. Multiply line 1 by line 5. The result is the net income attributable to the contribution to be recharacterized.
7. Add lines 1 and 6. The result is the amount of the IRA contribution plus the net income attributable to it to be recharacterized.

[IRS Publication 590, *Individual Retirement Arrangements (IRAs)* 2008 (see Appendix A)]

A special rule is provided for an IRA asset that is not normally valued on a daily basis. In this case, the fair market value of the asset at the beginning of the computation period is deemed to be the most recent, regularly determined, fair market value of the asset, determined as of a date that coincides with or precedes the first day of the computation period. [Treas. Reg. § 1.408A-5, Q&A-2(c)(1)]

> **Example.** Nancy has a Roth IRA worth $80,000. On April 1, 2009, Nancy makes a $160,000 conversion contribution to her Roth IRA. On January 31, 2010, she discovers that she is ineligible to make a Roth IRA conversion contribution for 2009 because her MAGI exceeded $100,000. Nancy requests that the IRA trustee recharacterize $160,000 from her Roth IRA, which is now worth $225,000, to a traditional IRA. The trustee must also transfer the net income gained along with the $160,000 to the traditional IRA.
>
> The adjusted opening balance is $240,000 ($80,000 + $160,000), and the adjusted closing balance is $225,000. Thus, the net income allocable to the $160,000 is a loss of $10,000 (i.e., $160,000 × (($225,000 − $240,000) ÷ $240,000).

In order to recharacterize the April 1, 2009, conversion contribution of $160,000 on January 31, 2010, the Roth IRA trustee transfers $150,000 ($160,000 – $10,000) from Nancy's Roth IRA to her traditional IRA.

The step-by-step calculation of net income is as follows:

1.	The amount of Nancy's IRA contribution for 2008 to be recharacterized	$ 160,000
2.	The fair market value of Nancy's IRA immediately prior to the *recharacterization* (including any distributions, transfers, or recharacterizations made while the contribution was in the account)	$ 225,000
3.	The fair market value of Nancy's IRA immediately prior to the time the *contribution* being recharacterized was made, including the amount of such contribution and any other contributions, transfers, or recharacterizations made while the contribution was in the account	$ 240,000
4.	Subtract line 3 from line 2.	(15,000)
5.	Divide line 4 by line 3. The result is a decimal	(.0625)
6.	Multiply line 1 by line 5. The result is the net income attributable to the contribution to be characterized.	($10,000)
7.	Add lines 1 and 6. This is the sum of the IRA contribution plus the net income attributable to it, which is the total amount to be recharacterized.	$ 150,000

[IRS Publication 590, *Individual Retirement Arrangements (IRAs)* 2008 (see Appendix A)]

Q 3:128   May an amount converted from a SIMPLE IRA or a SEP IRA to a Roth IRA be recharacterized?

Yes. An amount converted from a savings incentive match plan for employees (SIMPLE) IRA or a simplified employee pension plan (SEP) IRA to a Roth IRA may be recharacterized back to the SIMPLE IRA or SEP IRA. Employer contributions (including elective deferrals) under a SIMPLE IRA plan or a SEP cannot, however, be recharacterized as contributions to another IRA. [Treas. Reg. § 1.408A-5, Q&A-5]

Q 3:129   May an individual convert, recharacterize, and then reconvert the same contribution to an IRA?

Yes. An individual may convert an IRA contribution, recharacterize it, and then reconvert it. It should be noted, however, that special rules apply, depending on when the transaction takes place.

IRA owners who wish to reconvert must wait a fixed number of days before doing so. An IRA owner who converts an amount from a traditional IRA to a

Roth IRA during any taxable year and then transfers that amount back to a traditional IRA by means of a recharacterization may not reconvert that amount from the traditional IRA to a Roth IRA before the beginning of the next taxable year following the year of the conversion or, if later, the end of the 30-day period beginning on the day on which the owner transferred the amount from the Roth IRA back to a traditional IRA by means of a recharacterization. [Treas. Reg. § 1.408A-5, Q&A-9(a)(1)]

> **Example 1.** John converts his traditional IRA to a Roth IRA in January 2009. He recharacterizes the Roth IRA as a traditional IRA in February 2009. John cannot reconvert the traditional IRA to a Roth IRA until January 2010.

> **Example 2.** Mindy converts a traditional IRA to a Roth IRA in January 2009. She transfers the conversion amount back to a traditional IRA in a recharacterization on January 18, 2010. The recharacterization is effective for the 2009 taxable year, so Mindy cannot reconvert that amount until February 18, 2010 (i.e., the first day after the end of the 30-day period beginning on the day of the recharacterization).

Q 3:130 What are the consequences of failing to wait the required fixed number of days before making a reconversion?

A reconversion made before the later of the beginning of the next taxable year following the year of the conversion to a Roth IRA or the end of the 30-day period that begins on the day of the recharacterization (see Q 3:129) is treated as a failed conversion and is considered to be a distribution from the traditional IRA and a regular contribution to the Roth IRA. A failed conversion may be corrected by a subsequent recharacterization back to a traditional IRA. A failed conversion resulting from a failure to satisfy the statutory requirements for a conversion (e.g., the $100,000 MAGI limit), however, is treated as a conversion in determining when an IRA owner may make a reconversion. [Preamble to Treas. Reg. § 1.408A, 64 Fed. Reg. 5,597–5,611 (1999)] Accordingly, a conversion that fails to meet the statutory requirements may be recharacterized and potentially reconverted at a later date.

> **Example.** Wendy converts her traditional IRA to a Roth IRA in 2009. On January 18, 2010, she recharacterizes the Roth IRA as a traditional IRA because she realizes that her MAGI for 2009 will exceed $100,000. She cannot reconvert before February 18, 2010, but she inadvertently does so. Wendy's attempted reconversion is not treated as a conversion for purposes of the reconversion rules (although it is otherwise treated as a failed conversion), so it does not further delay her eligibility to reconvert. Therefore, Wendy may transfer the amount back to a traditional IRA in a recharacterization and reconvert it at any time on or after February 18, 2009.

Q 3:131 Is a recharacterization of an IRA contribution treated as a rollover for purposes of the one-rollover-per-year rule?

No. The recharacterization of an IRA contribution is never treated as a rollover for purposes of the one-rollover-per-year limit of Code Section 408(d)(3)(B). [Treas. Reg. § 1.408A-5, Q&A-8, 64 Fed. Reg. 5,597–5,611 (1999)]

Q 3:132 May an individual recharacterize a rollover or a contribution that has been transferred?

No. A rollover or a contribution that has been transferred may not be recharacterized. [Treas. Reg. § 1.408A-5, Q&A-10]

Example. In 2009, Ron receives a distribution from one traditional IRA and contributes the entire amount to another traditional IRA in a rollover contribution described in Code Section 408(d)(3). Ron may not elect to recharacterize the contribution by transferring the contribution amount plus net income to a Roth IRA, because an amount contributed to an IRA in a tax-free transfer may not be recharacterized. Ron may, however, convert (other than by recharacterization) the amount in the second traditional IRA to a Roth IRA at any time if the eligibility requirements are satisfied.

Q 3:133 May an election be made to recharacterize an IRA contribution on behalf of a deceased IRA owner?

Yes. The election to recharacterize an IRA contribution may be made by the executor, administrator, or other person charged with the duty of filing a deceased IRA owner's final federal income tax return. [Treas. Reg. § 1.408A-5, Q&A-6]

Q 3:134 Is a conduit IRA that is converted and then recharacterized still a conduit IRA?

Yes. A conduit IRA that is converted to a Roth IRA and subsequently recharacterized back to a traditional IRA retains its status as a conduit IRA. That is so because the effect of the recharacterization is to treat the amount recharacterized as if it had been transferred directly from the original conduit IRA to another conduit IRA. [Preamble to Treas. Reg. § 1.408A]

Q 3:135 Is a recharacterization subject to withholding?

No. A recharacterization is not a designated distribution under Code Section 3405 and therefore is not subject to federal income tax withholding. [Preamble to Treas. Reg. § 1.408A]

Q 3:136   How are recharacterizations and reconversions reported for federal income tax purposes?

A recharacterization or reconversion of an IRA must be reported on Form 1099-R, Distributions From Pensions, Annuities, Retirement or Profit-Sharing Plans, IRAs, Insurance Contracts, etc., and Form 5498, IRA Contribution Information.

Prior-year recharacterizations and same-year recharacterizations are separately coded; it follows then that the amounts may not be reported together on the same Form 1099-R. Similarly, because a recharacterization will have a different code than other reportable distributions, it may not be reported together with another reportable distribution on the same Form 1099-R. It should be noted, however, that all recharacterized contributions received by an IRA in the same year may be totaled and reported on one Form 5498. Alternatively, each recharacterized contribution may be reported on a separate Form 5498.

Note. These forms are discussed in chapter 7; see Q 7:91 (Form 1099-R) and Q 7:150 (Form 5498).

Excess Contributions

Q 3:137   What is an excess contribution to a traditional IRA?

An *excess contribution* to a traditional IRA is the amount that an individual contributes to his or her traditional IRAs for a year that is more than the smaller of the individual's taxable compensation for the year or $5,000 ($6,000 if the individual is age 50 or older). This limit applies whether the contributions are deductible or nondeductible. Contributions to a traditional IRA made in the year in which an individual reaches age 70½ (or thereafter) are also considered excess contributions. Excess contributions may also result from a spouse's contribution, an employer's contribution, or an improper rollover contribution. [I.R.C. § 408(a); Treas. Reg. § 1.408-4(c); IRS Publication 590, *Individual Retirement Arrangements (IRAs)* 2008 (see Appendix A)]

Q 3:138   What is an excess contribution to a Roth IRA?

The term *excess contribution* is often used to refer to any type of contribution to a Roth IRA that is in excess of the allowable amount. The Code specifically defines an excess contribution as any contribution to a Roth IRA for the taxable year (other than a qualified rollover contribution) in excess of the amount allowable as a contribution to a Roth IRA for that taxable year. [I.R.C. § 4973(f); IRS Publication 590, *Individual Retirement Arrangements (IRAs)* 2008 (see Appendix A)]

If an excess contribution is caused by an individual's contributing to both a traditional IRA and a Roth IRA, the excess contribution is considered to have occurred in the Roth IRA. That is the case because an individual's contributions are applied first to a traditional IRA and then to a Roth IRA. [Treas. Reg. § 1.408A-3, Q&A-3]

> **Example.** Gary, age 42, who is eligible to make either a full $5,000 Roth IRA contribution *or* a full $5,000 traditional IRA contribution, misunderstands the rules and contributes $5,000 to a Roth IRA *and* $5,000 to a traditional IRA for the same year. Gary has an excess contribution of $5,000 in the Roth IRA.

Q 3:139   How are excess contributions to a traditional or Roth IRA corrected?

An excess contribution to either type of IRA may be corrected without penalty if the excess is returned before the IRA owner's tax return filing due date, including extensions. The return of the excess must include any earnings attributable to the contribution. [I.R.C. § 408(d)(4); IRS Publication 590, *Individual Retirement Arrangements (IRAs)* 2008 (see Appendix A)] The earnings are deemed to have been earned and receivable in the taxable year in which the excess contribution was made.

Excess contributions to a traditional or Roth IRA may also be corrected after the due date for the tax return, but not without penalty, either by withdrawal (deductible contributions only) or recasting the excess amount as a regular contribution made in a subsequent year for which the maximum allowable contribution has not yet been made. (See chapter 7 for detailed discussion.)

In some cases, excess contributions in a Roth IRA can be recharacterized as contributions to a traditional IRA (see Q 3:121).

Q 3:140   What penalty applies to excess contributions to a traditional or Roth IRA?

A 6 percent penalty applies to excess contributions that remain in either type of IRA after the IRA owner's tax return filing due date, including extensions. The 6 percent applies to the amount of the excess and is imposed for each taxable year until the excess contribution amount is distributed. [I.R.C. § 4973] The earnings may remain in the IRA if the excess is not corrected until after the tax return filing due date, including extensions (i.e., if the penalty applies).

Saver's Tax Credit for IRA Contributions

Q 3:141   What is the saver's tax credit?

An individual who makes eligible contributions (see Qs 3:2, 3:4, 3:5) to either a traditional or a Roth IRA (or a combination of both) may be eligible for the saver's tax credit. The amount of the credit is based on income and filing status (see Q 3:146). For qualifying individuals, the credit rate can be as low as 10 percent and as high as 50 percent, depending on the individual's AGI. The lower the individual's income, the higher the credit rate. [I.R.C. § 25B; IRS Publication 590, *Individual Retirement Arrangements (IRAs)* 2008 (see Appendix A)]

The credit is nonrefundable, which means that it cannot exceed the tax otherwise payable for the year (disregarding other nonrefundable credits and the adoption credit). [I.R.C. § 25B]

Q 3:142   What are the eligibility requirements for claiming the saver's tax credit?

The eligibility requirements for claiming the saver's tax credit are as follows:

1. The taxpayer must be age 18 or older.
2. The taxpayer must not be a full-time student. A *full-time student* is an individual who at any time during some part of each of five calendar months (not necessarily consecutive) is a full-time student at a school or in an on-farm training course given by a school that has a regular teaching staff, a regular course of study, and a regularly enrolled body of students in attendance. The on-farm training course may also be sponsored by a state, county, or local government.
3. The taxpayer must not be claimed by another individual as an exemption on his or her individual or joint tax return (e.g., by a parent).
4. For 2009, the taxpayer must have AGI of $55,000 or less if his or her filing status is married filing jointly; $41,625 or less if his or her filing status is head of household; or $27,750 or less if his or her filing status is single, married filing separately, or qualifying widow or widower. For purposes of determining eligibility for the saver's tax credit, AGI is determined by adding back any exclusion or deduction claimed for the year for (1) foreign earned income, (2) foreign housing reimbursement, or (3) excludable income for residents of American Samoa and Puerto Rico.

[I.R.C. § 25B(b); Ann. 2001-106, 2001-2 C.B. 416; IRS News Release IR-2008-118 (Oct. 16, 2008); Notice 2008-102, 2008-45 I.R.B. 1106]

Q 3:143   What is an eligible contribution?

An *eligible contribution* is a contribution made to a traditional or Roth IRA (or a combination of both). Salary reduction contributions to a 401(k) plan (including a SIMPLE 401(k) plan), a Section 403(b) annuity, an eligible deferred compensation plan of a state or local government (a governmental 457 plan), a SIMPLE IRA plan, or a salary reduction SEP and voluntary after-tax contributions made to a tax-qualified retirement plan or Section 403(b) annuity are also considered eligible contributions.

Eligible contributions are reduced by the sum of any taxable distribution from a qualified retirement plan, traditional IRA, or Section 457 plan, and any distribution (whether or not taxable) from a Roth IRA received during the testing period (see below) that is not rolled over. (However, IRA contributions (and related income) returned before the tax return filing due date (including extensions) are not counted for this purpose.) [I.R.C. § 25B(c); S. Rep. No. 107-30 (Pub. L. No. 107-16) at page 91]

In addition, distributions received by the individual's spouse, if a joint tax return is filed for the year of distribution and for the year for which the credit is claimed, are treated as if received by the individual claiming the saver's tax credit. [I.R.C. § 25B(c)]

Q 3:144   What is the testing period?

The *testing period* consists of the year for which the saver's tax credit is claimed (the "credit year"), the period after the end of that year and before the due date (including extensions) for filing the tax return for that year, and the two years before the credit year. [I.R.C. § 25B(d)]

Q 3:145   What is the maximum eligible contribution?

After contributions are reduced (see Q 3:143), the maximum eligible contribution that can be taken into account to determine the credit is $2,000 per person. On a joint return, up to $2,000 per spouse can be considered.

Q 3:146   How is the amount of the credit determined?

The saver's credit is determined by multiplying the eligible contribution amount by the applicable credit rate. [I.R.C. § 25B] The income thresholds that determine a taxpayer's applicable credit rate are indexed annually for inflation; the levels effective for 2009 contributions are shown in Table 3-4 below. Since the maximum eligible contribution is $2,000 and the highest credit rate is 50 percent, the saver's tax credit cannot exceed $1,000 per person.

Table 3-4. Saver's Tax Credit Rates for 2009

Joint Filers	Heads of Households	All Others	Credit Rate
$0–$33,000	$0–$24,750	$0–$16,500	50%
$33,001–$36,000	$24,751–$27,000	$16,501–$18,000	20%
$36,001–$55,500	$27,001–$41,625	$18,001–$27,750	10%
Over $55,500	Over $41,625	Over $27,750	0%

[IRS News Release IR-2008-118 (Oct. 16, 2008); Notice 2008-102, 2008-45 I.R.B. 1106)]

Chapter 4

Distributions from Traditional IRAs

Martin Fleisher, Esq.
Jo Ann Lippe, Esq.

An IRA is a tax-deferred vehicle and assets in an IRA are generally taxed only on withdrawal. Accordingly, an IRA owner generally enjoys a long period of income tax deferral. A point is reached, however, when the benefit of tax deferral does not continue for all of the account: that is the date when required minimum distributions (RMDs) must commence. Usually this date is the April 1 following the calendar year in which the IRA owner attains age 70½ (the required beginning date or RBD), but distributions to beneficiaries may be required to start earlier in the event of the IRA owner's death. If a required distribution from the IRA is not made on a timely basis, the IRS can assess a penalty of 50 percent of the underpayment. Although the IRA owner may always commence taking distributions before the RBD, a 10 percent penalty may be imposed on withdrawals before attaining age 59½ if no exception applies.

Distributions from IRAs are generally taxed as ordinary income, but individuals may make a once-per-lifetime election to transfer funds tax free from a traditional IRA to a health savings account (HSA). Tax benefits are also available—on a temporary basis—for qualified reservist distributions, qualified hurricane distributions, and qualified recovery assistance distributions (a new type of tax-favored distribution available to qualifying individuals who were affected by the storms and tornadoes that ravaged Kansas in May 2007 and the Midwestern disaster areas in 2008).

Finally, IRA minimum distributions have been suspended for 2009, pursuant to the Worker, Retiree, and Employer Recovery Act of 2008 (WRERA). This means that most owners and beneficiaries of traditional IRAs do not have to take an RMD during 2009. A traditional IRA owner who attained age 70½ in 2008, however, is still required to take his or her first RMD by April 1, 2009. Because the calendar year 2009 is now disregarded for distribution purposes, the law also adds a sixth year to the distribution period of any IRA that is being distributed to beneficiaries according to the five-year rule.

Minimum Distributions During the IRA Owner's Lifetime

Required Beginning Date

Q 4:1   What distributions must be paid during the life of the traditional IRA owner?

Once the traditional IRA owner attains age 70½, he or she must take a minimum distribution from the account at least annually. [I.R.C. § 401(a)(9)] The required minimum distributions (RMDs) are calculated to amortize payment of the IRA over a number of years that is based on actuarial life expectancy (see Q 4:9).

However, most traditional IRA owners do not have to receive an RMD in 2009 (see Q 4:21). [I.R.C. § 401(a)(9)(H)(i)]

Q 4:2 What other distributions are permitted?

Subject to whatever contractual terms apply to the account, the owner may take distributions from a traditional IRA at any time. However, distributions that are taken before the calendar year in which the owner attains age 59½ are subject to a penalty unless an exception in Section 72(t) of the Internal Revenue Code (Code; I.R.C.) applies (see Qs 4:108, 4:109).

Q 4:3 When must the first minimum distribution be paid?

The first RMD must be taken during the period that starts on January 1 of the calendar year in which the IRA owner attains age 70½ and ends on the owner's required beginning date (RBD), which is April 1 of the next calendar year. [Treas. Reg. § 1.401(a)(9)-2, Q&A-2] Only distributions that are made during this period count toward payment of the first RMD.

Example. Seth was born on September 1, 1938. He attains age 70½ on March 1, 2009, and his RBD is April 1, 2010. Seth may take part or all of the first RMD at any time during 2009 and/or during the period from January 1 to April 1, 2010.

Q 4:4 When must subsequent required minimum distributions be paid?

All RMDs except the first one must be made by December 31 of the calendar year to which they are attributable. Only the first RMD, which is made for the calendar year in which the IRA owner attains age 70½, is allowed the three-month grace period that ends on the RBD. [Treas. Reg. § 1.401(a)(9)-5, Q&A-1(c)]

Q 4:5 Would an IRA owner ever receive two minimum distributions within the same calendar year?

Yes. The first RMD is for the calendar year in which the individual attains age 70½ and the second RMD is for the next calendar year. If the first RMD is paid during the three-month grace period that ends on the owner's RBD, the result is that two RMDs must be paid during the same calendar year. [Treas. Reg. § 1.401(a)(9)-2]

Example. Jamie attains age 70½ on July 31, 2009, and decides to wait until January 2010 to take his first RMD. His second RMD will also have to be distributed during 2010.

Q 4:6 Should an IRA owner wait until the three-month grace period to take the first minimum distribution?

Perhaps not. The bunching of income that result from receiving both the first and the second RMD during the same calendar year could push the recipient into a higher tax bracket. Delaying the first RMD payment also increases the size of the second RMD. This is because every RMD is calculated with respect to the value of the IRA at the end of the prior year (see Q 4:9), and in this case the value is not yet reduced by the first RMD. [Treas. Reg. § 1.408-8, Q&A-6]

Q 4:7 Are distributions from IRAs subject to the same commencement date rules as distributions from qualified plans?

No. Distributions from qualified plans for everyone but owners of at least 5 percent of the employer are not required until termination of employment regardless of an employee's age. For all IRA owners, distributions must commence by April 1 of the calendar year following the owner's attainment of age 70$\frac{1}{2}$—whether or not the owner has retired. Thus, an employee who continues to work beyond age 70$\frac{1}{2}$ is able to defer distributions from his or her employer's qualified plan until actual retirement, whereas distributions from such an employee's IRA would have to begin sooner.

Q 4:8 May an IRA owner withdraw more than the required minimum distribution from his or her IRA?

Yes. Code Section 401(a)(9) does not limit the amount an IRA owner may withdraw from an IRA as long as the first RMD is taken no later than the owner's RBD. An IRA owner is permitted to take distributions at any time in amounts greater than his or her RMD. [IRS Publication 590, *Individual Retirement Arrangements (IRAs)* 2008 (see Appendix A)]

Calculating Required Minimum Distributions

Q 4:9 How are required minimum distributions calculated during an IRA owner's lifetime?

The regulations provide a simple method for calculating RMDs. The RMD is determined for a particular year by dividing the IRA balance at the previous year-end (December 31) by an applicable divisor. The divisors are set forth in two tables—the Uniform Lifetime Table, which most IRA owners are required to use, and the Joint and Last Survivor Table for all others. [Treas. Reg. § 1.401(a)(9)-9]

Q 4:10 Which table does an IRA owner use to compute minimum distributions?

All IRA owners—with one exception—are required to use the Uniform Lifetime Table to compute RMDs. The exception is the IRA owner whose spouse is more than 10 years younger than the owner is, provided the spouse is also the owner's sole IRA beneficiary. IRA owners to whom this exception applies use the Joint and Last Survivor Table to compute their RMDs. [Treas. Reg. § 1.401(a)(9)-5, Q&A-4]

Q 4:11   What do the divisors in the Uniform Lifetime Table represent?

The divisors in the Uniform Lifetime Table represent the number of years over which an IRA is apportioned in order to calculate the RMD. They are based on the actuarially determined joint life expectancy of an IRA owner and a beneficiary who is 10 years younger than the owner. The applicable divisor for an RMD calculation is found next to the age, in years, that the IRA owner will attain during the distribution year. [IRS Publication 590, *Individual Retirement Arrangements (IRAs)* 2008 (see Appendix A)] The Uniform Table is reproduced as Table 4-1.

Table 4-1. The Uniform Table

Age	Applicable Divisor	Age	Applicable Divisor	Age	Applicable Divisor
70	27.4	86	14.1	102	5.5
71	26.5	87	13.4	103	5.2
72	25.6	88	12.7	104	4.9
73	24.7	89	12.0	105	4.5
74	23.8	90	11.4	106	4.2
75	22.9	91	10.8	107	3.9
76	22.0	92	10.2	108	3.7
77	21.2	93	9.6	109	3.4
78	20.3	94	9.1	110	3.1
79	19.5	95	8.6	111	2.9
80	18.7	96	8.1	112	2.6
81	17.9	97	7.6	113	2.4
82	17.1	98	7.1	114	2.1
83	16.3	99	6.7	115+	1.9
84	15.5	100	6.3		
85	14.8	101	5.9		

Example. Elaine turns 80 on July 10, 2010. As of December 31, 2009, the balance in her traditional IRA is $12,000. Elaine's minimum distribution for 2010 is $641.71 ($12,000 divided by 18.7, the applicable life expectancy divisor).

Q 4:12   How is the Joint and Last Survivor Table used to determine required minimum distributions?

The Joint and Last Survivor Table is used in determining the RMD from a traditional IRA for any year throughout which the IRA's sole beneficiary is the owner's spouse, and the spouse is more than 10 years younger than the owner. In that case, the owner's RMD is computed by dividing the IRA balance at the prior year-end by the applicable joint life expectancy that is set forth in the Joint and Last Survivor Table.

The Joint and Last Survivor Table takes into account not only the IRA owner's age to be attained during the distribution year, but also that of the beneficiary (the spouse). The period of their joint life expectancy is located in the table where the column that has the IRA owner's age intersects the row that has the spouse's age. The Joint and Last Survivor Table is found in Treasury Regulations Section 1.401(a)(9)-9, Q&A-3, and is also published in IRS Publication 590, *Individual Retirement Arrangements (IRAs)* 2008 (see Appendix A).

Example 1. Randall's only IRA beneficiary is his wife, Natalie. Randall will attain age 75 and Natalie age 50 in 2010. As of December 31, 2009, Randall's traditional IRA has a value of $20,000. The joint life expectancy of a 75-year-old IRA owner and a 50-year-old beneficiary, determined from the Joint and Last Survivor Table, is 34.7 years. Thus, Randall's RMD for 2010 is $576.37 ($20,000 divided by 34.7).

Example 2. The facts are the same as those in Example 1, except that Randall is only 5 years older than Natalie. The life expectancy divisor for calculating Randall's 2010 RMD is 22.9, determined from the Uniform Lifetime Table. Randall's RMD is $873.36 ($20,000 divided by 22.9).

Q 4:13   Can an IRA owner outlive his or her IRA by taking minimum distributions each year?

No. Both the Uniform Lifetime Table and the Joint and Last Survivor Table are recalculating tables; that is, the joint life expectancy is extended and recalculated each year as the IRA owner gets older. For example, at age 100, an individual's life expectancy divisor is 6.3 years. At age 115 and beyond, the life expectancy divisor is 1.9 years. Such a low factor would require the withdrawal of only 52.6 percent of the IRA. Thus, the IRA owner is never required to deplete the entire account.

Q 4:14   Is the life expectancy divisor corresponding to age 70, or to age 71, used to calculate the first minimum distribution?

The life expectancy divisor that applies to calculate the first RMD corresponds to the age the IRA owner will attain on his or her birthday during the same calendar year in which he or she reaches age 70½. [Treas. Reg. § 1.401(a)(9)-5, Q&A-4(a)] This rule applies regardless of which table—the Uniform Lifetime Table or the Joint and Last Survivor Table—is used to determine the divisor.

An individual whose birthday falls in the months from January through June celebrates his or her 70th birthday and also reaches age 70½ within the same calendar year. Such an individual uses the life expectancy divisor for age 70 to calculate his or her first RMD. By contrast, an individual born in any month from July through December does not attain age 70½ until the calendar year of his or her 71st birthday, so in that case the first RMD is calculated using the life expectancy divisor for age 71.

Example 1. Fran maintains a traditional IRA, and her son is the designated beneficiary. Because Fran was born in February 1940, she attains age 70 *and* age 70½ during 2010. Fran's first RMD is calculated using a life expectancy divisor of 27.4, which corresponds to age 70 in the Uniform Lifetime Table.

Example 2. Ryan, a widower, owns a traditional IRA. He was born in October 1940, and attains age 70½ in April 2011, which is also the year of his 71st birthday. For calculating Ryan's first RMD, a life expectancy divisor of 26.5 is used because that figure corresponds to age 71 in the Uniform Lifetime Table.

Q 4:15 How are minimum distributions calculated if an owner has multiple traditional IRAs?

A separate RMD calculation is performed for each traditional IRA that an individual owns, and the amounts are summed to determine the total minimum distribution requirement for the year. That total RMD may be distributed, however, from any one or more of the individual's traditional IRAs (see Q 4:16). [Treas. Reg. § 1.408-8, Q&A-9; IRS Publication 590, *Individual Retirement Arrangements (IRAs)* 2008 (see Appendix A)]

Q 4:16 May larger and more rapid distributions be made from some traditional IRAs than from others?

Yes. The owner may withdraw an amount larger than required from one traditional IRA, an amount smaller than required from another, and nothing from a third. The IRS requires only that the accounting be kept separate, that the total distribution be at least equal to the sum of the required minimums, and that the total distributed be reported as taxable income. Of course, if the total distribution is less than the sum of the minimums, the IRS may levy a 50 percent excise tax on the shortfall (see Q 4:104). [Treas. Reg. § 1.408-8, Q&A-9; IRS Publication 590, *Individual Retirement Arrangements (IRAs)* 2008 (see Appendix A)]

There may be several reasons to vary the size and the rate of distributions from an individual's various IRAs. Variations may be desirable for investment reasons (favoring those IRAs expected to perform best in the future) or to favor one beneficiary over another. Certain IRA investments are less liquid than others, and an owner of several IRAs may wish to retain the illiquid investments in one IRA and take distributions from more liquid investments in another IRA.

Q 4:17   If an IRA owner withdraws more than his or her RMD in one year, may the excess withdrawal be used to reduce a subsequent year's RMD?

No. Each year's RMD from an IRA is calculated using the value of the IRA on December 31 of the immediately preceding calendar year. Thus, an IRA owner who takes more than the RMD in 2009 may not apply the excess amount to decrease his or her RMD in 2010. Of course, withdrawals in excess of the RMD in a given calendar year will lower the IRA's value at year-end, thereby lowering the RMD in subsequent years. [IRS Publication 590, *Individual Retirement Arrangements (IRAs)* 2008 (see Appendix A)]

Q 4:18   Does a change in the traditional IRA owner's marital status during a calendar year affect the RMD calculations?

A change in a traditional IRA owner's marital status may affect his or her RMD calculations in two ways—either by resulting in a transfer of IRA assets due to divorce, or by altering an IRA owner's eligibility to use the Joint and Last Survivor Table for life expectancy determinations.

First, if a marriage ends by divorce, there may be a transfer of assets into or out of an owner's IRA pursuant to the divorce decree. RMDs for years after the transfer year would reflect the changed account value, but for the transfer year itself, the RMD does not change; it is still calculated with respect to the IRA value at the end of the prior year (before the transfer). [Treas. Reg. § 1.401(a)(9)-5, Q&A-3]

Second, a change in marital status can alter how life expectancy is determined for the RMD calculation, but not until the year after the event. Generally, to use the Joint and Last Survivor Table an owner must be married (to a spouse more than 10 years younger than the owner) and the spouse must be the owner's sole beneficiary for the entire year. [Treas. Reg. § 1.401(a)(9)-5, Q&A-4(b)(1)] However, if one spouse dies or the couple divorces, then eligibility to use the Joint and Last Survivor Table is based on the marital and beneficiary status as of January 1. [Treas. Reg. § 1.401(a)(9)-5, Q&A-4(b)(2); T.D. 8987 (Apr. 16, 2002); IRS Publication 590, *Individual Retirement Arrangements (IRAs)* 2008 (see Appendix A)]

Q 4:19   What is the effect on an IRA owner's RMD if the designated IRA beneficiary is older than the IRA owner?

None. The Uniform Table uses the same life expectancy factor regardless of the age of the beneficiary.

Q 4:20   What is the effect on an IRA owner's RMD if the designated IRA beneficiary is the owner's estate or a charity?

None. An IRA beneficiary's own life expectancy (or lack of one, in the case of an estate or charity) has no bearing on the life expectancy divisor applicable to the IRA owner.

Waiver of the Minimum Distribution for 2009

Q 4:21   Are minimum distributions required for 2009?

No. The Worker, Retiree, and Employer Recovery Act of 2008 [Pub. L. No. 110-458, § 201, 122 Stat. 5092] (WRERA), signed by President George W. Bush on December 23, 2008, suspends the minimum distribution requirements for 2009. Enacted in response to sharp declines in the stock market, the measure allows individuals who suffered severe losses in the value of their retirement accounts to avoid—temporarily—depleting them further.

This means that there is no RMD requirement for 2009 for any traditional IRA, Roth IRA, SEP IRA, or SIMPLE IRA. The RMD waiver applies to the owners and beneficiaries of such accounts. However, the RBD does not change for any individual. [WRERA § 201; I.R.C. § 401(a)(9)(H)]

Q 4:22   If a traditional IRA owner's RBD is in 2009, when must the first distribution be paid?

The first RMD still has to be paid by April 1, 2009. If a traditional IRA owner's RBD is April 1, 2009, the first distribution the owner must receive is the RMD for 2008—and 2008 RMDs are not suspended. [Notice 2009-9, 2009-5 I.R.B. 419]

Q 4:23   When is the first distribution required if a traditional IRA owner's RBD is in 2010?

The first RMD must be paid by December 31, 2010. But for the 2009 suspension, a traditional IRA owner whose RBD is April 1, 2010, would have received his or her first minimum distribution for 2009 (although payment could have been delayed until April 1, 2010), and the second minimum distribution for 2010 (payable by December 31, 2010). The RMD for 2009 is waived, but not the 2010 RMD. [Notice 2009-9, 2009-5 I.R.B. 419]

Q 4:24   What can an IRA owner or beneficiary do if a distribution was unnecessarily made?

An individual who took from any IRA all or a portion of the amount that would have been his or her 2009 RMD (but for the waiver) may roll these funds back into the IRA from which they were distributed, or into another IRA, within 60 days of the distribution. The taxable portion of any amount that is not rolled over must be included in the recipient's gross income. [Notice 2009-9, 2009-5 I.R.B. 419]

Caution. If more than one distribution was taken in 2009 (e.g., according to a systematic withdrawal plan), only one of the distributions can be rolled back into an IRA. The rollover rules do not allow the rollover of more than one distribution during any 12-month period (see Q 6:6).

Q 4:25 If an IRA is being distributed according to the five-year rule, is the distribution period affected?

Yes. For an IRA that is being distributed according to the five-year rule, the 2009 calendar year is entirely disregarded. In effect, the distribution period is extended to six years. [Notice 2009-9, 2009-5 I.R.B. 419]

Example. Mark died in 2008, and the beneficiary of his IRA is a charity, so the IRA must be fully distributed within five years from the end of the year after the calendar year of Mark's death. Since the distribution period is determined without regard to 2009, the IRA must be distributed by December 31, 2014.

Distributions After the IRA Owner's Death

Q 4:26 What is an important difference between lifetime distributions to a traditional IRA owner and distributions after the owner's death?

The traditional IRA owner is never required to fully deplete the IRA (see Q 4:13), but after the owner dies the IRA must be fully distributed to beneficiaries within a fixed term of years. There is one exception to this rule—the surviving spouse of the owner, if he or she is the sole IRA beneficiary, always uses a recalculated life expectancy to compute RMDs. [Treas. Reg. § 1.401(a)(9)-5, Q&A-5(c)(2)] This means that a traditional IRA left to the spouse has the opportunity to be stretched over the longest period of time (see chapter 8).

Q 4:27 Do the distribution requirements vary depending on when the owner dies?

Yes. Post-death distributions are calculated one way if the owner dies before his or her RBD, and another way if death occurs on or after the owner's RBD (see Qs 4:30, 4:36).

Q 4:28 Is the identity of the owner's beneficiary relevant to the calculation of post-death distributions?

Yes. The rules governing distributions after the death of the IRA owner differ depending on the type of beneficiary involved (i.e., spouse, non-spouse, individual, or non-individual).

Q 4:29 When is the identity of the ultimate beneficiary or beneficiaries determined?

The identity of the ultimate IRA beneficiary or beneficiaries is not determined until September 30 of the year following the year of the IRA owner's death.

Thus, if multiple primary and contingent beneficiaries have been named on an IRA owner's beneficiary designation form, the regulations permit disclaimers, cashouts, and divisions among beneficiaries during the period between the IRA owner's date of death and September 30 of the following year. Only the beneficiary or beneficiaries remaining on the September 30 deadline are relevant in determining the period over which distributions may be made (see Q 4:86). [Treas. Reg. § 1.401(a)(9)-4, Q&A-4]

General Rule—Death On or After the Required Beginning Date

Q 4:30 **If the owner dies after reaching his or her RBD for distributions, what distribution rules apply to the beneficiaries?**

When an IRA owner dies on or after the RBD, distributions to beneficiaries must commence by December 31 of the year following the year of the IRA owner's death. The identity of the IRA beneficiary or beneficiaries on September 30 of the year following the year of the IRA owner's death determines the distribution period over which minimum payments from the IRA are calculated. [Treas. Reg. § 1.401(a)(9)-4, Q&A-5, Q&A-6, Q&A-7] (For distributions after the beneficiary's death, see Qs 4:43–4:48.)

1. If the owner's surviving spouse is the sole beneficiary, the spouse has these options:

   (a) The spouse may elect to treat the IRA as his or her own, or may roll over the decedent's IRA to one that is titled in the spouse's name. In either case the distribution rules that govern owners would apply to the spouse, and minimum distributions based on the spouse's life expectancy (determined using the Uniform Lifetime Table) would not commence until his or her RBD. There is one exception to the spouse being treated the same as the owner—the RMD for the decedent's year of death is always calculated as if the decedent had survived, even if the spouse elects ownership that year. [Treas. Reg. § 1.408-8, Q&A-5; I.R.C. § 402(c)(9); Treas. Reg. § 1.401(a)(9)-5, Q&A-1, Treas. Reg. § 1.401(a)(9)-9, Q&A-2] (See Qs 4:33, 4:59, 4:62.)

   (b) If the spouse does not choose ownership treatment, distributions to the spouse would commence by December 31 of the year following the calendar year of the owner's death. The RMD for any year would be calculated by dividing the prior year-end IRA value by the spouse's recalculated life expectancy, based on the spouse's age on his or her birthday in the distribution year, and determined using the Single Life Table of Treasury Regulations Section 1.401(a)(9)-9, Q&A-1 [refer to Appendix A]. [IRS Publication 590, *Individual Retirement Arrangements (IRAs)* 2008 (see Appendix A); I.R.C. § 401(a)(9)(B)(iv); Treas. Reg. § 1.401(a)(9)-5, Q&A-5(c)(2); Treas. Reg. § 1.401(a)(9)-9, Q&A-1] (See Q 4:63.)

2. If the only beneficiary is an individual (other than the decedent's surviving spouse), the fixed distribution period for determining minimum distributions from the IRA is the longer of (a) the owner's life expectancy,

based on the owner's age on his or her birthday in the year of death, or (b) the beneficiary's life expectancy, based on the beneficiary's age on his or her birthday in the year after the year of the owner's death. The owner's and the beneficiary's life expectancies are both determined for this purpose using the Single Life Table. The RMD for any distribution year is calculated by reducing the applicable distribution period by one for each calendar year elapsed since the year after the year of the owner's death, and dividing the prior year-end IRA value by the result. [Treas. Reg. § 1.401(a)(9)-5, Q&A-5(a)(1), Q&A-6]

3. If there are multiple individual beneficiaries, distributions from the IRA are determined according to the method in paragraph 2, except that only the life expectancy of the oldest beneficiary is compared to that of the owner. (See Q 4:68.) [Treas. Reg. § 1.401(a)(9)-5, Q&A-7]

    Note. The life expectancy of each individual beneficiary may be used if the decedent's IRA is split into separate IRAs by December 31 of the year following the year of the IRA owner's death (see Q 4:87).

4. If any beneficiary is not an individual (e.g., the decedent's estate or a charity), and the non-individual beneficiary's interest has not been cashed out by December 31 of the year following the year of the IRA owner's death, the distribution period for the IRA is the IRA owner's life expectancy in the year of death, determined using the Single Life Table. RMDs are calculated by reducing the distribution period by one for each calendar year elapsed since the owner's death, and dividing the prior year-end IRA value by the result. [Treas. Reg. § 1.401(a)(9)-4; Treas. Reg. § 1.401(a)(9)-5] (See Qs 4:72, 4:73.)

Q 4:31 Must any IRA beneficiary receive a minimum distribution for 2009?

No. The suspension of RMDs for 2009 also applies to beneficiaries. [Notice 2009-9, 2009-5 I.R.B. 419]

Q 4:32 What happens if an IRA owner dies before withdrawing his or her RMD for the year of death?

If an IRA owner dies before taking his or her RMD for the year, the IRA owner's beneficiaries must withdraw the distribution before the end of the year in which the IRA owner's death occurs. [Treas. Reg. § 1.401(a)(9)-5, Q&A-4; IRS Publication 590, *Individual Retirement Arrangements (IRAs)* 2008 (see Appendix A)]

Q 4:33 Is the RMD for the year of death computed as if the owner had not died?

Yes. The rules for determining minimum distributions to beneficiaries of a traditional IRA do not take effect until the year following the year of the owner's death; then they are applied to the IRA balance at the end of the year of death.

A minimum distribution to the IRA beneficiary in the year of the IRA owner's death must be calculated as if the IRA owner had survived, even if the sole beneficiary is the surviving spouse who immediately elects to be treated as the owner. [Treas. Reg. § 1.401(a)(9)-5, Q&A-4; Treas. Reg. § 1.408-8, Q&A-5]

Thus, the distribution for the year of the owner's death is calculated by dividing the value of the IRA as of the end of the year before the death, by the life expectancy of an owner who is the age the decedent would have attained in the year of death. The life expectancy divisor is determined using the same table that would have applied had the owner survived—the Uniform Lifetime Table (for most owners) or the Joint and Last Survivor Table (for an owner whose spouse by marriage is more than 10 years younger than the owner and who is the sole IRA beneficiary throughout the year of death). [Treas. Reg. § 1.401(a)(9)-5, Q&A-4; Treas. Reg. § 1.401(a)(9)-9]

Example 1. Amelia dies on August 21, 2010, two weeks before her 80th birthday and without having received a distribution that year from her traditional IRA. The RMD for 2010 is paid to Amelia's beneficiary, her daughter, by December 31, 2010. It is calculated by dividing the IRA value as of year-end 2009 by the life expectancy, determined from the Uniform Table, of a person who attains age 80 during the distribution year.

Example 2. Keith, age 76, dies on January 10, 2011. His surviving spouse, Cheryl, is the sole beneficiary of Keith's IRA; she reaches her 72nd birthday in 2011. Cheryl elects to be treated as the owner of Keith's IRA by instructing the custodian, in August 2011, to retitle the account in her name. Nonetheless, the 2011 RMD, which had not been paid to Keith, is calculated based on Keith's life expectancy in 2011, not Cheryl's. The first RMD to be calculated with respect to Cheryl's life expectancy will be that for 2012.

Q 4:34   If the minimum distribution for the year of the owner's death is paid to a beneficiary, is the owner's estate or the beneficiary taxed on it?

The IRA beneficiary is subject to income tax on the RMD. However, the RMD constitutes income in respect of a decedent (IRD) under Code Section 691, so the beneficiary may deduct the portion of the estate tax that is attributable to inclusion of the distributed amount in the IRA owner's taxable estate. [I.R.C. § 691] (See Q 10:74.)

Q 4:35   What do the divisors in the Single Life Table represent?

The divisors in the Single Life Table represent the actuarial life expectancy, in years, of an individual at various ages. The Single Life Table is found in Treasury Regulations Section 1.401(a)(9)-9, Q&A-1, and is also published in IRS Publication 590, *Individual Retirement Arrangements (IRAs)* 2008 (see Appendix A).

General Rule—Death Before the Required Beginning Date

Q 4:36 What distribution rules apply to the beneficiaries if the IRA owner dies before his or her RBD?

When an IRA owner dies before the RBD, the distribution period for the IRA is determined differently than it would be for a death that occurs on or after the RBD. However, the distribution period still depends on the identity of the IRA beneficiary or beneficiaries as of September 30 of the year following the year of the IRA owner's death. [Treas. Reg. § 1.401(a)(9)-3; Treas. Reg. § 1.401(a)(9)-4, Q&A-5, Q&A-6, Q&A-7] (For distributions after the beneficiary's death, see Qs 4:43–4:48.)

1. If the owner's surviving spouse is the sole beneficiary, the spouse has several options:

   a. The spouse may take an action that causes the IRA to be governed by the distribution rules that apply to owners (i.e., elect to treat the decedent's IRA as the spouse's own, or roll over the decedent's IRA to one that is titled in the spouse's name). Minimum distributions would not be required until the spouse's RBD, and the RMD for any year would be calculated by dividing the prior year-end IRA balance by the spouse's recalculated life expectancy, as determined using the Uniform Lifetime Table and based on the spouse's age on the birthday in the distribution year. [Treas. Reg. § 1.408-8, Q&A-5; I.R.C. § 402(c)(9); Treas. Reg. § 1.401(a)(9)-5, Q&A-1, Treas. Reg. § 1.401(a)(9)-9, Q&A-2] (See Qs 4:33, 4:59, 4:62.)

   b. The spouse may elect to have the decedent's IRA fully distributed by December 31 of the fifth calendar year following the year of the owner's death. This is called the *five-year method*. [Treas. Reg. § 1.401(a)(9)-3, Q&A-4]

   c. If the spouse does not choose one of those methods, the default method would require minimum distributions to commence by the later of (i) the end of the calendar year following the year of the owner's death, or (ii) the end of the calendar year in which the owner would have attained age 70½. The RMD for any year would be calculated by dividing the prior year-end IRA balance by the spouse's recalculated life expectancy, based on the spouse's age on his or her birthday in the distribution year and determined using the Single Life Table. [I.R.C. § 401(a)(9)(iv); Treas. Reg. § 1.401(a)(9)-3, Q&A-3(b)]

2. If the sole beneficiary is an individual other than the surviving spouse, the beneficiary has two options:

   a. The beneficiary may elect to have the IRA fully distributed according to the five-year method. [Treas. Reg. § 1.401(a)(9)-3, Q&A-4; Treas. Reg. § 1.401(a)(9)-5, Q&A-5(b)]

   b. If the election is not made, minimum distributions to the beneficiary would commence by the end of the calendar year following the year of the owner's death. RMDs would be distributed over a fixed distribution period—the beneficiary's life expectancy, as determined using the

Single Life Table and based on the beneficiary's age on the birthday in the year after the calendar year of the owner's death. To calculate the RMD for any year, the applicable distribution period would be reduced by one for each calendar year elapsed since the year after the year of the owner's death, and the prior year-end IRA value would be divided by the result. [Treas. Reg. § 1.401(a)(9)-5, Q&A-5(b)]

3. If there are multiple individual beneficiaries, distributions from the IRA are determined according to the method in paragraph 2, except that only the life expectancy of the oldest beneficiary is compared to that of the owner. (See Q 4:68.)

   Note. If the decedent's IRA is split into separate IRAs by December 31 of the year following the death, the life expectancy of each individual beneficiary may be used. (See Q 4:87.)

4. If any beneficiary is not an individual (e.g., the decedent's estate or a charity), and the non-individual beneficiary's interest has not been cashed out by September 30 of the year following the year of the IRA owner's death, the IRA must be fully distributed according to the five-year method. [Treas. Reg. § 1.401(a)(9)-3, Q&A-4] (See Q 4:72.)

Q 4:37   Are beneficiaries allowed to skip the distribution for 2009?

Yes. The suspension of the RMD rules also applies to beneficiaries. [Notice 2009-9, 2009-5 I.R.B. 419]

Q 4:38   Does the RMD waiver for 2009 affect distributions under the five-year rule?

Yes. The distribution period is determined without regard to calendar year 2009. This has the effect of adding a sixth year to the distribution period of IRAs that are now being distributed according to this rule. [Notice 2009-9, 2009-5 I.R.B. ___]

   Example. Malcolm died in 2007 and his IRA is being distributed according to the five-year rule. The IRA must be fully distributed by December 31, 2013 (instead of 2012).

Q 4:39   If the five-year distribution rule applies after the IRA owner's death, must installment payments be made during that period?

No. If the decedent's IRA is required to be distributed within five calendar years following the year of death, all that matters is that no balance should remain undistributed at the end of that period. The entire IRA could be distributed in a single balloon payment at the end of the fifth year, but caution is advised—any portion of the IRA that remains undistributed after five years is penalized at the rate of 50 percent. [IRS Publication 590, *Individual Retirement Arrangements (IRAs)* 2008 (see Appendix A); I.R.C. § 4974(a); Priv. Ltr. Rul. 8718037 (Feb. 3, 1987)]

Q 4:40   If distributions to the designated nonspouse beneficiary have not commenced by December 31 of the calendar year following the owner's death, is it too late to use the life expectancy method for distributions?

Apparently not. In Private Letter Ruling 200811028 (Mar. 14, 2008), involving an IRA owner who had died before the RBD and designated a nonspouse beneficiary, the IRS allowed distributions according to the life expectancy method even though no RMDs had been paid to the beneficiary until the third calendar year after the year of the IRA owner's death. The RMDs for years one and two (as calculated under the life expectancy method) were distributed to the beneficiary in the third year, along with the RMD so calculated for that year, and the beneficiary paid the 50 percent excise tax on excess accumulations that applied under Code Section 4974 with respect to the untimely paid RMDs. Based on this ruling, it appears that the IRS would allow a designated nonspouse beneficiary to use the life expectancy method if all of the following conditions are satisfied:

1. Makeup distributions of all missed RMDs (as determined under the life expectancy method) are made, presumably before the last date for making a distribution under the five-year rule;

2. The beneficiary pays the 50 percent excise tax for each year in which there was an excess accumulation of untimely paid RMDs;

3. The IRA provisions do not prohibit distributions based on life expectancy; and

4. The beneficiary has not affirmatively elected the five-year method.

Determining Which General Rule Applies

Q 4:41   Which rules apply if an IRA owner dies after attaining age 70½ but before his or her RBD?

If an IRA owner dies before his or her RBD, it is immaterial whether he or she attained age 70½. The rules regarding death before the owner's RBD still apply (see Q 4:36).

This can be significant when the beneficiary is not an individual (e.g., the owner's estate or a charity). The payout to a non-individual in the case of death before the owner's RBD is subject to the five-year rule. If the IRA owner dies after reaching his or her RBD, the payout to a non-individual is based on the term certain period equal to the IRA owner's remaining life expectancy in the year of his or her death.

Q 4:42   Does it matter whether the IRA owner commenced receiving minimum distributions before death?

No. If an IRA owner dies before his or her RBD, it is irrelevant that distributions may already have started. The rules applicable to distributions on account of the IRA owner's death before the RBD still apply (see Q 4:36). [Treas. Reg. § 1.401(a)(9)-2, Q&A-6(a)]

Distributions After the Beneficiary's Death

Q 4:43 May an IRA beneficiary name his or her own beneficiary after the IRA owner's death?

Yes. An IRA beneficiary may name a new beneficiary who will succeed to the first beneficiary's interest in the event of the original IRA beneficiary's death. [*See* Treas. Reg. § 1.401(a)(9)-4.]

Q 4:44 How is the IRA distributed if a beneficiary survives the owner, but dies before September 30 of the year after the owner's year of death?

If a beneficiary survives the IRA owner but dies before September 30 of the year after the year of the owner's death (when the owner's designated beneficiaries are finally determined), and the beneficiary did not disclaim his or her interest in the IRA, then the deceased beneficiary continues to be recognized as a beneficiary for purposes of determining the distribution period for the IRA. The identity and life expectancy of the deceased beneficiary's successor to the IRA interest is irrelevant to this determination, so payments are made to the successor on the same basis that they would have been made to the deceased beneficiary. [Treas. Reg. § 1.401(a)(9)-4, Q&A-4(c)]

Example. Lauren maintains a traditional IRA, and her son, Reggie, is her only beneficiary. Lauren dies in 2010, and Reggie names his wife, Barbara, as his successor beneficiary for the IRA. Distributions to Reggie must commence by December 31, 2011, but Reggie dies that year in July. Distributions (now to Barbara) must still commence by the end of 2011, and the RMDs will be based on Reggie's single life expectancy as of his birthday in 2011.

Q 4:45 What happens if a beneficiary survives until September 30 of the year after the IRA owner's year of death, but dies before receiving his or her entire interest in the IRA?

If an IRA beneficiary (other than a spouse beneficiary who treats the inherited IRA as the spouse's own) survives until the date when the owner's designated beneficiaries are finally determined (September 30 of the year after the owner's year of death), but dies before receiving his or her entire interest in the IRA, and that beneficiary named a beneficiary of his or her own, then the balance of the deceased beneficiary's IRA interest is distributed to his or her successor beneficiary. The distribution period does not change, though. That remains constant even if the IRA has multiple beneficiaries and the deceased beneficiary's life expectancy was used to determine the distribution period. [Treas. Reg. § 1.401(a)(9)-5, Q&A-7(c)(2)]

If the deceased beneficiary did not name a beneficiary, the remaining payments would be made to the beneficiary's estate. Of course, the beneficiary's estate has the right to accelerate payments in order to close the estate.

Example. John is age 45 when his father dies in 2010. He is the primary beneficiary of his father's IRA. Distributions from his father's IRA are required to begin by December 31, 2011, based on a payout period of 37.9 years (i.e., John's single life expectancy in the year following his father's death, determined under the Single Life Table). John designates his older sister, Susan, as his beneficiary in the event that he dies before the payout term is completed. If John dies in 2015 after taking that year's RMD, Susan will be entitled to the remaining payments from the IRA and she will use a payout term of 32.9 years (John's 37.9 year term less the five years he survived). Susan's life expectancy does not enter into the calculation.

Q 4:46 If the surviving spouse is the IRA owner's sole beneficiary, and the spouse elects to be treated as the IRA owner, what happens when the spouse dies?

A surviving spouse who is an IRA owner's sole beneficiary and elects to treat the inherited IRA as the spouse's own is treated as the IRA owner for all purposes. In that case, the general rules that apply to distributions after the death of an owner will apply (see Qs 4:30, 4:36).

Q 4:47 If the IRA owner dies before his or her RBD, and the surviving spouse is his or her sole beneficiary, what happens if the spouse dies before distributions commence?

If an IRA owner dies before his or her RBD and his or her surviving spouse is the sole IRA beneficiary, but the spouse dies before the date on which distributions to the spouse must begin (see Q 4:36), the spouse is treated as the owner of the IRA in order to determine the distribution schedule. Consequently, the designated beneficiary of the IRA is not finally determined until September 30 of the year following the *spouse's* death, and the payout is determined with respect to that beneficiary's life expectancy. [Treas. Reg. § 1.401(a)(9)-4, Q&A-4(b); I.R.C. § 401(a)(9)(B)(iv); Treas. Reg. § 1.401(a)(9)-3, Q&A-5]

Example 1. Frank maintains a traditional IRA, and his wife, Sarah, is his only beneficiary. Frank dies in March 2010 at age 60, after his birthday that year, and Sarah names their son, Jack, as the beneficiary to succeed to her interest in the IRA. Minimum distributions to Sarah from Frank's IRA are not required until April 1, 2021 (Frank's RBD). Sarah dies in 2018. On September 30, 2019, the designated beneficiary of the IRA is finally determined to be Jack. Distributions to Jack must commence by December 31, 2019, and his single life expectancy in 2019 is used as the fixed distribution period for calculating RMDs.

Example 2. The facts are the same as those in Example 1, except that Sarah names a charity as her successor beneficiary. Frank's IRA is determined to have no designated beneficiary on September 30, 2019, and the IRA must be completely distributed to the charity by December 31, 2023.

Q 4:48   What happens if a beneficiary predeceases the IRA owner?

If the IRA beneficiary predeceases the IRA owner and no contingent beneficiary was named, the owner's estate may become the beneficiary by default. The IRA document should be consulted to determine whether the default applies. Accordingly, an IRA owner should always complete the contingent beneficiary section of the IRA beneficiary document and should discuss the effect of the designations with his or her tax advisor.

Beneficiaries

The Beneficiary Designation

Q 4:49   What designation must be made under the IRA document during the lifetime of an IRA owner?

An IRA owner should always designate a beneficiary. Although the beneficiary designation is irrelevant to calculating the owner's lifetime RMDs (other than allowing some owners to use the Joint and Last Survivor Table; see Q 4:12), it has lasting consequences after the IRA owner's death. An IRA trustee or custodian may have its own beneficiary provisions that provide for a result that is inconsistent with the wishes of the IRA owner. Thus, it is advisable that an IRA owner and his or her advisors review the IRA plan documents (see chapter 2) to determine whether they are appropriate. If there is more than one IRA, the plan documents of each IRA should be carefully examined because different IRA sponsors may have different provisions in their governing documents. An IRA owner may even find that certain beneficiary designations in the IRA plan documents have been made by default in the absence of the owner's instructions to the contrary. [Treas. Reg. § 1.401(a)(9)-4]

Q 4:50   May an IRA owner change his or her beneficiary designation at any time?

Yes. An IRA owner may change his or her beneficiary designation at any point during his or her lifetime.

Q 4:51   If the decedent's will names an IRA beneficiary but a different beneficiary is designated in the IRA agreement, which provision controls?

The beneficiary designation in the IRA contract is controlling. [Treas. Reg. § 1.401(a)(9)-4, Q&A-1] An IRA is not a probate asset, so the terms of a will do not have primacy in this matter.

Although the will does not control the identity of the designated beneficiary, it can still be very important to the disposition of an IRA. For example, an IRA owner could designate a trust (such as a marital trust) as the beneficiary, and establish the terms of the trust in the will.

Q 4:52   If the IRA beneficiary predeceases the IRA owner, who becomes the IRA beneficiary?

If a designated IRA beneficiary predeceases the IRA owner, the contingent beneficiary (if any) becomes the new IRA beneficiary. Alternatively, the IRA owner may name a new beneficiary. [Treas. Reg. § 1.401(a)(9)-4, Q&A-4(c)]

Q 4:53   Why is it important to name a successor beneficiary for the IRA?

The designation of a successor IRA beneficiary is important in the event that the primary beneficiary dies before the entire IRA is distributed. By naming a contingent beneficiary, the IRA owner can control the identity of the successor beneficiary. A contingent beneficiary should be named at the same time that the IRA owner designates the primary beneficiary or beneficiaries.

Q 4:54   Do the beneficiary forms of IRA trustees and custodians contain language affecting the choice of a contingent beneficiary?

Generally, yes. Many IRA trustees and custodians have beneficiary forms that provide for a contingent beneficiary in the event that the primary beneficiary dies and the IRA owner failed to designate a contingent beneficiary of his or her own choosing. A contingent beneficiary is typically the remaining primary beneficiary or an immediate descendant of the deceased primary beneficiary.

> **Practice Pointer.** It is a critical estate planning step for an IRA owner and his or her advisors to review the underlying beneficiary forms of the IRA trustee or custodian to determine whether any changes are appropriate. For example, the original IRA document may provide that when a beneficiary of the IRA dies, the deceased beneficiary's interest in the IRA passes to the original IRA owner's surviving beneficiaries rather than to the deceased beneficiary's heirs. This may not be the result the IRA owner desired.

Q 4:55   Can an IRA owner customize his or her own beneficiary form and have it accepted by the IRA trustee or custodian?

Yes; however, IRA trustees and custodians vary in their acceptance of customized IRA beneficiary documents. Most IRA trustees and custodians will allow an IRA owner to make simple changes regarding the designation of contingent beneficiaries and to override the default language in their own forms. Complex changes may pose a problem. In many situations, it may be appropriate for the IRA owner to contact the legal department of the IRA trustee or custodian to discuss the terms of a particular beneficiary designation. The IRA owner generally has the upper hand in any negotiations with an IRA trustee or custodian because he or she can move the IRA to a more liberal trustee or custodian.

Q 4:56   How are beneficiary designations made?

Designations under an IRA should be executed by the IRA owner and filed with the IRA trustee or custodian. Because there is no requirement that an IRA owner file any forms with the IRS relating to any election or designation, he or she should keep a copy of any elections or designations filed with his or her IRA trustee or custodian.

There are many different forms for beneficiary designations in use by IRA trustees and custodians, so an IRA owner should compare such forms for ideas as to wording. Most institutions allow some modification of their forms.

Caution. If an IRA owner prepares customized forms for beneficiary selection, he or she should submit the forms to the IRA trustee or custodian to ensure that they are not inconsistent with the underlying IRA plan document.

Q 4:57   Must the IRA owner specify each beneficiary by name?

No. The IRA owner may name a class of beneficiaries (such as "my children") who are identifiable at the time of his or her death. [Treas. Reg. 1.401(a)(9)-4, Q&A-1]

Q 4:58   Are there any rules regarding the mailing of designations?

No. Mailing procedures applicable to IRA designations are not governed by IRS rules. Nevertheless, the absence of specific rules suggests that extreme care should be exercised. Whether documents are sent via registered or certified mail or delivered by hand and whether a receipt is requested are matters of individual judgment, but special diligence might well be worth the extra effort.

Spouse as Beneficiary

Q 4:59   May the surviving spouse elect to treat the decedent's IRA as the spouse's own IRA?

The surviving spouse of a traditional IRA owner may elect to treat the decedent's IRA as his or her own IRA only if the surviving spouse is the sole beneficiary of the IRA and has unlimited rights to withdraw amounts from the IRA. The election can be made at any time after the death of the decedent spouse, and it results in the surviving spouse being treated as the IRA owner for all purposes. [Treas. Reg. § 1.408-8, Q&A-5]

Q 4:60 Can the surviving spouse make the election if a trust was named as the sole beneficiary, and the spouse is the sole beneficiary of the trust?

No, because such a spouse does not have unlimited rights to withdraw amounts from the IRA. However, a spouse who actually receives a distribution from the trust may roll that distribution over to an IRA in the spouse's name. [T.D. 8787 (Apr. 16, 2002); Treas. Reg. § 1.408-8, Q&A-5]

Q 4:61 How is the election made?

An eligible surviving spouse affirmatively makes the election by redesignating the decedent's IRA (i.e., changing the name to list the spouse as the owner, not beneficiary, of the account). Alternatively, the spouse is deemed to make the election if he or she makes a contribution to the decedent's IRA, or fails to withdraw any RMD that would be payable to the spouse as a beneficiary, rather than owner, of the IRA. [Treas. Reg. § 1.408-8, Q&A-5]

Q 4:62 Instead of making the election, can the surviving spouse roll over the decedent's IRA to an IRA that the spouse owns?

Yes, subject to the same requirements as for the election—i.e., the surviving spouse must be the sole beneficiary of the IRA and have an unlimited right to withdraw amounts from it. A rollover by such a spouse may occur any time after the death of the first spouse. [I.R.C. § 402(c)(9)]

Q 4:63 If the surviving spouse is over age 70½, is the spouse better off being treated as the owner or the beneficiary of the IRA?

In most cases (see the exception in Q 4:64), a surviving spouse who is older than age 70½ is better off being treated as the owner, rather than beneficiary, of the decedent's IRA. As the owner, the spouse has several advantages—RMDs are smaller (because the spouse's life expectancy is recalculated using the Uniform Lifetime Table, not the Single Life Table); the IRA can be stretched over a longer period of time when the spouse dies (because the spouse's beneficiary can use his or her own life expectancy, instead of the spouse's, to calculate RMDs); and conversion to a Roth IRA is possible (because only owners are eligible to convert inherited IRAs).

Example 1. Herman dies in 2009, having designated his wife, Rose, as his only IRA beneficiary. Rose attains age 75 in 2010, and elects to treat Herman's IRA as her own. Her RMD from the IRA for 2010 is calculated based on a life expectancy of 22.9 years, determined using the Uniform Lifetime Table. When Rose dies, her designated beneficiary will be able to calculate RMDs based on his or her own life expectancy.

Example 2. The facts are the same as those in Example 1, except that Rose neither elects to be treated as the owner of Herman's IRA, nor rolls over Herman's IRA to one of her own. Rose's RMD for 2010 is now calculated based on her life expectancy of 13.4 years, as determined using the Single Life Table. Although Rose's life expectancy is recalculated each year (e.g., for 2011 her RMD calculation uses the 12.7 year life expectancy of a person at age 76, according to the Single Life Table), Rose must take a larger RMD each year than she would have to take if she were the owner, rather than beneficiary, of the IRA. Moreover, after Rose dies, the successor beneficiary will have to calculate subsequent minimum distributions based on Rose's remaining life expectancy at the time of her death.

Q 4:64   In what situation might a surviving spouse older than age 70½ prefer to remain as the beneficiary of the inherited IRA?

If the IRA owner was younger than the surviving spouse, and the owner died before his or her RBD, and the surviving spouse wants to delay taking RMDs, the spouse should remain as the IRA beneficiary. As the beneficiary, the spouse could postpone all distributions from the IRA until the deceased owner's RBD. By contrast, a spouse older than age 70½ who assumes ownership of the IRA must immediately commence RMDs. [I.R.C. § 401(a)(9)(B)]

> **Example.**   Sam, age 72, is the IRA beneficiary of his spouse, Martha. Martha dies at age 60 in 2009. If Sam assumes ownership of Martha's IRA, he must withdraw an RMD by December 31, 2009. Otherwise, he could remain as the IRA beneficiary and delay RMDs for about 10 years, until the date that would have been Martha's RBD had she survived.

Q 4:65   If the spouse beneficiary is younger than age 59½ when the owner dies, is the spouse better off being treated as the owner or the beneficiary of the IRA?

A surviving spouse younger than age 59½ may be better offer continuing to be treated as the IRA beneficiary, rather than owner, for some time. If the spouse is treated as the IRA owner, any distribution before the spouse attains age 59½ would be subject to a 10 percent premature distribution penalty unless an exception to that penalty were found to apply (see Qs 4:108, 4:109). By contrast, distributions to the spouse as the beneficiary of the IRA would not be subject to the penalty. [I.R.C. § 72(t)(2)(A)(ii)]

Q 4:66   May a surviving spouse disclaim designation as the decedent spouse's IRA beneficiary?

Yes, a surviving spouse may disclaim designation as the decedent spouse's IRA beneficiary pursuant to the rules of Code Section 2518(a). The effect of disclaiming an IRA beneficiary designation is to make the contingent beneficiary the new primary beneficiary. Distributions to the contingent beneficiary are then made over such beneficiary's life expectancy, as determined in the year following the year of the IRA owner's death. [Treas. Reg. § 1.401(a)(9)-4, Q&A-4] (See Q 4:95.)

Practice Pointer. A disclaimer is a valuable tool if the surviving spouse wishes to benefit his or her children after the IRA owner's death: the children's life expectancies would be used in calculating future distributions.

Q 4:67   Do the rules governing IRAs tend to favor the choice of a spouse as the beneficiary of an IRA?

In some ways, yes. There are potential income tax advantages to naming a spouse as the IRA beneficiary in the following situations:

1. The spouse is more than 10 years younger than the IRA owner. This allows their actual joint life expectancies, rather than the life expectancy set forth in the Uniform Table, to be used during the IRA owner's lifetime.
2. A rollover to a new IRA will be the eventual outcome. Only a spouse may create a new IRA after the IRA owner's death.
3. The spouse will want to stretch the IRA for many years. Only a spouse beneficiary may annually recalculate his or her life expectancy to determine RMDs.

Nonspouse Individual Beneficiaries

Q 4:68   How are minimum distributions computed if there are multiple individual beneficiaries?

If the IRAs are not divided by September 30 of the year following the calendar year of the IRA owner's death, then only the shortest life expectancy (i.e., that of the oldest individual beneficiary) can be taken into account to compute RMDs. [Treas. Reg. § 1.401(a)(9)-5] (See Q 4:87.)

Thus, if the IRA owner dies before his or her RBD, the RMDs for all the beneficiaries would be calculated with respect to the oldest beneficiary's single life expectancy in the year following the calendar year of the owner's death. If the IRA owner dies on or after the owner's RBD, the same distribution period or, if longer, the period equal to the owner's single life expectancy on his or her birthday in the year of death, would be used. (See Qs 4:30, 4:36.)

Example 1. Walter dies on September 1, 2010, two months before he turns 72, having designated his brothers, Myron and Martin, as the equal beneficiaries of his traditional IRA. In 2010, Myron attains age 68, and Martin age 76. The IRA is not divided before December 31, 2011.

Walter's 2010 RMD, undistributed before his death, is calculated on the basis of his 25.6 year life expectancy in that year, as determined using the Uniform Table (and age 72). That RMD, and all subsequent distributions, will be divided equally between Myron and Martin.

The fixed distribution period for calculating RMDs for 2011 and beyond is determined by comparing Martin's (the older beneficiary's) life expectancy as of his birthday in *2011* (age 77), with Walter's life expectancy as of his birthday in *2010* (age 72). The Single Life Table is used for both, so that

Martin has an expectancy of 12.1 years and Walter's is 15.5 years. Walter's is longer, so the fixed distribution period for this IRA is 15.5 years.

The 2011 RMD is calculated by dividing the IRA value at the end of 2010 by 14.5 (15.5 minus one, since Walter's is the measuring life, and one year will have elapsed since the year of his death). For 2012, the divisor will be 13.5, and so on.

Example 2. The facts are the same as those in Example 1, except that Myron and Martin attain ages 65 and 68, respectively, in 2010.

The calculation of Walter's 2010 RMD does not change. The fixed distribution period for calculating subsequent RMDs is determined using the same method as in Example 1, but now Martin has a life expectancy of 17.8 years (for age 69) in 2011, which exceeds Walter's 15.5 year life expectancy for 2010. The fixed distribution period for this IRA is 17.8 years.

The divisor used to calculate the 2011 RMD is 17.8. It will be 16.8 for 2012, 15.8 for 2013, and so on.

Q 4:69 Must an individual who is the beneficiary of multiple IRAs withdraw minimum distributions from each, or can they be aggregated for purposes of withdrawing the total RMD?

Aggregation is permitted if the IRA owner holds multiple IRAs as the beneficiary of a single decedent, and they are being distributed under the life expectancy rule. IRAs of different decedents cannot be aggregated, however. Nor can an individual aggregate any IRAs that the individual holds as owner with any IRAs of which he or she is a beneficiary. [Treas. Reg. § 1.408-8, Q&A-9]

Example 1. Mel, age 73, has three separate IRAs. Each IRA has a separate beneficiary. The RMDs from each IRA, taking into account Mel's joint and last survivor expectancy with each separate beneficiary, are $3,900, $600, and $60, respectively. Mel may withdraw the total amount of $4,560 ($3,900 + $600 + $60) from one IRA or withdraw portions of it from several of the IRAs.

Example 2. Mel is the beneficiary of two IRAs—one that he inherited from his brother, and another inherited from his cousin. For 2010, Mel's RMD from his brother's IRA is $2,000 and that from his cousin's IRA is $1,500. Mel may not withdraw the total amount of $3,500 from one of the two IRAs, but must take the RMDs of $2,000 and $1,500 from the respective IRAs.

Example 3. The facts are the same as those in Example 1, except that Mel is also the beneficiary of two IRAs inherited from his mother. His 2010 RMD from one his mother's IRAs is $700 and his RMD from her other IRA is $1,900. Mel may withdraw the total amount of $2,600 ($700 + $1,900) from either of his mother's IRAs, or may withdraw portions of the total from both of them. However, Mel cannot take the RMD calculated for his mother's IRAs from either the IRA of his brother or that of his cousin.

Q 4:70   What options are available to an IRA beneficiary who continues to maintain the IRA in the name of the decedent?

The IRA must be retitled so it identifies both the deceased IRA owner and the beneficiary—for example, "Tom Smith as beneficiary of John Smith."

The beneficiary is also free to initiate a trustee-to-trustee transfer. Revenue Ruling 78-406 [1978-2 C.B. 157] states that such a transfer may be initiated by a bank trustee or an IRA owner. Private Letter Ruling 8716058 (Jan. 21, 1987) recognized that such a transfer can also be initiated by a designated beneficiary after the IRA owner's death.

Q 4:71   May a nonspouse beneficiary become the titled owner of an inherited IRA after the death of the IRA owner rather than remaining the IRA beneficiary?

No. A nonspouse beneficiary of an IRA is not allowed to transfer an inherited IRA to his or her own name because such a transfer would be treated by the IRS as a distribution. If a nonspouse beneficiary were to become the owner of an inherited IRA, the IRS would treat the entire amount of the IRA as a distribution to the beneficiary. [IRS Publication 590, *Individual Retirement Arrangements (IRAs)* 2008 (see Appendix A)]

Non-individual Beneficiaries

Q 4:72   What payout schedule applies after an IRA owner's death if a non-individual, such as the owner's estate or a charity, is the IRA beneficiary?

A non-individual, such as the owner's estate or a charity, has no life expectancy, so the distribution rules for individual beneficiaries (which rely on life expectancy) are not used. The IRA is considered to have no designated beneficiary, and the minimum payout schedule depends on whether the owner dies before or after reaching his or her RBD. [Treas. Reg. § 1.409(a)(9)-4] (For a special rule regarding trust beneficiaries, see Q 4:77.)

If an IRA owner dies before reaching his or her RBD and the beneficiary is a non-individual, the entire IRA must be distributed by December 31 of the calendar year in which the fifth anniversary of the IRA owner's death occurs (the *five-year rule*). [Treas. Reg. § 1.401(a)(9)-3, Q&A-4]

However, if the IRA owner dies on or after reaching his or her RBD, and the beneficiary is a non-individual, then the owner's life expectancy for the year of death (determined using the Single Life Table) is fixed as the length of the post-death distribution period. The RMD for the year of the owner's death is determined as if the owner had survived (see Q 4:33), but the divisor used to calculate subsequent RMDs is the length of the post-death distribution period reduced by one for each year that elapses since the year of the owner's death. [Treas. Reg. § 1.401(a)(9)-4; Treas. Reg. § 1.401(a)(9)-5, Q&A-5(c)(2)].

Example 1. Barney, age 68, dies on January 1, 2010, having named a charity as his beneficiary. His entire IRA must be distributed by December 31, 2015.

Example 2. Marie, age 75, dies on June 15, 2010, having named her estate as her IRA beneficiary. Under the Single Life Table, Marie's single life expectancy in the year of her death is 13.4 years. Thus, Marie's estate calculates distributions from her IRA beginning in 2011, using a divisor of 12.4 years (13.4 years minus one). The divisor will be 11.4 years in 2012, 10.4 years in 2013, and so on.

Q 4:73   If one of two IRA beneficiaries at the time of the IRA owner's death is a non-individual, how are post-death required minimum distributions from the IRA calculated?

The IRA has no designated beneficiary if any beneficiary is a non-individual, even if an individual beneficiary is also named. [Treas. Reg. § 1.401(a)(9)-4, Q&A-3] Consequently, the rules are the same as if the non-individual were the only beneficiary (see Q 4:72). However, if the non-individual beneficiary's interest in the IRA is fully distributed by September 30 of the year following the year of the IRA owner's death, then the remaining individual is the designated beneficiary, and the distribution period is determined according to the rules for individual beneficiaries (see Qs 4:27, 4:28, 4:86). [Treas. Reg. § 1.401(a)(9)-4, Q&A-4(a)]

Q 4:74   Does designating a non-individual beneficiary affect the calculation of traditional IRA distributions during the owner's lifetime?

No. An IRA owner who designates a non-individual as beneficiary still uses the Uniform Table to calculate lifetime RMDs. [Treas. Reg. § 1.401(a)(9)-5, Q&A-4]

Example. Gerald names his college alma mater as the beneficiary of his traditional IRA. In 2010, he attains age 79. He uses the Uniform Table to determine his RMD, dividing his IRA balance as of December 31, 2009, by the applicable life expectancy divisor of 19.5 years. Thus, only about 5 percent of his IRA must be distributed in 2010.

Q 4:75   May a trust be designated as the beneficiary of the IRA?

Yes. Designating a trust as the beneficiary of an IRA is an acceptable approach and one that is used in many circumstances. Such a designation does not constitute a distribution. [Priv. Ltr. Rul. 9253054 (Oct. 8, 1992)]

Q 4:76   When is having a trust as the beneficiary of an IRA advisable?

Having a trust as the beneficiary of an IRA might be advisable when significant sums of money are involved, including projected long-term investment growth of the IRA that spans two or more generations. For example, if grandchildren or great-grandchildren are named as beneficiaries, and their current ages are such that they might ultimately have control of money while they are minors or young adults (and thus, presumably, before financial maturity), the control exercised by a trustee might help conserve the assets. Another reason for having a trust beneficiary is to avoid the expense of establishing guardianships for beneficiaries who are minors. Furthermore, overall family estate tax planning considerations may dictate the choice of grandchildren over children or of children over a spouse.

The use of a trust need not be limited to grandchildren. Sometimes, special attention is given to the protection and assistance of disabled adult family members for whom the IRA owner wants to provide.

Note. Trustees need not be independent; they may be family members.

Q 4:77   Is a trust treated as a designated beneficiary by the IRS?

No. Only an individual may be treated as a designated beneficiary. [Treas. Reg. § 1.401(a)(9)-4, Q&A-5(a)] If certain requirements are satisfied, however, the beneficiaries of the trust will be treated as designated beneficiaries under the IRA for purposes of determining the distribution period under Code Section 401(a)(9).

Q 4:78   What requirements must be satisfied for a trust beneficiary to be treated as a designated beneficiary for minimum distribution purposes?

If the named beneficiary of an IRA is a trust, and four conditions are met, then the designated beneficiaries of the IRA are determined by "looking through" the trust. The normal rules are then applied to identify the IRA's designated beneficiary—i.e., the IRA has no designated beneficiary if any trust beneficiary is a non-individual, and if all the trust beneficiaries are individuals the oldest trust beneficiary's life expectancy is used to compute RMDs. The four requirements for a look-through trust are:

1. The trust must be a valid trust under state law, or one that would be valid but for the fact that there is no corpus.

2. The trust must be irrevocable or will, by its terms, become irrevocable upon the death of the IRA owner.

3. The beneficiary of the trust must be identifiable from the trust instrument.

4. The IRA owner must provide the IRA trustee or custodian with a copy of the trust instrument or, alternatively, a list of all the trust beneficiaries (including contingent and remainder beneficiaries) and agree to (a) provide a copy of the trust instrument to the IRA trustee or custodian upon

demand and (b) provide the IRA trustee or custodian with any amendments to the previously supplied information in the future. [Treas. Reg. § 1.401(a)(9)-4, Q&A-5(b), Q&A-6(a)]

The trust must actually be named as the IRA beneficiary for the look-through rule to apply. In Private Letter Ruling 200846028 (Nov. 14, 2008), the decedent IRA owner had written the phrase "as stated in wills" on the IRA beneficiary form, but the will did not mention the IRA. The will poured all of the estate residue, including the IRA, into an irrevocable trust, but the IRS ruled that the look-through rule did not apply, and the IRA had no designated beneficiary.

Q 4:79   When must the four requirements be satisfied for the trust beneficiary to be treated as a designated beneficiary for purposes of Code Section 401(a)(9)?

The four requirements listed above (see Q 4:78) must be satisfied by October 31 of the year immediately following the year of the IRA owner's death [Treas. Reg. § 1.401(a)(9)-4, Q&A-6(b)]. The only exception is when the IRA owner has named a trust as his or her beneficiary, the sole beneficiary of the trust is the owner's spouse, and the spouse is more than 10 years younger than the owner. In such a case, the four requirements must be satisfied no later than the IRA owner's RBD. If these requirements are satisfied, the actual joint life expectancy of the IRA owner and his or her spouse, rather than the life expectancy under the Uniform Table, may be used to determine RMDs (see Q 4:81).

Q 4:80   Is the requirement that a trust be irrevocable at the IRA owner's death satisfied if a testamentary trust arising under the owner's will is named as the IRA beneficiary?

Yes. A testamentary trust named as the IRA beneficiary will qualify as being irrevocable at the IRA owner's death, thereby enabling the trust beneficiaries to be treated as designated beneficiaries for minimum distribution purposes. [Treas. Reg. § 1.401(a)(9)-5, Q&A-7(c)(3)]

Q 4:81   Is the life expectancy of a trust beneficiary named as the IRA beneficiary relevant to the IRA owner in calculating his or her lifetime minimum distributions?

Generally, no. A trust beneficiary's life expectancy is not relevant to an IRA owner during his or her lifetime except in the limited circumstance when the IRA owner's spouse is the sole beneficiary of the trust and is more than 10 years younger than the IRA owner. In all other circumstances, the same Uniform Table life expectancy divisor based on the IRA owner's age will apply, regardless of the identity or life expectancy of the underlying trust beneficiary.

Q 4:82 Is the life expectancy of a remainder trust beneficiary relevant in determining the IRA owner's post-death distribution period?

Yes. In Revenue Ruling 2000-2 [2000-1 C.B. 305], modified by Revenue Ruling 2006-26 [2006-22 I.R.B. 939], the IRS stated that it will treat a remainder trust beneficiary as a co-beneficiary in determining the distribution period for RMDs if amounts are, or may be, accumulated for the remainder beneficiary's benefit during the life of the income beneficiary. This proposition has considerable relevance when the class of remainder beneficiaries includes a charity. In such a situation, the payout schedule will be accelerated because the life expectancy of an individual trust beneficiary cannot be used to determine post-death distributions (see Q 4:72). [Treas. Reg. § 1.401(a)(9)-5, Q&A-7(c)(3), Ex. 1]

Q 4:83 What is a qualified terminable interest property trust, and what happens when one is designated an IRA beneficiary?

A *qualified terminable interest property trust*, or QTIP trust, is a trust generally established by an individual to provide for life income to a surviving spouse with the remainder to the couple's children. Because a QTIP trust qualifies for the marital deduction, any trust assets remaining at the surviving spouse's death will be taxable in the second estate, even though the testator effectively controlled the subsequent distribution (see Qs 8:38–8:44).

If a QTIP trust is designated the beneficiary of an IRA, the trust receives distributions from the IRA, but the IRA continues to be held by its trustee or custodian even though it makes payments to the QTIP trust. IRA distributions to a QTIP trust vary according to whether the IRA owner dies before or after his or her RBD.

Practice Pointer. QTIP trusts have their own estate tax rules, and planning priorities must also be considered. Because many of the issues involving the use of a QTIP trust as an IRA beneficiary are complex, consulting a qualified legal advisor before a QTIP trust is implemented is strongly advised.

Q 4:84 If an IRA owner named a QTIP trust benefiting his or her spouse as the IRA beneficiary and dies before attaining age 70½ when must required minimum distributions from the IRA commence under Code Section 401(a)(9)?

It depends. If the IRA owner's spouse is the sole beneficiary of the QTIP trust, RMDs to the spouse must begin no later than December 31 of the year in which the IRA owner would have attained age 70½. [I.R.C. § 401(a)(9)(B)(iii)] If any IRA distributions are accumulated in the trust for remainder beneficiaries rather than being distributed to the spouse, the special rule of Code Section 401(a)(9)(B)(iii) is inapplicable and RMDs to the spouse must commence by December 31 of the year following the year of the IRA owner's death. [Treas. Reg. § 1.401(a)(9)-5, Q&A-7(c)(3), Ex. 1]

Q 4:85   When an IRA is split into a number of IRAs under a trustee-to-trustee transfer but the trustee does not change, does such a transfer constitute a distribution?

No. In Private Letter Ruling 8752061, an IRA owner who had four children directed the trustee to split the assets of the IRA among four new IRAs. The same bank to which the directions were issued continued as trustee. From the bank's point of view, such a procedure might amount to a mere bookkeeping transaction; however, in substance, a trustee-to-trustee transfer did occur. The IRS ruled that even though a new trustee was not named, four new IRAs were created. It was no more a distribution and new contribution than it would have been had the accounts been transferred to a new trustee. [Rev. Rul. 78-406, 1978-2 C.B. 157; Priv. Ltr. Ruls. 9331055 (May 13, 1993), 9226076 (Apr. 3, 1992), 8944058 (Aug. 10, 1989), 8752061 (Oct. 30, 1987)]

Post-Mortem Distribution Planning

Q 4:86   How does Treasury Regulations Section 1.401(a)(9) encourage post-mortem distribution planning?

Since the designated beneficiaries of an IRA are determined as of September 30 of the calendar year following the year of the owner's death, beneficiaries may be changed before that date through the use of qualified disclaimers, or removed by cashing out their interests. This is most common when a charity is one of the beneficiaries, so as to leave the IRA benefiting only individuals. [Treas. Reg. § 1.401(a)(9)-4, Q&A-4(a)]

The decedent's IRA may also be split into separate shares so as to maximize each beneficiary's distribution period. (See Qs 4:89–4:95 for a discussion of rules and deadlines applicable to qualified disclaimers.) The deadline for this, however, is December 31 of the calendar year following the year of the owner's death (i.e., three months following the final determination of the identity of beneficiaries). [Treas. Reg. § 1.409(a)(9)-8, Q&A-2(a)(2)]

Q 4:87   Why should an IRA that has multiple beneficiaries be divided into separate IRAs after the owner dies?

Having multiple individual IRA beneficiaries at the time of death will affect the determination of post-death IRA distributions unless certain actions are taken in a timely manner. If there is more than one beneficiary of the IRA on September 30 of the year following the year of the IRA owner's death, the shortest of the beneficiaries' life expectancies will be used to calculate post-death minimum distributions unless the IRA has been split into separate IRAs for each beneficiary before December 31 of the year following the year of the IRA owner's death. If the IRA is split, the payout schedule from each IRA is determined with reference to each beneficiary's own life expectancy. (See Qs 4:68, 4:73.) [Treas. Reg. § 1.401(a)(9)-8, Q&A-2(a)(2)]

Example. Ruth dies in 2009 at age 65, having named her daughter Amy (age 40), her son Bob (age 35), and a charity as equal beneficiaries of her single IRA. If nothing changes before September 30, 2010, the entire IRA would have to be distributed by December 31, 2014.

However, the trustee of Ruth's IRA could distribute the charity's entire share before September 30, 2010, leaving the IRA with two designated beneficiaries, Amy and Bob. The payout period would depend on whether or not the IRA is divided into separate accounts or shares by December 31, 2010. If there is no division of shares, the IRA will be distributed over the period of the shorter life expectancy (Amy's). But if the trustee allocates Bob's IRA interest to a separate account or share on or before December 31, 2010, then distributions to Bob will be based on his own life expectancy.

Q 4:88 Can one IRA with multiple beneficiaries be divided into separate IRAs for each beneficiary without adverse tax consequences?

Yes, provided the IRA remains titled in the name of the decedent both before and after the IRA is divided. If the IRA custodian inadvertently changes the name of the account from that of the deceased IRA owner to that of a beneficiary, the beneficiary's interest in the IRA will be considered distributed. Only a spouse beneficiary can create a new IRA in his or her own name after the death of the original IRA owner. A nonspouse beneficiary must continue to be listed as a beneficiary of the decedent's IRA even after it is divided. The IRA trustee or custodian will need the nonspouse beneficiary's Social Security number in order to file the appropriate Form 1099-R with the IRS for each distribution. [IRS Publication 590, *Individual Retirement Arrangements (IRAs)* 2008 (see Appendix A)]

Q 4:89 What is a qualified disclaimer of a beneficiary's interest in an IRA?

Under Code Section 2518(a), the IRS treats an IRA beneficiary making a qualified disclaimer as having predeceased the IRA owner. Thus, the disclaiming beneficiary's interest in the IRA would pass to the contingent IRA beneficiary. Under Code Section 2518(b), a *qualified disclaimer* is an irrevocable and unqualified refusal to accept an interest in property, but only if the following conditions are met:

1. The refusal is in writing.

2. The refusal is received by the IRA trustee or custodian within nine months of the IRA owner's death.

3. The disclaimant has not accepted the interest in the IRA or any of its benefits.

4. As a result of the refusal, the interest passes without direction either to the spouse of the decedent or to an individual other than the individual making the disclaimer.

Q 4:90   How can qualified disclaimers be used to maximize the tax benefits of an IRA after the death of the IRA owner?

If the primary IRA beneficiary named at the time of the IRA owner's death does not need the funds from the IRA and is older than the contingent IRA beneficiary, a qualified disclaimer will lengthen the payout term applicable to the IRA because the life expectancy of the younger contingent IRA beneficiary will be used to calculate minimum distributions.

Example. Fern dies in 2009, naming her husband Ralph, age 82, as her primary IRA beneficiary and her daughter Ellen, age 42, as her contingent IRA beneficiary. In the absence of a qualified disclaimer, Ralph may receive minimum distributions from the IRA beginning in 2010, based on an applicable divisor of 16.3 years, determined under the Uniform Table. If Ralph timely disclaims his interest in Fern's IRA, however, the IRA will pass to Ellen, and she can use her life expectancy of 40.7 years (the life expectancy of a 43-year-old beneficiary) to calculate RMDs from the IRA beginning in 2009 using the Single Life Table of Treasury Regulations Section 1.401(a)(9)-9, Q&A-1. Ellen's longer life expectancy will create lower minimum distributions, thereby maximizing the tax benefits of Fern's IRA.

In Private Letter Ruling 200208028 (Nov. 26, 2001), the eldest of five children disclaimed his interest in his parent's IRA. The other four children created four IRA subaccounts before the end of the year following the year of the parent's death. The IRS held that the life expectancy of the oldest child should be disregarded and that each of the other four children would be permitted to use his or her own life expectancy to determine minimum distributions from each subaccount.

Q 4:91   May a qualified disclaimer be made with respect to a portion of an IRA?

Yes. A beneficiary may elect to disclaim a specific pecuniary amount or a percentage of the IRA and claim ownership of the balance. The disclaimed portion will pass to the contingent beneficiary. The amount disclaimed and any income attributable to that amount must be segregated based on the fair market value of the assets on the date of the disclaimer or on a basis that fairly represents the value changes that have occurred between the IRA owner's date of death and the date of disclaimer. [Rev. Rul. 2005-36, 2005-26 I.R.B. 1368]

Q 4:92   May the IRA owner's surviving spouse make a qualified disclaimer after having received the RMD for the year of the owner's death?

Yes, provided the pre-disclaimer income attributable to the RMD is properly segregated as well. The following examples are based on Revenue Ruling 2005-36 [2005-26 I.R.B. 1368].

Example 1. Jack owned an IRA at the time of his death in January 2009. The primary beneficiary is his wife, Doris, and the contingent beneficiary is his daughter, Annette. Jack died before receiving his $10,000 RMD for 2009, so in February 2009 the IRA custodian pays the amount to Doris, who has decided not to waive the RMD for 2009. Shortly afterward, Doris executes a valid disclaimer of the pecuniary amount equal to $60,000 plus whatever income was earned in respect of that amount after the date of Jack's death. The IRA's value was $200,000 at Jack's date of death and $40,000 income was earned between that date and the date of the disclaimer. The income attributable to the $60,000 portion is $12,000 ($40,000 × ($60,000 ÷ $200,000)). Accordingly, $72,000 ($60,000 + $12,000) passes to Annette.

Example 2. The facts are the same as those in Example 1, except that Doris validly disclaims 30 percent of her remaining interest in the principal and income of the IRA after both the $10,000 RMD for 2009 and the income attributable to it since Jack's death have been removed. The income attributable to the RMD is $2,000 ($40,000 × ($10,000 ÷ $200,000)). The disclaimed amount, which passes to Annette, is $68,400 (.30 × ($200,000 + $40,000 – $10,000 – $2,000)).

Example 3. The facts are the same as those in Example 1, except that Doris validly disclaims the entire remaining balance in the IRA after reduction by the income earned since Jack's death in respect of the RMD she received. The IRA custodian segregates $2,000 for Doris' account, and the balance of the IRA passes to Annette.

Q 4:93 May an IRA owner's surviving spouse use a qualified disclaimer to maximize the portion of the IRA that will escape estate tax?

Yes. Using qualified disclaimers with respect to an IRA can effectively reduce a couple's exposure to estate tax.

Example. Sidney's total net worth of $5.5 million includes an IRA of $2.5 million. His wife, Sophie, is the primary beneficiary of his IRA, and a testamentary credit shelter trust with Sophie as the primary trust beneficiary is named the contingent beneficiary. If Sidney dies in 2009, his estate tax exclusion amount will be $3.5 million; however, Sidney has only $3 million of non-IRA assets with which to fund the testamentary credit shelter trust. Thus, if Sophie rolls over the entire $2.5 million IRA to a spousal IRA, her estate may be subject to increased estate taxes. Alternatively, Sophie could disclaim $500,000 of Sidney's IRA and roll over the $2 million balance. The $500,000 would then pass to the testamentary credit shelter trust and escape estate taxes at Sidney's death as well as at Sophie's death.

Q 4:94 When must a qualified disclaimer be made for it to be effective for estate and gift tax purposes?

A qualified disclaimer must be executed within nine months of the IRA owner's death to be effective for estate and gift tax purposes. If the disclaiming beneficiary misses this deadline, he or she is deemed to have made a taxable gift of the disclaimed property to the contingent beneficiary. Because such a gift would expose the disclaimant to gift taxes and would be deemed an IRA distribution subject to income tax, the nine-month deadline must be strictly observed.

Note. Treasury Regulations Section 1.401(a)(9)-4 contemplates a deadline of September 30 of the year following the year of the IRA owner's death for implementing various postmortem minimum distribution strategies; however, adhering to the separate nine-month deadline for performing a qualified disclaimer under Code Section 2518(b) will avoid triggering unwarranted income and gift tax consequences.

Q 4:95   If a surviving spouse executes a qualified disclaimer, is his or her life expectancy still used for calculating post-death distributions to a contingent beneficiary?

No. If a contingent beneficiary succeeds to an IRA by reason of a qualified disclaimer, such beneficiary's own life expectancy as determined in the year following the year of the IRA owner's death may be used for determining all post-death distributions from the IRA, and the disclaiming beneficiary's life expectancy is no longer relevant. [Treas. Reg. § 1.401(a)(9)-4, Q&A-4]

Taxation of Traditional IRA Distributions

Regular Tax on Distributions

Q 4:96   How are distributions from a traditional IRA taxed?

Distributions from a traditional IRA are governed by the annuity rules of Code Section 72. [I.R.C. § 402(d)(1)] In general, these rules permit the tax-free withdrawal of any nondeductible contributions, but tax as ordinary income all other amounts withdrawn. The ordering rules require that a portion of each distribution be allocated between basis and income. The basis allocation is made by aggregating all distributions made from the individual's traditional IRAs during the calendar year, and multiplying that amount by a fraction. The numerator of the fraction is the total amount of the individual's nondeductible contributions to all traditional IRAs (reduced by amounts that were previously recovered), and the denominator is the combined value of all the individual's traditional IRAs (determined as of the end of the calendar year and augmented by the current year distributions). [I.R.C. § 408(d)(2); HR Rep. No. 841, 99th Cong., 2d Sess. at II-379 (Conf. Rep. 1986)]

Example. Eve owns two traditional IRAs. All her contributions to IRA 1 were deductible, but her contributions to IRA 2 include $4,000 that are nondeductible. In October 2009, Eve withdraws her first IRA distribution in the amount of $1,000, and she takes it from IRA 1. At the end of 2009, the value of IRA 1 is $10,000 and the value of IRA 2 is $5,000. The portion of Eve's distribution that is allocated to nontaxable basis recovery is $250

($1,000 × ($4,000 ÷ ($10,000 + $1,000 + $5,000)). Eve recognizes $750 of ordinary income from this distribution.

In many cases, an individual will have made only deductible contributions to his or her traditional IRAs. All distributions such an individual receives from a traditional IRA would consist of ordinary income.

Various penalties may also apply to distributions from traditional IRAs. (See Q 4:106 (excess accumulation penalty) and Q 4:108 (early distribution penalty).)

Q 4:97   When does an IRA owner recognize a loss on a traditional IRA investment?

An IRA owner may only recognize a loss on a traditional IRA investment when all amounts have been distributed from all of his or her traditional IRA accounts. The amount of loss recognized on the final distribution is the aggregate amount of the owner's unrecovered basis in the IRAs (i.e., the total nondeductible contributions that were not returned in any distribution). The owner may claim the loss as a miscellaneous itemized deduction, subject to the applicable 2 percent-of-adjusted-gross-income limit. For purposes of calculating the alternative minimum tax, the loss must be added back to taxable income. [I.R.C. § 67; IRS Publication 590, *Individual Retirement Arrangements (IRAs)* 2008 (see Appendix A)]

Q 4:98   What is the effect if an owner of a traditional or Roth IRA sells stock or securities at a loss, and the IRA acquires substantially identical securities within 30 days before or after the sale?

If the individual is not a securities dealer acting in the ordinary course of business, the transaction is considered a wash sale and the IRA owner's loss is disallowed under Code Section 1091. Further, the owner's basis in the securities is entirely wasted, because it cannot be added to his or her basis in the IRA. [Rev. Rul. 2008-5, 2008-3 I.R.B. 271] As a result, the loss is never allowed, even upon liquidation of the IRA.

Caution. A transaction such as this may be a prohibited transaction that could invalidate the IRA (see Q 1:54). The IRS expressly warned in Revenue Ruling 2008-5 that the ruling does not address prohibited transaction issues under Code Section 4975. An IRA that is involved in a prohibited transaction loses its tax exempt status as of the first day of the year of the transaction, and all the IRA assets are deemed distributed on that day. [I.R.C. § 408(e)(2)]

Q 4:99   What are the tax consequences of converting a traditional IRA to a Roth IRA?

The term *conversion* refers to the movement of assets from a traditional IRA to a Roth IRA. There are several ways to accomplish a conversion, but in each case the transaction is viewed as a two-step process: the taxable distribution of all assets from the traditional IRA followed by the recontribution of those assets to the Roth IRA. The distribution from the traditional IRA is taxed in accordance with the annuity rules discussed in Q 4:9. (Conversions are discussed in detail in chapter 6.)

Q 4:100 How is the distribution taken into account if one of the converted assets is an annuity contract, or if an IRA annuity is converted?

The general rule is that the amount that is deemed to be distributed is the fair market value of the annuity contract on the date of the conversion. Until recently, no exceptions were allowed. However, Treasury Regulations Section 1.408A-4, issued in 2008, now provides that if a conversion is accomplished by surrendering the annuity for its cash value and reinvesting the entire cash proceeds in a Roth IRA, and all the contractual rights are extinguished in the surrender, then the amount that is deemed distributed is limited to the cash proceeds. [Treas. Reg. § 1.408A-4, Q&A-14]

The new regulation is a final rule that replaces Temporary Treasury Regulations Section 1.408A-4T. The temporary regulation included guidance for determining the fair market value of an annuity contract on the date of conversion; the final regulation adopts those methods with some changes. For conversions that occur before 2009, a taxpayer may elect to use the valuation methods provided in either regulation. [Treas. Reg. § 1.408A-4, Q&A-14(c)] Conversions after 2008 are controlled by the final regulation. Both the final and temporary regulations include the caveat that no method may be used to value an annuity if, because of the unusual nature of a particular contract, the method results in an approximation that is not reasonably close to the contract's full value.

The final regulation provides as follows:

1. The actual premiums paid for the annuity may be used to establish the contract's fair market value, if the conversion occurs soon after the contract is purchased.

2. If the same company that issued the annuity sells a comparable contract, the cost of the latter may be used to measure fair market value.

3. If there are no comparable contracts, fair market value may be established through an approximation based on the interpolated terminal reserve at the date of conversion, plus the proportionate part of the gross premium last paid before the date of the conversion that covers the period extending beyond that date.

4. For an annuity contract that has not yet been annuitized, a modified version of the accumulation methodology provided in Treasury Regulations Section 1.401(a)(9)-6, Q&A-12 may be used.

[Treas. Reg. § 1.408A-4, Q&A-14]

The methods under the temporary regulation, which are available for conversions before 2009, are generally similar, but also include a safe harbor

method that is described in Revenue Procedure 2006-13. [2006-3 I.R.B. 315]
[Temp. Treas. Reg. § 1.408A-4T, Q&A-14]

Conversions that involve annuity contracts are extremely complex. Individuals who undertake them should seek professional tax advice.

Q 4:101   What distributions from a traditional IRA are not taxable?

Distributions that are rolled over from a traditional IRA to another IRA or qualified plan are not taxable. Such rollovers may be accomplished by either a trustee-to-trustee transfer or a distribution and recontribution within a 60-day period (see chapter 6). As discussed in Q 4:96, distributions from traditional IRAs are also not taxable to the extent that they represent a return of the IRA owner's after-tax (i.e., nondeductible) contributions. A provision enacted under the Pension Protection Act of 2006 [Pub. L. No. 109-280, 120 Stat. 780] (PPA) excludes from income a qualified health savings account (HSA) funding distribution that is made from an IRA (see Qs 4:144–4:156). [I.R.C. § 408(d)(9)] Finally, an economic stimulus payment that the IRS directly deposited in 2008 to an individual's IRA may be withdrawn without adverse tax consequences until the due date (including extensions) for filing the 2008 income tax return. [Ann. 2008-44, 2008-20 I.R.B. 982]

Q 4:102   Is special tax treatment still available for qualified charitable distributions?

Yes. Since the start of 2006, certain IRA distributions made to charities that do not exceed $100,000 (qualified charitable distributions) have enjoyed special tax treatment. These provisions have been extended to include IRA distributions made through 2009. [I.R.C. § 408(d)(8)]

Q 4:103   Are IRA distributions subject to mandatory withholding?

No. IRA distributions are not subject to mandatory withholding. [I.R.C. § 3405(b)] Furthermore, regular federal income tax withholding may be waived. [I.R.C. § 3405(b)(2)] IRA distributions must, however, be taken into account in determining how much estimated tax (payable four times a year) is due. State estimated tax laws must also be considered.

50 Percent Excise Tax on Accumulated Distributions

Q 4:104   What is the penalty for taking a distribution that is less than the required minimum distribution?

A distribution from an IRA that is less than the RMD is subject to a 50 percent penalty tax. [I.R.C. § 4974(a)] The penalty applies only to the shortfall. The distribution that was in fact made may be offset against the gross amount required to be distributed, and only the difference between the RMD and the amount actually distributed is subject to the penalty.

Note. The penalty assessed for an insufficient distribution from an IRA is in addition to—and is not reduced by—the income tax that applies to the amount actually distributed.

Q 4:105 Is any relief possible from the 50 percent penalty on insufficient distributions from an IRA?

Yes. The IRS may waive or reduce the penalty for failure to take an RMD from an IRA upon a showing of reasonable cause and the IRA owner's effort to correct the error as soon as it was discovered. [I.R.C. § 4974(d)]

Q 4:106 When must a shortfall distribution from an IRA be corrected?

The IRS requires that the shortfall from the RMD be added to the RMD for the year following the year in which the minimum was not satisfied. The IRS does not allow the shortfall to be spread across the balance of the years of required distributions. Furthermore, the 50 percent penalty does not reduce in any way the amount that must be made up. The recipient must file Form 5329, Additional Taxes on Qualified Plans (Including IRAs) and Other Tax Favored Accounts, with his or her income tax return for the taxable year for which the minimum distribution was not taken, showing the 50 percent penalty for an excess accumulation in an IRA. The shortfall distribution is taxable in the year of distribution. [Treas. Reg. § 1.401(a)(9)-5, Q&A-8]

Q 4:107 Is the penalty ever automatically waived?

The 50 percent penalty is automatically waived in one case: the IRA owner is deceased, the sole beneficiary is an individual who should have received (but did not) a post-death RMD under the life-expectancy rule, and instead the IRA is entirely distributed in accordance with the five-year rule. [Treas. Reg. § 54.4974-2, Q&A-7(b)]

10 Percent Additional Tax on Early Distributions

Q 4:108 What is the 10 percent premature distribution penalty?

An IRA distribution that is not taken in a legislatively sanctioned manner is subject to an additional tax that is equal to 10 percent of the taxable amount distributed. [I.R.C. § 72(t)]

Q 4:109 Are there exceptions to the premature distribution penalty?

Yes. Qualified rollover distributions from IRAs are not subject to the premature distribution penalty, which is only imposed on the taxable part of a distribution. [I.R.C. § 72(t)(1)] For other IRA distributions, the following exceptions to the premature distribution penalty apply:

1. *Attainment of age 59½.* The distribution is made on or after the date on which the IRA owner attains age 59½. [I.R.C. § 72(t)(2)(A)(i)] (See Q 4:113.)

2. *Death.* The distribution is made to a beneficiary or to the IRA owner's estate on or after the death of the IRA owner. [I.R.C. § 72(t)(2)(A)(ii)] (See Q 4:111.)

3. *Disability.* The distribution is attributable to the IRA owner's becoming disabled (within the meaning of Code Section 72(m)(7)). [I.R.C. § 72(t)(2)(A)(iii)] (See Q 4:126.)

4. *First-time home purchase.* The distribution is a qualified first-time home-buyer distribution (also referred to as a qualified special purpose distribution). [I.R.C. § 72(t)(2)(F)] (See Qs 4:127–4:138.)

5. *Substantially equal periodic payments.* The distribution is part of a series of substantially equal periodic payments (payments made not less frequently than annually) made for the life (or life expectancy) of the IRA owner or the joint lives (or joint life expectancies) of the IRA owner and his or her designated beneficiary. [I.R.C. § 72(t)(2)(A)(iv)] (See Q 4:118.)

6. *Medical expenses in excess of 7.5 percent of adjusted gross income.* The distribution is used to pay medical expenses in excess of 7.5 percent of the IRA owner's AGI. [I.R.C. § 72(t)(2)(B)] (See Q 4:125.)

7. *Unemployed individual's purchase of health insurance.* The distribution is made after termination of employment and after the IRA owner has received unemployment compensation for 12 consecutive weeks under any federal or state unemployment compensation law by reason of such termination. [*See* I.R.C. § 72(t)(2)(D) for additional requirements.]

8. *Qualified higher education expenses.* The distribution is used for qualified higher education expenses. [I.R.C. § 72(t)(2)(E)] (See Qs 4:139–4:143.)

9. *Internal Revenue Service (IRS) levy.* The distribution is due to an IRS levy on the IRA. [I.R.C. § 72(t)(2)(A)(vii)]

10. *Qualified reservist distribution.* The distribution is to certain military reservists called to active duty. [I.R.C. § 72(t)(2)(G)] (See Q 4:157.)

11. *Direct-deposited economic stimulus payment.* The distribution is a timely withdrawal of an economic stimulus payment that was direct-deposited to an IRA in 2008 in accordance with instructions on the taxpayer's 2007 income tax return. [Ann. 2008-44, 2008-20 I.R.B. 982]

12. *Disaster related distributions.* The distribution is made to qualifying individuals affected by certain disasters (e.g., tornados). [I.R.C. § 1400Q] (See Qs 4:158–4:165.)

Q 4:110   Is a distribution still taxable if it is exempt from the penalty exception?

Yes. Distributions made under the penalty exception rules are taxable as made, even though there is no penalty.

Exception for Post-Death Distributions

Q 4:111   Is every traditional IRA distribution made to an IRA owner's beneficiary exempt from the penalty?

Yes, because the death exception applies to such distributions. The death exception does not, however, cover distributions to a surviving spouse who became the owner of the decedent spouse's IRA (see Q 4:59). The penalty applies to such distributions unless the spouse is older than age 59½ or another exception applies.

Q 4:112   Does the rule exempting IRA distributions from the premature distribution penalty after the death of the IRA owner apply without regard to the age of the IRA owner or the beneficiary at the time of death?

Yes. The exception from the premature distribution penalty for post-death distributions from an IRA applies without regard to the age of either the IRA owner or the IRA beneficiary. [I.R.C. § 72(t)(2)]

Example. Wanda, age 75, dies in 2009. Her daughter Irene, age 50, is the sole beneficiary of the IRA, and distributions to her must begin by the end of 2010. In 2010 and 2011, Irene takes only RMDs from the IRA, but in 2012 she withdraws $5,000 more than that year's RMD in order to purchase a boat. Although Irene will not attain age 59½ for several more years, none of the distributions to Irene are subject to the 10 percent premature distribution penalty because she is the beneficiary of a deceased IRA owner.

Exception for Distributions after Age 59½

Q 4:113   Is every traditional IRA distribution made to a recipient older than age 59½ exempt from the penalty?

Yes.

Q 4:114   May a pre-age-59½ distribution that is redeposited into an IRA within 60 days avoid the 10 percent premature distribution penalty?

Yes. Redepositing a distribution from an IRA made before age 59½ within 60 days of the distribution avoids the 10 percent penalty on premature distributions. What is accomplished is not a net withdrawal but a temporary interest-free loan of the withdrawn (and redeposited) amount. (See chapter 6.)

Exception for Substantially Equal Periodic Distributions

Q 4:115   If a surviving spouse younger than age 59½ chooses to own the decedent's IRA, what distribution options does the spouse have?

A spouse beneficiary who takes ownership of the IRA before attaining age 59½ can take substantially level periodic distributions, which are exempt from the 10 percent additional tax under Code Section 72(t). Qualifying distributions are determined based on the spouse beneficiary's life expectancy using one of the methods set forth in Revenue Ruling 2002-62 [2002-2 C.B. 710], and they must continue uninterrupted for at least five years and at least until the spouse attains age 59½. [I.R.C. § 72(t)(4)(A); Rev. Rul. 2002-62, 2002-2 C.B. 710] Alternatively, to avoid the 10 percent premature distribution penalty, the surviving spouse could leave the IRA in the decedent's name and take distributions at any time. These distributions would not be subject to the premature distribution penalty. [I.R.C. § 72(t)(2)(A)(ii)]

After the rollover to a spousal IRA is accomplished, the IRA belongs to the surviving spouse. Thus, the surviving spouse may make beneficiary designations without regard to the previous designations of the deceased spouse, and the life expectancy used in the distribution period is determined solely with reference to the surviving spouse's own age under the Uniform Table.

Q 4:116   What methods are approved to determine a series of substantially equal periodic distributions?

Three approved methods are set forth in Revenue Ruling 2002-62. [2002-2 C.B. 710] If the RMD method is used the result is a variable series of payments, because each year's payment depends on the IRA balance at the end of the prior year. The other methods (fixed amortization and fixed annuitization) generally result in a uniform series of payments. (See Q 4:119.)

Q 4:117   How long must the series of substantially equal periodic payments continue in order to avoid the 10 percent penalty on early distributions from an IRA?

To avoid the 10 percent penalty on early distributions from an IRA, the substantially equal periodic payments must continue without interruption for five years or until the IRA owner attains age 59½, whichever occurs later. The method for determining the calculation must not change. If it does, the IRS will treat the change as an impermissible modification and impose the 10 percent penalty on all distributions made before age 59½. [Priv. Ltr. Rul. 9821056 (Feb. 24, 1998)]

In *Benz v. Commissioner* [132 T.C. No. 15 (May 11, 2009)], the Tax Court held that a distribution for higher education expenses that separately qualifies for a Code Section 72(t) exception to the additional tax (see Q 4:139) does not modify a series of substantially equal periodic payments. The opinion suggests that other distributions for which statutory exceptions to the additional tax exist (e.g., qualified medical expense and first-time homebuyer distributions) are also permissible.

Substantially equal periodic distributions may start at any time before the owner attains age 59½ and may cease at the end of five years if the owner has then attained age 59½. If age 59½ has not been attained, the distributions must continue without interruption until such age is attained. If distributions commenced after the owner attained age 54½ but before age 59½, the distributions must continue beyond age 59½ in order to satisfy the five-year rule.

It should be noted that the five-year period does not end on the date of the fifth annual distribution, but rather closes at the end of the fifth year measured from the date of the first distribution. Thus, any payments made after the fifth annual payment and before the close of the fifth year would be deemed an impermissible modification. [Arnold v. Commissioner, 111 T.C. 250 (1998)]

Q 4:118   What penalty applies if the series of substantially equal periodic payments from an IRA is interrupted?

There is no penalty if the interruption of substantially equal periodic payments from an IRA is caused by disability or death. [Priv. Ltr. Rul. 9004042 (Dec. 9, 1989)] If, however, the reason for the interruption is to make a distribution that is not consistent with the established calculation pattern, the 10 percent penalty on premature distributions will be applied not only to that distribution but also to the whole series of distributions for which the Section 72 exemption was being claimed, to the extent the distributions were made before age 59½ (the recapture provision). [Priv. Ltr. Rul. 9821056 (Feb. 24, 1998)]

However, in the case where an individual under age 59½ was taking substantially equal periodic payments to avoid the 10 percent early withdrawal penalty, but due to an error by his IRA custodian took less than the RMD in one year, the IRS ruled that taking a make-up distribution in the next year to avoid the 10 percent penalty was not a modification of a series of substantially equal periodic payments under Code Section 72(t)(2)(A)(iv). [Priv. Ltr. Rul. 200503036 (Jan. 21, 2005)]

Practice Pointer. On account of the significant downturn in investment performance of most retirement assets beginning in 2000, the IRS issued Revenue Ruling 2002-62 [2002-2 C.B. 710], which allows taxpayers a one-time election to modify their amortization method under Code Section 72(t) without incurring a 10 percent premature distribution penalty.

Q 4:119   Must an IRA owner select an interest rate for the calculation of substantially equal payments?

It depends on the method chosen. The issue of an interest rate arises when an IRA owner who has not attained age 59½ seeks to make withdrawals that will not be subject to the 10 percent penalty under Code Section 72.

The simplest approach may be to parallel the method prescribed for RMDs in IRS Publication 590, *Individual Retirement Arrangements (IRAs)* 2008. (See Appendix A.) Under that method, no interest rate factor need be used—the IRA owner simply uses the life expectancy tables provided by the IRS. For example, if $40,000 is amortized over a life expectancy of 40 years, the first annual payment is $1,000; if at the end of the second year $39,000 is left to pay out over 39 years, the annual payment is $1,000 for that year; and so on. No interest is assumed, but whatever interest is earned (along with gain or loss, generally) is reflected in the balance remaining for amortization at each year-end.

The other alternatives for satisfying the Section 72(t)(2)(A)(iv) exception are as follows:

1. Fixed amortization—the IRA is evenly amortized based on the beneficiary's life expectancy and a reasonable interest factor; or

2. Fixed annuitization—payments are determined based on an annuity factor and a reasonable interest rate

[Notice 89-25, 1989-1 C.B. 662, *modified by* Rev. Rul. 2002-62, 2002-2 C.B. 710]

The IRS has issued a number of letter rulings dealing with the matter of an appropriate interest rate. The interest rate chosen must not exceed a rate considered reasonable at the date payment commences. [Priv. Ltr. Rul. 9021058 (Feb. 28, 1990)] In Private Letter Ruling 8946045 (Aug. 22, 1989), an assumed interest rate equal to 120 percent of the long-term federal rate on an annual basis (rounded off to the nearest 0.2 percent for the month immediately preceding the start of regular, systematic distributions) was deemed to be acceptable. An assumed interest rate of 9 percent for a distribution starting in 1988 was approved in Private Letter Ruling 8919052 (Feb. 15, 1989). In Private Letter Ruling 8921098 (undated), a rate of 5 percent was found not to exceed a reasonable interest rate for a distribution starting in 1989. That letter ruling included an example in which a 50-year-old having a life expectancy of 33.1 years and an account balance of $100,000 would satisfy Code Section 72, using 5 percent interest, by distributing $6,241 annually. In Private Letter Ruling 9312035 (Dec. 30, 1992), 8 percent was found not to be unreasonably high.

In Private Letter Ruling 9021058, the mortality table used was the 1983 IAM Male Mortality Table, and the interest rate was 8.5 percent. [*See also* Priv. Ltr. Ruls. 9240042 (July 9, 1992), 9231048 (May 5, 1992).] In Private Letter Ruling 9816028 (Jan. 21, 1998), the mortality table used was the UP-1984 Mortality Table, and the interest rate was 7.5 percent.

Note. For distributions first commencing on or after January 1, 2003, Revenue Ruling 2002-62 [2002-2 C.B. 710] mandates that the interest rate may not be more than 120 percent of the federal mid-term rate for either of the two months immediately preceding the month in which the distribution begins.

Q 4:120 Must the exact dollar amount calculated pursuant to the method chosen be paid out from the IRA each year in the case of an early distribution?

Yes. Once the calculation method for satisfying the 10 percent penalty exception under Code Section 72(t)(2) has been chosen and distributions have begun, the amount of all subsequent annual distributions must equal the exact dollar amount calculated pursuant to the method chosen. Any smaller or larger amount calculated pursuant to the method chosen would violate the substantially equal periodic payment exception. The calculation method chosen may incorporate an updated account balance, however. Thus, in Private Letter Ruling 200105066 (Nov. 9, 2000), the IRS permitted a taxpayer to multiply the applicable annuitization factor by the IRA value as of the close of the preceding year. This may be an important planning technique if IRA values decline on account of adverse market conditions.

Q 4:121 May a taxpayer incorporate increases in the cost of living in the calculation of substantially equal periodic payments under Code Section 72(t)(2)?

Yes. In Private Letter Ruling 9816028 (Jan. 21, 1998), the IRS permitted a taxpayer to apply a 3 percent cost-of-living factor to each distribution from an IRA so that the amount of the distribution would increase each year. Such methodology would, however, have to remain unchanged for the duration of the distributions; if it did not, the IRS could claim an impermissible modification and apply the recapture provision (see Q 4:118) for the 10 percent penalty.

Q 4:122 May distributions from an IRA be made through a fixed number of payments over a fixed time period to avoid the 10 percent premature distribution penalty?

Unless the determination of payments is based on actual life expectancy tables, the IRS will disallow a method of making a fixed number of payments from an IRA over a fixed period.

Q 4:123 If an individual has several IRAs, may pre-age-59½ distributions be made from one or more of the IRAs without taking distributions from others?

Yes. An individual may designate which of several IRAs are to be included in the annuitization calculation. For example, in Private Letter Ruling 9816028 (Jan. 21, 1998), a 49-year-old taxpayer was permitted to annuitize seven of his IRAs without annuitizing the others, but distributions could be made only from the seven accounts, and no distributions from the nonannuitized IRAs were permitted. It is interesting to note that the IRS permitted the gross annual distribution with respect to the seven annuitized IRAs to be made from any one or more of the seven specified IRAs in each year.

Q 4:124   What happens if a lump-sum distribution is made from an IRA after the owner attains age 59½ and after completion of five years of payments?

A lump-sum distribution from an IRA made after the owner attains age 59½ and after satisfaction of the Section 72 exception for annuity payments is not penalized, since the requirements of Code Section 72(t) would have already been satisfied. It is, however, still taxable at ordinary income rates.

Exception for Medical Expenses

Q 4:125   When must medical expenses be paid and incurred for a distribution to qualify for the medical expenses exception?

The exception only applies to an IRA distribution to the extent of the recipient's medical expenses that are deductible in the distribution year. Medical expenses are subject to various deductibility restrictions; one is that the deduction is only allowed for expenses actually paid during the year. [I.R.C. §§ 72(t)(2)(B); 213]

Thus, if medical expenses are rendered, and an IRA distribution is taken, in one year, but the expenses are not paid until a later year, the medical expenses exception to the 10 percent early distribution penalty does not apply. [Kimball v. Commissioner, T.C. Summary Opinion 2004-2 (Jan. 8, 2004)]

Nor does the exception apply if an individual takes an IRA distribution in one year to repay a loan of funds used in a prior year to pay medical expenses, because the loan repayment (the same-year event) is not the deductible event. [Bernard W. Evers v. Commissioner, T.C. Summary Opinion 2008-140 (Nov. 3, 2008)]

Exception for Disability Distributions

Q 4:126   How does the disability exclusion work to relieve an IRA owner from the penalty for early distributions?

An IRA owner may be exempted from the premature distribution penalty if he or she becomes seriously disabled. Under Code Section 72(m)(7), the disability must be any medically determinable physical or mental impairment that leaves the owner unable to engage in any substantial gainful activity. The impairment must also be expected to result in death or to be of long-continued and indefinite duration. [Priv. Ltr. Rul. 9249034 (Sept. 11, 1992)]

The existence of such a disability eliminates restrictions on distributions before age 59½. [I.R.C. § 72(t)(2)(A)(iii)] Thus, when a disability is established, distributions may be made in such manner as the IRA owner determines, including in a lump sum. Furthermore, if an exempt pattern of a series of substantially equivalent payments has commenced, it may be stopped or accelerated at that point. A reason for stopping might be that death appears so imminent that conserving the estate is preferable to receiving distributions.

Acceleration might also be used to help with a financial crunch. The reason for the alteration in the payment pattern is irrelevant for Section 72 purposes.

To be exempt under Code Section 72, distributions must be made after the individual is disabled. Uncorroborated testimony is insufficient to establish disability, and the mere fact that an individual may qualify for payment under a private disability insurance policy is also insufficient. [Kowsh v. Commissioner, T.C. Memo. 2008-204 (2008)]

However, the granting of disability benefits by the Social Security Administration on one date, based on evidence submitted on an earlier date, is proof of disability on the earlier date—so IRA distributions need not be delayed until benefits are actually granted to qualify for the exception. [Dart v. Commissioner (2008, Tax Ct.), T.C. Summ. Op. 2008-158, 2008 WL 5233290]

Exception for Qualified First-Time Homebuyer's Distributions

Q 4:127   What is a qualified first-time homebuyer distribution?

A *qualified first-time homebuyer distribution* from a traditional IRA is a distribution that is used to pay for the qualified acquisition costs associated with a first-time homebuyer's principal [I.R.C. § 72(t)(8)] The term *first-time homebuyer* is very broadly defined (see Q 4:129).

Q 4:128   What costs are classified as qualified acquisition costs for purposes of a qualified first-time homebuyer distribution?

For purposes of a qualified first-time homebuyer distribution, qualified acquisition costs include the costs of acquiring, constructing, or reconstructing a residence. They also include any usual or reasonable settlement, financing, or other closing costs. [I.R.C. § 72(t)(8)(C)]

Q 4:129   Who qualifies as a first-time homebuyer for purposes of a qualified first-time homebuyer distribution?

The term *first-time homebuyer* is generously defined. It covers any individual who did not (and, if married, whose spouse also did not) own a principal residence during the two year period that ends on the date when the residence at issue is acquired. Thus, ownership of a principal residence that ended more than two years earlier does not disqualify an individual. However, any type of present ownership interest held within the two-year period does eliminate use of the exception. [*See* I.R.C. § 72(t)(8)(D).]

For a married couple, the test of first-time home ownership applies separately to each spouse. Consequently, if one newlywed spouse already owned a principal residence during the two-year period, the exception does not apply when the *couple* jointly purchases a principal residence within the same period. [Olup v. Commissioner, T.C. Summ. Op. 2005-183 (Dec. 13, 2005)]

Finally, an interest counts as a present ownership interest if it is regarded as such under local law. Thus, individuals who used IRA distributions in 2004 to pay off a mortgage on their residence, contending that the mortgage company owned the property before the payoff, did not qualify for the first-time ownership exception because their joint tenancy interest in the residence (held since 1997) was already a present ownership interest under state law. [Sharma v. Commissioner, T.C. Summ. Op. 2008-98 (Aug. 7, 2008]

Q 4:130 What is the date of acquisition for purposes of a qualified first-time homebuyer distribution?

For purposes of a qualified first-time homebuyer distribution, the *date of acquisition* is the date on which a binding contract to acquire a principal residence is entered into or the date on which construction or reconstruction of such a principal residence begins. [I.R.C. § 72(t)(8)(D)(iii)]

Q 4:131 Must a qualified first-time homebuyer distribution be used by a certain time?

Yes. A qualified first-time homebuyer distribution must be used before the close of the 120th day after the day on which the distribution is received. [I.R.C. § 72(t)(8)(A)]

Q 4:132 Does the 60-day rollover period apply to a qualified first-time homebuyer distribution?

A distribution from an IRA must normally be rolled back into the IRA within 60 days (see chapter 6). That period is extended to 120 days for a qualified first-time homebuyer distribution if the rollover is due to the delay or cancellation of the purchase or construction of the residence. [I.R.C. § 72(t)(8)(E)] Congress granted the additional time because of the frequent delays and cancellations in home purchases.

> **Example.** Alex is single and has never before owned a principal residence. He enters into a purchase agreement to buy a home, with the closing scheduled for October. On August 20, Alex takes a $10,000 distribution from his IRA in anticipation of the October closing. Immediately before the closing, his real estate agent tells Alex that the closing will be delayed. In early December the closing has not yet occurred, and Alex becomes concerned about exceeding the 120-day period for completing the rollover. He may roll over the distribution amount back to the IRA by December 18 (120 days).

Q 4:133 Does the 12-month limitation apply to the rollover of a qualified first-time homebuyer distribution?

No, the prohibition against more than one rollover within a 12-month period does not apply to rollovers meeting the first-time homebuyer exception.

Q 4:134 What is a principal residence for purposes of a qualified first-time homebuyer distribution?

If an individual uses more than one property as a residence, which property is considered the individual's principal residence depends on the facts and circumstances of the case, including the good faith of the individual. A *principal residence*, for purposes of a qualified first-time homebuyer distribution, may include a houseboat, a house trailer, or stock held by a tenant-stockholder in a cooperative housing corporation. [Treas. Reg. §§ 1.121-3, 1.1034-1(d)(1)]

Q 4:135 For whom may a principal residence be purchased using a qualified first-time homebuyer distribution?

The qualified first-time homebuyer distribution exception is available to pay the qualified acquisition costs of a principal residence for the IRA owner or the owner's spouse, or a child, grandchild, or ancestor of the IRA owner or owner's spouse. It is important to note that the individual who must meet the definition of a first-time homebuyer is the person acquiring the home—not the IRA owner. [I.R.C. § 72(t)(8)(A)]

Q 4:136 Is there a dollar limit on qualified first-time homebuyer distributions?

Yes. There is a lifetime limit of $10,000 on qualified first-time homebuyer distributions. The limit applies to the IRA owner, not necessarily to the individual acquiring the home. [I.R.C. § 72(t)(8)(B)]

Example. Tamara, the daughter of Tom and Wanda, is a qualified first-time homebuyer. Tom and Wanda both have IRAs. Tom takes a $10,000 distribution from his IRA and gives the money to Tamara to purchase her first home. The next year, Tamara sells the home and moves to a rental apartment in a new city and lives there for three years. Tamara then finds a home she would like to purchase and asks her parents to help out with the down payment. Tom has already exhausted the $10,000 lifetime limit on first-time home-buyer distributions from his IRA. Wanda, however, may take a distribution from her IRA and give the funds to Tamara to acquire her home. Tamara is once again considered to be a qualified first-time homebuyer because she had no present ownership interest in a principal residence during the two-year period ending on the date of acquisition of her new home.

Q 4:137 May an individual take $10,000 from a traditional IRA and $10,000 from a Roth IRA under the first-time homebuyer exception?

Apparently not. The $10,000 lifetime limit on the first-time homebuyer exception appears to apply on a combined basis for all IRAs of an IRA owner. [I.R.C. § 72(t)(8)(B)]

Q 4:138   Does a qualified first-time homebuyer distribution count against the $10,000 lifetime limit if the distribution meets another exception to the 10 percent premature distribution penalty?

No. If an IRA owner who takes a qualified first-time homebuyer distribution meets one of the other exceptions to the 10 percent premature distribution penalty (see Q 4:109), the first-time homebuyer distribution does not count against the $10,000 lifetime limit on such distributions. [I.R.C. § 72(t)(2)]

Exception for Qualified Higher Education Expenses

Q 4:139   What are qualified higher education expenses?

For IRA distribution purposes, *qualified higher education expenses* include tuition, fees, books, supplies, and equipment required for the enrollment or attendance of a student at an eligible educational institution (see Q 4:142). For a "special needs beneficiary" (see Q 13:86), the cost of special needs services incurred for enrollment or attendance is also included. Room and board are qualified higher education expenses if the student is enrolled at least half time—generally the school's posted room and board charge, or, if greater, a fixed annual dollar amount (currently $2,500) for students living off campus and not at home. [I.R.C. § 529(e)(3); Notice 97-60, 1997-2 C.B. 310]

Particular books, supplies, or equipment (e.g., a laptop computer) may be considered necessary by the IRA owner or student, but an item's cost is not a qualified higher education expense unless the educational institution specifically requires the item. On that basis, the Tax Court recently held that a computer, housewares, appliances, furniture, and bedding purchased for an IRA owner's daughter were not qualified higher education expenses. Nor did book expenses qualify, because the purchased books were not shown to be required for courses, and payment for them was not substantiated. [Gorski v. Commissioner, T.C. Summ. Op. 2005-112]

Practice Pointer. An IRA owner should retain documentation (e.g., a course syllabus) to prove that specific items are required by the educational institution, as well as receipts to substantiate their expense.

Q 4:140   When must education expenses be incurred for a distribution to qualify for the exception?

The education expenses must be incurred in the year of the IRA distribution and not in a prior year. [Beckert v. Commissioner, T.C. Memo. 2005-162 (2005)]

Q 4:141   May an IRA owner use the qualified higher education expenses exception for members of his or her family?

Yes. Qualified higher education expenses are qualified expenses of the IRA owner, the owner's spouse, or any child or grandchild of the owner or the owner's spouse. [I.R.C. § 72(t)(7)]

Q 4:142   What is an eligible educational institution for purposes of qualified higher education expenses?

An *eligible educational institution* for purposes of qualified higher education expenses is any college, university, vocational school, or other postsecondary educational institution that is described in Section 481 of the Higher Education Act of 1965 [20 U.S.C. § 1088] and is therefore eligible to participate in the student aid programs administered by the Department of Education. The category includes all accredited public, nonprofit, and proprietary postsecondary institutions. [I.R.C. § 529(e)(5); Notice 97-60, 1997-2 C.B. 310]

Note. The traditional IRA, the Roth IRA, the Coverdell ESA, the HOPE Scholarship Credit, and the Lifetime Learning Credit all use the same eligibility requirements for educational institutions. [Notice 97-60, 1997-2 C.B. 310]

Q 4:143   Do other tax-favored education programs reduce the amount of education expenses available for penalty-free distributions from an IRA?

Yes. If a student does not need the assets from an IRA for qualified higher education expenses because funds are otherwise available, the exception for such expenses may not apply. Qualified higher education expenses paid with a Pell grant (or other tax-free scholarships), a tax-free distribution from a Coverdell ESA, veteran's educational assistance, or tax-free employer-provided educational assistance are *not* eligible for a penalty-free distribution from an IRA. [IRS Publication 590, *Individual Retirement Arrangements (IRAs)* 2008 (see Appendix A)]

On the other hand, qualified higher education expenses paid with an individual's earnings, a loan, a gift, an inheritance given to the student or the individual claiming the credit, or personal savings (including savings from a qualified state tuition program) are included in determining the amount of the IRA withdrawal that is not subject to the 10 percent premature distribution penalty.

Qualified Health Savings Account Funding Distributions

Q 4:144   What is the one-time-only exclusion from income for a qualified HSA funding distribution?

A one-time election is available that allows an eligible individual to withdraw funds from an IRA and roll them over tax free to an HSA to fund future medical expenses. The withdrawal must be a *qualified HSA funding distribution*, which is an otherwise taxable (but for this rule) distribution that is transferred to an HSA in a direct trustee-to-trustee transfer. For purposes of determining whether a distribution is "otherwise taxable," amounts distributed from a traditional IRA are treated as coming from income first (i.e., basis is not prorated). [I.R.C. § 408(d)(9); Joint Comm. Staff, Tech. Expln. of the Tax Relief and Health Care Act of 2006 (JCX-50-06), Dec. 7, 2006, p. 79] The qualified HSA funding distribution is also exempt from the 10 percent additional tax on premature IRA distributions. [I.R.C. § 408(d)(9)(E)]

Only one election is allowed for the lifetime of an individual, and it is irrevocable once made. An exception applies if the qualified HSA funding distribution is made during a month when, as of the first day of such month, the individual has self-only coverage under a high deductible health plan (HDHP). In that case, if the individual obtains family coverage that is in effect as of the first day of a later month in the same year, he or she may elect to make a second qualified HSA funding distribution during that later month. [I.R.C. § 408(d)(9)(C)]

Q 4:145 Who is an eligible individual?

An *eligible individual* is a person who, with respect to any month, is covered under an HDHP as of the first day of the month, and does not have duplicate coverage for any benefit under another, non-high-deductible health plan. Eligibility is determined under the rules that govern health savings accounts. [I.R.C. §§ 408(d)(9)(A), 223(c)]

A person must be an eligible individual at the time of the qualified HSA funding distribution, and must remain so throughout a testing period that starts with the month in which the distribution is made and ends on the last day of the twelfth month following that month. [Notice 2008-51, 2008-25 I.R.B. 1163]

Example Paul is 40 years old and has self-only coverage under an HDHP. On March 15, 2010, he transfers $3,000 from his traditional IRA to his HSA as a qualified HSA funding distribution. The testing period begins in March 2010 and ends on March 31, 2011.

Q 4:146 What is the dollar limitation on a qualified HSA funding distribution?

A qualified HSA funding distribution cannot exceed the maximum amount that the individual may contribute to the HSA for the same year. The HSA contribution limit depends on the contributor's age and the type of insurance coverage that is effective when the contribution is made. It is subject to annual increase for the cost of living. For 2009 and 2010, the limits are:

	2009	*2010*
Eligible individual with self-only coverage	$3,000	$3,050
Eligible individual with family coverage	$5,950	$6,150
Additional catch-up contribution for eligible individual age 55 or older during the taxable year	$1,000	$1,000

[I.R.C. § 223(g); Rev. Proc. 2008-29, 2008–22 I.R.B. 1039; Rev. Proc. 2009-29, 2009-22 I.R.B. 1050]

Q 4:147 If the exception for changed coverage applies and a second qualified HSA funding distribution is made, how is the testing period determined?

If an individual with self-only coverage under an HDHP rolls over a qualified HSA funding distribution, and later in the same year changes to family coverage under an HDHP and makes a second qualified HSA funding distribution, each of the contributions is subject to a separate testing period. Note that the combined distributions may not exceed the annual contribution limit for family coverage. [Notice 2008-51, 2008-25 I.R.B. ___]

Q 4:148 What happens if the transferor ceases to be an eligible individual at some point during the testing period?

If the individual fails to remain eligible throughout the testing period and the failure occurs for a reason other than the individual's death or disability, the qualified HSA funding distribution (but not the earnings on it) is includable in gross income when the failure occurs, and an additional tax equal to 10 percent of the includable amount is also payable. [I.R.C. § 408(d)(9)(D)] The early distribution penalty does not apply, however.

Example. On November 1, 2009, Ben, age 40, rolls over $2,000 from his IRA as a qualified HSA funding distribution. He excludes the $2,000 distribution from gross income for 2009 and does not have to pay an early distribution penalty. In February 2010, Ben terminates his coverage under the HDHP and ceases to be an eligible individual. For 2010, Ben must include the $2,000 in income and pay an additional tax of $200.

Q 4:149 To what year is a qualified HSA funding distribution attributable?

A qualified HSA funding distribution relates to the taxable year in which it is actually made. [Notice 2008-51, 2008-25 I.R.B. 1163]

Example. Trevor has family coverage under an HDHP in 2009 and 2010. He is eligible to contribute to an HSA in 2009, but forgets to do so. He realizes his mistake in February 2010. If he elects then to make his one-time qualified HSA funding distribution, he can roll over up an amount that will count against his 2010 HSA contribution limit. It is too late to designate the distribution for 2009.

Q 4:150 May an individual contribute a qualified HSA funding distribution to another person's HSA?

No. The qualified HSA funding distribution can only be deposited to an HSA that is owned by the distributing IRA's owner (or beneficiary, if it is an inherited IRA).

Example. Beth and Brian are married, and each has an HSA. Beth is also the beneficiary of an IRA she inherited from her father. She may elect to take her one-time qualified HSA funding distribution from the inherited IRA, but can only use it to fund her own HSA. She cannot use it to fund Brian's HSA.

Q 4:151 Can any type of IRA be the source of a qualified HSA funding distribution?

The funds may only be transferred from a traditional IRA or Roth IRA. They cannot be withdrawn from an ongoing SEP or SIMPLE. A SEP or SIMPLE is considered to be ongoing if there will be an employer contribution for the plan year ending with or within the taxable year of the IRA owner (or beneficiary, for an inherited IRA) in which the qualified HSA funding distribution would be made. [Notice 2008-51, 2008-25 I.R.B. 1163]

Q 4:152 May an individual combine amounts from two or more IRAs to make a qualified HSA funding distribution?

The qualified HSA funding distribution must come from a single IRA. If the individual desires to use funds from two or more IRAs for the funding distribution, an IRA-to-IRA transfer should be made first to consolidate the funds. [Notice 2008-51, 2008-25 I.R.B. 1163]

Q 4:153 How must funds be transferred to the HSA?

The funds must be transferred from the IRA to the HSA by means of a direct trustee-to-trustee transfer. [I.R.C. § 408(d)(9)(B)] This requirement is satisfied if a check drawn on the IRA made payable to the HSA trustee or custodian is delivered by the IRA owner. [Notice 2008-51, 2008-25 I.R.B. 1163]

Q 4:154 How does a qualified HSA funding distribution affect an owner's basis in the IRA?

A qualified HSA funding distribution removes income to the extent it does not exceed the total amount that would be included in gross income if there were a total distribution of all of the individual's IRAs. If the distribution exceeds that total amount, the excess does not carry over to the HSA as basis. [Notice 2008-51, 2008-25 I.R.B. 1163]

Example. Aaron's traditional IRA is held at Alpha Bank and all his contributions to it have been deductible. He owns a second traditional IRA at Beta Bank, which he funded with a single, nondeductible contribution of $2,000. On January 1, 2010, the Alpha and Beta IRAs are worth $18,000 and $3,000, respectively. Aaron withdraws $4,000 on that date from the Alpha IRA and elects to treat it as a qualified HSA funding distribution. Before the distribution, Aaron's IRAs consist in the aggregate of $2,000 of basis and $19,000 of income. The qualified HSA distribution removes $4,000 of that income.

Afterwards, the Alpha IRA is worth $14,000, the Beta IRA is worth $3,000, and Aaron still has a basis of $2,000 in his IRAs.

Q 4:155 Is the IRA trustee or custodian required to verify that a distribution meets the requirements for a qualified HSA funding distribution?

No. The IRA trustee or custodian may rely upon reasonable representations of the IRA owner or beneficiary that the requested distribution satisfies the requirements for a qualified HSA funding distribution. [Notice 2008-51, 2008-25 I.R.B. 1163]

Q 4:156 Is a qualified HSA funding distribution subject to withholding?

No. An individual who requests such a distribution is deemed to have elected out of withholding. [Notice 2008-51, 2008-25 I.R.B. 1163]

Exception for Qualified Reservist Distributions

Q 4:157 To what distributions does the qualified reservist exception apply?

The exception applies if (a) the reservist is ordered or called to active duty after September 11, 2001; (b) the order or call is for a period of more than 179 days or an indefinite period because the individual is a member of a *reserve component*; and (c) the reservist receives the distribution on or after the date of the order or call to active duty and by the close of the active duty period. The term "reserve component" means the Army National Guard of the United States, Army Reserve, Naval Reserve, Marine Corps Reserve, Air National Guard of the United States, Air Force Reserve, Coast Guard Reserve, or Reserve Corps of the Public Health Service. [IRS Publication 590, *Individual Retirement Arrangements (IRAs)* 2008 (see Appendix A)]

Special Tax Relief for Disaster Victims

Q 4:158 Is there tax relief for victims of a disaster who use IRA funds to cope with the emergency?

Yes, eligible individuals may, for a limited time, withdraw or borrow up to $100,000 from their IRAs and repay the amount taken without having to pay the taxes and penalties that normally apply. This benefit was first offered to the victims of hurricanes Katrina, Rita, and Wilma in 2005, and later extended to those of the storms, tornados, and flooding in Kansas (2007) and the Midwest (2008). [I.R.C. § 1400Q; Farm Act, Pub. L. No. 110-234, § 15345 (2008); Heartland Disaster Tax Relief Act, Pub. L. No. 110-343 § 702 (2008)]

Q 4:159   What tax relief is available?

Qualified hurricane distributions, *qualified recovery assistance distributions*, and *qualified disaster recovery assistance distributions*, defined in Code Section 1400Q, are tax-favored in several ways. They are exempt from the 10 percent penalty that ordinarily applies if the IRA owner is younger than age 59½. They are included ratably in gross income over a three-year period, giving recipients additional time to pay tax (though an election is available if the recipient prefers to include all the income in the first year). Finally, they may be rolled over on a tax-free basis at any time within the three-year (instead of 60-day) period that dates from the distribution. If an IRA owner pays tax on one of these distributions before rolling it over, the tax is recovered by filing an amended return. [I.R.C. § 1400Q]

> **Note.** Neither the 2008 Farm Act nor the Heartland Disaster Tax Relief Act of 2008 amends Code Section 1400Q, but each provides rules of interpreting it so that, for example, a reference to a qualified hurricane distribution is deemed to refer to a qualified recovery assistance distribution. Accordingly, Code Section 1400Q must be read in conjunction with Section 15345 of the Farm Act and Section 702 of the Heartland Disaster Tax Relief Act.

Q 4:160   What is a qualified hurricane distribution?

A *qualified hurricane distribution* meets four requirements:

1. It was made from an IRA (traditional, Roth, SEP, or SIMPLE), individual retirement annuity (other than an endowment contract) or other eligible qualified plan.
2. The recipient was an individual (*qualified individual*) whose principal place of abode was located in the hurricane disaster area for Hurricane Katrina on August 28, 2005, or for Hurricane Rita on September 23, 2005, or for Hurricane Wilma on October 23, 2005, and who suffered an economic loss resulting from that storm.
3. The distribution was made after August 24, 2005, for Hurricane Katrina, or after September 22, 2005, for Hurricane Rita, or after October 22, 2005, for Hurricane Wilma, and in all cases before January 1, 2007.
4. The distribution, when aggregated with all other qualified hurricane distributions received by the individual with respect to all three hurricanes, did not exceed $100,000.

[I.R.C. § 1400Q(a)]

Q 4:161   What is a qualified recovery assistance distribution?

A *qualified recovery assistance distribution* relates to the Kansas disaster area of 2007 and meets four requirements:

1. It is a distribution from an IRA (traditional, Roth, SEP, or SIMPLE), individual retirement annuity (other than an endowment contract), or other eligible qualified plan.

2. The recipient is an individual (*qualified individual*) whose principal place of abode on May 4, 2007, was located in the Kansas disaster area (as declared by President Bush), and who suffered an economic loss resulting from the storms on that date.

3. The distribution was made on or after May 4, 2007, and before January 1, 2009.

4. The distribution, when aggregated with all other qualified recovery assistance distributions received by the individual in all prior tax years, did not exceed $100,000.

[I.R.C. § 1400Q; 2008 Farm Act §§ 15345(b), (d)(5)]

The Kansas disaster area covers eight counties: Edwards, Kiowa, McPherson, Osage, Pottawatomie, Pratt, Smith, and Stafford. [Federal Disaster Declaration FEMA-1699-DR-KS (May 6, 2007)]

Q 4:162   What is a qualified disaster recovery assistance distribution?

A *qualified disaster recovery assistance distribution* relates to the Midwestern disaster area of 2008 and meets four requirements:

1. It is made from an IRA (traditional, Roth, SEP, or SIMPLE), individual retirement annuity (other than an endowment contract), or other eligible qualified plan.

2. The recipient is an individual (qualified individual) whose principal place of abode between May 20, 2008 and July 31, 2008, was located in the Midwestern disaster area (as declared by President Bush), and who suffered an economic loss resulting from the storms on that date.

3. The distribution is made on or after May 20, 2008, and before January 1, 2010.

4. The distribution, when aggregated with all other qualified disaster recovery assistance distributions received by the individual in all prior tax years, does not exceed $100,000.

[I.R.C. § 1400Q; Heartland Disaster Tax Relief Act of 2008 § 702]

The Midwestern disaster area covers ten states: Arkansas, Illinois, Indiana, Iowa, Kansas, Michigan, Minnesota, Missouri, Nebraska, and Wisconsin. [IRS Publication 4492-B, *Information for Affected Taxpayers in the Midwestern Disaster Area* 2009; IRS Publication 590, *Individual Retirement Arrangements (IRAs)* 2008 (see Appendix A)]

Q 4:163   What economic losses qualify for the disaster relief?

Examples of economic loss include, but are not limited to:

- Loss, damage to, or destruction of real or personal property from fire, flooding, looting, vandalism, theft, wind, or other cause;
- Loss related to displacement from one's home; and
- Loss of livelihood due to temporary or permanent layoffs.

[IRS Publication 590, *Individual Retirement Arrangements (IRAs)* 2008 (see Appendix A)]

Q 4:164   Can a qualified individual designate any distribution received from an IRA within the proper time period as a distribution under Code Section 1400Q?

Yes. Any IRA distribution received by a qualified individual within the allowable time frame could be designated as a qualified hurricane distribution, and the same is now true for qualified recovery assistance distributions and qualified disaster recovery assistance distributions. This applies whether the distribution is an RMD, one of a series of substantially equal periodic payments, or a distribution received by the qualified individual as the beneficiary of an IRA. [Notice 2005-92, § 4.G, 2005-2 C.B. 1165]

Q 4:165   What happens if the qualified individual dies before recognizing all the income from the distribution?

If a qualified individual dies before the full taxable amount of a qualified hurricane distribution, qualified recovery assistance distribution, or qualified disaster recovery assistance distribution has been included in gross income, then the remainder of the distribution must be included in gross income for the taxable year that includes the individual's death. [Notice 2005-92, § 4.G, 2005-51 I.R.B. 1165]

> **Example.** Carrie's home located in the Midwestern disaster area was destroyed by a tornado on May 20, 2008. On November 30, 2009, she takes a qualified recovery assistance distribution of $15,000 from her IRA. Carrie dies in June 2010, having included only $5,000 of the resulting income on her 2009 federal return. The remaining $10,000 of income must be included on Carrie's final income tax return for 2010.

Q 4:166   Must an IRA custodian verify that the distribution the IRA owner seeks to roll over qualifies under Code Section 1400Q?

Absent actual knowledge to the contrary, the IRA custodian may rely on reasonable representations from the distributee as to his or her principal place of abode on the date of the relevant storm and whether economic loss was suffered due to the storm. [Notice 2005-92, § 2.E., 2005-2 C.B. 1165]

Chapter 5

Roth IRA Distributions

Martin Fleisher, Esq.
Jo Ann Lippe, Esq.

Traditional IRAs, as well as qualified retirement plans, savings incentive match plans for employees, and tax-sheltered annuities, all offer up-front tax breaks and tax-deferred earnings on contributions. Distributions from all these plans, however, are subject to taxation. On the other hand, Roth IRA distributions are potentially tax free. Yet the complexity of Roth IRA distributions has frustrated many Roth IRA owners—especially when costly mistakes are made.

Only "qualified" distributions from Roth IRAs are tax free. To be qualified, distributions must (1) satisfy a five-year holding period and (2) be taken after the owner attains age 59½, dies, or becomes disabled, or be taken for the purchase of a first home. This chapter discusses the taxes and penalties applicable to Roth IRA distributions, the five-year holding period, and other requirements for tax-favored treatment of Roth IRA distributions.

Distributions in General

Q 5:1   What distributions are required from a Roth IRA?

None during the owner's lifetime. Unlike the owner of a traditional IRA, a Roth IRA owner never has to take distributions from his or her account. [I.R.C. § 408A(c)(5)] This feature makes the Roth IRA a useful estate-planning tool. Beneficiaries of a Roth IRA, however, are subject to minimum distribution requirements. (See Q 5:49.) If a Roth IRA beneficiary fails to take an RMD, a penalty of 50 percent is imposed on the amount that should have been distributed. [I.R.C. § 4974; Treas. Reg. § 54.4974-1]

> **Note.** The minimum distribution rules have been suspended for 2009 (see Q 5:51). [*See* Worker, Retiree, and Employer Recovery Act of 2008, § 201 (Pub. L. No. 110-458, 122 Stat. 5092–5120); I.R.C. § 401(a)(9)(H); Notice 2009-9, 2009-5 I.R.B. 419.]

Q 5:2   Does a distribution from a Roth IRA count toward a required minimum distribution for a traditional IRA?

No. An individual who is required to take minimum distributions from his or her traditional IRA (or SIMPLE IRA) may not choose to take such distributions from a Roth IRA.

Q 5:3   Are Roth IRA distributions exempt from federal income tax?

Many distributions are tax exempt. All *qualified distributions* (see Q 5:10), some *nonqualified distributions* (see Qs 5:10, 5:23), and certain other special distributions do not incur federal income tax (see Qs 5:5–5:9). Nonqualified Roth IRA distributions may be subject to federal income tax, and also to the 10 percent additional tax that applies to some premature distributions.

The tax treatment of a Roth IRA distribution generally depends on four factors: (1) the timing of the distribution, (2) the reason for the distribution, (3) the type of contributions distributed, and (4) whether the distribution is a return of contributions only or of contributions plus earnings. [*See* I.R.C. § 408A.]

Q 5:4   What taxes and penalties may apply to Roth IRA distributions?

Other taxes and penalties that may apply to Roth IRAs include the following:

State Income Taxes. Individual states may impose income tax on a distribution from a Roth IRA or on the annual earnings in a Roth IRA.

Excess Accumulation Penalty. Each failure to distribute a required minimum distribution (RMD) to a beneficiary results in a 50 percent penalty (see Q 5:52).

Penalty for Prohibited Transactions and Pledging Account as Security for a Loan. A Roth IRA is considered distributed if its owner engages in a prohibited transaction with respect to the Roth IRA or pledges the Roth IRA as security for a loan (see chapter 1).

Trustee or Custodian Penalties. The trustee or custodian of a Roth IRA may charge a penalty on early withdrawals. The trustee or custodian may also charge a back-end load or other fee in connection with the investment or account at the time of distribution.

Estate Taxes. The Roth IRA is considered part of the deceased owner's estate; therefore, estate taxes may apply (see chapters 9 and 10).

Q 5:5   Is a Roth IRA distribution taxable if it is rolled over to another Roth IRA?

No. Distributions from a Roth IRA are not included in gross income to the extent they are rolled over to another Roth IRA on a tax-free basis (see chapter 6). [Treas. Reg. § 1.408A-6, Q&A-1(c)]

Q 5:6   Are corrective distributions from a Roth IRA subject to tax?

Corrective distributions return previously made excess contributions (and their earnings) to a Roth IRA owner (see Q 3:139). The returned contributions are not taxable, but any income that is distributed is includable in the Roth IRA owner's gross income for the taxable year in which the contributions were made. [Treas. Reg. § 1.408A-6, Q&A-1(d)]

Q 5:7   Do qualified charitable distributions still enjoy special tax treatment?

Yes, but only through 2009. Originally for 2006 and 2007, and now also for 2008 and 2009, *qualified charitable distributions* are excluded from the income of any owner of a Roth or traditional IRA. A qualified charitable distribution is generally a distribution that is otherwise taxable, is made directly to a tax-qualified charity or private foundation by means of a trustee-to-trustee transfer, and is made on or after the date when the owner attains age 70½. The amount excluded from income for any year is capped at $100,000, taking into account all such distributions from any of the owner's Roth IRAs and traditional IRAs. This special treatment of qualified charitable distributions expires at the end of 2009. [I.R.C. § 408(d)(8); Pension Protection Act of 2006, § 1201 (Pub. L. No. 109-280, 120 Stat. 780 (Aug. 17, 2006)) (PPA); Tax Extenders and Alternative Minimum Tax Relief Act of 2008, § 205(a), Pub. L. 110-343 (Oct. 3, 2008)]

Q 5:8   What other special tax provisions apply to Roth IRA distributions?

A one-time only exclusion from income is available for a *qualified HSA funding distribution* (generally, a traditional or Roth IRA distribution that an eligible individual may use, subject to restrictions, to fund a health savings account (see Qs 4:144–4:156 for details).

Special tax relief is available for certain victims of hurricanes and other disasters, allowing them to use Roth or traditional IRA funds without being subject to the normal taxes and penalties that apply (see Qs 4:158–4:166 for details).

Finally, if an individual's economic stimulus payment was directly deposited in 2008 into an individual's Roth IRA, part or all of it may be withdrawn without adverse tax consequences if the withdrawal is made by the filing deadline (including extensions) for the 2008 income tax return. [Ann. 2008-44, 2008-20 I.R.B. 982]

Q 5:9 What rule applies to the withdrawal of an economic stimulus payment that was directly deposited in 2008 to a Roth IRA account?

An economic stimulus payment that was directly deposited in 2008 into an individual's Roth IRA may be withdrawn without adverse tax consequences until the deadline (including extensions) for filing the 2008 income tax return. [Ann. 2008-44, 2008-20 I.R.B. 982]

Qualified Distributions

Q 5:10 What is a qualified distribution from a Roth IRA?

A distribution from a Roth IRA is qualified if it meets both of the following requirements:

1. *Five-year holding period.* Roth IRAs are subject to a five-year holding period requirement, and qualified distributions cannot be made until after the period closes (see Qs 5:12–5:21). [Treas. Reg. § 1.408A-6, Q&A-1]

2. *Qualifying reason.* A distribution made after the close of the holding period is a qualified distribution if it is made for one of these reasons:

    a. Attainment of age 59½. The distribution is made on or after the date when the Roth IRA owner attains age 59½.

    b. Death. The distribution is made to a beneficiary, or to the Roth IRA owner's estate, after the owner's death.

    c. Disability. The distribution is attributable to the Roth IRA owner's becoming disabled (within the meaning of Code Section 72(m)(7)).

    d. First-time home purchase. The distribution is a "qualified first-time homebuyer distribution" (see Qs 5:27, 4:127–4:138).

[I.R.C. § 408A(d)(2); Treas. Reg. § 1.408A-6, Q&A-1]

Q 5:11 What tax benefits do qualified distributions from a Roth IRA enjoy?

Qualified distributions from a Roth IRA are exempt from all federal income taxes, including the 10 percent additional tax on premature distributions. [I.R.C. § 408A(d)(1)]

Five-Year Holding Period for Qualified Distribution Purposes

Q 5:12 When is the five-year holding period requirement satisfied for a Roth IRA?

The five-year holding period requirement is satisfied on the fifth anniversary of the first day of the year for which the initial Roth IRA contribution is made. Any type of contribution, whether a direct, rollover, or conversion contribution, is sufficient to commence the holding period—with one exception. A contribution that is returned as a corrective distribution is ignored and does not commence the holding period for qualified distribution purposes. [I.R.C. § 408A(d)(2)(B); Treas. Reg. § 1.408A-6, Q&A-2] If the initial contribution is made in 2009 (or in 2010 for the 2009 contribution year), the five-year holding period works as follows:

2009	First Year—Initial Contribution (made anytime between January 1, 2009, and April 15, 2010)
2010	Second Year
2011	Third Year
2012	Fourth Year
2013	Fifth Year
2014	Distributions meet five-year holding period requirement on January 1, 2014.

Q 5:13 Does a conversion contribution restart the five-year holding period for qualified distribution purposes?

No. A conversion contribution does not restart the five-year holding period that determines whether a Roth IRA distribution is qualified or nonqualified. Every conversion contribution does have its own five-year holding period requirement (see Q 5:31), but the purpose is different; it determines whether a conversion contribution that is returned in a *nonqualified* distribution is subject to a 10 percent additional tax. [S. Rep. No. 105-174, Pub. L. No. 105-206, 112 Stat. 58 (1998)]

Q 5:14 How is the five-year holding period tracked for subsequent contributions to a contributory Roth IRA?

The five-year holding period that applies for qualified distribution purposes starts when the first contribution is made. One significant benefit of that rule is that once the five-year period begins, it begins not only for the initial contribution but also for all future contributions. [Treas. Reg. § 1.408A-6, Q&A-2]

Example. Jane establishes a Roth IRA in 2005 with a $4,000 contribution. She also makes annual contributions to that Roth IRA for 2006 through 2009. In 2010, Jane takes a full distribution from the Roth IRA. She meets the five-year holding period requirement because the five-year holding period started in 2005, the year of her first contribution to a Roth IRA.

Q 5:15 How is the five-year holding period tracked if an individual establishes multiple contributory Roth IRAs?

The five-year holding period begins in the year of the first Roth IRA contribution regardless of whether future contributions are made to the same or different Roth IRAs. [Treas. Reg. § 1.408A-6, Q&A-2]

Example. Jason contributes $5,000 to his Roth IRA at ABC Bank in 2008. In 2009 he contributes $5,000 to a new Roth IRA at XYZ Credit Union. Jason's five-year holding period for the 2009 contribution begins in 2008, even though the Roth IRA to which it was made did not exist in 2008.

Q 5:16 Is the five-year holding period tracked to the day?

No. The five-year holding period is based on the year, not the day. It makes no difference whether the individual made the contribution on the first possible day to make a contribution for a tax year or on the last possible day. The five-year holding period starts in the year for which the first contribution is made and ends on January 1 of the year that is five years later. [Treas. Reg. § 1.408A-6, Q&A-2]

Example 1. Louise makes her 2007 Roth IRA contribution on January 1, 2007. Her five-year holding period begins in 2007 and will end on January 1, 2012. Any distribution taken on or after January 1, 2012, will have met the five-year holding period requirement.

Example 2. Lydia makes her Roth IRA contribution for 2009 on April 15, 2010. Her five-year holding period begins in 2009 and ends on January 1, 2014.

Q 5:17 Should an individual make a minimum contribution to a Roth IRA for the sole purpose of starting the five-year holding period?

Yes. An eligible individual who decides against making a full Roth IRA contribution in a particular year (e.g., 2009) should make a minimum contribution to begin his or her five-year holding period. For example, a $50 contribution to a Roth IRA in 2009 starts the holding period in 2009 as if it were a $5,000 contribution. In that way, if the individual does decide to contribute to a Roth IRA in the future, the five-year holding period will have already begun.

Q 5:18 Does the five-year holding period begin anew if an individual takes a full distribution from his or her Roth IRA?

Generally, no. The five-year holding period does not start over after a full distribution of a Roth IRA, unless the full distribution was due to a revocation during the seven-day period following establishment of the Roth IRA, a recharacterization (see Q 3:121), or the return of an excess contribution (see chapter 3). [Treas. Reg. § 1.408A-6, Q&A-2]

Example. Sam establishes a Roth IRA in 2006 by making a $2,000 contribution. In 2007 he withdraws the entire $2,000 plus all attributable earnings for a family emergency. (He does not remove the assets as an excess contribution or a recharacterization.) In 2009 Sam makes a $5,000 Roth IRA contribution. His five-year period started in 2006, the date of his first contribution to a Roth IRA.

Q 5:19 How is the five-year holding period requirement met for beneficiaries of a Roth IRA?

The beneficiary of a Roth IRA "steps into the shoes" of the deceased Roth IRA owner to determine when the five-year holding period begins. [Treas. Reg. § 1.408A-6, Q&A-7]

Example. Sean establishes a Roth IRA in 2009 and dies in 2010. The beneficiary, Sean's daughter Nicole, has the Roth IRA fully distributed in 2010. The distribution Nicole receives is not a qualified distribution because the five-year holding period begins with Sean's contribution in 2009 and runs until the end of 2013. To receive a qualified distribution from the Roth IRA, Nicole must wait until January 1, 2014.

Q 5:20 If a Roth IRA beneficiary also has his or her own IRA, are there two separate five-year holding periods?

Yes. An individual's five-year holding period for an inherited Roth IRA is determined independently of his or her five-year holding period for other Roth IRAs that are held as the owner. Consequently, a beneficiary in this position must keep track of two holding periods. Roth IRAs inherited from different decedents also have separate holding periods. [Treas. Reg. § 1.408A-6, Q&A-7]

Example. Melissa established a Roth IRA in 2008; her father established a Roth IRA in 2009 and named Melissa the beneficiary. He dies on March 13, 2013. The five-year holding period for Melissa's own Roth IRA has closed by that date (it began in 2008 and ended on January 1, 2013), but for the Roth IRA she inherits from her father the five-year holding period continues until January 1, 2014.

Q 5:21 How is the five-year holding period determined for a spouse beneficiary who also has his or her own Roth IRA?

The spouse is governed by the same rule that applies to nonspouse beneficiaries (see Q 5:20)—unless the spouse is the sole beneficiary and the spouse elects to treat the Roth IRA as his or her own. If the spouse does so, the inherited Roth IRA is treated for all purposes as one that the spouse owns, and whichever five-year holding period ends first—the one tracked from the decedent or the one tracked for the spouse's other Roth IRAs—becomes the five-year holding period that applies to all of them. [Treas. Reg. § 1.408A-6, Q&A-7]

> **Example 1.** Conrad establishes a Roth IRA in 2009 and dies in 2010. He leaves the assets to his wife, Betsy, who treats the IRA as her own. Betsy's five-year holding period starts in 2009.

> **Example 2.** Lisa establishes a Roth IRA in 2006. Her husband, John, establishes a Roth IRA in 2008 and names Lisa the beneficiary. In 2011 John dies. Lisa treats John's Roth IRA as her own. She immediately meets the five-year holding period requirement because her own start year (2006) was earlier than her husband's start year (2008).

> **Example 3.** The facts are the same as those in Example 2, except that Lisa established her Roth IRA in 2008 and John established his Roth IRA in 2006. When John dies, Lisa treats his Roth IRA as her own. For both of Lisa's Roth IRAs, the five-year holding period begins in 2006 (the earlier start year).

> **Example 4.** Barbara established a Roth IRA in 2005. Her husband, Norman, established a Roth IRA in 2007. In 2008, Norman dies, having named Barbara as beneficiary of his Roth IRA. Barbara elects *not* to treat Norman's Roth IRA as her own. She has two separate five-year holding periods: one for her own Roth IRA, starting in 2005, and one for the Roth IRA she inherits from Norman, with a start year of 2007.

Nonqualified Distributions

Q 5:22 What is a nonqualified distribution from a Roth IRA?

A *nonqualified distribution* from a Roth IRA is any distribution that either occurs within the five-year holding period (that applies for qualified distribution purposes), or does not satisfy one of the four qualifying reasons (attainment of age 59½, death, disability, or first-home purchase) (see Q 5:10). Nonqualified distributions are subject to federal income tax and may be subject to penalties.

> **Note.** An economic stimulus payment that was directly deposited to a Roth IRA in 2008 and withdrawn by the deadline (with extensions) for filing the Roth IRA owner's 2008 tax return is apparently *not* treated as a nonqualified distribution. (See Q 5:9.)

Q 5:23   Are all nonqualified distributions from a Roth IRA taxed and penalized?

No. Every nonqualified distribution from a Roth IRA must be analyzed to determine its component parts—which may include earnings, regular contributions, and conversion contributions—because each is taxed differently. Conversion contributions are further broken down to distinguish between amounts that were taxed at the time of conversion and amounts that were not. The components of a nonqualified Roth IRA distribution are determined according to a complex series of ordering and aggregation rules (see Qs 5:38–5:47).

Note. In a conversion of traditional IRA funds to a Roth IRA, only the previously untaxed amounts (earnings and deductible contributions) are included in the owner's gross income. Nondeductible contributions, which are made with previously taxed dollars, are not taxed again in a conversion. [Treas. Reg. § 1.408A-4, Q&A-7]

Q 5:24   How do the federal tax rules apply to the components of a nonqualified Roth IRA distribution?

The separate components of a nonqualified Roth IRA distribution are taxed as follows:

1. Earnings are taxed as ordinary income. They are also subject to the 10 percent additional tax on premature distributions, unless one of the exceptions in Code Section 72(t) applies. (See Q 5:27.) [Treas. Reg. § 1.408A-6, Q&A-4]

2. Regular contributions are excluded from gross income, and are also exempt from the 10 percent additional tax. [Treas. Reg. § 1.408A-6, Q&A-4]

3. Conversion contributions are excluded from gross income. However, each conversion contribution is subject to its own five-year holding period requirement. If a conversion contribution is prematurely returned, and the distribution is not protected by a Code Section 72(t) exception, then a 10 percent additional tax is levied on the part of the conversion contribution that was not taxed at conversion. (See Note in Q 5:23.) [Treas. Reg. § 1.408A-6, Q&A-5; I.R.C. § 72(t)]

Note. The five-year holding period requirement that applies to each conversion contribution is completely separate from the five-year holding period that determines whether or not a Roth IRA distribution is qualified or nonqualified (see Q 5:10).

10 Percent Additional Tax on Early Distributions

Q 5:25   What is the 10 percent additional tax on early distributions from a Roth IRA?

The 10 percent additional tax exists under the authority of Code Section 72(t) and its function is to discourage individuals from withdrawing retirement savings too early. Certain exceptions are available that allow an individual to withdraw distributions free of the additional tax (e.g., to pay for qualified medical expenses).

Q 5:26 Does the 10 percent additional tax apply to the entire amount of a nonqualified distribution from a Roth IRA?

Usually, no. The 10 percent additional tax applies only to two components of a nonqualified Roth IRA distribution—distributed earnings and prematurely returned conversion contributions that were not taxed at the time of conversion. (See Q 5:24.) That is significant because regular contributions are returned *first* and earnings are returned *last* from a Roth IRA (see Q 5:40). [Treas. Reg. § 1.408A-6, Q&A-4, Q&A-5]

Q 5:27 Do the same exceptions that apply to traditional IRAs also apply to Roth IRAs?

Yes. The same exceptions to the additional tax apply to both kinds of distributions; they are extensively discussed in chapter 4 (refer to Qs 4:108–4:166). Briefly, the exceptions are:

- *Attainment of age 59½.* The distribution is made on or after the date on which the Roth IRA owner attains age 59½. [I.R.C. § 408A(d)(2)(A)(i)]
- *Death.* The distribution is made to a beneficiary or to the Roth IRA owner's estate on or after the owner's death. [I.R.C. § 408A(d)(2)(A)(ii)]
- *Disability.* The distribution is attributable to the Roth IRA owner's becoming disabled (within the meaning of Code Section 72(m)(7)). [I.R.C. § 408A(d)(2)(A)(iii)]
- *First-time home purchase.* The distribution is a qualified first-time homebuyer distribution (also referred to as a qualified special purpose distribution). [I.R.C. §§ 72(t)(2)(F), 408A(d)(2)(A)(iv), 408A(d)(2)(A)(v)]
- *Substantially equal periodic payments.* The distribution is part of a series of substantially equal periodic payments (payments made not less frequently than annually) made for the life (or life expectancy) of the Roth IRA owner or the joint lives (or joint life expectancies) of the Roth IRA owner and his or her designated beneficiary. [I.R.C. § 72(t)(2)(A)(iv)]
- *Medical expenses in excess of 7.5 percent of adjusted gross income.* The distribution is used to pay medical expenses in excess of 7.5 percent of the Roth IRA owner's adjusted gross income (AGI). [I.R.C. § 72(t)(2)(B)]
- *Unemployed individual's purchase of health insurance.* The distribution is made after termination of employment and after the Roth IRA owner has received unemployment compensation for 12 consecutive weeks under any federal or state unemployment compensation law by reason of such termination. [*See* I.R.C. § 72(t)(2)(D) for additional requirements.]

- *Qualified higher education expenses.* The distribution is used for qualified higher education expenses. [I.R.C. § 72(t)(2)(E)]

- *Internal Revenue Service (IRS) levy.* The distribution is due to an IRS levy on the Roth IRA. [I.R.C. § 72(t)(2)(A)(vii)]

- *Qualified reservist distribution.* The distribution is to certain military reservists called to active duty (see Q 4:157). [I.R.C. § 72(t)(2)(G)(i)]

- *Direct-deposited economic stimulus payment.* The distribution is a timely withdrawal of an economic stimulus payment that was direct-deposited to an IRA in 2008 in accordance with instructions on the taxpayer's 2007 income tax return. [Ann. 2008-44, 2008-20 I.R.B. 982]

- *Disaster-related distributions.* The distribution is made to qualifying individuals affected by certain disasters (e.g., tornados). (See Qs 4:158–4:166.) [I.R.C. § 1400Q]

- *Qualified health savings account funding distribution.* The distribution is used (once per lifetime) to fund a health savings account (see Qs 4:144–4:156 for details).

Q 5:28   How do the qualifying reasons for a Roth IRA distribution overlap with the exceptions to the 10 percent additional tax?

Four of the exceptions to the 10 percent additional tax—attainment of age 59½, death, disability, and purchase of a first home—are also the qualifying reasons that partly determine whether a Roth IRA distribution is qualified or nonqualified (see Q 5:10). A Roth IRA distribution can have a qualifying reason and still be nonqualified (if the five-year holding period is still open). In that case, the 10 percent additional tax does not apply to the distribution, but distributed earnings are included in gross income. [Treas. Reg. § 1.408A-6, Q&A-5]

Q 5:29   What is the result if a distribution from a Roth IRA meets an exception to the 10 percent additional tax that is not one of the four qualifying reasons?

If a distribution from a Roth IRA meets an exception to the 10 percent additional tax but not one that is also a qualifying reason (see Q 5:10), the distribution is nonqualified regardless of when it is made. The 10 percent additional tax is not levied because a Code Section 72(t) exception applies, but any earnings that are distributed must be included in gross income. [Treas. Reg. § 1.408A-6, Q&A-5]

Example. Quentin, age 45, began contributing to a Roth IRA in 1999. In 2010, he withdraws funds and uses them to pay his daughter's college tuition. The withdrawal is a nonqualified distribution, and if earnings are part of the distribution they are taxed as ordinary income. The additional tax does not apply.

Q 5:30   Does a withdrawal of contributions from a Roth IRA count against the $10,000 lifetime limit on qualified first-time homebuyer distributions?

Apparently not. In a contributory Roth IRA, the original contribution amounts generally are available free of taxes and penalties at any time and for any reason. A Roth IRA owner should, one would think, be able to take a return of the original contribution amount, plus $10,000 in earnings, for a first-home purchase. The Code, however, does not specifically authorize distributions above $10,000 for such a purchase.

To avoid exceeding the lifetime limit, two distributions could be taken. The first would be a nonqualified distribution of the original contribution amount (*not* a qualified first-time homebuyer distribution). The second distribution would be a distribution of earnings and would be designated as a qualified first-time homebuyer distribution. Most likely, the two distributions would not need to be taken separately. The trustee or custodian of the Roth IRA would report the entire distribution as a premature distribution on Form 1099-R and the Roth IRA owner would have to allocate some portion of the distribution as a first-time homebuyer exception on his or her income tax return (on Forms 8606 and 5329).

> **Example.** Mike has been contributing $2,000 per year for six years to his Roth IRA to save for his first home. The Roth IRA balance is $16,000 ($12,000 in contributions and $4,000 in earnings). Mike would like to withdraw the entire balance to use to purchase his first home. He can do so by first taking a $12,000 nonqualified distribution to retrieve his contributions. That distribution would not be taxed or penalized because it would be a return of contributions. Mike could then take a second distribution of $4,000 as a qualified first-time homebuyer distribution. He would still have $6,000 available for additional first-time homebuyer distributions. (The result should be the same whether Mike takes one distribution or two.)

Distribution of Conversion Contributions

Q 5:31   How are conversion contributions taxed when they are returned in a nonqualified Roth IRA distribution?

Conversion contributions that are returned in a nonqualified Roth IRA distribution are excluded from gross income because they were previously taxed—in most cases at the conversion time, but earlier if the converted amount was a nondeductible contribution (see Note in Q 5:23). However, any that were not taxed until the conversion time—this includes all deductible contributions and earnings that were converted from the traditional IRA—must be held in the Roth IRA long enough to satisfy their own five-year requirement, or else the 10 percent additional tax may apply if they are returned in a nonqualified distribution. [Treas. Reg. § 1.408A-6, Q&A-5; Treas. Reg. § 1.408A-6, Q&A-10, Examples 6 & 9]

Note. A special rule allows the 10 percent additional tax to be applied in this way; usually, the additional tax only applies to the taxable part of an IRA distribution. [I.R.C. § 408A(d)(3)(F)(i)]

Example 1. Andy converts his $10,000 traditional IRA (his only IRA) to a Roth IRA in 2009. Andy's only contribution to his traditional IRA was a rollover of qualified plan assets, so the entire $10,000 is taxable at conversion. In 2010, Andy requests a distribution of $1,000. The distribution is nonqualified because neither requirement for a qualified distribution (five-year holding period and a qualifying reason) is satisfied. The distribution returns some of Andy's conversion contribution and is not taxable. (The Roth IRA ordering rules require that contributions be returned first; see Q 5:40.) However, since the conversion contribution was held in the Roth IRA for less than five years and no Code Section 72(t) exception applies, Andy must pay an additional tax of $100 (10 percent of $1,000).

Example 2. Rose converts her $20,000 traditional IRA (her only IRA) to a Roth IRA in 2009. Rose's traditional IRA was a nondeductible IRA consisting of $15,000 in after-tax contributions and $5,000 in earnings. Although Rose does not meet any exception to the 10 percent additional tax on early distributions, she takes a complete distribution of the $20,000 shortly after converting. Rose will be subject to the 10 percent penalty on $5,000, the amount includable in income as part of the conversion. Rose will not, however, be subject to the 10 percent penalty on the return of the $15,000 that is not includable in income as part of the conversion.

Q 5:32 What circumstances allow conversion contributions to be returned without the 10 percent additional tax applying?

The 10 percent additional tax *never* applies to these distributions of conversion contributions from a Roth IRA:

- Any qualified distribution of any conversion contribution
- Any nonqualified distribution of a conversion contribution that was nondeductible when contributed to the traditional IRA
- Any nonqualified distribution of a conversion contribution that was taxed in the conversion transaction, if a Code Section 72(t) exception applies
- Any nonqualified distribution of a conversion contribution that was taxed in the conversion transaction, if the distribution is made after the close of that contribution's five-year holding period in the Roth IRA

[I.R.C. § 408A(d)(3)(F); Treas. Reg. § 1.408A-6, Q&A-5, Q&A-8, and Q&A-10, Examples 6 & 9]

Example 1. Pete made a conversion contribution from a traditional IRA to a Roth IRA (his first Roth IRA) on February 25, 2006, and made a regular contribution for 2005 on the same date. For penalty purposes, the five-year holding period of the conversion contribution began on January 1, 2006. For qualified distribution purposes, the five-year holding period for Pete's Roth

IRA began on January 1, 2005. On January 3, 2010, Pete takes a complete distribution from the Roth IRA that qualifies as a first-time homebuyer distribution. The distribution is a qualified distribution that is not includable in Pete's income. Nor does the 10 percent penalty apply, because a qualified first-time homebuyer distribution is one of the 10 exceptions to the penalty.

Example 2. Margo, age 35, makes a $5,000 conversion contribution to her first Roth IRA on April 1, 2009. She makes no further contributions. On January 1, 2014, the value of the account has grown to $7,300, and Margo withdraws $5,000 to pay for a vacation. The distribution is nonqualified, but no amount is includable in Margo's income because the distribution is treated under the allocation rules as a return of the 2009 conversion contribution. Nor does the 10 percent penalty apply, because the five-year holding period for the conversion contribution ended on December 31, 2013, the day before the distribution.

Q 5:33 Is the special rule for premature Roth IRA distributions of conversion amounts altered if those amounts are kept in a separate Roth conversion IRA?

No. The 10 percent additional tax applies to premature distributions of conversion amounts whether or not the conversion amounts are placed in a separate Roth conversion IRA.

Q 5:34 May an individual complete a conversion, wait five years, and then take a full distribution of the conversion amount from the Roth IRA free of taxes and penalties?

Yes. Funds in a traditional IRA, which are relatively inaccessible, can be made far more accessible by converting them to a Roth IRA and waiting five years for a withdrawal. The regular income tax applies in either case (whether there is a simple distribution from the traditional IRA or a conversion), but the 10 percent additional tax is completely avoided.

Example. Edward is age 40 in 2009. He has $50,000 in a deductible traditional IRA that he expects to use to start a business. He is advised that none of the exceptions to the 10 percent additional tax will apply to the withdrawal. In 2009, Edward converts the traditional IRA to a Roth IRA and pays income tax on the conversion. On January 1, 2014, Edward takes his first distribution—$50,000—from the Roth IRA, which is now worth $60,000. The distribution only returns the previously taxed conversion contribution (see Q 5:40) and is excluded from income. The additional tax does not apply because the five-year holding requirement for the conversion contribution has been fulfilled.

Instead, Edward could leave the funds in the traditional IRA and simply withdraw them in 2014. That would defer the regular tax until 2014, but at the cost of the additional tax—an expense of $5,000 (10 percent of $50,000) that he does not have to pay using the conversion strategy.

Q 5:35 When does the five-year holding period begin for each conversion contribution?

The five-year holding period for a conversion contribution begins on January 1 of the year when that conversion occurred. [Treas. Reg. § 1.408A-6, Q&A-5(c)] The holding period of each contribution must be separately tracked. Making a conversion contribution does not, however, restart the five-year holding period that applies to determine whether distributions are qualified or nonqualified.

Example 1. In 2009, Stephanie converts her traditional IRA to a Roth IRA (Roth IRA-1) at Penny Bank. In 2010, Stephanie changes jobs and receives a distribution from her 401(k) plan that she rolls over to a traditional IRA. Later in 2010, she converts this new traditional IRA into a Roth IRA at Nickel Bank (Roth IRA-2). The 2009 conversion contribution is subject to a five-year holding period that begins on January 1, 2009, and ends on December 31, 2013. The holding period for the 2010 conversion contribution begins on January 1, 2010, and ends on December 31, 2014. However, the five-year holding period that applies for qualified distribution purposes begins on January 1, 2009, and applies to both Roth IRAs.

Example 2. Max establishes a Roth IRA in 2006 at Anchor Bank and immediately makes a $2,000 regular contribution. In 2007, he converts an existing traditional IRA into a Roth IRA at Safeway Credit Union. In 2008, he contributes $4,000 to a new Roth IRA at Mutual Funds, Inc. In 2009, Max converts another traditional IRA to a Roth IRA at Big Insurance Co. All of Max's Roth IRAs at Anchor Bank, Safeway Credit Union, Mutual Funds, Inc., and Big Insurance Co. share the same five-year holding period that begins in 2006 for qualified distribution purposes.

Q 5:36 How is the five-year holding period for conversion contributions determined if contributions from different-year conversions are commingled?

The five-year holding period is determined the same way, whether contributions from conversions that occur in different years are kept separate or are combined. Each conversion amount has its own five-year holding period that starts in the year of the conversion. [Treas. Reg. § 1.408A-6, Q&A-2, Q&A-4, Q&A-5] Separate accounting is required (using Form 8606, Nondeductible IRAs), but the assets themselves do not have to be separated. (See chapter 7 for discussion of Form 8606.)

Example. Denis completes a conversion from a traditional IRA to a Roth IRA in 2009. The five-year holding period begins in 2009. Denis completes a second conversion in 2011 and contributes the assets into the same Roth IRA. Denis's five-year holding period for purposes of qualified distributions begins in 2009 for both the 2009 and the 2011 conversion amounts. If Denis had maintained separate Roth conversion IRAs for the 2009 and 2011 conversion amounts, it would not have made any difference. For purposes of nonqualified distributions, however, Denis's five-year holding period begins in 2009 for the 2009 conversion amount and in 2011 for the 2011 conversion amount.

Q 5:37   If conversion contributions are segregated from regular contributions in separate Roth IRAs, is the five-year holding period for conversion contributions affected?

No. The five-year holding period is determined the same way whether annual contributions and conversion contributions are commingled in the same Roth IRA or kept separate.

Allocating Roth IRA Distributions for Tax Purposes

Q 5:38   How are the components of a nonqualified Roth IRA distribution allocated to determine their tax consequences?

The Code and Treasury regulations provide ordering and aggregation rules for determining the order in which regular contributions, taxable and nontaxable portions of conversion contributions, and earnings are returned in Roth IRA distributions.

Q 5:39   How does a Roth IRA owner keep track of contributions versus earnings in a Roth IRA?

A Roth IRA owner should save his or her Forms 5498, IRA Contribution Information, to keep track of Roth IRA contribution amounts.

Ordering Rules for Distributions

Q 5:40   What are the basic ordering rules for distributions from Roth IRAs?

Distributions from Roth IRAs are taken from contributions first and then from earnings, in the following order:

1. Direct (annual) contributions;
2. Conversion contributions—taken into account on a first-in, first-out basis, with the taxable portion (the amount required to be included in gross income because of conversion) distributed first, and the nontaxable portion (the nontaxable basis at the time of conversion) distributed second; and
3. Earnings.

[I.R.C. § 408A(d)(4)(B)]

Q 5:41   Which contribution is returned first from a nonqualified Roth IRA distribution?

When an individual takes a nonqualified distribution from a Roth IRA, his or her original contribution amount is returned first (i.e., before any earnings) for purposes of calculating penalties and taxes. [Treas. Reg. § 1.408A-6, Q&A-8]

Q 5:42   Why is the return of contributions first in a distribution from a Roth IRA significant?

The significance of the rule that calls for the return of contributions first in a distribution from a Roth IRA is that it gives the Roth IRA owner the ability to access the principal tax free and penalty free at any time and for any purpose. Many individuals object to making a commitment to retirement planning because most retirement plans trap assets until retirement or penalize early distributions. The Roth IRA overcomes that objection. If an emergency strikes or an opportunity arises, a Roth IRA owner may retrieve the amount of his or her principal.

Example. Dillon, age 30, contributes $5,000 to his Roth IRA in both 2008 and 2009. In 2009 Dillon takes a distribution of $10,000. His distribution will not be subject to taxes or penalties, because it is simply a return of his original contribution amount of $10,000. If Dillon withdrew his Roth IRA accumulated earnings of $150 as well, he would be subject to taxes and the 10 percent premature distribution penalty on the earnings amount (unless an exception applied).

Q 5:43   Are conversion contributions distributed from a Roth IRA before earnings?

Yes. All contributions—annual and conversion—are distributed from a Roth IRA before earnings (see Q 5:40).

Q 5:44   Are any particular conversion amounts returned first in a distribution from a Roth IRA?

Yes. Conversion amounts in a Roth IRA are returned on a first-in, first-out basis. [I.R.C. § 408A(d)(4)(B)]

Example. Karen converts her $10,000 traditional IRA to a Roth IRA in 2008. In 2009 she changes jobs and rolls over $25,000 from her qualified plan to a traditional IRA. Later in 2009, Karen converts that IRA, worth $26,000 at the time of conversion, to a Roth IRA. In 2010 Karen takes a distribution of $12,000. The distribution is considered to have come first from Karen's 2008 conversion amount—$10,000; the next $2,000 is considered to come from Karen's 2009 conversion amount.

Aggregation Rules for Distributions

Q 5:45   How are contributions and distributions grouped to determine the component parts of a single Roth IRA distribution?

These aggregation rules apply to the ordering of Roth IRA distributions:

1. All distributions from any of an individual's Roth IRAs made within a single year are treated as a single distribution. [Treas. Reg. § 1.408A-6, Q&A-9(a)]

2. Distributions are treated as occurring at the close of the year. This means that the earnings and contributions for the entire year are taken into account when allocating a distribution among the various sources.

3. To determine the total amount of regular contributions available for a distribution, an individual's regular contributions for that distribution year to all of his or her Roth IRAs are aggregated, and the sum is added to the undistributed total regular contributions made for prior taxable years. Regular contributions for a taxable year include contributions made in the following taxable year that are identified as made for the taxable year. [Treas. Reg. § 1.408A-6, Q&A-9(b)]

4. All conversion contributions made during the same taxable year to any of the individual's Roth IRAs are aggregated. [Treas. Reg. § 1.408A-6, Q&A-9(c)]

5. A distribution from an individual's Roth IRA that is rolled over to another Roth IRA of the individual is disregarded for purposes of determining the amount of both contributions and distributions. [Treas. Reg. § 1.408A-6, Q&A-9(d)]

6. Any amount distributed as a corrective distribution (including net income) is disregarded in determining the amount of contributions, earnings, and distributions. [Treas. Reg. § 1.408A-6, Q&A-9(e)]

7. If an individual recharacterizes a contribution made to a traditional IRA by transferring it to a Roth IRA, the contribution is treated as contributed to the Roth IRA on the same date and for the same taxable year that the contribution was made to the traditional IRA. [Treas. Reg. § 1.408A-6, Q&A-9(f)]

8. If an individual recharacterizes a regular or conversion contribution made to a Roth IRA by transferring the contribution to a traditional IRA, both the contribution to the Roth IRA and the recharacterizing transfer are disregarded in determining the contributions and distributions for the taxable year for which the original contribution was made to the Roth IRA. [Treas. Reg. § 1.408A-6, Q&A-9(g)]

9. If a contribution is made and then recharacterized, the effect of income or loss occurring after the contribution and before the recharacterization is disregarded. [Treas. Reg. § 1.408A-6, Q&A-9(h)]

Q 5:46   How are annual contributions returned in a distribution from a Roth IRA when an individual establishes multiple Roth IRAs?

The number of Roth IRAs established does not affect how Roth IRA annual contributions are returned in a distribution. Annual contributions are always returned before conversion contributions and earnings. [I.R.C. § 408A(d)(4)(B)(i)]

Example 1. Jennifer makes a $4,000 Roth IRA contribution at ABC Bank in 2007. In 2008 she makes a $5,000 Roth IRA contribution at XYZ Credit Union. In 2009 Jennifer's balance in ABC Bank has grown to $9,300 from interest payments, and she takes a distribution of $6,300. Jennifer will not owe taxes or penalties on the $6,300 distribution, because her contributions to all Roth IRAs totaled $9,000 and she has taken a distribution of only $6,300. Jennifer still has $2,700 in contributions (basis) remaining before taxes and penalties may apply to her Roth IRA distributions.

Example 2. Marie converted a $20,000 traditional IRA to a Roth IRA in 2005 and a $15,000 traditional IRA (in which she had a basis of $2,000) to another Roth IRA in 2006. She made no other contributions. In 2010, Marie takes a $30,000 nonqualified distribution. The distribution is treated as made from $20,000 of the 2005 conversion contribution and from $10,000 of the 2006 conversion contribution that was includable in gross income at conversion. As a result, for 2010 no amount is includable in gross income; however, because $10,000 is allocable to a conversion contribution made within the previous five taxable years, that amount is subject to the 10 percent premature distribution penalty under Code Section 72(t) as if the amount were includable in gross income for 2010, unless an exception applies. The result would be the same no matter which of Marie's Roth IRAs made the distribution.

Example 3. The facts are the same as those in Example 2, except that the $30,000 distribution occurs after Marie attains age 59½ and is therefore a qualified distribution. The result is the same as in Example 2, except that no amount is subject to the 10 percent premature distribution penalty under Code Section 72(t).

Q 5:47 How are nondeductible traditional IRA contributions that have been converted to a Roth IRA returned when only a partial distribution is taken from the Roth IRA?

Amounts that were includable in income as a result of the conversion are returned first in a distribution from a Roth IRA; these are the deductible contributions to the traditional IRA and the earnings that were taxed in the conversion. Amounts that were not includable in income as a result of the conversion (nondeductible contributions to the traditional IRA) are returned next from the Roth IRA. Earnings are returned last. [I.R.C. § 408A(d)(4)(B)]

Example. Diane converts her $20,000 traditional IRA (her only IRA) to a Roth IRA in 2009. Her traditional IRA consisted of $15,000 in nondeductible (after-tax) contributions and $5,000 in taxable earnings, so only the earnings were taxed at the time of conversion. Two years later, Diane takes a $6,000 distribution from the Roth IRA, and none of the exceptions to the 10 percent additional tax apply. The distribution returns a previously taxed conversion contribution, so it is excluded from Diane's gross income. But since the first $5,000 of the distribution was not taxed until the conversion, that amount is subject to the additional tax (10 percent of $5,000, or $500).

Post-Death Distributions

Q 5:48   What happens to the assets in a Roth IRA upon the death of the owner?

When a Roth IRA owner dies, the assets in the Roth IRA pass to the named beneficiaries. The trust or custodial agreement generally provides the rules concerning the naming of beneficiaries. Most trustees and custodians provide forms that request information concerning primary and contingent beneficiaries who will receive the assets in the event of the IRA owner's death.

The most common approach for trustees and custodians is to allow for the naming of one or more primary and contingent beneficiaries and to assign a percentage to each of the beneficiaries. The primary beneficiaries will receive all the assets unless all the primary beneficiaries predecease the Roth IRA owner. Generally, if one or more of the primary beneficiaries predecease the owner, the deceased primary beneficiary's share is reallocated among the surviving primary beneficiaries on a pro rata basis. A less common approach is to provide that if a primary beneficiary predeceases the owner, that beneficiary's share is given to his or her heirs (per stirpes). If no beneficiaries survive the owner or none are named, the assets generally are payable to the estate.

Practice Pointer. An individual concerned with beneficiary issues should carefully read the trust or custodial agreement for the Roth IRA. If appropriate, an attorney can draft a special beneficiary designation to be used with a standard Roth IRA agreement. The trustee or custodian would have to agree to accept the designation.

Q 5:49   How are the minimum distribution rules applied to Roth IRA beneficiaries?

The Roth IRA follows the traditional IRA rules concerning RMDs to beneficiaries, except the rules apply as though the Roth IRA owner had died before his or her required beginning date, and no RMD is distributed for the year of the owner's death. [Treas. Reg. § 1.408A-6, Q&A-14]

Consequently, the distribution period for the Roth IRA depends on the identity of the IRA beneficiary or beneficiaries as of September 30 of the year following the year of the Roth IRA owner's death. [Treas. Reg. § 1.401(a)(9)-3; Treas. Reg. § 1.401(a)(9)-4, Q&A-5, Q&A-6, Q&A-7] (For distributions after the beneficiary's death, see Qs 4:43–4:48.)

1. If the owner's surviving spouse is the sole beneficiary, the spouse has several options:

   a. The spouse may treat the Roth IRA as his or her own, or roll over the decedent's Roth IRA to one that is titled in the spouse's name. This is the way for the spouse to opt out the RMD requirements altogether, since an owner is not required to take RMDs from a Roth IRA. It is only an option if the spouse has the unlimited right to withdraw amounts from the Roth IRA. [Treas. Reg. § 1.408A-6, Q&A-14(b); Treas. Reg. § 1.408-8, Q&A-5(a)]

  b. The spouse may elect to have the decedent's Roth IRA distributed according to the five-year rule—i.e., a full distribution by December 31 of the fifth calendar year following the year of the owner's death. [IRS Publication 590, *Individual Retirement Arrangements (IRAs)* 2008 (see Appendix A)]

  c. The spouse may commence RMDs by the end of the year in which the owner would have attained age 70½ had he or she survived. For any year, the RMD would be calculated by dividing the prior year-end Roth IRA balance by the spouse's recalculated life expectancy, based on the spouse's age on his or her birthday in the distribution year and determined using the Single Life Table (see Example 2 in Q 4:63 for details). [Treas. Reg. § 1.408A-6, Q&A-14; IRS Publication 590, *Individual Retirement Arrangements (IRAs)* 2008 (see Appendix A)]

2. If the sole beneficiary is an individual other than the surviving spouse, the beneficiary has two options:

  a. The beneficiary may elect to have the IRA fully distributed according to the five-year rule. [Treas. Reg. § 1.401(a)(9)-3, Q&A-4; Treas. Reg. § 1.401(a)(9)-5, Q&A-5(b)]

  b. If the election is not made, RMDs would commence by the end of the calendar year following the year of the owner's death. RMDs would be distributed over a fixed distribution period—the beneficiary's life expectancy, as determined using the Single Life Table and based on the beneficiary's age on the birthday in the year after the calendar year of the owner's death. To calculate the RMD for any year, the applicable distribution period would be reduced by one for each calendar year elapsed since the year after the year of the owner's death, and the prior year-end Roth IRA value would be divided by the result (see example in Q 4:45 for details). [Treas. Reg. § 1.401(a)(9)-5, Q&A-5(b)]

3. If there are multiple individual beneficiaries, RMDs are determined according to the method in paragraph 2, except that only the life expectancy of the oldest beneficiary is compared to that of the owner. (See Q 4:68 for details.)

Note. If the decedent's Roth IRA is split into separate Roth IRAs by December 31 of the year following the death, the life expectancy of each individual beneficiary may be used. (See Q 4:87.)

4. If any beneficiary is not an individual (e.g., the decedent's estate or a charity), and the non-individual beneficiary's interest has not been cashed out by September 30 of the year following the year of the Roth IRA owner's death, the Roth IRA must be fully distributed according to the five-year rule. [Treas. Reg. § 1.401(a)(9)-3, Q&A-4] (See Q 4:29.)

Q 5:50   What are the default distribution presumptions for a Roth IRA?

If the sole designated beneficiary of a Roth IRA is the surviving spouse who has the unlimited right to make withdrawals, the default presumption is that the spouse will treat the IRA as his or her own. For any other designated beneficiary, distributions are automatically based on the oldest beneficiary's life expectancy, unless the five-year method is elected or the IRA expressly prohibits life expectancy distributions. If no beneficiary is designated, distributions are made according to the five-year method. [T.D. 8987 (Apr. 16, 2002); IRS Form 5305-RA, Article V]

> **Note.** Prototype documents may have different default provisions. The List of Required Modifications and Information Package (LRM) that the IRS issued in May 2007 contains sample language for post-death distributions that would alter the presumption of Form 5305-RA for a surviving spouse. Under the LRM provision, the default method for a surviving spouse who is the designated beneficiary would be distributions based on life expectancy.

Q 5:51   Are Roth IRA beneficiaries affected by the suspension of the RMD rules for 2009?

Yes, the suspension of the RMD rules for 2009 also applies to Roth IRA beneficiaries. Accordingly, any Roth IRA beneficiary may skip the RMD for 2009, and calendar year 2009 is disregarded for a Roth IRA that is being distributed according to the five-year rule. [Notice 2009-9, 2009-5 I.R.B. 419]

> **Example.** Philip died in 2008, and his Roth IRA is being distributed to a charitable beneficiary according to the five-year rule. Normally, that would require a full distribution by the end of 2013, but because 2009 is now disregarded the distribution deadline is December 31, 2014.

Q 5:52   What is the penalty for failing to take a required minimum distribution?

The 50 percent excess accumulation penalty is imposed on the amount by which the RMD for any year exceeds the total distributions that were made. [I.R.C. § 4973]

Q 5:53   May a Roth IRA beneficiary satisfy the minimum distribution requirements by taking a distribution from another Roth IRA?

A beneficiary may *only* use a distribution from one Roth IRA to satisfy the RMD requirement of another Roth IRA if both Roth IRAs are inherited from the same decedent. [Treas. Reg. § 1.408A-6, Q&A-15]

Q 5:54   If distributions to a designated beneficiary have not commenced by December 31 of the year after the Roth IRA owner's year of death, is it too late to avoid the five-year rule?

Apparently not, based on Private Letter Ruling 200811028 (Mar. 14, 2008) (discussed in Q 4:40). The designated beneficiary should be able to remedy the missed RMDs and use the life expectancy method if all of the following conditions are satisfied:

1. Makeup distributions of all missed RMDs (as determined under the life expectancy method) are made, presumably before the last date for making a distribution under the five-year rule;

2. The beneficiary pays the 50 percent excise tax for each year in which there was an excess accumulation of untimely paid RMDs;

3. The IRA provisions do not prohibit distributions based on life expectancy; and

4. The beneficiary has not affirmatively elected the five-year method.

Q 5:55   If an eligible surviving spouse treats the decedent's Roth IRA as the spouse's own, is the owner's death a qualifying reason for distributions to the spouse?

No. In this case, the distribution is treated as coming from the individual's own Roth IRA and not the deceased spouse's Roth IRA. Consequently, a distribution must have one of the other qualifying reasons (age 59½, disability, or first-time home purchase) to be classified as a qualified distribution. [Treas. Reg. § 1.408A-6, Q&A-3]

Q 5:56   How should a surviving spouse younger than age 59½ take distributions from a Roth IRA?

It depends. If the spouse will not need to use the Roth IRA funds and the goal is to preserve capital for future generations, a spouse younger than 59½ should roll over the Roth IRA or elect to treat the decedent's Roth IRA as the spouse's own. Otherwise, it may be beneficial to continue treatment as the beneficiary and take RMDs based on the spouse's recalculated life expectancy. The death exception of Code Section 72(t) applies if beneficiary status is retained, making all distributions to the spouse exempt from the 10 percent additional tax. A rollover could still be done later, perhaps when the spouse reaches age 59½.

Example. Gina, age 40, dies, leaving all her Roth IRA assets to her husband, George, also age 40. George treats the Roth IRA as his own. George then needs to take a distribution. He will owe the 10 percent premature distribution penalty because it is his Roth IRA and he is under age 59½ (and does not meet any other exception). If George had left the assets in Gina's Roth IRA and taken a distribution from the Roth IRA as a beneficiary, the distribution would have met the death distribution exception to the 10 percent premature distribution penalty.

Q 5:57   May a trustee or custodian that uses an IRS model form expand the spouse beneficiary's distribution options?

Possibly. The IRS requires model form users to adopt forms that are word-for-word identical. Yet the model form allows users to add provisions after the model articles, and the instructions even state that trustees and custodians may add language concerning the "beginning date of distributions." [IRS Form 5305-RA and Instructions]

Q 5:58   May a beneficiary take a full distribution from a Roth IRA?

Yes. The RMD rules are designed to ensure that assets do not remain in a tax-protected Roth IRA for too long a time. A beneficiary is always free to increase the distribution amount to an amount greater than the RMD amount.

Q 5:59   May the beneficiary of a traditional IRA convert it to a Roth IRA?

No, unless the sole beneficiary is the surviving spouse and the spouse has an unlimited right to withdraw amounts from the Roth IRA. Starting in 2010, any spouse may directly convert an inherited traditional IRA to a Roth IRA. Before then, the spouse may only do so if the eligibility requirements are met for conversion. A nonspouse beneficiary of a traditional IRA is not eligible to convert the inherited interest to a Roth IRA. [I.R.C. §§ 402(c)(11), 402(f)(2)(A)]

Q 5:60   Is post-mortem planning useful for Roth IRAs?

Yes. Post-mortem planning, using the same techniques that are available to traditional IRAs, may also be helpful with Roth IRAs (see Qs 4:86–4:95).

Q 5:61   How are the components of a Roth IRA allocated to multiple beneficiaries?

Each component of a Roth IRA (see Q 5:40) is allocated to each beneficiary on a pro rata basis. [Treas. Reg. § 1.408A-6, Q&A-11] The allocation determines the tax consequences if a nonqualified distribution is received.

Example. Dean, a Roth IRA owner, dies in 2008. His Roth IRA contains a regular contribution of $4,000, a conversion contribution of $6,000, and earnings of $1,000. Dean had named his four children as equal beneficiaries of the Roth IRA. Dee, Dean's youngest child, takes an immediate distribution of $2,500. It will be deemed to consist of $1,000 of regular contributions (.25 × $4,000) and $1,500 of conversion contributions (.25 × $6,000). Since Dee's share of the contributions has now been entirely distributed to her, all future distributions to Dee will include only earnings.

Miscellaneous Taxation Issues

Q 5:62   If property is distributed from a Roth IRA, how is its basis determined?

The basis of property distributed from a Roth IRA is its fair market value on the date of distribution, whether or not it is a qualified distribution.

Example. On the date of its distribution from a Roth IRA, one share of stock in XYZ Corp. has a fair market value of $40. For purposes of determining gain or loss on a subsequent sale, the XYZ share has a basis of $40. [Treas. Reg. § 1.408A-6, Q&A-16]

Q 5:63   What are the federal income tax consequences if an owner transfers his or her Roth IRA to another individual by gift?

A Roth IRA owner's transfer of his or her Roth IRA to another individual by gift constitutes an assignment of the owner's rights under the Roth IRA. At the time of the gift, the assets of the Roth IRA are deemed to be distributed to the owner and, accordingly, are treated as no longer held in a Roth IRA. [Treas. Reg. § 1.408A-6, Q&A-19]

Q 5:64   When does an IRA owner recognize a loss on a Roth IRA investment?

The owner of a Roth IRA may only recognize a loss on the investment when all amounts have been distributed from all of his or her Roth IRA accounts. The amount of loss recognized on the final distribution is the aggregate amount of the owner's unrecovered basis (i.e., contributions that were not returned in any distribution). The owner may claim the loss as a miscellaneous itemized deduction, subject to the applicable 2 percent-of-adjusted-gross-income limit. The loss must be added back to taxable income for purposes of calculating the alternative minimum tax. [IRS Publication 590, *Individual Retirement Arrangements (IRAs)* 2008 (see Appendix A)]

Q 5:65   Is basis in the Roth IRA affected if the owner sells stock or securities at a loss, and the Roth IRA acquires substantially identical securities within 30 days before or after the sale?

If the individual is not a securities dealer acting in the ordinary course of business, the transaction is considered a wash sale, the Roth IRA owner's loss is disallowed under Code Section 1091, and his or her basis in the stock or securities cannot be added to his or her in the IRA. As a result, the owner's loss on the investment is never allowed, even on liquidation of the Roth IRA. [Rev. Rul. 2008-5, 2008-3 I.R.B. 271]

Caution. A transaction such as this may be a prohibited transaction that could invalidate the IRA (see Q 1:54). The IRS expressly warned in Revenue Ruling 2008-5 that the ruling does not address issues under Code Section 4975.

Withholding

Q 5:66 Do the withholding rules apply to Roth IRA distributions?

Yes, even though many Roth IRA distributions are not taxable. Roth IRAs follow the same federal income tax withholding rules that apply to traditional IRAs. [Treas. Reg. § 1.408A-6, Q&A-12]

Q 5:67 May an individual waive federal income tax withholding?

Yes, recipients of Roth IRA distributions may waive federal income tax withholding. Many would do so because the tax on nonqualified distributions is often low (see Q 5:24). An individual completes Form W-4P, Withholding Certificate for Pension or Annuity Payments (or an acceptable substitute form), to waive federal income tax withholding.

Q 5:68 What rate of withholding applies to Roth IRAs?

The trustee or custodian of a Roth IRA must withhold 10 percent of the total distribution unless the Roth IRA owner has completed a withholding form (Form W-4P). If the owner completes Form W-4P, he or she may elect to have tax withheld at a rate of 10 percent or at any rate up to 100 percent. Alternatively, the owner may elect to waive withholding altogether. [I.R.C. § 3405]

Q 5:69 Will overwithholding occur in the case of the Roth IRA?

Too much tax may be withheld if the distributee does not appropriately instruct the Roth IRA custodian. Many IRA custodians allow a distributee to choose the precise percentage of tax to be withheld from a Roth IRA distribution. Others are more rigid and permit either no withholding or withholding of 10 percent or more, but nothing in between. In either case, a distributee is well advised to estimate the tax bill that the distribution will generate, calculate it as a percentage of the total, and adjust the withholding instruction accordingly.

Example. Glenda, age 60, converts her deductible traditional IRA containing $50,000 to a Roth IRA in 2007. The account grows to a value of $63,500 after two years. In 2009 (i.e., before meeting the five-year holding period requirement), Glenda takes a complete distribution. She will owe taxes on the $13,500 in earnings, and because Glenda is in the 28 percent tax bracket she would like to have $3,780 withheld from her Roth IRA distribution. If her Roth IRA custodian allows her to do so, Glenda will ask for that amount to be withheld, or request 6 percent withholding if a percentage must be stated (that would result in $3,810 of withheld tax). If the custodian requires her to either waive withholding altogether or elect to have 10 percent or more of the distribution withheld, Glenda should request two distributions—one in the amount of $3,780 (and request 100 percent withholding) and one for the remaining balance (and waive withholding).

Q 5:70   Is withholding necessary on trustee-to-trustee transfers between Roth IRAs?

No federal income tax withholding is required in the case of transfers between Roth IRAs. Accordingly, a Roth IRA owner need not complete Form W-4P to waive withholding in such an instance.

State Law Issues

Q 5:71   Do state income taxes apply to the Roth IRA?

The Roth IRA law exempts qualified distributions only from *federal* income tax. For state tax purposes, some states conform to the treatment under federal tax law but others do not. Each state's law must be consulted to determine how it applies to Roth IRA distributions. (See chapter 14 for further discussion.)

Chapter 6

Rollovers

Martin Fleisher, Esq.
Jo Ann Lippe, Esq.

Severe tax ramifications flow from the complicated legal restrictions that apply to rollovers. Those difficult and important issues are explored thoroughly in this chapter. Although the complex rollover rules vary somewhat depending on whether a rollover is made between IRAs of the same type, between IRAs of different types, or between an IRA and a qualified plan, the most basic rule applies to nearly all rollovers (other than direct rollovers): unless an exception applies, an individual has only 60 days from receipt of an IRA or qualified plan distribution to complete the rollover.

Overview

Q 6:1   What is an IRA rollover used for?

A rollover is basically a method of moving an individual's IRA or qualified plan assets from one financial institution to another or from one type of retirement plan to another. A rollover generally moves assets without changing the character of the account; in some cases, however, a rollover is meant to change the character of the account. All rollovers—with one exception—are tax free and penalty free. Direct rollovers from qualified plans to Roth IRAs (which have been allowed since the start of 2008) are taxed like conversions if the requirements are met.

Q 6:2   What are the different types of rollovers?

The most common types of rollovers are the following:

Traditional IRA to Traditional IRA. This type of rollover allows for the movement of assets in one traditional IRA to another.

Roth IRA to Roth IRA. This type of rollover allows for the movement of assets in one Roth IRA to another Roth IRA. The rules for Roth IRA rollovers are generally the same as those for traditional IRA rollovers.

Coverdell ESA (Coverdell Education Savings Account) to Coverdell ESA. This type of rollover allows the responsible individual to transfer assets from one IRA trustee or custodian to another on behalf of the designated beneficiary (see chapter 13).

Rollover to New Designated Beneficiary. The assets in a Coverdell ESA may be rolled over to a new designated beneficiary in the same family.

SIMPLE IRA to SIMPLE IRA. This type of rollover allows for the movement of assets in a SIMPLE IRA to another SIMPLE IRA. (SIMPLE is the acronym for savings incentive match plan for employees.)

SIMPLE IRA to Traditional IRA. Assets in a SIMPLE IRA may be rolled over to a traditional IRA after the participant in the SIMPLE meets a two-year holding period. An individual may want to accomplish such a rollover to combine SIMPLE IRA assets with traditional IRA assets.

SIMPLE IRA to Qualified Plan. Assets distributed from a SIMPLE IRA to an individual may be rolled over to a qualified plan after the participant in the SIMPLE IRA meets a two-year holding period.

Qualified Plan to IRA. Assets distributed from a qualified plan to an individual may usually be rolled over to an IRA. If the rollover is not a direct rollover (see below), the distributing plan will generally withhold tax at a rate of 20 percent on the amount of the distribution that is eligible for rollover.

Qualified Plan to Traditional IRA Direct Rollover. The assets distributed from a qualified plan may be directly rolled over to an IRA. A direct rollover is different from a rollover because in a direct rollover the individual never gains control of the assets. The assets are moved directly from the qualified plan trustee or custodian to the IRA trustee or custodian.

Qualified Plan to Roth IRA Direct Rollover. A direct rollover of assets from a qualified plan to a Roth IRA is permitted if the requirements for conversion are met.

Designated Roth Account to Roth IRA. Assets held in a designated Roth account (DRAC) within a qualified plan under Code Section 402A may be rolled over to a Roth IRA.

IRA to Qualified Plan and Other Plans. Assets held in a traditional IRA may be rolled over to a qualified plan, a tax-sheltered annuity under Section 403(b) of the Code, or a Section 457 governmental plan. None of these plans, however, is required to accept rollovers.

Rollover for Spouse Beneficiary to Treat Inherited IRA as Own. A spouse beneficiary of any type of IRA may treat the account as his or her own after the death of the IRA owner by rolling over the account to an account in his or her own name.

Rollover to Inherited IRA for Nonspouse Beneficiary. Assets are transferred to an IRA and held for a beneficiary whose rights are not the same as an owner's.

Traditional or Roth IRA to Health Savings Account. Eligible individuals are allowed a one-time-only rollover of IRA funds to a health savings account.

Q 6:3   How do a rollover, a direct rollover, and a transfer differ from one another?

An individual may move assets between various types of retirement plans by means of a rollover, a direct rollover, or a transfer. Each method has vastly different reporting and tax consequences. In addition, traditional IRAs may be converted to Roth IRAs using a method similar to the trustee-to-trustee transfer but requiring compliance with rules that are somewhat similar to those for a rollover (see chapter 3).

Rollover. A rollover occurs when an individual takes a distribution from his or her IRA or from a qualified plan and transfers the assets to another IRA or another qualified plan.

Direct Rollover. In a direct rollover, assets are moved directly from an employer's qualified plan, a deferred compensation plan of a state or local government (Section 457 plan), or a tax-sheltered annuity (Section 403(b) plan) to a traditional IRA. A direct rollover, which is similar to a transfer in some ways, is treated as a rollover even though the participant never receives the distribution. The participant does, however, direct where the distribution is to go and may even deliver the check.

Transfer. A transfer occurs when IRA assets are moved directly from one trustee or custodian to another trustee or custodian. The key feature distinguishing a transfer from a rollover is that in a transfer the individual never receives direct access to the assets being moved. At the direction of the IRA owner, the current IRA trustee or custodian sends the original IRA's assets directly to the new IRA trustee or custodian. If a check for the assets is issued, the check is made payable to the new IRA trustee or custodian as trustee or custodian for the individual's IRA. That procedure is significant; the reporting and tax rules that the Internal Revenue Service (IRS) imposes on transfers are often more lenient precisely because the assets are never within the control of the individual. For example, the 60-day turnaround requirement (see Q 6:6) is not applicable to transfers. Furthermore, transfers between like types of IRAs are generally not reported to the IRS.

Note. The terms *rollover* and *transfer* are often used interchangeably—in many cases, incorrectly.

Q 6:4   Why would an IRA owner want to roll over assets from one IRA to another IRA of the same type?

A rollover allows an IRA owner to move his or her assets to a new trustee or custodian. The decision to roll over assets from one IRA to another IRA of the same type generally is made because the owner is not satisfied with the investment performance of the original IRA or because the trustee or custodian has imposed new fees or terms unacceptable to the owner. Some owners carry out rollovers because they want to use their IRA funds outside the IRA during the 60-day period allowed for completing a rollover (see Q 6:6).

Q 6:5   What makes a trustee-to-trustee transfer a better choice than a rollover, and when may a rollover nevertheless be preferable?

One of the benefits of the trustee-to-trustee transfer is that there is no possibility of noncompliance with the 60-day rule or the 12-month rule (see Q 6:6). Accordingly, individuals are usually better served by having their IRA assets transferred directly via trustee-to-trustee transfer rather than via rollover.

A rollover is preferable when the IRA owner wants access to his or her assets during the 60 days immediately after the distribution or wants to transfer the funds as quickly as possible. Rollovers are usually quicker than trustee-to-trustee transfers.

Traditional IRA Rollovers and Transfers

Q 6:6 What are the rules for a rollover from a traditional IRA to a traditional IRA?

A rollover from one traditional IRA to another must be completed within 60 days of receipt of the distribution by the individual (60-day rule), and the individual is allowed only one rollover in each 12-month period (12-month rule). [I.R.C. §§ 408(d)(3)(A), 408(d)(3)(B)]

Q 6:7 Are there exceptions to the 60-day rule and the 12-month rule?

Yes, and they are:

1. The 60-day rule is automatically waived in certain cases involving error by the financial institution (see Q 6:18).

2. In certain hardship cases, the IRS waives the 60-day rule upon application by the taxpayer (see Q 6:19).

3. The rollover period is extended to 120 days and the 12-month rule does not apply to a qualified first-time homebuyer distribution if the funds are not used solely because of delay or cancellation of the contract (see Q 6:28).

4. A three-year rollover period applies to qualified hurricane distributions, qualified recovery assistance distributions, and qualified disaster recovery assistance distributions (see Qs 6:29, 6:30, 6:31).

5. An exception to the 60-day rule applies to frozen deposits, which are funds that cannot be withdrawn from a financial institution for certain reasons related to the bankruptcy or insolvency of a financial institution (see Q 6:32).

6. The 12-month rule does not apply to IRA distributions that the Federal Deposit Insurance Corporation (FDIC), as receiver for a failed custodial institution, initiates (see Q 6:33).

Operation of the Rollover Rules

Q 6:8 Is a direct rollover subject to the 60-day rule?

No. A direct rollover does not have to be made within 60 days of a distribution. For purposes of a direct rollover, the distribution and rollover are deemed to occur simultaneously; this makes the 60-day rule irrelevant. [Treas. Reg. § 1.402(c)-2, Q&A-1]

Q 6:9 If a rollover is not a direct rollover, when is the distribution deemed received for purposes of the 60-day rule?

The date on which a distribution is actually received is the start date of the 60-day period. [Treas. Reg. § 1.402(c)-2, Q&A-11] The end of the 60-day period may be adequately determined by postmark, but the IRS will not consider a distribution received by the employee on the date the transfer mailing is postmarked.

In one case, an employee was away on vacation, during which time his mail was being held at the post office. Promptly upon returning from vacation, the employee picked up his mail from the post office, and that date was deemed to be the date of receipt of the distribution. The decision noted that the mail was not picked up until the day after the employee's return from vacation because the employee had returned too late on his date of return to retrieve his mail. [Priv. Ltr. Rul. 8804014 (Oct. 27, 1987)]

In another case, a distribution check was received 10 months after it was issued because the trustee did not have the employee's correct address from the employer. Because the rollover was made 30 days after the check was finally received, it was timely. There was no indication that had the employee accidentally given an incorrect address the result would have been different. [Priv. Ltr. Rul. 8833043 (May 26, 1988)]

Q 6:10 When a distribution consists of more than one payment to the individual, how is the 60-day rule applied?

When separate payments are part of the same qualifying distribution, the 60-day rule is applied separately to each payment. [Treas. Reg. § 1.402(c)-2, Q&A-11]

Q 6:11 What rule applies when the last day of the 60-day period for completion of a rollover falls on a holiday or a weekend?

Although no clear rule exists, the Code provides that when the last day prescribed for performing any act falls on a Saturday, a Sunday, or a legal holiday, the performance of that act will be considered timely if it is performed on the next succeeding day that is not a Saturday, a Sunday, or a legal holiday. [I.R.C. § 7503]

Q 6:12 How is the 12-month period between rollovers determined?

The 12-month period during which a second rollover cannot be made starts on the date the IRA assets are distributed. [I.R.C. § 408(d)(3)(B)]

Example. Steve receives a distribution from his traditional IRA on December 5, 2009. He rolls over the money to another IRA on February 1, 2010. Steve may not make another rollover of the same IRA until December 6, 2010—the day after the 12-month period beginning on the date Steve received the distribution.

Q 6:13   How is the 12-month rule applied to an individual with more than one IRA?

The rule applies separately to each IRA owned by an individual. For example, suppose an individual has two IRAs, IRA-1 and IRA-2, and rolls over the assets of IRA-1 to a new IRA, IRA-3. That individual may roll over assets from IRA-2 to IRA-3, or to any other IRA (including IRA-1), within one year of the rollover distribution from IRA-1. The IRA owner cannot, however, within the one-year period, initiate another rollover that involves either IRA-1 or IRA-3. [IRS Publication 590, *Individual Retirement Arrangements (IRAs) 2008* (see Appendix A)]

Q 6:14   Does the suspension of minimum distribution requirements for 2009 mean that 2009 distributions may be returned without regard to the timing rules?

No. Distributions may be returned to IRAs but the normal rollover rules apply. Consequently, 2009 distributions that were made according to a systematic withdrawal program (e.g., on a quarterly or monthly basis) are each regarded separately, and only one of them made in 2009 may be returned to the same IRA or rolled over to another IRA. [I.R.C. § 408(d)(3)(B)]

Q 6:15   When an IRA is split into a number of IRAs under a trustee-to-trustee transfer but the trustee does not change, does such a transfer constitute a distribution or a rollover?

This is a rollover, not a taxable distribution. The trustee is not required to transfer assets to a different trustee in order to have the rollover rules apply. In Private Letter Ruling 8752061, an IRA owner who had four children directed the trustee to split the assets of the IRA among four new IRAs. The same bank to which the directions were issued continued as trustee. From the bank's point of view, such a procedure might amount to a mere bookkeeping transaction; however, in substance, a trustee-to-trustee transfer did occur. The IRS ruled that even though a new trustee was not named, four new IRAs were created, and the transaction was no more a distribution and new contribution than it would have been had the accounts been transferred to a new trustee. [Rev. Rul. 78-406, 1978-2 C.B. 157; Priv. Ltr. Ruls. 9331055 (May 13, 1993), 9226076 (Apr. 3, 1992), 8944058 (Aug. 10, 1989), 8752061 (Oct. 30, 1987)]

Q 6:16   Are rollovers from one traditional IRA to another traditional IRA allowed after the required beginning date for minimum distributions?

Yes, transfers from one traditional IRA to another traditional IRA are permitted at any time, but the RMD itself may not be rolled over. [I.R.C. § 402(c)]

Relief for Defective Rollovers

Q 6:17   What are the basic requirements to obtain an automatic or discretionary waiver of the 60-day rule?

The IRS extends the rollover period beyond 60 days in cases where failure to do so would be "against equity or good conscience, including casualty, disaster, or other events beyond the reasonable control of the individual." [I.R.C. § 408(d)(3)(I)] Revenue Procedure 2003-16 [2003-1 C.B. 359] sets forth guidance concerning the hardship cases for which the 60-day rule will be waived. Two categories of hardship cases exist: automatic waiver cases and cases for which a letter ruling must be obtained.

Q 6:18   What circumstances result in the automatic waiver of the 60-day rule?

The 60-day rule is automatically waived when four requirements are met: (1) the distribution occurred after 2001; (2) the taxpayer properly instructed the financial institution concerning the rollover and did everything it required; (3) solely because of error by the financial institution, the rollover was invalid; and (4) the rollover was completed within one year after the distribution. In all other cases, waivers must be granted in a letter ruling. [Rev. Proc. 2003-16, 2003-1 C.B. 359]

Q 6:19   What is the procedure to obtain a discretionary waiver of the 60-day rule?

To obtain a non-automatic waiver of the 60-day rule, the taxpayer must apply to the IRS for a letter ruling. The IRS considers all facts and circumstances related to the untimely rollover, including: errors by the financial institution; inability to complete a rollover because of death, disability, hospitalization, incarceration, restrictions imposed by a foreign country, or postal error; the intervention of a casualty or disaster; how the distributed funds were used before rollover; and the period of time since distribution.

The submission of a ruling request requires payment of a user fee and detailed paperwork concerning the retirement account and rollover circumstances. [Rev. Proc. 2009-8, 2009-1 I.R.B. 229] The paperwork can take many hours to complete and, in most cases, will involve additional professional fees. A variable user fee applies to such requests:

Rollover Amount	*User Fee*
Less than $50,000	$ 500
$50,000 or more, but less than $100,000	$1,500
$100,000 or more	$3,000

Since 2003, the IRS has been generous in granting waivers of the 60-day limit where (1) making a timely rollover was beyond the taxpayer's control or the taxpayer's mistakes were reasonable, and (2) the funds were available for rollover when the period expired. (See Qs 6:20–6:26 for discussion on how the IRS has ruled since it was granted authority to extend the 60-day rollover period.)

Q 6:20   How has the IRS ruled in cases relating to death of the IRA owner or another person?

The IRS has waived the 60-day deadline in several cases involving an IRA owner's death. In one case, an IRA owner withdrew funds from his IRA, parked them in a taxable account, and died less than 60 days later without completing the rollover. His widow discovered the problem some time later, but the IRS found her tardiness reasonable because she was in mourning and busy with funeral arrangements. [Priv. Ltr. Rul. 200415012 (Jan. 15, 2004)]

Waivers have been granted based on miscommunication between the surviving beneficiary and financial custodian. In one such case, a company that maintained IRAs was unaware an account owner had died seven months earlier and mailed to his address a routine form requesting updated personal information. The widow/beneficiary crossed out her husband's name, wrote "deceased [date], funds to go to [her name] IRA," changed the owner's personal information (date of birth, etc.) to describe herself, and returned the form. The company took it as a request to place the IRA funds in a taxable account established in her name as estate executor. Several months later, the widow learned from the accountant preparing the estate tax return that the new account was not an IRA. From her actions (substituting herself on the form as owner, leaving the funds untouched, and attempting to fix the error after discovery) the IRS discerned she meant to effect a distribution and rollover, and waived the deadline to allow her to complete the transaction. [Priv. Ltr. Rul. 200546048 (Nov. 18, 2005)]

In another case, the IRS showed leniency toward a surviving spouse who relied, to her detriment, on advice from the custodians of her deceased husband's investments. They advised her to cash in a particular investment without explaining it was an individual retirement annuity that she could roll into an IRA, and the IRS waived the 60-day rollover deadline. [Priv. Ltr. 200544030 (Nov. 4, 2005)]

Q 6:21   How has the IRS ruled in cases where failure to complete a rollover was related to disability or hospitalization?

In several cases the IRS has waived the 60-day rollover deadline for taxpayers either personally incapacitated by illness or disability or overwhelmed by the burden of caring for another person. One example of personal incapacity involves a 68-year-old retiree suffering from Alzheimer's disease who improperly withdrew IRA funds to help pay for a house. The IRS deemed the withdrawal beyond the taxpayer's reasonable control, and waived the 60-day limit to allow redeposit to an IRA. [Priv. Ltr. Rul. 200401025 (Nov. 5, 2003)] Other similar cases involve a taxpayer whose medical treatments interfered with timely completion of a rollover [Priv. Ltr. Rul. 200538029 (Sept. 23, 2005)]; a taxpayer whose psychiatric condition, which required in-patient monitoring, impaired her judgment and ability to make financial decisions [Priv. Ltr. Rul. 200602047 (Jan. 13, 2006)]; an individual with severe hearing loss who failed to use hearing aids at a meeting with his IRA custodian, with ensuing confusion regarding his intent [Priv. Ltr. Rul. 200410027 (Dec. 9, 2003)]; and taxpayers mentally impaired by strokes who were consequently confused about rollover requirements. [Priv. Ltr. Ruls. 200516021 (Apr. 22, 2005), 200507019 (Feb. 18, 2005), and 200603038 (Jan. 20, 2006)]

Other taxpayers have contended that they wished to complete a rollover but did not because they were preoccupied by a family member's medical crisis. One such taxpayer provided around-the-clock care for an elderly parent who was bedridden and suffered from dementia. The taxpayer withdrew funds from her IRA, intending to roll them over, but mistakenly deposited them to a non-IRA account two days after admitting her mother to the hospital for a serious condition. The IRS was satisfied the taxpayer intended a rollover because she never tapped the wrongly deposited funds and tried to correct the error as soon as her accountant discovered it. [Priv. Ltr. Rul. 200608025 (Feb. 24, 2006)] In another case, the IRS waived the deadline for a taxpayer who was preoccupied with caring for his severely disabled spouse and missed the 60-day rollover deadline by four days. [Priv. Ltr. Rul. 200516023 (Apr. 22, 2005)]

However, the IRS refused to waive the requirement for a taxpayer who claimed he missed the deadline because of concern about his daughter's delayed speech and motor skill development. The daughter's disability had been a concern for at least six months and continued throughout the rollover period, but the taxpayer still managed to carry out other financial transactions during the same time frame. The transactions included withdrawing a sum from his IRA several days before selling one beach rental property and purchasing another, using the amount withdrawn to fund closing costs, and depositing the entire check for the sale proceeds (which exceeded the IRA withdrawal) three weeks later without rolling any of it into an IRA. The IRS concluded that concern for his daughter did not excuse the father's failure to roll over the funds, because he had shown himself able to keep track of the other financial matters. [Priv. Ltr. Rul. 200540023 (Oct. 7, 2005)]

Q 6:22 In what situations has the IRS granted waivers because of errors or acts committed by financial institutions or other advisors?

Numerous private letter rulings concern errors and acts committed by financial institutions, ranging from mistakes, miscommunication, and bad advice to delay, unavailability, and misappropriation of funds. In all cases where a waiver was granted, the taxpayer could have completed a timely rollover but for the financial institution's negligence or erroneous action.

Mistake. Waivers were granted to allow rollovers past the 60-day limit where, for example, financial institutions improperly made IRA distributions [Priv. Ltr.

Ruls. 200401020 (Oct. 8, 2003), 200421008 (Feb. 27, 2004), 200524036 (June 17, 2005), 200551026 (Dec. 23, 2005)]; failed to follow the taxpayers' deposit or distribution instructions [Priv. Ltr. Ruls. 200401023 (Oct. 9, 2003), 200507020 (Feb. 18, 2005), 200550040 (Dec. 16, 2005), and 200608028 (Feb. 24, 2006)]; mistakenly accepted a distribution check that was clearly payable to another company [Priv. Ltr. Rul. 200546045 (Nov. 18, 2005)]; incorrectly prepared forms or mailed them to the wrong address [Priv. Ltr. Ruls. 200550041 (Dec. 16, 2005), 200549019 (Dec. 9, 2005), and 200545053 (Nov. 10, 2005)]; mailed the distribution check to the wrong address [Priv. Ltr. Ruls. 200550041 (Dec. 16, 2005)], 200549019 (Dec. 9, 2005)]; improperly withheld taxes [Priv. Ltr. Rul. 200527026 (July 8, 2005)]; or miscalculated the required minimum distribution (with waiver granted as to the excess) [Priv. Ltr. Ruls. 200443034 (Oct. 22, 2004), 200416015 (Jan. 22, 2004)].

Miscommunication. Miscommunication between the taxpayer and financial institution led to waivers in various rulings. [Priv. Ltr. Ruls. 200603034 (Jan. 20, 2006), 200551027 (Dec. 23, 2005), 200610030 (Mar. 10, 2006), 200542040 (Oct. 21, 2005)]

Bad advice or insufficient information. Rollover extensions were granted to taxpayers who relied on erroneous advice given by the financial institution [Priv. Ltr. Ruls. 200544026 (Nov. 4, 2005), 200610028 (Mar. 10, 2006), 200606052 (Feb. 10, 2006)]; by a financial advisor [Priv. Ltr. Ruls. 200609019 (Mar. 3, 2006), 200606053 (Feb. 10, 2006)], or by a government employee [Priv. Ltr. Rul. 200540022 (Oct. 7, 2005)]. In one case, a beneficiary/distributee received a waiver of the 60-day rollover rule because the distributing company failed to inform her the distribution came from an individual retirement annuity. [Priv. Ltr. Rul. 200602049 (Jan. 13, 2006)]

Delay or unavailability. Waivers were granted to taxpayers who did not complete timely rollovers because of a financial institution's delay or the unavailability of its personnel. [Priv. Ltr. Ruls. 200532061 (Aug. 12, 2005), 200550038 (Dec. 16, 2005)]

Misappropriation. Rollover waivers were granted to allow redeposit of IRA funds that had been misappropriated by individuals employed by the financial institution. [Priv. Ltr. Ruls. 200531030 (Aug. 5, 2005), 200327064 (Jul. 3, 2003)]

Q 6:23 In what circumstances does the error, act, or omission of a financial institution or advisor fail to justify the granting of a waiver?

To obtain a waiver, the taxpayer must show that the rollover would have occurred but for the erroneous intervention of the financial institution or advisor. For example, though a financial advisor incorrectly advised a taxpayer he had 90 days to complete a rollover, the mistake did not justify a waiver because the taxpayer did not have assets available for the rollover within either the 60-day period or the 90-day period. [Priv. Ltr. Rul. 200541050 (July 22, 2005)]

Q 6:24   Has the IRS granted waivers in cases where the taxpayer's own mistake prevented a timely rollover?

Yes. The IRS has granted waivers where circumstances indicated a rollover would have occurred but for a reasonable mistake of the taxpayer.

In Private Letter Ruling 200608026 (Nov. 28, 2005), the taxpayer maintained his IRA with a financial company and split the assets between two of the company's funds, a stock fund and a money market fund. In an Internet transaction, the taxpayer transferred assets from the stock fund to a non-IRA money market fund of the company, believing the latter to be the money market fund he held in his IRA. The mistake was discovered two days after the rollover period ended. The IRS viewed this mistake as reasonable and granted a waiver.

The IRS also granted a waiver to a taxpayer who the IRS described as having misunderstood the proper time frame for a rollover. Private Letter Ruling 200606055 (Feb. 10, 2006) is odd because the facts as related seem to show the taxpayer correctly understood the law. According to the ruling, the taxpayer asserted that her attempt to deposit rollover funds failed "due to an error on her part in computing the 60-day rollover period" (namely, "she believed that when the 60th day fell on a weekend or holiday, she had until the next business day to accomplish a rollover.") The IRS extended the rollover period because it found the taxpayer had acted in conformance with her belief (attempting the rollover two days after the period ended) and the funds remained available both during and after the rollover period. The ruling briefly mentions serious medical issues the taxpayer faced as additional justification for the waiver.

Note. The taxpayer's belief, as described in Private Letter Ruling 200606055 (Feb. 10, 2006), seems correct under Code Section 7503, so it is surprising that the IRS did not attribute the failed rollover to error by the financial institution in rejecting the deposit. The circumstances of the rejection are not described, however, and the taxpayer apparently did not ask the IRS to rule on the correctness of her belief.

Q 6:25   Has the IRS declined waiver requests because of taxpayer mistakes?

Yes. In such cases the IRS found the taxpayers' mistakes were unreasonable or otherwise did not justify a waiver.

In Private Letter Ruling 200609023 (Mar. 3, 2006), the IRS declined a waiver request because the taxpayer failed to exercise reasonable control. The taxpayer mistakenly believed the rollover period would remain open as long as he did not cash his distribution check, and did not bother to consult a tax professional. A waiver was similarly denied to the taxpayer who ignored company correspondence that contained his IRA distribution check [Priv. Ltr. Rul. 200601042 (Jan. 6, 2006)]. In another case, where the taxpayer did not make note of the 60-day rollover period and forgot he possessed a distribution check, the IRS refused the waiver request. [Priv. Ltr. Rul. 200602051 (Jan. 13, 2006)]

Other cases demonstrate that failure to appreciate adverse consequences of an IRA distribution does not justify a waiver of the 60-day rollover rule. One taxpayer owned both an IRA and a non-IRA annuity. Needing funds for a house purchase, he chose to use a distribution from the IRA because he knew that cashing out the annuity would trigger a financial penalty. Unfortunately, it was only after the rollover period ended that he learned the tax cost of his IRA distribution was far worse. [Priv. Ltr. Rul. 200546047 (Aug. 23, 2005)] Similarly, a 71-year-old man used funds withdrawn from his IRA to purchase charitable annuities for which he claimed income tax deductions. This taxpayer did not know the withdrawal was a taxable distribution until he filed his tax return, and that was too late for a rollover. [Priv. Ltr. Rul. 200526024 (Apr. 6, 2005)] After the death of a qualified plan participant, a beneficiary took a lump-sum distribution without asking the administrator not to withhold tax. She rolled over to her IRA the value of the funds minus the 20 percent withheld for tax. When the tax was refunded the following year, she tried to roll that over too, but the IRS refused to grant a waiver. [Priv. Ltr. Rul. 200613037 (Mar. 31, 2006)] Another individual suffered heart attacks and strokes and withdrew IRA funds he expected to need for medical expenses. He discovered later that insurance would cover the bills, and later still that he could have returned the funds to his IRA but the rollover period had closed. The IRS did not extend the deadline because it found a rollover was not intended when the distributions were taken. [Priv. Ltr. Rul. 200840057 (Oct. 3, 2008)] Finally, the IRS did not extend the rollover deadline for an individual who liquidated three IRAs because of alleged concerns about identity theft; he made no attempt to comply with the original deadline. [Priv. Ltr. Rul. 200904031 (Jan. 23, 2009)]

Q 6:26   How has the IRS ruled in other kinds of hardship cases?

The IRS waives the normal rollover deadline for taxpayers whose rollovers were interrupted by a casualty, disaster, or similar event, as long as the taxpayers could otherwise have completed them. Such rulings include:

1. A woman participated in rescue and assistance efforts during Hurricane Isabel and randomly bundled her mail during the storm to keep it dry. She did not expect to receive an IRA distribution check and, amidst the chaos, did not realize one had been mailed to her. [Priv. Ltr. Rul. 200453018 (Oct. 6, 2004)]

2. On the last day of the rollover period, a blizzard made a trip to the bank impractical and unsafe. [Priv. Ltr. Rul. 200406054 (Nov. 13, 2003)]

3. An individual could not complete a timely qualified plan-to-IRA rollover because he was working in a war zone located in a foreign country. [Priv. Ltr. Rul. 200502052 (Jan. 14, 2005)] The ruling indicates only that the taxpayer worked abroad in a war zone; it does not state that he was serving in a combat zone in support of the Armed Forces or acting under the Armed Forces' direction (e.g., as a contractor). Had the taxpayer been under the aegis of the Armed Forces, he would have been entitled to other relief in the performance of tax acts such as filing income, estate, or gift

tax returns or filing a claim for credit or refund. [IRS Publication 3, *Armed Forces' Tax Guide* (2008)]

4. A taxpayer in the process of selling one home and purchasing another used an IRA distribution to show proof of assets and pay closing costs. He intended to replace the funds using proceeds from the sale of the old home, which was scheduled to close within 60 days, but closing was delayed because Hurricane Frances struck and damaged the home. Soon afterward, the taxpayer tried to deposit the funds, but the bank rejected the rollover as untimely. Neither party realized that the IRS had granted special relief for victims of Hurricane Frances that extended the rollover period, and since the taxpayer had attempted to deposit the rollover within the extended period, a waiver was granted. [Priv. Ltr. Rul. 200543063 (Aug. 2, 2005)]

5. A taxpayer withdrew IRA funds that she intended to use for a first-time home purchase. The purchase fell through more than 60 days later, and the taxpayer's financial advisor erroneously told her it was too late to redeposit the funds; neither the taxpayer nor her advisor understood that a special 120-day rollover period applies to failed first-time home purchases. The taxpayer filed a waiver request, but the IRS did not consider it until after the close of the 120-day period. Since the taxpayer had filed the request within the 120-day period, the IRS granted the waiver. [Priv. Ltr. Rul. 200729038 (July 20, 2007)]

Hardship alone does not justify a waiver. The IRS is unsympathetic to taxpayers who cannot roll funds over on a timely basis because either the funds were spent in coping with an emergency, or an emergency delayed a transaction that was to have yielded timely replacement funds. One example is a ruling with facts similar to Private Letter Ruling 200543063 except that special relief was not granted to victims of this storm, and the taxpayer's replacement funds came too late. [Priv. Ltr. Rul. 200543063 (Aug. 2, 2005)] Another ruling concerns a couple who used retirement distributions to pay bills and other personal expenses while waiting for a Social Security determination on the wife's disability and unemployment, which came more than 60 days after the distributions were taken. [Priv. Ltr. Rul. 200549023 (Sept. 12, 2005)]

Q 6:27   Does the IRS have the last word on whether a defective rollover can be cured?

No, the courts do when cases go that far. In a line of decisions, the Tax Court has granted relief for imperfect rollover contributions if the taxpayer acted with full knowledge of the legal requirements, took all steps to comply that were reasonably within his or her control, and achieved substantial compliance. [Wood v. Commissioner, 93 T.C. 114 (1989)] On the other hand, if the defect is not merely "procedural" but concerns a "fundamental element" of the statutory requirements, the Tax Court has denied relief. Examples of that are failing to establish an IRA and merely depositing the distribution into a regular savings account. [Crow v. Commissioner, T.C. Memo. 1992-331 (1992 RIA T.C. Memo. ¶ 92,331), *aff'd without published opinion*, 987 F.2d 770 (5th Cir. 1993)]; and attempting to roll over an inherited IRA without using a direct, trustee-to-trustee transfer, though inherited IRAs cannot be transferred by other means. [Jankelovits v. Commissioner, T.C. Memo. 2008-285]

Statutory Exceptions to the Rollover Rules

Q 6:28   What exceptions apply to a qualified first-time homebuyer distribution that cannot be used for its intended purpose?

A *qualified first-time homebuyer distribution* is exempt from the early distribution penalty if it is used within 120 days of receipt to pay certain costs of purchasing a residence (see Q 4:127). However, if the distribution cannot be used for that purpose solely because of a delay or cancellation of the purchase or construction of the residence, the rollover period is extended to 120 days, and the 12-month rule does not apply. [I.R.C. § 72(t)(8)(E); Priv. Ltr. Rul. 200729038 (July 20, 2007)]

Q 6:29   Is there an exception to the 60-day rule for qualified hurricane distributions?

Yes. Pursuant to legislation enacted in 2005 after the disastrous hurricanes Katrina, Rita, and Wilma, *qualified hurricane distributions* were allowed special tax benefits. One benefit was the extension of the rollover period for qualified hurricane distributions to three years (see Q 4:160). The last date for making a qualified hurricane distribution was December 31, 2006, so some of the amounts remain eligible for rollover until December 31, 2009. [*See* I.R.C. § 1400Q.]

Q 6:30   What exception to the 60-day rule applies to qualified recovery assistance distributions?

Qualified recovery assistance distributions may also be rolled over within three years from the date of distribution. These distributions are available to qualifying individuals who were affected by the storms and tornados that ravaged Kansas on May 4, 2007, and must be taken before January 1, 2009 (see Q 4:161). [I.R.C. § 1400Q; Food, Conservation, and Energy Act of 2008, Pub. L. No. 110-234, § 15345, 122 Stat. 923 (2008)]

Q 6:31   What exception to the 60-day rule applies to qualified disaster recovery assistance distributions?

A three year rollover period is also allowed for *qualified disaster recovery assistance distributions,* which are available to qualifying individuals who were affected by the storms and tornados during the period May 20, 2008 to July 31, 2008, in the Midwestern disaster areas (Arkansas, Illinois, Indiana, Iowa, Kansas, Michigan, Minnesota, Missouri, Nebraska, and Wisconsin). The distributions must be taken before January 1, 2010 (see Q 4:162). [I.R.C. § 1400Q; Heartland Disaster Tax Relief Act of 2008, Pub. L. No. 110-343, § 702; IRS Publication 4492-B, *Information for Affected Taxpayers in the Midwestern*

Disaster Area 2009; IRS Publication 590, *Individual Retirement Arrangements (IRAs)* 2008 (see Appendix A)]

Q 6:32 What exception to the 60-day rule applies to frozen deposits?

An IRA distribution may be temporarily deposited in a non-IRA account during the rollover period. If it cannot be timely withdrawn because it has become a *frozen deposit*, special rules apply. A frozen deposit is an amount that cannot be withdrawn from a financial institution either because the institution is bankrupt or insolvent, or because the state in which it is located has restricted withdrawals on account of the bankruptcy or insolvency (or threat of either) of another financial institution in the state. In the event of a frozen deposit, the period during which the amount is a frozen deposit is not counted in the 60-day period. Also, the 60-day period cannot end earlier than 10 days after the deposit is no longer frozen. [I.R.C. §§ 408A(e), 408(d)(3)(F), 402(c)(7); IRS Publication 590, *Individual Retirement Arrangements (IRAs)* 2008 (see Appendix A)]

Q 6:33 What exception to the 12-month rule applies to IRA distributions that are solely initiated by the Federal Deposit Insurance Corporation?

The 12-month rule does not apply to an IRA distribution from a failed custodial institution if the Federal Deposit Insurance Corporation (FDIC), as receiver for the institution, initiates the distribution because the institution is insolvent and the FDIC cannot find a buyer for it. The exception does not apply if either the custodian or the depositor requests the distribution. Direct FDIC instruction or professional legal guidance may be necessary for the proper application of this rule. [IRS Publication 590, *Individual Retirement Arrangements (IRAs)* 2008 (see Appendix A)]

Roth IRAs

Transfers

Q 6:34 Are trustee-to-trustee transfers allowed between Roth IRAs?

Yes. A transfer is the movement of the assets from one Roth IRA to another without taking a distribution. In general, the transfer rules for traditional IRAs also apply to Roth IRAs. Transfers are permitted between Roth IRAs pursuant to revenue rulings, not pursuant to the Code or the Treasury regulations. [*See* Instructions for IRS Forms 1099, 1098, 5498, and W-2G (2009); Rev. Rul. 78-406, 1978-2 C.B. 157.]

Rollovers

Q 6:35   Are rollovers allowed between Roth IRAs?

Yes. A rollover takes place when one Roth IRA's assets are distributed directly to the Roth IRA owner and are then rolled over to another Roth IRA or rolled over back to the same Roth IRA. [Treas. Reg. § 1.408A-8, Q&A-1(b)(9)]

Q 6:36   Must a rollover between Roth IRAs be completed within 60 days?

Yes. Like a traditional IRA rollover (see Q 6:6), a Roth IRA rollover must be completed within 60 days of receipt of the distribution, except under the circumstances discussed earlier in this chapter (see Q 6:7). [I.R.C. § 408A(e)]

Q 6:37   Does the 12-month rule apply to rollovers between Roth IRAs?

Yes. Rollovers between Roth IRAs generally are limited to one for each IRA within a 12-month period (see Q 6:7). [I.R.C. § 408A(e)]

Note. First-time homebuyers enjoy an exception to the 12-month rule if a distribution is rolled over because of a delay in or cancellation of the purchase or construction of the residence. [I.R.C. § 72(t)(8)(E)]

Conversions

Q 6:38   What is a conversion?

The term *conversion* refers to the movement of assets from a traditional IRA to a Roth IRA. An individual is allowed to convert his or her traditional IRA to a Roth IRA if the individual meets the eligibility requirements and complies with the rules governing such a transaction. [I.R.C. § 408A(c)(3)(B)] (see Q 3:92).

Note. The term *conversion* is less frequently used to describe the changing of a traditional IRA contribution into a Roth IRA contribution before the individual's tax filing due date. Also known as a *contribution conversion* or a *recharacterization*, such a conversion is different from that under discussion here (see chapter 3).

Q 6:39   How is a conversion completed?

A conversion of a traditional IRA to a Roth IRA may be made in several ways and without taking a distribution. For example, an individual may make a conversion simply by notifying the IRA trustee or custodian of the conversion. Alternatively, an individual may make a conversion in connection with changing an IRA trustee or custodian through a rollover or trustee-to-trustee transfer and notify the new trustee or custodian that the recipient IRA is to be a Roth IRA.

Q 6:40   Is a conversion treated as a rollover or a transfer?

Regardless of how the transaction is actually completed, a conversion is treated as a rollover of traditional IRA assets to a Roth IRA for reporting and tax purposes. The IRS has made it clear that a conversion must be reported as a taxable distribution and should not be treated as a trustee-to-trustee transfer from a reporting perspective. [Instructions for IRS Forms 1099, 1098, 5498, and W-2G (2009)] The assets are treated as a distribution from the traditional IRA and then as a rollover contribution to the Roth IRA. [Treas. Reg. § 1.408A-4, Q&A-1(c)]

The law also contemplates that some individuals will simply convert their traditional IRAs to Roth IRAs without taking physical distribution of the assets. That may happen when an individual authorizes his or her existing IRA trustee or custodian to convert the traditional IRA to a Roth IRA. The transaction is considered a rollover even though the assets never leave the trustee's or custodian's control. The rule applies both to conversions within the same trustee or custodian and to conversions to a new trustee or custodian, even when the assets are moved directly between the traditional IRA and the Roth IRA as a convenience to the IRA owner.

> **Example.** Marc receives a brochure from Mutual Funds, Inc. advertising the Roth IRA and in particular the benefits of converting. Marc has a traditional IRA with Big Bank. He completes the conversion form included in the marketing material and returns it to Mutual Funds, Inc. Mutual Funds forwards the form to Big Bank. The form asks Big Bank to send Marc's IRA assets directly to Mutual Funds, Inc. Big Bank forwards the assets and treats the conversion as a taxable distribution. Mutual Funds treats the contribution as a rollover conversion contribution.

Q 6:41   Does the 60-day rule apply to rollover conversions?

Yes. Assets distributed from a traditional IRA must be rolled over to a Roth IRA within 60 days of receipt (see Q 6:6). [I.R.C. § 408A(e)]

If the assets move directly between trustees or custodians and the IRA owner never receives an actual distribution, it is less clear that the 60-day rule applies. An argument can be made that the 60-day rule applies only when the taxpayer actually receives distribution of the assets. (For exceptions to the 60-day rule, see Q 6:7.)

Q 6:42   Is there a limit on the number of conversions an individual may make each year?

No. Although rollovers of an IRA are generally limited to one per 12-month period (see Q 6:12), the 12-month rule does not apply in the case of a conversion from a traditional IRA to a Roth IRA. The IRS, however, limits the number of reconversions of the same assets to once a year (see chapter 5). [Treas. Reg. § 1.408A-5, Q&A-8]

Example. Sam has $100,000 in a traditional IRA invested in a mutual fund. He would like to convert the traditional IRA to a Roth IRA. Sam understands that the conversion is a taxable distribution, and he does not want to risk converting the entire amount in the traditional IRA at one time. Like other investors, Sam does not know whether the market is going up or down over the next 12 months. He decides to convert $10,000 for each of the 12 months in 2010 in order to obtain a rough yearly average of the stock price. He may do so because there is no limit on the number of conversions an individual may make in a year.

Miscellaneous

Q 6:43   What is the effect of taking a distribution from a Roth IRA and contributing it to a retirement plan other than a Roth IRA?

Any amount distributed from a Roth IRA and contributed to another type of retirement plan is treated as a distribution from the Roth IRA that is not a rollover contribution. This treatment also applies to any amount transferred from a Roth IRA to any other type of retirement plan, unless the transfer is a recharacterization of a Roth IRA contribution as a traditional IRA contribution. [Treas. Reg. § 1.408A-6, Q&A-17]

Q 6:44   What are the federal income tax consequences of a Roth IRA owner's transferring his or her Roth IRA to another individual by gift?

A Roth IRA owner's transfer of his or her Roth IRA to another individual by gift is considered an assignment of the owner's rights under the Roth IRA. At the time of the gift, the assets of the Roth IRA are deemed to be distributed to the owner and, accordingly, are treated as no longer held in a Roth IRA. [Treas. Reg. § 1.408A-6, Q&A-19]

Coverdell Education Savings Accounts

Transfers

Q 6:45   Are trustee-to-trustee transfers allowed between Coverdell ESAs?

Yes. A transfer is the movement of the assets from one Coverdell ESA to another without taking a distribution. In general, the transfer rules for traditional IRAs apply to Coverdell ESAs (see Qs 6:3, 6:5). The instructions for Form 5498-ESA, Coverdell ESA Contribution Information, indicate that direct trustee-to-trustee transfers from one Coverdell ESA to another Coverdell ESA are permitted and are to be reported on this form. If a distribution includes a trustee-to-trustee transfer, it is reported on Form 1099-Q, Payments from Qualified Education Programs (under Sections 529 and 530). [Instructions for IRS Forms 1099-Q and 5498-ESA (2009)]

Q 6:46 How is a trustee-to-trustee transfer accomplished between Coverdell ESAs?

Generally, the responsible individual will select a new trustee or custodian for the Coverdell ESA and complete a new Coverdell ESA agreement as well as a transfer form. The transfer form is forwarded to the current trustee or custodian with instructions to send the assets in the Coverdell ESA directly to the new trustee or custodian. The new trustee or custodian receives the assets directly and places them in the Coverdell ESA.

Other permissible methods of completing a transfer exist. The key feature of a transfer is that the responsible individual or designated beneficiary never has direct access to the funds. Because the assets move directly between financial institutions, no distribution is deemed to have occurred.

Rollovers

Q 6:47 Are rollovers allowed between Coverdell ESAs?

Yes. A rollover is simply a way of moving assets from one Coverdell ESA to another. A rollover takes place when assets in a Coverdell ESA are distributed and then rolled over to another Coverdell ESA or rolled over back to the same Coverdell ESA. [I.R.C. § 530(d)(5)]

Q 6:48 Does the 60-day rule apply to rollovers between Coverdell ESAs?

Yes. Like rollovers between traditional IRAs and between Roth IRAs (see Qs 6:6, 6:35), rollovers between Coverdell ESAs must be completed within 60 days of the date of distribution. [I.R.C. § 530(d)(5)]

Q 6:49 Does the 12-month rule apply to rollovers between Coverdell ESAs?

Yes. Rollovers between Coverdell ESAs are limited to one for each ESA in a 12-month period (see Q 6:12). [I.R.C. § 530(d)(5)]

Q 6:50 May the designated beneficiary of a Coverdell ESA be changed via a rollover?

Yes. The designated beneficiary of a Coverdell ESA may be changed from a child to a member of the designated beneficiary's family without triggering any tax consequences by using a rollover to complete the transaction. [I.R.C. § 530(d)(5)] The terms of the particular Coverdell ESA agreement must permit such a change, however. [Notice 97-60, 1997-2 C.B. 310] Each trustee or custodian controls whether such an option is available in the accounts it offers.

Moving Coverdell ESA Assets to a Roth IRA

Q 6:51 **May an amount be transferred directly from a Coverdell ESA to a Roth IRA or be distributed from a Coverdell ESA and rolled over to a Roth IRA?**

No. Amounts may not be transferred directly from, or rolled over from, a Coverdell ESA to a Roth IRA. A transfer of funds (or a distribution and rollover) from a Coverdell ESA to a Roth IRA is considered a distribution from the ESA and a regular contribution to the Roth IRA (rather than a qualified rollover contribution to the Roth IRA). [Treas. Reg. § 1.408A-6, Q&A-18]

Qualified Plan Rollovers to IRAs

Q 6:52 **Are both traditional IRAs and Roth IRAs eligible to receive rollovers from a qualified plan?**

Until 2008, only traditional IRAs could receive rollovers from a qualified plan. Now, qualified plan assets may also be rolled over to a Roth IRA, although the transaction is taxed like a conversion and—until 2010—the requirements for a conversion must be met (see Q 3:92). [I.R.C. § 408A(e); Notice 2008-30, 2008-12 I.R.B. 638; Treas. Reg. § 1.408A-4, Q&A-5]

Q 6:53 **What main events may trigger a decision to roll over assets from a qualified plan?**

The three main events that may trigger a decision to roll over assets from a qualified plan are as follows:

1. *Termination of employment.* Although an employer cannot force terminated employees to accept a lump-sum distribution unless an employee's vested account balance is less than $1,000 or a lesser threshold amount provided in the qualified plan, many employees prefer to take their money with them (and employers prefer that they do so for purposes of administration and responsibility). The employer may elect whether the threshold amount is determined with or without regard to amounts (including earnings) that a participant rolled over to the plan. [I.R.C. § 411(a)(11)(D)]

2. *Death.* When a plan participant dies, his or her surviving spouse often will roll over the participant's account to his or her own IRA. If the beneficiary is not the spouse, he or she (or a trust) may qualify to roll over the account to an inherited IRA.

3. *Disability.* Typically, the family of a disabled plan participant will need to evaluate resources and medical coverage, as well as proceeds of disability insurance, before deciding how much, if any, of the qualified plan distribution should be rolled over.

Current employees may also look to a rollover as a way to realign investment choices. It is important to note, however, that no plan is required to allow in-service withdrawals.

Q 6:54　May funds be rolled over from qualified plans during the required distribution period?

Yes. Even when an IRA owner is over age 70½, there is nothing to stop him or her from receiving a distribution from a qualified plan and rolling it over to an IRA. If the qualified plan is already making its own distributions on a required minimum distribution basis, such minimum distributions will not be eligible to be rolled over to an IRA or other qualified plan. If additional amounts are distributed from the qualified plan earlier than required or in addition to the RMD, however, the portion represented each year by such excess distributions may be rolled over. If the amount is rolled over directly, 20 percent mandatory withholding is avoided.

After-tax employee contributions distributed from qualified plans may also be rolled over to IRAs. Separate recordkeeping is required to track any after-tax contributions so that the subsequent withdrawal of such amounts from the IRA will retain their tax-free character.

Note. To be effective, a rollover from a qualified plan to an IRA must be completed by the time the IRA owner dies. In Private Letter Ruling 200204038 (Oct. 30, 2001), the IRS ruled that when an IRA owner directed his plan trustees to transfer his plan assets to his IRA but died before the transfer took place, the transfer could not be accomplished on a post-mortem basis.

Q 6:55　What types of distributions from a qualified plan may not be rolled over to an IRA?

The following distributions from a qualified plan may *not* be rolled over to an IRA:

1. A series of substantially equal annual distributions that are based either on the employee's life (or life expectancy) or on the joint lives (or joint life expectancies) of the employee and his or her designated beneficiary, or distributions that are payable for at least 10 years (see Q 6:56). [I.R.C. § 402(c)(4)(A)]

2. A required minimum distribution (RMD) under Code Section 401(a)(9) following the attainment of age 70½. [I.R.C. § 402(c)(4)(B)] (Generally, individuals who are over age 70½ but are still employed by the employer are not required to begin receiving minimum distributions, except for 5 percent owners. [I.R.C. § 401(a)(9)])

3. The portion of a distribution that is nontaxable for reasons other than being a return of *after-tax contributions* (e.g., the unrealized appreciation on employer stock). [I.R.C. § 402(c)(2)]

4. Hardship distributions (see Q 6:58). [I.R.C. § 402(c)(4)(C)]

5. Dividends that are deductible by the plan sponsor.

6. Loans from a qualified employer.

7. Corrective distributions from 401(k) plans.

[Treas. Reg. § 1.402(c)-2, Q&A-4]

Q 6:56 What determines whether payments are substantially equal periodic payments?

One of the exceptions to the 10 percent additional tax on early distributions applies to substantially equal periodic payments. These are IRA or qualified plan payments that are made at least annually (generally for at least five years) and are computed according to one of three methods—the RMD method, the fixed amortization method, or the fixed annuitization method (see Qs 4:115–4:124). Substantially equal periodic payments may not be rolled over to an IRA. [I.R.C. § 72(t)(2)(A)(ii); Rev. Rul. 2002-62, 2002-2 C.B. 710; Treas. Reg. § 1.402(c)-2, Q&A-5]

Q 6:57 What happens if a distribution from a qualified plan exceeds the minimum required by Code Section 401(a)(9)?

If a distribution from a qualified plan exceeds the minimum distribution required by Code Section 401(a)(9), the excess is subject to 20 percent withholding and is eligible for rollover. The portion representing the minimum distribution is taxable. [Treas. Reg. § 1.402(c)-2, Q&A-8; Notice 93-3, 1993-1 C.B. 293]

Q 6:58 Are hardship distributions from a 401(k) plan eligible for rollover to a traditional IRA?

No. Hardship distributions attributable to elective deferrals under 401(k) plans and non-401(k) plan contributions (e.g., employer profit sharing contributions) are not eligible for rollover to a traditional IRA. [I.R.C. § 402(c)(4)(C); Notice 99-5, 1999-1 C.B. 319; *modified by* Notice 2000-32, 2000-1 C.B. 1274]

In addition, Notice 99-5 provides that if another event permitting distribution, without regard to hardship, occurs (such as the employee's separation from service or attainment of age 59½), no amount distributed from a qualified plan after that event is ineligible for rollover treatment on account of its being a hardship distribution.

Q 6:59 May excess contributions returned from a 401(k) plan be rolled over to an IRA?

No. Contributions to a 401(k) plan that are in violation of the Section 415 or Section 401(k) nondiscrimination rules may not be rolled over to an IRA. [Treas. Reg. § 1.402(c)-2, Q&A-4]

Q 6:60   May amounts held in nonconduit IRAs be rolled over to qualified plans in which the IRA owner participates on a tax-free basis?

Yes, as long as the qualified plan contains provisions permitting such a rollover. The only restriction is that the amount rolled over from the IRA to the qualified plan may not contain after-tax contributions to the IRA. [I.R.C. § 408(d)(3)(A)(ii)]

Distribution of Noncash Property

Q 6:61   May a distribution of noncash property from a qualified plan be rolled over to an IRA?

Yes. Noncash property distributed from a qualified plan (whether or not cash is also received in the distribution) may be rolled over to an IRA. It should be noted, however, that each IRA sponsor has its own rules as to what types of property it will accept. [I.R.C. § 402(c)(1)(B), 402(c)(1)(C)]

Q 6:62   May an individual sell property received in a distribution and roll over the proceeds?

Yes. As long as the rollover is completed within 60 days of distribution, the proceeds of sale can be rolled over even if the value of the property changes from the date of distribution to the date of sale. [I.R.C. § 402(c)(6)(A), 402(c)(6)(B)] A property sale will not be taxable, even if there is an increase in value between the date of distribution and the date of rollover, as long as the entire proceeds of the sale are rolled over. [I.R.C. § 402(c)(6)(D)]

If a portion of the distribution is nontaxable (usually a return of after-tax contributions) and the property is sold and only a portion rolled over, the individual may designate which part of the cash or other property is attributable to the nontaxable portion and which part is treated as included in the rollover contribution. The designation, which must be made no later than the due date of the employee's income tax return (including extensions), is irrevocable. If no designation is made, the rollover amount must be allocated pro rata between the cash distribution and the value (determined as of the date of the distribution) of any property received. [I.R.C. § 402(c)(6)(C)]

Q 6:63   May the recipient of a distribution that is partly cash and partly property determine the cash equivalent of the property and roll over that cash equivalent?

No. [Rev. Rul. 87-77, 1987-2 C.B. 115]

Q 6:64   How is a distribution of employer securities treated?

The main option for a distribution of employer stock other than rollover is to pay tax on the cost basis of the stock to the distributing plan. The unrealized appreciation is not taxable until the stock is sold, and then only at capital gains rates. Alternatively, the stock (or the proceeds from the sale of the stock) may be rolled over. If the stock is sold and the proceeds are rolled over, there will be no capital gain. [I.R.C. § 402(c)(6)]

Withholding

Q 6:65   May a nondirect rollover from a qualified plan include a makeup of withholding?

Yes. A plan participant who receives a net distribution after tax withholding may add to the rollover the amount reduced by the withholding. The participant has the option of replacing all or part of the withholding to bring the rollover up to, but not higher than, the initial gross amount. Replacement of the withheld amount, for which the taxpayer will receive credit on his or her tax return, ensures that the largest possible rollover is made and the least tax paid. [Treas. Reg. § 1.402(c)-2, Q&A-11]

Transferring and Receiving Qualified Plans

Q 6:66   May a qualified plan refuse to accept rollovers?

Yes. Qualified plans are not required to *accept* rollovers. The law does, however, require that a qualified plan offer to make a rollover directly to another defined contribution plan or to an IRA. [Treas. Reg. § 1.401(a)(31)-1, Q&A-13; I.R.C. §§ 408A(c)(3)(B), 408A(d)(3)(B), 402(c)(11), 402(f)(2)(A)] As of 2010, qualified plans must also offer nonspouse beneficiaries the option to have a trustee-to-trustee transfer to an inherited IRA (see Q 6:82).

Q 6:67   Will a rollover be taxed if the trust from which the distribution was made is no longer a qualified plan?

There are two basic theories regarding the taxing of a distribution for a plan that was originally a qualified plan but becomes disqualified. Three circuit courts, the IRS, and now the Tax Court take the position that once a plan becomes disqualified, no amount is eligible for rollover or income averaging. [*See* Fazi v. Commissioner, 102 T.C. 695 (1994); Priv. Ltr. Rul. 9241008 (July 6, 1992).]

However, under a theory that was previously advanced by the Tax Court, and is still the position of the Second Circuit, it appears that a portion of the distribution is treated as a distribution from a qualified plan that is treated as eligible for rollover and income-averaging treatment (or capital gains treatment, if applicable) and the remainder of the distribution is currently taxable and is not eligible for rollover or averaging. Of course, one of the difficulties is determining what portion of the distribution can be rolled over or can be eligible for income averaging and what portion cannot. [Greenwald v. Commissioner, 366 F.2d 538, 18 A.F.T.R.2d ¶ 5,645 (2d Cir. 1996)] The Tax Court ruled in favor of the partial disqualification theory in *Baetens v. Commissioner* [777 F.2d 1160 (6th Cir. 1985)], although the Tax Court was later overruled by the Sixth Circuit. In *Fazi v. Commissioner* [102 T.C. 695 (1994)], the Tax Court reconsidered and reversed its original holding in *Baetans* and held that the entire distribution from a disqualified plan was taxable.

Q 6:68　As of what date must the distributing plan be qualified for a rollover to be effective?

When a rollover is contemplated, the distributing plan must be qualified, and its trust must be tax exempt, on the date that the distribution is made. A distribution made some time after the plan's termination will probably not be eligible to be rolled over. In one case, a distribution made four years after termination of the plan could not be rolled over. [Priv. Ltr. Rul. 9241008 (July 6, 1992)] In *Boggs v. Commissioner* [83 T.C. 132 (1984)], the Tax Court held that the portion of the distribution consisting of contributions made and trust earnings accrued before the date of a retroactive disqualification remained available for rollover, but subsequent portions were not available for rollover. In *Fazi v. Commissioner* [102 T.C. 695 (1994)], however, the Tax Court found that a distribution from a disqualified plan was taxable, and thus not eligible to be rolled over, even though it included contributions made when the plan was qualified. In *Fazi*, the court found that taxability of the distribution was determined at the time of the distribution rather than at the time the contributions were made. The entire rollover from the plan to Fazi's traditional IRA was disallowed.

Q 6:69　If a distribution is paid to a financial institution with the intention that the rollover be made to that institution's retirement account, is that enough to accomplish a rollover?

No. An intention to make a rollover is not sufficient. However, a waiver of the 60-day limit may be granted under such circumstances (see Qs 6:22, 6:23).

Q 6:70　May a distribution from a qualified plan be divided up and rolled over to more than one traditional IRA?

Yes. There is no requirement that a distribution from a qualified plan be rolled over to a single traditional IRA. As long as the 60-day rule is complied with (see Q 6:6), a lump-sum or other distribution may be divided up and rolled over to more than one traditional IRA. [Rev. Rul. 79-265, 1979-2 C.B. 186; Priv. Ltr. Rul. 8708041 (Nov. 25, 1986)]

In Private Letter Ruling 9217049 (Jan. 31, 1992), a distribution split between an IRA rolled over to a traditional IRA and a rollover to a 401(k) plan was approved. It may be noted that if a direct rollover is made, the 60-day requirement is eliminated because the distribution and rollover are effectively combined into one step, as long as the distributing plan does not bar a split direct rollover.

Q 6:71   Can a rollover maneuver by a 5 percent owner permit the deferral of his or her required minimum distributions?

Yes. Treasury Regulations Section 1.401(a)(9)-7, Q&A-2 provides that where amounts are distributed by one plan and rolled over to a receiving plan, "the benefit of the employee under the receiving plan is increased by the amount rolled over for purposes of determining the required minimum distribution" for the year following the year in which the amount rolled over is distributed.

Based on this ruling, the IRS approved a clever deferral maneuver by a taxpayer who was employed by one company in which he was a 5 percent owner and another in which he had no 5 percent ownership interest. The IRS permitted him to defer his RMDs past age 70½ from the plan sponsored by the company in which he was a 5 percent owner by rolling over his account balance to the plan maintained by the company in which he was not a 5-percent owner. This maneuver would result in the taxpayer deferring his RMD from the recipient plan until April 1 following the year he retires. [Priv. Ltr. Rul. 200453015 (Dec. 31, 2005)]

Q 6:72   May a surviving spouse roll over assets from the decedent's IRA into a qualified plan in which the spouse participates?

Yes. A surviving spouse who previously rolled over the decedent spouse's IRA to his or her IRA may roll back all or a portion of that IRA to a qualified plan in which he or she is a participant. [IRS Publication 590, *Individual Retirement Arrangements (IRAs)* 2008 (see Appendix A)]

Q 6:73   Should a qualified plan participant monitor the rollover process?

A qualified plan participant is well advised to monitor the rollover process. In one case, confusion arose about whether the recipient plan (not a traditional IRA) could or would receive a distribution. The employee relied on a letter from the transferor plan, received before 60 days had elapsed, stating that the application and the employee's check had been forwarded to the plan administrator of the transferee plan at its corporate office. After 60 days had passed without any notification from the transferee plan, the employee contacted a personnel officer at the transferee plan and learned that the check had not been received. Actually, had the check been received, it would not have been accepted because the employee was not eligible to participate in the new plan until the following January 1, the earliest date on which the check could have been accepted. It was then too late to effect a traditional IRA rollover. [Priv. Ltr. Rul. 8819074 (Feb. 17, 1988)]

This case demonstrates that a more efficient approach would have been for the employee to deal directly with the new employer, especially since he was employed within 10 days after terminating employment with his previous employer. If the employee had personally delivered the check to the new employer, he would have immediately learned about the issues involved and would have been able to take the appropriate action to avoid the problem.

Private Letter Ruling 8819074 clearly states that the employee has the burden of verifying whether the transferee plan permits the contemplated transfer, and that the employee is eligible for immediate participation in the transferee plan. This kind of problem may be avoided now that the IRS has the authority to extend the 60-day rollover period (see Q 6:17).

Security Agreements

Q 6:74   May an IRA that contains rollover assets be pledged as security for a liability of its owner?

No. An IRA, regardless of whether it is a rollover, cannot be pledged as security. [I.R.C. § 408(c)(4)] On the other hand, listing a traditional IRA on a balance sheet in support of a loan application apparently does not violate the nonassignability requirement.

Q 6:75   Are there circumstances in which an IRA may be pledged?

Yes. The IRS approved a pledge of an IRA rollover in one situation. Certain highly compensated participants in a qualified defined benefit plan are generally restricted from receiving benefits in a lump sum to prevent the premature depletion of the plan's assets should the plan terminate. [Treas. Reg. § 1.401(a)(4)-5(b)(3)] Some highly compensated participants nonetheless asked the IRS for permission to (1) take lump-sum distributions, (2) roll them over to IRAs, (3) pledge that the money would be repaid if the plan terminates without sufficient funds to cover all liabilities, and (4) pledge the rollover IRAs to secure repayment. The IRS agreed that such a pledge would not disqualify the IRAs. [*See* Priv. Ltr. Ruls. 8408063 (Nov. 23, 1983); 9514028 (Jan. 13, 1995).]

Special Rules

Q 6:76   May a distribution from a traditional IRA be rolled over if the recipient has already attained age 70½?

The rule requiring that minimum distributions from a traditional IRA start no later than April 1 of the calendar year following the IRA owner's attainment of age 70½ does not prevent an individual over that age from rolling over the portion of a distribution from a traditional IRA that exceeds the minimum distribution. Once the distribution is received, however, RMDs based on the new rollover amount must also commence. Nonetheless, the IRA is an effective tax shelter, because distributions may not be completed for a number of years. [Rev. Rul. 82-153, 1982-2 C.B. 86]

An individual who is over age 70½ is not permitted to make nonrollover contributions to a traditional IRA. In addition, an RMD under Code Section 401 (a)(9) may never be rolled over. Only amounts in excess of the RMD may be rolled over to a traditional IRA.

Note. An individual who is employed is not required to begin distributions from his or her qualified plan until retirement. That rule does not apply to 5 percent owners of a business, who are required to start taking distributions at age 70½ regardless of their employment status. [I.R.C. § 401(a)(9)]

Q 6:77 How may a distribution from a Keogh plan or tax-sheltered annuity be rolled over to an IRA?

An eligible rollover distribution from a Keogh plan maintained by a self-employed individual may be rolled over to another eligible retirement plan or to a traditional IRA. The rollover may include the entire lump-sum distribution or only part of it. [IRS Publication 590, *Individual Retirement Arrangements (IRAs)* 2008 (see Appendix A)] A self-employed individual is generally treated as an employee for rollover purposes. An eligible rollover distribution from a tax-sheltered annuity may be rolled over to a traditional IRA, to another tax-sheltered annuity [I.R.C. § 403(b)(8)(A)(ii)], to a qualified plan, or to a Section 457 plan sponsored by a state or local government. [I.R.C. § 402(c)(8)(B)]

Q 6:78 Can qualified reservist distributions be rolled over to an IRA?

Yes. An individual who receives a qualified reservist distribution (see Q 4:157) has two years, commencing immediately after the end of active duty, to restore the amount to an IRA. No deduction is allowed when a qualified reservist distribution is repaid to an IRA. However, any portion of a qualified reservist distribution that was taxable at receipt constitutes basis when it is repaid to the IRA. [I.R.C. § 72(t)(2)(G)]

Q 6:79 Can military death gratuities and payments received under the Servicemen's Group Life Insurance Program be rolled over to an IRA?

Yes. To the extent they are not contributed to a Coverdell ESA (see Q 13:51), military death gratuities and SGLI payments may be contributed to a Roth IRA. If contributed within one year of receipt, the funds are treated as qualified rollover contributions and the contribution is not subject to the modified adjusted gross income (MAGI) limits that normally (until 2010) restrict rollovers to a Roth IRA. [Heroes Earnings Assistance and Relief Tax (HEART) Act, § 109, Pub. L. No. 110-245, 122 Stat. 2316 (2008)]

Q 6:80 Can payments received in settlement of the *Exxon Valdez* litigation be rolled over to an IRA?

Individuals (or their death beneficiaries) who were plaintiffs in the *Exxon Valdez* litigation, which related to a disastrous 1989 oil spill, may generally roll over to a traditional IRA or Roth IRA (or other eligible retirement plan) up to $100,000 of the settlement payments they receive. [Tax Extenders and Alternative Minimum Tax Relief Act of 2008, § 504(b), Pub. L. No. 110-343, 122 Stat. 3765 (2008)); *In re Exxon Valdez*, No. 89-095-CV (HRH) (Consolidated) (D. Alaska)]

The settlement payments may be contributed whether they are received in a lump sum or on a periodic basis, but each must be contributed by the due date (unextended) for filing the return for the taxable year when the payment is made. The payment is treated as a qualified rollover distribution that is deposited into the IRA by a trustee-to-trustee transfer. The 12-month limit on rollover contributions (see Q 6:12) does not apply to these contributions.

If *Exxon Valdez* settlement payments are contributed to a traditional IRA, they are excluded from gross income and not taxed until distributed from the traditional IRA. Payments contributed to a Roth IRA are includible in gross income on receipt, but treated as investment in the contract (i.e., basis) and not taxed when later distributed from the Roth IRA. [Tax Extenders and Alternative Minimum Tax Relief Act of 2008, § 504(b)(3), Pub. L. No. 110-343, 122 Stat. 3765 (2008)]

Q 6:81 Can eligible airline employees roll over payments received in connection with the employer's bankruptcy proceeding?

Yes, under special relief that was granted in 2008 and only briefly available. The rule allows certain individuals to contribute a "qualified airline payment" to a Roth IRA within 180 days of its receipt (or by June 21, 2009, if later). [Worker, Retiree, and Employer Recovery Act of 2008, § 125, Pub. L. No. 110-458 (2008)]

The affected individuals are current and former employees of a commercial passenger airline carrier, who participated in a qualified defined benefit plan of the carrier that was terminated or became subject to benefit accrual under minimum funding rules. A *qualified airline payment* is generally money or other property paid to the employee in connection with a bankruptcy proceeding filed after September 11, 2001, and before January 1, 2007. The amount that may be contributed includes any withheld employment tax, but not amounts based on the future performance of the carrier. A payment contributed under this rule is treated as a qualified rollover contribution, and is not subject to the MAGI requirements that normally (until 2010) restrict rollovers to a Roth IRA. [Joint Comm. Staff, Tech. Expln. of H.R. 7327, *The Worker, Retiree, and Employer Recovery Act of 2008 as Passed by the House on Dec. 10, 2008*, p. 19 (JCX-85-08, Dec. 11, 2008)]

Beneficiaries

Q 6:82   May a nonspouse beneficiary roll over qualified plan b enefits to a traditional IRA?

Yes. A nonspouse designated beneficiary of a deceased qualified plan participant may now (since 2007) roll over the benefit in a tax-free transaction. [I.R.C. § 402(c)(11)] This is helpful because IRAs are simpler to deal with and have more flexible distribution provisions than many qualified plans. Usually, an IRA may be distributed over the beneficiary's life expectancy; that option is often unavailable if the benefit remains in a qualified plan.

The rollover is tax free if several conditions are satisfied. [I.R.C. 402(c)(11); Notice 2007-7, 2007-5 I.R.B. 395] First, a direct rollover is required; plan distributions are taxable if they pass through the nonspouse beneficiary's hands. As a practical matter, the direct transfer requirement means that many rollovers were unavailable in 2008 and 2009 because qualified plans were not then mandated to offer direct transfers and many did not allow them. Congress finally settled the matter by enacting a technical correction that requires qualified plans, effective January 2010, to offer direct transfers to nonspouse beneficiaries. [Worker, Retiree, and Employer Recovery Act of 2008, § 108(f)(2)(A), Pub. L. No. 110-458 (2008); I.R.C. § 402(f)(2)(A)]

The second requirement is that the receiving IRA must be titled so as to identify both the deceased participant and the beneficiary (e.g., "Tom Smith as beneficiary of John Smith") because it is treated for minimum distribution purposes as an inherited IRA (see Q 4:68–4:70).

Third, nonspouse beneficiaries may only roll over benefits from eligible retirement plans. Those are qualified plans under Code Section 401(a), annuity plans under Code Section 403(a) or (b), and governmental plans under Code Section 457(b).

Finally, if the decedent's named beneficiary is a trust, a direct rollover of the qualified plan benefits to an IRA on behalf of the trust is permitted provided the beneficiaries of the trust meet the requirements to be treated as the designated beneficiaries (see Q 4:78). [Notice 2007-7, Q&A-16, 2007-5 I.R.B. 395]

Q 6:83   May a nonspouse beneficiary roll over qualified plan benefits to a Roth IRA?

Yes, all of the same conditions described above for a direct rollover to a traditional IRA must be satisfied for rollover into a Roth IRA. In addition, until 2010 the requirements for a conversion must be met (see Q 3:92). [I.R.C. § 408A(e); Notice 2008-30, Q&A-7, 2008-12 I.R.B. 638]

Q 6:84   May a surviving spouse make a rollover when the beneficiary makes a disclaimer and the spouse then becomes the beneficiary?

Yes. In Private Letter Ruling 9247026 (Aug. 24, 1992), the trust beneficiaries of a trust that was named the beneficiary of a qualified plan death benefit made a disclaimer. As a result, the surviving spouse was entitled to the benefit and was permitted to make a rollover to a traditional IRA.

Q 6:85   When qualified plan benefits are paid to the employee's estate, is it possible to make a rollover?

No. The law provides that only a spouse beneficiary who is the sole beneficiary may roll over a deceased employee's benefits. [Priv. Ltr. Rul. 9229022 (Apr. 20, 1992)]

Q 6:86   If the beneficiary of an IRA is a marital trust or the decedent's estate, may the surviving spouse roll over the IRA or elect to treat it as his or her own IRA?

No, the spouse may roll over any distributions from the inherited IRA but may not elect to treat the inherited IRA as his or her own IRA (see Qs 10:41, 10:42, 10:49). [Priv. Ltr. Ruls. 200807025 (Feb. 15, 2008), 200615032 (Apr. 14, 2006)]

Q 6:87   May a rollover distribution include a required minimum distribution?

A distribution that includes an RMD may be rolled over only to the extent that the amount distributed exceeds the required minimum. The RMD portion may not be rolled over. [Priv. Ltr. Rul. 9211059 (Dec. 20, 1991); Notice 2007-7, Q&A-17, 2007-5 I.R.B. 395]

Note. The minimum distribution rules are suspended for 2009 (see Qs 4:21–4:25).

Q 6:88   If a decedent's traditional IRA is being rolled over to a surviving spouse's IRA, is there any mandatory withholding?

No. Traditional IRAs are not subject to the 20 percent withholding associated with qualified plan distributions. If the decedent's account was in a qualified plan or tax-sheltered annuity, however, a distribution to the surviving spouse would be subject to mandatory withholding unless it was directly rolled over to the surviving spouse's traditional IRA. Traditional IRAs are generally subject to 10 percent withholding on distributions unless the withholding is waived by the surviving spouse.

Q 6:89   **What is the result if a surviving spouse younger than age 59½ rolls over the deceased spouse's IRA to a spousal IRA and then takes a distribution?**

Once the funds are rolled over to the surviving spouse's IRA, they belong to the spouse as owner, not beneficiary, and the distribution-to-beneficiary exception to the Code Section 72(t) penalty would not apply upon a subsequent distribution to the spouse. Thus, the 10 percent penalty will apply unless the distribution qualifies under another exception (e.g., a first-time home-buyer's distribution). [Gee v. Commissioner, 127 T.C. 1 (2006)]

Practice Pointer. A surviving spouse who is younger than age 59½ may be better advised to delay rolling over a decedent spouse's IRA until the surviving spouse attains age 59½, so that distributions from the IRA may remain free of penalty.

Divorce

Q 6:90   **After rolling over a distribution to a traditional IRA, may an individual make a tax-free transfer to his or her spouse's traditional IRA?**

Unless a transfer to a spouse's traditional IRA is incident to divorce, it is treated as a taxable distribution from a traditional IRA followed by a recontribution to the spouse's traditional IRA. In Private Letter Ruling 8820086 (Feb. 25, 1988), the IRS declined to treat such a transfer as a tax-free spousal transfer pursuant to Code Section 1041(a), holding that Code Section 408 applies to traditional IRA transfers. In Private Letter Ruling 9344027 (Aug. 9, 1993), a separation agreement not incident to a legal separation or divorce was taxable to a traditional IRA owner who was dividing the traditional IRA in compliance with the agreement and community property rules. [*See also* I.R.C. § 408(d)(6); Priv. Ltr. Rul. 9006066 (Nov. 15, 1989) (regarding tax-free transfers incident to divorce).]

Q 6:91   **How is a transfer to a spouse's traditional IRA in conjunction with a divorce property settlement agreement treated?**

In Private Letter Ruling 8504079 (Oct. 31, 1984), A and B were in the process of obtaining a divorce, and it was proposed that the distribution from a qualified plan to A be transferred over by A's traditional IRA to a traditional IRA established for B as part of the agreement. The transfer was held to be nontaxable, and the traditional IRA was treated as belonging to B, incident to the divorce.

In Private Letter Ruling 8649053 (Sept. 10, 1986), a property settlement made pursuant to a marriage dissolution and incorporated into the final decree called for an equitable division of all in-force retirement accounts and annuities. The court issued a clarification, ordering the rollover of one ex-spouse's traditional

IRA assets to the other ex-spouse. Cash surrender proceeds of the Section 403(b) annuity contracts were rolled over to an existing traditional IRA owned by the first ex-spouse. That traditional IRA was then transferred to the second ex-spouse by way of a transfer of the traditional IRA assets. The IRS concluded that this transfer was nontaxable as a transfer of a traditional IRA incident to divorce. [*See also* Priv. Ltr. Rul. 9016077 (Jan. 25, 1990) (regarding an assignment to an ex-spouse).] A similar result was reached regarding an agreement that "merely" reclassified assets under a state marital property law. [Priv. Ltr. Rul. 9419036 (Feb. 16, 1994)]

Q 6:92   How may a rollover or a transfer be made in the context of a divorce?

There are six ways to make a rollover or transfer in the context of a divorce:

1. The traditional IRA may be continued and the name of the owner changed. (The traditional IRA trustee or custodian may require the new owner to sign a new traditional IRA document.)

2. A trustee-to-trustee transfer to a new or an existing traditional IRA may be directed.

3. When the receiving spouse is not receiving all the traditional IRA assets, the transferring spouse may direct the trustee or custodian to make a direct transfer of his or her portion to a new or an existing traditional IRA, changing the name of the owner of the traditional IRA from which the transfer has been made to the receiving spouse's name.

4. Assets may be withdrawn and transferred, by rollover within 60 days, to a new or an existing traditional IRA of the receiving spouse.

5. The assets may be given to the receiving spouse, who then contributes the assets by rollover, within 60 days, to his or her new or existing traditional IRA.

6. The receiving spouse may change the name on the transferring spouse's traditional IRA to the receiving spouse's name, after withdrawing assets not being transferred, and roll over those assets to another traditional IRA in the transferring spouse's name.

Q 6:93   What happens when a rollover occurs pursuant to a QDRO directing that the qualified plan account of one spouse be transferred to the other spouse?

If a court order meets the requirements of a qualified domestic relations order (QDRO) issued under Code Section 414(p), the spouse or former spouse of the plan participant is deemed to be the alternate payee and distributee. As such, the spouse or former spouse has the right to roll over a distribution from the qualified plan to a traditional IRA or have it directly transferred to a traditional IRA by the plan's trustee. The recipient spouse or former spouse will not be taxed if the distribution is directly rolled over, as long as the distribution is rolled over within 60 days.

In Private Letter Ruling 9327083 (Apr. 14, 1993), an ex-wife had a legitimate QDRO claim to half of the benefits accrued by her ex-husband under his employer's plan. Subsequently, the ex-husband remarried and rolled over the entire balance of his plan benefits to a traditional IRA. When he died, the traditional IRA went to his second wife. The first wife claimed her QDRO benefits under the original plan and received a settlement from the second wife. When the first wife wanted to treat the benefits as either a tax-free rollover based on the original QDRO or a transfer incident to divorce under the traditional IRA, the IRS refused to allow that treatment. The IRS said it was not considered a taxable distribution from the terminated traditional IRA or from the original plan, but rather a settlement of a separate claim.

Q 6:94 What happens if the entire QDRO distribution is not rolled over?

The portion of a QDRO distribution that is not rolled over is taxable in the year it is received. If it is not rolled over, special rules for lump-sum distributions may apply. [IRS Publications 590, *Individual Retirement Arrangements (IRAs)* 2008 (see Appendix A), and 575, *Pension and Annuity Income* 2008]

Q 6:95 How does the 10 percent premature distribution penalty apply to distributions incident to divorce?

Neither an alternate payee (spouse or former spouse of a participant receiving a distribution under a QDRO), a beneficiary (other than the spouse), nor a surviving spouse should be subject to the 10 percent premature distribution penalty, even if such a person is under age 59½. That is not the case, however, when a traditional IRA is divided pursuant to a divorce. The recipient spouse, if he or she is under age 59½, must keep the assets in a traditional IRA or be subject to the premature distribution penalty. [IRS Publications 590, *Individual Retirement Arrangements (IRAs)* 2008 (see Appendix A), and 575, *Pension and Annuity Income* 2008]

Q 6:96 Is a direct rollover permitted under a QDRO?

Yes. A direct rollover may be made to the traditional IRA or other eligible employer plan of a spouse or former spouse receiving a qualified plan distribution under a QDRO. Failure to elect a direct rollover will subject the spouse or former spouse to mandatory withholding. [I.R.C. § 402(e)(1)]

Rollovers and Transfers from SIMPLE IRAs

Q 6:97 May a SIMPLE IRA be rolled over or transferred to another SIMPLE IRA?

Yes. Rollovers and transfers between SIMPLE IRAs follow the same basic rules as rollovers and transfers between traditional IRAs (see Q 6:6). Unlike traditional IRAs, however, SIMPLE IRAs are subject to specific rules governing when the trustee or custodian may charge transfer or other fees in connection with a transfer from one SIMPLE IRA to another. [Notice 98-4, 1998-1 C.B. 269]

Q 6:98   May a SIMPLE IRA be rolled over to a traditional IRA?

Yes, but only after two years. For the two-year period beginning on the date that an employee first participated in a SIMPLE, the employee is not allowed to roll over or transfer assets from the SIMPLE to a traditional IRA. The date that the employee first participated in the SIMPLE is the date of the first deposit into the SIMPLE IRA. [Notice 98-4, 1998-1 C.B. 269] After the two-year period has elapsed, the SIMPLE IRA assets may be rolled over or transferred to a traditional IRA.

Q 6:99   How does the SIMPLE IRA differ from the traditional IRA during its first two years?

Distributions from a SIMPLE IRA occurring within the first two years that the individual participated in the SIMPLE are subject to a 25 percent penalty for individuals under age 59½, instead of the 10 percent penalty applicable to other IRAs. Accordingly, the law requires that the assets in the SIMPLE IRA remain separate from the assets in a traditional IRA for the first two years.

Q 6:100   May an individual transfer or roll over traditional IRA or qualified plan assets to a SIMPLE IRA?

No. SIMPLE IRAs are designed to receive only contributions made pursuant to a SIMPLE.

Q 6:101   May a SIMPLE IRA be rolled over to a qualified plan, a tax-sheltered annuity, or a deferred compensation plan of a state or local government?

Yes. After the expiration of the two-year period (see Q 6:98), an individual may make a tax-free rollover of a distribution from a SIMPLE IRA to a qualified plan, a tax-sheltered annuity (Section 403(b) plan), or a deferred compensation plan of a state or local government (Section 457 plan). [I.R.C. § 408(d)(3)(G)]

Rollovers from IRAs to Qualified Plans

Q 6:102   May IRA assets that were originally sourced from a qualified plan rollover be rolled over from the IRA to a qualified plan?

Yes. All assets in IRAs (except after-tax contributions) are eligible to be rolled over to qualified plans without regard to the original source of the funds (i.e., whether prior rollovers or IRA contributions). [I.R.C. § 408(d)(3)(A)]

Q 6:103   How are nondeductible contributions made by the IRA owner treated?

Funds in IRAs that are attributable to after-tax contributions may not be rolled over to qualified plans. [I.R.C. § 408(d)(3)(A)(ii)] However, the earnings on such after-tax contributions can be rolled over to a qualified plan.

Q 6:104   May IRA funds that are rolled over to a qualified plan be used to purchase life insurance?

Although IRAs are not permitted to purchase life insurance [I.R.C. § 408(a)(3)], IRA assets that are rolled over into a qualified plan can be used for that purpose if the plan permits.

Q 6:105   What steps must be taken to roll over IRA assets back to a qualified plan?

Because qualified plans are not required to permit rollbacks, the provisions of a qualified plan must be reviewed to determine whether IRA assets may be rolled over to the plan. A qualified plan may require that the IRA owner certify to the plan administrator that the IRA is eligible to be rolled over (i.e., none of its assets are attributable to after-tax contributions).

Note. A qualified plan will not lose its tax qualification if it inadvertently accepts an invalid rollover contribution from an IRA custodian as long as the plan administrator reasonably concludes that the rollover is permissible based on the documentation provided by the IRA owner. [Treas. Reg. § 1.401(a)(31)-1, Q&A-14]

Q 6:106   Is the IRA trustee or custodian required to withhold income taxes if funds are distributed to the IRA owner and rolled over to a qualified plan?

No. An IRA trustee or custodian is not required to withhold income taxes if funds are distributed to an IRA owner and rolled over to a qualified plan. Such a distribution would be a *nonperiodic distribution*, and the owner therefore would be able to waive 10 percent withholding by completing Form W-4P, Withholding Certificate for Pension or Annuity Payments, and requesting that no taxes be withheld (see chapter 7).

Q 6:107   If an IRA owner withdraws funds from an IRA, how long does he or she have to roll over the funds back to a qualified plan before they become taxable to the owner?

IRA funds withdrawn by an IRA owner must be rolled over to a qualified plan (or to another IRA) within 60 days of receipt of the distribution. Failure to adhere to the 60-day rule will trigger income tax on the amounts withdrawn. (See Qs 6:6–6:11.)

Q 6:108　If an IRA has received rollover distributions from two different qualified plans, may all the funds in the IRA be rolled over to a qualified plan?

As long as the qualified plans originally making the rollover distribution to the IRA did not hold after-tax contributions that were transferred to the IRA, and no after-tax contributions were made to the IRA, there are no restrictions regarding rolling over the IRA assets to a qualified plan.

> **Note.** Code Section 408(d)(3)(H) permits an IRA owner to apportion and retain the after-tax contributions in an IRA and roll over the remaining pretax amount to a qualified plan. Thus, the fact that an IRA contains after-tax contributions does not taint the entire IRA or prevent the rollover of the pretax portion of its assets to a qualified plan.

Q 6:109　May only a portion of an IRA's assets be rolled over to a qualified plan?

Yes. Code Section 408(d)(3)(A) provides that an IRA may distribute "any amount," and such amount may be rolled over to a qualified plan. Moreover, under Code Section 408(d)(3)(D), if only a portion of the amount withdrawn from an IRA is rolled over to a qualified plan and the rest of it is retained by the IRA owner, the IRS will treat the requirements of Code Section 408(d)(3)(A) as being satisfied for the portion that is rolled over to a qualified plan, provided the rollover is performed not later than the 60th day after the day on which the owner received the distribution. [Priv. Ltr. Rul. 9518019 (Feb. 6, 1995)]

Q 6:110　Is there a special aggregation rule for determining taxable amounts from multiple IRAs?

Yes. An individual may have multiple IRAs and may have made nondeductible contributions to one or more of them, or have after-tax contributions in one or more of them. The individual does not have to limit a rollover from any one of these IRAs to a qualified plan to the actual taxable amount in a particular IRA because the part being rolled over is considered to come from amounts in all IRAs, disregarding nondeductible contributions and after-tax contributions. [I.R.C. § 408(d)(3)(H)(ii)(II)] This is the exception to Code Section 408(d)(2)(A), which normally requires basis to be recovered pro rata when amounts are withdrawn from an IRA and the IRA owner has made nondeductible contributions or has after-tax contributions in any IRA.

> **Example.** Robert, age 53, is employed by ABC Company and participates in the ABC 401(k) Plan. His vested 401(k) account balance is approximately $145,000. The plan allows rollovers from traditional IRAs, and Robert has two IRAs. IRA-1 has a $60,000 balance (consisting of deductible contributions and earnings on these contributions) and IRA-2, which has a balance of $125,000 ($40,000 of which is a nontaxable investment in the contract derived from nondeductible contributions over the years and $85,000 of which is taxable contributions and earnings on all contributions). Because

Robert has a total taxable amount of $145,000 ($60,000 + $85,000), he can roll over up to $145,000 of any IRA funds to any eligible retirement plan. Robert decides to roll over all of IRA-2 to the ABC 401(k) Plan. In this manner, he is permitted to roll over the $40,000 of investment in the contract funds that had previously existed in IRA-2.

Q 6:111 Must an IRA owner be employed by the employer sponsoring the qualified plan that is receiving the rollover funds?

Yes. A qualified plan may allow only employees to be participants. Thus, a qualified plan is not permitted to accept a rollover from an independent contractor or an individual who does not otherwise have an employment relationship with the employer.

Q 6:112 May an IRA owner who is over age 70½ roll over assets to a qualified plan and begin to have contributions to that plan made on his or her behalf?

Yes. The prohibition against continued contributions after reaching age 70½ is applicable only to traditional IRAs. [I.R.C. § 219(d)] There are no similar age limitations for making contributions to a qualified plan. Thus, an IRA owner over age 70½ may roll over his or her IRA to a qualified plan and have contributions made to that plan. It should be noted, however, that if the IRA owner is over age 70½ and is a 5 percent owner with respect to the employer maintaining the qualified plan, the plan would have to make required minimum distributions (RMDs) under Code Section 401(a)(9) while such contributions are being made. It should also be noted that Code Section 408(d)(3)(E) prohibits RMDs from an IRA to be rolled over to a qualified plan. Only amounts that the IRA owner withdraws in excess of the RMD are permitted to be rolled over to an IRA.

Q 6:113 May IRA funds that are rolled over to a qualified plan be used to issue employer stock?

There does not seem to be a clear legal impediment, but the IRS considers such transactions as potentially abusive. In 2008, it issued guidelines for applying heightened scrutiny to so-called ROBS transactions (its acronym for "rollovers as business start-ups"). Briefly, these are transactions in which an IRA (or other retirement account) is rolled over to a new shell corporation's qualified plan, the plan acquires employer stock in exchange for the cash, and the corporation uses the cash to fund start-up costs of a new business. The IRS view is that the transactions may illegally circumvent the taxable distribution rules. [Memorandum from Michael D. Julianelle (Oct. 1, 2008), at *http://www.irs.gov/pub/irs-tege/rollover_guidelines.pdf*; IR-2009-41, *Beware of IRS' 2009 "Dirty Dozen" Tax Scams* (Apr. 13, 2009)]

Rollovers from Designated Roth Accounts to Roth IRAs

Q 6:114 What is a designated Roth account?

It is now possible for 401(k) and 403(b) plans to include a qualified Roth IRA contribution program, under which participants may elect to have part or all of their elective deferrals to the plan designated as after-tax Roth contributions. [I.R.C. § 402A; Prop. Treas. Reg. § 1.402A-1] Designated Roth IRA accounts (DRACs) are not subject to the income limitations that apply to Roth IRAs.

Note. A DRAC is not an IRA but a particular kind of after-tax account for accepting elective deferrals held in a qualified plan.

Q 6:115 Why may it be desirable to roll amounts over from a DRAC to a Roth IRA?

There are two advantages to rolling over amounts from a DRAC to a Roth IRA. DRACs are subject to lifetime RMDs, but Roth IRAs are exempted from those rules. [I.R.C. § 408A(c)(5)] Also, the rules for recovering basis (the employee's investment on which taxes have already been paid) are more favorable for a Roth IRA than for a DRAC. With a Roth IRA, basis comes out first, and distributions are tax free until basis has been entirely distributed. With a DRAC, a portion of the earnings, which are taxable, must be allocated to each distribution. [I.R.C. § 408A(d)(4)(B)] (See chapter 5 for a full discussion of the Roth IRA distribution rules.)

Q 6:116 Are there disadvantages in rolling amounts over from a DRAC to a Roth IRA?

There are disadvantages in some cases. One disadvantage of rolling over an amount from a DRAC to a Roth IRA is that the participant may have to start the five-year holding period for receiving tax-free qualified distributions all over again. The holding period that began when the DRAC owner first contributed to the DRAC does not carry over to the Roth IRA. The five-year holding period for a Roth IRA begins with the first year of contribution to any Roth IRA, so if the first year the individual contributes to any Roth IRA is the year of the DRAC rollover, the wait for a qualified distribution from that IRA will be five years. Of course, if the participant already fulfilled the five-year requirement for the Roth IRA, the rollover from the DRAC can be immediately distributed tax free from the Roth IRA even if the money was in the DRAC for less than five years. [Prop. Treas. Reg. § 1.408A-10, A-4(b)]

Example. Margaret establishes a DRAC in 2009, and in 2014 she takes a qualified distribution of $50,000, which she rolls into a new Roth IRA account (her first) established for that purpose. Although qualified distributions cannot be made from the Roth IRA until 2019, Margaret may withdraw up to $50,000 tax free at any time, because the ordering rules treat her basis as coming out first.

A second possible disadvantage is that the rules for basis allocation are unclear in the case of an unqualified distribution that is received from a DRAC where only part of the distribution is rolled over to a Roth IRA. [*See* Prop. Treas. Reg. § 1.402As-1, A-5(b).]

Q 6:117 How is a rollover from a DRAC to a Roth IRA accomplished?

Any participant (even one who is ineligible to make annual contributions to a Roth IRA or convert from a traditional IRA to a Roth IRA) can make a tax-free rollover from a DRAC to a Roth IRA. [Prop. Treas. Reg. § 1.408A-10, A-2] A rollover can be effected by a trustee-to-trustee transfer or by a 60-day distribution and recontribution. [Prop. Treas. Reg. § 1.402A-1, A-5(a); Notice 2009–68, 2009–39 I.R.B. ___]

Rollovers from IRAs to Health Savings Accounts

Q 6:118 May assets be rolled over tax free from an IRA to an HSA to fund future medical expenses?

Yes, but only once per lifetime and if an election is made. The participant must be an eligible individual, and the withdrawal from the IRA must be a qualified HSA funding distribution. If the requirements are satisfied, the rollover is made tax free and without penalty. The rules are extremely complicated, however (see Qs 4:144–4:156). [I.R.C. § 408(d)(9); Notice 2008-51, 2008-25 I.R.B. 1163]

Chapter 7

Disclosure, Filings, Penalties, and Withholding

Martin Fleisher, Esq.
Jo Ann Lippe, Esq.

Contributions to and distributions from IRAs must be reported both to the Internal Revenue Service (IRS) and to the IRA owner. Withholding is required, unless waived. This chapter explains how to comply with the IRS and Department of Labor reporting requirements applicable to IRA owners, employers, trustees, and custodians. Substantive issues that may affect reporting are examined, as are rules relating to regular IRA contributions, rollovers, transfers, inherited IRAs, revoked IRAs, and SEP and SIMPLE contributions. Disclosure requirements on the establishment of an IRA are reviewed, as is the seven-day waiting period during which the decision to establish an IRA may be revoked.

Disclosure

Q 7:1 Must a disclosure statement be provided to a prospective IRA owner?

Yes. When an IRA is being established, a full disclosure statement must be given to the prospective IRA owner (see Q 7:2) along with a complete set of IRA plan documents. The prospective IRA owner must then be given at least seven days in which to change his or her mind. [Treas. Reg. § 1.408-6(d)(4)(ii)] (During that period, financial and other data regarding the individual establishing the IRA may be completed.)

The foregoing rules also apply to IRAs that are established in connection with a simplified employee pension plan (SEP), a salary reduction simplified employee pension plan (SARSEP), or a savings incentive match plan for employees (SIMPLE). The Roth IRA and the Coverdell education savings account (Coverdell ESA) also require disclosure statements that are slightly different from a traditional IRA disclosure statement.

Q 7:2 What information must be included in the disclosure statement for a traditional IRA?

Information that must be included in the disclosure statement for a traditional IRA is as follows:

1. The requirements for establishing an IRA;
2. Financial projections that indicate whether the return on the IRA is guaranteed;
3. Deductibility rules;
4. Revocation rights, including the name, address, and telephone number of the personal representative of the trustee or custodian designated to receive revocations;
5. Distribution rules;
6. Prohibited transactions and their consequences;
7. Tax penalties;
8. Estate and gift tax consequences;
9. Whether approval of the IRS has been obtained and, if it has, that the approval does not deal with the financial merits or advisability of the taxpayer's adopting the plan;
10. Rollover availability;
11. Tax exemption;
12. Nonavailability of forward averaging or capital gains treatment;
13. Advice about commissions payable, expressed as a percentage of an assumed contribution; and
14. Any additional information required by Treasury regulations (that the statement must not be false or misleading).

[Treas. Reg. § 1.408-6(d)(4)(iii)–1.408-6(d)(4)(vii)]

Note The disclosure statement need not contain specific information pertaining to the benefited individual; however, it must be complete in all other respects. [*See* Treas. Reg. § 1.408-6(d)(4)(ii)(A)(2).]

Q 7:3   What are the rules for mailing an IRA disclosure statement?

Treasury regulations provide that if an IRA disclosure statement, a governing instrument, or an amendment to either is mailed to an individual, it will be deemed to have been received seven days after the date of mailing, unless there is contrary evidence. If the mailing is received in less than seven days before the earlier of the date of the IRA's establishment or the date of investment, the right of revocation must be granted. If an individual's written revocation is required or permitted, the postmark or certification date determines when the revocation was mailed. [Treas. Reg. § 1.408-6(d)(4)]

Generally, a disclosure statement is considered to be mailed on the date of the postmark stamped on the cover in which the document was properly mailed, even if it is received after the date normally required. [Prop. Treas. Reg. §§ 301.7502-1, 301.7502-2] The sender has the burden of proving when the postmark was made. (See Qs 7:42–7:55 for additional mailing rules.)

Revocation

Q 7:4 What may the prospective IRA owner do during the seven-day revocation period?

If a prospective IRA owner is given a disclosure statement on the same day his or her IRA is established, that individual has seven days after the establishment date to exercise his or her right of revocation. If the individual is given the disclosure statement at least seven days before the IRA is established, no additional revocation period is required. Within the seven-day revocation period, the prospective IRA owner may cancel the IRA plan agreement. Revocation may be accomplished orally or in writing, as specified in the IRA disclosure statement received.

If a timely revocation is received by the IRA trustee or custodian, the individual is entitled to receive the entire amount contributed without any adjustments for sales commissions, administrative fees (including certificate of deposit penalties), or fluctuation in the market value. [Treas. Reg. § 1.408-6(d)(4)]

Note. The traditional IRA and the Roth IRA follow the same rules concerning revocation. The Coverdell ESA is not subject to the revocation rules.

Q 7:5 Must the revocation of an IRA be reported?

Yes. IRA trustees and custodians must report contributions made and revoked on Form 5498, IRA Contribution Information (see Q 7:10), and all "revoked" distributions on Form 1099-R, Distributions From Pensions, Annuities, Retirement or Profit-Sharing Plans, IRAs, Insurance Contracts, etc. Form 5498 will, however, show the year-end fair market value as zero unless the transaction was initiated immediately before the end of the year and revoked early in the following year.

Note. In many cases, depending on the type of contribution being revoked, the revocation of an IRA has tax consequences.

Q 7:6 How may IRA trustees and custodians protect themselves during the seven-day revocation period?

To protect themselves from having to restore investment losses upon revocation, some IRA trustees and custodians do not allow initial contributions to be invested in anything other than a government-guaranteed investment or government-guaranteed security until the seven-day revocation period has expired. Unless the IRA document provides otherwise, investment gains do not have to be distributed from an IRA that is timely revoked.

Example. The IRA document sponsored by Friendly Mutual Funds provides that contributions made during the first seven days after an IRA is established will be invested in the Friendly U.S. Government Cash Fund. After the seven-day period, assets in the IRA may be transferred to any of the Friendly stock or bond funds. Friendly has limited its loss in the event that an IRA is revoked; it could even make a profit.

Reports to the IRS and the IRA Owner

Q 7:7   What report must be filed to advise the IRS about contributions that have been made to an IRA?

An IRA trustee or custodian is required to report IRA contributions to the IRS on Form 5498 (see Qs 7:136–7:147). Items reported include regular contributions, rollovers, SEP contributions, SIMPLE contributions, Roth conversion amounts, recharacterized contributions, and year-end fair market value.

Q 7:8   When must Form 5498 be filed?

Form 5498 must be filed on an annual basis. It is due by May 31 of the year following the year for which the contribution is made.

Q 7:9   Must Form 5498 be filed even if an IRA is closed before year-end or has no value at year-end because of investment loss?

Yes. Even if an IRA is closed before year-end, or has no value at year-end because of investment loss, Form 5498 must still be filed to report contributions made for the year.

Q 7:10   Must Form 5498 be filed even if an IRA is revoked by December 31?

If any reportable contributions were made during the year, even if an IRA is revoked by December 31 of that year, Form 5498 must be filed to report contributions made for the year.

Q 7:11   What must be reported on Form 5498 if an IRA is revoked in the year following its creation?

If at the end of the year in which a contribution was made the fair market value of an IRA is more than zero, that amount must be included on Form 5498, which must be filed to cover the year the IRA was created. That is the case even if the IRA is timely revoked in the following year.

Q 7:12   Must a report on the December 31 fair market value of the assets held by an IRA be provided to the IRA owner?

Yes. A December 31 fair market value report is required to be provided to the IRA owner in any written format no later than the following January 31.

Q 7:13 Does an IRA owner receive Form 5498?

Yes. Except as provided below, by the filing deadline for Form 5498 (see Q 7:8), each IRA owner must receive from the IRA trustee or custodian either the official IRS Form 5498 or a substitute Form 5498 that meets the requirements of IRS Publication 1179, *Rules and Specifications for Private Printing of Substitute Forms 1096, 1098, 1099, 5498, and W-2G.* Publication 1179 includes Revenue Procedure 2008-36 [2008-33 I.R.B. 340], which contains the requirements for the format, content, and furnishing of substitute statements to recipients; it is revised annually.

If the IRA trustee or custodian furnished the December 31 fair market value statement to the IRA owner by January 31 as required (see Q 7:12) and no reportable contributions to the IRA were made, the owner need not receive Form 5498. In such a case, however, the fair market value statement must contain a legend indicating which information is being provided to the IRS.

Q 7:14 How must distributions from an IRA be reported?

IRA distributions must be reported to the IRS on Form 1099-R (see Qs 7:84–7:109), which generally must be filed with the IRS by the trustee or custodian no later than February 28 (March 31 if filed electronically) following the calendar year for which distributions are being reported. For 2010, however, the paper filing deadline is March 1, 2010, because February 28 falls on a Sunday. A copy must be sent to the recipient of the distribution by January 31 following the calendar year being reported.

Q 7:15 What report must be filed when a trustee transfers an IRA to another trustee?

Generally, the receiving trustee does not file Form 5498 to report direct transfers between IRAs that involve no payment or distribution to the IRA owner. The transferring trustee would have been responsible for reporting the contributions when they were initially made. Moreover, the transferring IRA trustee does not report the transfer of assets on Form 1099-R, because no distribution has been made.

There are exceptions. If a SIMPLE IRA is transferred to a non-SIMPLE IRA before the employee has participated in the SIMPLE for a two-year period measured from the date the first SIMPLE contribution was deposited into the SIMPLE IRA, reporting is required on both Form 1099-R (as a taxable distribution) and Form 5498 (as a regular contribution). Reporting may also be required for recharacterizations made pursuant to a trustee-to-trustee transfer. (See Qs 7:89, 7:142.)

Q 7:16 Do reporting requirements differ when a transfer is made or received by an IRA custodian?

No. The IRA rules specifically allow for choosing a trustee or a custodian without any change in IRA attributes (see chapter 2).

Taxpayer Reporting of Distributions

Q 7:17 How does a taxpayer report receipt of distributions from an IRA?

Using the information provided on Form 1099-R, a taxpayer must report distributions received during the year from an IRA on lines 15a and 15b of Form 1040, U.S. Individual Income Tax Return (or lines 11a and 11b of Form 1040A), which is filed by the following April 15 or by a later, extended due date (see Qs 7:73–7:78).

Q 7:18 How does a taxpayer determine whether any portion of a distribution may be excluded from income because it was rolled over within 60 days to another IRA or to an employer plan?

An IRA-to-IRA rollover should be documented by corresponding copies of Forms 1099-R and 5498. A direct rollover from an employer's plan to an IRA should be represented by a Form 1099-R that is properly coded to show that the distribution is not taxable because it was directly rolled over; Form 5498 will report that the amount was rolled over to an IRA.

If a conduit IRA (an IRA consisting of assets transferred or rolled over from a qualified plan) is rolled over to another employer's plan, the taxpayer does not file Form 5498 to report the amount rolled over. Instead, the taxpayer should attach an explanation to his or her federal income tax return stating that the direct rollover was made to another employer's plan. If a conduit IRA is paid directly to the trustee (or custodian) of the employer's plan, it is reported on Form 1099-R. Code G is placed in box 7 to show that the funds were directly rolled over to an employer's plan.

Rollovers of traditional IRAs (excluding the portion of the IRA consisting of nondeductible IRA contributions) to any employer plan, including a qualified plan, a Section 403(b) plan, and a Section 457(b) plan, are to be reported on Form 1099-R using code G in box 7 (see Q 7:89).

Q 7:19 If any portion of an IRA distribution is not rolled over, is that portion automatically reported as a fully taxable distribution?

Not necessarily. The portion of an IRA distribution that was not rolled over is not automatically reported by the taxpayer as a fully taxable distribution if nondeductible contributions were made to the IRA. In that case, a calculation must be made to determine what portion of the distribution represents a return of after-tax money (i.e., money taxed before being contributed on a nondeductible basis). It should be noted, however, that the IRA trustee or custodian will report the amount as taxable; the taxpayer must file Form 8606, Nondeductible IRAs, to prove otherwise.

Q 7:20 Are other IRAs taken into account in the calculation of the portion of a distribution representing a return of after-tax money?

Yes. A taxpayer's entire traditional IRA portfolio (including SEP IRAs, rollovers, and SIMPLE IRAs) must be taken into account when calculating what portion of a distribution represents a return of after-tax contributions. That is so even if none of the other traditional IRAs includes any nondeductible contributions (i.e., those other IRAs were all 100 percent deductible when created; see Qs 7:164–7:175). Roth IRAs are treated separately for the purpose of calculating a return of after-tax money.

Withholding

Q 7:21 Is withholding reflected on Form 1099-R?

Yes. Form 1099-R reflects federal income tax withholding. It also provides for state and local tax information (see chapter 14).

Q 7:22 What is withheld from an IRA distribution?

Ten percent of a traditional IRA's nonperiodic taxable distributions (see Q 7:24) will be withheld unless the taxpayer waives withholding (see Q 7:23). [I.R.C. § 3405] Such withholding is referred to as "voluntary" withholding. Withholding does not apply to Roth IRA distributions. [I.R.C. § 3405(e)(1)]

No waiver is necessary, of course, when the distribution is an eligible rollover distribution and it is made directly from an employer plan to another employer plan or to an IRA. Thus, an IRA can be used to avoid "mandatory" withholding (see Q 7:25).

Q 7:23 How is withholding from an IRA distribution waived?

The IRA trustee or custodian should provide the taxpayer with Form W-4P, Withholding Certificate for Pension or Annuity Payments (or other acceptable form), so that the waiver can be executed before the distribution is made.

Q 7:24 What is a nonperiodic distribution?

For withholding purposes, a *nonperiodic distribution* is any distribution that is not a periodic distribution. A periodic distribution includes taxable annuity payments, such as a series of payments to be made for more than a year.

Q 7:25 Is there any mandatory withholding from an IRA?

There is generally no mandatory withholding from an IRA. However, withholding may be required if a taxpayer identification number (TIN) is missing or incorrect (see Qs 7:96, 7:97).

Penalties

Q 7:26   What role does Form 1099-R play in determining if penalties apply to an IRA distribution?

Form 1099-R is a statement provided to both the IRS and the recipient of IRA distributions made during the year (see Q 7:14). Box 7 of Form 1099-R contains a number of "reason codes" that notify the IRS of the tax treatment of the distributions and the year to which the statements relate. Those codes assist the taxpayer in determining whether Form 5329, Additional Taxes on Qualified Plans (Including IRAs) and Other Tax-Favored Accounts, must be prepared.

Q 7:27   What is the importance of Form 5329?

Form 5329 is used by a taxpayer to calculate excise taxes due (see Qs 7:29–7:41, 7:110–7:125). There are eight parts to Form 5329.

Part I. Part I is used to report the additional tax (10 percent) for distributions made before age 59½ that do not meet one of the exceptions allowed for IRAs (see Qs 7:29, 7:30).

Part II. Part II is used to report the additional tax (10 percent) on distributions from Coverdell ESAs not used for qualified educational expenses.

Part III. Part III is used to report the tax on excess contributions to traditional IRAs.

Part IV. Part IV is used to report the tax on excess contributions to Roth IRAs.

Part V. Part V is used to report the tax on excess contributions to Coverdell ESAs.

Part VI. Part VI is used to report the tax on excess contributions to Archer medical savings accounts (Archer MSAs).

Part VII. Part VII is used to report the tax on excess contributions to health savings accounts (HSAs).

Part VIII. Part VIII is used to report the tax on excess accumulations. Excess accumulations result when an individual fails to take a required minimum distribution (RMD) after age 70½ or death.

Q 7:28   In addition to "reason codes," what other information may be provided on Form 1099-R?

If a distribution from an IRA includes an annuity contract, its value will be shown on Form 1099-R even though it is not taxable until (and only as) distributions are received from the contract under Code Section 72. [Treas. Reg. § 1.408-4(e)] For purposes of applying Code Section 72 to a distribution from such a contract, the investment in the contract is zero.

The percentage of the total IRA distribution belonging to the recipient, if distribution is also made to another person or persons, may also be included on Form 1099-R.

Early Distributions

Q 7:29   How does Part I of Form 5329 specifically address the 10 percent penalty tax on early distributions?

Part I of Form 5329 (with accompanying instructions) begins by enumerating the types of IRA distributions that are to be considered. In each case, the distribution is one that has been received before the taxpayer has reached age 59½.

Distributions should be shown net of current-year contributions already withdrawn and earlier contributions withdrawn as excess, as explained in the form. Nondeductible contributions as determined on Form 8606 are also to be excluded.

Among the distributions to be summarized are the following:

1. Annuity contract distributions;
2. Modified endowment contract distributions; and
3. Distributions resulting from prohibited transactions.

Distributions can occur as a result of a prohibited transaction in various ways. If, for example, a taxpayer borrows from either an individual retirement account or an individual retirement annuity, such an action disqualifies the IRA as of the first day of the tax year in which the borrowing occurred. If the taxpayer was at that time younger than age 59½ (even if he or she was age 59½ or older when the borrowing actually occurred), the early distribution penalty applies.

The result is different if an individual retirement annuity is pledged as security for a loan.

If a pledge relates to an individual retirement annuity, the amount pledged is to be reported in Part I. Because the date of the pledge determines the age of the taxpayer, if the taxpayer is at that time under age 59½, a pre-age-59½ distribution of the IRA will be deemed to have occurred on the date of the pledge.

Investment of an IRA in a collectible is deemed a distribution of the IRA on the date of the investment. Collectibles include the following:

- Works of art
- Rugs or antiques
- Metals or gems
- Stamps or coins other than certain U.S. gold, silver, and platinum coins
- Certain gold, silver, platinum, and palladium bullion
- Alcoholic beverages
- Any other tangible personal property specified by the IRS

For detailed information about reporting prohibited transactions on Form 5330, Return of Excise Taxes Related to Employee Benefit Plans, see Qs 7:126 through 7:135.

Q 7:30 **What exceptions to the 10 percent penalty on premature distributions are recognized on line 2 in Part I of Form 5329?**

The exceptions to the 10 percent penalty on premature distributions that are recognized (and coded according to the exception number shown below) on line 2 in Part I of Form 5329 are as follows:

1. Distributions due to separation from service in or after the year the taxpayer reaches age 55 (does not apply to IRAs);

2. Substantially equal periodic payments [I.R.C. § 72(t)(2)(A)(iv)];

3. Distributions on account of disability, as defined by the IRS [I.R.C. § 72(t)(2)(A)(iii); Treas. Reg. § 1.712-17(f)];

4. Distributions due to death [I.R.C. § 72(t)(2)(A)(ii)];

5. Distributions for medical expenses under Code Section 213 to the extent that they do not exceed the amount allowable as an itemized deduction (even if the taxpayer does not itemize deductions) [I.R.C. § 72(t)(2)(B)];

6. Distributions made pursuant to a qualified domestic relations order (does not apply to IRAs) [I.R.C. § 72(t)(2)(C)];

7. Distributions made to unemployed individuals for health insurance premiums [I.R.C. § 72(t)(2)(D)];

8. Distributions made for qualified higher education expenses [I.R.C. § 72(t)(2)(E)];

9. Distributions made for a first-time home purchase, up to $10,000 [I.R.C. § 72(t)(2)(F)];

10. Distributions made pursuant to an IRS levy [I.R.C. § 72(t)(2)(A)(vii)];

11. Qualified distributions to reservists while serving on active duty for at least 180 days [I.R.C. § 72(t)(2)(G)];

12. Other—use code 12 if more than one exception applies, or if one of the following exceptions applies:

    • Distributions incorrectly indicated as early distributions by code 1, J or S in box 7 of Form 1099-R (include on line 2 the amount received by a taxpayer age 59½ or older);

    • Distributions from a Code Section 457 plan, which are not from a rollover from a qualified retirement plan;

    • Distributions already commenced and based on status as of March 1986; and

    • Distributions from annuity contracts allocable to investments in the contract before August 14, 1982.

Q 7:31 **If Form 1099-R incorrectly reported a distribution as being premature, how may that error be corrected?**

If a distribution was reported on Form 1099-R as being premature even though it was received after the taxpayer attained age 59½, Form 5329 should be used to correct the error. The taxpayer should include the distribution that was received after age 59½ on line 2 and enter exception number "12" in the space provided.

Distributions Not Used for Qualified Higher Education Expenses

Q 7:32 What are the exceptions to the additional tax on distributions from a Coverdell ESA that are not used for qualified higher education expenses?

Part II of Form 5329 is used to calculate the additional 10 percent tax on Coverdell ESA distributions not used for qualified higher education expenses. The additional tax does not apply to distributions that are

1. Due to the death or disability of the designated beneficiary;
2. Made on account of a scholarship, allowance, or payment described in Code Section 25A(g)(2);
3. Made to cover the cost of advanced education (as defined in title 10 of the U.S. Code, § 2005) for the beneficiary at a U.S. military academy); or
4. Taxable solely because the taxpayer chose to use a HOPE Scholarship Credit or a Lifetime Learning Credit.

The 10 percent additional tax also does not apply to excess contributions to a Coverdell ESA that are returned before the tax return filing due date.

Excess Contributions

Q 7:33 How does Part III of Form 5329 address excess contributions?

Part III of Form 5329 helps the IRS and the taxpayer trace the recovery of excess contributions and determine what portion was not corrected during the year and is thus to be taxed again at 6 percent. It is also used to calculate the tax on new overcontributions. (Returns of excess contributions before age 59½ may be taxed at 10 percent under Part I, unless an exception applies.)

Q 7:34 How does Form 5329 recognize the excess contributions subject to tax, and what are the reporting guidelines?

Form 5329 lists the following ways of recognizing excess contributions to an IRA:

1. Earlier-year excess contributions that were not previously eliminated;
2. Undercontributions for the current year that may be applied;
3. Certain withdrawals of prior-year excess contributions; and
4. Any other distributions made in the current year that are taxable.

[I.R.C. § 4973(b)]

Thus, if an IRA owner makes an excess contribution in any year, he or she is permitted to carry over that excess as a contribution made for a subsequent year for which he or she has not made the maximum allowable contribution. The carryover is reported on the owner's income tax return; it is not, however, reported to the IRS on Form 5498.

Q 7:35   How may excess contributions be corrected?

The three methods for correcting excess contributions to an IRA are discussed below. The examples under each method include reporting guidelines.

Method 1. *Withdrawing current-year contributions before that year's tax return due date.*

An individual is allowed to withdraw any contribution, whether it is deductible or nondeductible. The following rules must be met to effect the withdrawal. [Treas. Reg. § 1.408-11]

1. The excess or unwanted contribution as well as earnings attributable to it must be distributed to the individual no later than the deadline (including extensions) for filing the federal income tax return for the year in which the contribution was made.
2. The IRA owner may not deduct the excess or unwanted contribution.

Example. Harriet makes an IRA contribution for 2009 on January 10, 2010. She has until the deadline for filing her 2010 federal income tax return, including extensions, to remove the excess or unwanted contribution (whether or not deductible) because the contribution was made in 2010.

If the rules set forth above are satisfied, the distribution of the excess or unwanted contribution is not taxable; however, the accompanying earnings on the unwanted contribution are considered a taxable IRA distribution. In addition, if the IRA owner is under age 59½, the 10 percent premature distribution penalty will apply to the distribution of the earnings attributable to the unwanted contribution.

Net earnings. The formula for calculating the net income on a returned contribution or a recharacterized contribution is as follows:

$$\text{Net income}^1 = \text{Contribution}^2 \times \frac{(\text{Adjusted closing balance}^3 - \text{Adjusted opening balance}^4)}{\text{Adjusted opening balance}}$$

---

[1] Net income can be positive or negative.

[2] The amount of the contribution that is being returned or recharacterized.

[3] Adjusted closing balance (ACB) is the fair market value (FMV) of the IRA at the end of the computation period plus the amount of any distributions or transfers (including recharacterizations) made from the IRA during the computation period. Thus, the ACB is the value just prior to the distribution or recharacterization.

[4] Adjusted opening balance (AOB) is the FMV of the IRA at the beginning of the computation period, plus the amount of any contributions (including the contribution that is being returned) or transfers (including recharacterizations) made to the IRA during the computation period.

Example. On January 1, 2009, Arnold, who is age 49 and a calendar-year taxpayer, contributes $6,000 to a traditional IRA established for his benefit. On April 3, 2010, when the account value is $6,420, Arnold realizes he was only entitled to contribute $5,000 for 2009, and asks for the $1,000 excess contribution to be returned. The earnings attributable to the excess contribution must also be returned. Arnold's adjusted opening balance (AOB) is $6,000, and his adjusted closing balance (ACB) is $6,420. The net income attributable to the returned contribution is $70 ($1,000 × ($6,420 − $6,000) ÷ $6,000). Consequently, Arnold's total distribution from the IRA will be $1,070, and on his 2009 return he will deduct $5,000 for his IRA contribution and include earnings of $70 in gross income. Arnold will also pay a premature distribution penalty of $7 for 2009.

Method 2. *Withdrawing true excess contributions after the tax return due date.* (This procedure does not apply to withdrawing nondeductible contributions.)

After the time to file an IRA owner's federal income tax return has expired, the excess contribution may be withdrawn under the following rules:

1. Because the tax return due date has passed, the owner is immediately subject to the 6 percent excise tax penalty, applied first to the year in which the excess contribution was made and then to each subsequent year until the excess is corrected.

2. Only the excess amount is withdrawn; earnings attributable to the excess are not required to be distributed, as they were under Method 1.

3. The owner does not deduct the excess contribution amount.

As noted above, Method 2 does not apply to a nondeductible contribution that is not a true excess contribution. Thus, if an IRA owner had made a nondeductible contribution and did not withdraw the nondeductible amount plus the earnings attributable (as described above), the owner must attach Form 8606 to the tax return and report the amount as a nondeductible contribution.

The $5,000 Rule. Whereas the principal amount of an excess contribution being withdrawn under Method 1 is always treated as a nontaxable IRA distribution, that is not always the case under Method 2. That is, under Method 2, if the principal amount of an excess contribution is withdrawn after the tax return filing deadline for the year in which the excess contribution was made, it will not be taxable—provided the IRA owner's total aggregate contributions during the year in which the excess contribution was made did not exceed $5,000. If, however, the owner's total contributions during the year did exceed $5,000, the principal amount of the excess contribution withdrawn under Method 2 is taxable; and if the owner is not yet age 59½, that amount may be subject to the 10 percent premature distribution penalty. Because an owner may not deduct an excess contribution, such a situation would result in double taxation. [I.R.C. § 408(d)(5)]

Example. Lewis, age 43, inadvertently contributes $5,500 to his IRA for 2009. His contribution limit for the year, however, is $5,000. Thus, Lewis has made a $500 excess contribution. If he does not correct the excess by using Method 1 (withdrawal by the filing deadline, plus extensions, for his tax return for the year in which the excess contribution was made), Lewis is immediately subject to the 6 percent excess contribution penalty on the $500 excess.

If Lewis withdraws the $500 on October 31, 2010, under Method 2 the $500 is taxable to him for the year in which the distribution occurs and may also be subject to the 10 percent premature distribution penalty because he is not yet age 59½. Because the contribution amount is in excess of $5,000 and Lewis does not get a deduction for the excess contribution, he is paying taxes twice on the same money. If eligible, Lewis may be better off using Method 3 (see below), even though he would have to pay a 6 percent penalty.

Under Method 2, the following would occur:

1. Lewis would report the distribution on his Form 1040 for 2009 (the year in which the excess contribution was made) as follows—

   a. $5,000 as a regular contribution and

   b. $30 ($500 × 6%) as the excess contribution penalty.

2. Lewis would complete Form 5329 (and attach it to Form 1040). He would complete Part III and report the 6 percent excess contribution penalty of $30, if applicable.

3. The trustee or custodian would

   a. Report the full amount contributed ($5,500) on Form 5498 for 2009 (the year in which the excess contribution was made) and

   b. Report the gross distribution as $500 and the taxable distribution as zero on Form 1099-R (2009 version).

Because no earnings attributable to the $500 excess are required to be distributed, the IRA trustee or custodian would not be required to determine the taxable distribution (as was required under Method 1 when earnings were distributed). Nevertheless, the instructions for Form 1099-R indicate that the gross amount must be reported in box 1 and zero entered in box 2a. Code P or 8 does not apply to a distribution of an excess contribution after the tax return filing deadline (because no earnings are distributed). The trustee or custodian would use the premature distribution code (code 1) because of Lewis's age.

Exceptions to the $5,000 Rule. There are two exceptions to the $5,000 rule applicable to corrections of true excess contributions after the due date of the individual's federal income tax return:

1. If an employer makes an excess contribution to an employee's IRA under a SEP or SARSEP arrangement, the $5,000 amount is increased by the excess SEP contribution.

2. If an individual makes an excess rollover contribution based on erroneous information received from his or her employer with respect to the amount eligible to be rolled over, the $5,000 amount is increased by the portion of the rollover contribution attributable to the erroneous information.

Method 3. *Treating a previous-year excess as a regular contribution made in a subsequent year for which the IRA owner had not made the maximum allowable contribution.*

Under Method 3, there is no distribution from the IRA. The IRA owner merely undercontributes in the first subsequent year in which he or she has not made the maximum allowable contribution, until the excess amount is exhausted. Still, as in the case of Method 2, the owner is immediately subject to the 6 percent excess contribution penalty because a corrective distribution did not occur on a timely basis (see Method 1). The 6 percent penalty is applied first to the year in which the excess contribution was made and then to any uncorrected excess amount remaining in each subsequent year until the excess amount is exhausted. [I.R.C. § 219(f)(6)]

Practice Pointer. The 6 percent penalty may be less costly than the result under Method 1. With Method 1, the IRA owner has a taxable distribution of the earnings attributable to the excess amount, a possible 10 percent premature distribution penalty assessed on earnings, and a possible early withdrawal penalty or other fee assessed by the trustee or custodian. The owner should consult his or her tax or legal advisor.

Note. Under Method 3, the IRA owner must be eligible to make a regular IRA contribution for the subsequent year.

Example. Lucy, age 23, makes a contribution to her IRA in the amount of $5,000 for 2009. Her compensation for the year was only $4,200. Therefore, she has made a 2009 excess IRA contribution of $800.

If Lucy decides not to withdraw the $800 excess under Method 1, she is immediately subject to the 6 percent excess contribution penalty for the year in which the excess contribution was made. Lucy's compensation for 2010 is $9,000, making her eligible to contribute the maximum of $5,000. Lucy makes a new contribution of $4,200 for 2010 and applies the prior-year excess amount of $800 toward her overall limit of $5,000 for 2010. Because she uses up her entire prior-year excess in the following year, the 6 percent penalty is not reapplied.

Under Method 3, the following would occur:

1. Lucy would report the contribution on her Form 1040 for 2009 (the year in which the excess contribution was made) as follows—

   a. $4,200 as a regular contribution and

   b. $48 ($800 × 6%) as the excess contribution penalty.

2. Lucy would complete Form 5329 (and attach it to Form 1040). She would complete Part III and report the excess contribution penalty of $48.

3. The trustee or custodian would report the full amount contributed ($5,000) on Form 5498 for 2009 (the year in which the excess contribution was made). No further reporting would be required from the trustee or custodian, because no distributions were made.

4. Lucy would report $5,000 ($4,200 + $800) as a regular contribution on her Form 1040 for 2010.

Q 7:36 What official guidance has been provided regarding distributions?

Notice 2000-39 [2000-2 C.B. 132] and the regulations provided the following information regarding distributions from an IRA:

1. "Net income" may include a negative number; therefore, investment losses may be allocated to an excess or recharacterized contribution.
2. Earnings are determined based on an IRA's entire balance, not on an investment account balance within the IRA.
3. Recharacterized contributions are taken into account for the period they are actually held in a traditional IRA or Roth IRA for purposes of calculating earnings.
4. If an IRA owner has made regular contributions to an IRA, the last contribution made is deemed to be the contribution being distributed (i.e., the last-in, first-out method).
5. If an individual maintains multiple IRAs, the earnings calculation is made with respect to the IRA designated by the individual and the corrective distribution must be made from that IRA.
6. An individual who has an IRA must recharacterize the dollar amount of his or her account balance. Property (e.g., a specific number of shares of stock) may not be recharacterized.

Q 7:37 Who is responsible for calculating net income and what is the formula?

The IRA trustee or custodian is responsible for calculating the net income to distribute with the IRA owner's excess contribution. [Treas. Reg. § 1.408-11(d)]

The formula for calculating the net income on a returned contribution or a recharacterized contribution is:

$$\text{Net income}^1 = \text{Contribution}^2 \times \frac{(\text{Adjusted closing balance}^3 - \text{Adjusted opening balance}^4)}{\text{Adjusted opening balance}}$$

---

[1] Net income can be positive or negative.

[2] The amount of the contribution that is being returned or recharacterized.

[3] Adjusted closing balance (ACB) is the fair market value (FMV) of the IRA at the end of the computation period plus the amount of any distributions or transfers (including recharacterizations) made from the IRA during the computation period. Thus, the ACB is the value just prior to the distribution or recharacterization.

[4] Adjusted opening balance (AOB) is the FMV of the IRA at the beginning of the computation period, plus the amount of any contributions (including the contribution that is being returned) or transfers (including recharacterizations) made to the IRA during the computation period.

The computation period is the period beginning immediately prior to the time that the contribution being returned or recharacterized was made to the IRA and ending immediately prior to the removal of the contribution (or transfer in the case of a recharacterization).

The preamble to the regulations implies that if an IRA is valued on a daily basis, for purposes of determining the AOB the computation period begins the exact day before the contribution was made that is being returned or recharacterized. If the IRA is not valued on a daily basis, for purposes of determining the AOB the FMV at the beginning of the computation period is deemed to be the most recent, regularly determined, FMV of the asset as of a date that coincides with or precedes the first day of the computation period (i.e., the most recent statement value). The IRS believes that if an IRA asset is normally valued on a daily basis, these values must be used so that the calculation of the amount of net income is based on the actual earnings and losses during the time the IRA actually held the contribution. The IRS also believes that using the most recent statement value would produce anomalous results.

Two regulations control the calculation of net income associated with returned contributions:

1. Regulation Section 1.408-11 governs the net income calculation for returned contributions under Code Section 408(d)(4). Returned contributions can be either excess contributions or "unwanted" contributions made to a traditional IRA or to a Roth IRA.

2. Regulation Section 1.408A-5, QA-2(c) governs the net income calculation for recharacterized contributions. Recharacterized contributions include regular contributions made to a traditional IRA or a Roth IRA or conversions made to a Roth IRA.

In general, both regulations are identical except in the following areas:

1. For returned contributions under Code Section 408(d)(4), where a series of regular contributions were made, the contribution being returned is deemed to be the last contribution made, up to the amount of the contribution identified as the amount to be distributed.

2. For recharacterized contributions under Code Section 408A(d)(6), where a series of contributions were made that are eligible for recharacterization, the IRA owner can choose by date and by dollar amount which contribution, or portion thereof, is to be recharacterized. (However, the IRA owner may not identify by a specific asset acquired with those dollars.)

The regulations clarify that the net income calculation is performed only on "the IRA" containing the particular contribution being returned or recharacterized, and that IRA is the IRA from which the distribution or recharacterizing transfer must be made. Although the regulations do not specifically define the term "the IRA," it is the author's interpretation that this means all assets associated with the particular IRA agreement and for which a separate Form 5498 is issued.

The regulations also clarify that if regular and conversion contributions are commingled in a single Roth IRA, the calculation of net income must be performed on the entire IRA, and any net income, including losses, must be prorated.

Example 1. Shannon contributes $1,600 to her traditional IRA on May 1, 2009; immediately before the contribution, the FMV of the IRA was $4,800. On February 1, 2010, Shannon requests a distribution under Code Section 408(d)(4) to return $400 of that contribution. The FMV of her IRA on February 1, 2010, is $7,600. During the computation period (May 1, 2009, through February 1, 2010), no other contributions are made and no distributions are taken.

The AOB is $6,400 ($4,800 + $1,600) and the ACB is $7,600. The earnings attributable to the excess are determined as follows:

$$\text{Net income} = \$400 \times \frac{(\$7,600 - \$6,400)}{\$6,400} = \$75$$

Therefore, the distribution must be $475, of which $75 is taxable to Shannon on her 2009 tax return.

Example 2. Beginning in 2009, Jackie contributes $500 to a Roth IRA on the 15th of each month through payroll deduction. As a result, she makes an excess contribution of $1,000 for 2009. The last two contributions made for 2009 are the excess contributions. The balance in Jackie's IRA immediately before the first excess contribution (on November 15) is $11,000 and the balance immediately before the second excess contribution (on December 15) is $12,100. On March 1, 2010, Jackie requests a distribution of the $1,000 excess contribution plus earnings thereon. The balance of the IRA immediately before the corrective distribution on March 1, 2010, is $16,000. No distributions were taken during the computation period November 15, 2009, through March 1, 2010. The only other contributions made during the computation period consisted of $1,000 ($500 × 2), contributed on January 15, 2010, and February 15, 2010.

The earnings attributable to the excess contribution are calculated as follows:

For the excess contribution of $500 on November 15, 2009, the AOB is $13,000 ($11,000 + (4 × $500)), and the ACB is $16,000.

$$\text{Net income} = \$500 \times \frac{(\$16,000 - \$13,000)}{\$13,000} = \$115$$

For the excess contribution of $500 on December 15, 2009, the AOB is $13,600 ($12,100 + (3 × $500)); the ACB is $16,000.

$$\text{Net income} = \$500 \times \frac{(\$16,000 - \$13,600)}{\$13,600} = \$88$$

Therefore, the total to be distributed on March 1, 2010, is $1,203 ($500 + $500 + $115 + $88). Of this amount $203 is taxable to Jackie on her 2009 tax return.

Example 3. Carl has both a traditional IRA and a Roth IRA. On March 1, 2009, the FMV of Carl's Roth IRA is $80,000. On that day, he converts his traditional IRA with an FMV of $160,000 to a Roth IRA and transfers it to his existing Roth IRA. A year later, when the FMV of the Roth IRA has declined to $225,000, Carl finds he was ineligible to make the 2009 conversion; he requests that the $160,000 conversion contribution be recharacterized back to the traditional IRA. The computation period is March 1, 2009, through March 1, 2010.

On March 1, 2009, the AOB of Carl's Roth IRA is $240,000 ($80,000 + $160,000), and the ACB is $225,000.

$$\text{Net income} = \$160,000 \times \frac{(\$225,000 - \$240,000)}{\$240,000}$$

$$= \$160,000 \times \frac{-\$15,000}{\$240,000} = -\$10,000$$

Consequently, the net loss attributable to the $160,000 contribution is $10,000. The total amount to be recharacterized is $150,000 ($160,000 − $10,000).

Example 4. Sharon has a traditional IRA that holds 100 shares each of Down Corp. and Up Corp. stock, On April 1, 2009, each block of shares is worth $50,000, and Sharon decides to convert them both to a Roth IRA. Six months after the conversion, the Down shares have lost value, and the Up shares have gained. Sharon wants to recharacterize only the Down Corp. shares (and avoid paying the conversion tax based on the high FMV of $50,000 on the conversion date), but she may not do so. She may only select the specific dollar amount to recharacterize. On the day of recharacterization, the Down shares are worth $40,000 and the Up shares are worth $70,000. No other contributions or distributions have been made during the computation period.

To recharacterize $50,000 of the converted assets, Sharon must also recharacterize net income of $5,000, determined as follows:

The AOB is $100,000, and the ACB is $110,000.

$$\text{Net income} = \$50,000 \quad \times \quad \frac{(\$110,000 - \$100,000)}{\$100,000} \quad = \$5,000$$

Therefore, the total amount transferred in the recharacterization is $55,000.

If Sharon recharacterizes only $40,000 of the amount converted (the FMV of the Down shares on the distribution date), her net income will be $4,000, determined as follows:

The AOB is $100,000, and the ACB is $110,000.

$$\text{Net income} = \$40,000 \quad \times \quad \frac{(\$110,000 - \$100,000)}{\$100,000} \quad = \$4,000$$

In this case, $44,000 must be transferred back to the traditional IRA.

Note that the determination of the amount to be recharacterized and the earnings attributable to it is not affected by whether a recharacterization is made with the transfer of the Down shares of stock or the Up shares of stock. The fact that the Down shares alone generated the loss is not taken into account when calculating attributable net income for recharacterization purposes.

A better strategy would have been for Sharon to do two separate conversions—one of the Up shares, and the other of the Down shares. That way, she could have recharacterized the Down assets without also dragging the profitable Up shares (and their income) back to the traditional IRA.

Q 7:38   How are excess contributions to a Roth IRA or a Coverdell ESA reported on Form 5329?

Part IV of Form 5329 is used to report the tax on excess contributions to a Roth IRA, and Part V of Form 5329 is used to report the tax on excess contributions to a Coverdell ESA. If the excess contribution is withdrawn, no penalty will apply provided (1) the withdrawal is made by the tax return filing due date (including extensions) and (2) the withdrawal includes any income earned on the withdrawn contributions.

Q 7:39   How is the 6 percent penalty tax on excess contributions applied?

The penalty tax is computed as 6 percent of the total excess contribution remaining at the end of the year. However, it may not exceed 6 percent of the IRA or Coverdell ESA value as determined at the end of the year. [I.R.C. § 4973(a)]

Excess Accumulations

Q 7:40 How does Part VIII of Form 5329 address the 50 percent penalty tax on excess accumulations?

The instructions for Form 5329 confirm that the IRS may excuse the 50 percent penalty tax (see Qs 4:104, 5:52) on excess accumulations resulting from the failure of the IRA owner to take RMDs if the owner shows that reasonable error has occurred and the owner is taking appropriate steps to correct the shortfall. The IRS suggests that if an IRA owner believes that he or she qualifies for relief, Form 5329 should nevertheless be filed, the tax paid, and a letter of explanation attached. The IRS will respond with a refund check if it grants the request. An IRA owner will, of course, want to consult a tax advisor to determine whether such an approach is the best, or the only, one to take.

Reporting Form 5329 Penalties on Form 1040

Q 7:41 Does the filing of Form 5329 affect what is to be reported on Form 1040?

Yes. With respect to Part I of Form 5329, because a distribution may be fully taxable even if it is not subject to the 10 percent premature distribution penalty, the distribution (but not the penalty) should be reported in full on lines 15a and 15b of Form 1040. The penalty tax, if applicable, is reported on line 60 of Form 1040.

Parts III–V of Form 5329 reflect the fact that any excess contribution may be left in an IRA as long as the 6 percent penalty is regularly (annually) paid. Nonetheless, a taxable distribution reported on line 15b of Form 1040 should reflect the elimination of an excess contribution.

General Filing Information

Q 7:42 How may additional information about IRS forms reporting be obtained?

There are a variety of ways to obtain information about IRS forms reporting, including forms and publications, telephone queries, and FIRE (see below).

Forms and Publications. To order IRS forms and publications, taxpayers can call (800) TAX-FORM (i.e., (800) 829-3676).

Telephone Queries. The IRS operates a centralized telephone site to answer questions about reporting on Forms W-2, W-3, 1099, and other information returns. For questions related to reporting on information returns, taxpayers can call (304) 263-8700. For questions about magnetic media filing of Forms W-2, taxpayers can call (800) 772-1213 for the telephone number of the local Social Security magnetic media coordinator or visit the Web site *www.SocialSecurity.gov.*

Filing Information Returns Electronically (FIRE). To reach FIRE, taxpayers can call (866) 455-7438. With a personal computer and a modem, taxpayers accessing FIRE can obtain electronic and magnetic media filing specifications, some IRS and Social Security Administration forms and publications, correct Social Security number data, and general topics of interest about information reporting.

An enormous amount of information is also available from the IRS Web site (*www.irs.gov*).

Q 7:43   How is a compliance deadline met if it falls on a weekend or legal holiday?

Generally, if the due date for a specific act of compliance or for filing a return falls on a Saturday, Sunday, or legal holiday, the act or filing is considered timely if it is performed on the earliest succeeding day that is not a Saturday, Sunday, or legal holiday. [I.R.C. § 7503; Treas. Reg. § 301.7503-1(a)]

Q 7:44   What is a legal holiday?

The term *legal holiday* refers to any of the legal holidays in the District of Columbia, as follows:

- New Year's Day, January 1
- Dr. Martin Luther King Jr.'s Birthday, the third Monday in January
- Inauguration Day, January 20, in a Presidential inauguration year
- Presidents' Day, the third Monday in February
- Memorial Day, the last Monday in May
- Independence Day, July 4
- Labor Day, the first Monday in September
- Columbus Day, the second Monday in October
- Veterans Day, November 11
- Thanksgiving Day, the fourth Thursday in November
- Christmas Day, December 25

[I.R.C. § 7503; Treas. Reg. § 301.7503-1(b); D.C. Code Ann. § 28-2701 (1985)]

Q 7:45   What rule applies if the local IRS office is closed on a compliance deadline date?

If the local IRS office is closed because of a legal holiday recognized throughout the state, territory, or possession in which the office is located, the term *legal holiday* also includes the local holiday. [Treas. Reg. § 301.7503-1(b)]

Q 7:46   When is a mailed document or payment deemed to be filed or paid?

Generally, a document or payment is considered to be filed or paid on the date of the postmark stamped on the cover in which the document or payment was properly mailed. Thus, if the cover containing the document or payment bears a timely postmark, the document or payment is considered timely filed or paid even if it is received after the date it is normally required to be received (see Qs 7:42–7:55). [Prop. Treas. Reg. §§ 301.7502-1, 301.7502-2]

Q 7:47   What date controls if a document or payment is considered not timely filed or paid?

If a document or payment is considered not timely filed or paid (see Qs 7:48, 7:49), the date of the postmark stamped on the cover in which it was mailed will *not* be considered the filing or payment date. For purposes of computing any penalties and additions to tax, the date that the document or payment is received will be taken as the date filed or paid.

Q 7:48   Must a document actually be received to be considered timely filed?

It depends on the method of delivery. For a document (but not a payment; see Q 7:49) sent by registered or certified mail, proof that the document was properly registered or that a postmarked certified mail sender's receipt was properly issued for it and that the envelope or wrapper was properly addressed to an agency, officer, or office constitutes prima facie evidence that the document was delivered to that agency, officer, or office. Private delivery companies would also satisfy this requirement (see Q 7:50).

Q 7:49   Must a payment actually be received to be considered timely paid?

Yes. Whether made in the form of currency or other medium, a payment is not treated as paid unless it is actually received and accounted for. If, for example, a check is used as the form of payment, the check does not constitute payment unless it is honored upon presentation.

Q 7:50   What are the requirements for a valid mailing?

Documents or payments must be mailed to the IRS in accordance with the following criteria:

1. The documents or payments must be enclosed in an envelope or other appropriate wrapper and be properly addressed to the agency, officer, or office with which the document is required to be filed or to which the payment is required to be made.
2. Sufficient postage must be affixed.
3. The documents or payments must be deposited within the prescribed time in the mail with the domestic mail service of the U.S. Postal Service (including mail transmitted within, among, and between the United States, its possessions, and Army-Air Force (APO) and Navy (FPO) post

offices). [Treas. Reg. § 301.7502-1] (The mail services of other countries are not considered.)

The IRS has designated four private delivery companies, also called designated delivery services, that last-minute filers may use and have the same assurance as those who use the U.S. Postal Service that a return mailed on time is considered filed on time. Those companies and the specific types of delivery services that qualify are as follows:

1. DHL Worldwide Express (DHL)—DHL "Same Day" Service, DHL Next Day 10:30 a.m., DHL Next Day 12:00 p.m., DHL Next Day 3:00 p.m., and DHL 2nd Day Service

2. Federal Express (FedEx)—FedEx Priority Overnight, FedEx Standard Overnight, FedEx 2nd Day, FedEx International Priority, and FedEx International First

3. United Parcel Service (UPS)—UPS Next Day Air, UPS Next Day Air Saver, UPS 2nd Day Air, UPS 2nd Day Air A.M., UPS Worldwide Express Plus, and UPS Worldwide Express

[2009 General Instructions for Forms 1099, 1098, 3921, 3922, 5498, and W-2G]

Only the specific types of delivery services identified qualify, not other services offered by the companies listed (e.g., FedEx Saturday or FedEx 3rd Business Day delivery).

Q 7:51   What happens if the postmarked date is wrong or not legible?

If a postmarked date is wrong or illegible, the person required to submit the document or payment has the burden of proving when the postmark was made.

Q 7:52   Can the risk that a document or a payment will not be postmarked on the day that it is posted be overcome?

The risk of an incorrect postmark may be overcome by use of registered, certified, or express mail.

Q 7:53   What is the postmark date for U.S. registered mail?

If a document or payment is sent by U.S. registered mail, the date of registration of the document or payment is treated as the postmark date.

Q 7:54   What is the postmark date for U.S. certified mail?

If a document or payment is sent by U.S. certified mail and the sender's receipt is postmarked by the postal employee to whom that document or payment is presented, the date of the U.S. postmark on the receipt is treated as the postmark date of the document or payment.

Q 7:55   What rules apply to postmarks of foreign postal services?

Special rules apply if the postmark on an envelope or wrapper is made by a foreign postal service. When the document or payment is received later than it would have been received if it had been duly mailed and postmarked by the U.S. Postal Service, it is treated as having been received when a document or payment so mailed and so postmarked would ordinarily be received. Still, the person required to file or pay must establish that the document or payment was in fact timely deposited in the mail before the last collection of the mail from the place of deposit. That person must also show that the delay in receipt was the result of a delay in the transmission of the mail and must explain the cause of that delay. [Prop. Treas. Reg. § 301.7502-1(c)(2)(iii)]

Form 990-T

Q 7:56   What is the purpose of Form 990-T?

In general, Form 990-T, Exempt Organization Business Income Tax Return (and proxy tax under section 6033(e)), is used by tax-exempt organizations and by certain IRAs to report their unrelated business taxable income under Code Section 511 and to obtain a refund of income tax held on undistributed long-term capital gains. [I.R.C. §§ 408(e)(1), 852; Treas. Reg. § 1.408-1(b)]

> **Example.** Cathy establishes a large rollover IRA. She purchases shares in an actively managed mutual fund. Gains from trading are reported to her on Form 2439, Notice to Shareholder of Undistributed Long-Term Capital Gains. To obtain a refund of income tax paid on undistributed long-term capital gains, the IRA trustee should make a regulated investment company (RIC) filing on Form 990-T.

Failure to recover undistributed long-term capital gains tax may result in liability to the IRA owner. (For detailed information on Form 990-T and RIC filings, see Qs 7:56–7:72.)

Q 7:57   What is unrelated business taxable income?

Unrelated business taxable income is the taxable income derived from any trade or business that is regularly carried on and not substantially related to an IRA's exempt purpose or function, such as engaging in a business for profit. [I.R.C. §§ 512, 513]

> **Example.** Myra establishes a large rollover IRA. She purchases an interest in a real estate limited partnership. The partnership invests all its assets in real estate. The partnership borrows $9 out of every $10 it invests in real estate. As a result of the leveraging, the IRA is subject to a tax on its unrelated business taxable income.

Q 7:58   What is the threshold amount for filing Form 990-T?

Form 990-T is not required to be filed unless an IRA has gross income of $1,000 or more from an unrelated trade or business.

Q 7:59   When must Form 990-T be filed?

Form 990-T must be filed by the 15th day of the fourth month after the end of the tax year.

Q 7:60   Who must sign Form 990-T?

Form 990-T must be signed and dated by the trustee or custodian of the IRA.

Q 7:61   May the IRA trustee or custodian request an extension of time to file for filing Form 990-T?

Yes. An IRA trustee or custodian may request an extension of time to file Form 990-T by using Form 2758, Application for Extension of Time to File Certain Excise, Income, Information, and Other Returns. The extension of time to file Form 990-T is not granted automatically.

Q 7:62   When must any tax due under Form 990-T be paid?

The IRA trustee or custodian must pay the tax due in full when Form 990-T is filed, but no later than the 15th day of the fifth month after the end of the tax year. The trustee or custodian may be required to use the electronic funds transfer (EFT) system.

Q 7:63   Is interest charged on any underpayment of taxes due under Form 990-T?

Yes. Interest is charged on taxes due under Form 990-T not paid by the due date even if an extension of time to file is granted. Interest is also charged on penalties imposed for failure to file, negligence, fraud, gross valuation overstatements, and substantial understatements of tax from the due date (including extensions) to the date of payment. The interest charge is figured at the underpayment rate determined under Code Section 6621(a)(2).

Q 7:64   What is the penalty for a late filing of Form 990-T?

An IRA trustee or custodian that fails to file Form 990-T when due (including extensions of time to file) is subject to a penalty of 5 percent of the unpaid tax for each month or part of a month the return is late, up to a maximum of 25 percent of the unpaid tax, unless it can show reasonable cause for the delay. A trustee or custodian filing after the due date (including extensions) must attach an explanation to the return. The minimum penalty for a return that is more than

60 days late is the lesser of the tax due or $135. The penalty will not be imposed if it is shown that the failure to file on time was due to reasonable cause. A statement should be attached to a late return explaining the reasonable cause.

Q 7:65   What is the penalty for late payment of tax due under Form 990-T?

In general, the penalty for late payment of taxes is usually 0.5 percent of the unpaid tax for each month or part of a month the tax is unpaid. The penalty may not exceed 25 percent of the unpaid tax. As described above (see Q 7:64), a penalty will not be imposed if the filer can show that the failure to file on time was due to reasonable cause.

Q 7:66   Which parts of Form 990-T must be completed?

All filers of Form 990-T must complete the applicable items in the heading area at the top of page 1 and the signature area on page 2. Except in the case of a RIC filing (see Q 7:67), Part I, Column (A), lines 1 through 13, on page 1 should be completed. If the amount on line 13 of Column (A), is $10,000 or less, only line 13 of Columns (B) and (C), lines 29 through 34 of Part II, and Parts III through V should be completed. Filers who enter $10,000 or less on line 13 of Column (A), do not have to complete Schedules A through K (however, they should refer to applicable schedules when completing Column (A) and in determining the deductible expenses to include on line 13 of Column (B)). If the amount on line 13 of Column (A) is more than $10,000, all lines and schedules that apply should be completed.

Q 7:67   Which parts of Form 990-T should be completed in a regulated investment company filing?

To obtain a refund of income tax paid on undistributed long-term capital gains (only), the IRA trustee or custodian should make a regulated investment company (RIC) filing on Form 990-T as follows:

1. Write "Claim for refund shown on Form 2439" at the top of the form;
2. Complete the heading (using the name and employer identification number (EIN) of the exempt trustee or custodian);
3. Enter the credit on line 44g;
4. Sign the return; and
5. Attach Copy B of Form 2439, Notice to Shareholder of Undistributed Long-Term Capital Gains.

Q 7:68   May a trustee or custodian of multiple IRAs that are invested in regulated investment companies file a composite return?

Yes. Instead of filing a separate Form 990-T for each IRA, an IRA trustee or custodian may file a composite return to claim a refund under Code Section

852(b) for IRAs that are invested in RICs that elected to retain a long-term capital gain.

Q 7:69   How is a composite filing accomplished?

A composite filing for multiple IRAs that have invested in RICs is accomplished as follows:

1. The trustee or custodian must apply to its Internal Revenue Service Center for a special EIN on Form SS-4, Application for Employer Identification Number (EIN). The special EIN will be effective only for making a composite claim for refund of tax under Code Section 852(b) on behalf of the IRAs administered by the trustee. (The trustee or custodian should *not* apply for a separate specialized EIN for each year it makes a claim for refund.)

2. The trustee or custodian must indicate that the application is for a special EIN by writing "Notice 90-18" at the top of the Form SS-4.

3. The trustee or custodian must attach a list of the IRAs for which the claim is being made, showing the names and Social Security numbers of the persons who established the IRAs and the allocated shares of tax paid by the RICs.

4. The IRAs must be grouped according to the RIC in which each IRA has made an investment.

5. Form 2439 must be attached for each RIC according to such grouping.

6. The trustee or custodian must write at the top of the Form 990-T, "Composite return for each Notice 90-18."

7. The trustee must enter the special EIN assigned for the composite return (and only that EIN) in the block provided for EINs.

Q 7:70   Under what circumstances is a composite return not available to an IRA trustee or custodian?

A composite return may be filed only by a common trustee or custodian of more than one IRA. It may not be filed by a person acting merely as a nominee (owner of record) of RIC shares owned by an IRA.

Furthermore, an IRA that has unrelated business taxable income may not be included in the claim for refund on the composite return. The trustee or custodian of such an IRA must file a separate Form 990-T for the IRA reporting the income on that return and claiming a credit for any RIC that elected to retain a long-term capital gain.

Q 7:71   To whom will the refund check awarded under Form 990-T be issued?

The IRS will issue a refund check awarded under Form 990-T to the IRA trustee (or custodian).

Q 7:72   What is the responsibility of the IRA trustee or custodian with respect to the refund issued under Form 990-T?

The trustee or custodian must allocate the refund issued under Form 990-T to the IRA trusts in accordance with the amounts due as shown on the composite return. [Notice 90-18, 1990-1 C.B. 327]

Form 1040

Q 7:73   How does an individual report an IRA distribution?

If the recipient of an IRA distribution is an individual, that individual must report the distribution on his or her federal income tax return. Form 1040 filers use lines 15a and 15b; Form 1040A filers use lines 11a and 11b.

For a distribution that is fully taxable, the entire amount is reported on line 15b (or 11b). The amount should be the same as that reported in box 1 of Form 1099-R. Line 15a (or 11a) is not used for a fully taxable IRA distribution.

For a distribution that is not fully taxable, the gross amount is entered on line 15a (or 11a), and the portion that is taxable is entered on line 15b (or 11b). The gross amount should be the same as the amount reported in box 1 of Form 1099-R, and the taxable amount should be the same as the amount in box 2a of Form 1099-R.

If the payer checked "Tax Amount Not Determined" in box 2b of Form 1099-R, it indicates the payer was unsure of what taxable amount to report in box 2a. That should alert the recipient to check with his or her accountant for assistance in determining the taxable amount.

Note. A qualified health savings account (HSA) distribution does not require special reporting on Form 1099-R. [2009 Instructions for Forms 1099-R and 5498]

Q 7:74   Is there an exception to using line 15 of Form 1040 (or line 11 of Form 1040A) to report an IRA distribution?

Yes. There is one exception to using line 15 of Form 1040 (or line 11 of Form 1040A) to report an IRA distribution. For corrective distributions of excess deferrals, excess contributions, or disallowed deferrals, plus income allocable thereto under a SARSEP, the recipient must report those amounts on the wage line of the tax return for the appropriate year (line 7 of Form 1040 or Form 1040A). The principal amount is taxable in the year it was deferred; the income allocable thereto is taxable in the year it was distributed.

In most corrective distribution cases, therefore, the payer must issue separate Forms 1099-R because parts of the distribution may be taxed in two or three different years.

Q 7:75   How does a taxpayer request the direct deposit of a tax refund into his or her IRA?

An individual may directly deposit a tax refund into his or her IRA at a bank or other financial institution (such as a mutual fund, brokerage firm, or credit union). The direct deposit is reported on either Form 1040 or Form 1040A. This is accomplished as follows:

- If the refund is to be directly deposited into only one individual retirement account, complete lines 74b through 74d on Form 1040 (or lines 45b through 45d on Form 1040A). Box 74a on Form 1040 (or box 45a on Form 1040A) should not be checked when reporting the deposit of a refund into one IRA.

- If the purpose is to split the direct deposit among two or three individual retirement accounts or other accounts, check the box on line 74a of Form 1040 (or on line 45a of Form 1040A) and attach Form 8888 (see Q 7:176).

Q 7:76   What forms are used to report corrective distributions under SEP IRAs?

An individual reports corrective distributions under SEP IRAs on line 7 of Form 1040 or Form 1040A.

Various forms are used to report corrective distributions to SEP or SARSEP participants:

- Excess salary deferrals (deferrals exceeding the dollar limit on elective contributions, generally $16,500 for 2009) are reported as part of total deferral on Form W-2, Wage and Tax Statement.

- Excess contributions (contributions failing the 125 percent actual deferral percentage test) are reported on Form 1099-R.

- Disallowed deferrals (deferrals failing the 50 percent participation rate requirement) are reported on Form 1099-R.

- Deferrals of an ineligible employer (deferrals failing the "fewer than 26 employees in previous year" requirement) are reported on Form 1099-R.

- Nonexcluded contributions (contributions of more than the applicable dollar amount under Code Section 402(h)(2)(B) if the plan is integrated or 25 percent of compensation or earned income) are reported on Form W-2.

- Amounts that exceed the $49,000 limit for 2009 or 100 percent of compensation limit under Code Section 415 are reported on Form W-2.

Q 7:77   How is a rollover of SEP IRA assets reported on Form 1040 (or Form 1040A)?

A SEP IRA owner should report a rollover from one IRA to another IRA on lines 15a and 15b of Form 1040 (or lines 11a and 11b of Form 1040A). This is because the investment vehicle for a SEP IRA is an IRA, and the basic IRA rules apply. The total distribution should be entered on line 15a of Form 1040 (or line

11a of Form 1040A). If the total on line 15a was rolled over, zero should be entered on line 15b of Form 1040 (or line 11b of Form 1040A). If the total was not rolled over, the part not rolled over should be entered on line 15b of Form 1040 (or line 11b of Form 1040A). The owner uses Form 8606 to figure the taxable part to enter on line 15b of Form 1040 (or line 11b of Form 1040A). Nondeductible contributions that were made to an IRA that is rolled over should be reported on line 15b of Form 1040 (or line 11b of Form 1040A).

Q 7:78   How is a rollover from a SEP IRA reported if the monies are rolled over to an employer plan?

Funds in SEP IRAs may be rolled over to an employer plan (including a qualified plan, a Section 403(b) account, or a governmental Section 457(b) account).

The taxpayer should make sure first that the employer's plan has been amended to accept such rollovers. If the plan has been amended, the taxpayer may request a direct rollover from the SEP IRA to the employer's plan, and the SEP IRA plan would report the transaction with the code G in box 7 of Form 1099-R. No reporting of the rollover contribution is required of the employer's plan.

If, however, the taxpayer requests the rollover of the SEP IRA funds, the SEP IRA trustee would report the distribution on Form 1099-R, using code 1 (if the taxpayer is under age 59½) or code 7 (if the taxpayer is age 59½ or older), since the trustee would not know whether the taxpayer will in fact roll over the amount within 60 days.

Once the rollover is completed, the SEP IRA assets will take on the characteristics of the plan into which they have been rolled. This means that if the SEP IRA is rolled over into a qualified plan, the assets would become subject to the qualified plan rules (e.g., loans may be taken from the monies; the premature distribution exceptions would be those for qualified plans; and so forth).

Obtaining Form W-2

Q 7:79   What should be done if Form W-2 is incorrect or lost?

If Form W-2 is incorrect or lost, the employee-taxpayer should request another from his or her employer.

Q 7:80   What should be done if an employer fails to issue Form W-2 by January 31?

If an employee does not receive Form W-2 by January 31, the employee should ask his or her employer for the form. Even if Form W-2 is not received from the employer, the employee-taxpayer may be responsible for including the proper amount in income.

Q 7:81   What should be done if Form W-2 is not received by February 15?

An employee who has not received Form W-2 by February 15 should call TeleTax at 800-829-4477 (enter topic 154). An employee may also obtain information by accessing TeleTax topics at the IRS's Web site (*www.irs.gov*).

Q 7:82   Is there a special Form W-2 or Form 1040 help line for people with impaired hearing?

Yes, In the continental United States, as well as in Alaska, Hawaii, Puerto Rico, and the U.S. Virgin Islands, persons with impaired hearing who have access to a teletypewriter/telecommunications device for the deaf (TTY/TDD equipment) can call (800) 829-4059 for assistance regarding Form W-2 or Form 1040. This number is answered only by TTY/TDD equipment.

Q 7:83   What information may be needed when requesting assistance from the IRS in obtaining Form W-2?

When a taxpayer requests assistance from the IRS in obtaining Form W-2, an IRS representative may ask for the following information:

- Employer's name
- Employer's address
- Employer's telephone number
- EIN or taxpayer identification number (TIN) (if known)
- Employee's address
- Employee's Social Security number
- Employee's daytime telephone number
- Dates of employment
- Estimate of missing income amount or amount of federal income tax withheld

Note. The information just listed may also be used for requesting taxpayer assistance on general tax matters that affect Form 1040.

Form 1099-R

Reporting Distributions on Form 1099-R

Q 7:84   What are a trustee's or custodian's reporting requirements with respect to IRA distributions?

A trustee's or custodian's reporting obligations with respect to IRA distributions are twofold: certain information must be reported to the recipient of the distribution and to the IRS. [I.R.C. § 408(i); Treas. Reg. § 1.408-7] Except for certain *de minimis* distributions, all distributions are required to be reported, even when the IRA owner exercises his or her right to revoke the initial establishment of the plan.

Q 7:85 What are the deadlines for filing Form 1099-R with the IRS and providing it to distributees?

Form 1099-R, Distributions From Pensions, Annuities, Retirement or Profit-Sharing Plans, Insurance Contracts, etc., must generally be provided to the recipient of the distribution no later than January 31 following the calendar year during which the distribution was made, but for 2009 forms the due date is February 1, 2010. Form 1099-R must generally be transmitted to the IRS no later than February 28 following the calendar year during which the distribution was made, but for 2009 forms the due date is March 1, 2010. Leap years are ignored for such deadlines. [Ann. 91-179, 1991-49 I.R.B. 78] If a trustee or custodian files electronically, the electronic filing is due to the IRS by March 31 following the calendar year in which the distribution was made.

Q 7:86 How may an extension of time to file Forms 1099-R with the IRS be requested?

For paper, magnetic media, or electronic filing, an IRA trustee or custodian should request an extension of time to file Forms 1099-R with the IRS by completing Form 8809, Application for Extension of Time to File Information Returns, and sending it to the following address:

Enterprise Computing Center—Martinsburg
Information Reporting Program
Attn: Extension of Time Coordinator
240 Murall Drive
Kearneysville, WV 25430

The IRS suggests that Form 8809 be filed as soon as the need for an extension becomes apparent. In any case, Form 8809 must be filed no later than the due date of the return (February 28 usually, but March 1, 2009 for 2009 returns) for the IRS to consider granting the extension. If the IRS approves the extension request, the IRA trustee or custodian will be granted an additional 30 days to file. If more time to file is needed, the trustee or custodian should request an additional 30 days by submitting another Form 8809 before the end of the initial extension period.

Note. An approved extension request will apply only to the due date for filing Forms 1099-R with the IRS. Such approval will not extend the due date for providing statements to the recipients of the distributions (see Q 7:87).

Q 7:87 How may an extension of time to provide Forms 1099-R to recipients of the distributions be requested?

To request an extension of time for providing Forms 1099-R to the recipients of the distributions, the IRA trustee or custodian should send a letter to the Enterprise Computing Center—Martinsburg (see Q 7:86).

The letter must include all of the following:

- Payer's name
- Payer's TIN
- Payer's address
- Type of return
- A statement that the request is for an extension for providing statements to recipients
- Reason for the delay
- Signature of payer or authorized agent

The request must be postmarked by the due date of the return—generally January 1, but February 1, 2010, for 2009 returns. If the request for extension is approved, an additional 30 days to furnish the recipient statements will be granted.

Q 7:88 What changes were made to Form 1099-R for 2009?

The following changes relevant to IRAs were made to the 2009 Form 1099-R:

1. Instructions are included for reporting qualified charitable distributions, which may be made through December 31, 2009.
2. The instructions modify the reporting of distributions from traditional or SEP IRAs. Box 2a should be left blank, unless otherwise noted in Form 1099-R's instructions. "Taxable amount not determined" should be checked in box 2b.
3. For how to treat partial exchanges of annuity contracts under Code Sections 72 and 1035, individuals are referred to Revenue Procedure 2008-24 [2008-13 I.R.B. 684].
4. Filers are instructed to continue using code 1 to report qualified reservist distributions.
5. For plan years beginning after 2007, excess contributions and excess aggregate contributions plus earnings are taxable in the year distributed.

Q 7:89 How is the 2009 Form 1099-R to be completed?

The following are box-by-box instructions for correctly completing the 2009 Form 1099-R.

Box 1. Gross Distribution.

All Plans (Including Governmental Section 457(b) Plans): Report the total amount of the distribution before any taxes were withheld, but do *not* include any fees that were charged, such as CD penalties for early withdrawal. For a distribution of property other than cash, report the FMV of the property on the date of distribution.

Recharacterizations: Recharacterizations of eligible IRA contributions are reportable on Form 1099-R. Enter the amount of the recharacterized IRA contribution, plus earnings, in this box. In the case of a loss on the recharacterized contribution, enter the actual amount recharacterized in this box. Recharacterizations *must* be accomplished via a trustee-to-trustee transfer rather than by a distribution followed by a rollover.

The IRA *from* which the recharacterized amount is being transferred is referred to as the "First IRA"; therefore, the trustee or custodian of the First IRA must issue Form 1099-R. (The trustee or custodian of the First IRA must also report the original contribution and its character on Form 5498 issued with respect to the First IRA.)

If the First IRA is a traditional IRA, the only type of contribution to it that is eligible to be recharacterized as a Roth IRA contribution is a regular contribution. If the First IRA is a Roth IRA, either a regular contribution or a conversion contribution to it may be recharacterized as a contribution to a traditional IRA.

Earnings (or losses) attributable to the recharacterized contribution must be included in the transfer. Prior-year recharacterizations and same-year recharacterizations must be reported on separate Forms 1099-R because different reporting codes apply for box 7. Code R is used for a prior-year recharacterization; code N is used for a same-year recharacterization.

A *prior-year recharacterization* is a recharacterization of a contribution made *for* 2008 and recharacterized in 2009, even if the 2008 contribution was made in 2009. A recharacterization of a conversion that came from a traditional IRA in 2008, but was not converted until 2009 (but within the requisite 60-day period) is treated as a prior-year recharacterization for reporting purposes.

A *same-year recharacterization* is a recharacterization of a contribution made *for* 2009 and recharacterized in 2009.

Conversions and Reconversions: The trustee or custodian must report an IRA that is converted or reconverted to a Roth IRA, even if the conversion is accomplished as a trustee-to-trustee transfer or is internally converted with the same trustee.

Revocations: If a regular or conversion contribution is made to an IRA that is revoked within the plan's first seven days, and the contribution is distributed, the gross amount of the distribution is reported in box 1, the taxable portion in box 2a, and the appropriate code in box 7. This applies to

- a regular contribution made to a traditional or Roth IRA,
- a conversion contribution made to a Roth IRA,
- a rollover or transfer to a traditional IRA or Roth IRA, and
- an employer contribution to a SEP IRA or SIMPLE IRA.

Table 7-1 shows the appropriate code or codes to enter in box 7 when reporting the revocation of a contribution to an IRA and the amount to be entered in box 2a of Form 1099-R. The gross amount of the revoked contribution is reported in box 1 of the form.

Table 7-1. Contribution Revocations

Source of Contribution	Box 2a	Box 7
Regular contribution to a traditional IRA without earnings	0	Code 8 regardless of age
Regular contribution to a traditional IRA with earnings	Earnings	Code 1 regardless of age
Regular contribution to a Roth IRA without earnings	0	Code J regardless of age
Regular contribution to a Roth IRA with earnings	Earnings	Code J regardless of age
Rollover or transfer to a traditional IRA	Same as box 1	Code 1 if under age 59½; code 7 if at least age 59½
Rollover or transfer to a Roth IRA	Same as box 1	Code J regardless of age
Conversion to a Roth IRA without earnings	0	Code J regardless of age
Conversion to a Roth IRA with earnings	Earnings	Code J regardless of age
SEP IRA or SIMPLE IRA	Same as box 1	Code S if SIMPLE IRA established less than 2 years; otherwise, code 1 if under age 59½; code 7 if at least age 59½

Box 2a. Taxable Amount.

Enter the taxable amount (usually the same amount as is reported in box 1), but leave the box blank if unable to reasonably obtain the data needed to compute the taxable amount.

If a traditional IRA is rolled over to the trustee or custodian of or is transferred to an employer's plan, enter 0 (zero).

If a regular traditional IRA contribution is recharacterized as a regular contribution to a Roth IRA, enter 0 (zero).

For a corrective distribution described in Code Section 408(d)(4), enter only the earnings attributable to the returned contribution in this box. However, in accordance with Treasury Regulations Section 1.408-11, the amount of the returned contribution can be reduced by any losses attributable to the contribution. In the case of a loss, enter 0 (zero) in this box. A Section 408(d)(4) distribution is a distribution of an excess (or unwanted) contribution paid to the individual no later than the deadline for filing the federal income tax return (including extensions) for the year *during which* (not *for which*) such contribution was made. Such distribution must include the earnings (or loss) attributable to the returned contribution. Earnings are taxable in the year *during which* the contribution was made rather than in the year they are distributed. The IRS suggests that the trustee or custodian advise the participant at the time of the distribution of the year in which the earnings are taxable.

For a corrective distribution described in Code Section 408(d)(5), enter 0 (zero) in this box. A Section 408(d)(5) distribution is a distribution of a "true" excess contribution paid to an individual after the deadline for filing the federal income tax return (including extensions) for the year *during which* such contribution was made. Such corrective distribution of an excess contribution after the tax return filing deadline does *not* include the earnings or loss attributable to it.

For a corrective distribution of certain excess contributions to a SARSEP, parts of the distribution may be taxable in more than one year. Thus, in many cases, two Forms 1099-R are required to show when the different parts are taxable. Note that the correction procedures and reporting requirements for excess SARSEP contributions (excess deferrals, excess contributions, or disallowed deferrals) are different from those for the return of any other excess IRA contributions. The IRS suggests that the trustee or custodian advise the participant at the time of the distribution of the year or years in which the distribution is taxable.

If a traditional IRA (including a SEP IRA) or a SIMPLE IRA is converted or reconverted to a Roth IRA (regardless of the conversion method used), report in this box the same amount as that entered in box 1.

If a regular contribution made to a traditional IRA is timely revoked (usually within the first seven days from the date the plan is established) and no earnings are distributed, enter 0 (zero) in this box. If earnings are distributed in the revoked distribution, enter only the earnings. If the trustee (or custodian) knows that the taxpayer deducted the regular contribution, report in this box the same amount as that entered in box 1.

If a rollover, direct rollover, or transfer made to a traditional IRA is timely revoked, report in this box the same amount as that entered in box 1.

If a contribution made to a SEP IRA or SIMPLE IRA is timely revoked, report in this box the same amount as that entered in box 1.

Roth IRAs: Box 2a is generally left blank for all Roth IRA distributions, with a few exceptions. Note that leaving a box blank is different from entering 0 (zero).

If a regular Roth IRA contribution or a conversion is recharacterized to a traditional IRA, enter 0 (zero) in this box.

If an excess (or unwanted) contribution made to a Roth IRA (including the earnings attributable to the contribution) is distributed by the deadline for filing the individual's federal income tax return (including extensions) for the year *during* which the contribution was made, enter only the earnings in this box. If there are no earnings, enter 0 (zero) in this box. This type of distribution is treated and reported in the same manner as that described under Code Section 408(d)(4).

If a regular contribution made to a Roth IRA is timely revoked (usually within the first seven days from the date the plan is established) and no earnings are distributed, enter 0 (zero) in this box. If earnings in the revoked IRA are distributed, enter only the earnings in this box.

If a conversion to a Roth IRA is timely revoked and no earnings are distributed, enter 0 (zero) in this box. If earnings in the revoked IRA are distributed, enter only the earnings in this box.

If a rollover or transfer made from one Roth IRA to another Roth IRA is timely revoked, report in this box the same amount as that entered in box 1.

If a distribution is made from the "Deemed IRA" portion of an employer's plan, *see* the explanation under the following section, "Qualified Plans and Section 403(b) Plans."

Qualified Plans and Section 403(b) Plans: Generally, the trustee must enter the taxable amount of the distribution in this box. If, however, the trustee is unable to reasonably obtain the data needed to compute the taxable amount, leave this box blank. The trustee must make every effort to compute the taxable amount.

Do not include in this box 2a any excludable or tax-deferred amounts reportable in box 5 (after-tax employee contributions), box 6 (net unrealized appreciation in employer's securities), or box 8 (current actuarial value of an annuity contract that is part of a lump-sum distribution).

For a direct rollover to a traditional IRA, enter 0 (zero). If part of the distribution is paid as a direct rollover and part is distributed to the participant, the trustee must issue two Forms 1099-R to report each part.

For a distribution of deductible voluntary employee contributions, the trustee must file a separate Form 1099-R and report in this box the same amount as that entered in box 1, unless that amount was part of a direct rollover to another plan or traditional IRA.

For periodic distributions where the employee made after-tax contributions and the payments began in 1998 or later, the trustee *must* use the simplified method described under Code Section 72(d) to compute the taxable amount. Special rules apply for payments that began after November 18, 1996, and before 1998, as well as for payments that began before November 19, 1996. [*See* Notice 98-2, 1998-1 C.B. 266; IRS Publication 575, *Pension and Annuity Income for Use in Preparing 2008 Returns.*]

For corrective distributions of excess deferrals under a 401(k) plan or a 403(b) plan, excess contributions, and/or excess aggregate contributions, report in this box on Form 1099-R for the year of the distribution regardless of when the distribution is taxable to the participant. If the excess and the earnings are taxable in two different years, two Forms 1099-R must be issued to designate the year in which each part is taxable. The participant must be advised at the time of the distribution of the year or years in which the distribution is taxable and that an amended tax return may be necessary.

If a distribution is made to reduce the participant's excess annual additions under Code Section 415, report in this box the same amount as that entered in box 1, but reduced by the portion (if any) that represents the participant's after-tax contributions.

If a participant defaults on a loan, the loan requirements under Code Section 72(p) are not satisfied, or the loan exceeds the maximum permissible loan amount, the participant has a "deemed" distribution that must be reported here using the normal taxation rules, including basis recovery. Such deemed distribution may also be subject to the 10 percent premature distribution penalty under Code Section 72(t). It should be noted, however, that interest that accrues after the deemed distribution is not an additional loan and thus is not reportable on Form 1099-R. Deemed distributions are given the code L and are not eligible for rollover.

On the other hand, if a participant's accrued benefit is reduced (offset) to repay a loan, the offset amount is reported like any other actual distribution, using either code 1 or code 7 depending on the participant's age. Loan offset amounts are eligible for rollover if the participant makes up the offset loan amount from other sources.

Deemed IRAs Under an Employer's Plan: An employer's plan (qualified plan, 403(b) plan, or governmental 457 plan) can permit participants to make "deemed" traditional as well as Roth IRA contributions to the plan. In general, the deemed IRA portion of the plan follows the rules applicable to the traditional IRA or Roth IRA, and the other portion of the plan follows the rules applicable to the employer's plan for purposes of taxation, required minimum distributions, premature distribution exceptions and withholding. Thus, distributions of the deemed IRA portion of the plan and distributions of the other portion of the plan must be reported on separate Forms 1099-R.

The Form 1099-R reporting the distribution from the deemed IRA portion of the plan uses the distribution codes applicable to traditional or Roth IRAs, as applicable. If the participant has *both* a deemed traditional IRA and a deemed Roth IRA, distributions from the two types of IRAs must be reported on separate Forms 1099-R.

Governmental Section 457(b) Plans: Generally, the taxable amount of the distribution must be entered in this box. If, however, the payer is unable to reasonably obtain the data needed to compute the taxable amount, this box should be left blank. The payer must make every effort to compute the taxable amount.

For a direct rollover to another plan, enter 0 (zero) in this box. If part of the distribution is paid as a direct rollover and part is distributed to the participant, two Forms 1099-R must be issued to report each part.

A distribution from a governmental Section 457(b) plan, although taxable, is not subject to the 10 percent premature distribution penalty under Code Section 72(t). However, if an amount was rolled over to a receiving 457 plan that was subject to the 10 percent premature distribution penalty, distributions from the rollover portion must be reported on a Form 1099-R separate from distributions attributable to the non-rollover portion. If the distribution consists solely of amounts that are attributable to the non-rollover portion, enter the amount in this box and enter code 2 in box 7. If the distribution consists solely of amounts that are attributable to the rollover portion, enter the amount in this box, and enter in box 7 either code 1 or code 7, depending on the age of the participant.

Box 2b. Taxable Amount Not Determined.

Enter an "X" in box 2b only if it is not possible to reasonably obtain the data needed to compute the taxable amount. If this box is marked, leave box 2a blank unless reporting a traditional IRA, SEP IRA, or SIMPLE IRA distribution.

If the distribution is from a traditional IRA (SEP or SIMPLE) the payer must enter an amount (which could be zero) in box 2a even if this box 2b is marked.

If the distribution is from a Roth IRA, this box generally should be marked and box 2a left blank (unless the distribution is a return of an excess contribution plus earnings, a recharacterization, or a revocation, as explained in box 2a).

Do *not* mark this box if the distribution is a return of an excess contribution plus earnings from a Roth IRA. In such a case, the earnings are taxable (and reported in box 2a), and thus the taxable amount is determined.

Do *not* mark this box if the Form 1099-R is reporting a recharacterization transfer from a Roth IRA to a traditional IRA. In that case, 0 (zero) is entered in box 2a, and thus the taxable amount is determined to be zero.

Do *not* mark this box if the distribution is a revocation of a Roth IRA. In this case, either the earnings or 0 (zero) will be entered in box 2a, and thus the taxable amount is determined.

Second Box 2b. Total Distribution.

Enter an "X" in this box 2b only if the payment shown in box 1 is a total distribution. (A total distribution is one or more distributions within one tax year in which the entire balance of the account is distributed.) If periodic or installment payments are made, mark in this box the year in which the final payment is made.

Box 3. Capital Gain (Included in Box 2a).

This box does not apply to IRAs, SEPs, or SIMPLEs and should be left blank.

Box 4. Federal Income Tax Withheld.

Enter any federal income tax withheld. This withholding is subject to the deposit rules and to Form 945, Annual Return of Withheld Federal Income Tax. No withholding is required until the annual aggregate distribution exceeds $200.

Traditional IRAs (Including SEP IRAs) and SIMPLE IRAs: All IRA distributions that are "payable upon demand" are generally subject to a flat 10 percent withholding rate, unless the recipient elects to have more than 10 percent withheld. If the recipient is eligible for and elects no withholding, leave this box blank.

For individual retirement *annuities*, the issuer of the annuity contract generally withholds under the periodic payment rules.

For withholding purposes, assume that the entire amount of any IRA distribution is taxable, except for the distribution of contributions under Code Section 408(d)(4), in which case only the earnings are taxable, and for Section 408(d)(5) distributions of excess contributions.

A traditional IRA that is converted (or reconverted) to a Roth IRA is subject to withholding, unless the recipient is eligible for and elects no withholding. This is true regardless of the method used for the conversion (transfer or rollover) and even if the conversion is accomplished within the same financial institution.

Roth IRAs: Most Roth IRA distributions are exempt from any federal income tax withholding. Therefore, there should be no withholding on Roth IRA distributions, except in the case of a returned contribution plus earnings under Code Section 408(d)(4) or a revoked contribution plus earnings. Such earnings are always treated as taxable distributions—even when they otherwise meet the definition of a *qualified distribution*. [I.R.C. § 408A(d)(2)(C); Treas. Reg. § 1.408A-6, Q&A-1(d)] Thus, withholding applies only on the earnings being distributed. Of course, the recipient can elect no withholding on the earnings.

Recharacterizations: Do not withhold on any IRA recharacterization. Recharacterizations are not treated as distributions.

Qualified Plans, Section 403(b) Plans, and Governmental Section 457(b) Plans: Eligible rollover distributions from a qualified plan, Section 403(b) plan, or governmental Section 457(b) plan that are not paid as a direct rollover are subject to mandatory withholding at the rate of 20 percent. If part of an eligible rollover distribution is paid in a direct rollover and the other part is distributed to the participant, the portion distributed is subject to 20 percent mandatory withholding on the taxable amount. All other distributions from a qualified plan, Section 403(b) plan, or governmental Section 457(b) plan are subject to 10 percent withholding (for nonperiodic distributions) or to the wage tables in Circular E (for periodic distributions).

If a distribution from an employer's qualified plan consists solely of employer securities and $200 or less in cash in lieu of fractional shares, no withholding is required. Employer securities (excluding the net unrealized appreciation) and plan loan offset amounts that are part of an eligible rollover distribution must be included in the amount multiplied by the 20 percent. However, the amount to be withheld may not exceed the sum of the cash and the fair market value of property (excluding employer securities and plan loan offset amounts).

If the trustee knows the amount of after-tax employee contributions, if there were any, no withholding is applied to that amount, since it is reasonable to believe that the amount is not includable in the employee's gross income.

All Plans: If a payee fails to furnish his or her taxpayer identification number (TIN), or if the IRS notifies the payer before any distribution that the TIN furnished is incorrect, the payee may not claim exemption from the withholding requirements (see Qs 7:96, 7:97).

Note. Backup withholding under Code Section 3406 does not apply to any retirement plan distribution.

Box 5. Employee Contributions/Designated Roth Contributions or Insurance Premiums.

Box 5 does not apply to IRAs, SEPs, or SIMPLEs.

Box 6. Net Unrealized Appreciation in Employer's Securities.

Box 6 does not apply to IRAs, SEPs, or SIMPLEs.

Box 7. Distribution Code.

Enter the code or codes appropriate for the type of distribution made. In certain cases, double codes must be entered. For example, for a corrective distribution of an excess contribution plus earnings from a traditional IRA where the earnings are taxable in the prior year and the participant is under age $59\frac{1}{2}$, enter double code 1P in box 7. For a direct rollover from an employer's qualified plan, Section 403(b) plan, or governmental Section 457(b) plan to a traditional IRA or employer's plan for the surviving spouse of a deceased participant, enter double code 4G.

Only three numeric combinations are permitted: codes 8 and 1, 8 and 2, or 8 and 4. If two other numeric codes are applicable, more than one Form 1099-R must be filed. For example, if a participant takes a premature distribution during the first part of 2006 and takes another distribution on or after attaining age $59\frac{1}{2}$, two Forms 1099-R must be issued. The premature distribution would be coded 1 and the normal distribution would be coded 7.

If a second code is applicable, it is listed under each of the following code descriptions. When an alpha code and a numeric code are used, either code may be placed first (see Table 7-1 above).

Code 1. Early Distribution, No Known Exception. Indicates that the employee or taxpayer is under age $59\frac{1}{2}$ and none of the exceptions to the 10 percent premature distribution penalty are *known* to apply.

Use code 1 even if the distribution is made for any of the following reasons:

- Medical expenses (applies to IRAs, qualified plans, and Section 403(b) plans)
- Qualified higher education expenses (applies only to IRAs)
- First-time homebuyer expenses (applies only to IRAs)

- Health insurance premiums paid by certain unemployed individuals (applies only to IRAs)
- Qualified reservist distribution

In such cases, the taxpayer may file Form 5329 with his or her federal income tax return to indicate that the 10 percent premature distribution penalty does not apply.

Also use code 1 in these cases:

- If the recipient of the distribution is age 59½ or older and modifies a series of substantially equal periodic payments within five years of the first payment
- For a Section 408(d)(5) distribution if the taxpayer is under age 59½ (See the description of Section 408(d)(5) corrective distributions in the discussion under "Box 2a. Taxable Amounts")

Distributions from a governmental Section 457(b) plan are not subject to the 10 percent premature distribution penalty. Thus, code 1 is not applicable to Section 457(b) plan distributions in most cases. However, if assets from a governmental Section 457(b) plan are rolled over to another plan (e.g., a traditional IRA) that is subject to that penalty, subsequent distributions from the plan that received the governmental Section 457(b) plan's assets will be subject to the 10 percent premature distribution penalty unless the participant satisfies one of the exceptions. Moreover, if a plan distribution subject to the 10 percent premature distribution penalty is rolled over to a Section 457(b) plan, subsequent distributions from that Section 457(b) plan, to the extent they are attributable to the amounts rolled over, will be subject to the 10 percent premature distribution penalty. If the distribution consists solely of assets attributable to the Section 457(b) plan, use code 2. If the distribution consists solely of assets attributable to a rollover contribution from any plan that is subject to the 10 percent penalty, use code 1. (Use code 7 if the taxpayer is age 59½ or older.) If the distribution comprises amounts from both sources, the plan trustee must file a separate Form 1099-R for each part.

If applicable, use code 1 in conjunction with code 8, B, D, L, or P.

Code 2. Early Distribution, Exception Applies (as defined in Code Section 72(q), 72(t), or 72(v)). Code 2 is used only for the following specific reasons:

1. A traditional IRA, SEP IRA, or SIMPLE IRA is converted to a Roth IRA, and the participant is under age 59½.

2. A pre-age 59½ distribution is made from the participant's employer's plan or the participant's IRA because of an IRS levy under Code Section 6331.

3. A distribution from a governmental Section 457(b) is made that is not subject to the 10 premature distribution penalty under Code Section 72(t). If the distribution consists solely of assets attributable to the Section 457(b) plan, use code 2. If the distribution consists solely of assets attributable to a rollover contribution from any plan that is subject to the

10 percent premature distribution tax rules, use code 1 (or code 7 if the taxpayer is age 59½ or older). If the distribution is made up of amounts from both sources, file a separate Form 1099-R for each amount distributed, unless code 2 can be entered on each form.

4. A distribution is made from a qualified plan or Section 403(b) plan due to the participant's separation from service during or after the calendar year during which the participant attains the age of 55.

5. A distribution is one of a series of substantially equal payments (as described in Code Section 72(q), (t), or (v)).

6. Any other distribution that is subject to an exception under Code Section 72(t) that is not required to be reported using code 1, 3, or 4 (for example, dividends distributed from an ESOP). Also, as described under code 1, if the trustee knows that the distribution under a QDRO meets all the applicable rules.

If applicable, use one of the following codes in addition to code 2: code 8, B, D, or P.

Code 3. Disability. Use code 3 if the employee or taxpayer is disabled. The instructions for Form 1099-R refer to *disability* as defined under Code Section 72(m)(7). Thus, a taxpayer must be disabled under Code Section 72(m)(7) to avoid the 10 percent premature distribution penalty. Because many employer plans use a definition of disability different from the definition under Code Section 72(m)(7), a taxpayer may be subject to the 10 percent premature distribution penalty even though he or she meets the plan's definition of disability.

For reporting purposes, code 3 should be used only if the taxpayer is disabled under Code Section 72(m)(7). Do not use any other code with code 3.

Code 4. Death. Use code 4 regardless of the age of the deceased participant or beneficiary to indicate that the distribution was made to the decedent's beneficiary, including an estate or trust. For example, for a trustee-to-trustee transfer of assets on behalf of a nonspouse beneficiary to an inherited IRA, code 4 is used to identify the distribution. If applicable, use one of the following codes in addition to code 4: code 8, A, B, D, G, H, L, or P.

Code 5. Prohibited Transaction. If the trustee or custodian knows that the participant or beneficiary of any IRA has engaged in a prohibited transaction (as defined under Code Section 4975(c)), or there has been improper use of the account (as defined under Code Section 408(e)(2)), it is required to report the "deemed" distribution on Form 1099-R. If the prohibited transaction involves a Roth IRA, use code 5 (instead of code J) regardless of the taxpayer's age. Code 5 means that the account is no longer an IRA, and no other code should be used with it.

Code 6. Section 1035 Exchange. Use code 6 to indicate the tax-free exchange of life insurance, annuity, or endowment contracts under Code Section 1035. For a Section 1035 exchange that is in part taxable, file a separate Form 1099-R to report the taxable amount.

A tax-free Section 1035 exchange is the exchange of

1. A life insurance contract for another life insurance contract, endowment, or annuity contract;

2. An endowment contract for an annuity contract or for another endowment contract that provides for regular payments to begin no later than they would have begun under the old contract; or

3. An annuity contract for another annuity contract.

The distribution of other property or the cancellation of a contract loan at the time of the exchange may be taxable and reportable on a separate Form 1099-R.

All Section 1035 exchanges are reportable on Form 1099-R, except when

1. The exchange occurs within the same insurance company;

2. The exchange is solely a contract-for-contract exchange that does not result in a designated distribution; and

3. The insurance company maintains adequate records of the policyholder's basis in the contracts.

Do not use any other code with code 6.

Code 7. Normal Distribution. Use code 7 for a normal distribution from a plan to indicate that the taxpayer is age 59½ or older, unless code 5, 8, 9, D, E, F, G, L, N, P, or R applies. Also use code 7 if a traditional IRA (including a SEP IRA) or a SIMPLE IRA is converted to a Roth IRA and the participant is age 59½ or older.

Do not use code 7 for any Roth IRA distribution.

Use code 7 for a Section 408(d)(5) distribution if the taxpayer is age 59½ or older.

Also use code 7 to report a distribution from a life insurance contract, annuity contract, or endowment contract and to report income from a failed life insurance contract.

If code A applies to the distribution (see below), the double code 7A may be used. Generally, if no other code applies to the distribution, use code 7.

Code 8. Excess Contributions Plus Earnings/Excess Deferrals (and/or Earnings) Taxable in 2009. Use code 8 for a corrective distribution of an excess contribution plus earnings from a traditional IRA, SEP IRA, or Roth IRA when the earnings are taxable in the year of distribution. For a Roth IRA, use the double code 8J regardless of the taxpayer's age.

Example. A taxpayer contributes $5,000 to a traditional IRA in 2009 and, after realizing he is ineligible to make the contribution, withdraws the $5,000 plus $100 of earnings attributable to the contribution before the end of the year. On the taxpayer's 2009 Form 1099-R, the IRA trustee or custodian should enter $5,100 in box 1, $100 in box 2a, and code 8 in box 7 because the earnings included in the distribution are taxable in the year of the distribution (2009).

If the participant is under age 59½, use the double code 81 to indicate that the IRA earnings are subject to the 10 percent premature distribution penalty. If the participant is age 59½ or older, use code 8.

For a revoked IRA, see Table 7-1 above.

Code 8 also applies to corrective distributions of excess deferrals, excess contributions, and excess aggregate contributions under a 401(k) plan or a 403(b) plan, or disallowed deferrals (under a SARSEP), unless code P or code D applies. These corrective distributions could be taxable in more than one year; in such a case, separate Forms 1099-R must be issued reporting the year in which each part is taxable and using code 8, D, or P, whichever applies.

For all plans, if applicable, use one of the following codes in addition to code 8: code 1, 2, 4, B, or J.

Code 9. Cost of Current Life Insurance Protection. Use code 9 to report premiums paid by an employee's trust under a qualified plan for current life or other insurance protection taxable to plan participants or their beneficiaries. These costs are reported in boxes 1 and 2a. However, do not report these costs and a distribution on the same Form 1099-R; use a separate form for each. Do not use any other code with code 9.

Code A. May Be Eligible for 10-Year Tax Option. This code does not apply to IRAs, SEPs, or SIMPLEs.

Code B. Designated Roth Account Distribution. This code does not apply to IRAs, SEPs, or SIMPLEs.

Code D. Excess Contributions Plus Earnings/Excess Deferrals Taxable in 2007]. This code does not apply to IRAs, SEPs, or SIMPLEs.

Code E. Distributions under Employee Plans Compliance Resolution System (EPCRS). This code does not apply to IRAs, SEPs, or SIMPLEs..

Code F. Charitable Gift Annuity. This code does not apply to IRAs, SEPs, or SIMPLEs.

Code G. Direct Rollover and Rollover Contribution. Use code G when benefits in an employer's qualified plan, 403(b) plan, or governmental 457(b) plan are paid to the participant's traditional IRA in a direct rollover. Code G also applies to direct rollovers of a traditional IRA or SIMPLE IRA to an employer's qualified plan, 403(b) plan, or governmental 457(b) plan that accepts such rollovers. If assets in a traditional IRA or SIMPLE IRA are paid directly to the IRA owner, do not use code G. Instead, use code 1 or code 7, depending on the age of the IRA owner. If the employer's plan pays part of the employee's benefit in a direct rollover to an IRA and part is distributed to the employee, the trustee or custodian must issue two Forms 1099-R to report the different parts.

Use double code 4G to indicate a direct rollover to an IRA by a beneficiary of a deceased plan participant, and use double code BG to indicate a direct rollover of a designated Roth account distribution to a Roth IRA.

Code H. Direct Rollover of a Designated Roth Account Distribution to a Roth IRA. This new code may be used with code 4, if appropriate.

Code J. Early Distribution from a Roth IRA. Use code J generally to report any distribution from a Roth IRA that is made before the participant attains age 59½, dies, or become disabled. (For Roth IRA distributions after one of those events, use Code Q or T). In some cases, the taxpayer will need to file Form 5329 to indicate that the 10 percent premature distribution penalty does not apply. Use code 5 instead if the Roth IRA engages in a prohibited transaction, or code 2 for an IRS levy.

If applicable, one of the following codes may be used in addition to code J to indicate the reason for the distribution: code 8 or code P. For a revoked Roth IRA, see Table 7-1 above.

Code L. Loans Treated as Deemed Distributions Under Code Section 72(p). This code does not apply to IRAs, SEPs, or SIMPLEs.

Code N. Recharacterized IRA Contribution Made for 2009. Use code N to indicate a recharacterization of a contribution made for 2009 and recharacterized in 2009 to another type of IRA by a trustee-to-trustee transfer or with the same trustee or custodian. (See the discussion under box 1.) Do not use any other code with code N.

Code P. Excess Contributions Plus Earnings/Excess Deferrals Taxable in 2008. Use code P to indicate that the distribution is taxable in the prior year. (See the discussions under box 2a and code 8 above.) For corrective distributions of excess contributions plus earnings for any IRA (including a Roth IRA), the IRS suggests that the trustee or custodian advise the payee, at the time of the distribution, that the earnings are taxable in the year *in which* the contributions were made.

Example. A taxpayer made a regular contribution of $5,000 to a Roth IRA on November 12, 2008. Because the taxpayer's MAGI exceeded the limit in 2008, the taxpayer had an excess Roth IRA contribution. On April 5, 2009, a corrective distribution that included earnings of $250 was made. On the taxpayer's 2009 Form 1099-R, the Roth IRA trustee enters $4,250 in box 1 and $250 in box 2a. Regardless of the taxpayer's age, the double code JP is entered in box 7. Code P indicates that the earnings distributed are taxable in the prior year (2008).

If applicable, use one of the following codes in addition to code P: code 1, 2, 4, B or J.

Code Q. Qualified Distribution from a Roth IRA. This code applies if it is known that the recipient meets the five-year holding period requirement and also has a qualifying reason (attainment of age 59½, death of the owner and distribution to beneficiary, or disability).

Do not use any other code with code Q. If any other code (such as code 8 or P) applies, use code J.

Code R. Recharacterized IRA Contribution Made for 2008. Use code R to indicate a recharacterization of a contribution made for 2008 and recharacterized in 2009 to another type of IRA by a trustee-to-trustee transfer or with the same trustee or custodian. (See the discussion of box 1 above.)

Do not use any other code with code R.

Code S. Early Distribution from a SIMPLE IRA in First Two Years, No Known Exception. Use code S to report a distribution from a SIMPLE IRA in the first two years if the participant has not reached age 59½ and none of the exceptions under Code Section 72(t) are known to apply. The two-year period begins on the day contributions are first deposited in the individual's SIMPLE IRA by the employer. Code S indicates that the 25 percent tax under Code Section 72(t)(6) may apply unless the amount is rolled over to another SIMPLE IRA.

Do not use code S if code 3 or 4 applies.

Use code 7 if the participant is age 59½ or older. Do not use any other code with code S.

Code T. Roth IRA Distribution, Exception Applies. Use code T for a distribution from a Roth IRA if it is not known whether the five-year holding period requirement has been satisfied but it is known that there is a qualifying reason for the distribution (i.e., the owner is at least age 59½ or is disabled, or the Roth IRA owner died and the distribution is to a beneficiary).

Do not use any other code with code T.

Code U. Dividends distributed from an ESOP under Code Section 404(k). This code does not apply to IRAs, SEPs, or SIMPLEs.

IRA/SEP/SIMPLE Checkbox. Enter an "X" in the IRA/SEP/SIMPLE checkbox if the distribution is from a traditional IRA, SEP IRA, or SIMPLE IRA, including an IRA that is converted to a Roth IRA. It is not necessary to mark the box for a distribution from a Roth IRA or any recharacterization transfer.

Box 8. Other.

Enter the current actuarial value of an annuity contract that is part of a lump-sum distribution. Do not include such value in box 1 or box 2a. To determine the value of an annuity contract, show the value as an amount equal to the current actuarial value of the annuity contract, reduced by an amount equal to the excess of the employee's contributions over the cash and other property (not including the annuity contract) distributed. If an annuity contract is part of a multiple-recipient lump-sum distribution, enter in box 8, along with the current actuarial value, the percentage of the total annuity contract each Form 1099-R represents.

Box 9a. Percentage of Total Distribution.

This box does not apply to IRAs, SEPs, or SIMPLEs.

Box 9b. Total Employee Contributions.

This box does not apply to IRAs, SEPs, or SIMPLEs.

Boxes 10–15. State and Local Tax Withheld.

These boxes and copies 1 and 2 of Form 1099-R are provided for convenience only and need not be completed for the IRS. The state and local information boxes can be used to report distributions and taxes for two states or localities separated by the dotted line.

Unnumbered Boxes.

The following information is contained in unnumbered boxes:

1. Payer's name, address, and ZIP code.

2. Payer's federal identification number. The same name, address, and EIN used to remit federal income tax withheld and to file Form 945 must be entered here.

3. Recipient's identification number. This box must reflect the taxpayer identification number (TIN) of the person or entity receiving the distribution. In the case of a distribution to an estate or trust, the estate's or trust's TIN is used, not the Social Security number of the decedent. For multiple beneficiary recipients, a separate Form 1099-R is prepared for each beneficiary.

4. Recipient's name, address, and ZIP code. This box reflects the name of the recipient as it is shown on his or her Social Security card. In the case of a distribution made to a beneficiary, the recipient is the beneficiary, not the deceased participant. In some cases, the beneficiary recipient is not an individual (i.e., it may be an estate, a charity, or a university). The appropriate name and TIN of the entity should be provided, not the name and Social Security number of the deceased participant.

5. Account number. The account number box must be completed if the payer has multiple accounts for a recipient for whom it is filing more than one Form 1099-R. Otherwise, designation of an account number is encouraged.

The account number must be unique in order to identify the specific "plan" being reported. The recipient's TIN cannot be used for this purpose. Also, in cases where multiple reportable distributions are made from the same plan for different reasons that require separate Forms 1099-R, the account number must be able to identify the specific Form 1099-R. The purpose of the account number box is to identify the proper form if a correction is filed.

For example, assume that the following distributions were all made during 2009 from the same traditional IRA (Account No. 23456789):

March distribution was a premature distribution (code 1 applies)

June distribution was converted to a Roth IRA (code 2 applies)

IRA owner attains age 59$\frac{1}{2}$ on July 14, 2008

September distribution was a return of an excess contribution for 2009 (code 8 applies)

November distribution was a normal distribution (code 7 applies)

Although four distributions were made from the same "plan," separate Forms 1099-R are required because different codes apply. In this example, it would be acceptable to enter "Account No. 123456789" and designate the distributions using numbers (e.g., -1, -2, -3, and -4) or letters (e.g., -A, -B, -C, and -D) or some other sequence.

Filing Corrected Forms 1099-R

Q 7:90   How are corrected Forms 1099-R filed?

All corrections to reporting forms for a year must be submitted to the IRS in accordance with special rules. For Form 1099-R, those rules are explained in IRS Publication 1220, *Specifications for Filing Forms 1098, 1099, 5498, and W-2G Electronically or Magnetically with IBM 3480, 3490, 3590, and AS400 compatible tape cartridges*. Revised each year, Publication 1220 may be ordered by calling (800) 829-3676.

Form 1099-R is subject to the three-tiered penalty structure applicable to other reporting forms. A section of the Form 1099-R instructions emphasizes the requirement to file a corrected Form 1099-R with the IRS if the form has already been filed and an error is later discovered.

Example. Chuck makes a direct rollover to an eligible recipient plan, and Form 1099-R is filed with the IRS, reporting that none of the direct rollover is taxable by entering a zero in box 2a. It is later discovered that part of the direct rollover was not eligible to be rolled over; that is, part of the distribution consisted of Chuck's RMD. The original Form 1099-R must be corrected by issuing a new Form 1099-R.

Corrections should be filed as soon as possible. Those filed after August 1 may be subject to the maximum penalty of $50 for each return; those filed on or before August 1 may be subject to a lesser penalty. If a payer discovers errors after August 1, however, it may still be required to file corrections so that it will not be subject to a penalty for intentional disregard of the filing requirements.

All fields in a corrected Form 1099-R must be completed with the accurate information, not only the data fields needing correction. Completing some types of corrections, such as the correction of an erroneous Social Security number, requires two separate steps. A payer should submit corrections only for the returns filed in error, not all the returns filed. Corrected statements should be furnished to recipients as soon as possible. [IRS Publication 1220]

If a payer discovers errors for previous years that affect a large number of payees, in addition to sending the IRS the corrected forms and notifying the payees, a letter containing the following information should be sent to IRS Magnetic Media Coordinator:

- Name and address of payer
- Type of error (explained clearly)
- Tax year

- Payer tax identification number
- Transmitter control code
- Type of return
- Number of payees affected

The IRS will forward the information to the appropriate IRS office in an attempt to prevent erroneous notices from being sent to the payees. The corrections must be submitted on a paper information return document or filed magnetically or electronically. The payer should provide the correct tax year in box 2 of Form 4804, Transmittal of Information Returns Reported Magnetically/ Electronically, and the external media label. [IRS Publication 1220]

If submitting prior-year data or corrections, the payer should use the record format for the current year and submit on separate media; it should, however, use the actual year designation of the correction in field positions 2 and 3 or positions 3 and 4 for 8-inch diskette filing. If filing is done electronically, a separate transmission must be made for each tax year. [IRS Publication 1220]

In general, a filer should submit corrections for returns to be filed within the last three calendar years (four years if the payment is a reportable payment subject to backup withholding under Code Section 3406). [IRS Publication 1220]

If the corrected Forms 1099-R are being submitted on paper documents, the filer should place an "X" in the corrected box at the top of a new Form 1099-R. For paper transmissions, the accompanying paper transmittal form, Form 1096, must be marked "corrected" at the top. For magnetic media submissions, the procedures contained in the IRS revenue procedure for that year should be followed.

Magnetic Media and Electronic Filing Requirements

Q 7:91   What are the magnetic media or electronic filing requirements for original and corrected Forms 1099-R?

If a payer is required to file 250 or more Forms 1099-R, the original submission must be made via an approved magnetic media submission or filed electronically. The 250-forms requirement applies separately to original and corrected returns. Thus, for example, if the count for the payer's original submission was 1,000 and the count for its corrections is 225, the original submission must be made via magnetic media or filed electronically, whereas the corrections may be submitted either (1) on paper forms or (2) on magnetic media or filed electronically. Form 4804, Transmittal of Information Returns Reported Magnetically/Electronically, must accompany the submission.

The due date for magnetic media reporting of Form 1099-R is the same date as for paper reporting (generally February 28, but March 1, 2010, for 2009 forms). The due date for electronic filing is March 31.

All information returns filed magnetically should be sent to the following address:

Enterprise Computing Center—Martinsburg
Information Reporting Program
230 Murall Drive
Kearneysville, WV 25430

Note. A magnetic media or electronic filer should not file paper copies in addition to the magnetic media or electronic filing.

Q 7:92   How is IRS approval to file magnetically or electronically obtained?

Form 4419, Application for Filing Information Returns Magnetically or Electronically, must be filed at least 30 days (45 days for some electronic filing) before the due date of Form 1099-R. (Only one Form 4419 need be filed for all types of returns that will be filed electronically or on magnetic media.) Once the payer has received approval, annual approvals are not required.

The IRS will provide a written reply to the applicant and further instructions at the time of the approval, usually within 30 days. A magnetic media reporting package, which includes all of the necessary transmittals (Form 4804, labels, and instructions), will be sent to an approved filer each year.

Q 7:93   May an organization request that it not be required to file electronically or on magnetic media?

Yes. Form 8508, Request for Waiver From Filing Information Returns on Magnetic Media (Forms W-2, W-2G, 1099 Series, 5498, and 8027), may be submitted requesting an undue hardship waiver from electronic or magnetic media filing for a period of time not to exceed one tax year. Waiver requests must be filed at least 45 days before the return is due and should be sent to the following address:

Enterprise Computing Center—Martinsburg
Information Reporting Program
240 Murall Drive
Kearneysville, WV 25430

Noncompliance Penalties

Q 7:94   What penalties apply if a filer fails to transmit Forms 1099-R via magnetic media or electronically when required or fails to follow the paper document format?

Failure to transmit Forms 1099-R via magnetic media or electronically when required and failure to follow the paper document format are treated as failures to file the form unless the filer has an approved waiver on file or can establish reasonable cause or, in some cases, due diligence.

In general, for corrections submitted within 30 days after the required filing date (see Q 7:85), the penalty is $15 for each failure, with a maximum annual penalty of $75,000 ($25,000 for small businesses). For corrections submitted on or before August 1 of the calendar year in which the required filing date occurs, the penalty is $30 for each failure, with a maximum annual penalty of $150,000 ($50,000 for small businesses). Corrections submitted after August 1 are subject to $50 for each failure, with a maximum annual penalty of $250,000 ($100,000 for small businesses). In the case of intentional disregard of the filing requirements, however, a penalty of $100 for each failure may be imposed.

Note. A small business is a business that has annual gross receipts of $5 million or less for the three most recent tax years ending before the calendar year in which Form 1099-R is due. Also, special penalty rules apply to certain *de minimis* failures and certain payers with gross receipts of not more than $5 million.

Q 7:95 How does the IRS identify a missing or correct taxpayer identification number when Form 1099-R is filed?

Form 1099-R is included in the Information Returns Name/TIN Matching Program. Consequently, the IRS performs a verification check when Form 1099-R is filed to determine whether the name/TIN combination reported on the form matches information in the Social Security Administration's files. If the information does not match, the IRS sends Notice 972CG, *Notice of Proposed Civil Penalty*, to the filer of the information statement.

Notice 972CG lists each submission in which a name/TIN combination is missing or incorrect, states the proposed penalty, and explains how the filer should respond. Details concerning this procedure are explained in IRS Publication 1586, *Reasonable Cause Regulations and Requirements for Missing and Incorrect Name/TINs* (Rev. 9/2007).

Q 7:96 What actions must a payer take if a taxpayer identification number is missing from Form 1099-R?

The payer is required to take these actions if there is no TIN associated with the name on an IRA:

1. When the IRA is opened, the payer must complete an initial solicitation. A solicitation is a request (made by mail, telephone, or approved electronic means) that the payee furnish a correct TIN. If no TIN is received after the initial solicitation, immediately begin backup withholding on reportable payments.

2. Complete a first annual solicitation if a TIN is not provided in response to the initial solicitation. The first annual solicitation must generally be made by December 31 of the year in which the account was opened. However, for accounts opened during December, the first annual solicitation must be made by January 31 of the following year.

3. If the first annual solicitation does not result in the provision of a TIN, a second annual solicitation must be completed by December 31 of the year immediately following the calendar year in which the account was opened.

4. The rate of withholding required when a TIN is missing depends upon the type of payment made from the IRA. If the payment is an eligible rollover distribution that is not directly paid to an eligible retirement plan, 20 percent must be withheld. If the payment is not an eligible rollover distribution, and the payment is nonperiodic (see Q 7:24), 10 percent withholding is required. Finally, for a periodic payment that is not an eligible rollover distribution, withholding is required based on the wage withholding tables, using the rate that applies for a single individual who claims zero withholding allowances.

[IRS Publication 1586, *Reasonable Cause Regulations and Requirements for Missing and Incorrect Name/TINs* (Rev. 9/2007)]

Q 7:97   What must a payer do if the taxpayer identification number on a Form 1099-R is incorrect?

The payer must do the following when notified by the IRS that it filed a Form 1099-R providing an incorrect TIN:

1. Within 30 business days after receiving Notice 972CG, the payer must complete a first annual solicitation.

2. If the payee responds to the first annual solicitation within 45 days, and confirms that the previously provided name/TIN combination is correct, the payer may continue to treat the payee's prior withholding election as valid.

3. If the payee responds to the first annual solicitation within 45 days and furnishes a different name/TIN combination, any existing withholding election based on the prior name/TIN combination must be disregarded. The payee may submit a new withholding election by completing Form W-4P (or a substitute form). The new withholding election will be effective no later than January 1, May 1, July 1, or October 1 after it is received, as long as it is received at least 30 days before that date. [Treas. Reg. § 35.3405-1, Q&A D-21] Until a new withholding election is made, the payer must withhold from distributions based on the wage withholding rate that applies to a married individual claiming three withholding allowances.

4. If the payee does not respond to the first annual solicitation within 45 days, the payer must withhold from any distribution at the appropriate rate.

5. Alternatively, upon receipt of a Notice 972CG in which the IRS notifies the payer of an incorrect name/TIN combination, the payer may choose to disregard any prior withholding elections made by the payees whose name/TIN combinations are identified as incorrect in that notice. In that

event, the payer should consider those payees to have no withholding election in effect until new withholding elections are received.

6. The payer must complete a second annual solicitation within the same time frame as required for the first annual solicitation if it is notified of an incorrect name/TIN combination in any calendar year following the first notification (apparently, within 30 business days of receiving the second Notice 972CG).

[IRS Publication 1586, *Reasonable Cause Regulations and Requirements for Missing and Incorrect Name/TINs* (Rev. 9/2007)]

CD Penalty

Q 7:98 How is an early withdrawal certificate of deposit penalty treated?

In no event will the assessment of an early withdrawal certificate of deposit (CD) penalty or other permissible transaction fees be included as part of the gross distribution amount. The reportable distribution amount is *net* of the CD penalty or fee.

Example 1. Beth requests a distribution from her IRA in the amount of $1,000. This is *not* a withdrawal of an unwanted contribution, plus earnings. The trustee institution imposes an early withdrawal CD penalty of $50. The trustee gives Beth a check for $1,000 and takes the $50 CD penalty from the remaining IRA balance. The reportable distribution is $1,000, even though $1,050 came out of Beth's IRA. Any withholding is assessed on the reportable distribution amount of $1,000.

Example 2. The facts are the same as those in Example 1, except the trustee reduces the $1,000 by the $50 CD penalty, resulting in a check to Beth of $950 net. The reportable distribution is $950, even though $1,000 came out of Beth's IRA. Withholding is assessed on the reportable distribution amount of $950.

Intended Rollover of IRA Distribution

Q 7:99 How is a distribution reported when an IRA owner indicates that a rollover will be made?

There is no "rollover" code. Therefore, when making a distribution to an IRA owner who indicates that he or she will roll over the amount to another IRA, the trustee or custodian should use code 1 if the distributee is under age 59½ or code 7 if the distributee is age 59½ or older.

Note. Because the receiving IRA trustee or custodian will produce a Form 5498 indicating the amount rolled over, the distributee must reflect the rollover transaction on the appropriate line of his or her federal income tax return. [Ann. 90-56, 1990-16 I.R.B. 22]

Reporting Revoked IRAs

Q 7:100   Must a revoked IRA be reported?

Yes. Revenue Procedure 91-70 [1991-2 C.B. 899] outlines the reporting requirements for an IRA that is timely revoked and provides that even when the option to revoke the IRA is exercised by an individual, the IRS reporting requirements still apply. (See Qs 2:19, 2:46.)

Q 7:101   Do distribution reporting requirements vary according to the type of IRA contribution being revoked?

Yes. Proper distribution reporting depends on the type of IRA contribution being revoked. For details, see the discussion of box 1 in Q 7:89.

Renewing Investments

Q 7:102   Are renewed investments treated as distributions?

No. Whenever existing investments (e.g., CDs) within an IRA are renewed or reinvested in some other form of investment, no distribution occurs. Therefore, no Form 1099-R is issued in such cases, and, accordingly, Form 5498 would not report the renewed investments as contributions.

Fees Deducted from IRAs

Q 7:103   Are fees deducted from an IRA treated as a distribution?

No. When fees such as annual maintenance fees or transaction fees are deducted from an IRA, those amounts are not treated as distributions and are not reportable on Form 1099-R. In addition, once fees are deducted from the plan, a participant may not reimburse those amounts back to the plan. That is, if fees are reimbursed to the plan, they are treated as regular IRA contributions, and they must be reported in box 1 of Form 5498. Such amounts would thus count toward the IRA owner's contribution limit for the year. [Priv. Ltr. Ruls. 9124037 (Mar. 19, 1991), 9124036 (Mar. 19, 1991), 8830061 (May 4, 1988)]

Miscellaneous Rules

Q 7:104   How is Form 1099-R filed when two corporations merge?

When two corporations merge and the surviving corporation becomes the owner of all the assets and assumes all the liabilities of the absorbed corporation, the reporting requirements are met if the surviving corporation files Forms 1099-R for both corporations.

In Revenue Procedure 99-50 [1999-2 C.B. 757], the IRS outlined procedures that permit a successor business to combine all information reporting following a merger or an acquisition. Revenue Procedure 99-50 covers information reporting with respect to several forms, including Form 1099-R.

The provisions of Revenue Procedure 99-50 apply only when all of the following conditions are met:

1. One business entity (the successor) acquires from another business entity (the predecessor) substantially all of the property (a) used in the trade or business of the predecessor or (b) used in a separate unit of a trade or business of the predecessor;

2. During the pre-acquisition portion of the calendar year in which the acquisition occurs, the predecessor is required to file any of the information returns covered in the revenue procedure (including Form 1099-R);

3. During the post-acquisition portion of the acquisition year, the predecessor or the separate unit of the predecessor does not make or receive any reportable payments and does not withhold or collect any tax;

4. The requirements described in Section 5 of the revenue procedure (relating to the "alternative procedure") are met; and

5. The IRS instructions to the appropriate forms do not prohibit use of the alternative procedure.

[Rev. Proc. 99-50, § 4, 1999-2 C.B. 757]

For the successor to file combined information reporting using the alternate procedure, the following requirements must be satisfied:

1. Both the predecessor and the successor must agree that the successor assumes the predecessor's entire information reporting obligations for the appropriate forms to which their agreement applies. In such case, the predecessor is relieved of its information reporting obligations for reportable transactions occurring in the acquisition year only to the extent that the agreement meets, and the successor satisfies, the requirements of Revenue Procedure 99-50.

2. The predecessor and the successor must agree on the specific forms to which the alternative procedure applies.

3. On each Form 1099-R, the successor must combine (a) any payments made or received on account of a person by the predecessor in the pre-acquisition portion of the acquisition year with (b) any payments made or received on account of that person by the successor in that year, if any, and must report the aggregate amount on account of that person for that year.

4. On each Form 1099-R, the successor must also combine the amount of any income tax withheld for a person by the predecessor in the preacquisition portion of the acquisition year with the amount withheld for that person by the successor in that year and must report the aggregate amount withheld for the year.

5. The successor must file a statement with the IRS indicating that the Forms 1099-R are being filed on a combined basis in accordance with Revenue Procedure 99-50. If any income tax has been withheld by the predecessor during the acquisition year and reported by the predecessor on Form 945, the total of the withholding amounts shown on the successor's Forms

1099-R for that year will exceed the total of the withholding amounts shown on the successor's Form 945. Therefore, the statement that must be filed with the IRS must reflect the amount of any income tax that has been withheld by the predecessor and by the successor for each type of form.

6. The statement required to be filed with the IRS must include the name, address, telephone number, and EIN of both the successor and the predecessor, and the name and telephone number of the person responsible for preparing the statement.

7. Unless otherwise directed by the form's instructions, the statement for Forms 1099-R must be mailed on or before the due date for such forms to the following address:

Enterprise Computing Center—Martinsburg
Attn: Chief, Information Returns Branch
Mail Stop 360
230 Murall Dr.
Kearneysville, WV 25430

Q 7:105   How long should copies of Form 1099-R be kept?

Copies of information returns filed with the IRS (including Form 1099-R) should be kept for at least three years from the due date of the return.

Q 7:106   May Form 1099-R be enclosed in the same envelope with other forms?

Maybe. If a trustee or custodian combines Forms 1099-R with returns for interest, dividend, and royalty payments, strict mailing requirements must be followed. For example, no enclosures are permitted for promotional material or a quarterly or annual report. Even a sentence on the year-end statement describing new services being offered is not permitted. Logos are permitted on the envelope and on any nontax enclosures. If, however, Form 1099-R is being mailed without such forms, a combined mailing may be allowed. Payee statements that are related may be included in the same envelope; related forms include Form 1099, Form 1098, and Form 5498 (or the account balance on a Form 5498). In addition, Form W-2 may also be included in the single mailing because it is related to the payee statements. [Notice 87-17, 1987-1 C.B. 454]

Q 7:107   Must Form 1099-R be sent by first-class mail?

Yes. Postal regulations require packages of IRS forms (including Form 1099-R) to be sent by first-class mail.

Practice Pointer. If so many Forms 1099-R are being sent to the IRS that they must be packaged separately, the sender should write the payer's name and TIN on each package, number the packages consecutively, and place Form 1099 in package number one.

Q 7:108   Must the account number box on Form 1099-R be completed?

Yes. The account number is a unique identifier; it must not appear anywhere else on the form, and it must not be a Social Security number. In the event that multiple reportable distributions are made from the same plan for different reasons that require separate Forms 1099-R, and the payer files a corrected form, the account number will allow the IRS to identify the specific Form 1099-R that is being corrected.

Q 7:109   Are there any other requirements that trustees or other payers of distributions should be aware of?

Yes. The instructions for Form 1099-R contain the following important reminders:

Trustee-to-Trustee Transfers. Form 1099-R is not to be used to report direct transfers between trustees for the same type of plan (i.e., traditional IRA to traditional IRA (including SEP IRA to SEP IRA), SIMPLE IRA to SIMPLE IRA, Roth IRA to Roth IRA, qualified plan to qualified plan, 403(b) plan to 403(b) plan, and 457 plan to 457 plan). However, recharacterization transfers must be reported on Form 1099-R.

The trustee must report as a taxable distribution on Form 1099-R any trustee-to-trustee transfer from a SIMPLE IRA to any IRA (other than another SIMPLE IRA) during the two-year period beginning on the day employer contributions are first deposited in the participant's SIMPLE IRA. The IRS needs this information because tax-free transfers (and rollovers) are not permitted from a SIMPLE IRA to an IRA other than another SIMPLE IRA during the first two years regardless of the participant's age. Since the original SIMPLE IRA trustee will know that assets are transferring to a non-SIMPLE IRA before the two-year period has expired, it can prepare and file Form 1099-R.

Roth Conversions. If a traditional IRA (including a SEP IRA) or SIMPLE IRA is converted to a Roth IRA, it must be reported even if the assets are transferred in a trustee-to-trustee transfer or the assets are transferred within the same financial institution. A SIMPLE IRA is not eligible to convert to a Roth IRA until the participant has satisfied the two-year holding period applicable to SIMPLE IRAs.

Divorces. Under a qualified plan, 403(b) plan, or governmental 457(b) plan, a distribution to a spouse or former spouse made pursuant to a QDRO must be reported on Form 1099-R in the name and with the TIN of the spouse or former spouse. A payment from a qualified plan, 403(b) plan, or governmental 457(b) plan to a nonspouse alternate payee under a QDRO must be reported in the name and with the TIN of the participant.

However, for a transfer pursuant to a divorce or legal separation under any IRA, including a Roth IRA, a transfer under a QDRO is not considered a distribution and is not reportable on Form 1099-R. Any distribution from the IRA of the recipient spouse is taxable to him or her and is reportable on Form 1099-R.

Nonresident Aliens. If income tax is withheld under Code Section 3405 (the normal retirement plan withholding section), the distribution and withholding must be reported on Form 1099-R and the annual withholding return must be filed with Form 945. If income tax is withheld under Code Section 1441 (the nonresident alien section), the distribution and withholding must be reported on Forms 1042-S and 1042.

Attaching Form 1099-R to Tax Return. Recipients of distributions from an IRA are required to attach Form 1099-R to their federal income tax returns *only if* federal income tax withholding is shown in box 4.

How to Treat an IRA Plan for Reporting Distributions. An IRA includes all investments under one IRA plan or account. Thus, only one Form 1099-R is filed for all distributions from all investments that are paid in one year to one recipient under one plan, unless different codes must be entered in box 7. The trustee, custodian, or other payer need not file a separate Form 1099-R for each distribution under the same plan using the same code. If multiple distributions from an IRA are made during a year one recipient and all the distributions use the same code in box 7, only one Form 1099-R should be filed.

When Form 1099-R Is Not Required. Form 1099-R is not required when aggregate distributions to an individual during the year are less than $10. Negative amounts also need not be entered in any box on the form (e.g., Form 1099-R is not required for a distribution of worthless property). However, the recipient of a negative amount may enter 0 (zero) in boxes 1 and 2a, and, in the case of an employer's plan, enter any after-tax employee contributions in box 5.

Form 5329

Q 7:110   Who must file Form 5329?

An IRA owner generally must file Form 5329, Additional Taxes on Qualified Retirement Plans (Including IRAs) and Other Tax-Favored Accounts, if any of the following applies (for exceptions, see Q 7:111):

1. An early distribution was made from a Roth IRA, the amount on Form 8696, line 23, is more than zero, and the owner is required to enter an amount that is more than zero on line 1.

2. An exception to the tax on early IRA distributions applies, and distribution code 1 is shown in box 7 of Form 1099-R or the distribution code shown is incorrect. (Part I must be completed.)

3. An excess contribution was made to a traditional IRA (Part III must be completed), to a Roth IRA (Part IV must be completed), to a Coverdell ESA (Part V must be completed), to an MSA (Part VI must be completed), to an HSA (Part VII must be completed), to a qualified retirement plan (including IRAs) (Part VII must be completed), or there is a tax due from an excess contribution on line 17, 25, 33, 41, 49, or 53 of the 2006 Form 5329.

4. A distribution from a Coverdell ESA was made in excess of amounts spent for qualified higher education expenses.

5. RMDs from an IRA were not made by April 1 of any year following attainment of age 70½. (Part VIII must be completed.)

Q 7:111 Are there any exceptions to filing Form 5329?

Yes. Form 5329 need not be filed if any of the following applies:

1. Only the 10 percent tax is owed on early distributions (distribution code 1 must be shown in box 7 of Form 1099-R). (If Form 1040 is filed, 10 percent of the taxable part of the distribution should be entered on line 60 and "no" written under the heading "Other Taxes" to the left of line 60 to indicate that Form 5329 does not have to be filed.)

2. An early distribution was received from an IRA, but the distributee meets an exception to the tax (distribution code 2, 3, or 4 must be correctly shown on Form 1099-R).

3. The taxable part of all qualifying distributions was rolled over.

Q 7:112 How is Form 5329 filed?

Form 5329 should be attached to Form 1040, and both forms should be filed by the due date of Form 1040 (including extensions).

Q 7:113 Might Form 5329 have to be filed when Form 1040 does not have to be filed?

Yes. Although Form 1040 may not need to be filed, if tax is owed on Form 5329 or if the form is required to be filed even though no tax is due, Form 5329 must be completed and filed with the IRS at the time and place Form 1040 would have been required to be filed.

If Form 5329 alone is being filed, the taxpayer should include his or her address on page 1 and his or her signature and the date on page 2. The taxpayer should enclose (but not attach) a check or money order payable to the United States Treasury for the total of any taxes due. The taxpayer's Social Security number and "[year for which the form is being filed] Form 5329" should be included on the check or money order.

Q 7:114 Which Form 5329 is used to pay a tax for a previous year?

To pay a tax for a previous year, that year's version of Form 5329 must be used. For example, to pay tax for 2009, the 2009 version of the form must be used.

Q 7:115 How should Form 5329 be filed if tax is owed for a previous year?

If tax is owed for a previous year because of an early distribution, Part I of Form 5329 for that year should be completed and attached to Form 1040X,

Amended U.S. Income Tax Return. The taxpayer should include the distribution as additional income on Form 1040X if it has not previously been reported. If a tax other than the tax on early distributions for a previous year is owed, Form 5329 should be filed by itself for that year. The other tax (e.g., excess contribution penalty tax) would be paid on Form 5329 for the current year.

The taxpayer's signature and the date should appear on page 2 of Form 5329. A check or money order payable to the United States Treasury for the amount of tax due must be enclosed. The taxpayer's Social Security number and "[year for which the form is being filed] Form 5329" should be included on the check or money order.

Q 7:116   How should Form 5329 be prepared if both spouses owe penalty taxes and are filing a joint return?

Each spouse must complete a separate Form 5329 for taxes attributable to his or her own IRA or SEP IRA. If both spouses owe penalty taxes and are filing a joint return, they should enter the combined total tax from Forms 5329 on Form 1040, line 60.

Q 7:117   How is line 1 of Form 5329 completed if the taxpayer engaged in a prohibited transaction?

If a prohibited transaction took place—for example, borrowing from an IRA or pledging an individual retirement annuity as security for a loan—the IRA is no longer qualified as an IRA on the first day of the tax year the borrowing or pledging occurred. The IRA owner is considered to have received a distribution of the entire value of his or her IRA at that time.

If the taxpayer was under age 59½ on the first day of the year, the entire value of the account or annuity should be reported on line 1 of Form 5329.

Q 7:118   Must Form 5329 be filed if an IRA invests in collectibles?

Yes. If an IRA trustee or custodian invested IRA funds in collectibles, the IRA owner is considered to have received a distribution equal to the cost of those collectibles. If the owner was under age 59½ when the funds were invested, the cost of the collectibles is included on line 1 of Form 5329. Collectibles generally include works of art, rugs, antiques, metals, gems, stamps, coins, alcoholic beverages, and certain other tangible personal property purchased after 1981.

Nevertheless, an IRA trustee or custodian may invest IRA funds in U.S. one-ounce, one-half-ounce, one-quarter-ounce, and one-tenth-ounce gold coins; one-ounce silver coins; and certain platinum coins minted after September 30, 1986. Certain state-issued coins are also permissible IRA investments. [I.R.C. § 408(m)(3)]

Furthermore, a registered security such as a mutual fund share is not treated as a collectible, even if the fund holds coins or precious metals. Nonetheless, if the issuer distributes coins or metals to the IRA in a redemption of shares or otherwise, it will cause the IRA to acquire a prohibited collectible unless the foregoing exception applies. [Priv. Ltr. Rul. 200732026 (Oct. 8, 2007)]

Note. The IRA owner must include the total cost of the collectibles in income on line 15b of his or her Form 1040. [I.R.C. § 408(m)]

Q 7:119   May the 50 percent excess accumulations tax for failure to withdraw the required minimum distribution from an IRA be waived?

Yes. The IRS may waive the 50 percent excise tax on excess accumulations in an IRA if certain conditions are satisfied (see Q 7:40). To request such relief, Form 5329 must be filed, any excise tax must be paid, and a letter of explanation must be attached. If the IRS grants the request, it will send out a refund. (Special rules apply if the IRA is unable to make an RMD because of the insolvency of an insurance company.) [I.R.C. § 4974(d); Rev. Proc. 92-10, 1992-1 C.B. 661, *clarified by* Rev. Proc. 92-16, 1992-1 C.B. 673 and Rev. Proc. 95-52, 1995-2 C.B. 439]

Q 7:120   What conditions must be satisfied to qualify an IRA for exemption from the 50 percent excess accumulations excise tax?

Either of two conditions must be satisfied to qualify an IRA for exemption from the 50 percent excess accumulations excise tax:

1. The assets in the IRA must include an affected investment (see Q 7:121); or
2. The shortfall in RMDs must have been the result of reasonable error, and reasonable steps must have been taken to remedy the shortfall.

Q 7:121   What is an affected investment?

An *affected investment* is an annuity contract or a guaranteed investment contract (GIC) (with an insurance company) for which payments under the terms of the contract have been reduced or suspended because of state insurer delinquency proceedings against the contracting insurance company. [Rev. Proc. 92-10, 1992-1 C.B. 661, *clarified by* Rev. Proc. 92-16, 1992-1 C.B. 673 and Rev. Proc. 95-52, 1995-2 C.B. 439]

Q 7:122   Which assets must be used to satisfy the minimum distribution requirement if an IRA contains an affected investment?

If an IRA includes assets in addition to the affected investment, all IRA assets, including the available portion (see Q 7:123) of the affected investment, must be used to satisfy as much as possible of the minimum distribution requirement. If the affected investment is the only asset in the IRA, as much as possible of the RMD must come from the available portion, if any, of the affected investment.

Q 7:123   What is the available portion of an affected investment?

The *available portion* of an affected investment is the amount of payments remaining after they have been reduced or suspended because of state insurer delinquency proceedings.

Q 7:124   What action must be taken if the reduction or suspension of payments under an annuity contract or a GIC is canceled?

If the payments under an annuity contract or a GIC increase because all or part of the reduction or suspension is canceled, the amount of any shortfall in a previous distribution pursuant to the delinquency proceedings must be made up by December 31 of the calendar year following the year in which increased payments were received.

Q 7:125   Is the estate tax increased if there are excess accumulations in an IRA?

No. An addition to the estate tax was once levied equal to 15 percent of the decedent's excess retirement accumulation as of the date of death. It was repealed in 1997. [I.R.C. § 4980A, repealed by Taxpayer Relief Act of 1997, Pub. L. No. 105-34, § 1073(a)]

Form 5330

Q 7:126   What is the purpose of Form 5330?

With regard to an IRA, a SEP, or a SARSEP, Form 5330, Return of Excise Taxes Related to Employee Benefit Plans, is used to report the 10 percent excise tax on the following:

- Nondeductible employer contributions to SEPs, SARSEPs, and SIMPLEs [I.R.C. § 4972(d)(1)(A)(ii)]
- Prohibited transactions [I.R.C. §§ 4975(a), 4975(e)(1)]
- Excess contributions to plans with a cash or deferred arrangement (CODA) [I.R.C. §§ 4979(a), 4979(e)(4)]

The nondeductible contributions are computed as of the end of the employer's tax year. The current-year nondeductible contributions are equal to the amount contributed during the employer's tax year in excess of the amount of contributions allowable as a deduction under Code Section 404. In addition, prior-year nondeductible SEP contributions continue to be subject to the 10 percent excise tax annually until eliminated by a carryforward deduction in years after the nondeductible contributions are made.

Q 7:127   May more than one type of excise tax be reported on the same Form 5330?

Yes. Generally, a single return may be filed for different excise taxes with the same due date. Thus, an employer may use one Form 5330 to report the prohibited transaction tax and the tax on nondeductible employer contributions. It should be noted, however, that more than one "person" may be required to file Form 5330 in the event of a prohibited transaction.

Note. The due date for the payment of tax on excess contributions to plans with CODAs falls after the due date for the payment of taxes on prohibited transactions and nondeductible employer contributions. Furthermore, the IRS requires a separate filing for reporting the tax on excess contributions to plans with CODAs.

Q 7:128   Who must file Form 5330?

Form 5330 must be filed by the following:

1. Any employer that is liable for the tax under Code Section 4972 for nondeductible contributions to SEPs, SARSEPs, and SIMPLEs;

2. Any disqualified person (see Q 7:130) who is liable for the tax under Code Section 4975 for participating in a prohibited transaction (other than a fiduciary acting only as such or an individual (or his or her beneficiary) who engages in a prohibited transaction with respect to his or her IRA); and

3. Any employer that is liable for the tax under Code Section 4979 on excess contributions to plans with a CODA.

Q 7:129   Why is an individual (or his or her beneficiary) who engages in a prohibited transaction with respect to his or her IRA not required to file Form 5330?

Form 5330 need not be filed by an individual (or his or her beneficiary) who engages in a prohibited transaction with respect to his or her IRA because by that action the IRA is disqualified. As a result, the IRA itself becomes taxable (see Q 7:29).

Q 7:130   Who is a disqualified person?

A *disqualified person* is any one of the following:

1. A fiduciary;
2. A person providing services to the plan;
3. An employer, any of whose employees are covered by the plan;
4. An employee organization, any of whose members are covered by the plan;
5. Any direct or indirect owner of 50 percent or more of
   a. The combined voting power of all classes of stock entitled to vote,
   b. The total value of shares of all classes of stock of a corporation,
   c. The capital interest or the profits interest of a partnership,

   d. The beneficial interest of a trust or unincorporated enterprise that is an employer or an employee organization described in item 3 or 4, respectively, or

   e. Any direct or indirect owner of 50 percent or more of (i) the combined voting power of all classes of stock entitled to vote or the total value of shares of all classes of stock of a corporation, (ii) the capital interest or the profits interest of a partnership, or (iii) the beneficial interest of a trust or unincorporated enterprise that is an employer or an employee organization described in item 3 or 4, respectively;

6. A family member of any individual described in item 1, 2, 3, or 5 (a family member is a spouse, an ancestor, a lineal descendant, or a spouse of a lineal descendant);

7. A corporation, partnership, or trust or estate of which (or in which) any direct or indirect owner holds 50 percent or more of the interest described in item 5e(i), (ii), or (iii) (for purposes of (iii), the beneficial interest of the trust or estate is owned directly or indirectly or held by persons described in items 1 through 5);

8. An officer or director (or an individual having powers or responsibilities similar to those of an officer or director), 10 percent or more shareholder, or highly compensated employee (earning 10 percent or more of the yearly wages of an employer) of a person described in item 3, 4, 5, or 7; or

9. A 10 percent or more (in capital or profits) partner or joint venturer of a person described in item 3, 4, 5, or 7.

Q 7:131   When must Form 5330 be filed?

Form 5330 must be filed by the last day of the seventh month after the end of the tax year of the employer or other person that must file the return for the tax on nondeductible contributions to SEPs and SARSEPs and for the tax on engaging in a prohibited transaction.

Q 7:132   How may an extension to file Form 5330 be requested?

Form 5558, Application for Extension of Time to File Certain Employee Plan Returns, can be filed to request an extension of time to file Form 5330. If the request is approved, an extension of up to six months may be granted.

Q 7:133   What is the penalty for not filing Form 5330 by the due date?

If Form 5330 is not filed by the due date, including extensions, there may be a penalty of 5 percent of the unpaid tax for each month or part of a month the return is late, up to a maximum of 25 percent of the unpaid tax. The minimum penalty for a return that is more than 60 days late is the lesser of the tax due or $100.

The penalty for late filing will not be imposed if failure to file on time can be shown to have a reasonable cause. A request for abatement of any late filing penalties requires a statement explaining the reasonable cause to be attached to Form 5330.

Q 7:134   What is the penalty for late payment of tax due on Form 5330?

If the tax due on Form 5330 is not paid when due, there may be a penalty of 0.5 percent of the unpaid tax for each month or part of a month the tax is not paid, up to a maximum of 25 percent of the unpaid tax. This penalty may also apply to any additional tax not paid within 10 days of the date of the notice and demand for payment. The penalty will not be imposed if it can be shown that the failure to pay on time was for reasonable cause.

Q 7:135   May interest and other penalties be charged if the tax due under Form 5330 is not paid by the due date?

Yes. Even if an extension of time to file is granted (see Q 7:132), interest (determined under Code Section 6621) is charged on taxes not paid by the due date. Interest is also charged on penalties imposed for failure to file, negligence, fraud, gross valuation overstatements, and substantial understatements of tax from the due date (including extensions) to the date of payment. Interest and penalties will be billed separately after the return is filed.

Form 5498

Reporting Contributions on Form 5498

Q 7:136   What is Form 5498 used to report?

Each year, IRA trustees and custodians must submit IRA contribution information to the IRS. Form 5498 is used for that purpose. (See also Qs 7:7–7:13.) [I.R.C. § 408(i); Prop. Treas. Reg. § 1.408-5]

Q 7:137   Must Form 5498 be filed even if an IRA is closed or revoked before the end of the year or has no value at year-end?

Yes. Form 5498 must be filed if any reportable activity occurred during the year.

Q 7:138   What is the due date for filing Form 5498?

Form 5498 must be filed with the IRS generally by May 31 of each year.

Q 7:139   How may an extension to file Form 5498 with the IRS be requested?

For paper, magnetic media, or electronic filing, an extension to file Forms 5498 with the IRS may be requested by completing Form 8809, Request for Extension of Time to File Information Returns, and sending it to the following address:

Enterprise Computing Center—Martinsburg
Information Reporting Program
Attn: Extension of Time Coordinator
240 Murall Drive
Kearneysville, WV 25430

The IRS suggests that Form 8809 be filed as soon as the need becomes apparent; in any case, Form 8809 must be filed no later than the due date of the return (see Q 7:8) for the IRS to consider granting the extension. If the IRS approves the extension request, an additional 30 days to file will be granted. If more time to file is needed, an additional 30 days may be requested by submitting another Form 8809 before the end of the initial extension period.

Note. The approved extension request will apply only to the due date for filing the returns with the IRS. Such approval will not extend the due date for providing statements to IRA owners.

Q 7:140   How may an extension to provide Forms 5498 to IRA owners be requested?

If it is necessary to request an extension for providing Forms 5498 to IRA owners, a letter should be sent to the IRS-Martinsburg Computing Center (see Q 7:139). The letter must include the following:

- Payer's name
- Payer's TIN
- Payer's address
- Type of return
- A statement that the request is for an extension for providing statements to recipients
- Reason for the delay
- Payer's signature

The request must be postmarked by the due date of the return (May 31). If the request for extension is approved, an additional 30 days to furnish the statements to IRA owners will be granted.

Q 7:141   What changes were made to Form 5498 for 2009?

The following changes were made to Form 5498 for 2009:

1. Form 5498 has been enlarged and reformatted; new boxes are included for information that formerly was reported in the blank box next to box 10.

2. Filers are now directed to the IRS Web site for information on the disaster relief available for "federally declared disaster areas" (the replacement term for "presidentially declared disaster areas").

3. Instructions are provided for reporting contributions now treated as rollovers under new provisions of law—military death gratuities and servicemembers' group life insurance (SGLI) payments contributed to Roth IRAs; qualified settlement income received in connection with the Exxon Valdez litigation and contributed to traditional or Roth IRAs; and qualifying payments from commercial passenger airline carriers to qualified employees or their beneficiaries who contribute them to Roth IRAs.

4. Guidance is provided concerning the suspension of the minimum distribution requirements for 2009.

Q 7:142   How is the 2009 Form 5498 completed?

The following are box-by-box instructions for correctly completing the 2009 Form 5498.

Box 1: Regular Contributions (Other Than Amounts in Boxes 2–4, 8–10, 13a, 14a, and 15a). Enter all contributions to a traditional IRA made in 2009 and from January 1 through April 15, 2010, that are designated for 2009. Regular contributions include catch-up contributions made by eligible individuals who are age 50 or older by December 31, 2009. Report catch-up contributions made to a traditional IRA in this box.

Report gross contributions, including excess contributions, even if the excess contributions are subsequently withdrawn. Also include in box 1 a regular traditional IRA contribution even if the regular contribution (plus earnings) has been recharacterized as a regular Roth IRA contribution.

For excess contributions that are being treated by the IRA owner as a regular contribution made in a subsequent year, do *not* report the contribution on Form 5498 for the subsequent year. It will have been reported on the Form 5498 for the year the contribution was originally made to the IRA.

Report in this box any regular traditional IRA contributions (referred to as *employee contributions*) made to an IRA under a SEP. Such contributions are treated as the employee's regular traditional IRA contributions for the year and not as employer contributions to the SEP.

These contributions are *not* reported in box 1: contributions to a SIMPLE IRA (box 9), contributions to a Roth IRA (box 10), rollover contributions (box 2), conversion contributions (box 3), and recharacterized contributions (box 4).

Box 2: Rollover Contributions. Box 2 is for entry of rollover contributions, and contributions treated as rollover contributions, to any IRA during 2009. This includes 60-day rollover contributions made from one IRA to another, direct or indirect rollovers from a qualified plan (including a governmental Section

457(b) plan) or Section 403(b) plan to a traditional or Roth IRA, and contributions of military death gratuities, SGLI payments, qualified settlement income received in connection with the Exxon Valdez litigation, and airline payment amounts. If the rollover consists of property other than cash, value the property on the day it is received by the payer (which may differ from its value on the day it was distributed from the original plan).

Box 3: Roth IRA Conversion Amount. Enter the amount converted (or reconverted) from a traditional IRA, SEP IRA, or SIMPLE IRA (that has met the two-year period requirement) to a Roth IRA during 2009, regardless of how the conversion (or reconversion) was accomplished.

Box 4: Recharacterized Contributions. Report in this box a recharacterization transfer from a traditional IRA to a Roth IRA or from a Roth IRA to a traditional IRA, plus earnings. All recharacterization transfers received by the same IRA during the same year are aggregated and reported on a single Form 5498. Mark the appropriate checkbox in box 7 to indicate the type of IRA that received the recharacterization transfer.

Box 5: Fair Market Value of Account. Enter in this box the fair market value (FMV) of a traditional IRA, SEP, SIMPLE IRA, or Roth IRA as of December 31, 2009. This value includes all assets of the plan. An IRA *plan* refers to all the assets under the trust or custodial agreement (or, in the case of an individual retirement annuity, the value of the annuity contract). The December 31, 2009, FMV does not include regular contributions made in 2010 for 2009.

If an individual has signed only one IRA agreement but has various investments, only one Form 5498 should be issued. If the individual has more than one IRA agreement (e.g., one agreement for regular contributions, a second agreement for SEP contributions, and a third for a rollover from an employer's plan), three Forms 5498 must be issued because the individual has three traditional IRA plans.

Traditional IRAs must be reported separately from Roth IRAs. Likewise, SIMPLE IRAs must be reported on a separate Form 5498.

Box 6: Life Insurance Cost Included in Box 1. This box is used for endowment contracts only. Enter the amount included in box 1 allocable to the cost of life insurance.

Box 7: Checkboxes. This series of checkboxes is used to identify the type of IRA for which contributions are being reported.

IRA Checkbox. Check this box if the Form 5498 is being filed to report information about a traditional IRA, including a conduit IRA.

SEP Checkbox. Check this box if the Form 5498 is being filed to report information about a SEP IRA account. If it is not known whether the account is a SEP IRA, mark the "IRA" checkbox.

SIMPLE Checkbox. Check this box if the Form 5498 is being filed to report information about a SIMPLE IRA account.

Roth IRA Checkbox. Check this box if the Form 5498 is being filed to report information about any Roth IRA.

Box 8: SEP Contributions. In box 8, report any amount that the employer contributed to a SEP IRA *during* 2009; amounts contributed by a self-employed individual to his or her own account, and salary deferral contributions made under a SARSEP, are treated as employer contributions for this purpose. Contributions made in 2009 for 2008 are included, but not contributions made in 2010 for 2009. The trustee or custodian does *not* report based on the employer's tax year for which the contributions have been made. Report the dollar amount of employer SEP contributions paid to the IRA during the year.

Employee contributions to a SEP are not reported in box 8. Since they are treated as regular IRA contributions that are subject to—or deemed subject to—the 100 percent of compensation or $5,000 limit of Code Section 219, they are reported in box 1.

Box 9: SIMPLE Contributions. Enter any amount that the employer contributed to a SIMPLE IRA (including salary deferrals and employer matching or nonelective contributions) *during* 2009. The trustee or custodian does *not* report based on the employer's tax year for which these contributions are being made. Report the dollar amount of employer SIMPLE contributions paid to the SIMPLE IRA during the year.

Box 10: Roth IRA Contributions. Enter any regular contributions made to a Roth IRA in 2009 and from January 1 through April 15, 2010, that are designated for 2009.

Box 11: Check if RMD for 2010. Check this box on the *2009* Form 5498 if a traditional IRA owner must take an RMD in 2010.

Boxes 12a and 12b: RMD Date and Amount. The IRA trustee or custodian must give advance notice to participants of the dates and amounts of RMDs to be paid in 2010. Boxes 12a and 12b may be used for this purpose, but alternative means of notice are also available. Instead of using boxes 12a and 12b in this way, the trustee or custodian may provide the information in a separate Form 5498, or in a separate RMD statement delivered to the participant before January 31, 2010, in accordance with Alternative One or Alternative Two (see Qs 7:178–7:185).

Note. The authors recommend that the trustee or custodian do both—send the annual RMD statement, and provide the information in boxes 12a and 12b of Form 5498.

Boxes 13a, 13b, and 13c: Postponed Contribution. Enter in box 13a the amount of any postponed contribution made in 2009 for a prior year. If contributions are made for more than one prior year, each prior year's postponed contribution must be reported on a separate form. The year for which the postponed contribution was made is entered in box 13b. Finally, in box 13c, enter the code for the reason for the participant's postponed contribution:

- For participants' service in the combat zone or hazardous duty area, enter: AF—Allied Force; JE—Joint Endeavor; EF—Enduring Freedom; IF—Iraqi Freedom.

- For participants who are "affected taxpayers," as described in an IRS News Release relating to a federally designated disaster area, enter FD.

For details about these postponed contributions, see Q 7:144.

Boxes 14a and 14b: Repayments. These boxes are used to report any repayment of a qualified reservist distribution or of a designated disaster distribution (for example, a qualified hurricane distribution). The amount repaid is reported in box 14a, and the code for the type of payment is entered in box 14b—code QR for the repayment of a qualified reservist distribution, or code DD for repayment of a federally designated disaster distribution.

Boxes 15a and 15b: Other Contributions. Enter in box 15a the amount of special catch-up contributions made (maximum of $3,000) under the special rules that apply to qualifying individuals who lost retirement savings in the collapse of the Enron Corporation (see Qs 3:31, 3:32). Code BK is entered in box 15b.

Q 7:143   What additional reporting requirements does a trustee have if the IRA owner is age 70½ or older?

Notice 2002-27 [2002-1 C.B. 814], *modified by* Notice 2009-9 2009-5 I.R.B. 419] requires trustees, custodians, and issuers to send a notice annually to each participant who must receive an RMD that either states the amount of the RMD, or offers to calculate it for the participant. The statement must generally be received by the participant by January 31 (for 2010, the deadline is February 1 (see Q 7:43)). This reporting applies to traditional IRAs, including regular IRAs, rollover IRAs, SEP IRAs, and SIMPLE IRAs. (See Qs 7:17–7:185.)

Note. For 2009, RMBs are suspended (see Qs: 4.21–4.25); accordingly, special reporting requirements apply for 2008 and 2009. First, according to Notice 2009-9 [2009-5 I.R.B. 419] trustees, custodians and other issuers were not required to provide the information that Notice 2002-27 would otherwise require with respect to 2009 RMDs. Instead, Notice 2009-9 sets forth two methods for notifying participants about the suspension of 2009 RMDs: The first method is to calculate the 2009 RMD but show the actual RMD for 2009 as zero, or explain the 2009 waiver and report the RMD that would have been required had there not been a waiver. The second method is for preparers not to check the box in the 2008 Forms 5498 that indicates an RMD is required for 2009. Finally, since the waiver of 2009 RMDs was enacted so late in 2008, Notice 2009-9 extends the time allowed for issuers to fulfill the special reporting requirements—until March 31, 2009.

Q 7:144   What is the reporting procedure for contributions made during the extended time periods allowed for military personnel in certain combat zones?

Individuals who serve in or support the Armed Forces in a designated combat zone or qualified hazardous duty area may make IRA contributions for a prior year after the normal contribution due date (i.e., April 15 of the following calendar year). "IRA contributions" for this purpose encompass contributions to a traditional IRA, Roth IRA, SEP IRA, or SIMPLE IRA. The additional time allowed includes the time that the individual was in the designated zone or area plus at least 180 days. The individual must designate the contribution for a prior year. If a qualifying individual makes an IRA contribution after April 15 and designates the contribution for a prior year, the trustee or custodian must report the contribution either on Form 5498 for the year for which the contribution was made or on Form 5498 for a subsequent year.

If the trustee or custodian reports the contribution for the year in which it is made, no special reporting is required. The contribution is included in the appropriate box on the original Form 5498 or, if an original form had been filed for that individual, on a corrected Form 5498.

If the contribution is reported on Form 5498 for a subsequent year, the trustee or custodian must include the year for which the contribution was made, the amount of the contribution, and one of the following indicators: "JE" for Joint Endeavor for the Persian Gulf area; "AF" for Allied Force for the Kosovo area; "EF" for Enduring Freedom for Afghanistan, Uzbekistan, Kyrgyzstan, Pakistan, Tajikistan, Jordan, and Somalia; or "IF" for Iraqi Freedom for the Arabian Peninsula Areas (the Persian Gulf, the Red Sea, the Gulf of Oman, the portion of the Arabian Sea that lies north of 10 degrees north latitude and west of 68 degrees east longitude, the Gulf of Aden, and the total land areas of Iraq, Kuwait, Saudi Arabia, Oman, Bahrain, Qatar, and the United Arab Emirates and the airspace above such locations).

The information is entered on Form 5498 in boxes 13a, 13b, and 13c (see Q 7:142).

Q 7:145   Must Form 5498 be filed if no contributions were made and a total distribution was made during the year?

No. If a total distribution was made during the year and no reportable contributions were made, Form 5498 need not be filed. Neither must an annual statement be furnished. It should be noted, however, that special rules apply in the year of an IRA owner's death (see Q 7:162) and in the case of a revoked IRA (see discussion of box 1 in Q 7:89).

Q 7:146   Are separate Forms 5498 required for each investment under a single IRA plan?

No. It is not necessary to file a separate Form 5498 for each investment under one IRA plan. For example, if a participant has three CDs under one IRA plan, only one Form 5498 is required for all contributions and the fair market values of the CDs under the plan. In contrast, if an individual has established more than one IRA plan with the same financial organization, a separate Form 5498 must be filed for each plan.

Because the definition of an individual retirement account includes all assets within the same trust or custodial agreement, a trustee or custodian should reflect all information that is associated with that same agreement on one Form 5498. On the other hand, in an individual retirement annuity, each contract is a separate plan.

Q 7:147   How should the "Account Number" box on Form 5498 be completed?

The "Account Number" box is provided on Form 5498 to identify the IRA being reported. This number (which must be unique so that it will distinguish the specific IRA) is especially important if an individual maintains more than one IRA at the same organization—for example, one plan for regular contributions and a separate plan for rollover contributions. The individual's Social Security number may *not* be used here. If the trustee or custodian later needs to correct a Form 5498 (see Q 7:150) and the account number box was completed on the original submission, the box *must* be completed on the corrected return for the IRS to correct the form properly.

Annual Participant Statement

Q 7:148   What are the rules applicable to the annual participant statement vis-à-vis Form 5498?

In certain cases, information is required to be reported to an IRA owner (or his or her beneficiaries). Information must also be reported to a nonspouse designated beneficiary of qualified plan benefits that were directly rolled over to an inherited IRA. The information that must be reported in these cases is frequently referred to as the *annual participant statement*. Two general rules and a special rule apply to the annual participant statement.

1. In general, a copy of the Form 5498 that is submitted to the IRS must be provided to the participant. The deadline for providing that copy to the participant is generally May 31 , the same deadline as that for submission to the IRS.

2. The IRA participant must receive an *additional report* before that deadline. Generally, by January 31 of each year (February 1 in 2010), the trustee or custodian of any IRA, SEP, or SIMPLE must provide the participant with a statement of the preceding December 31 fair market value in any written format. That is the same fair market value that will eventually be reflected in box 5 of Form 5498 submitted to the IRS by May 31.

3. The trustee or custodian of a SIMPLE IRA must provide a statement of account activity by January 31 (February 1 in 2010). The instructions for Form 5498 do not provide a definition of the term *account activity* because the IRS chief counsel has not yet issued one. The Forms and Publications Division has indicated informally that until such guidance is issued, a good-faith interpretation of *account activity* may be used.

Q 7:149 Must Form 5498 be filed when the IRA trustee, custodian, or issuer has furnished a timely statement of the fair market value of the IRA to the IRA owner and no contributions were made to the IRA by the owner?

No. If the IRA trustee, custodian, or issuer furnished a timely statement of the fair market value (FMV) of an IRA to the IRA owner and no contributions were made to the IRA by the participant for the previous year, the trustee, custodian, or issuer need not furnish another statement (or Form 5498) to the participant. Nevertheless, Form 5498 must be filed with the IRS by May 31 to report the preceding December 31 FMV of the IRA. That is true for beneficiary accounts under the inherited IRA rules.

If the trustee, custodian, or issuer does not furnish another statement to the IRA owner, because no contributions were made for the year, the December 31 FMV statement must contain a legend designating which information is being furnished to the IRS, although the FMV statement itself has no required format.

Many organizations comply with the FMV statement and Form 5498 requirements in the following manner:

1. In January, they produce and mail the official Form 5498 (or a substitute that meets the specifications of IRS Publication 1179) for the previous year. The previous year-end value will be available from the system for any IRA owner who has already made the previous year's regular contribution, made a rollover or direct rollover contribution during the previous year, or received an employer's SEP contribution or SIMPLE contribution during the previous year.

2. After April 15, they produce the official Form 5498 (or a substitute that meets the specifications of IRS Publication 1179) only for those IRA owners who made a previous-year regular contribution between January 1 and April 15 of the following year. Only those owners need to receive a mailing before the May 31 deadline.

3. They transmit the entire tape (both the January information and the later information) to the IRS via the approved magnetic media at the same time, after April 15 but before the May 31 deadline.

Practice Pointer. Because reporting requirements change every year, it is always a good idea to discuss those requirements with the filer's data processor at least once each year.

Filing Corrected Forms 5498

Q 7:150   How are corrected Forms 5498 submitted?

Sometimes it is necessary to correct a Form 5498 after the original has been submitted to the IRS. Although Form 5498 is not subject to the three-tiered penalty structure applicable to other reporting forms, all corrections for a year should be submitted to the IRS in accordance with the rules that apply to corrected Forms 1099-R (see Q 7:90).

Magnetic Media and Electronic Filing Requirements

Q 7:151   What are the magnetic media or electronic filing requirements for original and corrected Forms 5498?

If a trustee or custodian is required to file 250 or more Forms 5498, the original submission must be made via an approved magnetic media submission or filed electronically. The 250-forms count applies separately to the original and the corrected Forms 5498. For example, if the count for the original submission was 1,000 and the count for the corrections is 225, the original submission must be made via magnetic media or filed electronically, whereas the corrections may be submitted either on paper forms or on magnetic media or filed electronically.

Q 7:152   May an organization request that it not be required to file electronically or on magnetic media?

Yes. Form 8508 may be submitted requesting an undue hardship waiver from electronic or magnetic media filing for a period of time not to exceed one tax year (see Q 7:93). Waiver requests must be filed at least 45 days before the return is due.

Q 7:153   Is it necessary to obtain IRS approval to file Forms 5498 magnetically or electronically?

Yes. The requirements for requesting approval for magnetic media or electronic filing of Forms 5498 are similar to those for Form 1099-R (see Qs 7:92, 7:93).

Q 7:154   What is the due date for filing Form 5498 magnetically or electronically?

The due date for magnetic media or electronic filing of Forms 5498 is the same as that for paper reporting—generally May 31.

Q 7:155   Where are magnetic media filings for Forms 5498 made?

All information returns filed magnetically (including Forms 5498) should be sent to the following address:

Enterprise Computing Center—Martinsburg
Information Reporting Program
240 Murall Drive
Kearneysville, WV 25430

Form 4804, Transmittal of Information Returns Reported Magnetically/Electronically, must accompany the submissions.

Noncompliance Penalties

Q 7:156 What penalties may apply to a trustee or custodian required to file Form 5498?

The following penalties apply to a trustee or custodian required to file Form 5498:

1. A $50 penalty applies to each failure to timely file a Form 5498.
2. A $50 penalty applies to each failure to timely furnish a statement to a participant as required.
3. For a trustee or custodian filing on paper returns, a $50 penalty applies to each failure to furnish paper forms that are machine scannable.

Any of the penalties listed above may be waived if the failure to perform was due to reasonable cause and not to willful neglect.

For intentional disregard of the filing and correct information requirements, a penalty of $100 for each failure may be imposed. [I.R.C. § 6693; Treas. Reg. § 1.408-5] Failure to transmit Forms 5498 electronically or via magnetic media when required and failure to follow the paper submission format are treated as failure to file the form, unless the trustee or custodian has an approved waiver on file or can establish reasonable cause or, in some cases, due diligence.

Miscellaneous Rules

Q 7:157 Does Form 5498 indicate which amounts, if any, are deductible?

No. Form 5498 does not address the issue of whether a contribution is deductible or nondeductible or whether the amount is excludable from income under Code Section 402(h).

Q 7:158 Must an IRA owner inform the trustee or custodian, the issuer, or his or her employer whether an IRA contribution is deductible?

No. An IRA owner is not required to inform the IRA trustee or custodian, the issuer, or his or her employer whether a contribution is deductible or nondeductible.

Q 7:159   How is Form 5498 filed when two corporations merge or are otherwise combined?

A combined reporting procedure may be used if the following requirements are both met:

1. The successor business acquires from the predecessor business substantially all the property used in the predecessor's trade or business (or used in a separate unit of the predecessor's trade or business).

2. With respect to some or all of the predecessor's information reporting responsibilities, the predecessor and successor agree that the predecessor must report amounts, including withholding, on information returns for the pre-acquisition portion of the acquisition year, but not for the post-acquisition portion of the acquisition year.

If the combined reporting procedure is available, the successor files one Form 1099 or 5498 for each recipient combining the predecessor's and successor's reportable amounts (including any withholding), and the predecessor does not need to report the amounts.

The successor must also file a statement with the IRS indicating the forms that are being filed on a combined basis under Revenue Procedure 99-50. [1999-2 C.B. 757] The statement must include the predecessor's and successor's names, addresses, telephone numbers, and EINs, as well as the name and telephone number of the person responsible for preparing the statement, and must reflect separately the amount of federal income tax withheld by the predecessor and by the successor for each type of form being filed on a combined basis. The statement must be sent separately for Forms 1099 and 5498 by the forms' due dates to:

Enterprise Computing Center—Martinsburg
Attn: Chief, Information Returns Branch
Mail Stop 360
230 Murall Dr.
Kearneysville, WV 25430

[2009 General Instructions for Forms 1099, 1098, 3921, 3922, 5498, and W-2G]

Q 7:160   How long should copies of Form 5498 be kept?

Copies of information returns filed with the IRS (including Form 5498) should be kept for at least three years from the due date of the return.

Q 7:161   May Form 5498 be enclosed in the same envelope with other forms?

Maybe. If a trustee or custodian combines Form 5498 with returns for interest, dividend, and royalty payments, strict mailing requirements must be followed. For example, no enclosures are permitted for promotional material or a quarterly or annual report. Even a sentence on the year-end statement describing new services being offered is not permitted. Logos are permitted on the envelope and on any nontax enclosures. If, however, Form 5498 is being mailed without any related forms, a combined mailing may be allowed. Payee statements that are related may be included in a single mailing; related forms include Form 1099 and Form 1098. In addition, Forms W-2 and W-2P may be included in the single mailing because they are related to the payee statements. [Notice 87-17, 1987-1 C.B. 454]

Q 7:162 What are the special Form 5498 reporting requirements for a deceased IRA owner?

In the year of an IRA owner's death, Form 5498 (and the year-end FMV information due generally by January 31, but by February 1 in 2010) must be issued in both the decedent's name and that of each beneficiary.

A spouse beneficiary (unless the spouse makes the IRA his or her own IRA) is treated as any other beneficiary for the special reporting purposes. If the spouse makes the IRA his or her own in the year of the IRA owner's death, the filer should report on Form 5498 and the annual statement without the beneficiary designation (see below).

On the decedent's Form 5498 and annual statement, either the FMV of the IRA on the date of death is entered, or the alternate reporting method is used and the FMV as of the end of the year in which the decedent died is reported.

Under the alternative method detailed in Revenue Procedure 89-52 [1989-2 C.B. 632], any FMV reported on the beneficiary's Form 5498 should not also be reported on the decedent's Form 5498 for that year. Consequently, the value of the decedent's account as of the end of the year will frequently be zero—even though money remains in the account.

Under the alternative method, therefore, for the year during which the IRA owner dies, the trustee or custodian will prepare a Form 5498 in the name (and Social Security number) of the original owner reflecting any current-year contributions (box 1 information), any rollover contributions (box 2 information), and the FMV as zero (box 5 information). The SEP checkbox will be marked if an employer SEP contribution is made during the year of death (box 8 information). No further Form 5498 will be issued in the name of the deceased IRA owner.

> **Note.** Usually, no Form 5498 is required if a zero is entered in box 5, unless specific instructions indicate otherwise. Here, money actually remains in the account at year-end; therefore, zero must be entered.

In addition, for the year in which an IRA owner died, the trustee (or custodian) will prepare a Form 5498 in the name of *each* primary beneficiary reflecting the beneficiary's Social Security number. The beneficiary's Form 5498 must be styled, for example, as "Brian Young as beneficiary of Steve Gates." The only information to be reported on the beneficiary's Form 5498 will be the FMV of *that* beneficiary's portion of the decedent's IRA as of year-end. The trustee or custodian will continue issuing a Form 5498 on behalf of the beneficiary until the IRA is reduced to zero.

If a beneficiary takes a total distribution of his or her share of the IRA in the year of the IRA owner's death, it is not necessary to file Form 5498 or furnish an annual statement for that beneficiary. (A Form 1099-R in the name of the beneficiary reporting the amount of the death distribution must still be issued, however.)

If the trustee or custodian has no knowledge of the death of the IRA owner until after the reporting deadline, no corrective filing of the Form 5498 is required for that year. Be that as it may, the trustee or custodian should probably prepare Forms 5498 for the year it became aware of the IRA owner's death, provided the IRA has not yet been withdrawn by the beneficiary.

Revenue Procedure 89-52 also states that if the trustee or custodian uses this alternative method, it must inform the executor of the decedent's estate of his or her right to receive the IRA's FMV as of the IRA owner's death. Form 5498 has language on the reverse of Copy B, the participant's copy, which refers to the executor's right to request the IRA's FMV as of the IRA participant's date of death.

If the trustee or custodian is sending a substitute statement to participants in lieu of the official Form 5498, the following two sentences should be added to the reverse of the participant's copy (which is a requirement when substitute statements are prepared):

> However, if a decedent is shown as the participant on this form, it may be the FMV on the date of death. If a decedent's name is shown as the participant and the FMV is zero, the executor or administrator of the decedent's estate may request a date-of-death valuation from the financial institution.

Example. Diane Smith had an IRA with Big Bank. The beneficiaries of her IRA were her three nephews: Ian, Joe, and Kevin O'Brien. During the year before Diane's death, a direct rollover in the amount of $75,000 was added to Diane's IRA from her 401(k) plan. Diane died during the same year, but after the direct rollover occurred. Joe and Kevin took a total distribution of their beneficial interests in the IRA; Ian decided to have his portion paid out over a five-year period.

In the year of Diane's death there will be two Forms 5498 issued. First, a Form 5498 will be issued in Diane Smith's name and Social Security number with $75,000 reported in box 2 for the rollover from her 401(k) plan and a zero in box 5 under the alternative method for reporting FMV. Ian will receive a Form 5498 with his Social Security number and styled "Ian O'Brien as beneficiary of Diane Smith," with $25,000 fair market value reported in box 5. That dollar amount represents Ian's one-third beneficial interest in his aunt's IRA. There will be no Forms 5498 issued for Joe and Kevin, because each took a total distribution of his beneficial interest in the IRA before year-end.

Joe will receive a Form 1099-R with his Social Security number and styled "Joe O'Brien as beneficiary of Diane Smith," reflecting the $25,000 death distribution he received from his aunt's IRA during the year. Kevin will also receive a Form 1099-R with his Social Security number and styled "Kevin O'Brien as beneficiary of Diane Smith," reflecting the $25,000 death distribution he received from his aunt's IRA during the year.

Q 7:163   How is Form 5498 used to report the direct rollover to an IRA of qualified plan assets to a nonspouse beneficiary of a deceased participant?

If a nonspouse beneficiary of a deceased qualified plan participant rolls over inherited assets directly to an IRA established for that purpose (or directly converts the assets to a Roth IRA), the receiving IRA is treated as an inherited IRA, and the procedures described above (see Q 7:162) apply.

Note. A trustee-to-trustee transfer is required to roll over or convert the inherited interest of a nonspouse beneficiary to a traditional or Roth IRA. When reporting the transfer on Form 1099-R, code 4 would be entered in box 7.

Form 8606

Q 7:164   Which form is used to determine the portion of an IRA distribution that is a tax-free return of nondeductible contributions?

Form 8606, Nondeductible IRAs, is used to determine the portion of an IRA distribution that is a tax-free return of nondeductible contributions. It must be filed with an IRA owner's federal tax return (Form 1040) unless there have been no nondeductible contributions to the owner's traditional IRA or IRAs and the owner has no Roth IRAs. If a portion of a current contribution is nondeductible, Form 8606 starts or continues the data history that will be needed to determine the nontaxable portion of a distribution when it occurs.

Practice Pointer. It is likely that Form 8606 will be needed long after the individual tax return is discarded. Therefore, Form 8606 or the information it contains should be kept as part of a permanent tax record (see Q 7:167).

Q 7:165   Is Form 8606 also used for reporting nondeductible contributions to the Roth IRA?

Yes. Parts II and III of Form 8606 are used to report nondeductible contributions to the Roth IRA and the Coverdell ESA:

1. *Conversion section.* Part II is used for figuring the taxable amount of conversions from a traditional IRA or a SIMPLE IRA to a Roth IRA. Part II is also used to show a recharacterization of amounts that were converted to a Roth IRA.

2. *Roth IRA distribution section.* Part III is used for reporting distributions from a Roth IRA and to report a recharacterization involving a Roth IRA contribution.

Q 7:166   Must an IRA owner file Form 8606 if neither a nondeductible traditional IRA contribution nor a traditional IRA distribution occurs in a particular year?

If an IRA owner has never made a nondeductible contribution to a traditional IRA, there is no need to file Form 8606. If, however, there is a history of nondeductible contributions to preserve, there seems to be no harm in filing Form 8606 to keep the file current, even if the owner did not make a nondeductible contribution or take a distribution in a particular year. Whether to file Form 8606 under such circumstances is a matter for the owner's tax preparer to determine.

If an IRA owner is not filing a Form 1040 for the year, but nondeductible contributions or distributions (or both) have occurred, Form 8606 must still be filed—at the time and place the Form 1040 would have been filed.

Q 7:167   What recordkeeping is suggested for Form 8606 filers?

In the instructions for Form 8606, the IRS provides a list of records that are to be kept:

1. Page 1 of each year's Form 1040 for years in which nondeductible contributions were made to a traditional IRA;
2. Confirmation of contributions through a file of Forms 5498 received regarding each year's IRA contribution to a traditional IRA or Roth IRA;
3. Forms 5498 or similar statements to confirm year-end values for each year in which a distribution occurred;
4. Forms 1099-R and W-2P for each year in which a distribution was received. (Form W-2P, formerly used for partial distributions from IRAs, was discontinued and has been replaced by Form 1099-R.); and
5. Forms 8606 and any supporting statements, attachments and worksheets for all applicable years.

Practice Pointer. It is advisable to maintain a separate IRA file that contains photocopies of the items needed for filing Form 8606, rather than removing the items from the IRA owner's general tax return files.

Q 7:168   Should information similar to that needed to file Form 8606 be kept for all IRAs, even those for which Form 8606 never needs to be filed?

It is a good idea to maintain information similar to that needed to file Form 8606 for both types of IRAs (traditional and Roth), even though it is not required, before a distribution occurs for any IRA that has received nondeductible contributions. That is so because the rules for allocating nondeductible and deductible portions of an IRA take into account all of an individual's IRAs. (It should be noted, however, that Forms 8606 are prepared separately for each type of IRA (traditional and Roth) and for each spouse, even though the parties may be filing jointly.)

The rules require that when a distribution is made all IRAs of the same type be combined, so that the IRA owner is prevented from making distributions from the IRA with the heaviest nondeductible contributions, thereby delaying taxability.

Q 7:169 Does the taxpayer report after-tax monies that were rolled over from an employer plan into a traditional IRA?

Yes, also on Form 8606. The instructions to Form 8606 provide for amounts rolled over from any nontaxable portion of a qualified employer plan to a traditional or SEP IRA to be entered on Line 2. The legend on Line 2 of the form merely reads, "Enter your total basis in traditional IRAs."

Example. Prior to 2009, Sam had made nondeductible contributions of $10,000 to a traditional IRA. During 2009, Sam made a $5,000 current-year IRA contribution that is all nondeductible, and he rolled over to the IRA $5,000 of the after-tax employee contributions that he had made to his employer's qualified plan. On Sam's 2009 Form 8606, Lines 1, 2, and 3 would be completed as follows:

Line 1: $5,000 (2009 regular contribution)

Line 2: $15,000 ($10,000 basis for prior years + $5,000 after-tax rolled over amount)

Line 3: $20,000

Q 7:170 Why may it become crucial to maintain separate Form 8606 records for each IRA owned when IRAs have separate beneficiaries?

If an IRA owner dies owning more than one traditional IRA, the beneficiary of one of the IRAs might wish to continue that IRA and not accelerate its distribution. If the decedent had made nondeductible contributions, the basis would not have been fully recovered, and at least some of it would remain because the IRA itself remains. In that event, Form 8606 must continue to be filed for distributions from the inherited IRA, which is effectively owned by the beneficiary.

If, for example, there were two traditional IRAs and separate beneficiaries, the beneficiary of each IRA would file a separate Form 8606. The decedent's basis would therefore need to be split between the two traditional IRAs; separately maintained Form 8606 records would facilitate that process. If either beneficiary also maintained one or more IRAs that were not inherited, distributions from such IRAs would be combined under the IRA owner's Form 8606, but not with the Form 8606 of the inherited traditional IRA, which would continue to have its own separate basis.

Q 7:171   What penalties may arise from a failure to follow the requirements of Form 8606?

Unless reasonable cause can be established, a $50 fine results from failing to file Form 8606 in a year when nondeductible contributions are made. Further, unless reasonable cause is shown, there is a $100 fine for each overstatement of nondeductible contributions on Form 8606.

Q 7:172   In addition to the penalties for failing to file Form 8606 correctly, what other consequences may result from the failure to follow the requirements of Form 8606?

An IRA owner who fails to file Form 8606 correctly may lose out on recovery of basis. In the absence of evidence to the contrary, the IRS will assume that all distributions are of amounts previously deducted and that the entire distribution is fully taxable.

Q 7:173   When is basis fully recovered?

Basis should be fully recovered automatically when the final distribution from all IRAs of an individual has occurred. That may happen many years hence. In any event, it would seem reasonable to correct any mathematical errors in the final distribution by applying the basis recovery formula so that 100 percent of the unapplied nondeductible contributions is used as a setoff at that time. If there has been a loss, the unamortized basis may become a deductible loss. [IRS Publication 590, *Individual Retirement Arrangements (IRAs)* 2008 (see Appendix A)]

Q 7:174   What is the procedure to follow when redesignating a nondeductible contribution as a deductible contribution?

To change a nondeductible contribution to a deductible contribution, the IRA owner must file a new Form 8606 along with Form 1040X, Amended U.S. Individual Income Tax Return.

Q 7:175   How are distributions from IRAs reflected on Form 1040 (Form 1040A)?

Total taxable distributions from IRAs are entered on line 15b of Form 1040 (line 11b of Form 1040A). If the distribution has been rolled over, line 15a of Form 1040 (line 11a of Form 1040A) will show the total distributed, and line 15b (line 11a of Form 1040A) will show only the portion not rolled over reduced by the basis recovery amount calculated on Form 8606, which will in effect be used to subtract the nondeductible contributions from the amount shown on line 15b (line 11b of Form 1040A).

Form 8888

Q 7:176   What is the purpose of Form 8888?

A taxpayer who is due a refund of income tax may instruct the IRS to deposit the refund directly into one, two, or three IRAs, mutual funds, or other financial accounts. The instruction is given on Form 1040 or 1040A if the entire refund is to be deposited in a single account (see Q 7:75). Form 8888 is required if the taxpayer wants the direct deposit to be split among two or three accounts. The IRS will not deposit a tax refund into more than three accounts, and taxpayers may not request partial payment of a refund by check.

The financial accounts designated on Form 8888 must be in the taxpayer's own name (or the spouse's name if a joint return is filed). Direct deposit is allowed into a traditional IRA, Roth IRA, or SEP IRA, but not a SIMPLE IRA. The year for which the IRA contribution is to be made should be indicated on the form. It will not be valid for such year, however, unless it is actually deposited to the account by the due date of the return (without regard to extensions).

Example. Irene completes her income tax return for 2009 and determines that a $5,000 tax refund is due. She attaches Form 8888, instructing the IRS to deposit $3,000 to her Roth IRA at Bank X and $2,000 to her Roth IRA at Bank Y, and designating the amounts as 2009 IRA contributions. Irene files the return on March 1, 2010, allowing ample time for the IRS to make the direct deposits before the April 15, 2010 deadline for 2009 IRA contributions. She also confirms with the financial institutions that the deposits were actually made in time.

If a requested deposit is not actually made by the contribution deadline for the designated year, it will not qualify as a contribution for that year and the taxpayer must file an amended return.

Some banks and financial institutions do not permit deposit of joint refunds to individual accounts. If a deposit is rejected for this reason, the IRS will mail a check to the taxpayer.

If an income tax refund that was directly deposited to an IRA is later adjusted due to math errors on the return or offset by other obligations of the taxpayer, the IRA contribution must also be adjusted. For detailed discussion of these matters, see Qs 3:44 to 3:47.

Forms 8915 and 8930

Q 7:177   **What forms are used to report distributions and repayments for qualifying individuals who suffered economic harm from natural disasters?**

Form 8915 is used by qualifying individuals who suffered economic harm from the Kansas storms and tornadoes on May 4, 2007. These individuals were entitled to withdraw amounts (called *qualified recovery assistance distributions*) from their IRAs or other retirement plans on a tax-advantaged basis. Form 8915 is also used by qualifying individuals who suffered economic harm from hurricane Katrina, Rita, or Wilma occurring between August 24 and October 22, 2005. The withdrawn amounts were called *qualified hurricane distributions.*

Form 8930 is used by qualifying individuals who suffered economic harm as a result of the severe storms, tornados, and flooding that occurred in the Midwestern disaster areas from May 2 to June 5, 2008 (called *qualified disaster recovery assistance distributions*).

These three types of distributions are subject to income deferral (ratable inclusion over a three-year period), tax-free rollover treatment for amounts redeposited within three years, and exemption from withholding tax and the 10 percent premature distribution penalty at the time of distribution. A recipient of either a qualified recovery assistance distribution, a qualified hurricane distribution or a qualified disaster recovery assistance distribution uses Form 8915 to report the distribution itself and also any deferred income from or repayments of the distribution. A recipient of a qualified disaster recovery assistance distribution uses Form 8930 to report the required information applicable to this disaster. An additional requirement for IRA owners who received a qualified distribution for the purchase or construction of a main home in the Midwestern disaster area that was repaid, in whole or in part, before March 4, 2009, is to report this information on Form 8930. The form recommends that individual who are required to file Form 8606 (see Q 7:164) should complete that form before completing Form 8930.

Both Form 8915 and Form 8930 are filed with the taxpayer's Form 1040, 1040A or 1040NR. If the individual is not required to file an income tax return, but is required to file Form 8915, then the individual must file, sign, and send the required form to the IRS at the same time and location where his or her Form 1040, 1040A, or 1040NR would have been filed.

Required Minimum Distribution Statement

Q 7:178   **What are the requirements for sending an RMD Statement?**

Code Section 408(i) delegates authority to the Secretary of the Treasury to require that the trustee, custodian, or issuer of an IRA (hereinafter the "IRA trustee") report on IRAs. In addition, Treasury Regulations Section 1.408-8,

Q&A-10 provides that the IRA trustee must report information regarding RMDs in accordance with guidance published by the IRS.

Concerned that large numbers of IRA owners were not complying with RMD requirements, the IRS issued Notice 2002-27 [2002-1 C.B. 814], *modified by* Notice 2009-9 [2009-5 I.R.B. 419], which provides guidance to taxpayers on the reports that trustees are required to make regarding RMDs from individual retirement accounts and individual retirement annuities. Notice 2002-27 provides that if an RMD is required for a calendar year after 2002, and the IRA owner is alive at the beginning of the year, the trustee that held the IRA as of December 31 of the prior year must provide a statement to the IRA owner by January 31 of the calendar year regarding the RMD in accordance with either of two alternatives (see Qs. 7:180, 7:181). These alternatives are not required for 2009, since there are no RMDs for 2009. [Notice 2009-9, 2009-5 I.R.B. 419]

These reporting requirements apply to traditional IRA, rollover IRAs, SEP IRAs, and SIMPLE IRAs. Currently, there are no IRS reporting requirements of any kind for beneficiary IRAs (including Roth IRAs) and accounts under Section 403(b) plans. However, if the IRS determines in the future that RMD reporting applies to those types of accounts, it will issue additional guidance that will be effective prospectively.

Q 7:179 What are the reporting requirements to the IRA owner?

If the IRA owner is alive at the beginning of the year and is required to take an RMD for that year, the IRA trustee as of the prior December 31 must provide a statement to the IRA owner by January 31 (February 1 in 2010) regarding the RMD for that year under one of two alternatives. This requirement coincides with the requirement that a statement of the IRA's FMV as of December 31 must be provided to the IRA owner by the following January 31. The RMD statement can be provided along with the FMV statement. [Under both alternatives, the RMD statement must inform the IRA owner that the trustee will be reporting to the IRS (on the 2009 Form 5498) the RMDs for calendar year 2010 that the IRA owner is required to receive.]

Note. For a discussion of the special statement concerning the suspension of RMD requirements for 2009, which supplanted the usual RMD statement, see Q 7:142.

Q 7:180 What is Alternative One?

Alternative One is the option for the trustee to furnish the IRA owner with a statement of the amount of the RMD with respect to the IRA for the calendar year and the date by which such amount must be distributed. [Notice 2002-27 (2002-18 I.R.B. 814), *modified by* Notice 2009-59, 2009-5 I.R.B. 419] The trustee must calculate the RMD amount with respect to each separate IRA maintained by the IRA owner, based on the following criteria for all IRA owners:

1. Use the December 31 account balance without any adjustments for contributions received by that IRA after December 31. This balance will

be the same as the amount required to be reported on the year-end FMV statement.

2. Use the Uniform Lifetime Table to determine the IRA owner's life expectancy, based on the IRA owner's attained age during the calendar year for which the RMD is being determined, even though the IRA owner's spouse may be the sole beneficiary and is more than 10 years younger than the IRA owner.

Example. Robert, who attained age 73 in 2009, maintains an IRA with Lone Tree Bank as trustee. Lone Tree Bank has opted for Alternative One in meeting its RMD reporting obligation. On December 31, 2009, the FMV of Robert's IRA is $85,000. Based on Robert's attained age in 2009, his life expectancy factor from the Uniform Lifetime Table is 24.7. The December 31, 2009, FMV statement that Lone Tree Bank is required to furnish to Robert by January 31, 2010, indicates that Robert's RMD for 2010 is $3,441 ($85,000 ÷ 24.7). The statement also indicates that the RMD must be distributed from this IRA or any other traditional IRA for which Robert is the owner no later than December 31, 2010. Finally, the FMV statement informs Robert that Lone Tree Bank will be required to report on his 2010 Form 5498 (provided to Robert and the IRS during 2011) that Robert will receive an RMD *for* calendar year 2011.

Q 7:181   What is Alternative Two?

Alternative Two is the option for the trustee to provide the IRA owner with a statement that (1) informs the IRA owner that an RMD with respect to the IRA is required for the calendar year and the date by which such amount must be distributed; and (2) includes an offer to furnish to the IRA owner, upon request, a calculation of the amount of the RMD with respect to the IRA for that calendar year.

Alternative Two does not prescribe a date by which the trustee must provide the IRA owner with the calculated amount. It may be concluded, therefore, that there is no required date for providing the calculation to the IRA owner, although such calculation should be provided within a reasonable time after the IRA owner's request. Alternative Two also does not specifically permit the calculation of the RMD to be determined under the same criteria for all IRA owners as is permitted under Alternative One. Thus, it can be assumed that if the trustee uses Alternative Two, it should calculate the actual RMD based on the facts of the particular IRA owner.

Q 7:182   What must the trustee report to the IRS concerning the RMD?

The trustee indicates on Form 5498 that an RMD will be required for the next calendar year (see discussion of box 11 in Q 7:142).

Q 7:183   Can both Alternative One and Alternative Two be used in the same year?

Yes. Notice 2003-3 [2003-1 C.B. 285] clarified that a trustee may use Alternative One and Alternative Two simultaneously. That is, the trustee may use Alternative One for some IRA owners and Alternative Two for other IRA owners.

Q 7:184   Are there any special rules if annuity payments have not commenced on an irrevocable basis?

Yes. If annuity payments under an individual retirement annuity have not yet commenced on an irrevocable basis (except for acceleration), the IRA issuer must determine the entire interest under the annuity contract as the sum of the value of the account as of December 31 of the prior year plus the actuarial value of any additional benefits (in excess of the account value) provided under the contract.

Q 7:185   May RMD statements be provided electronically?

Yes. Notice 2003-3 [2003-1 C.B. 258] provides that an IRA trustee may satisfy the RMD statement requirement by transmitting such statement electronically. The electronic transmission of an IRA owner's RMD statement must comply with the procedures described in Treasury Regulations Section 31.6051-1T for filing Form W-2 electronically. These procedures include the consent requirements described in the regulations under Code Section 6051.

For purposes of these procedures, the term *furnisher* means the IRA trustee, custodian, or issuer, and the term *recipient* means the IRA owner.

1. *Consent.* The recipient must affirmatively consent to receive the RMD statement electronically and must not have withdrawn that consent before the RMD statement is furnished. The consent must be made electronically in a manner that demonstrates that the recipient can access the information in the format in which it will be furnished to the recipient. If a change in hardware or software required to access the RMD statement creates a risk that the recipient will not be able to access the information, the furnisher must provide the recipient with a notice prior to changing the hardware or software. That notice must describe the revised hardware or software and inform the recipient that a new consent to the revised electronic format must be provided to the furnisher. After implementing the revised hardware or software, the furnisher must obtain a new consent from the recipient to receive the RMD statement electronically.

2. *Disclosure.* Prior to, or at the time of, a recipient's consent, the furnisher must provide the recipient with a disclosure statement in which:

    a. The recipient is informed that the RMD statement will be furnished on paper if the recipient does not consent to receiving it electronically.

   b. The recipient is informed of the scope and duration of the consent (e.g., whether the consent applies to the RMD statement every year until consent is withdrawn, or only to the RMD statement required to be furnished by January 31 immediately following the date on which the consent is given).

   c. The recipient is informed of procedures for obtaining a paper copy of the RMD statement after giving consent for an electronic version.

   d. The recipient is informed that he or she may withdraw consent at any time by furnishing the withdrawal in writing, either electronically or on paper, to the person whose name, mailing address, telephone number, and e-mail address is provided in the disclosure statement, and the furnisher must confirm the withdrawal in writing, either electronically or on paper. A withdrawal of consent does not apply to an RMD statement that was furnished electronically before the withdrawal of consent is furnished.

   e. The recipient is informed of the conditions under which a furnisher will cease furnishing statements electronically to the recipient (e.g., termination of the account subject to RMD reporting).

   f. The recipient is informed of the procedures for updating the information needed by the furnisher to contact the recipient.

   g. The recipient is provided with a description of the hardware and software needed to access, print, and retain the RMD statement, and the date when the information will no longer be available on the Web site.

3. *Format*. The electronic version of the RMD statement must contain all required information and comply with applicable revenue procedures relating to substitute statements to recipients.

4. *Posting*. The furnisher must post the RMD statement on a Web site accessible to the recipient on or before the deadline for providing the annual RMD statement (January 31 of the year to which the RMD applies).

5. *Notice Requirements*. The furnisher must notify the recipient that the RMD statement is posted on a Web site no later than the due date for that year's RMD statement. The notice may be delivered by U.S. mail, electronic mail, or in person. The notice must provide instructions on how to access and print the statement, and must include the following legend in capital letters: IMPORTANT TAX RETURN DOCUMENT AVAILABLE. If the notice is provided by electronic mail, the foregoing statement should be on the subject line of the e-mail and the message sent with high importance.

If an electronic notice is returned as undeliverable, and the correct electronic address cannot be obtained from the furnisher's records or from the recipient, the furnisher must then furnish the notice by mail or in person within 30 days after the electronic notice is returned.

The furnisher must also notify a recipient of any corrected RMD statement information posted on its Web site within 30 days of such posting. Such notice must be furnished by mail or in person if (1) an electronic notice of the original posting of the RMD statement was returned as undeliverable or (2) the recipient did not provide a new e-mail address.

6. *Retention*. The furnisher must provide access to the RMD statements posted on its Web site through October 15 of the year following the calendar year to which the statement relates. The furnisher must also provide access to corrected RMD statements on the Web site for the same time period or, if later than that date, for 90 days after the corrected statements are posted.

Chapter 8

Estate and Tax Planning for Traditional IRAs

Martin Fleisher, Esq.
Jo Ann Lippe, Esq.

An IRA can be a valuable component of an individual's total estate plan. Through rollovers, successful investments, and tax-free accumulation, an individual's IRA or IRAs may even come to represent a major portion of a family's assets. The income tax consequences of owning a traditional IRA are an important consideration in estate planning. Careful planning is needed to ensure that delayed distributions do not cause the imposition of excise taxes for failure to withdraw the required minimum amount each year.

This chapter discusses income and estate tax planning and administration in connection with traditional IRAs, including how traditional IRAs are affected by various trust arrangements.

Estate Planning in General

Q 8:1   How should estate planning decisions be made?

Estate planning decisions depend on the size of the expected estate, although the complexities can be great even when the estate is small. When an estate is large (e.g., over $3 million), planning often starts much earlier than it would for a smaller estate. Depending on the size of the estate, it may be necessary to call in experts—attorneys, accountants, and, in some cases, actuaries. Financial planners and life insurance specialists may also be consulted.

The strategy that provides the greatest flexibility after an IRA owner's death is to designate the surviving spouse as the primary beneficiary, because he or she can perform a spousal rollover of the decedent's IRA or, alternatively, disclaim in favor of a younger beneficiary. An IRA owner may also give the IRA directly to his or her children, bypassing the spouse. Leaving the IRA to a trust may also be appropriate (see Q 8:31). Whether an IRA goes directly to a beneficiary, to a trust, or to the owner's estate, it may be advisable to designate tiers of beneficiaries in order to avoid the possibility that unforeseen deaths will accelerate distributions after the death of the IRA owner. Therefore, even for an estate that is less than the applicable estate tax exemption amount (see Q 8:7), the taxpayer may need professional advice.

Both tax and nontax goals factor into a well-considered estate plan. At times, these goals will conflict with one another. For example, income tax deferral is generally maximized by taking only minimum distributions from an IRA, but a beneficiary may have needs that are best met by withdrawing a lump-sum distribution.

Q 8:2   How do IRAs differ from other assets in estate planning?

IRAs are distinguished from other assets in an estate because they can generate tax deferral for the life of the IRA beneficiary after the death of the IRA owner. Thus, an IRA should be considered in the context of an individual's overall estate to determine whether it will merely create an income stream for the life of the IRA owner or whether it can preserved over the lifetime of its beneficiaries. Under current law, an IRA that a decedent owned at the time of his or her death may not be rolled over to another IRA—unless the sole beneficiary is the surviving spouse, and the spouse has an unlimited right to withdraw amounts from the IRA. [Treas. Reg. § 1.408-8, Q&A-5]

Q 8:3   How do Roth IRAs differ from traditional IRAs in regard to estate planning?

Qualified distributions to a Roth IRA beneficiary are exempt from income tax. This potential for tax-free withdrawal of distributions can make a Roth IRA more valuable to a beneficiary than a traditional IRA of equal size. On the other hand, the tax advantage of the Roth IRA is lost if a charity is made the beneficiary. For detailed discussion of estate planning strategies involving Roth IRAs, including conversion of traditional IRAs to Roth IRAs, see chapters 9 and 10.

Q 8:4 Is IRA estate planning too speculative and complex to justify the effort?

When IRA owners die, their families sometimes cash in the IRAs and pay the income taxes even when funds are not needed for current support. That is extremely short-sighted: continuing the IRA and deferring taxes will generally produce significant savings. A well-advised IRA owner will allow his or her family to choose to cash in an inherited IRA, but not require it by failing to make proper beneficiary designations.

Q 8:5 What undesirable outcomes may result from inattention to the details of the IRA document and election forms supplied by an institutional IRA trustee or custodian?

An institutional IRA trustee or custodian may restrict the selection of alternative beneficiaries. Such a provision should be challenged. If the IRA owner's designated beneficiary does not survive the IRA owner, the IRA will generally pass to the owner's estate. Because the estate is not a person and thus has no life expectancy, the IRA may have to be distributed within five years of the owner's death or be distributed over the remaining life expectancy of the IRA owner, depending on whether the owner dies before or after his or her required beginning date (RBD).

Certain institutional forms may require faster payouts to IRA beneficiaries than the law allows, especially if the IRA owner dies before his or her RBD. Other forms may restrict a beneficiary's right to transfer assets to a new IRA trustee or custodian or to appoint an outside investment manager to direct the investment of the IRA. Such policies indicate that the institution is reluctant to be involved in administrative issues that could be complex and time-consuming.

An IRA owner will want to ensure that his or her intentions are carried out. More important, an IRA owner will want to ensure that his or her successors—whether executor, trustee, spouse, or child—will not be trapped into unplanned or undesired constructive or default elections. If an IRA trustee or custodial institution does not properly tailor or amend its forms, the IRA owner should find an institution that is more cooperative in tailoring a new IRA and, if necessary, undertake a trustee-to-trustee transfer of an existing IRA.

Income Tax and Estate Tax Considerations

Q 8:6 Are IRAs subject to federal estate tax?

Yes. An IRA is part of the IRA owner's gross estate and is taxed in the same manner as qualified plan benefits.

Q 8:7　What is the maximum federal estate tax rate for 2009?

The estate of an individual who dies in 2009 is subject to a maximum federal estate tax rate of 45 percent. The amount that is excludable from the taxable estate is $3.5 million. [I.R.C. § 2001(b)(2)] Generally, this means that with proper planning a married couple can pass assets worth $7 million to their heirs free of the estate tax.

Q 8:8　What will happen to the federal estate tax after 2009?

Pursuant to law enacted in 2001, the federal estate tax is set to expire in 2010—for one year only—and then spring back into existence on January 1, 2011, using the same tax rates (up to 55 percent) and exemption amount ($1 million) that were effective in 2001. This peculiar state of affairs was the result of the Congressional budget machinations used to gain passage of the law. [Economic Growth and Tax Relief Reconciliation Act of 2001, Pub. L. No. 107-16, 115 Stat. 38 (2001), or EGTRRA]

It had been widely expected, however, that Congress would change this result and it now appears likely that the estate tax law as in effect for 2009 will be made permanent. President Obama's budget proposal for fiscal year 2010 provides for that change, as does the joint Congressional budget resolution for fiscal year 2010 that the U.S. Senate and House of Representatives passed on April 29, 2009. [S. Con. Res. 13, 111th Cong. (Apr. 29, 2009)]

Q 8:9　If the IRA owner's estate receives the balance of the IRA following the owner's death, is that balance subject to income tax?

Yes. IRA distributions are treated as income in respect of a decedent (IRD) under Section 691 of the Internal Revenue Code (Code; I.R.C.) and thus may be subject to income tax. If estate tax is also imposed on the distribution, however, the recipient of the distribution is entitled to a deduction under Code Section 691(c)(1) against the income tax for the portion of the net federal estate tax that resulted from the same distribution.

Q 8:10　How may immediate income taxation be avoided when ownership of an IRA changes from the decedent to the beneficiary?

Income is only recognized as distributions are made from the IRA, so the way to achieve income tax deferral is by keeping the IRA intact. If the IRA is distributed when its ownership passes from the decedent to the beneficiary, the beneficiary must pay tax on the distribution. An exception is made for an IRA distributed to the decedent's surviving spouse, who has 60 days to roll over the IRA to his or her own IRA. [I.R.C. § 402(c)(9)]

Q 8:11   May income taxation of an inherited IRA be delayed indefinitely?

No. There is a point at which distributions from an inherited IRA (and income tax on the IRA) must begin; there is a further point at which all distributions from the IRA must be completed (see chapter 4).

Q 8:12   What can an IRA beneficiary do to take full advantage of the opportunity for income tax deferral?

An IRA beneficiary can prolong income tax deferral by maintaining his or her inherited IRA for as long as the minimum distribution rules permit (see chapter 4). According to these rules an IRA must generally be amortized over the period of a beneficiary's life expectancy, or in some cases fully distributed within five years after the owner's death. [Treas. Reg. § 1.401(a)(9)-5]

For example, if the owner began receiving required minimum distributions (RMDs) on reaching age 70½, after his or her death such distributions may continue to his or her beneficiary. The period for distributions to the IRA beneficiary is generally determined with reference to the beneficiary's age in the year following the year of the IRA owner's death. Because a nonspouse beneficiary is not permitted to roll over an IRA to a new IRA in his or her own name, the IRA must be continued in the name of the deceased IRA owner. The beneficiary will be taxed as distributions are received, and the IRA trustee or custodian will generally report those distributions to the Internal Revenue Service (IRS) under the beneficiary's Social Security number (SSN) or taxpayer identification number (TIN).

IRA trustees and custodians are required to notify both the IRS and the IRA owner (or beneficiary) of the amount of the RMD for the year as calculated under Code Section 401(a)(9). [Treas. Reg. § 1.408-8, Q&A-10; Notice 2002-27, 2002-1 C.B. 814] Alternatively, IRA trustees and custodians may provide a statement to the IRA owner that a minimum distribution is required and offer to provide the IRA owner with a calculation on request. In Notice 2003-3 [2003-1 C.B. 258] the IRS provided additional guidance on how these statements may be transmitted electronically to the IRA owner.

Note. The RMD rules have been suspended for 2009 (see Qs 4:21–4:25).

Q 8:13   Does the size of the expected estate play a role in determining whether to plan for income tax savings or estate tax savings?

Yes. Wealth accumulation over the applicable estate tax exemption amount (see Q 8:7) may require estate planning to limit the estate taxes on the surviving spouse and other family members. For estates worth less than the estate tax exemption amount, estate planning is generally not as important. Estates of any size, however, may benefit from income tax planning. (For more discussion of large estates, see Qs 8:61–8:68 and chapter 10.)

Q 8:14   What happens if the IRA owner named his or her estate as the IRA beneficiary and a provision in the IRA owner's will requires that the IRA be cashed in and that the proceeds go into a trust?

Unfortunately, if the owner's will stipulates that the IRA must be cashed in and the proceeds placed in a trust, the IRA, upon liquidation, will become fully taxable—as income to the estate. That will be the case even if the trust distributes the proceeds to the same person who would ultimately have received the IRA. Wills should never be drafted with such a requirement.

It makes sense not to liquidate an IRA, even if some of the proceeds will be needed before mandatory distributions begin. If the IRA remains intact, larger-than-required distributions may still be taken and the undistributed balance will be left sheltered from income tax for future distribution.

Q 8:15   What happens when an IRA owner names his or her estate as the beneficiary but the will neither specifically refers to the IRA nor enumerates it as a specific asset?

If an IRA is not made part of a specific dollar bequest and is not required to be liquidated, no immediate income tax is due at the time of death. Distributions from the IRA to the estate must be made either under the five-year rule if distributions to the IRA owner have not begun or over the IRA owner's remaining life expectancy if minimum distributions have begun (see Qs 4:26–4:42). [Treas. Reg. § 1.401(a)(9)-8, Q&A-11]

Naming the estate as beneficiary without further testamentary instruction generally causes the payout period for the IRA to be shorter than what is possible using other planning options.

Q 8:16   For what reason other than a testamentary provision may an IRA be liquidated?

An IRA may be cashed in if the owner's estate needs cash to pay creditors or estate taxes or to satisfy pecuniary bequests. If the full value of an IRA is not needed immediately, however, cash to be raised from any IRA should come from partial withdrawals rather than from liquidating the entire IRA—to avoid full income taxation.

Q 8:17   How is an IRA taxed for federal estate tax purposes when it is part of an offset to the decedent's gross estate?

A decedent's IRA is not necessarily included in his or her net taxable estate if the IRA is part of an offset to the gross estate. The principal offsets applicable to the taxation of an estate are:

1. The applicable estate tax exemption amount (see Q 8:7), regardless of how the property is devised; and

2. The marital deduction, which completely eliminates tax on property or other assets left to the surviving spouse.

Q 8:18 Is there a limit on the amount of the marital deduction?

No. If the IRA owner's surviving spouse is given full dominion and control of an asset, there is a total offset or deduction based on the full value of the property received. That is, there is no federal estate tax on whatever amounts are directed to the spouse.

Beneficiaries

Q 8:19 What are the possible classes of beneficiaries of an IRA?

The major classes of beneficiaries of an IRA are:

1. The IRA owner's surviving spouse;
2. An individual or individuals other than the IRA owner's surviving spouse;
3. The IRA owner's estate;
4. A charity; and
5. One or more trusts.

Q 8:20 What special rights does the IRA owner's surviving spouse have when he or she is the designated beneficiary?

The IRA owner's surviving spouse is the only beneficiary who need not continue the IRA under the deceased owner's name in order to continue to defer distributions. The surviving spouse may elect at any time after the IRA owner's death to roll over the decedent's IRA to an IRA in the surviving spouse's own name, or to treat the IRA as the spouse's own (see Q 8:21). [Treas. Reg. § 1.408-8, Q&A-5]

If the owner's surviving spouse is younger than age 70½, distributions from the IRA that the surviving spouse has made his or her own are not mandatory until the spouse has reached age 70½ (see chapter 4). After age 70½, the spouse will receive minimum distributions as determined using the Uniform Lifetime Table. The distribution period that was applicable to the decedent is discontinued and replaced by the distribution schedule that is based on the surviving spouse's age and is determined using the Uniform Table set forth in Treasury Regulations Section 1.401(a)(9)-9, Q&A-2 (see Q 4:11). When the surviving spouse becomes the new owner of the IRA, he or she should name new primary and contingent beneficiaries using the IRA beneficiary designation form. If a new beneficiary is not designated, and the surviving spouse—the new owner—dies before minimum distributions are required to begin, the IRA will be payable to the spouse's estate and in that case the five-year rule will govern its distribution (see Q 4:36). [Treas. Reg. § 1.401(a)(9)-3; Priv. Ltr. Rul. 200644022 (Nov. 3, 2006)]

In any event, the RMD for the calendar year of the decedent's death is computed as though the decedent had survived to the end of that year. To the extent that RMD was not distributed to the decedent before death, it must be distributed to the surviving spouse (or other beneficiary). [Treas. Reg. § 1.408(a)(9)-5, Q&A-4]

Q 8:21   How may an IRA owner's surviving spouse elect to change the distribution pattern and treat the IRA as his or her own?

There are two ways in which a surviving spouse may elect to treat the decedent's IRA as his or her own and consequently change the distribution pattern of the decedent's IRA:

1. Make an affirmative election to do so by redesignating the IRA as an account in the name of the surviving spouse as IRA owner, rather than as beneficiary; or
2. Make a deemed election to do so, either by making a contribution to the IRA or by allowing an amount that would have to be distributed to the spouse as beneficiary to remain undistributed.

The first method is highly recommended. The election can be made at any time after the decedent's death. However, a surviving spouse is only eligible to treat the decedent's IRA as his or her own if the spouse is the sole beneficiary of the IRA and has an unlimited right to withdraw amounts from it. [Treas. Reg. § 1.408-8, Q&A-5]

See detailed discussion of these issues in chapter 4.

Q 8:22   Should a surviving spouse roll over the decedent's IRA to a new IRA as soon as possible after the death of the IRA owner?

In most cases, the surviving spouse should roll over the IRA as soon as possible in order to gain the maximum flexibility concerning distributions. However, the spouse may do better to retain the status of beneficiary for a while in two cases: if the spouse is older than age 70½ and also significantly older than the IRA owner at the time of the owner's death, or if the spouse is younger than age 59½ at that time. (See Qs 4:63–4:65.)

In making the decision, the surviving spouse should review every option with an IRA planning advisor to determine the likely tax ramifications. Questions that the surviving spouse should also address include the following:

1. Should the surviving spouse commingle the decedent spouse's IRA with his or her own IRA?
2. Whom should the surviving spouse name as the new beneficiary of the decedent spouse's IRA?
3. Did the decedent spouse withdraw his or her minimum distribution from the IRA in the year of death?

4. What are the rules applicable to multiple IRAs for minimum distribution purposes?

5. Should the surviving spouse execute a qualified disclaimer with respect to all or a portion of the decedent's IRA?

Q 8:23   May death beneficiaries direct trustee-to-trustee transfers and create subaccounts without creating taxable distributions?

Ordinarily, trustee-to-trustee transfers and the creation of subaccounts by death beneficiaries do not create taxable distributions. [*See* Priv. Ltr. Ruls. 9504045 (Nov. 2, 1994), 9305025 (Nov. 12, 1992).] It is important, however, to review the IRA document to be certain that such transfers have not been restricted. Such a restriction could have been made inadvertently if the IRA owner executed a standard document used by the IRA trustee or custodian or if the owner issued specific instructions restricting such transfers. In general, the IRA owner should resolve the matter in advance. The beneficiaries should find out what has been specified and, if appropriate, seek a trustee-to-trustee transfer.

Q 8:24   What happens if an individual is not timely notified by an IRA trustee or custodian that he or she is a beneficiary of an IRA?

If an individual is not timely notified of his or her beneficiary status, the default payout schedule applicable to an IRA beneficiary is based on the beneficiary's life expectancy rather than the five-year rule. [Treas. Reg. § 1.401(a)(9)-3, Q&A-4] However, an IRA document may still provide more restrictive provisions and therefore control the distribution option.

Q 8:25   Why may it be important to create separate IRAs for each ultimate beneficiary?

When more than one beneficiary is chosen, it often makes sense to split an IRA, by trustee-to-trustee transfer or sometimes by IRA-to-IRA rollover, into a separate IRA (or several separate IRAs) for each beneficiary. Not only can that simplify administration, it also facilitates a personalized investment and distribution pattern and avoids the older-beneficiary rule (for nonspouse beneficiaries) in determining life expectancy. When a trust beneficiary is selected, creating a separate trust for each ultimate beneficiary may be advisable, unless administrative costs are prohibitive.

IRA beneficiaries have until December 31 of the year following the year of the IRA owner's death to split the IRA into separate IRAs for each beneficiary (see Q 4:86). [Treas. Reg. § 1.401(a)(9)-8, Q&A-2(a)(2)] Doing so allows each beneficiary to use his or her own life expectancy to determine the required distribution in the year the IRA is split and in all future years. Of course, an IRA owner could divide the IRA into multiple IRAs before his or her death to prevent the IRA beneficiaries from missing the December 31 deadline.

.26   Should an IRA owner name contingent beneficiaries?

Yes. Generally, the IRA owner should name alternative and contingent beneficiaries so that distributions may continue as long as possible after the death of the primary beneficiary. The use of contingent beneficiaries is also important under certain disclaimer strategies whereby the primary beneficiary disclaims all or a portion of the IRA in favor of the person who the owner had named as the contingent beneficiary. If a timely disclaimer is made, the contingent beneficiary uses his or her own life expectancy to determine post-death IRA payments even though he or she was not the primary beneficiary when the IRA owner died. This is so whether the IRA owner died before or after his or her RBD. For a disclaimer to be effective under federal estate and gift tax law, however, it must be performed within nine months of the decedent's death. [I.R.C. § 2518(b)]

Q 8:27   How are minimum distributions calculated for the contingent beneficiary after the primary IRA beneficiary dies?

The consequence depends on the primary beneficiary's identity and when his or her death occurs. (See Qs 4:43–4:48.)

Trusts in General

Q 8:28   How is a trust designated as the beneficiary of an IRA?

A trust beneficiary of an IRA may be designated by completing the IRA beneficiary designation form and by naming the trust as the primary beneficiary. If a trust is to be used, it must be validly established and either be irrevocable from the beginning or become irrevocable, by its terms, no later than at the death of the IRA owner. In addition, a copy of the trust should be filed with the IRA administrator, or the administrator should be provided with a list of the trust beneficiaries, including contingent and remainder beneficiaries. [Treas. Reg. § 1.401(a)(9)-4, Q&A-5(b)]

Establishing a trust does not prevent subsequent adjustments to the IRA. Such adjustments may include the following:

- Creating a new trust to become the beneficiary
- Trustee-to-trustee transfers of the IRA
- Early termination of the IRA or faster-than-required distributions
- IRA-to-IRA rollovers (no more than once a year for each IRA)

Q 8:29   Apart from the protection of minors, what are the justifications for naming a trust as the IRA beneficiary?

When a trust is named as IRA beneficiary, the trustee becomes a conduit between the IRA trustee or custodian and the owner's beneficiaries, ensuring that necessary notices, filings, and tax payments are made. The conduit nature of the irrevocable trusteeship allows the beneficiaries to enjoy the advantages of delayed distributions much as if they had been directly named as beneficiaries.

An IRA owner may be able to ensure professional management of the IRA assets after his or her death by naming a trust as the IRA beneficiary and selecting an expert trustee.

A trust may serve as a buffer between the beneficiaries and their creditors. Of course, the degree of protection afforded by the trust depends on state law and on the trust's provisions (e.g., a spendthrift provision).

An IRA owner may name contingent IRA beneficiaries through a trust, to ensure that they receive distributions from the IRA after the death of the primary beneficiary. In the absence of a trust, the primary beneficiary may be able to change the beneficiary designation on the IRA or withdraw accelerated amounts from the IRA to defeat the interests of the contingent beneficiaries.

Without a trust, beneficiaries taking under a will may be left with the estate tax liability owed on other IRAs even when they are directly passing outside of the will. That may be contrary to the intent of the decedent. There may also be conflicts about which devisee is entitled to the income tax deduction for estate tax imposed on the IRA. A well-chosen trustee is in a position to work with the executor to iron out such complications by applying coordinated provisions of the will, trust, and IRA designation of the trust as beneficiary to achieve an equitable and appropriate result.

Finally, a *special-needs trust* may be established and funded with an IRA to provide for the care of a disabled family member. If the trust is properly established, the individual can receive the benefit of the assets without being disqualified from receiving government benefits on account of the disability. (See Qs 10:45–10:48.)

Q 8:30 If a marital trust is the beneficiary of a traditional IRA, may the surviving spouse elect to treat it as the spouse's own traditional IRA?

No. The spouse may not do so, even it the spouse is the sole beneficiary of the trust, because the spouse does not have an unlimited right to withdraw amounts from the IRA. [Treas. Reg. § 1.408-8, Q&A-5]

Q 8:31 If a marital trust is the beneficiary of a traditional IRA, may the surviving spouse roll over distributions from the trust to the spouse's own traditional IRA?

Yes. The Preamble to the final regulations under Code Section 408 [T.D. 8787 (Apr. 16, 2002)] states that a surviving spouse who *actually receives* a distribution from an IRA of the decedent spouse is permitted to roll that distribution over to an IRA in the surviving spouse's name (except to the extent it is an RMD), even if the distribution is paid from a trust that the surviving spouse controls as both trustee and beneficiary.

Note. In various subsequent private letter rulings, the IRS reaches the seemingly contradictory conclusion that a surviving spouse who can compel a distribution of the IRA from a trust may roll it over, but may not elect to treat the IRA as the spouse's own without undergoing that formal distribution step. [*E.g.*, Priv. Ltr. Rul. 200424011 (Mar. 17, 2004), Priv. Ltr. Rul. 200644028 (Nov. 3, 2006)]

Q 8:32 How is a traditional IRA distributed if it is allocated to a revocable or testamentary trust that has one or more individual beneficiaries?

The distribution period depends on whether the IRA owner died before or after his or her RBD and other terms of the trust. If the trust meets the "see-through" requirements of the regulations, then the trust beneficiaries (not the trust itself) are treated as having been designated as the IRA beneficiaries, and the distribution period is determined accordingly (see chapter 4). The see-through requirements are:

1. The trust must be a valid trust under state law, or would be valid but for the fact that there is no corpus.

2. The trust must be irrevocable or will, by its terms, become irrevocable upon the death of the IRA owner.

3. The beneficiaries of the trust must be identifiable from the trust instrument.

4. The trustee must provide the IRA trustee or custodian with a copy of the trust instrument or, alternatively, the IRA trustee or custodian must receive a list of all trust beneficiaries (including contingent and remainder beneficiaries), and the trustee of the trust must agree to supply the IRA trustee or custodian with a copy of the trust agreement on demand.

[Treas. Reg. § 1.401(a)(9)-4, Q&A-5(b), Q&A-6(b)]

If all four requirements are satisfied, the distribution period is based on the life expectancy of the oldest trust beneficiary for purposes of calculating RMDs under Code Section 401(a)(9). If any one of the requirements is not satisfied, the owner is considered to have no designated beneficiary. In that case, the IRA must be distributed according to the five-year rule if the owner died before his or her RBD, or based on the IRA owner's single-life expectancy in the year of IRA death (not a beneficiary's life expectancy) if the owner died on or after the RBD (see chapter 4). [Treas. Reg. § 1.401(a)(9)-4, Q&A-3]

Note. The preamble to the final Treasury Regulations issued in April 2002 makes it clear that a testamentary trust meeting the above requirements would qualify the trust beneficiary as a designated beneficiary for RMD purposes. Example 1 and Example 2 in Treasury Regulations Section 1.401(a)(9)-5, Q&A-7(c)(2), confirm this result.

Q 8:33   Can an IRA be payable to a trust for a minor and accumulate IRA distributions until the child reaches majority?

Yes. As long as annual IRA distributions are made from the IRA to the trust, the terms of the trust can provide that the trustee has the discretion to pass through the distributions to the beneficiary currently or accumulate the distributions in the trust until a future date. If the trust accumulates the distributions, it must pay income tax on those distributions at ordinary income tax rates.

Q 8:34   What IRA distribution schedule would apply if a trust has the discretion to accumulate rather than distribute the annual IRA distributions?

The applicable distribution schedule depends on the identity of the contingent trust beneficiaries. For example, if the terms of a trust provide the trustee with discretion to accumulate distributions and provide that such accumulations will be paid to an older beneficiary upon the death of the primary beneficiary, the applicable distribution schedule will be based on the life expectancy of the older beneficiary. [Priv. Ltr. Rul. 200228025 (Apr. 18, 2002)] This is because the older contingent beneficiary's entitlement to distributions is dependent upon the trustee's exercise of discretion to accumulate the IRA distribution in the trust and not merely on the death of the primary beneficiary. If, under the terms of the trust, the accumulated distribution can pass to a younger beneficiary only upon the death of the primary beneficiary, the applicable distribution schedule would be based on the life expectancy of the primary beneficiary. [See Priv. Ltr. Rul. 200235038 (June 4, 2002); Treas. Reg. § 1.401(a)(9)-5, Q&A-7(c)(1).]

Q 8:35   Can the decedent's IRA be made available to the surviving spouse during the spouse's lifetime, but excluded from the spouse's estate when he or she dies?

Yes. The IRA owner can create an exemption (also called a credit shelter or bypass) trust under which the trustee distributes amounts for the reasonable needs of the surviving spouse pursuant to specific language sanctioned by the IRS. Ultimate control of the remaining trust assets—beyond the lifetime of the surviving spouse—is beyond the power of the surviving spouse to determine because there is no power of appointment for the surviving spouse to exercise. Consequently, when the surviving spouse dies, the assets still in the trust are also excluded from his or her estate.

Caution. The increases of the estate tax exemption amount (from $1 million to $3.5 million) during this decade, coupled with the recent, widespread decline in most asset values, may present a problem for estate plans that were crafted to take maximum advantage of the exemption amount. The portion of an estate that is allocated to the exemption assets may now be too large. Estate plans should be reviewed on a regular basis.

Q 8:36   Can a trust qualify for the marital deduction?

Yes. An asset that qualifies for the marital deduction is included in the spouse's estate when the spouse dies (unless the asset is dissipated), and a trust may be designed for that purpose. To qualify for the marital deduction, the trust must contain a provision that gives the surviving spouse enough power that the property will be part of his or her taxable estate at his or her death.

Use of a marital trust may be recommended for both tax and nontax reasons.

Qualified Terminable Interest Property Trusts

Q 8:37   Can a marital trust be designed that does not give broad power to the surviving spouse?

Yes. Qualified terminable interest property (QTIP) provisions may be used to limit the power of the surviving spouse. During his or her lifetime, the surviving spouse is the sole income beneficiary of the trust, and trust income cannot be appointed to anyone else. The spouse may also require the trust to be invested in income-producing property.

The QTIP trust may be treated as a marital deduction trust even though the surviving spouse lacks complete dominion over the corpus. An election to use the marital deduction means that the trust property will be included in the estate of the surviving spouse.

If an IRA passes to a QTIP trust upon the death of the IRA owner, the QTIP beneficiary does not have the right to name a new IRA beneficiary—the terms of the QTIP trust would control such designation. In addition, naming a QTIP trust as the IRA beneficiary requires the IRA to remain in the name of the decedent after the death of the owner, because a spousal rollover would not be permitted.

Revenue Ruling 2006-26 [2006-22 I.R.B. 939] lays out a clear roadmap for structuring a QTIP trust that is also the beneficiary of an IRA.

Q 8:38   If a QTIP trust is named as the IRA beneficiary to benefit the IRA owner's second spouse and to preserve the IRA for the owner's children from a previous marriage after that spouse's death, what are the likely tax consequences at the time of the death of the second spouse?

A QTIP trust for a second spouse is often erroneously employed as a strategy to preserve the IRA assets that remain at the time of the second spouse's death for the original IRA owner's children from a previous marriage. Although a QTIP strategy may work well with other after-tax assets of the owner that may pass to his or her second spouse, such a strategy involving pretax IRA assets may not achieve the original objective of preserving those assets for the children of an earlier marriage. For an example of the erosion of a large IRA due to estate and income taxes, see Q 10:73.

Q 8:39 Does a QTIP trust have to distribute the entire IRA distribution to the surviving spouse?

No. Although an IRA must distribute RMDs to a QTIP trust beginning in the year after the death of the IRA owner, there is no requirement that the surviving spouse receive a distribution of more than the IRA income from the QTIP trust. [Rev. Rul. 2006-26 (2006-22 I.R.B. 939)] Thus, a QTIP trust could accumulate the difference between the RMD and the IRA income within the trust for the remainder beneficiary, although income tax would become payable by the trust on the amount retained.

Q 8:40 If a QTIP trust is named as IRA beneficiary and provides for distributions of income to a surviving spouse only at his or her direction, is the surviving spouse treated as the designated beneficiary for minimum distribution purposes?

It depends on the identity of the remainder beneficiary under the QTIP trust. The surviving spouse is not considered to be the sole designated beneficiary if amounts may be accumulated in the trust for the benefit of anyone else. If there are no non-individual beneficiaries or potential beneficiaries, RMDs may be determined based on the beneficiary with the shortest life expectancy (generally, the surviving spouse) using the Single Life Table (of Treasury Regulations Section 1.401(a)(9)-9, Q&A-1) on a non-recalculating basis. After the death of the surviving spouse, RMDs with respect to any undistributed balance of the trust will continue to be calculated in the same way and will be distributed to the trust over the same period. [Rev. Rul. 2006-26, 2006-22 I.R.B. 939]

Note. The Single Life Table is reproduced in IRS Publication 590, *Individual Retirement Arrangements* (2008) (see Appendix A).

If any amounts retained in the trust are ultimately payable to charity, the trust has a beneficiary that is not an individual and consequently there is no designated beneficiary. As a result, if an IRA owner dies with charitable remainder beneficiaries before reaching his or her RBD, payments from the IRA to the QTIP trust may only be based on the five-year rule: there is no life expectancy against which to calculate lifetime payments. If such an IRA owner dies after reaching his or her RBD, the QTIP trust is entitled to a payout for a distribution period based on the IRA owner's remaining life expectancy in the year of death. [Rev. Rul. 2006-26, 2006-22 I.R.B. 939]

Q 8:41 Under what circumstances will an IRA and the trust that has been named the beneficiary of the IRA qualify for the marital deduction?

The IRA and the trust will qualify for the marital deduction if the surviving spouse has a qualifying income interest for life in both the IRA and the trust, and the election is made to treat each as QTIP. The surviving spouse must have the right to compel the trustee to invest both the IRA and the non-IRA assets of the trust in a manner that is reasonably productive of income. [Rev. Rul. 2006-26, 2006-22 I.R.B. 939]

Q 8:42 How must the amount of income from the trust and the IRA be determined if the surviving spouse is to have a qualifying income interest for life in each?

At least annually, the trustee must *separately* determine the amount of income from the IRA assets and the amount of income from the non-IRA assets. Each amount must either be distributed annually to the surviving spouse or be subject annually to the surviving spouse's power of withdrawal. [Rev. Rul. 2006-26, 2006-22 I.R.B. 939]

Q 8:43 How do state-law provisions governing the allocation between a trust's income and principal bear on qualification for the marital deduction when a trust is the beneficiary of an IRA?

The following provisions of law have the effects described:

- *State-law provisions similar to Section 104(a) of the Uniform Principal and Income Act (UPIA).* UPIA Section 104(a) authorizes a trustee to make adjustments between income and principal if necessary to satisfy the trustee's duty of impartiality between the income and remainder beneficiaries. An allocation of income from the non-IRA assets or from the IRA made under this type of provision is reasonable and does not disqualify the trust or the IRA from QTIP status. [Rev. Rul. 2006-26, Situation 1, 2006-22 I.R.B. 939]

- *State-law provisions similar to UPIA Section 409(c).* UPIA Section 409(c) in effect requires the trustee to allocate 10 percent of a RMD to income and 90 percent to principal. This is not a reasonable allocation because the RMD amount is unrelated to the amount of income an IRA produces in a year. Thus, if the applicable law contains such a provision, the IRA cannot qualify as QTIP unless the trust instrument specifically requires the trustee to distribute, at minimum, all the income the IRA produces. [Rev. Rul. 2006-26, Situation 1, 2006-22 I.R.B. 939]

- *State-law provisions similar to UPIA Section 409(d).* UPIA Section 409(d) implicitly recognizes that the 90/10 allocation of a RMD may not be adequate for QTIP purposes. In effect, UPIA Section 409(d) mandates the trustee to allocate more than 10 percent of the RMD to income if the greater allocation is necessary to allow the trust to qualify as QTIP. The IRS has stated that a provision like UPIA Section 409(d) "may not" be enough to qualify the arrangement under the QTIP rules. [Rev. Rul. 2006-26, Situation 1, 2006-22 I.R.B. 939]

- *State-law unitrust provisions.* State law may provide for the amount of income to be determined (if so allowed by the trust instrument or if the interested parties consent) by applying a unitrust percentage to the fair market value of the trust, determined annually. The IRS considers a unitrust percentage to be a reasonable allocation of income from either the non-IRA assets or from the IRA if it is not less than 3 percent or more than 5 percent. [Rev. Rul. 2006-26, Situation 2, 2006-22 I.R.B. 939]

- *Law of a state that has not enacted the UPIA.* The IRA and trust may both qualify as QTIP if the state has not enacted the UPIA and the trustee is required to follow state law regarding the allocation of receipts and disbursements to income and principal without modification. [Rev. Rul. 2006-26, Situation 3, 2006-22 I.R.B. 939]

The following must also be true for the trust and the IRA to qualify for the marital deduction:

1. At least annually, the trustee must separately determine the amount of income from the non-IRA assets and the amount of income from the IRA.

2. At least annually, either all the income from the non-IRA assets must be distributed to the surviving spouse, or the spouse must be able to require the trustee to withdraw such amount and distribute it to the spouse.

3. At least annually, either all the IRA income must be distributed to the spouse, or the spouse must be able to require the trustee to withdraw all the IRA income (or the RMD, if greater) and distribute at least the IRA income to the spouse.

4. If the spouse does not exercise the power with respect to the IRA, the trustee must only withdraw the RMD and is required to allocate it to principal.

5. The QTIP election must be made with respect to both the trust and the IRA.

[Rev. Rul. 2006-26, 2006-22 I.R.B. 939]

Placement of IRAs in the Estate

Q 8:44 May IRAs be directed by a will to one or more segments of an estate?

Yes, a.will may allocate IRAs to specific segments of an estate, but the will should always be drafted to be consistent with the beneficiary designation on the IRA form.

Q 8:45 If the decedent's estate is the designated IRA beneficiary, can the executor assign the right to receive distributions to different residuary beneficiaries of the estate?

Yes. If the decedent IRA owner's estate is the designated IRA beneficiary, the executor has the discretion to allocate the IRA to different beneficiaries. Such allocations do not cause the IRA to become taxable to the estate. [Treas. Reg. § 1.691(a)-4(b)] For example, in Private Letter Ruling 200234019 (May 13, 2002), an executor assigned IRA assets to the charitable residuary beneficiaries while the individual residuary beneficiaries received nonretirement plan assets. The IRS concluded that such assignment did not cause the estate to have taxable income, and that the ultimate distribution of the IRA to the charities would be tax free because the charities had tax-exempt status under Code Section 501(c)(3).

Q 8:46 If the decedent's estate is the designated IRA beneficiary, what post-death payout schedule from the IRA would be applicable if the executor assigned the rights to IRA distributions to the residuary beneficiaries of the estate?

If the IRA owner died *on or after* his or her RBD, the payout schedule would be the term certain period equal to the number of years remaining in the IRA owner's single life expectancy in the year of death. If the IRA owner died *before* his or her RBD, the payout schedule would be subject to the five-year rule (i.e. the entire IRA must be distributed by the end of the fifth calendar year following the year of the IRA owner's death). (See chapter 4.)

In Private Letter Ruling 200343030 (July 31, 2003), the IRS ruled that where a decedent who had died at age 71 failed to name a designated IRA beneficiary but had named his three children as his IRA beneficiaries under his will, the estate executor was permitted to assign equal one-third interests in the IRA to each of the children. Each child was then permitted to withdraw amounts from the IRA over a term of years equal to their father's remaining single life expectancy of 16.3 years.

Q 8:47 Why would an executor of an estate assign the rights to IRA distributions to the residuary beneficiaries of the estate?

By assigning the rights to distributions from the IRA to the residuary beneficiaries of the IRA owner's estate, the estate would no longer be required to remain open until the entire IRA balance is distributed. The estate would be able to complete all of its tax filings and file a final return.

Q 8:48 In which part of the estate should IRAs be placed?

Where to place IRAs in an estate is a complex question for which there can be no uniform answer. If the IRAs will be depleted by taxes on distributions of principal and income, that may argue in favor of placing the IRAs in the portion of the estate that will be subject to estate tax on the death of the beneficiary (e.g., the surviving spouse). On the other hand, if the IRAs can be maintained without more than minimum distributions in a trust that comes within the applicable estate tax exemption amount (see Q 8:7), and the trust beneficiary's life expectancy can be used to calculate distributions after the death of the IRA owner, placing the IRAs in the exemption trust might produce a more favorable tax result. Projections are complex and never perfect. Furthermore, tax considerations are not the only concern.

Payment of Taxes

Q 8:49   What part of an estate pays estate and inheritance taxes?

The will generally specifies how estate and inheritance taxes are apportioned among beneficiaries. For example, a will could require bequests to be determined from the after-tax estate; that may have a prorating effect depending on how the bequests are drafted. Another method may call for taxes to be paid from the residual part of an estate (the portion remaining after initial distributions are made). That method shifts the tax burden to the residuary beneficiaries and may require them to pay taxes that are attributable to other beneficiaries' gifts. A third approach is to earmark specific assets to be used for tax payments. The earmark limits the executor's freedom to choose assets for the satisfaction of bequests, and is problematic if the chosen assets lose significant value after the will is drafted or are not even held in the estate when death occurs. However, it is very useful in combination with a life insurance policy, the proceeds of which are designated to pay the decedent's final taxes. Finally, a will could explicitly require taxes to be prorated among the beneficiaries. In the absence of any testamentary direction, taxes would be allocated as required by state law.

Q 8:50   May an IRA, which is devised directly by beneficiary designation and outside of the probate estate, be used to pay the estate tax?

This can occur. An IRA is included in the estate for estate tax purposes, even though it is devised outside the probate estate. If the probate estate lacks sufficient liquid assets to pay the estate tax, the IRA may be used as a source of payment. The estate tax apportionment provisions of the decedent's will, or state law in their absence, dictate which portion of the estate will bear the liability for estate taxes.

Q 8:51   What is the effect if a trust is named as the IRA beneficiary, and the trust instrument authorizes the trustee to distribute IRA assets in order to pay the debts, expenses, and taxes of the estate?

If trust assets are used to pay debts, expenses, and taxes of the estate, the IRS may take the position that the estate is a trust beneficiary. This could pose a problem if there also are individual trust beneficiaries. In such a circumstance, the payout schedule from the IRA would be significantly shortened (the five-year rule would apply) because an estate has no life expectancy, and in the case of a trust with multiple beneficiaries, the life expectancy of the beneficiary with the shortest life expectancy must be used to determine the payout schedule. (See chapter 4.)

Q 8:52   Can an IRA beneficiary trust document be drafted to permit the trustee to pay debts, expenses, and taxes of the estate without affecting the payout schedule to the remaining trust beneficiaries?

Yes, if the trustee's power to distribute trust assets for payment of debts, expenses, and taxes of the estate is limited to the time period between the IRA owner's date of death and September 30 of the year following death. Since the regulations under Code Section 401(a)(9) disregard any beneficiary who is entirely cashed out from the IRA by September 30 of the year following the IRA owner's death, the IRA owner's estate would no longer be relevant in determining the appropriate payout schedule to the remaining IRA beneficiaries. This strategy may not be appropriate, however, if exposing the trust assets to the estate's debts, expenses, or taxes would otherwise defeat the IRA owner's dispositive plan.

Earlier-Than-Planned Liquidation of IRAs

Q 8:53   What happens if an IRA becomes part of the portion of the estate used to pay taxes?

An IRA that is cashed out to pay estate taxes becomes subject to income tax because the distribution constitutes income in respect of a decedent (IRD) under Code Section 691. [Rev. Rul. 92-47, 1992-1 C.B. 198]

In Private Letter Ruling 9132021 (May 2, 1991), the agreement governing the IRA after the death of the IRA owner provided that if the primary IRA beneficiary died before the receipt of all distributions from the IRA, the remaining installments would be paid to seven contingent beneficiaries. After the death of the primary beneficiary, the executor of the primary beneficiary's estate sought contributions from the contingent IRA beneficiaries for the federal and state estate taxes attributable to the inclusion of the IRA in the primary beneficiary's estate. Accordingly, funds were paid directly from the IRA to the estate for payment of taxes. The IRS ruled that the amounts paid from the IRA to the estate constituted IRD and were includable in the contingent beneficiaries' gross incomes for the taxable year during which the distributions were made from the IRA.

Q 8:54   Is income tax on the cash-out of an IRA a tax that can be avoided?

No. The cash-out merely accelerates the imposition of income tax. Even though the cash-out is immediately taxed, it may be preferable to deferral. Subsequent taxation will be affected by the taxpayer's situation at a later date. For example, an estate may be in a lower income tax bracket than the heirs of the estate. In addition, tax rates might be higher or lower at a later date. The availability of tax deductions, now versus later, should also be considered.

Q 8:55   How is income in respect of a decedent taxed to the IRA beneficiary?

Income in respect of a decedent (IRD) is included in an IRA beneficiary's gross income and may be offset by a portion of the federal estate tax imposed on the IRA at the time of the IRA owner's death. Under Code Section 691(c), the net federal estate tax (after the credit for state death taxes) is deductible as a miscellaneous itemized deduction on the IRA beneficiary's Schedule A.

Q 8:56   May an IRA beneficiary claim a deduction for the estate tax attributable to income in respect of a decedent, if the income is recognized in a year that precedes the year of the estate tax payment?

Yes. In Private Letter Ruling 200011023 (Dec. 15, 1999), the IRS stated that neither the Code nor the regulations require that estate tax be paid before the recipient of IRD is allowed to claim a deduction. Since the estate tax return and the applicable taxes are not due until nine months after the death of an IRA owner, this ruling permits an IRA beneficiary to claim a deduction for prospective estate taxes in situations in which amounts must be withdrawn from the IRA immediately following the IRA owner's death.

Q 8:57   What happens if an IRA is used to satisfy a specific pecuniary bequest?

If a will or trust instrument provides for the gift of a specific sum (a pecuniary bequest) to any beneficiary, using an IRA to satisfy the bequest causes the estate or trust to recognize income in respect of a decedent equal to the value that is transferred. [See IRS Chief Counsel Advice 200644020; I.R.C. § 691] This is a very unfavorable result.

An IRA owner can avoid the problem, however—by naming IRA beneficiaries directly (rather than passing the IRA through a trust or estate), by gifting a fractional share (rather than a specific sum of money), or by specifying in the will or trust instrument that IRA assets are to be transferred to the beneficiary. [See I.R.C. § 691(a)(2)]

Q 8:58   What happens if IRAs have to be split between different sections of the estate?

Splitting an IRA between different sections of an estate triggers income tax if it requires any liquidation of the IRA. If an IRA can be split without a liquidation, income tax deferral continues according to the age and the identity of the IRA beneficiary. The IRS has ruled that the assignment of all or a portion of an IRA to different residuary beneficiaries of an estate does not cause an acceleration of income tax either to the estate or to the beneficiaries. [Priv. Ltr. Rul. 200234019 (May 13, 2002)] The beneficiaries would be taxed when funds are withdrawn from the IRA. [Treas. Reg. § 1.691(a)-4(b)]

Q 8:59   Can the executor change the allocation of estate assets to avoid liquidating an IRA, or to redirect it to another beneficiary?

Yes, if the will authorizes the executor to do so (and provided the direction is consistent with the beneficiary designation in the IRA contract). Such authority is commonly given to an executor, along with authority to make the reasonable valuations that may be needed to avoid a liquidation.

The executor may also be authorized to allocate entire IRAs to the devisees who most want them, and to direct other assets that do not generate income tax upon distribution to the other beneficiaries.

Q 8:60   May the value of an IRA be discounted for estate tax purposes to reflect the fact that income taxes will ultimately be paid when the funds are distributed?

No. In a Technical Advice Memorandum, the IRS has ruled that the value of an IRA for estate tax purposes is the IRA's gross asset value on the date of death, and that value may not be discounted to reflect future income taxes on distributions. [Tech. Adv. Mem. 200247001 (Nov. 22, 2002)] Thus, even though an independent appraisal firm had valued the decedent's IRA at a discount to reflect future income taxes, the IRS concluded that Code Section 691 was intended to provide a statutory remedy and counterbalance to the double taxation of IRAs, because federal estate taxes are deductible by the beneficiary in calculating the income tax on IRA distributions (see Qs 8:53–8:56).

Strategies for Large Estates

Q 8:61   Is it realistic to plan for IRAs that exceed $3 million?

Yes. IRAs may contain more than $3 million in assets, primarily as a result of sizable rollovers from qualified plans. Such rollovers, which are often made before the IRA owner's retirement, should be made directly to avoid mandatory 20 percent withholding from the qualified plan. Individuals may prefer (although they are not required) to hold retirement savings in their own IRAs rather than have them held in an employer's plan.

Q 8:62   If a married couple's estate is larger than the estate tax exemption amount, what can be done to avoid or lessen tax on the estate of the second to die?

One way to avoid or lessen tax on the estate of the second to die when a couple's estate exceeds the estate tax exemption amount (see Q 8:7) is to make property transfers while both spouses are alive and to divide the property between them in such a way that the sizes of their respective estates are relatively equal. Another approach is to provide for the transfer of the applicable estate tax exemption amount into a bypass trust under which the property will not be taxed in the estate of the survivor. The trust bypasses the second estate by making a direct transfer, at the time of the second spouse's death, to children and other beneficiaries.

Q 8:63 Why should an IRA owner consider naming a charity as the beneficiary of the IRA rather than having other assets in his or her estate designated for a charitable bequest?

Besides the philanthropic reasons for benefiting a charity at death, naming a charity as the beneficiary of a traditional IRA is a wise choice because traditional IRA assets are pretax assets. Such assets are less costly to leave to charity from a tax standpoint than are other assets in an individual's estate.

Example. Vernon, age 80, has a net worth of $600,000 composed entirely of Z Corporation stock. He wants to leave half of his estate to his alma mater, Corinth College, after his death and the remaining half to his daughter, Elena. Vernon holds 10,000 shares of Z Corporation stock with a current value of $300,000 outside his IRA. In addition, Vernon has an IRA worth $300,000, also in 10,000 shares of Z Corporation stock.

Vernon bequeaths the 10,000 shares of Z Corporation stock that he owns outright to Corinth College and names Elena his IRA beneficiary. At Vernon's death, Elena must pay income tax on $300,000 if she withdraws all the funds from the IRA at that time. If Elena is in the 35 percent income tax bracket, the after-tax value of her inheritance would amount to $195,000 (i.e., $300,000 less $105,000 of income taxes). Corinth College receives $300,000 of Z Corporation shares.

If Vernon had named Corinth College rather than Elena as his IRA beneficiary, the college would have benefited from the entire $300,000 because it is tax exempt under Code Section 501(c)(3). Elena's inheritance would have amounted to $300,000 without diminution for income tax or capital gains tax. [*See generally* I.R.C. § 1014 (dealing with a step-up in basis at death).] Thus, Vernon would have increased Elena's inheritance by $105,000 (without any cost to Corinth College) by having his IRA pass to the college rather than to his daughter after his death.

Q 8:64 If an IRA owner benefits a charity at death, should the charity be named on the IRA beneficiary designation form, or should the owner name his or her estate as the IRA beneficiary and provide for the charity under the terms of his or her will?

The charity should be designated the IRA beneficiary on the appropriate IRA beneficiary designation form because the tax consequences of doing so are less complicated than if the IRA owner's estate is named as the beneficiary and the will allocates it to the charity. If a charity is named as the direct IRA beneficiary, the IRA will not be treated as a probate asset and will pass directly to the charity. In that event, no income tax consequences will be triggered, because the IRA owner's estate is not involved in the transfer. If, however, the IRA is left to the

IRA owner's estate, the IRA assets will be distributed to the estate and be taxed as income in respect of a decedent (IRD) under Code Section 691. [*See* Priv. Ltr. Rul. 200221011 (Feb. 12, 2002).]

As a result of income tax deduction limitations involving gifts to charity under Code Section 170, the estate may not be able to claim an immediate income tax deduction for the entire amount of the IRA passing to the charity. However, in Private Letter Ruling 200234019 (Aug. 23, 2002) the IRS permitted the executor of an estate that had been named as the beneficiary of the decedent's IRA to assign the decedent's IRA interest directly to a charity, thereby bypassing the estate and avoiding taxable income from being generated.

> **Practice Pointer.** Although the IRS may grant a favorable ruling request permitting IRA assets to be assigned by an executor of an estate directly to a charity, IRA owners and their advisors should continue to name the charity as the beneficiary in the IRA beneficiary designation form. This would avoid having to involve the estate executor in the charitable decision-making process and would avoid having the IRA assets possibly being treated as taxable income to the estate. It would also result in a lower probate estate subject to statutory executor fees under state law.

Q 8:65   Why may an IRA owner want to skip a generation and name his or her grandchild as the IRA beneficiary?

If an IRA owner's children are financially well off and do not need to inherit the entirety of the owner's estate, the use of generation-skipping strategies will result in significant estate tax savings to the owner's family over time. In addition, the use of an IRA in a generation-skipping strategy will result in a significant amount of tax-deferred compounding within the IRA over the lifetime of a grandchild. This technique is particularly powerful when a Roth IRA is used (see chapter 9).

If a grandchild is properly named as the IRA owner's designated beneficiary at the time of the owner's death, that grandchild will be able to calculate minimum distributions after the death of the grandparent based on the grandchild's remaining life expectancy.

> **Example.** Beatrice, age 85, named her grandson, Michael, as her IRA beneficiary after Sidney, her husband, died in 2003. Beatrice dies in 2011, when Michael is age 28. Michael calculates his RMDs using his life expectancy of 55.3 years based on the Uniform Lifetime Table. Thus, distributions to Michael can be spread over a period of 55.3 years.

> **Note.** The Code limits the amount of a decedent's assets that may skip a generation. Amounts in excess of that limit are subject to special generation-skipping taxes. [I.R.C. §§ 2601, 2602] The maximum generation-skipping amount coincides with the applicable estate tax exclusion amount in effect for the calendar year. [I.R.C. § 2631] For 2009, the maximum amount that is exempt from generation-skipping taxes is $3.5 million.

Q 8:66 How is generation skipping performed with IRA assets if there are several grandchildren?

If an IRA owner has several grandchildren and there is a wide disparity in ages among those grandchildren, consideration should be given to establishing separate IRAs for each grandchild to avoid having the grandchildren miss a critical deadline after the grandparent's death. That is because the IRS requires that after the death of the IRA owner, RMDs must be based on the life expectancy of the oldest beneficiary if the IRA is not split into separate IRAs by Dcember 31 of the year following the year of the IRA owner's death. [Treas. Reg. § 1.401(a)(9)-8, Q&A-2(a)(2)] If separate IRAs are established before the IRA owner's death, each grandchild will automatically be able to determine RMDs based on his or her own life expectancy.

Q 8:67 May a trust for grandchildren be named as the IRA beneficiary as part of a generation-skipping strategy?

Yes. A trust for minor grandchildren may be named as the IRA beneficiary, but the strategy only works if the trust is made to satisfy the "see-through" requirements (see Q 8:32). Assuming it is, the IRA will be distributed based on the oldest beneficiary's (grandchild's) life expectancy. [Treas. Reg. § 1.401(a)(9)-4, Q&A-5(b), Q&A-6(b)]

Q 8:68 If a trust for grandchildren is named as the IRA beneficiary, will grandchildren who are born after the owner dies be eligible to receive payments from the IRA after the death of the owner?

Yes. A designated beneficiary need not be specified by name in an IRA as long as the individual who is to be the beneficiary is identifiable under the IRA as of the date of the IRA owner's death. The members of a class of beneficiaries capable of expansion or contraction are treated as being identifiable if it is possible to identify the class member who has the shortest life expectancy. Thus, grandchildren who are born after the owner dies are eligible to receive payments because they cannot have a shorter life expectancy than any beneficiary who was identifiable when the owner died. [Treas. Reg. § 1.401(a)(9)-4, Q&A-1]

Chapter 9

Estate and Tax Strategies for Roth IRAs

Martin Fleisher, Esq.
Jo Ann Lippe, Esq.

Both traditional and Roth IRAs are subject to estate taxes, but Roth IRAs can be distributed tax-free to beneficiaries and are not subject to minimum distribution requirements during an owner's lifetime. These economic advantages, combined with a surviving spouse's ability to treat an inherited IRA as his or her own, make the Roth IRA an excellent vehicle for accumulating and transferring wealth to heirs. However, many individuals have substantial holdings in traditional IRAs and pre-tax qualified plan interests. This chapter is designed to help IRA owners and beneficiaries understand the various income tax and estate planning strategies that conversion to a Roth IRA offers.

Whether it makes sense for an individual to convert a traditional IRA to a Roth IRA depends on a variety of factors, including the individual's age, current and future income tax brackets, need for the IRA funds, estate planning objectives, and ability to pay the accelerated income taxes that will become due on conversion.

The year 2010 is an opportune time for Roth IRA conversions. Eligibility requirements for conversions that previously disqualified many individuals are eliminated as of 2010. Even the sharp decline of market values during 2009 may, at least temporarily, provide a silver lining in the form of reduced recognition of conversion income (and lower conversion tax).

Moreover, a special rule provides tax deferral only for conversions that occur in 2010. None of the conversion income is recognized in 2010, half is recognized in 2011, and the other half in 2012.

Overview

Q 9:1 What are the key planning considerations for Roth IRA conversions?

A Roth IRA is a valuable component of an individual's retirement and estate plans. Often, however, an individual has (or inherits) retirement funds that are invested in pre-tax qualified employer plans and traditional IRAs. Those assets can be converted to Roth IRAs (subject to some restrictions) but the cost of doing so is high. Whether conversion is useful in a particular situation generally depends on the answers to these questions:

- Are assets available for payment of the conversion tax that are not invested in tax deferred accounts? Conversion is rarely worthwhile if tax favored assets must be withdrawn to pay tax.

- Does the owner expect to withdraw the account funds at some point, or is the goal to build wealth for the owner's death beneficiaries? Minimum distributions need not be withdrawn during the owner's lifetime if the account is converted to a Roth IRA. Conversions are also most valuable if the funds remain invested in the Roth IRA for a long time.

- Funds cannot remain invested forever; when they are finally withdrawn will the owner's or the beneficiary's income tax rate be higher or lower than the rate that presently applies to the holder? Conversion makes economic sense if the tax rate at conversion is lower than it will be at withdrawal.

- Does the owner or beneficiary want to remove assets from his or her estate in order to reduce the estate tax that will eventually apply? If so, conversion is an efficient strategy because paying the conversion tax removes assets, while the conversion can eliminate future income tax on account distributions.

Q 9:2   How do recent changes affect Roth IRA planning?

The planning landscape for Roth IRAs is experiencing rapid and favorable changes. As of 2010, the eligibility requirements for a conversion (based on income and marital status) no longer apply. Also, it is now clear that qualified plan (but not IRA) nonspouse beneficiaries may convert to Roth IRAs, as long as beneficiaries use the direct trustee-to-trustee transfer method and the Roth IRA is titled in the deceased owner's name. (Before 2010, qualified plans did not have to offer nonspouse beneficiaries the option of a trustee-to-trustee transfer.) Uncertainty about the future of the federal estate tax seems now to be resolving, so that conversions are becoming easier to plan (see Q 8:8). Even the market declines of 2009 mean that, at least temporarily, conversions may result in less recognized income and lower conversion tax. Finally, a special rule allows tax on conversions that occur in 2010 to be deferred so that half is not recognized until 2011 and the other half in 2012 (see Q 9:4). [I.R.S. Notice 2008-30, Q&A-7, 2008-12 I.R.B. 638]

The Basics of Conversions

Q 9:3   What are the benefits of converting a traditional IRA to a Roth IRA?

When a traditional IRA is converted to a Roth IRA, all subsequent *qualified distributions* (see Q 5:10), whether to the owner or the owner's death beneficiary, are free of income tax. That is, the tax benefit of a Roth IRA is back-loaded. In a traditional IRA, the tax benefit is front-loaded (because contributions are tax deductible).

A second benefit of converting a traditional IRA to a Roth IRA is that there are no mandatory lifetime distributions from a Roth IRA. [I.R.C. § 408A(c)(5)] Only beneficiaries of a Roth IRA are subject to the minimum distribution rules. Consequently, an owner may leave funds in a Roth IRA for many years, allowing them to compound tax free.

Note. The RMD rules have been suspended for 2009 (see Qs 4:21–4:25).

Q 9:4   What is the immediate tax cost of a conversion?

There is an immediate tax cost when an IRA or a pre-tax qualified plan interest is converted to a Roth IRA. The conversion is treated as a taxable distribution of assets from the traditional IRA or qualified plan, followed by a rollover contribution to the Roth IRA. [Treas. Reg. § 1.408A-4, Q&A-1] If nondeductible contributions were made to the traditional IRA or qualified plan, they are excluded from income on the conversion; otherwise, the converted assets are included in the owner's or beneficiary's gross income for the year of the conversion. [I.R.C. §§ 408A(d)(3)(A)(i), 408A(d)(3)(C); Treas. Reg. § 1.408A-4, Q&A-7]]

A special deferral rule applies to conversions that occur in 2010, the year when the eligibility requirements for conversions are eliminated. For a conversion in 2010 (unless the individual elects otherwise), half the conversion income is recognized in 2011 and the other half in 2012. An income acceleration rule will apply if the converted amounts are distributed before 2012. [I.R.C. § 408A(d)(3)]

Q 9:5   Does the 10 percent additional tax apply if an individual younger than age 59½ converts a traditional IRA to a Roth IRA?

No. The 10 percent additional tax under Code Section 72(t)(2) does not apply to amounts converted from a traditional IRA to a Roth IRA. [I.R.C. § 408A(d)(3)(A)]

Q 9:6   What assets should be used to pay the conversion tax?

If possible, the conversion tax should be paid from nonretirement plan sources, so the undiminished retirement account funds can continue to grow tax free. Withdrawing IRA or qualified plan funds to pay a conversion tax also triggers the 10 percent additional tax if the individual taking the distribution is younger than age 59½. A conversion that can only be managed by using tax favored funds for the conversion tax is probably not advantageous unless the converted assets can be left to compound in the Roth IRA for a long time.

Q 9:7   What IRA assets may be converted to Roth IRAs?

Generally, assets held by an owner, but not a beneficiary, in a traditional IRA, a simplified employee pension arrangement (SEP), or a savings incentive match plan for employees (SIMPLE IRA) may be converted to a Roth IRA (see chapters 11 and 12). However, any required minimum distribution (RMD) for the conversion year from a traditional IRA, SEP, or SIMPLE IRA must be paid to the individual; it may not be converted to a Roth IRA. [I.R.C §§ 408A(e), 408(d)(3), 408A(c)(3)(B), 408A(d)(3)(B); Treas. Reg. § 1.408A-4, Q&A-6]

There is no requirement that assets remain in a traditional IRA or SEP for any length of time before they are converted to a Roth IRA. Assets may not be converted from a SIMPLE IRA, however, during the first two years of an individual's first participation in any SIMPLE of the employer. [Treas. Reg. § 1.408A-4, Q&A-4]

Example 1. Jerry's traditional IRA has a value of $1.1 million on December 31, 2009. During 2010, he must receive a minimum distribution of $50,000 from the IRA (his RMD based on attaining age 76 during the distribution year). He may convert the rest ($1,050,000) to a Roth IRA in 2010.

Example 2. David, age 17, earns $10,000 during 2009 working as a golf caddie after school and on weekends. He contributes $5,000 to a traditional IRA on April 10, 2010, and claims a deduction on his 2009 income tax return. If he wants to convert the IRA to a Roth IRA the very next day, he may do so.

Q 9:8   What other plan assets may be converted to Roth IRAs?

Assets may be converted to Roth IRAs from a qualified plan, Section 403(b) annuity, or a Section 457 plan, provided in each case that a distribution is allowed by the plan provisions. [I.R.C. §§ 408A(e), 457(e)(16); I.R.S. Notice 2008-30, 2008-12 I.R.B. 638]

Note. Assets held in a designated Roth account (DRAC) of a qualified plan may be rolled over to a Roth IRA. This is not a conversion, however, and the rollover is not taxed. A DRAC is like a Roth IRA in that contributions are not deductible and distributions may generally be tax free. (See Qs 6:114–6:118.)

Q 9:9   Who is eligible to convert assets?

Starting in 2010, the conversion option is available to any owner of an IRA. [I.R.C. §§ 402(c)(11), 402(f)(2)(A)] Before 2010, a conversion is only possible if the individual satisfies eligibility requirements based on income and marital status (see Q 9:4). [I.R.C. § 408A(e)]

The ability to convert is not restricted by age. An individual older than age 70½, who is no longer able to make regular contributions to a traditional IRA, may convert it to a Roth IRA and continue to make annual contributions.

Participation in a qualified plan also does not disqualify an individual from converting assets to a Roth IRA.

Q 9:10   Are qualified plan and IRA beneficiaries treated differently for Roth IRA purposes?

Apparently yes. There may be a drafting error in the law, but at present a nonspouse beneficiary of a qualified retirement plan may directly roll over the interest into a Roth IRA if the beneficiary is eligible for a Roth IRA conversion (which all beneficiaries will be starting in 2010). However, nonspouse beneficiaries of traditional IRAs cannot roll them over into Roth IRAs. [I.R.S. Notice 2008-30, Q&A-7, 2008-12 I.R.B. 638]

Q 9:11   How are Roth IRA distributions taxed after a conversion?

If conversion contributions are distributed from the Roth IRA generally within five years, the 10 percent additional tax of Code Section 72(t) may apply. Otherwise, conversion has no effect on the distribution rules that govern Roth

IRAs. These rules are complicated, however. (For an extensive discussion of Roth IRA distributions, including distributions of conversion contributions, see chapter 5.)

Q 9:12 What are the eligibility requirements for conversions before 2010?

For conversions before 2010, two eligibility requirements apply—the individual's modified adjusted gross income (MAGI) cannot exceed $100,000 for the year of conversion, and married individuals must file a joint income tax return unless they live apart for that entire year. [I.R.C. §§ 408A(c)(3)(B)(ii), 219(g)(4); Treas. Reg. § 1.408A-4, Q&A-2] For this purpose, individuals who are married on December 31 are treated as being married for the entire year. (For discussion of the eligibility requirements that apply until 2010, see Qs 3:92–3:98).

Q 9:13 Can a conversion be recharacterized?

Yes. A conversion is reversed by recharacterizing the assets and their post-conversion earnings back to a traditional IRA. A recharacterization may be done for any reason until six months after the due date (plus extensions) for filing the individual's tax return for the year of the conversion. A recharacterization of assets is valid only if the earnings are included. [I.R.C. § 408A(d)(6); Treas. Reg. § 1.408A-5]

A conversion may be recharacterized after the income tax return for the conversion year is filed, as long as the recharacterization deadline is met. In that case, the individual must amend the income tax return to remove the "undone" conversion income. [Ann. 99-57, 1999-1 C.B. 1256]

The IRS may, upon petition for a letter ruling, extend the recharacterization deadline. The IRS has discretion to grant extensions that do not prejudice the government's interests, for individuals who act reasonably and in good faith. The regulations provide that an individual is generally deemed to act reasonably and in good faith if he or she reasonably relies on a qualified tax professional, and that person fails to make (or advise the taxpayer of the ability to make) a particular election. [Treas. Reg. § 301.9100-3] For example, in Private Letter Ruling 200128058 (Apr. 16, 2001), the IRS extended the deadline for a recharacterization for an individual who demonstrated that his accountant was unaware of the $100,000 MAGI limit and the recharacterization deadline. Relief was also granted in Private Letter Ruling 200423030 (Mar. 9, 2004), to an individual who received conflicting advice from two tax advisors about his eligibility to recharacterize a conversion.

For a general discussion of recharacterizations, see Qs 3:120–3:136.

Q 9:14   If a conversion to a preexisting Roth IRA is recharacterized, how are the earnings computed?

The net income to be recharacterized is determined by allocating to the conversion contribution a pro rata portion of the earnings accrued by the Roth IRA during the period the Roth IRA held the contribution. [Notice 2000-39, 2000-2 C.B. 132] The method is described in detail in Q 3:120.

Example 1. On July 1, 2009, Donald converts $160,000 from his traditional IRA to a preexisting Roth IRA; the Roth IRA holds assets worth $80,000 immediately before the conversion. In February 2010 Donald discovers he was ineligible for a 2009 conversion because his MAGI was too high, so he asks the Roth IRA trustee to recharacterize the $160,000 conversion contribution. At that time, the value of the Roth IRA has declined to $225,000. The net loss attributable to the $160,000 conversion contribution is $10,000, calculated as follows:

$$\text{Net income (loss)} = \$160,000 \times \frac{(\$225,000 - \$240,000)}{\$240,000} = (-\$10,000)$$

The $10,000 loss is offset against the $160,000 conversion contribution, so the total amount recharacterized is $150,000.

Example 2. The facts are the same as those in Example 1, except that the value of Donald's Roth IRA has increased to $270,000 when he requests the recharacterization. The total amount that must be transferred back to the traditional IRA is now $180,000 (the $160,000 conversion contribution plus earnings of $20,000). The $20,000 earnings are calculated as follows:

$$\text{Net income} = \$160,000 \times \frac{(\$270,000 - \$240,000)}{\$240,000} = \$20,000$$

Q 9:15   May an individual convert, recharacterize, and reconvert all within the same taxable year?

No. If assets are converted from a traditional IRA to a Roth IRA and then recharacterized back to the traditional IRA, they may not subsequently be reconverted back to a Roth IRA until the start of the next calendar year or 30 days after the recharacterization, whichever is later. [Treas. Reg. § 1.408A-5, Q&A-9(a)(1)]

Example. Joan converted her traditional IRA to a Roth IRA on April 1, 2009. If she recharacterizes the conversion on November 30, 2009, she cannot reconvert that amount to a Roth IRA before January 1, 2010. If Joan recharacterizes the Roth IRA conversion during December 2009, she must wait at least 30 days before reconverting the traditional IRA to a Roth IRA.

Conversion Strategies

General

Q 9:16 Should a spouse beneficiary of a decedent's Roth IRA roll it over to a new Roth IRA?

In most cases, a spouse beneficiary should roll over the inherited Roth IRA to a Roth IRA in the spouse's name (or treat the inherited Roth IRA as the spouse's own; see Q 5:49) as soon as practicable after the Roth IRA owner dies. This offers two great advantages. First, it frees the spouse of the need to take lifetime distributions. Second, it allows the Roth IRA to be extended over the longest period of time. When the spouse dies after becoming the owner, distributions can be made over the life expectancy of the spouse's beneficiary. If the spouse did not become the owner, the distribution period for the Roth IRA would be the spouse's remaining life expectancy in the year of death; the life expectancy of the spouse's beneficiary would be irrelevant. (See Qs 4:45; 5:49.)

> **Note.** A surviving spouse who is the Roth IRA beneficiary and wants to take distributions is better off retaining the status of beneficiary, rather than owner, until he or she attains age 59½ (see Q 5:56).

Q 9:17 After a conversion, who should be named as the Roth IRA beneficiary?

Purely from an income tax planning standpoint, the individual with the longest life expectancy should be named the beneficiary of a Roth IRA. Since payments can be stretched out over the life expectancy of the beneficiary after the Roth IRA owner dies, tax free compounding has the greatest value for the youngest beneficiary. If various assets of a Roth IRA owner will be left to parents, siblings, and children when he or she dies, then all else being equal, the Roth IRA should be left to the children.

However, many considerations enter into the choice of beneficiary. For extensive discussion of choosing particular individuals or entities (including trusts) as Roth IRA beneficiaries, and how the minimum distribution rules apply in each case, see Qs 5:48–5:61 and Qs 4:49–4:95.

Q 9:18 Should an individual who converts assets to a Roth IRA adjust his or her estimated tax payments for the year of the conversion?

Yes. Because the amount converted from a traditional IRA to a Roth IRA constitutes taxable income, a taxpayer should adjust his or her estimated tax payments (or, alternatively, wage withholding). Failure to adjust estimated tax payments will result in interest penalties under Code Section 6654. In Legal Memorandum 200105062 (Feb. 2, 2001), the IRS refused to grant a waiver of the underpayment of an estimated tax penalty on the conversion to a Roth IRA because such waivers are granted only in unusual circumstances such as casualty or disaster.

Q 9:19 If a Roth IRA owner dies shortly after converting to the Roth IRA, may an election to recharacterize the conversion be made by his or her executor?

Yes, provided the recharacterization is completed on a timely basis—that is, before the extended due date for filing the decedent's federal income tax return for the taxable year of the conversion. [Treas. Reg. § 1.408A-5, Q&A-6(c)]

Strategies for Reducing MAGI (before 2010)

Q 9:20 What planning strategies are available to help reduce a taxpayer's MAGI?

At this point, the best planning strategy is probably to wait until 2010 to convert to a Roth IRA. However, any of these actions might lower an individual's MAGI sufficiently for a conversion in 2009:

1. Defer the sale of investments that have increased in value into years other than the year of the conversion to a Roth IRA.

2. Defer salary or bonuses into future years.

3. Maximize contributions to an employer's 401(k) plan in the year of the Roth IRA conversion.

4. If self-employed, establish a Keogh plan to reduce MAGI.

5. Change the investment portfolio to include municipal bonds for the year of the conversion.

6. Retain income in a C corporation during the year of the conversion.

7. Defer commencement of Social Security benefits until the year after the conversion to a Roth IRA.

8. Purchase a tax-deferred variable annuity or make deposits to a variable life insurance contract.

9. Sell investments that have declined in value to generate a $3,000 capital loss to offset ordinary income or to offset capital gains.

10. Determine whether any adjustments to MAGI can be maximized (e.g., moving expenses, penalties for early withdrawal of savings, health insurance for the self-employed, or alimony payments).

Q 9:21 What should be done if it is determined after conversion that MAGI exceeded the $100,000 limit?

If it turns out that MAGI exceeds $100,000, the conversion may be undone by recharacterizing it in a timely manner (see Q 9:13). [Ann. 99-57, 1999-1 C.B. 1256]

Strategies for Reducing Income Tax

Q 9:22 Are there ways to mitigate the impact of the conversion tax?

The impact of the conversion tax may be reduced by deferring income recognition (only for conversions in 2010), spreading out conversions, and timing conversions to take advantage of deductions or lower income tax rates.

Q 9:23 Why is it beneficial to convert assets in 2010?

The conversion tax is deferred for conversions that occur in 2010. Generally, none of the conversion income is recognized in 2010, half is recognized in 2011, and the other half in 2012 (see Q 9:4). [I.R.C. § 408A(d)(3)] Tax deferral is not available for any other conversion year.

Q 9:24 How may conversions be timed for an income tax advantage?

Sometimes conversions can be timed to take advantage of offsetting deductions or a lower marginal income tax rate. For example, a year in which a sole proprietor recognizes a business loss might be an opportune time to convert to a Roth IRA, because the ordinary loss may offset income from the conversion. A beneficiary who inherits a traditional IRA may be able to claim a Code Section 691(c) deduction that partly offsets the income recognized from converting it to an inherited Roth IRA; that deduction would be for the portion of any estate tax payable that is attributable to including the traditional IRA in the deceased individual's estate. Finally, an individual whose income (and tax bracket) are expected to rise in the future should convert, if possible, before that happens.

Q 9:25 May only a portion of a taxpayer's IRA be converted to a Roth IRA?

Yes. Code Section 408A(d)(3) applies to any amount that is transferred from a traditional IRA to a Roth IRA, and there is no requirement that the entire IRA be converted to a Roth IRA. Conversions may be done in stages to avoid bunching all the income into a single year.

Q 9:26 May conversions be made from the same traditional IRA to different Roth IRAs during the same 12-month period?

Yes. There is no limit on the number of Roth IRAs that a taxpayer may create during the year by converting traditional IRA assets to Roth IRAs.

Q 9:27   If assets decline in value shortly after conversion, can paying a conversion tax based on the higher asset value on the conversion date be avoided?

Yes. The conversion may be recharacterized in a timely manner—within six months after the deadline, with extensions, for filing the tax return for the conversion year (see Q 9:13). [Treas. Reg. § 1.408A-5, Q&A-1]

Q 9:28   Are there tax advantages to converting IRA assets into more than one Roth IRA?

Yes. A conversion must be recharacterized in its entirety, so if several assets are transferred in a single conversion and one asset loses value before the recharacterization deadline (see Q 9:13), either all or none of the assets must be recharacterized. Instead, if assets are segregated for conversion into separate Roth IRAs, one conversion could be recharacterized without affecting the others. [I.R.S. Notice 2000-39, 2000-2 CB 132]

Example 1. Martin converts $100,000 cash from a traditional IRA to a Roth IRA. Half of the cash is invested in Stock A and the other half in Stock B. Shortly after the conversion, Stock A's value declines to $20,000, and Stock B's value increases to $80,000. If Martin recharacterizes the conversion, all of the assets (including Stock B's $30,000 of earnings) must be transferred back to a traditional IRA.

Example 2. The facts are the same as those in Example 1, except that Martin converts $50,000 into one Roth IRA that invests in Stock A, and $50,000 into another Roth IRA that invests in Stock B. When Stock A's value falls to $20,000, Martin only recharacterizes one of the conversions (the one that involves Stock A). The amount returned to a traditional IRA is only $20,000; Stock B (worth $80,000) remains in a Roth IRA.

Q 9:29   Should a charity be named the beneficiary of a Roth IRA?

No; that would waste the key benefit of a Roth IRA—that distributions are generally received tax free by the recipient. A charity is a tax exempt entity, and receives equal value whether the asset is a traditional or Roth IRA. For the estate, the estate tax charitable deduction is the same whether a traditional or Roth IRA is donated. What tips the balance is that the heirs of the deceased are better off receiving a Roth IRA than a traditional IRA because they will receive all Roth IRA distributions free of any income tax.

Q 9:30   What are the federal income tax consequences if a Roth IRA owner transfers his or her Roth IRA to another individual by gift?

A transfer of a Roth IRA to another individual constitutes an assignment of the Roth IRA owner's rights under the Roth IRA and is treated as a distribution of the Roth IRA assets to the original owner. Accordingly, the assets would be treated as no longer held within a Roth IRA. [Treas. Reg. § 1.408A-6, Q&A-19]

Strategies for Reducing Estate Tax

Q 9:31   Why is the Roth IRA a more valuable estate planning vehicle than the traditional IRA?

The Roth IRA is an extremely flexible vehicle for performing estate planning. Unlike the traditional IRA, the Roth IRA does not generate income in respect of a decedent (IRD) for the Roth IRA designated beneficiaries under Code Section 691, because all post-death distributions to the beneficiaries are free of income tax. Further, after the death of the Roth IRA owner, the designated beneficiaries may receive distributions from the Roth IRA free of income tax over their remaining lifetimes. Thus, the creation of a Roth IRA for a second or third generation would likely be the most valuable asset that the Roth IRA owner could pass to his or her heirs.

Q 9:32   Does converting a traditional IRA to a Roth IRA save estate taxes for high net worth taxpayers?

In most cases, yes, because paying the conversion tax removes assets from the overall estate. If the individual dies shortly after the conversion and before paying the conversion tax, the unpaid tax is deductible in calculating the estate tax.

Example, part 1. Sarah's net worth of $3,850,000 consists of the following assets:

Investments	$ 2,850,000
Traditional IRA	$ 1,000,000

If Sarah were to die in 2009, her estate tax would be calculated as follows:

Net Worth	$3,850,000
Estate Tax Exempt Amount	$3,500,000
Taxable Estate	$ 350,000
Estate Tax @ 45%	$ 157,500

If Sarah converted her IRA to a Roth IRA in 2009, her net worth and estate tax would be calculated as follows:

Investments	$ 2,850,000
Roth IRA	$ 1,000,000
Roth IRA Tax Liability @ 35%	($ 350,000)
Net Worth	$ 3,500,000
Estate Tax Exempt Amount	$ 3,500,000
Estate Tax	-0-

Thus, $157,500 of estate taxes will be saved if Sarah converts her IRA to a Roth IRA. Furthermore, converting a traditional IRA to a Roth IRA may increase the economic benefit of the entire inheritance to the heirs of the deceased.

Example, part 2. Although $157,500 of estate taxes is saved as a result of the Roth IRA conversion, Sarah's net worth when she dies will now consist of only a $1 million Roth IRA plus $2,500,000 of investment assets, because $350,000 of the outside investment assets are used to pay the income tax on conversion. Without the conversion, Sarah's heirs would receive the $1 million traditional IRA and outside investments of $2,692,000 ($2,850,000 less the estate tax of $157,500). In other words, the heirs would receive $192,500 more in assets without the Roth IRA conversion.

Still, the income tax that Sarah's heirs would pay on distributions from a $1 million traditional IRA exceeds (in present value terms) the $192,500 reduction of their inheritance that results from the conversion. They receive a much greater economic benefit if they inherit a $1,000,000 Roth IRA that generates no income tax liability over their lifetimes.

Q 9:33 Why else should income taxes be paid before federal and state estate taxes?

It is generally better to pay income taxes before paying estate taxes rather than the reverse. Income taxes paid on a conversion before death reduce, dollar for dollar, the IRA value on which both federal and estate taxes are calculated. On the other hand, federal and estate taxes do not have the same effect on reducing the future income tax payable on a traditional IRA distribution, which is taxed as IRD. That is because a beneficiary who receives IRD is allowed to deduct only the portion of the federal—but not the state—estate tax payment that results from including the IRD in the estate. [I.R.C. § 691(c)]

Q 9:34 Is a Roth IRA an appropriate vehicle to use for generation-skipping transfers upon death?

Yes. Because younger beneficiaries of a Roth IRA have the opportunity to take RMDs based on their life expectancies, using a Roth IRA in a generation-skipping strategy can produce enormous tax benefits through tax free compounding.

Table 9-1 sets forth the total tax free payments that would be made from a $2 million Roth IRA to potential beneficiaries with alternative life expectancies of 30 years, 40 years, 50 years, and 60 years, at rates of return of 8 percent, 10 percent, and 12 percent on the Roth IRA funds.

Table 9-1. Distributions from a $2 Million Roth IRA
After Death of Roth IRA Owner

Total Number of Years of Distributions	Appreciation Rate		
	8%	10%	12%
30 Years	$ 8,171,708	$ 12,093,813	$ 18,077,806
40 Years	$14,011,519	$ 24,394,205	$ 43,068,980
50 Years	$24,821,076	$ 51,302,907	$107,751,023
60 Years	$45,169,609	$111,444,670	$279,443,752

Strategies for Building Capital and Extending the Roth IRA

Q 9:35　Should an individual convert pre-tax retirement assets to a Roth IRA if the primary goal is to allow wealth to build in the IRA for many years?

Yes. Assets can remain in a Roth IRA much longer than in a traditional IRA or other pre-tax convertible account, because distributions do not have to be made from a Roth IRA during the owner's lifetime.

Q 9:36　How may the distribution period of an IRA be extended for a long period of time?

With proper planning, a Roth IRA (more so than a traditional IRA) can be made to endure for generations, especially if the owner forgoes taking lifetime distributions. Ideally, an owner would establish the Roth IRA as early as possible, convert into it any pre-tax IRAs or qualified plan interests, and make regular annual contributions. The owner's spouse, if any, could be designated as the primary beneficiary, and upon the owner's death the spouse would roll over the decedent's Roth IRA or treat it as the spouse's own; that would free the spouse from the minimum distribution requirements. The spouse would designate a young beneficiary (or class of beneficiaries, such as the grandchildren) to succeed to the Roth IRA. Finally, when the spouse dies, RMDs would commence, and minimum distributions could extend over the long period of the beneficiary's life expectancy.

Q 9:37　If an owner is reluctant to pay a large conversion tax because the funds it would require may be needed later on, is conversion planning still possible?

Yes. Conversion can be enormously beneficial even if it does not occur until late in the owner's life or after the owner has died. An owner who is unsure whether conversion is affordable could invest a pool of funds that could be drawn on for living expenses as needed, but used later to pay the conversion tax if not required for another use. If unspent at the owner's death, the funds could be bequeathed to the beneficiary of the convertible interest, to allow him or her to proceed with the conversion.

Chapter 10

Income and Estate Planning Concerns for Large IRA Balances

Martin Fleisher, Esq.
Jo Ann Lippe, Esq.

As an IRA balance increases on account of rollovers from a qualified plan (or plans), special attention should be given to the unique character of these assets in order to achieve the optimum tax results. Without proper planning, a large IRA balance could be subject to two levels of tax—estate and income—at death, which could consume over 75 percent of the account. With proper planning, an IRA could be maintained to provide tax-deferred income to the IRA owner and successive generations of his or her family for over 70 years. Such planning includes a review of the beneficiary designations, the strategies available to spouse and nonspouse beneficiaries, the benefits of leaving all or a portion of an IRA to a charity or private foundation, and the use of life insurance to prefund anticipated estate tax attributable to a large IRA.

The regulations under Section 401(a)(9) of the Internal Revenue Code substantially revised and simplified the minimum distribution requirements that apply during the IRA owner's lifetime and after his or her death. These changes increased the importance of estate planning for large IRA balances, because many strategies may now be undertaken after the IRA owner's death that were not permissible under the prior proposed regulations. In addition, the minimum distribution requirements now applicable to all IRA owners (regardless of the identity of their beneficiary or beneficiaries) allow significantly smaller amounts to be paid out during the owner's lifetime, which generally permits larger IRA balances to be accumulated for beneficiaries.

General Rules

Q 10:1   How can an individual project the size of his or her IRA balance at age 70½?

The projected rate of return on IRA assets is the most important consideration in any special planning for an individual with a large IRA balance. Because IRA assets compound on a tax-deferred basis, a projection of future IRA values at various rates of return may (and should) be performed.

One way to estimate the future size of an IRA is to consider the number of years required for an investment to double at various rates of return, as shown in the following table.

Table 10-1. Doubling Rate of Investments

Rate of Return	Number of Years for Investment to Double in Value
1%	69.7
2%	35.0
3%	23.4
4%	17.7
5%	14.2
6%	11.9
7%	10.2

Table 10-1. Doubling Rate of Investments (*cont'd*)

Rate of Return	Number of Years for Investment to Double in Value
8%	9.0
9%	8.0
10%	7.3
11%	6.6
12%	6.1

For example, if an individual, age 58, has $1 million in an IRA that earns 6 percent per year for the next 12 years, this individual at age 70½ should have an IRA balance of roughly $2 million.

Note. If an individual is contributing to a 401(k) plan into which an employer is also making contributions, the value of the employer's contributions must be taken into account when projecting the individual's IRA balance because those contributions are likely to make their way into the individual's IRA after he or she terminates employment.

Q 10:2   Why does IRA planning require consideration of both IRA and qualified plan benefits?

The Internal Revenue Code (Code; I.R.C.) encourages the rollover of qualified plan balances to IRAs by generally imposing a 10 percent premature additional tax on funds that are distributed before the participant attains age 59½. For this reason, qualified plan benefits that an individual receives as a lump sum are typically rolled over to an IRA.

A high-income employee who receives a lump-sum distribution from a qualified plan when employment is terminated would probably roll it over to an IRA to defer income tax and avoid the 10 percent additional tax. Large rollovers to IRAs may also occur if an employer terminates a qualified plan. Over the course of an employee's career, it is likely that he or she will roll over several qualified plan distributions to IRAs.

Q 10:3   Why do large IRA balances require special income tax planning?

Large IRA balances require special income tax planning to prevent an acceleration of income tax after the death of the IRA owner on account of poorly prepared beneficiary designations or inappropriate minimum distribution elections.

Q 10:4   Why does a large IRA balance require special estate planning?

After the death of an IRA owner, an IRA passes to a named IRA beneficiary (or beneficiaries) under operation of law and does not become part of the IRA owner's probate estate. A critical part of proper estate planning is to review the

IRA owner's beneficiary designations, because they will override contrary terms of his or her will.

The same level of care employed in drafting an individual's will should be applied to drafting the IRA beneficiary designation. Provision should be made for contingent IRA beneficiaries in the event of the death of the primary beneficiary. If the IRA owner wishes to control the amount of the payout to the primary beneficiary and the identity of contingent beneficiaries who will receive the remaining IRA funds in the event of the primary beneficiary's death, consideration should be given to naming a trust as the IRA beneficiary.

If the IRA beneficiary is not the IRA owner's surviving spouse, the provisions of the IRA owner's will should be reviewed to determine who will bear the responsibility for the estate tax that will become due on account of such designation.

Q 10:5 What estate planning problems may arise if an IRA represents the majority of a taxpayer's net worth?

If an IRA exceeds 50 percent of an individual's net worth, there may not be sufficient non-IRA assets at death to pay the estate taxes. In that case, the IRA beneficiaries may be forced to withdraw funds from the IRA on a taxable basis to pay estate taxes. The acceleration of estate and income taxes in the same year can cause the aggregate tax on the IRA to exceed 75 percent—a staggering result (see Q 10:73). The IRS has held that the value of an IRA at death may not be discounted for estate tax purposes to reflect the liability for income taxes that will become payable by the IRA beneficiaries in the future. [*See* Tech. Adv. Mem. 2002-47-001 (Nov. 22, 2002).]

Estate Tax Exemption Amount

Q 10:6 For 2009, what are the maximum federal estate tax rate and the estate tax exemption amount?

The estate of an individual who dies in 2009 is subject to a maximum federal estate tax rate of 45 percent. The amount that is excludable from the taxable estate is $3.5 million. [I.R.C. § 2001(b)(2)] The first $3.5 million of assets in an individual's estate are exempt from federal tax. Generally, this means that with proper planning a married couple can pass assets worth $7 million to their heirs free of the estate tax.

Q 10:7 What will happen to the federal estate tax after 2009?

Pursuant to law enacted in 2001, the federal estate tax is set to expire in 2010—for one year only—and then spring back into existence on January 1, 2011, using the same tax rates (up to 55 percent) and exemption amount ($1 million) that were effective in 2001 (see Q 8:8). It now appears likely that the provisions of the estate tax law as they are in effect for 2009 will be made permanent. President Obama's budget proposal for fiscal year 2010 provides for that change of law, and so does the joint Congressional budget resolution for fiscal year 2010 that the U.S. Senate and House of Representatives passed on April 29, 2009. The President's Budget for Fiscal Year 2010, OMB, Updated Summary Tables (May 2009), Table S-7, Bridge from Budget Enforcement Act Baseline to Baseline Projection of Current Policy, p. 15, n. 1 (*http://www.whitehouse. gov/omb/budget/fy2010/assets/summary.pdf*); S. Cong. Res. 13 (111th Congress, April 29, 2009)]

Q 10:8 How may an estate plan be designed to take advantage of the estate tax exemption if the IRA is the only significant asset in the taxpayer's name?

Often, an IRA is the only asset in an estate to exceed the amount of the estate tax exemption. For a husband and wife to take advantage of the $3.5 million exemption from federal estate tax applicable for 2009 (and probably also later years) and pass $7 million of assets to their heirs without estate tax, each spouse must hold $3.5 million in his or her own name.

To take full advantage of the estate tax exemption using IRA assets, an individual must designate an exemption trust as his or her IRA beneficiary (see Q 8:35). If the IRA owner's surviving spouse is the oldest beneficiary of the exemption trust and the trust satisfies the requirements of the final regulations under Code Section 401(a)(9) (see Q 10:9), the surviving spouse will be permitted to use his or her own remaining life expectancy (after the IRA owner's death) to calculate his or her lifetime distributions from the IRA.

The final regulations under Code Section 401(a)(9) require that certain conditions be satisfied for the underlying trust beneficiary to be recognized as a designated beneficiary for purposes of required minimum distributions (RMDs) from the IRA. [Treas. Reg. § 1.401(a)(9)-4, Q&A-5(b), Q&A-6] If any condition is not satisfied, the distribution of IRA assets to an exemption trust after the death of the IRA owner may not be based on the surviving spouse's remaining life expectancy. Instead, because a nonconforming trust is treated by the IRS as having no life expectancy of its own, the payout method would depend on whether the IRA owner died before or after his or her required beginning date (RBD) (see Qs 4:130, 4:136).

Example 1. Greg, a married taxpayer, has a family net worth of $5.5 million, $2.5 million of which is in his traditional IRA. The remaining $3 million is in the name of his spouse, Jill. Greg dies in 2008, having named Jill as the direct beneficiary of his IRA. No federal estate tax applies because Greg's entire estate qualifies for the marital deduction. Jill rolls over the $2.5 million inherited IRA to an IRA in her own name and designates their children as the IRA beneficiaries. If the value of the estate remains the same and Jill dies in 2009, only $3.5 million of Jill's $5.5 million estate is exempt from federal estate tax (see Q 10:6). Estate tax is levied on the $2 million balance of Jill's estate.

Example 2. The facts are the same as those in Example 1, except that Greg names two beneficiaries for the IRA—Jill, and an irrevocable inter vivos exemption trust whose beneficiary is Jill during her lifetime, and then the children. When Greg dies in 2008, the trust's share of the traditional IRA is $2 million (the federal estate tax exemption amount that year), and Jill directly inherits the rest ($500,000). No federal estate tax is due on Greg's estate because it is entirely covered by the estate tax exemption amount and the marital deduction.

Jill rolls over her directly inherited interest in the traditional IRA to one in her own name and designates the children as beneficiaries. The exemption trust satisfies the requirements of Code Section 401(a)(9) (see Q 10:9), so Jill is treated as the designated beneficiary of the trust's share of the IRA, and RMDs are paid to the trust (and distributed to Jill) based on her recalculated life expectancy (see Qs 4:30, 4:36, 5:49). When Jill dies in 2009, the exemption trust is excluded from her estate so Jill's estate is worth only $3.5 million (her $500,000 IRA and other assets worth $3 million). Jill's estate is entirely covered by the exemption amount and no federal estate tax is payable.

Q 10:9   What requirements must be met for the underlying beneficiary of a trust that is named as the IRA beneficiary to be treated as a designated beneficiary for required minimum distribution purposes?

For the trust beneficiary to be treated as a designated beneficiary for RMD purposes after the death of the IRA owner (i.e., for the trust to be a "see-through" trust), the following requirements must be met no later than October 31 of the year following the year of the IRA owner's death:

1. The trust must be a valid trust under state law, or one that would be valid but for the fact that there is no corpus;

2. The trust must be irrevocable or must, by its terms, become irrevocable upon the death of the IRA owner;

3. The beneficiaries of the trust must be identifiable from the trust document; and

4. Before his or her RBD, the IRA owner must have provided the IRA trustee or custodian with the trust instrument or, alternatively, the IRA owner must have met and certified certain other substantiation and notification requirements.

[Treas. Reg. § 1.401(a)(9)-4, Q&A-5(b), Q&A-6(b)]

These requirements must be satisfied before the IRA owner's RBD if the trust beneficiary is the IRA owner's spouse and the spouse is more than 10 years younger than the IRA owner. Because the distribution period in such a case could be based on the actual recalculated joint life expectancy of the IRA owner and spouse (and not on the shorter life expectancy determined from the Uniform Table under Treasury Regulations Section 1.401(a)(9)-5, Q&A-4), the spouse would have to qualify as a designated beneficiary at the time of the IRA owner's RBD. [*See* Treas. Reg. § 1.401(a)(9)-4, Q&A-6(a).]

Q 10:10   What is the result if the trust does not satisfy the see-through requirements of the regulations?

Only individuals may be designated beneficiaries, so if the IRA beneficiary is a trust that does not qualify under the see-through rules, there is no designated beneficiary for the trust's interest. That portion of the IRA must be paid out over the shortest distribution period allowed. If the trust's interest is in a traditional IRA and the owner dies before his or her RBD, or if the trust's interest is in a Roth IRA, then the IRA must be entirely distributed within five years after the owner's death. Otherwise (i.e., the trust's interest is in a traditional IRA and the owner dies on or after the RBD), minimum distributions are calculated based on the fixed period of the owner's life expectancy in the year of death. (See Qs 4:30, 4:36, 5:49.) The trust beneficiary's life expectancy is completely irrelevant.

Example. Mike maintains a large traditional IRA. He names two beneficiaries for it—an inter vivos trust, intended to qualify under Code Section 401(a)(9), that will inherit the part of the IRA valued at the estate tax exemption amount for the year of Mike's death, and his wife, Elsa, who will inherit the rest. Mike dies in 2009 before his RBD. Unfortunately, the trust instrument is poorly drafted (it does not become irrevocable upon Mike's death), and because the look-through rules are not satisfied there is no designated beneficiary for the trust's share of the IRA ($3.5 million). That part of the IRA must be fully distributed to the trust within five years after Mike's death.

Q 10:11   If an exemption trust is correctly named as an IRA beneficiary and the IRA owner dies on or after his or her required beginning date, how is the IRA distributed after the surviving spouse dies?

If an IRA is payable to an exemption trust that satisfies the "see-through" requirements of Treasury Regulations Section 1.401(a)(9)-4, Q&A-5(b) (see Q 10:9), then upon the death of the surviving spouse who was treated as the designated beneficiary of the IRA, the distribution period for the IRA is the remaining term of years in the surviving spouse's distribution period. Thus, if the surviving spouse was age 65 after the death of the IRA owner and, therefore, had a life expectancy of 21 years, the subsequent death of the surviving spouse before the expiration of the 21-year period will permit distributions to the exemption trust for the balance of the original 21-year period. [Treas. Reg. § 1.401(a)(9)-5, Q&A-7(c)]

Q 10:12   How may a disclaimer be used with a testamentary exemption trust?

If an IRA owner names his or her spouse as the primary IRA beneficiary and a testamentary exemption trust as the contingent beneficiary, the surviving spouse may disclaim the decedent's IRA and have the beneficiary of the exemption trust become the designated IRA beneficiary. Although the designated beneficiaries are not determined until September 30 of the year following the year of the IRA owner's death, the disclaimer must be made within nine months after the owner's death. Otherwise, the disclaimer is not effective for estate and gift tax purposes. [I.R.C. § 2518(b); Treas. Reg. § 1.401(a)(9)-4, Q&A-4(a)]

In General Counsel Memorandum 39858, the IRS sanctioned the use of qualified disclaimers with IRAs and held that a properly executed disclaimer is not an impermissible assignment of income, nor does it violate the nonforfeitability requirement of Code Section 408(a)(4). For income tax and estate planning purposes, the disclaiming party is treated as having predeceased the IRA owner, and the IRA's contingent beneficiary is elevated to primary beneficiary status.

Q 10:13   Does designating an exemption trust as the primary or contingent IRA beneficiary violate the irrevocability requirement of a see-through trust?

No. The testamentary trust named as the IRA owner's beneficiary may use the life expectancy of the underlying trust beneficiary to determine post-death minimum distributions. [*See* Preamble to Treas. Reg. § 1.401(a)(9), 67 Fed. Reg. 18,988–19,028 (2002); Treas. Reg. § 1.401(a)(9)-5, Q&A-7(c)(3).] Of course, the various requirements applicable to all trusts named as beneficiaries must be satisfied on a timely basis (see Q 10:9). [Treas. Reg. § 1.401(a)(9)-4, Q&A-5(b)]

Q 10:14   Is a traditional IRA the optimum asset to use for taking full advantage of a taxpayer's estate tax exemption amount?

No. A traditional IRA is generally one of the least attractive assets for funding an estate tax exemption because income taxes have not yet been paid on the IRA assets. Other financial assets get a stepped-up basis at the owner's death under Code Section 1014, but not IRAs because distributions are treated as income in respect of the decedent.

Example. Les, who is in the 35 percent income tax bracket, has a traditional IRA worth $3 million. His IRA would be worth only $1,225,000 after taxes if it were totally distributed. At an assumed estate tax rate of 45 percent, using the IRA to fund the exemption amount effectively produces aggregate tax savings of only $1,023,750. If Les had other financial assets to fund the $3 million estate tax exemption (applicable in 2008), his effective tax savings would be $1,575,000.

It is clear from the preceding example that using a taxpayer's traditional IRA to fund the estate tax exemption amount produces a significantly smaller overall tax benefit than using other financial assets.

Practice Pointer. If a taxpayer's estate has no other significant assets, using a traditional IRA to fund the estate tax exemption amount is always better than forgoing the exemption entirely.

Q 10:15 What are other potential disadvantages of using an IRA to fund an exemption trust?

One potential disadvantage of using an IRA to fund a taxpayer's estate tax exemption amount is that the IRA may not be rolled over by the surviving spouse to a new spousal IRA. As a result, the annual post-death distributions from an IRA that are used to fund the estate tax exemption amount will be larger than the annual distributions from a spousal rollover IRA. That is the case for a traditional IRA simply because the calculation of distributions from an IRA used to fund the estate tax exemption amount will, in most cases, be based on the surviving spouse's remaining single life expectancy. By contrast, in the case of a spousal rollover to a new traditional IRA, the surviving spouse may use the Uniform Table to calculate his or her RMDs. If a Roth IRA is used to fund the exemption trust, the spouse's inability to treat the Roth IRA as his or her own also means that RMDs must be taken during the spouse's lifetime, rather than allowed to accumulate for beneficiaries (see Q 9:16).

Q 10:16 Is there a benefit to using a Roth IRA to fund an exemption trust?

Yes. Roth IRA distributions to a beneficiary are tax free (unlike distributions from a traditional IRA), so funding a decedent's exemption trust with a Roth IRA is an excellent way to transfer wealth to heirs (see Qs 10:57, 10:59).

Distributions

After the Traditional IRA Owner's Required Beginning Date

Q 10:17 How are a traditional IRA owner's required minimum distributions determined?

Unless the owner's spouse is the sole beneficiary of the IRA and the spouse is more than 10 years younger than the IRA owner, the regulations require that the applicable divisors set forth in the Uniform Table be used for calculating the IRA owner's RMDs. The life expectancy factors in the table are premised on the assumption that the IRA owner's beneficiary is exactly 10 years younger than the IRA owner, regardless of the beneficiary's actual age. Thus, if an IRA owner who is age 70½ names a beneficiary who is age 90, he or she may use a life expectancy period of 27.4 years in the first year of distributions under the Uniform Table even though the joint life expectancy of the owner and the beneficiary is closer to 17 years.

It should be noted that if a spouse beneficiary is more than 10 years younger than the owner of the traditional IRA joint life expectancy is recalculated based on the actual ages of the spouses.

Q 10:18 **If an IRA owner dies at age 85 in 2008 after having named his or her grandchild and a charity as equal beneficiaries, can the grandchild use his or her own life expectancy to determine the distribution period?**

The distribution of a beneficiary's interest in an IRA before September 30 of the year following the year of the IRA owner's death renders such a beneficiary's life expectancy irrelevant in the calculation of post-death distributions to the remaining IRA beneficiaries. [Treas. Reg. § 1.401(a)(9)-4, Q&A-4(a)] Thus, if the charity's interest in the IRA is fully distributed before September 30, 2008, the grandchild as the sole remaining beneficiary may use his or her own life expectancy in determining the IRA owner's post-death distributions.

Q 10:19 **Should a traditional IRA owner wait until April 1 of the year following his or her attainment of age 70½ to withdraw the first required minimum distribution?**

It may be advisable for a traditional IRA owner to wait until April 1 of the year following his or her attainment of age 70½ to take the first RMD because the three-month grace period between December 31 and April 1 provides an extra year of tax deferral. However, waiting until April of the year following the attainment of age 70½ results in the taxpayer being required to take two distributions in the same year: the first year's distribution by April 1 and the second year's distribution by December 31, which could cause some income to be taxed at a higher marginal rate.

Moreover, the RMD for a traditional IRA's second distribution year will be higher if the IRA owner uses the three-month grace period, because taking the RMD in the first year reduces the account balance used in determining the RMD for the second year. [Treas. Reg. § 1.408-8, Q&A-6]

Before the IRA Owner Attains Age 59½

Q 10:20 **What strategy can a traditional or Roth IRA owner use to eliminate his or her exposure to the 10 percent premature distribution penalty?**

Under Code Section 72(t)(2)(A)(iv), the IRS allows an IRA owner to avoid the 10 percent penalty on withdrawals made before age 59½ by making a series of substantially equal periodic payments over his or her life expectancy or over the joint life expectancy of the owner and his or her designated beneficiary. The distributions must continue without interruption until age 59½ or for five years, whichever is longer. There is no minimum age that an owner must attain to qualify under this exception.

In Notice 89-25, Q&A-12 [1989-1 C.B. 662], the IRS approved three calculation methods under which payments from an IRA will be considered substantially equal periodic payments:

1. *The required distribution method.* Any method acceptable for calculating RMDs under Code Section 401(a)(9). (The preamble to the final regulations under Code Section 401(a)(9) provides that a taxpayer is permitted to switch to the factors contained in the Uniform Table after beginning annuitization based on the 1987 proposed regulations. Such a change is not considered an impermissible modification.)

2. *The fixed amortization method.* Any method under which the amount to be distributed annually is determined by amortizing the IRA owner's account balance over a number of years equal to the life expectancy of the owner or the joint life expectancy of the owner and beneficiary at an interest rate that does not exceed a reasonable interest rate on the date payments commence. For example, at an interest rate of 8 percent, a 50-year-old IRA owner with a life expectancy of 34.2 years and an account balance of $100,000 could satisfy Code Section 72(t)(2)(A)(iv) by distributing $8,400 annually, derived by amortizing $100,000 over 34.2 years at 8 percent interest.

3. *The fixed annuitization method.* Any method under which the annual payment is determined by dividing the IRA owner's account balance by an annuity factor (the present value of an annuity of $1 per year beginning at the owner's age attained in the first distribution year and continuing for the life of the owner), with the annuity factor derived using a reasonable mortality table and using an interest rate that does not exceed a reasonable interest rate on the date payments commence.

Note. In Revenue Ruling 2002-62 [2002-2 C.B. 710], the IRS modified the provisions of Notice 89-25 to permit a taxpayer who had chosen either the fixed amortization method or the fixed annuitization method to make a one-time election to switch to the required distribution method. This modification would have the effect of lowering the amount of the annual distribution.

The IRS permits the Section 72(t) calculation methods to be applied on an IRA-to-IRA basis; that is, an individual who maintains multiple IRAs is permitted to annuitize any one or more of the IRAs in determining substantially equal periodic payments. Thus, in Private Letter Ruling 9816028 (Jan. 16, 1998), distributions from seven of a taxpayer's 10 IRAs were held to satisfy this requirement.

Caution. For distributions commencing on or after January 1, 2003, Revenue Ruling 2002-62 requires that the interest rate used not exceed 120 percent of the federal mid-term rate for either of the two months immediately preceding the month in which the distributions begin.

Q 10:21   Will the substantially equal periodic payment requirement be satisfied if each year's distribution is increased by a predetermined cost-of-living factor?

Yes. In Private Letter Ruling 9816028 (Jan. 16, 1998), the IRS concluded that the application of a 3 percent cost-of-living factor to each distribution would not violate the requirement that the distributions be substantially equal periodic payments.

Q 10:22   If investment returns on an IRA exceed the expected return, may the IRA owner modify the method for calculating substantially equal periodic payments to produce higher annual distributions?

No. In Private Letter Ruling 9821056 (Feb. 24, 1998), the IRS held that a change in the calculation method to account for greater than expected investment returns would constitute an impermissible modification of substantially equal periodic payments and would result in the application of the 10 percent premature distribution penalty. Under Code Section 72(t)(4)(A), the only modifications that are permitted are those attributable to the taxpayer's death or disability. (See, however, Revenue Ruling 2002-62, discussed in Q 10:20.) In Private Letter Ruling 200105066 (Nov. 9, 2000), the IRS permitted a taxpayer to calculate substantially equal periodic payments based on an updated account balance each year. The key to the ruling is that this methodology was established from the beginning and therefore was not a modification of a previously established method.

Q 10:23   If substantially equal periodic payments from an IRA have commenced, may the IRA owner cease making distributions by rolling over the IRA to a qualified plan without incurring the 10 percent premature distribution penalty?

No. Ceasing to take IRA distributions either before attaining age 59½ or within five years of commencing distributions, whichever is later, constitutes an impermissible modification of substantially equal periodic payments and would result in the imposition of the 10 percent premature distribution penalty. This would be the case even if the reason for the cessation of distributions was a rollover of the IRA to a qualified plan. [Priv. Ltr. Rul. 9818055 (Feb. 2, 1998)]

Before the Traditional IRA Owner's Required Beginning Date

Q 10:24   If a traditional IRA owner dies before his or her required beginning date, having named an individual as his or her beneficiary, under what circumstances would the five-year rule apply to the distributions from the IRA?

The five-year rule applies only when the IRA document mandates this method of distribution. [Treas. Reg. § 1.401(a)(9)-3, Q&A-4(a)(1)] Thus, an individual beneficiary is permitted to use his or her remaining life expectancy in determining post-death distributions.

Note. If any IRA beneficiary is not an individual on September 30 of the year following the year of the IRA owner's death, the five-year rule is still applicable. In such cases, all distributions must be made no later than

December 31 of the year in which the fifth anniversary of the IRA owner's death occurs. [Treas. Reg. § 1.401(a)(9)-3, Q&A-2, Q&A-4(a)(2)]

Q 10:25   If distributions to the nonspouse beneficiary have not commenced by December 31 of the calendar year following the owner's death, can the life expectancy method still be used for distributions?

Yes, based on a favorable ruling that the IRS granted in 2008. [*See* Priv. Ltr. Rul. 200811028 (Mar. 14, 2008), discussed at Q 4:40.] The life expectancy method should still be available if the following requirements are met:

1. Makeup distributions of all missed RMDs (as determined under the life expectancy method) are made, presumably before the last date for making a distribution under the five-year rule;

2. The beneficiary pays the 50 percent excise tax for each year in which there was an excess accumulation of untimely paid RMDs;

3. The IRA provisions do not prohibit distributions based on life expectancy; and

4. The beneficiary has not affirmatively elected the five-year method.

Beneficiaries

Nonspouse Beneficiary

Q 10:26   What precautions should a nonspouse beneficiary take to avoid an acceleration of income taxes after the death of the IRA owner?

A nonspouse beneficiary should make sure that the inherited traditional IRA or Roth IRA is not retitled in his or her name. If the IRA is retitled, the IRS will take the position that the entire IRA has been distributed inasmuch as a nonspouse beneficiary may not roll over the decedent's IRA to a new IRA in the beneficiary's name. After the death of the IRA owner, the retitling of the account should include a reference to the decedent. For example, a proper retitling could read: "First City Bank as Custodian for Joseph Smith, deceased, for benefit of Mary Smith, beneficiary." The beneficiary's Social Security number must be supplied to the IRA custodian or trustee for annual tax reporting purposes.

Q 10:27   If a nonspouse beneficiary of an IRA effects a trustee-to-trustee transfer of his or her interest in the IRA, in whose name should the new IRA be established?

A nonspouse beneficiary who effects a trustee-to-trustee transfer of his or her interest in an IRA must establish the new IRA in the name of the original deceased IRA owner; otherwise, the IRA will be treated as though it were distributed in its entirety to the beneficiary. That is, the beneficiary must remain the beneficiary of the newly created account. [Priv. Ltr. Ruls. 9810033 (Dec. 10, 1997), 9810032 (Dec. 10, 1997)]

Q 10:28 May a nonspouse IRA beneficiary name his or her own beneficiary to continue to receive distributions from the decedent spouse's IRA until the nonspouse beneficiary's life expectancy has expired?

Yes. A beneficiary may designate a subsequent beneficiary for distributions that would occur after the death of the initial beneficiary. [Treas. Reg. § 1.401(a)(9)-5, Q&A-7(c)(2)] In addition, if the designated beneficiary whose life expectancy is being used to calculate the distribution period dies, his or her remaining life expectancy will be used to determine the distribution period applicable to the subsequent beneficiary, regardless of the life expectancy of the subsequent beneficiary. Thus, even if the subsequent beneficiary is older than the deceased designated beneficiary (or has no life expectancy, as in the case of an estate or charity), the applicable distribution period is the deceased beneficiary's remaining life expectancy.

Q 10:29 If an IRA owner's estate is named the IRA beneficiary, may the executor of the estate assign the right to receive IRA payments to the beneficiaries of the estate?

Yes. Assigning the right to receive IRA distributions to the beneficiaries of the IRA owner's estate does not accelerate the payment of income tax on the IRA. [*See* I.R.C. § 691(a)(2); Treas. Reg. § 1.691(a)-4(b)(2).]

However, such an assignment also does not lengthen the distribution period even if the assignment occurs before September 30 of the year following the year of the IRA owner's death. Thus, if the traditional IRA owner died before his or her RBD, the entire IRA must be distributed according to the five-year rule (see Q 10:24). If the traditional IRA owner died after attaining his or her RBD, the distribution period is the IRA owner's remaining life expectancy in the year of his or her death. [Treas. Reg. § 1.401(a)(9)-5, Q&A-5(c)(3), Q&A-6(a)] (See Q 10:31.)

Q 10:30 If the executor of the IRA owner's estate assigns to the beneficiaries of the estate the right to receive IRA distributions, can the beneficiaries establish separate IRAs with their respective shares?

Yes, as long as the separate IRAs are created by trustee-to-trustee transfer. Since nonspouse beneficiaries are not permitted to roll over funds to a new IRA by taking a withdrawal and redepositing the funds within 60 days, a trustee-to-trustee transfer to a new IRA is the only permissible method of establishing a new IRA account. In Private Letter Ruling 200343030 (July 31, 2003), the IRS ruled that once the estate's interest in the decedent's IRA has been assigned to the decedent's beneficiaries under his will, the transfer of funds from the decedent's IRA performed by trustee-to-trustee transfer to an inherited IRA is not a taxable distribution to the estate or to the beneficiary. The inherited IRA would be retitled, for example, "John Smith, deceased, f/b/o Susan Smith, beneficiary thereof."

Q 10:31 What is the advantage to having the executor of an estate assign the right to IRA distributions to the beneficiaries of the estate?

The primary advantage of assigning IRA distributions to the estate beneficiaries is that it allows the estate to close its affairs and file final tax returns. In the absence of such assignment, an estate must remain open solely for the purpose of transferring distributions from the IRA to the estate beneficiaries. From a minimum distribution standpoint, however, the assignment by the estate to an individual beneficiary does not lengthen the payout schedule. For a decedent dying after his or her RBD, the payout schedule remains the decedent's remaining single life expectancy as calculated in the year of his or her death. The IRA beneficiary subtracts one from the life expectancy in each subsequent year to determine the appropriate divisor for calculating minimum distributions.

Surviving Spouse

Q 10:32 What timely actions must a spouse beneficiary of an IRA take if he or she is over age 70½ at the time of the IRA owner's death?

Upon the death of the IRA owner, a surviving spouse who is over age 70½ must do the following on a timely basis:

1. Decide whether to roll over the IRA to his or her own IRA;
2. Determine who the beneficiaries of the spousal IRA are; and
3. Decide whether to establish separate IRAs for each beneficiary.

Q 10:33 When should a spouse beneficiary not perform a spousal rollover after the death of the IRA owner?

If the spouse beneficiary of the deceased IRA owner is younger than age 59½ and will need to make immediate use of a large portion of the IRA, a spousal rollover should not be performed. An immediate distribution from the spousal IRA would be subject to the 10 percent premature distribution penalty under Code Section 72(t). As long as the IRA remains in the name of the IRA owner, such a distribution to the IRA beneficiary would not be subject to the 10 percent penalty. [See I.R.C. § 72(t)(2)(A)(ii).]

Q 10:34   When might it be advisable for a spouse beneficiary to roll over a portion of the decedent's IRA to a spousal IRA and retain the balance in the decedent's IRA?

For maximum flexibility, a spouse beneficiary who is younger than age 59½ and who needs to withdraw a large portion of the decedent's IRA for his or her own living expenses may consider rolling over only a portion of the deceased spouse's IRA to a spousal IRA. Doing so would shelter the portion not rolled over from the 10 percent premature distribution penalty at the time of withdrawal. The surviving spouse would be able to name his or her own beneficiary for the IRA created with the amount rolled over, thereby making it possible for the IRA to continue after his or her death for a longer duration. After the surviving spouse attains age 59½, he or she may then roll over the balance of the decedent's IRA to a spousal IRA. The final regulations make it clear that a surviving spouse's election to roll over the decedent spouse's IRA to a spousal IRA may be made at any time. [Treas. Reg. § 1.408-8, Q&A-5]

Q 10:35   What happens if an IRA owner fails to withdraw the required minimum distribution in the year of his or her death?

If a traditional IRA owner dies without withdrawing the RMD in the year of his or her death, his or her surviving spouse may not roll over that portion of the IRA to which the distribution is attributable. [Priv. Ltr. Rul. 9211059 (Dec. 20, 1991)] Thus, before making a spousal rollover, the surviving spouse must withdraw the RMD from the decedent's traditional IRA to avoid the 50 percent penalty under Code Section 4974 based on the amount that should have been withdrawn in the year of death. [Treas. Reg. § 1.408-8, Q&A-5(a)]

> **Note.** The 50 percent penalty may be waived by the IRS if the owner's failure to withdraw the RMD was the result of reasonable error and reasonable steps were taken to remedy the shortfall. [I.R.C. § 4974(d)]

Q 10:36   If a traditional IRA owner fails to withdraw the RMD in the year of his or her death, does the amount of that distribution belong to the decedent IRA owner's estate or to the IRA beneficiary?

The RMD that is not taken in the year of the traditional IRA owner's death belongs to the IRA beneficiary, because an IRA is not an asset of the decedent's probate estate. The right to the IRA would pass by operation of law to the IRA beneficiary. In many situations this distinction is important because the IRA beneficiaries and the beneficiaries of the decedent's estate may be entirely different classes of individuals.

Q 10:37   If a spouse beneficiary of an IRA names two of his or her children as successor beneficiaries, may each child use his or her own life expectancy in determining required minimum distributions from the IRA after the death of the spouse beneficiary?

Yes, provided the IRA is divided into two separate IRAs for each child by December 31 of the year following the year of the spouse beneficiary's death. [Treas. Reg. § 1.401(a)(9)-8, Q&A-2(a)(2)] If the children fail to divide a traditional IRA by the December 31 deadline, the RMDs would be calculated using the life expectancy of the older child.

Q 10:38   Is it advisable for a spouse beneficiary with multiple IRA beneficiaries to divide the IRA into separate accounts before his or her death?

Yes, such a division is advisable if the spouse beneficiary is concerned that his or her beneficiaries may not act before the December 31 deadline or that the IRA trustee or custodian may not permit such action. If, however, the surviving spouse's beneficiaries are knowledgeable about the law and the importance of prompt action, and the IRA trustee or custodian permits the division of the account after death, there is no advantage under the final regulations to dividing the IRA into separate accounts before the spouse beneficiary's death.

Q 10:39   If a spouse beneficiary rolls over the decedent's IRA to a spousal rollover IRA, what happens if the spouse beneficiary remarries and names a new spouse as his or her IRA beneficiary?

The spouse beneficiary's new spouse is treated as a nonspouse beneficiary, and the delayed commencement rules of Code Section 401(a)(9)(B)(iv) are not available to the new spouse upon the death of the spouse beneficiary. [Treas. Reg. § 1.401(a)(9)-3, Q&A-5] Thus, distributions to the new spouse must begin by December 31 of the year following the year of the death of the spouse beneficiary and may not be postponed to the year in which the spouse beneficiary would have attained age 70½. The new spouse may not effect a rollover to a new IRA.

Q 10:40   If a spouse beneficiary rolls over the decedent spouse's traditional IRA to a spousal IRA, may he or she subsequently roll over that IRA to a qualified plan in which he or she participates?

Yes. [See I.R.C. § 408(d)(3)(A).] Thus, the commingling of a rollover IRA with a traditional IRA funded with annual contributions no longer prevents the IRA from being rolled over to a qualified plan.

Note. A Roth IRA may not be rolled over to a qualified plan. [Treas. Reg. § 1.408A-6, Q&A-17]

Trusts

Q 10:41   If a marital trust is the beneficiary of a IRA, may the surviving spouse elect to treat it as his or her own IRA?

No. A surviving spouse may only elect to treat the decedent's IRA as his or her own IRA if the surviving spouse is the sole beneficiary of the IRA and has an unlimited right to withdraw amounts from it. According to Treasury Regulations Section 1.408-8, Q&A-5, these requirements are not met if a trust is the beneficiary of the decedent's IRA, even if the surviving spouse is the sole beneficiary of the trust. [Priv. Ltr. Rul. 200644028 (Nov. 3, 2006)]

Q 10:42   If a marital trust is the beneficiary of a IRA, may the surviving spouse roll over distributions from the trust to his or her own IRA?

Yes. The Preamble to the final regulations under Code Section 408 [T.D. 8787 (Apr. 16, 2002)] states that a surviving spouse who *actually receives* a distribution from an IRA of the decedent spouse is permitted to roll that distribution over to an IRA in the surviving spouse's name (except to the extent it is a required minimum distribution), even if the distribution is paid from a trust that the surviving spouse controls as both trustee and beneficiary. [Priv. Ltr. Rul. 200644028 (Nov. 3, 2006)]

> **Note.** In Private Letter Ruling 200644028 (Nov. 3, 2006) and others like it (e.g., Private Letter Ruling 200424011 (Mar. 17, 2004)), the IRS reaches the seemingly contradictory conclusion (see Q 10:49) that a surviving spouse who can compel a distribution of the IRA from a trust may roll it over, but may not elect to treat the IRA as his or her own IRA without undergoing that formal distribution step.

Q 10:43   Can an IRA be transferred to the owner's surviving spouse in a manner that qualifies the transfer for the estate tax marital deduction yet also restricts the spouse's power over the property?

Yes. A qualified terminable interest property (QTIP) trust may be used to accomplish this objective (see Qs 8:37–8:43).

Q 10:44   Should a surviving spouse name an IRA beneficiary through an irrevocable inter vivos trust rather than directly?

A surviving spouse should name an irrevocable inter vivos trust as an IRA beneficiary rather than directly naming an individual as the IRA beneficiary in the following circumstances:

1. If the IRA beneficiary is a minor or otherwise unable to make sound financial and tax decisions with respect to the IRA, a trust will offer valuable protection.

2. An IRA that is held through a trust will not be considered part of the beneficiary's marital estate in the event of the beneficiary's divorce.

3. An IRA that is held through a trust can be continued by contingent trust beneficiaries after the primary beneficiary's death rather than pass in accordance with the primary beneficiary's will.

4. An IRA that is held through a trust will not be subject to estate tax at the time of the beneficiary's death. It can be continued by the trust's contingent beneficiaries after the death of the original trust beneficiary without triggering an estate tax. (If the contingent beneficiaries are the grandchildren of the surviving spouse, however, generation-skipping issues could be raised at the time of the surviving spouse's death.)

Q 10:45 What is a special-needs trust?

A special-needs trust can be a valuable tool for parents who are trying to plan for the future of a disabled child. The trust can be funded with inheritances, life insurance, and family gifts—including an inherited IRA. Setting up a special-needs trust can make it possible for a disabled adult to draw on family funds for supplemental needs while still receiving government assistance. Government programs such as the federal Supplemental Security Income program and Medicaid support only basic needs such as food, clothing, and medical care and generally only accept people with less than $2,000 in assets.

Q 10:46 May an inherited IRA be payable to a special-needs trust?

Yes, a parent can leave an IRA to a special-needs trust and name the trust as the beneficiary of the IRA. The rules applicable to a special-needs trust are detailed and the trust should be prepared so as to provide supplemental benefits for the disabled individual without disqualifying him or her from government benefit programs.

Both traditional and Roth IRAs may be left to the trust. In fact, it may be advisable to convert the traditional IRA to a Roth IRA because the withdrawals from the Roth IRA would generally be tax free. Therefore, the trust would owe no taxes on any distributions it held (although it would have to pay tax on additional earnings).

Q 10:47 How may a parent leave an IRA to benefit an adult disabled child?

The best option for a parent who wants to leave an IRA to benefit an adult disabled child is to ensure that the trust qualifies as a "see-through trust" for minimum distribution purposes. In that event, IRA distributions can be stretched out over the life expectancy of the oldest beneficiary (ideally, the disabled individual or a sibling). For a special-needs trust to qualify as a see-through trust, the following are required:

- The terms of the trust must provide for it to terminate upon the death of the oldest beneficiary and be paid outright at such time to individual beneficiaries.
- The trust must be valid under state law.
- The trust either is irrevocable or will be irrevocable upon the death of the IRA owner.
- Beneficiaries of the trust who are beneficiaries with respect to the trust's interest in the IRA are identifiable from the trust instruments.
- The IRA custodian must be in possession of the trust document and informed of any amendments.

Q 10:48   Is there a way that a disabled child can preserve both an inherited IRA and his or her qualification for government benefits where the parent dies and leaves the IRA outright to the child?

Successful post-mortem planning was applied to such a situation in Private Letter Ruling 200620025 (May 19, 2006). The IRA owner had named his four sons as equal beneficiaries of his IRA. One son was disabled, and direct receipt of his share would have disqualified him from receiving Medicaid benefits. The son's guardian was able to avoid that result by transferring, by means of a court order, the son's IRA share to a trust that was designed to meet the requirements of a supplemental needs trust. Assets placed in such a trust are not considered to belong to the individual for Medicaid qualification purposes.

The Decedent's Estate

Q 10:49   If the estate is named as the IRA beneficiary and the spouse is both the executor and the sole beneficiary of the estate, may the spouse roll over the IRA or elect to treat it as his or her own IRA?

Relying on Treasury Regulation Section 1.408-8, Q&A-5 (as it does in the trust-as-beneficiary context), the IRS has concluded that a surviving spouse may not elect to treat an IRA that passes through the estate as his or her own, even if the spouse is the sole executor and has authority to allocate the IRA to a portion of the estate of which the spouse is the sole beneficiary. On the other hand, a surviving spouse who *actually receives* a distribution of the IRA from the estate (even if the spouse, as executor, has authority to compel it) may roll over the distribution to an IRA in the spouse's name. [Priv. Ltr. Rul. 200644031 (Nov. 3, 2006)]

Charity

Q 10:50   Why should a charitable bequest be made by naming a charity as the beneficiary of a traditional IRA rather than by using other assets in the estate for such purpose?

By using traditional IRA assets to make a charitable bequest, an individual uses pretax assets rather than after-tax assets in the estate to meet his or her charitable objectives. The charity is not taxed on the IRA distributions, and a bequest of other assets to the family—assets that do not yield income in respect of a decedent (IRD), and that do get a step-up in basis at death—is more valuable to them (see Qs 8:63, 8:64).

Q 10:51   If an IRA owner has multiple beneficiaries, including a charity, what should be done after the owner's death to extend the distribution period to the individual beneficiaries?

The charity's interest in the IRA should be cashed out before September 30 of the year following the year of the IRA owner's death. If the September 30 deadline is met, the charity is disregarded in determining the payout term to the remaining IRA beneficiaries. If the September 30 deadline is not met, the payout from the IRA will be greatly accelerated (see Qs 4:30, 4:36, 5:49).

Q 10:52   What distribution period applies to an IRA that is payable to a trust if one of the remainder beneficiaries is a charity?

In what may be viewed as a trap for the unwary, the IRS treats a remainder beneficiary as a co-beneficiary if amounts are accumulated in the trust for the remainder beneficiary during the life of the primary trust beneficiary. [Treas. Reg. § 1.401(a)(9)-5, Q&A-7(c)(3)] Thus, if an IRA is payable to a trust that may accumulate amounts for a charity, the IRA owner will be treated as having no designated beneficiary, and the IRA distribution period will be accelerated (see Qs 4:30, 4:36, 5:49).

Q 10:53   What are the advantages and disadvantages of naming a charitable remainder trust as a traditional IRA beneficiary?

A traditional IRA owner may name a charitable remainder trust (CRT) as the IRA beneficiary by completing the appropriate IRA beneficiary forms with the IRA trustee or custodian. Upon the IRA owner's death, all the IRA assets would be distributed to the CRT without triggering an income tax. The decedent owner's estate would receive an estate tax deduction equal to the present value of the charity's remainder interest. The disadvantage of leaving a traditional IRA to a CRT is that CRT beneficiaries may not access the principal of the trust, and distributions to the CRT are not treated as income in respect of a decedent (IRD), thereby making the distributions ineligible for the IRD deduction (see Q 10:76).

Continuing the IRA for Future Generations

Q 10:54 How may an IRA be continued to benefit members of future generations if the owner's surviving spouse is named as beneficiary?

Upon the death of an IRA owner who had previously named his or her spouse as the IRA beneficiary, the surviving spouse is permitted to roll over the decedent's IRA to a new spousal IRA and name their children or grandchildren as the new IRA beneficiaries. When the surviving spouse dies, the IRA can continue to generate distributions for subsequent generations because the children's or grandchildren's life expectancies would be used to determine post-death distributions.

Q 10:55 How does naming a contingent beneficiary ensure the preservation of an IRA for a subsequent generation?

Naming a contingent beneficiary is an important step in ensuring the continuation of an IRA. If an IRA owner dies shortly after the death of his or her primary beneficiary without having named a contingent beneficiary, the terms of the IRA document may control and provide for a default beneficiary. Often, the default beneficiary is the IRA owner's estate. By naming a contingent beneficiary, the IRA owner ensures that his or her IRA will continue pursuant to his or her wishes and will enable the contingent beneficiary to use his or her own life expectancy for determining post-death distributions.

Q 10:56 Can an IRA owner designate the beneficiary who will receive distributions from his or her IRA if the primary beneficiary dies before distributions are completed?

Yes. This is an aspect of IRAs that is often overlooked in the estate planning process. If an IRA owner does not name the beneficiary who will succeed his or her primary beneficiary, the IRA document may control the identity of subsequent beneficiaries. Often, when an IRA owner names multiple beneficiaries, the IRA documents provide that the interest of a deceased beneficiary will pass to the remaining beneficiaries. Because this outcome may run counter to the desires of the IRA owner, it is important that the IRA owner complete a beneficiary designation form after the death of his or her primary beneficiary.

IRA Assets and Generation Skipping

Q 10:57 What are the benefits of using IRA assets for generation skipping?

If a grandparent dies after naming a grandchild as a traditional IRA beneficiary, the distributions to the grandchild can be spread out over the grandchild's remaining life expectancy. In such a situation, the value of tax-deferred compounding can be astonishing. For example, an IRA worth $1 million left to a 10-year-old beneficiary could provide distributions of over $40 million to the grandchild if RMDs are made over the life expectancy of the grandchild and the IRA funds are invested at an 8 percent rate of return. The grandchild would also be able to claim a deduction for the portion of the grandparent's federal estate taxes attributable to the IRA pursuant to Code Section 691(c).

Passing a Roth IRA to one's grandchildren is an excellent generation-skipping strategy, because all future distributions will be free of income tax. In addition, the minimum distribution requirements do not apply during the Roth IRA owner's lifetime.

Practice Pointer. Because generation-skipping taxes are not triggered by bequests that do not exceed $3.5 million (for 2009, and possibly later years), an IRA that is not worth more than $3.5 million at the time of the IRA owner's death may be an ideal asset to use for a generation-skipping strategy.

Q 10:58   When must a generation-skipping strategy be implemented in order to be effective for required minimum distribution purposes?

A generation-skipping strategy may be implemented at any time before the IRA owner's death by merely amending the IRA beneficiary form.

Q 10:59   Should a grandparent consider converting a traditional IRA to a Roth IRA as part of a strategy for stretching distributions over the lifetime of grandchildren after the death of the grandparent?

Yes. Once the traditional IRA is converted to a Roth IRA, the RMD elections that were applicable to the IRA are no longer relevant—Roth IRAs are not subject to RMDs during the lifetime of the Roth IRA owner. Moreover, future distributions to the beneficiaries of the Roth IRA would be free of income tax. (For discussion of conversions, see chapters 3 and 9.)

Q 10:60   How are qualified disclaimers used in a generation-skipping strategy?

If an IRA beneficiary who does not need the funds from the IRA after the death of the IRA owner executes a qualified disclaimer within nine months of the IRA owner's death, the IRA passes to the contingent IRA beneficiary. The contingent beneficiary may then use his or her own life expectancy to determine minimum distributions. For this strategy to work, however, the person must already be a contingent beneficiary when the IRA owner dies.

Example. Marie dies in 2009 at age 96 with an IRA valued at $3.5 million. Marie had named her son, Jack, age 70, as her primary beneficiary; her grandson, Donald, age 45, as the contingent beneficiary upon Jack's death;

and her great-granddaughter, Rachel, age 23, as the contingent beneficiary upon Donald's death. Both Jack and Donald are wealthy and do not need Marie's $3.5 million IRA; they also recognize that the IRA will have the greatest value if it can be allowed to compound tax free over the longest possible period. To make that possible, Jack and Donald execute qualified disclaimers within nine months after Marie's death. The result is that they are treated as having predeceased Marie, and the IRA passes to Rachel. Minimum distributions may now be calculated based on Rachel's life expectancy as of the year after Marie's death (58 years).

Note. The regulations encourage this strategy by allowing the identity of the ultimate IRA beneficiary to be determined as late as September 30 of the year following the year of an IRA owner's death. [Treas. Reg. § 1.401(a)(9)-4, Q&A-4(a)]

Q 10:61   What generation-skipping strategies involve IRA assets and life insurance?

Rather than apply the $3.5 million generation-skipping exemption against $3.5 million of IRA assets at the death of the IRA owner, greater advantages may be obtained by withdrawing funds from the IRA and making gifts to grandchildren for purchasing life insurance on the IRA owner. If the $3.5 million generation-skipping exemption is applied against the annual premium on the insurance rather than against the ultimate death benefit, a death benefit of significantly more than $3.5 million can likely be acquired (depending, of course, on the age and insurability of the IRA owner). That death benefit, even when in excess of $3.5 million, would escape generation-skipping tax because only the annual premium (and not the ultimate face amount of coverage) would count against the $3.5 million generation-skipping exemption.

Life Insurance as a Funding Vehicle

Q 10:62   What role can second-to-die life insurance play in the strategy of continuing a large IRA for a second or third generation?

Second-to-die life insurance is an excellent source of liquidity at the death of either the IRA owner or his or her spouse (whoever dies second) to provide the cash necessary to pay estate taxes that become due. With second-to-die life insurance, IRA assets do not have to be prematurely withdrawn by the children or grandchildren to pay the estate tax attributable to the IRA. Using the insurance proceeds to pay the estates taxes allows the IRA to be continued for the lives of the owner's heirs.

Because IRA assets that must be withdrawn to pay estate taxes upon the death of the second spouse to die may leave less than 25 percent of the IRA remaining for beneficiaries (see example in Q 10:73), an optimum pension and estate planning strategy would be for the owner to make accelerated withdrawals from the IRA and use the distributions to make gifts to his or her children or grandchildren (or both). Those gifts could be used to pay the premiums on a second-to-die policy to prefund estate taxes attributable to the IRA. For example, the gift tax exclusion amount for 2009 is $13,000, so if there are five beneficiaries the owner could gift $13,000 to each of them in 2009 without incurring gift tax. [Rev. Proc. 2008-66, 2008-45 I.R.B. 1107] The gifts are also helpful to estate planning because they remove assets from the owner's estate that would otherwise be subject to estate tax when the owner dies.

Q 10:63   May IRA assets be used as a source of premiums to purchase a second-to-die life insurance policy in an IRA?

No. IRA assets may not be invested in a life insurance contract. [I.R.C. § 408(a)(3)] Obviously, however, IRA assets may be withdrawn from the IRA in order to acquire second-to-die life insurance outside the IRA. It is also possible to roll over traditional IRA assets to a qualified plan in which the IRA owner participates in order to purchase insurance with pretax dollars. Such a rollover may be made to the current employer's qualified plan or to a newly adopted Keogh plan covering the IRA owner. Because life insurance is not a prohibited investment under the qualified plan rules, such a strategy may be advisable if the IRA owner is still actively employed or has self-employment income with which to establish a Keogh plan.

Q 10:64   Who should own the second-to-die insurance policy to ensure that the death benefit proceeds are ultimately free of estate taxes?

In order for the proceeds from a second-to-die insurance policy to be received free of estate tax, those insured under the policy may not retain any incidents of ownership in the policy at the time of death. To meet that requirement, an irrevocable life insurance trust is created to own the policy from the outset. The premium payments to the insurance company are made by the trustee of the trust. The funds that are used for premium payments are generally obtained by having the insured make gifts to the trust each year. As long as the trust beneficiaries have the right to withdraw the gifts during the *Crummey* notification period each year, the insured's gifts to the trust qualify as gifts of a "present interest" for gift tax purposes. (The *Crummey* notification period gets its name from the Ninth Circuit case that sanctioned such an arrangement, *Crummey v. Commissioner* [397 F.2d 82 (9th Cir. 1968)].) Thus, the insured may count the premium payments against his or her $13,000 per donee (for 2009) gifting allowance under Code Section 2503(b).

Instead of having an insurance trust own the policy, it is often easier to have the children of the insured person own the policy directly. If the children are responsible adults, such a strategy avoids a significant amount of paperwork and legal fees during the insured's remaining lifetime. The disadvantages of this strategy are that the insurance policy is subject to the children's creditors, could be part of the children's marital estates if the children divorce, and could pass outside the insured's immediate family if a child predeceases the insured.

Q 10:65 Under what circumstances should a married IRA owner consider acquiring a single life insurance policy on his or her own life, rather than a second-to-die insurance policy on the lives of the owner and spouse?

If a married IRA owner wishes to pass all or a portion of his or her IRA assets to his or her children rather than to his or her spouse at death, a single life policy may be used as a funding source for the estate taxes that will become due. Without life insurance, the owner's children might be forced to withdraw funds prematurely from the IRA to obtain cash for paying the estate taxes. Such a withdrawal would defeat the strategy of bypassing the owner's spouse as the IRA beneficiary.

Caution. Either the children or an irrevocable life insurance trust should own the policy. If the policy is payable to the estate and the estate pays the taxes on the IRA, the estate could be deemed the IRA beneficiary—making the proceeds subject to estate tax.

Q 10:66 Should the surviving spouse consider acquiring a life insurance policy to prefund estate tax that will be payable when the spouse dies and the IRA is transferred to the children or grandchildren?

For various reasons, the original IRA owner may not want to acquire a second-to-die insurance policy. After a married IRA owner dies, however, a surviving spouse who is the sole IRA beneficiary may roll over the decedent's IRA to one in the spouse's name, designate the children or grandchildren as beneficiaries, and acquire insurance on his or her life so that later, when the spouse dies, the beneficiaries will be able to pay the estate taxes without draining the IRA.

This is a good strategy for a surviving spouse who has adequate financial resources and is not likely to exhaust the IRA during the spouse's lifetime. Acquiring a single life insurance policy with IRA withdrawals ensures the continuation of the IRA after the surviving spouse's death because there will be ample funds from the insurance to pay estate taxes attributable to the IRA. The insurance policy should be owned by the spouse's heirs either directly or through an irrevocable life insurance trust so that the insurance proceeds will be received free of estate taxes.

Q 10:67 Why does life insurance planning have special significance for IRA owners with large IRA balances?

Using IRA withdrawals to fund an insurance policy that is held outside the IRA owner's estate changes the future form of an investment from a highly taxed asset to one that not only grows tax free during the owner's life but is also transferred, when the owner dies, without being diminished by estate taxes. Once it is clear that the owner is not likely to exhaust the IRA during his or her lifetime, the proper focus from an estate tax standpoint should be on strategies to preserve the IRA for subsequent generations.

This use of a life insurance policy also allows an IRA owner's will to be drafted to apportion the estate tax liability attributable to the IRA to the IRA beneficiaries (instead of charging it against the owner's residual estate). That is a critical factor where the residuary legatees under the will are not the same individuals as the IRA beneficiaries.

Because a second-to-die life insurance policy creates an immediate pool of assets at the death of the IRA owner or the spouse, whichever is later, it is uniquely suited to individuals who wish to preserve their IRAs for the benefit of their children or grandchildren.

Q 10:68 What tax and financial factors are relevant in determining whether life insurance makes sense as part of an overall strategy to preserve an IRA for heirs?

The higher the insured's estate tax bracket, the more valuable life insurance is as an estate planning strategy (see schedule in Q 10:7). Life insurance is not needed to fund federal estate tax if none will be due (i.e., if the IRA owner and spouse will each have assets worth less than the applicable estate tax exemption amount when they die).

A cost-benefit analysis should be done to compare insurance with alternative investments. For example, instead of using IRA withdrawals to fund insurance premiums, the IRA owner could use them to make gifts to his or her children, and the children could invest the gifts in mutual funds. It is useful to consider the after-tax rate of return that mutual funds would have to earn to produce the same pool of assets as the insurance.

Example. Tony, age 55, is an IRA owner whose spouse, Ann, is age 53. Ann will probably have IRA assets of over $6 million when she attains age 70. The total estate tax that the IRA will generate is likely to exceed $2 million. Tony wants to know whether it makes sense to acquire a second-to-die life insurance policy to prefund the estate tax liability and preserve the IRA so it can be continued for their children after both Ann and Tony die. Tony is advised that a single premium of $200,000 will fund a $2 million second-to-die policy on his and Ann's lives. To analyze the financial effect of paying $200,000 to buy a $2 million second-to-die life insurance policy, Tony needs to determine the after-tax rate of return that a non-insurance investment (e.g., a diversified equity-based mutual fund) would have to yield to produce $2 million at stated five-year intervals, as follows.

Year of Second Death	After-Tax Rate of Return Required
5	60.0%
10	25.5%
15	16.9%
20	12.1%
25	9.5%
30	8.0%
35	6.8%
40	6.0%

If Tony thinks that an after-tax return of 8 percent is achievable by the mutual fund over the long term, either he or Ann would have to survive 30 years for the original $200,000 investment to grow to $2 million. If both Tony and Ann die before the end of the 30-year period, a mutual fund that earns 8 percent after tax is inferior to the second-to-die insurance policy. If either Tony or Ann survives beyond 30 years, the mutual fund that earns 8 percent after tax outperforms the insurance investment. The attractiveness of the insurance investment is that the $2 million pool of assets is available as soon as the policy is acquired. Thus, Tony can be assured that adequate funds will be available from the outset to preserve the IRA for another generation.

Q 10:69   **May life insurance be used as an alternative to designating a qualified terminable interest property trust for the IRA owner's surviving spouse as an IRA beneficiary?**

Yes. Using a QTIP trust as an IRA beneficiary is usually proposed when the IRA owner has remarried and wants to preserve the IRA for the children of his or her first marriage. The primary problem in implementing this strategy is that if assets remain in the IRA or QTIP trust at the time of the second spouse's death, the liability for the estate tax triggered by such assets will likely be apportioned by the second spouse to the QTIP trust beneficiaries (the IRA owner's children). As a result, the ultimate value of a traditional IRA held by a QTIP trust after estate and income taxes are paid is generally equal to about 25 percent of the IRA (or for a Roth IRA, 55 percent) at the time of the second spouse's death.

For this reason, it often makes sense to acquire an insurance policy on the life of the IRA owner and to name his or her children as the owners and beneficiaries of the ultimate death benefit. Premiums for such a policy should come from additional IRA withdrawals, and the IRA should be left to the second spouse outright rather than through a QTIP trust. Such a strategy has the following advantages over the QTIP trust:

1. If the policy is owned by the IRA owner's children, they will receive the insurance proceeds free of estate tax and they will not have to wait until the death of the owner's second spouse to inherit assets from their parent.

2. The surviving spouse will be able to name his or her own IRA beneficiaries and potentially have the IRA continued by those beneficiaries after his or her death.

Q 10:70   Does it make sense to use life insurance to replace the value of a traditional IRA that is left to a charitable beneficiary?

Yes. Traditional IRA assets are the most tax-efficient assets for making charitable bequests; such assets in the hands of the IRA owner's heirs would be taxed as income in respect of a decedent. Therefore, a traditional IRA owner who is charitably inclined should amend his or her IRA beneficiary designations to satisfy charitable bequests with IRA assets. Such designations will have the effect of making charitable bequests with assets that otherwise may be worth 25 cents on the dollar to heirs (i.e., the estate and income taxes on every dollar of IRA assets may total 75 cents).

An IRA owner who makes a charitable bequest with his or her traditional IRA may acquire a single life insurance policy or a second-to-die insurance policy and may make premium payments on the policy by making gifts of IRA withdrawals to his or her children. In that way, the children will receive an insured death benefit free of estate tax (if the policy is owned by the children directly or through an irrevocable insurance trust), and the estate will receive a charitable deduction for the IRA assets passing to the charitable beneficiary.

Tax Strategies

Q 10:71   May a taxpayer with a large IRA balance withdraw an IRA for 60 days each year and roll over the balance to a new IRA for the purpose of obtaining an interest-free loan from the IRA?

Yes. By combining two rules—the 60-day rollover provision and the once-yearly rollover limitation—it is possible to withdraw all or a portion of an IRA for 60 days and redeposit the same proceeds into a new IRA. Such a step may be taken if the IRA owner needs funds on a short-term basis and does not wish to borrow from a lending institution.

It is important that the IRA owner redeposit the same proceeds back into the IRA. If the owner received the distribution in cash and purchased stock during the 60-day period after withdrawal, the stock may not be redeposited into the IRA. [I.R.C. § 401(c)(1)] In *Lemishow v. Commissioner* [110 T.C. 110 (1998)], an

IRA owner purchased stock with a distribution of cash from an IRA and Keogh plan and rolled over the stock back to the IRA within 60 days. The Tax Court held that the rollover was improper and that the owner was subject to income tax on the amount impermissibly rolled over to the IRA.

Q 10:72   Should a participant in a qualified plan who has named a nonspouse beneficiary seek to have his or her qualified plan balance transferred to an IRA before death?

Effective in 2007, there is no reason to do so (see Q 6:83). A nonspouse beneficiary may now roll over inherited qualified plan benefits to an IRA established in the name of the decedent (assuming the plan allows it).

Calculation of Aggregate Estate and Income Taxes on Large IRA Balances

Q 10:73   If the top tax brackets for 2009 are assumed for estate and income tax purposes, how large might the combined tax be on a large IRA balance after the deaths of both the IRA owner and his or her spouse?

At the top tax brackets for 2008, the combined estate and income tax liability on a traditional IRA that is withdrawn at death can approach 80 percent.

Example. Carla, a resident of a state that imposes a 16 percent state estate tax (for estates in excess of $10 million) dies in 2009 with $3.5 million in her traditional IRA. If the entire IRA is withdrawn by Carla's heirs to generate enough funds to pay the federal and state estate taxes, the net amount remaining would be only $732,200, calculated as follows:

IRA assets	$3,500,000
ESTATE TAX CALCULATION	
(A deduction is allowed for federal estate tax purposes for state estate taxes actually paid.)	
State estate tax on IRA ($3,500,000 × 16%)	$ 560,000
Value of IRA as reduced by state estate tax	$2,940,000
Maximum federal estate tax bracket equals 45%	
Federal estate tax on IRA ($2,940,000 × 45%)	$1,323,000
Total estate taxes ($560,000 + $1,323,000)	$1,883,000
INCOME TAX CALCULATION	
Total distribution	$3,500,000

Code Section 691(c) deduction for federal estate taxes	$1,323,000
Less: Code Section 68 limitation on itemized deductions ($3,500,000 × 1%)	($ 35,000)
Adjusted itemized deduction	$1,288,000
IRA income net of Section 691(c) deduction ($3,500,000 less $1,288,000)	$2,212,000
Combined federal and state income taxes (at an assumed aggregate 40% rate)	$ 884,800

SUMMARY OF TAXES

Total distribution	$3,500,000
Estate taxes	$1,883,000
Income taxes	$ 884,800
TOTAL TAXES	$2,767,800
Net to heirs	$ 732,200
Percentage of original IRA	20.92%

Calculation of Income in Respect of a Decedent

Q 10:74   How are distributions from a traditional IRA after the death of the IRA owner taxed to the IRA beneficiaries?

Distributions from a traditional IRA after the death of the IRA owner are taxable as income in respect of a decedent under Code Section 691. Such funds are characterized in the same manner in the hands of an IRA beneficiary as they would have been had the decedent lived and received the IRA funds himself or herself.

If the traditional IRA generates an estate tax in the estate of the decedent, Code Section 691(c) allows the IRA beneficiary taking a distribution from the IRA to deduct against the distribution the portion of the federal estate tax attributable to including the IRA in the decedent's estate. The deduction is claimed by the beneficiary on Schedule A, Itemized Deductions, of Form 1040, U.S. Individual Income Tax Return, as a miscellaneous itemized deduction that is not subject to the 2 percent of adjusted gross income (AGI) offset, but is subject to reduction under Code Section 68 (see Q 10:77). The beneficiary must itemize deductions to claim the IRD deduction. It is important to note that Code Section 691(c) permits an income tax deduction only for the federal estate tax and not for the state estate tax.

Note. Distributions to Roth IRA beneficiaries are not taxable income, so those recipients are not allowed a Code Section 691(c) deduction.

Q 10:75   May an IRA beneficiary claim a deduction for federal estate taxes attributable to an IRA before the estate tax is paid?

Yes. In Field Service Advice 200011023, the IRS allowed an IRD deduction to be taken by a beneficiary even though no estate tax had yet been paid. Because an estate tax return does not have to be filed until nine months after the decedent's death, the IRS does not require such filing (and payment of tax) as a precondition for allowing the IRD deduction.

> **Example.** Margaret, age 82, dies on October 1, 2009, before withdrawing her RMD for 2009 from her IRA. In December 2009, Margaret's son, Arnold, as her IRA beneficiary, withdraws the RMD that Margaret would have withdrawn had she lived. Arnold must include the distribution in his 2009 income when he files his tax return by April 15, 2009. On his 2008 federal income tax return, Arnold may claim an IRD deduction for a portion of the federal estate taxes that will be attributable to the IRA distribution even though Margaret's federal estate tax return and estate tax payment are not due until July 1, 2009 (nine months after her death).

Q 10:76   If a charitable remainder trust is named as the beneficiary of a decedent's traditional IRA, may the trust beneficiaries claim a deduction for the estate tax attributable to ordinary income distributed by the trust?

No. The IRS held in Private Letter Ruling 199901023 (Oct. 8, 1998) that because distributions from a traditional IRA to a CRT are treated as "first-tier" ordinary income, annuity payments from the CRT to the CRT beneficiaries would be treated as income first. In so doing, the IRS concluded that an IRD deduction is not distributed from a CRT as part of first-tier income. The effect of the ruling would be to waste the IRD deduction because the CRT is tax exempt and has no use for a tax deduction.

Q 10:77   How is a high-income IRA beneficiary's deduction of the estate tax on IRA assets included in the decedent's estate limited by Code Section 68?

An IRA beneficiary's deduction of the estate tax attributable to a receipt of IRD may be limited by Code Section 68. If the beneficiary's AGI exceeds a base amount (nominally $100,000, but adjusted annually for inflation) for the distribution year, the allowable itemized deductions (including the IRD deduction) must be reduced by a percentage of the excess amount. For 2009, the base amount is $166,800 ($83,400 for married taxpayers filing separately). [Rev. Proc. 2008-66, 2008-45 I.R.B. 1107] The percentage applied to determine the reduction has undergone a phaseout from 3 percent (its level in 2005), to 2 percent in 2006 and 2007, and 1 percent in 2008 and 2009. Like the estate tax, the percentage is supposed to be fully phased out for 2010 only (i.e., the percentage reduction will be zero) and then bounce back in 2011 to the pre-phaseout level of 3 percent. [I.R.C. § 68(f), 68(g)] Congress will likely change that schedule, however.

The Section 68 itemized deduction limits may be triggered if an individual beneficiary withdraws a large amount from the inherited traditional IRA to defray estate taxes in the decedent's estate. However, Code Section 68 does not apply to the tax return of an estate or trust. [I.R.C. § 68(e)] Therefore, it may be advantageous in certain situations to change the beneficiary designation of an IRA to an estate or trust if the IRA cannot otherwise be continued by an individual beneficiary.

IRAs Versus Qualified Plans

Q 10:78   Is an IRA more flexible than a qualified plan as a tool for deferring distributions for subsequent generations?

The IRA is much more flexible than a qualified plan, except in one respect. Unlike an inherited qualified plan interest, which a nonspouse beneficiary may convert to a Roth IRA, an inherited qualified plan interest cannot be converted to a Roth IRA by a nonspouse beneficiary. Otherwise, IRAs have many advantages over qualified plans:

1. To maintain its qualified status, a qualified plan must be amended throughout its existence for all changes in the law. To date, IRAs have not been subject to the continued amendment and requalification concerns that have plagued qualified plans.

2. Form 5500, Annual Return/Report of Employee Benefit Plan, must be filed each year for a qualified plan that has at least $100,000 in assets.

3. A beneficiary of a qualified plan may not vary the distribution amount each year depending on his or her financial needs.

4. A beneficiary of a qualified plan may not be offered the same investment choices and discretion that are possible with an IRA.

5. A qualified plan may not allow a beneficiary to designate a contingent beneficiary to receive the balance of payments upon the death of the primary beneficiary.

6. A qualified plan may not be permitted to continue at all if the employer maintaining the plan ceases to exist.

7. A qualified plan may lose its qualified status if the plan sponsor violates the rules for tax qualification under Code Section 401(a), creating an immediate income tax on the remaining plan benefits.

8. Both spouse and nonspouse beneficiaries of qualified plan interests are eligible to roll their interests over to IRAs and benefit from the greater flexibility that is possible with an IRA (see chapter 6).

Chapter 11

Simplified Employee Pension Plans

Martin Fleisher, Esq.
Jo Ann Lippe, Esq.

The simplified employee pension (SEP) plan was created so that small employers could use the IRA funding technique to provide retirement benefits for their employees without being subject to the complex disclosure, funding, and approval requirements of a qualified ERISA plan. A SEP may be adopted by any employer, whether a corporation, a limited liability company, a limited liability partnership, or a sole proprietorship. Once a SEP is in place, all eligible employees of the employer must be covered by the SEP, even seasonal and part-time workers.

An employer may permit eligible employees to make elective contributions under its SEP; this type of SEP is commonly called a salary reduction SEP (SARSEP). Although SARSEPs were repealed by the Small Business Job Protection Act of 1996 (SBJPA), a SARSEP established before January 1, 1997, may continue to receive contributions under current rules, and employees of the employer hired after December 31, 1996, may participate in the SARSEP in accordance with such rules.

Overview

Q 11:1   What is a simplified employee pension plan?

A *simplified employee pension plan* (SEP) is a written arrangement or program that allows an employer to make tax-deductible contributions to its employees' IRAs. [I.R.C. § 408(k)(1); Prop. Treas. Reg. § 1.408-7] Technically, a SEP is an individual retirement account or individual retirement annuity (IRA) that must meet additional requirements. [I.R.C. § 408(k)(1); Prop. Treas. Reg. § 1.408-7(a)] Internal Revenue Code (Code) Sections 408(a), (b), and (c) set forth the requirements for a valid IRA that is part of a SEP arrangement. Code Sections 408(k)(2) through 408(k)(5) and Code Section 416(c)(2) (if the plan is top heavy) are specific to SEPs. A SEP may be established by a corporate or a noncorporate employer. Generally, each IRA into which SEP contributions are made is in the name of the employee—as is any other IRA—and is known variously as a SEP IRA, a SEP, or, simply, a traditional IRA.

Typically, an employee selects, establishes, and maintains the IRA into which employer SEP contributions are made. Group IRAs, which may be established by an employer or by an employee association under Section 408(c) of the Internal Revenue Code (Code), may qualify as SEPs if additional requirements are met.

Employers that adopt SEPs frequently use IRAs that are sponsored by financial institutions to satisfy some of the underlying IRA requirements applicable to SEPs (SEP IRAs); such IRAs form an essential part of the employer's SEP. [Prop. Treas. Reg. § 1.408-7(b)]

The legislation that enacted SEPs, effective in 1979, appears to have envisioned a combined IRA with SEP provisions in one document. As it came to be, the Internal Revenue Service (IRS) released separate documents in the form of model plans. Both documents, however, are inextricably tied to the existence of a valid SEP.

Q 11:2   What is a salary reduction SEP, or SARSEP?

A *salary reduction SEP* (also called a SARSEP) is a SEP that includes an elective salary deferral feature. SARSEPs have been repealed, meaning that new SARSEPs cannot now be established. Some SARSEPs are grandfathered, however, and, subject to restrictions, participants in those plans are still able to make elective (salary reduction) contributions, including catch-up contributions, with pretax dollars (see Q 11:65).

Q 11:3   What limits apply to a SEP?

The following contribution, income exclusion, deduction, and compensation limits apply to a SEP for tax years beginning in 2009.

Contribution limits. Four limits apply:

1. The total contributions to a participant's account (not including catch-up contributions made by or on behalf of the participant) may not exceed $49,000 (or $54,500, including catch-up contributions, for a participant who is at least 50 years of age during the year) or, if less, 100 percent of compensation. The dollar limits are reduced for highly compensated employees (HCEs) if the SEP is integrated with Social Security (see Qs 11:58, 11:68). [I.R.S. News Release IR-2008-118 (Oct. 16, 2008); I.R.C. §§ 415(k)(4), 415(a)(2), 402(h)(2)(B)]

2. A SARSEP participant's elective deferrals cannot exceed $16,500 ($22,000 for a catch-up eligible participant) or, if less, 25 percent of compensation. [I.R.S. News Release IR-2008-118 (Oct. 16, 2008); I.R.C. §§ 402(h)(2), 414(v)(3)(A); Treas. Reg. § 1.414(v)-1(c)(2)(i).

3. SEP contributions that fail the 125 percent nondiscrimination test of Code Section 408(k)(6)(A)(iii) must be withdrawn from the SEP IRAs of highly compensated employees (HCEs).

4. Under a SARSEP, deferrals are disallowed unless at least 50 percent of the eligible participants elect deferral. [I.R.C. § 408(k)(6)(A)(ii)]

Exclusion limit. Contributions allocated to an individual's SEP IRA are excludable from income except to the extent they exceed 25 percent of that participant's includable taxable compensation (as determined without reduction for catch-up contributions). (Catch-up contributions are always excludable.) The 25 percent exclusion limit for regular contributions is computed using each participant's compensation for the calendar year in which the plan year began. [I.R.C. § 402(h)(2)]

Deduction limit. All of an employer's SEP contributions (excluding elective deferrals) are deductible up to the deduction limit, which is 25 percent of the aggregate plan year compensation (including, for this purpose, all elective deferrals) of all plan participants. Elective (including catch-up) contributions are also deductible without regard to compensation. Contributions that exceed the exclusion limit and therefore must be included in participants' income may nonetheless be deductible. [I.R.C. § 402(h)(1)(C)]

Covered compensation. In applying the above limits, any individual's compensation over $245,000 is ignored. [I.R.C. § 408(k)(3)(C); I.R.S. News Release IR-2008-118 (Oct. 16, 2008)]

Q 11:4   Are the above limits adjusted for inflation?

Yes. Cost-of-living adjustments are applied annually to increase the total contribution limit ($49,000) by $1,000 increments, the covered compensation limit ($245,000) by $5,000 increments, the elective deferral limit ($16,500) by $500 increments, and the catch-up contribution limit ($5,500) by $500 increments. (Figures in parentheses are as adjusted for 2009.) [I.R.C. §§ 402(g)(4), 402(h)(2), 414(v)(3)(A); Treas. Reg. § 1.414(v)-1(c)]

Q 11:5   What elements must an IRA contain to be treated as a SEP?

An IRA must contain the following elements to be treated as a SEP:

1. Top-heavy contribution requirements [I.R.C. § 408(k)(1)(B)];
2. Minimum participation requirements [I.R.C. § 408(k)(2)];
3. Nondiscriminatory allocation requirements [I.R.C. § 408(k)(3)];
4. Unlimited access to nonelective contributions [I.R.C. § 408(k)(4)];
5. Written allocation formula [I.R.C. § 408(k)(5)]; and
6. Restrictions on the withdrawal of elective contributions to a SARSEP before March 15 or an earlier written determination by the employer that amounts deferred by HCEs comply with applicable limits [I.R.C. § 408(k)(6)(F)].

Q 11:6   Must each eligible employee of an employer that establishes a SEP have an IRA?

Yes. (See Q 11:40.) Failure of an eligible employee to have a valid SEP IRA may result in disqualification of the employer's SEP. That is, the employer may lose tax deductions for the employees who are covered, and the employees who thought they were covered may be taxed on the amounts contributed. The employees may also be subject to a 6 percent penalty for excess contributions to their IRAs. [Prop. Treas. Reg. § 1.408-7(d)(1); Notice 81-1, 1981-1 C.B. 610]

An employer may assist an employee in establishing an IRA if an employee has not already done so. Indeed, an employer may execute any necessary documents on behalf of an employee who is entitled to a SEP contribution if the employee is unable or unwilling to execute such documents or if the employee has terminated service and the employer is unable to locate him or her. [Prop. Treas. Reg. § 1.408-7(d)(2)]

Example. Mort, an employee of Aardvarks, Inc., who is eligible to receive a SEP contribution, dies before establishing an IRA. Aardvarks may establish an IRA in Mort's name. Mort's estate will be designated as the beneficiary of the IRA or the default option under the IRA, if any, will be selected. (An interest-bearing investment is generally chosen for an IRA established in such a manner.)

Note. The IRS has the authority to require reports with respect to employees who cannot be located, but so far it has not done so. [Prop. Treas. Reg. § 1.408-9(c)]

Q 11:7   May a SEP use an individual retirement annuity method of funding?

Yes. Either an individual retirement trust (or custodial account) or an individual retirement annuity (which must be a nontransferable annuity or endowment contract issued by an insurance company) may be used to fund a SEP.

Q 11:8   Can a Roth IRA be part of a SEP arrangement?

No. However, amounts may be withdrawn from the SEP and converted to a Roth IRA (see Qs 11:94, 11:95).

Q 11:9   Which investments may be used for a SEP?

Generally, a SEP may invest in anything permitted for IRAs. The SEP IRA documentation will spell out the investments that the SEP sponsor allows.

Q 11:10   How does a SEP differ from a qualified plan?

A *qualified plan* is a plan that satisfies the requirements of Code Section 401(a); the SEP rules are in Code Section 408. Because SEPs are not qualified under Code Section 401(a) or 403(a), distributions from SEPs do not qualify for the favorable tax treatment that is available to certain qualifying lump-sum distributions from qualified plans (e.g., 10-year forward income averaging and capital gains treatment). [I.R.C. § 402(d)]

Q 11:11   Is a SARSEP the same as a 401(k) plan?

No. First, a SARSEP is not a qualified plan; thus, many of the rules that apply to 401(k) plans do not apply to SARSEPs. Second, the nondiscrimination test for a SARSEP is not as liberal as that for 401(k) plans. Only the 125 percent rule applies, and the test is administered differently.

Q 11:12   What are the advantages of using a SEP?

An employer that maintains a SEP or SARSEP generally does not have to file Form 5500, Annual Return/Report of Employee Benefit Plan, when the employer uses the alternative methods of compliance. Further, instead of the summary description required with a qualified plan, the employer may use a copy of Form 5305-SEP or Form 5305A-SEP (see Q 11:17) to describe its SEP or SARSEP.

Under current law, the Secretary of the Treasury has the authority to require an employer that contributes to a SEP to provide simplified reports with respect to those contributions. Those reports could appropriately include information as to compliance with the requirements that apply to SEPs, including the contribution limits. [Joint Comm. on Taxation, *Technical Explanation of the Job Creation and Worker Assistance Act of 2002* (JCX-12-02) (Mar. 6, 2002)] Because the IRS is concerned that many employers are not covering all of their eligible employees, it is likely that simplified reports will eventually be mandated for SEPs.

Other advantages of choosing a SEP over a qualified plan include the following:

1. Reduction of outside consultant fees and other professional expenses that normally accompany a retirement plan of the non-SEP variety;
2. Ease of establishing a SEP (i.e., no need for IRS approval);
3. Possibility of using a SEP to increase the permissible funding in an IRA;
4. Ease of shifting investment selection responsibility to the employee;
5. Freedom to decide whether to contribute at all (the SEP contribution is completely discretionary) and to vary the contribution amounts within the statutory limits; and
6. Option of establishing a SEP after the tax year (qualified plans must be established by the end of the tax year).

Q 11:13 What are the disadvantages of using a SEP?

The disadvantages of using a SEP include the following:

1. Employees have full and immediate vesting and withdrawal rights.
2. It is often necessary to cover part-time and seasonal employees.
3. Individual and overall contribution limits may be lower than those for a qualified plan.

[I.R.C. §§ 101(b), 219(g), 402(d), 408(d), 408(k)(1)]

Q 11:14 Are SEP contributions subject to Social Security, Medicare, and unemployment taxes?

Nonelective SEP contributions made by an employer are not subject to Social Security, Medicare, or unemployment taxes. In the case of a SARSEP, however, elective contributions (including catch-up elective contributions) are subject to Social Security, Medicare, and unemployment taxes.

Q 11:15   Is a tax credit available to employers that establish a SEP for the first time?

Yes. A small business that adopts a SEP (or a SIMPLE) can generally claim an income tax credit for 50 percent of the first $1,000 in administrative and retirement-education expenses incurred for each of the first three years of the plan. The credit is available only to employers that did not have more than 100 employees with compensation in excess of $5,000 during the previous tax year. The employer must also have had at least one nonhighly compensated employee (NHCE) (see Q 11:68). The credit is taken as a general business credit on the employer's tax return. The other 50 percent of the expenses may be taken as a business deduction. [I.R.C. § 45E] The income tax credit is claimed on Form 8881, Credit for Small Employer Plan Startup Costs. [IRS Publication 560, *Retirement Plans for Small Business (SEP, SIMPLE, and Qualified Plans)* (2008)]

Practice Pointer. The 50 percent of qualifying expenses that is effectively offset by the tax credit is not deductible; the other 50 percent of the qualifying expenses (and other expenses) is deductible to the extent permitted under current law.

Q 11:16   Can the credit for administrative and retirement-education expenses be claimed if a SEP is terminated and another SEP adopted the following year?

No. The tax credit for the administrative and retirement-education expenses of establishing a SEP is not allowed if substantially the same employees are covered under a new plan adopted within the three-taxable-year period immediately preceding the first taxable year for which an employer could claim the new-plan credit. [I.R.C. § 45E(c)(2)]

SEP Forms

Model Forms

Q 11:17   What IRS model forms may be used to establish a SEP?

IRS approval of a SEP is not necessary if one of the IRS model SEP forms—Form 5305-SEP, Simplified Employee Pension-Individual Retirement Accounts Contribution Agreement, or Form 5305A-SEP, Salary Reduction and Other Elective Simplified Employee Pension-Individual Retirement Accounts Contribution Agreement—is used to establish the plan. (When a salary reduction feature is incorporated, Form 5305A-SEP or other IRS-approved document (see Q 11:21), not Form 5305-SEP, must be used.) Whichever form is used, it is to be kept by the employer and not filed with the IRS. [Rev. Proc. 2009-8, § 4.02(3), 2009-1 I.R.B. 229]

Form 5305-SEP and Form 5305A-SEP work in tandem with Form 5305, Individual Retirement Trust Account, or Form 5305-A, Individual Retirement

Custodial Account (or other IRA models approved by the IRS). The SEP simply expands the contributions that may be made to an IRA.

Q 11:18   May Form 5305-SEP and Form 5305A-SEP be used for all SEPs?

No. Form 5305-SEP may not be used if any of the following is the case:

1. The employer currently maintains a qualified plan (see Qs 11:19, 11:27). (This restriction does not prevent an employer from maintaining another SEP.)
2. The employer is not willing to pay the cost of the SEP contribution.
3. Any eligible employee does not have an IRA.
4. The employer uses the services of any leased employees. [I.R.C. § 414(n)]
5. The employer is not willing to include all eligible employees, including those employees of related, controlled, and affiliated employers (see Q 11:37).

Model Form 5305A-SEP may not be used if any of the following is the case:

1. The employer has leased employees as defined in Code Section 414(n)(2).
2. The employer currently maintains a qualified plan. (This restriction does not prevent an employer from also maintaining a model SEP (Form 5305-SEP) or other SEP to which either elective or nonelective contributions may be made.)
3. The employer had more than 25 employees eligible to participate in the SEP at any time during the prior calendar year.
4. The employer has an eligible employee who does not have an IRA.
5. The employer is a state or local government or a tax-exempt organization.
6. The employer has any eligible employees whose taxable year is not the calendar year.

Note. Since 1996, new SARSEPs cannot be established. If a SEP that permitted elective deferrals was established before 1997, however, the employer may continue to maintain the SEP for years after 1996 and amend it for tax law changes.

Q 11:19   May Form 5305-SEP or Form 5305A-SEP be used if an employer maintains a qualified plan?

No. Neither Form 5305-SEP nor Form 5305A-SEP may be used by an employer that maintains a qualified plan (see Q 11:27). A prototype SEP that is preapproved by the IRS National Office may be used instead (see Q 11:21).

Q 11:20   When must amended Forms 5305-SEP and 5305A-SEP be substituted for earlier versions?

There have been several versions of the IRS model SEP forms.

Form 5305-SEP was revised in December 2004.

Form 5305A-SEP was revised in June 2006.

Existing prototype SEP documents must be amended, approved, and adopted by the employer within 180 days after the plan receives IRS approval.

Practice Pointer. Organizations that provide amended documents to clients may want to consider a mailing to adopting employers informing them of their responsibility to notify eligible employees of plan amendments as required by plan provisions.

Note. The most recent version of the model SEP (Form 5305-SEP), issued in June 2006, does not require that the form be executed by an employer that had previously adopted a SEP using the model form. However, the new version of the model SEP should be used by an employer that initially establishes a SEP.

Practice Pointer. Like its predecessor, the current version of Form 5305-SEP may be used by an employer that has a terminated defined benefit plan.

Prototypes

Q 11:21   May a prototype be used to establish a SEP?

Yes. A SEP may be established using an IRS-approved master or prototype IRA. Features not allowed in a model plan may be included in a prototype or individually designed plan (see Q 11:27). Prototype SEPs are generally offered to employers by financial institutions, which may also provide administrative and technical services to employers.

Qualifying organizations may file Form 5306-A, Application for Approval of Prototype Simplified Employee Pension (SEP), with the IRS for approval of a prototype SEP (see Q 11:22) The IRS will not issue opinion letters on prototype SEPs that consolidate a SEP and an IRA into one document.

A prototype SEP may also be drafted and submitted by a mass submitter to the IRS National Office for approval. Once approved, the prototype plan may be sponsored by banks or other financial institutions for their customers.

Q 11:22   What types of organizations qualify to sponsor a prototype SEP?

An organization seeking to qualify as a sponsor of a prototype SEP must be one of the following:

- A trade or professional organization (other than an employee association) having characteristics similar to those described in Treasury Regulations Section 1.501(c)(6)-1;

- A bank (as defined in Code Section 581);
- An insured credit union (within the meaning of Section 101(6) of the Federal Credit Union Act);
- A regulated investment company (as defined in Code Section 851);
- An investment advisor under a contract with one or more regulated investment companies;
- A principal underwriter that has a principal underwriting contract with one or more regulated investment companies; or
- A person that, under the Treasury regulations, may act as a trustee or custodian of an IRA (nonbank trustee or custodian).

When the sponsoring organization is an insurance company, the IRS will issue an opinion letter, if requested to do so, as to whether a specific prototype individual annuity contract, within the meaning of the regulations, meets the requirements of Code Section 408(b).

Practice Pointer. A copy of the IRS opinion letter approving the prototype SEP must be furnished to employers using that agreement.

Q 11:23 May an employer that adopts a prototype SEP document rely on the opinion letter received from the IRS by the prototype sponsor?

Yes. If a particular employer adopts a prototype SEP arrangement in accordance with the form approved by the IRS and observes its provisions, that employer may rely on the opinion letter as long as

1. SEP contributions are made to a model IRA or an IRS-approved master or prototype IRA and
2. Contributions under the SEP arrangement do not (in combination with another SEP arrangement or any terminated qualified defined benefit plan of the employer) fail to satisfy the requirements of Code Section 415 (see Qs 11:77, 11:78).

Q 11:24 May a prototype SEP be used by an employer that currently maintains a master or prototype defined contribution plan?

Yes. If an employer maintains a master or prototype defined contribution plan, the plan document most likely contains language that will coordinate contributions under that plan with any other master or prototype defined contribution plan or SEP maintained by the same employer. [*See, e.g.,* Defined Contribution Listing of Required Modifications and Information Package (LRM), item 31 (8-2005).] If a qualified plan does not contain language that coordinates contributions made under it with a SEP and is maintained with a SEP, it may not satisfy Code Section 415.

Q 11:25   How may a sponsor of a prototype SEP ensure relief from ERISA's reporting requirements?

Under Title I of the Employee Retirement Income Security Act of 1974 (ERISA), relief from the annual reporting requirements is *not* available to an employer that selects, recommends, or in any other way influences employees to choose a particular IRA or type of IRA to which contributions under the SEP will be made if those IRAs are subject to restrictions that prohibit the withdrawal of funds for any period (other than restrictions imposed by the Code that apply to all IRAs). If, however, an employer that sponsors a nonmodel (i.e., prototype) SEP selects the IRAs to which contributions will be made and such IRAs make available to participants an option that imposes a restriction on withdrawals, the plan administrator for that SEP (generally the employer) is not precluded from using the alternative method of compliance under Department of Labor (DOL) Regulations Section 2520.104-49, provided:

1. Other meaningful investment options that do not restrict withdrawals are available to participants;

2. The employer does not select, recommend, or otherwise influence any participant's choice of an available investment option under the IRAs; and

3. All other conditions of the regulation are satisfied.

[DOL Adv. Op. 82-3A; DOL Reg. §§ 2520.104-48(c), 2520.104-49(a)(1)(iv); IRS Forms 5305-SEP, 5305A-SEP]

> **Example.** The Five Cents Savings Bank (the Bank) establishes a nonmodel SEP for its employees. The terms of the SEP require all eligible employees to establish their IRAs with the Bank. In most other respects, the terms of the IRA and SEP follow Form 5305 and Form 5305-SEP, which contain no restrictions on withdrawals, and the Bank has added no withdrawal restrictions. Investments under the plan are at the direction of the participant and are not under the control of any other person.
>
> Through its IRAs, the Bank offers various investment options, including regular savings, term certificates, and "special notice accounts," to participants. Neither the regular savings nor the term certificates impose any restrictions on withdrawals by the participant; however, the special notice accounts do not allow withdrawal of funds held on deposit for less than 90 days.
>
> The Bank is not precluded from using the alternative method of compliance for its SEP, because meaningful investment options that do not restrict withdrawals are available to participants. The Bank does not select, recommend, or otherwise influence any participant's choice of an investment option available under the IRAs, and all other conditions of the applicable regulation are satisfied. [DOL Adv. Ops. 82-61A, 82-3A]

Q 11:26   How is compensation determined for a fiscal-year prototype SEP?

For a plan year that is not a calendar year in a prototype SEP, the applicable compensation limit (see Q 11:3) is the limit for the calendar year in which the fiscal year begins. Thus, for example, for a plan year beginning on July 1, 2008, the compensation limit is the 2008 limit of $230,000. [I.R.S. News Release IR-2007-171 (Oct. 18, 2007)]

Individually Designed Forms

Q 11:27   How may a SEP be established if an employer has a defined benefit plan or a defined contribution plan?

An employer that has a defined benefit plan or a defined contribution plan is not eligible to use the IRS model forms or IRS-approved prototype plan documents. It is not, however, necessarily precluded from establishing a SEP.

The IRS National Office has a procedure for issuing rulings and opinion letters on IRAs and the acceptability of the form of an individually designed SEP or SARSEP: an employer may submit a letter ruling request to the IRS.

If an employer that is adopting a SEP has ever maintained a qualified defined benefit plan (that is now terminated covering any of the same employees covered by the SEP, the employer may request a letter ruling stating whether the SEP (in combination with the terminated defined benefit plan) satisfies the requirements of Code Section 415.

Employers that have other defined contribution or defined benefit plans may apply to the appropriate IRS district office for a determination letter under the procedures set forth in Revenue Procedure 2009-6 [2009-1 I.R.B. 189]. If the other plans are prototype qualified defined contribution plans, however, a determination letter will not normally be issued unless there are special circumstances involving Code Section 415 and the employer cannot otherwise rely on the prototype's favorable opinion letter (see Q 11:30).

Q 11:28   Is there a procedure for obtaining IRS approval of an individually designed SEP or SARSEP?

Yes. An employer may submit a request for a letter ruling to the National Office of the IRS regarding the acceptability of an individually designed SEP or SARSEP arrangement. The IRS imposes a one-time user fee of $9,000. [Rev. Proc. 2009-8, 2009-1 I.R.B. 229]

Approval for Combined Plans and Prior Plans

Q 11:29   May an employer that adopts more than one SEP obtain IRS approval of its SEP documents?

Yes. If an adopting employer maintains more than one SEP covering any of the same employees, the employer may request a letter ruling as to whether the SEP, in combination with the other SEP (or SEPs), satisfies the requirements of Code Section 415 (see Qs 11:77, 11:78).

Q 11:30   May a prototype or model SEP be combined with a prototype or model SARSEP?

Yes. The instructions contained in the IRS model documents (Forms 5305-SEP and 5305A-SEP) permit SEPs and SARSEPs to be used with one another. Multiple SEPs or SARSEPs are also permitted. Similar rules apply to SEPs and SARSEPs established with IRS-approved prototypes. It should be noted, however, that if an employer has ever maintained a defined benefit pension plan that is now terminated, the employer may request a letter ruling from the IRS confirming that the requirements of 415 are satisfied.

Q 11:31   May a prototype or individually designed SEP or SARSEP be used in conjunction with a qualified defined contribution plan without violating Code Section 415?

Yes. Language coordinating Code Section 415 with a SEP or SARSEP is contained in the qualified plan (non-SEP) documents and should be followed. The SEP limits are not deemed to have been exceeded merely because an employer has made a contribution to a qualified plan.

Q 11:32   May an employer that once maintained a defined benefit plan (now terminated) request IRS approval of a SEP document?

Yes. If an adopting employer ever maintained a qualified defined benefit plan that is now terminated and that plan covers any of the same employees covered by the employer's SEP, the employer *may* request a letter ruling stating whether the SEP (in combination with the terminated defined benefit plan) satisfies the requirements of Code Section 415.

Participation

Eligible Employees

Q 11:33   Which employees are eligible for inclusion in a SEP?

All employees who have attained age 21, worked for the employer during at least three of the immediately preceding five years, and received at least $550 (for 2009) in compensation during the year must be eligible to participate in a SEP. [I.R.C. § 408(k)(2); I.R.S. News Release IR-2008-118 (Oct. 16, 2008)] The age and service requirements are satisfied if they are met at any time during the plan year. [Prop. Treas. Reg. § 1.408-7(d)(1)]

Note. Eligible employees who die or terminate employment before the employer contribution is made for the year in which death or termination occurred must be included in the allocation of that contribution based on compensation received in that year (see Q 11:6).

An employer may implement more liberal eligibility rules, including a lower age limit; however, it may be difficult for a minor to establish an IRA. [I.R.C. § 408(k)(1)]

> **Example 1.** Gladiator Corporation maintains a SEP for its employees. The plan year is the calendar year, and the SEP requires that participants be at least age 21 and have performed services for at least three of the immediately preceding five calendar years.

Jane worked for Gladiator in 2006, 2007, and 2008, while attending college. She never worked more than 25 days in any one year. In October 2009, Jane begins to work for Gladiator on a full-time basis; she earns $5,000 from Gladiator in 2009. Jane turns 21 on December 31, 2009. She is entitled to share in any SEP contributions made by Gladiator with respect to 2009. As of December 31, 2009, Jane meets the minimum age and service requirements because she worked for Gladiator in three of the five years preceding 2009. [Prop. Treas. Reg. § 1.408-7(d)(5)] Had Jane started working for Gladiator in 2008, she would not have satisfied the plan's three-year eligibility requirement, because she would have completed only two years of prior service as of December 31, 2009.

> **Example 2.** Wizard Software, Inc., adopted a SEP that required an employee to have performed services for at least three of the immediately preceding five calendar years. Tommy had been continuously employed by Wizard since 1982 and shared in Wizard's SEP contribution for each year through 2005. Tommy performed no service during 2006, 2007, and 2008. Tommy returned to employment in 2009. He is not entitled to share in Wizard's contributions for 2009 because he worked during only two of the immediately preceding five years—2004 and 2005.

> **Example 3.** Timely Telexes adopted a SEP that requires an employee to have performed services for at least three of the immediately preceding five calendar years and earn $550 in the current year. Sandra, the owner's spouse, has performed services for Timely Telexes every year since the business started in 1980 but has never received any compensation. At the end of 2009, she received $600 in compensation. Sandra is eligible to participate in the SEP for the 2009 plan year.

> **Example 4.** Great Falls, Inc. maintains a grandfathered SARSEP that required an employee to be age 21 to qualify for participation. The plan is maintained on a calendar-year basis. Joy will attain age 21 on December 31, 2009. Her participation commences on January 1, 2009, the first day of the plan year that contains her date of eligibility.

> **Example 5.** Neurology Partners established a SEP on April 1, 2010, for the prior calendar year (2009). The SEP document has a minimum service requirement of three years and a minimum compensation requirement of $550. Laura has worked part-time at Neurology Partners since the business was formed in 1990. She earned $550 in 2009, but never earned more than $200 in any prior year. Laura is eligible to participate in the SEP in 2009. She will also participate in 2010 and thereafter, as long as she continues to earn

compensation at least equal to the minimum compensation requirement (if any is specified in the plan) for that year.

Example 6. Candace, the sole proprietor of Datamatron, established a SEP with no age, compensation, or service requirements. The legal age to contract in the state where Datamatron is located is age 18. Henry, a vocational student in a work-study program, is age 16, and none of the financial institutions near him will establish an IRA for a minor. Henry's failure to establish an IRA places Datamatron's SEP in danger of disqualification (see Q 11:40). Candace could eliminate that risk by specifying an age requirement of 18 years for participation in the SEP, thus excluding Henry from eligibility until such time as he can set up an IRA.

Q 11:34 May an employee be eligible for a SEP even though new contributions to the employee's own IRA are not allowed because the employee will attain age 70½ before the end of the year?

Yes. Code Section 219(d), which prohibits annual IRA contributions beyond age 70½, does not apply to SEP or SARSEP contributions. [I.R.C. § 219(b)(2)] A SEP is thus a way for a person age 70½ or older to participate in an IRA.

Nevertheless, distributions of SEP contributions must begin no later than the April 1 following the year in which a participant attains age 70½. The RMD formula is applied to the new IRA balance, even though it results from post-age-70½ contributions through the SEP.

Q 11:35 May a person who is employed on the effective date of the plan be treated as satisfying the age and/or service requirements specified in the SEP?

Yes. The IRS has allowed a prototype plan sponsor to include a provision that allows an employer to waive the age and/or service requirement for an individual employed on the effective date of the plan.

Q 11:36 May leased employees be included in a SEP?

Yes. A prototype SEP may be established by an employer that uses the services of a leased employee. In general, any leased employees who are not employees of the employer but who are required to be treated as employees under Code Section 414(n) must be included in the plan if they are otherwise eligible. The language of the prototype should be examined to make sure the plan sponsor includes as an option in the adoption agreement a restriction relating to leased employees.

The LRM for a combination prototype (i.e., for a SEP and a SARSEP contained in one prototype) restricts the use of the SARSEP portion of the plan if the employer uses the services of leased employees. In such a case, the employer may use an individually designed plan.

Excludable Employees

Q 11:37   Must employees of related entities be included in an employer's SEP?

Yes. For purposes of a SEP, *service* includes service with any related entity; that is, service with an entity under common control or with a member of a controlled group must be aggregated. Service with a member of an affiliated service group must also be counted. [I.R.C. §§ 414(b), 414(c), 414(m)(4)(B); Treas. Reg. § 1.414(m)-3(a)(5); Priv. Ltr. Ruls. 9033061 (May 24, 1990), 9026056 (Apr. 3, 1990), 8945070 (Aug. 17, 1989), 8928008 (Nov. 12, 1989)] All members of a controlled group must exist simultaneously. The operation of Code Section 414(b), (c), and (m) and the regulations thereunder "necessarily require that controlled group members exist concurrently." [Priv. Ltr. Rul. 9541041 (Jul. 21, 1995)]

> **Example 1.** The Rusty Sleigh Company has a SEP. On December 31, 2009, Rusty Sleigh comes under common control with Slick Sleds Company. Employees of Slick Sleds who satisfy the plan's age, service, and compensation requirements become eligible to participate in the SEP for 2009 on the same basis as Rusty Sleigh's employees.

> **Example 2.** Kitty Corporation has 20 employees and sponsors a calendar year SARSEP. Only Kitty's employees are eligible to participate. On November 3, 2009, Cat Company (Catco) acquires all of Kitty Corporation's stock, and the two companies become a controlled group. Catco has 100 employees, most of whom have worked at the company at least four years. On January 1, 2010, Kitty Corporation's SARSEP will no longer satisfy the requirement that it employed fewer than 26 eligible employees throughout the prior plan year. Moreover, the plan fails to satisfy the 50 percent participation requirements of the Code for 2009—namely, participation by all employees over age 21 who have at least $550 in compensation (the 2009 limit, as adjusted for cost-of-living increases) and who have been credited with service during any three of the immediately preceding five years. The only alternative is to discontinue contributions under the plan as soon as possible. There are no transition or grace period rules for SEP plans.

Prototype and model SEP documents may be used in related employer situations. Individually designed SEPs that provide for coverage of a related employer's employees have also been accepted by the IRS. [Priv. Ltr. Ruls. 200003057 (Oct. 29, 2000), 9709008 (Dec. 7, 1996), 9026056 (Apr. 3, 1990)]

Q 11:38   May otherwise eligible employees be excluded from a SEP?

Yes. The categories of otherwise eligible employees who may be excluded from a SEP are:

1. Employees whose retirement benefits were collectively bargained for in good faith and who are under a union agreement with the employer; and

2. Nonresident alien employees with no U.S. source income from the employer.

[I.R.C. § 408(k)(2)]

In addition, the IRS permits a sponsor of a prototype SEP or SARSEP to provide provisions regarding the exclusion of "acquired" employees (during a transition period) (see Q 11:39).

Q 11:39   May an employee "acquired" by acquisition or other similar transaction be excluded from participation in a SEP or SARSEP?

Yes. The IRS permits a sponsor of a prototype SEP or SARSEP to include a provision that excludes acquired employees from participation during a transition period. An *acquired employee* is an employee who would be employed by another employer that has been involved in an acquisition or other similar transaction with the employer had the transaction not occurred. The plan may provide that an acquired employee would not be eligible to become a participant in the SEP during a transition period beginning on the date of the transaction and ending on the last day of the first plan year beginning after the transaction. For the exclusion to apply, the minimum coverage requirements (see Q 11:33) must have been met before the acquisition and coverage under the plan must not significantly change during the transition period other than by reason of the change in members of the group. [I.R.C. § 410(b)(6)(C)(i); Treas. Reg. §§ 1.410(b)-2(a), 1,410(b)-2(b)]

Required Participation

Q 11:40   May an employer demand that each eligible employee participate in its SEP?

Yes. Form 5305-SEP indicates that an employer may require an employee to participate in its SEP as a condition of employment (see Q 11:42).

Q 11:41   May an employer that maintains a SEP require an eligible employee to make elective contributions?

No. An employer may not require or pressure an employee to make elective contributions under a *SARSEP*. An employee may, however, be required to sign an investment form and any other documents that are necessary to create an IRA required to be used under a *SEP*.

Q 11:42   Must an employee acquiesce to becoming a participant in a SEP if the employee does not understand the concept of such a plan?

At least one state court has addressed the issue of whether an employee may be forced to participate in a SEP that he or she does not understand. In

Schultz v. Production Stamping Corp. [434 N.W.2d 780 (Wis. 1989)], the court held that ERISA does not require that a summary plan description be given to an employee before SEP coverage is imposed.

That ruling was less broad than it would seem on its face because, in *Schultz,* the employer did distribute to employees a copy of Form 5305-SEP, which was the plan document. In addition, a meeting was held, at which the plaintiff-employee asked no questions. The employee signed up, but her husband persuaded her to go back the next day and cross her name out. The employer warned the employee that she would be fired, and she was. The court, reversing an award of $173,000 in damages, concluded that it was reasonable for the employer to take the position it did because one employee should not have the power to destroy the pension of all the other employees. (The explanation portion of the standard SEP plan document confirms that the employer may terminate an uncooperative employee.)

The court also had to rule on the issue of whether, in Wisconsin, such a discharge would be impermissible as a matter of public policy. Again, the court noted that the employer's disclosure exceeded the minimum requirements of ERISA; there could be no bar to a dismissal authorized by ERISA.

Of course, where possible, educating employees about a SEP before it is put into place would be the better practice. In *Schultz,* however, there were special circumstances. The decision to adopt the SEP was made on April 10, and the employer needed to complete the paperwork within a few days.

Q 11:43   Why are the SEP participation rules so strict?

The SEP was conceived as a way for small employers to use their employees' own IRAs as vehicles for a pension arrangement that would involve little administrative work once contributions were made to those IRAs. To allow less than 100 percent participation would necessitate compliance with complex provisions that usually require actuarial and other professional help—exactly the opposite of what was intended.

Q 11:44   What harm might an employee suffer by being forced to participate in a SEP?

One consequence of SEP participation is the possible reduction of the deduction that would otherwise be available for an employee's own IRA contributions. Such a reduction could occur because participation in a SEP invokes the IRA deduction limits that apply above certain income levels when the IRA owner or his or her spouse actively participates in certain retirement plans, including qualified plans and SEPs (see Q 3:48). This disadvantage might be counterbalanced by an employer's contributions to a SEP, depending on the size and regularity of those contributions. Of course, the nondeductibility of an IRA contribution is taken into account when distributions are made, and, at that time, the appropriate portion is treated as a tax-free return of contributions.

Employer Contributions

Limits

Q 11:45 How does Code Section 415 limit annual additions to a SEP plan?

Code Section 415 limits the annual additions that may be allocated to an individual's account in any *limitation year*. [I.R.C. § 415(c)(1)] The limitation year of a SEP is the calendar year unless another 12-month period is designated in the plan document. Nearly every plan designates the plan year as its limitation year.

Q 11:46 Must an employer contribute to a SEP every year?

No. SEP contributions, determined on a year-to-year basis, are discretionary. If an integrated SEP (see Q 11:58) or a SARSEP is top heavy, however, a minimum contribution may have to be made to all non-key employees.

Q 11:47 To be nondiscriminatory, must the allocation of the SEP contribution be uniform in relationship to the compensation of all employees?

Not necessarily. Code Section 408(k)(3)(C) clearly indicates that contributing the same percentage of compensation for all SEP participants is not discriminatory. All that is required is that contributions be based on a written allocation formula that does not discriminate in favor of HCEs (see Q 11:86). That leaves open the possibility that another formula might be approved (see Q 11:66).

SEPs that are integrated with Social Security are also permitted (see Q 11:58) because an integrated plan takes into account employer-paid benefits.

Q 11:48 Is a flat hourly contribution rate nondiscriminatory?

Possibly not. For instance, in Private Letter Ruling 8441067 (July 12, 1984), a SEP that had called for a contribution of 60 cents per hour was amended by the employer in two respects. First, the highly compensated group was limited to 160 hours of credited hours per month. Second, the non-highly compensated group was guaranteed an additional credit at the end of each calendar year to the extent necessary to ensure that each member of the group received, as a percentage of compensation, no less than the percentage credited to the member of the highly compensated group being credited with the highest percentage of compensation. The IRS ruled that the SEP, as amended, was not discriminatory. [*See also* Priv. Ltr. Rul. 8824019 (Mar. 17, 1988).]

Q 11:49   What restrictions may an employer not place on its SEP contributions?

The following restrictions on an employer's SEP contributions are *not* permitted:

1. An employer may not in any way restrict an employee's right to a contribution made by the employer.

2. An employer may not condition a contribution on an employee's making contributions or on an employee's maintaining any balance in his or her account.

3. An employer may not prohibit withdrawals.

Q 11:50   What form of contribution is acceptable for a SEP?

Contributions to a SEP must be in the form of money (cash, check, or money order). In-kind (property) contributions are not permitted (except by rollover from another retirement plan). [I.R.C. § 408(a)(1)]

Q 11:51   May a SEP contribution be made even if there are no profits in a particular year?

Yes. Contributions may be made to a SEP in excess of profits for the year or even in the absence of profits. A contribution on behalf of a self-employed individual (including a partner in a partnership) may not, however, create a net operating loss; that is, the contribution may not exceed the individual's earned income (determined without regard to the deduction for the contribution). Contributions made to nonowner-employees may, however, exceed the owner's earned income and create a net loss from self-employment. [I.R.C. §§ 404(a)(8)(C), 404(h)(2); Temp. Treas. Reg. § 1.404(a)(8)-1T]

> **Example 1.** Theo's sole proprietorship has no employees and makes a 26 percent SEP contribution for 2009. There is no carryforward. The excess employer SEP contribution is not deductible on Theo's tax return for 2009. Theo should include the excess amount on line 7 of his Form 1040 for 2009.

> **Example 2.** Max, a sole proprietor, makes a 25 percent SEP contribution for himself and all eligible employees. Max overestimated his earned income; in fact, he had no earned income for the year. The contributions made on behalf of only the nonowner-employees create a net operating loss that Max may use to offset personal income. Any balance attributable to the nonowner-employees may be carried forward.

Q 11:52   When must SEP contributions be made?

A SEP may be based on a calendar year or on an employer's fiscal year. Further, a SEP may be established after an employer's fiscal year-end; that is, an employer has until the due date of the business's tax return, including extensions, to establish and make contributions to a SEP for the taxable year. [I.R.C. §§ 404(h)(1)(B), 6072(a), 6072(b)] Contributions made by that due date and made for the prior year are treated as made on the last day of the business's taxable year.

Note. The employer is required to provide the employee with a written statement indicating the amount of the employer's contribution for the year. This statement must be furnished within 30 days of the contribution or by January 31 of the year following the "calendar year for which the contribution is made." [Prop. Treas. Reg. § 1.408-9(b)] SEP contributions are not coded by year when reported to the IRS by the trustee or custodian.

Example. Maxgate maintains a calendar year SEP. Its federal income tax return for the 2009 tax year is due on March 15, 2010. On February 1, 2010, Maxgate makes its 2009 contribution and notifies the trustee that the contribution is being made for the prior year. On April 5, 2010, Maxgate's bookkeeper discovers that the company had already made its 2009 contribution on January 25, 2010, and that the SEP is now overfunded by $10,000. Although the SEP trustee will report both contributions as being made in 2010, there is no requirement that the report indicate for which year the contributions are made. Arguably, a SEP contribution made between January 1 and April 15, 2010, could be for either 2009 or 2010. Maxgate might not have a problem at all, unless participant compensation for 2009 cannot support the additional $10,000 contribution.

Although it was issued a few years prior to the existence of SEPs, Revenue Ruling 76-28 [1976-1 C.B. 106, *modified slightly by* Revenue Ruling 76-77, 1976-1 C.B. 107], would appear to support the reasoning in the preceding example, because the language of Code Section 404(h) is similar to the "special rules for SEPs" under Code Section 404 regarding the time contributions are deemed made. [I.R.C. §§ 404(h), 404(a)(6)] On the other hand, the IRS might consider whether employees were notified that the contribution was made for the current year or prior taxable year. In the example, Maxgate's contribution notice to its employees would be required by January 31, 2009, or within 30 days after the contribution is made.

All contributions to a SEP are plan assets. [DOL Reg. § 2510.3-102(a)] ERISA regulations generally require employee contributions to a SARSEP to be deposited as soon as they can reasonably be segregated from the employer's general assets, but in any event within 15 business days after the end of the month in which the payroll deduction is made. [DOL Reg. § 2510.3-102] Thus, the 15-day period (30 days in the case of a SIMPLE) is not a safe harbor. Under some circumstances, one day may be sufficient time to segregate and deposit contributions.

Compensation and Related Issues

Q 11:53   May compensation that is paid after a limitation year be used for the prior limitation year?

It depends. In general, compensation may only be taken into account for a limitation year if it is actually paid or made available to the employee within the limitation year. [Treas. Reg. § 1.415(c)-2(e)(1)(i)] However, compensation paid after the limitation year may be used if all of the following circumstances are met:

1. The plan provides that compensation for a limitation year includes amounts earned during the year but paid afterward solely because of the timing of pay periods and pay dates.

2. The compensation at issue was earned during the limitation year but is paid in the first few weeks of the succeeding year.

3. All such amounts are included on a uniform and consistent basis with respect to all similarly situated employees.

4. The same amount is not included in more than one limitation year.

[Treas. Reg. § 1.415(c)-2(e)(2)]

Example. Jean defers part of her salary into her employer's SARSEP during 2009. The plan contains a provision like that just described. On January 15, 2010, Jean receives a check for the pay period that ends on December 31, 2009. Jean may defer from the check received on January 15, 2010, for the 2009 limitation year.

Q 11:54 May severance payments be treated as compensation for purposes of making elective deferrals under a SARSEP?

Generally not. Most severance payments are not considered compensation and cannot be used for elective deferrals. However, certain payments made after the termination from employment may be treated as compensation under a plan, and in that case elective deferrals may be taken from them (see Q 11:55). [*See* Treas. Reg. § 1.415(c)-2(e)(3).]

Q 11:55 What amounts received after termination from employment are treated as compensation for elective deferral purposes?

An amount paid after termination from employment is treated as compensation, and may be used for elective deferral purposes under a SARSEP, if it is paid during the limitation year in which severance occurs or, if later, within $2\frac{1}{2}$ months after the severance date, and is one of the following kinds of payments:

1. Regular compensation for services that would have been paid before severance if the employment had continued. Examples include pay for service during regular hours, overtime pay, commissions and bonuses.

2. Cashing out payments for accrued sick, vacation, or other leave, but only if the employee could have used the leave had the employment continued, and the plan specifically treats such payments as compensation for Code Section 415 purposes.

3. Payments pursuant to a nonqualified unfunded deferred compensation plan, but only if the employee would have received such amounts at the same time had the employment continued, and the plan specifically treats such payments as compensation for Code Section 415 purposes.

[Treas. Reg. § 1.415(c)-2(e)(3)]

Q 11:56   May payments made after severance from employment by reason of qualified military service be treated as compensation?

Yes. Amounts must generally be paid or treated as paid prior to severance from employment in order to be taken into account as compensation. [Treas. Reg. § 1.415(c)-2(e)(ii)] However, a plan can provide for this general rule not to apply to payments to an individual who does not currently perform services for the employer by reason of qualified military service, to the extent those payments do not exceed the amounts the individual would have received had he or she continued to perform services for the employer rather than entering qualified military service. [Treas. Reg. § 1.415(c)-2(e)(4)]

Qualified military service means any service in the uniformed services (as defined in chapter 43 of title 38, United States Code) by any individual, if such individual is entitled to reemployment rights under such chapter with respect to such service. [I.R.C. § 414(u)(1); Treas. Reg. § 1.415(c)-2(e)(4)]

Example. Ben, an employee of The Bender Company, is a member of the National Guard and called to active military service for the period July 2009 through December 2010. Bender's corporate policy is to supplement the military pay of its employees who are deployed in the military, and the pay supplements are treated as compensation under the terms of Bender's SEP. The pay supplements Ben receives in 2009 and 2010 are taken into account when Bender allocates its SEP contributions for those years.

Q 11:57   May salary continuation payments for disabled participants be treated as compensation?

Yes. A rule almost identical to the one described above (see Q 11:56) applies with respect to contributions on behalf of disabled employees. The employee must be disabled within the meaning of Code Section 22(e)(3), which requires total and permanent *inability* to engage in any substantial gainful activity by reason of any medically determinable physical or mental impairment which can be expected to result in death or which has lasted or can be expected to last for a continuous period of not less than 12 months. In that case the employer is permitted to base a SEP contribution on the amount of compensation the participant would have received if he or she were paid at the rate of compensation received immediately before becoming permanently and totally disabled. [Treas. Reg. § 1.415(c)-2(e)(4)] Also, the participant must be nonhighly compensated (under Code Section 414(q)) (see Q 11:68) or the plan sponsor must make contributions for all disabled participants. [I.R.C. § 415(c)(3)(C)]

Q 11:58   How does Social Security integration affect SEP contributions and the $49,000 limit?

In theory, the integration rules avoid the duplication of benefits by not requiring that contributions be made twice on the same compensation. Social Security integration (sometimes called *permitted disparity*) is allowable under the same rules that apply to defined contribution plans. That is, the contribution based on compensation above the taxable wage base (TWB) for the current year may not be more than twice the rate that is applied to the portion of compensation subject to the base. Furthermore, under current rules, the spread may never exceed 5.7 percent. For example, instead of providing a flat 8 percent of pay for each participant, a SEP could provide 5 percent on the portion of pay covered by Social Security ($106,800 for 2009) [Notice 2008-103, 2008-46 IRB 1156] and 10 percent on the portion in excess of pay covered by Social Security.

Generally, only one plan of an employer may be integrated. Form 5305A-SEP does not provide for integration.

The spread or disparity rate depends on the integration level selected for the plan year. The maximum percentage rate of 5.7 percent may be used when the plan is integrated at the TWB or when the integration amount is set at 20 percent or less of the TWB. If the integration level is set above $10,000 (or 20 percent of the TWB if that amount is greater) and below the TWB, the maximum spread factor of 5.7 percent must be reduced. [Treas. Reg. § 1.401(1)-2d] Table 11-1 summarizes these rules.

Table 11-1.   Adjusting the Maximum Disparity Rate

If the Integration Level Is More Than	But Not More Than	The 5.7% Maximum Disparity Rate Is Reduced To
The greater of $10,000 or 20% of the TWB	80% of the TWB	4.3%
80% of the TWB	An amount less than 100% of the TWB	5.4%

Calculated from the 2009 TWB of $106,800, the maximum 5.7 percent spread would be as shown in Table 11-2.

Table 11-2.   Adjustments Based on 2009 TWB of $106,800

If the Integration Level Is More Than	But Not More Than	The 5.7% Maximum Disparity Rate
$ 0	$ 21,360	Remains at 5.7%
$21,360	$ 85,440	Is reduced to 4.3%
$85,440	$106,800	Is reduced to 5.4%
NA	$106,800	Remains at 5.7%

Caution. Code Section 402(h)(2)(B), regarding the exclusion of an employer's SEP contribution, provides for a reduction of the dollar limit ($49,000 for 2009) if the plan is integrated with Social Security. The reduction to the $49,000 annual contribution limit in an integrated SEP is equal to the plan's spread (disparity) percentage multiplied by the amount of the HCE's compensation not in excess of the plan's integration level or the TWB, whichever is less. Compensation in excess of $245,000 (the 2009 limit) is not considered. In the case of an NHCE, the $49,000 limit is not reduced.

For 2009, the maximum offset applicable to an HCE produces a limit of $42,912 ($49,000 − (the maximum integration level of $106,800 × .057)).

Practice Pointer. An employer with few employees (or employees who do not earn significant amounts) may have to determine the additional non-owner cost to provide an owner with a $49,000 contribution rather than the reduced limit. The additional cost of the nonowner contributions may be insignificant, especially if there is more than one owner.

Example 1. The Darn Knit Store established a prototype SEP for its employees. Under the plan, SEP contributions are integrated with Social Security. The plan's integration level is set at $10,000 for 2009 and uses the maximum permitted spread of 5.7 percent. Donna Darn, the owner, has W-2 compensation of $245,000. Mona, the only employee, earns $10,000. Darn Knit contributes the smallest amount ($49,860) that will result in an allocation to Donna of $48,430 (her maximum for 2009; i.e., $49,000 − (.057 × $10,000)). When the contribution is expressed as a formula, it results in a contribution of 14.3 percent of compensation plus 5.7 percent of compensation (the spread) in excess of $10,000 (the integration level).

Donna receives a contribution of $48,430 ($245,000 × .143) + (($245,000 − $10,000) × .057). Mona would receive $1,430 ($10,000 × .143).

If the plan were *not* integrated, Donna could receive a contribution of $49,000 ($245,000 × .20), and Mona could receive $2,000 ($10,000 × .20).

Analysis. The difference in plan costs is $1,140 ($51,000 − $49,860). For Donna to receive an additional $570 under a nonintegrated plan, it would require an additional nonowner contribution of an equal amount. From Donna's point of view, the additional cost is only 50 percent effective ($570 ÷ $1,140), so an integrated plan may be a better alternative for the Darn Knit Store.

Example 2. Beaver Hat Shop established a SEP for its employees. Under the plan, contributions are integrated with Social Security. The plan's integration level is set at the TWB for 2009 ($106,800) and uses the maximum permitted spread of 5.7 percent. Clarence, the owner, has W-2 compensation of $245,000. Joe, the only employee, earns $15,000. Beaver Hat contributes the smallest amount ($45,057) that will result in an allocation of $42,912 to Clarence (his maximum for 2009; i.e., $49,000 − (.057 × $106,800)). When the contribution is expressed as a formula, it results in a contribution of 14.3 percent of compensation plus 5.7 percent of compensation (the spread) in excess of $10600 (the integration level).

Clarence receives a contribution of $42,912 (($245,000 × .143) + ($245,000 − $106,800) × .057)). Joe would receive $2,145 ($15,000 × .143).

Hypothetically, if the plan were *not* integrated, Clarence could receive a contribution of $49,000 ($245,000 × .20), and Joe could receive $3,000 ($15,000 × .20).

Analysis. The difference in plan costs is $6,943 ($52,000 − $45,057). For Clarence to receive an additional $6,088 under a nonintegrated plan, it would require an additional nonowner contribution of $855. From Clarence's point of view, the additional cost is 87.7 percent effective ($6,088 ÷ $6,943), so a nonintegrated plan may be a better alternative for the Beaver Hat Shop.

Example 3. The facts are the same as those in Example 2, except that Beaver Hat Shop has five employees, each with compensation of $30,000. Clarence receives the same contribution of $42,912. Each of the employees receives $4,290 ($30,000 × .143).

Hypothetically, if the plan were *not* integrated, Clarence could receive a contribution of $49,000, and each of the employees could receive $6,000 ($30,000 × .2).

Analysis. The difference in plan costs is $14,638 ($79,000 − $64,362). For Clarence to receive an additional $6,088 under a nonintegrated plan, an additional nonowner contribution of $8,550 (($6,000 − $4,290) × 5) is required. Because there are more employees and/or higher levels of compensation, Clarence would only receive 41.6 percent ($6,088 ÷ $14,638) of the additional $14,638. Clarence is likely to find the integrated plan the more efficient method of allocating employer contributions.

In the above examples, the contribution of the HCE is being reduced, while NHCE contributions are not being reduced. NHCEs are merely receiving the allocation percentage provided under the integrated plan. Of the amounts contributed by the employers in the above examples, only the NHCE allocations would be increased.

Contributions for Self-Employed Individuals

Q 11:59   May an unincorporated business owner who has no employees establish a SEP?

Yes. An owner of an unincorporated business is known as a self-employed individual. A self-employed individual in effect wears two hats: that of employer and that of employee. If the business has no employees, the self-employed individual's participation in a SEP is sufficient.

Q 11:60   How is a self-employed individual's contribution to a SEP determined?

A self-employed individual's *compensation* for qualified plan and SEP purposes is defined as his or her earned income. [I.R.C. § 408(k)(7)(B)] Under Code Section 401(c)(2), the term *earned income* for a self-employed individual (including partners in a partnership) refers to the net earnings from self-employment in a trade or business in which the personal services of an individual are a material income-producing factor. Earned income is determined on the last day of the business's taxable year. Generally, after several adjustments, up to $245,000 of earned income may be considered for plan purposes for plan years starting in 2009. [I.R.C. §§ 401(a)(17), 404(*l*)]

The phrase *net earnings from self-employment* is defined in Code Section 1402(a), relating to taxes on self-employment income. Under Code Section 401(c)(2), net earnings from self-employment must be reduced by all contributions made by or on behalf of the owner, and the deduction under Code Section 164(f) for half of the self-employment tax must be known. It should also be noted that the owner's share of the allowable contribution expense for nonowner-employees is subtracted from business income before calculation of the amount of net earnings from self-employment.

In general, an individual's earned income is the amount subject to federal income tax.

Practice Pointer. Calculating earned income for both plan and self-employment tax purposes can be extremely complicated because the owner's compensation fluctuates as the plan is being designed. Even practitioners with a thorough understanding of how plan limits are applied and how earned income is calculated will find the process of designing plans, calculating contributions, and applying limits a complex, if not impossible, task. Until there is a legislative change, the practitioner must use caution. Custom illustrations and spreadsheet software are available to practitioners who need to design plans for unincorporated business owners with common-law employees.

Q 11:61 How do guaranteed payment partners and ineligible owners affect the calculation of a self-employed individual's plan compensation?

Ineligible owners and guaranteed payment partners cause additional factors to be considered when designing a plan. Although an ineligible owner does not receive a contribution, their pro rata share of the nonowner contribution expense must be set aside and not allocated to remaining participating owners. A guaranteed payment partner is promised a stated amount, which is not reduced by nonowner contributions. The nonowner contribution expense is only allocated to regular partners. Generally, the nonowner contribution expense is allocated among all regular partners in proportion to their pre-plan earned income. In some cases, there is a written agreement that specifies how nonowner contribution expense is to be allocated among regular partners. (See Q 11:62 for an example illustrating additional external factors that may affect the calculation of an owner's plan compensation.)

Q 11:62 How does W-2 income or unrelated gains or losses from self-employment affect the calculation of a self-employed individual's plan compensation?

A self-employed individual who also has W-2 wages receives a credit for contributions to Social Security and a reduction of his or her self-employment tax. The reduction in self-employment tax has the effect of increasing earned income. Similarly, an unrelated loss from self-employment also has the effect of reducing self-employment tax and increasing earned income. In both instances, the individual will receive a larger contribution. Conversely, an unrelated gain from self-employment has the effect of increasing self-employment tax and reducing earned income, resulting in the partner receiving a smaller contribution. When there is an unrelated gain from self-employment, the self-employment tax must be apportioned between the entities.

Example. Unusual Facts, a partnership, maintains a SEP plan for its employees. The partnership makes a 25 percent contribution of $97,632.75 to the plan for 2009. There are three nonowner-employees with wages of $4,000 each. The following chart shows the eligibility status of the owners, payment arrangements, pre-plan earned income, allocation of nonowner contributions, one half of the self-employment tax deduction, allocation of the 2009 contribution, and the compensation on which the allocation was made.

Table 11-3. Maximum Disparity—Partnership Example

Employee Name/ Status	A Pre-Plan Compensation	B Share of $3,000 Nonowner Contribution Expense	C Self-Employment Income for SE Tax	D Half of the Self-Employment Tax Deduction	E 25% Contribution
Owners					
Joe Normal	$ 110,000	$ 600	$109,400	$8,086.55	$20,262.69
Lou—has $20,000 of W-2 income from an unrelated entity	110,000	600	109,400	6,846.55*	20,510.69
Tom—has a $10,000 loss from self-employment from an unrelated entity	110,000	600	99,400	7,022.39	18,475.52

Table 11-3. Maximum Disparity—Partnership Example (cont'd)

Employee Name/ Status	A Pre-Plan Compensation	B Share of $3,000 Nonowner Contribution Expense	C Self- Employment Income for SE Tax	D Half of the Self- Employment Tax Deduction	E 25% Contribution
Tim—has a $10,000 gain from self-employment from an unrelated entity	110,000	600	119,400	7,535.42**	22,372.92
Abe—is ineligible to participate	110,000	600	n/a	n/a	Ineligible
Roz—is a guaranteed payment partner with $70,000 of guaranteed payment	70,000	none allocated	70,000	4,945.34	13,010.93
Nonowners					
Employees (combined)	$ 12,000	n/a	n/a	n/a	$3,000

* In computing his self-employment tax, Lou is allowed a $2,480 credit for the amount of Social Security tax paid on his wages ($20,000 × 12.4% = $2,480).

** Tim's total deduction for self-employment tax on $119,400 ($110,000 + $10,000 − $600) is $8,220.46. To determine what portion is attributable to earned income from this entity, the total deduction is multiplied by .9167 (pre-plan earned income of $110,000, divided by $120,000 (the sum of the pre-plan earned income and outside earned income)). The result, $8,220.46, is the amount of Tim's deduction for self-employment tax that is taken into account for purposes of determining his SEP contribution.

Practice Pointer. Frequently, partners have different tax preparers. Information from the uncompleted federal income tax returns of some partners may be needed to compute the contributions to be made under the plan and to complete the federal income tax returns of the partnership, which, in turn, are needed for the completion of the federal income tax returns of the individual partners. When all the partners and the partnership use the same tax preparer, return preparation is facilitated and confidentiality issues are minimized.

Deduction of Employer Contributions

Q 11:63　When is a SEP contribution deductible by an employer?

Although there are other limits that may apply to contributions under a SEP (see Q 11:1), it is generally true that employer contributions are deductible by an employer in accordance with the following rules:

1. In the case of a plan maintained by a calendar-year business on a calendar-year basis, contributions are deductible for that calendar year.
2. Contributions made to plans maintained on the basis of the employer's fiscal taxable year are deductible for that fiscal taxable year.
3. When a fiscal-year business maintains a plan on a calendar-year basis, contributions are deductible for the fiscal taxable year that includes the last day of the calendar plan year.

[I.R.C. §§ 402(h), 404(h)]

> **Example 1.** Clarity Corporation is a calendar-year taxpayer that adopts a calendar-year SEP for 2009. Contributions made with respect to the 2009 SEP plan year are deductible by Clarity on its 2009 federal corporate income tax return.

> **Example 2.** The Timely Reporting Corporation adopts a SEP with a plan year that corresponds to its fiscal taxable year, ending on June 30. Contributions made with respect to the plan year ending on June 30, 2009, are deductible by Timely when it files its federal corporate income tax return for its fiscal taxable year ending June 30, 2009.

> **Example 3.** Westside Co.'s taxable year ends on the last day of February. Westside adopts a SEP with a calendar-year plan year. On March 5, 2009, Westside makes a 2009 SEP contribution. Westside will claim its deduction on its federal corporate income tax return for its fiscal taxable year ending February 28, 2010.

Q 11:64　May SEP contributions that are nondeductible in one year be deducted in future years?

Yes. The amount contributed in excess of the amount deductible by an employer for a taxable year is deductible in succeeding taxable years (in order of time), subject, of course, to the 25 percent limit. [I.R.C. § 404(h)(1)(C)]

> **Example.** Crane Corporation, a calendar-year business, establishes a SEP for its 2009 taxable year and contributes 10 percent at that time. On March 1, 2010, the business accidentally makes a 26 percent contribution for the previous taxable year (2009) and a 15 percent contribution for the current year (2010). If no more contributions are made for 2010, the amount of the 2009 excess (11 percent) may be deductible on Crane's 2010 tax return (10 percent) and 2011 tax return (1 percent). The amount carried forward may also be subject to a nondeductible contribution penalty of 10 percent.

Elective Deferrals (for Salary Reduction SEPs)

Q 11:65   Have SARSEPs been repealed?

Yes, meaning that an employer can no longer *initiate* a SARSEP plan. However, a SARSEP that an employer established before January 1, 1997, may continue to receive contributions under present-law rules, and employees of that employer who were hired after December 31, 1996, may participate in that SARSEP in accordance with those rules. [I.R.C. § 408(k)(6)(H)] (See Q 11:37 regarding recently related employers.)

> **Example 1.** Sound Company has had a SEP since 1991. It established a SARSEP effective January 1, 1996, and all employees elected to participate. Sound can continue to maintain its SARSEP after December 31, 1996, because it has been grandfathered.

> **Example 2.** Light Company has never maintained a retirement program. As of December 31, 1996, it had established a SARSEP using Form 5305A-SEP. None of the employees established an IRA. Because Light did not completely establish a SARSEP by December 31, 1996, the grandfather rules do not apply to it (or to any successor company).

Q 11:66   What requirements must a SEP meet to include a salary reduction feature?

To qualify as a SARSEP, a SEP plan must have no more than 25 eligible employees, and at least 50 percent of the employees must elect the SARSEP feature. The 25-employee test is ordinarily measured by the employer's experience in the preceding year.

Q 11:67   What is the 125 percent rule?

Under the 125 percent rule, also referred to as the actual deferral percentage (ADP) test, the percentage of total compensation elected to be deferred by each eligible HCE for the current year cannot exceed the average of the individual percentages, computed separately, for all eligible NHCEs multiplied by 1.25. [I.R.C. § 408(k)(6)(A)(iii)] (See Q 11:75 for the treatment of catch-up contributions for purposes of the ADP test.)

> **Example 1.** Nutmeg Corporation's employees earn the following amounts and defer the following percentages for 2009:

NHCE 1	$10,000/8%
NHCE 2	$10,000/4%
NHCE 3	$10,000/4%
NHCE 4	$10,000/0%

Nutmeg Corporation maintains a prototype SARSEP that defines compensation for ADP testing purposes as gross compensation (before reduction for elective deferrals). The average of the NHCEs' deferral percentages is computed as follows:

$$(8\% \ + \ 4\% \ + \ 4\% \ + \ 0\%) \ \div \ 4 \ = \ 4\%$$

The amount that may be deferred by each eligible HCE is computed as follows:

$4\% \times 1.25 = 5\%$, up to \$16,500 for 2009, plus catch-up contribution if eligible

Example 2. If an eligible HCE is over age 50 on December 31, 2009, that employee may defer 5 percent of total compensation, up to \$20,500, plus a catch-up contribution of \$5,000.

Note. The percentage that an eligible HCE may defer is not dependent (as is generally the case in a 401(k) plan) on the percentages or dollar amounts that other HCEs elect to defer.

Example 3. Sunfish Corporation maintains a SARSEP for its non-key employees using Form 5305A-SEP. Sunfish has three NHCEs, who elect to defer 2 percent, 3 percent, and 4 percent, respectively. The only other eligible employee is the company's owner, Marsha, and she contributes her allowed maximum of 3.75 percent (the average of the ADPs of each eligible NHCE, determined separately for each employee, multiplied by 1.25). Because Marsha, a key employee, is a plan participant, the SARSEP is deemed top heavy, and Sunfish must contribute 3 percent (i.e., the lesser of 3 percent or 3.75 percent) to each non-key employee who has made an excess SEP contribution. Elective contributions must be reduced if the 25 percent of includable compensation limit is exceeded (see Q 11:80).

Example 4. Bonefish Corporation maintains a SARSEP for its employees using Form 5305A-SEP. All employees of Bonefish are under age 50. Each of the company's three NHCEs elects to defer 1 percent. The only other eligible employee is the company's owner, Arthur, and he contributes his allowed maximum of 1.25 percent (the average of the ADPs of each eligible NHCE, determined separately for each employee, multiplied by 1.25). Because Arthur, a key employee, is a plan participant, the SARSEP is deemed top heavy, and Bonefish must contribute 1.25 percent (i.e., the lesser of 3 percent or 1.25 percent) to each non-key employee. Normal elective contributions (but not catch-up contributions) must be reduced if the 25 percent of includable compensation limit is exceeded (see Q 11:80).

Caution. In a model SARSEP (Form 5305A-SEP), the term *compensation* generally excludes elective contributions that are made by the participant to the plan. Under the model document, the ADP percentage for an employee who deferred \$400 from gross wages of \$10,000 would be 4.166667 percent (\$400 ÷ \$9,600) rather than 4 percent (\$400 ÷ \$10,000) as used in this example. It should be noted that the 25 percent participant exclusion limit is always based on reduced compensation.

Q 11:68   What is a highly compensated employee for purposes of a SEP?

For 2009, a *highly compensated employee* is an individual who

1. Was a 5 percent owner at any time during the current year or preceding ("look back") year or
2. Received from the employer during the preceding year (2008) compensation exceeding $110,000 (the 2009 limit is used) and in the preceding year, if the employer so elected, was in the top-paid group.

[I.R.C. § 414(q)(1); I.R.S. News Release IR 2008-118 (Oct. 16, 2008)]

Note. Even though a prototype SEP may not have been amended to reflect the new definition of HCE, an employer must apply the new definition in its operation of the plan.

An employee is in the top-paid group for any year if the employee is in the group consisting of the top 20 percent of the employees of the employer when the employees are ranked on the basis of compensation paid to employees during that year. Ownership for purposes of determining key employee status is determined in accordance with the attribution rules of Code Section 318. A 5 percent owner is an individual who owns directly or indirectly *more than* 5 percent of the business. [I.R.C. § 414(q)(2)]

Q 11:69   Is the salary reduction in a SARSEP treated as an employer or employee contribution?

Like the salary reduction in a 401(k) plan, the salary reduction in a SARSEP is treated as an employer contribution for deduction purposes and is included with other employer contributions, the total (excluding catch-up contribution) being subject to the overall SEP deduction limit of 25 percent or (for 2009) $49,000 ($54,500 with catch-up contributions) per participant, whichever is less.

Q 11:70   What are catch-up contributions?

Catch-up contributions generally are elective deferrals made by a catch-up eligible participant to a SARSEP that exceed an otherwise applicable limit and that are treated as catch-up contributions under the plan, but only to the extent they do not exceed the maximum amount of catch-up contributions permitted for the taxable year (see Q 11:3).

Q 11:71   What is a catch-up eligible participant?

A *catch-up eligible participant* is a participant who is otherwise eligible to make elective deferrals under a SARSEP and is age 50 or older. [I.R.C. § 414(v)(5); Treas. Reg. § 1.414(v)-1(g)(3)]

Q 11:72   How is a participant projected to reach age 50 by the end of the calendar year treated?

A participant who will reach age 50 before the end of the calendar year is treated as having attained age 50 as of January 1 of that year. [Treas. Reg. § 1.414(v)-1(g)(3)(ii)]

Q 11:73   Which elective deferrals are treated as catch-up contributions?

Elective deferrals in excess of an applicable limit are treated as catch-up contributions only to the extent that the elective deferrals do not exceed the catch-up contribution limit for the calendar year reduced by elective deferrals previously treated as catch-up contributions for the calendar year (i.e., contributions that were determined to be catch-up contributions for a plan year that ended within the calendar year). [I.R.C. § 414(v)(2)(B)]

Q 11:74   Are catch-up contributions subject to the otherwise applicable limits under a SEP?

No. If an elective deferral is treated as a catch-up contribution, it is not subject to the otherwise applicable limits under a SEP and the plan will not be treated as failing otherwise applicable nondiscrimination requirements because of the catch-up contributions. Under the Code and regulations, catch-up contributions are not taken into account in applying the limits of certain Code Sections, including Code Sections 401(a)(30), 402(h), 403(b), 404(h), 408, 415, and 457(b)(2) (determined without regard to 457(b)(3)), to other contributions or benefits under the plan offering catch-up contributions or under any other plan of the employer. [Treas. Reg. § 1.414(v)-1(d)(1)]

Q 11:75   How are catch-up contributions treated for purposes of ADP testing?

Any elective deferral for the plan year that is treated as a catch-up contribution because it exceeds a statutory or employer-provided limit is disregarded in calculating a participant's actual deferral percentage (ADP) under a SARSEP. [Treas. Reg. § 1.414(v)-1(d)(2)(i)]

Caution. Because an amount treated as a catch-up contribution is not taken into account in calculating the ADP, the ADP may have to be recalculated if unanticipated catch-up amounts are determined to exist for any participating non-highly compensated employee (NHCE).

Q 11:76   How are catch-up contributions treated for purposes of the 25 percent of includable compensation exclusion limit under Code Section 402(h)?

Catch-up contributions are treated as includable compensation for purposes of the 25 percent of includable compensation exclusion limit (see Q 11:80). Thus, the compensation is not reduced by catch-up contributions when applying the percentage exclusion limits. Catch-up contributions are separately excludable from a participant's gross income in addition to the amount determined under the 25 percent participant exclusion limit. [I.R.C. § 414(v)(3)(A)]

Q 11:77   How are catch-up contributions treated for purposes of the 100 percent limit under Code Section 415?

Catch-up contributions are not taken into account in determining whether the 100 percent limit under Code Section 415 has been exceeded. [I.R.C. § 414(v)(3)(A)(i)]

Q 11:78   How are catch-up contributions treated for purposes of the $49,000 limit under Code Section 415?

The $49,000 limit (for 2009) under Code Section 415 may be exceeded for allowable catch-up contributions. [I.R.C. § 414(v)(3)(A)(i)]

Q 11:79   How are catch-up contributions treated for purposes of the 25 percent of aggregate compensation deduction limit?

Catch-up contributions are separately deductible. [I.R.C. § 404(n)] They do not reduce the compensation on which the percentage deduction limit is applied.

Participants' Exclusion of Contributions

Q 11:80   Is there a separate limit on the amount of contributions made by an employer that may be excluded from an employee's gross income?

Yes. Contributions that are deductible by an employer (see Q 11:63) are not necessarily excludable from an employee's gross income. Thus, the portion of a fully deductible contribution that exceeds a participant's individually computed exclusion limit, although deductible, is nonetheless included in the affected participant's gross income for the taxable year.

Contributions that do not exceed 25 percent of taxable compensation are generally excluded from the employee's taxable compensation. For the purpose of the exclusion limit, compensation is considered only if it is included in the employee's gross income. The year to be used in determining an employee's compensation for purposes of the 25 percent exclusion limit seems to be the SEP's plan year, generally the calendar year. The Section 415 limit, which is also part of Code Section 402(h)(2)(A), would clearly be applied on such a plan-year basis. Elective contributions in excess of $16,500 ($22,000 with catch-up contributions) must be included by the participant in gross income on Form 1040 or Form 1040A for 2009, notwithstanding the 25 percent exclusion limit under Code Section 402(h). [Treas. Reg. § 1.402(g)-1(a)]

The 25 percent exclusion limit is determined after subtracting normal elective salary reduction contributions (but not catch-up contributions) from compensation. Code Section 402(h)(2)(A), referring to Section 414(s) compensation, includes such compensation only to the extent that it is includable in the employee's gross income. Code Section 414(v) does not require that catch-up contributions reduce compensation upon which the 25 percent exclusion limit is computed. Elective salary reduction SEP contributions, within limits, are separately excludable from gross income.

Example. Reddy Corporation maintains a SEP for its employees. The plan year is the calendar year. Lisa, age 40, a nonowner-employee, earns $10,000 and makes an elective contribution of $2,196 for 2009. If no other contributions are made, the 25 percent exclusion limit of $2,000 is computed as follows:

$$(\$10,000 \times .25) \div 1.25 = \$2,000$$

$$\text{Proof: } (\$10,000 - \$2,000) \times .25 = \$2,000$$

Reddy should report $196 in box 1 on Lisa's Form W-2 for 2009. It is unclear whether other amounts have to be withheld.

Q 11:81 How might a SEP interfere with the deductibility of an employee's IRA contributions?

Although a SEP is not a Section 401(a) qualified plan, participating in a SEP may cause IRA contributions to be nondeductible if an employee's modified adjusted gross income (MAGI) exceeds the limits applicable to various types of joint or individual returns (see chapter 3). Of course, if an employee (or the spouse of an employee) is already covered by a qualified plan (or by another SEP), the employee's IRA deductions may have already been limited without regard to the existence of the SEP.

Q 11:82 How can an employee receive an exclusion from income for a contribution that his or her employer makes?

To receive an exclusion from income for a contribution made by his or her employer, an employee must have elected to make salary reduction contributions. That procedure works in much the same way as it does in a 401(k) plan, but it is permitted only if the SEP qualifies for a salary reduction feature (see Q 11:66).

Direct Employee Contributions to a SARSEP

Q 11:83   May an employee contribute directly to his or her IRA under a SARSEP?

Yes, under a SARSEP an employee may contribute either directly if the plan allows it, or indirectly through payroll deduction. In any event, an employee's direct and indirect SEP IRA contributions, plus any IRA contributions otherwise made by the employee, may not exceed the annual contribution limit.

Q 11:84   May an employee use a spouse's IRA to fund his or her SEP IRA contribution?

No. If an employee used his or her spouse's IRA to fund the employee's SEP IRA, the SEP would fail to meet the participation requirements of Code Section 408(k). Furthermore, the contribution would be included in the employee's gross income, and it would be subject to the IRA contribution and deduction limits of Code Sections 219 and 408. [Notice 81-1, Q&A-7, 1981-1 C.B. 610]

Q 11:85   Is the saver's tax credit available for employee contributions to a SARSEP?

Yes, certain individuals may receive a nonrefundable low-income taxpayer contribution credit for a percentage of their contributions to a SARSEP. The credit is based on a sliding scale percentage of up to $2,000 contributed to a SEP (or SIMPLE IRA). The credit is in addition to the possible tax deduction (or any other tax benefit) that the contribution gives the taxpayer. [I.R.C. §§ 25B(a), 25B(b)]

To be eligible for the contribution tax credit, an employee must be 18 years of age or older and must not be a full-time student or be claimed as a dependent on another taxpayer's tax return. [I.R.C. § 25B(c)(1)]

The amount of the credit for any year is reduced by any distribution taken during the *testing period,* which consists of the two preceding tax years, the tax year, and the period after the tax year and before the due date of the federal income tax return of the employee (and spouse if a joint return is filed) for the tax year, including extensions. [I.R.C. § 25B(d)] (See chapter 3 for a full discussion of the credit.)

Excess Contributions to a SEP or SARSEP

Q 11:86   What are the consequences when an employer contributes more than the deductible limit to a SEP?

As noted above (see Q 11:3), an employer's contribution for 2009 under a SEP may not exceed $49,000 ($54,500 with catch-up contributions) or 100 percent of a participant's pre-plan compensation (including an elective contribution excluded from income under a Section 125 plan, a Section 457(b) plan, or a qualified transportation fringe benefit under Code Section 132(f)(4)). The entire SEP is likely to be disqualified under Code Section 415 if the annual limit on contributions (other than catch-up contributions) is exceeded. [I.R.C. § 415(c)(3)(D)]

Unless corrected, nondeductible contributions are subject to a 10 percent annual tax. [I.R.C. § 4972(d)(1)(A)(iii)]

Note. Correction for such an excess contribution is possible. The excess amount should be treated as wages reported to the employee on Form W-2. [Ann. 97-41, 1997-16 I.R.B. 28] The employee should withdraw the excess amount by the due date of his or her tax return to avoid any penalty.

Caution. Elective deferrals made by a catch-up eligible participant that exceed an otherwise applicable limit are treated as catch-up contributions under the plan, but only to the extent they do not exceed the maximum amount of catch-up contributions permitted for the calendar year (see Q 11:50).

Q 11:87   What types of excess elective contributions could arise with a SARSEP?

Three types of excess elective contributions may result under a SARSEP:

1. *Excess elective deferrals*, which are elective deferrals exceeding the taxpayer's elective deferral limit under Code Section 402(g)—for 2009, $16,500, plus catch-up contributions for individuals who are age 50 or older on December 31 of the tax year;

2. *Excess SEP contributions*, which are SEP contributions failing the 125 percent nondiscrimination test of Code Section 408(k)(6)(A)(iii) and generally affect only HCEs; and

3. *Disallowed deferrals*, which are deferrals failing the 50 percent participation rate requirement of Code Section 408(k)(6)(A)(ii).

Q 11:88   What information must be included in an employer's notification to employees regarding excess SEP contributions, and when must the notification be made?

Excess SEP contributions are SEP contributions that fail the 125 percent nondiscrimination test of Code Section 408(k)(6)(A)(iii); these generally affect only HCEs. An employer's notification of excess SEP contributions to any affected employees must specifically state the following in a manner calculated to be understood by the average plan participant:

1. The amount of the excess contributions attributable to the employee's elective deferrals;

2. The calendar year for which the excess contributions were made;

3. That the excess contributions are includable in the affected employee's gross income for the specified calendar year; and

4. That failure to withdraw the excess SEP contributions and income attributable to it by April 15 of the tax year following the year of notification may result in significant penalties.

The employer's notification must be made within two and one-half months after the end of the plan year (generally, March 15). An employer's failure to notify affected employees of excess SEP contributions or disallowed deferrals in no way alters the fact that the amounts are includable in the employees' gross income and may also be subject to the IRA contribution limits (and thus may be considered excess IRA contributions). Although, in a sense, the employer has 12 months to act, failure to make a proper and timely notification within two and one-half months will cost the employer a 10 percent penalty under Code Section 4979. [I.R.C. § 4979(f); Treas. Reg. §§ 54.4979-1(a)(4)(i), 54.4979-1(a)(4)(ii)]

> **Note.** It is unclear whether the correction period is shortened by one year when the notification of an excess SEP contribution or disallowed deferral is made during the year that the excess elective SARSEP contribution was made.

Distributions

Q 11:89 Must distributions from a SEP commence no later than April 1 following the calendar year in which the employee attains age 70½?

Yes. The same rules that apply to traditional IRAs apply to SEP IRAs; the 50 percent penalty on underdistributions likewise applies.

If an individual newly covered under a SEP reaches age 70½ before the end of the first year of coverage, a portion of the first year's contribution made during the year may have to be included in the minimum amount distributed, probably starting no later than the following year. That outcome is similar to the outcome under the rule that applies in the case of a rollover to an IRA when the individual reaches age 70½ in the year of the rollover (see Q 11:34).

Q 11:90 Does the suspension of the minimum distribution rules for 2009 also apply to SEPs and SARSEPs?

Yes. Generally, this means there is no required minimum distribution (RMD) for 2009, and calendar year 2009 is disregarded for SEPs and SARSEPs that have distributions to beneficiaries according to the five-year rule. (See discussion at Qs 4:21–4:25.)

Q 11:91 May employer contributions to a SEP or SARSEP be withdrawn by an employee?

Generally, yes. Employer contributions to a SEP or SARSEP may be withdrawn by an employee. Elective contributions made to a SARSEP, however, may not be withdrawn or transferred to a traditional IRA, a Roth IRA, or a SEP IRA by any HCE until March 15 of the following year or an earlier determination by the employer that the special 125 percent nondiscrimination test (see Q 11:67) has been satisfied. The trustee or custodian of the IRA may enforce the restriction; failure to do so could result in penalties to the employee and possible loss of SEP status for the arrangement.

Until the employer determines that the 125 percent nondiscrimination test has been satisfied, any transfer or distribution from a SARSEP of restricted funds (salary reduction contributions and income attributable to such contributions) by an HCE is subject to tax and may be subject to the 10 percent premature distribution penalty, regardless of whether an exception to the penalty would otherwise apply. [I.R.C. § 408(k)(6)(F)] Indeed, any distribution, transfer, or rollover of the restricted funds before the earlier of employer certification or March 15 following the end of the plan year will not be treated as an excess contribution permitted to be withdrawn without penalty. [*See* IRS Form 5305A-SEP, Instructions for the Employer—Restrictions on Withdrawals, at 4, and Instructions for the Employee—Excess SEP Contributions (containing references to HCEs), at 7; *but see* Model Elective SEP Deferral Form, at 5 (containing a restriction applicable to all employees) (June 2006).]

> **Practice Pointer.** The tax, if any, is reported in Part I of Form 5329, Additional Taxes on Qualified Plans (Including IRAs) and Other Tax-Favored Accounts.

Under Code Section 408(k)(6)(F), the Secretary of the Treasury has broad discretion to issue reporting and other requirements to "insure" that contributions (and any income allocable thereto) are not withdrawn until the 125 percent nondiscrimination test has been satisfied. Although the rules and legislative history of Code Section 408(k)(6)(F) are quite vague, it could easily be inferred that the tax applies to any employee (not only to an HCE) who withdraws restricted funds. [I.R.C. §§ 408(d)(7)(A), 408(k)(6)(G); TAMRA § 1011(f)(1)-1011(f)(5)]

Rollovers, Conversions, and Recharacterizations

Q 11:92 May a distribution from a terminated qualified plan be rolled over to a SEP maintained by the same employer?

Yes. In Private Letter Ruling 8630068 (Apr. 30, 1986), an employer created a SEP to replace the employer's profit sharing plan, which was being terminated. The IRS permitted a rollover of a participant's full account balance (excluding nontaxable amounts) within 60 days of receipt to be made to the employee's IRA under the SEP. The combination of the rollover with future SEP contributions was held to be permissible.

Q 11:93   Is a direct transfer of an eligible rollover distribution to a SEP permitted?

Yes. In Private Letter Ruling 8033090 (May 23, 1980), a rollover of a discontinued Keogh to a SEP was permitted, but a trustee-to-trustee transfer was not. The Unemployment Compensation Amendments of 1992 amended the Code to allow for the direct transfer of an eligible rollover distribution. Private Letter Ruling 8033090 is therefore obsolete. Note, however, that the IRS uses the term *transfer* to sometimes mean simply a movement of assets, which includes rollovers and transfers. Therefore, the direct transfer allowed under the Unemployment Compensation Amendments of 1992 is a direct rollover and a reportable transaction. [I.R.C. § 401(a)(31); Priv. Ltr. Ruls. 200138030 (June 28, 2002), 9608041 (Dec. 1, 1995), 9547047 (Sept. 1, 1995)]

Q 11:94   May a SEP IRA be converted to a Roth IRA?

Yes. Amounts held in a SEP IRA may be converted to a Roth IRA. [Treas. Reg. § 1.408A-4]

Q 11:95   May SEP IRA contributions be made to a SEP IRA that has been converted to a Roth IRA?

It depends. The conversion may be accomplished by redesignating the SEP IRA as a Roth IRA. If the conversion is accomplished by means of a redesignation, the SEP IRA becomes a Roth IRA and ceases to be part of a SEP; thus, no SEP contributions may be made to the Roth IRA. [Treas. Reg. § 1.408A-4] However, if the conversion is accomplished by means of transferring the SEP IRA assets to a separate and distinct Roth IRA maintained by the same trustee or a different trustee, then the SEP IRA does not become a Roth IRA, and it may still receive employer contributions. [Treas. Reg. § 1.408A-4 Q&A-1(b)]

Q 11:96   May employer contributions under a SEP be recharacterized?

No. Employer contributions under a SEP may not be recharacterized. [Treas. Reg. § 1.408A-5]

Miscellaneous Rules

Q 11:97   What aspects of state law other than income tax might apply to SEPs?

Once contributions are made into a SEP IRA, certain aspects of state law may apply—for example, estate, inheritance, and gift taxes, as well as the rules of escheat and applicability of power-of-attorney documents. Intangible property taxes on account balances (or values) may be imposed. Some states impose taxes on the annual income or the realized gains (or both) generated by a SEP IRA. As a general rule, the validity of a trust is determined under state law.

Escheat law. The ERISA status of SEP IRAs under applicable escheat law cannot be definitely determined. Treasury Regulations Section 1.411(a)-4(b)(6) provides that a benefit "lost by reason of escheat under applicable state law will not be deemed an impermissible forfeiture." That regulation does not apply to SEPs, however, and it provides no guidance as to whether a particular application of state escheat law is preempted under ERISA Section 514. Most states provide for an unclaimed or abandoned IRA to escheat to the state after a number of years, and many documents provide for compliance by the trustee or custodian with such laws.

Q 11:98 Are SEP IRA assets subject to the claims of creditors or the IRS in a non-bankruptcy situation?

Nearly all states grant creditor protection for assets held in an IRA, including a SEP IRA. Most states, however, do not offer any protection from creditors for assets held in an IRA that is established and maintained by a participating employee for the holding of SEP contributions. The Sixth Circuit affirmed a district court order holding that an attorney's SEP was subject to garnishment to satisfy a judgment for violating ERISA. [Lampkins v. Golden, 90 A.F.T.R. 2d 2002-5303 (6th Cir. 2002), 27 Employee Benefits Cas. (BNA) 1587 (2002-1 U.S.T.C. ¶ 50216, 28 Fed. Appx. 409 (6th Cir. Jan. 17, 2002) (unpublished)] The status of assets held in an employer IRA under Code Section 408(c) has not been determined; however, in the authors' opinion, a participant's interest should be treated no differently than a regular, "self-settled" IRA.

Note. The IRS can enforce a federal lien against an IRA. [I.R.C. § 6334] Amounts distributed from an IRA, even if used to satisfy a federal lien, are generally (but not always) subject to the premature distribution penalty if the IRA owner is under age 59½. [Chief Counsel Notice N(36)000-2 (Jan. 21, 2000)]

Q 11:99 Are SEP IRA and SIMPLE IRA plans subject to the ERISA bonding requirements?

It depends. In most cases, an employer that handles funds or other property belonging to an ERISA plan is required to be bonded. For this purpose, a SEP is generally treated as an ERISA plan. The basic standard is determined by the possibility of risk of loss in each situation; thus, it is based on the facts and circumstances in each situation. The amount of a bond is determined at the beginning of each year. It may not be less than 10 percent of the amount of funds handled, and the minimum bond is $1,000. Contributions made by withholding from an employee's salary are not considered funds or other property of a SEP IRA or SIMPLE IRA plan for purposes of the bonding provisions as long as they are retained in, and not segregated in any way from, the general assets of the withholding employer. Because contributions employers make into traditional or SIMPLE IRAs established by individual employees, once made, are outside the control of the employer, bonding would not generally apply. [ERISA §§ 404(c), 412; DOL Reg. §§ 2510.3-3, 2550.412-5]

Q 11:100   Has the IRS indicated any concern that the rules governing SEPs are not always clear and are sometimes not being followed?

Yes. The IRS has issued examination guidelines in response to its concern that the rules governing SEPs are not always clear and, therefore, not always followed. [IRM 4.72.17 (July 31, 2002)]

Q 11:101   How is a SEP or SARSEP terminated?

A SEP may be terminated by an amendment prepared by the employer. Employees must be given notice of the amendment. Because contributions are generally discretionary, a formal termination is rarely used to terminate a SEP. To discontinue elective contributions under a SARSEP, however, an employer would have to formally terminate the elective portion of the plan.

Chapter 12

SIMPLE IRA Arrangements

Martin Fleisher, Esq.
Jo Ann Lippe, Esq.

The savings incentive match plan for employees (SIMPLE) a simplified tax-favored retirement plan for small employers that is available under Section 408(p) of the Internal Revenue Code (Code). Employees may choose to make salary reduction contributions to a SIMPLE individual retirement account or annuity (IRA) rather than receive those amounts as part of their regular compensation. The employer makes a matching contribution or nonelective contribution on behalf of eligible employees.

SIMPLE IRAs are established in conjunction with the SIMPLE adopted by an employer. All contributions are deposited with a financial institution authorized to accept IRA deposits. The employer may stipulate the financial institution that employees must use to establish their SIMPLE IRAs.

This chapter examines the basics of a SIMPLE established in the form of an IRA, employer and employee eligibility, employee notifications, salary reduction arrangements, summary descriptions, the time and manner of making contributions and elections, and the administrative requirements and deposit rules for financial institutions and employers. It also discusses how to use Form 5305-SIMPLE and Form 5304-SIMPLE, whether an employer should use a model form or a prototype document, and the establishment of a SIMPLE IRA by eligible employees. SIMPLE IRAs are compared with 401(k) plans that employ some of the SIMPLE rules to satisfy nondiscrimination requirements.

Basic Concepts

Q 12:1 What is a SIMPLE IRA plan?

A *SIMPLE IRA plan* (more simply referred to as a SIMPLE) is a written agreement established by an employer under Section 408(p) of the Internal Revenue Code (Code) that provides a simplified tax-favored retirement plan for small employers.

A *SIMPLE IRA* is an individual retirement account or an individual retirement annuity established by an individual (an employee or former employee) that satisfies the following rules in addition to the rules for traditional IRAs:

1. The vesting requirements of Code Section 408(p)(3) (see Q 12:80);

2. The participation requirements of Code Section 408(p)(4) (see Q 12:43);

3. The administrative requirements of Code Section 408(p)(5) (see Q 12:82); and

4. The requirement that a qualified salary reduction arrangement exist under which, and only under which, contributions may be made (see Q 12:56).

[I.R.C. § 408(p)(1)]

If an employer establishes a SIMPLE, each eligible employee may choose to have the employer make payments as contributions under the plan or to receive those payments directly in cash. An employer that opts to establish a SIMPLE must make either matching contributions or nonelective contributions.

The only contributions that can be made to a SIMPLE IRA are salary reduction contributions elected by the employee (see Q 12:11), employer matching or nonelective contributions, and rollovers or transfers from another SIMPLE IRA. [Notice 98-4, Q&A A-2, 1998-1 C.B. 269]

Q 12:2 Why did Congress create the SIMPLE?

Congress created the SIMPLE to provide a "simple" tax-favored retirement plan for small employers. The law provides a number of ways for individuals to save for retirement on a tax-favored basis, including employer-sponsored retirement plans such as qualified plans and simplified employee pension plans (SEPs). To receive tax-favored treatment, however, such plans must comply with many rules, including in some cases nondiscrimination and administrative rules. A SIMPLE entails none of the top-heavy or complex discrimination rules or administrative burdens associated with a qualified plan. Thus, for some employers a SIMPLE may be a less burdensome alternative than other types of deferred compensation arrangements.

Q 12:3 Does the SIMPLE replace the SARSEP?

No. The SIMPLE does not entirely replace the salary reduction simplified employee pension plan (SARSEP). For example, for 2009 the maximum contribution that may be made for any employee under a SIMPLE (including employer contributions (see Q 12:58)) is generally $23,000 ($28,000 if the employee is age 50 or older), compared to $49,000 ($54,500 if the employee is age 50 or older) under a SEP or a SARSEP. [I.R.C. §§ 408(p)(2)(E), 415(k)(4); I.R.S. News Release IR-2008-118 (Oct. 16, 2008)] Furthermore, employer matching or nonelective contributions are mandatory under a SIMPLE, but not under a SARSEP. For most employers, however, there is no real choice, since no new SARSEP can be established after 1996 (see chapter 11).

Q 12:4 What are the design parameters of a SIMPLE IRA?

A SIMPLE IRA may be based on either of two Internal Revenue Service (IRS) model forms or on an individually designed prototype approved by the IRS.

Eligible employees use Form 5305-S, SIMPLE Individual Retirement Trust Account, or model Form 5305-SA, SIMPLE Individual Retirement Custodial Account, to establish SIMPLE IRAs (see Q 12:20). These model forms are quite similar to the IRS model forms used to establish traditional IRAs (Forms 5305 and 5305-A). A model SIMPLE IRA, however, may be used only in connection with a contribution made under a SIMPLE or to receive a transfer or rollover from another SIMPLE IRA.

A model or prototype SIMPLE must be used with an IRS model SIMPLE IRA (Form 5305-S or 5305-SA) or an IRS-approved prototype SIMPLE IRA. [Rev. Proc. 97-29, 1997-1 C.B. 698; Rev. Proc. 87-50, 1987-2 C.B. 647]

Note. SIMPLE IRAs established using IRS model forms remain SIMPLE IRAs even after two years of participation (see Q 12:109); that is, they do not become traditional IRAs and cannot accept traditional IRA contributions after that time. A similar restriction applies to prototype SIMPLE IRAs. [SIMPLE IRA—Listing of Required Modifications and Information Package (Mar. 2002)] Thus, a traditional IRA contribution, transfer, or rollover from a qualified plan or a Section 403(b) arrangement to a SIMPLE IRA is not permitted. A SIMPLE IRA can generally be rolled over, but there are several restrictions (see Qs 12:123–12:128).

Q 12:5   Must a SIMPLE be maintained on a calendar-year basis?

Yes. Thus, employer eligibility to establish a SIMPLE (see Qs 12:29–12:42) and SIMPLE contributions (see Qs 12:55–12:72) are determined on a calendar-year basis. [I.R.C. § 408(p)(6)(C)] Nevertheless, a SIMPLE may be started during the year (see Q 12:13).

Q 12:6   Must a SIMPLE be in writing?

Yes. Both a SIMPLE and its requisite qualified salary reduction arrangement must be in writing. [I.R.C. §§ 408(a)–408(c), 408(p)(1), 408(p)(2)(A)]

Q 12:7   Who may be covered under a SIMPLE?

Only employees may be covered under a SIMPLE maintained by an employer. For purposes of a SIMPLE, *employee* means a common-law employee of the employer; the term also includes self-employed individuals and leased employees described in Code Section 414(n). [I.R.C. § 408(p)(6)(B)] It follows that an independent contractor is not treated as an employee. A household employee may also be covered under a SIMPLE (see Q 12:43). [I.R.C. § 4972(c)(6)]

Q 12:8   May contributions made under a SIMPLE be made to any type of IRA?

No. Contributions made under a SIMPLE may be made only to a SIMPLE IRA. Conversely, the only contributions that may be made to a SIMPLE IRA are contributions under a SIMPLE and rollovers or transfers from another SIMPLE IRA. [Notice 98-4, Q&A A-2, 1998-1 C.B. 269]

Q 12:9   May SIMPLE IRA contributions be made to an employer-sponsored IRA under Code Section 408(c)?

Probably. Accounts established by employers and certain associations of employees under Code Section 408(c)—commonly referred to as group IRAs or employer-sponsored IRAs—are usually treated as individual retirement accounts as described in Code Section 408(a). No guidance, however, has been issued on whether SIMPLE IRA contributions may be made to a group SIMPLE IRA. [See Treas. Reg. §§ 1.408A-2, 1.408A-3 (relating to Roth IRAs).] In most cases, group IRAs are submitted to the IRS for advance approval as to form.

Q 12:10   Is a SIMPLE IRA subject to tax?

A SIMPLE IRA is not generally subject to tax. It is, however, subject to tax on unrelated business taxable income that exceeds $1,000. [*See* I.R.C. §§ 408(e), 511.]

Further, if a SIMPLE IRA owner engages in a prohibited transaction, such as borrowing an account's assets or pledging the account as security for a loan, the account ceases to be treated as a SIMPLE IRA. The 15 percent prohibited transaction tax does not apply if the account ceases to be a SIMPLE IRA; instead, all amounts in the account become subject to tax. [I.R.C. §§ 408(e)(1)–408(e)(3), 4975(c)(3)]

Qualified Salary Reduction Arrangement

Q 12:11   What is a qualified salary reduction arrangement?

A *qualified salary reduction arrangement*, one of the basic requirements of a SIMPLE, is a written agreement that allows an eligible employee (see Q 12:43) of an eligible employer (see Q 12:29) to make elective salary reduction contributions to a SIMPLE IRA and requires the employer to make either a matching contribution or a 2 percent nonelective contribution to the SIMPLE IRA. All contributions are fully vested, and there can be no conditions restricting withdrawals. [I.R.C. § 408(p)]

Note. A nonelective contribution feature appears to be a permissive document feature—that is, it does not have to be included in a prototype plan document.

The salary reduction amount that the employee elects must be expressed as a percentage of compensation or a dollar amount, and it may not exceed a total of $11,500 ($14,000 with catch-up contribution) for 2009 (see Q 12:57). [I.R.C. § 408(p)(2)(A)(ii)]

The employer may choose each year whether to make a matching contribution or a nonelective contribution to the SIMPLE IRA, but must contribute one or the other. If the employer chooses to make a matching contribution, the employer's contribution must equal the amount that the employee elects to defer, subject to a cap. The cap is determined as the *applicable percentage* of the employee's compensation. [I.R.C. § 408(p)(2)(A)(iii)] The applicable percentage is generally 3 percent, but under certain circumstances the employer may elect a lower percentage (not less than 1 percent) for the year for all employees eligible to participate in the plan (see Q 12:62). [I.R.C. § 408(p)(2)(C)(ii)] Alternatively, if the employer chooses to make a nonelective contribution, the employer's contribution is equal to 2 percent of the employee's compensation. [I.R.C. § 408(p)(2)(B)]

Q 12:12   How long does a qualified salary reduction arrangement remain in effect?

In general, a qualified salary reduction arrangement replaces any earlier arrangements and remains in effect as long as the individual who is a party to the arrangement remains an eligible employee under the SIMPLE or until the employee requests that salary reduction contributions be discontinued, the plan is terminated, or the employee provides the employer with a new salary reduction arrangement as permitted under the SIMPLE.

An eligible employee must be permitted to terminate a salary reduction arrangement at any time (see Q 12:77). The termination request must be in writing and become effective as soon as practicable after receipt of the request by the employer or, if later, the date specified in the termination request. [I.R.C. § 408(p)(5)(B)]

Establishing a SIMPLE

Q 12:13   Must an employer establish its initial SIMPLE on January 1?

Not necessarily. An existing employer may establish a SIMPLE effective on any date between January 1 and October 1, inclusive, if the employer (or any predecessor employer; see Q 12:14) did not previously maintain a SIMPLE (see Q 12:41). If, however, an employer or predecessor employer previously maintained a SIMPLE, it may establish a SIMPLE effective only on January 1 (see Q 12:42). [Notice 98-4, Q&A K-1, 1998-1 C.B. 269]

Q 12:14   What is a predecessor employer?

The term *predecessor employer* has not been defined for SIMPLE purposes. However, a regulation under Code Section 415 (which does not apply to SIMPLE IRAs) generally would find the existence of a predecessor employer if:

1. A plan maintained by the current employer continues a benefit that a participant accrued while performing services for a former employer, or
2. The current employer constitutes (taking facts and circumstances into account) a continuation of all or a portion of the trade or business of a former entity that predated the current employer.

[Treas. Reg. § 1.415(f)-1(c); *see* Treasury Decision 9319 (Apr. 5, 2007).]

Q 12:15   When is a SIMPLE considered adopted?

If a model form (Form 5305-SIMPLE or Form 5304-SIMPLE) is used to establish a SIMPLE (see Q 12:19), the plan is considered adopted when all appropriate boxes and blanks have been completed and the form has been executed by an employer and a designated financial institution (DFI). In the case of a prototype, a SIMPLE is considered adopted when all instructions for the adoption of the prototype have been followed.

Q 12:16 What is the effective date of a SIMPLE?

In general, the effective date of a SIMPLE is the date that its provisions become effective.

For SIMPLEs established using Form 5305-SIMPLE or Form 5304-SIMPLE, as well as for prototype SIMPLEs, January 1 is the effective date. In the first year an employer adopts a SIMPLE, however, the effective date may be any date from January 1 through October 1 of the applicable year. Unless the plan provides for additional election periods (see Q 12:77), an employee's election to participate may be set to expire on the day before the plan's effective date.

Q 12:17 When must a SIMPLE IRA be established for an employee?

A SIMPLE IRA must be established for an employee on or before the first date by which a contribution is required to be deposited into the employee's SIMPLE IRA. [Notice 98-4, Q&A K-2, 1998-1 C.B. 269]

Q 12:18 Is IRS approval of a SIMPLE or a SIMPLE IRA required?

No. A favorable opinion letter or letter ruling from the IRS regarding a SIMPLE or a SIMPLE IRA is not required as a condition of receiving favorable tax treatment; however, the form of a nonapproved plan may not be relied on by either an adopting employer or an employee (see Q 12:20). Without IRS approval, clearly there is no assurance that the form of the document establishing a SIMPLE or a SIMPLE IRA will guarantee the deferral of income taxes and the deductibility of employer contributions.

A prototype or model SIMPLE must be used with an IRS model SIMPLE IRA (Form 5305-S or 5305-SA) or an IRS-approved prototype SIMPLE IRA (see Q 12:19). [Rev. Proc. 87-50, 1987-2 C.B. 647; Rev. Proc. 97-29, 1997-1 C.B. 698]

Q 12:19 Has the IRS made available model SIMPLE and SIMPLE IRA forms ?

Yes. The IRS has issued four model forms pertaining to SIMPLEs; they are similar to the model forms used to establish traditional IRAs (Forms 5305 and 5305-A). The forms were last revised in September 2008.

Form 5305-SIMPLE—Savings Incentive Match Plan for Employees of Small Employers (SIMPLE) (For Use With a Designated Financial Institution). This form provides small employers with a way to adopt a SIMPLE by using a model plan document, notification to employees, and salary reduction arrangement. It is for use by employers that require that all contributions be made to SIMPLE IRAs established for participants at a DFI. [I.R.S. News Release IR-96-46 (Oct. 31, 1996)]

Form 5304-SIMPLE—Savings Incentive Match Plan for Employees of Small Employers (SIMPLE) (Not Subject to the Designated Financial Institution Rules). This form provides small employers with a way to adopt a SIMPLE by using a model plan document, notification to employees, and salary reduction arrangement. It is for use by employers that permit plan participants to select the financial institutions at which their SIMPLE IRAs are established. [I.R.S. News Release IR-96-55 (Dec. 30, 1996)]

Form 5305-S—SIMPLE Individual Retirement Trust Account. This form provides eligible employees and financial institutions with a model trust account that meets the requirements of Code Sections 408(a) and 408(p). A SIMPLE IRA is established after the form is fully executed by both the participant and the trustee.

Form 5305-SA—SIMPLE Individual Retirement Custodial Account. This form provides eligible employees and financial institutions with a model custodial account that meets the requirements of Code Sections 408(a) and 408(p). A SIMPLE IRA is established after the form is fully executed by both the participant and the custodian.

Q 12:20 May a model SIMPLE be submitted by an adopting employer for approval by the IRS?

No. An eligible employer that adopts one of the IRS model SIMPLE forms and follows its terms is assured that the plan meets the requirements of Code Section 408(p). Because automatic approval has been granted, no ruling, opinion, or determination letter from the IRS regarding the SIMPLE is necessary, and none will be issued.

Q 12:21 Must Form 5305-SIMPLE or Form 5304-SIMPLE be used to establish a SIMPLE?

No. A SIMPLE may be established using Form 5305-SIMPLE, Form 5304-SIMPLE, or any other document that satisfies the statutory requirements (see Qs 12:1, 12:4, 12:18). [I.R.C. § 408(p)(2)(A)]

Q 12:22 Why may a SIMPLE not be adopted after October 1?

An employer generally may not adopt a SIMPLE after October 1 for at least two reasons:

1. To lessen the likelihood of overlapping election periods (see Q 12:73), which could occur, for example, if the election period for the second year starts on November 2 (60 days before the beginning of any year); and
2. To prevent possible abuses when the plan is adopted late in the year.

Example. On December 25, Swift Manufacturing established a SIMPLE providing for a 3 percent matching contribution. Although all Swift employees are eligible to participate (and have received summary descriptions, forms, notices, and elections), only one, the company's president, elects to participate. Arguably, the adoption is not a valid one, because the "necessary opportunity to participate" did not occur. [SBJPA § 1421(a); S. Rep. No. 104-281 on H.R. Rep. No. 3448, II (June 18, 1996)]

Special rules apply to new employers that come into existence after October 1 (see Q 12:41).

Q 12:23 May an employer amend Form 5305-SIMPLE or Form 5304-SIMPLE?

Yes, an employer may amend Form 5305-SIMPLE or Form 5304-SIMPLE. It should be noted, however, that an employer may amend only the entries inserted in the blanks or boxes on those forms. A SIMPLE IRA plan established using an IRS-approved prototype document (fill-ins and optional provisions) may also be amended.

An amendment to a SIMPLE can be made effective only at the beginning of a calendar year and must conform to the content of the plan notice (see Q 12:82) for that calendar year. Thus, an amendment that conforms to the plan notice may be made effective as of the beginning of that calendar year. [*See* SIMPLE IRAs Listing of Required Modifications and Information Package (LRM), item 18 (Mar. 2002).]

Q 12:24 May Form 5305-SIMPLE and Form 5304-SIMPLE be reproduced and used without making any reference to the IRS or its forms?

Very possibly. Rules exist for the use of IRS model forms for SEPs and SARSEPs. It is likely that similar rules apply to SIMPLEs that use Form 5305-SIMPLE or Form 5304-SIMPLE. If so, the provisions of the model forms may be reproduced on the letterhead of an employer or in pamphlets that omit all reference to the IRS and its forms (see Qs 12:21, 12:25).

Q 12:25 May the IRS model SIMPLE IRA forms be reproduced and reduced in size?

Yes. Form 5305-S and Form 5305-SA may be reproduced and reduced in size—for example, to passbook size.

Q 12:26 When should an employer *not* use Form 5305-SIMPLE to establish a SIMPLE?

An employer should *not* use Form 5305-SIMPLE in any of the following circumstances:

1. The form does not meet the employer's needs and objectives. (A prototype SIMPLE may contain more flexible provisions that better suit the needs and objectives of the employer. A prototype may also offer greater protection to the financial institution that sponsors the plan document or invests the contributions.)

2. Employees are to be given the right to choose a financial institution that will initially receive contributions; that is, the employer will not be designating or selecting the financial institution. (Form 5304-SIMPLE may be used in this case.)

3. Nonresident alien employees receiving no earned income from the employer that constitutes income from sources within the United States are to be eligible under the plan (see Q 12:44).

4. The employer wants to establish a SIMPLE in the form of a qualified 401(k) plan.

Q 12:27 Will the IRS issue an opinion letter approving or rejecting the form of a document intended to be a prototype SIMPLE?

Yes. Form 5306-A, Application for Approval of Prototype Simplified Employee Pension (SEP) or Savings Incentive Match Plan for Employees of Small Employers (SIMPLE IRA Plan), is used to request IRS approval of a prototype SIMPLE.

Q 12:28 Is there a fee for requesting IRS approval of a prototype SIMPLE?

Yes. The IRS imposes a user fee for the review of plan documents and their amendments. [Rev. Proc. 2009-8, 2009-1 I.R.B. 229] The fee is determined by the document type and use and the type of sponsor.

Employer Eligibility

Q 12:29 May any employer establish a SIMPLE?

No. A SIMPLE may be established only by an employer that had no more than 100 employees who earned $5,000 or more in compensation (see Qs 12:30–12:34, 12:38) during the preceding calendar year (the 100-employee limit). [I.R.C. § 408(p)(2)(C)(i)]

Q 12:30 May any employees be excluded for the purpose of the 100-employee limit?

No. For purposes of the 100-employee limit, all employees employed at any time during the prior calendar year are taken into account, regardless of whether they are eligible to participate in the SIMPLE. Thus, certain unionized employees who are excludable under the rules of Code Section 410(b)(3), nonresident alien employees, and employees who have not met the plan's minimum eligibility requirements (see Q 12:44) must be taken into account. Employees also include self-employed individuals who received earned income from the employer during the year. [I.R.C. §§ 401(c)(1), 408(p)(2)(C)(i)(I), 408(p)(4)(A)]

An employer may adopt a SIMPLE for non-collectively bargained employees without violating the exclusive plan requirement (see Q 12:39) even though the employer also maintains a qualified plan for collectively bargained employees. [I.R.C. § 408(p)(2)(D)(i)] All employees, however, are taken into account for the purpose of determining whether an employer has 100 or fewer employees.

Q 12:31   How are leased employees treated for purposes of the 100-employee limit?

If an employer has leased employees who are required to be treated as its own employees under Code Section 414(n), the leased employees must be treated as employees of the employer for purposes of the employer's eligibility to establish a SIMPLE (see Q 12:29). [I.R.C. §§ 414(b), 414(c), 414(m), 414(n), 414(o)]

Q 12:32   How are related employers treated for purposes of the 100-employee limit?

Certain related employers (trades or businesses under common control) must be treated as a single employer. As a result, individuals working for related employers are treated as if they were employed by a single employer for purposes of satisfying the SIMPLE requirements, including the 100-employee limit.

Related employers include the following:

- A controlled group of corporations under Code Section 414(b)
- A partnership or sole proprietorship under common control under Code Section 414(c)
- An affiliated service group under Code Section 414(n)

Example. Pam owns Peach, a computer rental agency that has 80 employees, each of whom received more than $5,000 in compensation in 2009. Pam also owns Pear, a company that repairs computers and has 60 employees, each of whom received more than $5,000 in compensation in 2009. Pam is the sole proprietor of both businesses. Code Section 414(c) provides that the employees of partnerships and sole proprietorships that are under common control are treated as employees of a single employer. Thus, for purposes of the SIMPLE rules, all 140 employees are treated as being employed by Peach. As a result, neither Peach nor Pear is eligible to establish a SIMPLE for 2010.

Q 12:33   Is a grace period available to an employer that ceases to satisfy the 100-employee limit?

Yes. An employer that previously maintained a SIMPLE for at least one year is treated as satisfying the 100-employee limit for the two calendar years immediately following the calendar year for which it last satisfied that requirement. [I.R.C. § 408(p)(2)(C)(i)(II)] A special transition rule applies if the failure to satisfy the 100-employee limit results from an acquisition, disposition, or similar transaction involving the employer (see Q 12:34).

Example. Train Associates employed 90 individuals during 2007 and 2008. It establishes a SIMPLE for 2009 for employees who earned at least $5,000 during any two previous years. During 2009, Train hires 50 additional employees. All employees earn at least $5,000. If it were not for the grace period, Train would not be eligible to maintain a SIMPLE for 2010, because it employed more than 100 employees earning at least $5,000. However, as a result of the grace period, Train is permitted to maintain the SIMPLE for 2009 and 2010.

Q 12:34 What transition rule applies to the 100-employee limit?

If the failure to satisfy the 100-employee limit is the result of an acquisition, disposition, or similar transaction involving the employer, the qualified plan transition rule for coverage when there is an acquisition or disposition replaces the two-year grace period. That is, the grace period runs through the end of the year following the acquisition or disposition. [I.R.C. §§ 408(p)(2)(D)(iii)(II), 408(p)(10), 410(b)(6)(C)]

Q 12:35 May an employer make contributions under a SIMPLE for a calendar year if it maintains a qualified plan?

No. An employer-maintained SIMPLE must be the only plan of the employer. An employer may not make contributions under a SIMPLE for a calendar year if the employer, or a predecessor employer, maintains a qualified plan (see Q 12:36) under which any of its employees receives an allocation of contributions (in the case of a defined contribution plan) or has an increase in a benefit accrued or treated as an accrued benefit under Code Section 411(d)(6) (in the case of a defined benefit plan) for any plan year beginning or ending in that calendar year. If such a contribution is made, all SIMPLE contributions become excess contributions and should be treated as wages by the employer on Form W-2, Wage and Tax Statement. Nonetheless, an employer may maintain a qualified plan covering collectively bargained employees only (see Q 12:30). Employees covered under such a plan must be excluded from participation in the SIMPLE (see Q 12:44). [I.R.C. § 408(p)(2)(D)]

Certain types of contributions are disregarded; that is, they are not treated as contributions (see Q 12:37).

Q 12:36 What types of employer-sponsored plans are considered to be qualified plans for the purpose of denying a SIMPLE contribution?

For the purpose of denying a SIMPLE contribution, *qualified plan* means a plan, contract, pension, or trust described in Code Section 219(g)(5) as follows:

1. A qualified pension, profit sharing, or stock bonus plan under Code Section 401(a) that includes a tax-exempt trust under Code Section 501(a);

2. An annuity plan under Code Section 403(a);

3. A tax-sheltered annuity contract described in Code Section 403(b);

4. A governmental plan (i.e., a plan established by the United States, a state, an agency of a state, or a political subdivision of a state) other than an eligible deferred compensation plan under Code Section 457(b);

5. Certain trusts funded solely with employee contributions under Code Section 501(c)(18);

6. A SEP or SARSEP within the meaning of Code Section 408(k); and

7. A SIMPLE IRA within the meaning of Code Section 408(p).

[I.R.C. §§ 219(g)(5)(A), 408(p)(2)(D)]

It follows from item 7 that an employer may not maintain more than one SIMPLE without losing its deductions.

Q 12:37   What contributions are disregarded in determining whether a contribution has been made to a qualified plan?

Except to the extent that forfeitures replace otherwise-required contributions, forfeitures, transfers, and rollovers are disregarded in determining whether a contribution has been made to a qualified plan. [Notice 98-4, Q&A B-3, 1998-1 C.B. 269]

Q 12:38   Are tax-exempt organizations and governmental entities permitted to establish SIMPLEs?

Yes. The IRS permits tax-exempt organizations and governmental entities to establish SIMPLEs (in contrast to its explicit refusal to permit such employers to establish SARSEPs). [I.R.C. § 408(k)(6)(E); Priv. Ltr. Ruls. 8833047 (May 27, 1988), 8824019 (Mar. 17, 1988)]

Excludable contributions may be made to the SIMPLE IRAs of employees of tax-exempt organizations and governmental entities on the same basis as contributions may be made for employees of other eligible employers. [Notice 98-4, Q&A B-4, 1998-1 C.B. 269] It should be noted, however, that a governmental entity may not maintain a SIMPLE in the form of a 401(k) plan. [I.R.C. § 401(k)(4)(B)(ii)]

Q 12:39   May an employer maintain a SIMPLE and an eligible plan under Code Section 457(b) without violating the only-plan-of-the-employer rule?

Yes. Contributions made under a Section 457 plan do not violate the only-plan-of-the-employer rule, because such a plan is not a qualified plan; furthermore, a Section 457 plan is not treated as a qualified plan for the purpose of denying SIMPLE contributions (see Q 12:36). [I.R.C. §§ 219(g)(5)(A), 219(g)(5)(B), 408(p)(2)(D)(ii)] The limits under an eligible Section 457(b) plan are not reduced by the amount of elective employer contributions deferred by an employee under a SIMPLE (or 401(k) SIMPLE). [I.R.C. § 457(c)]

Q 12:40   May a new employer establish a SIMPLE?

Yes. A new employer could qualify as an employer eligible to establish a SIMPLE; however, the employer would have to adopt extremely liberal eligibility requirements. Otherwise, the plan would have no participants.

In the case of a new employer, it is unclear whether the IRS may require that the 100-employee limit be satisfied during the first 30 days that the business was in existence (as it does for the less-than-25 rule for SARSEPs). [Rev. Proc. 91-44, § VI.D, 1991-2 C.B. 733, *modified by* Rev. Proc. 2008-8, 2008-1 I.R.B. 233] Arguably, a new employer qualifies because it had no employees in the previous year.

Q 12:41   How is a new employer that comes into existence after October 1 treated?

The requirement that a SIMPLE become effective on any date from January 1 through October 1 does not apply to a new employer that comes into existence after October 1 of the year the SIMPLE is established if the employer establishes the SIMPLE as soon as administratively feasible after it comes into existence.

Note. The IRS model SIMPLE forms do not allow for an adoption date later than October 1 of the applicable year (see Q 12:22).

Q 12:42   May an employer that terminates a SIMPLE start another SIMPLE in the same taxable year?

No. If an employer (or predecessor employer; see Q 12:14) previously maintained a SIMPLE, it may establish a SIMPLE effective only on January 1. [Notice 98-4, Q&A K-1, 1998-1 C.B. 269]

Employee Eligibility

Q 12:43   Which employees are eligible to participate in a SIMPLE?

All employees of the employer who received at least $5,000 in compensation from the employer during any two preceding calendar years (whether or not consecutive) and who are reasonably expected to receive at least $5,000 in compensation during the calendar year are eligible to participate in the SIMPLE for the calendar year. The term *reasonably expected* is not defined. [I.R.C. § 408(p)(4)(A), 408(p)(6)(B)]

Example. Harry's employer maintains a SIMPLE in 2010. The plan uses the most restrictive service provision (two years) and compensation threshold ($5,000) that the law allows to determine eligibility. Harry earned $10,000 in

2003 and 2004 but did not perform any services during 2005, 2006, or 2007. During 2008 and 2009, Harry earned $4,000 each year. Harry is reasonably expected to earn $7,000 in 2010. He is eligible to participate in 2010 because he can reasonably be expected to earn at least $5,000 in compensation during the current year and he earned at least $5,000 in two previous years (2003 and 2004).

Certain employees may be excluded from participation (see Q 12:44), although a SIMPLE may not impose an age requirement.

Caution. Independent contractors are not considered employees. Employers should note, however, that in many cases part-time employees are misidentified as independent contractors. [*See* Treas. Reg. § 31.3401(c)-1(b); Rev. Rul. 87-41, 1987-1 C.B. 296.]

An employer can make contributions on behalf of domestic and similar workers other than the employer or a member of the employer's family but cannot deduct such contributions because they are not made in connection with the employer's trade or business. A 10 percent excise tax is normally levied on employers that make nondeductible contributions to a SIMPLE IRA, but these contributions do not trigger it. This is because an exemption exists for contributions that are nondeductible solely because they do not qualify as trade or business expenses. [I.R.C. § 4972(c)(6)]

Note. This provision is intended to apply only to employers that have paid and continue to pay all applicable employment taxes, but the statute does not include this limitation. [EGTRRA § 637; H.R. Conf. Rep. No. 107-51, pt. 1 (2001)] Similar provisions were not made for a SEP or SARSEP covering only a domestic or household worker. Thus, the nondeductible contribution to a SEP or grandfathered SARSEP (see Q 12:3) may be subject to a 10 percent penalty. [I.R.C. § 4972(d)(1)(A)(iv)]

Q 12:44 May an employee be excluded from participation in a SIMPLE?

Yes. An employer, at its option, may exclude from eligibility for a SIMPLE any employee described in Code Section 410(b)(3). [I.R.C. § 408(p)(4)(B)] The plan document must affirmatively exclude such employees by classification.

The following employees may be excluded:

1. An employee who is included in a unit of employees covered by an agreement that the Secretary of Labor finds to be a collective bargaining agreement between employee representatives and one or more employers, if there is evidence that retirement benefits were the subject of good-faith bargaining between such employee representatives and such employer or employers;

2. In the case of a trust established or maintained pursuant to an agreement that the Secretary of Labor finds to be a collective bargaining agreement between air pilots represented in accordance with Title II of the Railway Labor Act and one or more employers, all employees *not* covered by that agreement; and

3. An employee who is a nonresident alien and who received no earned income (within the meaning of Code Section 911(d)(2)) from the employer that constitutes income from sources within the United States (within the meaning of Code Section 861(a)(3); see Q 12:134).

The related employer rules (see Q 12:32) and leased employee rules (see Q 12:31) apply for purposes of Code Section 408(p). Thus, for example, if two related employers must be aggregated under the rules of Code Section 414(b), all employees of either employer who satisfy the eligibility criteria must be allowed to participate in the SIMPLE.

The IRS model SIMPLE forms (see Q 12:19) automatically exclude from participation nonresident alien employees receiving no earned income from an employer that constitutes income from sources within the United States, but allow an employer to choose whether to exclude employees covered under a collective bargaining agreement in which retirement benefits were the subject of good-faith bargaining.

Q 12:45 May an employer impose less restrictive eligibility requirements for its SIMPLE?

Yes. An employer may impose less restrictive eligibility requirements for its SIMPLE by eliminating or reducing the previous-year compensation requirements, the current-year compensation requirements, or both. An employer could, for instance, allow participation for employees who received $2,500 in compensation during any preceding calendar year.

Note. Plane Company, an eligible employer, establishes a SIMPLE in 2009. All employees who received any compensation from Plane during any one preceding year are eligible. Joe worked for Plane in 2008; therefore, he is eligible to participate in 2009.

Q 12:46 May an employer impose more restrictive eligibility requirements for its SIMPLE?

No. An employer may not impose conditions for participating in a SIMPLE that are more restrictive than those set forth by the SBJPA and the IRS.

Q 12:47 May an employer use a rolling eligibility period to exclude employees who become eligible?

It is unclear at this time whether a SIMPLE may be amended each year to increase the number of years of service needed to participate.

Example. Marvin, the owner and only employee of a newly established small business, creates a SIMPLE in 2009 using an IRS model SIMPLE form. The plan does not have a service requirement. A new employee, Carl, is hired in June, and Marvin amends the plan to provide for one year of service so that Carl will not be eligible to participate until the following year. In 2010, Marvin amends the plan again, this time effective January 1, 2011. The amendment is timely and conforms to the summary plan description (see Q 12:82) previously provided to eligible employees (i.e., himself only). The new amendment provides for a two-year service requirement. Again, Carl is ineligible. It is not known whether such a rolling eligibility period will pass IRS scrutiny, but given that such serial amendments would be prohibited in a qualified plan it seems unlikely that they would pass muster under a SIMPLE.

Q 12:48 May an employee participate in a SIMPLE if he or she also participates in a plan of an unrelated employer for the same year?

Yes. An employee may participate in a SIMPLE if he or she also participates in a plan of an unrelated employer in the same year. The employee's salary reduction contributions are subject to the limitations of Code Section 402(g), which provides an aggregate limit for 2009 on the exclusion for elective deferrals for any individual of $16,500 ($22,000 for employees who have reached age 50 by the end of the year. (See Qs 12:36 and 12:39 for a discussion of participation in a Section 457 plan.) [I.R.S. News Release IR-2008-118 (Oct. 16, 2008)] Individuals who participate in a SIMPLE IRA plan and a deferred compensation plan, as described in Code Section 457(b), are not subject to the contribution coordination rules. [I.R.C. § 457(c); EGTRRA § 611(d)]

> **Note.** An employer that establishes a SIMPLE is not responsible for monitoring compliance with the dollar limitations under Code Section 402(g) if the SIMPLE is the only plan maintained by the employer. [Notice 98-4, Q&A C-3, 1998-1 C.B. 269]

Q 12:49 How are rehired employees and employees who are eligible to participate immediately on initial hire treated for SIMPLE purposes?

An employee eligible to participate upon becoming first employed and a rehired employee must be permitted under a special rule to make or modify a salary reduction election under a SIMPLE during the 60-day period that begins on the day the plan notice is provided to the employee and that includes the day the employee becomes an eligible employee or the day before (see Qs 12:73, 12:75). The notice must normally be provided by the employer immediately before the employee's 60-day election period and not on the date participation commences (see Q 12:73).

> **Example.** Stacy, an eligible employee, was a participant in her employer's SIMPLE until she severed her employment and cancelled her salary reduction agreement in January 2009. She was rehired on May 1. On May 1 Stacy was provided notice of the opportunity to make an election. The 60-day period that started on May 1 includes the day Stacy became an eligible employee. If it were not for the special rule, Stacy would have to wait until the following year (2010), which would be the first year in which the 60-day period could begin on a date that included the day she became an eligible employee (or the day before).

Compensation

Q 12:50 What definition of *compensation* applies for purposes of a SIMPLE for a person who is not a self-employed individual?

For purposes of a SIMPLE, *compensation* for a person who is not a self-employed individual generally means the amount described in Code Section 6051(a)(3) (i.e., wages, tips, and other compensation from the employer subject to income tax withholding under Code Section 3401(a)) and amounts described in Code Section 6051(a)(8), including elective deferrals made under a SIMPLE and compensation deferred under an eligible Section 457 plan. [I.R.C. §§ 408(p)(6)(A)(i), 3401(a), 6051(a)(3), 6051(a)(8)] (See also Q 12:134 regarding nonresident alien crews of foreign transportation vessels.) As of 2009, *compensation* also includes differential pay that an employer provides during an employee's period of active duty in the U.S. uniformed services extending more than 30 days, to make up for some or all of the wages that would be paid if the services were provided to the employer. [I.R.C. § 219(f)(1)]

For purposes of applying the 100-employee limit and determining whether an employee is eligible to participate in a SIMPLE by virtue of previous amounts of compensation, an employee's compensation also includes his or her elective deferrals under a 401(k) plan, a SARSEP, or a Section 403(b) annuity contract. [I.R.C. §§ 408(p)(6)(A), 6051(a)(3), 6051(a)(8)]

Example 1. Ian, an eligible employee of Nuts and Bolts, Inc., earned $10,000 and elected to defer 5 percent of that amount into his employer's SIMPLE. Although only $9,500 is reported on his Form W-2, Ian's compensation for plan purposes is $10,000 ($9,500 + $500). If Nuts and Bolts elected to make a 2 percent nonelective contribution for the year, Ian would receive $200 ($10,000 × .02).

Example 2. Donna has been a full-time employee of the Giant Motor Company for 18 years. Her annual salary is $36,000. Shortly before the plan's election period (November 2 to December 31), Donna requests and is granted an 11-month personal leave of absence to start on January 1, 2010. For 2010, Donna is reasonably expected to earn only $3,000 and is not eligible to participate in the SIMPLE that year if Giant Motor imposes a current compensation requirement in excess of $3,000.

Example 3. The facts are the same as those in Example 2, except that (1) on January 2, 2010, Donna decides not to take the leave of absence, (2) Giant Motor elects to make the 2 percent nonelective contribution, and (3) Giant Motor's SIMPLE requires that an employee have $5,000 of current compensation to participate, but only $2,000 of previous compensation to be eligible. Donna is not entitled to receive a nonelective contribution for 2010 because she was not an eligible employee; that is, during the election period for 2010 (the 60-day period immediately preceding the first day of 2010), it was not reasonably expected that Donna would earn $5,000 in current (2010) compensation.

Note. In the authors' opinion, compensation earned before the effective date of a SIMPLE should not be disregarded absent clear indication from the IRS to the contrary.

Q 12:51   What definition of *compensation* applies for purposes of a SIMPLE for a self-employed individual?

For purposes of a SIMPLE, *compensation* for a self-employed individual means net earnings from self-employment determined under Code Section 1402(a), without regard to Code Section 1402(c)(6), before subtracting any contributions made under the SIMPLE on behalf of the individual. [I.R.C. § 408(p)(6)(A)] Thus, for example, a sole proprietor who has $10,000 of personal service income from self-employment and is the only participant in a SIMPLE will make a contribution to the SIMPLE based on compensation of $9,235 – ($10,000 × (1 – .0765)). For purposes of a SIMPLE, self-employed individuals generally may use the amount on line 4 in Section A, or line 6 in Section B, of Schedule SE (Form 1040) as their compensation. [I.R.C. § 408(p)(6)(A)(ii)]

Note. IRS model documents (Forms 5304-SIMPLE and 5305-SIMPLE) specifically include in the definition of "compensation" amounts paid for domestic service in a private home, local college, club, or local chapter of a college fraternity or sorority.

Q 12:52   Must an unincorporated business owner's net earnings from self-employment be reduced by the owner's matching and nonelective contributions made on behalf of nonowner employees?

Yes. Employer matching and nonelective contributions made on behalf of nonowner-employees (common-law employees) are deducted as an expense of the business, and this results in a reduction of an owner's net earnings from self-employment. [I.R.C. §§ 404(a), 404(h), 404(k), 404(m), 1402(a)]

Q 12:53   Can SIMPLE contributions for a self-employed nonowner-employee create a loss for that self-employed individual?

Yes. [I.R.C. § 1402(a)] Contributions made on behalf of nonowner-employees in an unincorporated business reduce the owner's income. A distributable loss could result.

Q 12:54   Can a matching or nonelective contribution to a SIMPLE made on behalf of a self-employed individual create a deductible loss or an excess contribution?

The IRS has not issued any guidance with regard to the matter; that is, it is unclear whether a self-employed individual may claim a loss for the required matching contribution (or, alternatively, the nonelective contribution) made on his or her behalf. This situation may arise if compensation is insufficient to support a self-employed person's contributions under a SIMPLE.

> **Example.** Jane, a self-employed individual with no other employees, has compensation (after all adjustments; see Q 12:51) of $4,000. Her SIMPLE provides for a matching contribution (up to 3 percent of compensation). Jane contributes $4,000 and also receives a $120 matching contribution. The combined contributions exceed her compensation by $120. It is not clear whether Jane can deduct the $120 matching contribution, nor whether the 10 percent excise tax applies to it.

> **Note.** In the case of a qualified defined contribution plan, contributions that exceed a self-employed individual's earned income are not deductible by reason of Code Section 404(a)(8)(C). That provision does not apply, however, to a SIMPLE.

Contributions

Q 12:55   What contributions must an employer make under a SIMPLE?

Under a SIMPLE, the employer must make salary reduction contributions that the employees elect (see Q 12:61). In addition, the employer must make employer matching contributions (see Q 12:57) or employer nonelective contributions (see Q 12:65).

Q 12:56   What is a salary reduction contribution?

A *salary reduction contribution* is a contribution made pursuant to an employee's voluntary election via a qualified salary reduction arrangement (see Qs 12:11–12:12) to have an amount contributed to his or her SIMPLE IRA rather than have the amount paid directly to the employee in cash. An employee must be permitted to elect to have salary reduction contributions made at the level he or she specifies, expressed as a percentage of compensation for the year. Additionally, an employer may permit an employee to express the level of salary reduction contributions as a specific dollar amount (see Q 12:60). [Notice 98-4, Q&A D-2, 1998-2 I.R.B. 26]

Q 12:57   What is the maximum annual limit imposed by the IRS on the amount of salary reduction contributions made by any one employee to a SIMPLE IRA?

A participant in a SIMPLE may defer the lesser of 100 percent of compensation or $11,500 ($14,000 if age 50 or older) for 2009. The participant will receive a matching contribution of 3 percent of compensation (or less if permitted) or receive a nonelective contribution equal to 2 percent of compensation. [I.R.C. § 408(p)] If the nonelective contribution is made, only compensation up to the limit in Code Section 401(a)(17) is taken into account; for 2009, that limit is

$245,000. [I.R.C. § 408(p)(2)(B)(ii); I.R.S. News Release IR-2008-118 (Oct. 16, 2008)]

Example. Gloria, age 55, participates in a SIMPLE. For 2009, her compensation is $600,000 and she defers the maximum of $14,000. If Gloria's employer matches her deferrals at 3 percent of compensation, Gloria's matching contribution would be $14,000 ($600,000 × .03 = $18,000, but capped at $14,000, the amount of her deferrals). Alternatively, if Gloria's employer uses the 2 percent nonelective option, Gloria's nonelective contribution would be $4,900 ($245,000 compensation limit × .02).

Q 12:58 May an employer place restrictions on the amount of an employee's annual salary reduction contributions to a SIMPLE IRA?

No. An employer may not place any restrictions on the amount of an employee's annual salary reduction contributions to a SIMPLE IRA (e.g., by limiting the contribution percentage), except to the extent needed to comply with the annual limit imposed by the IRS (see Qs 12:57, 12:59). [Notice 98-4, Q&A D-2, 1998-1 C.B. 269]

Q 12:59 Are elective deferrals limited to the amount the employee would have received in cash after FICA and FUTA taxes are deducted?

The IRS has not issued any guidance regarding limits on elective deferral amounts vis-à-vis taxes imposed under the Federal Insurance Contributions Act (FICA) and the Federal Unemployment Tax Act (FUTA) (see Q 12:105). It is unclear whether an employer may limit the amount that must be deposited to the portion that remains after applicable taxes and other amounts have been deducted from wages (see Q 12:58). The question may arise when a low-paid employee elects to defer more than the amount of his or her net payroll check. Because only the net amount would have been received in cash (see Q 12:56), arguably, only the net amount is available for deferral by the employee. [I.R.C. § 408(p)(2)(A)(i)(II)]

Q 12:60 How must elective deferrals under a SIMPLE be expressed?

The amount deferred under a SIMPLE by an employee must be expressed as a percentage of compensation (including bonuses) or a specific dollar amount. [I.R.C. § 408(p)(2)(A)(ii)] The following language is appropriate for elective deferrals:

> Subject to the requirements of the employer's SIMPLE plan, I authorize (a) _____ percent, or (b) $_____ (which equals _____ percent of my current rate of pay) to be withheld from my pay for each pay period and contributed to my SIMPLE IRA as a salary reduction contribution.

[IRS Form 5305-SIMPLE]

The deferral language set out above is also suitable for a self-employed individual whose compensation is determined at the end of the business's taxable year. [Treas. Reg. § 1.401(k)-1(a)(6)(B)(ii), 1.401(k)-1(b)(4)(B)(iii)]

Note. A partner may not make a cash or deferred election with respect to compensation for a partnership taxable year after the last day of that year because a partner's compensation is deemed currently available on the last day of the partnership's taxable year. [Treas. Reg. § 1.401(k)-1(a)(6)(B)(ii)] Periodic advances made by partners throughout the year, pursuant to an election of the partner, are "elective contributions," assuming the plan otherwise satisfies the applicable requirements of Code Section 408(p). [Priv. Ltr. Rul. 200247052 (Aug. 28, 2002); *see also* Treas. Reg. § 1.401(k)-1(a)(3)(i), 1.401(k)-1(g)(3).] Although no guidance has ever been issued, arguably a sole proprietor can make elective contributions of "advances" pursuant to an election to defer compensation made before the end of the year.

Q 12:61   May an employee choose not to make contributions to a SIMPLE?

Yes. Participating in a SIMPLE must be voluntary. An employee must elect to participate and may not be required to do so. A participant may discontinue contributions at any time during the calendar year (see Q 12:77). [I.R.C. § 408(p)(5)(B)]

Note. A SIMPLE IRA must be established for those years in which the employer elects to make a nonelective contribution to eligible employees. The employer must sign the documents establishing a SIMPLE IRA on behalf of any employee who refuses to sign establishing documents.

Q 12:62   May an employer make a matching contribution of less than 3 percent?

Yes. The 3 percent matching contribution required from the employer may be reduced for a calendar year at the election of the employer, but only under the following conditions:

1. The matching contribution percentage is not reduced below 1 percent;

2. The matching contribution percentage is not reduced for more than two years out of the five-year period that ends with (and includes) the year for which the election is effective (see Q 12:63); and

3. Employees are notified of the reduced matching contribution percentage within a reasonable period of time (see Q 12:83) before the 60-day election period during which employees may enter into salary reduction arrangements (see Q 12:73).

[I.R.C. § 408(p)(2)(C)(ii)]

Q 12:63 If no qualified salary reduction arrangement was in effect for a prior year, or a 2 percent nonelective contribution was made, how is the prior year treated for purposes of the two-years-out-of-five test?

In either case, the prior year is treated as one for which a 3 percent matching contribution was made. [See I.R.C. §§ 408(p)(2)(C)(ii)(III), 408(p)(2)(B)(i).]

Example 1. After graduation in 2001, Alex formed the Alpha Company. Alpha established a SIMPLE in 2009. It may make a contribution of less than 3 percent (but not less than 1 percent) to the SIMPLE during any two years out of the five-year period 2009 through 2013 because it is deemed to have made a 3 percent matching contribution for all earlier years.

Example 2. The facts are the same as those in Example 1. During the first five years, Alpha elects to make the following contributions to its SIMPLE:

2009—1 percent alternative matching contribution

2010—3 percent matching contribution

2011—2 percent nonelective contribution

2012—3 percent matching contribution

2013—2 percent alternative matching contribution

2014—Alpha may make an alternative matching contribution of less than 3 percent (but not less than 1 percent) for the 2014 plan year. If it does so, it will not be able to elect that alternative again until 2018.

Example 3. The facts are the same as those in Example 2. Alpha elects to make a 2 percent nonelective contribution for 2014. It may elect to make an alternative matching contribution once during the next three years because the 2009 plan year has rolled away; that is, it is no longer a part of the five-year contribution history ending with the current year. For purposes of the five-year contribution history, both 2011 and 2014 are treated as years for which the limit is 3 percent.

Q 12:64 Are matching contributions subject to the annual dollar limit in the case of a self-employed individual?

No. Matching contributions to a SIMPLE IRA for a self-employed individual are not subject to the annual dollar limit on elective deferrals ($14,000 for 2008, including a $2,500 catch-up contribution) (see Q 12:57). [I.R.C. §§ 402(g)(8), 408(p)(8), 408(p)(9)]

Q 12:65 What is a nonelective contribution?

A *nonelective contribution* is an employer contribution that is not subject to a voluntary cash or deferred option. For example, a unilateral decision by the employer to reduce an employee's compensation and to make a contribution of all or part of the reduction amount is considered a nonelective contribution.

Q 12:66 How may an employer make nonelective contributions under a SIMPLE?

As an alternative to making matching contributions under a SIMPLE (see Q 12:57), an employer may make nonelective contributions (see Q 12:65) equal to 2 percent of each eligible employee's compensation (presumably, for the entire calendar year). For this purpose, only compensation up to the limit in Code Section 401(a)(17) is taken into account. [I.R.C. § 408(p)(2)(B)(ii)] Thus, for 2009 the maximum compensation taken into account to determine the 2 percent nonelective contribution is $245,000. [I.R.S. News Release IR-2008-118 (Oct. 16, 2008)]

The employer's nonelective contributions must be made for each eligible employee, regardless of whether the employee elects to make salary reduction contributions for the calendar year. The employer may, but is not required to, limit nonelective contributions to eligible employees who have at least $5,000 (or some lower amount selected by the employer) of compensation for the year.

An employer may substitute the 2 percent nonelective contribution for the matching contribution for a year only if

1. Eligible employees are notified that a 2 percent nonelective contribution will be made instead of a matching contribution and
2. That notice is provided within a reasonable period of time (see Q 12:83) before the 60-day election period during which employees may enter into salary reduction arrangements (see Q 12:73).

Q 12:67 What happens if an employer fails to make the matching or nonelective contributions that it agreed to make?

The IRS has not issued guidance regarding an employer's failure to make the contributions it agreed to make to a SIMPLE. It is possible the plan would not qualify as a SIMPLE for the year and all contributions would be reported to the employees as regular wages on Form W-2, thus creating excess contributions in the employees' SIMPLE IRAs; in the case of a self-employed individual, no deduction would be allowed. The Voluntary Correction Procedures for SIMPLE IRA plans allow employers to correct operational failures.

Caution. State law may create additional employer liability if agreed-to contributions are not made.

It is unclear what happens if an employee does not remove the excess contribution (i.e., contribution that should be treated as wages) or, for that matter, by what date excess contributions have to be removed (removed because traditional IRA contributions are not permitted to be made to a SIMPLE IRA). Also unclear is what happens if an inadvertent error occurs (see Qs 12:129–12:131).

Q 12:68   **May an employee elect not to receive matching or nonelective contributions?**

No. An eligible employee may not opt out of a SIMPLE. An employer must make the matching contribution (or, alternatively, the nonelective contribution) as indicated in the notification to all eligible employees meeting the compensation requirements (if any are specified). [I.R.C. § 408(p)(4)(A)]

Q 12:69   **May contributions be made from compensation earned before the date a qualified salary reduction arrangement is executed?**

No. A salary reduction election may not apply to compensation that an employee received, or had a right to immediately receive, before execution of the qualified salary reduction arrangement.

Q 12:70   **May contributions be made to a SIMPLE IRA for an employee who is age 70½ or older?**

Yes. Contributions to a SIMPLE IRA are not subject to a maximum age requirement. [I.R.C. §§ 219(d)(1), 408(b)(4)]

Q 12:71   **Are contributions to a SIMPLE IRA excluded from the employee's gross income?**

Yes, assuming compliance with the applicable requirements. [I.R.C. § 402(k)]

If the SIMPLE IRA fails to meet statutory requirements (participation, vesting, administrative, and qualified salary reduction arrangement), it is unclear whether and in what year contributions would have to be included in the employee's gross income. Such contributions may not be treated as traditional IRA contributions because a SIMPLE may not be used as a traditional IRA (see Q 12:8).

Q 12:72   **Is a SIMPLE subject to minimum funding standards?**

No. The minimum funding standards under ERISA and Code Section 412 do not apply to a SIMPLE. Under ERISA, employee deferrals must be deposited in a timely manner (see Q 12:87).

Employee Elections

Q 12:73   **When must an employee be given the right to enter into a qualified salary reduction arrangement?**

For an existing SIMPLE, an eligible employee must be given the right to enter into a qualified salary reduction arrangement for a calendar year during the

60-day period immediately preceding January 1 of such year (i.e., November 2 to December 31 of the preceding calendar year). A special rule applies in other situations.

In addition to the election period before the beginning of any year, there is a 60-day period before an employee first becomes eligible to participate. Thus, for the year in which the employee first becomes eligible to make salary reduction contributions, the period during which the employee may make or modify an election is a 60-day period that includes either the date he or she becomes eligible or the day before. This special rule is especially useful for rehired former participants, new employees, and new plans (see Q 12:49).

Furthermore, for the year in which the employee first becomes eligible to make salary reduction contributions, the employee must be able to commence those contributions as soon as he or she becomes eligible, regardless of whether the 60-day period has ended, but no earlier than the plan's effective date.

In all cases, the SIMPLE may provide for additional periods during which an employee may make a salary reduction election or modify an election. [I.R.C. § 408(p)(5)(C); Notice 98-4, Q&As E-1, E-2, 1998-1 C.B. 269]

Example 1. On November 1, 2008, Precision Company decides to establish its first retirement plan. It adopts a SIMPLE with no service or compensation requirements for its 40 employees. The plan is duly adopted and effective on January 1, 2009. Employees are given a summary description, a model notification to eligible employees, and a model qualified salary reduction arrangement on November 1, 2008. The 60-day period starts on November 2 and ends on December 31, 2008. Here, the 60-day period includes the "day before" (December 31) the date the employee becomes eligible. Although contributions may be discontinued at any time (see Q 12:77), no modifications are permitted after the 60-day election period unless the plan provides for additional opportunities to modify (or make) an election to defer compensation.

Example 2. In May 2009, Big Bucks, Inc. decides to establish its first retirement plan. It adopts a SIMPLE with no compensation or service requirements for its 60 employees. The plan is duly adopted on May 25, but it states an effective date of June 1, 2009. Employees are given a summary description, a model notification to eligible employees, and a model qualified salary reduction arrangement on June 2. The 60-day period starts on June 3. The summary description and other notices must be given before the employees' 60-day election period (see Q 12:82). Salary reduction contributions may start as soon as administratively feasible but not earlier than June 3 (the day after notification and delivery of the summary description). The plan may provide for salary deferrals to start at some later date during the year. Here, the 60-day period includes the date the employees become eligible (June 3). Employees of Big Bucks may make or modify an election during the 60-day period that ends on August 2, 2009.

Example 3. Crawdad Company establishes a SIMPLE effective as of July 1, 2009; each eligible employee becomes eligible to make salary reduction contributions on that date. The 60-day period must begin no later than July 1 and may not end before August 30, 2009.

Q 12:74 May an employee modify his or her salary reduction elections under a SIMPLE during the 60-day election period?

Yes. During the 60-day election period (see Q 12:73), an employee may modify his or her salary reduction elections without restrictions (including reducing the amount subject to any salary reduction arrangement to zero). Even an employee who commences participation during an election period may cancel or modify a previous election.

Any such modification of an election is prospective and should be implemented by the employer as soon as administratively feasible or in accordance with the documentation submitted to the employer.

Q 12:75 May a SIMPLE provide an election period that is longer than 60 days?

Yes. Nothing precludes a SIMPLE from providing periods longer than 60 days for permitting employees to enter into qualified salary reduction arrangements or to modify earlier arrangements.

Q 12:76 May a SIMPLE provide additional election periods?

Yes. Nothing precludes a SIMPLE from providing additional election periods—for instance, quarterly election periods during the 30 days before each calendar quarter.

Q 12:77 Does an employee have the right to terminate a qualified salary reduction arrangement outside a SIMPLE's election period?

Yes. An employee must be given the right to terminate a qualified salary reduction arrangement for a calendar year at any time during the year. The plan may provide that an employee who terminates participation outside of the normal cycle provided under the plan may not elect to resume participation until the beginning of the next year. [I.R.C. § 408(p)(5)(B)] If, however, an employee terminates participation in accordance with the provisions (if any) adopted by the employer, the employee could resume participation in accordance with the normal cycle (if available) without having to wait until the following year.

Example 1. Lunar Company's SIMPLE permits participants to elect to make a salary reduction contribution or modify an earlier election on the first day of any month. Cecil terminates his participation in the SIMPLE on August 1.

On September 1 he again elects to make salary reduction contributions, to start as soon as possible.

Example 2. Solar Inc.'s SIMPLE permits participants to elect to make a salary reduction contribution or modify an earlier election during the first week of any month. The plan provides that a participant who terminates participation outside of the normal cycle (which must be permitted) may not participate until the following year. Larry terminates his participation in the SIMPLE in the third week of August 2009. Larry may not participate in Solar's SIMPLE until 2010.

Q 12:78 May a SIMPLE permit an employee to change his or her salary reduction election outside of the 60-day election period?

Yes. A SIMPLE plan may permit (but is not required to permit) an individual to make changes to his or her qualified salary reduction arrangement during the year (i.e., increase or reduce the contribution percentage) at times other than during the 60-day election period (see Q 12:76).

Q 12:79 Must an employer allow an employee to select the financial institution to which the employer will make all SIMPLE IRA contributions on behalf of the employee?

Generally, yes. Under Code Section 408(p), an employer must permit an employee to select the financial institution for the SIMPLE IRA to which the employer will make all contributions on behalf of the employee. There is an exception, however, that allows an employer to require that all contributions be made to a designated financial institution (see Qs 12:110–12:117).

Vesting Requirements

Q 12:80 Must contributions under a SIMPLE be nonforfeitable?

Yes. All contributions under a SIMPLE must be fully vested and nonforfeitable when made. [I.R.C. §§ 408(a)(4), 408(b)(4), 408(p)(3)]

Q 12:81 May an employer impose any restrictions or penalties on withdrawals by an employee from a SIMPLE IRA?

No. An employer may not require an employee to retain any portion of the contributions in his or her SIMPLE IRA or otherwise impose any withdrawal restrictions. [I.R.C. § 408(p)(3); Treas. Reg. § 1.408-6(d)(4)(ii)]

Notice and Reporting Requirements

Q 12:82   What notice must an employer provide to eligible employees before the 60-day election period can begin?

Two formal notifications must be given to each eligible employee under a SIMPLE before the 60-day election period (see Q 12:73) may generally begin:

1. *Summary description.* A summary description must be provided before the 60-day election period (see Q 12:92). If using IRS model SIMPLE forms, an employer may satisfy this requirement by giving the employee a copy of Form 5305-SIMPLE or Form 5304-SIMPLE (whichever is applicable). The form must be completed and must include a copy of the procedures for withdrawals and transfers from the SIMPLE IRA received from the financial institution that established the SIMPLE IRA. The employer receives the summary description from the trustee (see Q 12:92). The notification to eligible employees must also indicate whether it will provide a matching contribution up to 3 percent of compensation, a matching contribution percentage that is between 1 and 3 percent of compensation, or a nonelective contribution equal to 2 percent of compensation.

2. *Notification to eligible employees.* Each employee must be notified before his or her 60-day election period (see Q 12:73) that the employee may make or change salary reduction elections during that period. If applicable, this notification must disclose an employee's ability to select the financial institution that will serve as the trustee of the employee's SIMPLE IRA (see Q 12:79).

[I.R.C. §§ 408(*l*)(2)(C), 6693(c); ERISA § 101(g)]

Practice Pointer. An employer that uses either of the IRS model SIMPLE forms is not required to use the model salary reduction arrangement (for employees' salary reduction elections) or the model notification to eligible employees. Nevertheless, the arrangement and notice used must satisfy all statutory requirements.

Q 12:83   What is a reasonable period for providing the notification regarding a reduced matching contribution or a nonelective contribution in lieu of a matching contribution?

An employer is deemed to have provided the notification regarding a reduced matching contribution (see Q 12:62) or a nonelective contribution in lieu of a matching contribution (see Q 12:66) within a reasonable period of time before the 60-day election period if, immediately before the 60-day election period, the notification is included with the notification of an employee's opportunity to enter into a salary reduction arrangement. [I.R.C. § 408(p)(2)(C)(ii)(II)] Thus, a reasonable period of time can be as short as one day. [Notice 98-4, Q&A G-2, 1998-1 C.B. 269]

Q 12:84   May an employer change the matching contribution percentage once the 60-day election period has begun?

No. An employer may not change the matching contribution percentage after the 60-day election period has begun; that is, the percentage must be communicated to employees before the election period. (The same is true for an employer's election to make a nonelective contribution.)

> **Example.** Ezra adopts a SIMPLE for his business that provides for a dollar-for-dollar matching contribution (not to exceed 1 percent of compensation). None of Ezra's employees participates. Realizing he can take advantage of the situation, Ezra increases the matching contribution to 3 percent of compensation and makes that contribution for the current year. Ezra will have to await further guidance from the IRS on how to correct the excess contributions that were made to the plan.

Q 12:85   What reporting penalties apply if an employer fails to provide any of the notices required for a SIMPLE?

If an employer fails to provide any of the notices required for a SIMPLE (see Q 12:82), it will be liable under the Code for a penalty of $50 per day until the notices are provided. If an employer can show that the failure is attributable to reasonable cause, however, the penalty will not be imposed.

If an employee is permitted to select the trustee for his or her SIMPLE IRA (see Q 12:79) and is so notified (see Q 12:82), and the name and address of the trustee and its withdrawal procedures are not available at the time the employer is required to provide the summary description, the employer is deemed to have shown reasonable cause for failure to provide that information to eligible employees. [I.R.C. §§ 408(*l*)(2)(C), 6693(c)(1)]

Q 12:86   What if an eligible employee is unwilling or unable to establish a SIMPLE IRA?

If an eligible employee is unwilling or unable to establish a SIMPLE IRA with any financial institution before the date on which the SIMPLE contribution is required to be made to his or her SIMPLE IRA, the employer may execute the necessary documents to establish a SIMPLE IRA on the employee's behalf with a financial institution selected by the employer. [Notice 98-4, Q&A G-4, 1998-1 C.B. 269] Under such circumstances, the employee's estate should be named beneficiary of the SIMPLE IRA if the plan does not provide for a default beneficiary.

Q 12:87   When is an employer required to make salary reduction contributions under a SIMPLE?

A matching or nonelective contribution to a SIMPLE IRA is timely if deposited with the financial institution by the due date for filing the employer's income tax return, including extensions, for the taxable year that includes the last day of the calendar year for which the contributions are made. [I.R.C. § 408(p)(5)(A)(ii)] Salary reduction contributions, however, must be deposited as soon as they can reasonably be segregated from the employer's general assets, but in any event no later than 15 business days after the end of the month in which the contributions would otherwise have been payable in cash to the SIMPLE IRA participant. [DOL Reg. § 2510.3-102]

Note. A salary reduction contribution that is not timely for ERISA purposes may nonetheless be deductible for tax purposes (see Q 12:108).

Q 12:88   Must an employer file a Form 5500 annual return/report for a SIMPLE?

No. An employer is not required to file any annual information returns, such as Form 5500 or Form 5500-EZ, for a SIMPLE. [I.R.C. §§ 408(i), 408(l)(2)(A); ERISA § 101(g)]

Q 12:89   What must an employer that maintains a SIMPLE report to the IRS?

An employer that maintains a SIMPLE must report to the IRS which eligible employees are active participants in the plan and the amount of the employees' salary reduction contributions to the SIMPLE on Form W-2. Salary reduction contributions are subject to Social Security, Medicare, railroad retirement, and federal unemployment taxes (see Qs 12:59, 12:105, 12:106).

Form W-2, Box 12. The salary reduction contribution (elective deferral) is reported in box 12, marked with code S. If the elective deferral limit was exceeded, the excess contribution must be included The instructions on the back of copy C of Form W-2 (2009) for code S state: "Employee salary reduction contributions under a section 408(p) SIMPLE (not included in box 1)." That language differs from the language used in the instructions for code F relating to SARSEPs, which does not contain the phrase "(not included in box 1)." Presumably, excess contributions to a SIMPLE are treated as wages and included in boxes 1, 3, and 5.

Example. Hillary, an employee of Cosmic Enterprises, earned $20,000 and elected to defer $3,000 to a SIMPLE IRA. Cosmic Enterprises made a 2 percent nonelective contribution ($400) for the year. Thus, $3,000 is reported in box 12, preceded by code S (S 3000.00).

Note. The employer's nonelective (or matching) contribution is not reported on Form W-2.

No more than four codes should be entered in box 12. If more than four items need to be reported in box 12, a payer should use a separate Form W-2 or a substitute Form W-2 to report the additional items. Reporting instructions for magnetic media filing may differ from the paper reporting instructions. For example, more than four entries in box 12 of an individual's wage report are permitted on magnetic tape, but not on any single paper Form W-2.

Form W-2, Box 13. A taxpayer who is a participant in a SIMPLE is treated as an active participant for the purpose of claiming a deduction for the contribution made to an IRA. Thus, special limits may apply to the amount of IRA contributions that the taxpayer may deduct (see Q 12:132). The employer indicates active participation by checking the "Retirement plan" box. The "Retirement plan" box is also checked if the taxpayer is a participant in a SIMPLE for any part of the year. Further, if the taxpayer is a statutory employee, the "Statutory employee" box should be checked.

Practice Pointer. An employer must retain books and records relating to a SIMPLE as long as their contents may become material in the administration of any federal tax law. A SIMPLE participant should keep a copy of copy C of Form W-2 for at least three years after the due date for filing his or her federal income tax return.

Q 12:90 Must the employer report matching and nonelective contribution amounts to the IRS?

No. Matching and nonelective contribution amounts are not required to be reported on Form W-2 or otherwise. [Notice 98-4, Q&A I-1, 1998-1 C.B. 269]

Q 12:91 How are deductions for SIMPLE contributions claimed?

Elective and nonelective contributions made on behalf of a self-employed individual (including a partner in a partnership) to a SIMPLE are claimed on Form 1040, U.S. Individual Income Tax Return (line 28). The deduction for SIMPLE contributions made on behalf of nonowner-employees is claimed on the business's Form 1065, U.S. Partnership Return of Income (line 18), if the organization is taxed as a partnership. An unincorporated business other than a partnership claims the deduction for SIMPLE contributions made on behalf of a nonowner-employee on Schedule C, Profit or Loss From Business (Sole Proprietorship) (line 19), or Schedule F, Profit or Loss From Farming (line 25), of Form 1040. If the organization is taxed as a corporation, the deduction for owners and nonowners is claimed on the corporation's federal income tax return, Form 1120 (line 23) or Form 1120-S (line 17).

Note. The line numbers indicated are from the 2008 versions of those forms.

Trustee Administrative Requirements

Q 12:92 What information must a SIMPLE IRA trustee provide to an employer?

Each year, a SIMPLE IRA trustee must provide the employer sponsoring the SIMPLE with a summary description containing the following information:

1. Name and address of the employer and of the trustee;
2. Requirements for eligibility for participation;

3. Benefits provided with respect to the SIMPLE;

4. Time and method of making elections with respect to the SIMPLE; and

5. Procedures for, and effects of, withdrawals (including rollovers) from the SIMPLE IRA.

The trustee must provide the summary description to the employer early enough to allow the employer to meet its notification obligation to its employees (see Q 12:82). A trustee is not, however, required to provide the summary description for the SIMPLE before agreeing to be the trustee of a SIMPLE IRA. [Notice 98-4, Q&A H-1(2), 1998-1 C.B. 269]

A trustee may satisfy its obligation for a SIMPLE established using Form 5305-SIMPLE or Form 5304-SIMPLE by providing an employer with a current copy of the model form, with instructions; the information required for completion of Article VI of the model form (regarding the procedure for withdrawal); and the name and address of the financial institution. The trustee should provide guidance to the employer concerning the need to complete the first two pages of the model form in accordance with its plan's terms and to distribute completed copies to eligible employees. A procedure similar to that used for the model forms applies to prototype SIMPLEs. [Notice 98-4, Q&A G-1(4), 1998-1 C.B. 269]

An employer is relieved from providing the procedures for withdrawal if the information is provided directly to the employee by the financial institution.

Q 12:93   What is the penalty if a SIMPLE IRA trustee fails to timely provide an employer with a summary description?

Under the Code, a SIMPLE IRA trustee that fails to provide an employer with a summary description of the plan incurs a $50 penalty for each day the failure continues, unless the trustee shows that the failure is a result of reasonable cause. [I.R.C. § 6693(c); Notice 98-4, Q&A H-1(3), 1998-1 C.B. 269]

To the extent that the employer or trustee provides the information contained in a summary description (see Q 12:92) by the deadline prescribed by law (see Q 12:82) to the employee for whom the SIMPLE IRA is established, the trustee of that SIMPLE IRA is deemed to have shown reasonable cause for failure to provide that information to the employer. Thus, for example, if an employer provides its name and address and other necessary information and the effects of withdrawal to all eligible employees in a SIMPLE, and the trustee provides its name and address and its procedures for withdrawal to each eligible employee for whom a SIMPLE IRA is established with the trustee under the SIMPLE, the trustee will be deemed to have shown reasonable cause for failing to provide the employer with that information. [Notice 98-4, Q&As G-1, H-1, 1998-1 C.B. 269]

Q 12:94   What is a transfer SIMPLE IRA?

A *transfer SIMPLE IRA* is a SIMPLE IRA established by an employee to hold assets from another SIMPLE IRA. [Notice 98-4, Q&A H-1, 1998-1 C.B. 269]

Q 12:95   Is the trustee of a transfer SIMPLE IRA required to provide a summary description to the employer?

No. [Notice 98-4, Q&A H-1, 1998-1 C.B. 269]

Q 12:96   What information must a SIMPLE IRA trustee or custodian provide to participants in a SIMPLE?

Within 31 days after the close of each calendar year, a SIMPLE IRA trustee must provide each individual on whose behalf an account is maintained with a statement of the individual's account balance as of the close of that calendar year and the account activity during that calendar year. A trustee or custodian that fails to provide any individual with such a statement incurs a $50 penalty under the Code for each day the failure continues, unless the trustee or custodian shows that the failure is attributable to reasonable cause.

A SIMPLE IRA trustee must also provide any other information required to be furnished to IRA holders, such as disclosure statements for individual retirement plans referred to in Treasury Regulations Section 1.408-6. [I.R.C. § 408(i)]

Q 12:97   What information must a SIMPLE IRA trustee or custodian provide to the IRS?

Code Section 408(i) requires the trustee or custodian of a SIMPLE IRA to make reports regarding the SIMPLE IRA to the IRS. Form 5498, IRA Contribution Information, is used to report the amount of contributions and rollovers (including a direct rollover) to a SIMPLE IRA and the fair market value of the account or annuity. [Ann. 97-10, 1997-10 I.R.B. 64] A trustee or custodian that fails to file the reports incurs a $50 penalty under the Code for each failure, unless it is shown that the failure is attributable to reasonable cause. [I.R.C. § 6693(c); Notice 98-4, Q&A H-1(3), 1998-1 C.B. 269] A copy of Form 5498 for 2009 must be furnished to the participant and the information provided to the IRS by March 31, 2010.

Box 2. This box is used to report any rollover contributions made during the prior year (2008), including a direct rollover, to an IRA, SEP, or SIMPLE IRA.

Box 5. This box is used to report the fair market value of the SIMPLE IRA as of December 31, 2009.

Box 7. This is a checkbox used to indicate an IRA, SEP, SIMPLE, or Roth IRA.

Box 9. This box is used to report the amount of any SIMPLE IRA contributions made during the prior year (2008).

Box 11. This box is used to indicate that an RMD is required for the following year. However, an RMD may be required even if the box is not checked.

Form 5498 does not address the issues of whether a contribution is deductible or nondeductible, the taxable year for which the contribution is made, and whether the amount is excludable from income under the Code.

Q 12:98   Must distributions from a SIMPLE IRA be reported on Form 1099-R?

Yes. Pursuant to Code Section 6047 and Treasury Regulations Section 35.3405-1, the payer of a designated distribution from an IRA must report the distribution on Form 1099-R, Distributions From Pensions, Annuities, Retirement or Profit-Sharing Plans, IRAs, Insurance Contracts, etc. Inasmuch as a distribution from a SIMPLE IRA is a designated distribution from an IRA, it must be reported on Form 1099-R.

The penalty under the Code for failure to report a designated distribution from an IRA (including a SIMPLE IRA) is $50 for each failure (but not more than $50,000) unless the failure is attributable to reasonable cause (rather than willful neglect). [I.R.C. §§ 6047(f), 6704]

(See chapter 7 for a discussion of distribution codes for Form 1099-R.)

Q 12:99   Is special coding required for reporting a SIMPLE IRA distribution to a participant during the initial two-year period after that participant began participating in a SIMPLE?

Yes. A SIMPLE IRA trustee or custodian is required to report on Form 1099-R a distribution to a participant made during the initial two-year period after that participant began participating in a SIMPLE. Code S is used in box 7 (see chapter 7).

The SIMPLE IRA trustee or custodian is permitted to prepare that report on the basis of its own records with respect to the SIMPLE IRA. A trustee or custodian may, but is not required to, take into account other adequately substantiated information regarding the date on which an individual first participated in any SIMPLE maintained by the individual's employer. [Notice 98-4, Q&A H-5, 1998-1 C.B. 269]

Distributions

Q 12:100   Do the required minimum distribution rules for individuals age 70½ or older apply to a SIMPLE IRA?

Yes. The required minimum distribution (RMD) rules generally require that a traditional IRA commence distributions beginning when an individual attains age 70½. [I.R.C. §§ 408(a)(6), 408(b)(4), 408(p)(1)]. Contributions may be made for an employee who is age 70½ or older (see Q 12:70). All the rules that govern distributions from a traditional IRA during the owner's lifetime apply to SIMPLE IRAs. (See chapter 4.)

Q 12:101   Does the suspension of the minimum distribution rules for 2009 apply to SIMPLE IRAs?

Yes. Generally, this means there is no RMD for 2009, and calendar year 2009 is disregarded for SIMPLE IRAs that are being distributed to beneficiaries according to the five-year rule. (For details, see Qs 4:21–4:25.) [Notice 2009-9, 2009-5 I.R.B. 419]

Q 12:102   May required minimum distributions from a SIMPLE IRA be postponed until the calendar year in which an individual retires?

No. The delayed payout rules applicable to a qualified plan under Code Section 401(a)(9)(C) do not apply to any type of IRA, including a SIMPLE IRA. The normal age 70½ traditional IRA distribution rules apply. [I.R.C. § 401(a)(9)(C); Notice 96-67, 1996-2 C.B. 235]

Q 12:103   How are distributions made to beneficiaries after the SIMPLE IRA owner dies?

All the rules that govern post-death distributions of a traditional IRA apply to SIMPLE IRAs. (See chapter 4.)

Tax Treatment

Q 12:104   Are contributions to a SIMPLE IRA excludable from federal income and thus not subject to federal income tax withholding?

Yes. This is true for both salary reduction contributions and an employer's matching or nonelective contributions. [I.R.C. §§ 402(k), 3401(a)(12)(D); Notice 98-4, Q&A I-1, 1998-1 C.B. 269]

Q 12:105   Are salary reduction contributions to a SIMPLE IRA subject to other taxes?

Yes. Salary reduction contributions to a SIMPLE IRA are subject to FICA and FUTA taxes as well as the tax imposed under the Railroad Retirement Tax Act (RRTA). [I.R.C. §§ 3121(a)(5)(H), 3306(b)(5)(H); Notice 98-4, Q&A I-1, 1998-1 C.B. 269]

Q 12:106   Are matching and nonelective contributions to a SIMPLE IRA subject to FICA, FUTA, or RRTA taxes?

No. Matching and nonelective contributions to a SIMPLE IRA are not subject to FICA, FUTA, or RRTA taxes. [I.R.C. §§ 3121(a)(5)(H), 3121(v)(2)(C), 3231(e)(8)(B), 3306(b)(5)(H); Notice 98-4, Q&A I-1, 1998-2 I.R.B. 26]

Q 12:107   Are employer contributions under a SIMPLE deductible by an employer?

Within prescribed limits, all SIMPLE contributions are deductible by an employer. Elective salary reduction contributions made by employees are treated as employer contributions for deduction purposes.

Q 12:108   When must an employer make contributions under a SIMPLE to claim a deduction for such contributions for its current taxable year?

Contributions to SIMPLEs are deductible in the fiscal taxable year of the employer with or within which the calendar year for which the contributions were made ends. [I.R.C. § 404(m)(1), 404(m)(2)(A)] Contributions are therefore deductible by the employer in accordance with the following rules:

1. In the case of a SIMPLE maintained by a calendar-year business, contributions are deductible for that calendar year.

2. When a fiscal-year business maintains a SIMPLE, contributions are deductible for the fiscal taxable year that includes the last day of the SIMPLE plan year (i.e., December 31).

Example 1. Webster Corporation's taxable year ends on November 30. Webster adopts a SIMPLE for 2009. On January 10, 2010 (just before its tax return due date), Webster makes a nonelective contribution to all employees for the 2009 plan year. Webster may claim a deduction for its contribution on its federal income tax return for the taxable year ending on November 30, 2009.

Example 2. Complex Corporation, whose taxable year ends on November 30, adopts a SIMPLE for 2009. On August 30, 2009, Complex files Form 8736 and receives an automatic six-month extension to file its federal income tax return. Thus, its 2009 federal income tax return, normally due on February 15, 2010, is due on August 16, 2010. Then, on August 10, 2010, Complex makes a matching contribution to all employees for the 2009 plan year. For its contribution made on August 10, 2010, Complex may claim a deduction on its federal income tax return for the taxable year ending on November 30, 2009.

An entity that is tax exempt has until the due date of its Form 990, Exempt Organization Business Income Tax Return (generally, the 15th day of the fifth month following the close of its accounting period), to make any contributions required of it under the plan.

Note. Salary reduction contributions may be timely for tax purposes but not for ERISA purposes (see Q 12:87).

Q 12:109   What are the tax consequences when amounts are distributed from a SIMPLE IRA?

SIMPLE IRA distributions are generally treated for income tax purposes like traditional IRA distributions—i.e., they are taxable except to the extent of pro rata basis recovery, the 50 percent excess accumulation penalty applies to missed RMDs, and premature distributions that are not protected by a Code Section 72(t) exception are subject to the additional tax. (See chapter 4.) However, the additional tax applies at a special rate—25 percent rather than 10 percent—if the distribution is made during the first two years of an individual's participation in his or her employer's SIMPLE. [I.R.C. §§ 408(d), 4974(a), 72(t)(6)] The two-year period that is governed by the special rule starts on the first day on which the employer makes a contribution to the individual's SIMPLE IRA, and ends exactly two years later. [Notice 98-4, Q&A I-2, 1998-1 C.B. 269]

Note. The rules that govern conversions and rollovers of SIMPLE IRAs are somewhat different from those for traditional IRAs (see Qs 12:123–12:128).

Designated Financial Institutions

Q 12:110　What is a designated financial institution?

A *designated financial institution*, or DFI, is a trustee or custodian for a SIMPLE that agrees to maintain IRAs on behalf of all individuals receiving contributions under the SIMPLE and to deposit those contributions into the SIMPLE IRAs of each eligible employee as soon as practical. The DFI must also agree to transfer the participant's account balance in a SIMPLE IRA to another SIMPLE IRA without cost or penalty to the participant. [I.R.C. § 408(p)(7)]

Only certain financial institutions (banks, savings and loan associations, insured credit unions), insurance companies that issue insurance contracts, and IRS-approved nonbank trustees may serve as DFIs under a SIMPLE. [I.R.C. § 408(n)]

Practice Pointer. An employer that does not want to use a DFI should not use Form 5305-SIMPLE to establish a SIMPLE.

Q 12:111　May an employer designate a particular financial institution to which all contributions under a SIMPLE will be made?

Yes. Instead of making SIMPLE contributions to the financial institution selected by each eligible employee (see Q 12:79), an employer may require that all contributions on behalf of all eligible employees under its SIMPLE be made to SIMPLE IRAs at a DFI (see Q 12:110) if the following requirements are met:

1. The employer and the financial institution agree that the financial institution will be a DFI under Code Section 408(p)(7) for the SIMPLE.
2. The financial institution agrees that if a participant so requests, the participant's balance will be transferred without cost or penalty to another SIMPLE IRA, or, after the two-year period, to any IRA at a financial institution selected by the participant.
3. Each participant is given written notification describing the procedures under which, if a participant so requests, the participant's balance will be

transferred without cost or penalty to another SIMPLE IRA, or, after the two-year period, to any IRA at a financial institution selected by the participant.

[I.R.C. § 408(p)(7)]

Example 1. A representative of Lucky Investment Financial Institution approaches Top Brass Manufacturing Company concerning the establishment of a SIMPLE. Top Brass agrees to establish a SIMPLE for its eligible employees. Because Top Brass would prefer to avoid writing checks to more than one financial institution on behalf of employees, it is interested in making all contributions under its SIMPLE to a single financial institution. Top Brass and Lucky Investment agree that Lucky Investment will be a DFI, and Lucky Investment agrees that if a participant so requests, it will transfer the participant's balance, without cost or penalty, to another SIMPLE IRA, or, after the two-year period, to any IRA at a financial institution selected by the participant.

A SIMPLE IRA is established for each participating employee of Top Brass at Lucky Investment. Each participant is provided with a written description of how and when the participant may direct that the participant's balance attributable to contributions made to Lucky Investment be transferred without cost or penalty to a SIMPLE IRA, or, after the two-year period, to any IRA at another financial institution selected by the participant. Lucky Investment Financial Institution is a DFI, and Top Brass Manufacturing Company may require that all contributions on behalf of all eligible employees be made to SIMPLE IRAs at Lucky Investment.

Example 2. A representative of Metro Financial Institution approaches Mirror Company concerning the establishment of a SIMPLE. Mirror invites Metro to make a presentation on its investment options for SIMPLE IRAs to Mirror's employees. Each eligible employee receives notification that he or she must select the financial institution that will serve as the trustee of the employee's SIMPLE IRA (see Q 12:79). All eligible employees of Mirror voluntarily select Metro to serve as the trustee of the SIMPLE IRAs to which Mirror will make all contributions on behalf of the employees. Metro is not a DFI merely because all eligible employees of Mirror selected it to serve as the trustee of their SIMPLE IRAs and Mirror consequently makes all contributions to Metro. Therefore, Metro is not required to transfer SIMPLE IRA balances without cost or penalty.

Example 3. The facts are the same as those in Example 2, except that two employees of Mirror Company who made salary reduction elections, Lance and Gwen, failed to establish SIMPLE IRAs to receive SIMPLE contributions on their behalf before the first date on which Mirror is required to make a contribution to their SIMPLE IRAs (see Q 12:108). Mirror establishes SIMPLE IRAs at Metro Financial Institution for Lance and Gwen and contributes the amount required to their accounts. Metro is not a DFI merely because Mirror establishes SIMPLE IRAs on behalf of Lance and Gwen.

Q 12:112   May the period during which a participant may transfer his or her SIMPLE IRA balance without cost or penalty be limited?

Yes. Code Section 408(p)(7) will not be violated merely because a participant may transfer his or her SIMPLE IRA balance without cost or penalty only during a reasonable period of time each year.

A participant will be deemed to have been given a *reasonable* period of time in which to transfer his or her SIMPLE IRA balance without cost or penalty if, for each calendar year, the participant has until the end of a 60-day period (see Q 12:73) to request a transfer, without cost or penalty, of his or her balance for the calendar year following that 60-day period (or, for the year in which an employee becomes eligible to make salary reduction contributions, for the balance of that year) and subsequent calendar years.

Example 1. Orange Computer first establishes a SIMPLE plan effective January 1, 2009, and intends to make all contributions to Starship Financial Institution, which has agreed to serve as a DFI. For the 2009 calendar year, Orange Computer provides the 60-day election period beginning November 2, 2008, and notifies each participant that the participant may request that his or her balance attributable to future contributions be transferred from Starship to a SIMPLE IRA at a financial institution that the participant selects. The notification states that the transfer will be made without cost or penalty if the participant contacts Starship Financial Institution before January 1, 2009. For the 2009 calendar year, the requirements of Code Section 408(p)(7) will not be violated merely because participants are given only a 60-day period in which to request a transfer of their balances without cost or penalty.

Example 2. The facts are the same as those in Example 1. Linda, a participant, does not request a transfer of her balance by December 31, 2008, but requests a transfer of her current balance to another SIMPLE IRA on July 1, 2009. Linda's current balance would not be required to be transferred without cost or penalty, because she did not request such a transfer before January 1, 2009. During the 60-day period preceding the 2010 calendar year, Linda may, however, request a transfer without cost or penalty of her balance attributable to contributions made for the 2010 calendar year and for all future calendar years (but not her balance attributable to contributions for the 2009 calendar year).

Example 3. The facts are the same as those in Example 1. Under the terms of his employer's SIMPLE, Eli, a participant, becomes an eligible employee on June 1, 2009; for Eli, the 60-day period (see Q 12:73) begins on that date. Eli will be deemed to have been given a reasonable amount of time in which to request a transfer, without cost or penalty, of his balance attributable to contributions for the balance of the 2009 calendar year if Starship Financial Institution allows such a request to be made by July 31, 2009.

Q 12:113   How is any limit on the time or manner in which a participant may transfer his or her SIMPLE IRA balance without cost or penalty disclosed?

If the time or manner in which a participant may transfer his or her SIMPLE IRA balance without cost or penalty (see Q 12:115) is limited, any such limitation (see Q 12:114) must be disclosed as part of a written notification regarding a DFI. In the case of a SIMPLE established using Form 5305-SIMPLE, if the summary description requirement is being satisfied by providing a completed copy of pages one and two of that form, Article VI of Form 5305-SIMPLE (Procedures for Withdrawal) must contain a clear explanation of any such limitation.

Q 12:114   Is there a limit on the frequency with which a participant's SIMPLE IRA balance must be transferred without cost or penalty?

Yes. To satisfy Code Section 408(p)(7), if a participant acts within applicable reasonable time limits (see Q 12:112), if any, to request a transfer of his or her SIMPLE IRA balance, the participant's balance must be transferred on a reasonably frequent basis. A participant's balance will be deemed to be so-transferred if it is transferred on a monthly basis. [Notice 98-4, Q&A J-3, 1998-1 C.B. 269]

Q 12:115   When is a transfer of a SIMPLE IRA balance deemed to be made without cost or penalty?

A transfer of a SIMPLE IRA balance is deemed to be made without cost or penalty if no liquidation, transaction, redemption, or termination fee; commission; load (front-end or back-end); surrender charge; or similar fee or charge is imposed with respect to the balance being transferred. A transfer will not fail to be made without cost or penalty merely because contributions that a participant has elected to have transferred without cost or penalty are required to be invested in one specified investment option until transferred, even though a variety of investment options are available with respect to contributions that participants have not elected to transfer.

Example 1. Sound Financial Institution agrees to be a DFI for the SIMPLE IRA maintained by Cement Company. Cement provides a 60-day election period (see Q 12:73) beginning on November 2 of each year, and each participant is notified that he or she may request, before the end of the 60-day period, a transfer of his or her future contributions from Sound without cost or penalty to a SIMPLE IRA, or, after the two-year period (see Qs 12:123–12:125), to any IRA at a financial institution selected by the participant. The notification states that a participant's contributions that are to be transferred without cost or penalty will be invested in a specified investment option and will be transferred to the financial institution selected by the participant on a monthly basis.

Sound Financial Institution offers various investment options for its SIMPLE IRAs, including investment options with a sales charge. Any participant who does not elect to have his or her balance transferred to another financial institution may invest the contributions made on his or her behalf in any investment option available to holders of SIMPLE IRAs at Sound. Contributions that a participant has elected to have transferred are automatically invested, before transfer, in a specified investment option that has no sales charge. The requirement that a participant's balance be transferred without cost or penalty will not be violated.

Example 2. The facts are the same as those in Example 1. Sound Financial Institution generally charges its IRAs a reasonable annual administration fee. Sound also charges that fee with respect to SIMPLE IRAs, including SIMPLE IRAs from which balances must be transferred in accordance with participants' transfer elections. The requirement that participants' balances be transferred without cost or penalty will not be violated merely because a reasonable *annual* administration fee is charged to SIMPLE IRAs from which balances must be transferred in accordance with participants' transfer elections.

[Notice 98-4, Q&A J-4, 1998-1 C.B. 269]

Q 12:116   Is the without-cost-or-penalty requirement violated if a designated financial institution charges an employer for the transfer of a participant's SIMPLE IRA balance?

No. The without-cost-or-penalty requirement for the transfer of a SIMPLE IRA balance (see Q 12:115) is not violated merely because a DFI charges an *employer* an amount that takes into account the financial institution's responsibility to transfer balances on participants' requests or otherwise charges an employer for transfers requested by participants. [Notice 98-4, Q&A J-5, 1998-1 C.B. 269]

Q 12:117   May an employer pass on any SIMPLE IRA transfer charge or penalty to its employees?

No. If a DFI SIMPLE IRA transfer charge or penalty is passed through to the participants, the without-cost-or-penalty requirement is violated and the employer may not require that a DFI be used under such circumstances.

Fiduciary Responsibility

Q 12:118   Is an employer or other fiduciary responsible when an employee or beneficiary exercises control over the assets in a SIMPLE IRA?

No. An employer or any other plan fiduciary will not be liable under ERISA when an employee or beneficiary exercises control over the assets in a SIMPLE IRA.

Q 12:119 When is an employee or beneficiary treated as exercising control over a SIMPLE IRA?

An employee or beneficiary is treated as exercising control over the assets in a SIMPLE IRA on the earliest of

1. An affirmative election among investment options with respect to the initial investment of any contribution;
2. A rollover to any other SIMPLE IRA; or
3. One year after the SIMPLE IRA is established.

[ERISA § 404(c)(2)]

An employer must also forward elective contributions to the trustee or custodian of the SIMPLE IRA on a timely basis (see Q 12:108).

Tax Credits for Employers and Employees

Q 12:120 Are there tax incentives for employers to establish a SIMPLE for the first time?

Yes. A small business that adopts a new SIMPLE can generally claim an income tax credit for 50 percent of the first $1,000 in administrative and retirement-education expenses incurred for each of the first three years of the plan. The credit is available only to employers that did not have more than 100 employees with compensation in excess of $5,000 during the previous tax year. The employer must also have had at least one NHCE. The credit is taken as a general business credit on the employer's tax return. The other 50 percent of the expenses may be taken as a business deduction. [I.R.C. § 45E] The income tax credit is claimed on Form 8881, Credit for Small Employer Startup Costs. [IRS Publication 560, *Retirement Plans for Small Business (SEP, SIMPLE, and Qualified Plans)* (2008)]

The maximum credit amount is $500 for the first year and each of the two taxable years immediately following the first year. Thus, the credit is limited to $1,500 over a three-year period. [I.R.C. § 45E(b); EGTRRA § 637; H.R. Conf. Rep. No. 107-51, pt. 1 (2001)]

> **Practice Pointer.** The credit cannot be carried back to years before 2003. The 50 percent of qualifying expenses that is effectively offset by the tax credit is not deductible; the other 50 percent of the qualifying expenses (as well as other expenses) is deductible to the extent otherwise permitted under current law.

Q 12:121 Can a credit for administrative and retirement-education expenses be claimed if a SIMPLE is terminated and another SIMPLE adopted in the following year?

The administrative and retirement-education expenses credit is not allowed if substantially the same employees are covered under a new plan adopted within the three-taxable-year period immediately preceding the first taxable year for which an employer could claim the new-plan credit. [I.R.C. § 45E(c)(2)]

Q 12:122   What is the saver's credit for employee contributions to a SIMPLE IRA?

An employee who makes salary reduction contributions to a SIMPLE IRA may be eligible for the saver's tax credit. This credit, originally effective from 2002 through 2006, was extended and made permanent by the Pension Protection Act of 2006 [Pub. L. No. 109-280, 120 Stat. 780]. The amount of the credit is based on income and filing status, and ranges from 10 percent to 50 percent, depending on the individual's AGI. The lower the individual's income, the higher the credit rate. [I.R.C. § 25B; IRS Publication 590, *Individual Retirement Arrangements (IRAs)* 2008 (see Appendix A)] (For further discussion of the saver's tax credit, see Qs 3:141–3:146.)

Rollovers, Conversions, and Recharacterizations

Q 12:123   Are rollovers permitted from a SIMPLE IRA?

Yes. During the two-year period that begins when contributions are first deposited into the participant's SIMPLE IRA, distributions may only be rolled over to another SIMPLE IRA. After that, distributions may also be rolled over to another qualified plan, Section 403(b) annuity or custodial account plan, or governmental Section 457(b) plan in which the SIMPLE IRA owner participates. [I.R.C. §§ 408(d)(3)(A)(ii); 408(d)(3)(G)]

Q 12:124   May an amount be transferred from a SIMPLE IRA to another IRA in a trustee-to-trustee transfer?

Yes.

Q 12:125   What happens if an amount is paid from a SIMPLE IRA directly to the trustee or custodian of an IRA that is not a SIMPLE IRA during the two-year period?

If, during the two-year period, an amount is paid from a SIMPLE IRA directly to the trustee or custodian of an IRA or other plan that is not a SIMPLE IRA (i.e., a qualified plan, a governmental Section 403(b) plan, a traditional IRA, or a Roth IRA), the payment is neither a tax-free trustee-to-trustee transfer nor a rollover contribution. Rather, the payment is a distribution from the SIMPLE IRA and a contribution to the other IRA or other plan that does not qualify as a rollover contribution. The amount, if paid to a traditional or Roth IRA, is treated as an annual IRA contribution and is subject to the IRA contribution limits (see Q 12:132).

Q 12:126   May a SIMPLE IRA be converted to a Roth IRA?

Yes. Amounts held in a SIMPLE IRA may be converted to a Roth IRA. Such a conversion may be accomplished, however, only after the expiration of the two-year period (see Qs 12:123–12:125). [Treas. Reg. § 1.408A-4, Q&A-4(b); Notice 98-4, 1998-1 C.B. 269]

Q 12:127   May contributions under a SIMPLE be made to a SIMPLE IRA that has been converted to a Roth IRA?

It depends. The conversion may be accomplished by redesignating the SIMPLE IRA as a Roth IRA (see Q 12:126). If the conversion is accomplished by means of a redesignation, the SIMPLE IRA becomes a Roth IRA and ceases to be part of a SIMPLE; thus, no SIMPLE contributions may be made to the Roth IRA [Treas. Reg. § 1.408A-4] However, if the conversion is accomplished by means of transferring the assets from the SIMPLE IRA to a separate and distinct Roth IRA maintained by the same trustee or a different trustee, then the SIMPLE IRA is not a Roth IRA and may still receive employer contributions. [Treas. Reg. § 1.408A-4, Q&A-4(b), -4(c)]

Q 12:128   May an amount contributed by an employer under a SIMPLE be recharacterized?

No. Employer contributions (including elective contributions) under a SIMPLE may not be recharacterized. [Treas. Reg. § 1.408A-5, Q&A-5]

Excess Contributions

Q 12:129   What is an excess SIMPLE IRA contribution?

An *excess SIMPLE IRA contribution* is an employer contribution or salary reduction contribution that is made in excess of the permitted amounts. Contributions are also excess contributions if the employer does not qualify to establish or maintain a SIMPLE (see Qs 12:29, 12:57).

Q 12:130   What action is required if an excess contribution is made?

The excess contribution must be corrected. An excess employer contribution is not deductible by the employer. It is corrected by returning the excess contribution (with earnings) to the employer and reporting the distribution as nontaxable on Form 1099-R. An excess salary reduction contribution is corrected by distributing the amount (with earnings) to the participant, filing Form 1099-R to report the distribution as includable in the participant's gross income for the year of the distribution, and notifying the participant that no part of the corrective distribution is eligible for a rollover. [*The Fix Is In—Common Plan Mistakes—"Simple" Retirement Arrangements—SEPs, SARSEPs and SIMPLE IRA*

Plans, available on the IRS Web site at *http://www.irs.gov/retirement/sponsor/article/0,,id = 157615,00.html.*]

Q 12:131   What are the tax consequences of making an excess contribution to a SIMPLE IRA?

Both the employer and the participant may realize tax consequences if an excess contribution is made to a SIMPLE IRA.

If there is an excess employer contribution, the employer cannot deduct it. The excess contribution is not taxed on its return to the employer, but the earnings included in the corrective distribution are included in the employer's gross income. [I.R.C. §§ 408(d)(4),(5)]

When an excess salary reduction contribution is corrected, the distribution (including the excess contribution and its earnings) is generally taxable to the participant for the year of the distribution. It is taxable for the year of the contribution, however, if the distribution is made by the participant's deadline (including extensions) for filing his or her tax return for the year for which the contribution was made. Also, the Code Section 72(t) additional tax on premature distributions is generally levied on the distribution if the participant is younger than age 59½. The additional tax is computed as a percentage of the entire distribution (not just the earnings), at the rate of 25 percent if the distribution is made during the individual's first two years of participation in the SIMPLE, or 10 percent if it occurs later (see Q 12:109). [I.R.C. §§ 408(d), 72(t)].

For either type of excess contribution, the participant must pay a 6 percent excise tax for each year in which an excess contribution remains in the SIMPLE IRA. There is one exception—the excise tax is avoided with respect to an excess contribution that is returned, with earnings, by the participant's filing deadline (including extensions) for the tax return for the year for which the excess contribution was made. [I.R.C. § 4973(a)]

Miscellaneous Rules

Q 12:132   May an employee who actively participates in a SIMPLE contribute to a traditional or Roth IRA in the same year?

Individuals who actively participate in a SIMPLE may also contribute to traditional and Roth IRAs subject to the rules that normally govern those accounts (see Qs 3:49, 3:81). However, active participation in a SIMPLE does affect the deductibility of any traditional IRA contribution (see Qs 3:48, 3:51). [I.R.C. § 219(g)(5)] For this purpose, nonelective contributions made after the end of the year are treated as though made on the last day of the previous year because they are not discretionary. [Notice 87-16, 1987-1 C.B. 446, *clarified by* Notice 89-25 1989-1 C.B. 662, *and modified by* Notice 98-49, 1998-2 C.B. 365; I.R.C. § 219(g)(5)(A)(vi)]

Example 1. Reliance Corporation established a SIMPLE IRA plan and elected to make a 2 percent nonelective contribution instead of a matching contribution for 2009. The nonelective contribution is made in January 2010. Employees will be treated as active participants for 2009.

Example 2. Beehive Corporation establishes a cash-bonus SIMPLE. Under the SIMPLE, employees may elect in writing to have all or a portion of their annual bonuses treated as elective contributions under the SIMPLE or to receive their bonuses in cash on December 31. The employees who make elective contributions based on their 2009 bonuses are treated as active participants for 2009 even though the amounts may be deposited into their SIMPLE IRAs after the end of the year.

Q 12:133   If an employer that maintains a 401(k) plan wants to terminate the plan in favor of a SIMPLE, is the SIMPLE a defined contribution plan to which the 401(k) plan assets must be rolled over?

No. Under Code Section 401(k)(10)(A)(i), when a 401(k) plan terminates, participants may not receive a distribution of their account balances if the employer maintains a successor defined contribution plan (other than an employee stock ownership plan (ESOP)). Treasury Regulations Section 1.401(k)-1(d)(3) indicates that a plan is a *successor plan* only if it exists at any time during the period beginning on the date of plan termination and ending 12 months after distribution of all assets from the terminated plan. A SIMPLE IRA is not treated as an "alternative defined contribution plan" for this purpose. [Treas. Reg. § 1.401(k)-1(d)(4)]

Q 12:134   Is compensation paid to a nonresident alien considered income earned in the United States?

Only amounts subject to income tax withholding are treated as compensation. If a nonresident alien is a regular member of a crew of a foreign vessel engaged in transportation between the United States and a foreign country or a possession of the United States, compensation received by the nonresident alien is not considered U.S. source income for purposes of a SIMPLE IRA or any qualified retirement plan, SEP, 401(k) SIMPLE, or SARSEP. [I.R.C. § 861(a)(3)]

Q 12:135   Are SIMPLE IRAs subject to the claims of creditors?

It depends. A SIMPLE IRA is generally protected from the reach of creditors under the Federal Bankruptcy Code. However, state law will likely apply in a non-bankruptcy situation. For bankruptcy purposes a SIMPLE IRA is not generally treated as an ERISA plan.

Q 12:136   May defects in a SIMPLE IRA plan be corrected under any of the IRS compliance programs?

Yes. The Voluntary Corrections Procedures for SIMPLE IRA plans allows an employer to correct certain qualification failures (i.e., plan document failure, operational failure, demographic failure, and employee eligibility failure) if certain requirements are satisfied. [Rev. Proc. 2006-27, § 3.01, 2006-22 I.R.B. 945]

Bonding

Q 12:137   Are SIMPLE IRA plans subject to ERISA bonding requirements?

Possibly. In most cases, an employer that handles funds or other property that belongs to an ERISA plan is required to be bonded. The basic standard is determined by the possibility of risk of loss in each situation; thus, it is based on the facts and circumstances of each situation. The amount of a bond is determined at the beginning of each year. The bond amount may not be less than 10 percent of the amount of funds handled. The minimum bond amount is $1,000. Contributions made by withholding from an employee's salary are not considered funds or other property of a SIMPLE IRA plan for purposes of the bonding provisions as long as they are retained in, and not segregated in any way from, the general assets of the withholding employer. Because employer contributions are made into SIMPLE IRAs established by each employee (and are outside of the control of an employer, once made), bonding would not generally apply. [ERISA §§ 404(c), 412; DOL Reg. §§ 2510.3-3, 2550.412-5]

Chapter 13

Coverdell Education Savings Account

Martin Fleisher, Esq.
Jo Ann Lippe, Esq.

The Coverdell education savings account (Coverdell ESA), formerly called the Education IRA, was originally created to encourage saving for *higher* education expenses through the granting of federal tax benefits. It was subsequently expanded to cover expenses for secondary and elementary school education. Like contributions to a Roth IRA, contributions to a Coverdell ESA are not tax deductible, but qualified distributions are tax free.

Contributions may be made to a Coverdell ESA on behalf of any child who is under age 18, or on behalf of any special needs beneficiary, regardless of the relationship of the contributor to the child or the beneficiary. Contributions to a Coverdell ESA are limited to $2,000 per *child* (not per contributor) annually, and all contributors must meet certain income limits. Assets in a Coverdell ESA that are not used or needed for educational purposes by the time the child reaches age 30 (unless the child is a special needs beneficiary) must be distributed or rolled over to another family member's Coverdell ESA.

As shown in this chapter, the Coverdell ESA provides an attractive vehicle for saving for a child's education, as well as a tool for a family's financial planning.

Overview

Q 13:1   What is the Coverdell ESA?

The Coverdell ESA is a vehicle that allows individuals to save for a child's postsecondary, secondary, and elementary school education expenses on a tax-favored basis. Earnings are allowed to grow tax free within the account, and withdrawals for the child's qualified education expenses are also tax free. Contributions to a Coverdell ESA, like contributions to a Roth IRA, are not tax deductible.

Q 13:2   Is the Coverdell ESA ever used as an individual retirement account?

No. The Coverdell ESA is not a retirement planning tool, most obviously because an individual may not leave the assets in the account until retirement age. In general, any assets remaining in a Coverdell ESA must be fully distributed no later than 30 days after the designated beneficiary reaches age 30, or must be transferred to a new designated beneficiary; however, special needs beneficiaries (see Q 13:75) are permitted to leave assets in their Coverdell ESAs past age 30. [I.R.C. § 530(b)(1)(E)]

Coverdell ESA Versus IRAs

Q 13:3   What are the key similarities between the Coverdell ESA and the traditional IRA or the Roth IRA?

The following discussion highlights key similarities between the rules applicable to the Coverdell ESA and those applicable to the traditional IRA or the Roth IRA.

Trustee or Custodial Requirements. The Coverdell ESA shares with the traditional IRA and the Roth IRA the requirement that assets be held by a trustee or custodian. The rules relating to a Coverdell ESA trustee or custodian are the same as the rules relating to the traditional or Roth IRA trustee or custodian.

Cash Contributions. Coverdell ESA contributions must be made in cash, like traditional IRA and Roth IRA contributions. [I.R.C. § 530(b)(1)(A)(i)]

Contribution Deadline. Like contributions to a traditional IRA or Roth IRA, contributions to a Coverdell ESA may be made until the tax filing due date for the tax year, excluding extensions (generally April 15 of the following year). [I.R.C. § 530(b)(4)]

Tax-Deferred Growth of Earnings. Earnings in a Coverdell ESA, traditional IRA, and Roth IRA all grow federal income tax deferred while protected in the account. Distributions from a Coverdell ESA and a Roth IRA may also be free from federal income taxes.

Investments. Although the investment rules for the Coverdell ESA are not fully explained in the law, the investment options permissible for the Coverdell ESA appear to be the same as those allowed for the traditional IRA and the Roth IRA. Those would include certificates of deposit (CDs), time accounts, stocks, mutual funds, bonds, other securities, and most other investment vehicles. The Coverdell ESA is specifically prohibited from investing in life insurance. [I.R.C. § 530(b)(1)(C)] If an ESA is pledged as security for a loan, the portion pledged will be treated as distributed. [I.R.C. §§ 530(e), 408(e)(4)] Assets in a Coverdell ESA may not be commingled with the assets of other property (except in a common investment fund) or involved in prohibited transactions. [I.R.C. §§ 530(b)(1)(D), 530(e)(2), 408(e)(2)]

Movement of Assets Between Like Accounts. The assets in a Coverdell ESA can be moved to a new Coverdell ESA via a rollover or transfer following rules similar to those for the traditional IRA and the Roth IRA. [I.R.C. § 530(d)(5)]

Q 13:4 What are the differences between the Coverdell ESA and the traditional IRA and the Roth IRA?

Some of the many differences between the Coverdell ESA and the traditional IRA and the Roth IRA are indicated below.

Purpose of the Account. The Coverdell ESA is not a retirement savings account like the traditional IRA or a general savings account like the Roth IRA. The Coverdell ESA is used exclusively to save for education.

Eligibility. Both the income limits and the overall eligibility rules are different for the Coverdell ESA and the Roth IRA. For example, the Roth IRA has no age limitations, whereas contributions to a Coverdell ESA must be for a designated beneficiary under age 18. [I.R.C. § 530(b)(1)(A)(ii)]

Contribution Amount. Coverdell ESA contributions are limited to $2,000 per child per year (excluding rollovers from another Coverdell ESA and eligible contributions of military death gratuities and payments under the Servicemen's

Group Life Insurance program). [I.R.C. § 530(b)(1)(A)(iii)] This amount, unlike the contribution amount for IRAs, is not indexed to inflation.

Tax Treatment of Contributions. Contributions to a Coverdell ESA are treated the same as contributions to a Roth IRA; that is, they are not tax deductible. Contributions to a Coverdell ESA, however, count as part of the contributor's annual gift tax exclusion. [I.R.C. § 530(d)(3)]

Tax Treatment of Distributions. Distributions from a Coverdell ESA are tax free only if they are used for qualified education expenses (see Qs 13:77–13:82). Other distributions are subject to a pro rata return of principal and earnings and those earnings are subject to tax and a penalty. The Roth IRA generally allows for all contributions to be returned before earnings (see Qs 5:40–5:43).

Full Distribution at Age 30. The assets in a Coverdell ESA must be fully distributed by the time the designated beneficiary attains age 30 or within 30 days thereafter, unless he or she is a special needs beneficiary. [I.R.C. § 530(b)(1)(E)] The age limit also does not apply in the case of a rollover contribution for the benefit of a special needs beneficiary or when there is a change in beneficiaries to a special needs beneficiary. The traditional IRA does not require distributions to commence until the owner attains age 70½. For the Roth IRA, distributions need not commence until the owner's death (see Q 5:1).

Change in Beneficiary. The beneficiary of a Coverdell ESA may be changed to a family member of the original beneficiary who has not yet attained age 30 (see Q 13:18). Except in cases of death or divorce, a Roth IRA and a traditional IRA may not change ownership.

Movement of Assets Between Different Plan Types. Assets in a Coverdell ESA may be moved only to another Coverdell ESA. In certain circumstances, assets may be moved between Roth IRAs, traditional IRAs, and qualified plans (see chapter 6).

Parties to the Agreement. Unlike the traditional IRA or the Roth IRA, the Coverdell ESA generally is established by one person for the benefit of another. In many cases, a third party may control the account.

Reporting. Form 1099-Q, Payments from Qualified Education Programs (Under Sections 529 and 530), and Form 5498-ESA, Coverdell ESA Contribution Information, are used to report information about a Coverdell ESA to the IRS. In contrast, Form 1099-R, Distributions from Pensions, Annuities, Retirement or Profit-Sharing Plans, IRAs, Insurance Contracts, etc., and Form 5498, IRA Contribution Information, are used to report information for the traditional IRA or the Roth IRA.

Parties

Q 13:5   Who are the parties to a Coverdell ESA?

In most cases, there are at least three parties to the establishment of a Coverdell ESA: a child (designated beneficiary), a contributor (grantor or depositor), and a financial institution (trustee or custodian). The Coverdell ESA agreement entered into between the contributor and the trustee or custodian should define the various parties and their rights and obligations.

The IRS model Coverdell ESA forms (Form 5305-E, Coverdell Education Savings Trust Account, and Form 5305-EA, Coverdell Education Savings Custodial Account) and the Internal Revenue Code (Code) provide the following terms and definitions:

1. *Designated beneficiary.* The Code refers to the child on whose behalf a Coverdell ESA is established as the designated beneficiary. [I.R.C. § 530(b)(1)] (Usually, the designated beneficiary for a traditional IRA or Roth IRA is the person receiving the assets after the death of the IRA owner.)

2. *Trustee or custodian.* The financial institution accepting a Coverdell ESA contribution is the trustee or custodian. [I.R.C. § 530(b)(1)(B) (trustee); Notice 97-60, 1997-2 C.B. 310 (custodian)]

3. *Grantor or depositor.* The individual making the contribution on behalf of the child is the grantor or depositor. Corporations and other entities are also permitted to contribute to Coverdell ESAs. The individual or entity making the contribution may be referred to by other terms, including *contributor.*

4. *Responsible individual.* On the IRS model forms, the person who controls the Coverdell ESA on behalf of the designated beneficiary is referred to as the responsible individual. Drafters of prototype documents may use a different term.

5. *Successor responsible individual.* The successor responsible individual is the person named by the responsible individual to succeed him or her in the case of death or incapacity.

6. *Death beneficiary.* Although the Code does not contain the term *death beneficiary,* the term is used in the model forms to describe the person who is named to receive the IRA assets after the death of the designated beneficiary.

Q 13:6 May prototype documents alter the roles of the parties to a Coverdell ESA?

To a limited extent, drafters of prototype Coverdell ESA documents may change the terminology and roles for the various parties to the Coverdell ESA. The roles of the trustee or custodian and of the designated beneficiary are well established in the law and not subject to much change by a prototype drafter. The provisions designating the responsible individual and the responsible individual's role and responsibilities are more apt to be changed in a prototype document.

Responsible Individual

Q 13:7   Who is a responsible individual?

The IRS model forms for the Coverdell ESA use the term *responsible individual* to describe the person who controls the Coverdell ESA on behalf of the designated beneficiary (the child). Under the model forms, the responsible individual generally must be the child's parent or legal guardian, at least until the child reaches the age of majority. [IRS Forms 5305-E, 5305-EA]

Q 13:8   Who selects the responsible individual?

When an IRA model Coverdell ESA form is used to establish a Coverdell ESA, the original contributor (grantor or depositor) selects the responsible individual for the ESA and, if necessary, a successor responsible individual. Prototype Coverdell ESA documents may provide differently.

Q 13:9   May a mother and a father jointly serve as the responsible individual?

No. Only one person may serve as the responsible individual for a Coverdell ESA. [IRS Forms 5305-E, 5305-EA]

Q 13:10   What powers does the responsible individual possess?

The responsible individual has the power to redirect the investments of the Coverdell ESA and the power to direct the IRA trustee or custodian regarding the investment of all additional contributions (including the earnings on the contributions). In addition, he or she may direct the trustee or custodian regarding the administration, management, and distribution of the account and transfer the account's assets to another trustee or custodian in order to change the investment selections or acquire different terms in the trust or custodial agreement. [IRS Forms 5305-E, 5305-EA]

Example. Grandfather makes a $2,000 Coverdell ESA contribution on behalf of Grandson at Bank XYZ and selects a five-year CD earning 3 percent annually. Grandfather names Grandson's Mother as the responsible individual. Shortly after Mother receives notification of her role as responsible individual, she transfers the assets in the Coverdell ESA to ABC Mutual Fund and invests in an international index fund. Bank XYZ imposes a loss-of-earnings penalty on the Coverdell ESA CD because Mother withdrew the assets before maturity. Grandfather becomes angry at Mother's actions and demands that the assets be transferred back to Bank XYZ and placed back into the CD. Neither ABC Mutual Fund nor Bank XYZ may honor Grandfather's request. Grandfather has no authority over the Coverdell ESA. Mother, as the responsible individual, may complete the transfer of the Coverdell ESA assets.

The responsible individual also has the power (unless the contributor restricts this power when the Coverdell ESA is established) to change the beneficiary designation at any time. The new beneficiary must be a qualifying member of the formerly designated beneficiary's family who is younger than age 30 (or a special needs beneficiary). [IRS Forms 5305-E and 5305-EA] (See Q 13:18.)

Q 13:11 What happens if the responsible individual predeceases the designated beneficiary?

If the responsible individual becomes incapacitated or dies while the designated beneficiary is a minor (as determined under state law), the successor responsible individual assumes the role of responsible individual. [IRS Forms 5305-E, 5305-EA]

Q 13:12 Who is a successor responsible individual?

A *successor responsible individual* is the person named in a witnessed writing to succeed the responsible individual. If no successor is named, the successor responsible individual is the designated beneficiary's other parent or successor guardian. [IRS Forms 5305-E, 5305-EA]

Q 13:13 When may the designated beneficiary serve as the responsible individual?

The terms of a Coverdell ESA's trust or custodial agreement may provide that upon the child's reaching the age of majority (age 18 or 21, as prescribed by state law) the child becomes the responsible individual. Alternatively, the terms of the agreement may provide that the initial responsible individual will continue to serve in that capacity after the child attains the age of majority. [IRS Forms 5305-E, 5305-EA]

Q 13:14 Are individuals who use a prototype document to establish a Coverdell ESA compelled to follow the rules concerning the responsible individual?

Probably not. Trustees and custodians who draft their own prototype documents should be able to draft their own rules regarding the individual controlling a Coverdell ESA. Accordingly, the rules for the responsible individual may apply only to users of IRS model Coverdell ESA forms. The IRS has not yet issued a listing of required modifications (LRM) or a process for submitting prototype Coverdell ESA documents.

Contributor

Q 13:15 What is a grantor or depositor?

A *grantor* or *depositor* is the individual who makes the Coverdell ESA contribution on behalf of the child and may be referred to as the *contributor*. The contributor may be any individual (including the designated beneficiary) or a corporation or other entity (including a tax-exempt entity). Until the IRS issues guidance, it is difficult to know how contributions by non-individuals are to work. It is important to note, however, that the contributor may not serve as the responsible individual under the IRS model Coverdell ESA forms unless he or she is the child's parent or legal guardian. [IRS Forms 5305-E, 5305-EA]

Q 13:16　What powers does the contributor have?

Under the IRS model Coverdell ESA forms, the contributor may select the initial trustee or custodian, the initial investment, the initial terms of the trust or custodial account (including whether or not the responsible individual has power to change the designated beneficiary), and the responsible individual. After the Coverdell ESA is established and the first investment made for the designated beneficiary, the contributor loses control over the Coverdell ESA.

Note. A contributor may have more authority under a (non-IRS model) prototype document.

Q 13:17　May a contributor make additional contributions to a Coverdell ESA to which the contributor made the initial contribution?

Yes. A contributor may make additional contributions to the Coverdell ESA; however, only the initial contribution permits the contributor to make certain choices concerning the account. If the contributor wants additional rights with respect to future contributions, he or she may establish a new Coverdell ESA with the new contributions.

Changing the Designated Beneficiary

Q 13:18　May the designated beneficiary of a Coverdell ESA be changed?

Yes, if the change is allowed under the terms of the particular Coverdell ESA agreement. In that case, the responsible individual may change the designated beneficiary from one child to a member of that child's family without triggering any tax consequences. [I.R.C. § 530(d)(6); Notice 97-60, 1997-2 C.B. 310] The new designated beneficiary must be under age 30, unless he or she is considered a special needs beneficiary. (The age 18 limit applies to the annual contributions to the ESA for the designated beneficiary, not to transfers to a new designated beneficiary.) [I.R.C. §§ 530(d)(6), 530(d)(6)]

It may also be possible to change the designated beneficiary upon the death of the original designated beneficiary (see Q 13:76).

Q 13:19　Do the IRS model Coverdell ESA forms provide an option that prohibits changing the designated beneficiary?

Yes. The IRS model Coverdell ESA forms provide the following options:

The responsible individual ＿＿＿ may or ＿＿＿ may not change the beneficiary designated under this agreement to another member of the designated beneficiary's family described in Section 529(e)(2) in accordance with the trustee's procedures.

Example. Grandfather makes a Coverdell ESA contribution on behalf of his grandson, Jimmy. Grandfather names his son, Jimmy's dad, as the responsible individual. Jimmy has always been Grandfather's favorite grandson, and Grandfather does not want the Coverdell ESA assets transferred to one of his other grandchildren. Grandfather could check the box stipulating that the responsible individual may not change the designated beneficiary.

Q 13:20   Who is considered a member of the same family for purposes of a Coverdell ESA?

For the purpose of changing a designated beneficiary under a Coverdell ESA, members of the same family include the following:

1. The spouse of the designated beneficiary;
2. A son or daughter of the designated beneficiary or a descendant of either;
3. A brother, sister, stepbrother, or stepsister of the designated beneficiary;
4. The father or mother of the designated beneficiary or an ancestor of either;
5. A stepfather or stepmother of the designated beneficiary;
6. A son or daughter of a brother or sister of the designated beneficiary;
7. A brother or sister of the father or mother of the designated beneficiary;
8. A son-in-law, daughter-in-law, father-in-law, mother-in-law, brother-in-law, or sister-in-law of the designated beneficiary;
9. An individual (other than the spouse of the designated beneficiary) who, for the taxable year of the designated beneficiary, has as his or her principal abode the home of the designated beneficiary and is a member of the designated beneficiary's household;
10. A spouse of any individual listed above; and
11. A first cousin of the designated beneficiary (but not his or her spouse).

[I.R.C. § 152(a); *see also* I.R.C. §§ 529(e)(2), 530(d)(6); IRS Publication 970, *Tax Benefits for Education* 2008.]

Q 13:21   What would prompt a change in the designated beneficiary of a Coverdell ESA?

The designated beneficiary of a Coverdell ESA may be changed because the original beneficiary did not have any education expenses.

Example. Erica has $2,000 left in her Coverdell ESA after she graduates from college. The responsible individual may transfer the full $2,000 balance to a Coverdell ESA for Erica's younger sister, Stacey, who is still in high school, without any taxes being owed on the transfer. [IRS Publication 970, *Tax Benefits for Education* 2008]

Eligibility

Contributor Eligibility

Q 13:22 Who is eligible to make a Coverdell ESA contribution on behalf of an eligible child?

Any individual may contribute to a Coverdell ESA if his or her modified adjusted gross income (MAGI) is less than $110,000 ($220,000 for married taxpayers filing jointly) (see Q 13:26). It is unclear whether there is an income limit for corporations and other such entities. [I.R.C. § 530(c)(1)]

Q 13:23 Must a contributor have earned income to be eligible to contribute to a Coverdell ESA?

No. A contributor need not have earned income to contribute to a Coverdell ESA. The absence of an earned income requirement is notable because the rules for both the traditional IRA and the Roth IRA require that the IRA owner have earned income.

Q 13:24 May a child contribute to a Coverdell ESA on his or her own behalf?

Yes. A child may make a contribution to a Coverdell ESA for himself or herself. [Notice 97-60, 1997-2 C.B. 310] The absence of an earned income requirement will make most children under the age of 18 eligible to make their own Coverdell ESA contributions. In contrast, most children are not eligible to make a traditional or Roth IRA contribution because most children do not have earned income.

Q 13:25 May an ineligible parent give $2,000 to a child and then have the child make his or her own Coverdell ESA contribution?

Perhaps. The ability of a child to make his or her own contribution to a Coverdell ESA may make it easy to circumvent the income limit eligibility rules. Whether the IRS will challenge the interpretation that allows an ineligible parent to give $2,000 to his or her child to establish a Coverdell ESA is unknown. Similarly, a friend or other relative could make the contribution and be reimbursed by the parents. In any event, the maximum contribution amount of $2,000 imposes a built-in limit on the benefits of the Coverdell ESA.

Q 13:26 What are the income limits regarding eligibility to contribute to a Coverdell ESA?

To qualify to make a contribution to a Coverdell ESA, an individual's MAGI must fall below certain limits, as described below.

Married, Filing Jointly. A married couple filing a joint return with MAGI of $190,000 or less is entitled to make up to a full $2,000 Coverdell ESA contribution. Married joint filers with MAGI of more than $190,000 but less than $220,000 may make partial Coverdell ESA contributions. The range between $190,000 and $220,000 is called the *phaseout range* because the ability to contribute to a Coverdell ESA is phased out as an individual's MAGI increases. Married couples filing jointly whose MAGI falls within the phaseout range determine the amount of their contributions by using a reduced Coverdell ESA contribution calculation (see Q 13:29). Married joint filers with MAGI of $220,000 or more are not eligible to make Coverdell ESA contributions.

Married, Filing Separate Returns. Married individuals filing separate returns are treated as single filers (*see* below) for the purpose of eligibility to contribute to a Coverdell ESA. This is in contrast to the contribution requirements for both the traditional IRA and the Roth IRA, which provide threshold limits for married couples filing separately that are substantially lower than the single-filer thresholds.

Single Filers. Single filers with MAGI of $95,000 or less may make up to a full $2,000 Coverdell ESA contribution. Single filers with MAGI of more than $95,000 but less than $110,000 may make partial Coverdell ESA contributions (see Qs 13:28, 13:29). Single filers with MAGI of $110,000 or more are not eligible to contribute to a Coverdell ESA.

Table 13-1 summarizes the income limits based on filing status. The law does not provide for these limits to be adjusted for inflation.

Table 13-1. Coverdell ESA Income Limits

MAGI	Single	Married, Filing Jointly
Less than $95,000	Full contribution	Full contribution
$95,001–$109,999	Partial contribution	Full contribution
$110,000–$190,000	No contribution	Full contribution
$190,001–$219,999	No contribution	Partial contribution
$220,000 or over	No contribution	No contribution

Example 1. Alice is single and has MAGI of $60,000 for the tax year. Because her MAGI is below the $95,000 limit, Alice may make a full $2,000 Coverdell ESA contribution on behalf of any child.

Example 2. Bruce is married and files a joint federal income tax return. His MAGI (which includes his spouse's income) is $350,000, which is more than the $220,000 limit. Therefore, Bruce is not eligible to make a Coverdell ESA contribution.

Example 3. Ken, a single filer, would like to establish and contribute $2,000 to a Coverdell ESA for his daughter, Barbara. Ken's MAGI in 2008 is $100,000. He will be able to make only a partial Coverdell ESA contribution (see Q 13:29).

Q 13:27   What is modified adjusted gross income?

Modified adjusted gross income, or MAGI, for purposes of determining eligibility to make a Coverdell ESA contribution, is an individual's adjusted gross income (AGI) from his or her federal income tax return, with certain modifications. For most taxpayers, MAGI will be the same as AGI. The modifications made to AGI are slightly different for the Coverdell ESA than for the traditional IRA or the Roth IRA.

For the Coverdell ESA income limits, an individual's AGI must be *increased* by the following exclusions:

1. Foreign earned income of U.S. citizens or residents living abroad;

2. Housing costs of U.S. citizens or residents living abroad; and

3. Income from sources in Puerto Rico, Guam, American Samoa, or the Northern Mariana Islands.

[I.R.C. § 530(c)(2)]

Q 13:28   How are partial contribution amounts to a Coverdell ESA determined when an individual's income falls within the phaseout range?

If an individual's MAGI falls within the phaseout range (partial contribution range), the maximum contribution amount must be calculated. The calculation proportionately reduces the amount of the contribution over the phaseout range. For example, if an individual's income falls exactly at the midpoint of the phaseout range for his or her filing status, he or she would be entitled to make one-half of a full Coverdell ESA contribution, or $1,000.

Q 13:29   What is the partial contribution formula for Coverdell ESA contributions?

The IRS guidance for determining the amount of a partial Coverdell ESA contribution states that to figure the maximum contribution to a Coverdell ESA, $2,000 should be multiplied by a fraction, the numerator of which is the individual's MAGI minus $95,000 ($190,000 in the case of a joint return) and the denominator of which is $15,000 ($30,000 in the case of a joint return). The result should then be subtracted from $2,000. The final figure is the *maximum* amount that an individual whose MAGI is within the phaseout range may contribute to a Coverdell ESA for any one child.

Example. Mark, who is single, had MAGI of $96,500 for 2009. His maximum contribution to a Coverdell ESA for any one child is $1,800, determined as follows.

1. $96,500 − $95,000 = $1,500

2. $1,500 ÷ $15,000 = 10%

3. 10% × $2,000 = $200
4. $2,000 − $200 = $1,800

[*See* IRS Publication 970, *Tax Benefits for Education* 2008.]

Q 13:30   Is the partial Coverdell ESA contribution amount rounded?

No. Although rounding to the nearest dollar is allowed for federal income tax returns, the contributions to a Coverdell ESA may not be rounded. This prohibition distinguishes the treatment of Coverdell ESA contributions from contributions to a traditional IRA and a Roth IRA, which are rounded to the nearest $10. (If the amount is between $0 and $200, it is rounded up to $200.)

Q 13:31   Does active participation in a retirement plan affect contributions to a Coverdell ESA?

No. An individual may actively participate in a 401(k) plan or any other type of defined contribution or defined benefit plan without affecting his or her ability to make a Coverdell ESA contribution. The contributor's income and the child's eligibility (see Qs 13:26–13:30, 13:32–13:35) are the only limiting factors in making a Coverdell ESA contribution.

Designated Beneficiary Eligibility

Q 13:32   What is the age limit for the designated beneficiary of a Coverdell ESA?

No contribution may be made for a designated beneficiary after he or she attains age 18, unless he or she is a special needs beneficiary (see Q 13:75). [I.R.C. § 530(b)(1)(A)(ii)]

Q 13:33   May a child participate in both a state prepaid tuition program and a Coverdell ESA?

Yes. A child may receive a contribution to his or her Coverdell ESA for a year and have contributions made to a qualified state prepaid tuition program on his or her behalf. [I.R.C. § 530(d)(2)(C)(ii)]

Q 13:34   Must a child have a Social Security number or a taxpayer identification number to establish a Coverdell ESA?

Yes. The trustee or custodian of a Coverdell ESA is required to report certain information to the government using the child's Social Security number (SSN) or taxpayer identification number (TIN). Most trustees and custodians will require the child's SSN or TIN at the time the Coverdell ESA is established; others will require it to be provided within a certain number of days after establishment.

Q 13:35   Is an unborn child eligible to be the designated beneficiary of a Coverdell ESA?

No. A child must be born in order to be the designated beneficiary for a Coverdell ESA. (Code Section 530(b)(1) uses the word *individual* to clarify the issue.)

Contributions

Annual Contributions

Q 13:36   How much may be contributed annually to a Coverdell ESA?

No more than $2,000 may be contributed to Coverdell ESAs on behalf of a single beneficiary in one year. There is no limit on the number of Coverdell ESAs that may be established for one beneficiary, but the accounts are aggregated for purposes of this annual limit.

The $2,000 limit does not apply to rollovers from another Coverdell ESA (see Qs 13:46–13:50), or to certain transfers of military gratuities and life insurance proceeds paid under the Servicemembers' Group Life Insurance (SGLI) program (see Q 13:51).

Q 13:37   Is there a minimum contribution amount for a Coverdell ESA?

No. An individual may make as small a contribution to a Coverdell ESA as he or she wants. The trustee or custodian, however, may place a minimum contribution requirement on its accounts.

Q 13:38   May more than one individual make a contribution to a Coverdell ESA for the same child?

Yes. Any number of eligible individuals may make contributions to a Coverdell ESA for the same child; however, the total contribution on behalf of the child in any year may not exceed $2,000. [I.R.C. § 530(b)(1)(A)(iii)]

Q 13:39   May an individual make Coverdell ESA contributions on behalf of several children?

Yes. An eligible individual may make Coverdell ESA contributions on behalf of any number of designated beneficiaries. The individual's contributions for each child may not exceed the limit on contributions based on the contributor's MAGI (see Qs 13:26–13:30), but there is no limit on the amount of aggregate contributions that the individual may make.

Example. Carol and Fred have four children, file a joint federal income tax return, and have MAGI of $80,000. They may make a $2,000 contribution for each of their four children.

Q 13:40   What is the deadline for making contributions to a Coverdell ESA?

A grantor's contribution to a Coverdell ESA for any calendar year must be made by April 15 of the following year, which is also the deadline for traditional and Roth IRA contributions. [I.R.C. § 530(b)(4)]

Q 13:41   Is the Coverdell ESA contribution limit coordinated with the traditional IRA or Roth IRA limits?

No. The Coverdell ESA is independent of the traditional IRA and the Roth IRA. Therefore, an individual may establish both a traditional IRA or a Roth IRA and a Coverdell ESA. Furthermore, an individual may make a full $5,000 contribution to a traditional IRA or a Roth IRA and remain eligible to make a $2,000 contribution to a Coverdell ESA. It is also important to note that a child may have the maximum contribution made to a Coverdell ESA on his or her behalf and remain eligible to make the maximum annual contribution to a traditional IRA or Roth IRA (if the child has earned income).

Example. Paula makes a $5,000 contribution to her Roth IRA. She may also make a $2,000 contribution to a Coverdell ESA on behalf of her daughter, Iris. Iris may make her own $5,000 contribution to a Roth IRA if she has sufficient earned income.

Q 13:42   May an individual combine a Coverdell ESA with his or her traditional IRA or Roth IRA?

No. Contributions to a Coverdell ESA must be maintained separately from contributions to a traditional IRA or Roth IRA. [I.R.C. § 530(b)(1)]

Q 13:43   May an annual Coverdell ESA contribution be made in securities or other property?

No. Annual Coverdell ESA contributions must be made in cash. [I.R.C. § 530(b)(1)(A)(i)]

Example. Steve and Linda bought stock that is now worth $1,000. They would like to transfer the stock directly to the Coverdell ESAs of their daughters, Mindy and Margaret. That is not permissible. Steve and Linda must sell the stock or liquidate other assets to raise cash for the Coverdell ESA contributions.

Q 13:44   Can a federal income tax refund be directly deposited into a Coverdell ESA?

Yes. A taxpayer may instruct the IRS to deposit a tax refund directly into a Coverdell ESA. Amounts directly deposited to a Coverdell ESA remain subject, however, to the annual contribution limit.

Q 13:45 In 2008, did the IRS deposit some economic stimulus payments directly into Coverdell ESAs?

Yes. Most taxpayers were eligible to receive an economic stimulus payment in 2008 from the U.S. Treasury. In making the payment (really an advance refund of the income tax payable for 2008), the IRS followed any refund instruction that the taxpayer had designated on the 2007 income tax return if the instruction was for deposit of the refund to a single financial account. The account so designated may have been an IRA, a Coverdell ESA, a health savings account, or other tax-favored account.

Nonetheless, the IRS recognized that some taxpayers may have wanted to receive the economic stimulus payment in cash, rather than by direct deposit to an account such as an IRA. Without special tax relief, the withdrawal of a stimulus payment from an IRA or Coverdell ESA would subject the taxpayer to tax and penalties. Consequently, the IRS announced in 2008 that it would allow a taxpayer to withdraw—free of Code restrictions that would otherwise apply—all or part of an economic stimulus payment that was directly deposited into a tax-favored account, if the payment is withdrawn by a specified time. For a stimulus payment that was directly deposited into a Coverdell ESA, a withdrawal qualifies for this relief if it occurs by the *later* of June 1, 2009, or the deadline (including extensions) for filing the taxpayer's 2008 income tax return. [Ann. 2008-44, 2008-20 I.R.B. 982; IRS Publication 970, *Tax Benefits for Education* 2008]

> **Caution.** If the stimulus payment was directly deposited into a tax-favored account other than a Coverdell ESA (such as an IRA), the deadline for a qualifying withdrawal is simply the due date (including extensions) of the 2008 return. [Ann. 2008-44, 2008-20 I.R.B. 982; IRS Publication 970, *Tax Benefits for Education* 2008]

Rollover and Transfer Contributions

Q 13:46 Are trustee-to-trustee transfers allowed between Coverdell ESAs?

Yes. Trustee-to-trustee transfers are allowed between Coverdell ESAs. Such a transfer is the movement of assets from one Coverdell ESA to another without taking a distribution. Transfers are significant because they avoid the rule that limits rollovers to one every 12 months and the rule that requires a rollover to be completed within 60 days.

Trustee-to-trustee transfers are permitted between traditional IRAs pursuant to a revenue ruling—not pursuant to the Code or its regulations. [Rev. Rul. 78-406, 1978-2 C.B. 157] Although the revenue ruling does not apply to the Coverdell ESA, the IRS instructions to Form 5498-ESA indicate that trustee-to-trustee transfers are permitted and must be reported in box 2 on Form 5498-ESA. [Instructions for Form 5498-ESA (2009)]

Q 13:47   How is a trustee-to-trustee transfer accomplished?

Generally, to accomplish a trustee-to-trustee transfer, the responsible individual selects a new trustee or custodian for the Coverdell ESA and completes a new Coverdell ESA agreement as well as a transfer form. That transfer form is forwarded to the current trustee or custodian with instructions to send the assets in the Coverdell ESA directly to the new trustee (or custodian). The new trustee or custodian then receives the assets directly and places them in the Coverdell ESA.

The key feature of a transfer is that the responsible individual or designated beneficiary never has direct access to the funds in the Coverdell ESA. Because the assets are moved directly between financial organizations, no distribution is deemed to have occurred. Nevertheless, the transfer must be reported on Form 5498-ESA.

Q 13:48   May assets be rolled over from one Coverdell ESA to another?

Yes. Assets from one Coverdell ESA may be rolled over to another Coverdell ESA. A rollover takes place when the Coverdell ESA assets are paid directly to the responsible individual (or whoever controls the Coverdell ESA) and then are rolled over to a new Coverdell ESA (which may or may not be maintained by the original trustee or custodian). [I.R.C. § 530(d)(5)] In addition, a rollover can be made from certain U.S. savings bonds to a Coverdell ESA. [Instructions for Form 5498-ESA (2009)]

Q 13:49   Must a rollover between Coverdell ESAs be completed within 60 days?

Yes. Like traditional IRA and Roth IRA rollovers, Coverdell ESA rollovers must be completed within 60 days after the date of distribution. A hardship exception will be made, however, in cases where the completion of a Coverdell ESA rollover within the 60 days would be against equity or good conscience (e.g., following a casualty, a disaster, or other event beyond the reasonable control of the individual). [I.R.C. § 530(d)(5)] (See chapter 6 for a more complete discussion of the 60-day rule.)

Q 13:50   Is there a limit on how often rollovers may occur between Coverdell ESAs?

Yes. Rollovers between Coverdell ESAs are limited to one every 12 months. [I.R.C. § 530(d)(5)]

Military Death Gratuities and SGLI Payments

Q 13:51   Can military death gratuities and proceeds paid under the Servicemembers Group Life Insurance program be deposited to Coverdell ESAs without regard to the $2,000 limit and the income phaseout for contributor eligibility?

Yes. The Heroes Earnings Assistance and Relief Act of 2008 [Pub. L. No. 110-245, § 109] introduced a new provision of law that allows the recipient of an eligible military death gratuity, or of life insurance proceeds paid under the Servicemembers Group Life Insurance (SGLI) program of the U.S. Veterans Administration, to transfer all or a part of the payment to one or more Roth IRAs and Coverdell ESAs without regard to the dollar limits that normally apply. For transfers to Coverdell ESAs, this means that neither the $2,000 annual contribution limit nor the income phaseout rule for determining contributor eligibility applies.

There is no limit on the frequency of such contributions, but an individual's aggregate contributions under this rule to all Roth IRAs and Coverdell ESAs cannot exceed the sum of his or her gratuity and SGLI payments received plus the regular $2,000 annual contribution. [I.R.C. § 530(d)(9)] Contributed amounts are included in the cost basis of the respective account. [I.R.C. § 530(d)(9)]

The new rule is effective for military gratuities and SGLI payments that relate to deaths from injuries occurring after June 16, 2008, and amounts must be contributed to Roth IRAs or Coverdell ESAs within one year from their date of receipt by a beneficiary. A transition rule allows gratuities and SGLI payments made in respect of deaths from injuries occurring after October 6, 2001, and before June 17, 2008 (the enactment date), to be contributed with the same result by June 17, 2009. [Pub. L. No. 110-245, § 109(d)]

Note. The military death gratuity is a $100,000 payment made by the U.S. Department of Defense to eligible survivors of a servicemember who has died during active duty or in other specified circumstances. SGLI is a life insurance program offered by the U.S. Veterans Administration that provides certain members of the uniformed services with coverage up to $400,000. [U.S. Department of Defense Publication, *A Survivor's Guide to Benefits: Taking Care of Our Own* (2009)]

Excess Contributions

Q 13:52   What excise tax is payable if excess contributions are made on behalf of a designated beneficiary?

The designated beneficiary of a Coverdell ESA is required to pay an excise tax equal to 6 percent of the excess contributions in his or her Coverdell ESAs at the end of the year. An exception applies to an excess contribution that is withdrawn, with its earnings, before the beginning of the sixth month following the year of contribution. Accordingly, a calendar-year taxpayer has until May 31, 2010, to withdraw an excess contribution that is made for 2009. If an excess contribution is timely withdrawn, the excise tax does not apply but the withdrawn earnings are included in the gross income of the beneficiary for the year of the contribution. [I.R.C. §§ 4973(a), 530(d)(4)(C)] An excess contribution that is not withdrawn in time to apply the exception remains subject to the excise tax each year until it is removed. [I.R.C. § 4973(e)]

Note. An excess contribution for 2008 that is attributable to the direct deposit of a taxpayer's economic stimulus payment to the Coverdell ESA, can be corrected without incurring excise tax by withdrawing the stimulus payment before the later of June 1, 2009, or the taxpayer's deadline (including extensions) for filing the 2008 return (see Q 13:45).

Q 13:53   What is an excess contribution?

An *excess contribution* is generally any contribution, excluding rollovers, that exceeds the prescribed contribution limits. Thus, if aggregate contributions on behalf of a designated beneficiary exceed $2,000 per year or, if less, the combined maximum contributions that the donors were eligible to make that year, the surplus amount is an excess contribution. Undistributed excess contributions may be "absorbed" by unused contribution capacity in a later year. They are not absorbed, though, by unused contribution capacity from a former year. [I.R.C. § 4973(e)(1)]

For any year, the excess contributions that are subject to the 6 percent excise tax are determined as the sum of two amounts:

1. The current year's excess contribution, which is the amount by which the aggregate current year contributions of all donors to Coverdell ESAs having the same designated beneficiary exceeds the lesser of $2,000 or the combined maximum contributions that donors were eligible to make.

2. The preceding year's unmitigated excess contribution, which is the amount of excess contributions that were subject to excise tax in the preceding year, reduced (but not below zero) by (a) distributions (not including rollovers) during the current year from the beneficiary's Coverdell ESAs, and (b) the amount, if any, by which the current year's contributions are less than the maximum amount that the donors could have contributed.

[I.R.C. § 4973(e)(1)]

Example. In 2008, Ray's mother, Elena, and grandfather, Thomas, respectively contribute $500 and $2,000 to Coverdell ESAs on Ray's behalf. Neither contribution is restricted by the MAGI limits, but in combination they result in a $500 excess contribution for 2008. There is no distribution before June 1, 2009, so Ray has to pay a $30 excise tax when he files his 2008 tax return. For 2009, Elena contributes nothing and Thomas contributes $1,500, which is $500 less than his individual contribution limit based on MAGI. The excess contribution from 2008 is now absorbed and exempt from further excise tax.

Q 13:54   Is a contribution made on behalf of an ineligible individual subject to excise tax?

A contribution made for an individual who is ineligible—that is, an individual over age 18 who is not a special needs beneficiary (see Q 13:75)—must be removed from the account, with earnings, but it appears the excise tax would not apply. Code Section 4973(e), which defines excess contributions for purposes of the excise tax, does not describe this kind of improper contribution.

Q 13:55   Are excess contributions likely in a Coverdell ESA?

Yes. There is a high risk of excess contributions in a Coverdell ESA. Anyone can make a contribution on behalf of a child without knowing what others are doing. The responsible individual will be notified of the establishment of the Coverdell ESA; however, a child could have several responsible individuals who are not communicating with one another.

> **Example.** Marge and her former husband, Rick, have joint custody over their son, Jim. Marge makes a $2,000 contribution in 2009 on behalf of Jim and names herself as the responsible individual. Rick's parents also establish a Coverdell ESA and make a $2,000 contribution for Jim. Those grandparents name Rick as the responsible individual. Unless Rick and Marge are communicating with one another, the excess may go unnoticed. The IRS may well catch the error and send a penalty letter to Jim. If Rick and Marge do discover the excess contribution by June 1, 2010, the excess contribution (plus earnings) may be removed without penalty.

Q 13:56   How are excess contributions discovered?

Excess contributions made on behalf of a designated beneficiary may be discovered by any of the recipients of Form 5498-ESA, which is the form that must be prepared by each trustee who maintains a Coverdell ESA (see Qs 13:103–13:106). Thus, the IRS, the beneficiary, and/or the beneficiary's parents may discover excess contributions made on behalf of the designated beneficiary when they receive the Form 5498-ESA. The person completing the tax return for a designated beneficiary who files a tax return may also discover the excess contributions if he or she receives all of the beneficiary's Forms 5498.

Q 13:57   Who receives the money when an excess contribution from a Coverdell ESA is returned?

It is not clear who receives the money when an excess contribution from a Coverdell ESA is returned. As noted below (see Q 13:91), the instructions to the IRS model Coverdell ESA forms specifically provide that language may be added concerning the treatment of excess contributions. Some forms providers have added language in the Coverdell ESA agreement to the effect that the responsible individual shall have the authority to remove the excess and use the money as he or she deems appropriate.

Example. Joey has loving grandparents on both sides of his family. Each set of grandparents makes a $2,000 Coverdell ESA contribution for Joey in 2009. The correction method required is clearly removal of $2,000 plus earnings. Which contribution is the excess? How is it corrected? Who gets the money? None of these questions can be definitively answered.

Distributions

Q 13:58   May a distribution be taken from a Coverdell ESA at any time for any reason?

Yes. The responsible individual is able to access the Coverdell ESA assets at any time and for any reason, just as an IRA owner can access IRA assets. If the distribution is not a qualified distribution, however, it may be subject to taxes and penalties. The investment vehicle may also impose early withdrawal penalties or other restrictions on early withdrawal.

Q 13:59   Which distributions from a Coverdell ESA are tax free and penalty free?

Only two kinds of distributions are free from federal income tax and penalties:

1. Distributions used to pay for qualified education expenses (see Qs 13:77–13:82). [I.R.C. § 530(d)(2)]
2. A distribution that returns a directly deposited economic stimulus payment to the taxpayer who was entitled to receive it (i.e., the contributor to the Coverdell ESA), before the later of June 1, 2009, and the taxpayer's deadline (including extensions) for filing the 2008 return. [Ann. 2008-44, 2008-20 I.R.B. 982] However, the terms of the Coverdell ESA may not permit a distribution to the contributor, and if the distribution is made to the beneficiary, it is not clear that the tax relief afforded by Announcement 2008-44 would apply. [IRS Publication 970, *Tax Benefits for Education* 2008]

Q 13:60   What taxes and penalties might apply to distributions from a Coverdell ESA?

Distributions from a Coverdell ESA are potentially subject to a variety of taxes and penalties if they are not tax free. The principal tax is the federal income tax. The penalty generally associated with Coverdell ESAs is an additional 10 percent penalty imposed on the taxable portion of any distribution (see Qs 13:62–13:64). [I.R.C. § 530(d)(4)]

Other taxes and penalties, including the following, may apply:

1. *State income taxes.* State income taxes may apply to a distribution from a Coverdell ESA or to the annual earnings in a Coverdell ESA.

2. *Excise tax (6 percent) on excess contributions.* (See Qs 13:52–13:57.)

3. *Prohibited transactions and pledging account as security for a loan.* If a Coverdell ESA engages in a prohibited transaction, or if it is pledged as security for a loan, it is considered distributed. This results in the distribution's being taxable and subject to the 10 percent penalty. [I.R.C. §§ 530(e), 4975]

4. *Trustee or custodian penalties.* The trustee or custodian of a Coverdell ESA may charge a loss-of-earnings penalty on early withdrawals. The trustee or custodian may also charge a back-end load or other fee in connection with the investment or account at the time of distribution.

5. *Estate taxes.* The Coverdell ESA is considered part of a deceased designated beneficiary's estate, and estate taxes may apply (see chapters 9 and 10).

6. *Unrelated business income tax.* The Coverdell ESA is subject to the unrelated business income tax imposed by Code Section 511.

[Joint Comm. on Taxation, *Description of Senate Finance Committee Chairman's Remarks Relating to Reform and Restructuring of the IRS* (JCX-17-98) (Mar. 26, 1998)]

Q 13:61   What are the exceptions to the 10 percent penalty on Coverdell ESA distributions?

A distribution from a Coverdell ESA is not subject to the 10 percent penalty, even if it is otherwise subject to federal income tax, provided it meets one of the following exceptions:

1. *Death.* The distribution is made to the estate of the designated beneficiary upon his or her death. [I.R.C. § 530(d)(4)(B)(i)]

2. *Disability.* The distribution is attributable to the designated beneficiary's being disabled (within the meaning of Code Section 72(m)(7)). This generally means that the individual cannot perform substantial gainful activity as a result of a mental or physical condition that is expected to last for an indefinite duration or result in death. [I.R.C. § 530(d)(4)(B)(ii)]

3. *Scholarship.* The distribution is made in a year when an otherwise nontaxable scholarship, allowance, or payment that covers eligible education expenses is received by the designated beneficiary (see Q 13:65). [I.R.C. § 530(d)(4)(B)(iii)]

4. *Waiver.* The tax-free nature of the distribution is waived so that the individual or his or her parents can claim the HOPE Scholarship Credit or Lifetime Learning Credit (see Q 13:80). [I.R.C. § 530(d)(4)(B)(iv); IRS Publication 970, *Tax Benefits for Education* 2008]

5. *Attendance at a U.S. Military Academy.* The distribution is made because the designated beneficiary attends a U.S. military academy (e.g., West Point). This exception applies only to the extent that the amount of the distribution does not exceed the costs of advanced education [Title 10 of the U.S. Code] at the applicable academy. [IRS Publication 970, *Tax Benefits for Education* 2008]

6. *Excess Contribution.* The distribution of an excess 2009 contribution (and any earnings on it) is made before June 1, 2010. The distribution earnings must be included in gross income for the year in which the excess contribution was made. [I.R.C. § 530(d)(4)(C); IRS Publication 970, *Tax Benefits for Education* 2008]

Q 13:62 Is the 10 percent penalty imposed on distributions from a Coverdell ESA the same penalty imposed on premature distributions from a traditional IRA or Roth IRA?

No. The Coverdell ESA penalty is the same amount as the premature distribution penalty (10 percent) and follows some of the same rules, but it is a different penalty, as described in Code Section 530(d)(4). The rules and exceptions applicable to traditional IRAs, Roth IRAs, and qualified plans, which are contained in Code Section 72, do *not* apply to Coverdell ESAs.

Q 13:63 Does the 10 percent penalty apply to the entire amount of the distribution from a Coverdell ESA?

No. The 10 percent penalty applies only to the taxable portion of a distribution from a Coverdell ESA. The return on contribution amounts is not taxable and is thus not subject to the 10 percent penalty. [I.R.C. § 530(d)(4)(A)]

Example. Donna, age 19, serves as the responsible individual for her own Coverdell ESA. She has $2,200 in her account, which represents a $2,000 contribution (principal or basis) plus $200 in earnings. She takes a distribution of the entire $2,200 to take a vacation unrelated to education. Donna will owe taxes and penalties on the $200 in earnings ($54 in taxes, assuming a 27 percent tax bracket, plus a $20 penalty).

Q 13:64 What are the income tax consequences of a distribution from a Coverdell ESA that is not used for qualified education expenses but does meet one of the other exceptions to the 10 percent penalty?

Any earnings on a distribution from a Coverdell ESA that is not used for qualified education expenses (see Qs 13:77–13:82) but meets another exception to the 10 percent penalty are subject to federal income tax.

Q 13:65 What is a qualified scholarship?

A *qualified scholarship* includes a scholarship excludable from gross income, an educational assistance allowance, or a payment for the designated beneficiary's education expenses that is excludable from gross income under any law of the United States to the extent the Coverdell ESA distribution is not more than the scholarship, allowance, or payment. [I.R.C. § 25A(g)(2); IRS Publication 970, *Tax Benefits for Education* 2008]

Congress did not think it fair to impose a penalty on a designated beneficiary who withdraws assets from a Coverdell ESA to pay for qualified education expenses and then receives a scholarship to cover the same education expenses. Accordingly, the 10 percent penalty does not apply to those amounts, but ordinary income tax does. Of course, if the scholarship does not cover all of the beneficiary's education expenses, the remaining expenses can be paid using the Coverdell ESA distribution, which will not be subject to tax or penalty to the extent it is so used. [I.R.C. § 530(d)(4)(B)(iii); IRS Publication 970, *Tax Benefits for Education* 2008]

Q 13:66   Are contributions returned first in a Coverdell ESA?

No. Distributions from a Coverdell ESA consist of a ratio of contributions and earnings. A calculation must be performed to determine the ratio of contributions to earnings in any distribution. The calculation is similar to that required for a traditional IRA when nondeductible contributions have been made. [I.R.C. § 530(d)(2)(B)]

Q 13:67   How is the taxable portion of a distribution from a Coverdell ESA determined?

Generally, if the total withdrawals from a Coverdell ESA for a tax year are more than the designated beneficiary's qualified education expenses (see Qs 13:77–13:82), a portion of the amount withdrawn is taxable to the beneficiary.

The taxable portion is the amount that represents earnings that have accumulated tax free in the Coverdell ESA. The taxable amount may be figured by performing the following steps:

1. Multiply the amount withdrawn by a fraction, the numerator of which is the total contributions in the account and the denominator of which is the total balance in the account before the withdrawals.

2. Subtract the amount figured in Step 1 from the total amount withdrawn during the year. This is the amount of earnings included in the withdrawals.

3. Multiply the amount of earnings figured in Step 2 by a fraction, the numerator of which is the qualified education expenses paid during the year and the denominator of which is the total amount withdrawn during the year.

4. Subtract the amount figured in Step 3 from the amount figured in Step 2. This is the amount the beneficiary must include in income.

Example 1. Hans takes a $6,000 distribution from a Coverdell ESA to which $10,000 has been contributed. The balance in the account before the withdrawal was $12,000. Hans had $4,500 of qualified education expenses for the year. The taxable portion of the distribution is computed as follows:

1. $6,000 × ($10,000 ÷ $12,000) = $5,000
2. $6,000 − $5,000 = $1,000

3. $1,000 × ($4,500 ÷ $6,000) = $750
4. $1,000 − $750 = $250

Hans must include $250 in income as withdrawn earnings not used for qualified education expenses. [IRS Publication 970, *Tax Benefits for Education* 2008]

Example 2. Ivy is the beneficiary of a Coverdell ESA with a balance of $10,000, of which $4,000 represents principal (i.e., contributions) and $6,000 represents earnings. A distribution of $2,000 is made in 2009 from the account. Of that distribution, $800 will be treated as a return of principal (which is not includable in Ivy's gross income) and $1,200 will be treated as accumulated earnings. If Ivy's qualified education expenses for 2009 are at least equal to the total amount of the distribution (i.e., principal plus earnings), the entire earnings portion of the distribution is excludable under Code Section 530. If Ivy's qualified education expenses for 2009 are less than $2,000, however, only a portion of the earnings is excludable from her gross income under Code Section 530. Thus, if Ivy incurs only $1,500 of qualified education expenses in 2009, only $900 of the earnings will be excludable from her gross income under Code Section 530 (i.e., an exclusion will be provided for the pro rata portion of the earnings based on the ratio that the $1,500 of qualified education expenses bears to the $2,000 distribution), and the remaining $300 of the earnings portion of the distribution will be includable in Ivy's gross income. [IRS Publication 970, *Tax Benefits for Education* 2008]

Note. Form 8606, Nondeductible IRAs and Coverdell ESAs, must be used to determine the taxation of distributions from Coverdell ESAs.

Q 13:68   What is the effect of receiving a taxable distribution from a Coverdell ESA that has no earnings to distribute?

If the Coverdell ESA has no earnings to distribute, the entire distribution would be reported as a return of contributions, and no tax would result.

Q 13:69   If there is a loss on investments within the Coverdell ESA, is it deductible by the beneficiary?

Losses within a Coverdell ESA are not deductible until all amounts have been finally distributed. At that point, the beneficiary may be allowed a deduction on his or her income tax return for the amount of any contributions that have not been returned. The loss would be claimed as a miscellaneous itemized deduction and subject to the 2-percent-of-adjusted-gross-income limit. [IRS Publication 970, *Tax Benefits for Education* 2008; I.R.C. § 67]

Q 13:70   Does the trustee or custodian track the contributions and earnings in a Coverdell ESA?

No. The trustee or custodian of a Coverdell ESA is not responsible for tracking the amount of contributions and earnings in the account, except when a distribution has been made and Form 1099-Q must be filed with the IRS. The responsible individual or the person completing the tax return for the designated beneficiary must determine the amount of contributions and earnings. [Instructions to Form 1099-Q; IRS Forms 5305-E, 5305-EA]

Q 13:71   Is federal income tax withholding required from a Coverdell ESA?

No, federal income tax withholding is not required from a Coverdell ESA.

Q 13:72   What happens to the assets remaining in a Coverdell ESA after the designated beneficiary finishes his or her education?

There are two options. The amount remaining in a Coverdell ESA after the designated beneficiary completes his or her post-secondary education may be paid to the designated beneficiary. It will be subject to both federal income tax and the additional 10 percent penalty on the portion of the amount withdrawn that represents earnings (if no exception to the penalty applies) (see Qs 13:60–13:64).

Alternatively, the amount in the designated beneficiary's Coverdell ESA may be withdrawn and rolled over to another Coverdell ESA for the benefit of a member of the designated beneficiary's family (see Q 13:20) who has not yet attained age 30. The amount rolled over will not be taxable. [I.R.C. § 530(d)(5); Notice 97-60, 1997-2 C.B. 310]

Q 13:73   Is the Coverdell ESA a better choice than the traditional IRA or the Roth IRA for a parent who wishes to save for a child's education?

Although a parent is permitted to make both a Roth IRA (or traditional IRA) contribution and a Coverdell ESA contribution, for financial reasons one or the other may need to be selected. If the parent will not have attained age 59½ when the account's assets will be needed for education expenses, then a Roth IRA is not an optimal choice because its major tax benefit is that qualified distributions are tax free. As discussed elsewhere (see chapter 5), Roth IRA distributions are qualified only if they are (1) made on or after the date on which the individual attains age 59½ (2) made to a beneficiary (or to the estate of the Roth IRA owner) on or after the death of the Roth IRA owner, (3) attributable to the individual's being disabled, or (4) qualified first-time homebuyer distributions. Thus, a distribution taken before age 59½ will likely be taxable and the major benefit of the Roth IRA will be lost.

If the parent will be over age 59½ at the time of distribution, a Roth IRA is ideal, because it gives the parent tax-free distributions without the Coverdell ESA's requirement that accumulated assets be used for education expenses. Moreover, the Roth IRA's assets count less directly against the student when he or she is applying for financial aid. A Roth IRA may even be suitable for a parent who will be under age 59½ at the time of distribution, because contributions (but not earnings) may be withdrawn income tax free. If a parent knew that the Roth IRA's contributions without earnings would be sufficient to fund a child's education, the earnings could be retained for the parent's retirement. Otherwise, the Coverdell ESA or the traditional IRA may be a better choice. Distributions from a Coverdell ESA will be tax free (the major tax benefit of the Coverdell ESA). Distributions from a traditional IRA will be taxable but free of the 10 percent excise tax on premature distributions because the traditional IRA permits an exception for qualified education expenses. Because distributions from a traditional IRA will always be taxable, the intrinsic tax benefit will not be lost (as would be the case if Roth IRA distributions were taken prematurely).

Distributions at Age 30

Q 13:74   Is a full distribution required when the designated beneficiary of a Coverdell ESA attains age 30?

Usually. A full distribution of a Coverdell ESA is required when the designated beneficiary reaches age 30, *unless* he or she is a special needs beneficiary or the responsible individual elects to transfer the assets to another member of the designated beneficiary's family. [I.R.C. § 530(b)(1)(E)]

Q 13:75   What is a special needs beneficiary?

Treasury regulations are expected to be issued to define a *special needs beneficiary* as an individual who requires additional time to complete his or her education because of a physical, mental, or emotional condition (including a learning disability). [H.R. Conf. Rep. No. 107-84 § IV.A (2001)]

Distributions After Death

Q 13:76   What happens to the assets in a Coverdell ESA upon the death of the designated beneficiary?

The Code provides that upon the death of the designated beneficiary, any balance to the credit of the beneficiary is deemed distributed within 30 days after the date of death. [I.R.C. § 530(b)(1)(E)] Furthermore, the Code clearly allows for another member of the family to assume the assets upon the death of the designated beneficiary. [I.R.C. § 530(d)(7)]

Both IRS model Coverdell ESA forms read as follows:

> Any balance to the credit of the designated beneficiary shall be distributed within 30 days of the date of such designated beneficiary's death unless the designated death beneficiary is a family member of the

designated beneficiary who is under 30 on the date of death. In such a case, the family member shall become the designated beneficiary as of the date of death.

The Code further provides that death beneficiaries are not subject to the 10 percent penalty (see Q 13:61). [I.R.C. § 530(d)(4)]

Qualified Education Expenses

Q 13:77   What are qualified education expenses?

The definition of *qualified education expenses* varies according to whether the expenses are for elementary or secondary school education or for higher education.

The following are qualified education expenses for elementary and secondary school education and for higher education:

- Tuition, fees, academic tutoring, special needs services in the case of a special needs beneficiary, books, supplies, and other equipment required for the enrollment or attendance of the designated beneficiary at a public, private, or religious school. [I.R.C. §§ 529(e)(3)(A)(i), 530(b)(4)(A)(i)]
- Room and board. [I.R.C. §§ 529(e)(3)(B), 530(b)(4)(A)(ii)]
- The purchase of any computer technology or equipment or Internet access or any related service, if the equipment, technology, or service is used by the beneficiary and his or her family during any of the years the beneficiary is in school (not including computer software designed for sports, games, or hobbies unless the software is educational in nature). [I.R.C. § 530(b)(4)(A)(iii)]
- Amounts contributed to a qualified state tuition program. [I.R.C. § 529(e)(3)(B)(i)]

The following are qualified education expenses only in the following instances:

- Expenses for room and board at a higher education institution for students who attend an eligible educational institution at least half time (see Q 13:78), but limited to one of the following: (1) the school's posted room and board charge or (2) $2,500 per year for students living off campus and not at home. [I.R.C. § 529(e)(3)(B)]
- Expenses for uniforms, transportation, and supplementary items or services (including extended day programs) that are required by an elementary or secondary school in connection with enrollment or attendance. [I.R.C. § 530(b)(4)(A)(ii)]

[*See also* IRS Publication 970, *Tax Benefits for Education* 2008.]

Q 13:78   When is a student considered to be enrolled at least half time?

A student is considered to be enrolled at least half time if he or she is enrolled for at least half of the full-time academic workload for the course of study the student is pursuing as determined under the standards of the institution where the student is enrolled. The institution's standard for a full-time workload must equal or exceed the standards established by the Department of Education under the Higher Education Act. [Notice 97-60, 1997-2 C.B. 310; 34 C.F.R. § 674.2(b)]

Q 13:79   What is an eligible educational institution?

The definition of *eligible educational institution* includes virtually all accredited public, nonprofit, and proprietary postsecondary, secondary, and elementary institutions. If the institution is eligible to participate in the student aid programs administered by the Department of Education, it is an eligible institution. [Notice 97-60, 1997-2 C.B. 310; 20 U.S.C. § 1088] Verification of a school's status as an eligible educational institution is available online at *http://www.fafsa.ed.gov/FOTWWebApp/FSLookupServlet.*

Q 13:80   Does having a Coverdell ESA affect qualification for the HOPE Scholarship Credit or the Lifetime Learning Credit?

The HOPE Scholarship Credit and the Lifetime Learning Credit help families pay for higher education. The credits may be claimed by the student, the student's parents (if the student is a dependent), or the student's spouse on the federal income tax return. The credits are phased out for individuals making above certain income levels.

A student can claim the HOPE Scholarship Credit or the Lifetime Learning Credit in the same year that he or she receives a tax-free distribution from a Coverdell ESA. The student's parents are also permitted to claim either credit in the same year that the student receives a tax-free distribution from a Coverdell ESA. The distribution, however, may not be used for the same education expense for which the credit is claimed. [Notice 97-60, 1997-2 C.B. 310; I.R.C. § 530(d)(2)(C)]

Q 13:81   May a beneficiary receive distributions from both a Coverdell ESA and a qualified tuition program in the same year?

Yes, but if the combined distributions are more than the beneficiary's qualified education expenses, the expenses must be allocated between the Coverdell ESA and the qualified tuition program (also known as a *529 plan*) so that the taxable portion of each distribution may be determined. [*See* IRS Publication 970, *Tax Benefits for Education* 2008.]

Q 13:82   What happens if the designated beneficiary of a Coverdell ESA does not incur any qualified education expenses?

If the designated beneficiary of a Coverdell ESA never incurs any qualified education expenses, the responsible individual (who may be the designated beneficiary) has two options. The assets in the Coverdell ESA may be paid to the designated beneficiary—but they will be subject to taxes and the 10 percent penalty (see Q 13:60). Alternatively, the assets may be rolled over to a Coverdell ESA whose designated beneficiary is a member of the original designated beneficiary's family (see Q 13:20). [Notice 97-60, 1997-2 C.B. 310]

Trustees and Custodians

Q 13:83   What institutions may serve as trustees or custodians of Coverdell ESAs?

Any financial organization authorized to accept traditional IRA contributions will automatically be approved to accept Coverdell ESA contributions and act as a trustee or custodian. Thus, banks, credit unions, savings associations, insurance companies, mutual funds, brokerages, and other financial institutions already approved by the IRS to offer IRAs are automatically approved by the IRS to offer Coverdell ESAs. Any other organization must submit an application to the IRS for approval to serve as a trustee or custodian of a Coverdell ESA in accordance with the procedures set forth in Treasury Regulations Section 1.408-2(e) and Section 3.09 of Revenue Procedure 2009-4. [2009-1 I.R.B. 118]

Note. Individuals may not serve as Coverdell ESA trustees or custodians.

Q 13:84   May federal credit unions offer the Coverdell ESA?

Yes. Federal credit unions were initially barred from offering the Coverdell ESA because of a National Credit Union Administration (NCUA) rule that allows credit unions to offer only IRAs authorized by Code Section 408. The NCUA, however, amended its rules so that federal credit unions could offer the Coverdell ESA. [12 C.F.R. §§ 724, 701 (1998); *see also* NCUA Ltr. No. 98-CU-5 (Feb. 20, 1998).]

Note. The NCUA considers Coverdell ESAs to be insured member accounts. They are insured under Code of Federal Regulations Section 745.9-1 and will be added to other irrevocable trust accounts for insurance purposes. [NCUA Ltr. No. 98-CU-5 (Feb. 20, 1998)]

Documentation

Q 13:85   How is a Coverdell ESA established?

Like a traditional IRA or a Roth IRA, a Coverdell ESA must be established as a trust or custodial account. That process requires the use of either of two IRS model Coverdell ESA forms—Form 5305-E, Coverdell Education Savings Trust Account, or Form 5305-EA, Coverdell Education Savings Custodial Account—or a prototype document, along with a plain-language disclosure statement.

Q 13:86   What are the trust requirements for a Coverdell ESA?

The document creating and governing the trust for a Coverdell ESA must be in writing and must satisfy the following requirements:

1. The trust must be created and organized in the United States.
2. The trustee must be a bank or an entity approved by the IRS.
3. The trust must provide that the trustee may accept only a contribution that
    a. Is in cash;
    b. Is made before the beneficiary reaches age 18; and
    c. Would not result in total contributions for the tax year (not including rollover contributions) of more than the legal maximum (currently $2,000).
4. Money in the account cannot be invested in life insurance contracts.
5. Money in the account cannot be combined with other property except in a common trust fund or common investment fund.

[I.R.C. § 530; *see also* IRS Publication 970, *Tax Benefits for Education* 2008.]

Q 13:87   What is the difference between the two IRS model Coverdell ESA forms?

The two IRS model Coverdell ESA forms are nearly identical; the only difference is the use of a few words. *Trust* and *grantor* are used in Form 5305-E to describe, respectively, the financial institution accepting the contribution and the person making the contribution. In Form 5305-EA, the terms *custodian* and *depositor* are used. Trust departments and trust companies generally select the trust agreement (Form 5305-E); all other financial institutions generally use the custodial agreement (Form 5305-EA).

Q 13:88   What is the advantage of using the IRS model Coverdell ESA forms?

The advantage of using the IRS model forms to establish a Coverdell ESA is that they are automatically approved. Trustees and custodians using the model Coverdell ESA forms are not required to submit any application or user fee to the IRS.

Q 13:89   Who is entitled to a copy of the IRS model Coverdell ESA form?

If a trustee or custodian chooses to use an IRS model Coverdell ESA form, it must provide a copy of the model form to the contributor (grantor or depositor) and to the responsible individual if the responsible individual is someone other than the contributor.

Example. Jane opens a Coverdell ESA at ABC Bank for her friend's daughter, Ann. Jane selects her friend, Susan (Ann's mother), as the responsible individual. ABC Bank must provide a copy of the IRS model Coverdell ESA form to Jane and Susan.

Q 13:90   What do the IRS model Coverdell ESA forms contain?

The IRS model Coverdell ESA forms—Form 5305-E and Form 5305-EA—have the same look and organization as the IRS model forms for the traditional IRA and the Roth IRA. The forms contain the following:

1. Contributor information: the name and the Social Security number (SSN) or individual taxpayer identification number (TIN) of the person establishing the Coverdell ESA.

2. Designated beneficiary information: the name, SSN or TIN, date of birth, and address of the designated beneficiary.

3. Responsible individual information: the name and address of the responsible individual.

4. Trustee or custodian information: the name and address of the trustee or custodian.

5. Contribution information: the amount of the initial contribution.

6. Legal document: the required IRS provisions that must be adopted word for word in Articles I through X of the form.

7. Instructions: a description of how to use the form.

8. Signature lines: signature lines for the contributor (grantor or depositor), the trustee or custodian, and a witness.

Neither of the IRS model Coverdell ESA forms contains a disclosure statement, but each indicates that one is required.

Q 13:91   May trustees or custodians add language to the IRS model Coverdell ESA forms?

Yes. While the language in the IRS model Coverdell ESA forms may not be changed, the IRS allows trustees and custodians to *add* their own language to the forms.

The additional language may begin at Article X (as many articles as desired may be added). The additional language may include definitions, investment powers, voting rights, exculpatory provisions, amendment and termination procedures, processes for removal of the trustee or custodian, trustee's or custodian's fees, state law requirements, treatment of excess contributions, and a discussion of prohibited transactions with the contributor, designated beneficiary, and responsible individual. [General Instructions to Forms 5305-E and 5305-EA]

Q 13:92   May the trustee or custodian preselect the options on the IRS model Coverdell ESA form?

Yes. If a particular Coverdell ESA trustee or custodian in lieu of the contributor wants to select the options on the IRS model, it may do so. For example, the trustee or custodian may decide that administration will be easier if all the Coverdell ESAs it services are the same or that certain options confuse its customers. Whatever its reasons, the trustee or custodian may preselect the options.

Q 13:93   What is required in the disclosure statement for a Coverdell ESA?

The IRS requires that the trustee or custodian of a Coverdell ESA provide the grantor and the responsible individual with a plain-language disclosure explaining the Coverdell ESA. [IRS Forms 5305-E, 5305-EA] There are no regulations that discuss the disclosure requirements for Coverdell ESAs, but the IRS model Coverdell ESA forms indicate that providing the contributor with a copy of IRS Notice 97-60 [1997-2 C.B. 310] is considered providing a sufficient disclosure statement.

Q 13:94   Who is required to receive the disclosure statement for a Coverdell ESA?

The contributor (grantor or depositor) must receive a disclosure statement at the time the Coverdell ESA is established. The trustee or custodian must also provide a copy to the responsible individual if the responsible individual is not the same person as the contributor. [IRS Forms 5305-E and 5305-EA]

Q 13:95   Is a financial disclosure statement required for a Coverdell ESA?

Not at this time. Regulations requiring financial disclosure statements for both the traditional IRA and the Roth IRA do not apply to the Coverdell ESA.

Q 13:96   What taxpayer identification numbers are required?

The SSN of the contributor (grantor or depositor) and the SSN of the designated beneficiary will serve as the identification numbers. (The designated beneficiary's SSN is the identification number of the Coverdell ESA.) If the contributor is a nonresident alien and does not have an identification number, "Foreign" should be written in the block where the number is requested. [General Instructions to Forms 5305-E and 5305-EA]

An employer identification number (EIN) is required for a Coverdell ESA for which a return is filed to report unrelated business taxable income. An EIN is also required for a common fund created for Coverdell ESAs. [General Instructions to Forms 5305-E and 5305-EA]

Q 13:97   Is Form W-9 TIN certification required for a Coverdell ESA?

No. The Coverdell ESA trustee or custodian must collect the designated beneficiary's SSN or TIN; however, it is not necessary to use Form W-9, Request for Taxpayer Identification Number and Certification, to do so. The trustee or custodian may determine that information in a manner convenient to the trustee or custodian.

Q 13:98   Who must sign an IRS model Coverdell ESA form?

An IRS model Coverdell ESA form must be signed by both the contributor (grantor or depositor) and the trustee or custodian. A witness's signature may also be necessary pursuant to state law.

Q 13:99   Must the responsible individual sign an IRS model Coverdell ESA form?

No. An IRS model Coverdell ESA form does not provide a signature line for the responsible individual. The lack of a signature line creates some concern over whether the responsible individual is bound under the terms of the agreement. Some trustees and custodians are requiring the responsible individual to sign and return a copy of the model form or are requiring the responsible individual to sign a signature card or other acknowledgment form.

Note. The responsible individual signs the IRS model Coverdell ESA form (as grantor or depositor) in the case of a rollover or a transfer of the Coverdell ESA.

Q 13:100   May a trustee or custodian create a prototype Coverdell ESA document?

Presumably. The IRS generally allows trustees and custodians to draft prototype IRA documents; however, the IRS is not yet accepting any prototype Coverdell ESAs for approval and has not yet established an approval process.

Q 13:101   May a Coverdell ESA be revoked?

Whether a Coverdell ESA may be revoked is unclear. Regulations applicable to the traditional IRA provide that the IRA owner has the right to revoke an IRA within seven days after receiving the disclosure statement. [Treas. Reg. § 1.408-6(d)(4)] Those regulations have not yet been extended to the Coverdell ESA.

Q 13:102   How many Coverdell ESAs may one individual establish?

There is no limit on the number of Coverdell ESAs an individual may establish; however, the total annual contribution to all Coverdell ESAs of any one designated beneficiary is limited to $2,000. [IRS Publication 970, *Tax Benefits for Education* 2008]

Reporting

Q 13:103 What forms must Coverdell ESA trustees and custodians complete for the IRS?

Coverdell ESA trustees and custodians are required to provide two primary reports to the IRS: Form 1099-Q to report distributions (including earnings and the basis portions of the distributions) taken during the calendar year (not necessary if there are no distributions) and Form 5498-ESA to report contributions and earnings in the account. (A trustee's or custodian's other reports may satisfy as substitutes for Form 5498-ESA.) The Code gives the IRS the authority to require additional reporting in the future. [I.R.C. § 530(h)] (See chapter 7 for a discussion of reporting requirements.)

Q 13:104 What are Coverdell ESA trustees and custodians required to provide to the contributor?

After the initial establishment of the Coverdell ESA, the trustee or custodian is not required to provide any reports to the contributor (grantor or depositor), unless the contributor is also the responsible individual.

Q 13:105 What is reported on Form 5498-ESA?

Form 5498-ESA is used for reporting contributions or rollovers to a Coverdell ESA. The form consists of a series of boxes. The trustee or custodian enters the amount of a Coverdell ESA contribution in box 1 and the amount of a rollover contribution in box 2.

Q 13:106 When is Form 5498-ESA due?

Form 5498-ESA is a three-part form. Copy A is filed with the IRS by May 31 of the year following the year for which the contribution was made. Copy B is distributed to the beneficiary by April 30 of such year. Copy C is retained by the trustee or custodian of the Coverdell ESA. [Instructions for IRS Form 5498-ESA]

Q 13:107 How are distributions from a Coverdell ESA reported?

Distributions from a Coverdell ESA are reported to the IRS on Form 1099-Q, which must be filed no later than February 28 of the year following the year of distribution. A copy of the form must be sent to the recipient of the distribution no later than January 31 of the year following the year of distribution. [Instructions for Forms 1099, 1098, 5498, and W-2G] Distributions include refunds, payments upon death or disability, and withdrawals of excess contributions plus earnings. The trustee or custodian reports the distribution as follows:

1. The gross distribution (including the amount of any excess contributions and earnings thereon distributed to the recipient during the calendar year) is reported in box 1.

2. The amount of earnings on excess contributions is reported in box 2. This amount is computed using the method for calculating the net income attributable to IRA contributions that are distributed as a returned contribution (i.e., in accordance with Code Section 408(d)(4) under IRS Notice 2000-39 [2000-2 C.B. 132] and Proposed Treasury Regulations Section 1.408-11). Box 2 can be left blank if the distribution does not include earnings on excess contributions.

3. The basis (i.e., the gross distribution minus earnings, or the amount in box 2 subtracted from box 1) is reported in box 3. If no earnings on excess contribution are distributed, box 3 can be left blank.

4. If the Coverdell ESA suffers a loss in a year that is not the final year of distributions from the account, or there are no earnings for a year, zero is entered in box 2. A loss is entered in box 2 only for the final year of distributions for the account.

5. When a trustee-to-trustee transfer is made from one Coverdell ESA directly to another Coverdell ESA or to a qualified tuition program, box 4 is checked. Box 4 can be left blank if the trustee or custodian does not know whether the distribution was a trustee-to-trustee transfer.

6. In box 5, the trustee or custodian checks the Coverdell-ESA option.

7. Box 6 is checked if the recipient is not the designated beneficiary.

8. In the blank space below boxes 5 and 6, the trustee or custodian must state that box 2 includes earnings on excess contributions (when box 2 includes such earnings), report the fair market value of the Coverdell ESA as of December 31, and refer recipients of Form 1099-Q to IRS Publication 970, *Tax Benefits for Education* 2008, for the calculation of the earnings portion of the distribution.

[Instructions to 2009 Form 1099-Q, Payments From Qualified Education Programs (Under Sections 529 and 530); Notice 2003-53, 2003-2 C.B. 362]

Q 13:108 How should the withdrawal of a directly deposited economic stimulus payment from a Coverdell ESA be reported?

The financial institution should report the distribution just like any other. The taxpayer whose stimulus payment is withdrawn does not report the distribution if it is made by the later of June 1, 2009, or the taxpayer's deadline (including extensions) for filing the 2008 income tax return, because in that case the deposit and withdrawal are both disregarded for tax purposes. [Ann. 2008-44, 2008-20 I.R.B. 982; IRS Publication 970, *Tax Benefits for Education* 2008] If any part of the stimulus payment remains in the Coverdell ESA after that date, upon its later withdrawal the distribution will be taxed to the beneficiary and reported in accordance with the normal rules that govern Coverdell ESA distributions (see Qs 13:58–13:76).

Q 13:109   Are Coverdell ESA trustees and custodians required to compute the taxable portion of a Coverdell ESA distribution?

Yes. The trustee or custodian of a Coverdell ESA is required to compute the taxable and nontaxable portions of a Coverdell ESA distribution. [Instructions to Forms 1099-R and 5498-ESA; *see* IRS Notice 2003-53, 2003-2 C.B. 362.]

Q 13:110   How is the 10 percent penalty on distributions from a Coverdell ESA reported and paid?

The 10 percent penalty on distributions from a Coverdell ESA is reported and paid using Form 5329, Additional Taxes on Qualified Plans (Including IRAs) and Other Tax-Favored Accounts (see chapter 7).

Q 13:111   How are contributions and earnings tracked in a Coverdell ESA?

The responsible individual should save the Forms 5498-ESA to keep track of contributions. The IRS requires that the taxable amount of a distribution be reported on line 21 of Form 1040 for the year in which any distribution is made from a Coverdell ESA. [Instructions to 2008 Form 1040, Individual Tax Return] A distribution may not be taxable if it was used to pay for qualified educational expenses (see Qs 13:77–13:82). [*See* IRS Publication 970, *Tax Benefits for Education* 2008.]

Chapter 14

State Tax Rules Regarding IRAs

Anthony P. Curatola

Individuals in 43 states and the District of Columbia pay some form of state income tax. Of course, states differ in how they tax retirement income, whether before or after retirement; whether from qualified retirement plans, traditional IRAs, Roth IRAs, or nonqualified retirement plans; and whether as a lump sum or as an annuity. The purpose of this chapter, therefore, is to provide insight into the state income tax treatment of retirement income. It should be noted, however, that income tax laws—state and federal—are ever-changing. For example, the Economic Growth and Tax Relief Reconciliation Act of 2001 (EGTRRA) changed the federal law on contribution limits to, distributions from, and even transfers between qualified retirement plans (including IRAs) beginning in 2002. The Job Creation and Worker Assistance Act of 2002 (JCWAA) made a number of technical corrections to several tax provisions in EGTRRA; the Katrina Emergency Tax Relief Act of 2005 (KETRA) and Gulf Opportunity Zone Act of 2005 (GOZA) provided special relief for those affected by hurricanes; and the Pension Protection Act of 2006 (PPA) provided special relief for qualified charitable contributions and early distributions for reservists called to active duty. Some states adopted the provisions in the year of enactment; others adopted them in later years; and still others, pending their legislative sessions, have not yet adopted them.

Traditional IRA Contributions

Q 14:1   Do all states permit a deduction for traditional IRA contributions?

No. Three states do not permit a deduction for traditional IRA contributions: Massachusetts, New Jersey, and Pennsylvania. Seven states (Alaska, Florida, Nevada, South Dakota, Texas, Washington, and Wyoming) do not have a state personal income tax, and two states (New Hampshire and Tennessee) have a state personal income tax on interest and dividends only. The remaining 38 states and the District of Columbia permit a deduction for contributions made to a traditional IRA on a taxpayer's state income tax form.

Q 14:2   Do states that permit a deduction for traditional IRA contributions follow the federal tax law?

In general, yes. The majority of those states use the federal income tax return information as a starting point, applying their own rates and some state adjustments. When changes in federal tax law occur, however, the states do not always respond immediately or in the same manner. For example, although contributions to a traditional IRA have been deductible on the federal tax return since 1975, they have been deductible in Alabama and the District of Columbia only since 1982, and in Minnesota only since 1985 (see Qs 14:9, 14:10).

EGTRRA increased the contribution limit for traditional IRAs and Roth IRAs to $3,000 beginning in 2002 (see Q 3:4), increased it to $4,000 in 2005, and increased it again to $5,000 in 2008. It allows an even higher contribution limit for taxpayers who are age 50 or over by December 31 of the current year (see Qs 3:4, 3:5). Unfortunately, not all states adopted the provisions of EGTRRA immediately after its enactment. For example, the Governor of Wisconsin did not sign conforming legislation until July 26, 2002 (the legislation was made retroactive to January 1, 2002). Similarly, the Arkansas General Assembly, which also was not scheduled to meet in 2002, did not sign conforming legislation until February 26, 2003 (the legislation was made retroactive to January 1, 2002).

Q 14:3   Do states that permit a deduction for traditional IRA contributions generally follow the federal tax law on nondeductible contributions?

Yes. States that permit a deduction for contributions to traditional IRAs generally follow the federal tax law on nondeductible contributions.

Q 14:4   Do states that permit a deduction for traditional IRA contributions generally follow the federal tax law on catch-up contributions?

Yes. States that permit an income tax deduction for traditional IRA contributions generally follow the federal tax law on catch-up contributions.

Q 14:5   Do states tax earnings on traditional IRA contributions in the year of accrual?

No. Earnings on traditional IRA contributions are taxed only in the year of distribution.

Traditional IRA Distributions

Q 14:6   How are traditional IRA distributions taxed by states?

In most states, distributions from a traditional IRA that are included on the recipient's federal income tax return are also included on his or her state income tax return. The exceptions include states that do not permit a deduction for a contribution to a traditional IRA (e.g., Massachusetts and New Jersey) or permit, in some years, a lesser or greater deduction for a traditional IRA contribution (e.g., Arkansas, California, District of Columbia, Georgia, and Minnesota). Although Pennsylvania does not permit a deduction for contributions to a traditional IRA, that state also does not tax any form of retirement income received by a retiree (see Q 14:9).

Illinois (as of 1989), and Mississippi (as of 1994) exclude retirement benefits from gross income, including traditional IRA distributions received by a retiree, spouse, or other beneficiary at the death of the primary retiree. [35 Ill. Comp. Stat. Ann. 5/203(a); Miss. Code Ann. § 27-7-15(4)(*l*)] Other states provide an exclusion amount for retirement income, including IRA distributions (see Q 14:8).

Q 14:7   Does state taxation of distributions apply to traditional IRAs in the same way that it does to other types of retirement benefits?

Most states tax distributions from a traditional IRA and a qualified plan in the same manner. Of course, there are some exceptions whereby qualified retirement benefits receive preferential treatment.

Three states (Louisiana, Michigan, and Ohio) do not tax lump-sum distributions from qualified plans if the taxpayer elects 10-year forward averaging for federal income tax calculations.

Note. Only taxpayers born before 1936 are eligible for 10-year averaging.

States that have their own version of the federal 10-year averaging rules are Delaware (Form 329), Kentucky (Form 4972-K), Minnesota (Sch M1LS), New York (Form IT-230), and South Carolina (Form SC4972). Arkansas, California, and North Dakota were included in this group of states in prior years.

Lump-sum distributions from traditional IRAs have never been eligible for forward averaging for federal income tax calculations.

Q 14:8   Do states tax a lump-sum distribution from a traditional IRA differently than they tax an annuity distribution from a traditional IRA?

Generally, no. New York, however, allows a $20,000 annual exclusion for annuity distributions, including annuity distributions from traditional IRAs. Lump-sum distributions from IRAs now qualify for the annual exclusion, but payments derived from contributions made after retirement do not. [*See* NY State Dep't of Taxation and Finance Publication 36, "General Information for Senior Citizens and Retired Persons" (Dec. 2007), page 16.] Interestingly, lump-sum payments from an HR 10 (Keogh) plan qualify for the exclusion, but only if the taxpayer does not use federal Form 4972, Tax on Lump-Sum Distributions (from Qualified Plans of Participants Born Before January 2, 1936).

Q 14:9   What is the state income tax effect on a distribution from a traditional IRA if a state does not permit a deduction for a traditional IRA contribution?

Currently, there are only three states with a personal income tax that do not permit a deduction for a traditional IRA contribution (Massachusetts, New Jersey, and Pennsylvania).

For a Pennsylvania resident, a retirement distribution is not taxable if it is made after the person has reached normal retirement age, or age 59½. Otherwise, the distribution, less previously taxed contributions, is totally taxable.

A Massachusetts or New Jersey resident must maintain records of all contributions to his or her traditional IRA. Because a traditional IRA owned by a resident of those states may have two bases, separate records are needed to determine which portion of the traditional IRA distribution is subject to federal tax and which portion is subject to state tax. In the case of a New Jersey resident, New Jersey Income Tax Publication Bulletin GIT-2, *IRA Withdrawals* (rev. December 2007), provides that the taxpayer must calculate the New Jersey taxable portion of a periodic distribution annually. The calculation specifics, however, are given in New Jersey Income Tax Publication Bulletin GIT-1, *Pension and Annuity* (rev. December 2008), and provide that a taxpayer must use the Three-Year Rule Method, if qualified, or the General Rule Method. The Three-Year Method allows a person to recover previously taxed contributions before including any distribution amount in New Jersey gross income if it can be totally recovered within three years. Otherwise, the General Rule applies, which prorates the previously taxed contribution over the taxpayer's expected return on the contract. These methods are discussed in detail in Publication Bulletin GIT-1 at *http://www.state.nj.us/treasury/taxation/pdf/pubs/tgi-ee/git1.pdf*. A Massachusetts resident, on the other hand, may recover previously taxed contributions before including any distribution amounts in Massachusetts gross income. [Instructions for Form 1, Schedule X, p. 18]

Q 14:10   What is the state income tax effect on a distribution from a traditional IRA if a state permitted a greater or lesser deduction than the federal deduction for a traditional IRA contribution?

A few states have permitted a deduction that, in some years, was different from the federal deduction. As a result, an IRA owned by a taxpayer in those states has two bases: one for federal purposes and one for state purposes. Therefore, taxpayers in those states need to keep separate records to determine which portion of the distribution is subject to federal tax and which portion is subject to state tax (see Qs 14:6, 14:9).

Q 14:11   Does a taxpayer's state basis in a traditional IRA transfer to another state when the taxpayer takes a distribution from the traditional IRA as a resident of that other state?

Generally, no. South Carolina, for example, issued Private Letter Ruling 89-4 (Apr. 7, 1989) holding that "a resident individual is fully taxable on withdrawals from an IRA although amounts contributed [by the individual] while residing in Pennsylvania were non-deductible."

However, Oregon and (as of 1996) Virginia permit a resident taxpayer a subtraction for distributions from a traditional IRA, Keogh, or simplified employee pension (SEP) plan for the contributions to the plan that have already been taxed by another state. Oregon allows the subtraction only if several conditions are satisfied. [*See* 1999 Or. Laws 746, § 316.680(1)(g); Or. Admin. R. 150-316.159.]

California provides a partial step-up in basis to a taxpayer's IRA assets upon establishing residency in the state. Beginning in 2002, the IRA basis for California purposes is the taxpayer's IRA contributions in excess of $1,500 that were made in years 1982 through 1986. This rule applies to taxpayers regardless of when they established residency in the state. [*See* State of California Franchise Tax Board Publication 1100 (Rev. 04-2005) online at *http://www.ftb.ca.gov/forms/misc/1100.pdf*.]

Q 14:12   If a state denies a deduction for a traditional IRA contribution, will the IRA owner (when retired) be able to claim that state's state tax basis after he or she has moved to a state that allows a deduction for a traditional IRA contribution?

The answer varies from state to state. Three states (Massachusetts, New Jersey, and Pennsylvania) do not permit a deduction for a contribution to an IRA. Depending on the state of relocation, the retired IRA owner may or may not be permitted an adjustment for the state tax basis in the IRA that he or she would have had if he or she had not moved (see Q 14:11). If such an adjustment is granted, only the accumulated earnings on the IRA will be taxed by the state to which the IRA owner has moved.

Q 14:13   Is double taxation of a traditional IRA distribution possible at the state level?

Yes. Double taxation is possible on part but not all of a distribution from a traditional IRA. This is true even after the enactment of the ban on source taxes (see Q 14:21). In certain situations, the amount of a traditional IRA contribution can be taxed twice. For example, if the owner of a traditional IRA residing in a state that does not permit a deduction for a traditional IRA contribution moves to another state upon retirement, and the new state of residence does not recognize the prior state's state basis in the IRA, the contribution portion of any distribution from the IRA will be taxed by the new state of residence. Since the contribution has already been taxed by the former state of residence, it will have been taxed twice. [*See, e.g.,* South Carolina Priv. Ltr. Rul. 89-4 (Apr. 7, 1989).]

Q 14:14   Is negative taxation of a traditional IRA distribution possible at the state level?

Yes. Negative taxation is possible on part but not all of a distribution from a traditional IRA. Negative taxation can occur with respect to the IRA contribution amount. For example, if the owner of a traditional IRA residing in a state that permits a deduction for a traditional IRA contribution moves at retirement to a state that does not have a state income tax, the contribution portion of any distribution from the owner's traditional IRA will not be taxed by the new state of residence. The contribution will have been awarded a tax subsidy in the former state of residence and no tax cost in the current state of residence.

Q 14:15   Do traditional IRA distributions qualify for a state's pension exclusion?

It depends. The taxable portion of a traditional IRA distribution is generally eligible for the pension exclusion in states that have a pension exclusion provision; however, not all states have a pension exclusion provision, and the amount and eligibility requirements in the states that have one generally vary. For example, South Carolina provides a $3,000 annual deduction per spouse for retirement income received before age 65 and a $10,000 annual deduction per spouse at age 65 or over. [S.C. Code Ann. § 12-6-1170] Delaware provides a pension exclusion of up to $12,500 per person for taxpayers who are age 60 or older and up to $2,000 per person for taxpayers who are under age 60. [Del. Code Ann. tit. 30, § 1106] (See Q 14:38.)

Q 14:16   Where can a state's retirement exclusion amount be found?

The quickest way to locate a state's retirement exclusion amount and criteria for exclusion is the state's Web site. See a list of state Web sites in Q 14:77.

For a broad-based appreciation of the treatment of IRA distributions by state, readers should consult Curatola & Trewin, *Taxation of Retirement Income: A State Analysis*, State Tax Notes, 2031–41 (June 12, 2000). Because state tax laws change frequently, state Web sites should be consulted for the most up-to-date provisions.

Q 14:17   Is an individual's age for qualifying under a state's pension exclusion provision determined on December 31 of the taxable year or January 1 of the following year?

It depends on the state. Colorado residents qualify if they are over age 55 as of December 31 of the taxable year. Virginia provides an exclusion of $6,000 if the taxpayer is age 62, 63, or 64 on January 1 of the following year; the exclusion amount increases to $12,000 if the taxpayer is age 65 or older on January 1 of the following year. Delaware and South Carolina, on the other hand, do not stipulate the date and, as a result, the taxpayer's age is presumably determined on December 31 of the taxable year (see Q 14:38).

Q 14:18   Do states treat traditional IRA rollovers or direct transfers to another IRA as taxable distributions?

No. All states treat rollovers, direct transfers, and trustee-to-trustee transfers as nontaxable transactions. It should be noted, however, that some states give favorable tax treatment to distributions from qualified retirement plans. Thus, a rollover to a traditional IRA from a qualified retirement plan may defer taxation but result in taxation at a less favorable state income tax rate when distributions are taken from the IRA.

For example, a taxpayer who takes a lump-sum distribution from a qualified plan in Louisiana (or Michigan or Ohio) and elects 10-year forward averaging for federal income tax calculations would pay no state income tax on the distribution. If the same taxpayer rolls over the distribution from the qualified plan to a traditional IRA, the withdrawal from the traditional IRA in a later year will be treated as ordinary income on both the federal and state tax returns. (For other situations with similar state laws, see Q 14:7.)

Q 14:19   Do states conform to the federal tax laws concerning traditional IRA rollovers or direct transfers to a qualified plan?

For the most part. Massachusetts, for example, follows federal law for workplace retirement plans, effective January 1, 2002, including the provisions of Internal Revenue Code (Code) Sections 72 and 401 through 420 (but excluding Code Sections 402A (elective deferral of Roth IRA contributions) and 408(q) (deemed IRAs)) and Sections 457, 3401, and 3405. [Mass. Dept. of Rev., MATIR 02-18, I.D (Nov. 6, 2002)] Some states are unable to conform to federal tax law until their next legislative session. In these situations, the state legislature must decide to conform to the tax law either prospectively or retroactively. Moreover, the state's department of revenue must decide whether or not to issue a position statement on how taxpayers should handle such a situation on the current-year tax return (see Q 14:43). In the case of EGTRRA, Massachusetts signed conforming legislation on July 25, 2002; Wisconsin signed on July 26, 2002; and Arkansas signed on February 26, 2003. At the time the 2008 tax forms and instructions were printed, Minnesota indicated on its Web site "What's new for individuals?" that it had not yet adopted the federal changes enacted after February 13, 2008. Those changes included the Heroes Earned Assistance and Relief Tax (HEART) Act of 2008; The Heartland, Habitat, Harvest, and Horticulture Act of 2008; The Emergency Economic Stabilization Act of 2008; and The Housing Assistance Tax Act of 2008. The notice indicated that some or all of these federal provisions may be adopted during the 2009 Minnesota Legislative Session. The Web site was updated on April 20, 2009, to say that the legislation enacted April 3, 2009, adopted the federal tax provisions enacted from February 13 through December 31, 2008, with certain exceptions. [*See http://www.taxes.state.mn.us/taxes/individ/other_supporting_content/whats_ new_08.shtml#P77_5160.*]

Q 14:20   Is a distribution from a traditional IRA taxable by the IRA owner's former state of residence when the individual moves out of the state and claims residency in another state?

The answer depends on the former state of residence and on the year in which the distribution was made (i.e., after 1995 or before 1996). Another important factor is the relationship that the taxpayer has or has not maintained with the former state of residency. These issues are discussed in the following sections.

Tax on Post-1995 Distributions Received from Traditional IRAs by Former Residents

Q 14:21   If an individual moves out of a state permanently, does that end the possibility that the former state of residence will tax a traditional IRA distribution made to that individual in the new domicile?

Yes, for traditional IRA distributions made after 1995. Public Law No. 104-95 (Jan. 10, 1996), which is known as the ban on source taxes, prevents states and the District of Columbia from taxing former residents on retirement income from qualified retirement plans, traditional IRAs, and, in some cases, nonqualified retirement plans. The law is effective for distributions received in 1996 and thereafter.

Q 14:22   What is a domicile?

A *domicile* is a residence intended as an individual's permanent and primary home. Whether a residence qualifies as a domicile may be verified in a number of ways, including the following:

- The amount of time the individual is physically present in the residence
- The home address listed on the individual's
  - Car registration,
  - Driver's license,
  - Voter registration, and
  - State and federal tax returns (as well as where the returns are filed)
- The location of the individual's
  - Real estate holdings,
  - Club memberships,
  - Business connections, and
  - Polling place

All facts and circumstances are considered. Unless care is exercised, a dispute over the location of the domicile may lead to expensive litigation. [*See, e.g.,* Reichstetter, New York Division of Tax Appeals, DTA No. 818356 (Oct. 31, 2002).]

Other factors that may be relevant in determining an individual's state of domicile are the location of the individual's checking account, savings account, stockbroker, and cemetery plot.

The Idaho State Tax Commission has prepared a nine-page brochure titled *Residency Status and Idaho Source Income,* TC00260 (Feb. 12, 1998), which provides a lengthy discussion of this topic, with illustrations. The brochure is available on the Web at *http://tax.idaho.gov/pdf/publications/TC00260%20 Residency%20Brochure.pdf.*

Minnesota has prepared Income Tax Fact Sheet 1 for Residency determination. This fact sheet provides the criteria for individuals, military personnel, students, and non-U.S. citizens as well as a number of examples to illustrate some of the more complex issues. The fact sheet is available on the state's Web site at *http://www.taxes.state.mn.us/individ/other_supporting_ content/inctaxfs1.shtml.*

Q 14:23   What is a source state?

The term *source state* refers to the state in which an individual's traditional IRA was initially established, or in which the individual's pension was earned or funded. A source state seeks to tax the income that was deferred and, in most cases, to tax the tax benefit that was given while the individual was working or living in the source state.

Q 14:24 May an individual continue to have a residence in a state in which he or she formerly had a domicile?

Yes. Maintaining such a residence, however, may demonstrate that the individual continues to be domiciled in that state and, therefore, may still be considered a resident of that state. A possible outcome is that the individual's traditional IRA distributions may be taxable by the former state of domicile (the source state) because the individual is not deemed to be a "former resident," as required for relief under federal law. From a tax standpoint, therefore, it is even more desirable now than it was previously to cleanly sever ties with the source state (to establish "former residency" status) and keep contacts with the source state to a minimum.

A person can have more than one residence but can have only one domicile. The difficulty is that a person must prove that he or she has taken up a new domicile and, in so doing, has abandoned the former domicile.

The two examples that follow are taken from the Minnesota Income Tax Fact Sheet 1 for residency determination and provide an appreciation for this issue. [See *http://www.taxes.state.mn.us/individ/other_supporting_content/inctaxfs1. shtml.*]

> **Example 1.** Laura lives in Minnesota for five months and in Arizona for seven months. Because she was a Minnesota resident before she began spending time in Arizona, Laura continues to be a full-year Minnesota resident until she takes steps to change her residency.

> **Example 2.** Patrick retired, sold his permanent home in Minnesota, and lives the life of a nomad, traveling around the country in a recreational vehicle. Even though he abandoned his Minnesota home, Patrick is still considered to be a full-year Minnesota resident until he establishes residency in another state.

Q 14:25 Does it matter whether a traditional IRA distribution is taken out of the state in the year of the move rather than in subsequent years?

Yes. Most states include a distribution from a traditional IRA in a taxpayer's gross income if the taxpayer takes the distribution while he or she is still a resident of the state. In addition, if a taxpayer maintains residency (e.g., by voting or keeping a residence) in a state, the distribution could be taxed by that state even if the distribution was taken after the taxpayer moved out of the state. For example, New York law leans toward the automatic taxation of distributions that are received before the end of the year of relocation. To ensure that a distribution is not taxable by the former state of residence, a taxpayer would be wise to delay the distribution until the year after the relocation (see Q 14:24).

Q 14:26   Are all forms of nonqualified retirement income protected by the ban on source taxes?

No. The ban on source taxes shelters nonqualified retirement income from any plan, program, or arrangement described in Code Section 3121(v)(2)(C) only if such income is part of a series of substantially equal periodic payments made not less frequently than annually for

- The life or life expectancy of the recipient (or joint lives or joint life expectancies of the recipient and his or her designated beneficiary), or
- A period of not less than 10 years.

In addition, income from a nonqualified plan is protected by the ban on source taxes if the plan was established solely to provide benefits in excess of the qualified plan limits and the benefits are paid after the employee terminates.

The effect of a nonqualified plan on the ban on sources taxes raises some questions. For example, does the term *terminate* have the same meaning as *separate from service*, which is found in Code Section 402? Does a nonqualified plan that provides a participant with the option to take a lump-sum payment or an annuity payment satisfy the ban on source taxes if the employer's qualified plan provides only an annuity option? These and other questions are still to be resolved.

Wisconsin highlights this issue in Publication 106, *Wisconsin Tax Information for Retirees* (January 2009), which states:

> If you worked in Wisconsin but are now a resident of another state, payments you received from a *nonqualified* pension or annuity or a *nonqualified* deferred compensation plan are taxable by Wisconsin unless (1) the distribution is paid out in annuity form over your life expectancy or for a period of not less than 10 years or (2) the distribution is paid in either an annuity form or lump-sum from arrangements known commonly as "mirror plans."

[*See http://www.dor.state.wi.us/pubs/pb106.pdf.*]

Tax on Pre-1996 Distributions Received from Traditional IRAs by Former Residents

Q 14:27   If an individual leaves a state entirely, does that end the possibility that the individual will be taxed by the former state of residence on a distribution made to that individual in the new state of residence?

Not necessarily. Public Law No. 104-95 (Jan. 10, 1996), the ban on source taxes (see Q 14:21), is effective for IRA distributions taken *after* 1995. Thus, complete relocation does not necessarily end the possibility that an individual will be taxed by his or her former state of residence on IRA distributions taken before January 1, 1996.

It is true that the state from which the individual departed may no longer be able to claim him or her as a resident, and, as a nonresident, the individual may leave behind no assets on which taxes can be levied. The former resident may not even be physically present to be served with process. Nevertheless, there have been cases where state tax authorities successfully moved against former residents in their new domiciles.

Q 14:28 If an individual maintains a residence in his or her former state of residence, will that individual cease to be taxed by the former state on IRA distributions made in the new state of residence?

It depends. Maintaining a residence may demonstrate that the individual continues to be domiciled in the former state. As such, the individual may be deemed to be a current resident, not a former resident (see Q 14:24). For example, Publication 88 (December 2008, page 6), *General Tax Information for New York State Nonresidents and Part-Year Residents*, discusses this issue in depth and states that:

> If your domicile is not New York State you are considered a New York State nonresident. However, you are a New York State resident for income tax purposes if your domicile is not New York State, but you maintain a permanent place of abode in New York State for more than 11 months of the year and spend 184 days or more (any part of a day is a day for this purpose) in New York State during the tax year.

Q 14:29 May a taxpayer's former state of residence attach assets in the taxpayer's new state of residence?

Yes. Nevertheless, a number of states—including Arizona, Colorado, Illinois, Louisiana, New Mexico, New York, Oregon (to a limited extent), and Virginia— have adopted legislation that specifically precludes judgments against retirement income and bars states from such action against former residents, particularly involving retirement income.

Q 14:30 On what theory may a state tax an individual after his or her change of domicile from that state to another state?

The theory is quite clear. The individual, having been allowed by the state in which he or she was domiciled to deduct contributions and to defer tax on earnings accruing on the contributions (which are otherwise taxable income) should not be allowed to avoid that state's tax permanently by moving to another state.

Q 14:31 What is the claim of the state to which the taxpayer moves?

Domicile or residency in a state is a valid basis for a state to impose an income tax. By claiming domicile or residency, a taxpayer enjoys various services and privileges provided by the new state—roads, police, firefighting, social services, welfare, and the protection of its laws. Because most of a retiree's income may come from Social Security benefits, IRA distributions, or pension payments, there might be little other income for the new state of domicile to tax to support its efforts on behalf of the new resident.

Q 14:32   Which states have sought to tax former residents and in what ways?

Various states have sought to tax different types of retirement income of former residents. California and Oregon have attempted to tax traditional IRA and pension distributions. New York has attempted to tax distributions from non-annuity IRAs. [*See, e.g.*, Wolf, New York Division of Tax Appeals, Tax Appeals Tribunal, DTA No. 812738 (Mar. 7, 1996).] Minnesota, New York, and Vermont have claimed authority to tax non-IRA distributions.

Q 14:33   How long is the statute of limitations for seeking tax on a traditional IRA distribution received by a former state resident?

The answer is unclear. The general rule is three years; however, the three-year statute of limitations applies only to timely filed tax returns. An individual who has not filed a state tax return for pre-1996 retirement income should not rely on the three-year statute of limitations. The reason is that if a state tax return has not been filed for a prior year, the clock has not begun to run. Thus, a state may be within its rights to seek tax on those prior distributions.

Q 14:34   How is tax apportioned when more than one state makes a claim on an individual's distributions based on being the source state?

In Iowa, it had been proposed that the allocation for a state be based on the number of years the taxpayer worked in that state. This would have been calculated using a fraction whose denominator was the number of years lived in all states. Iowa rescinded those proposed rules, which would have become effective in 1993. Furthermore, in 1994 Iowa acted to end its taxation of pensions received by former residents.

Roth IRA Distributions

Q 14:35   How are Roth IRA distributions taxed by states?

In most states, Roth IRA distribution amounts that are included on or excluded from the federal income tax return are likewise included on or excluded from the state income tax return. Pennsylvania holds that "distributions are includable in income to the extent that contributions were not previously included if made before the individual for whom the account is maintained obtains age 59 and retires from service or if the plan makes no provision for payments at regularly recurring intervals continuing at least until the participant's death." [Pa. Ltr. Rul. PIT-98-048] Similarly, Massachusetts excludes from gross income distributions from a Roth IRA so long as the taxpayer is at least age 59½ but adds the provision that the account must be at least five years old. [TIR 98-02]

Q 14:36   Do states treat Roth IRA rollovers or direct transfers to another Roth IRA as taxable distributions?

No. All states treat rollovers, direct transfers, and trustee-to-trustee transfers as nontaxable transfers. Rollovers between Roth IRAs may be made only once every 365 days, whereas direct rollovers (i.e., trustee-to-trustee transfers) may be made as often as trustees will permit.

Q 14:37   Is a taxable Roth IRA distribution taxable by a former state of residence if an individual moves out of the state and claims residency in another state?

The answer is no if the taxable distribution occurs in a year other than the year in which the taxpayer relocates. The answer also depends on the state and the timing of the distribution if the distribution occurs in the year in which the taxpayer is a part-year resident of the source state. In New York, for example, if a taxable distribution from a Roth IRA is received during the change-of-residence year, the income portion of the distribution is included in the recipient's New York AGI for the change-of-residence year. If the individual receives the taxable distribution when he or she is a resident of New York, the income portion of the distribution is included in New York source income. If the taxable distribution is received when the individual is not a resident of New York, the income portion of the distribution is not included in New York source income. [N.Y. TSB-M-98(7)I (Dec. 24, 1998)]

Q 14:38   Do Roth IRA distributions qualify for a state's pension exclusion?

The portion of a Roth IRA distribution that is taxable is generally eligible for a state's pension exclusion; the portion of a Roth IRA distribution that is not taxable is generally not eligible for a state's pension exclusion (see Qs 14:15–14:17). Not all states have a pension exclusion provision.

Special Purpose Distributions

Q 14:39   Are distributions from a traditional IRA for a first-time home purchase taxable at the state level?

Generally, yes. In most states, traditional IRA distribution amounts that are included in the gross income of an individual's federal income tax return are likewise included in the gross income reported on the individual's state income tax return (see Q 14:6). Many states have specifically adopted the provisions of the IRA regulations of 1997 and 1998. Although other states have not specifically adopted those regulations, they base their state taxable income on the taxpayer's federal return, giving the taxpayer the same result.

Federal law includes in gross income any taxable distribution amounts from traditional IRAs used for first-time home purchases but exempts up to $10,000 of that taxable amount from the 10 percent premature distribution penalty.

Q 14:40 Are distributions from a Roth IRA for a first-time home purchase taxable at the state level?

Generally, no. Most states exclude from taxation Roth IRA distributions that are excluded from federal income taxation (see Q 14:35). Contributions returned to a Roth IRA are never taxable. Beginning in 2003, earnings distributed from a Roth IRA are exempted for "qualified" first-time home purchases.

Of the states that do not follow the federal treatment of IRAs, Massachusetts and New Jersey have adopted the federal treatment of Roth IRA qualified distributions. Massachusetts, for example, issued TIR 98-02, which states that distributions [from Roth IRAs] are tax free so long as the taxpayer is at least age 59½ (or disabled, or a first-time homebuyer) and the account is at least five years old. New Jersey provides conformity in its statute. [NJ § 54A: 6-28.b.(4)] At present, Pennsylvania taxes all distributions from any type of IRA after the recovery of contributions unless the distribution is received after the participant attains age 59½.

Q 14:41 Are distributions from a traditional IRA or Roth IRA for education expenses taxable at the state level?

Generally, yes. The distributed amount is included in state gross income. Federal income tax law, however, exempts from the 10 percent premature distribution penalty taxable IRA distribution amounts that are used to pay "qualified education expenses" of the taxpayer or the taxpayer's spouse, children, or grandchildren. [I.R.C. § 72(t)(7)]

Michigan, for example, provides that for tax years that begin after December 31, 1999, a taxpayer may deduct, to the extent included in AGI, the amount of a distribution from an IRA that qualifies under Code Section 408 as long as that distribution is used to pay "qualified higher education expenses" as that term is defined in the Michigan Education Savings Program Act (MESP). [MCL § 206.30(1)(y)]

Q 14:42 Are distributions from a traditional IRA for medical expenses taxable at the state level?

Yes. Many states, however, allow deductions for contributions to medical savings accounts (MSAs) and tax-free withdrawals from such accounts.

Q 14:43   Do states conform to special short-term provisions of the federal income tax law for distributions from traditional or Roth IRAs?

In general, yes. But because of their respective legislative schedules, not all states adopt federal income tax provisions immediately. For example, North Carolina's Department of Revenue (DOR) announced that it would follow the changes made by the Deficit Reduction Act of 2005 [Pub. L. No. 109-171, 120 Stat. 4 (Feb 8, 2006)], Heroes Earned Retirement Opportunities Act [Pub. L. No. 109-227, 120 Stat. 385 (May 29, 2006)], Pension Protection Act of 2006 [Pub. L. No. 109-280, 120 Stat. 780 (Aug. 17, 2006)], and Tax Relief and Health Care Act of 2006 [Pub. L. No. 109-432, 120 Stat. 2922 (Dec. 20, 2006)] for 2006 filers. The North Carolina DOR also stated that if the state's General Assembly elected not to adopt some or all of the provisions during its 2007 legislative session, the DOR would assess any income tax plus applicable interest due as a result of a taxpayer using provisions not adopted by the General Assembly in determining the taxpayer's income tax liability. [*See* Important Notice About 2006 Federal Tax Legislation (Jan. 4, 2007) at *http://www.dor.state.nc.us.*]

Minnesota, on the other hand, reported on its Web site "What's new for individuals?" that it had not yet adopted the federal changes enacted after February 13, 2008, which included the Heroes Earned Assistance and Relief Tax Act of 2008; The Heartland, Habitat, Harvest, and Horticulture Act of 2008; The Emergency Economic Stabilization Act of 2008; and The Housing Assistance Tax Act of 2008. The notice indicated that some or all of these federal provisions may be adopted during the 2009 Minnesota Legislative Session. On April 20, 2009, this Web site was updated to say that the legislation enacted on April 3, 2009 adopted the federal tax provisions enacted from February 13 through December 31, 2008, with certain exceptions. [*See http://www.taxes.state.mn.us/taxes/individ/other_supporting_content/whats_new_08.shtml#P77_5160.*]

Prior to March 1, 2009, South Carolina reported on its Web site "SC Conformity Issues for tax year 2008" that "S.C. Code Ann. § 12-6-40(A)(1)(a) recognizes the IRC as amended through December 31, 2007, including the effective dates, except where otherwise provided." Thus, a taxpayer faced with a conformity issue has two legitimate choices: File a return making an adjustment for the conformity issue or wait to file a return, requesting an extension of time if necessary, until conformity occurs. Historically, conformity has occurred in all years as far back as 1986. [*See http://www.sctax.org/default.htm.*]

Q 14:44   Do states provide a tax credit comparable to the saver's credit under Code Section 25B?

In general, no.

Q 14:45   Do all states permit taxpayers age 70½ or older to make up to $100,000 tax-free qualified charitable gifts from their IRA?

No. Many states have conformed to the provisions provided under the Pension Protection Act of 2006 [Pub. L. No. 109-280, 120 Stat. 780], known as the PPA. In those states, taxpayers who are age 70½ or older can exclude from income up to $100,000 of distributions from their traditional and Roth IRAs for qualified charitable gifts in tax years 2006 and 2007. California, for example, did not adopt all of the provisions under the PPA, but it did adopt the tax-free distribution provision for IRA distributions for charitable gifts. [*See http://www. ftb.ca.gov/forms/updates/conformity.html*] New Jersey, on the other hand, announced that it would not adopt this provision (*see* New Jersey Income Tax Publication Bulletin GIT-2, *IRA Withdrawals* (rev. December 2007)).

On March 8, 2009, South Carolina reported on its Web site "SC Conformity Issues for tax year 2008" that "S.C. Code Ann. § 12-6-40(A)(1)(a) recognizes the IRC as amended through December 31, 2007, including the effective dates, except where otherwise provided." Many federal tax provisions were enacted or extended in 2008 and made applicable to the 2008 tax year. Listed on this Web site are just some of the conformity issues and how they should be dealt with prior to conformity through December 31, 2008, provided that the provision is not otherwise excepted. In particular, the tax-free treatment of the qualified IRA distributions to charity should be added back to South Carolina income. [*See http://www.sctax.org/default.htm.*]

Wisconsin's legislative session meets in the first half of 2009, which means that taxpayers in that state did not know until action was taken on the budget as to whether the provision of the Emergency Economic Stabilization Act of 2008 [Pub. L. No. 110-343] was adopted and whether it was retroactive to 2008. Wisconsin's Web site, as of March 6, 2009, reported that when filing their 2008 Wisconsin income tax returns, taxpayers who donated an IRA distribution to charity must complete 2008 Wisconsin Schedule I to include the IRA distribution in Wisconsin income. To calculate the Wisconsin itemized deduction credit, taxpayers use the amount of charitable deduction that would have been allowed on federal Schedule A without considering Public Law No. 110-343. In addition, because the Wisconsin Legislature is in session during the first half of 2009, the 2009 Budget Bill was not signed into law until June 29, 2009. As part of this law, the provision relating to IRAs was adopted retroactively for Wisconsin. Since Wisconsin adopts this provision retroactively, taxpayers who included in income an IRA distribution that was donated to charity may file an amended return (Form 1X) to remove such amount from income and to adjust the itemized deduction credit. In general, taxpayers must check individual state Web sites (see Q 14:77) to learn the specifics as provided by the Department of Revenue.

Q 14:46 Did all states conform to the GOZA and KETRA provisions for taxpayers taking early distributions from an IRA?

No. However, those states specifically addressed by GOZA and KETRA did adopt the provisions. It should be noted that although Alabama, Florida, Louisiana, and Mississippi are identified in these acts, Florida is not germane to this discussion because the state does not have an individual income tax. Mississippi provides that early distributions from retirement accounts withdrawn as a result of Hurricane Katrina are excluded from Mississippi gross income. [*See http://www.mstc.state.ms.us/katrina/ketra2005.html.*] Louisiana adopted the federal treatment since it begins its calculation with the taxpayer's federal adjusted gross income.

Q 14:47 Have all states conformed to the Pension Protection Act provision relating to reservists called to active duty who elect to take an early distribution?

Yes, with some limitations. Wisconsin adopted this provision (PPA § 827) retroactively in 2007. Minnesota adopted on March 7, 2008, the federal tax provisions enacted after May 18, 2006, retroactive to the federal effective date, with a few exceptions (see Q 14:43). (See, e.g., recent Minnesota tax law changes, updated April 11, 2008, on the state's Web site, *http://www. taxes. state.mn.us.*) California adopted the provision beginning on January 1, 2005 (but not retroactive to January 11, 2001, as provided by the PPA). [*See http://www.ftb.ca.gov/law/legis/06FedTax.pdf.*]

Q 14:48 Do all states permit taxpayers who participated in an employer's 401(k) plan that went bankrupt to make additional contributions to their IRAs?

It depends on the state and its conformity date. For example, California has a conformity date of January 1, 2005, and it has not incorporated amendments made to Code Section 219(b) by the Pension Protection Act of 2006 (PPA) that allow qualifying individuals who participated in a bankrupt employer's 401(k) plan to make additional IRA contributions of up to $3,000 for each year from 2007 through 2009.

Conversion Rollovers to Roth IRAs

Q 14:49 Do states follow the federal income tax rules for conversion rollovers to Roth IRAs?

In general, yes. There are, however, some notable exceptions. Massachusetts and New Jersey include in state gross income only the Massachusetts or New Jersey taxable portion of the conversion distribution, which in general differs from the federal taxable portion (see Qs 14:1, 14:6). Illinois and Pennsylvania do not include the taxable portion of a qualified conversion in state gross income. The position of both states is consistent with the fact that both exclude from state gross income distributions from qualified traditional IRAs. [Ill. Admin. R. 97-99; Pa. Ltr. Rul. PIT-98-048]

Q 14:50 Did states follow the four-year averaging rule for 1998 conversion rollovers?

In general, yes. New Jersey, however, provided a taxpayer some flexibility in this area. If a New Jersey resident elected four-year averaging for a 1998 conversion on his or her federal income tax return, the taxpayer had to elect four-year averaging on his or her New Jersey tax return. If, however, the taxpayer elected to include the entire taxable income portion from a 1998 conversion on his or her federal income tax return, the taxpayer could choose either the all-inclusion method or the four-year averaging method on his or her New Jersey income tax return.

Another state that allowed for flexibility is Illinois. An Illinois resident could exclude from state gross income any amount included in AGI for federal income tax purposes due to a conversion rollover.

Note. This issue will become relevant again in tax year 2010, when taxpayers can elect to convert IRAs into Roth IRAs and ratably recognize the income in tax years 2011 and 2012.

Q 14:51   Do states permit taxpayers to apply exclusion amounts for retirement income to the taxable portion of a conversion rollover?

It depends on the state. Iowa, Kentucky, and North Carolina, for example, permit taxpayers who are eligible to elect retirement exclusion to apply the exclusion to all or part of the taxable portion of a conversion rollover. Illinois and Pennsylvania (see Q 14:49) exclude the entire taxable portion of a conversion rollover.

Colorado, for example, provides in "FYI—Pension/Annuity Subtraction" that the rollover amount included in federal adjusted gross income as an IRA distribution qualifies for the pension subtraction in the year the amount is received in gross income if the taxpayer is age 55 or older as of December 31 of that year. More importantly, this provision applies whether the rollover is reported in full in the year of the conversion or reported over a four-year period. In light of this provision, one can only conclude that the two-year carryover provision for conversions in 2010 will receive similar treatment. (See Q 14:50.)

Q 14:52   If an individual moves to another state and during that year converts a traditional IRA to a Roth IRA, is that individual required to include the taxable portion of the conversion in his or her state gross income?

It depends on the state and the timing of the conversion. Oregon, for example, requires the entire taxable amount of a conversion to a Roth IRA to be included in state gross income if the taxpayer is a resident of Oregon at the time of the conversion. Kentucky requires that the entire taxable amount be included in state gross income in the case of an "inbound" taxpayer who has already moved into the state, or an "outbound" taxpayer who has not yet left the state, at the time of the conversion. [Ky. Tax Alert, Vol. 18, No. 1 (Jan. 1999)]

Iowa requires a taxpayer who resides in the state for part of the year to include only the portion of the taxable amount of the conversion attributable to the months of residence. For this purpose, a month is a period longer than half a month spent in Iowa. Thus, a taxpayer who spends 16 or more days of the month (15 days for February) in Iowa is credited with being a resident of Iowa for that month. [Iowa Reg. Rule 701 40.54(2)]

California, like Iowa, taxes the portion of the current year's taxable income based on the taxpayer's residency in the state. However, California's allocation is based on residency days, not residency months.

Q 14:53 If an individual moved out of a state during the four-year averaging period for a 1998 conversion rollover and took up residency in another state, could the former state of residence tax the conversion rollover?

It depended on the state. New York, for example, required the inclusion of any remaining deferred taxable portion from the conversion on the individual's part-year state tax return. Thus, the tax was collected before the individual left the state.

Iowa's allocation was based on residency months, and California's allocation was based on residency days (see Q 14:52).

Wisconsin, on the other hand, did not require the inclusion of any remaining deferred taxable portion from a 1988 conversion upon a person's moving out of the state. Rather, the state required the former resident to continue filing state income tax returns in the proper year. For taxpayers who moved into the state during the four-year averaging period, none of the deferred conversion amount was subject to Wisconsin income tax. [See Wis. Tax Bull. No. 112 (Jan. 1999).]

Colorado provides in "FYI—Pension/Annuity Subtraction" that the rollover amount included in federal adjusted gross income as an IRA distribution qualifies for the pension subtraction in the year the amount is received in gross income if the taxpayer is age 55 or older as of December 31 of that year. This provision applies whether the rollover is reported in full in the year of the conversion or reported over a four-year period. In light of this provision, it would appear that a taxpayer would report income over 2011 and 2012 for a 2010 conversion but claim the deduction on the entire conversion amount in 2011. If the taxpayer relocates in 2012, however, the question will be whether any part of the pension subtraction taken in 2011 must be added back to income as a result of the income being partly reported in 2011 and 2012.

SEP IRAs and SIMPLE IRAs

Q 14:54 Do all states permit a deduction for employer contributions to SEP IRA and SIMPLE IRA plans?

Yes, with a few notable exceptions. Contributions made by self-employed individuals to SEP IRA and SIMPLE IRA plans on behalf of themselves are not deductible for personal income tax purposes in Pennsylvania [Reg. 101.6], New

Jersey [Reg. 18:35-2.5], and Massachusetts. [Dep't of Revenue, Dir. 99-7, May 28, 1999] However, contributions made by employers on behalf of their employees are deductible.

Q 14:55   Do all states permit a deduction for employee contributions to SEP IRA and SIMPLE IRA plans?

No. Self-employed taxpayers and employees in some states are not eligible to deduct from their state gross income the amounts employers contributed to SEP IRA and SIMPLE IRA plans on their behalf (see Q 14:54).

In the case of Massachusetts, the deductibility rules are more complicated for tax years prior to 2002. The deductible amount for Massachusetts purposes is limited to the elective deferrals of an individual that is permitted under EGTRRA for federal tax purposes in the current year under the 1998 Code. Hence, any excess deferral amounts contributed by a Massachusetts taxpayer are included in Massachusetts gross income even though it is excluded from federal gross income. [TIR 02-7] For tax years beginning on or after January 1, 2002, Massachusetts follows the federal treatment for elective and nonelective employer contributions, employer matching contributions, and catch-up contributions for SEP IRA and SIMPLE IRA plans, but not for self-employed contributions. [TIR 02-18]

For tax years beginning on or after January 1, 2002, all amounts of retirement plan contributions and distributions that are excluded from gross income under the sections of the current Code enumerated are excluded from Massachusetts gross income. In the case of contributions to and distributions from qualified plans, 401(k) plans, 403(b) plans, 457 plans, SEPs, and SIMPLE IRAs, the amount excluded from Massachusetts gross income is the amount excluded from federal gross income by the current Code. Thus, for those plans, Massachusetts conforms to federal law in the treatment of elective deferrals, catch-up contributions, and qualified rollovers of plan proceeds. [TIR 02-18 (Nov. 6, 2002)]

Q 14:56   Do all states permit a deduction for contributions to a SIMPLE IRA plan on behalf of a domestic employee?

No. The majority of states conform to the federal income tax rules; thus, they would not permit a deduction for such contributions. New Jersey and Pennsylvania do not permit a deduction in any case (see Q 14:54).

Q 14:57   Do all states permit a deduction for catch-up contributions to SEP IRA and SIMPLE IRA plans by individuals age 50 or older?

No. Catch-up contribution amounts are not deductible from gross income for New Jersey, Pennsylvania, and Massachusetts. (See Q 14:54.)

Q 14:58   Do states tax earnings on contributions to SEP IRA and SIMPLE IRA plans in the year of accrual?

No. Earnings on contributions to SEP IRA and SIMPLE IRA plans are taxed only in the year of distribution. (See Q 14:5.)

Penalties

Q 14:59   Do some states concentrate on penalizing wealthy, self-employed individuals more than retired employees?

State laws do not make any discernible distinction. Regulators and enforcers, however, seem to be more vocal when the recipient of a distribution has control over the timing of personal transactions and defers the realization and receipt of an asset due for distribution so that it can be "earned" in the lower-tax or no-tax state to which he or she has moved. Transactions that occur shortly before a move, and even in the same tax year, are highly suspect.

Q 14:60   Do states tax and impose penalties on distributions that are taken before the IRA owner attains age 59½?

Yes. Treatment varies from state to state. Some states provide different exclusion amounts for retirement benefits, including IRA distributions, that are received before a stated age. The stated age may be 55, 59½, or 66, depending on the state.

Moreover, some states determine the attainment of age as of December 31 of the taxable year; others determine it as of January 1 of the following year. (See Qs 14:15, 14:17.)

Q 14:61   Why should the age of a recipient at the time of distribution be a factor?

Congress provided tax incentives to encourage individuals to participate in qualified retirement plans and IRAs and thereby have resources available at retirement. To discourage people from withdrawing funds from a retirement plan for nonretirement purposes, Congress placed an additional 10 percent penalty on certain early (pre-age-59½) distributions.

Q 14:62   Do states have their own version of the federal early distribution tax found in Code Section 72(t)?

Some states penalize monies withdrawn "early" from qualified plans and IRAs. (The definition of *early* varies among the states.) For example, Alabama, Colorado, Hawaii, Illinois, Indiana, Michigan, Minnesota, Mississippi, Montana, New Jersey, New York, Pennsylvania, and South Carolina require the taxpayer to include the distribution amount in gross income.

Other states impose an additional state tax that is a percentage of the federal premature distribution tax found in Code Section 72(t) (e.g., 10 percent in Arkansas, 15 percent in Maine, 29.6 percent in Nebraska, and 33 percent in Wisconsin). California simply levies a 2.5 percent tax on the taxable distribution amount.

Q 14:63 Can an IRA owner deduct from federal income tax penalties imposed by a state on distributions that are taken before he or she attains age 59½?

Yes. The Office of Chief Counsel issued IRS Memorandum 20072201F on June 1, 2007, which ruled in the case of California's penalty. The Office of Chief Counsel held, in part, that "since it is apparent that the 2 percent additional amount is properly considered a tax, it is deductible under IRC § 164."

Therefore, one must assume that if the California penalty is deductible, then the Arkansas, Maine, Nebraska, and Wisconsin penalties also must be deductible.

Q 14:64 Are there any exceptions to the state penalties on distributions before age 59½?

Yes, but the exceptions vary among the states. Pennsylvania, for example, does not penalize a retirement distribution that is made after the recipient has reached normal retirement age in his or her profession or age 59½. Other states follow the federal tax provisions, which contain several exceptions to the 10 percent premature distribution penalty (e.g., a distribution made to an employee who is disabled or as part of a series of substantially equal periodic payments).

Health Savings Accounts

Q 14:65 Do all states permit a deduction for contributions to a health savings account?

No. Four states do not recognize health savings accounts (HSAs): Alabama, California, New Jersey, and Wisconsin. Seven states (Alaska, Florida, Nevada, South Dakota, Texas, Washington, and Wyoming) do not have a state personal income tax, and two states (New Hampshire and Tennessee) have a state personal income tax on interest and dividends only. The remaining 37 states and the District of Columbia permit a deduction for contributions made to an HSA.

Q 14:66 Do states that permit a deduction for contributions to a health savings account follow the federal tax law?

Yes. Those states use the federal adjusted gross income (AGI) as a starting point for calculating state income.

Q 14:67 What is the state income tax effect on a rollover from a medical savings account to a health savings account?

Generally, a rollover from a medical savings account (MSA) to an HSA is tax free. If the state follows the federal regulation, the rollover will be tax free. There are four states that do not apply this rule (see Q 14:65).

In California, the rollover from an MSA to an HSA is treated as a nonqualified MSA distribution and is subjected to income tax plus a 10 percent penalty. For a Wisconsin resident, a rollover from an MSA to an HSA results in a taxable transaction.

Even though New Jersey does not recognize HSAs, the state allows an exclusion for amounts distributed from an MSA.

Q 14:68 Are distributions from health savings accounts taxed by the states?

In general, HSA distributions are not taxable. Amounts distributed from an HSA that are used to pay the qualified medical expenses of the account beneficiary are not subject to tax. The four states that do not recognize HSA accounts are the exceptions (see Q 14:65).

Q 14:69 Do states tax earnings on health savings accounts?

No. Earnings from HSAs are excluded from a state's gross income, except for those four states that do not permit a deduction for HSA contributions (see Q 14:65).

Withholding and Estimated Taxes

Q 14:70 Do states practice mandatory withholding?

Not all states practice mandatory withholding, which was introduced in federal tax law in 1992 for certain distributions from qualified retirement plans but not from IRAs.

Q 14:71 Do states have mandatory withholding on distributions from IRAs?

Generally, no. Most states follow the federal rule that allows a taxpayer to waive withholding on a distribution from an IRA. A few states, however, have mandatory withholding: Georgia (if the payments are periodic) [Ga. Code § 48-7-101(h)], Iowa (if federal income tax is withheld) [Iowa Reg. Rule 701, 46.1(422)], and Oregon (unless the taxpayer opts out of withholding) [Or. Admin. R. 150-316.189(6)].

Q 14:72   Does the IRA trustee withhold state income tax on IRA distributions?

The IRA trustee usually follows the directions of the IRA owner. The IRA owner may elect either to pay estimated tax on the distribution or to have the trustee withhold tax on the distribution. Of course, any underpayment penalty incurred is the responsibility of the IRA owner.

Q 14:73   Is the IRA owner responsible for making estimated tax payments on IRA distributions?

Yes, unless the IRA owner directs the IRA trustee to withhold taxes on the distributions (see Q 14:72). If the withholding amounts are adequate, there should be no need to make estimated tax payments. Any underpayment penalty incurred is the responsibility of the IRA owner.

Q 14:74   How are IRA trustees reacting to the myriad withholding rules that have evolved?

In light of the ban on source taxes (see Q 14:21), IRA trustees should be less frequently caught between the IRA owner's source state and his or her current state of residence. Withholding has not been a major issue for post-1995 distributions from IRAs, simplified employee pension plans, or savings incentive match plans for employees.

Future State Legislation

Q 14:75   Is further taxation of retirement benefits by states possible?

Additional income taxes are always possible. Studies on the tax dollars lost by federal and state governments through employee benefits programs are published continually. IRAs continue to be popular among wage earners as a result of the recent federal tax law changes. For tax years 2008 and 2009, the limit for spousal IRA contributions increased from $8,000 to $10,000 (total for both spouses, if younger than 50) and $10,000 to $12,000 (total for both spouses, if age 50 or older).

On the other hand, state treasuries may actually experience a revenue increase as a result of the tax law changes passed by Congress. The Roth IRA has been available to wage earners since 1998. Contributions to a Roth IRA are nondeductible, but withdrawals and distributions are nontaxable. If taxpayers divert to Roth IRAs part of their contributions to qualified plans (e.g., 401(k) plans), federal AGI and state gross income will increase. Hence, state income tax revenue will increase. Further, many taxpayers converted their traditional IRAs to Roth IRAs in 1998. The taxable portion of the conversion was included in federal AGI and in state gross income over four years. State income tax revenues were expected to increase and did increase during the period 1995 through 2001. In fact, individual income tax revenues increased at an average of 9 percent per year, peaking at 12.3 percent in FY 2000. This trend, however, reversed itself in 2002 (decrease of 11.4 percent) and 2003 (decrease of 2.4 percent). State tax revenues from individuals increased in fiscal years 2004 (9.5 percent), 2005 (12.4 percent), 2006 (11.8 percent), 2007 (7.2 percent), and 2008 (5.5 percent). [*See* U.S. Census Bureau, Quarterly Summary of State and Local Government Tax Revenues, Table 2, at *http://www.census.gov/govs/www/qtax.html*.]

Choosing a State for Retirement

Q 14:76   Do individuals choose a state for retirement on the basis of whether their retirement income from IRAs and other sources will be taxed more favorably, or possibly not at all?

State income taxation of retirement income is surely a factor in the choice of a state in which to retire, but should not be the only factor considered. Property tax rates, sales tax levels, and old-age exemptions are also important. Some people would argue that taxation of any kind should be one of the last things to consider in selecting a retirement community. Location of one's family, health facilities, and recreational areas are sometimes regarded as more important considerations than taxes.

Q 14:77   Where can one obtain income tax information about a state?

One quick way of obtaining information about a state's income tax and current and previous tax forms is to check the state's revenue department Web site:

State	Web Site
Alabama	www.ador.state.al.us
Alaska	N/A
Arizona	www.revenue.state.az.us
Arkansas	www.arkansas.gov/dfa
California	www.ftb.ca.gov
Colorado	www.colorado.gov/revenue
Connecticut	www.ct.gov/drs/site/
Delaware	revenue.delaware.gov
District of Columbia	www.cfo.dc.gov
Florida	N/A
Georgia	www.etax.dor.ga.gov
Hawaii	www.state.hi.us/tax
Idaho	www.tax.idaho.gov/index.html

State	Web Site
Illinois	www.revenue.state.il.us
Indiana	www.in.gov/dor
Iowa	www.state.ia.us/tax
Kansas	www.ksrevenue.org
Kentucky	www.revenue.ky.gov
Louisiana	www.rev.state.la.us
Maine	www.state.me.us/revenue
Maryland	www.comp.state.md.us
Massachusetts	www.mass.gov
Michigan	www.michigan.gov/treasury
Minnesota	www.taxes.state.mn.us
Mississippi	www.mstc.state.ms.us
Missouri	dor.mo.gov
Montana	www.mt.gov/revenue
Nebraska	www.revenue.state.ne.us
Nevada	N/A
New Hampshire	www.nh.gov/revenue
New Jersey	www.state.nj.us/treasury/taxation
New Mexico	www.tax.state.nm.us
New York	www.tax.state.ny.us
North Carolina	www.dor.state.nc.us
North Dakota	www.nd.gov/tax
Ohio	www.tax.ohio.gov
Oklahoma	www.oktax.state.ok.us
Oregon	www.oregon.gov/DOR
Pennsylvania	www.revenue.state.pa.us
Rhode Island	www.tax.ri.gov
South Carolina	www.sctax.org
South Dakota	N/A
Tennessee	tn.us/revenue
Texas	N/A
Utah	www.tax.utah.gov
Vermont	www.state.vt.us/tax
Virginia	www.tax.virginia.gov
Washington	www.dor.wa.gov
West Virginia	www.wvtax.gov
Wisconsin	www.dor.state.wi.us
Wyoming	N/A

Appendix A

IRS Publication 590—Individual Retirement Arrangements (IRAs) (2008)

Department of the Treasury
Internal Revenue Service

Publication 590
Cat. No. 15160X

Individual Retirement Arrangements (IRAs)

For use in preparing

2008 Returns

Get forms and other information faster and easier by:

Internet www.irs.gov

Jan 30, 2009

Contents

What's New for 2008

Traditional IRA contribution and deduction limit. The contribution limit to your traditional IRA for 2008 increased to the smaller of the following amounts:

- $5,000, or
- Your taxable compensation for the year.

If you were age 50 or older before 2009, the most that can be contributed to your traditional IRA for 2008 is the smaller of the following amounts:

- $6,000, or
- Your taxable compensation for the year.

For more information, see *How Much Can Be Contributed?* in chapter 1.

Roth IRA contribution limit. If contributions on your behalf are made only to Roth IRAs, your contribution limit for 2008 is generally the smaller of:

- $5,000, or
- Your taxable compensation for the year.

If you were age 50 or older before 2009 and contributions on your behalf were made only to Roth IRAs, your contribution limit for 2008 is generally the smaller of:

- $6,000, or
- Your taxable compensation for the year.

However, if your modified adjusted gross income (AGI) is above a certain amount, your contribution limit may be reduced. For more information, see *How Much Can Be Contributed?* under *Can You Contribute to a Roth IRA?* in chapter 2.

Modified AGI limit for traditional IRA contributions increased. For 2008, if you were covered by a retirement plan at work, your deduction for contributions to a traditional IRA is reduced (phased out) if your modified AGI is:

- More than $85,000 but less than $105,000 for a married couple filing a joint return or a qualifying widow(er),
- More than $53,000 but less than $63,000 for a single individual or head of household, or
- Less than $10,000 for a married individual filing a separate return.

If you either lived with your spouse or file a joint return, and your spouse was covered by a retirement plan at work, but you were not, your deduction is phased out if your modified AGI is more than $159,000 but less than $169,000. If your modified AGI is $169,000 or more, you cannot take a deduction for contributions to a traditional IRA. See *How Much Can You Deduct?* in chapter 1.

Modified AGI limit for Roth IRA contributions increased. For 2008, your Roth IRA contribution limit is reduced (phased out) in the following situations.

- Your filing status is married filing jointly or qualifying widow(er) and your modified AGI is at least $159,000. You cannot make a Roth IRA contribution if your modified AGI is $169,000 or more.
- Your filing status is single, head of household, or married filing separately and you did not live with your spouse at any time in 2008 and your modified AGI is at least $101,000. You cannot make a Roth IRA contribution if your modified AGI is $116,000 or more.
- Your filing status is married filing separately, you lived with your spouse at any time during the year, and your modified AGI is more than -0-. You cannot make a Roth IRA contribution if your modified AGI is $10,000 or more.

See *Can You Contribute to a Roth IRA?* in chapter 2.

Modified AGI limit for retirement savings contributions credit increased. For 2008, you may be able to claim the retirement savings contributions credit if your modified adjusted gross income (AGI) is not more than:

- $53,000 if your filing status is married filing jointly,
- $39,750 if your filing status is head of household, or
- $26,500 if your filing status is single, married filing separately, or qualifying widow(er).

See *Can you claim the credit?* in chapter 5.

Rollovers from qualified retirement plans. Beginning in 2008, you can roll over (convert) amounts from a qualified retirement plan to a Roth IRA. For more information, see *Rollover From Employer's Plan Into a Roth IRA* in chapter 2.

Economic stimulus payments. Economic stimulus payments directly deposited in your IRA or other tax-favored account in 2008 may be withdrawn tax-free and penalty-free. See *Tax-Free Withdrawals of Economic Stimulus Payments* under *When Can You Withdraw or Use Assets?* in chapter 1 for more information.

Military death gratuities and servicemembers' group life insurance (SGLI) payments. If you received a military death gratuity or SGLI payment with respect to a death from injury that occurred after October 6, 2001, you may roll over some or all of the amount received to your Roth IRA. For more information, see *Military Death Gratuities and Servicemembers' Group Life Insurance (SGLI) Payments* in chapter 2.

Tax relief for the Kansas disaster area. Special rules may apply if you received a distribution from your IRA and your main home was located in the Kansas disaster area on the date the disaster occurred, and you sustained an economic loss due to the storms and tornadoes.

Special rules may also apply if you received a distribution to purchase or construct a main home in the Kansas disaster area, but the home was not purchased or constructed because of the storms and tornadoes.

For more information, see *Tax Relief for the Kansas Disaster Area*, in chapter 5.

Tax relief for the Midwestern disaster areas. Special rules may apply if you received a distribution from your IRA and your main home was located in a Midwestern disaster area on the date the disaster occurred, and you sustained an economic loss due to the severe storms, tornadoes, or flooding.

Special rules may also apply if you received a distribution to purchase or construct a main home in a Midwestern disaster area, but the home was not purchased or constructed because of the severe storms, tornadoes, or flooding.

For more information, see *Tax Relief for the Midwestern Disaster Areas* in chapter 5.

Rollover of Exxon Valdez settlement income. If you received qualified settlement income in connection with the Exxon Valdez litigation, you may roll over the amount received, or part of the amount received, to your traditional or Roth IRA. For more information, see *Rollover of Exxon Valdez Settlement Income* in chapter 1.

Rollover of airline payments. If you are a qualified airline employee, you may contribute any portion of an airline payment paid to you by a commercial passenger airline carrier under a Federal bankruptcy court order to your Roth IRA. For more information, see *Rollover of Airline Payments* in chapter 2.

What's New for 2009

Modified AGI limit for traditional IRA contributions increased. For 2009, if you are covered by a retirement plan at work, your deduction for contributions to a traditional IRA is reduced (phased out) if your modified AGI is:

- More than $89,000 but less than $109,000 for a married couple filing a joint return or a qualifying widow(er),
- More than $55,000 but less than $65,000 for a single individual or head of household, or
- Less than $10,000 for a married individual filing a separate return.

If you either live with your spouse or file a joint return, and your spouse is covered by a retirement plan at work, but you are not, your deduction is phased out if your modified AGI is more than $166,000 but less than $176,000. If your modified AGI is $176,000 or more, you cannot take a deduction for contributions to a traditional IRA. See *How Much Can You Deduct?* in chapter 1.

Modified AGI limit for Roth IRA contributions increased. For 2009, your Roth IRA contribution limit is reduced (phased out) in the following situations.

- Your filing status is married filing jointly or qualifying widow(er) and your modified AGI is at least $166,000. You cannot make a Roth IRA contribution if your modified AGI is $176,000 or more.
- Your filing status is single, head of household, or married filing separately and you did not live with your spouse at any time in 2009 and your modified AGI is at least $105,000. You cannot make a Roth IRA contribution if your modified AGI is $120,000 or more.
- Your filing status is married filing separately, you lived with your spouse at any time during the year, and your modified AGI is more than -0-. You cannot make a Roth IRA contribution if your modified AGI is $10,000 or more.

See *Can You Contribute to a Roth IRA?* in chapter 2.

Modified AGI limit for retirement savings contributions credit increased. For 2009, you may be able to claim the retirement savings contributions credit if your modified AGI is not more than:

- $55,500 if your filing status is married filing jointly,
- $41,625 if your filing status is head of household, or
- $27,750 if your filing status is single, married filing separately, or qualifying widow(er).

See *Can you claim the credit?* in chapter 5.

Temporary waiver of required minimum distribution rules. No minimum distribution is required from your traditional or Roth IRA for 2009. See *Temporary waiver of required minimum distribution rules for 2009* in chapter 1.

Reminders

Simplified employee pension (SEP). SEP IRAs are not covered in this publication. They are covered in Publication 560, Retirement Plans for Small Business.

Deemed IRAs. A qualified employer plan (retirement plan) can maintain a separate account or annuity under the plan (a deemed IRA) to receive voluntary employee contributions. If the separate account or annuity otherwise meets the requirements of an IRA, it will be subject only to IRA rules. An employee's account can be treated as a traditional IRA or a Roth IRA.

For this purpose, a "qualified employer plan" includes:

- A qualified pension, profit-sharing, or stock bonus plan (section 401(a) plan),
- A qualified employee annuity plan (section 403(a) plan),

- A tax-sheltered annuity plan (section 403(b) plan), and
- A deferred compensation plan (section 457 plan) maintained by a state, a political subdivision of a state, or an agency or instrumentality of a state or political subdivision of a state.

Contributions to both traditional and Roth IRAs. For information on your combined contribution limit if you contribute to both traditional and Roth IRAs, see *Roth IRAs and traditional IRAs* under *How Much Can Be Contributed?* in chapter 2.

Statement of required minimum distribution (RMD). If an RMD is required from your IRA, the trustee, custodian, or issuer that held the IRA at the end of the preceding year must either report the amount of the RMD to you, or offer to calculate it for you. The report or offer must include the date by which the amount must be distributed. The report is due January 31 of the year in which the minimum distribution is required. It can be provided with the year-end fair market value statement that you normally get each year. No report is required for section 403(b) contracts (generally tax-sheltered annuities) or for IRAs of owners who have died.

Waiver of RMD for 2009. You are not required to take an RMD for 2009.

IRA interest. Although interest earned from your IRA is generally not taxed in the year earned, it is not tax-exempt interest. Do not report this interest on your return as tax-exempt interest.

Hurricane tax relief. Special rules apply to the use of retirement funds (including IRAs) by qualified individuals who suffered an economic loss as a result of Hurricane Katrina, Rita, or Wilma. While qualified hurricane distributions can no longer be made, special rules apply to the repayment of these distributions. See *Hurricane-Related Relief*, in chapter 4, for information on these special rules.

Photographs of missing children. The Internal Revenue Service is a proud partner with the National Center for Missing and Exploited Children. Photographs of missing children selected by the Center may appear in this publication on pages that would otherwise be blank. You can help bring these children home by looking at the photographs and calling 1-800-THE-LOST (1-800-843-5678) if you recognize a child.

Introduction

This publication discusses individual retirement arrangements (IRAs). An IRA is a personal savings plan that gives you tax advantages for setting aside money for retirement.

What are some tax advantages of an IRA? Two tax advantages of an IRA are that:

- Contributions you make to an IRA may be fully or partially deductible, depending on which type of IRA you have and on your circumstances, and
- Generally, amounts in your IRA (including earnings and gains) are not taxed until distributed. In some cases, amounts are not taxed at all if distributed according to the rules.

What's in this publication? This publication discusses traditional, Roth, and SIMPLE IRAs. It explains the rules for:

- Setting up an IRA,
- Contributing to an IRA,
- Transferring money or property to and from an IRA,
- Handling an inherited IRA,
- Receiving distributions (making withdrawals) from an IRA, and
- Taking a credit for contributions to an IRA.

It also explains the penalties and additional taxes that apply when the rules are not followed. To assist you in complying with the tax rules for IRAs, this publication contains worksheets, sample forms, and tables, which can be found throughout the publication and in the appendices at the back of the publication.

How to use this publication. The rules that you must follow depend on which type of IRA you have. Use Table I-1 to help you determine which parts of this publication to read. Also use Table I-1 if you were referred to this publication from instructions to a form.

Comments and suggestions. We welcome your comments about this publication and your suggestions for future editions.

You can write to us at the following address:

Internal Revenue Service
Individual Forms and Publications Branch
SE:W:CAR:MP:T:I
1111 Constitution Ave. NW, IR-6526
Washington, DC 20224

We respond to many letters by telephone. Therefore, it would be helpful if you would include your daytime phone number, including the area code, in your correspondence.

You can email us at *taxforms@irs.gov*. (The asterisk must be included in the address.) Please put "Publications Comment" on the subject line. Although we cannot respond individually to each email, we do appreciate your feedback and will consider your comments as we revise our tax products.

Publication 590 (2008)

Ordering forms and publications. Visit www.irs.gov/formspubs to download forms and publications, call 1-800-829-3676, or write to the address below and receive a response within 10 days after your request is received.

Internal Revenue Service
1201 N. Mitsubishi Motorway
Bloomington, IL 61705-6613

Tax questions. If you have a tax question, check the information available on www.irs.gov or call 1-800-829-1040. We cannot answer tax questions sent to either of the above addresses.

Table I-1. Using This Publication

IF you need information on ...	THEN see ...
traditional IRAs	chapter 1.
Roth IRAs	chapter 2, and parts of chapter 1.
SIMPLE IRAs	chapter 3.
disaster-related relief (including hurricane, Midwestern, and Kansas)	chapter 4.
the credit for qualified retirement savings contributions (the saver's credit)	chapter 5.
how to keep a record of your contributions to, and distributions from, your traditional IRA(s)	appendix A.
SEP IRAs and 401(k) plans	Publication 560.
Coverdell education savings accounts (formerly called education IRAs)	Publication 970.
IF for 2008, you • received *social security* benefits, • had taxable compensation, • contributed to a traditional IRA, and • you or your spouse was covered by an employer retirement plan, and you want to...	THEN see ...
first figure your modified adjusted gross income (AGI)	appendix B worksheet 1.
then figure how much of your traditional IRA contribution you can deduct	appendix B worksheet 2.
and finally figure how much of your social security is taxable	appendix B. worksheet 3.

Useful Items

You may want to see:

Publications

❏ **560** Retirement Plans for Small Business (SEP, SIMPLE, and Qualified Plans)

❏ **571** Tax-Sheltered Annuity Plans (403(b) Plans)

❏ **575** Pension and Annuity Income

❏ **939** General Rule for Pensions and Annuities

❏ **4492** Information for Taxpayers Affected by Hurricanes Katrina, Rita, and Wilma

❏ **4492-A** Information for Taxpayers Affected by the May 4, 2007, Kansas Storms and Tornadoes

❏ **4492-B** Information for Affected Taxpayers in the Midwestern Disaster Areas

Forms (and instructions)

❏ **W-4P** Withholding Certificate for Pension or Annuity Payments

❏ **1099-R** Distributions From Pensions, Annuities, Retirement or Profit-Sharing Plans, IRAs, Insurance Contracts, etc.

❏ **5304-SIMPLE** Savings Incentive Match Plan for Employees of Small Employers (SIMPLE)–Not for Use With a Designated Financial Institution

❏ **5305-S** SIMPLE Individual Retirement Trust Account

❏ **5305-SA** SIMPLE Individual Retirement Custodial Account

❏ **5305-SIMPLE** Savings Incentive Match Plan for Employees of Small Employers (SIMPLE)–for Use With a Designated Financial Institution

❏ **5329** Additional Taxes on Qualified Plans (Including IRAs) and Other Tax-Favored Accounts

❏ **5498** IRA Contribution Information

❏ **8606** Nondeductible IRAs

❏ **8815** Exclusion of Interest From Series EE and I U.S. Savings Bonds Issued After 1989

❏ **8839** Qualified Adoption Expenses

❏ **8880** Credit for Qualified Retirement Savings Contributions

❏ **8915** Qualified Hurricane Retirement Plan Distributions and Repayments

❏ **8930** Qualified Disaster Recovery Assistance Retirement Plan Distributions and Repayments

See chapter 6 for information about getting these publications and forms.

Table I-2. **How Are a Traditional IRA and a Roth IRA Different?**
This table shows the differences between traditional and Roth IRAs. Answers in the middle column apply to traditional IRAs. Answers in the right column apply to Roth IRAs.

Question	Answer	
	Traditional IRA?	**Roth IRA?**
Is there an age limit on when I can set up and contribute to a	Yes. You must not have reached age 70½ by the end of the year. See *Who Can Set Up a Traditional IRA?* in chapter 1.	No. You can be any age. See *Can You Contribute to a Roth IRA?* in chapter 2.
If I earned more than $5,000 in 2008 ($6,000 if I was 50 or older by the end of 2008), is there a limit on how much I can contribute to a	Yes. For 2008, you can contribute to a traditional IRA up to: • $5,000, or • $6,000 if you were age 50 or older by the end of 2008. There is no upper limit on how much you can earn and still contribute. See *How Much Can Be Contributed?* in chapter 1.	Yes. For 2008, you may be able to contribute to a Roth IRA up to: • $5,000, or • $6,000 if you were age 50 or older by the end of 2008, but the amount you can contribute may be less than that depending on your income, filing status, and if you contribute to another IRA. See *How Much Can Be Contributed?* and Table 2-1 in chapter 2.
Can I deduct contributions to a	Yes. You may be able to deduct your contributions to a traditional IRA depending on your income, filing status, whether you are covered by a retirement plan at work, and whether you receive social security benefits. See *How Much Can You Deduct?* in chapter 1.	No. You can never deduct contributions to a Roth IRA. See *What Is a Roth IRA?* in chapter 2.
Do I have to file a form just because I contribute to a	Not unless you make nondeductible contributions to your traditional IRA. In that case, you must file Form 8606. See *Nondeductible Contributions* in chapter 1.	No. You do not have to file a form if you contribute to a Roth IRA. See *Contributions not reported* in chapter 2.
Do I have to start taking distributions when I reach a certain age from a	Yes. You must begin receiving required minimum distributions by April 1 of the year following the year you reach age 70½. See *When Must You Withdraw Assets? (Required Minimum Distributions)* in chapter 1.	No. If you are the original owner of a Roth IRA, you do not have to take distributions regardless of your age. See *Are Distributions Taxable?* in chapter 2. However, if you are the beneficiary of a Roth IRA, you may have to take distributions. See *Distributions After Owner's Death* in chapter 2.
How are distributions taxed from a	Distributions from a traditional IRA are taxed as ordinary income, but if you made nondeductible contributions, not all of the distribution is taxable. See *Are Distributions Taxable?* in chapter 1.	Distributions from a Roth IRA are not taxed as long as you meet certain criteria. See *Are Distributions Taxable?* in chapter 2.
Do I have to file a form just because I receive distributions from a	Not unless you have ever made a nondeductible contribution to a traditional IRA. If you have, file Form 8606.	Yes. File Form 8606 if you received distributions from a Roth IRA (other than a rollover, qualified charitable distribution, one-time distribution to fund an HSA, recharacterization, certain qualified distributions, or a return of certain contributions).

Note. You may be able to contribute up to $8,000 if you participated in a 401(k) plan and the employer who maintained the plan went into bankruptcy in an earlier year. For more information, see *Catch-up contributions in certain employer bankruptcies* in chapter 1 for traditional IRAs and in chapter 2 for Roth IRAs.

1.

Traditional IRAs

What's New for 2008

Traditional IRA contribution and deduction limit. The contribution limit to your traditional IRA for 2008 increased to the smaller of the following amounts:

- $5,000, or
- Your taxable compensation for the year.

If you were age 50 or older before 2009, the most that can be contributed to your traditional IRA for 2008 is the smaller of the following amounts:

- $6,000, or
- Your taxable compensation for the year.

For more information, see *How Much Can Be Contributed?* in this chapter.

Modified AGI limit for traditional IRA contributions increased. For 2008, if you were covered by a retirement plan at work, your deduction for contributions to a traditional IRA is reduced (phased out) if your modified AGI is:

- More than $85,000 but less than $105,000 for a married couple filing a joint return or a qualifying widow(er),
- More than $53,000 but less than $63,000 for a single individual or head of household, or
- Less than $10,000 for a married individual filing a separate return.

For 2008, if you either lived with your spouse or file a joint return, and your spouse was covered by a retirement plan at work, but you were not, your deduction is phased out if your modified AGI is more than $159,000 but less than $169,000. If your modified AGI is $169,000 or more, you cannot take a deduction for contributions to a traditional IRA. See *How Much Can You Deduct?* in this chapter.

Economic stimulus payments. Economic stimulus payments directly deposited in your traditional IRA in 2008 may be withdrawn tax-free and penalty-free. See *Tax-Free Withdrawals of Economic Stimulus Payments* under *When Can You Withdraw or Use Assets?* in this chapter.

Rollover of Exxon Valdez settlement income. If you received qualified settlement income in connection with the Exxon Valdez litigation, you may roll over the amount received, or part of the amount received, to your traditional IRA. For more information, see *Rollover of Exxon Valdez Settlement Income* in this chapter.

What's New for 2009

Modified AGI limit for traditional IRA contributions increased. For 2009, if you are covered by a retirement plan at work, your deduction for contributions to a traditional IRA is reduced (phased out) if your modified AGI is:

- More than $89,000 but less than $109,000 for a married couple filing a joint return or a qualifying widow(er),
- More than $55,000 but less than $65,000 for a single individual or head of household, or
- Less than $10,000 for a married individual filing a separate return.

If you either live with your spouse or file a joint return, and your spouse is covered by a retirement plan at work, but you are not, your deduction is phased out if your modified AGI is more than $166,000 but less than $176,000. If your modified AGI is $176,000 or more, you cannot take a deduction for contributions to a traditional IRA. See *How Much Can You Deduct?* in this chapter.

Temporary waiver of required minimum distribution rules. No minimum distribution is required from your traditional IRA for 2009. See *Temporary waiver of required minimum distribution rules* in this chapter.

Introduction

This chapter discusses the original IRA. In this publication the original IRA (sometimes called an ordinary or regular IRA) is referred to as a "traditional IRA." The following are two advantages of a traditional IRA:

- You may be able to deduct some or all of your contributions to it, depending on your circumstances.
- Generally, amounts in your IRA, including earnings and gains, are not taxed until they are distributed.

What Is a Traditional IRA?

A traditional IRA is any IRA that is not a Roth IRA or a SIMPLE IRA.

Who Can Set Up a Traditional IRA?

You can set up and make contributions to a traditional IRA if:

- You (or, if you file a joint return, your spouse) received taxable compensation during the year, and
- You were not age 70½ by the end of the year.

Chapter 1 **Traditional IRAs**   Page 7

You can have a traditional IRA whether or not you are covered by any other retirement plan. However, you may not be able to deduct all of your contributions if you or your spouse is covered by an employer retirement plan. See *How Much Can You Deduct*, later.

Both spouses have compensation. If both you and your spouse have compensation and are under age 70½, each of you can set up an IRA. You cannot both participate in the same IRA. If you file a joint return, only one of you needs to have compensation.

What Is Compensation?

Generally, compensation is what you earn from working. For a summary of what compensation does and does not include, see Table 1-1. Compensation includes all of the items discussed next (even if you have more than one type).

Wages, salaries, etc. Wages, salaries, tips, professional fees, bonuses, and other amounts you receive for providing personal services are compensation. The IRS treats as compensation any amount properly shown in box 1 (Wages, tips, other compensation) of Form W-2, Wage and Tax Statement, provided that amount is reduced by any amount properly shown in box 11 (Nonqualified plans). Scholarship and fellowship payments are compensation for IRA purposes only if shown in box 1 of Form W-2.

Commissions. An amount you receive that is a percentage of profits or sales price is compensation.

Self-employment income. If you are self-employed (a sole proprietor or a partner), compensation is the net earnings from your trade or business (provided your personal services are a material income-producing factor) reduced by the total of:

- The deduction for contributions made on your behalf to retirement plans, and
- The deduction allowed for one-half of your self-employment taxes.

Compensation includes earnings from self-employment even if they are not subject to self-employment tax because of your religious beliefs.

Self-employment loss. If you have a net loss from self-employment, do not subtract the loss from your salaries or wages when figuring your total compensation.

Alimony and separate maintenance. For IRA purposes, compensation includes any taxable alimony and separate maintenance payments you receive under a decree of divorce or separate maintenance.

Nontaxable combat pay. If you were a member of the U.S. Armed Forces, compensation includes any nontaxable combat pay you received. This amount should be reported in box 12 of your 2008 Form W-2 with code Q.

If you received nontaxable combat pay in 2004 or 2005, and the treatment of the combat pay as compensation

means that you can contribute more for those years than you already have, you can make additional contributions to an IRA for 2004 or 2005 by May 28, 2009. The contributions will be treated as having been made on the last day of the year you designate. If you have already filed your return for a year for which you make a contribution, you must file Form 1040X, Amended U.S. Individual Income Tax Return, by the latest of:

- 3 years from the date you filed your original return for the year for which you made the contribution,
- 2 years from the date you paid the tax due for the year for which you made the contribution, or
- 1 year from the date on which you made the contribution.

Table 1-1. **Compensation for Purposes of an IRA**

Includes ...	Does not include ...
wages, salaries, etc.	earnings and profits from property.
commissions.	interest and dividend income.
self-employment income.	pension or annuity income.
alimony and separate maintenance.	deferred compensation.
nontaxable combat pay.	income from certain partnerships.
	any amounts you exclude from income.

What Is Not Compensation?

Compensation does not include any of the following items.

- Earnings and profits from property, such as rental income, interest income, and dividend income.
- Pension or annuity income.
- Deferred compensation received (compensation payments postponed from a past year).
- Income from a partnership for which you do not provide services that are a material income-producing factor.
- Any amounts (other than combat pay) you exclude from income, such as foreign earned income and housing costs.

When Can a Traditional IRA Be Set Up?

You can set up a traditional IRA at any time. However, the time for making contributions for any year is limited. See *When Can Contributions Be Made*, later.

How Can a Traditional IRA Be Set Up?

You can set up different kinds of IRAs with a variety of organizations. You can set up an IRA at a bank or other financial institution or with a mutual fund or life insurance company. You can also set up an IRA through your stockbroker. Any IRA must meet Internal Revenue Code requirements. The requirements for the various arrangements are discussed below.

Kinds of traditional IRAs. Your traditional IRA can be an individual retirement account or annuity. It can be part of either a simplified employee pension (SEP) or an employer or employee association trust account.

Individual Retirement Account

An individual retirement account is a trust or custodial account set up in the United States for the exclusive benefit of you or your beneficiaries. The account is created by a written document. The document must show that the account meets all of the following requirements.

- The trustee or custodian must be a bank, a federally insured credit union, a savings and loan association, or an entity approved by the IRS to act as trustee or custodian.

- The trustee or custodian generally cannot accept contributions of more than the deductible amount for the year. However, rollover contributions and employer contributions to a simplified employee pension (SEP) can be more than this amount.

- Contributions, except for rollover contributions, must be in cash. See *Rollovers*, later.

- You must have a nonforfeitable right to the amount at all times.

- Money in your account cannot be used to buy a life insurance policy.

- Assets in your account cannot be combined with other property, except in a common trust fund or common investment fund.

- You must start receiving distributions by April 1 of the year following the year in which you reach age 70½. See *When Must You Withdraw Assets? (Required Minimum Distributions)*, later.

Individual Retirement Annuity

You can set up an individual retirement annuity by purchasing an annuity contract or an endowment contract from a life insurance company.

An individual retirement annuity must be issued in your name as the owner, and either you or your beneficiaries who survive you are the only ones who can receive the benefits or payments.

An individual retirement annuity must meet all the following requirements.

- Your entire interest in the contract must be nonforfeitable.

- The contract must provide that you cannot transfer any portion of it to any person other than the issuer.

- There must be flexible premiums so that if your compensation changes, your payment can also change. This provision applies to contracts issued after November 6, 1978.

- The contract must provide that contributions cannot be more than the deductible amount for an IRA for the year, and that you must use any refunded premiums to pay for future premiums or to buy more benefits before the end of the calendar year after the year in which you receive the refund.

- Distributions must begin by April 1 of the year following the year in which you reach age 70½. See *When Must You Withdraw Assets? (Required Minimum Distributions)*, later.

Individual Retirement Bonds

The sale of individual retirement bonds issued by the federal government was suspended after April 30, 1982. The bonds have the following features.

- They stop earning interest when you reach age 70½. If you die, interest will stop 5 years after your death, or on the date you would have reached age 70½, whichever is earlier.

- You cannot transfer the bonds.

If you cash (redeem) the bonds before the year in which you reach age 59½, you may be subject to a 10% additional tax. See *Age 59½ Rule* under *Early Distributions*, later. You can roll over redemption proceeds into IRAs.

Simplified Employee Pension (SEP)

A simplified employee pension (SEP) is a written arrangement that allows your employer to make deductible contributions to a traditional IRA (a SEP IRA) set up for you to receive such contributions. Generally, distributions from SEP IRAs are subject to the withdrawal and tax rules that apply to traditional IRAs. See Publication 560 for more information about SEPs.

Employer and Employee Association Trust Accounts

Your employer or your labor union or other employee association can set up a trust to provide individual retirement accounts for employees or members. The requirements for individual retirement accounts apply to these traditional IRAs.

Required Disclosures

The trustee or issuer (sometimes called the sponsor) of your traditional IRA generally must give you a disclosure statement at least 7 days before you set up your IRA. However, the sponsor does not have to give you the statement until the date you set up (or purchase, if earlier) your IRA, provided you are given at least 7 days from that date to revoke the IRA.

The disclosure statement must explain certain items in plain language. For example, the statement should explain when and how you can revoke the IRA, and include the name, address, and telephone number of the person to receive the notice of cancellation. This explanation must appear at the beginning of the disclosure statement.

If you revoke your IRA within the revocation period, the sponsor must return to you the entire amount you paid. The sponsor must report on the appropriate IRS forms both your contribution to the IRA (unless it was made by a trustee-to-trustee transfer) and the amount returned to you. These requirements apply to all sponsors.

How Much Can Be Contributed?

There are limits and other rules that affect the amount that can be contributed to a traditional IRA. These limits and rules are explained below.

Community property laws. Except as discussed later under *Spousal IRA Limit*, each spouse figures his or her limit separately, using his or her own compensation. This is the rule even in states with community property laws.

Brokers' commissions. Brokers' commissions paid in connection with your traditional IRA are subject to the contribution limit. For information about whether you can deduct brokers' commissions, see *Brokers' commissions*, later under *How Much Can You Deduct*.

Trustees' fees. Trustees' administrative fees are not subject to the contribution limit. For information about whether you can deduct trustees' fees, see *Trustees' fees*, later under *How Much Can You Deduct*.

Qualified reservist repayments. If you were a member of a reserve component and you were ordered or called to active duty after September 11, 2001, you may be able to contribute (repay) to an IRA amounts equal to any qualified

reservist distributions (defined later under *Early Distributions*) you received. You can make these repayment contributions even if they would cause your total contributions to the IRA to be more than the general limit on contributions. To be eligible to make these repayment contributions, you must have received a qualified reservist distribution from an IRA or from a section 401(k) or 403(b) plan or a similar arrangement.

Limit. Your qualified reservist repayments cannot be more than your qualified reservist distributions, explained under *Early Distributions*, later.

When repayment contributions can be made. You cannot make these repayment contributions later than the date that is 2 years after your active duty period ends.

No deduction. You cannot deduct qualified reservist repayments.

Reserve component. The term "reserve component" means the:

- Army National Guard of the United States,
- Army Reserve,
- Naval Reserve,
- Marine Corps Reserve,
- Air National Guard of the United States,
- Air Force Reserve,
- Coast Guard Reserve, or
- Reserve Corps of the Public Health Service.

Figuring your IRA deduction. The repayment of qualified reservist distributions does not affect the amount you can deduct as an IRA contribution.

Reporting the repayment. If you repay a qualified reservist distribution, include the amount of the repayment with nondeductible contributions on line 1 of Form 8606, Nondeductible IRAs.

Example. In 2008, your IRA contribution limit is $5,000. However, because of your filing status and AGI, the limit on the amount you can deduct is $3,500. You can make a nondeductible contribution of $1,500 ($5,000 - $3,500). In an earlier year you received a $3,000 qualified reservist distribution, which you would like to repay this year.

For 2008, you can contribute a total of $8,000 to your IRA. This is made up of the maximum deductible contribution of $3,500; a nondeductible contribution of $1,500; and a $3,000 qualified reservist repayment. You contribute the maximum allowable for the year. Since you are making a nondeductible contribution ($1,500) and a qualified reservist repayment ($3,000), you must file Form 8606 with your return and include $4,500 ($1,500 + $3,000) on line 1 of Form 8606. The qualified reservist repayment is not deductible.

 Contributions on your behalf to a traditional IRA reduce your limit for contributions to a Roth IRA. See chapter 2 for information about Roth IRAs.

General Limit

For 2008, the most that can be contributed to your traditional IRA generally is the smaller of the following amounts:

- $5,000 ($6,000 if you are age 50 or older), or
- Your taxable compensation (defined earlier) for the year.

This general limit may be increased to $8,000 if you participated in a 401(k) plan maintained by an employer who went into bankruptcy in an earlier year. For more information, see *Catch-up contributions in certain employer bankruptcies* later.

Note. This limit is reduced by any contributions to a section 501(c)(18) plan (generally, a pension plan created before June 25, 1959, that is funded entirely by employee contributions).

This is the most that can be contributed regardless of whether the contributions are to one or more traditional IRAs or whether all or part of the contributions are nondeductible. (See *Nondeductible Contributions*, later.) Qualified reservist repayments do not affect this limit.

Examples. George, who is 34 years old and single, earns $24,000 in 2008. His IRA contributions for 2008 are limited to $5,000.

Danny, an unmarried college student working part time, earns $3,500 in 2008. His IRA contributions for 2008 are limited to $3,500, the amount of his compensation.

More than one IRA. If you have more than one IRA, the limit applies to the total contributions made on your behalf to all your traditional IRAs for the year.

Annuity or endowment contracts. If you invest in an annuity or endowment contract under an individual retirement annuity, no more than $5,000 ($6,000 if you are age 50 or older) can be contributed toward its cost for the tax year, including the cost of life insurance coverage. If more than this amount is contributed, the annuity or endowment contract is disqualified.

Catch-up contributions in certain employer bankruptcies. If you participated in a 401(k) plan and the employer who maintained the plan went into bankruptcy, you may be able to contribute an additional $3,000 to your IRA. For this to apply, the following conditions must be met.

- You must have been a participant in a 401(k) plan under which the employer matched at least 50% of your contributions to the plan with stock of the company.
- You must have been a participant in the 401(k) plan 6 months before the employer went into bankruptcy.
- The employer (or a controlling corporation) must have been a debtor in a bankruptcy case in an earlier year.
- The employer (or any other person) must have been subject to indictment or conviction based on business transactions related to the bankruptcy.

 If you choose to make these catch-up contributions, the higher contribution and deduction limits for individuals who are age 50 or older do not apply. The most you can contribute to your IRA is the smaller of $8,000 or your taxable compensation for the year.

Worksheet 1-2 and Worksheet 2 in Appendix B. If you qualify to make the catch-up contributions described above due to an employer bankruptcy, you must use the additional instructions below when completing Worksheet 1-2 or Worksheet 2 in Appendix B, shown later.

On line 4 of the worksheet, use the percentage below that applies to you.

- Married filing jointly or qualifying widow(er) and you are covered by an employer plan, multiply line 3 by 40% (.40).
- All others, multiply line 3 by 80% (.80).

On line 6 of the worksheet, enter contributions made, or to be made for 2008, but do not enter more than $8,000.

Spousal IRA Limit

For 2008, if you file a joint return and your taxable compensation is less than that of your spouse, the most that can be contributed for the year to your IRA is the smaller of the following two amounts:

1. $5,000 ($6,000 if you are age 50 or older), or
2. The total compensation includible in the gross income of both you and your spouse for the year, reduced by the following two amounts.

   a. Your spouse's IRA contribution for the year to a traditional IRA.

   b. Any contributions for the year to a Roth IRA on behalf of your spouse.

This means that the total combined contributions that can be made for the year to your IRA and your spouse's IRA can be as much as $10,000 ($11,000 if only one of you is age 50 or older or $12,000 if both of you are age 50 or older).

This limit may be increased to $8,000 for each spouse who participated in a 401(k) plan maintained by an employer who went into bankruptcy in an earlier year. For more information, see *Catch-up contributions in certain employer bankruptcies* earlier.

Note. This traditional IRA limit is reduced by any contributions to a section 501(c)(18) plan (generally, a pension plan created before June 25, 1959, that is funded entirely by employee contributions).

Example. Kristin, a full-time student with no taxable compensation, marries Carl during the year. Neither was age 50 by the end of 2008. For the year, Carl has taxable compensation of $30,000. He plans to contribute (and deduct) $5,000 to a traditional IRA. If he and Kristin file a joint return, each can contribute $5,000 to a traditional IRA. This is because Kristin, who has no compensation, can add Carl's compensation, reduced by the amount of his IRA contribution, ($30,000 − $5,000 = $25,000) to her own compensation (-0-) to figure her maximum contribution to a traditional IRA. In her case, $5,000 is her contribution limit, because $5,000 is less than $25,000 (her compensation for purposes of figuring her contribution limit).

Filing Status

Generally, except as discussed earlier under *Spousal IRA Limit*, your filing status has no effect on the amount of allowable contributions to your traditional IRA. However, if during the year either you or your spouse was covered by a retirement plan at work, your deduction may be reduced or eliminated, depending on your filing status and income. See *How Much Can You Deduct*, later.

Example. Tom and Darcy are married and both are 53. They both work and each has a traditional IRA. Tom earned $3,800 and Darcy earned $48,000 in 2008. Because of the spousal IRA limit rule, even though Tom earned less than $6,000, they can contribute up to $6,000 to his IRA for 2008 if they file a joint return. They can contribute up to $6,000 to Darcy's IRA. If they file separate returns, the amount that can be contributed to Tom's IRA is limited to $3,800.

Less Than Maximum Contributions

If contributions to your traditional IRA for a year were less than the limit, you cannot contribute more after the due date of your return for that year to make up the difference.

Example. Rafael, who is 40, earns $30,000 in 2008. Although he can contribute up to $5,000 for 2008, he contributes only $3,000. After April 15, 2009, Rafael cannot make up the difference between his actual contributions for 2008 ($3,000) and his 2008 limit ($5,000). He cannot contribute $2,000 more than the limit for any later year.

More Than Maximum Contributions

If contributions to your IRA for a year were more than the limit, you can apply the excess contribution in one year to a later year if the contributions for that later year are less than the maximum allowed for that year. However, a penalty or additional tax may apply. See *Excess Contributions*, later under *What Acts Result in Penalties or Additional Taxes*.

When Can Contributions Be Made?

As soon as you set up your traditional IRA, contributions can be made to it through your chosen sponsor (trustee or other administrator). Contributions must be in the form of

money (cash, check, or money order). Property cannot be contributed. However, you may be able to transfer or roll over certain property from one retirement plan to another. See the discussion of rollovers and other transfers later in this chapter under *Can You Move Retirement Plan Assets*.

 You can make a contribution to your IRA by having your income tax refund (or a portion of your refund), if any, paid directly to your traditional IRA, Roth IRA, or SEP IRA. For details, see the instructions for your income tax return or Form 8888, Direct Deposit of Refund to More Than One Account.

Contributions can be made to your traditional IRA for each year that you receive compensation and have not reached age 70½. For any year in which you do not work, contributions cannot be made to your IRA unless you receive alimony, nontaxable combat pay or file a joint return with a spouse who has compensation. See *Who Can Set Up a Traditional IRA*, earlier. Even if contributions cannot be made for the current year, the amounts contributed for years in which you did qualify can remain in your IRA. Contributions can resume for any years that you qualify.

Contributions must be made by due date. Contributions can be made to your traditional IRA for a year at any time during the year or by the due date for filing your return for that year, not including extensions. For most people, this means that contributions for 2008 must be made by April 15, 2009, and contributions for 2009 must be made by April 15, 2010.

Nontaxable combat pay. If you received nontaxable combat pay in 2004 or 2005, and the treatment of the combat pay as compensation means that you can contribute more for those years than you already have, you can make additional contributions to an IRA for 2004 or 2005 by May 28, 2009. The contributions will be treated as having been made on the last day of the year you designate. If you have already filed your return for a year for which you make a contribution, you must file Form 1040X, Amended U.S. Individual Income Tax Return, by the latest of:

- 3 years from the date you filed your original return for the year for which you made the contribution,

- 2 years from the date you paid the tax due for the year for which you made the contribution, or

- 1 year from the date on which you made the contribution.

Age 70½ rule. Contributions cannot be made to your traditional IRA for the year in which you reach age 70½ or for any later year.

You attain age 70½ on the date that is six calendar months after the 70th anniversary of your birth. If you were born on or before June 30, 1938, you cannot contribute for 2008 or any later year.

Designating year for which contribution is made. If an amount is contributed to your traditional IRA between January 1 and April 15, you should tell the sponsor which year (the current year or the previous year) the contribution is for. If you do not tell the sponsor which year it is for, the sponsor can assume, and report to the IRS, that the contribution is for the current year (the year the sponsor received it).

Filing before a contribution is made. You can file your return claiming a traditional IRA contribution before the contribution is actually made. Generally, the contribution must be made by the due date of your return, not including extensions.

Contributions not required. You do not have to contribute to your traditional IRA for every tax year, even if you can.

How Much Can You Deduct?

Generally, you can deduct the lesser of:

- The contributions to your traditional IRA for the year, or
- The general limit (or the spousal IRA limit, if applicable) explained earlier under *How Much Can Be Contributed*.

However, if you or your spouse was covered by an employer retirement plan, you may not be able to deduct this amount. See *Limit if Covered by Employer Plan*, later.

 You may be able to claim a credit for contributions to your traditional IRA. For more information, see chapter 5.

Catch-up contributions. If the requirements listed earlier at *Catch-up contributions in certain employer bankruptcies* under *How Much Can Be Contributed?* are met and you choose to make those catch-up contributions, you cannot use the higher contribution and deduction limits for individuals who are age 50 or older.

Trustees' fees. Trustees' administrative fees that are billed separately and paid in connection with your traditional IRA are not deductible as IRA contributions. However, they may be deductible as a miscellaneous itemized deduction on Schedule A (Form 1040). For information about miscellaneous itemized deductions, see Publication 529, Miscellaneous Deductions.

Brokers' commissions. These commissions are part of your IRA contribution and, as such, are deductible subject to the limits.

Full deduction. If neither you nor your spouse was covered for any part of the year by an employer retirement plan, you can take a deduction for total contributions to one or more of your traditional IRAs of up to the lesser of:

- $5,000 ($6,000 if you are age 50 or older), or
- 100% of your compensation.

This limit may be increased to $8,000 if you participated in a 401(k) plan maintained by an employer who went into

bankruptcy in an earlier year. For more information, see *Catch-up contributions in certain employer bankruptcies* earlier.

This limit is reduced by any contributions made to a 501(c)(18) plan on your behalf.

Spousal IRA. In the case of a married couple with unequal compensation who file a joint return, the deduction for contributions to the traditional IRA of the spouse with less compensation is limited to the lesser of:

1. $5,000 ($6,000 if the spouse with the lower compensation is age 50 or older), or

2. The total compensation includible in the gross income of both spouses for the year reduced by the following three amounts.

   a. The IRA deduction for the year of the spouse with the greater compensation.

   b. Any designated nondeductible contribution for the year made on behalf of the spouse with the greater compensation.

   c. Any contributions for the year to a Roth IRA on behalf of the spouse with the greater compensation.

This limit may be increased to $8,000 if the spouse with the lower compensation participated in a 401(k) plan maintained by an employer who went into bankruptcy in an earlier year. For more information, see *Catch-up contributions in certain employer bankruptcies* earlier.

This limit is reduced by any contributions to a section 501(c)(18) plan on behalf of the spouse with the lesser compensation.

Note. If you were divorced or legally separated (and did not remarry) before the end of the year, you cannot deduct any contributions to your spouse's IRA. After a divorce or legal separation, you can deduct only the contributions to your own IRA. Your deductions are subject to the rules for single individuals.

Covered by an employer retirement plan. If you or your spouse was covered by an employer retirement plan at any time during the year for which contributions were made, your deduction may be further limited. This is discussed later under *Limit if Covered by Employer Plan*. Limits on the amount you can deduct do not affect the amount that can be contributed.

Are You Covered by an Employer Plan?

The Form W-2 you receive from your employer has a box used to indicate whether you were covered for the year. The "Retirement Plan" box should be checked if you were covered.

Reservists and volunteer firefighters should also see *Situations in Which You Are Not Covered*, later.

If you are not certain whether you were covered by your employer's retirement plan, you should ask your employer.

Federal judges. For purposes of the IRA deduction, federal judges are covered by an employer plan.

For Which Year(s) Are You Covered?

Special rules apply to determine the tax years for which you are covered by an employer plan. These rules differ depending on whether the plan is a defined contribution plan or a defined benefit plan.

Tax year. Your tax year is the annual accounting period you use to keep records and report income and expenses on your income tax return. For almost all people, the tax year is the calendar year.

Defined contribution plan. Generally, you are covered by a defined contribution plan for a tax year if amounts are contributed or allocated to your account for the plan year that ends with or within that tax year. However, also see *Situations in Which You Are Not Covered*, later.

A defined contribution plan is a plan that provides for a separate account for each person covered by the plan. In a defined contribution plan, the amount to be contributed to each participant's account is spelled out in the plan. The level of benefits actually provided to a participant depends on the total amount contributed to that participant's account and any earnings and losses on those contributions. Types of defined contribution plans include profit-sharing plans, stock bonus plans, and money purchase pension plans.

Example. Company A has a money purchase pension plan. Its plan year is from July 1 to June 30. The plan provides that contributions must be allocated as of June 30. Bob, an employee, leaves Company A on December 31, 2007. The contribution for the plan year ending on June 30, 2008, is made February 15, 2009. Because an amount is contributed to Bob's account for the plan year, Bob is covered by the plan for his 2008 tax year.

A special rule applies to certain plans in which it is not possible to determine if an amount will be contributed to your account for a given plan year. If, for a plan year, no amounts have been allocated to your account that are attributable to employer contributions, employee contributions, or forfeitures, by the last day of the plan year, and contributions are discretionary for the plan year, you are not covered for the tax year in which the plan year ends. If, after the plan year ends, the employer makes a contribution for that plan year, you are covered for the tax year in which the contribution is made.

Example. Mickey was covered by a profit-sharing plan and left the company on December 31, 2007. The plan year runs from July 1 to June 30. Under the terms of the plan, employer contributions do not have to be made, but if they are made, they are contributed to the plan before the due date for filing the company's tax return. Such contributions are allocated as of the last day of the plan year, and allocations are made to the accounts of individuals who have any service during the plan year. As of June 30, 2008, no contributions were made that were allocated to the June 30, 2008 plan year, and no forfeitures had been allocated within the plan year. In addition, as of that date, the company was not obligated to make a contribution for such plan year and it was impossible to determine whether or not a contribution would be made for the plan year. On December 31, 2008, the company decided to contribute to the plan for the plan year ending June 30, 2008. That contribution was made on February 15, 2009. Mickey is an active participant in the plan for his 2009 tax year but not for his 2008 tax year.

No vested interest. If an amount is allocated to your account for a plan year, you are covered by that plan even if you have no vested interest in (legal right to) the account.

Defined benefit plan. If you are eligible to participate in your employer's defined benefit plan for the plan year that ends within your tax year, you are covered by the plan. This rule applies even if you:

- Declined to participate in the plan,
- Did not make a required contribution, or
- Did not perform the minimum service required to accrue a benefit for the year.

A defined benefit plan is any plan that is not a defined contribution plan. In a defined benefit plan, the level of benefits to be provided to each participant is spelled out in the plan. The plan administrator figures the amount needed to provide those benefits and those amounts are contributed to the plan. Defined benefit plans include pension plans and annuity plans.

Example. Nick, an employee of Company B, is eligible to participate in Company B's defined benefit plan, which has a July 1 to June 30 plan year. Nick leaves Company B on December 31, 2007. Because Nick is eligible to participate in the plan for its year ending June 30, 2008, he is covered by the plan for his 2008 tax year.

No vested interest. If you accrue a benefit for a plan year, you are covered by that plan even if you have no vested interest in (legal right to) the accrual.

Situations in Which You Are Not Covered

Unless you are covered by another employer plan, you are not covered by an employer plan if you are in one of the situations described below.

Social security or railroad retirement. Coverage under social security or railroad retirement is not coverage under an employer retirement plan.

Benefits from previous employer's plan. If you receive retirement benefits from a previous employer's plan, you are not covered by that plan.

Reservists. If the only reason you participate in a plan is because you are a member of a reserve unit of the armed forces, you may not be covered by the plan. You are not covered by the plan if both of the following conditions are met.

1. The plan you participate in is established for its employees by:

   a. The United States,

   b. A state or political subdivision of a state, or

   c. An instrumentality of either (a) or (b) above.

2. You did not serve more than 90 days on active duty during the year (not counting duty for training).

Volunteer firefighters. If the only reason you participate in a plan is because you are a volunteer firefighter, you may not be covered by the plan. You are not covered by the plan if both of the following conditions are met.

1. The plan you participate in is established for its employees by:

   a. The United States,

   b. A state or political subdivision of a state, or

   c. An instrumentality of either (a) or (b) above.

2. Your accrued retirement benefits at the beginning of the year will not provide more than $1,800 per year at retirement.

Limit if Covered by Employer Plan

As discussed earlier, the deduction you can take for contributions made to your traditional IRA depends on whether you or your spouse was covered for any part of the year by an employer retirement plan. Your deduction is also affected by how much income you had and by your filing status. Your deduction may also be affected by social security benefits you received.

Reduced or no deduction. If either you or your spouse was covered by an employer retirement plan, you may be entitled to only a partial (reduced) deduction or no deduction at all, depending on your income and your filing status.

Your deduction begins to decrease (phase out) when your income rises above a certain amount and is eliminated altogether when it reaches a higher amount. These amounts vary depending on your filing status.

To determine if your deduction is subject to the phaseout, you must determine your modified adjusted gross income (AGI) and your filing status, as explained later under *Deduction Phaseout*. Once you have determined your modified AGI and your filing status, you can use Table 1-2 or Table 1-3 to determine if the phaseout applies.

Social Security Recipients

Instead of using Table 1-2 or Table 1-3 and Worksheet 1-2, Figuring Your Reduced IRA Deduction for 2008, later, complete the worksheets in Appendix B of this publication if, for the year, all of the following apply.

- You received social security benefits.

- You received taxable compensation.

- Contributions were made to your traditional IRA.

- You or your spouse was covered by an employer retirement plan.

Use the worksheets in Appendix B to figure your IRA deduction, your nondeductible contribution, and the taxable portion, if any, of your social security benefits. Appendix B includes an example with filled-in worksheets to assist you.

Table 1-2. **Effect of Modified AGI[1] on Deduction if You Are Covered by a Retirement Plan at Work**

If you are covered by a retirement plan at work, use this table to determine if your modified AGI affects the amount of your deduction.

IF your filing status is ...	AND your modified adjusted gross income (modified AGI) is ...	THEN you can take ...
single or head of household	$53,000 or less	a full deduction.
	more than $53,000 but less than $63,000	a partial deduction.
	$63,000 or more	no deduction.
married filing jointly or qualifying widow(er)	$85,000 or less	a full deduction.
	more than $85,000 but less than $105,000	a partial deduction.
	$105,000 or more	no deduction.
married filing separately[2]	less than $10,000	a partial deduction.
	$10,000 or more	no deduction.

[1] Modified AGI (adjusted gross income). See *Modified adjusted gross income (AGI),* later.
[2] If you did not live with your spouse at any time during the year, your filing status is considered Single for this purpose (therefore, your IRA deduction is determined under the "Single" filing status).

Table 1-3. **Effect of Modified AGI[1] on Deduction if You Are NOT Covered by a Retirement Plan at Work**

If you are not covered by a retirement plan at work, use this table to determine if your modified AGI affects the amount of your deduction.

IF your filing status is ...	AND your modified adjusted gross income (modified AGI) is ...	THEN you can take ...
single, head of household, or qualifying widow(er)	any amount	a full deduction.
married filing jointly or separately with a spouse who *is not* covered by a plan at work	any amount	a full deduction.
married filing jointly with a spouse who *is* covered by a plan at work	$159,000 or less	a full deduction.
	more than $159,000 but less than $169,000	a partial deduction.
	$169,000 or more	no deduction.
married filing separately with a spouse who *is* covered by a plan at work[2]	less than $10,000	a partial deduction.
	$10,000 or more	no deduction.

[1] Modified AGI (adjusted gross income). See *Modified adjusted gross income (AGI),* later.
[2] You are entitled to the full deduction if you did not live with your spouse at any time during the year.

 For 2009, if you are not covered by a retirement plan at work and you are married filing jointly with a spouse who is covered by a plan at work, your deduction is phased out if your modified AGI is more than $166,000 but less than $176,000. If your AGI is $176,000 or more, you cannot take a deduction for a contribution to a traditional IRA.

Deduction Phaseout

The amount of any reduction in the limit on your IRA deduction (phaseout) depends on whether you or your spouse was covered by an employer retirement plan.

Covered by a retirement plan. If you are covered by an employer retirement plan and you did not receive any social security retirement benefits, your IRA deduction

may be reduced or eliminated depending on your filing status and modified AGI, as shown in Table 1-2.

 For 2009, if you are covered by a retirement plan at work, your IRA deduction will not be reduced (phased out) unless your modified AGI is:

- *More than $55,000 but less than $65,000 for a single individual (or head of household),*
- *More than $89,000 but less than $109,000 for a married couple filing a joint return (or a qualifying widow(er)), or*
- *Less than $10,000 for a married individual filing a separate return.*

If your spouse is covered. If you are not covered by an employer retirement plan, but your spouse is, and you did not receive any social security benefits, your IRA deduction may be reduced or eliminated entirely depending on your filing status and modified AGI as shown in Table 1-3.

Filing status. Your filing status depends primarily on your marital status. For this purpose, you need to know if your filing status is single or head of household, married filing jointly or qualifying widow(er), or married filing separately. If you need more information on filing status, see Publication 501, Exemptions, Standard Deduction, and Filing Information.

Lived apart from spouse. If you did not live with your spouse at any time during the year and you file a separate return, your filing status, for this purpose, is single.

Modified adjusted gross income (AGI). You can use Worksheet 1-1 to figure your modified AGI. If you made contributions to your IRA for 2008 and received a distribution from your IRA in 2008, see *Both contributions for 2008 and distributions in 2008,* later.

 Do not assume that your modified AGI is the same as your compensation. Your modified AGI may include income in addition to your compensation such as interest, dividends, and income from IRA distributions.

Form 1040. If you file Form 1040, refigure the amount on the page 1 "adjusted gross income" line without taking into account any of the following amounts.

- IRA deduction.
- Student loan interest deduction.
- Tuition and fees deduction.
- Domestic production activities deduction.
- Foreign earned income exclusion.
- Foreign housing exclusion or deduction.
- Exclusion of qualified savings bond interest shown on Form 8815.
- Exclusion of employer-provided adoption benefits shown on Form 8839.

Worksheet 1-1. **Figuring Your Modified AGI**
Use this worksheet to figure your modified AGI for traditional IRA purposes.

1.	Enter your adjusted gross income (AGI) from Form 1040, line 38; Form 1040A, line 22; or Form 1040NR, line 36, figured without taking into account the amount from Form 1040, line 32; Form 1040A, line 17; or Form 1040NR, line 31	1. _____
2.	Enter any student loan interest deduction from Form 1040, line 33; Form 1040A, line 18; or Form 1040NR, line 32	2. _____
3.	Enter any tuition and fees deduction from Form 1040, line 34 or Form 1040A, line 19	3. _____
4.	Enter any domestic production activities deduction from Form 1040, line 35, or Form 1040NR, line 33	4. _____
5.	Enter any foreign earned income exclusion and/or housing exclusion from Form 2555, line 45, or Form 2555-EZ, line 18	5. _____
6.	Enter any foreign housing deduction from Form 2555, line 50	6. _____
7.	Enter any excludable savings bond interest from Form 8815, line 14	7. _____
8.	Enter any excluded employer-provided adoption benefits from Form 8839, line 30 . . .	8. _____
9.	Add lines 1 through 8. This is your **Modified AGI** for traditional IRA purposes	9. _____

This is your modified AGI.

Form 1040A. If you file Form 1040A, refigure the amount on the page 1 "adjusted gross income" line without taking into account any of the following amounts.

- IRA deduction.
- Student loan interest deduction.
- Tuition and fees deduction.
- Exclusion of qualified savings bond interest shown on Form 8815.

This is your modified AGI.

Form 1040NR. If you file Form 1040NR, refigure the amount on the page 1 "adjusted gross income" line without taking into account any of the following amounts.

- IRA deduction.
- Student loan interest deduction.
- Domestic production activities deduction.
- Exclusion of qualified savings bond interest shown on Form 8815.
- Exclusion of employer-provided adoption benefits shown on Form 8839.

This is your modified AGI.

Income from IRA distributions. If you received distributions in 2008 from one or more traditional IRAs and your traditional IRAs include only deductible contributions, the distributions are fully taxable and are included in your modified AGI.

Both contributions for 2008 and distributions in 2008. If all three of the following apply, any IRA distributions you received in 2008 may be partly tax free and partly taxable.

- You received distributions in 2008 from one or more traditional IRAs,
- You made contributions to a traditional IRA for 2008, and
- Some of those contributions may be nondeductible contributions. (See *Nondeductible Contributions* and Worksheet 1-2, later.)

If this is your situation, you must figure the taxable part of the traditional IRA distribution before you can figure your modified AGI. To do this, you can use Worksheet 1-5, Figuring the Taxable Part of Your IRA Distribution.

If at least one of the above does not apply, figure your modified AGI using Worksheet 1-1.

How To Figure Your Reduced IRA Deduction

If you or your spouse is covered by an employer retirement plan and you did not receive any social security benefits, you can figure your reduced IRA deduction by using Worksheet 1-2, Figuring Your Reduced IRA Deduction for 2008. The instructions for both Form 1040 and Form 1040A include similar worksheets that you can use instead of the worksheet in this publication. If you file Form 1040NR, use the worksheet in this publication.

If you or your spouse is covered by an employer retirement plan, and you received any social security benefits, see *Social Security Recipients*, earlier.

Chapter 1   **Traditional IRAs**   Page 17

Note. If you were married and both you and your spouse contributed to IRAs, figure your deduction and your spouse's deduction separately.

Reporting Deductible Contributions

If you file Form 1040, enter your IRA deduction on line 32 of that form. If you file Form 1040A, enter your IRA deduction on line 17 of that form. If you file Form 1040NR, enter your IRA deduction on line 31 of that form. You cannot deduct IRA contributions on Form 1040EZ or Form 1040NR-EZ.

Self-employed. If you are self-employed (a sole proprietor or partner) and have a SIMPLE IRA, enter your deduction for allowable plan contributions on Form 1040, line 28. If you file Form 1040NR, enter your deduction on line 27 of that form.

Nondeductible Contributions

Although your deduction for IRA contributions may be reduced or eliminated, contributions can be made to your IRA of up to the general limit or, if it applies, the spousal IRA limit. The difference between your total permitted contributions and your IRA deduction, if any, is your nondeductible contribution.

Example. Tony is 29 years old and single. In 2008, he was covered by a retirement plan at work. His salary is $57,312. His modified AGI is $65,000. Tony makes a $5,000 IRA contribution for 2008. Because he was covered by a retirement plan and his modified AGI is above $63,000, he cannot deduct his $5,000 IRA contribution. He must designate this contribution as a nondeductible contribution by reporting it on Form 8606.

Repayment of reservist, hurricane, disaster recovery assistance, and recovery assistance distributions. Nondeductible contributions may include repayments of qualified reservist, hurricane, disaster recovery assistance, and recovery assistance distributions. For more information, see *Qualified reservist repayments* under *How Much Can Be Contributed?* earlier and chapter 4, *Disaster-Related Relief*.

Form 8606. To designate contributions as nondeductible, you must file Form 8606. (See the filled-in Forms 8606 in this chapter.)

You do not have to designate a contribution as nondeductible until you file your tax return. When you file, you can even designate otherwise deductible contributions as nondeductible contributions.

You must file Form 8606 to report nondeductible contributions even if you do not have to file a tax return for the year.

 A Form 8606 is not used for the year that you make a rollover from a qualified retirement plan to a traditional IRA and the rollover includes nontaxable amounts. In those situations, a Form 8606 is completed for the year you take a distribution from that IRA.

See Form 8606 *under* Distributions Fully or Partly Taxable *later.*

Failure to report nondeductible contributions. If you do not report nondeductible contributions, all of the contributions to your traditional IRA will be treated like deductible contributions when withdrawn. All distributions from your IRA will be taxed unless you can show, with satisfactory evidence, that nondeductible contributions were made.

Penalty for overstatement. If you overstate the amount of nondeductible contributions on your Form 8606 for any tax year, you must pay a penalty of $100 for each overstatement, unless it was due to reasonable cause.

Penalty for failure to file Form 8606. You will have to pay a $50 penalty if you do not file a required Form 8606, unless you can prove that the failure was due to reasonable cause.

Tax on earnings on nondeductible contributions. As long as contributions are within the contribution limits, none of the earnings or gains on contributions (deductible or nondeductible) will be taxed until they are distributed.

Cost basis. You will have a cost basis in your traditional IRA if you made any nondeductible contributions. Your cost basis is the sum of the nondeductible contributions to your IRA minus any withdrawals or distributions of nondeductible contributions.

 Commonly, distributions from your traditional IRAs will include both taxable and nontaxable (cost basis) amounts. See Are Distributions Taxable? *later, for more information.*

 Recordkeeping. There is a recordkeeping worksheet, *Appendix A, Summary Record of Traditional IRA(s) for 2008,* that you can use to keep a record of deductible and nondeductible IRA contributions.

Examples — Worksheet for Reduced IRA Deduction for 2008

The following examples illustrate the use of Worksheet 1-2, Figuring Your Reduced IRA Deduction for 2008.

Example 1. For 2008, Tom and Betty file a joint return on Form 1040. They are both 39 years old. They are both employed and Tom is covered by his employer's retirement plan. Tom's salary is $57,000 and Betty's is $30,555. They each have a traditional IRA and their combined modified AGI, which includes $2,000 interest and dividend income, is $89,555. Because their modified AGI is between $85,000 and $105,000 and Tom is covered by an employer plan, Tom is subject to the deduction phaseout discussed earlier under *Limit if Covered by Employer Plan.*

For 2008, Tom contributed $5,000 to his IRA and Betty contributed $5,000 to hers. Even though they file a joint return, they must use separate worksheets to figure the IRA deduction for each of them.

Tom can take a deduction of only $3,870.

Worksheet 1-2. **Figuring Your Reduced IRA Deduction for 2008**

(Use only if you or your spouse is covered by an employer plan and your modified AGI falls between the two amounts shown below for your coverage situation and filing status.)

Note. If you were married and both you and your spouse contributed to IRAs, figure your deduction and your spouse's deduction separately.

Certain employer bankruptcies. See *Catch-up contributions in certain employer bankruptcies* earlier, for instructions to complete lines 4 and 6 of this worksheet.

IF you ...	AND your filing status is ...	AND your modified AGI is over ...	THEN enter on line 1 below ...
are **covered** by an employer plan	single or head of household	$53,000	$63,000
	married filing jointly or qualifying widow(er)	$85,000	$105,000
	married filing separately	$0	$10,000
are **not covered** by an employer plan, but your spouse is **covered**	married filing jointly	$159,000	$169,000
	married filing separately	$0	$10,000

1. Enter applicable amount from table above . . . . 1. _____

2. Enter your **modified AGI** (that of both spouses, if married filing jointly) . . . . 2. _____

    Note. If line 2 is equal to or more than the amount on line 1, **stop here.**
    Your IRA contributions are not deductible. See *Nondeductible Contributions*.

3. Subtract line 2 from line 1. **If line 3 is $10,000 or more ($20,000 or more if married filing jointly or qualifying widow(er) and you are covered by an employer plan), stop here.** You can take a full IRA deduction for contributions of up to $5,000 ($6,000 if you are age 50 or older) or 100% of your (and if married filing jointly, your spouse's) compensation, whichever is less ... 3. _____

4. Multiply line 3 by the percentage below that applies to you. If the result is not a multiple of $10, round it to the next highest multiple of $10. (For example, $611.40 is rounded to $620.) However, if the result is less than $200, enter $200.

    - Married filing jointly or qualifying widow(er) **and** you are covered by an employer plan, multiply line 3 by 25% (.25) (by 30% (.30) if you are age 50 or older).
    - All others, multiply line 3 by 50% (.50) (by 60% (.60) if you are age 50 or older). } . . . . 4. _____

5. Enter your compensation minus any deductions on Form 1040, line 27 (one-half of self-employment tax) and line 28 (self-employed SEP, SIMPLE, and qualified plans); or on Form 1040NR, line 27 (self-employed SEP, SIMPLE, and qualified plans). If you are filing a joint return and your compensation is less than your spouse's, include your spouse's compensation reduced by his or her traditional IRA and Roth IRA contributions for this year. If you file Form 1040 or Form 1040NR, do not reduce your compensation by any losses from self-employment . . . . 5. _____

6. Enter contributions made, or to be made, to your IRA for 2008 but **do not** enter more than $5,000 ($6,000 if you are age 50 or older). If contributions are more than $5,000 ($6,000 if you are age 50 or older), see *Excess Contributions*, later. . . . . 6. _____

7. **IRA deduction.** Compare lines 4, 5, and 6. Enter the smallest amount (or a smaller amount if you choose) here and on the Form 1040, 1040A, or 1040NR line for your IRA, whichever applies. If line 6 is more than line 7 and you want to make a nondeductible contribution, go to line 8 . . . . . 7. _____

8. **Nondeductible contribution.** Subtract line 7 from line 5 or 6, whichever is smaller. Enter the result here and on line 1 of your Form 8606 . . . . 8. _____

He can choose to treat the $3,870 as either deductible or nondeductible contributions. He can either leave the $1,130 ($5,000 – $3,870) of nondeductible contributions in his IRA or withdraw them by April 15, 2009. He decides to treat the $3,870 as deductible contributions and leave the $1,130 of nondeductible contributions in his IRA.

Using Worksheet 1-2, Figuring Your Reduced IRA Deduction for 2008, Tom figures his deductible and nondeductible amounts as shown on Worksheet 1-2, Figuring Your Reduced IRA Deduction for 2008—Example 1 Illustrated.

Betty figures her IRA deduction as follows. Betty can treat all or part of her contributions as either deductible or nondeductible. This is because her $5,000 contribution for 2008 is not subject to the deduction phaseout discussed earlier under *Limit if Covered by Employer Plan*. She does not need to use Worksheet 1-2, Figuring Your Reduced IRA Deduction for 2008, because their modified AGI is not within the phaseout range that applies. Betty decides to treat her $5,000 IRA contributions as deductible.

The IRA deductions of $3,870 and $5,000 on the joint return for Tom and Betty total $8,870.

Example 2. For 2008, Ed and Sue file a joint return on Form 1040. They are both 39 years old. Ed is covered by his employer's retirement plan. Ed's salary is $45,000. Sue had no compensation for the year and did not contribute to an IRA. Sue is not covered by an employer plan. Ed contributed $5,000 to his traditional IRA and $5,000 to a traditional IRA for Sue (a spousal IRA). Their combined modified AGI, which includes $2,000 interest and dividend income and a large capital gain from the sale of stock, is $161,555.

Because the combined modified AGI is $105,000 or more, Ed cannot deduct any of the contribution to his traditional IRA. He can either leave the $5,000 of nondeductible contributions in his IRA or withdraw them by April 15, 2009.

Sue figures her IRA deduction as shown on Worksheet 1-2, Figuring Your Reduced IRA Deduction for 2008—Example 2 Illustrated.

What if You Inherit an IRA?

If you inherit a traditional IRA, you are called a beneficiary. A beneficiary can be any person or entity the owner chooses to receive the benefits of the IRA after he or she dies. Beneficiaries of a traditional IRA must include in their gross income any taxable distributions they receive.

Inherited from spouse. If you inherit a traditional IRA from your spouse, you generally have the following three choices. You can:

1. Treat it as your own IRA by designating yourself as the account owner.

2. Treat it as your own by rolling it over into your traditional IRA, or to the extent it is taxable, into a:

   a. Qualified employer plan,

   b. Qualified employee annuity plan (section 403(a) plan),

   c. Tax-sheltered annuity plan (section 403(b) plan),

   d. Deferred compensation plan of a state or local government (section 457 plan), or

3. Treat yourself as the beneficiary rather than treating the IRA as your own.

Treating it as your own. You will be considered to have chosen to treat the IRA as your own if:

- Contributions (including rollover contributions) are made to the inherited IRA, or

- You do not take the required minimum distribution for a year as a beneficiary of the IRA.

You will only be considered to have chosen to treat the IRA as your own if:

- You are the sole beneficiary of the IRA, and

- You have an unlimited right to withdraw amounts from it.

However, if you receive a distribution from your deceased spouse's IRA, you can roll that distribution over into your own IRA within the 60-day time limit, as long as the distribution is not a required distribution, even if you are not the sole beneficiary of your deceased spouse's IRA. For more information, see *When Must You Withdraw Assets? (Required Minimum Distributions)*, later.

Inherited from someone other than spouse. If you inherit a traditional IRA from anyone other than your deceased spouse, you cannot treat the inherited IRA as your own. This means that you cannot make any contributions to the IRA. It also means you cannot roll over any amounts into or out of the inherited IRA. However, you can make a trustee-to-trustee transfer as long as the IRA into which amounts are being moved is set up and maintained in the name of the deceased IRA owner for the benefit of you as beneficiary.

Like the original owner, you generally will not owe tax on the assets in the IRA until you receive distributions from it. You must begin receiving distributions from the IRA under the rules for distributions that apply to beneficiaries.

IRA with basis. If you inherit a traditional IRA from a person who had a basis in the IRA because of nondeductible contributions, that basis remains with the IRA. Unless you are the decedent's spouse and choose to treat the IRA as your own, you cannot combine this basis with any basis you have in your own traditional IRA(s) or any basis in traditional IRA(s) you inherited from other decedents. If you take distributions from both an inherited IRA and your IRA, and each has basis, you must complete separate Forms 8606 to determine the taxable and nontaxable portions of those distributions.

Federal estate tax deduction. A beneficiary may be able to claim a deduction for estate tax resulting from certain distributions from a traditional IRA. The beneficiary can

Worksheet 1-2. **Figuring Your Reduced IRA Deduction for 2008—Example 1 Illustrated**

(Use only if you or your spouse is covered by an employer plan and your modified AGI falls between the two amounts shown below for your coverage situation and filing status.)

Note. If you were married and both you and your spouse contributed to IRAs, figure your deduction and your spouse's deduction separately.

Certain employer bankruptcies. See *Catch-up contributions in certain employer bankruptcies* earlier, for instructions to complete lines 4 and 6 of this worksheet.

IF you ...	AND your filing status is ...	AND your modified AGI is over ...	THEN enter on line 1 below ...	
are **covered** by an employer plan	single or head of household	$53,000	$63,000	
	married filing jointly or qualifying widow(er)	$85,000	$105,000	
	married filing separately	$0	$10,000	
are **not covered** by an employer plan, but your spouse is **covered**	married filing jointly	$159,000	$169,000	
	married filing separately	$0	$10,000	

1. Enter applicable amount from table above . . . . **1.**   <u>105,000</u>

2. Enter your ***modified AGI*** (that of both spouses, if married filing jointly) . . . . **2.**   <u>89,555</u>

    Note. If line 2 is equal to or more than the amount on line 1, **stop here.**
    Your IRA contributions are not deductible. See *Nondeductible Contributions.*

3. Subtract line 2 from line 1. **If line 3 is $10,000 or more ($20,000 or more if married filing jointly or qualifying widow(er) and you are covered by an employer plan), stop here.** You can take a full IRA deduction for contributions of up to $5,000 ($6,000 if you are age 50 or older) or 100% of your (and if married filing jointly, your spouse's) compensation, whichever is less . . . **3.**   <u>15,445</u>

4. Multiply line 3 by the percentage below that applies to you. If the result is not a multiple of $10, round it to the next highest multiple of $10. (For example, $611.40 is rounded to $620.) However, if the result is less than $200, enter $200.

    • Married filing jointly or qualifying widow(er) **and** you are covered by an employer plan, multiply line 3 by 25% (.25) (by 30% (.30) if you are age 50 or older).
    • All others, multiply line 3 by 50% (.50) (by 60% (.60) if you are age 50 or older).   } . . . . **4.**   <u>3,870</u>

5. Enter your compensation minus any deductions on Form 1040, line 27 (one-half of self-employment tax) and line 28 (self-employed SEP, SIMPLE, and qualified plans); or on Form 1040NR, line 27 (self-employed SEP, SIMPLE, and qualified plans). If you are filing a joint return and your compensation is less than your spouse's, include your spouse's compensation reduced by his or her traditional IRA and Roth IRA contributions for this year. If you file Form 1040 or Form 1040NR, do not reduce your compensation by any losses from self-employment . . . . **5.**   <u>57,000</u>

6. Enter contributions made, or to be made, to your IRA for 2008 but **do not** enter more than $5,000 ($6,000 if you are age 50 or older). If contributions are more than $5,000 ($6,000 if you are age 50 or older), see *Excess Contributions*, later. . . . . **6.**   <u>5,000</u>

7. **IRA deduction.** Compare lines 4, 5, and 6. Enter the smallest amount (or a smaller amount if you choose) here and on the Form 1040, 1040A, or 1040NR line for your IRA, whichever applies. If line 6 is more than line 7 and you want to make a nondeductible contribution, go to line 8 . . . . . **7.**   <u>3,870</u>

8. **Nondeductible contribution.** Subtract line 7 from line 5 or 6, whichever is smaller. Enter the result here and on line 1 of your Form 8606 . . . . **8.**   <u>1,130</u>

Worksheet 1-2. Figuring Your Reduced IRA Deduction for 2008—Example 2 Illustrated

(Use only if you or your spouse is covered by an employer plan and your modified AGI falls between the two amounts shown below for your coverage situation and filing status.)

Note. If you were married and both you and your spouse contributed to IRAs, figure your deduction and your spouse's deduction separately.

Certain employer bankruptcies. See *Catch-up contributions in certain employer bankruptcies* earlier, for instructions to complete lines 4 and 6 of this worksheet.

IF you ...	AND your filing status is ...	AND your modified AGI is over ...	THEN enter on line 1 below ...		
are **covered** by an employer plan	single or head of household	$53,000	$63,000		
	married filing jointly or qualifying widow(er)	$85,000	$105,000		
	married filing separately	$0	$10,000		
are **not covered** by an employer plan, but your spouse is **covered**	married filing jointly	$159,000	$169,000		
	married filing separately	$0	$10,000		

1. Enter applicable amount from table above **1.** 169,000

2. Enter your ***modified AGI*** (that of both spouses, if married filing jointly) **2.** 161,555

   Note. If line 2 is equal to or more than the amount on line 1, **stop here.**
   Your IRA contributions are not deductible. See *Nondeductible Contributions*.

3. Subtract line 2 from line 1. **If line 3 is $10,000 or more ($20,000 or more if married filing jointly or qualifying widow(er) and you are covered by an employer plan), stop here.** You can take a full IRA deduction for contributions of up to $5,000 ($6,000 if you are age 50 or older) or 100% of your (and if married filing jointly, your spouse's) compensation, whichever is less . . . **3.** 7,445

4. Multiply line 3 by the percentage below that applies to you. If the result is not a multiple of $10, round it to the next highest multiple of $10. (For example, $611.40 is rounded to $620.) However, if the result is less than $200, enter $200.

   - Married filing jointly or qualifying widow(er) **and** you are covered by an employer plan, multiply line 3 by 25% (.25) (by 30% (.30) if you are age 50 or older).
   - All others, multiply line 3 by 50% (.50) (by 60% (.60) if you are age 50 or older). } **4.** 3,730

5. Enter your compensation minus any deductions on Form 1040, line 27 (one-half of self-employment tax) and line 28 (self-employed SEP, SIMPLE, and qualified plans); or on Form 1040NR, line 27 (self-employed SEP, SIMPLE, and qualified plans). If you are filing a joint return and your compensation is less than your spouse's, include your spouse's compensation reduced by his or her traditional IRA and Roth IRA contributions for this year. If you file Form 1040 or Form 1040NR, do not reduce your compensation by any losses from self-employment **5.** 40,000

6. Enter contributions made, or to be made, to your IRA for 2008 but **do not** enter more than $5,000 ($6,000 if you are age 50 or older). If contributions are more than $5,000 ($6,000 if you are age 50 or older), see *Excess Contributions*, later. **6.** 5,000

7. **IRA deduction.** Compare lines 4, 5, and 6. Enter the smallest amount (or a smaller amount if you choose) here and on the Form 1040, 1040A, or 1040NR line for your IRA, whichever applies. If line 6 is more than line 7 and you want to make a nondeductible contribution, go to line 8 . . . . . **7.** 3,730

8. **Nondeductible contribution.** Subtract line 7 from line 5 or 6, whichever is smaller. Enter the result here and on line 1 of your Form 8606 . . . . **8.** 1,270

deduct the estate tax paid on any part of a distribution that is income in respect of a decedent. He or she can take the deduction for the tax year the income is reported. For information on claiming this deduction, see *Estate Tax Deduction* under *Other Tax Information* in Publication 559, Survivors, Executors, and Administrators.

Any taxable part of a distribution that is not income in respect of a decedent is a payment the beneficiary must include in income. However, the beneficiary cannot take any estate tax deduction for this part.

A surviving spouse can roll over the distribution to another traditional IRA and avoid including it in income for the year received.

More information. For more information about rollovers, required distributions, and inherited IRAs, see:

- *Rollovers*, later under *Can You Move Retirement Plan Assets,*

- *When Must You Withdraw Assets? (Required Minimum Distributions)*, later, and

- The discussion of IRA beneficiaries later under *When Must You Withdraw Assets? (Required Minimum Distributions).*

Can You Move Retirement Plan Assets?

You can transfer, tax free, assets (money or property) from other retirement programs (including traditional IRAs) to a traditional IRA. You can make the following kinds of transfers.

- Transfers from one trustee to another.

- Rollovers.

- Transfers incident to a divorce.

This chapter discusses all three kinds of transfers.

Transfers to Roth IRAs. Under certain conditions, you can move assets from a traditional IRA or from a designated Roth account to a Roth IRA. For more information about these transfers, see *Converting From Any Traditional IRA Into a Roth IRA*, later, and *Can You Move Amounts Into a Roth IRA?* in chapter 2.

Transfers to Roth IRAs from other retirement plans. Beginning in 2008, under certain conditions, you can move assets from a qualified retirement plan to a Roth IRA. For more information, see *Can You Move Amounts Into a Roth IRA?* in chapter 2.

Trustee-to-Trustee Transfer

A transfer of funds in your traditional IRA from one trustee directly to another, either at your request or at the trustee's request, is not a rollover. Because there is no distribution to you, the transfer is tax free. Because it is not a rollover, it

is not affected by the 1-year waiting period required between rollovers. This waiting period is discussed later under *Rollover From One IRA Into Another*.

For information about direct transfers from retirement programs other than traditional IRAs, see *Direct rollover option*, later.

Rollovers

Generally, a rollover is a tax-free distribution to you of cash or other assets from one retirement plan that you contribute to another retirement plan. The contribution to the second retirement plan is called a "rollover contribution."

Note. An amount rolled over tax free from one retirement plan to another is generally includible in income when it is distributed from the second plan.

Kinds of rollovers to a traditional IRA. You can roll over amounts from the following plans into a traditional IRA:

- A traditional IRA,

- An employer's qualified retirement plan for its employees,

- A deferred compensation plan of a state or local government (section 457 plan), or

- A tax-sheltered annuity plan (section 403 plan).

Treatment of rollovers. You cannot deduct a rollover contribution, but you must report the rollover distribution on your tax return as discussed later under *Reporting rollovers from IRAs* and *Reporting rollovers from employer plans.*

Rollover notice. A written explanation of rollover treatment must be given to you by the plan (other than an IRA) making the distribution.

Kinds of rollovers from a traditional IRA. You may be able to roll over, tax free, a distribution from your traditional IRA into a qualified plan. These plans include the Federal Thrift Savings Fund (for federal employees), deferred compensation plans of state or local governments (section 457 plans), and tax-sheltered annuity plans (section 403(b) plans). The part of the distribution that you can roll over is the part that would otherwise be taxable (includible in your income). Qualified plans may, but are not required to, accept such rollovers.

Tax treatment of a rollover from a traditional IRA to an eligible retirement plan other than an IRA. Ordinarily, when you have basis in your IRAs, any distribution is considered to include both nontaxable and taxable amounts. Without a special rule, the nontaxable portion of such a distribution could not be rolled over. However, a special rule treats a distribution you roll over into an eligible retirement plan as including only otherwise taxable amounts if the amount you either leave in your IRAs or do not roll over is at least equal to your basis. The effect of this special rule is to make the amount in your traditional IRAs that you can roll over to an eligible retirement plan as large as possible.

Eligible retirement plans. The following are considered eligible retirement plans.

- Individual retirement arrangements (IRAs).
- Qualified trusts.
- Qualified employee annuity plans under section 403(a).
- Deferred compensation plans of state and local governments (section 457 plans).
- Tax-sheltered annuities (section 403(b) annuities).

Time Limit for Making a Rollover Contribution

You generally must make the rollover contribution by the 60th day after the day you receive the distribution from your traditional IRA or your employer's plan. However, see *Extension of rollover period*, later.

The IRS may waive the 60-day requirement where the failure to do so would be against equity or good conscience, such as in the event of a casualty, disaster, or other event beyond your reasonable control.

Rollovers completed after the 60-day period. In the absence of a waiver, amounts not rolled over within the 60-day period do not qualify for tax-free rollover treatment. You must treat them as a taxable distribution from either your IRA or your employer's plan. These amounts are taxable in the year distributed, even if the 60-day period expires in the next year. You may also have to pay a 10% additional tax on early distributions as discussed later under *Early Distributions*.

Unless there is a waiver or an extension of the 60-day rollover period, any contribution you make to your IRA more than 60 days after the distribution is a regular contribution, not a rollover contribution.

Example. You received a distribution in late December 2008 from a traditional IRA that you do not roll over into another traditional IRA within the 60-day limit. You do not qualify for a waiver. This distribution is taxable in 2008 even though the 60-day limit was not up until 2009.

Automatic waiver. The 60-day rollover requirement is waived automatically only if all of the following apply.

- The financial institution receives the funds on your behalf before the end of the 60-day rollover period.
- You followed all the procedures set by the financial institution for depositing the funds into an eligible retirement plan within the 60-day period (including giving instructions to deposit the funds into an eligible retirement plan).
- The funds are not deposited into an eligible retirement plan within the 60-day rollover period solely because of an error on the part of the financial institution.

- The funds are deposited into an eligible retirement plan within 1 year from the beginning of the 60-day rollover period.
- It would have been a valid rollover if the financial institution had deposited the funds as instructed.

Other waivers. If you do not qualify for an automatic waiver, you can apply to the IRS for a waiver of the 60-day rollover requirement. You apply by following the procedures for applying for a letter ruling. Those procedures are stated in a revenue procedure generally published in the first Internal Revenue Bulletin of the year. You must also pay a user fee with the application. For how to get that revenue procedure, see chapter 6.

In determining whether to grant a waiver, the IRS will consider all relevant facts and circumstances, including:

- Whether errors were made by the financial institution (other than those described under *Automatic waiver*, earlier),
- Whether you were unable to complete the rollover due to death, disability, hospitalization, incarceration, restrictions imposed by a foreign country or postal error,
- Whether you used the amount distributed (for example, in the case of payment by check, whether you cashed the check), and
- How much time has passed since the date of distribution.

Amount. The rules regarding the amount that can be rolled over within the 60-day time period also apply to the amount that can be deposited due to a waiver. For example, if you received $6,000 from your IRA, the most that you can deposit into an eligible retirement plan due to a waiver is $6,000.

Extension of rollover period. If an amount distributed to you from a traditional IRA or a qualified employer retirement plan is a frozen deposit at any time during the 60-day period allowed for a rollover, two special rules extend the rollover period.

- The period during which the amount is a frozen deposit is not counted in the 60-day period.
- The 60-day period cannot end earlier than 10 days after the deposit is no longer frozen.

Frozen deposit. This is any deposit that cannot be withdrawn from a financial institution because of either of the following reasons.

- The financial institution is bankrupt or insolvent.
- The state where the institution is located restricts withdrawals because one or more financial institutions in the state are (or are about to be) bankrupt or insolvent.

Rollover From One IRA Into Another

You can withdraw, tax free, all or part of the assets from one traditional IRA if you reinvest them within 60 days in the same or another traditional IRA. Because this is a rollover, you cannot deduct the amount that you reinvest in an IRA.

 You may be able to treat a contribution made to one type of IRA as having been made to a different type of IRA. This is called recharacterizing the contribution. See Recharacterizations in this chapter for more information.

Waiting period between rollovers. Generally, if you make a tax-free rollover of any part of a distribution from a traditional IRA, you cannot, within a 1-year period, make a tax-free rollover of any later distribution from that same IRA. You also cannot make a tax-free rollover of any amount distributed, within the same 1-year period, from the IRA into which you made the tax-free rollover.

The 1-year period begins on the date you receive the IRA distribution, not on the date you roll it over into an IRA.

Example. You have two traditional IRAs, IRA-1 and IRA-2. You make a tax-free rollover of a distribution from IRA-1 into a new traditional IRA (IRA-3). You cannot, within 1 year of the distribution from IRA-1, make a tax-free rollover of any distribution from either IRA-1 or IRA-3 into another traditional IRA.

However, the rollover from IRA-1 into IRA-3 does not prevent you from making a tax-free rollover from IRA-2 into any other traditional IRA. This is because you have not, within the last year, rolled over, tax-free, any distribution from IRA-2 or made a tax-free rollover into IRA-2.

Exception. There is an exception to the rule that amounts rolled over tax free into an IRA cannot be rolled over tax free again within the 1-year period beginning on the date of the original distribution. The exception applies to a distribution which meets all three of the following requirements.

1. It is made from a failed financial institution by the Federal Deposit Insurance Corporation (FDIC) as receiver for the institution.

2. It was not initiated by either the custodial institution or the depositor.

3. It was made because:

    a. The custodial institution is insolvent, and

    b. The receiver is unable to find a buyer for the institution.

The same property must be rolled over. If property is distributed to you from an IRA and you complete the rollover by contributing property to an IRA, your rollover is tax free only if the property you contribute is the same property that was distributed to you.

Partial rollovers. If you withdraw assets from a traditional IRA, you can roll over part of the withdrawal tax free and keep the rest of it. The amount you keep will generally be taxable (except for the part that is a return of nondeductible contributions). The amount you keep may be subject to the 10% additional tax on early distributions discussed later under *What Acts Result in Penalties or Additional Taxes*.

Required distributions. Amounts that must be distributed during a particular year under the required distribution rules (discussed later) are not eligible for rollover treatment.

Inherited IRAs. If you inherit a traditional IRA from your spouse, you generally can roll it over, or you can choose to make the inherited IRA your own as discussed earlier under *What if You Inherit an IRA*.

Not inherited from spouse. If you inherit a traditional IRA from someone other than your spouse, you cannot roll it over or allow it to receive a rollover contribution. You must withdraw the IRA assets within a certain period. For more information, see *When Must You Withdraw Assets*, later.

Reporting rollovers from IRAs. Report any rollover from one traditional IRA to the same or another traditional IRA on Form 1040, lines 15a and 15b; Form 1040A, lines 11a and 11b; or Form 1040NR, lines 16a and 16b.

Enter the total amount of the distribution on Form 1040, line 15a; Form 1040A, line 11a; or Form 1040NR, line 16a. If the total amount on Form 1040, line 15a; Form 1040A, line 11a; or Form 1040NR, line 16a, was rolled over, enter zero on Form 1040, line 15b; Form 1040A, line 11b; or Form 1040NR, line 16b. If the total distribution was not rolled over, enter the taxable portion of the part that was not rolled over on Form 1040, line 15b; Form 1040A, line 11b; or Form 1040NR, line 16b. Put "Rollover" next to line 15b, Form 1040; line 11b, Form 1040A; or line 16b, Form 1040NR. See the forms' instructions.

If you rolled over the distribution into a qualified plan (other than an IRA) or you make the rollover in 2009, attach a statement explaining what you did.

For information on how to figure the taxable portion, see *Are Distributions Taxable*, later.

Rollover From Employer's Plan Into an IRA

You can roll over into a traditional IRA all or part of an eligible rollover distribution you receive from your (or your deceased spouse's):

- Employer's qualified pension, profit-sharing or stock bonus plan,

- Annuity plan,

- Tax-sheltered annuity plan (section 403(b) plan), or

- Governmental deferred compensation plan (section 457 plan).

A qualified plan is one that meets the requirements of the Internal Revenue Code.

Chapter 1 **Traditional IRAs** Page 25

Eligible rollover distribution. Generally, an eligible rollover distribution is any distribution of all or part of the balance to your credit in a qualified retirement plan except the following.

1. A required minimum distribution (explained later under *When Must You Withdraw Assets? (Required Minimum Distributions)*).

2. A hardship distribution.

3. Any of a series of substantially equal periodic distributions paid at least once a year over:

    a. Your lifetime or life expectancy,

    b. The lifetimes or life expectancies of you and your beneficiary, or

    c. A period of 10 years or more.

4. Corrective distributions of excess contributions or excess deferrals, and any income allocable to the excess, or of excess annual additions and any allocable gains.

5. A loan treated as a distribution because it does not satisfy certain requirements either when made or later (such as upon default), unless the participant's accrued benefits are reduced (offset) to repay the loan.

6. Dividends on employer securities.

7. The cost of life insurance coverage.

Your rollover into a traditional IRA may include both amounts that would be taxable and amounts that would not be taxable if they were distributed to you, but not rolled over. To the extent the distribution is rolled over into a traditional IRA, it is not includible in your income.

 Any nontaxable amounts that you roll over into your traditional IRA become part of your basis (cost) in your IRAs. To recover your basis when you take distributions from your IRA, you must complete Form 8606 for the year of the distribution. See Form 8606 *under* Distributions Fully or Partly Taxable *later.*

Rollover by nonspouse beneficiary. A direct transfer from a deceased employee's qualified pension, profit-sharing or stock bonus plan, annuity plan, tax-sheltered annuity (section 403(b)) plan, or governmental deferred compensation (section 457) plan to an IRA set up to receive the distribution on your behalf can be treated as an eligible rollover distribution if you are the designated beneficiary of the plan and not the employee's spouse. The IRA is treated as an inherited IRA. For more information about inherited IRAs, see *What if You Inherit an IRA*, earlier.

Written explanation to recipients. Before making an eligible rollover distribution, the administrator of a qualified employer plan must provide you with a written explanation. It must tell you about all of the following.

- Your right to have the distribution paid tax free directly to a traditional IRA or another eligible retirement plan.

- The requirement to withhold tax from the distribution if it is not paid directly to a traditional IRA or another eligible retirement plan.

- The tax treatment of any part of the distribution that you roll over to a traditional IRA or another eligible retirement plan within 60 days after you receive the distribution.

- Other qualified employer plan rules, if they apply, including those for lump-sum distributions, alternate payees, and cash or deferred arrangements.

- How the plan receiving the distribution differs from the plan making the distribution in its restrictions and tax consequences.

The plan administrator must provide you with this written explanation no earlier than 90 days and no later than 30 days before the distribution is made.

However, you can choose to have a distribution made less than 30 days after the explanation is provided as long as both of the following requirements are met.

- You are given at least 30 days after the notice is provided to consider whether you want to elect a direct rollover.

- You are given information that clearly states that you have this 30-day period to make the decision.

Contact the plan administrator if you have any questions regarding this information.

Withholding requirement. Generally, if an eligible rollover distribution is paid directly to you, the payer must withhold 20% of it. This applies even if you plan to roll over the distribution to a traditional IRA. You can avoid withholding by choosing the direct rollover option, discussed later.

Exceptions. The payer does not have to withhold from an eligible rollover distribution paid to you if either of the following conditions apply.

- The distribution and all previous eligible rollover distributions you received during your tax year from the same plan (or, at the payer's option, from all your employer's plans) total less than $200.

- The distribution consists solely of employer securities, plus cash of $200 or less in lieu of fractional shares.

 The amount withheld is part of the distribution. If you roll over less than the full amount of the distribution, you may have to include in your income the amount you do not roll over. However, you can make up the amount withheld with funds from other sources.

Other withholding rules. The 20% withholding requirement does not apply to distributions that are not eligible rollover distributions. However, other withholding rules apply to these distributions. The rules that apply depend on whether the distribution is a periodic distribution or a nonperiodic distribution. For either of these types of distributions, you can still choose not to have tax withheld. For more information, see Publication 575.

Direct rollover option. Your employer's qualified plan must give you the option to have any part of an eligible rollover distribution paid directly to a traditional IRA. The plan is not required to give you this option if your eligible rollover distributions are expected to total less than $200 for the year.

Withholding. If you choose the direct rollover option, no tax is withheld from any part of the designated distribution that is directly paid to the trustee of the traditional IRA.

If any part is paid to you, the payer must withhold 20% of that part's taxable amount.

Choosing an option. Table 1-4 may help you decide which distribution option to choose. Carefully compare the effects of each option.

Table 1-4. Comparison of Payment to You Versus Direct Rollover

Affected item	Result of a payment to you	Result of a direct rollover
withholding	The payer must withhold 20% of the taxable part.	There is no withholding.
additional tax	If you are under age 59½, a 10% additional tax may apply to the taxable part (including an amount equal to the tax withheld) that is not rolled over.	There is no 10% additional tax. See *Early Distributions.*
when to report as income	Any taxable part (including the taxable part of any amount withheld) not rolled over is income to you in the year paid.	Any taxable part is not income to you until later distributed to you from the IRA.

TIP
If you decide to roll over any part of a distribution, the direct rollover option will generally be to your advantage. This is because you will not have 20% withholding or be subject to the 10% additional tax under that option.

If you have a lump-sum distribution and do not plan to roll over any part of it, the distribution may be eligible for special tax treatment that could lower your tax for the distribution year. In that case, you may want to see Publication 575 and Form 4972, Tax on Lump-Sum Distributions, and its instructions to determine whether your distribution qualifies for special tax treatment and, if so, to figure your tax under the special methods.

You can then compare any advantages from using Form 4972 to figure your tax on the lump-sum distribution with any advantages from rolling over all or part of the distribution. However, if you roll over any part of the lump-sum distribution, you cannot use the Form 4972 special tax treatment for any part of the distribution.

Contributions you made to your employer's plan. You can roll over a distribution of voluntary deductible employee contributions (DECs) you made to your employer's plan. Prior to January 1, 1987, employees could make and deduct these contributions to certain qualified employers' plans and government plans. These are not the same as an employee's elective contributions to a 401(k) plan, which are not deductible by the employee.

If you receive a distribution from your employer's qualified plan of any part of the balance of your DECs and the earnings from them, you can roll over any part of the distribution.

No waiting period between rollovers. The once-a-year limit on IRA-to-IRA rollovers does not apply to eligible rollover distributions from an employer plan. You can roll over more than one distribution from the same employer plan within a year.

IRA as a holding account (conduit IRA) for rollovers to other eligible plans. If you receive an eligible distribution from your employer's plan, you can roll over part or all of it into one or more conduit IRAs. You can later roll over those assets into a new employer's plan. You can use a traditional IRA as a conduit IRA. You can roll over part or all of the conduit IRA to a qualified plan, even if you make regular contributions to it or add funds from sources other than your employer's plan. However, if you make regular contributions to the conduit IRA or add funds from other sources, the qualified plan into which you move funds will not be eligible for any optional tax treatment for which it might have otherwise qualified.

Property and cash received in a distribution. If you receive both property and cash in an eligible rollover distribution, you can roll over part or all of the property, part or all of the cash, or any combination of the two that you choose.

The same property (or sales proceeds) must be rolled over. If you receive property in an eligible rollover distribution from a qualified retirement plan you cannot keep the property and contribute cash to a traditional IRA in place of the property. You must either roll over the property or sell it and roll over the proceeds, as explained next.

Sale of property received in a distribution from a qualified plan. Instead of rolling over a distribution of property other than cash, you can sell all or part of the property and roll over the amount you receive from the sale (the proceeds) into a traditional IRA. You cannot keep the property and substitute your own funds for property you received.

Example. You receive a total distribution from your employer's plan consisting of $10,000 cash and $15,000 worth of property. You decide to keep the property. You can roll over to a traditional IRA the $10,000 cash received, but you cannot roll over an additional $15,000 representing the value of the property you choose not to sell.

Treatment of gain or loss. If you sell the distributed property and roll over all the proceeds into a traditional IRA, no gain or loss is recognized. The sale proceeds (including any increase in value) are treated as part of the distribution and are not included in your gross income.

Example. On September 4, Mike received a lump-sum distribution from his employer's retirement plan of $50,000 in cash and $50,000 in stock. The stock was not stock of his employer. On September 24, he sold the stock for $60,000. On October 4, he rolled over $110,000 in cash ($50,000 from the original distribution and $60,000 from the sale of stock). Mike does not include the $10,000 gain from the sale of stock as part of his income because he rolled over the entire amount into a traditional IRA.

Note. Special rules may apply to distributions of employer securities. For more information, see Publication 575.

Partial rollover. If you received both cash and property, or just property, but did not roll over the entire distribution, see *Rollovers* in Publication 575.

Life insurance contract. You cannot roll over a life insurance contract from a qualified plan into a traditional IRA.

Distributions received by a surviving spouse. If you receive an eligible rollover distribution (defined earlier) from your deceased spouse's eligible retirement plan (defined earlier), you can roll over part or all of it into a traditional IRA. You can also roll over all or any part of a distribution of deductible employee contributions (DECs).

Distributions under divorce or similar proceedings (alternate payees). If you are the spouse or former spouse of an employee and you receive a distribution from a qualified employer plan as a result of divorce or similar proceedings, you may be able to roll over all or part of it into a traditional IRA. To qualify, the distribution must be:

- One that would have been an eligible rollover distribution (defined earlier) if it had been made to the employee, and

- Made under a qualified domestic relations order.

Qualified domestic relations order. A domestic relations order is a judgment, decree, or order (including approval of a property settlement agreement) that is issued under the domestic relations law of a state. A "qualified domestic relations order" gives to an alternate payee (a spouse, former spouse, child, or dependent of a participant in a retirement plan) the right to receive all or part of the benefits that would be payable to a participant under the plan. The order requires certain specific information, and it cannot alter the amount or form of the benefits of the plan.

Tax treatment if all of an eligible distribution is not rolled over. Any part of an eligible rollover distribution that you keep is taxable in the year you receive it. If you do not roll over any of it, special rules for lump-sum distributions may apply. See Publication 575. The 10% additional tax on early distributions, discussed later under *What Acts Result in Penalties or Additional Taxes*, does not apply.

Keogh plans and rollovers. If you are self-employed, you are generally treated as an employee for rollover purposes. Consequently, if you receive an eligible rollover distribution from a Keogh plan (a qualified plan with at least one self-employed participant), you can roll over all or part of the distribution (including a lump-sum distribution) into a traditional IRA. For information on lump-sum distributions, see Publication 575.

More information. For more information about Keogh plans, see Publication 560.

Distribution from a tax-sheltered annuity. If you receive an eligible rollover distribution from a tax-sheltered annuity plan (section 403(b) plan), you can roll it over into a traditional IRA.

Receipt of property other than money. If you receive property other than money, you can sell the property and roll over the proceeds as discussed earlier.

Rollover from bond purchase plan. If you redeem retirement bonds that were distributed to you under a qualified bond purchase plan, you can roll over tax free into a traditional IRA the part of the amount you receive that is more than your basis in the retirement bonds.

Reporting rollovers from employer plans. Enter the total distribution (before income tax or other deductions were withheld) on Form 1040, line 16a; Form 1040A, line 12a; or Form 1040NR, line 17a. This amount should be shown in box 1 of Form 1099-R. From this amount, subtract any contributions (usually shown in box 5 of Form 1099-R) that were taxable to you when made. From that result, subtract the amount that was rolled over either directly or within 60 days of receiving the distribution. Enter the remaining amount, even if zero, on Form 1040, line 16b; Form 1040A, line 12b; or Form 1040NR, line 17b. Also, enter "Rollover" next to line 16b on Form 1040; line 12b of Form 1040A; or line 17b of Form 1040NR.

Rollover of Exxon Valdez Settlement Income

If you are a qualified taxpayer and you received qualified settlement income, you can contribute all or part of the amount received to an eligible retirement plan which includes a traditional IRA. The amount contributed cannot exceed $100,000 (reduced by the amount of qualified settlement income contributed to an eligible retirement plan in prior tax years) or the amount of qualified settlement income received during the tax year. Contributions for the year can be made until the due date for filing your return, not including extensions.

Qualified settlement income that you contribute to a traditional IRA will be treated as having been rolled over in a direct trustee-to-trustee transfer within 60 days of the distribution. The amount contributed is not included in your income at the time of the contributions and is not considered to be investment in the contract. Also, the 1-year waiting period between rollovers does not apply.

Qualified taxpayer. You are a qualified taxpayer if you are:

- A plaintiff in the civil action *In re Exxon Valdez*, No. 89-095-CV (HRH) (Consolidated) (D.Alaska), or

- The beneficiary of the estate of a plaintiff who acquired the right to receive qualified settlement income and who is the spouse or immediate relative of that plaintiff.

Qualified settlement income. Qualified settlement income is any interest and punitive damage awards which are:

- Otherwise includible in income, and

- Received in connection with the civil action *In re Exxon Valdez*, No. 89-095-CV (HRH) (Consolidated) (D.Alaska) (whether pre- or post-judgment and whether related to a settlement or judgment).

Qualified settlement income can be received as periodic payments or as a lump sum. See Publication 525, Taxable and Nontaxable Income, for information on how to report qualified settlement income.

Transfers Incident To Divorce

If an interest in a traditional IRA is transferred from your spouse or former spouse to you by a divorce or separate maintenance decree or a written document related to such a decree, the interest in the IRA, starting from the date of the transfer, is treated as your IRA. The transfer is tax free. For information about transfers of interests in employer plans, see *Distributions under divorce or similar proceedings (alternate payees)* under *Rollover From Employer's Plan Into an IRA*, earlier.

Transfer methods. There are two commonly-used methods of transferring IRA assets to a spouse or former spouse. The methods are:

- Changing the name on the IRA, and

- Making a direct transfer of IRA assets.

Changing the name on the IRA. If all the assets are to be transferred, you can make the transfer by changing the name on the IRA from your name to the name of your spouse or former spouse.

Direct transfer. Under this method, you direct the trustee of the traditional IRA to transfer the affected assets directly to the trustee of a new or existing traditional IRA set up in the name of your spouse or former spouse.

If your spouse or former spouse is allowed to keep his or her portion of the IRA assets in your existing IRA, you can direct the trustee to transfer the assets you are permitted to keep directly to a new or existing traditional IRA set up in

your name. The name on the IRA containing your spouse's or former spouse's portion of the assets would then be changed to show his or her ownership.

 If the transfer results in a change in the basis of the traditional IRA of either spouse, both spouses must file Form 8606 and follow the directions in the instructions for that form.

Converting From Any Traditional IRA Into a Roth IRA

You can convert amounts from a traditional IRA into a Roth IRA if, for the tax year you make the withdrawal from the traditional IRA, both of the following requirements are met.

- Your modified AGI for Roth IRA purposes (see *Modified AGI* in chapter 2) is not more than $100,000.

- You are not a married individual filing a separate return.

Note. If you did not live with your spouse at any time during the year and you file a separate return, your filing status, for this purpose, is single.

Allowable conversions. You can withdraw all or part of the assets from a traditional IRA and reinvest them (within 60 days) in a Roth IRA. The amount that you withdraw and timely contribute (convert) to the Roth IRA is called a conversion contribution. If properly (and timely) rolled over, the 10% additional tax on early distributions will not apply.

You must roll over into the Roth IRA the same property you received from the traditional IRA. You can roll over part of the withdrawal into a Roth IRA and keep the rest of it. The amount you keep will generally be taxable (except for the part that is a return of nondeductible contributions) and may be subject to the 10% additional tax on early distributions. See *When Can You Withdraw or Use Assets*, later for more information on distributions from traditional IRAs and *Early Distributions*, later, for more information on the tax on early distributions.

Periodic distributions. If you have started taking substantially equal periodic payments from a traditional IRA, you can convert the amounts in the traditional IRA to a Roth IRA and then continue the periodic payments. The 10% additional tax on early distributions will not apply even if the distributions are not qualified distributions (as long as they are part of a series of substantially equal periodic payments).

Required distributions. You cannot convert amounts that must be distributed from your traditional IRA for a particular year (including the calendar year in which you reach age 70½) under the required distribution rules (discussed in this chapter).

Income. You must include in your gross income distributions from a traditional IRA that you would have had to include in income if you had not converted them into a Roth IRA. You do not include in gross income any part of a distribution from a traditional IRA that is a return of your basis, as discussed under *Are Distributions Taxable*, later in this chapter.

 If you must include any amount in your gross income, you may have to increase your withholding or make estimated tax payments. See Publication 505, Tax Withholding and Estimated Tax.

Recharacterizations

You may be able to treat a contribution made to one type of IRA as having been made to a different type of IRA. This is called recharacterizing the contribution.

To recharacterize a contribution, you generally must have the contribution transferred from the first IRA (the one to which it was made) to the second IRA in a trustee-to-trustee transfer. If the transfer is made by the due date (including extensions) for your tax return for the year during which the contribution was made, you can elect to treat the contribution as having been originally made to the second IRA instead of to the first IRA. If you recharacterize your contribution, you must do all three of the following.

- Include in the transfer any net income allocable to the contribution. If there was a loss, the net income you must transfer may be a negative amount.

- Report the recharacterization on your tax return for the year during which the contribution was made.

- Treat the contribution as having been made to the second IRA on the date that it was actually made to the first IRA.

No deduction allowed. You cannot deduct the contribution to the first IRA. Any net income you transfer with the recharacterized contribution is treated as earned in the second IRA. The contribution will not be treated as having been made to the second IRA to the extent any deduction was allowed for the contribution to the first IRA.

Conversion by rollover from traditional to Roth IRA. For recharacterization purposes, if you receive a distribution from a traditional IRA in one tax year and roll it over into a Roth IRA in the next year, but still within 60 days of the distribution from the traditional IRA, treat it as a contribution to the Roth IRA in the year of the distribution from the traditional IRA.

Effect of previous tax-free transfers. If an amount has been moved from one IRA to another in a tax-free transfer, such as a rollover, you generally cannot recharacterize the amount that was transferred. However, see *Traditional IRA mistakenly moved to SIMPLE IRA*, later.

Recharacterizing to a SEP IRA or SIMPLE IRA. Roth IRA conversion contributions from a SEP IRA or SIMPLE IRA can be recharacterized to a SEP IRA or SIMPLE IRA (including the original SEP IRA or SIMPLE IRA).

Traditional IRA mistakenly moved to SIMPLE IRA. If you mistakenly roll over or transfer an amount from a traditional IRA to a SIMPLE IRA, you can later recharacterize the amount as a contribution to another traditional IRA.

Recharacterizing excess contributions. You can recharacterize only actual contributions. If you are applying excess contributions for prior years as current contributions, you can recharacterize them only if the recharacterization would still be timely with respect to the tax year for which the applied contributions were actually made.

Example. You contributed more than you were entitled to in 2008. You cannot recharacterize the excess contributions you made in 2008 after April 15, 2009, because contributions after that date are no longer timely for 2008.

Recharacterizing employer contributions. You cannot recharacterize employer contributions (including elective deferrals) under a SEP or SIMPLE plan as contributions to another IRA. SEPs are discussed in Publication 560. SIMPLE plans are discussed in chapter 3.

Recharacterization not counted as rollover. The recharacterization of a contribution is not treated as a rollover for purposes of the 1-year waiting period described earlier in this chapter under *Rollover From One IRA Into Another*. This is true even if the contribution would have been treated as a rollover contribution by the second IRA if it had been made directly to the second IRA rather than as a result of a recharacterization of a contribution to the first IRA.

Reconversions

You cannot convert and reconvert an amount during the same tax year or, if later, during the 30-day period following a recharacterization. If you reconvert during either of these periods, it will be a failed conversion.

Example. If you convert an amount from a traditional IRA to a Roth IRA and then transfer that amount back to a traditional IRA in a recharacterization in the same year, you may not reconvert that amount from the traditional IRA to a Roth IRA before:

- The beginning of the year following the year in which the amount was converted to a Roth IRA or, if later,

- The end of the 30-day period beginning on the day on which you transfer the amount from the Roth IRA back to a traditional IRA in a recharacterization.

How Do You Recharacterize a Contribution?

To recharacterize a contribution, you must notify both the trustee of the first IRA (the one to which the contribution was actually made) and the trustee of the second IRA (the one to which the contribution is being moved) that you have elected to treat the contribution as having been made to the second IRA rather than the first. You must make the notifications by the date of the transfer. Only one notification is required if both IRAs are maintained by the same trustee. The notification(s) must include all of the following information.

- The type and amount of the contribution to the first IRA that is to be recharacterized.

- The date on which the contribution was made to the first IRA and the year for which it was made.

- A direction to the trustee of the first IRA to transfer in a trustee-to-trustee transfer the amount of the contribution and any net income (or loss) allocable to the contribution to the trustee of the second IRA.

- The name of the trustee of the first IRA and the name of the trustee of the second IRA.

- Any additional information needed to make the transfer.

In most cases, the net income you must transfer is determined by your IRA trustee or custodian. If you need to determine the applicable net income on IRA contributions made after 2008 that are recharacterized, use Worksheet 1-3. See Regulations section 1.408A-5 for more information.

Worksheet 1-3. **Determining the Amount of Net Income Due To an IRA Contribution and Total Amount To Be Recharacterized**

1. Enter the amount of your IRA contribution for 2009 to be recharacterized .... **1.**	
2. Enter the fair market value of the IRA immediately prior to the recharacterization (include any distributions, transfers, or recharacterization made while the contribution was in the account) ..... **2.**	
3. Enter the fair market value of the IRA immediately prior to the time the contribution being recharacterized was made, including the amount of such contribution and any other contributions, transfers, or recharacterizations made while the contribution was in the account...... **3.**	
4. Subtract line 3 from line 2 .... **4.**	
5. Divide line 4 by line 3. Enter the result as a decimal (rounded to at least three places) .... **5.**	
6. Multiply line 1 by line 5. This is the net income attributable to the contribution to be recharacterized .... **6.**	
7. Add lines 1 and 6. This is the amount of the IRA contribution plus the net income attributable to it to be recharacterized .... **7.**	

Example. On April 1, 2009, when her Roth IRA is worth $80,000, Allison makes a $160,000 conversion contribution to the Roth IRA. Subsequently, Allison discovers that she was ineligible to make a Roth conversion contribution in 2009 and so she requests that the $160,000 be recharacterized to a traditional IRA. Pursuant to this request, on April 1, 2010, when the IRA is worth $225,000, the Roth IRA trustee transfers to a traditional IRA the $160,000 plus allocable net income. No other contributions have been made to the Roth IRA and no distributions have been made.

The adjusted opening balance is $240,000 ($80,000 + $160,000) and the adjusted closing balance is $225,000. Thus the net income allocable to the $160,000 is ($10,000) ($160,000 x (($225,000 − $240,000) ÷ $240,000)). Therefore in order to recharacterize the April 1, 2009, $160,000 conversion contribution on April 1, 2010, the Roth IRA trustee must transfer from Allison's Roth IRA to her traditional IRA $150,000 ($160,000 − $10,000). This is shown on the following worksheet.

Worksheet 1-3. **Example—Illustrated**

1. Enter the amount of your IRA contribution for 2009 to be recharacterized .... **1.**	160,000
2. Enter the fair market value of the IRA immediately prior to the recharacterization (include any distributions, transfers, or recharacterization made while the contribution was in the account) ..... **2.**	225,000
3. Enter the fair market value of the IRA immediately prior to the time the contribution being recharacterized was made, including the amount of such contribution and any other contributions, transfers, or recharacterizations made while the contribution was in the account...... **3.**	240,000
4. Subtract line 3 from line 2 .... **4.**	(15,000)
5. Divide line 4 by line 3. Enter the result as a decimal (rounded to at least three places) .... **5.**	(.0625)
6. Multiply line 1 by line 5. This is the net income attributable to the contribution to be recharacterized .... **6.**	(10,000)
7. Add lines 1 and 6. This is the amount of the IRA contribution plus the net income attributable to it to be recharacterized .... **7.**	150,000

Timing. The election to recharacterize and the transfer must both take place on or before the due date (including extensions) for filing your tax return for the year for which the contribution was made to the first IRA.

Extension. Ordinarily you must choose to recharacterize a contribution by the due date of the return or the due date plus extensions. However, if you miss this deadline, you can still recharacterize a contribution if:

- Your return was timely filed for the year the choice should have been made, and

- You take appropriate corrective action within 6 months from the due date of your return excluding extensions. For returns due April 15, 2009, this period ends on October 15, 2009. When the date for doing any act for tax purposes falls on a Saturday, Sunday, or legal holiday, the due date is delayed until the next business day.

Appropriate corrective action consists of:

- Notifying the trustee(s) of your intent to recharacterize,

- Providing the trustee with all necessary information, and

- Having the trustee transfer the contribution.

Once this is done, you must amend your return to show the recharacterization. You have until the regular due date for amending a return to do this. Report the recharacterization on the amended return and write "Filed pursuant to section 301.9100-2" on the return. File the amended return at the same address you filed the original return.

Decedent. The election to recharacterize can be made on behalf of a deceased IRA owner by the executor, administrator, or other person responsible for filing the decedent's final income tax return.

Election cannot be changed. After the transfer has taken place, you cannot change your election to recharacterize.

Same trustee. Recharacterizations made with the same trustee can be made by redesignating the first IRA as the second IRA, rather than transferring the account balance.

Reporting a Recharacterization

If you elect to recharacterize a contribution to one IRA as a contribution to another IRA, you must report the recharacterization on your tax return as directed by Form 8606 and its instructions. You must treat the contribution as having been made to the second IRA.

Example. On June 1, 2008, Christine properly and timely converted her traditional IRAs to a Roth IRA. At the time, she and her husband, Lyle, expected to have modified AGI of $100,000 or less for 2008. In December, Lyle received an unexpected bonus that increased his and Christine's modified AGI to more than $100,000. In January 2009, to make the necessary adjustment to remove the unallowable conversion, Christine set up a traditional IRA with the same trustee. Also in January 2009, she instructed the trustee of the Roth IRA to make a trustee-to-trustee transfer of the conversion contribution made to the Roth IRA (including net income allocable to it since the conversion) to the new traditional IRA. She also notified the trustee that she was electing to recharacterize the contribution to the Roth IRA and treat it as if it had been contributed to the new traditional IRA. Because of the recharacterization, Lyle and Christine have no taxable income from the conversion to report for 2008, and the resulting rollover to a traditional IRA is not treated as a rollover for purposes of the one-rollover-per-year rule.

More than one IRA. If you have more than one IRA, figure the amount to be recharacterized only on the account from which you withdraw the contribution.

When Can You Withdraw or Use Assets?

You can withdraw or use your traditional IRA assets at any time. However, a 10% additional tax generally applies if you withdraw or use IRA assets before you are age 59½. This is explained under *Age 59½ Rule* under *Early Distributions,* later.

You generally can make a tax-free withdrawal of contributions if you do it before the due date for filing your tax return for the year in which you made them. This means that, even if you are under age 59½, the 10% additional tax may not apply. These withdrawals are explained next.

Contributions Returned Before Due Date of Return

If you made IRA contributions in 2008, you can withdraw them tax free by the due date of your return. If you have an extension of time to file your return, you can withdraw them tax free by the extended due date. You can do this if, for each contribution you withdraw, both of the following conditions apply.

- You did not take a deduction for the contribution.

- You withdraw any interest or other income earned on the contribution. You can take into account any loss on the contribution while it was in the IRA when calculating the amount that must be withdrawn. If there was a loss, the net income earned on the contribution may be a negative amount.

In most cases, the net income you must withdraw is determined by the IRA trustee or custodian. If you need to determine the applicable net income on IRA contributions made after 2008 that are returned to you, use Worksheet 1-4. See Regulations section 1.408-11 for more information.

Worksheet 1-4. **Determining the Amount of Net Income Due To an IRA Contribution and Total Amount To Be Withdrawn From the IRA**

1. Enter the amount of your IRA contribution for 2009 to be returned to you........................... **1.** _____
2. Enter the fair market value of the IRA immediately prior to the removal of the contribution, plus the amount of any distributions, transfers, and recharacterizations made while the contribution was in the IRA .... **2.** _____
3. Enter the fair market value of the IRA immediately before the contribution was made, plus the amount of such contribution and any other contributions, transfers, and recharacterizations made while the contribution was in the IRA .... **3.** _____
4. Subtract line 3 from line 2 .... **4.** _____
5. Divide line 4 by line 3. Enter the result as a decimal (rounded to at least three places)...................... **5.** _____
6. Multiply line 1 by line 5. This is the net income attributable to the contribution to be returned................... **6.** _____
7. Add lines 1 and 6. This is the amount of the IRA contribution plus the net income attributable to it to be returned to you........................... **7.** _____

Worksheet 1-4. **Example—Illustrated**

1. Enter the amount of your IRA contribution for 2009 to be returned to you........................... **1.** 400
2. Enter the fair market value of the IRA immediately prior to the removal of the contribution, plus the amount of any distributions, transfers, and recharacterizations made while the contribution was in the IRA **2.** 7,600
3. Enter the fair market value of the IRA immediately before the contribution was made, plus the amount of such contribution and any other contributions, transfers, and recharacterizations made while the contribution was in the IRA **3.** 6,400
4. Subtract line 3 from line 2 .... **4.** 1,200
5. Divide line 4 by line 3. Enter the result as a decimal (rounded to at least three places)...................... **5.** .1875
6. Multiply line 1 by line 5. This is the net income attributable to the contribution to be returned................... **6.** 75
7. Add lines 1 and 6. This is the amount of the IRA contribution plus the net income attributable to it to be returned to you........................... **7.** 475

Last-in first-out rule. If you made more than one regular contribution for the year, your last contribution is considered to be the one that is returned to you first.

Example. On May 1, 2009, when her IRA is worth $4,800, Cathy makes a $1,600 regular contribution to her IRA. Cathy requests that $400 of the May 1, 2009, contribution be returned to her. On February 2, 2010, when the IRA is worth $7,600, the IRA trustee distributes to Cathy the $400 plus net income attributable to the contribution. No other contributions have been made to the IRA for 2009 and no distributions have been made.

The adjusted opening balance is $6,400 ($4,800 + $1,600) and the adjusted closing balance is $7,600. The net income due to the May 1, 2009, contribution is $75 ($400 x ($7,600 − $6,400) ÷ $6,400). Therefore, the total to be distributed on February 2, 2010, is $475. This is shown on the following worksheet.

Earnings Includible in Income

You must include in income any earnings on the contributions you withdraw. Include the earnings in income for the year in which you made the contributions, not the year in which you withdraw them.

> Generally, except for any part of a withdrawal that is a return of nondeductible contributions (basis), any withdrawal of your contributions after the due date (or extended due date) of your return will be treated as a taxable distribution. Excess contributions can also be recovered tax free as discussed under What Acts Result in Penalties or Additional Taxes, later.

Early Distributions Tax

The 10% additional tax on distributions made before you reach age 59½ does not apply to these tax-free withdrawals of your contributions. However, the distribution of interest or other income must be reported on Form 5329 and, unless the distribution qualifies as an exception to the age 59½ rule, it will be subject to this tax. See Early Distributions under What Acts Result in Penalties or Additional Taxes, later.

Excess Contributions Tax

If any part of these contributions is an excess contribution for 2007, it is subject to a 6% excise tax. You will not have to pay the 6% tax if any 2007 excess contribution was withdrawn by April 15, 2008 (plus extensions), and if any 2008 excess contribution is withdrawn by April 15, 2009 (plus extensions). See *Excess Contributions* under *What Acts Result in Penalties or Additional Taxes,* later.

 You may be able to treat a contribution made to one type of IRA as having been made to a different type of IRA. This is called recharacterizing the contribution. See Recharacterizations *earlier for more information.*

Tax-Free Withdrawals of Economic Stimulus Payments

If you received an economic stimulus payment in 2008 that was directly deposited to your traditional IRA, you can choose to treat the payment either as a 2008 contribution (subject to traditional IRA contribution and deduction limits), or you may choose to withdraw all or part of the payment. If you choose to withdraw the payment, or a portion of the payment, that portion is treated as neither contributed to nor distributed from your IRA. The amount withdrawn is not included in your income and is not subject to additional tax or penalty. The withdrawal must be made by the due date for filing your 2008 tax return, including extensions. For most people that would be April 15, 2009.

If you do withdraw all or part of the payment from your IRA, you will receive a Form 1099-R showing the amount of the distribution. Include the distribution on Form 1040, line 15a; Form 1040A, line 11a; or Form 1040NR, line 16a. Do not make an entry on Form 1040, line 15b; Form 1040A, line 11b; or Form 1040NR, line 16b, but enter "ESP" in the space next to the line. For more information, see the instructions for your tax return.

When Must You Withdraw Assets? (Required Minimum Distributions)

You cannot keep funds in a traditional IRA indefinitely. Eventually they must be distributed. If there are no distributions, or if the distributions are not large enough, you may have to pay a 50% excise tax on the amount not distributed as required. See *Excess Accumulations,* later under *What Acts Result in Penalties or Additional Taxes.* The requirements for distributing IRA funds differ, depending on whether you are the IRA owner or the beneficiary of a decedent's IRA.

Required minimum distribution. The amount that must be distributed each year is referred to as the required minimum distribution.

Distributions not eligible for rollover. Amounts that must be distributed (required minimum distributions) during a particular year are not eligible for rollover treatment.

Temporary waiver of required minimum distribution rules for 2009. For 2009, you are not required to take a minimum distribution from your traditional IRA. This waiver applies to IRA participants as well as to beneficiaries. The waiver also applies to you if you turn 70½ in 2009 and delay your 2009 required minimum distribution until April 1, 2010. The waiver does not apply to minimum required distributions for 2008, even if you turned 70½ in 2008 and choose to take the 2008 required minimum distribution by April 1, 2009.

If you are a beneficiary receiving distributions over a 5-year period, you can now waive the distribution for 2009, effectively taking distributions over a 6-year rather than a 5-year period.

If you received a distribution in 2009 that would otherwise be a required minimum distribution, you can roll over that amount into another IRA or eligible retirement plan within 60 days of the distribution. The plan administrator is permitted, but not required to offer a direct rollover of that amount. Also, the distribution is not subject to the 20% income tax withholding requirement.

IRA Owners

If you are the owner of a traditional IRA, you must start receiving distributions from your IRA by April 1 of the year following the year in which you reach age 70½. April 1 of the year following the year in which you reach age 70½ is referred to as the required beginning date.

Distributions by the required beginning date. You must receive at least a minimum amount for each year starting with the year you reach age 70½ (your 70½ year). If you do not (or did not) receive that minimum amount in your 70½ year, then you must receive distributions for your 70½ year by April 1 of the next year.

If an IRA owner dies after reaching age 70½, but before April 1 of the next year, no minimum distribution is required because death occurred before the required beginning date.

If you reach age 70½ in 2009, you are not required to receive your first distribution by April 1, 2010. Your first required distribution however must be made for 2010 by December 31, 2010.

 Even if you begin receiving distributions before you reach age 70½, you must begin calculating and receiving required minimum distributions by your required beginning date.

More than minimum received. If, in any year, you receive more than the required minimum distribution for that year, you will not receive credit for the additional amount when determining the minimum required distributions for future years. This does not mean that you do not reduce your IRA account balance. It means that if you receive more than your required minimum distribution in one year, you cannot treat the excess (the amount that is more than the required minimum distribution) as part of your required minimum distribution for any later year. However, any amount distributed in your 70½ year will be credited toward the amount that must be distributed by April 1 of the following year.

Distributions after the required beginning date. The required minimum distribution for any year after the year you turn 70½ must be made by December 31 of that later year.

Example. You reach age 70½ on August 20, 2008. For 2008, you must receive the required minimum distribution from your IRA by April 1, 2009. For 2009, you are not required to take a required minimum distribution. Your next required minimum distribution would be for 2010 which you must receive by December 31, 2010.

Distributions from individual retirement account. If you are the owner of a traditional IRA that is an individual retirement account, you or your trustee must figure the required minimum distribution for each year. See *Figuring the Owner's Required Minimum Distribution*, later.

Distributions from individual retirement annuities. If your traditional IRA is an individual retirement annuity, special rules apply to figuring the required minimum distribution. For more information on rules for annuities, see Regulations section 1.401(a)(9)-6. These regulations can be read in many libraries and IRS offices.

Change in marital status. For purposes of figuring your required minimum distribution, your marital status is determined as of January 1 of each year. If your spouse is a beneficiary of your IRA on January 1, he or she remains a beneficiary for the entire year even if you get divorced or your spouse dies during the year. For purposes of determining your distribution period, a change in beneficiary is effective in the year following the year of death or divorce.

Change of beneficiary. If your spouse is the sole beneficiary of your IRA, and he or she dies before you, your spouse will not fail to be your sole beneficiary for the year that he or she died solely because someone other than your spouse is named a beneficiary for the rest of that year. However, if you get divorced during the year and change the beneficiary designation on the IRA during that same year, your former spouse will not be treated as the sole beneficiary for that year.

Figuring the Owner's Required Minimum Distribution

Figure your required minimum distribution for each year by dividing the IRA account balance (defined next) as of the close of business on December 31 of the preceding year by the applicable distribution period or life expectancy.

IRA account balance. The IRA account balance is the amount in the IRA at the end of the year preceding the year for which the required minimum distribution is being figured.

Contributions. Contributions increase the account balance in the year they are made. If a contribution for last year is not made until after December 31 of last year, it increases the account balance for this year, but not for last year. Disregard contributions made after December 31 of last year in determining your required minimum distribution for this year.

Outstanding rollovers and recharacterizations. The IRA account balance is adjusted by outstanding rollovers and recharacterizations of Roth IRA conversions that are not in any account at the end of the preceding year.

For a rollover from a qualified plan or another IRA that was not in any account at the end of the preceding year, increase the account balance of the receiving IRA by the rollover amount valued as of the date of receipt.

If a conversion contribution or failed conversion contribution is contributed to a Roth IRA and that amount (plus net income allocable to it) is transferred to another IRA in a subsequent year as a recharacterized contribution, increase the account balance of the receiving IRA by the recharacterized contribution (plus allocable net income) for the year in which the conversion or failed conversion occurred.

Distributions. Distributions reduce the account balance in the year they are made. A distribution for last year made after December 31 of last year reduces the account balance for this year, but not for last year. Disregard distributions made after December 31 of last year in determining your required minimum distribution for this year.

Example 1. Laura was born on October 1, 1937. She is an unmarried participant in a qualified defined contribution plan. She reaches age 70½ in 2008. Her required beginning date is April 1, 2009. As of December 31, 2007, her account balance was $26,500. No rollover or recharacterization amounts were outstanding. Using Table III in Appendix C, the applicable distribution period for someone her age (71) is 26.5 years. Her required minimum distribution for 2008 is $1,000 ($26,500 ÷ 26.5). That amount is distributed to her on April 1, 2009.

For 2009, Laura does not have to take a required minimum distribution. Her next distribution would be for 2010 which she must receive by December 31, 2010.

Example 2. Joe, born October 1, 1937, reached 70½ in 2008. His wife (his beneficiary) turned 56 in September 2008. He must begin receiving distributions by April 1, 2009. Joe's IRA account balance as of December 31, 2007, is $30,100. Because Joe's wife is more than 10 years younger than Joe and is the sole beneficiary of his IRA, Joe uses Table II in Appendix C. Based on their ages at year end (December 31, 2008), the joint life expectancy for Joe (age 71) and his wife (age 56) is 30.1 years. The required minimum distribution for 2008, Joe's first distribution year (his 70½ year), is $1,000 ($30,100 ÷ 30.1). This amount is distributed to Joe on April 1, 2009.

Distribution period. This is the maximum number of years over which you are allowed to take distributions from the IRA. The period to use for 2008 is listed next to your age as of your birthday in 2008 in Table III in Appendix C.

Life expectancy. If you must use Table I, your life expectancy for 2009 is listed in the table next to your age as of your birthday in 2009. If you use Table II, your life expectancy is listed where the row or column containing your age as of your birthday in 2009 intersects with the row or column containing your spouse's age as of his or her birthday in 2009. Both Table I and Table II are in Appendix C.

Distributions during your lifetime. Required minimum distributions during your lifetime are based on a distribution period that generally is determined using Table III (Uniform Lifetime) in Appendix C. However, if the sole beneficiary of your IRA is your spouse who is more than 10 years younger than you, see *Sole beneficiary spouse who is more than 10 years younger,* later.

To figure the required minimum distribution for 2008, divide your account balance at the end of 2007 by the distribution period from the table. This is the distribution period listed next to your age (as of your birthday in 2008) in Table III in Appendix C, unless the sole beneficiary of your IRA is your spouse who is more than 10 years younger than you.

Example. You own a traditional IRA. Your account balance at the end of 2007 was $100,000. You are married and your spouse, who is the sole beneficiary of your IRA, is 6 years younger than you. You turn 75 years old in 2008. You use Table III. Your distribution period is 22.9. Your required minimum distribution for 2008 is $4,367 ($100,000 ÷ 22.9).

Sole beneficiary spouse who is more than 10 years younger. If the sole beneficiary of your IRA is your spouse and your spouse is more than 10 years younger than you, use the life expectancy from Table II (Joint Life and Last Survivor Expectancy).

The life expectancy to use is the joint life and last survivor expectancy listed where the row or column containing your age as of your birthday in 2008 intersects with the row or column containing your spouse's age as of his or her birthday in 2008.

You figure your required minimum distribution for 2008 by dividing your account balance at the end of 2007 by the life expectancy from Table II (Joint Life and Last Survivor Expectancy) in Appendix C.

Example. You own a traditional IRA. Your account balance at the end of 2007 was $100,000. You are married and your spouse, who is the sole beneficiary of your IRA, is 11 years younger than you. You turn 75 in 2008 and your spouse turns 64. You use Table II. Your joint life and last survivor expectancy is 23.6. Your required minimum distribution for 2008 is $4,237 ($100,000 ÷ 23.6). For 2009, you do not have to take a required minimum distribution.

Distributions in the year of the owner's death. The required minimum distribution for the year of the owner's death depends on whether the owner died before the required beginning date.

If the owner died before the required beginning date, see *Owner Died Before Required Beginning Date,* later under *IRA Beneficiaries.*

If the owner died on or after the required beginning date, the required minimum distribution for the year of death generally is based on Table III (Uniform Lifetime) in Appendix C. However, if the sole beneficiary of the IRA is the owner's spouse who is more than 10 years younger than the owner, use the life expectancy from Table II (Joint Life and Last Survivor Expectancy).

Note. You figure the required minimum distribution for the year in which an IRA owner dies as if the owner lived for the entire year.

IRA Beneficiaries

 IRA beneficiaries do not have to take required minimum distributions for 2009.

The rules for determining required minimum distributions for beneficiaries depend on whether the beneficiary is an individual. The rules for individuals are explained below. If the owner's beneficiary is not an individual (for example, if the beneficiary is the owner's estate), see *Beneficiary not an individual,* later.

Surviving spouse. If you are a surviving spouse who is the sole beneficiary of your deceased spouse's IRA, you may elect to be treated as the owner and not as the beneficiary. If you elect to be treated as the owner, you determine the required minimum distribution (if any) as if you were the owner beginning with the year you elect or are deemed to be the owner. However, if you become the owner in the year your deceased spouse died, you are not required to determine the required minimum distribution for that year using your life; rather, you can take the deceased owner's required minimum distribution for that year (to the extent it was not already distributed to the owner before his or her death).

Taking balance within 5 years. A beneficiary who is an individual may be required to take the entire account by the end of the fifth year following the year of the owner's death. If this rule applies, no distribution is required for any year before that fifth year.

For 2009, the distribution can be waived, effectively taking distributions over a 6-year period.

Owner Died On or After Required Beginning Date

If the owner died on or after his or her required beginning date, and you are the designated beneficiary, you generally must base required minimum distributions for years after the year of the owner's death on the longer of:

- Your single life expectancy as shown on Table I, or

- The owner's life expectancy as determined under *Death on or after required beginning date,* under *Beneficiary not an individual,* later.

Appendix A

Owner Died Before Required Beginning Date

If the owner died before his or her required beginning date, base required minimum distributions for years after the year of the owner's death generally on your single life expectancy.

If the owner's beneficiary is not an individual (for example, if the beneficiary is the owner's estate), see *Beneficiary not an individual*, later.

Date the designated beneficiary is determined. Generally, the designated beneficiary is determined on September 30 of the calendar year following the calendar year of the IRA owner's death. In order to be a designated beneficiary, an individual must be a beneficiary as of the date of death. Any person who was a beneficiary on the date of the owner's death, but is not a beneficiary on September 30 of the calendar year following the calendar year of the owner's death (because, for example, he or she disclaimed entitlement or received his or her entire benefit), will not be taken into account in determining the designated beneficiary. An individual may be designated as a beneficiary either by the terms of the plan or, if the plan permits, by affirmative election by the employee specifying the beneficiary.

Death of a beneficiary. If a person who is a beneficiary as of the owner's date of death dies before September 30 of the year following the year of the owner's death without disclaiming entitlement to benefits, that individual, rather than his or her successor beneficiary, continues to be treated as a beneficiary for determining the distribution period.

Death of surviving spouse. If the designated beneficiary is the owner's surviving spouse, and he or she dies before he or she was required to begin receiving distributions, the surviving spouse will be treated as if he or she were the owner of the IRA. However, this rule does not apply to the surviving spouse of a surviving spouse.

More than one beneficiary. If an IRA has more than one beneficiary or a trust is named as beneficiary, see *Miscellaneous Rules for Required Minimum Distributions*, later.

Figuring the Beneficiary's Required Minimum Distribution

How you figure the required minimum distribution depends on whether the beneficiary is an individual or some other entity, such as a trust or estate.

Beneficiary an individual. If the beneficiary is an individual, to figure the required minimum distribution for 2008, divide the account balance at the end of 2007 by the appropriate life expectancy from Table I (Single Life Expectancy) in Appendix C. Determine the appropriate life expectancy as follows.

- *Spouse as sole designated beneficiary.* Use the life expectancy listed in the table next to the spouse's age (as of the spouse's birthday in 2008). If the owner died before the year in which he or she

reached age 70½, distributions to the spouse do not need to begin until the year in which the owner would have reached age 70½.

- *Other designated beneficiary.* Use the life expectancy listed in the table next to the beneficiary's age as of his or her birthday in the year following the year of the owner's death, reduced by one for each year since the year following the owner's death.

Example. Your father died in 2007. You are the designated beneficiary of your father's traditional IRA. You are 53 years old in 2008. You use Table I and see that your life expectancy in 2008 is 31.4. If the IRA was worth $100,000 at the end of 2007, your required minimum distribution for 2008 is $3,185 ($100,000 ÷ 31.4). For 2009, you do not have to take a required minimum distribution. If the value of the IRA at the end of 2009 was again $100,000, your required minimum distribution for 2010 would be $3,401 ($100,000 ÷ 29.4). Instead of taking yearly distributions, you could choose to take the entire distribution in 2013 or earlier.

Beneficiary not an individual. If the beneficiary is not an individual, determine the required minimum distribution for 2008 as follows.

- *Death on or after required beginning date.* Divide the account balance at the end of 2007 by the appropriate life expectancy from Table I (Single Life Expectancy) in Appendix C. Use the life expectancy listed next to the owner's age as of his or her birthday in the year of death, reduced by one for each year after the year of death.

- *Death before required beginning date.* The entire account must be distributed by the end of the fifth year following the year of the owner's death. No distribution is required for any year before that fifth year.

For 2009, the distribution can be waived, effectively taking distributions over a 6-year period.

Example. The owner died in 2007 at the age of 80. The owner's traditional IRA went to his estate. The account balance at the end of 2007 was $100,000. In 2008, the required minimum distribution was $10,870 ($100,000 ÷ 9.2). (The owner's life expectancy in the year of death, 10.2, reduced by one.) If the owner had died in 2007 at the age of 70, the entire account would have to be distributed by the end of 2013.

Which Table Do You Use To Determine Your Required Minimum Distribution?

 For 2009, you do not have to take a required minimum distribution.

There are three different tables. You use only one of them to determine your required minimum distribution for each traditional IRA. Determine which one to use as follows.

Reminder. In using the tables for lifetime distributions, marital status is determined as of January 1 each year. Divorce or death after January 1 is generally disregarded until the next year. However, if you divorce and change the beneficiary designation in the same year, your former spouse cannot be considered your sole beneficiary for that year.

Table I (Single Life Expectancy). Use Table I for years after the year of the owner's death if either of the following apply.

- You are an individual and a designated beneficiary, but not both the owner's surviving spouse and sole designated beneficiary.

- You are not an individual and the owner died on or after the required beginning date.

Surviving spouse. If you are the owner's surviving spouse and sole designated beneficiary, and the owner had not reached age 70½ when he or she died, and you do not elect to be treated as the owner of the IRA, you do not have to take distributions (and use *Table I*) until the year in which the owner would have reached age 70½.

Table II (Joint Life and Last Survivor Expectancy). Use Table II if you are the IRA owner and your spouse is both your sole designated beneficiary and more than 10 years younger than you.

Note. Use this table in the year of the owner's death if the owner died after the required beginning date and this is the table that would have been used had he or she not died.

Table III (Uniform Lifetime). Use Table III if you are the IRA owner and your spouse is not both the sole designated beneficiary of your IRA and more than 10 years younger than you.

Note. Use this table in the year of the owner's death if the owner died after the required beginning date and this is the table that would have been used had he or she not died.

No table. Do not use any of the tables if the designated beneficiary is not an individual and the owner died before the required beginning date. In this case, the entire distribution must be made by the end of the fifth year following the year of the IRA owner's death.

This rule also applies if there is no designated beneficiary named by September 30 of the year following the year of the IRA owner's death.

5-year rule. If you are an individual, you can elect to take the entire account by the end of the fifth year following the year of the owner's death. If you make this election, do not use a table.

For 2009, the distribution can be waived, effectively taking distributions over a 6-year period.

What Age(s) Do You Use With the Table(s)?

The age or ages to use with each table are explained below.

Table I (Single Life Expectancy). If you are a designated beneficiary figuring your first distribution, use your age as of your birthday in the year distributions must begin. This is usually the calendar year immediately following the calendar year of the owner's death. After the first distribution year, reduce your life expectancy by one for each subsequent year. If you are the owner's surviving spouse and sole designated beneficiary, this is generally the year in which the owner would have reached age 70½. After the first distribution year, use your age as of your birthday in each subsequent year.

Example. You are the owner's designated beneficiary figuring your first required minimum distribution. Distributions must begin in 2008. You become 57 years old in 2008. You use Table I. Your distribution period for 2008 is 27.9 years. For 2009, you do not have to take a required minimum distribution. Your distribution period for 2010 is 25.9 (27.9 – 2).

Example. You are the owner's surviving spouse and the sole designated beneficiary. The owner would have turned age 70½ in 2008. Distributions must begin in 2008. You become 69 years old in 2008. You use Table 1. Your distribution period for 2008 is 17.8. For 2009, you do not have to take a required minimum distribution. For 2010, when you are 71 years old, your distribution period is 16.3.

No designated beneficiary. In some cases, you need to use the owner's life expectancy. You need to use it when the owner dies on or after the required beginning date and there is no designated beneficiary as of September 30 of the year following the year of the owner's death. In this case, use the owner's life expectancy for his or her age as of the owner's birthday in the year of death and reduce it by one for each subsequent year.

Table II (Joint Life and Last Survivor Expectancy). For your first distribution by the required beginning date, use your age and the age of your designated beneficiary as of your birthdays in the year you become age 70½. Your combined life expectancy is at the intersection of your ages.

If you are figuring your required minimum distribution for 2008, use your ages as of your birthdays in 2008. For each subsequent year, use your and your spouse's ages as of your birthdays in the subsequent year. For 2009, you do not have to take a required minimum distribution.

Table III (Uniform Lifetime). For your first distribution by your required beginning date, use your age as of your birthday in the year you become age 70½.

If you are figuring your required minimum distribution for 2008, use your age as of your birthday in 2008. For each subsequent year, use your age as of your birthday in the subsequent year. For 2009, you do not have to take a required minimum distribution.

Miscellaneous Rules for Required Minimum Distributions

The following rules may apply to you.

Installments allowed. The yearly required minimum distribution can be taken in a series of installments (monthly, quarterly, etc.) as long as the total distributions for the year are at least as much as the minimum required amount.

More than one IRA. If you have more than one traditional IRA, you must determine a separate required minimum distribution for each IRA. However, you can total these minimum amounts and take the total from any one or more of the IRAs.

Example. Sara, born August 1, 1937, became 70½ on February 1, 2008. She has two traditional IRAs. She must begin receiving her IRA distributions by April 1, 2009. On December 31, 2007, Sara's account balance from IRA A was $10,000; her account balance from IRA B was $20,000. Sara's brother, age 64 as of his birthday in 2008, is the beneficiary of IRA A. Her husband, age 78 as of his birthday in 2008, is the beneficiary of IRA B.

Sara's required minimum distribution from IRA A is $377 ($10,000 ÷ 26.5 (the distribution period for age 71 per Table III)). The amount of the required minimum distribution from IRA B is $755 ($20,000 ÷ 26.5). The amount that must be withdrawn by Sara from her IRA accounts by April 1, 2009, is $1,132 ($377 + $755).

For 2009, Sara does not have to take a required minimum distribution from any of her IRAs.

More than minimum received. If, in any year, you receive more than the required minimum amount for that year, you will not receive credit for the additional amount when determining the minimum required amounts for future years. This does not mean that you do not reduce your IRA account balance. It means that if you receive more than your required minimum distribution in one year, you cannot treat the excess (the amount that is more than the required minimum distribution) as part of your required minimum distribution for any later year. However, any amount distributed in your 70½ year will be credited toward the amount that must be distributed by April 1 of the following year.

Multiple individual beneficiaries. If as of September 30 of the year following the year in which the owner dies there is more than one beneficiary, the beneficiary with the shortest life expectancy will be the designated beneficiary if both of the following apply.

- All of the beneficiaries are individuals, and
- The account or benefit has not been divided into separate accounts or shares for each beneficiary.

Separate accounts. Separate accounts with separate beneficiaries can be set up at any time, either before or after the owner's required beginning date. If separate accounts with separate beneficiaries are set up, the separate accounts are not combined for required minimum distribution purposes until the year after the separate accounts are established, or if later, the date of death. As a general rule, the required minimum distribution rules separately apply to each account. However, the distribution period for an account is separately determined (disregarding beneficiaries of the other account(s)) only if the account was set up by the end of the year following the year of the owner's death.

The separate account rules cannot be used by beneficiaries of a trust.

Trust as beneficiary. A trust cannot be a designated beneficiary even if it is a named beneficiary. However, the beneficiaries of a trust will be treated as having been designated as beneficiaries if all of the following are true.

1. The trust is a valid trust under state law, or would be but for the fact that there is no corpus.

2. The trust is irrevocable or will, by its terms, become irrevocable upon the death of the owner.

3. The beneficiaries of the trust who are beneficiaries with respect to the trust's interest in the owner's benefit are identifiable from the trust instrument.

4. The IRA trustee, custodian, or issuer has been provided with either a copy of the trust instrument with the agreement that if the trust instrument is amended, the administrator will be provided with a copy of the amendment within a reasonable time, or all of the following.

   a. A list of all of the beneficiaries of the trust (including contingent and remaindermen beneficiaries with a description of the conditions on their entitlement).

   b. Certification that, to the best of the owner's knowledge, the list is correct and complete and that the requirements of (1), (2), and (3) above, are met.

   c. An agreement that, if the trust instrument is amended at any time in the future, the owner will, within a reasonable time, provide to the IRA trustee, custodian, or issuer corrected certifications to the extent that the amendment changes any information previously certified.

   d. An agreement to provide a copy of the trust instrument to the IRA trustee, custodian, or issuer upon demand.

The deadline for providing the beneficiary documentation to the IRA trustee, custodian, or issuer is October 31 of the year following the year of the owner's death.

If the beneficiary of the trust is another trust and the above requirements for both trusts are met, the beneficiaries of the other trust will be treated as having been designated as beneficiaries for purposes of determining the distribution period.

The separate account rules cannot be used by beneficiaries of a trust.

Annuity distributions from an insurance company. Special rules apply if you receive distributions from your traditional IRA as an annuity purchased from an insurance company. See Regulations sections 1.401(a)(9)-6 and 54.4974-2. These regulations can be found in many libraries and IRS offices.

Are Distributions Taxable?

In general, distributions from a traditional IRA are taxable in the year you receive them.

Failed financial institutions. Distributions from a traditional IRA are taxable in the year you receive them even if they are made without your consent by a state agency as receiver of an insolvent savings institution. This means you must include such distributions in your gross income unless you roll them over. For an exception to the 1-year waiting period rule for rollovers of certain distributions from failed financial institutions, see *Exception* under *Rollover From One IRA Into Another,* earlier.

Exceptions. Exceptions to distributions from traditional IRAs being taxable in the year you receive them are:

- Rollovers,

- Qualified charitable distributions, discussed below,

- Tax-free withdrawals of contributions, discussed earlier, and

- The return of nondeductible contributions, discussed later under *Distributions Fully or Partly Taxable.*

 Although a conversion of a traditional IRA is considered a rollover for Roth IRA purposes, it is not an exception to the rule that distributions from a traditional IRA are taxable in the year you receive them. Conversion distributions are includible in your gross income subject to this rule and the special rules for conversions explained earlier and in chapter 2.

Qualified charitable distributions. A qualified charitable distribution (QCD) is a nontaxable distribution made directly by the trustee of your IRA (other than a SEP or SIMPLE IRA) to an organization eligible to receive tax-deductible contributions. You must have been at least age 70½ when the distribution was made. Also, you must have the same type of acknowledgement of your contribution that you would need to claim a deduction for a charitable contribution. See *Records To Keep* in Publication 526, *Charitable Contributions.* Your total QCDs for the year cannot be more than $100,000. If you file a joint return, your spouse can also have a QCD of up to $100,000. However, the amount of the QCD is limited to the amount of the distribution that would otherwise be included in income. If your IRA includes nondeductible contributions, the distribution is first considered to be paid out of otherwise taxable income.

 A qualified charitable distribution will count towards your minimum required distribution.

Example. On November 1, 2008, Jeff, age 75, directed the trustee of his IRA to make a distribution of $25,000 directly to a qualified 501(c)(3) organization (a charitable organization eligible to receive tax-deductible contributions). The total value of Jeff's IRA is $30,000 and consists of $20,000 of deductible contributions and earnings and $10,000 of nondeductible contributions (basis). Since Jeff is at least age 70½ and the distribution is made directly by the trustee to a qualified organization, the part of the distribution that would otherwise be includible in Jeff's income ($20,000) is a qualified charitable distribution (QCD). In this case, Jeff has made a QCD of $20,000 (his deductible contributions and earnings). Because Jeff made a distribution of nondeductible contributions from his IRA, he must file Form 8606, Nondeductible IRAs, with his return. Jeff includes the total distribution ($25,000) on line 15a of Form 1040. He completes Form 8606 to determine the amount to enter on line 15b of Form 1040 and the remaining basis in his IRA. Jeff enters -0- on line 15b. He also enters "QCD" next to line 15b to indicate a qualified charitable distribution. After the distribution, his basis in his IRA is $5,000. If Jeff itemizes his deductions and files Schedule A with Form 1040, the $5,000 portion of the distribution attributable to the nondeductible contributions can be deducted as a charitable contribution, subject to AGI limits. He cannot take a charitable contribution deduction for the $20,000 portion of the distribution that was not included in his income.

 You cannot claim a charitable contribution deduction for any QCD not included in your income.

Ordinary income. Distributions from traditional IRAs that you include in income are taxed as ordinary income.

No special treatment. In figuring your tax, you cannot use the 10-year tax option or capital gain treatment that applies to lump-sum distributions from qualified employer plans.

Distributions Fully or Partly Taxable

Distributions from your traditional IRA may be fully or partly taxable, depending on whether your IRA includes any nondeductible contributions.

Fully taxable. If only deductible contributions were made to your traditional IRA (or IRAs, if you have more than one), you have no basis in your IRA. Because you have no basis in your IRA, any distributions are fully taxable when received. See *Reporting and Withholding Requirements for Taxable Amounts,* later.

Partly taxable. If you made nondeductible contributions or rolled over any after-tax amounts to any of your traditional IRAs, you have a cost basis (investment in the contract) equal to the amount of those contributions. These nondeductible contributions are not taxed when they are distributed to you. They are a return of your investment in your IRA.

Only the part of the distribution that represents nondeductible contributions and rolled over after-tax amounts (your cost basis) is tax free. If nondeductible contributions have been made or after-tax amounts have been rolled over to your IRA, distributions consist partly of nondeductible contributions (basis) and partly of deductible contributions, earnings, and gains (if there are any). Until all of your basis has been distributed, each distribution is partly nontaxable and partly taxable.

Form 8606. You must complete Form 8606, and attach it to your return, if you receive a distribution from a traditional IRA and have ever made nondeductible contributions or rolled over after-tax amounts to any of your traditional IRAs. Using the form, you will figure the nontaxable distributions for 2008, and your total IRA basis for 2008 and earlier years. See the illustrated Forms 8606 in this chapter.

Note. If you are required to file Form 8606, but you are not required to file an income tax return, you still must file Form 8606. Complete Form 8606, sign it, and send it to the IRS at the time and place you would otherwise file an income tax return.

Figuring the Nontaxable and Taxable Amounts

If your traditional IRA includes nondeductible contributions and you received a distribution from it in 2008, you must use Form 8606 to figure how much of your 2008 IRA distribution is tax free.

Contribution and distribution in the same year. If you received a distribution in 2008 from a traditional IRA and you also made contributions to a traditional IRA for 2008 that may not be fully deductible because of the income limits, you can use Worksheet 1-5 to figure how much of your 2008 IRA distribution is tax free and how much is taxable. Then you can figure the amount of nondeductible contributions to report on Form 8606. Follow the instructions under *Reporting your nontaxable distribution on Form 8606,* next, to figure your remaining basis after the distribution.

Reporting your nontaxable distribution on Form 8606. To report your nontaxable distribution and to figure the remaining basis in your traditional IRA after distributions, you must complete Worksheet 1-5 before completing Form 8606. Then follow these steps to complete Form 8606.

1. Use Worksheet 1-2 or the IRA Deduction Worksheet in the Form 1040 or 1040A instructions to figure your deductible contributions to traditional IRAs to report on Form 1040, line 32; Form 1040A, line 17; or Form 1040NR, line 31.

2. After you complete Worksheet 1-2 or the IRA deduction worksheet in the form instructions, enter your

nondeductible contributions to traditional IRAs on line 1 of Form 8606.

3. Complete lines 2 through 5 of Form 8606.

4. If line 5 of Form 8606 is less than line 8 of Worksheet 1-5, complete lines 6 through 15 of Form 8606 and stop here.

5. If line 5 of Form 8606 is equal to or greater than line 8 of Worksheet 1-5, follow instructions 6 and 7, next. Do not complete lines 6 through 12 of Form 8606.

6. Enter the amount from line 8 of Worksheet 1-5 on lines 13 and 17 of Form 8606.

7. Complete line 14 of Form 8606.

8. Enter the amount from line 9 of Worksheet 1-5 (or, if you entered an amount on line 11, the amount from that line) on line 15a of Form 8606.

Example. Rose Green has made the following contributions to her traditional IRAs.

Year	Deductible	Nondeductible
2001	2,000	-0-
2002	2,000	-0-
2003	2,000	-0-
2004	1,000	-0-
2005	1,000	-0-
2006	1,000	-0-
2007	700	300
Totals	$9,700	$300

In 2008, Rose, whose IRA deduction for that year may be reduced or eliminated, makes a $2,000 contribution that may be partly nondeductible. She also receives a distribution of $5,000 for conversion to a Roth IRA. She completed the conversion before December 31, 2008, and did not recharacterize any contributions. At the end of 2008, the fair market values of her accounts, including earnings, total $20,000. She did not receive any tax-free distributions in earlier years. The amount she includes in income for 2008 is figured on Worksheet 1-5, Figuring the Taxable Part of Your IRA Distribution—Illustrated.

The Form 8606 for Rose, Illustrated, shows the information required when you need to use Worksheet 1-5 to figure your nontaxable distribution. Assume that the $500 entered on Form 8606, line 1, is the amount Rose figured using instructions 1 and 2 given earlier under *Reporting your nontaxable distribution on Form 8606.*

Recognizing Losses on Traditional IRA Investments

If you have a loss on your traditional IRA investment, you can recognize (include) the loss on your income tax return, but only when all the amounts in all your traditional IRA accounts have been distributed to you and the total distributions are less than your unrecovered basis, if any.

Your basis is the total amount of the nondeductible contributions in your traditional IRAs.

Chapter 1 **Traditional IRAs** Page 41

You claim the loss as a miscellaneous itemized deduction, subject to the 2%-of-adjusted-gross-income limit that applies to certain miscellaneous itemized deductions on Schedule A, Form 1040. Any such losses are added back to taxable income for purposes of calculating the alternative minimum tax.

Example. Bill King has made nondeductible contributions to a traditional IRA totaling $2,000, giving him a basis at the end of 2007 of $2,000. By the end of 2008, his IRA earns $400 in interest income. In that year, Bill receives a distribution of $600 ($500 basis + $100 interest), reducing the value of his IRA to $1,800 ($2,000 + $400 − $600) at year's end. Bill figures the taxable part of the distribution and his remaining basis on Form 8606 (illustrated).

In 2009, Bill's IRA has a loss of $500. At the end of that year, Bill's IRA balance is $1,300 ($1,800 − $500). Bill's remaining basis in his IRA is $1,500 ($2,000 − $500). Bill receives the $1,300 balance remaining in the IRA. He can claim a loss for 2009 of $200 (the $1,500 basis minus the $1,300 distribution of the IRA balance).

Other Special IRA Distribution Situations

Two other special IRA distribution situations are discussed below.

Distribution of an annuity contract from your IRA account. You can tell the trustee or custodian of your traditional IRA account to use the amount in the account to buy an annuity contract for you. You are not taxed when you receive the annuity contract (unless the annuity contract is being converted to an annuity held by a Roth IRA). You are taxed when you start receiving payments under that annuity contract.

Tax treatment. If only deductible contributions were made to your traditional IRA since it was set up (this includes all your traditional IRAs, if you have more than one), the annuity payments are fully taxable.

If any of your traditional IRAs include both deductible and nondeductible contributions, the annuity payments are taxed as explained earlier under *Distributions Fully or Partly Taxable*.

Cashing in retirement bonds. When you cash in retirement bonds, you are taxed on the entire amount you receive. Unless you have already cashed them in, you will be taxed on the entire value of your bonds in the year in which you reach age 70½. The value of the bonds is the amount you would have received if you had cashed them in at the end of that year. When you later cash in the bonds, you will not be taxed again.

Reporting and Withholding Requirements for Taxable Amounts

If you receive a distribution from your traditional IRA, you will receive Form 1099-R, or a similar statement. IRA distributions are shown in boxes 1 and 2a of Form 1099-R. A number or letter code in box 7 tells you what type of distribution you received from your IRA.

Number codes. Some of the number codes are explained below. All of the codes are explained in the instructions for recipients on Form 1099-R.

1—Early distribution, no known exception.

2—Early distribution, exception applies.

3—Disability.

4—Death.

5—Prohibited transaction.

7—Normal distribution.

8—Excess contributions plus earnings/excess deferrals (and/or earnings) taxable in 2008.

 If code 1, 5, or 8 appears on your Form 1099-R, you are probably subject to a penalty or additional tax. If code 1 appears, see Early Distributions, later. If code 5 appears, see Prohibited Transactions, later. If code 8 appears, see Excess Contributions, later.

Letter codes. Some of the letter codes are explained below. All of the codes are explained in the instructions for recipients on Form 1099-R.

B—Designated Roth account distribution.

D—Excess contributions plus earnings/excess deferrals taxable in 2006.

G—Direct rollover of a distribution (other than a designated Roth account distribution) to a qualified plan, a section 403(b) plan, a governmental section 457(b) plan or an IRA.

J—Early distribution from a Roth IRA.

N—Recharacterized IRA contribution made for 2008 and recharacterized in 2008.

P—Excess contributions plus earnings/excess deferrals taxable in 2007.

Q—Qualified distribution from a Roth IRA.

R—Recharacterized IRA contribution made for 2007 and recharacterized in 2008.

S—Early distribution from a SIMPLE IRA in the first 2 years, no known exception.

T—Roth IRA distribution, exception applies.

If the distribution shown on Form 1099-R is from your IRA, SEP IRA, or SIMPLE IRA, the small box in box 7 (labeled *IRA/SEP/SIMPLE*) should be marked with an "X."

Worksheet 1-5. Figuring the Taxable Part of Your IRA Distribution
Use only if you made contributions to a traditional IRA for 2008 and have to figure the taxable part of your 2008 distributions to determine your modified AGI. See *Limit if Covered by Employer Plan*. Form 8606 and the related instructions will be needed when using this worksheet.
Note. When used in this worksheet, the term **outstanding rollover** refers to an amount distributed from a traditional IRA as part of a rollover that, as of December 31, 2008, had not yet been reinvested in another traditional IRA, but was still eligible to be rolled over tax free.

1. Enter the basis in your traditional IRAs as of December 31, 2007 . . . .   **1.** _____

2. Enter the total of all contributions made to your traditional IRAs during 2008 and all contributions made during 2009 that were for 2008, **whether or not deductible**. Do not include rollover contributions properly rolled over into IRAs. Also, do not include certain returned contributions described in the instructions for line 7, Part I, of Form 8606. . . . .   **2.** _____

3. Add lines 1 and 2 . . . .   **3.** _____

4. Enter the value of all your traditional IRAs as of December 31, 2008 (include any outstanding rollovers from traditional IRAs to other traditional IRAs). Subtract any repayments of qualified disaster recovery assistance or recovery assistance distributions . . . .   **4.** _____

5. Enter the total distributions from traditional IRAs (including amounts converted to Roth IRAs that will be shown on line 16 of Form 8606) received in 2008. (Do not include outstanding rollovers included on line 4 or any rollovers between traditional IRAs completed by December 31, 2008. Also, do not include certain returned contributions described in the instructions for line 7, Part I, of Form 8606.) Include any repayments of qualified disaster recovery assistance or recovery assistance distributions . . . .   **5.** _____

6. Add lines 4 and 5 . . . .   **6.** _____

7. Divide line 3 by line 6. Enter the result as a decimal (rounded to at least three places).

   If the result is 1.000 or more, enter 1.000 . . . .   **7.** _____

8. **Nontaxable portion of the distribution.**
   Multiply line 5 by line 7. Enter the result here and on lines 13 and 17 of Form 8606 . . .   **8.** _____

9. **Taxable portion of the distribution (before adjustment for conversions).**
   Subtract line 8 from line 5. Enter the result here and if there are no amounts converted to Roth IRAs, **stop here** and enter the result on line 15a of Form 8606 . . . .   **9.** _____

10. Enter the amount included on line 9 that is allocable to amounts converted to Roth IRAs by December 31, 2008. (See *Note* at the end of this worksheet.) Enter here and on line 18 of Form 8606 . . . .   **10.** _____

11. **Taxable portion of the distribution (after adjustments for conversions).**
    Subtract line 10 from line 9. Enter the result here and on line 15a of Form 8606 . . . . .   **11.** _____

Note. If the amount on line 5 of this worksheet includes an amount converted to a Roth IRA by December 31, 2008, you must determine the percentage of the distribution allocable to the conversion. To figure the percentage, divide the amount converted (from line 16 of Form 8606) by the total distributions shown on line 5. To figure the amounts to include on line 10 of this worksheet and on line 18, Part II of Form 8606, multiply line 9 of the worksheet by the percentage you figured.

 If code D, J, P, or S appears on your Form 1099-R, you are probably subject to a penalty or additional tax. If code D appears, see Excess Contributions, later. If code J appears, see Early Distributions, later. If code P appears, see Excess Contributions, later. If code S appears, see Additional Tax on Early Distributions in chapter 3.

Withholding. Federal income tax is withheld from distributions from traditional IRAs unless you choose not to have tax withheld.

The amount of tax withheld from an annuity or a similar periodic payment is based on your marital status and the number of withholding allowances you claim on your withholding certificate (Form W-4P). If you have not filed a certificate, tax will be withheld as if you are a married individual claiming three withholding allowances.

Generally, tax will be withheld at a 10% rate on nonperiodic distributions.

IRA distributions delivered outside the United States. In general, if you are a U.S. citizen or resident

Worksheet 1-5. **Figuring the Taxable Part of Your IRA Distribution—Illustrated**

Use only if you made contributions to a traditional IRA for 2008 and have to figure the taxable part of your 2008 distributions to determine your modified AGI. See *Limit if Covered by Employer Plan.* Form 8606 and the related instructions will be needed when using this worksheet.

Note. When used in this worksheet, the term **outstanding rollover** refers to an amount distributed from a traditional IRA as part of a rollover that, as of December 31, 2008, had not yet been reinvested in another traditional IRA, but was still eligible to be rolled over tax free.

1. Enter the basis in your traditional IRAs as of December 31, 2007 . . . . **1.**	300
2. Enter the total of all contributions made to your traditional IRAs during 2008 and all contributions made during 2009 that were for 2008, **whether or not deductible**. Do not include rollover contributions properly rolled over into IRAs. Also, do not include certain returned contributions described in the instructions for line 7, Part I, of Form 8606. . . . . . . **2.**	2,000
3. Add lines 1 and 2 . . . . **3.**	2,300
4. Enter the value of all your traditional IRAs as of December 31, 2008 (include any outstanding rollovers from traditional IRAs to other traditional IRAs). Subtract any repayments of qualified disaster recovery assistance or recovery assistance distributions **4.**	20,000
5. Enter the total distributions from traditional IRAs (including amounts converted to Roth IRAs that will be shown on line 16 of Form 8606) received in 2008. (Do not include outstanding rollovers included on line 4 or any rollovers between traditional IRAs completed by December 31, 2008. Also, do not include certain returned contributions described in the instructions for line 7, Part I, of Form 8606.) Include any repayments of qualified disaster recovery assistance or recovery assistance distributions . . . . **5.**	5,000
6. Add lines 4 and 5 . . . . **6.**	25,000
7. Divide line 3 by line 6. Enter the result as a decimal (rounded to at least three places). If the result is 1.000 or more, enter 1.000 . . . . **7.**	.092
8. **Nontaxable portion of the distribution.** Multiply line 5 by line 7. Enter the result here and on lines 13 and 17 of Form 8606 . . . . . . **8.**	460
9. **Taxable portion of the distribution (before adjustment for conversions).** Subtract line 8 from line 5. Enter the result here and if there are no amounts converted to Roth IRAs, **stop here** and enter the result on line 15a of Form 8606 . . . . **9.**	4,540
10. Enter the amount included on line 9 that is allocable to amounts converted to Roth IRAs by December 31, 2008. (See *Note* at the end of this worksheet.) Enter here and on line 18 of Form 8606. . . . . **10.**	4,540
11. **Taxable portion of the distribution (after adjustments for conversions).** Subtract line 10 from line 9. Enter the result here and on line 15a of Form 8606 . . . . **11.**	0

Note. If the amount on line 5 of this worksheet includes an amount converted to a Roth IRA by December 31, 2008, you must determine the percentage of the distribution allocable to the conversion. To figure the percentage, divide the amount converted (from line 16 of Form 8606) by the total distributions shown on line 5. To figure the amounts to include on line 10 of this worksheet and on line 18, Part II of Form 8606, multiply line 9 of the worksheet by the percentage you figured.

alien and your home address is outside the United States or its possessions, you cannot choose exemption from withholding on distributions from your traditional IRA.

To choose exemption from withholding, you must certify to the payer under penalties of perjury that you are not a U.S. citizen, a resident alien of the United States, or a tax-avoidance expatriate.

Even if this election is made, the payer must withhold tax at the rates prescribed for nonresident aliens.

More information. For more information on withholding on pensions and annuities, see *Pensions and Annuities* in chapter 1 of Publication 505, Tax Withholding and

Estimated Tax. For more information on withholding on nonresident aliens and foreign entities, see Publication 515, Withholding of Tax on Nonresident Aliens and Foreign Entities.

Reporting taxable distributions on your return. Report fully taxable distributions, including early distributions, on Form 1040, line 15b (no entry is required on line 15a); Form 1040A, line 11b (no entry is required on line 11a); or Form 1040NR, line 16b (no entry is required on line 16a). If only part of the distribution is taxable, enter the total amount on Form 1040, line 15a; Form 1040A, line 11a; or Form 1040NR, line 16a, and enter the taxable part on

Form 1040, line 15b; Form 1040A, line 11b; or Form 1040NR, line 16b. You cannot report distributions on Form 1040EZ or Form 1040NR-EZ.

Estate tax. Generally, the value of an annuity or other payment receivable by any beneficiary of a decedent's traditional IRA that represents the part of the purchase price contributed by the decedent (or by his or her former employer(s)), must be included in the decedent's gross estate. For more information, see the instructions for Schedule I, Form 706, United States Estate (and Generation-Skipping Transfer) Tax Return.

In 2009, repeat footnote at bottom of page 1 of Rose Green's illustrated F8606 at the bottom of page 2 of her 8606.

What Acts Result in Penalties or Additional Taxes?

The tax advantages of using traditional IRAs for retirement savings can be offset by additional taxes and penalties if you do not follow the rules. There are additions to the regular tax for using your IRA funds in prohibited transactions. There are also additional taxes for the following activities.

- Investing in collectibles.
- Making excess contributions.
- Taking early distributions.
- Allowing excess amounts to accumulate (failing to take required distributions).

There are penalties for overstating the amount of nondeductible contributions and for failure to file Form 8606, if required.

This chapter discusses those acts that you should avoid and the additional taxes and other costs, including loss of IRA status, that apply if you do not avoid those acts.

Prohibited Transactions

Generally, a prohibited transaction is any improper use of your traditional IRA account or annuity by you, your beneficiary, or any disqualified person.

Disqualified persons include your fiduciary and members of your family (spouse, ancestor, lineal descendant, and any spouse of a lineal descendant).

The following are examples of prohibited transactions with a traditional IRA.

- Borrowing money from it.
- Selling property to it.
- Receiving unreasonable compensation for managing it.
- Using it as security for a loan.
- Buying property for personal use (present or future) with IRA funds.

Fiduciary. For these purposes, a fiduciary includes anyone who does any of the following.

- Exercises any discretionary authority or discretionary control in managing your IRA or exercises any authority or control in managing or disposing of its assets.
- Provides investment advice to your IRA for a fee, or has any authority or responsibility to do so.
- Has any discretionary authority or discretionary responsibility in administering your IRA.

Effect on an IRA account. Generally, if you or your beneficiary engages in a prohibited transaction in connection with your traditional IRA account at any time during the year, the account stops being an IRA as of the first day of that year.

Effect on you or your beneficiary. If your account stops being an IRA because you or your beneficiary engaged in a prohibited transaction, the account is treated as distributing all its assets to you at their fair market values on the first day of the year. If the total of those values is more than your basis in the IRA, you will have a taxable gain that is includible in your income. For information on figuring your gain and reporting it in income, see *Are Distributions Taxable*, earlier. The distribution may be subject to additional taxes or penalties.

Borrowing on an annuity contract. If you borrow money against your traditional IRA annuity contract, you must include in your gross income the fair market value of the annuity contract as of the first day of your tax year. You may have to pay the 10% additional tax on early distributions, discussed later.

Pledging an account as security. If you use a part of your traditional IRA account as security for a loan, that part is treated as a distribution and is included in your gross income. You may have to pay the 10% additional tax on early distributions, discussed later.

Trust account set up by an employer or an employee association. Your account or annuity does not lose its IRA treatment if your employer or the employee association with whom you have your traditional IRA engages in a prohibited transaction.

Owner participation. If you participate in the prohibited transaction with your employer or the association, your account is no longer treated as an IRA.

Taxes on prohibited transactions. If someone other than the owner or beneficiary of a traditional IRA engages in a prohibited transaction, that person may be liable for certain taxes. In general, there is a 15% tax on the amount of the prohibited transaction and a 100% additional tax if the transaction is not corrected.

Loss of IRA status. If the traditional IRA ceases to be an IRA because of a prohibited transaction by you or your beneficiary, you or your beneficiary are not liable for these excise taxes. However, you or your beneficiary may have

Form **8606**

Department of the Treasury
Internal Revenue Service (99)

Nondeductible IRAs

► See separate instructions.

► Attach to Form 1040, Form 1040A, or Form 1040NR.

OMB No. 1545-0074

20**08**

Attachment
Sequence No. **48**

Name. If married, file a separate form for each spouse required to file Form 8606. See page 5 of the instructions.

Rose Green

Your social security number

001 | 00 | 0000

Fill in Your Address Only If You Are Filing This Form by Itself and Not With Your Tax Return ►

Home address (number and street, or P.O. box if mail is not delivered to your home)

City, town or post office, state, and ZIP code

Apt. no.

Part I   **Nondeductible Contributions to Traditional IRAs and Distributions From Traditional, SEP, and SIMPLE IRAs**

Complete this part only if one or more of the following apply.
- You made nondeductible contributions to a traditional IRA for 2008.
- You took distributions from a traditional, SEP, or SIMPLE IRA in 2008 **and** you made nondeductible contributions to a traditional IRA in 2008 or an earlier year. For this purpose, a distribution does not include a rollover (other than a repayment of a qualified disaster recovery assistance distribution), qualified charitable distribution, one-time distribution to fund an HSA, conversion, recharacterization, or return of certain contributions.
- You converted part, but not all, of your traditional, SEP, and SIMPLE IRAs to Roth IRAs in 2008 (excluding any portion you recharacterized) **and** you made nondeductible contributions to a traditional IRA in 2008 or an earlier year.

1	Enter your nondeductible contributions to traditional IRAs for 2008, including those made for 2008 from January 1, 2009, through April 15, 2009 (see page 5 of the instructions)	**1**	*500*
2	Enter your total basis in traditional IRAs (see page 6 of the instructions)	**2**	*300*
3	Add lines 1 and 2	**3**	*800*

In 2008, did you take a distribution from traditional, SEP, or SIMPLE IRAs, or make a Roth IRA conversion?   **No** ──► Enter the amount from line 3 on line 14. Do not complete the rest of Part I.   **Yes** ──► Go to line 4.

4	Enter those contributions included on line 1 that were made from January 1, 2009, through April 15, 2009	**4**	*0*
5	Subtract line 4 from line 3	**5**	*800*
6	Enter the value of **all** your traditional, SEP, and SIMPLE IRAs as of December 31, 2008, plus any outstanding rollovers. Subtract any repayments of qualified disaster recovery assistance distributions. If the result is zero or less, enter -0- (see page 6 of the instructions) .	**6**	
7	Enter your distributions from traditional, SEP, and SIMPLE IRAs in 2008. **Do not** include rollovers (other than repayments of qualified disaster recovery assistance distributions), qualified charitable distributions, a one-time distribution to fund an HSA, conversions to a Roth IRA, certain returned contributions, or recharacterizations of traditional IRA contributions (see page 6 of the instructions) . . .	**7**	
8	Enter the net amount you converted from traditional, SEP, and SIMPLE IRAs to Roth IRAs in 2008. **Do not** include amounts converted that you later recharacterized (see page 7 of the instructions). Also enter this amount on line 16	**8**	
9	Add lines 6, 7, and 8	**9**	
10	Divide line 5 by line 9. Enter the result as a decimal rounded to at least 3 places. If the result is 1.000 or more, enter "1.000" . . .	**10**	× .
11	Multiply line 8 by line 10. This is the nontaxable portion of the amount you converted to Roth IRAs. Also enter this amount on line 17 . . .	**11**	
12	Multiply line 7 by line 10. This is the nontaxable portion of your distributions that you did not convert to a Roth IRA	**12**	
13	Add lines 11 and 12. This is the nontaxable portion of all your distributions	**13**	*460* *
14	Subtract line 13 from line 3. This is **your total basis in traditional IRAs for 2008 and earlier years**	**14**	*340*
15a	Subtract line 12 from line 7	**15a**	
b	Amount on line 15a attributable to qualified disaster recovery assistance distributions (see page 7 of the instructions). Also enter this amount on Form 8930, line 13	**15b**	
c	**Taxable amount.** Subtract line 15b from line 15a. If more than zero, also include this amount on Form 1040, line 15b; Form 1040A, line 11b; or Form 1040NR, line 16b . . . . **Note:** You may be subject to an additional 10% tax on the amount on line 15c if you were under age 59½ at the time of the distribution (see page 7 of the instructions).	**15c**	*0*

For Privacy Act and Paperwork Reduction Act Notice, see page 9 of the instructions.   Cat. No. 63966F   Form **8606** (2008)

*From Worksheet in Publication 590

Page 46   Chapter 1   **Traditional IRAs**

Form 8606 (2008)   Page **2**

| **Part II** | **2008 Conversions From Traditional, SEP, or SIMPLE IRAs to Roth IRAs** |

Complete this part if you converted part or all of your traditional, SEP, and SIMPLE IRAs to a Roth IRA in 2008 (excluding any portion you recharacterized).

Caution: *If your modified adjusted gross income is over $100,000 **or** you are married filing separately and you lived with your spouse at any time in 2008, you **cannot** convert any amount from traditional, SEP, or SIMPLE IRAs to Roth IRAs for 2008. If you erroneously made a conversion, you must recharacterize (correct) it (see page 7 of the instructions).*

16	If you completed Part I, enter the amount from line 8. Otherwise, enter the net amount you converted from traditional, SEP, and SIMPLE IRAs to Roth IRAs in 2008. **Do not** include amounts you later recharacterized back to traditional, SEP, or SIMPLE IRAs in 2008 or 2009 (see page 7 of the instructions)	**16**	5,000
17	If you completed Part I, enter the amount from line 11. Otherwise, enter your basis in the amount on line 16 (see page 7 of the instructions)	**17**	460
18	**Taxable amount.** Subtract line 17 from line 16. Also include this amount on Form 1040, line 15b; Form 1040A, line 11b; or Form 1040NR, line 16b	**18**	4,540 *

| **Part III** | **Distributions From Roth IRAs** |

Complete this part only if you took a distribution from a Roth IRA in 2008. For this purpose, a distribution does not include a rollover (other than a repayment of a qualified disaster recovery assistance distribution), qualified charitable distribution, one-time distribution to fund an HSA, recharacterization, or return of certain contributions (see page 7 of the instructions).

19	Enter your total nonqualified distributions from Roth IRAs in 2008 including any qualified first-time homebuyer distributions (see page 7 of the instructions).	**19**	
20	Qualified first-time homebuyer expenses (see page 7 of the instructions). **Do not** enter more than $10,000	**20**	
21	Subtract line 20 from line 19. If zero or less, enter -0- and skip lines 22 through 25	**21**	
22	Enter your basis in Roth IRA contributions (see page 8 of the instructions)	**22**	
23	Subtract line 22 from line 21. If zero or less, enter -0- and skip lines 24 and 25. If more than zero, you may be subject to an additional tax (see page 8 of the instructions)	**23**	
24	Enter your basis in conversions from traditional, SEP, and SIMPLE IRAs and rollovers from qualified retirement plans to a Roth IRA (see page 8 of the instructions)	**24**	
25a	Subtract line 24 from line 23. If zero or less, enter -0- and skip lines 25b and 25c	**25a**	
b	Amount on line 25a attributable to qualified disaster recovery assistance distributions (see page 8 of the instructions). Also enter this amount on Form 8930, line 14	**25b**	
c	**Taxable amount.** Subtract line 25b from line 25a. If more than zero, also include this amount on Form 1040, line 15b; Form 1040A, line 11b; or Form 1040NR, line 16b	**25c**	

| **Sign Here Only If You Are Filing This Form by Itself and Not With Your Tax Return** | Under penalties of perjury, I declare that I have examined this form, including accompanying attachments, and to the best of my knowledge and belief, it is true, correct, and complete. Declaration of preparer (other than taxpayer) is based on all information of which preparer has any knowledge. |

▶ _____   ▶ _____
Your signature   Date

Paid Preparer's Use Only	Preparer's signature	▶		Date		Check if self-employed ☐	Preparer's SSN or PTIN
	Firm's name (or yours if self-employed), address, and ZIP code	▶				EIN	
						Phone no. ( )	

Form **8606** (2008)

Form **8606**	**Nondeductible IRAs**	OMB No. 1545-0074
	▶ See separate instructions.	**2008**
Department of the Treasury Internal Revenue Service (99)	▶ Attach to Form 1040, Form 1040A, or Form 1040NR.	Attachment Sequence No. **48**

Name. If married, file a separate form for each spouse required to file Form 8606. See page 5 of the instructions.

Bill King

Your social security number
002 · 00 · 0000

Fill in Your Address Only If You Are Filing This Form by Itself and Not With Your Tax Return ▶

Home address (number and street, or P.O. box if mail is not delivered to your home)

Apt. no.

City, town or post office, state, and ZIP code

Part I	**Nondeductible Contributions to Traditional IRAs and Distributions From Traditional, SEP, and SIMPLE IRAs**

Complete this part only if one or more of the following apply.

- You made nondeductible contributions to a traditional IRA for 2008.
- You took distributions from a traditional, SEP, or SIMPLE IRA in 2008 **and** you made nondeductible contributions to a traditional IRA in 2008 or an earlier year. For this purpose, a distribution does not include a rollover (other than a repayment of a qualified disaster recovery assistance distribution), qualified charitable distribution, one-time distribution to fund an HSA, conversion, recharacterization, or return of certain contributions.
- You converted part, but not all, of your traditional, SEP, and SIMPLE IRAs to Roth IRAs in 2008 (excluding any portion you recharacterized) **and** you made nondeductible contributions to a traditional IRA in 2008 or an earlier year.

1	Enter your nondeductible contributions to traditional IRAs for 2008, including those made for 2008 from January 1, 2009, through April 15, 2009 (see page 5 of the instructions)	**1**	0
2	Enter your total basis in traditional IRAs (see page 6 of the instructions)	**2**	2,000
3	Add lines 1 and 2	**3**	2,000

> In 2008, did you take a distribution from traditional, SEP, or SIMPLE IRAs, or make a Roth IRA conversion? — **No** ──▶ Enter the amount from line 3 on line 14. Do not complete the rest of Part I.
> — **Yes** ──▶ Go to line 4.

4	Enter those contributions included on line 1 that were made from January 1, 2009, through April 15, 2009	**4**	0
5	Subtract line 4 from line 3	**5**	2,000
6	Enter the value of **all** your traditional, SEP, and SIMPLE IRAs as of December 31, 2008, plus any outstanding rollovers. Subtract any repayments of qualified disaster recovery assistance distributions. If the result is zero or less, enter -0- (see page 6 of the instructions) .	**6**	1,800
7	Enter your distributions from traditional, SEP, and SIMPLE IRAs in 2008. **Do not** include rollovers (other than repayments of qualified disaster recovery assistance distributions), qualified charitable distributions, a one-time distribution to fund an HSA, conversions to a Roth IRA, certain returned contributions, or recharacterizations of traditional IRA contributions (see page 6 of the instructions) . . .	**7**	600
8	Enter the net amount you converted from traditional, SEP, and SIMPLE IRAs to Roth IRAs in 2008. **Do not** include amounts converted that you later recharacterized (see page 7 of the instructions). Also enter this amount on line 16	**8**	
9	Add lines 6, 7, and 8	**9**	2,400
10	Divide line 5 by line 9. Enter the result as a decimal rounded to at least 3 places. If the result is 1.000 or more, enter "1.000" . . .	**10**	× . 833
11	Multiply line 8 by line 10. This is the nontaxable portion of the amount you converted to Roth IRAs. Also enter this amount on line 17 . . .	**11**	
12	Multiply line 7 by line 10. This is the nontaxable portion of your distributions that you did not convert to a Roth IRA	**12**	500
13	Add lines 11 and 12. This is the nontaxable portion of all your distributions	**13**	500
14	Subtract line 13 from line 3. This is **your total basis in traditional IRAs for 2008 and earlier years**	**14**	1,500
15a	Subtract line 12 from line 7	**15a**	100
b	Amount on line 15a attributable to qualified disaster recovery assistance distributions (see page 7 of the instructions). Also enter this amount on Form 8930, line 13	**15b**	
c	**Taxable amount.** Subtract line 15b from line 15a. If more than zero, also include this amount on Form 1040, line 15b; Form 1040A, line 11b; or Form 1040NR, line 16b	**15c**	100

Note: You may be subject to an additional 10% tax on the amount on line 15c if you were under age 59½ at the time of the distribution (see page 7 of the instructions).

For Privacy Act and Paperwork Reduction Act Notice, see page 9 of the instructions.   Cat. No. 63966F   Form **8606** (2008) to pay other taxes as discussed under *Effect on you or your beneficiary*, earlier.

Exempt Transactions

The following two types of transactions are not prohibited transactions if they meet the requirements that follow.

- Payments of cash, property, or other consideration by the sponsor of your traditional IRA to you (or members of your family).

- Your receipt of services at reduced or no cost from the bank where your traditional IRA is established or maintained.

Payments of cash, property, or other consideration. Even if a sponsor makes payments to you or your family, there is no prohibited transaction if all three of the following requirements are met.

1. The payments are for establishing a traditional IRA or for making additional contributions to it.

2. The IRA is established solely to benefit you, your spouse, and your or your spouse's beneficiaries.

3. During the year, the total fair market value of the payments you receive is not more than:

   a. $10 for IRA deposits of less than $5,000, or

   b. $20 for IRA deposits of $5,000 or more.

If the consideration is group term life insurance, requirements (1) and (3) do not apply if no more than $5,000 of the face value of the insurance is based on a dollar-for-dollar basis on the assets in your IRA.

Services received at reduced or no cost. Even if a sponsor provides services at reduced or no cost, there is no prohibited transaction if all of the following requirements are met.

- The traditional IRA qualifying you to receive the services is established and maintained for the benefit of you, your spouse, and your or your spouse's beneficiaries.

- The bank itself can legally offer the services.

- The services are provided in the ordinary course of business by the bank (or a bank affiliate) to customers who qualify but do not maintain an IRA (or a Keogh plan).

- The determination, for a traditional IRA, of who qualifies for these services is based on an IRA (or a Keogh plan) deposit balance equal to the lowest qualifying balance for any other type of account.

- The rate of return on a traditional IRA investment that qualifies is not less than the return on an identical investment that could have been made at the same time at the same branch of the bank by a

customer who is not eligible for (or does not receive) these services.

Investment in Collectibles

If your traditional IRA invests in collectibles, the amount invested is considered distributed to you in the year invested. You may have to pay the 10% additional tax on early distributions, discussed later.

Collectibles. These include:

- Artworks,

- Rugs,

- Antiques,

- Metals,

- Gems,

- Stamps,

- Coins,

- Alcoholic beverages, and

- Certain other tangible personal property.

Exception. Your IRA can invest in one, one-half, one-quarter, or one-tenth ounce U.S. gold coins, or one-ounce silver coins minted by the Treasury Department. It can also invest in certain platinum coins and certain gold, silver, palladium, and platinum bullion.

Excess Contributions

Generally, an excess contribution is the amount contributed to your traditional IRAs for the year that is more than the smaller of:

- $5,000 ($6,000 if you are age 50 or older), or

- Your taxable compensation for the year.

This limit may be increased to $8,000 if you participated in a 401(k) plan maintained by an employer who went into bankruptcy in an earlier year. For more information, see *Catch-up contributions in certain employer bankruptcies* earlier.

The taxable compensation limit applies whether your contributions are deductible or nondeductible.

Contributions for the year you reach age 70½ and any later year are also excess contributions.

An excess contribution could be the result of your contribution, your spouse's contribution, your employer's contribution, or an improper rollover contribution. If your employer makes contributions on your behalf to a SEP IRA, see Publication 560.

Tax on Excess Contributions

In general, if the excess contributions for a year are not withdrawn by the date your return for the year is due (including extensions), you are subject to a 6% tax. You must pay the 6% tax each year on excess amounts that remain in your traditional IRA at the end of your tax year. The tax cannot be more than 6% of the combined value of all your IRAs as of the end of your tax year.

The additional tax is figured on Form 5329. For information on filing Form 5329, see *Reporting Additional Taxes*, later.

Example. For 2008, Paul Jones is 45 years old and single, his compensation is $31,000, and he contributed $5,500 to his traditional IRA. Paul has made an excess contribution to his IRA of $500 ($5,500 minus the $5,000 limit). The contribution earned $5 interest in 2008 and $6 interest in 2009 before the due date of the return, including extensions. He does not withdraw the $500 or the interest it earned by the due date of his return, including extensions.

Paul figures his additional tax for 2008 by multiplying the excess contribution ($500) shown on Form 5329, line 16, by .06, giving him an additional tax liability of $30. He enters the tax on Form 5329, line 17, and on Form 1040, line 59. See Paul's filled-in Form 5329.

Excess Contributions Withdrawn by Due Date of Return

You will not have to pay the 6% tax if you withdraw an excess contribution made during a tax year and you also withdraw any interest or other income earned on the excess contribution. You must complete your withdrawal by the date your tax return for that year is due, including extensions.

How to treat withdrawn contributions. Do not include in your gross income an excess contribution that you withdraw from your traditional IRA before your tax return is due if both of the following conditions are met.

- No deduction was allowed for the excess contribution.
- You withdraw the interest or other income earned on the excess contribution.

You can take into account any loss on the contribution while it was in the IRA when calculating the amount that must be withdrawn. If there was a loss, the net income you must withdraw may be a negative amount.

In most cases, the net income you must transfer will be determined by your IRA trustee or custodian. If you need to determine the applicable net income you need to withdraw, you can use the same method that was used in Worksheet 1-3, earlier.

How to treat withdrawn interest or other income. You must include in your gross income the interest or other income that was earned on the excess contribution. Report it on your return for the year in which the excess contribution was made. Your withdrawal of interest or other income may be subject to an additional 10% tax on early distributions, discussed later.

Form 1099-R. You will receive Form 1099-R indicating the amount of the withdrawal. If the excess contribution was made in a previous tax year, the form will indicate the year in which the earnings are taxable.

Example. Maria, age 35, made an excess contribution in 2008 of $1,000, which she withdrew by April 15, 2009, the due date of her return. At the same time, she also withdrew the $50 income that was earned on the $1,000. She must include the $50 in her gross income for 2008 (the year in which the excess contribution was made). She must also pay an additional tax of $5 (the 10% additional tax on early distributions because she is not yet 59½ years old), but she does not have to report the excess contribution as income or pay the 6% excise tax. Maria receives a Form 1099-R showing that the earnings are taxable for 2008.

Excess Contributions Withdrawn After Due Date of Return

In general, you must include all distributions (withdrawals) from your traditional IRA in your gross income. However, if the following conditions are met, you can withdraw excess contributions from your IRA and not include the amount withdrawn in your gross income.

- Total contributions (other than rollover contributions) for 2008 to your IRA were not more than $5,000 ($6,000 if you are age 50 or older or $8,000 for certain individuals whose employers went into bankruptcy).
- You did not take a deduction for the excess contribution being withdrawn.

The withdrawal can take place at any time, even after the due date, including extensions, for filing your tax return for the year.

Excess contribution deducted in an earlier year. If you deducted an excess contribution in an earlier year for which the total contributions were not more than the maximum deductible amount for that year ($2,000 for 2001 and earlier years, $3,000 for 2002 through 2004 ($3,500 if you were age 50 or older), $4,000 for 2005 ($4,500 if you were age 50 or older), $4,000 for 2006 or 2007 ($5,000 if you were age 50 or older)), you can still remove the excess from your traditional IRA and not include it in your gross income. To do this, file Form 1040X, Amended U.S. Individual Income Tax Return, for that year and do not deduct the excess contribution on the amended return. Generally, you can file an amended return within 3 years after you filed your return, or 2 years from the time the tax was paid, whichever is later.

Excess due to incorrect rollover information. If an excess contribution in your traditional IRA is the result of a rollover and the excess occurred because the information the plan was required to give you was incorrect, you can withdraw the excess contribution. The limits mentioned above are increased by the amount of the excess that is due to the incorrect information. You will have to amend

Form **5329**	**Additional Taxes on Qualified Plans (Including IRAs) and Other Tax-Favored Accounts**	OMB No. 1545-0074
Department of the Treasury Internal Revenue Service (99)	▶ Attach to Form 1040 or Form 1040NR. ▶ See separate instructions.	**2008** Attachment Sequence No. **29**

Name of individual subject to additional tax. If married filing jointly, see instructions.

Paul Jones

Your social security number 003 : 00 : 0000

Fill in Your Address Only If You Are Filing This Form by Itself and Not With Your Tax Return ▶

Home address (number and street), or P.O. box if mail is not delivered to your home — Apt. no.

City, town or post office, state, and ZIP code

If this is an amended return, check here ▶ ☐

If you **only** owe the additional 10% tax on early distributions, you may be able to report this tax directly on Form 1040, line 59, or Form 1040NR, line 54, without filing Form 5329. See the instructions for Form 1040, line 59, or for Form 1040NR, line 54.

Part I Additional Tax on Early Distributions

Complete this part if you took a taxable distribution (other than a qualified disaster recovery assistance or qualified recovery assistance distribution), before you reached age 59½, from a qualified retirement plan (including an IRA) or modified endowment contract (unless you are reporting this tax directly on Form 1040 or Form 1040NR—see above). You may also have to complete this part to indicate that you qualify for an exception to the additional tax on early distributions or for certain Roth IRA distributions (see instructions).

1	Early distributions included in income. For Roth IRA distributions, see instructions	**1**	
2	Early distributions included on line 1 that are not subject to the additional tax (see instructions). Enter the appropriate exception number from the instructions: _____	**2**	
3	Amount subject to additional tax. Subtract line 2 from line 1	**3**	
4	**Additional tax.** Enter 10% (.10) of line 3. Include this amount on Form 1040, line 59, or Form 1040NR, line 54	**4**	

Caution: If any part of the amount on line 3 was a distribution from a SIMPLE IRA, you may have to include 25% of that amount on line 4 instead of 10%.

Part II Additional Tax on Certain Distributions From Education Accounts

Complete this part if you included an amount in income, on Form 1040 or Form 1040NR, line 21, from a Coverdell education savings account (ESA) or a qualified tuition program (QTP).

5	Distributions included in income from Coverdell ESAs and QTPs	**5**	
6	Distributions included on line 5 that are not subject to the additional tax (see instructions)	**6**	
7	Amount subject to additional tax. Subtract line 6 from line 5	**7**	
8	Additional tax. Enter 10% (.10) of line 7. Include this amount on Form 1040, line 59, or Form 1040NR, line 54	**8**	

Part III Additional Tax on Excess Contributions to Traditional IRAs

Complete this part if you contributed more to your traditional IRAs for 2008 than is allowable or you had an amount on line 17 of your 2007 Form 5329.

9	Enter your excess contributions from line 16 of your 2007 Form 5329 (see instructions). If zero, go to line 15		**9**	
10	If your traditional IRA contributions for 2008 are less than your maximum allowable contribution, see instructions. Otherwise, enter -0-	**10**		
11	2008 traditional IRA distributions included in income (see instructions)	**11**		
12	2008 distributions of prior year excess contributions (see instructions)	**12**		
13	Add lines 10, 11, and 12		**13**	
14	Prior year excess contributions. Subtract line 13 from line 9. If zero or less, enter -0-		**14**	
15	Excess contributions for 2008 (see instructions)		**15**	500
16	Total excess contributions. Add lines 14 and 15		**16**	500
17	**Additional tax.** Enter 6% (.06) of the **smaller** of line 16 **or** the value of your traditional IRAs on December 31, 2008 (including 2008 contributions made in 2009). Include this amount on Form 1040, line 59, or Form 1040NR, line 54		**17**	30

Part IV Additional Tax on Excess Contributions to Roth IRAs

Complete this part if you contributed more to your Roth IRAs for 2008 than is allowable or you had an amount on line 25 of your 2007 Form 5329.

18	Enter your excess contributions from line 24 of your 2007 Form 5329 (see instructions). If zero, go to line 23		**18**	
19	If your Roth IRA contributions for 2008 are less than your maximum allowable contribution, see instructions. Otherwise, enter -0-	**19**		
20	2008 distributions from your Roth IRAs (see instructions)	**20**		
21	Add lines 19 and 20		**21**	
22	Prior year excess contributions. Subtract line 21 from line 18. If zero or less, enter -0-		**22**	
23	Excess contributions for 2008 (see instructions)		**23**	
24	Total excess contributions. Add lines 22 and 23		**24**	
25	**Additional tax.** Enter 6% (.06) of the **smaller** of line 24 **or** the value of your Roth IRAs on December 31, 2008 (including 2008 contributions made in 2009). Include this amount on Form 1040, line 59, or Form 1040NR, line 54		**25**	

For Privacy Act and Paperwork Reduction Act Notice, see page 6 of the instructions. Cat. No. 13329Q Form **5329** (2008)

Chapter 1 **Traditional IRAs**   Page 51

your return for the year in which the excess occurred to correct the reporting of the rollover amounts in that year. Do not include in your gross income the part of the excess contribution caused by the incorrect information.

Deducting an Excess Contribution in a Later Year

You cannot apply an excess contribution to an earlier year even if you contributed less than the maximum amount allowable for the earlier year. However, you may be able to apply it to a later year if the contributions for that later year are less than the maximum allowed for that year.

You can deduct excess contributions for previous years that are still in your traditional IRA. The amount you can deduct this year is the lesser of the following two amounts.

- Your maximum IRA deduction for this year minus any amounts contributed to your traditional IRAs for this year.

- The total excess contributions in your IRAs at the beginning of this year.

This method lets you avoid making a withdrawal. It does not, however, let you avoid the 6% tax on any excess contributions remaining at the end of a tax year.

To figure the amount of excess contributions for previous years that you can deduct this year, see Worksheet 1-6.

Worksheet 1-6. **Excess Contributions Deductible This Year**

Use this worksheet to figure the amount of excess contributions from prior years you can deduct this year.

1. Maximum IRA deduction for the current year	1.	_____
2. IRA contributions for the current year	2.	_____
3. Subtract line 2 from line 1. If zero (0) or less, enter zero	3.	_____
4. Excess contributions in IRA at beginning of year	4.	_____
5. Enter the lesser of line 3 or line 4. This is the amount of excess contributions for previous years that you can deduct this year	5.	_____

Example. Teri was entitled to contribute to her traditional IRA and deduct $1,000 in 2007 and $1,500 in 2008 (the amounts of her taxable compensation for these years). For 2007, she actually contributed $1,400 but could deduct only $1,000. In 2007, $400 is an excess contribution subject to the 6% tax. However, she would not have to pay the 6% tax if she withdrew the excess (including any earnings) before the due date of her 2007 return. Because Teri did not withdraw the excess, she owes excise tax of $24 for 2007. To avoid the excise tax for 2008, she can correct the $400 excess amount from 2007 in 2008 if her actual contributions are only $1,100 for 2008 (the allowable deductible contribution of $1,500 minus the $400 excess from 2007 she wants to treat as a deductible contribution in 2008). Teri can deduct $1,500 in 2008 (the $1,100 actually contributed plus the $400 excess contribution from 2007). This is shown on the following worksheet.

Worksheet 1-6. **Example—Illustrated**

Use this worksheet to figure the amount of excess contributions from prior years you can deduct this year.

1. Maximum IRA deduction for the current year	1.	1,500
2. IRA contributions for the current year	2.	1,100
3. Subtract line 2 from line 1. If zero (0) or less, enter zero	3.	400
4. Excess contributions in IRA at beginning of year	4.	400
5. Enter the lesser of line 3 or line 4. This is the amount of excess contributions for previous years that you can deduct this year	5.	400

Closed tax year. A special rule applies if you incorrectly deducted part of the excess contribution in a closed tax year (one for which the period to assess a tax deficiency has expired). The amount allowable as a traditional IRA deduction for a later correction year (the year you contribute less than the allowable amount) must be reduced by the amount of the excess contribution deducted in the closed year.

To figure the amount of excess contributions for previous years that you can deduct this year if you incorrectly deducted part of the excess contribution in a closed tax year, see Worksheet 1-7.

Worksheet 1-7. Excess Contributions Deductible This Year if Any Were Deducted in a Closed Tax Year

Use this worksheet to figure the amount of excess contributions for prior years that you can deduct this year if you incorrectly deducted excess contributions in a closed tax year.

1. Maximum IRA deduction for the current year	1. _____
2. IRA contributions for the current year	2. _____
3. If line 2 is less than line 1, enter any excess contributions that were deducted in a closed tax year. Otherwise, enter zero (0)	3. _____
4. Subtract line 3 from line 1	4. _____
5. Subtract line 2 from line 4. If zero (0) or less, enter zero	5. _____
6. Excess contributions in IRA at beginning of year	6. _____
7. Enter the lesser of line 5 or line 6. This is the amount of excess contributions for previous years that you can deduct this year	7. _____

Early Distributions

You must include early distributions of taxable amounts from your traditional IRA in your gross income. Early distributions are also subject to an additional 10% tax, as discussed later.

Early distributions defined. Early distributions generally are amounts distributed from your traditional IRA account or annuity before you are age 59½, or amounts you receive when you cash in retirement bonds before you are age 59½.

Age 59½ Rule

Generally, if you are under age 59½, you must pay a 10% additional tax on the distribution of any assets (money or other property) from your traditional IRA. Distributions before you are age 59½ are called early distributions.

The 10% additional tax applies to the part of the distribution that you have to include in gross income. It is in addition to any regular income tax on that amount.

A number of exceptions to this rule are discussed below under *Exceptions*. Also see *Contributions Returned Before Due Date of Return*, earlier.

 You may have to pay a 25%, rather than a 10%, additional tax if you receive distributions from a SIMPLE IRA before you are age 59½. See Additional Tax on Early Distributions under When Can You Withdraw or Use Assets? in chapter 3.

After age 59½ and before age 70½. After you reach age 59½, you can receive distributions without having to pay the 10% additional tax. Even though you can receive distributions after you reach age 59½, distributions are not required until you reach age 70½. See *When Must You Withdraw Assets? (Required Minimum Distributions)*, earlier.

Exceptions

There are several exceptions to the age 59½ rule. Even if you receive a distribution before you are age 59½, you may not have to pay the 10% additional tax if you are in one of the following situations.

- You have unreimbursed medical expenses that are more than 7.5% of your adjusted gross income.

- The distributions are not more than the cost of your medical insurance.

- You are disabled.

- You are the beneficiary of a deceased IRA owner.

- You are receiving distributions in the form of an annuity.

- The distributions are not more than your qualified higher education expenses.

- You use the distributions to buy, build, or rebuild a first home.

- The distribution is due to an IRS levy of the qualified plan.

- The distribution is a qualified reservist distribution.

Most of these exceptions are explained below.

Note. Distributions that are timely and properly rolled over, as discussed earlier, are not subject to either regular income tax or the 10% additional tax. Certain withdrawals of excess contributions after the due date of your return are also tax free and therefore not subject to the 10% additional tax. (See *Excess Contributions Withdrawn After Due Date of Return*, earlier.) This also applies to transfers incident to divorce, as discussed earlier under *Can You Move Retirement Plan Assets*.

Receivership distributions. Early distributions (with or without your consent) from savings institutions placed in receivership are subject to this tax unless one of the above exceptions applies. This is true even if the distribution is from a receiver that is a state agency.

Unreimbursed medical expenses. Even if you are under age 59½, you do not have to pay the 10% additional tax on distributions that are not more than:

- The amount you paid for unreimbursed medical expenses during the year of the distribution, minus

- 7.5% of your adjusted gross income (defined later) for the year of the distribution.

You can only take into account unreimbursed medical expenses that you would be able to include in figuring a deduction for medical expenses on Schedule A, Form 1040. You do not have to itemize your deductions to take advantage of this exception to the 10% additional tax.

Adjusted gross income. This is the amount on Form 1040, line 38; Form 1040A, line 22; or Form 1040NR, line 36.

Medical insurance. Even if you are under age 59½, you may not have to pay the 10% additional tax on distributions during the year that are not more than the amount you paid during the year for medical insurance for yourself, your spouse, and your dependents. You will not have to pay the tax on these amounts if all of the following conditions apply.

- You lost your job.
- You received unemployment compensation paid under any federal or state law for 12 consecutive weeks because you lost your job.
- You receive the distributions during either the year you received the unemployment compensation or the following year.
- You receive the distributions no later than 60 days after you have been reemployed.

Disabled. If you become disabled before you reach age 59½, any distributions from your traditional IRA because of your disability are not subject to the 10% additional tax.

You are considered disabled if you can furnish proof that you cannot do any substantial gainful activity because of your physical or mental condition. A physician must determine that your condition can be expected to result in death or to be of long, continued, and indefinite duration.

Beneficiary. If you die before reaching age 59½, the assets in your traditional IRA can be distributed to your beneficiary or to your estate without either having to pay the 10% additional tax.

However, if you inherit a traditional IRA from your deceased spouse and elect to treat it as your own (as discussed under *What if You Inherit an IRA*, earlier), any distribution you later receive before you reach age 59½ may be subject to the 10% additional tax.

Annuity. You can receive distributions from your traditional IRA that are part of a series of substantially equal payments over your life (or your life expectancy), or over the lives (or the joint life expectancies) of you and your beneficiary, without having to pay the 10% additional tax, even if you receive such distributions before you are age 59½. You must use an IRS-approved distribution method and you must take at least one distribution annually for this exception to apply. The "required minimum distribution method," when used for this purpose, results in the exact amount required to be distributed, not the minimum amount.

There are two other IRS-approved distribution methods that you can use. They are generally referred to as the "fixed amortization method" and the "fixed annuitization method." These two methods are not discussed in this publication because they are more complex and generally require professional assistance. For information on these methods, see Revenue Ruling 2002-62, which is on page 710 of Internal Revenue Bulletin 2002-42 at *www.irs.gov/ pub/irs-irbs/irb02-42.pdf*.

Recapture tax for changes in distribution method under equal payment exception. You may have to pay an early distribution recapture tax if, before you reach age 59½, the distribution method under the equal periodic payment exception changes (for reasons other than your death or disability). The tax applies if the method changes from the method requiring equal payments to a method that would not have qualified for the exception to the tax. The recapture tax applies to the first tax year to which the change applies. The amount of tax is the amount that would have been imposed had the exception not applied, plus interest for the deferral period.

You may have to pay the recapture tax if you do not receive the payments for at least 5 years under a method that qualifies for the exception. You may have to pay it even if you modify your method of distribution after you reach age 59½. In that case, the tax applies only to payments distributed before you reach age 59½.

Report the recapture tax and interest on line 4 of Form 5329. Attach an explanation to the form. Do not write the explanation next to the line or enter any amount for the recapture on lines 1 or 3 of the form.

One-time switch. If you are receiving a series of substantially equal periodic payments, you can make a one-time switch to the required minimum distribution method at any time without incurring the additional tax. Once a change is made, you must follow the required minimum distribution method in all subsequent years.

Higher education expenses. Even if you are under age 59½, if you paid expenses for higher education during the year, part (or all) of any distribution may not be subject to the 10% additional tax. The part not subject to the tax is generally the amount that is not more than the qualified higher education expenses (defined later) for the year for education furnished at an eligible educational institution (defined later). The education must be for you, your spouse, or the children or grandchildren of you or your spouse.

When determining the amount of the distribution that is not subject to the 10% additional tax, include qualified higher education expenses paid with any of the following funds.

- Payment for services, such as wages.
- A loan.
- A gift.
- An inheritance given to either the student or the individual making the withdrawal.
- A withdrawal from personal savings (including savings from a qualified tuition program).

Do not include expenses paid with any of the following funds.

- Tax-free distributions from a Coverdell education savings account.
- Tax-free part of scholarships and fellowships.
- Pell grants.
- Employer-provided educational assistance.
- Veterans' educational assistance.
- Any other tax-free payment (other than a gift or inheritance) received as educational assistance.

Qualified higher education expenses. Qualified higher education expenses are tuition, fees, books, supplies, and equipment required for the enrollment or attendance of a student at an eligible educational institution. They also include expenses for special needs services incurred by or for special needs students in connection with their enrollment or attendance. In addition, if the individual is at least a half-time student, room and board are qualified higher education expenses.

Eligible educational institution. This is any college, university, vocational school, or other postsecondary educational institution eligible to participate in the student aid programs administered by the U.S. Department of Education. It includes virtually all accredited, public, nonprofit, and proprietary (privately owned profit-making) postsecondary institutions. The educational institution should be able to tell you if it is an eligible educational institution.

First home. Even if you are under age 59½, you do not have to pay the 10% additional tax on up to $10,000 of distributions you receive to buy, build, or rebuild a first home. To qualify for treatment as a first-time homebuyer distribution, the distribution must meet all the following requirements.

1. It must be used to pay qualified acquisition costs (defined later) before the close of the 120th day after the day you received it.

2. It must be used to pay qualified acquisition costs for the main home of a first-time homebuyer (defined later) who is any of the following.

   a. Yourself.

   b. Your spouse.

   c. Your or your spouse's child.

   d. Your or your spouse's grandchild.

   e. Your or your spouse's parent or other ancestor.

3. When added to all your prior qualified first-time homebuyer distributions, if any, total qualifying distributions cannot be more than $10,000.

 If both you and your spouse are first-time homebuyers (defined later), each of you can receive distributions up to $10,000 for a first home without having to pay the 10% additional tax.

Qualified acquisition costs. Qualified acquisition costs include the following items.

- Costs of buying, building, or rebuilding a home.
- Any usual or reasonable settlement, financing, or other closing costs.

First-time homebuyer. Generally, you are a first-time homebuyer if you had no present interest in a main home during the 2-year period ending on the date of acquisition of the home which the distribution is being used to buy, build, or rebuild. If you are married, your spouse must also meet this no-ownership requirement.

Date of acquisition. The date of acquisition is the date that:

- You enter into a binding contract to buy the main home for which the distribution is being used, or
- The building or rebuilding of the main home for which the distribution is being used begins.

Qualified reservist distributions. A qualified reservist distribution is not subject to the additional tax on early distributions.

Definition. A distribution you receive is a qualified reservist distribution if the following requirements are met.

- You were ordered or called to active duty after September 11, 2001.
- You were ordered or called to active duty for a period of more than 179 days or for an indefinite period because you are a member of a reserve component.
- The distribution is from an IRA or from amounts attributable to elective deferrals under a section 401(k) or 403(b) plan or a similar arrangement.
- The distribution was made no earlier than the date of the order or call to active duty and no later than the close of the active duty period.

Reserve component. The term "reserve component" means the:

- Army National Guard of the United States,
- Army Reserve,
- Naval Reserve,
- Marine Corps Reserve,
- Air National Guard of the United States,
- Air Force Reserve,
- Coast Guard Reserve, or
- Reserve Corps of the Public Health Service.

Additional 10% tax

The additional tax on early distributions is 10% of the amount of the early distribution that you must include in your gross income. This tax is in addition to any regular income tax resulting from including the distribution in income.

Use Form 5329 to figure the tax. See the discussion of Form 5329, later, under *Reporting Additional Taxes* for information on filing the form.

Example. Tom Jones, who is 35 years old, receives a $3,000 distribution from his traditional IRA account. Tom does not meet any of the exceptions to the 10% additional tax, so the $3,000 is an early distribution. Tom never made any nondeductible contributions to his IRA. He must include the $3,000 in his gross income for the year of the distribution and pay income tax on it. Tom must also pay an additional tax of $300 (10% × $3,000). He files Form 5329. See the filled-in Form 5329.

 Early distributions of funds from a SIMPLE retirement account made within 2 years of beginning participation in the SIMPLE are subject to a 25%, rather than a 10%, early distributions tax.

Nondeductible contributions. The tax on early distributions does not apply to the part of a distribution that represents a return of your nondeductible contributions (basis).

Excess Accumulations (Insufficient Distributions)

You cannot keep amounts in your traditional IRA indefinitely. Generally, you must begin receiving distributions by April 1 of the year following the year in which you reach age 70½. The required minimum distribution for any year after the year in which you reach age 70½ must be made by December 31 of that later year.

Temporary waiver for 2009. No minimum distribution is required from your IRA for 2009.

Tax on excess. If distributions are less than the required minimum distribution for the year, discussed earlier under *When Must You Withdraw Assets? (Required Minimum Distributions)*, you may have to pay a 50% excise tax for that year on the amount not distributed as required.

Reporting the tax. Use Form 5329 to report the tax on excess accumulations. See the discussion of Form 5329, later, under *Reporting Additional Taxes*, for more information on filing the form.

Request to waive the tax. If the excess accumulation is due to reasonable error, and you have taken, or are taking, steps to remedy the insufficient distribution, you can request that the tax be waived. If you believe you qualify for this relief, attach a statement of explanation and complete Form 5329 as instructed under *Waiver of tax* in the Instructions for Form 5329.

Exemption from tax. If you are unable to take required distributions because you have a traditional IRA invested in a contract issued by an insurance company that is in state insurer delinquency proceedings, the 50% excise tax does not apply if the conditions and requirements of Revenue Procedure 92-10 are satisfied. Those conditions and requirements are summarized below. Revenue Procedure 92-10 is in Cumulative Bulletin 1992-1. To obtain a copy of this revenue procedure, see *Mail* in chapter 6. You can also read the revenue procedure at most IRS offices and at many public libraries.

Conditions. To qualify for exemption from the tax, the assets in your traditional IRA must include an affected investment. Also, the amount of your required distribution must be determined as discussed earlier under *When Must You Withdraw Assets*.

Affected investment defined. Affected investment means an annuity contract or a guaranteed investment contract (with an insurance company) for which payments under the terms of the contract have been reduced or suspended because of state insurer delinquency proceedings against the contracting insurance company.

Requirements. If your traditional IRA (or IRAs) includes assets other than your affected investment, all traditional IRA assets, including the available portion of your affected investment, must be used to satisfy as much as possible of your IRA distribution requirement. If the affected investment is the only asset in your IRA, as much of the required distribution as possible must come from the available portion, if any, of your affected investment.

Form **5329**	**Additional Taxes on Qualified Plans (Including IRAs) and Other Tax-Favored Accounts**	OMB No. 1545-0074
Department of the Treasury Internal Revenue Service (99)	▶ Attach to Form 1040 or Form 1040NR. ▶ See separate instructions.	**20**08 Attachment Sequence No. **29**

Name of individual subject to additional tax. If married filing jointly, see instructions.
Tom Jones

Your social security number
004 : 00 : 0000

Fill in Your Address Only If You Are Filing This Form by Itself and Not With Your Tax Return ▶

Home address (number and street), or P.O. box if mail is not delivered to your home

Apt. no.

City, town or post office, state, and ZIP code

If this is an amended return, check here ▶ ☐

If you **only** owe the additional 10% tax on early distributions, you may be able to report this tax directly on Form 1040, line 59, or Form 1040NR, line 54, without filing Form 5329. See the instructions for Form 1040, line 59, or for Form 1040NR, line 54.

Part I | **Additional Tax on Early Distributions**

Complete this part if you took a taxable distribution (other than a qualified disaster recovery assistance or qualified recovery assistance distribution), before you reached age 59½, from a qualified retirement plan (including an IRA) or modified endowment contract (unless you are reporting this tax directly on Form 1040 or Form 1040NR—see above). You may also have to complete this part to indicate that you qualify for an exception to the additional tax on early distributions or for certain Roth IRA distributions (see instructions).

1	Early distributions included in income. For Roth IRA distributions, see instructions	**1**	3,000
2	Early distributions included on line 1 that are not subject to the additional tax (see instructions). Enter the appropriate exception number from the instructions: _____	**2**	0
3	Amount subject to additional tax. Subtract line 2 from line 1	**3**	3,000
4	**Additional tax.** Enter 10% (.10) of line 3. Include this amount on Form 1040, line 59, or Form 1040NR, line 54	**4**	300

Caution: If any part of the amount on line 3 was a distribution from a SIMPLE IRA, you may have to include 25% of that amount on line 4 instead of 10% (see instructions).

Part II | **Additional Tax on Certain Distributions From Education Accounts**

Complete this part if you included an amount in income, on Form 1040 or Form 1040NR, line 21, from a Coverdell education savings account (ESA) or a qualified tuition program (QTP).

5	Distributions included in income from Coverdell ESAs and QTPs	**5**	
6	Distributions included on line 5 that are not subject to the additional tax (see instructions) . .	**6**	
7	Amount subject to additional tax. Subtract line 6 from line 5	**7**	
8	**Additional tax.** Enter 10% (.10) of line 7. Include this amount on Form 1040, line 59, or Form 1040NR, line 54	**8**	

Part III | **Additional Tax on Excess Contributions to Traditional IRAs**

Complete this part if you contributed more to your traditional IRAs for 2008 than is allowable or you had an amount on line 17 of your 2007 Form 5329.

9	Enter your excess contributions from line 16 of your 2007 Form 5329 (see instructions). If zero, go to line 15		**9**	
10	If your traditional IRA contributions for 2008 are less than your maximum allowable contribution, see instructions. Otherwise, enter -0-	**10**		
11	2008 traditional IRA distributions included in income (see instructions)	**11**		
12	2008 distributions of prior year excess contributions (see instructions)	**12**		
13	Add lines 10, 11, and 12		**13**	
14	Prior year excess contributions. Subtract line 13 from line 9. If zero or less, enter -0- . . .		**14**	
15	Excess contributions for 2008 (see instructions)		**15**	
16	Total excess contributions. Add lines 14 and 15		**16**	
17	**Additional tax.** Enter 6% (.06) of the **smaller** of line 16 **or** the value of your traditional IRAs on December 31, 2008 (including 2008 contributions made in 2009). Include this amount on Form 1040, line 59, or Form 1040NR, line 54		**17**	

Part IV | **Additional Tax on Excess Contributions to Roth IRAs**

Complete this part if you contributed more to your Roth IRAs for 2008 than is allowable or you had an amount on line 25 of your 2007 Form 5329.

18	Enter your excess contributions from line 24 of your 2007 Form 5329 (see instructions). If zero, go to line 23		**18**	
19	If your Roth IRA contributions for 2008 are less than your maximum allowable contribution, see instructions. Otherwise, enter -0- . . .	**19**		
20	2008 distributions from your Roth IRAs (see instructions)	**20**		
21	Add lines 19 and 20		**21**	
22	Prior year excess contributions. Subtract line 21 from line 18. If zero or less, enter -0- . . .		**22**	
23	Excess contributions for 2008 (see instructions).		**23**	
24	Total excess contributions. Add lines 22 and 23		**24**	
25	**Additional tax.** Enter 6% (.06) of the **smaller** of line 24 **or** the value of your Roth IRAs on December 31, 2008 (including 2008 contributions made in 2009). Include this amount on Form 1040, line 59, or Form 1040NR, line 54		**25**	

For Privacy Act and Paperwork Reduction Act Notice, see page 6 of the instructions.   Cat. No. 13329Q   Form **5329** (2008)

Chapter 1 **Traditional IRAs**   Page 57

Available portion. The available portion of your affected investment is the amount of payments remaining after they have been reduced or suspended because of state insurer delinquency proceedings.

Make up of shortfall in distribution. If the payments to you under the contract increase because all or part of the reduction or suspension is canceled, you must make up the amount of any shortfall in a prior distribution because of the proceedings. You make up (reduce or eliminate) the shortfall with the increased payments you receive.

You must make up the shortfall by December 31 of the calendar year following the year that you receive increased payments.

Reporting Additional Taxes

Generally, you must use Form 5329 to report the tax on excess contributions, early distributions, and excess accumulations. If you must file Form 5329, you cannot use Form 1040A, Form 1040EZ, or Form 1040NR-EZ.

Filing a tax return. If you must file an individual income tax return, complete Form 5329 and attach it to your Form 1040 or Form 1040NR. Enter the total additional taxes due on Form 1040, line 59, or on Form 1040NR, line 54.

Not filing a tax return. If you do not have to file a return, but do have to pay one of the additional taxes mentioned earlier, file the completed Form 5329 with the IRS at the time and place you would have filed Form 1040 or Form 1040NR. Be sure to include your address on page 1 and your signature and date on page 2. Enclose, but do not attach, a check or money order payable to the United States Treasury for the tax you owe, as shown on Form 5329. Write your social security number and "2008 Form 5329" on your check or money order.

Form 5329 not required. You do not have to use Form 5329 if either of the following situations exist.

- Distribution code 1 (early distribution) is correctly shown in box 7 of Form 1099-R. If you do not owe any other additional tax on a distribution, multiply the taxable part of the early distribution by 10% and enter the result on Form 1040, line 59, or on Form 1040NR, line 54. Put "No" to the left of the line to indicate that you do not have to file Form 5329. However, if you owe this tax and also owe any other additional tax on a distribution, do not enter this 10% additional tax directly on your Form 1040 or Form 1040NR. You must file Form 5329 to report your additional taxes.

- If you rolled over part or all of a distribution from a qualified retirement plan, the part rolled over is not subject to the tax on early distributions.

2.

Roth IRAs

What's New for 2008

Roth IRA contribution limit. If contributions on your behalf are made only to Roth IRAs, your contribution limit for 2008 is generally the lesser of:

- $5,000, or
- Your taxable compensation for the year.

If you were age 50 or older before 2009 and contributions on your behalf were made only to Roth IRAs, your contribution limit for 2008 is generally the lesser of:

- $6,000, or
- Your taxable compensation for the year.

However, if your modified AGI is above a certain amount, your contribution limit may be reduced. For more information, see *How Much Can Be Contributed?* under *Can You Contribute to a Roth IRA?* in this chapter.

Modified AGI limit for Roth IRA contributions increased. For 2008, your Roth IRA contribution limit is reduced (phased out) in the following situations.

- Your filing status is married filing jointly or qualifying widow(er) and your modified AGI is at least $159,000. You cannot make a Roth IRA contribution if your modified AGI is $169,000 or more.

- Your filing status is single, head of household, or married filing separately and you did not live with your spouse at any time in 2008 and your modified AGI is at least $101,000. You cannot make a Roth IRA contribution if your modified AGI is $116,000 or more.

- Your filing status is married filing separately, you lived with your spouse at any time during the year, and your modified AGI is more than -0-. You cannot make a Roth IRA contribution if your modified AGI is $10,000 or more.

See *Can You Contribute to a Roth IRA?* in this chapter.

Rollovers from other retirement plans. Beginning in 2008, you can rollover amounts from a qualified retirement plan to a Roth IRA. For more information, see *Rollover From Employer's Plan Into a Roth IRA* in this chapter.

Economic stimulus payments. Economic stimulus payments directly deposited in your Roth IRA in 2008 may be withdrawn tax-free and penalty-free. See *Tax-free withdrawals of economic stimulus payments* under *Are Distributions Taxable?* later.

Military death gratuities and servicemembers' group life insurance (SGLI) payments. If you received a military death gratuity or SGLI payment with respect to a death from injury that occurred after October 6, 2001, you may roll over some or all of the amount received to your Roth IRA. For more information, see *Military Death Gratuities and Servicemembers' Group Life Insurance (SGLI) Payments* in this chapter.

Rollover of Exxon Valdez settlement income. If you received qualified settlement income in connection with the Exxon Valdez litigation, you may roll over the amount received, or part of the amount received, to your Roth IRA. For more information, see *Rollover of Exxon Valdez Settlement Income* in this chapter.

Rollover of airline payments. If you are a qualified airline employee, you may contribute any portion of an airline payment paid to you by a commercial passenger airline carrier under a Federal bankruptcy court order to your Roth IRA. For more information, see *Rollover of Airline Payments* in this chapter.

What's New for 2009

Modified AGI limits for Roth IRA contributions increased. For 2009, your Roth IRA contribution limit is reduced (phased out) in the following situations.

- Your filing status is married filing jointly or qualifying widow(er) and your modified AGI is at least $166,000. You cannot make a Roth IRA contribution if your modified AGI is $176,000 or more.

- Your filing status is single, head of household, or married filing separately and you did not live with your spouse at any time in 2009 and your modified AGI is at least $105,000. You cannot make a Roth IRA contribution if your modified AGI is $120,000 or more.

- Your filing status is married filing separately, you lived with your spouse at any time during the year, and your modified AGI is more than -0-. You cannot make a Roth IRA contribution if your modified AGI is $10,000 or more.

See *Can You Contribute to a Roth IRA ?* in this chapter.

Temporary waiver of required minimum distribution rules. No minimum distribution is required from your Roth IRA for 2009. See *Temporary waiver of required minimum distribution rules for 2009* in this chapter.

Reminder

Deemed IRAs. For plan years beginning after 2002, a qualified employer plan (retirement plan) can maintain a separate account or annuity under the plan (a deemed IRA) to receive voluntary employee contributions. If the separate account or annuity otherwise meets the requirements of an IRA, it will be subject only to IRA rules. An employee's account can be treated as a traditional IRA or a Roth IRA.

For this purpose, a "qualified employer plan" includes:

- A qualified pension, profit-sharing, or stock bonus plan (section 401(a) plan),

- A qualified employee annuity plan (section 403(a) plan),

- A tax-sheltered annuity plan (section 403(b) plan), and

- A deferred compensation plan (section 457 plan) maintained by a state, a political subdivision of a state, or an agency or instrumentality of a state or political subdivision of a state.

Introduction

Regardless of your age, you may be able to establish and make nondeductible contributions to an individual retirement plan called a Roth IRA.

Contributions not reported. You do not report Roth IRA contributions on your return.

What Is a Roth IRA?

A Roth IRA is an individual retirement plan that, except as explained in this chapter, is subject to the rules that apply to a traditional IRA (defined below). It can be either an account or an annuity. Individual retirement accounts and annuities are described in chapter 1 under *How Can a Traditional IRA Be Set Up.*

To be a Roth IRA, the account or annuity must be designated as a Roth IRA when it is set up. A deemed IRA can be a Roth IRA, but neither a SEP IRA nor a SIMPLE IRA can be designated as a Roth IRA.

Unlike a traditional IRA, you cannot deduct contributions to a Roth IRA. But, if you satisfy the requirements, qualified distributions (discussed later) are tax free. Contributions can be made to your Roth IRA after you reach age 70½ and you can leave amounts in your Roth IRA as long as you live.

Traditional IRA. A traditional IRA is any IRA that is not a Roth IRA or SIMPLE IRA. Traditional IRAs are discussed in chapter 1.

When Can a Roth IRA Be Set Up?

You can set up a Roth IRA at any time. However, the time for making contributions for any year is limited. See *When Can You Make Contributions*, later under *Can You Contribute to a Roth IRA.*

Can You Contribute to a Roth IRA?

Generally, you can contribute to a Roth IRA if you have taxable compensation (defined later) and your modified AGI (defined later) is less than:

- $169,000 for married filing jointly or qualifying widow(er),

- $116,000 for single, head of household, or married filing separately and you did not live with your spouse at any time during the year, and

- $10,000 for married filing separately and you lived with your spouse at any time during the year.

 You may be eligible to claim a credit for contributions to your Roth IRA. For more information, see chapter 5.

Is there an age limit for contributions? Contributions can be made to your Roth IRA regardless of your age.

Table 2-1. **Effect of Modified AGI on Roth IRA Contribution**
This table shows whether your contribution to a Roth IRA is affected by the amount of your modified adjusted gross income (modified AGI).

IF you have taxable compensation and your filing status is ...	AND your modified AGI is ...	THEN ...
married filing jointly or **qualifying widow(er)**	less than $159,000	you can contribute up to $5,000 ($6,000 if you are age 50 or older) as explained under How Much Can Be Contributed.
	at least $159,000 but less than $169,000	the amount you can contribute is reduced as explained under Contribution limit reduced.
	$169,000 or more	you cannot contribute to a Roth IRA.
married filing separately and you lived with your spouse at any time during the year	zero (-0-)	you can contribute up to $5,000 ($6,000 if you are age 50 or older) as explained under How Much Can Be Contributed.
	more than zero (-0-) but less than $10,000	the amount you can contribute is reduced as explained under Contribution limit reduced.
	$10,000 or more	you cannot contribute to a Roth IRA.
single, **head of household,** or **married filing separately** and you did not live with your spouse at any time during the year	less than $101,000	you can contribute up to $5,000 ($6,000 if you are age 50 or older) as explained under How Much Can Be Contributed.
	at least $101,000 but less than $116,000	the amount you can contribute is reduced as explained under Contribution limit reduced.
	$116,000 or more	you cannot contribute to a Roth IRA.

Note. You may be able to contribute up to $8,000 if you participated in a 401(k) plan maintained by an employer who went into bankruptcy in an earlier year. See Catch-up contributions in certain employer bankruptcies, later.

For 2009, the amounts in Table 2-1 increase. For 2009, your Roth IRA contribution limit is reduced (phased out) in the following situations.

- Your filing status is married filing jointly or qualifying widow(er) and your modified AGI is at least $166,000. You cannot make a Roth IRA contribution if your modified AGI is $176,000 or more.

- Your filing status is married filing separately, you lived with your spouse at any time during the year, and your modified AGI is more than -0-. You cannot make a Roth IRA contribution if your modified AGI is $10,000 or more.

- Your filing status is different than either of those described above and your modified AGI is at least $105,000. You cannot make a Roth IRA contribution if your modified AGI is $120,000 or more.

Can you contribute to a Roth IRA for your spouse?
You can contribute to a Roth IRA for your spouse provided the contributions satisfy the spousal IRA limit discussed in chapter 1 under *How Much Can Be Contributed*, you file jointly, and your modified AGI is less than $169,000.

Compensation. Compensation includes wages, salaries, tips, professional fees, bonuses, and other amounts received for providing personal services. It also includes commissions, self-employment income, nontaxable combat pay, and taxable alimony and separate maintenance payments. For more information, see *What Is Compensation?* under *Who Can Set Up a Traditional IRA?* in chapter 1.

Modified AGI. Your modified AGI for Roth IRA purposes is your adjusted gross income (AGI) as shown on your return modified as follows.

1. Subtracting the following.

   a. Roth IRA conversions included on Form 1040, line 15b; Form 1040A, line 11b; or Form 1040NR, line 16b. *Conversions* are discussed under *Can You Move Amounts Into a Roth IRA*, later.

   b. Roth IRA rollovers from qualified retirement plans included on Form 1040, line 16b; Form 1040A, line 12b; or Form 1040NR, line 17b.

   c. Minimum required distributions from IRAs (for conversions and rollovers from qualified retirement plans only).

2. Add the following deductions and exclusions:

   a. Traditional IRA deduction,

   b. Student loan interest deduction,

   c. Tuition and fees deduction,

   d. Domestic production activities deduction,

   e. Foreign earned income exclusion,

   f. Foreign housing exclusion or deduction,

   g. Exclusion of qualified bond interest shown on Form 8815, and

   h. Exclusion of employer-provided adoption benefits shown on Form 8839.

You can use Worksheet 2-1 to figure your modified AGI.

 Do not subtract conversion income or minimum required distributions from IRAs when figuring your other AGI-based phaseouts and taxable income, such as your deduction for medical and dental expenses. Subtract them from AGI only for the purpose of figuring your modified AGI for Roth IRA purposes.

How Much Can Be Contributed?

The contribution limit for Roth IRAs generally depends on whether contributions are made only to Roth IRAs or to both traditional IRAs and Roth IRAs.

Roth IRAs only. If contributions are made only to Roth IRAs, your contribution limit generally is the lesser of:

- $5,000 ($6,000 if you are age 50 or older), or
- Your taxable compensation.

This limit may be increased to $8,000 if you participated in a 401(k) plan maintained by an employer who went into bankruptcy in an earlier year. For more information, see *Catch-up contributions in certain employer bankruptcies* later.

However, if your modified AGI is above a certain amount, your contribution limit may be reduced, as explained later under *Contribution limit reduced*.

Roth IRAs and traditional IRAs. If contributions are made to both Roth IRAs and traditional IRAs established for your benefit, your contribution limit for Roth IRAs generally is the same as your limit would be if contributions were made only to Roth IRAs, but then reduced by all contributions for the year to all IRAs other than Roth IRAs. Employer contributions under a SEP or SIMPLE IRA plan do not affect this limit.

This means that your contribution limit is the lesser of:

- $5,000 ($6,000 if you are age 50 or older) minus all contributions (other than employer contributions under a SEP or SIMPLE IRA plan) for the year to all IRAs other than Roth IRAs, or
- Your taxable compensation minus all contributions (other than employer contributions under a SEP or SIMPLE IRA plan) for the year to all IRAs other than Roth IRAs.

This limit may be increased to $8,000 if you participated in a 401(k) plan maintained by an employer who went into bankruptcy in an earlier year. For more information, see *Catch-up contributions in certain employer bankruptcies* later.

However, if your modified AGI is above a certain amount, your contribution limit may be reduced, as explained later under *Contribution limit reduced*.

Simplified employee pensions (SEPs) are discussed in Publication 560. Savings incentive match plans for employees (SIMPLEs) are discussed in chapter 3.

Catch-up contributions in certain employer bankruptcies. If you participated in a 401(k) plan and the employer who maintained the plan went into bankruptcy, you may be able to contribute an additional $3,000 to your Roth IRA. For this to apply, the following conditions must be met.

- You must have been a participant in a 401(k) plan under which the employer matched at least 50% of your contributions to the plan with stock of the company.

- You must have been a participant in the 401(k) plan 6 months before the employer went into bankruptcy.

- The employer (or a controlling corporation) must have been a debtor in a bankruptcy case in an earlier year.

Chapter 2 **Roth IRAs** Page 61

- The employer (or any other person) must have been subject to indictment or conviction based on business transactions related to the bankruptcy.

 If you choose to make these catch-up contributions, the higher contribution limits for individuals who are age 50 or older do not apply. The most that can be contributed to your Roth IRA is the smaller of $8,000 or your taxable compensation for the year.

Repayment of reservist, hurricane, disaster recovery assistance, and recovery assistance distributions. You can repay qualified reservist, qualified hurricane, qualified disaster recovery assistance, and qualified recovery assistance distributions even if the repayments would cause your total contributions to the Roth IRA to be more than the general limit on contributions. However, the total repayments cannot be more than the amount of your distribution.

Worksheet 2-1. **Modified Adjusted Gross Income for Roth IRA Purposes**
Use this worksheet to figure your modified adjusted gross income for Roth IRA purposes.

1. Enter your adjusted gross income from Form 1040, line 38; Form 1040A, line 22; or Form 1040NR, line 36	1. _____
2. Enter any income resulting from the conversion of an IRA (other than a Roth IRA) to a Roth IRA, a rollover from a qualified retirement plan to a Roth IRA, and a minimum required distribution from an IRA (for conversions and rollovers from qualified retirement plans only)	2. _____
3. Subtract line 2 from line 1	3. _____
4. Enter any traditional IRA deduction from Form 1040, line 32; Form 1040A, line 17; or Form 1040NR, line 31	4. _____
5. Enter any student loan interest deduction from Form 1040, line 33; Form 1040A, line 18; or Form 1040NR, line 32	5. _____
6. Enter any tuition and fees deduction from Form 1040, line 34 or Form 1040A, line 19 . .	6. _____
7. Enter any domestic production activities deduction from Form 1040, line 35, or Form 1040NR, line 33	7. _____
8. Enter any foreign earned income exclusion and/or housing exclusion from Form 2555, line 45, or Form 2555-EZ, line 18	8. _____
9. Enter any foreign housing deduction from Form 2555, line 50	9. _____
10. Enter any excludable qualified savings bond interest from Form 8815, line 14	10. _____
11. Enter any excluded employer-provided adoption benefits from Form 8839, line 30	11. _____
12. Add the amounts on lines 3 through 11	12. _____

13. Enter:
    • $169,000 if married filing jointly or qualifying widow(er),
    • $10,000 if married filing separately and you lived with your spouse at any time during the year, or
    • $116,000 for all others . . . .
	13. _____

Is the amount on line 12 more than the amount on line 13?
If yes, see the note below.
If no, the amount on line 12 is your *modified adjusted gross income* for Roth IRA purposes.

Note. If the amount on line 12 is more than the amount on line 13 and you have other income or loss items, such as social security income or passive activity losses, that are subject to AGI-based phaseouts, you can refigure your AGI solely for the purpose of figuring your modified AGI for Roth IRA purposes. When figuring your modified AGI for conversion purposes, refigure your AGI without taking into account any income from conversions or minimum required distributions from IRAs. (If you receive social security benefits, use *Worksheet 1* in *Appendix B* to refigure your AGI.) Then go to list item 2 under *Modified AGI* earlier or line 3 above in *Worksheet 2-1* to refigure your modified AGI. If you do not have other income or loss items subject to AGI-based phaseouts, your modified adjusted gross income for Roth IRA purposes is the amount on line 12 above.

Note. If you make repayments of qualified reservist distributions to a Roth IRA, increase your basis in the Roth IRA by the amount of the repayment. If you make repayments of qualified hurricane, qualified disaster recovery assistance, or qualified recovery assistance distributions to a Roth IRA, the repayment is first considered to be a repayment of earnings. Any repayments of qualified hurricane, qualified disaster recovery assistance, or qualified recovery assistance distributions in excess of earnings will increase your basis in the Roth IRA by the amount of the repayment in excess of earnings. For more information, see *Qualified reservist repayments* under *How Much Can Be Contributed?* in chapter 1 and chapter 4, *Disaster-Related Relief.*

Contribution limit reduced. If your modified AGI is above a certain amount, your contribution limit is gradually reduced. Use Table 2-1 to determine if this reduction applies to you.

Figuring the reduction. If the amount you can contribute must be reduced, figure your reduced contribution limit as follows.

1. Start with your modified AGI.

2. Subtract from the amount in (1):

    a. $159,000 if filing a joint return or qualifying widow(er),

    b. $-0- if married filing a separate return, and you lived with your spouse at any time during the year, or

    c. $101,000 for all other individuals.

3. Divide the result in (2) by $15,000 ($10,000 if filing a joint return, qualifying widow(er), or married filing a separate return and you lived with your spouse at any time during the year).

4. Multiply the maximum contribution limit (before reduction by this adjustment and before reduction for any contributions to traditional IRAs) by the result in (3).

5. Subtract the result in (4) from the maximum contribution limit before this reduction. The result is your reduced contribution limit.

You can use Worksheet 2-2 to figure the reduction.

Worksheet 2-2. **Determining Your Reduced Roth IRA Contribution Limit**

Before using this worksheet, check Table 2-1 *to determine whether or not your Roth IRA contribution limit is reduced. If it is, use this worksheet to determine how much it is reduced.*

1. Enter your modified AGI for Roth IRA purposes	**1.** _____
2. Enter: • $159,000 if filing a joint return or qualifying widow(er), • $-0- if married filing a separate return and you lived with your spouse at any time in 2008, or • $101,000 for all others	**2.** _____
3. Subtract line 2 from line 1	**3.** _____
4. Enter: • $10,000 if filing a joint return or qualifying widow(er) or married filing a separate return and you lived with your spouse at any time during the year, or • $15,000 for all others	**4.** _____
5. Divide line 3 by line 4 and enter the result as a decimal (rounded to at least three places). If the result is 1.000 or more, enter 1.000	**5.** _____
6. Enter the lesser of: • $5,000 ($6,000 if you are age 50 or older, or $8,000 for certain employer bankruptcies), or • Your taxable compensation . . .	**6.** _____
7. Multiply line 5 by line 6	**7.** _____
8. Subtract line 7 from line 6. Round the result up to the nearest $10. If the result is less than $200, enter $200	**8.** _____
9. Enter contributions for the year to other IRAs	**9.** _____
10. Subtract line 9 from line 6	**10.** _____
11. Enter the lesser of line 8 or line 10. This is your **reduced Roth IRA contribution limit**	**11.** _____

 Round your reduced contribution limit up to the nearest $10. If your reduced contribution limit is more than $0, but less than $200, increase the limit to $200.

Example. You are a 45-year-old, single individual with taxable compensation of $113,000. You want to make the maximum allowable contribution to your Roth IRA for 2008. Your modified AGI for 2008 is $102,000. You have not contributed to any traditional IRA, so the maximum contribution limit before the modified AGI reduction is $5,000. Using the steps described earlier, you figure your reduced Roth IRA contribution of $4,670 as shown on the following worksheet.

Worksheet 2-2. Example—Illustrated

Before using this worksheet, check Table 2-1 to determine whether or not your Roth IRA contribution limit is reduced. If it is, use this worksheet to determine how much it is reduced.

1. Enter your modified AGI for Roth IRA purposes	1.	102,000
2. Enter: • $159,000 if filing a joint return or qualifying widow(er), • $-0- if married filing a separate return and you lived with your spouse at any time in 2008, or • $101,000 for all others	2.	101,000
3. Subtract line 2 from line 1	3.	1,000
4. Enter: • $10,000 if filing a joint return or qualifying widow(er) or married filing a separate return and you lived with your spouse at any time during the year, or • $15,000 for all others	4.	15,000
5. Divide line 3 by line 4 and enter the result as a decimal (rounded to at least three places). If the result is 1.000 or more, enter 1.000	5.	.067
6. Enter the lesser of: • $5,000 ($6,000 if you are age 50 or older, or $8,000 for certain employer bankruptcies), or • Your taxable compensation . . .	6.	5,000
7. Multiply line 5 by line 6	7.	335
8. Subtract line 7 from line 6. Round the result up to the nearest $10. If the result is less than $200, enter $200	8.	4,670
9. Enter contributions for the year to other IRAs	9.	0
10. Subtract line 9 from line 6	10.	5,000
11. Enter the lesser of line 8 or line 10. This is your **reduced Roth IRA contribution limit**	11.	4,670

When Can You Make Contributions?

You can make contributions to a Roth IRA for a year at any time during the year or by the due date of your return for that year (not including extensions).

 You can make contributions for 2008 by the due date (not including extensions) for filing your 2008 tax return. This means that most people can make contributions for 2008 by April 15, 2009.

What if You Contribute Too Much?

A 6% excise tax applies to any excess contribution to a Roth IRA.

Excess contributions. These are the contributions to your Roth IRAs for a year that equal the total of:

1. Amounts contributed for the tax year to your Roth IRAs (other than amounts properly and timely rolled over from a Roth IRA or properly converted from a traditional IRA or rolled over from a qualified retirement plan, as described later) that are more than your contribution limit for the year (explained earlier under *How Much Can Be Contributed*), plus

2. Any excess contributions for the preceding year, reduced by the total of:

   a. Any distributions out of your Roth IRAs for the year, plus

   b. Your contribution limit for the year minus your contributions to all your IRAs for the year.

Withdrawal of excess contributions. For purposes of determining excess contributions, any contribution that is withdrawn on or before the due date (including extensions) for filing your tax return for the year is treated as an amount not contributed. This treatment only applies if any earnings on the contributions are also withdrawn. The earnings are considered earned and received in the year the excess contribution was made.

Applying excess contributions. If contributions to your Roth IRA for a year were more than the limit, you can apply the excess contribution in one year to a later year if the contributions for that later year are less than the maximum allowed for that year.

Can You Move Amounts Into a Roth IRA?

You may be able to convert amounts from either a traditional, SEP, or SIMPLE IRA into a Roth IRA. You may be able to roll over amounts from a qualified retirement plan to a Roth IRA. You may be able to recharacterize contributions made to one IRA as having been made directly to a different IRA. You can roll amounts over from a designated Roth account or from one Roth IRA to another Roth IRA.

Conversions

You can convert a traditional IRA to a Roth IRA. The conversion is treated as a rollover, regardless of the conversion method used. Most of the rules for rollovers, described in chapter 1 under *Rollover From One IRA Into Another*, apply to these rollovers. However, the 1-year waiting period does not apply.

Conversion methods. You can convert amounts from a traditional IRA to a Roth IRA in any of the following three ways.

- **Rollover.** You can receive a distribution from a traditional IRA and roll it over (contribute it) to a Roth IRA within 60 days after the distribution.

- **Trustee-to-trustee transfer.** You can direct the trustee of the traditional IRA to transfer an amount from the traditional IRA to the trustee of the Roth IRA.

- **Same trustee transfer.** If the trustee of the traditional IRA also maintains the Roth IRA, you can direct the trustee to transfer an amount from the traditional IRA to the Roth IRA.

Same trustee. Conversions made with the same trustee can be made by redesignating the traditional IRA as a Roth IRA, rather than opening a new account or issuing a new contract.

More information. For more information on conversions, see *Converting From Any Traditional IRA Into a Roth IRA* in chapter 1.

Rollover From Employer's Plan Into a Roth IRA

Prior to 2008, you could only roll over (convert) amounts from either a traditional, SEP, or SIMPLE IRA into a Roth IRA. Beginning in 2008, you can roll over into a Roth IRA all or part of an eligible rollover distribution your receive from your (or your deceased spouse's):

- Employer's qualified pension, profit-sharing or stock bonus plan (including a 401(k) plan),
- Annuity plan,
- Tax-sheltered annuity plan (section 403(b) plan), or
- Governmental deferred compensation plan (section 457 plan).

Any amount rolled over is subject to the same rules for converting a traditional IRA into a Roth IRA. See *Converting From Any Traditional IRA Into a Roth IRA* in chapter 1. Also, the rollover contribution must meet the rollover requirements that apply to the specific type of retirement plan.

Income. You must include in your gross income distributions from a qualified retirement plan that you would have had to include in income if you had not rolled them over into a Roth IRA. You do not include in gross income any part of a distribution from a qualified retirement plan that is a return of contributions (after-tax contributions) to the plan that were taxable to you when paid.

Example. In July of 2008, you decide to roll over $50,000 from your 401(k) plan to your Roth IRA. You have no after-tax contributions. For 2008, you must include in income $50,000.

 If you must include any amount in your gross income, you may have to increase your withholding or make estimated tax payments. See Publication 505, Tax Withholding and Estimated Tax.

Rollover methods. You can roll over amounts from a qualified retirement plan to a Roth IRA in one of the following ways.

- **Rollover.** You can receive a distribution from a qualified retirement plan and roll it over (contribute) to a Roth IRA within 60 days after the distribution. Since the distribution is paid directly to you, the payer generally must withhold 20% of it.

- **Direct rollover option.** Your employer's qualified plan must give you the option to have any part of an eligible rollover distribution paid directly to a Roth IRA. Generally, no tax is withheld from any part of the designated distribution that is directly paid to the trustee of the Roth IRA.

For more information on eligible rollover distributions from qualified retirement plans and withholding, see *Rollover From Employer's Plan Into an IRA* in chapter 1.

How to report. A rollover to a Roth IRA is not a tax-free distribution other than any after-tax contributions you made. Report a rollover from a qualified retirement plan to a Roth IRA on Form 1040, lines 16a and 16b; Form 1040A, lines 12a and 12b; or Form 1040NR, lines 17a and 17b.

Enter the total amount of the distribution before income tax or deductions were withheld on Form 1040, line 16a; Form 1040A, line 12a; or Form 1040NR, line 17a. This amount is shown in box 1 of Form 1099-R. From this amount, subtract any contributions (usually shown in box 5 of Form 1099-R) that were taxable to you when made. Enter the remaining amount, even if zero, on Form 1040, line 16b; Form 1040A, line 12b; or Form 1040NR, line 17b.

Military Death Gratuities and Servicemembers' Group Life Insurance (SGLI) Payments

If you received a military death gratuity or SGLI payment with respect to a death from injury that occurred after October 6, 2001, you can contribute (roll over) all or part of the amount received to your Roth IRA. The contribution is treated as a qualified rollover contribution.

The amount you can roll over to your Roth IRA cannot exceed the total amount that you received reduced by any part of that amount that was contributed to a Coverdell ESA or another Roth IRA. Any military death gratuity or

Chapter 2   **Roth IRAs**   Page 65

SGLI payment contributed to a Roth IRA is disregarded for purposes of the 1-year waiting period between rollovers.

The rollover must be completed before the end of the 1-year period beginning on the date you received the payment. However, if you received a military death gratuity or SGLI payment with respect to a death from injury that occurred after October 6, 2001, and before June 17, 2008, you have until June 17, 2009, to make the contribution to your Roth IRA.

The amount contributed to your Roth IRA is treated as part of your cost basis (investment in the contract) in the Roth IRA that is not taxable when distributed.

Failed Conversions and Rollovers

If, when you converted amounts from a traditional IRA or SIMPLE IRA into a Roth IRA or when you rolled over amounts from a qualified retirement plan into a Roth IRA, you expected to have modified AGI of $100,000 or less and a filing status other than married filing separately, but your expectations did not come true, you have made a failed conversion or failed rollover.

Results of failed conversions and failed rollovers. If the converted or rolled over amount (contribution) is not recharacterized (explained in chapter 1), the contribution will be treated as a regular contribution to the Roth IRA and subject to the following tax consequences.

- A 6% excise tax per year will apply to any excess contribution not withdrawn from the Roth IRA.

- The distributions from the traditional IRA or qualified retirement plan must be included in your gross income.

- The 10% additional tax on early distributions may apply to any distribution.

How to avoid. You must move the amount converted or rolled over (including all earnings from the date of conversion or roll over) into a traditional IRA by the due date (including extensions) for your tax return for the year during which you made the conversion or roll over to the Roth IRA. You do not have to include this distribution (withdrawal) in income.

Rollover From a Roth IRA

You can withdraw, tax free, all or part of the assets from one Roth IRA if you contribute them within 60 days to another Roth IRA. Most of the rules for rollovers, described in chapter 1 under *Rollover From One IRA Into Another*, apply to these rollovers. However, rollovers from retirement plans other than Roth IRAs are disregarded for purposes of the 1-year waiting period between rollovers.

A rollover from a Roth IRA to an employer retirement plan is not allowed.

A rollover from a designated Roth account can only be made to another designated Roth account or to a Roth IRA.

Rollover of Exxon Valdez Settlement Income

If you are a qualified taxpayer and you received qualified settlement income, you can contribute all or part of the amount received to an eligible retirement plan which includes a Roth IRA. The rules for contributing qualified settlement income to a Roth IRA are the same as the rules for contributing qualified settlement income to a traditional IRA with the following exception. Qualified settlement income that is contributed to a Roth IRA, or to a designated Roth account, will be:

- Included in your taxable income for the year the qualified settlement income was received, and

- Treated as part of your cost basis (investment in the contract) in the Roth IRA that is not taxable when distributed.

For more information, see *Rollover of Exxon Valdez Settlement Income* in chapter 1.

Rollover of Airline Payments

If you are a qualified airline employee, you may contribute any portion of an airline payment you receive to a Roth IRA. The contribution must be made within 180 days from the date you received the payment, or before June 23, 2009, whichever is later. The contribution will be treated as a qualified rollover contribution and the modified AGI limits that generally apply to Roth IRA rollovers do not apply to airline payments. The rollover contribution is included in income to the extent it would be included in income if it were not part of the rollover contribution. Also, any reduction in the airline payment amount on account of employment taxes shall be disregarded when figuring the amount you can contribute to your Roth IRA.

Airline payment. An airline payment is any payment of money or other property that is paid to a qualified airline employee from a commercial airline carrier. The payment also must be made both:

- Under the approval of an order of federal bankruptcy court in a case filed after September 11, 2001, and before January 1, 2007, and

- In respect of the qualified airline employee's interest in a bankruptcy claim against the airline carrier, any note of the carrier (or amount paid in lieu of a note being issued), or any other fixed obligation of the carrier to pay a lump sum amount.

An airline payment amount shall not include any amount payable on the basis of the carrier's future earnings or profits.

Qualified airline employee. A qualified airline employee is an employee or former employee of a commercial airline carrier who was a participant in a qualified defined benefit plan maintained by the carrier which was terminated or became subject to restrictions under Section 402(b) of the Pension Protection Act of 2006.

For more information, see Form 8935, Airline Payment Report. This form will be sent to you within 90 days following an airline payment, or by March 23, 2009, whichever is later. The form will indicate the amount of the airline payment that is eligible to be rolled over to a Roth IRA.

Are Distributions Taxable?

You do not include in your gross income qualified distributions or distributions that are a return of your regular contributions from your Roth IRA(s). You also do not include distributions from your Roth IRA that you roll over tax free into another Roth IRA. You may have to include part of other distributions in your income. See *Ordering Rules for Distributions*, later.

Basis of distributed property. The basis of property distributed from a Roth IRA is its fair market value (FMV) on the date of distribution, whether or not the distribution is a qualified distribution.

Withdrawals of contributions by due date. If you withdraw contributions (including any net earnings on the contributions) by the due date of your return for the year in which you made the contribution, the contributions are treated as if you never made them. If you have an extension of time to file your return, you can withdraw the contributions and earnings by the extended due date. The withdrawal of contributions is tax free, but you must include the earnings on the contributions in income for the year in which you made the contributions.

What Are Qualified Distributions?

A qualified distribution is any payment or distribution from your Roth IRA that meets the following requirements.

1. It is made after the 5-year period beginning with the first taxable year for which a contribution was made to a Roth IRA set up for your benefit, and

2. The payment or distribution is:

   a. Made on or after the date you reach age 59½,

   b. Made because you are disabled,

   c. Made to a beneficiary or to your estate after your death, or

   d. One that meets the requirements listed under *First home* under *Exceptions* in chapter 1 (up to a $10,000 lifetime limit).

Additional Tax on Early Distributions

If you receive a distribution that is not a qualified distribution, you may have to pay the 10% additional tax on early distributions as explained in the following paragraphs.

Distributions of conversion and certain rollover contributions within 5-year period. If, within the 5-year period starting with the first day of your tax year in which you convert an amount from a traditional IRA or rollover an amount from a qualified retirement plan to a Roth IRA, you take a distribution from a Roth IRA, you may have to pay the 10% additional tax on early distributions. You generally must pay the 10% additional tax on any amount attributable to the part of the amount converted or rolled over (the conversion or rollover contribution) that you had to include in income. A separate 5-year period applies to each conversion and rollover. See *Ordering Rules for Distributions*, later, to determine the amount, if any, of the distribution that is attributable to the part of the conversion or rollover contribution that you had to include in income.

The 5-year period used for determining whether the 10% early distribution tax applies to a distribution from a conversion or rollover contribution is separately determined for each conversion and rollover, and is not necessarily the same as the 5-year period used for determining whether a distribution is a qualified distribution. See *What Are Qualified Distributions*, earlier.

For example, if a calendar-year taxpayer makes a conversion contribution on February 25, 2008, and makes a regular contribution for 2007 on the same date, the 5-year period for the conversion begins January 1, 2008, while the 5-year period for the regular contribution begins on January 1, 2007.

Unless one of the exceptions listed later applies, you must pay the additional tax on the portion of the distribution attributable to the part of the conversion or rollover contribution that you had to include in income because of the conversion or rollover.

You must pay the 10% additional tax in the year of the distribution, even if you had included the conversion or rollover contribution in an earlier year. You also must pay the additional tax on any portion of the distribution attributable to earnings on contributions.

Other early distributions. Unless one of the exceptions listed below applies, you must pay the 10% additional tax on the taxable part of any distributions that are not qualified distributions.

Exceptions. You may not have to pay the 10% additional tax in the following situations.

- You have reached age 59½.

- You are disabled.

- You are the beneficiary of a deceased IRA owner.

- You use the distribution to pay certain qualified first-time homebuyer amounts.

- The distributions are part of a series of substantially equal payments.

- You have significant unreimbursed medical expenses.

- You are paying medical insurance premiums after losing your job.

- The distributions are not more than your qualified higher education expenses.

- The distribution is due to an IRS levy of the qualified plan.

Figure 2-1.   **Is the Distribution From Your Roth IRA a Qualified Distribution?**

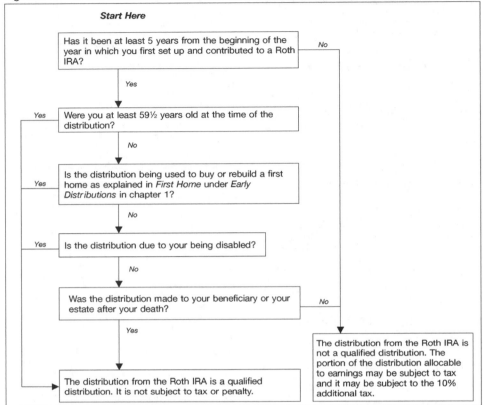

- The distribution is a qualified reservist distribution.
- The distribution is a qualified disaster recovery assistance distribution.
- The distribution is a qualified recovery assistance distribution.

Most of these exceptions are discussed earlier in chapter 1 under *Early Distributions*.

Tax-free withdrawal of economic stimulus payments.
You may choose to withdraw an economic stimulus payment that was directly deposited to your Roth IRA in 2008. If you choose to withdraw any or all of the payment, that portion of the payment is treated as neither contributed nor distributed from your IRA. The amount withdrawn is not included in your income and is not subject to additional tax or penalty. The withdrawal must be made by the due date for filing your 2008 tax return, including extensions. For most people that would be April 15, 2009.

If you do withdraw all or part of the payment from your IRA, you will receive a Form 1099-R showing the amount of the distribution. Include the distribution on Form 1040, line 15a; Form 1040A, line 11a; or Form 1040NR, line 16a. Do not make an entry on Form 1040, line 15b; Form 1040A, line 11b; or Form 1040NR, line 16b, but enter "ESP" in the space next to the line. For more information see the instructions for your tax return.

Ordering Rules for Distributions

If you receive a distribution from your Roth IRA that is not a qualified distribution, part of it may be taxable. There is a set order in which contributions (including conversion contributions and rollover contributions from qualified retirement plans) and earnings are considered to be distributed from your Roth IRA. For these purposes, disregard the withdrawal of excess contributions and the earnings on them (discussed earlier under *What if You Contribute Too Much*. Order the distributions as follows.

1. Regular contributions.

2. Conversion and rollover contributions, on a first-in-first-out basis (generally, total conversions and rollovers from the earliest year first). See *Aggregation (grouping and adding) rules*, later. Take these conversion and rollover contributions into account as follows:

   a. Taxable portion (the amount required to be included in gross income because of the conversion or rollover) first, and then the

   b. Nontaxable portion.

3. Earnings on contributions.

Disregard rollover contributions from other Roth IRAs for this purpose.

Aggregation (grouping and adding) rules. Determine the taxable amounts distributed (withdrawn), distributions, and contributions by grouping and adding them together as follows.

- Add all distributions from all your Roth IRAs during the year together.

- Add all regular contributions made for the year (including contributions made after the close of the year, but before the due date of your return) together. Add this total to the total undistributed regular contributions made in prior years.

- Add all conversion and rollover contributions made during the year together. For purposes of the ordering rules, in the case of any conversion or rollover in which the conversion or rollover distribution is made in 2008 and the conversion or rollover contribution is made in 2009, treat the conversion or rollover contribution as contributed before any other conversion or rollover contributions made in 2009.

Add any recharacterized contributions that end up in a Roth IRA to the appropriate contribution group for the year that the original contribution would have been taken into account if it had been made directly to the Roth IRA.

Disregard any recharacterized contribution that ends up in an IRA other than a Roth IRA for the purpose of grouping (aggregating) both contributions and distributions. Also disregard any amount withdrawn to correct an excess contribution (including the earnings withdrawn) for this purpose.

Example. On October 15, 2003, Justin converted all $80,000 in his traditional IRA to his Roth IRA. His Forms 8606 from prior years show that $20,000 of the amount converted is his basis.

Justin included $60,000 ($80,000 − $20,000) in his gross income.

On February 23, 2008, Justin made a regular contribution of $5,000 to a Roth IRA. On November 7, 2008, at age 60, Justin took a $7,000 distribution from his Roth IRA.

The first $5,000 of the distribution is a return of Justin's regular contribution and is not includible in his income.

The next $2,000 of the distribution is not includible in income because it was included previously.

How Do You Figure the Taxable Part?

To figure the taxable part of a distribution that is not a qualified distribution, complete Worksheet 2-3.

Worksheet 2-3. Figuring the Taxable Part of a Distribution (Other Than a Qualified Distribution) From a Roth IRA

1. Enter the total of all distributions made from your Roth IRA(s) (other than qualified charitable distributions or a one-time distribution to fund an HSA) during the year . . . . 1. _____

2. Enter the amount of qualified distributions made during the year 2. _____

3. Subtract line 2 from line 1 . . . . . . 3. _____

4. Enter the amount of distributions made during the year to correct excess contributions made during the year. (Do not include earnings.) 4. _____

5. Subtract line 4 from line 3 . . . . . . 5. _____

6. Enter the amount of distributions made during the year that were contributed to another Roth IRA in a qualified rollover contribution (other than a repayment of a qualified disaster recovery assistance or recovery assistance distribution) . . . . 6. _____

7. Subtract line 6 from line 5 . . . . . . 7. _____

8. Enter the amount of *all* prior distributions from your Roth IRA(s) (other than qualified charitable distributions or a one-time distribution to fund an HSA) whether or not they were qualified distributions . . . . 8. _____

9. Add lines 3 and 8 . . . . 9. _____

10. Enter the amount of the distributions included on line 8 that were previously includible in your income . . . . 10. _____

11. Subtract line 10 from line 9 . . . . . 11. _____

12. Enter the total of all your contributions to all of your Roth IRAs . . . . 12. _____

13. Enter the total of all distributions made (this year and in prior years) to correct excess contributions. (Include earnings.) . . . . 13. _____

14. Subtract line 13 from line 12. (If the result is less than 0, enter 0.) . . . . 14. _____

15. Subtract line 14 from line 11. (If the result is less than 0, enter 0.) . . . . 15. _____

16. Enter the smaller of the amount on line 7 or the amount on line 15. This is the **taxable part of your distribution** . . . . 16. _____

Must You Withdraw or Use Assets?

You are not required to take distributions from your Roth IRA at any age. The minimum distribution rules that apply to traditional IRAs do not apply to Roth IRAs while the owner is alive. However, after the death of a Roth IRA owner, certain of the minimum distribution rules that apply to traditional IRAs also apply to Roth IRAs as explained later under *Distributions After Owner's Death*.

Minimum distributions. You cannot use your Roth IRA to satisfy minimum distribution requirements for your traditional IRA. Nor can you use distributions from traditional IRAs for required distributions from Roth IRAs. See *Distributions to beneficiaries*, later.

Recognizing Losses on Investments

If you have a loss on your Roth IRA investment, you can recognize the loss on your income tax return, but only when all the amounts in all of your Roth IRA accounts have been distributed to you and the total distributions are less than your unrecovered basis.

Your basis is the total amount of contributions in your Roth IRAs.

You claim the loss as a miscellaneous itemized deduction, subject to the 2%-of-adjusted-gross-income limit that applies to certain miscellaneous itemized deductions on Schedule A, Form 1040. Any such losses are added back to taxable income for purposes of calculating the alternative minimum tax.

Distributions After Owner's Death

If a Roth IRA owner dies, the minimum distribution rules that apply to traditional IRAs apply to Roth IRAs as though the Roth IRA owner died before his or her required beginning date. See *When Can You Withdraw or Use Assets?* in chapter 1.

Distributions to beneficiaries. Generally, the entire interest in the Roth IRA must be distributed by the end of the fifth calendar year after the year of the owner's death unless the interest is payable to a designated beneficiary over the life or life expectancy of the designated beneficiary. (See *When Must You Withdraw Assets? (Required Minimum Distributions)* in chapter 1.) If you are a beneficiary receiving distributions over a 5-year period, you can waive the distribution for 2009, effectively taking distributions over a 6-year rather than a 5-year period.

If paid as an annuity, the entire interest must be payable over a period not greater than the designated beneficiary's life expectancy and distributions must begin before the end of the calendar year following the year of death. Distributions from another Roth IRA cannot be substituted for these distributions unless the other Roth IRA was inherited from the same decedent.

If the sole beneficiary is the spouse, he or she can either delay distributions until the decedent would have reached age 70½ or treat the Roth IRA as his or her own.

Temporary waiver of required minimum distribution rules for 2009. No minimum distributions are required for 2009. The waiver applies to post-death minimum distributions required for Roth IRA beneficiaries in the same way it applies to traditional IRA beneficiaries. See *Temporary waiver of required minimum distribution rules for 2009* in chapter 1.

Combining with other Roth IRAs. A beneficiary can combine an inherited Roth IRA with another Roth IRA maintained by the beneficiary only if the beneficiary either:

- Inherited the other Roth IRA from the same decedent, or

- Was the spouse of the decedent and the sole beneficiary of the Roth IRA and elects to treat it as his or her own IRA.

Distributions that are not qualified distributions. If a distribution to a beneficiary is not a qualified distribution, it is generally includible in the beneficiary's gross income in the same manner as it would have been included in the owner's income had it been distributed to the IRA owner when he or she was alive.

If the owner of a Roth IRA dies before the end of:

- The 5-year period beginning with the first taxable year for which a contribution was made to a Roth IRA set up for the owner's benefit, or

- The 5-year period starting with the year of a conversion contribution from a traditional IRA or a rollover from a qualified retirement plan to a Roth IRA,

each type of contribution is divided among multiple beneficiaries according to the pro-rata share of each. See *Ordering Rules for Distributions*, earlier in this chapter under *Are Distributions Taxable*.

Example. When Ms. Hibbard died in 2008, her Roth IRA contained regular contributions of $4,000, a conversion contribution of $10,000 that was made in 2004, and earnings of $2,000. No distributions had been made from her IRA. She had no basis in the conversion contribution in 2004.

When she established her Roth IRA, she named each of her 4 children as equal beneficiaries. Each child will receive one-fourth of each type of contribution and one-fourth of the earnings. An immediate distribution of $4,000 to each child will be treated as $1,000 from regular contributions, $2,500 from conversion contributions, and $500 from earnings.

In this case, because the distributions are made before the end of the applicable 5-year period for a qualified distribution, each beneficiary includes $500 in income for 2008. The 10% additional tax on early distributions does not apply because the distribution was made to the beneficiaries as a result of the death of the IRA owner.

Tax on excess accumulations (insufficient distributions). If distributions from an inherited Roth IRA are less than the required minimum distribution for the year, discussed in chapter 1 under *When Must You Withdraw Assets? (Required Minimum Distributions)*, you may have to pay a 50% excise tax for that year on the amount not distributed as required. For the tax on excess accumulations (insufficient distributions), see *Excess Accumulations (Insufficient Distributions)* under *What Acts Result in Penalties or Additional Taxes?* in chapter 1. If this applies to you, substitute "Roth IRA" for "traditional IRA" in that discussion.

3.

Savings Incentive Match Plans for Employees (SIMPLE)

Introduction

This chapter is for employees who need information about savings incentive match plans for employees (SIMPLE plans). It explains what a SIMPLE plan is, contributions to a SIMPLE plan, and distributions from a SIMPLE plan.

Under a SIMPLE plan, SIMPLE retirement accounts for participating employees can be set up either as:

- Part of a 401(k) plan, or

- A plan using IRAs (SIMPLE IRA).

This chapter only discusses the SIMPLE plan rules that relate to SIMPLE IRAs. See Publication 560 for information on any special rules for SIMPLE plans that do not use IRAs.

 If your employer maintains a SIMPLE plan, you must be notified, in writing, that you can choose the financial institution that will serve as trustee for your SIMPLE IRA and that you can roll over or transfer your SIMPLE IRA to another financial institution. See Rollovers and Transfers Exception, later under When Can You Withdraw or Use Assets.

What Is a SIMPLE Plan?

A SIMPLE plan is a tax-favored retirement plan that certain small employers (including self-employed individuals) can set up for the benefit of their employees. See Publication 560 for information on the requirements employers must satisfy to set up a SIMPLE plan.

A SIMPLE plan is a written agreement (salary reduction agreement) between you and your employer that allows you, if you are an eligible employee (including a self-employed individual), to choose to:

- Reduce your compensation (salary) by a certain percentage each pay period, and

- Have your employer contribute the salary reductions to a SIMPLE IRA on your behalf. These contributions are called salary reduction contributions.

All contributions under a SIMPLE IRA plan must be made to SIMPLE IRAs, not to any other type of IRA. The SIMPLE IRA can be an individual retirement account or an individual retirement annuity, described in chapter 1. Contributions are made on behalf of eligible employees. (See *Eligible Employees,* later.) Contributions are also subject to various limits. (See *How Much Can Be Contributed on Your Behalf,* later.)

In addition to salary reduction contributions, your employer must make either matching contributions or nonelective contributions. See *How Are Contributions Made,* later.

 You may be able to claim a credit for contributions to your SIMPLE. For more information, see chapter 5.

Eligible Employees

You must be allowed to participate in your employer's SIMPLE plan if you:

- Received at least $5,000 in compensation from your employer during any 2 years prior to the current year, and

- Are reasonably expected to receive at least $5,000 in compensation during the calendar year for which contributions are made.

Self-employed individual. For SIMPLE plan purposes, the term employee includes a self-employed individual who received earned income.

Excludable employees. Your employer can exclude the following employees from participating in the SIMPLE plan.

- Employees whose retirement benefits are covered by a collective bargaining agreement (union contract).

- Employees who are nonresident aliens and received no earned income from sources within the United States.

- Employees who would not have been eligible employees if an acquisition, disposition, or similar transaction had not occurred during the year.

Compensation. For purposes of the SIMPLE plan rules, your compensation for a year generally includes the following amounts.

- Wages, tips, and other pay from your employer that is subject to income tax withholding.

- Deferred amounts elected under any 401(k) plans, 403(b) plans, government (section 457) plans, SEP plans, and SIMPLE plans.

Self-employed individual compensation. For purposes of the SIMPLE plan rules, if you are self-employed, your compensation for a year is your net earnings from self-employment (Schedule SE (Form 1040), Section A, line 4, or Section B, line 6) before subtracting any contributions made to a SIMPLE IRA on your behalf.

For these purposes, net earnings from self-employment include services performed while claiming exemption from self-employment tax as a member of a group conscientiously opposed to social security benefits.

How Are Contributions Made?

Contributions under a salary reduction agreement are called salary reduction contributions. They are made on your behalf by your employer. Your employer must also make either matching contributions or nonelective contributions.

Salary reduction contributions. During the 60-day period before the beginning of any year, and during the 60-day period before you are eligible, you can choose salary reduction contributions expressed either as a percentage of compensation, or as a specific dollar amount (if your employer offers this choice). You can choose to cancel the election at any time during the year.

Salary reduction contributions are also referred to as "elective deferrals."

Your employer cannot place restrictions on the contributions amount (such as by limiting the contributions percentage), except to comply with the salary reduction contributions limit, discussed under *How Much Can Be Contributed on Your Behalf,* later.

Matching contributions. Unless your employer chooses to make nonelective contributions, your employer must make contributions equal to the salary reduction contributions you choose (elect), but only up to certain limits. See *How Much Can Be Contributed on Your Behalf,* later. These contributions are in addition to the salary reduction contributions and must be made to the SIMPLE IRAs of all eligible employees (defined earlier) who chose salary reductions. These contributions are referred to as matching contributions.

Matching contributions on behalf of a self-employed individual are not treated as salary reduction contributions.

Nonelective contributions. Instead of making matching contributions, your employer may be able to choose to make nonelective contributions on behalf of all eligible employees. These nonelective contributions must be made on behalf of each eligible employee who has at least $5,000 of compensation from your employer, whether or not the employee chose salary reductions.

One of the requirements your employer must satisfy is notifying the employees that the election was made. For other requirements that your employer must satisfy, see Publication 560.

How Much Can Be Contributed on Your Behalf?

The limits on contributions to a SIMPLE IRA vary with the type of contribution that is made.

Salary reduction contributions limit. Salary reduction contributions (employee-chosen contributions or elective deferrals) that your employer can make on your behalf under a SIMPLE plan are limited to $10,500 for 2008.

 If you are a participant in any other employer plans during 2008 and you have elective salary reductions or deferred compensation under those plans, the salary reduction contributions under the SIMPLE plan also are included in the annual limit of $15,500 for 2008 on exclusions of salary reductions and other elective deferrals.

You, not your employer, are responsible for monitoring compliance with these limits.

Additional elective deferrals can be contributed to your SIMPLE if:

- You reached age 50 by the end of 2008, and
- No other elective deferrals can be made for you to the plan for the year because of limits or restrictions, such as the regular annual limit.

The most that can be contributed in additional elective deferrals to your SIMPLE is the lesser of the following two amounts.

- $2,500 for 2008, or
- Your compensation for the year reduced by your other elective deferrals for the year.

The additional deferrals are not subject to any other contribution limit and are not taken into account in applying other contribution limits. The additional deferrals are not subject to the nondiscrimination rules as long as all eligible participants are allowed to make them.

Matching employer contributions limit. Generally, your employer must make matching contributions to your SIMPLE IRA in an amount equal to your salary reduction contributions. These matching contributions cannot be more than 3% of your compensation for the calendar year. See *Matching contributions less than 3%,* later.

Example 1. In 2008, Joshua was a participant in his employer's SIMPLE plan. His compensation, before SIMPLE plan contributions, was $41,600 ($800 per week). Instead of taking it all in cash, Joshua elected to have 12.5% of his weekly pay ($100) contributed to his SIMPLE IRA. For the full year, Joshua's salary reduction contributions were $5,200, which is less than the $10,500 limit on these contributions.

Under the plan, Joshua's employer was required to make matching contributions to Joshua's SIMPLE IRA. Because his employer's matching contributions must equal Joshua's salary reductions, but cannot be more than 3% of his compensation (before salary reductions) for the year, his employer's matching contribution was limited to $1,248 (3% of $41,600).

Example 2. Assume the same facts as in *Example 1,* except that Joshua's compensation for the year was $357,142 and he chose to have 2.94% of his weekly pay contributed to his SIMPLE IRA.

In this example, Joshua's salary reduction contributions for the year (2.94% × $357,142) were equal to the 2008 limit for salary reduction contributions ($10,500). Because 3% of Joshua's compensation ($10,714) is more than the amount his employer was required to match ($10,500), his employer's matching contributions were limited to $10,500.

In this example, total contributions made on Joshua's behalf for the year were $21,000, the maximum contributions permitted under a SIMPLE IRA for 2008.

Matching contributions less than 3%. Your employer can reduce the 3% limit on matching contributions for a calendar year, but only if:

1. The limit is not reduced below 1%,
2. The limit is not reduced for more than 2 years out of the 5-year period that ends with (and includes) the year for which the election is effective, and
3. Employees are notified of the reduced limit within a reasonable period of time before the 60-day election period during which they can enter into salary reduction agreements.

For purposes of applying the rule in item (2) in determining whether the limit was reduced below 3% for the year, any year before the first year in which your employer (or a former employer) maintains a SIMPLE IRA plan will be treated as a year for which the limit was 3%. If your employer chooses to make nonelective contributions for a year, that year also will be treated as a year for which the limit was 3%.

Nonelective employer contributions limit. If your employer chooses to make nonelective contributions, instead of matching contributions, to each eligible employee's SIMPLE IRA, contributions must be 2% of your compensation for the entire year. For 2008, only $230,000 of your compensation can be taken into account to figure the contribution limit.

Your employer can substitute the 2% nonelective contribution for the matching contribution for a year, if both of the following requirements are met.

- Eligible employees are notified that a 2% nonelective contribution will be made instead of a matching contribution.

- This notice is provided within a reasonable period during which employees can enter into salary reduction agreements.

Example 3. Assume the same facts as in *Example 2,* except that Joshua's employer chose to make nonelective contributions instead of matching contributions. Because his employer's nonelective contributions are limited to 2% of up to $230,000 of Joshua's compensation, his employer's contribution to Joshua's SIMPLE IRA was limited to $4,600. In this example, total contributions made on Joshua's behalf for the year were $15,100 (Joshua's salary reductions of $10,500 plus his employer's contribution of $4,600).

Traditional IRA mistakenly moved to SIMPLE IRA. If you mistakenly roll over or transfer an amount from a traditional IRA to a SIMPLE IRA, you can later recharacterize the amount as a contribution to another traditional IRA. For more information, see *Recharacterizations* in chapter 1.

Recharacterizing employer contributions. You cannot recharacterize employer contributions (including elective deferrals) under a SEP or SIMPLE plan as contributions to another IRA. SEPs are discussed in Publication 560. SIMPLE plans are discussed in this chapter.

Converting from a SIMPLE IRA. Generally, you can convert an amount in your SIMPLE IRA to a Roth IRA under the same rules explained in chapter 1 under *Converting From Any Traditional IRA Into a Roth IRA.*

However, you cannot convert any amount distributed from the SIMPLE IRA during the 2-year period beginning on the date you first participated in any SIMPLE IRA plan maintained by your employer.

When Can You Withdraw or Use Assets?

Generally, the same distribution (withdrawal) rules that apply to traditional IRAs apply to SIMPLE IRAs. These rules are discussed in chapter 1.

Your employer cannot restrict you from taking distributions from a SIMPLE IRA.

Are Distributions Taxable?

Generally, distributions from a SIMPLE IRA are fully taxable as ordinary income. If the distribution is an early distribution (discussed in chapter 1), it may be subject to the additional tax on early distributions. See *Additional Tax on Early Distributions,* later.

Rollovers and Transfers Exception

Generally, rollovers and trustee-to-trustee transfers are not taxable distributions.

Two-year rule. To qualify as a tax-free rollover (or a tax-free trustee-to-trustee transfer), a rollover distribution (or a transfer) made from a SIMPLE IRA during the 2-year period beginning on the date on which you first participated in your employer's SIMPLE plan must be contributed (or transferred) to another SIMPLE IRA. The 2-year period begins on the first day on which contributions made by your employer are deposited in your SIMPLE IRA.

After the 2-year period, amounts in a SIMPLE IRA can be rolled over or transferred tax free to an IRA other than a SIMPLE IRA, or to a qualified plan, a tax-sheltered annuity plan (section 403(b) plan), or deferred compensation plan of a state or local government (section 457 plan).

Additional Tax on Early Distributions

The additional tax on early distributions (discussed in chapter 1) applies to SIMPLE IRAs. If a distribution is an early distribution and occurs during the 2-year period following the date on which you first participated in your employer's SIMPLE plan, the additional tax on early distributions is increased from 10% to 25%.

If a rollover distribution (or transfer) from a SIMPLE IRA does not satisfy the 2-year rule, and is otherwise an early distribution, the additional tax imposed because of the early distribution is increased from 10% to 25% of the amount distributed.

4.

Disaster-Related Relief

Hurricane-Related Relief

Special rules applied to withdrawals from and repayments to certain retirement plans (including IRAs) for taxpayers who suffered an economic loss as a result of Hurricane Katrina, Rita, or Wilma. While qualified hurricane distributions cannot be made after December 31, 2006, the special rules still apply to repayments of these distributions.

If you received a qualified hurricane distribution, it is taxable, but is not subject to the 10% additional tax on early distributions. The taxable amount is figured in the same manner as other IRA distributions. However, the distribution is included in income ratably over 3 years unless you elected to report the entire amount in the year of distribution. You can repay the distribution and not be taxed on the distribution. See *Qualified Hurricane Distributions*, later.

Form 8915, Qualified Hurricane Retirement Plan Distributions and Repayments, is used to report qualified hurricane distributions and repayments.

For information on other tax provisions related to these hurricanes, see Publication 4492, Information for Taxpayers Affected by Hurricanes Katrina, Rita, and Wilma.

Qualified Hurricane Distributions

A qualified hurricane distribution is any distribution you received in 2005 or 2006 from an eligible retirement plan (including IRAs) if all of the following conditions apply.

1. The distribution was made:

   a. After August 24, 2005, and before January 1, 2007, for Hurricane Katrina.

   b. After September 22, 2005, and before January 1, 2007, for Hurricane Rita.

   c. After October 22, 2005, and before January 1, 2007, for Hurricane Wilma.

2. Your main home was located in a qualified hurricane disaster area listed below on the date shown for that area.

   a. August 28, 2005, for the Hurricane Katrina disaster area. For this purpose, the Hurricane Katrina disaster area includes the states of Alabama, Florida, Louisiana, and Mississippi.

   b. September 23, 2005, for the Hurricane Rita disaster area. For this purpose, the Hurricane Rita disaster area includes the states of Louisiana and Texas.

   c. October 23, 2005, for the Hurricane Wilma disaster area. For this purpose, the Hurricane Wilma disaster area includes the state of Florida.

3. You sustained an economic loss because of Hurricane Katrina, Rita, or Wilma and your main home was in that hurricane disaster area on the date shown in item (2) for that hurricane. Examples of an economic loss include, but are not limited to (a) loss, damage to, or destruction of real or personal property from fire, flooding, looting, vandalism, theft, wind, or other cause; (b) loss related to displacement from your home; or (c) loss of livelihood due to temporary or permanent layoffs.

If you met all these conditions, you generally could have designated any distribution (including periodic payments and required minimum distributions) from an eligible retirement plan as a qualified hurricane distribution, regardless of whether the distribution was made on account of Hurricane Katrina, Rita, or Wilma. Qualified hurricane distributions were permitted without regard to your need or the actual amount of your economic loss.

Distribution limit. The total of your qualified hurricane distributions from all plans for 2005 and 2006 was limited to $100,000. If you had distributions in excess of $100,000 from more than one type of plan, such as a 401(k) plan and an IRA, you could have allocated the $100,000 limit among the plans, any way you chose.

Example. In 2005, you received a distribution of $50,000. In 2006, you received a distribution of $125,000. Both distributions met the requirements for a qualified hurricane distribution. If you decided to treat the entire $50,000 received in 2005 as a qualified hurricane distribution, only $50,000 of the 2006 distribution could have been treated as a qualified hurricane distribution.

Main home. Generally, your main home is the home where you live most of the time. A temporary absence due to special circumstances, such as illness, education, business, military service, evacuation, or vacation will not change your main home.

Eligible retirement plan. An eligible retirement plan can be any of the following.

- A qualified pension, profit-sharing, or stock bonus plan (including a 401(k) plan).

- A qualified annuity plan.

- A tax-sheltered annuity contract.

- A governmental section 457 deferred compensation plan.

- A traditional, SEP, SIMPLE, or Roth IRA.

Additional 10% tax. Qualified hurricane distributions are not subject to the 10% additional tax (including the 25% additional tax for certain distributions from SIMPLE IRAs) on early distributions from qualified retirement plans (including IRAs). However, any distributions you received in excess of the $100,000 qualified hurricane distribution limit may have been subject to the additional tax on early distributions.

Repayment of Qualified Hurricane Distributions

Most qualified hurricane distributions are eligible for repayment to an eligible retirement plan. Payments received as a beneficiary (other than a surviving spouse), periodic payments (other than from IRAs), and required minimum distributions are not eligible for repayment. Periodic payments, for this purpose, are payments that are for (a) a period of 10 years or more, (b) your life or life expectancy, or (c) the joint lives or joint life expectancies of you and your beneficiary. For distributions eligible for repayment, you have 3 years from the day after the date you received the distribution to repay all or part to any plan, annuity, or IRA to which a rollover can be made. Within the time allowed, you may make as many repayments as you choose. The total amount repaid cannot be more than the amount of your qualified hurricane distributions. Amounts repaid are treated as a qualified rollover and are not included in income. The way you report repayments depends on whether you reported the distributions under the 3-year method, or you elected to report the distributions in the year of distribution.

Repayment of distributions if reporting under the 1-year election. If you elected to include all of your qualified hurricane distributions received in a year in income for that year and then repay any portion of the distributions during the allowable 3-year period, the amount repaid will reduce the amount included in income for the year of distribution. If the repayment is made after the due date (including extensions) for your return for the year of distribution, you will need to file a revised Form 8915 with an amended return. See *Amending Your Return*, later.

Repayment of distributions if reporting under the 3-year method. If you are reporting the distribution in income over the 3-year period and you repay any portion of the distribution to an eligible retirement plan before filing your 2008 tax return by the due date (including extensions) for that return, the repayment will reduce the portion of the distribution that was included in income in 2008. After 2008, qualified hurricane distributions are no longer required to be included in income. If, during 2008, you repay more than is otherwise includible in income for 2008, the excess may be carried back to reduce the amount included in income for that year.

Example. John received a $90,000 qualified hurricane distribution from his pension plan on November 15, 2006. He does not elect to include the entire distribution in his 2006 income. Without any repayments, he would include $30,000 of the distribution in income on each of his 2006, 2007, and 2008 returns. On November 10, 2008, John repays $45,000 to an IRA. He makes no other repayments during the allowable 3-year period. John may report the distribution and repayment in either of the following ways.

- Report $0 in income on his 2008 return, and file an amended return for 2006 to carry the excess repayment of $15,000 ($45,000 - $30,000) back to reduce the amount previously included in income to $15,000 ($30,000 - $15,000), or

- Report $0 in income on his 2008 return, and file an amended return for 2007 to carry the excess repayment of $15,000 ($45,000 - $30,000) back to reduce the amount previously included in income to $15,000 ($30,000 - $15,000).

Repayment of qualified hurricane distribution to a Roth IRA. If you make a repayment of a qualified hurricane distribution to a Roth IRA, the repayment is first considered to be a repayment of earnings. Any repayment of a qualified hurricane distribution in excess of earnings will increase your basis in the Roth IRA by the amount of the repayment in excess of earnings.

Example. In 2005, Ned takes a $30,000 qualified hurricane distribution from a Roth IRA. The $30,000 is the total value of the Roth IRA. He has $20,000 in basis (contributions) and $10,000 represents earnings. He elects to include the entire distribution in income for 2005. In 2005, he reports the distribution on Form 8606 and Form 8915 and determines that the taxable portion of the distribution is $10,000 ($30,000 - $20,000).

In 2008, Ned makes a $15,000 repayment of the 2005 qualified hurricane distribution to his Roth IRA. He will file an amended return for 2005 for the $10,000 taxable portion of the distribution that was included in income. $5,000 of the $15,000 repayment will represent basis in his Roth IRA for future distributions. $10,000 will be included in income when distributed in the future.

Amending Your Return

If, after filing your original return, you make a repayment, the repayment may reduce the amount of your qualified hurricane distributions that were previously included in income. Depending on when a repayment is made, you may need to file an amended tax return to refigure your taxable income.

If you make a repayment by the due date of your original return (including extensions), include the repayment on your amended return.

If you make a repayment after the due date of your original return (including extensions), include it on your amended return only if either of the following apply.

- You elected to include all of your qualified hurricane distributions in income for 2006 (not over 3 years) on your original return.

- You received a qualified hurricane distribution in 2006 and included it in income over 3 years, you can amend your 2006, 2007, or 2008 return, if applicable to carry the repayment back.

Example. You received a qualified hurricane distribution in the amount of $90,000 on October 15, 2006. You choose to spread the $90,000 over 3 years ($30,000 in income for 2006, 2007, and 2008). On November 19, 2008, you make a repayment of $45,000. For 2008, none of the qualified hurricane distribution is includible in income. The excess repayment of $15,000 can be carried back to 2006 or 2007.

File Form 1040X, Amended U.S. Individual Income Tax Return, to amend a return you have already filed. Generally, Form 1040X must be filed within 3 years after the date the original return was filed, or within 2 years after the date the tax was paid, whichever is later.

Tax Relief for the Kansas Disaster Area

Introduction

New rules provide for tax-favored withdrawals, repayments, and loans from certain retirement plans for taxpayers who suffered economic losses as a result of the storms and tornadoes that began on May 4, 2007.

If you received a qualified recovery assistance distribution, it is taxable, but is not subject to the 10% additional tax on early distributions. The taxable amount is figured in the same manner as other IRA distributions. However, the distribution is included in income over 3 years unless you elect to report the entire amount in the year of distribution. You can repay the distribution and not be taxed on the distribution. See *Qualified Recovery Assistance Distributions*, later.

The 2006 Form 8915, Qualified Hurricane Retirement Plan Distributions and Repayments, is modified and used to report qualified recovery assistance distributions and repayments. For information on other tax provisions related to the storms and tornadoes that began on May 4, 2007, see Publication 4492-A, Information for Taxpayers Affected By the May 4, 2007, Kansas Storms and Tornadoes.

Qualified Recovery Assistance Distributions

A qualified recovery assistance distribution is any distribution you received and designated as such from an eligible retirement plan if all of the following apply.

1. The distribution was made after May 3, 2007, and before January 1, 2009.

2. Your main home was located in the Kansas disaster area on May 4, 2007.

3. You sustained an economic loss because of the storms and tornadoes. Examples of an economic loss include, but are not limited to:

   a. Loss, damage to, or destruction of real or personal property from fire, flooding, looting, vandalism, theft, wind, or other cause;

   b. Loss related to displacement from your home; or

   c. Loss of livelihood due to temporary or permanent layoffs.

If (1) through (3) above apply, you can generally designate any distribution (including periodic payments and required minimum distributions) from an eligible retirement plan as a qualified recovery assistance distribution, regardless of whether the distribution was made on account of the storms or tornadoes. Qualified recovery assistance distributions are permitted without regard to your need or the actual amount of your economic loss.

The total of your qualified recovery assistance distributions from all plans is limited to $100,000. If you have distributions in excess of $100,000 from more than one type of plan, such as a 401(k) plan and an IRA, you can allocate the $100,000 limit among the plans any way you choose.

A reduction or offset after May 3, 2007, of your account balance in an eligible retirement plan in order to repay a loan can also be designated as a qualified recovery assistance distribution.

Kansas disaster area. The Kansas disaster area covers the Kansas counties of Barton, Clay, Cloud, Comanche, Dickinson, Edwards, Ellsworth, Kiowa, Leavenworth, Lyon, McPherson, Osage, Osborne, Ottawa, Phillips, Pottawatomie, Pratt, Reno, Rice, Riley, Saline, Shawnee, Smith, and Stafford.

Eligible retirement plan. An eligible retirement plan can be any of the following.

- A qualified pension, profit-sharing, or stock bonus plan (including a 401(k) plan).

- A qualified annuity plan.

- A tax-sheltered annuity contract.

- A governmental section 457 deferred compensation plan.

- A traditional, SEP, SIMPLE, or Roth IRA.

Taxation of Qualified Recovery Assistance Distributions

Qualified recovery assistance distributions are included in income in equal amounts over three years. However, you can elect to include the entire distribution in your income in the year it was received.

Qualified recovery assistance distributions are not subject to the additional 10% tax (or the additional 25% tax for certain distributions from SIMPLE IRAs) on early distributions from qualified retirement plans (including IRAs). However, any distributions you receive in excess of the $100,000 qualified recovery assistance distribution limit may be subject to the additional tax on early distributions.

For more information, see *How To Report Qualified Recovery Assistance Distributions* in Publication 4492-A.

Repayment of Qualified Recovery Assistance Distributions

If you choose, you generally can repay any portion of a qualified recovery assistance distribution that is eligible for tax-free rollover treatment to an eligible retirement plan. Also, you can repay a qualified recovery assistance distribution made because of a hardship from a retirement plan. However, see *Exceptions* later for qualified recovery assistance distributions you cannot repay.

Chapter 4   **Disaster-Related Relief**   Page 77

You have three years from the day after the date you received the distribution to make a repayment. Amounts that are repaid are treated as a qualified rollover and are not included in income. Also, a repayment to an IRA is not counted when figuring the one-rollover-per-year limit. See Publication 4492-A for more information on how to report repayments.

Exceptions. You cannot repay the following types of distributions.

1. Qualified disaster recovery assistance distributions received as a beneficiary (other than a surviving spouse).

2. Required minimum distributions.

3. Periodic payments (other than from an IRA) that are for:

   a. A period of 10 years or more,

   b. Your life or life expectancy, or

   c. The joint lives or joint life expectancies of you and your beneficiary.

How To Report Qualified Recovery Assistance Distributions

2007 Qualified Recovery Assistance Distributions. If you received a distribution after May 3, 2007, from an eligible retirement plan, you may be able to designate it as a qualified recovery assistance distribution. Detailed instructions for reporting these distributions on Form 8915 and Form 8606 are provided in Publication 4492-A.

2008 Qualified Recovery Assistance Distributions. If you received a distribution in 2008 from an eligible retirement plan, you may be able to designate it as a qualified recovery assistance distribution. See *Qualified Recovery Assistance Distributions* earlier. You will need to complete and attach Form 8915 and Form 8606 (if required) to your 2008 income tax return for any qualified recovery assistance distributions. See *Form 8915* and *Form 8606* in Publication 4492-A for instructions on completing the forms for this purpose.

Repayment of Qualified Distributions for the Purchase or Construction of a Main Home

If you received a qualified distribution to purchase or construct a main home in the Kansas disaster area, you can repay part or all of that distribution after May 3, 2007, but no later than October 22, 2008, to an eligible retirement plan. For this purpose, an eligible retirement plan is any plan, annuity, or IRA to which a qualified rollover can be made.

To be a qualified distribution, the distribution must meet all of the following requirements.

1. The distribution is a hardship distribution from a 401(k) plan, a hardship distribution from a tax-sheltered annuity contract, or a qualified first-time homebuyer distribution from an IRA.

2. The distribution was received after November 4, 2006, and before May 5, 2007.

3. The distribution was to be used to purchase or construct a main home in the Kansas disaster area that was not purchased or constructed because of the storms and tornadoes.

Amounts that are repaid before October 23, 2008, are treated as a qualified rollover and are not included in income. Also, for purposes of the one-rollover-per-year limit for IRAs, a repayment to an IRA is not considered a qualified rollover.

A qualified distribution not repaid before October 23, 2008, may be taxable for 2006 or 2007 and subject to the additional 10% tax (or the additional 25% tax for certain SIMPLE IRAs) on early distributions.

You must file Form 8915 if you received a qualified distribution that you repaid, in whole or in part, before October 23, 2008. See *How to report,* next, for information on completing Form 8915.

How to report. To report the repayment of a qualified distribution for the purchase or construction of a main home that was not purchased or constructed due to the storms and tornadoes, use the 2005 Form 8915, Part IV. Instructions for modifying the form for this purpose are provided in Publication 4492-A.

Amended return. If you repaid part or all of a qualified distribution by October 22, 2008, you will need to file an amended return for that part of a distribution that was previously included in income.

Loans From Qualified Plans

The following benefits are available to qualified individuals.

- Increases to the limits for distributions treated as loans from employer plans.

- A 1-year suspension for payments due on plan loans.

Qualified individual. You are a qualified individual if your main home on May 4, 2007, was located in the Kansas disaster area and you had an economic loss because of the storms and tornadoes. Examples of an economic loss include, but are not limited to:

- Loss, damage to, or destruction of real or personal property from fire, flooding, looting, vandalism, theft, wind, or other cause,

- Loss related to displacement from your home, or

- Loss of livelihood due to temporary or permanent layoffs.

Limits on plan loans. The $50,000 limit for distributions treated as plan loans is increased to $100,000. In addition, the limit based on 50% of your vested accrued benefit is increased to 100% of that benefit. If your home was located in the Kansas disaster area, the higher limits apply only to loans received during the period beginning on May 22, 2008, and ending on December 31, 2008.

One-year suspension of loan payments. Payments on plan loans outstanding after May 3, 2007, may be suspended for 1 year by the plan administrator. To qualify for the suspension, the due date for any loan payment must occur during the period beginning on May 4, 2007, and ending on December 31, 2008.

Tax Relief for the Midwestern Disaster Areas

Introduction

New rules provide for tax-favored withdrawals, repayments, and loans from certain retirement plans for taxpayers who suffered economic losses as a result of the severe storms, tornadoes, and flooding that occurred in the Midwestern disaster areas.

If you received a qualified disaster recovery assistance distribution, it is taxable, but is not subject to the 10% additional tax on early distributions. The taxable amount is figured in the same manner as other IRA distributions. However, the distribution is included in income over 3 years unless you elect to report the entire amount in the year of distribution. You can repay the distribution and not be taxed on the distribution. See *Qualified Disaster Recovery Assistance Distributions*, later.

Form 8930, Qualified Disaster Recovery Assistance Retirement Plan Distributions and Repayments, is used to report qualified disaster recovery assistance distributions and repayments.

For information on other tax provisions related to these severe storms, tornadoes, or flooding, see Publication 4492-B, Information for Affected Taxpayers in the Midwestern Disaster Areas. Tables 1 and 2 in Publication 4492-B list the affected counties by state and applicable disaster date that are included in the Midwestern disaster areas.

Qualified Disaster Recovery Assistance Distributions

A qualified disaster recovery assistance distribution is any distribution you received from an eligible retirement plan if all of the following apply.

1. The distribution was made on or after the applicable disaster date and before January 1, 2010.

2. Your main home was located in a Midwestern disaster area on the applicable disaster date.

3. You sustained an economic loss because of the severe storms, tornadoes, or flooding and your main

home was in a Midwestern disaster area on the applicable disaster date. Examples of an economic loss include, but are not limited to:

   a. Loss, damage to, or destruction of real or personal property from fire, flooding, looting, vandalism, theft, wind, or other cause,

   b. Loss related to displacement from your home, or

   c. Loss of livelihood due to temporary or permanent layoffs.

If (1) through (3) above apply, you can generally designate any distribution (including periodic payments and required minimum distributions) from an eligible retirement plan as a qualified disaster recovery assistance distribution, regardless of whether the distribution was made on account of the severe storms, tornadoes, or flooding. Qualified disaster recovery assistance distributions are permitted without regard to your need or the actual amount of your economic loss.

The total of your qualified disaster recovery assistance distributions from all plans is limited to $100,000. If you have distributions in excess of $100,000 from more than one type of plan, such as a 401(k) plan and an IRA, you may allocate the $100,000 limit among the plans any way you choose.

A reduction or offset (on or after the applicable disaster date) of your account balance in an eligible retirement plan in order to repay a loan can also be designated as a qualified disaster recovery assistance distribution.

Eligible retirement plan. An eligible retirement plan can be any of the following.

- A qualified pension, profit-sharing, or stock bonus plan (including a 401(k) plan).

- A qualified annuity plan.

- A tax-sheltered annuity contract.

- A governmental section 457 deferred compensation plan.

- A traditional, SEP, SIMPLE, or Roth IRA.

Main home. Generally, your main home is the home where you live most of the time. A temporary absence due to special circumstances, such as illness, education, business, military service, evacuation, or vacation, will not change your main home.

Taxation of Qualified Disaster Recovery Assistance Distributions

Qualified disaster recovery assistance distributions are included in income in equal amounts over three years. However, if you elect, you can include the entire distribution in your income in the year it was received.

Qualified disaster recovery assistance distributions are not subject to the additional 10% tax (or the additional 25% tax for certain distributions from SIMPLE IRAs) on early distributions from qualified retirement plans (including IRAs). However, any distributions you receive in excess of the $100,000 qualified disaster recovery assistance distribution limit may be subject to the additional tax on early distributions.

For more information, see Form 8930.

Repayment of Qualified Disaster Recovery Assistance Distributions

If you choose, you generally can repay any portion of a qualified disaster recovery assistance distribution that is eligible for tax-free rollover treatment to an eligible retirement plan. Also, you can repay a qualified disaster recovery assistance distribution made on account of a hardship from a retirement plan. However, see *Exceptions* below for qualified disaster recovery assistance distributions you cannot repay.

You have three years from the day after the date you received the distribution to make a repayment. Amounts that are repaid are treated as a qualified rollover and are not included in income. Also, a repayment to an IRA is not counted when figuring the one-rollover-per-year limit. See Form 8930 for more information on how to report repayments.

Exceptions. You cannot repay the following types of distributions.

1. Qualified disaster recovery assistance distributions received as a beneficiary (other than a surviving spouse).

2. Required minimum distributions.

3. Periodic payments (other than from an IRA) that are for:

    a. A period of 10 years or more,

    b. Your life or life expectancy, or

    c. The joint lives or joint life expectancies of you and your beneficiary.

Repayment of Qualified Distributions for the Purchase or Construction of a Main Home

If you received a qualified distribution to purchase or construct a main home in a Midwestern disaster area, you can repay part or all of that distribution on or after the applicable disaster date, but no later than March 3, 2009, to an eligible retirement plan. For this purpose, an eligible retirement plan is any plan, annuity, or IRA to which a qualified rollover can be made.

To be a qualified distribution, the distribution must meet all of the following requirements.

1. The distribution is a hardship distribution from a 401(k) plan, a hardship distribution from a

tax-sheltered annuity contract, or a qualified first-time homebuyer distribution from an IRA.

2. The distribution was received within 6 months prior to the day after the applicable disaster date.

3. The distribution was to be used to purchase or construct a main home in a Midwestern disaster area that was not purchased or constructed because of the severe storms, tornadoes, or flooding.

Amounts that are repaid before March 4, 2009, are treated as a qualified rollover and are not included in income. Also, for purposes of the one-rollover-per-year limit for IRAs, a repayment to an IRA is not considered a qualified rollover.

A qualified distribution not repaid before March 4, 2009, may be taxable for 2007 or 2008 and subject to the additional 10% tax (or the additional 25% tax for certain SIMPLE IRAs) on early distributions.

You must file Form 8930 if you received a qualified distribution that you repaid, in whole or in part, before March 4, 2009.

Loans From Qualified Plans

The following benefits are available to qualified individuals.

- Increases to the limits for distributions treated as loans from employer plans.

- A 1-year suspension for payments due on plan loans.

Qualified individual. You are a qualified individual if your main home was located in a Midwestern disaster area on the applicable disaster date and you had an economic loss because of the severe storms, tornadoes, or flooding. Examples of an economic loss include, but are not limited to:

- Loss, damage to, or destruction of real or personal property from fire, flooding, looting, vandalism, theft, wind, or other cause,

- Loss related to displacement from your home, or

- Loss of livelihood due to temporary or permanent layoffs.

Limits on plan loans. The $50,000 limit for distributions treated as plan loans is increased to $100,000. In addition, the limit based on 50% of your vested accrued benefit is increased to 100% of that benefit. If your main home was located in a Midwestern disaster area, the higher limits apply only to loans received during the period beginning on October 3, 2008, and ending on December 31, 2009.

One-year suspension of loan payments. Payments on plan loans outstanding on or after the applicable disaster date, may be suspended for 1 year by the plan administrator. To qualify for the suspension, the due date for any loan payment must occur during the period beginning on the applicable disaster date and ending on December 31, 2009.

5.

Retirement Savings Contributions Credit (Saver's Credit)

What's New for 2008

Modified AGI limit for retirement savings contributions credit increased. For 2008, you may be able to claim the retirement savings contributions credit if your modified AGI is not more than:

- $53,000 if your filing status is married filing jointly,

- $39,750 if your filing status is head of household, or

- $26,500 if your filing status is single, married filing separately, or qualifying widow(er).

What's New for 2009

Modified AGI limit for retirement savings contributions credit increased. For 2009, you may be able to claim the retirement savings contributions credit if your modified AGI is not more than:

- $55,500 if your filing status is married filing jointly,

- $41,625 if your filing status is head of household, or

- $27,750 if your filing status is single, married filing separately, or qualifying widow(er).

Introduction

You may be able to take a tax credit if you make eligible contributions (defined later) to a qualified retirement plan, an eligible deferred compensation plan, or an individual retirement arrangement (IRA). You may be able to take a credit of up to $1,000 (up to $2,000 if filing jointly). This credit could reduce the federal income tax you pay dollar for dollar.

Can you claim the credit? If you make eligible contributions to a qualified retirement plan, an eligible deferred compensation plan, or an IRA, you can claim the credit if all of the following apply.

1. You were born before January 2, 1991.

2. You are not a full-time student. (explained later).

3. No one else, such as your parent(s), claims an exemption for you on their tax return.

4. Your adjusted gross income (defined later) is not more than:

a. $53,000 if your filing status is married filing jointly,

b. $39,750 if your filing status is head of household, or

c. $26,500 if your filing status is single, married filing separately, or qualifying widow(er).

Full-time student. You are a full-time student if, during some part of each of 5 calendar months (not necessarily consecutive) during the calendar year, you are either:

- A full-time student at a school that has a regular teaching staff, course of study, and regularly enrolled body of students in attendance, or

- A student taking a full-time, on-farm training course given by either a school that has a regular teaching staff, course of study, and regularly enrolled body of students in attendance, or a state, county, or local government.

You are a full-time student if you are enrolled for the number of hours or courses the school considers to be full time.

Adjusted gross income. This is generally the amount on line 38 of your 2008 Form 1040; line 22 of your 2008 Form 1040A; or line 36 of your 2008 Form 1040NR. However, you must add to that amount any exclusion or deduction claimed for the year for:

- Foreign earned income,

- Foreign housing costs,

- Income for bona fide residents of American Samoa, and

- Income from Puerto Rico.

Eligible contributions. These include:

1. Contributions to a traditional or Roth IRA,

2. Salary reduction contributions (elective deferrals, including amounts designated as after-tax Roth contributions) to:

a. A 401(k) plan (including a SIMPLE 401(k)),

b. A section 403(b) annuity,

c. An eligible deferred compensation plan of a state or local government (a governmental 457 plan),

d. A SIMPLE IRA plan, or

e. A salary reduction SEP, and

3. Contributions to a section 501(c)(18) plan.

They also include voluntary after-tax employee contributions to a tax-qualified retirement plan or section 403(b) annuity. For purposes of the credit, an employee contribution will be voluntary as long as it is not required as a condition of employment.

Reducing eligible contributions. Reduce your eligible contributions (but not below zero) by the total distributions you received during the testing period. (defined later) from any IRA, plan, or annuity included above under *Eligible* *contributions.* Also reduce your eligible contributions by any distribution from a Roth IRA that is not rolled over, even if the distribution is not taxable.

Do not reduce your eligible contributions by any of the following.

1. The portion of any distribution which is not includible in income because it is a trustee-to-trustee transfer or a rollover distribution.

2. Any distribution that is a return of a contribution to an IRA (including a Roth IRA) made during the year for which you claim the credit if:

   a. The distribution is made before the due date (including extensions) of your tax return for that year,

   b. You do not take a deduction for the contribution, and

   c. The distribution includes any income attributable to the contribution.

3. Loans from a qualified employer plan treated as a distribution.

4. Distributions of excess contributions or deferrals (and income attributable to excess contributions and deferrals).

5. Distributions of dividends paid on stock held by an employee stock ownership plan under section 404(k).

6. Distributions from an IRA that are converted to a Roth IRA.

7. Distributions from a military retirement plan.

Distributions received by spouse. Any distributions your spouse receives are treated as received by you if you file a joint return with your spouse both for the year of the distribution and for the year for which you claim the credit.

Testing period. The testing period consists of the year for which you claim the credit, the period after the end of that year and before the due date (including extensions) for filing your return for that year, and the 2 tax years before that year.

Example. You and your spouse filed joint returns in 2006 and 2007, and plan to do so in 2008 and 2009. You received a taxable distribution from a qualified plan in 2006 and a taxable distribution from an eligible deferred compensation plan in 2007. Your spouse received taxable distributions from a Roth IRA in 2008 and tax-free distributions from a Roth IRA in 2009 before April 15. You made eligible contributions to an IRA in 2008 and you otherwise qualify for this credit. You must reduce the amount of your qualifying contributions in 2008 by the total of the distributions you received in 2006, 2007, 2008, and 2009.

Maximum eligible contributions. After your contributions are reduced, the maximum annual contribution on which you can base the credit is $2,000 per person.

Effect on other credits. The amount of this credit will not change the amount of your refundable tax credits. A refundable tax credit, such as the earned income credit or the refundable amount of your child tax credit, is an amount that you would receive as a refund even if you did not otherwise owe any taxes.

Maximum credit. This is a nonrefundable credit. The amount of the credit in any year cannot be more than the amount of tax that you would otherwise pay (not counting any refundable credits or the adoption credit) in any year. If your tax liability is reduced to zero because of other nonrefundable credits, such as the Hope credit, then you will not be entitled to this credit.

How to figure and report the credit. The amount of the credit you can get is based on the contributions you make and your credit rate. Your credit rate can be as low as 10% or as high as 50%. Your credit rate depends on your income and your filing status. See Form 8880 to determine your credit rate.

The maximum contribution taken into account is $2,000 per person. On a joint return, up to $2,000 is taken into account for each spouse.

Figure the credit on Form 8880. Report the credit on line 51 of your Form 1040; line 32 of your Form 1040A; or line 46 of your Form 1040NR and attach Form 8880 to your return.

6.

How To Get Tax Help

You can get help with unresolved tax issues, order free publications and forms, ask tax questions, and get information from the IRS in several ways. By selecting the method that is best for you, you will have quick and easy access to tax help.

Contacting your Taxpayer Advocate. The Taxpayer Advocate Service (TAS) is an independent organization within the IRS whose employees assist taxpayers who are experiencing economic harm, who are seeking help in resolving tax problems that have not been resolved through normal channels, or who believe that an IRS system or procedure is not working as it should.

You can contact the TAS by calling the TAS toll-free case intake line at 1-877-777-4778 or TTY/TDD 1-800-829-4059 to see if you are eligible for assistance. You can also call or write to your local taxpayer advocate, whose phone number and address are listed in your local telephone directory and in Publication 1546, Taxpayer Advocate Service – Your Voice at the IRS. You can file Form 911, Request for Taxpayer Advocate Service Assistance (And Application for Taxpayer Assistance Order), or ask an IRS employee to complete it on your behalf. For more information, go to *www.irs.gov/advocate.*

Low Income Taxpayer Clinics (LITCs). LITCs are independent organizations that provide low income taxpayers with representation in federal tax controversies with the

IRS for free or for a nominal charge. The clinics also provide tax education and outreach for taxpayers who speak English as a second language. Publication 4134, Low Income Taxpayer Clinic List, provides information on clinics in your area. It is available at *www.irs.gov* or at your local IRS office.

Free tax services. To find out what services are available, get Publication 910, IRS Guide to Free Tax Services. It contains lists of free tax information sources, including publications, services, and free tax education and assistance programs. It also has an index of over 100 TeleTax topics (recorded tax information) you can listen to on your telephone.

Accessible versions of IRS published products are available on request in a variety of alternative formats for people with disabilities.

Free help with your return. Free help in preparing your return is available nationwide from IRS-trained volunteers. The Volunteer Income Tax Assistance (VITA) program is designed to help low-income taxpayers and the Tax Counseling for the Elderly (TCE) program is designed to assist taxpayers age 60 and older with their tax returns. Many VITA sites offer free electronic filing and all volunteers will let you know about credits and deductions you may be entitled to claim. To find the nearest VITA or TCE site, call 1-800-829-1040.

As part of the TCE program, AARP offers the Tax-Aide counseling program. To find the nearest AARP Tax-Aide site, call 1-888-227-7669 or visit AARP's website at *www.aarp.org/money/taxaide*.

For more information on these programs, go to *www.irs.gov* and enter keyword "VITA" in the upper right-hand corner.

 Internet. You can access the IRS website at *www.irs.gov* 24 hours a day, 7 days a week to:

- *E-file* your return. Find out about commercial tax preparation and *e-file* services available free to eligible taxpayers.

- Check the status of your 2008 refund. Go to *www.irs.gov* and click on *Where's My Refund*. Wait at least 72 hours after the IRS acknowledges receipt of your e-filed return, or 3 to 4 weeks after mailing a paper return. If you filed Form 8379 with your return, wait 14 weeks (11 weeks if you filed electronically). Have your 2008 tax return available because you will need to know your social security number, your filing status, and the exact whole dollar amount of your refund.

- Download forms, instructions, and publications.

- Order IRS products online.

- Research your tax questions online.

- Search publications online by topic or keyword.

- View Internal Revenue Bulletins (IRBs) published in the last few years.

- Figure your withholding allowances using the withholding calculator online at *www.irs.gov/individuals*.

- Determine if Form 6251 must be filed using our Alternative Minimum Tax (AMT) Assistant.

- Sign up to receive local and national tax news by email.

- Get information on starting and operating a small business.

 Phone. Many services are available by phone.

- *Ordering forms, instructions, and publications.* Call 1-800-829-3676 to order current-year forms, instructions, and publications, and prior-year forms and instructions. You should receive your order within 10 days.

- *Asking tax questions.* Call the IRS with your tax questions at 1-800-829-1040.

- *Solving problems.* You can get face-to-face help solving tax problems every business day in IRS Taxpayer Assistance Centers. An employee can explain IRS letters, request adjustments to your account, or help you set up a payment plan. Call your local Taxpayer Assistance Center for an appointment. To find the number, go to *www.irs.gov/localcontacts* or look in the phone book under *United States Government, Internal Revenue Service*.

- *TTY/TDD equipment.* If you have access to TTY/TDD equipment, call 1-800-829-4059 to ask tax questions or to order forms and publications.

- *TeleTax topics.* Call 1-800-829-4477 to listen to pre-recorded messages covering various tax topics.

- *Refund information.* To check the status of your 2008 refund, call 1-800-829-1954 during business hours or 1-800-829-4477 (automated refund information 24 hours a day, 7 days a week). Wait at least 72 hours after the IRS acknowledges receipt of your e-filed return, or 3 to 4 weeks after mailing a paper return. If you filed Form 8379 with your return, wait 14 weeks (11 weeks if you filed electronically). Have your 2008 tax return available so you can provide your social security number, your filing status, and the exact whole dollar amount of your refund. Refunds are sent out weekly on Fridays. If you check the status of your refund and are not given the date it will be issued, please wait until the next week before checking back.

- *Other refund information.* To check the status of a prior year refund or amended return refund, call 1-800-829-1954.

Evaluating the quality of our telephone services. To ensure IRS representatives give accurate, courteous, and professional answers, we use several methods to evaluate

Chapter 6 **How To Get Tax Help** Page 83

the quality of our telephone services. One method is for a second IRS representative to listen in on or record random telephone calls. Another is to ask some callers to complete a short survey at the end of the call.

 Walk-in. Many products and services are available on a walk-in basis.

- *Products.* You can walk in to many post offices, libraries, and IRS offices to pick up certain forms, instructions, and publications. Some IRS offices, libraries, grocery stores, copy centers, city and county government offices, credit unions, and office supply stores have a collection of products available to print from a CD or photocopy from reproducible proofs. Also, some IRS offices and libraries have the Internal Revenue Code, regulations, Internal Revenue Bulletins, and Cumulative Bulletins available for research purposes.

- *Services.* You can walk in to your local Taxpayer Assistance Center every business day for personal, face-to-face tax help. An employee can explain IRS letters, request adjustments to your tax account, or help you set up a payment plan. If you need to resolve a tax problem, have questions about how the tax law applies to your individual tax return, or you are more comfortable talking with someone in person, visit your local Taxpayer Assistance Center where you can spread out your records and talk with an IRS representative face-to-face. No appointment is necessary—just walk in. If you prefer, you can call your local Center and leave a message requesting an appointment to resolve a tax account issue. A representative will call you back within 2 business days to schedule an in-person appointment at your convenience. If you have an ongoing, complex tax account problem or a special need, such as a disability, an appointment can be requested. All other issues will be handled without an appointment. To find the number of your local office, go to *www.irs. gov/localcontacts* or look in the phone book under *United States Government, Internal Revenue Service.*

 Mail. You can send your order for forms, instructions, and publications to the address below. You should receive a response within 10 days after your request is received.

Internal Revenue Service
1201 N. Mitsubishi Motorway
Bloomington, IL 61705-6613

 DVD for tax products. You can order Publication 1796, IRS Tax Products DVD, and obtain:

- Current-year forms, instructions, and publications.
- Prior-year forms, instructions, and publications.
- Tax Map: an electronic research tool and finding aid.
- Tax law frequently asked questions.
- Tax Topics from the IRS telephone response system.
- Internal Revenue Code—Title 26 of the U.S. Code.
- Fill-in, print, and save features for most tax forms.
- Internal Revenue Bulletins.
- Toll-free and email technical support.
- Two releases during the year.
  – The first release will ship the beginning of January 2009.
  – The final release will ship the beginning of March 2009.

Purchase the DVD from National Technical Information Service (NTIS) at *www.irs.gov/cdorders* for $30 (no handling fee) or call 1-877-233-6767 toll free to buy the DVD for $30 (plus a $6 handling fee).

 Small Business Resource Guide 2009. This online guide is a must for every small business owner or any taxpayer about to start a business. This year's guide includes:

- Helpful information, such as how to prepare a business plan, find financing for your business, and much more.
- All the business tax forms, instructions, and publications needed to successfully manage a business.
- Tax law changes for 2009.
- Tax Map: an electronic research tool and finding aid.
- Web links to various government agencies, business associations, and IRS organizations.
- "Rate the Product" survey—your opportunity to suggest changes for future editions.
- A site map of the guide to help you navigate the pages with ease.
- An interactive "Teens in Biz" module that gives practical tips for teens about starting their own business, creating a business plan, and filing taxes.

The information is updated during the year. Visit *www. irs.gov* and enter keyword "SBRG" in the upper right-hand corner for more information.

Appendices

To help you complete your tax return, use the following appendices that include worksheets, sample forms, and tables.

1. **Appendix A** — Summary Record of Traditional IRA(s) for 2008 and Worksheet for Determining Required Minimum Distributions.

2. **Appendix B** — Worksheets you use if you receive social security benefits and are subject to the IRA deduction phaseout rules. A filled-in example is included.

   a. Worksheet 1, Computation of Modified AGI.

   b. Worksheet 2, Computation of Traditional IRA Deduction for 2008.

   c. Worksheet 3, Computation of Taxable Social Security Benefits.

   d. Comprehensive Example and completed worksheets.

3. **Appendix C** — Life Expectancy Tables. These tables are included to assist you in computing your required minimum distribution amount if you have not taken all your assets from all your traditional IRAs before age 70½.

   a. Table I (Single Life Expectancy).

   b. Table II (Joint Life and Last Survivor Expectancy).

   c. Table III (Uniform Lifetime).

Appendix A. Summary Record of Traditional IRA(s) for 2008

Keep for Your Records

Name _____

I was ☐ covered ☐ not covered by my employer's retirement plan during the year.

I became 59½ on _____ (month) (day) (year)

I became 70½ on _____ (month) (day) (year)

Contributions

Name of traditional IRA	Date	Amount contributed for 2008	Check if rollover contribution	Fair Market Value of IRA as of December 31, 2008, from Form 5498
1.				
2.				
3.				
4.				
5.				
6.				
7.				
8.				
Total				

Total contributions deducted on tax return . . . . $ _____

Total contributions treated as nondeductible on Form 8606 . . . . $ _____

Distributions

Name of traditional IRA	Date	Amount of Distribution	Reason (for example, retirement, rollover, conversion, withdrawal of excess contributions)	Income earned on IRA	Taxable amount reported on income tax return	Nontaxable amount from Form 8606, line 13
1.						
2.						
3.						
4.						
5.						
6.						
7.						
8.						
Total						

Basis of all traditional IRAs for 2008 and earlier years (from Form 8606, line 14) . . . . $ _____

Note. *You should keep copies of your income tax return, and Forms W-2, 8606, and 5498.*

Appendix A. (Continued) Worksheet for Determining Required Minimum Distributions

Keep for Your Records

1. Age	70½	71½	72½	73½	74½
2. Year age was reached					
3. Value of IRA at the close of business on December 31 of the year immediately prior to the year on line 2[1]					
4. Distribution period from Table III or life expectancy from Life Expectancy Table I or Table II[2]					
5. Required distribution (divide line 3 by line 4)[3]					

1. Age	75½	76½	77½	78½	79½
2. Year age was reached					
3. Value of IRA at the close of business on December 31 of the year immediately prior to the year on line 2[1]					
4. Distribution period from Table III or life expectancy from Life Expectancy Table I or Table II[2]					
5. Required distribution (divide line 3 by line 4)[3]					

1. Age	80½	81½	82½	83½	84½
2. Year age was reached					
3. Value of IRA at the close of business on December 31 of the year immediately prior to the year on line 2[1]					
4. Distribution period from Table III or life expectancy from Life Expectancy Table I or Table II[2]					
5. Required distribution (divide line 3 by line 4)[3]					

1. Age	85½	86½	87½	88½	89½
2. Year age was reached					
3. Value of IRA at the close of business on December 31 of the year immediately prior to the year on line 2[1]					
4. Distribution period from Table III or life expectancy from Life Expectancy Table I or Table II[2]					
5. Required distribution (divide line 3 by line 4)[3]					

[1]If you have more than one IRA, you must figure the required distribution separately for each IRA.
[2]Use the appropriate life expectancy or distribution period for each year and for each IRA.
[3]If you have more than one IRA, you must withdraw an amount equal to the total of the required distributions figured for each IRA. You can, however, withdraw the total from one IRA or from more than one IRA.
Note. For 2009, you are not required to take a minimum distribution.

Appendix B. Worksheets for Social Security Recipients Who Contribute to a Traditional IRA

If you receive social security benefits, have taxable compensation, contribute to your traditional IRA, and you or your spouse is covered by an employer retirement plan, complete the following worksheets. (See *Are You Covered by an Employer Plan?* in chapter 1.)

Use Worksheet 1 to figure your modified adjusted gross income. This amount is needed in the computation of your IRA deduction, if any, which is figured using Worksheet 2.

The IRA deduction figured using Worksheet 2 is entered on your tax return.

Worksheet 1
Computation of Modified AGI
(For use only by taxpayers who receive social security benefits)

Filing Status — Check only one box:
☐ **A.** Married filing jointly
☐ **B.** Single, Head of Household, Qualifying Widow(er), or Married filing separately and *lived apart* from your spouse during the *entire year*
☐ **C.** Married filing separately and *lived with* your spouse at *any time* during the year

1. Adjusted gross income (AGI) from Form 1040 or Form 1040A (not taking into account any social security benefits from Form SSA-1099 or RRB-1099, any deduction for contributions to a traditional IRA, any student loan interest deduction, any tuition and fees deduction, any domestic production activities deduction, or any exclusion of interest from savings bonds to be reported on Form 8815) . . . . 1. _____

2. Enter the amount in box 5 of all Forms SSA-1099 and Forms RRB-1099 . . . . 2. _____

3. Enter one-half of line 2 . . . . 3. _____

4. Enter the amount of any foreign earned income exclusion, foreign housing exclusion, U.S. possessions income exclusion, exclusion of income from Puerto Rico you claimed as a bona fide resident of Puerto Rico, or exclusion of employer-provided adoption benefits . . . . 4. _____

5. Enter the amount of any tax-exempt interest reported on line 8b of Form 1040 or 1040A 5. _____

6. Add lines 1, 3, 4, and 5 . . . . 6. _____

7. Enter the amount listed below for your filing status.
   - **$32,000** if you checked box **A** above.
   - **$25,000** if you checked box **B** above.
   - **$0** if you checked box **C** above. . . . . 7. _____

8. Subtract line 7 from line 6. If zero or less, enter 0 on this line . . . . 8. _____

9. If line 8 is zero, **stop here**. None of your social security benefits are taxable.
   If line 8 is more than 0, enter the amount listed below for your filing status.
   - **$12,000** if you checked box **A** above.
   - **$9,000** if you checked box **B** above.
   - **$0** if you checked box **C** above . . . . 9. _____

10. Subtract line 9 from line 8. If zero or less, enter 0 . . . . 10. _____

11. Enter the smaller of line 8 or line 9 . . . . 11. _____

12. Enter one-half of line 11 . . . . 12. _____

13. Enter the smaller of line 3 or line 12 . . . . 13. _____

14. Multiply line 10 by .85. If line 10 is zero, enter 0 . . . . 14. _____

15. Add lines 13 and 14 . . . . 15. _____

16. Multiply line 2 by .85 . . . . 16. _____

17. **Taxable benefits** to be included in modified AGI for traditional IRA deduction purposes.
    Enter the smaller of line 15 or line 16 . . . . 17. _____

18. Enter the amount of any employer-provided adoption benefits exclusion and any foreign earned income exclusion and foreign housing exclusion or deduction that you claimed . . 18. _____

19. **Modified AGI** for determining your reduced traditional IRA deduction — add lines 1, 17, and 18. Enter here and on line 2 of Worksheet 2, next . . . . 19. _____

Publication 590 (2008)

Appendix B. (Continued)

Worksheet 2 Computation of Traditional IRA Deduction For 2008 (For use only by taxpayers who receive social security benefits)		
IF your filing status is ...	**AND** your modified AGI is over ...	**THEN** enter on line 1 below ...
married filing jointly or qualifying widow(er)	$85,000*	$105,000
married filing jointly (you are not covered by an employer plan but your spouse is)	$159,000*	$169,000
single, or head of household	$53,000*	$63,000
married filing separately**	$0*	$10,000

*If your modified AGI is **not** over this amount, you can take an IRA deduction for your contributions of up to the lesser of $5,000 ($6,000 if you are age 50 or older or $8,000 for certain employer bankruptcies) or your taxable compensation. Skip this worksheet, proceed to Worksheet 3, and enter your IRA deduction on line 2 of Worksheet 3.

If you did **not live with your spouse **at any time** during the year, consider your filing status as single.
Note. If you were married and you or your spouse worked and you both contributed to IRAs, figure the deduction for each of you separately.
Certain employer bankruptcies. See _Catch-up contributions in certain employer bankruptcies_ in chapter 1 for instructions to complete lines 4 and 6 of this worksheet.

1. Enter the applicable amount from above .... 1. _____
2. Enter your **modified AGI** from Worksheet 1, line 19 .... 2. _____
   Note. If line 2 is equal to or more than the amount on line 1, **stop here;** your traditional IRA contributions are not deductible. Proceed to Worksheet 3.
3. Subtract line 2 from line 1 .... 3. _____
4. Multiply line 3 by the percentage below that applies to you. If the result is not a multiple of $10, round it to the next highest multiple of $10. (For example, $611.40 is rounded to $620.) However, if the result is less than $200, enter $200.
   - Married filing jointly or qualifying widow(er) **and** you are covered by an employer plan, multiply line 3 by 25% (.25) (by 30% (.30) if you are age 50 or older).
   - All others, multiply line 3 by 50% (.50) (by 60% (.60) if you are age 50 or older). .... 4. _____
5. Enter your compensation minus any deductions on Form 1040, line 27 (one-half of self-employment tax) and line 28 (self-employed SEP, SIMPLE, and qualified plans). If you are the lower-income spouse, include your spouse's compensation reduced by his or her traditional IRA and Roth IRA contributions for this year .... 5. _____
6. Enter contributions you made, or plan to make, to your traditional IRA for 2008, but do not enter more than $5,000 ($6,000 if you are age 50 or older) .... 6. _____
7. **Deduction.** Compare lines 4, 5, and 6. Enter the smallest amount here (or a smaller amount if you choose). Enter this amount on the Form 1040 or 1040A line for your IRA. (If the amount on line 6 is more than the amount on line 7, complete line 8.) ... 7. _____
8. **Nondeductible contributions.** Subtract line 7 from line 5 or 6, whichever is smaller. Enter the result here and on line 1 of your Form 8606, _Nondeductible IRAs_. .... 8. _____

Appendix B. (Continued)

Worksheet 3
Computation of Taxable Social Security Benefits
(For use by taxpayers who receive social security benefits and take a traditional IRA deduction)

Filing Status — Check only one box:

☐ **A.** Married filing jointly

☐ **B.** Single, Head of Household, Qualifying Widow(er), or Married filing separately and *lived apart* from your spouse during the *entire year*

☐ **C.** Married filing separately and *lived with* your spouse at *any time* during the year

1. Adjusted gross income (AGI) from Form 1040 or Form 1040A (not taking into account any IRA deduction, any student loan interest deduction, any tuition and fees deduction, any domestic production activities deduction, any social security benefits from Form SSA-1099 or RRB-1099, or any exclusion of interest from savings bonds to be reported on Form 8815) . . . . **1.** _____
2. Deduction(s) from line 7 of Worksheet(s) 2 . . . . **2.** _____
3. Subtract line 2 from line 1 . . . . **3.** _____
4. Enter amount in box 5 of all Forms SSA-1099 and Forms RRB-1099 . . . . **4.** _____
5. Enter one-half of line 4 . . . . **5.** _____
6. Enter the amount of any foreign earned income exclusion, foreign housing exclusion, exclusion of income from U.S. possessions, exclusion of income from Puerto Rico you claimed as a bona fide resident of Puerto Rico, or exclusion of employer-provided adoption benefits . . . . **6.** _____
7. Enter the amount of any tax-exempt interest reported on line 8b of Form 1040 or 1040A . . . . **7.** _____
8. Add lines 3, 5, 6, and 7 . . . . **8.** _____
9. Enter the amount listed below for your filing status.

   • **$32,000** if you checked box **A** above.
   • **$25,000** if you checked box **B** above.
   • **$0** if you checked box **C** above. . . . . **9.** _____
10. Subtract line 9 from line 8. If zero or less, enter 0 on this line. . . . . **10.** _____
11. If line 10 is zero, **stop here**. None of your social security benefits are taxable. If line 10 is more than 0, enter the amount listed below for your filing status.

    • **$12,000** if you checked box **A** above.
    • **$9,000** if you checked box **B** above.
    • **$0** if you checked box **C** above. . . . . **11.** _____
12. Subtract line 11 from line 10. If zero or less, enter 0 . . . . **12.** _____
13. Enter the smaller of line 10 or line 11 . . . . **13.** _____
14. Enter one-half of line 13 . . . . **14.** _____
15. Enter the smaller of line 5 or line 14 . . . . **15.** _____
16. Multiply line 12 by .85. If line 12 is zero, enter 0 . . . . **16.** _____
17. Add lines 15 and 16 . . . . **17.** _____
18. Multiply line 4 by .85 . . . . **18.** _____
19. **Taxable social security benefits.** Enter the smaller of line 17 or line 18 . . . . **19.** _____

Appendix B. (Continued)

Comprehensive Example
Determining Your Traditional IRA Deduction and
the Taxable Portion of Your Social Security Benefits

John Black is married and files a joint return. He is 65 years old and had 2008 wages of $78,500. His wife did not work in 2008. He also received social security benefits of $10,000 and made a $6,000 contribution to his traditional IRA for the year. He had no foreign income, no tax-exempt interest, and no adjustments to income on lines 23 through 36 on his Form 1040. He participated in a section 401(k) retirement plan at work.

John completes worksheets 1 and 2. Worksheet 2 shows that his 2008 IRA deduction is $4,500. He must either withdraw the contributions that are more than the deduction (the $1,500 shown on line 8 of Worksheet 2), or treat the excess amounts as nondeductible contributions (in which case he must complete Form 8606 and attach it to his Form 1040).

The completed worksheets that follow show how John figured his modified AGI to determine the IRA deduction and the taxable social security benefits to report on his Form 1040.

Worksheet 1
Computation of Modified AGI
(For use only by taxpayers who receive social security benefits)

Filing Status — Check only one box:
☑ **A.** Married filing jointly
☐ **B.** Single, Head of Household, Qualifying Widow(er), or Married filing separately and *lived apart* from your spouse during the *entire year*
☐ **C.** Married filing separately and *lived with* your spouse at *any time* during the year

1. Adjusted gross income (AGI) from Form 1040 or Form 1040A (not taking into account any social security benefits from Form SSA-1099 or RRB-1099, any deduction for contributions to a traditional IRA, any student loan interest deduction, any tuition and fees deduction, any domestic production activities deduction, or any exclusion of interest from savings bonds to be reported on Form 8815)	1.	78,500
2. Enter the amount in box 5 of all Forms SSA-1099 and Forms RRB-1099	2.	10,000
3. Enter one-half of line 2	3.	5,000
4. Enter the amount of any foreign earned income exclusion, foreign housing exclusion, U.S. possessions income exclusion, exclusion of income from Puerto Rico you claimed as a bona fide resident of Puerto Rico, or exclusion of employer-provided adoption benefits	4.	0
5. Enter the amount of any tax-exempt interest reported on line 8b of Form 1040 or 1040A	5.	0
6. Add lines 1, 3, 4, and 5	6.	83,500
7. Enter the amount listed below for your filing status. • **$32,000** if you checked box **A** above. • **$25,000** if you checked box **B** above. • **$0** if you checked box **C** above.	7.	32,000
8. Subtract line 7 from line 6. If zero or less, enter 0 on this line	8.	51,500
9. If line 8 is zero, **stop here**. None of your social security benefits are taxable. If line 8 is more than 0, enter the amount listed below for your filing status. • **$12,000** if you checked box **A** above. • **$9,000** if you checked box **B** above. • **$0** if you checked box **C** above	9.	12,000
10. Subtract line 9 from line 8. If zero or less, enter 0	10.	39,500
11. Enter the smaller of line 8 or line 9	11.	12,000
12. Enter one-half of line 11	12.	6,000
13. Enter the smaller of line 3 or line 12	13.	5,000
14. Multiply line 10 by .85. If line 10 is zero, enter 0	14.	33,575
15. Add lines 13 and 14	15.	38,575
16. Multiply line 2 by .85	16.	8,500
17. **Taxable benefits** to be included in modified AGI for traditional IRA deduction purposes. Enter the smaller of line 15 or line 16	17.	8,500
18. Enter the amount of any employer-provided adoption benefits exclusion and any foreign earned income exclusion and foreign housing exclusion or deduction that you claimed	18.	0
19. **Modified AGI** for determining your reduced traditional IRA deduction — add lines 1, 17, and 18. Enter here and on line 2 of Worksheet 2, next	19.	87,000

A-93

Appendix B. (Continued)

Worksheet 2
Computation of Traditional IRA Deduction For 2008
(For use only by taxpayers who receive social security benefits)

IF your filing status is ...	AND your modified AGI is over ...	THEN enter on line 1 below ...
married filing jointly or qualifying widow(er)	$85,000*	$105,000
married filing jointly (you are not covered by an employer plan but your spouse is)	$159,000*	$169,000
single, or head of household	$53,000*	$63,000
married filing separately**	$0*	$10,000

*If your modified AGI is **not** over this amount, you can take an IRA deduction for your contributions of up to the lesser of $5,000 ($6,000 if you are age 50 or older or $8,000 for certain employer bankruptcies) or your taxable compensation. Skip this worksheet, proceed to Worksheet 3, and enter your IRA deduction on line 2 of Worksheet 3.

If you did **not live with your spouse **at any time** during the year, consider your filing status as single.

Note. If you were married and you or your spouse worked and you both contributed to IRAs, figure the deduction for each of you separately.

Certain employer bankruptcies. See *Catch-up contributions in certain employer bankruptcies* in chapter 1 for instructions to complete lines 4 and 6 of this worksheet.

1.	Enter the applicable amount from above	1.	105,000
2.	Enter your **modified AGI** from Worksheet 1, line 19	2.	87,000
	Note. If line 2 is equal to or more than the amount on line 1, **stop here;** your traditional IRA contributions are not deductible. Proceed to Worksheet 3.		
3.	Subtract line 2 from line 1	3.	18,000
4.	Multiply line 3 by the percentage below that applies to you. If the result is not a multiple of $10, round it to the next highest multiple of $10. (For example, $611.40 is rounded to $620.) However, if the result is less than $200, enter $200.		
	• Married filing jointly or qualifying widow(er) **and** you are covered by an employer plan, multiply line 3 by 25% (.25) (by 30% (.30) if you are age 50 or older). • All others, multiply line 3 by 50% (.50) (by 60% (.60) if you are age 50 or older).	4.	5,400
5.	Enter your compensation minus any deductions on Form 1040, line 27 (one-half of self-employment tax) and line 28 (self-employed SEP, SIMPLE, and qualified plans). If you are the lower-income spouse, include your spouse's compensation reduced by his or her traditional IRA and Roth IRA contributions for this year	5.	78,500
6.	Enter contributions you made, or plan to make, to your traditional IRA for 2008, but do not enter more than $5,000 ($6,000 if you are age 50 or older)	6.	6,000
7.	**Deduction.** Compare lines 4, 5, and 6. Enter the smallest amount here (or a smaller amount if you choose). Enter this amount on the Form 1040 or 1040A line for your IRA. (If the amount on line 6 is more than the amount on line 7, complete line 8.) . . .	7.	5,400
8.	**Nondeductible contributions.** Subtract line 7 from line 5 or 6, whichever is smaller. Enter the result here and on line 1 of your Form 8606, *Nondeductible IRAs*.	8.	600

Appendix B. (Continued)

Worksheet 3
Computation of Taxable Social Security Benefits
(For use by taxpayers who receive social security benefits and take a traditional IRA deduction)

Filing Status — Check only one box:

☑ **A.** Married filing jointly

☐ **B.** Single, Head of Household, Qualifying Widow(er), or Married filing separately and *lived apart* from your spouse during the *entire year*

☐ **C.** Married filing separately and *lived with* your spouse at *any time* during the year

1. Adjusted gross income (AGI) from Form 1040 or Form 1040A (not taking into account any IRA deduction, any student loan interest deduction, any tuition and fees deduction, any domestic production activities deduction, any social security benefits from Form SSA-1099 or RRB-1099, or any exclusion of interest from savings bonds to be reported on Form 8815)	1.	78,500
2. Deduction(s) from line 7 of Worksheet(s) 2	2.	5,400
3. Subtract line 2 from line 1	3.	73,100
4. Enter amount in box 5 of all Forms SSA-1099 and Forms RRB-1099	4.	10,000
5. Enter one-half of line 4	5.	5,000
6. Enter the amount of any foreign earned income exclusion, foreign housing exclusion, exclusion of income from U.S. possessions, exclusion of income from Puerto Rico you claimed as a bona fide resident of Puerto Rico, or exclusion of employer-provided adoption benefits	6.	0
7. Enter the amount of any tax-exempt interest reported on line 8b of Form 1040 or 1040A	7.	0
8. Add lines 3, 5, 6, and 7	8.	78,100
9. Enter the amount listed below for your filing status.		
• **$32,000** if you checked box **A** above.		
• **$25,000** if you checked box **B** above.		
• **$0** if you checked box **C** above.	9.	32,000
10. Subtract line 9 from line 8. If zero or less, enter 0 on this line.	10.	46,100
11. If line 10 is zero, **stop here**. None of your social security benefits are taxable. If line 10 is more than 0, enter the amount listed below for your filing status.		
• **$12,000** if you checked box **A** above.		
• **$9,000** if you checked box **B** above.		
• **$0** if you checked box **C** above.	11.	12,000
12. Subtract line 11 from line 10. If zero or less, enter 0	12.	34,100
13. Enter the smaller of line 10 or line 11	13.	12,000
14. Enter one-half of line 13	14.	6,000
15. Enter the smaller of line 5 or line 14	15.	5,000
16. Multiply line 12 by .85. If line 12 is zero, enter 0	16.	28,985
17. Add lines 15 and 16	17.	33,985
18. Multiply line 4 by .85	18.	8,500
19. **Taxable social security benefits.** Enter the smaller of line 17 or line 18	19.	8,500

Appendix C. Life Expectancy Tables

Table I (Single Life Expectancy) (For Use by Beneficiaries)			
Age	Life Expectancy	Age	Life Expectancy
0	82.4	28	55.3
1	81.6	29	54.3
2	80.6	30	53.3
3	79.7	31	52.4
4	78.7	32	51.4
5	77.7	33	50.4
6	76.7	34	49.4
7	75.8	35	48.5
8	74.8	36	47.5
9	73.8	37	46.5
10	72.8	38	45.6
11	71.8	39	44.6
12	70.8	40	43.6
13	69.9	41	42.7
14	68.9	42	41.7
15	67.9	43	40.7
16	66.9	44	39.8
17	66.0	45	38.8
18	65.0	46	37.9
19	64.0	47	37.0
20	63.0	48	36.0
21	62.1	49	35.1
22	61.1	50	34.2
23	60.1	51	33.3
24	59.1	52	32.3
25	58.2	53	31.4
26	57.2	54	30.5
27	56.2	55	29.6

Appendix C. (Continued)

Table I (Single Life Expectancy) (For Use by Beneficiaries)			
Age	**Life Expectancy**	**Age**	**Life Expectancy**
56	28.7	84	8.1
57	27.9	85	7.6
58	27.0	86	7.1
59	26.1	87	6.7
60	25.2	88	6.3
61	24.4	89	5.9
62	23.5	90	5.5
63	22.7	91	5.2
64	21.8	92	4.9
65	21.0	93	4.6
66	20.2	94	4.3
67	19.4	95	4.1
68	18.6	96	3.8
69	17.8	97	3.6
70	17.0	98	3.4
71	16.3	99	3.1
72	15.5	100	2.9
73	14.8	101	2.7
74	14.1	102	2.5
75	13.4	103	2.3
76	12.7	104	2.1
77	12.1	105	1.9
78	11.4	106	1.7
79	10.8	107	1.5
80	10.2	108	1.4
81	9.7	109	1.2
82	9.1	110	1.1
83	8.6	111 and over	1.0

Publication 590 (2008)

IRA Answer Book

Appendix C. Life Expectancy Tables (Continued)

Table II
(Joint Life and Last Survivor Expectancy)
(For Use by Owners Whose Spouses Are More Than 10 Years Younger and Are the Sole Beneficiaries of Their IRAs)

Ages	20	21	22	23	24	25	26	27	28	29
20	70.1	69.6	69.1	68.7	68.3	67.9	67.5	67.2	66.9	66.6
21	69.6	69.1	68.6	68.2	67.7	67.3	66.9	66.6	66.2	65.9
22	69.1	68.6	68.1	67.6	67.2	66.7	66.3	65.9	65.6	65.2
23	68.7	68.2	67.6	67.1	66.6	66.2	65.7	65.3	64.9	64.6
24	68.3	67.7	67.2	66.6	66.1	65.6	65.2	64.7	64.3	63.9
25	67.9	67.3	66.7	66.2	65.6	65.1	64.6	64.2	63.7	63.3
26	67.5	66.9	66.3	65.7	65.2	64.6	64.1	63.6	63.2	62.8
27	67.2	66.6	65.9	65.3	64.7	64.2	63.6	63.1	62.7	62.2
28	66.9	66.2	65.6	64.9	64.3	63.7	63.2	62.7	62.1	61.7
29	66.6	65.9	65.2	64.6	63.9	63.3	62.8	62.2	61.7	61.2
30	66.3	65.6	64.9	64.2	63.6	62.9	62.3	61.8	61.2	60.7
31	66.1	65.3	64.6	63.9	63.2	62.6	62.0	61.4	60.8	60.2
32	65.8	65.1	64.3	63.6	62.9	62.2	61.6	61.0	60.4	59.8
33	65.6	64.8	64.1	63.3	62.6	61.9	61.3	60.6	60.0	59.4
34	65.4	64.6	63.8	63.1	62.3	61.6	60.9	60.3	59.6	59.0
35	65.2	64.4	63.6	62.8	62.1	61.4	60.6	59.9	59.3	58.6
36	65.0	64.2	63.4	62.6	61.9	61.1	60.4	59.6	59.0	58.3
37	64.9	64.0	63.2	62.4	61.6	60.9	60.1	59.4	58.7	58.0
38	64.7	63.9	63.0	62.2	61.4	60.6	59.9	59.1	58.4	57.7
39	64.6	63.7	62.9	62.1	61.2	60.4	59.6	58.9	58.1	57.4
40	64.4	63.6	62.7	61.9	61.1	60.2	59.4	58.7	57.9	57.1
41	64.3	63.5	62.6	61.7	60.9	60.1	59.3	58.5	57.7	56.9
42	64.2	63.3	62.5	61.6	60.8	59.9	59.1	58.3	57.5	56.7
43	64.1	63.2	62.4	61.5	60.6	59.8	58.9	58.1	57.3	56.5
44	64.0	63.1	62.2	61.4	60.5	59.6	58.8	57.9	57.1	56.3
45	64.0	63.0	62.2	61.3	60.4	59.5	58.6	57.8	56.9	56.1
46	63.9	63.0	62.1	61.2	60.3	59.4	58.5	57.7	56.8	56.0
47	63.8	62.9	62.0	61.1	60.2	59.3	58.4	57.5	56.7	55.8
48	63.7	62.8	61.9	61.0	60.1	59.2	58.3	57.4	56.5	55.7
49	63.7	62.8	61.8	60.9	60.0	59.1	58.2	57.3	56.4	55.6
50	63.6	62.7	61.8	60.8	59.9	59.0	58.1	57.2	56.3	55.4
51	63.6	62.6	61.7	60.8	59.9	58.9	58.0	57.1	56.2	55.3
52	63.5	62.6	61.7	60.7	59.8	58.9	58.0	57.1	56.1	55.2
53	63.5	62.5	61.6	60.7	59.7	58.8	57.9	57.0	56.1	55.2
54	63.5	62.5	61.6	60.6	59.7	58.8	57.8	56.9	56.0	55.1
55	63.4	62.5	61.5	60.6	59.6	58.7	57.8	56.8	55.9	55.0
56	63.4	62.4	61.5	60.5	59.6	58.7	57.7	56.8	55.9	54.9
57	63.4	62.4	61.5	60.5	59.6	58.6	57.7	56.7	55.8	54.9
58	63.3	62.4	61.4	60.5	59.5	58.6	57.6	56.7	55.8	54.8
59	63.3	62.3	61.4	60.4	59.5	58.5	57.6	56.7	55.7	54.8

Publication 590 (2008)

A-98

Appendix C. (Continued)

	Table II (continued) (Joint Life and Last Survivor Expectancy) (For Use by Owners Whose Spouses Are More Than 10 Years Younger and Are the Sole Beneficiaries of Their IRAs)									
Ages	20	21	22	23	24	25	26	27	28	29
60	63.3	62.3	61.4	60.4	59.5	58.5	57.6	56.6	55.7	54.7
61	63.3	62.3	61.3	60.4	59.4	58.5	57.5	56.6	55.6	54.7
62	63.2	62.3	61.3	60.4	59.4	58.4	57.5	56.5	55.6	54.7
63	63.2	62.3	61.3	60.3	59.4	58.4	57.5	56.5	55.6	54.6
64	63.2	62.2	61.3	60.3	59.4	58.4	57.4	56.5	55.5	54.6
65	63.2	62.2	61.3	60.3	59.3	58.4	57.4	56.5	55.5	54.6
66	63.2	62.2	61.2	60.3	59.3	58.4	57.4	56.4	55.5	54.5
67	63.2	62.2	61.2	60.3	59.3	58.3	57.4	56.4	55.5	54.5
68	63.1	62.2	61.2	60.2	59.3	58.3	57.4	56.4	55.4	54.5
69	63.1	62.2	61.2	60.2	59.3	58.3	57.3	56.4	55.4	54.5
70	63.1	62.2	61.2	60.2	59.3	58.3	57.3	56.4	55.4	54.4
71	63.1	62.1	61.2	60.2	59.2	58.3	57.3	56.4	55.4	54.4
72	63.1	62.1	61.2	60.2	59.2	58.3	57.3	56.3	55.4	54.4
73	63.1	62.1	61.2	60.2	59.2	58.3	57.3	56.3	55.4	54.4
74	63.1	62.1	61.2	60.2	59.2	58.2	57.3	56.3	55.4	54.4
75	63.1	62.1	61.1	60.2	59.2	58.2	57.3	56.3	55.3	54.4
76	63.1	62.1	61.1	60.2	59.2	58.2	57.3	56.3	55.3	54.4
77	63.1	62.1	61.1	60.2	59.2	58.2	57.3	56.3	55.3	54.4
78	63.1	62.1	61.1	60.2	59.2	58.2	57.3	56.3	55.3	54.4
79	63.1	62.1	61.1	60.2	59.2	58.2	57.2	56.3	55.3	54.3
80	63.1	62.1	61.1	60.1	59.2	58.2	57.2	56.3	55.3	54.3
81	63.1	62.1	61.1	60.1	59.2	58.2	57.2	56.3	55.3	54.3
82	63.1	62.1	61.1	60.1	59.2	58.2	57.2	56.3	55.3	54.3
83	63.1	62.1	61.1	60.1	59.2	58.2	57.2	56.3	55.3	54.3
84	63.0	62.1	61.1	60.1	59.2	58.2	57.2	56.3	55.3	54.3
85	63.0	62.1	61.1	60.1	59.2	58.2	57.2	56.3	55.3	54.3
86	63.0	62.1	61.1	60.1	59.2	58.2	57.2	56.2	55.3	54.3
87	63.0	62.1	61.1	60.1	59.2	58.2	57.2	56.2	55.3	54.3
88	63.0	62.1	61.1	60.1	59.2	58.2	57.2	56.2	55.3	54.3
89	63.0	62.1	61.1	60.1	59.1	58.2	57.2	56.2	55.3	54.3
90	63.0	62.1	61.1	60.1	59.1	58.2	57.2	56.2	55.3	54.3
91	63.0	62.1	61.1	60.1	59.1	58.2	57.2	56.2	55.3	54.3
92	63.0	62.1	61.1	60.1	59.1	58.2	57.2	56.2	55.3	54.3
93	63.0	62.1	61.1	60.1	59.1	58.2	57.2	56.2	55.3	54.3
94	63.0	62.1	61.1	60.1	59.1	58.2	57.2	56.2	55.3	54.3
95	63.0	62.1	61.1	60.1	59.1	58.2	57.2	56.2	55.3	54.3
96	63.0	62.1	61.1	60.1	59.1	58.2	57.2	56.2	55.3	54.3
97	63.0	62.1	61.1	60.1	59.1	58.2	57.2	56.2	55.3	54.3
98	63.0	62.1	61.1	60.1	59.1	58.2	57.2	56.2	55.3	54.3
99	63.0	62.1	61.1	60.1	59.1	58.2	57.2	56.2	55.3	54.3

Appendix C. (Continued)

Ages	20	21	22	23	24	25	26	27	28	29
					Table II (continued) (Joint Life and Last Survivor Expectancy) (For Use by Owners Whose Spouses Are More Than 10 Years Younger and Are the Sole Beneficiaries of Their IRAs)					
100	63.0	62.1	61.1	60.1	59.1	58.2	57.2	56.2	55.3	54.3
101	63.0	62.1	61.1	60.1	59.1	58.2	57.2	56.2	55.3	54.3
102	63.0	62.1	61.1	60.1	59.1	58.2	57.2	56.2	55.3	54.3
103	63.0	62.1	61.1	60.1	59.1	58.2	57.2	56.2	55.3	54.3
104	63.0	62.1	61.1	60.1	59.1	58.2	57.2	56.2	55.3	54.3
105	63.0	62.1	61.1	60.1	59.1	58.2	57.2	56.2	55.3	54.3
106	63.0	62.1	61.1	60.1	59.1	58.2	57.2	56.2	55.3	54.3
107	63.0	62.1	61.1	60.1	59.1	58.2	57.2	56.2	55.3	54.3
108	63.0	62.1	61.1	60.1	59.1	58.2	57.2	56.2	55.3	54.3
109	63.0	62.1	61.1	60.1	59.1	58.2	57.2	56.2	55.3	54.3
110	63.0	62.1	61.1	60.1	59.1	58.2	57.2	56.2	55.3	54.3
111	63.0	62.1	61.1	60.1	59.1	58.2	57.2	56.2	55.3	54.3
112	63.0	62.1	61.1	60.1	59.1	58.2	57.2	56.2	55.3	54.3
113	63.0	62.1	61.1	60.1	59.1	58.2	57.2	56.2	55.3	54.3
114	63.0	62.1	61.1	60.1	59.1	58.2	57.2	56.2	55.3	54.3
115+	63.0	62.1	61.1	60.1	59.1	58.2	57.2	56.2	55.3	54.3

Table II (continued)
(Joint Life and Last Survivor Expectancy)
(For Use by Owners Whose Spouses Are More Than 10 Years Younger and Are the Sole Beneficiaries of Their IRAs)

Ages	30	31	32	33	34	35	36	37	38	39
30	60.2	59.7	59.2	58.8	58.4	58.0	57.6	57.3	57.0	56.7
31	59.7	59.2	58.7	58.2	57.8	57.4	57.0	56.6	56.3	56.0
32	59.2	58.7	58.2	57.7	57.2	56.8	56.4	56.0	55.6	55.3
33	58.8	58.2	57.7	57.2	56.7	56.2	55.8	55.4	55.0	54.7
34	58.4	57.8	57.2	56.7	56.2	55.7	55.3	54.8	54.4	54.0
35	58.0	57.4	56.8	56.2	55.7	55.2	54.7	54.3	53.8	53.4
36	57.6	57.0	56.4	55.8	55.3	54.7	54.2	53.7	53.3	52.8
37	57.3	56.6	56.0	55.4	54.8	54.3	53.7	53.2	52.7	52.3
38	57.0	56.3	55.6	55.0	54.4	53.8	53.3	52.7	52.2	51.7
39	56.7	56.0	55.3	54.7	54.0	53.4	52.8	52.3	51.7	51.2
40	56.4	55.7	55.0	54.3	53.7	53.0	52.4	51.8	51.3	50.8
41	56.1	55.4	54.7	54.0	53.3	52.7	52.0	51.4	50.9	50.3
42	55.9	55.2	54.4	53.7	53.0	52.3	51.7	51.1	50.4	49.9
43	55.7	54.9	54.2	53.4	52.7	52.0	51.3	50.7	50.1	49.5
44	55.5	54.7	53.9	53.2	52.4	51.7	51.0	50.4	49.7	49.1
45	55.3	54.5	53.7	52.9	52.2	51.5	50.7	50.0	49.4	48.7
46	55.1	54.3	53.5	52.7	52.0	51.2	50.5	49.8	49.1	48.4
47	55.0	54.1	53.3	52.5	51.7	51.0	50.2	49.5	48.8	48.1
48	54.8	54.0	53.2	52.3	51.5	50.8	50.0	49.2	48.5	47.8

Publication 590 (2008)

Appendix C. (Continued)

Table II (continued)
(Joint Life and Last Survivor Expectancy)
(For Use by Owners Whose Spouses Are More Than 10 Years Younger and Are the Sole Beneficiaries of Their IRAs)

Ages	30	31	32	33	34	35	36	37	38	39
49	54.7	53.8	53.0	52.2	51.4	50.6	49.8	49.0	48.2	47.5
50	54.6	53.7	52.9	52.0	51.2	50.4	49.6	48.8	48.0	47.3
51	54.5	53.6	52.7	51.9	51.0	50.2	49.4	48.6	47.8	47.0
52	54.4	53.5	52.6	51.7	50.9	50.0	49.2	48.4	47.6	46.8
53	54.3	53.4	52.5	51.6	50.8	49.9	49.1	48.2	47.4	46.6
54	54.2	53.3	52.4	51.5	50.6	49.8	48.9	48.1	47.2	46.4
55	54.1	53.2	52.3	51.4	50.5	49.7	48.8	47.9	47.1	46.3
56	54.0	53.1	52.2	51.3	50.4	49.5	48.7	47.8	47.0	46.1
57	54.0	53.0	52.1	51.2	50.3	49.4	48.6	47.7	46.8	46.0
58	53.9	53.0	52.1	51.2	50.3	49.4	48.5	47.6	46.7	45.8
59	53.8	52.9	52.0	51.1	50.2	49.3	48.4	47.5	46.6	45.7
60	53.8	52.9	51.9	51.0	50.1	49.2	48.3	47.4	46.5	45.6
61	53.8	52.8	51.9	51.0	50.0	49.1	48.2	47.3	46.4	45.5
62	53.7	52.8	51.8	50.9	50.0	49.1	48.1	47.2	46.3	45.4
63	53.7	52.7	51.8	50.9	49.9	49.0	48.1	47.2	46.3	45.3
64	53.6	52.7	51.8	50.8	49.9	48.9	48.0	47.1	46.2	45.3
65	53.6	52.7	51.7	50.8	49.8	48.9	48.0	47.0	46.1	45.2
66	53.6	52.6	51.7	50.7	49.8	48.9	47.9	47.0	46.1	45.1
67	53.6	52.6	51.7	50.7	49.8	48.8	47.9	46.9	46.0	45.1
68	53.5	52.6	51.6	50.7	49.7	48.8	47.8	46.9	46.0	45.0
69	53.5	52.6	51.6	50.6	49.7	48.7	47.8	46.9	45.9	45.0
70	53.5	52.5	51.6	50.6	49.7	48.7	47.8	46.8	45.9	44.9
71	53.5	52.5	51.6	50.6	49.6	48.7	47.7	46.8	45.9	44.9
72	53.5	52.5	51.5	50.6	49.6	48.7	47.7	46.8	45.8	44.9
73	53.4	52.5	51.5	50.6	49.6	48.6	47.7	46.7	45.8	44.8
74	53.4	52.5	51.5	50.5	49.6	48.6	47.7	46.7	45.8	44.8
75	53.4	52.5	51.5	50.5	49.6	48.6	47.7	46.7	45.7	44.8
76	53.4	52.4	51.5	50.5	49.6	48.6	47.6	46.7	45.7	44.8
77	53.4	52.4	51.5	50.5	49.5	48.6	47.6	46.7	45.7	44.8
78	53.4	52.4	51.5	50.5	49.5	48.6	47.6	46.6	45.7	44.7
79	53.4	52.4	51.5	50.5	49.5	48.6	47.6	46.6	45.7	44.7
80	53.4	52.4	51.4	50.5	49.5	48.5	47.6	46.6	45.7	44.7
81	53.4	52.4	51.4	50.5	49.5	48.5	47.6	46.6	45.7	44.7
82	53.4	52.4	51.4	50.5	49.5	48.5	47.6	46.6	45.6	44.7
83	53.4	52.4	51.4	50.5	49.5	48.5	47.6	46.6	45.6	44.7
84	53.4	52.4	51.4	50.5	49.5	48.5	47.6	46.6	45.6	44.7
85	53.3	52.4	51.4	50.4	49.5	48.5	47.5	46.6	45.6	44.7
86	53.3	52.4	51.4	50.4	49.5	48.5	47.5	46.6	45.6	44.6
87	53.3	52.4	51.4	50.4	49.5	48.5	47.5	46.6	45.6	44.6
88	53.3	52.4	51.4	50.4	49.5	48.5	47.5	46.6	45.6	44.6

Appendix C. (Continued)

Ages	30	31	32	33	34	35	36	37	38	39
89	53.3	52.4	51.4	50.4	49.5	48.5	47.5	46.6	45.6	44.6
90	53.3	52.4	51.4	50.4	49.5	48.5	47.5	46.6	45.6	44.6
91	53.3	52.4	51.4	50.4	49.5	48.5	47.5	46.6	45.6	44.6
92	53.3	52.4	51.4	50.4	49.5	48.5	47.5	46.6	45.6	44.6
93	53.3	52.4	51.4	50.4	49.5	48.5	47.5	46.6	45.6	44.6
94	53.3	52.4	51.4	50.4	49.5	48.5	47.5	46.6	45.6	44.6
95	53.3	52.4	51.4	50.4	49.5	48.5	47.5	46.5	45.6	44.6
96	53.3	52.4	51.4	50.4	49.5	48.5	47.5	46.5	45.6	44.6
97	53.3	52.4	51.4	50.4	49.5	48.5	47.5	46.5	45.6	44.6
98	53.3	52.4	51.4	50.4	49.5	48.5	47.5	46.5	45.6	44.6
99	53.3	52.4	51.4	50.4	49.5	48.5	47.5	46.5	45.6	44.6
100	53.3	52.4	51.4	50.4	49.5	48.5	47.5	46.5	45.6	44.6
101	53.3	52.4	51.4	50.4	49.5	48.5	47.5	46.5	45.6	44.6
102	53.3	52.4	51.4	50.4	49.5	48.5	47.5	46.5	45.6	44.6
103	53.3	52.4	51.4	50.4	49.5	48.5	47.5	46.5	45.6	44.6
104	53.3	52.4	51.4	50.4	49.5	48.5	47.5	46.5	45.6	44.6
105	53.3	52.4	51.4	50.4	49.4	48.5	47.5	46.5	45.6	44.6
106	53.3	52.4	51.4	50.4	49.4	48.5	47.5	46.5	45.6	44.6
107	53.3	52.4	51.4	50.4	49.4	48.5	47.5	46.5	45.6	44.6
108	53.3	52.4	51.4	50.4	49.4	48.5	47.5	46.5	45.6	44.6
109	53.3	52.4	51.4	50.4	49.4	48.5	47.5	46.5	45.6	44.6
110	53.3	52.4	51.4	50.4	49.4	48.5	47.5	46.5	45.6	44.6
111	53.3	52.4	51.4	50.4	49.4	48.5	47.5	46.5	45.6	44.6
112	53.3	52.4	51.4	50.4	49.4	48.5	47.5	46.5	45.6	44.6
113	53.3	52.4	51.4	50.4	49.4	48.5	47.5	46.5	45.6	44.6
114	53.3	52.4	51.4	50.4	49.4	48.5	47.5	46.5	45.6	44.6
115+	53.3	52.4	51.4	50.4	49.4	48.5	47.5	46.5	45.6	44.6

Ages	40	41	42	43	44	45	46	47	48	49
40	50.2	49.8	49.3	48.9	48.5	48.1	47.7	47.4	47.1	46.8
41	49.8	49.3	48.8	48.3	47.9	47.5	47.1	46.7	46.4	46.1
42	49.3	48.8	48.3	47.8	47.3	46.9	46.5	46.1	45.8	45.4
43	48.9	48.3	47.8	47.3	46.8	46.3	45.9	45.5	45.1	44.8
44	48.5	47.9	47.3	46.8	46.3	45.8	45.4	44.9	44.5	44.2
45	48.1	47.5	46.9	46.3	45.8	45.3	44.8	44.4	44.0	43.6
46	47.7	47.1	46.5	45.9	45.4	44.8	44.3	43.9	43.4	43.0
47	47.4	46.7	46.1	45.5	44.9	44.4	43.9	43.4	42.9	42.4

Table II (continued)
(Joint Life and Last Survivor Expectancy)
(For Use by Owners Whose Spouses Are More Than 10 Years Younger and Are the Sole Beneficiaries of Their IRAs)

Publication 590 (2008)

Appendix C. (Continued)

					Table II (continued) (Joint Life and Last Survivor Expectancy) (For Use by Owners Whose Spouses Are More Than 10 Years Younger and Are the Sole Beneficiaries of Their IRAs)					
Ages	40	41	42	43	44	45	46	47	48	49
48	47.1	46.4	45.8	45.1	44.5	44.0	43.4	42.9	42.4	41.9
49	46.8	46.1	45.4	44.8	44.2	43.6	43.0	42.4	41.9	41.4
50	46.5	45.8	45.1	44.4	43.8	43.2	42.6	42.0	41.5	40.9
51	46.3	45.5	44.8	44.1	43.5	42.8	42.2	41.6	41.0	40.5
52	46.0	45.3	44.6	43.8	43.2	42.5	41.8	41.2	40.6	40.1
53	45.8	45.1	44.3	43.6	42.9	42.2	41.5	40.9	40.3	39.7
54	45.6	44.8	44.1	43.3	42.6	41.9	41.2	40.5	39.9	39.3
55	45.5	44.7	43.9	43.1	42.4	41.6	40.9	40.2	39.6	38.9
56	45.3	44.5	43.7	42.9	42.1	41.4	40.7	40.0	39.3	38.6
57	45.1	44.3	43.5	42.7	41.9	41.2	40.4	39.7	39.0	38.3
58	45.0	44.2	43.3	42.5	41.7	40.9	40.2	39.4	38.7	38.0
59	44.9	44.0	43.2	42.4	41.5	40.7	40.0	39.2	38.5	37.8
60	44.7	43.9	43.0	42.2	41.4	40.6	39.8	39.0	38.2	37.5
61	44.6	43.8	42.9	42.1	41.2	40.4	39.6	38.8	38.0	37.3
62	44.5	43.7	42.8	41.9	41.1	40.3	39.4	38.6	37.8	37.1
63	44.5	43.6	42.7	41.8	41.0	40.1	39.3	38.5	37.7	36.9
64	44.4	43.5	42.6	41.7	40.8	40.0	39.2	38.3	37.5	36.7
65	44.3	43.4	42.5	41.6	40.7	39.9	39.0	38.2	37.4	36.6
66	44.2	43.3	42.4	41.5	40.6	39.8	38.9	38.1	37.2	36.4
67	44.2	43.3	42.3	41.4	40.6	39.7	38.8	38.0	37.1	36.3
68	44.1	43.2	42.3	41.4	40.5	39.6	38.7	37.9	37.0	36.2
69	44.1	43.1	42.2	41.3	40.4	39.5	38.6	37.8	36.9	36.0
70	44.0	43.1	42.2	41.3	40.3	39.4	38.6	37.7	36.8	35.9
71	44.0	43.0	42.1	41.2	40.3	39.4	38.5	37.6	36.7	35.9
72	43.9	43.0	42.1	41.1	40.2	39.3	38.4	37.5	36.6	35.8
73	43.9	43.0	42.0	41.1	40.2	39.3	38.4	37.5	36.6	35.7
74	43.9	42.9	42.0	41.1	40.1	39.2	38.3	37.4	36.5	35.6
75	43.8	42.9	42.0	41.0	40.1	39.2	38.3	37.4	36.5	35.6
76	43.8	42.9	41.9	41.0	40.1	39.1	38.2	37.3	36.4	35.5
77	43.8	42.9	41.9	41.0	40.0	39.1	38.2	37.3	36.4	35.5
78	43.8	42.8	41.9	40.9	40.0	39.1	38.2	37.2	36.3	35.4
79	43.8	42.8	41.9	40.9	40.0	39.1	38.1	37.2	36.3	35.4
80	43.7	42.8	41.8	40.9	40.0	39.0	38.1	37.2	36.3	35.4
81	43.7	42.8	41.8	40.9	39.9	39.0	38.1	37.2	36.2	35.3
82	43.7	42.8	41.8	40.9	39.9	39.0	38.1	37.1	36.2	35.3
83	43.7	42.8	41.8	40.9	39.9	39.0	38.0	37.1	36.2	35.3
84	43.7	42.7	41.8	40.8	39.9	39.0	38.0	37.1	36.2	35.3
85	43.7	42.7	41.8	40.8	39.9	38.9	38.0	37.1	36.2	35.2
86	43.7	42.7	41.8	40.8	39.9	38.9	38.0	37.1	36.1	35.2
87	43.7	42.7	41.8	40.8	39.9	38.9	38.0	37.0	36.1	35.2

Appendix C. (Continued)

Table II (continued) (Joint Life and Last Survivor Expectancy) (For Use by Owners Whose Spouses Are More Than 10 Years Younger and Are the Sole Beneficiaries of Their IRAs)									
Ages	40	41	42	43	44	45	46	47	48	49
88	43.7	42.7	41.8	40.8	39.9	38.9	38.0	37.0	36.1	35.2
89	43.7	42.7	41.7	40.8	39.8	38.9	38.0	37.0	36.1	35.2
90	43.7	42.7	41.7	40.8	39.8	38.9	38.0	37.0	36.1	35.2
91	43.7	42.7	41.7	40.8	39.8	38.9	37.9	37.0	36.1	35.2
92	43.7	42.7	41.7	40.8	39.8	38.9	37.9	37.0	36.1	35.1
93	43.7	42.7	41.7	40.8	39.8	38.9	37.9	37.0	36.1	35.1
94	43.7	42.7	41.7	40.8	39.8	38.9	37.9	37.0	36.1	35.1
95	43.6	42.7	41.7	40.8	39.8	38.9	37.9	37.0	36.1	35.1
96	43.6	42.7	41.7	40.8	39.8	38.9	37.9	37.0	36.1	35.1
97	43.6	42.7	41.7	40.8	39.8	38.9	37.9	37.0	36.1	35.1
98	43.6	42.7	41.7	40.8	39.8	38.9	37.9	37.0	36.0	35.1
99	43.6	42.7	41.7	40.8	39.8	38.9	37.9	37.0	36.0	35.1
100	43.6	42.7	41.7	40.8	39.8	38.9	37.9	37.0	36.0	35.1
101	43.6	42.7	41.7	40.8	39.8	38.9	37.9	37.0	36.0	35.1
102	43.6	42.7	41.7	40.8	39.8	38.9	37.9	37.0	36.0	35.1
103	43.6	42.7	41.7	40.8	39.8	38.9	37.9	37.0	36.0	35.1
104	43.6	42.7	41.7	40.8	39.8	38.8	37.9	37.0	36.0	35.1
105	43.6	42.7	41.7	40.8	39.8	38.8	37.9	37.0	36.0	35.1
106	43.6	42.7	41.7	40.8	39.8	38.8	37.9	37.0	36.0	35.1
107	43.6	42.7	41.7	40.8	39.8	38.8	37.9	37.0	36.0	35.1
108	43.6	42.7	41.7	40.8	39.8	38.8	37.9	37.0	36.0	35.1
109	43.6	42.7	41.7	40.7	39.8	38.8	37.9	37.0	36.0	35.1
110	43.6	42.7	41.7	40.7	39.8	38.8	37.9	37.0	36.0	35.1
111	43.6	42.7	41.7	40.7	39.8	38.8	37.9	37.0	36.0	35.1
112	43.6	42.7	41.7	40.7	39.8	38.8	37.9	37.0	36.0	35.1
113	43.6	42.7	41.7	40.7	39.8	38.8	37.9	37.0	36.0	35.1
114	43.6	42.7	41.7	40.7	39.8	38.8	37.9	37.0	36.0	35.1
115+	43.6	42.7	41.7	40.7	39.8	38.8	37.9	37.0	36.0	35.1

Table II (continued) (Joint Life and Last Survivor Expectancy) (For Use by Owners Whose Spouses Are More Than 10 Years Younger and Are the Sole Beneficiaries of Their IRAs)									
Ages	50	51	52	53	54	55	56	57	58	59
50	40.4	40.0	39.5	39.1	38.7	38.3	38.0	37.6	37.3	37.1
51	40.0	39.5	39.0	38.5	38.1	37.7	37.4	37.0	36.7	36.4
52	39.5	39.0	38.5	38.0	37.6	37.2	36.8	36.4	36.0	35.7
53	39.1	38.5	38.0	37.5	37.1	36.6	36.2	35.8	35.4	35.1
54	38.7	38.1	37.6	37.1	36.6	36.1	35.7	35.2	34.8	34.5
55	38.3	37.7	37.2	36.6	36.1	35.6	35.1	34.7	34.3	33.9
56	38.0	37.4	36.8	36.2	35.7	35.1	34.7	34.2	33.7	33.3

Publication 590 (2008)

Appendix C. (Continued)

Table II (continued)
(Joint Life and Last Survivor Expectancy)
(For Use by Owners Whose Spouses Are More Than 10 Years Younger and Are the Sole Beneficiaries of Their IRAs)

Ages	50	51	52	53	54	55	56	57	58	59
57	37.6	37.0	36.4	35.8	35.2	34.7	34.2	33.7	33.2	32.8
58	37.3	36.7	36.0	35.4	34.8	34.3	33.7	33.2	32.8	32.3
59	37.1	36.4	35.7	35.1	34.5	33.9	33.3	32.8	32.3	31.8
60	36.8	36.1	35.4	34.8	34.1	33.5	32.9	32.4	31.9	31.3
61	36.6	35.8	35.1	34.5	33.8	33.2	32.6	32.0	31.4	30.9
62	36.3	35.6	34.9	34.2	33.5	32.9	32.2	31.6	31.1	30.5
63	36.1	35.4	34.6	33.9	33.2	32.6	31.9	31.3	30.7	30.1
64	35.9	35.2	34.4	33.7	33.0	32.3	31.6	31.0	30.4	29.8
65	35.8	35.0	34.2	33.5	32.7	32.0	31.4	30.7	30.0	29.4
66	35.6	34.8	34.0	33.3	32.5	31.8	31.1	30.4	29.8	29.1
67	35.5	34.7	33.9	33.1	32.3	31.6	30.9	30.2	29.5	28.8
68	35.3	34.5	33.7	32.9	32.1	31.4	30.7	29.9	29.2	28.6
69	35.2	34.4	33.6	32.8	32.0	31.2	30.5	29.7	29.0	28.3
70	35.1	34.3	33.4	32.6	31.8	31.1	30.3	29.5	28.8	28.1
71	35.0	34.2	33.3	32.5	31.7	30.9	30.1	29.4	28.6	27.9
72	34.9	34.1	33.2	32.4	31.6	30.8	30.0	29.2	28.4	27.7
73	34.8	34.0	33.1	32.3	31.5	30.6	29.8	29.1	28.3	27.5
74	34.8	33.9	33.0	32.2	31.4	30.5	29.7	28.9	28.1	27.4
75	34.7	33.8	33.0	32.1	31.3	30.4	29.6	28.8	28.0	27.2
76	34.6	33.8	32.9	32.0	31.2	30.3	29.5	28.7	27.9	27.1
77	34.6	33.7	32.8	32.0	31.1	30.3	29.4	28.6	27.8	27.0
78	34.5	33.6	32.8	31.9	31.0	30.2	29.3	28.5	27.7	26.9
79	34.5	33.6	32.7	31.8	31.0	30.1	29.3	28.4	27.6	26.8
80	34.5	33.6	32.7	31.8	30.9	30.1	29.2	28.4	27.5	26.7
81	34.4	33.5	32.6	31.8	30.9	30.0	29.2	28.3	27.5	26.6
82	34.4	33.5	32.6	31.7	30.8	30.0	29.1	28.3	27.4	26.6
83	34.4	33.5	32.6	31.7	30.8	29.9	29.1	28.2	27.4	26.5
84	34.3	33.4	32.5	31.7	30.8	29.9	29.0	28.2	27.3	26.5
85	34.3	33.4	32.5	31.6	30.7	29.9	29.0	28.1	27.3	26.4
86	34.3	33.4	32.5	31.6	30.7	29.8	29.0	28.1	27.2	26.4
87	34.3	33.4	32.5	31.6	30.7	29.8	28.9	28.1	27.2	26.4
88	34.3	33.4	32.5	31.6	30.7	29.8	28.9	28.0	27.2	26.3
89	34.3	33.3	32.4	31.5	30.7	29.8	28.9	28.0	27.2	26.3
90	34.2	33.3	32.4	31.5	30.6	29.8	28.9	28.0	27.1	26.3
91	34.2	33.3	32.4	31.5	30.6	29.7	28.9	28.0	27.1	26.3
92	34.2	33.3	32.4	31.5	30.6	29.7	28.8	28.0	27.1	26.2
93	34.2	33.3	32.4	31.5	30.6	29.7	28.8	28.0	27.1	26.2
94	34.2	33.3	32.4	31.5	30.6	29.7	28.8	27.9	27.1	26.2
95	34.2	33.3	32.4	31.5	30.6	29.7	28.8	27.9	27.1	26.2
96	34.2	33.3	32.4	31.5	30.6	29.7	28.8	27.9	27.0	26.2

Appendix C. (Continued)

Table II (continued)
(Joint Life and Last Survivor Expectancy)
(For Use by Owners Whose Spouses Are More Than 10 Years Younger and Are the Sole Beneficiaries of Their IRAs)

Ages	50	51	52	53	54	55	56	57	58	59
97	34.2	33.3	32.4	31.5	30.6	29.7	28.8	27.9	27.0	26.2
98	34.2	33.3	32.4	31.5	30.6	29.7	28.8	27.9	27.0	26.2
99	34.2	33.3	32.4	31.5	30.6	29.7	28.8	27.9	27.0	26.2
100	34.2	33.3	32.4	31.5	30.6	29.7	28.8	27.9	27.0	26.1
101	34.2	33.3	32.4	31.5	30.6	29.7	28.8	27.9	27.0	26.1
102	34.2	33.3	32.4	31.4	30.5	29.7	28.8	27.9	27.0	26.1
103	34.2	33.3	32.4	31.4	30.5	29.7	28.8	27.9	27.0	26.1
104	34.2	33.3	32.4	31.4	30.5	29.6	28.8	27.9	27.0	26.1
105	34.2	33.3	32.3	31.4	30.5	29.6	28.8	27.9	27.0	26.1
106	34.2	33.3	32.3	31.4	30.5	29.6	28.8	27.9	27.0	26.1
107	34.2	33.3	32.3	31.4	30.5	29.6	28.8	27.9	27.0	26.1
108	34.2	33.3	32.3	31.4	30.5	29.6	28.8	27.9	27.0	26.1
109	34.2	33.3	32.3	31.4	30.5	29.6	28.7	27.9	27.0	26.1
110	34.2	33.3	32.3	31.4	30.5	29.6	28.7	27.9	27.0	26.1
111	34.2	33.3	32.3	31.4	30.5	29.6	28.7	27.9	27.0	26.1
112	34.2	33.3	32.3	31.4	30.5	29.6	28.7	27.9	27.0	26.1
113	34.2	33.3	32.3	31.4	30.5	29.6	28.7	27.9	27.0	26.1
114	34.2	33.3	32.3	31.4	30.5	29.6	28.7	27.9	27.0	26.1
115+	34.2	33.3	32.3	31.4	30.5	29.6	28.7	27.9	27.0	26.1

Table II (continued)
(Joint Life and Last Survivor Expectancy)
(For Use by Owners Whose Spouses Are More Than 10 Years Younger and Are the Sole Beneficiaries of Their IRAs)

Ages	60	61	62	63	64	65	66	67	68	69
60	30.9	30.4	30.0	29.6	29.2	28.8	28.5	28.2	27.9	27.6
61	30.4	29.9	29.5	29.0	28.6	28.3	27.9	27.6	27.3	27.0
62	30.0	29.5	29.0	28.5	28.1	27.7	27.3	27.0	26.7	26.4
63	29.6	29.0	28.5	28.1	27.6	27.2	26.8	26.4	26.1	25.7
64	29.2	28.6	28.1	27.6	27.1	26.7	26.3	25.9	25.5	25.2
65	28.8	28.3	27.7	27.2	26.7	26.2	25.8	25.4	25.0	24.6
66	28.5	27.9	27.3	26.8	26.3	25.8	25.3	24.9	24.5	24.1
67	28.2	27.6	27.0	26.4	25.9	25.4	24.9	24.4	24.0	23.6
68	27.9	27.3	26.7	26.1	25.5	25.0	24.5	24.0	23.5	23.1
69	27.6	27.0	26.4	25.7	25.2	24.6	24.1	23.6	23.1	22.6
70	27.4	26.7	26.1	25.4	24.8	24.3	23.7	23.2	22.7	22.2
71	27.2	26.5	25.8	25.2	24.5	23.9	23.4	22.8	22.3	21.8
72	27.0	26.3	25.6	24.9	24.3	23.7	23.1	22.5	22.0	21.4
73	26.8	26.1	25.4	24.7	24.0	23.4	22.8	22.2	21.6	21.1
74	26.6	25.9	25.2	24.5	23.8	23.1	22.5	21.9	21.3	20.8
75	26.5	25.7	25.0	24.3	23.6	22.9	22.3	21.6	21.0	20.5

Publication 590 (2008)

Appendix C. (Continued)

Ages	60	61	62	63	64	65	66	67	68	69
	Table II (continued)									
	(Joint Life and Last Survivor Expectancy)									
	(For Use by Owners Whose Spouses Are More Than 10 Years Younger and Are the Sole Beneficiaries of Their IRAs)									
76	26.3	25.6	24.8	24.1	23.4	22.7	22.0	21.4	20.8	20.2
77	26.2	25.4	24.7	23.9	23.2	22.5	21.8	21.2	20.6	19.9
78	26.1	25.3	24.6	23.8	23.1	22.4	21.7	21.0	20.3	19.7
79	26.0	25.2	24.4	23.7	22.9	22.2	21.5	20.8	20.1	19.5
80	25.9	25.1	24.3	23.6	22.8	22.1	21.3	20.6	20.0	19.3
81	25.8	25.0	24.2	23.4	22.7	21.9	21.2	20.5	19.8	19.1
82	25.8	24.9	24.1	23.4	22.6	21.8	21.1	20.4	19.7	19.0
83	25.7	24.9	24.1	23.3	22.5	21.7	21.0	20.2	19.5	18.8
84	25.6	24.8	24.0	23.2	22.4	21.6	20.9	20.1	19.4	18.7
85	25.6	24.8	23.9	23.1	22.3	21.6	20.8	20.1	19.3	18.6
86	25.5	24.7	23.9	23.1	22.3	21.5	20.7	20.0	19.2	18.5
87	25.5	24.7	23.8	23.0	22.2	21.4	20.7	19.9	19.2	18.4
88	25.5	24.6	23.8	23.0	22.2	21.4	20.6	19.8	19.1	18.3
89	25.4	24.6	23.8	22.9	22.1	21.3	20.5	19.8	19.0	18.3
90	25.4	24.6	23.7	22.9	22.1	21.3	20.5	19.7	19.0	18.2
91	25.4	24.5	23.7	22.9	22.1	21.3	20.5	19.7	18.9	18.2
92	25.4	24.5	23.7	22.9	22.0	21.2	20.4	19.6	18.9	18.1
93	25.4	24.5	23.7	22.8	22.0	21.2	20.4	19.6	18.8	18.1
94	25.3	24.5	23.6	22.8	22.0	21.2	20.4	19.6	18.8	18.0
95	25.3	24.5	23.6	22.8	22.0	21.1	20.3	19.6	18.8	18.0
96	25.3	24.5	23.6	22.8	21.9	21.1	20.3	19.5	18.8	18.0
97	25.3	24.5	23.6	22.8	21.9	21.1	20.3	19.5	18.7	18.0
98	25.3	24.4	23.6	22.8	21.9	21.1	20.3	19.5	18.7	17.9
99	25.3	24.4	23.6	22.7	21.9	21.1	20.3	19.5	18.7	17.9
100	25.3	24.4	23.6	22.7	21.9	21.1	20.3	19.5	18.7	17.9
101	25.3	24.4	23.6	22.7	21.9	21.1	20.2	19.4	18.7	17.9
102	25.3	24.4	23.6	22.7	21.9	21.1	20.2	19.4	18.6	17.9
103	25.3	24.4	23.6	22.7	21.9	21.0	20.2	19.4	18.6	17.9
104	25.3	24.4	23.5	22.7	21.9	21.0	20.2	19.4	18.6	17.8
105	25.3	24.4	23.5	22.7	21.9	21.0	20.2	19.4	18.6	17.8
106	25.3	24.4	23.5	22.7	21.9	21.0	20.2	19.4	18.6	17.8
107	25.2	24.4	23.5	22.7	21.8	21.0	20.2	19.4	18.6	17.8
108	25.2	24.4	23.5	22.7	21.8	21.0	20.2	19.4	18.6	17.8
109	25.2	24.4	23.5	22.7	21.8	21.0	20.2	19.4	18.6	17.8
110	25.2	24.4	23.5	22.7	21.8	21.0	20.2	19.4	18.6	17.8
111	25.2	24.4	23.5	22.7	21.8	21.0	20.2	19.4	18.6	17.8
112	25.2	24.4	23.5	22.7	21.8	21.0	20.2	19.4	18.6	17.8
113	25.2	24.4	23.5	22.7	21.8	21.0	20.2	19.4	18.6	17.8
114	25.2	24.4	23.5	22.7	21.8	21.0	20.2	19.4	18.6	17.8
115+	25.2	24.4	23.5	22.7	21.8	21.0	20.2	19.4	18.6	17.8

Appendix C. (Continued)

Table II (continued)
(Joint Life and Last Survivor Expectancy)
(For Use by Owners Whose Spouses Are More Than 10 Years Younger and Are the Sole Beneficiaries of Their IRAs)

Ages	70	71	72	73	74	75	76	77	78	79
70	21.8	21.3	20.9	20.6	20.2	19.9	19.6	19.4	19.1	18.9
71	21.3	20.9	20.5	20.1	19.7	19.4	19.1	18.8	18.5	18.3
72	20.9	20.5	20.0	19.6	19.3	18.9	18.6	18.3	18.0	17.7
73	20.6	20.1	19.6	19.2	18.8	18.4	18.1	17.8	17.5	17.2
74	20.2	19.7	19.3	18.8	18.4	18.0	17.6	17.3	17.0	16.7
75	19.9	19.4	18.9	18.4	18.0	17.6	17.2	16.8	16.5	16.2
76	19.6	19.1	18.6	18.1	17.6	17.2	16.8	16.4	16.0	15.7
77	19.4	18.8	18.3	17.8	17.3	16.8	16.4	16.0	15.6	15.3
78	19.1	18.5	18.0	17.5	17.0	16.5	16.0	15.6	15.2	14.9
79	18.9	18.3	17.7	17.2	16.7	16.2	15.7	15.3	14.9	14.5
80	18.7	18.1	17.5	16.9	16.4	15.9	15.4	15.0	14.5	14.1
81	18.5	17.9	17.3	16.7	16.2	15.6	15.1	14.7	14.2	13.8
82	18.3	17.7	17.1	16.5	15.9	15.4	14.9	14.4	13.9	13.5
83	18.2	17.5	16.9	16.3	15.7	15.2	14.7	14.2	13.7	13.2
84	18.0	17.4	16.7	16.1	15.5	15.0	14.4	13.9	13.4	13.0
85	17.9	17.3	16.6	16.0	15.4	14.8	14.3	13.7	13.2	12.8
86	17.8	17.1	16.5	15.8	15.2	14.6	14.1	13.5	13.0	12.5
87	17.7	17.0	16.4	15.7	15.1	14.5	13.9	13.4	12.9	12.4
88	17.6	16.9	16.3	15.6	15.0	14.4	13.8	13.2	12.7	12.2
89	17.6	16.9	16.2	15.5	14.9	14.3	13.7	13.1	12.6	12.0
90	17.5	16.8	16.1	15.4	14.8	14.2	13.6	13.0	12.4	11.9
91	17.4	16.7	16.0	15.4	14.7	14.1	13.5	12.9	12.3	11.8
92	17.4	16.7	16.0	15.3	14.6	14.0	13.4	12.8	12.2	11.7
93	17.3	16.6	15.9	15.2	14.6	13.9	13.3	12.7	12.1	11.6
94	17.3	16.6	15.9	15.2	14.5	13.9	13.2	12.6	12.0	11.5
95	17.3	16.5	15.8	15.1	14.5	13.8	13.2	12.6	12.0	11.4
96	17.2	16.5	15.8	15.1	14.4	13.8	13.1	12.5	11.9	11.3
97	17.2	16.5	15.8	15.1	14.4	13.7	13.1	12.5	11.9	11.3
98	17.2	16.4	15.7	15.0	14.3	13.7	13.0	12.4	11.8	11.2
99	17.2	16.4	15.7	15.0	14.3	13.6	13.0	12.4	11.8	11.2
100	17.1	16.4	15.7	15.0	14.3	13.6	12.9	12.3	11.7	11.1
101	17.1	16.4	15.6	14.9	14.2	13.6	12.9	12.3	11.7	11.1
102	17.1	16.4	15.6	14.9	14.2	13.5	12.9	12.2	11.6	11.0
103	17.1	16.3	15.6	14.9	14.2	13.5	12.9	12.2	11.6	11.0
104	17.1	16.3	15.6	14.9	14.2	13.5	12.8	12.2	11.6	11.0
105	17.1	16.3	15.6	14.9	14.2	13.5	12.8	12.2	11.5	10.9
106	17.1	16.3	15.6	14.8	14.1	13.5	12.8	12.2	11.5	10.9
107	17.0	16.3	15.6	14.8	14.1	13.4	12.8	12.1	11.5	10.9
108	17.0	16.3	15.5	14.8	14.1	13.4	12.8	12.1	11.5	10.9
109	17.0	16.3	15.5	14.8	14.1	13.4	12.8	12.1	11.5	10.9

Publication 590 (2008)

Appendix C. (Continued)

Table II (continued)
(Joint Life and Last Survivor Expectancy)
(For Use by Owners Whose Spouses Are More Than 10 Years Younger and Are the Sole Beneficiaries of Their IRAs)

Ages	70	71	72	73	74	75	76	77	78	79
110	17.0	16.3	15.5	14.8	14.1	13.4	12.7	12.1	11.5	10.9
111	17.0	16.3	15.5	14.8	14.1	13.4	12.7	12.1	11.5	10.8
112	17.0	16.3	15.5	14.8	14.1	13.4	12.7	12.1	11.5	10.8
113	17.0	16.3	15.5	14.8	14.1	13.4	12.7	12.1	11.4	10.8
114	17.0	16.3	15.5	14.8	14.1	13.4	12.7	12.1	11.4	10.8
115+	17.0	16.3	15.5	14.8	14.1	13.4	12.7	12.1	11.4	10.8

Table II (continued)
(Joint Life and Last Survivor Expectancy)
(For Use by Owners Whose Spouses Are More Than 10 Years Younger and Are the Sole Beneficiaries of Their IRAs)

AGES	80	81	82	83	84	85	86	87	88	89
80	13.8	13.4	13.1	12.8	12.6	12.3	12.1	11.9	11.7	11.5
81	13.4	13.1	12.7	12.4	12.2	11.9	11.7	11.4	11.3	11.1
82	13.1	12.7	12.4	12.1	11.8	11.5	11.3	11.0	10.8	10.6
83	12.8	12.4	12.1	11.7	11.4	11.1	10.9	10.6	10.4	10.2
84	12.6	12.2	11.8	11.4	11.1	10.8	10.5	10.3	10.1	9.9
85	12.3	11.9	11.5	11.1	10.8	10.5	10.2	9.9	9.7	9.5
86	12.1	11.7	11.3	10.9	10.5	10.2	9.9	9.6	9.4	9.2
87	11.9	11.4	11.0	10.6	10.3	9.9	9.6	9.4	9.1	8.9
88	11.7	11.3	10.8	10.4	10.1	9.7	9.4	9.1	8.8	8.6
89	11.5	11.1	10.6	10.2	9.9	9.5	9.2	8.9	8.6	8.3
90	11.4	10.9	10.5	10.1	9.7	9.3	9.0	8.6	8.3	8.1
91	11.3	10.8	10.3	9.9	9.5	9.1	8.8	8.4	8.1	7.9
92	11.2	10.7	10.2	9.8	9.3	9.0	8.6	8.3	8.0	7.7
93	11.1	10.6	10.1	9.6	9.2	8.8	8.5	8.1	7.8	7.5
94	11.0	10.5	10.0	9.5	9.1	8.7	8.3	8.0	7.6	7.3
95	10.9	10.4	9.9	9.4	9.0	8.6	8.2	7.8	7.5	7.2
96	10.8	10.3	9.8	9.3	8.9	8.5	8.1	7.7	7.4	7.1
97	10.7	10.2	9.7	9.2	8.8	8.4	8.0	7.6	7.3	6.9
98	10.7	10.1	9.6	9.2	8.7	8.3	7.9	7.5	7.1	6.8
99	10.6	10.1	9.6	9.1	8.6	8.2	7.8	7.4	7.0	6.7
100	10.6	10.0	9.5	9.0	8.5	8.1	7.7	7.3	6.9	6.6
101	10.5	10.0	9.4	9.0	8.5	8.0	7.6	7.2	6.9	6.5
102	10.5	9.9	9.4	8.9	8.4	8.0	7.5	7.1	6.8	6.4
103	10.4	9.9	9.4	8.8	8.4	7.9	7.5	7.1	6.7	6.3
104	10.4	9.8	9.3	8.8	8.3	7.9	7.4	7.0	6.6	6.3
105	10.4	9.8	9.3	8.8	8.3	7.8	7.4	7.0	6.6	6.2
106	10.3	9.8	9.2	8.7	8.2	7.8	7.3	6.9	6.5	6.2
107	10.3	9.8	9.2	8.7	8.2	7.7	7.3	6.9	6.5	6.1
108	10.3	9.7	9.2	8.7	8.2	7.7	7.3	6.8	6.4	6.1
109	10.3	9.7	9.2	8.7	8.2	7.7	7.2	6.8	6.4	6.0
110	10.3	9.7	9.2	8.6	8.1	7.7	7.2	6.8	6.4	6.0
111	10.3	9.7	9.1	8.6	8.1	7.6	7.2	6.8	6.3	6.0
112	10.2	9.7	9.1	8.6	8.1	7.6	7.2	6.7	6.3	5.9
113	10.2	9.7	9.1	8.6	8.1	7.6	7.2	6.7	6.3	5.9
114	10.2	9.7	9.1	8.6	8.1	7.6	7.1	6.7	6.3	5.9
115+	10.2	9.7	9.1	8.6	8.1	7.6	7.1	6.7	6.3	5.9

Appendix C. (Continued)

					Table II (continued) (Joint Life and Last Survivor Expectancy) (For Use by Owners Whose Spouses Are More Than 10 Years Younger and Are the Sole Beneficiaries of Their IRAs)					
AGES	90	91	92	93	94	95	96	97	98	99
90	7.8	7.6	7.4	7.2	7.1	6.9	6.8	6.6	6.5	6.4
91	7.6	7.4	7.2	7.0	6.8	6.7	6.5	6.4	6.3	6.1
92	7.4	7.2	7.0	6.8	6.6	6.4	6.3	6.1	6.0	5.9
93	7.2	7.0	6.8	6.6	6.4	6.2	6.1	5.9	5.8	5.6
94	7.1	6.8	6.6	6.4	6.2	6.0	5.9	5.7	5.6	5.4
95	6.9	6.7	6.4	6.2	6.0	5.8	5.7	5.5	5.4	5.2
96	6.8	6.5	6.3	6.1	5.9	5.7	5.5	5.3	5.2	5.0
97	6.6	6.4	6.1	5.9	5.7	5.5	5.3	5.2	5.0	4.9
98	6.5	6.3	6.0	5.8	5.6	5.4	5.2	5.0	4.8	4.7
99	6.4	6.1	5.9	5.6	5.4	5.2	5.0	4.9	4.7	4.5
100	6.3	6.0	5.8	5.5	5.3	5.1	4.9	4.7	4.5	4.4
101	6.2	5.9	5.6	5.4	5.2	5.0	4.8	4.6	4.4	4.2
102	6.1	5.8	5.5	5.3	5.1	4.8	4.6	4.4	4.3	4.1
103	6.0	5.7	5.4	5.2	5.0	4.7	4.5	4.3	4.1	4.0
104	5.9	5.6	5.4	5.1	4.9	4.6	4.4	4.2	4.0	3.8
105	5.9	5.6	5.3	5.0	4.8	4.5	4.3	4.1	3.9	3.7
106	5.8	5.5	5.2	4.9	4.7	4.5	4.2	4.0	3.8	3.6
107	5.8	5.4	5.1	4.9	4.6	4.4	4.2	3.9	3.7	3.5
108	5.7	5.4	5.1	4.8	4.6	4.3	4.1	3.9	3.7	3.5
109	5.7	5.3	5.0	4.8	4.5	4.3	4.0	3.8	3.6	3.4
110	5.6	5.3	5.0	4.7	4.5	4.2	4.0	3.8	3.5	3.3
111	5.6	5.3	5.0	4.7	4.4	4.2	3.9	3.7	3.5	3.3
112	5.6	5.3	4.9	4.7	4.4	4.1	3.9	3.7	3.5	3.2
113	5.6	5.2	4.9	4.6	4.4	4.1	3.9	3.6	3.4	3.2
114	5.6	5.2	4.9	4.6	4.3	4.1	3.9	3.6	3.4	3.2
115+	5.5	5.2	4.9	4.6	4.3	4.1	3.8	3.6	3.4	3.1

Publication 590 (2008)

Appendix C. (Continued)

AGES	100	101	102	103	104	105	106	107	108	109
Table II (continued)										
(Joint Life and Last Survivor Expectancy)										
(For Use by Owners Whose Spouses Are More Than 10 Years Younger and Are the Sole Beneficiaries of Their IRAs)										
100	4.2	4.1	3.9	3.8	3.7	3.5	3.4	3.3	3.3	3.2
101	4.1	3.9	3.7	3.6	3.5	3.4	3.2	3.1	3.1	3.0
102	3.9	3.7	3.6	3.4	3.3	3.2	3.1	3.0	2.9	2.8
103	3.8	3.6	3.4	3.3	3.2	3.0	2.9	2.8	2.7	2.6
104	3.7	3.5	3.3	3.2	3.0	2.9	2.7	2.6	2.5	2.4
105	3.5	3.4	3.2	3.0	2.9	2.7	2.6	2.5	2.4	2.3
106	3.4	3.2	3.1	2.9	2.7	2.6	2.4	2.3	2.2	2.1
107	3.3	3.1	3.0	2.8	2.6	2.5	2.3	2.2	2.1	2.0
108	3.3	3.1	2.9	2.7	2.5	2.4	2.2	2.1	1.9	1.8
109	3.2	3.0	2.8	2.6	2.4	2.3	2.1	2.0	1.8	1.7
110	3.1	2.9	2.7	2.5	2.3	2.2	2.0	1.9	1.7	1.6
111	3.1	2.9	2.7	2.5	2.3	2.1	1.9	1.8	1.6	1.5
112	3.0	2.8	2.6	2.4	2.2	2.0	1.9	1.7	1.5	1.4
113	3.0	2.8	2.6	2.4	2.2	2.0	1.8	1.6	1.5	1.3
114	3.0	2.7	2.5	2.3	2.1	1.9	1.8	1.6	1.4	1.3
115+	2.9	2.7	2.5	2.3	2.1	1.9	1.7	1.5	1.4	1.2

AGES	110	111	112	113	114	115+
Table II (continued)						
(Joint Life and Last Survivor Expectancy)						
(For Use by Owners Whose Spouses Are More Than 10 Years Younger and Are the Sole Beneficiaries of Their IRAs)						
110	1.5	1.4	1.3	1.2	1.1	1.1
111	1.4	1.2	1.1	1.1	1.0	1.0
112	1.3	1.1	1.0	1.0	1.0	1.0
113	1.2	1.1	1.0	1.0	1.0	1.0
114	1.1	1.0	1.0	1.0	1.0	1.0
115+	1.1	1.0	1.0	1.0	1.0	1.0

Appendix C. Uniform Lifetime Table

Table III
(Uniform Lifetime)

(For Use by:
- Unmarried Owners,
- Married Owners Whose Spouses Are Not More Than 10 Years Younger, and
- Married Owners Whose Spouses Are Not the Sole Beneficiaries of Their IRAs)

Age	Distribution Period	Age	Distribution Period
70	27.4	93	9.6
71	26.5	94	9.1
72	25.6	95	8.6
73	24.7	96	8.1
74	23.8	97	7.6
75	22.9	98	7.1
76	22.0	99	6.7
77	21.2	100	6.3
78	20.3	101	5.9
79	19.5	102	5.5
80	18.7	103	5.2
81	17.9	104	4.9
82	17.1	105	4.5
83	16.3	106	4.2
84	15.5	107	3.9
85	14.8	108	3.7
86	14.1	109	3.4
87	13.4	110	3.1
88	12.7	111	2.9
89	12.0	112	2.6
90	11.4	113	2.4
91	10.8	114	2.1
92	10.2	115 and over	1.9

Publication 590 (2008)

Index

To help us develop a more useful index, please let us know if you have ideas for index entries. See "Comments and Suggestions" in the "Introduction" for the ways you can reach us.

■

Internal Revenue Code Sections

[References are to question numbers.]

Treasury Regulations Sections

[References are to question numbers.]

Temporary Treasury Regulations

Temp. Treas. Reg. §

Proposed Treasury Regulations

Prop. Treas. Reg. §

Revenue Procedures and Rulings

[References are to question numbers.]

Revenue Procedures

Rev. Proc.

87-50, 1987-2 C.B. 647 . . . . 12:4, 12:18
89-52, 1989-2 C.B. 632 . . . . 7:162
91-18, 1991-1 C.B. 522 . . . . 3:30
91-70, 1991-2 C.B. 899 . . . . 7:100
92-10, 1992-1 C.B. 661 . . . . 7:119, 7:121
92-16, 1992-1 C.B. 673 . . . . 7:119
92-38, 1992-1 C.B. 859 . . . . 2:36
95-52, 1995-2 C.B. 439 . . . . 7:119,
7:121
97-29, 1997-1 C.B. 698 . . . . 12:4, 12:18
98-59, 1998-2 C.B. 727 . . . . 2:18, 2:56
99-50, 1999-2 C.B. 757 . . . . 7:104, 7:159
2003-16, 2003-4 C.B. 803 . . . . 6:17, 6:18
2006-13, 2006-3 I.R.B. 315 . . . . 4:100
2006-27, 2006-22 I.R.B. 945 . . . . . . 2:63, 12:136
2007-49, 2007-30 I.R.B. 141 . . . . 2:63
2007-66, 2007-45 I.R.B. 970 . . . . 3:2, 3:4
2008-8, 2008-1 I.R.B. 233 . . . . 12:40
2008-24, 2008-13 I.R.B. 684 . . . . 7:88
2008-29, 2008-22 I.R.B. 1039 . . . . 4:146
2008-36, 2008-33 I.R.B. 340 . . . . 7:13
2008-50, 2008-35 I.R.B. 464 . . . . 2:63
2008-51, 2008-25 I.R.B. 1163 . . . . 4:145
2008-66, 2008-45 I.R.B. 1107 . . . . . 10:62, 10:77
2009-4, 2009-1 I.R.B. 118 . . . . 2:18,
13:83
2009-6, 2009-1 I.R.B. 189 . . . . 11:27

Rev. Proc.

2009-8, 2009-1 I.R.B. 229 . . . . 2:14, 2:23,
6:19, 11:17, 12:28
2009-29, 2009-22 I.R.B. 1050 . . . . 4:146

Revenue Rulings

Rev. Rul.

76-28, 1976-1 C.B. 106 . . . . 11:52
76-77, 1976-1 C.B. 107 . . . . 11:52
78-406, 1978-2 C.B. 157 . . . . . . 4:70, 4:85, 6:15,
6:34, 13:46
79-265, 1979-2 C.B. 186 . . . . 6:70
79-286, 1979-2 C.B. 121 . . . . 3:24
82-153, 1982-2 C.B. 86 . . . . 6:76
84-18, 1984-1 C.B. 88 . . . . 3:39, 3:40
86-78, 1986-1 C.B. 208 . . . . 2:58
86-142, 1986-2 C.B. 60 . . . . 3:9
87-41, 1987-1 C.B. 296 . . . . 12:43
87-77, 1987-2 C.B. 115 . . . . 6:63
92-47, 1992-1 C.B. 198 . . . . 8:53
2000-2, 2000-1 I.R.B. 305 . . . . 4:82
2002-62, 2002-2 C.B. 710 . . . 4:116, 4:118, 4:119,
10:20, 10:22
2005-36, 2005-26 I.R.B. 1368 . . . . . . 4:91, 4:92
2006-26, 2006-22 I.R.B. 939 . . . . 4:82, 8:37,
8:39–8:43
2008-5, 2008-3 I.R.B. 271 . . . . . . 1:55, 4:98, 5:65

IRS Announcements, Notices, and General Counsel Memoranda

[References are to question numbers.]

Announcements

Ann.

90-56, 1990-16 I.R.B. 22	7:99
91-179, 1991-49 I.R.B. 78	7:85
97-41, 1997-16 I.R.B. 28	11:86
97-122, 1997-50 I.R.B. 63	2:56, 3:86
99-2, 1999-1 C.B. 305	2:61
99-57, 1999-1 C.B. 1256 . . . . . . 3:123, 9:13, 9:21
2001-106, 2001-44 I.R.B. 416	3:142
2008-44, 2008-20 I.R.B. 982 . . 3:45, 4:101, 4:109, 5:8, 5:9, 5:27, 13:45, 13:59, 13:108

Notices

Notice

81-1, 1981-1 C.B. 610	11:6
87-16, 1987-1 C.B. 446 . . . . 3:50, 3:53–3:56, 3:60, 12:132
87-17, 1987-1 C.B. 454	7:107, 7:161
89-25, 1989-1 C.B. 662 . . . . 3:50, 4:119, 10:20, 12:132
90-18, 1990-1 C.B. 327	7:69, 7:72
93-3, 1993-1 C.B. 293	6:57
96-67, 1996-2 C.B. 235	12:102
97-60, 1997-2 C.B. 310 . . 4:139, 4:142, 6:50, 13:5, 13:18, 13:24, 13:72, 13:78–13:80, 13:82, 13:93
98-2, 1998-1 I.R.B. 266	7:89

Notice

98-4, 1998-1 I.R.B. 269 . . . . . . 6:97, 6:98, 12:109, 12:126
98-4, Q&A A-2, 1998-1 I.R.B. 269 . . . . . 12:1, 12:8
98-4, Q&A B-3, 1998-1 I.R.B. 269	12:37
98-4, Q&A B-4, 1998-1 I.R.B. 269	12:38
98-4, Q&A E-1, 1998-1 I.R.B. 269	12:73
98-4, Q&A E-2, 1998-1 I.R.B. 269	12:73
98-4, Q&A G-1, 1998-1 I.R.B. 269	12:93
98-4, Q&A G-1(4), 1998-1 I.R.B. 269	12:92
98-4, Q&A G-2, 1998-1 I.R.B. 269	12:83
98-4, Q&A G-4, 1998-1 I.R.B. 269	12:86
98-4, Q&A H-1, 1998-1 I.R.B. 269 . . . 12:93–12:95
98-4, Q&A H-1(2), 1998-1 I.R.B. 269	12:92
98-4, Q&A H-1(3), 1998-1 I.R.B. 269	12:93
98-4, Q&A H-5, 1998-1 C.B. 269	12:99
98-4, Q&A I-1, 1998-1 I.R.B. 269 . . . . 12:90, 12:104–12:106
98-4, Q&A J-3, 1998-1 I.R.B. 269	12:114
98-4, Q&A J-4, 1998-1 I.R.B. 269	12:115
98-4, Q&A J-5, 1998-1 I.R.B. 269	12:116
98-4, Q&A K-1, 1998-1 I.R.B. 269	12:13
98-4, Q&A K-2, 1998-1 I.R.B. 269	12:17
98-49, 1998-2 C.B. 365 . . . . 3:50, 12:132
99-5, 1999-1 C.B. 319	6:58
99-30, 1999-1 C.B. 1135	3:27
2000-32, 2000-1 C.B. 1274	6:58
2000-39, 2000-2 C.B. 132 . . . . . . 7:36, 9:14, 9:28, 13:107
2002-17, 2002-1 C.B. 567	3:27
2002-27, 2002-18 I.R.B. 814 . . . . . . 7:143, 7:178, 7:180, 8:12
2003-3, 2003-2 C.B. 258 . . . . 7:183, 7:185, 8:12

Private Letter Rulings

[References are to question numbers.]

Priv. Ltr. Rul.

Priv. Ltr. Rul.

Internal Revenue Service Forms and Publications

[References are to question numbers.]

IRS Forms

Form No.

Form No.

IRS Publications

ERISA Sections and Advisory Opinions

[References are to question numbers.]

Department of Labor Regulations and Advisory Opinions

[References are to question numbers.]

DOL Regulations

DOL Advisory Opinions

Cases

[References are to question numbers.]

Index

References are to question numbers.

A

Accounts
FDIC coverage for retirement accounts. *See* Federal Deposit Insurance Corporation (FDIC)
fees,   3:9, 7:103
health saving accounts. *See* Health savings accounts (HSAs)
joint. *See* Joint accounts
review,   2:11
Roth IRA account-opening questions, 2:41–2:46
subaccounts,   8:23
traditional IRA account-opening questions, 2:1–2:12

Accrued benefits, coverage rules,   3:57

Acquired employees,   11:38, 11:39

Active participation. *See* Participation rules

Adjusted gross income. *See* Modified adjusted gross income (MAGI)

Administration
QTIP,   8:37–8:43
SIMPLE IRA,   12:82–12:91
trustee,   12:92–12:99
ultimate beneficiary, identifying,   4:28, 4:29

Adopting traditional or Roth IRA, Ch. 2
distribution provisions,   2:31–2:34
Roth IRA
account-opening questions,   2:41–2:46
documentation,   2:4, 2:5, 2:47–2:60
traditional IRA
account-opening questions,   2:1–2:12
additional provisions for,   2:34–2:40
documentation,   2:4, 2:5, 2:18–2:40
elections for,   2:30
trustee and custodian issues,   2:13–2:17

Age 30, Coverdell ESA distributions at, 13:74, 13:75

Age 59½
conversion and early withdrawal penalty, 1:8, 1:42, 7:89, 9:5, 9:6
distributions
before death,   1:8
redepositing,   4:114, 14:60
reporting,   7:89
state tax penalties,   14:60–14:64
early distributions correction,   4:114, 7:31
education expenses, IRA comparison, 13:73
surviving spouse, distribution before,   4:65, 4:111, 4:115–4:124, 6:89

Age 70½
additions to or creation of new IRAs,   1:2, 1:15
charitable donations,   14:45
contributions to traditional IRA,   1:2, 1:15, 3:3
distributions,   2:32, 8:20
large IRA balance,   10:19
minimum, Roth IRAs,   1:2
qualified charitable. *See* Charities
excess contributions,   3:137
individual over, Roth IRA contribution,   1:2, 1:15, 3:85
large IRA balance at,   10:1
minimum distributions. *See* Minimum distributions
rollovers after,   6:76
SEP arrangements
distribution commencement,   11:89
eligibility,   11:34
SIMPLE IRA, contributions after,   12:70
surviving spouse,   4:63, 8:20

Age of IRA owner. *See headings above starting with "Age"*

E

F

I

T